THE NEW INTERNATIONAL
GREEK TESTAMENT COMMENTARY

Editors
I. Howard Marshall
and
Donald A. Hagner

The Epistle to the
ROMANS

The Epistle to the
ROMANS

A Commentary on the Greek Text

Richard N. Longenecker

WILLIAM B. EERDMANS PUBLISHING COMPANY

GRAND RAPIDS, MICHIGAN

Published 2016 by
Wm. B. Eerdmans Publishing Co.
2140 Oak Industrial Drive N.E., Grand Rapids, Michigan 49505

Printed in the United States of America

22 21 20 19 18 17 16   7 6 5 4 3 2 1

Library of Congress Cataloging-in-Publication Data

Longenecker, Richard N.
The Epistle to the Romans: a commentary on the Greek text / Richard N. Longenecker.
    pages   cm.   — (The New International Greek Testament commentary)
Includes bibliographical references.
ISBN 978-0-8028-2448-6 (cloth: alk. paper)
1. Bible. Romans — Commentaries.   I. Title.

BS2665.53.L66   2015
227′.107 — dc23

2015030832

www.eerdmans.com

Contents

The Concluding Sections of the Letter 1053

Foreword

Although there have been many series of commentaries on the English text of the New Testament in recent years, very few attempts have been made to cater particularly to the needs of students of the Greek text. The present initiative to fill this gap by the publication of the New International Greek Testament Commentary is very largely due to the vision of W. Ward Gasque, who was one of the original editors of the series. At a time when the study of Greek is being curtailed in many schools of theology, we hope that the NIGTC will demonstrate the continuing value of studying the Greek New Testament and will be an impetus in the revival of such study.

The volumes of the NIGTC are for students who want something less technical than a full-scale critical commentary. At the same time, the commentaries are intended to interact with modern scholarship and to make their own scholarly contribution to the study of the New Testament. The wealth of detailed study of the New Testament in articles and monographs continues without interruption, and the series is meant to harvest the results of this research in an easily accessible form. The commentaries include, therefore, extensive bibliographies and attempt to treat all important problems of history, exegesis, and interpretation that arise from the New Testament text.

One of the gains of recent scholarship has been the recognition of the primarily theological character of the books of the New Testament. The volumes of the NIGTC attempt to provide a theological understanding of the text, based on historical-critical-linguistic exegesis. It is not their primary aim to apply and expound the text for modern readers, although it is hoped that the exegesis will give some indication of the way in which the text should be expounded.

Within the limits set by the use of the English language, the series aims to be international in character, though the contributors have been chosen not primarily in order to achieve a spread between different countries but above all because of their specialized qualifications for their particular tasks.

The supreme aim of this series is to serve those who are engaged in the ministry of the Word of God and thus to glorify God's name. Our prayer is that it may be found helpful in this task.

I. Howard Marshall
Donald A. Hagner

Preface

Paul's letter to believers in Jesus at Rome has always been highly regarded within the Christian church. It has been, in fact, the most highly acclaimed writing of the NT throughout the entire course of Christian history. It is so because it has been, in very large measure, the heartland of Christian thought, life, and proclamation.

THE VITALITY OF ROMANS FOR CHRISTIAN PIETY AND PRACTICE

In 386 Augustine, having been unable to overcome his sexual addiction, was converted to Christ when he read Rom 13:13b-14: "Not in orgies and drunkenness, not in sexual immorality and debauchery, not in dissension and jealousy. But clothe yourselves with the Lord Jesus Christ, and do not think about how to gratify the desires of your sinful nature." Later, in 400, in speaking of his conversion experience when reading this passage, he wrote: "No further would I read, nor had I any need; for instantly, at the end of this sentence, a clear light flooded my heart and all the darkness of doubt vanished away."[1]

In 1515 Martin Luther found Paul's teaching on "the righteousness of God" and "justification by faith" in Rom 1:17 to be the catalyst for his spiritual rebirth, an open door into "paradise," and "a gateway to heaven," and so the beginning of his own religious revolution — which, of course, eventuated in the Protestant Reformation. In his earlier days as an Augustinian monk he pondered deeply, with both consternation and sorrow, the meaning of the phrase *iustitia Dei* ("the justice of God") in his Latin Bible (though in Greek the phrase is δικαιοσύνη θεοῦ, which is better translated "the righteousness of God"). Later in 1545, recalling the resolution of his own spiritual struggles when he came to a proper understanding of this passage, Luther wrote (with the translation of the Latin

---

1. Augustine, *Confessions* 8.12.29; cf. 9.2.

xi

iustitia Dei, "the justice of God," in the text, and that of the Greek δικαιοσύνη θεοῦ, "the righteousness of God," in brackets):

> I greatly longed to understand Paul's Epistle to the Romans, and nothing stood in the way but that one expression, "the justice ['righteousness'] of God," because I took it to mean that justice ['righteousness'] whereby God is just ['righteous'] and deals justly ['righteously'] in punishing the unjust ['unrighteous']. My situation was that, although an impeccable monk, I stood before God as a sinner troubled in conscience, and I had no confidence that my merit would assuage him. Therefore I did not love a just ['righteous'] and angry God, but rather hated and murmured against him. Yet I clung to the dear Paul and had a great yearning to know what he meant.
>
> Night and day I pondered until I saw the connection between the justice ['righteousness'] of God and the statement that "the just ['righteous'] will live by his faith." Then I grasped the truth that the justice ['righteousness'] of God is that righteousness whereby, through grace and sheer mercy, he justifies us by faith. Thereupon I felt myself to be reborn and to have gone through open doors into paradise. The whole of Scripture took on a new meaning, and whereas before "the justice ['righteousness'] of God" had filled me with hate, now it became to me inexpressibly sweet in greater love. This passage of Paul became to me a gateway to heaven.[2]

On May 24, 1738, John Wesley, having heard Luther's "Preface to the Epistle to the Romans" read by someone at the Aldersgate Street Mission in London, wrote in his journal:

> About a quarter before nine [that evening], while he [Martin Luther] was describing the change which God works in the heart through faith in Christ, I felt my heart strangely warmed. I felt I did trust in Christ, in Christ alone for my salvation: an assurance was given me that He had taken away my sins, even mine, and saved me from the law of sin and death.[3]

And in 1918 Karl Barth, who was then a young Swiss pastor, related in the Preface to his *Römerbrief* his own reaction to Romans in the following words: "The reader will detect for himself that it has been written with a joyful sense of discovery. The mighty voice of Paul was new to me; and if to me, no doubt to many others also" — which is the response of many people today when first seriously reading Romans.[4]

---

2. M. Luther, "Preface to Latin Writings," in *Luther's Works,* 55 vols., general editors J. Pelikan (vols. 1-30) and H. T. Lehmann (vols. 31-55) (St. Louis: Concordia, 1972), 34.336-37; see also *idem,* "Table Talk," *ibid.,* 54.193, 309, 442.

3. J. Wesley, "Journal and Diaries I (1735-38)," in *Works of John Wesley* (Nashville: Abingdon, 1988), 18.249-50.

4. K. Barth, *The Epistle to the Romans,* 2.

THE CENTRALITY OF ROMANS FOR CHRISTIAN THEOLOGY

The letter to the Romans has also been central in the formulation and proclamation of Christian doctrine throughout the church's history. In 1540 John Calvin wrote regarding Romans:

> Among many other notable virtues the Epistle has one in particular, which is never sufficiently appreciated; it is this: If we have gained a true understanding of this Epistle, we have an open door to all the most profound treasures of Scripture.[5]

In 1886 Charles Bigg, then the Regius Professor of Ecclesiastical History at Oxford University, asserted: "The Pauline reactions describe the critical epochs of theology and the Church."[6] And Adolf Harnack, in concluding his chapter on "The Presuppositions of the History of Dogma," picked up on Bigg's thesis and expanded it as follows:

> One might write a history of dogma as a history of the Pauline reactions in the Church, and in doing so would touch on all the turning points of the history. Marcion after the Apostolic Fathers; Irenaeus, Clement and Origen after the Apologists; Augustine after the Fathers of the Greek Church; the great Reformers of the middle ages from Agobard to Wessel in the bosom of the mediaeval Church; Luther after the Scholastics; Jansenism after the council of Trent. Everywhere it has been Paul, in these men, who produced the Reformation. Paulinism has proved to be a ferment in the history of dogma, a basis it has never been. Just as it had that significance in Paul himself, with reference to Jewish Christianity, so it has continued to work through the history of the Church.[7]

It may, of course, be questioned whether Marcion in the mid-second century or Cornelius Jansen in the early seventeenth century were really "turning points" in the history of Christianity. Likewise, it may be debated whether Paul's thought was only "a ferment" and never "a basis" for the church's theology. Further, one might wonder why John Chrysostom and his colleagues in the late fourth and early fifth centuries receive no mention in Harnack's listing. Nonetheless, it remains true to say that whenever and wherever there has been a serious study of Paul's letters there has occurred in the church some type of renewal, reformation, or revolution.

All this is particularly true with regard to Paul's letter to the Christians

---

5. J. Calvin, "Theme of the Epistle of Paul to the Romans," trans. R. Mackenzie, in *Calvin's New Testament Commentaries*, 12 vols., ed. D. W. Torrance and T. F. Torrance (Edinburgh: Oliver & Boyd, 1960; Grand Rapids: Eerdmans, 1961), 8.5.

6. C. Bigg, *The Christian Platonists of Alexandria* (Oxford: Clarendon, 1886; repr. 1913), 53.

7. A. Harnack, *The History of Dogma*, trans. N. Buchanan (Boston: Little, Brown, 1901), 136.

at Rome. "In fact," as Joseph Fitzmyer has aptly noted, "one can almost write the history of Christian theology by surveying the ways in which Romans has been interpreted."[8]

CHALLENGES IN THE STUDY OF ROMANS

Yet despite its status in the church and its importance for Christian thought, life, and proclamation, Romans is probably the most difficult of all the NT letters to analyze and interpret. It hardly can be called a simple writing.

In the winter of 394-395 Augustine began to write a commentary on Romans. But after commenting on the first seven verses of chapter one,[9] he felt unable to proceed, saying that the project was just too large for him and that he would return to easier tasks.[10] In the early sixteenth century Erasmus, introducing his *Paraphrase of Romans,* said of Romans: "The difficulty of this letter equals and almost surpasses its utility!" — citing both Origen and Jerome as early Church Fathers who had also found the letter exceedingly difficult to understand.[11] As Erasmus saw it, this difficulty can be attributed to three causes: (1) the style of "speech" or language used, for "nowhere else is the order of speech more confused; nowhere is the speech more split by the transposition of words; nowhere is the speech more incomplete through absence of an apodosis," (2) the "obscurity of things which are hard to put into words," or the content of the letter itself, for "no other letter is handicapped by more frequent rough spots or is broken by deeper chasms," and (3) the "frequent and sudden change of masks" or stances on the part of the author, for "he considers now the Jews, now the Gentiles, now both; sometimes he addresses believers, sometimes doubters; at one point he assumes the role of a weak man, at another of a strong; sometimes that of a godly man, sometimes of an ungodly man."[12]

Indeed, 2 Pet 3:16 bears eloquent testimony to the church's mingled attitudes of (1) deep respect for Paul's letters generally (and Romans in particular), yet also (2) real difficulties in trying to understand them, and (3) a realization of possibilities for serious misinterpretation, when it says of Paul's letters that they "contain some things that are hard to understand, which ignorant and unstable people distort, as they do the other Scriptures, to their own destruction." In fact, despite all its appearances of being straightforward and clear, no other NT writing presents greater difficulties with respect to "style," "stance," and "audience" (to recall Erasmus's three categories of difficulty) than does Romans. Likewise, no other NT writing challenges the interpreter with as many problems of provenance, purpose, character, incorporation of tradition, rhetorical

---

8. Fitzmyer, *Romans,* xiii.
9. See Augustine, *Epistolae ad Romanos inchoata Expositio, PL* 35.2087-2106.
10. See Augustine, *Retractationes* 1.25.
11. Erasmus, *Opera* 7.777.
12. Erasmus, *Opera* 7.777-78.

genre, modes of persuasion, epistolary type, style, structure, flow of argument, and exegesis as does Romans.

Nonetheless, despite all its difficulties and problems, no other letter in the NT is as important as Romans for (1) the thought, piety, and living of Christians, (2) the theology, health, and ministry of the Christian church, and (3) the reformation and renewal of the church's doctrine and practice, which reforms and renewals must constantly be carried forward within the church of every time, place, and circumstance. It is, therefore, incumbent on all present-day commentators who work on this most important NT letter to attempt to spell out a proper interpretation of what is written, striving always (1) to build on the work of past commentators, but also to be informed by significant studies and insights of interpreters today, (2) to be critical, exegetical, and constructive in the analysis of what is written but also pastoral in its application, and (3) to set a course for the future that will promote a better understanding of this most famous of Paul's letters and a more relevant contextualization of its message.

Abbreviations

General

Ep(p)	Letter(s)
ET	English Translation
fl.	*floruit* (flourished)
FS	Festschrift
LXX	Septuagint
mg.	margin
MS(S)	manuscript(s)
MT	Masoretic Text
n.d.	no date
NT	New Testament
OT	Old Testament
par	parallel passage
TR	Textus Receptus
vid	*videtur* (it seems or apparently; used to indicate that the reading is not certain, especially in a damaged manuscript)

Bible Translations: Contemporary English Versions

ASV	American Standard Version
AV	Authorized Version
BV	*The New Testament: Berkeley Version* (Gerritt Verkuyl)
CEV	Contemporary English Version
Goodspeed	*An American Translation* (Edgar J. Goodspeed)
JB	The Jerusalem Bible
KJV	The Holy Bible. King James Version
Knox	*The New Testament of Our Lord and Saviour Jesus Christ, Newly Translated from the Vulgate Latin* (John Knox)
LB	Living Bible

Moffatt	*The Holy Bible. A New Translation* (James Moffatt)
NABRNT	New American Bible, Revised New Testament
NASB	New American Standard Bible
NEB	New English Bible
NET	New English Translation
NIV	New International Version
NJB	New Jerusalem Bible
NKJV	New King James Version
NLT	*New Living Translation* (revision of *The Living Bible*)
NRSV	New Revised Standard Version
Phillips	*The New Testament in Modern English / Letters to Young Churches* (J. B. Phillips)
REB	Revised English Bible
RSV	Revised Standard Version
TEV	Today's English Version / *Good News for Modern Man*
TNIV	Today's New International Version
Weymouth	*The New Testament in Modern Speech* (Richard F. Weymouth)
Williams	*The New Testament: A Private Translation in the Language of the People* (Charles B. Williams)

Texts

GNT[2, 3, 4]	*The Greek New Testament.* 2nd rev. ed. Stuttgart: Deutsche Bibelgesellschaft / United Bible Societies; 3rd rev. ed.; 4th rev. ed. 1993.
NA[27]	*Novum Testamentum Graece post Eberhard Nestle et Erwin Nestle.* 27th ed. Stuttgart: Deutsche Bibelgesellschaft, 1993.
Kittel	*Biblia Hebraica,* ed. R. Kittel. Stuttgart: Privilegierte Württembergische Bibelanstalt, 1929.
Rahlfs	*Septuaginta,* 2 vols., ed. A. Rahlfs. Stuttgart: Privilegierte Württembergische Bibelanstalt, 1935.
UBS[4]	*The Greek New Testament,* United Bible Societies, 4th ed.
W-H	*The New Testament in the Original Greek,* with *Introduction* and *Appendix,* 2 vols., B. F. Westcott and F. J. A. Hort. Cambridge-London, 1881; 2nd ed. 1896.

Pseudepigrapha

Apoc Ab	*Apocalypse of Abraham*
Barn	*Barnabas*
1 En	*1 Enoch*

Jub	*Jubilees*
Let Aris	*Letter of Aristeas*
Pss Sol	*Psalms of Solomon*
2 Bar	*2 Baruch*
2 En	*2 Enoch*
Sib Or	*Sibylline Oracles*
T Ab	*Testament of Abraham*
T Benj	*Testament of Benjamin*
T Dan	*Testament of Dan*
T Gad	*Testament of Gad*
T Jos	*Testament of Joseph*
T Jud	*Testament of Judah*
T Levi	*Testament of Levi*
T Naph	*Testament of Naphtali*
T Reub	*Testament of Reuben*

Epigraphic and Papyrological Publications

POxy	*Oxyrhynchus Papyri,* ed. B. P. Grenfell and A. S. Hunt. London, 1898-.
SbGU	*Sammelbuch griechischer Urkunden aus Ägypten,* ed. Friedrich Preisigke, et al. Wiesbaden, 1915-93.

Rabbinic Works

b.	Babylonian Talmud
Baba Mes.	*Baba Meṣiʿa*
Baba Qam.	*Baba Qamma*
Ber.	*Berakot*
Git.	*Giṭṭin*
y.	Jerusalem Talmud
Ketub.	*Ketubbot*
m.	Mishnah
Mak.	*Makkot*
Meg.	*Megillah*
Mek.	*Mekilta*
Midr.	Midrash
Naz.	*Nazir*
Ned.	*Nedarim*
Pesiq. R.	*Pesiqta Rabbati*
Qidd.	*Qiddušin*
Shabb.	*Shabbat*

Tanch.	*Tanḥuma*
Ter.	*Terumot*
Yebam.	*Yebamot*

Grammatical, Syntactical, and Lexical Aids

ATRob A Grammar of the Greek New Testament in the Light of Historical Research, A. T. Robertson. London: Hodder & Stoughton; New York: Doran, 2nd ed. revised and enlarged, 1915; repr. Nashville: Broadman, 1934.

BAG A Greek-English Lexicon of the New Testament and Other Early Christian Literature, W. Bauer, W. F. Arndt, and F. W. Gingrich. Chicago: University of Chicago Press, 1957.

BDB A Hebrew and English Lexicon of the Old Testament, with an Appendix Containing the Biblical Aramaic, F. Brown, S. R. Driver, and C. A. Briggs. Oxford: Clarendon, 1907; corrected 1952.

BDF A Greek Grammar of the New Testament and Other Early Christian Literature Literature, F. Blass, A. Debrunner, and R. W. Funk. Chicago: University of Chicago Press, 1961 (ET from 1913 German 4th. ed).

Burton Syntax of the Moods and Tenses in New Testament Greek, E. D. Burton, 3rd ed. Chicago: University of Chicago Press, 1898.

D-M A Manual Grammar of the Greek New Testament, H. E. Dana and J. R. Mantey. Toronto: Macmillan, 1927.

EDNT Exegetical Dictionary of the New Testament, ed. H. Balz, G. Schneider. ET: Grand Rapids: Eerdmans, 1990-93.

LSJM A Greek-English Lexicon, H. G. Liddell and R. Scott; revised by H. S. Jones and R. McKenzie. Oxford: Clarendon, 1968.

M-G A Concordance of the Greek Testament, ed. W. F. Moulton and A. S. Geden. Edinburgh: T. & T. Clark, 1897; 4th ed. revised by H. K. Moulton, 1963.

M-M The Vocabulary of the Greek Testament, Illustrated from the Papyri and Other Non-Literary Sources, James Hope Moulton and George Milligan. London: Hodder and Stoughton, 1930.

Moule An Idiom-Book of New Testament Greek, C. F. D. Moule. Cambridge: Cambridge University Press, 2nd ed. 1959.

M-T A Grammar of New Testament Greek, J. H. Moulton and N. Turner. Edinburgh: T. & T. Clark: Vol. 1, *Prolegomena* (3rd ed., 1908); Vol. 2, *Accidence and Word-Formation with an Appendix on Semitisms in the New Testament,* by J. H.

	Moulton and W. F. Howard (1919, 1929); Vol. 3, *Syntax,* by N. Turner (1963); Vol. 4, *Style,* by N. Turner (1976).
Porter	*Verbal Aspect in the Greek of the New Testament, with Reference to Tense and Mood,* S. E. Porter. New York: Peter Lang, 1989.
Thrall	*Greek Particles in the New Testament. Linguistic and Exegetical Studies,* M. E. Thrall. Leiden: Brill, 1962.

Reference Works

ANF	*The Ante-Nicene Fathers,* ed. A. Roberts and J. Donaldson; American edition, 10 vols., ed. A. C. Coxe. Grand Rapids: Eerdmans, 1987.
APOT	*Apocrypha and Pseudepigrapha of the Old Testament,* ed. R. H. Charles (1913, repr. 1963).
CCLat	*Corpus christianorum, series latina*
CIJ	*Corpus inscriptionum Judaicarum,* 2 vols., ed. J. B. Frey (1936-52).
CSEL	*Corpus scriptorum ecclesiasticorum latinorum,* Vienna Academy (1866ff.).
GCS	*Die griechische christliche Schriftsteller der ersten Jahrhunderte*
JE	*The Jewish Encyclopedia,* 12 vols., ed. I. Singer. New York: Ktav, 1901-1906.
NPNF	*The Nicene and Post-Nicene Fathers of the Christian Church,* ed. P. Schaff, 14 vols. Buffalo: Christian Literature, 1886-90.
NTA	*New Testament Apocrypha,* 2 vols., ed. W. Schneemelcher, trans. R. McL. Wilson. London: Lutterworth, 1963, 1965.
OTP	*The Old Testament Pseudepigrapha,* 2 vols., ed. J. H. Charlesworth (1983, 1985).
PG	*Patrologia graeca,* 162 vols., ed. Jacques-Paul Migne (1857-86).
PL	*Patrologia latina,* 221 vols., ed. Jacques-Paul Migne (1844-66).
Statistik	R. Morgenthaler, *Statistik des neuetestamentlichen Wortschatzes.* Zurich and Frankfurt-am-Main: Gotthelf Verlag, 1958.
Str-Bil	*Kommentar zum Neuen Testament aus Talmud und Midrasch,* 5 vols, H. L. Strack and P. Billerbeck. Munich: Beck, 1922-1961.
TDNT	*Theological Dictionary of the New Testament,* 9 vols., ed. G. Kittel and G. Friedrich, trans. G. W. Bromiley. Grand Rapids: Eerdmans, 1964-74 (ET of *TWNT*).

TWNT	*Theologisches Wörterbuch zum Neuen Testament,* 10 vols., ed. G. Kittel (vols. 1-4) and G. Friedrich (vols. 5-10). Stuttgart: Kohlhammer, 1933-1978.

Series (Commentaries, Texts, and Studies)

AASF	Annales Academiae scientarum Fennicae
AB	Anchor Bible
ABD	Anchor Bible Dictionary
ACNT	Augsburg Commentary on the New Testament
ACCS	Ancient Christian Commentary on Scripture
AGAJU	Arbeiten zür Geschichte des antiken Judentums und des Urchristentums
AnBib	Analecta Biblica
ANRW	Aufstieg und Niedergang der Römischen Welt
ANTF	Arbeiten zür neutestamentlichen Textforschung
ATANT	Abhandlungen zür Theologie des Alten und Neuen Testaments
BASORSup	Bulletin of the American Schools of Oriental Research: Supplement Series
BBET	Beiträge zur biblischen Exegese und Theologie
BECNT	Baker Exegetical Commentary on the New Testament
BEvT	Beiträge zur evangelischen Theologie
BFCT	Beiträge zur Förderung christlicher Theologie
BHT	Beiträge zur historischen Theologie
BJS	Brown Judaic Studies
BNTC	Black's New Testament Commentary
BST	Bible Speaks Today
BTN	Bibliotheca Theologica Norvegica
BZNW	Beiheft zur Zeitschrift für die neutestamentliche Wissenschaft
CB	Clarendon Bible
CBBC	Cokesbury Basic Bible Commentary
CBC	Cambridge Bible Commentary
CBNT	Coniectanea Biblica New Testament
CCSL	Corpus christianorum, Series Latina
CGTSC	Cambridge Greek Testament for Schools and Colleges
CNT	Commentaire du Nouveau Testament
CR	Corpus reformatorum
CRJNT	Compendia rerum Judaicarum ad novum Testamentum
CTS	Cambridge Texts and Studies
DJD	Discoveries in the Judean Desert
DSB	Daily Study Bible

EBC	Expositor's Bible Commentary
EGT	Expositor's Greek Testament
EKKNT	Evangelisch-katholischer Kommentar zum Neuen Testament
EPC	Epworth Preacher's Commentaries
EtBib	Etudes bibliques
Exp	Expositor
ExpB	Expositor's Bible
FBBS	Facet Books, Biblical Series
FRLANT	Forschungen zur Religion und Literatur des Alten und Neuen Testaments
GNC	Good News Commentary
HBK	Herders Bibelkommentar
Herm	Hermeneia
HNT	Handbuch zum Neuen Testament
HNTC	Harper's New Testament Commentary
HTKNT	Herders theologischer Kommentar zum Neuen Testament
IB	Interpreter's Bible
ICC	International Critical Commentary
Interp	Interpretation
IntCC	Interpreter's Concise Commentary
JBC	Jerome Biblical Commentary
JSNT.SS	Journal for the Study of the New Testament. Supplement Series
JSOT.SS	Journal for the Study of the Old Testament. Supplement Series
KEKNT	Kritisch-exegetischer Kommentar über das Neue Testament
KNT	Kommentar zum Neuen Testament
KPG	Knox Preaching Guides
LBBC	Layman's Bible Book Commentary
LBC	Layman's Bible Commentary
LCC	Library of Christian Classics
LCL	Loeb Classical Library
LEC	Library of Early Christianity
MCNT	Meyer's Commentary on the New Testament
MK	Meyer Kommentar
MKEKNT	Meyer kritisch-exegetischer Kommentar über das Neue Testament
MNTC	Moffatt New Testament Commentary
MNTS	McMaster New Testament Studies
MTS	Marburger Theologische Studien
NAC	New American Commentary
NCB	New Century Bible
NDIEC	New Documents Illustrating Early Christianity, 5 vols.

NEchB	Neue Echter Bibel
NIBC	New International Biblical Commentary
NICNT	New International Commentary on the New Testament
NJBC	New Jerome Biblical Commentary
NovTSup	Novum Testamentum Supplement
NTAbh	Neutestamentliche Abhandlungen
NTC	New Testament Commentary
NTD	Das Neue Testament Deutsch
NTM	New Testament Message
NTRG	New Testament Reading Guide
NTSR	New Testament for Spiritual Reading
NTTS	New Testament Tools and Studies
OBT	Overtures to Biblical Theology
PC	Pillar Commentary
PFES	Publications of the Finnish Exegetical Society
PNTC	Pelican New Testament Commentaries
RGRW	Religions in the Graeco-Roman World
RNT	Regensburger Neues Testament
SacPag	Sacra Pagina
SB	Sources bibliques
SBJ	La sainte bible de Jérusalem
SBL.DS	Society of Biblical Literature — Dissertation Series
SBL.SBS	Society of Bible Literature — Sources for Biblical Study
SBLSemStud	Society of Biblical Literature — Semeia Studies
SBLTT:ECLS	Society of Biblical Literature — Texts and Translations: Early Christian Literature Series
SBL.WAW	Society of Biblical Literature — Writings from the Ancient World
SBS	Stuttgarter Bibelstudien
SBT	Studies in Biblical Theology
SD	Studies and Documents
SJLA	Studies in Judaism in Late Antiquity
SNT	Studien zum Neuen Testament
SNTS.MS	Studiorum Novi Testamenti Societas — Monograph Series
SchrifNT	Schriften des Neuen Testaments
SGC	Study Guide Commentaries
StudBL	Studies in Biblical Literature
SUNT	Studien zur Umwelt des Neuen Testaments
SVRH	Schriften des Vereins für Reformationsgeschichte
TB	Theologische Bücherei
TBC	Torch Bible Commentary
TH	Théologie historique
THKNT	Theologischer Handkommentar zum Neuen Testament
TNTC	Tyndale New Testament Commentaries

TPINTC	Trinity Press International New Testament Commentary
TU	Texte und Untersuchungen
UMS.HS	University of Michigan Studies, Humanistic Series
VS	Verbum salutis
VTSup	Vetus Testamentum Supplements
WBC	Word Biblical Commentary
WMANT	Wissenschaftliche Monographien zum Alten und Neuen Testament
WUNT	Wissenschaftliche Untersuchungen zum Neuen Testament

Journals

ABR	*Australian Biblical Review*
AJA	*American Journal of Archaeology* (New York)
AJP	*American Journal of Philology* (Baltimore)
ATR	*Anglican Theological Review* (Evanston)
AusBR	*Australian Biblical Review* (Melbourne)
AUSS	*Andrews University Seminary Studies* (Berrien Springs, MI)
BARev	*Biblical Archaeology Review*
BBR	*Bulletin for Biblical Research* (Winona Lake, IN)
BEvT	*Beiträge zür evangelischen Theologie*
Bib	*Biblica* (Rome)
BibR	*Biblical Research* (Chicago)
BibT	*Bible Translator* (London)
Bijdr	*Bijdragen* (Amsterdam/Heverlee)
BJRL	*Bulletin of the John Rylands University Library* (Manchester)
BLit	*Bibel und Liturgie* (Klosterneuburg)
BSac	*Bibliotheca Sacra* (Dallas)
BTB	*Biblical Theology Bulletin* (St. Bonaventure, NY)
BTZ	*Berliner Theologische Zeitschrift*
BZ	*Biblische Zeitschrift* (Freiburg — Paderborn)
CBQ	*Catholic Biblical Quarterly* (Washington)
Christus	*Christus* (Paris)
CJT	*Canadian Journal of Theology* (Toronto)
CP	*Classical Philology*
CQR	*Church Quarterly Review* (London)
CurTM	*Currents in Theology and Mission* (Chicago)
EpR	*Epworth Review* (London)
EtBib	*Études bibliques* (Paris)
ETL	*Ephemerides theologicae lovanienses* (Louvain-Leuven)
EvQ	*Evangelical Quarterly* (Manchester — Aberdeen)
EvT	*Evangelische Theologie*
ExpT	*Expository Times* (Banstead)

Greg	*Gregorianum* (Rome)
HBT	*Horizons in Biblical Theology*
HeyJ	*Heythrop Journal* (London)
HibJ	*Hibbert Journal* (Liverpool)
HTR	*Harvard Theological Review* (Cambridge)
HUCA	*Hebrew Union College Annual* (Cincinnati)
IBS	*Irish Biblical Studies* (Belfast)
IJST	*International Journal of Systematic Theology*
Int	*Interpretation* (Richmond)
ITQ	*Irish Theological Quarterly* (Maynooth)
JAAR	*Journal of the American Academy of Religion* (Chico)
JAC	*Jahrbuch für Antike und Christentum* (Münster)
JAOS	*Journal of the American Oriental Society* (New Haven)
JBL	*Journal of Biblical Literature*
	(Philadelphia-Missoula-Chico-Decatur)
JETS	*Journal of the Evangelical Theological Society*
JJS	*Journal of Jewish Studies* (London — Oxford)
JP	*Journal of Philology*
JQR	*Jewish Quarterly Review* (Philadelphia)
JR	*Journal of Religion* (Chicago)
JRE	*Journal of Religious Ethics*
JRH	*Journal of Religious History*
JRS	*Journal of Roman Studies* (London)
JSJ	*Journal for the Study of Judaism* (Leiden)
JSNT	*Journal for the Study of the New Testament* (Sheffield)
JSOT	*Journal for the Study of the Old Testament* (Sheffield)
JTS	*Journal of Theological Studies* (Oxford)
JTSA	*Journal of Theology for Southern Africa*
Jud	*Judaica*
LexTQ	*Lexington Theological Quarterly* (Lexington)
LouvSt	*Louvain Studies* (Louvain)
LumVie	*Lumière et Vie* (Lyon)
MDB	*Le Monde de la Bible*
MQR	*The Mennonite Quarterly Review*
MTZ	*Münchener theologische Zeitschrift* (Munich)
Neot	*Neotestamentica* (Pretoria)
NKZ	*Neue kirchliche Zeitschrift*
NovT	*Novum Testamentum* (Leiden)
NRT	*Nouvelle Revue théologique* (Tournai)
NTS	*New Testament Studies* (Cambridge)
NTT	*Norsk Teologisk Tidsskrift*
Numen	*Numen: International Review for the History of Religions*
	(Leiden)
OrT	*Oral Tradition*

PRS	*Perspectives in Religious Studies*
PSBSup	*Princeton Seminary Bulletin Supplement*
PTR	*Princeton Theological Review*
RB	*Revue biblique* (Paris — Jerusalem)
RBén	*Revue bénédictine* (Maredsous)
RBR	*Ricerche bibliche e religiose* (Milan)
ResQ	*Restoration Quarterly* (Abilene)
RevApol	*Revue apologétique*
RevExp	*Review and Expositor* (Louisville)
RevistB	*Revista bíblica* (Buenos Aires)
RHPR	*Revue d'histoire et de philosophie religieuses* (Strasbourg)
RSPT	*Revue des sciences philosophiques et théologiques* (Paris)
RSR	*Recherches des sciences religieuses* (Strasbourg)
RTR	*Reformed Theological Review* (Melbourne)
SEÅ	*Svensk exegetisk årsbok* (Uppsala)
Semeia	*Semeia. An Experimental Journal for Biblical Criticism* (Missoula-Chico-Decatur)
SHAW	*Sitzungsberichte der Heidelberger Akademie der Wissenschaft Philosophisch-historische Klasse*
SJT	*Scottish Journal of Theology* (Edinburgh)
SR	*Studies in Religion*
ST	*Studia theologica* (Lund — Aarhus — Oslo)
STK	*Svensk teologisk Kvartalskrift*
TB	*Tyndale Bulletin* (Cambridge)
TBei	*Theologische Beiträge* (Wuppertal)
TBlä	*Theologische Blätter*
TEvan	*Theologia Evangelica* (Pretoria)
TJT	*Toronto Journal of Theology* (Toronto)
TLZ	*Theologische Literaturzeitung* (Leipzig — Berlin)
TP	*Theologie und Philosophie*
TPAPA	*Transactions and Proceedings of the American Philological Association*
TS	*Theological Studies*
TSK	*Theologische Studien und Kritiken*
TTijd	*Theologisch Tijdschrift*
TTZ	*Trierer theologische Zeitschrift* (Trier)
TV	*Theologia Viatorum*
TZ	*Theologische Zeitschrift* (Basel)
TZT	*Tübingen Zeitschrift für Theologie* (Tübingen)
VC	*Vigiliae christianae* (Amsterdam)
VD	*Verbum domini*
VT	*Vetus Testamentum* (Leiden)
WesTJ	*Wesleyan Theological Journal*
WTJ	*Westminster Theological Journal* (Philadelphia)

WW	*Word and World* (St. Paul)
ZEE	*Zeitschrift für evangelische Ethik*
ZKG	*Zeitschrift für Kirchengeschichte* (Stuttgart)
ZKT	*Zeitschrift für katholische Theologie* (Innsbruck)
ZNW	*Zeitschrift für die neutestamentliche Wissenschaft* (Berlin)
ZST	*Zeitschrift für systematische Theologie*
ZTK	*Zeitschrift für Theologie und Kirche* (Tübingen)
ZWT	*Zeitschrift für wissenschaftliche Theologie*

Bibliography of Selected Commentaries and Commentary Materials

Note: References to the following commentaries and commentary materials will be by authors' names and abbreviated titles.

I. THE PATRISTIC PERIOD

Major Greek Fathers (listed chronologically)

Origen (c. 185-254). *Commentarium in epistulam b. Pauli ad Romanos* (Rufinus's abridged Latin translation, *PG* 14.833-1291).

———. *Commentarii in Epistulam ad Romanos,* 5 vols., ed. T. Heither. Freiburg-im-Breisgau: Herder, 1990-95 *(CER).*

———. *Commentary on the Epistle to the Romans,* trans. T. P. Scheck. Washington: Catholic University Press of America, 2001.

———. *The Writings of Origen,* trans. F. Crombie, in *Ante-Nicene Christian Library,* vols. 10 and 23, ed. A. Roberts and J. Donaldson. Edinburgh: T. & T. Clark, 1869.

Diodore of Tarsus (died c. 390). "Fragments of a Commentary on Romans," in *Die Pauluskommentare aus der griechischen Kirche,* ed. K. Staab. Münster: Aschendorff, 1933, 83-112.

John Chrysostom (c. 347-407). *Homilia XXXII in Epistolam ad Romanos* (*PG* 60.391-682).

———. "The Homilies of St. John Chrysostom on the Epistle of St. Paul the Apostle to the Romans," in *NPNF,* 11.329-564 (cf. also *PG* 64.1037-38; 51.155-208).

Theodore of Mopsuestia (c. 350-428). *In epistolam Pauli ad Romanos commentarii fragmenta* (*PG* 66.787-876).

———. Fragments of a Commentary on Romans, in *Die Pauluskommentare aus der Griechischen Kirche,* ed. K. Staab. Münster: Aschendorff, 1933, 113-72.

Cyril of Alexandria (died c. 444). *Explanatio in Epistulam ad Romanos* (*PG* 74.773-856).

Theodoret of Cyrrhus (393-466). *Interpretatio in Epistulam ad Romanos* (*PG* 82.43-226).

Gennadius of Constantinople (died c. 471). *Epistulam ad Romanos* (fragments), in *Pauluskommentare aus der griechischen Kirche,* ed. K. Staab. Münster: Aschendorff, 1933.

Major Latin Fathers (listed chronologically)

Tertullian (c. 145-220). *Adversus Marcionem* (*PL* 2.263-555).

―――. *Adversus Valentinianos* (*PL* 2.558-662).

―――. "The Five Books against Marcion" and "Against the Valentinians," in *ANF*, 3.269-475, 503-20.

Ambrosiaster (wrote c. 366-384). *Commentarium in epistulam beati Pauli ad Romanos* (*PL* 17.47-197; *CSEL* 81.1).

Augustine (c. 354-430). *Expositio quarundam propositionum ex epistola ad Romanos* (*PL* 35.2063-88).

―――. *Epistolae ad Romanos inchoata expositio* (*PL* 35.2087-2106).

―――. *Augustine on Romans: Propositions from the Epistle to the Romans. Unfinished Commentary on the Epistle to the Romans,* ed. and trans. P. A. Landes. SBLTT: ECLS 23.6; Chico: Scholars, 1982.

―――. *Retractationes* (*CSEL* 84.183-85).

―――. *De diversis quaestionibus octoginta tribus* (*PL* 40.11-101).

―――. *De diversis quaestionibus ad Simplicianum* (*PL* 40.102-47).

Pelagius (c. 354-420). *In Epistolam ad Romanos* (*PL* 30.646-718).

―――. *Pelagius's Commentary on St. Paul's Epistle to the Romans. Translated with Introduction and Notes,* by T. de Bruyn. Oxford: Clarendon, 1993.

II. THE REFORMATION PERIOD

Major Roman Catholic Commentators (listed chronologically)

Thomas Aquinas (1225-74). "Expositio in omnes sancti Pauli epistolas. Epistola ad Romanos," in *Opera omnia,* 25 vols. Parma: Fiaccadori, 1852-73; repr. New York: Musurgia, 1948-50, 13.3-156.

Desiderius Erasmus (1469-1536). *The Collected Works of Erasmus,* vol. 42: *Paraphrases on Romans and Galatians,* trans. J. B. Payne, A. Rabil, Jr., and W. S. Smith, Jr.; ed. R. D. Sider. Toronto: University of Toronto Press, 1984.

―――. *Annotations on Romans,* ed. R. D. Sider et al. Toronto: University of Toronto Press, 1994.

Major Protestant Commentators (listed chronologically)

Martin Luther (1483-1546). *Luthers Werke,* 61 vols. Weimar: Böhlaus, 1883-1983: vol. 56 (Glossae & Scholia), 1938; vol. 57 (Nachschriften), 1939.

―――. *Luther's Works,* 55 vols., general editors J. Pelikan (vols. 1-30) and H. T. Lehmann (vols. 31-55): vol. 25, "Lectures on Romans: Glosses and Scholia," trans. W. G. Tillmanns and J. A. O. Preus, ed. H. C. Oswald. St. Louis: Concordia, 1972.

―――. *Commentary on the Epistle to the Romans. A New Translation,* trans. and ed. J. T. Mueller. Grand Rapids: Zondervan, 1954.

―――. *Luther: Lectures on Romans, Newly Translated and Edited* by W. Pauck. LCC 15; London: SCM; Philadelphia: Westminster, 1961.

Philipp Melanchthon (1497-1560). *Melanchthons Werke in Auswahl,* 7 vols., ed. R. Stupperich. Gütersloh: Mohn, 1951-75, 5.25-371.

———. *Loci Communes Theologici,* trans. J. A. O. Preuss. St. Louis: Concordia, 1992.

———. *Commentary on Romans,* trans. F. Kramer. St. Louis: Concordia, 1992.

Martin Bucer (1491-1551). "In epistolam ad Romanos," in *Metaphrases et enarrationes epistolarum d. Pauli apostoli.* Strasbourg: Rihel, 1536; repr. Basel: Pernan, 1562, 1-507.

John Calvin (1509-64). *Commentarii in omnes epistolas Pauli apostoli.* Strasbourg: Rihel, 1539.

———. *Commentarius in epistolam Pauli ad Romanos,* ed. T. H. L. Parker. Leiden: Brill, 1981.

———. *Commentary on the Epistle of Paul the Apostle to the Romans,* trans. J. Owen. Edinburgh: Calvin Translation Society, 1844; repr. Grand Rapids: Eerdmans, 1947.

———. *The Epistles of Paul the Apostle to the Romans and to the Thessalonians,* trans. R. Mackenzie, in *Calvin's Commentaries,* 12 vols., ed. D. W. Torrance and T. F. Torrance. Edinburgh: Oliver & Boyd, 1960; Grand Rapids: Eerdmans, 1961, 8.5-328.

———. *Calvin's New Testament Commentaries,* trans. and ed. T. H. L. Parker. London: SCM; Grand Rapids: Eerdmans, 1971.

Bengel, Johann A. (1687-1752). *Gnomon Novi Testament,* 2 vols. Tübingen: Fues, 1742; ET: *Gnomon of the New Testament,* 2 vols., trans. C. T. Lewis and M. R. Vincent. Philadelphia: Perkinpine & Higgins, 1860, 1862; repr. as *New Testament Word Studies,* Grand Rapids: Kregel, 1978.

Wesley, John (1703-91). *Explanatory Notes upon the New Testament.* London: Epworth, 1950 (repr. of 1754 edition).

III. THE MODERN CRITICAL PERIOD (LISTED ALPHABETICALLY)

Achtemeier, Paul J. *Romans. A Bible Commentary for Teaching and Preaching.* Interp; Atlanta: John Knox, 1985.

Althaus, Paul. *Der Brief an der Römer übersetzt und erklärt.* NTD; Göttingen: Vandenhoeck & Ruprecht, 1978.

Barclay, William. *The Letter to the Romans.* Daily Study Bible; Edinburgh: St. Andrews, 1955; Philadelphia: Westminster, 1975, repr. 1978.

Barrett, C. Kingsley. *A Commentary on the Epistle to the Romans.* BNTC / HNTC; London: Black; New York: Harper & Row, 1957; 2nd ed. Peabody: Hendrickson, 1991.

Barth, Karl. *The Epistle to the Romans,* trans. E. C. Hoskyns. London/New York: Oxford University Press, 1933; original German publication: *Der Römerbrief.* Zollikon-Zurich: Evangelischer Verlag, 1919; ET from Sixth Edition. Munich: Kaiser, 1929; rev. ed. by H. Schmitt, Zurich: Theologischer Verlag, 1985.

Best, Ernest. *The Letter of Paul to the Romans.* CBC; Cambridge: Cambridge University Press, 1967.

Billerbeck, Paul. *Kommentar zum Neuen Testament aus Talmud und Midrasch,* 6 vols. Munich: Beck, 1926-63, vol. 3 (4th ed. 1965), 1-320.

Black, Matthew. *Romans.* NCB; London: Oliphants; Grand Rapids: Eerdmans, 1973; 2nd ed. 1989.

Bray, Gerald, ed. *Romans,* in *Ancient Christian Commentary on Scripture,* general editor T. C. Oden, vol. VI. Downers Grove: InterVarsity, 1998.

Brown, Raymond E. "Letter to the Romans," in his *An Introduction to the New Testament.* New York: Doubleday, 1997, 559-84.

Bruce, Frederick F. *The Epistle of Paul to the Romans: An Introduction and Commentary.* TNTC; London: Tyndale; Grand Rapids: Eerdmans, 1963; 2nd ed., 1969; repr. Leicester: Inter-Varsity; Grand Rapids: Eerdmans, 1985.

Brunner, Emil. *The Letter to the Romans: A Commentary,* trans. H. A. Kennedy. London: Lutterworth; Philadelphia: Westminster, 1959; ET from *Der Römerbrief übersetzt und erklärt.* Stuttgart: Oncken, 1938; repr. 1956.

Byrne, Brendan. *Romans.* SacPag; Collegeville: Liturgical, 1996.

Craig, Gerald R. "The Epistle to the Romans" (Exposition), in *The Interpreter's Bible,* 12 vols, ed. G. A. Buttrick et al. New York: Abingdon, 1954, 9.379-668.

Cranfield, Charles E. B. *A Critical and Exegetical Commentary on the Epistle to the Romans.* ICC; 2 vols. Edinburgh: T. & T. Clark, 1975, 1979.

Denney, James. *St. Paul's Epistle to the Romans.* EGT; London: Hodder & Stoughton, 1900, 2.555-725; repr. Grand Rapids: Eerdmans, 1970, 1983.

Dodd, Charles Harold. *The Epistle of Paul to the Romans.* MNTC; London: Hodder & Stoughton, 1932; rev. ed. London: Collins, 1959.

Dunn, James D. G. *Romans.* WBC; 2 vols. Dallas: Word, 1988-89.

Fitzmyer, Joseph A. *Romans: A New Translation with Introduction and Commentary.* AB; New York: Doubleday, 1993.

Gaugler, Ernst. *Der Brief an die Römer,* 2 vols. Zurich: Zwingli, 1945; repr. 1958.

Gifford, Edward H. *The Epistle of St. Paul to the Romans, with Notes and Introduction.* London: Murray, 1881; repr. 1886.

Godet, Frédéric. *Commentary on St. Paul's Epistle to the Romans,* 2 vols., trans. A. Cusin. Edinburgh: T. & T. Clark, 1880-81; New York: Funk & Wagnalls, 1883; repr. Grand Rapids: Kregel, 1977; ET from *Commentaire sur l'épître aux Romains,* 2 vols. Paris: Sandoz & Rischbacher; Geneva: Desrogis, 1879; repr. Geneva: Labor et Fides, 1879-81.

Gore, Charles. *St. Paul's Epistle to the Romans: A Practical Exposition,* 2 vols. London: Murray; New York: Scribners, 1899-1900; repr. 1907.

Haldane, Robert. *Exposition of the Epistle to the Romans,* 3 vols. Edinburgh: Whyte, 1839; repr. New York: Carter, 1853; repr. in one volume as *Commentary on Romans,* Grand Rapids: Kregel, 1988.

Hamilton, Floyd E. *The Epistle to the Romans: An Exegetical and Devotional Commentary.* Philadelphia: Presbyterian and Reformed, 1958.

Harrison, Everett F., and Donald A. Hagner. "Romans," in *The Expositor's Bible Commentary,* rev. ed., 13 vols., ed. T. Longman and D. E. Garland. Grand Rapids: Zondervan, 2008, 11.19-237.

Harrisville, Roy A. *Romans.* ACNT; Minneapolis: Augsburg, 1980.

Hendriksen, William. *Exposition of Paul's Epistle to the Romans,* 2 vols. NTC; Grand Rapids: Baker; Edinburgh: Banner of Truth, 1980-81.

Hodge, Charles. *A Commentary on the Epistle to the Romans.* Philadelphia: Grigg & Elliot, 1835; 2nd ed. Philadelphia: Claxton, 1864; repr. New York: Armstrong, 1896; Grand Rapids: Eerdmans, 1980.

Huby, Joseph. *Saint Paul. Épître aux Romains. Traduction et commentaire.* VS; Paris: Beauchesne, 4th ed. 1940; new ed., rev. S. Lyonnet, 1957.

Hunter, Archibald M. *The Epistle to the Romans: Introduction and Commentary.* TBC; London: SCM, 1955; repr. with subtitle *The Law of Love,* 1968, 1977.

Jewett, Robert. *Romans: A Commentary.* Hermeneia; Minneapolis: Fortress, 2007.

Johnson, Luke Timothy. *Reading Romans: A Literary and Theological Commentary.* Macon: Smyth & Helwys, 2001.

Käsemann, Ernst. *Commentary on Romans,* trans. G. W. Bromiley. London: SCM; Grand Rapids: Eerdmans, 1980; ET from *An die Römer.* HNT; Tübingen: Mohr-Siebeck, 1973; 4th ed 1980.

Kertelge, Karl. *The Epistle to the Romans,* trans. F. McDonagh. NTSR; London: Sheed & Ward; New York: Herder & Herder, 1972; ET from *Der Brief an die Römer.* Düsseldorf: Patmos, 1971.

Knox, John. "The Epistle to the Romans" (Introduction and Exegesis), in *The Interpreter's Bible,* 12 vols., ed. G. A. Buttrick et al. New York: Abingdon, 1954, 9.353-668.

Kühl, Ernst. *Der Brief des Paulus an die Römer.* Leipzig: Quell & Meyer, 1913.

Kuss, Otto. *Der Römerbrief übersetzt und erklärt,* 3 vols. (on chs. 1-11). Regensburg: Pustet, 1957, 1959, 1978.

Lagrange, Marie-Joseph. *Saint Paul. Épître aux Romains.* EtBib; Paris: Gabalda, 1916; 4th ed. (with addenda) 1931; repr. 1950.

Leenhardt, Franz J. *The Epistle of Saint Paul to the Romans: A Commentary,* trans. H. Knight. London: Lutterworth; Cleveland: World, 1961; ET from *L'Épître de saint Paul aux Romains.* CNT; Neuchatel-Paris: Delachaux et Niestlé, 1957; 2nd ed. Geneva: Labor et Fides, 1981.

Lenski, Richard C. H. *The Interpretation of St. Paul's Epistle to the Romans.* Columbus: Lutheran Book Concern, 1936; repr. Minneapolis: Augsburg, 1961.

Liddon, Henry P. *Explanatory Analysis of St. Paul's Epistle to the Romans.* London: Longmans, Green, 1893; repr. Grand Rapids: Zondervan, 1961.

Lietzmann, Hans. *Die Briefe des Apostels Paulus an die Römer.* HNT 8; Tübingen: Mohr-Siebeck, 1906; 2nd ed. 1928; 3rd ed. 1933; 5th ed. 1971.

Lightfoot, Joseph B. *Notes on Epistles of St. Paul from Unpublished Commentaries.* London: Macmillan, 1895, 237-305 (on chs. 1-7); repr. Grand Rapids: Zondervan, 1957.

Lohse, Eduard. *Der Brief an die Römer.* KEKNT; Göttingen: Vandenhoeck & Ruprecht, 2003.

Lyonnet, Stanislaus. *Les Épîtres de Saint Paul aux Galates, aux Romains.* SBJ; Paris: Cerf, 1953; 2nd ed. 1959, 45-136.

Manson, Thomas W. "Romans," in *Peake's Commentary on the Bible,* 2nd ed., ed. M. Black and H. H. Rowley. London: Nelson, 1962, 940-53.

Matera, Frank J. *Romans,* Grand Rapids: Baker Academic, 2010.

Metzger, Bruce M. *A Textual Commentary on the Greek New Testament.* New York: United Bible Societies, 1971; 1975 (corrected edition); 2nd rev. ed. Stuttgart: Deutsche Bibelgesellschaft, 1994.

Meyer, Heinrich A. W. *Critical and Exegetical Handbook to the Epistle to the Romans,* 2 vols. MCNT; New York: Funk & Wagnalls, 1884; rev. ed. by W. P. Dickson and T. Dwight, 1889; ET from *Der Brief an die Römer.* MKEKNT; Göttingen: Vandenhoeck & Ruprecht, 1836; 5th ed. 1872.

Michel, Otto. *Der Brief an die Römer.* MKEKNT; Göttingen: Vandenhoeck & Ruprecht, 1955; 14th ed. 1978.

Moo, Douglas J. *The Epistle to the Romans.* NICNT; Grand Rapids: Eerdmans, 1996.

Morris, Leon. *The Epistle to the Romans.* PC; Leicester: Inter-Varsity; Grand Rapids: Eerdmans, 1988.

BIBLIOGRAPHY OF SELECTED COMMENTARIES

Murray, John. *The Epistle to the Romans: The English Text with Introduction, Exposition, and Notes,* 2 vols. NICNT; Grand Rapids: Eerdmans, 1959, 1965.

Nygren, Anders. *Commentary on Romans,* trans. C. C. Rasmussen. Philadelphia: Fortress, 1949, 1972; London: SCM, 1952; ET from *Der Römerbrief.* Göttingen: Vandenhoeck & Ruprecht, 1951, which was translated from *Pauli Brev till Romarna.* Stockholm: Svenska Kyrkans Diakonistyrelses Bokförlag, 1944.

O'Neill, John C. *Paul's Letter to the Romans.* PNTC; Harmondsworth-Baltimore: Penguin, 1975.

Robertson, Archibald T. "The Epistle to the Romans," in *Word Pictures in the New Testament,* 4 vols. New York: Smith, 1931, 4.320-430.

Robinson, John A. T. *Wrestling with Romans.* London: SCM; Philadelphia: Westminster, 1979.

Sanday, William, and Arthur C. Headlam. *A Critical and Exegetical Commentary on the Epistle to the Romans.* ICC; Edinburgh: T. & T. Clark; New York: Scribner, 1895, 2nd ed. 1896, 5th ed. 1902; repr. 1922, 1958, 1962.

Schelkle, Karl Hermann. *Paulus Lehrer der Väter. Die altkirchliche Auslegung von Römer 1-11.* Düsseldorf: Patmos, 1956.

————. *The Epistle to the Romans: Theological Meditations.* New York: Herder and Herder, 1964; ET of *Meditationen über den Römerbrief.* Einsiedeln: Benziger Verlag.

Schlatter, Adolf. *Romans: The Righteousness of God,* trans. S. S. Schatzmann. Peabody: Hendrickson, 1995; ET from *Gottes Gerechtigkeit. Ein Kommentar zum Römerbrief.* Stuttgart: Calwer, 1935, 3rd ed. 1959, 4th ed. 1965; 6th ed. (with preface by P. Stuhlmacher), 1991.

Schlier, Heinrich. *Der Römerbrief. Kommentar.* HTKNT; Freiburg/Basel/Vienna: Herder, 1977.

Schmidt, Hans W. *Der Brief des Paulus an die Römer.* THKNT; Berlin: Evangelische Verlagsanstalt, 1963, 3rd ed. 1972.

Schmithals, Walter. *Der Römerbrief. Ein Kommentar.* Gütersloh: Mohn, 1988.

Schreiner, Thomas R. *Romans.* BECNT; Grand Rapids: Baker, 1998.

Shedd, William G. T. *A Critical and Doctrinal Commentary upon the Epistle of St. Paul to the Romans.* New York: Scribner's, 1879; repr. Grand Rapids: Zondervan, 1967.

Stuhlmacher, Peter. *Paul's Letter to the Romans: A Commentary,* trans. S. J. Hafemann. Louisville: Westminster John Knox, 1994; ET from *Der Brief an die Römer übersetzt und erklart.* NTD; Göttingen: Vandenhoeck & Ruprecht, 1989.

Talbert, Charles H. *Romans.* Macon: Smyth & Helwys, 2002.

Taylor, Vincent. *The Epistle to the Romans.* EPC; London: Epworth, 1955, 2nd ed. 1962.

Weiss, Bernhard. *Der Brief an die Römer.* MK; Göttingen: Vandenhoeck & Ruprecht, 1881, 4th ed. 1891.

Wilckens, Ulrich. *Der Brief an die Römer,* 3 vols. EKKNT; Zurich: Benziger; Neukirchen-Vluyn: Neukirchener Verlag, 1978, 1980, 1982.

Witherington, Ben, III, with Darlene Hyatt. *Paul's Letter to the Romans: A Socio-Rhetorical Commentary.* Grand Rapids: Eerdmans, 2004.

Wright, N. Thomas. "The Messiah and the People of God: A Study in Pauline Theology with Particular Reference to the Argument of the Epistle to the Romans." D.Phil. Dissertation, University of Oxford, 1980.

Zahn, Theodor. *Der Brief des Paulus an die Römer ausgelegt.* KNT; Leipzig: Deichert, 1910, 2nd ed. 1925.

Zeller, Dieter. *Der Brief an die Römer. Übersetzt und erklärt.* RNT; Regensburg: Pustet, 1985.

Ziesler, John A. *Paul's Letter to the Romans.* TPINTC; London: SCM; Philadelphia: Trinity, 1989.

Bibliography of Supplemental Monographs, Articles, and Other Materials

Note: References to the following monographs, articles, and other materials will be by authors' names and abbreviated titles.

Abbot, Ezra. "On the Construction of Romans ix.5," *JBL* 1 (1881) 87-154.

———. "Recent Discussions of Romans ix.5," *JBL* 2 (1883) 90-112.

Abegg, Martin G. "Paul, 'Works of the Law' and MMT," *BARev* 20 (1994) 52-55, 81.

Achtemeier, Paul J. "'Some Things in Them Hard to Understand': Reflections on an Approach to Paul," *Int* 38 (1984) 254-67.

———. "Romans 3:1-8: Structure and Argument," in *Christ and His Communities: Essays in Honor of Reginald H. Fuller,* ed. A. J. Hultgren and B. Hall. Cincinnati: Forward Movement Publications, 1990, 77-87.

———. "Apropos the Faith of/in Christ: A Response to Hays and Dunn," in *Pauline Theology.* Vol. 4: *Looking Back, Pressing On,* ed. E. E. Johnson and D. M. Hay. Atlanta: Scholars, 1997, 82-92.

Aland, Kurt. "Das Verhältnis von Kirche und Staat in der Frühzeit," *ANRW* 11.23.1 (1979) 60-246.

———. *Neutestamentliche Entwürfe.* Munich: Kaiser, 1979.

Aland, Kurt, and Barbara Aland. *The Text of the New Testament: An Introduction to the Critical Editions and to the Theory and Practice of Modern Textual Criticism,* trans. E. F. Rhodes. Leiden: Brill; Grand Rapids: Eerdmans, 1987; 2nd rev. ed. 1989.

Albl, Martin C. *"And Scripture Cannot Be Broken": The Form and Function of the Early Testimonia Collections.* NovTSup 96; Leiden: Brill, 1999.

Aletti, Jean-Noël. "L'Argumentation paulinienne en Rm 9," *Bib* 68 (1987) 41-56.

———. "Rm 1,18–3,20. Incohérence ou cohérence de l'argumentation paulinienne?" *Bib* 69 (1988) 47-62.

Allen, Leslie C. "The Old Testament Background of (ΠΡΟ)ΟΡΙΖΕΙΝ in the New Testament," *NTS* 17 (1970) 104-8.

Allison, Dale C., Jr. "The Pauline Epistles and the Synoptic Gospels: The Pattern of the Parallels," *NTS* 28 (1982) 1-32.

———. "Jesus and the Covenant: A Response to E. P. Sanders," in *The Historical Jesus: A Sheffield Reader,* ed. C. A. Evans and S. E. Porter. Sheffield: Sheffield Academic, 1995, 61 82.

Arzt, Peter. "The 'Epistolary Introductory Thanksgiving' in the Papyri and in Paul," *NovT* 36 (1994) 29-46.

Aune, David E. *The New Testament in Its Literary Environment.* Philadelphia: Westminster, 1987, 158-225.

————, ed. *Greco-Roman Literature and the New Testament: Selected Forms and Genres.* SBL.SBS 21; Atlanta: Scholars, 1988.

————. "Romans as a *Logos Protreptikos* in the Context of Ancient Religious and Philosophical Propaganda," in *Paulus als Missionar und Theologe und das antike Judentum,* ed. M. Hengel and U. Heckel. WUNT 58; Tübingen: Mohr Siebeck, 1991, 91-124; abbreviated version: "Romans as a *Logos Protrepikos,*" in Donfried, ed., *Romans Debate* (1991), 278-96.

————. *The Westminster Dictionary of New Testament and Early Christian Literature and Rhetoric.* Louisville: Westminster John Knox, 2003.

Aus, Roger D. "Paul's Travel Plans to Spain and the 'Full Number of the Gentiles' of Rom 11:25," *NovT* 21 (1979) 232-62.

Avigad, Nahman. "Jewish Ritual Baths," in *Discovering Jerusalem.* Israel: "Shikmona" Publishing Company & Israel Exploration Society, 1983, esp. 139-43.

Bacon, Benjamin W. "The Doxology at the End of Romans," *JBL* 18 (1899) 167-76.

Bahr, Gordon J. "The Subscriptions in the Pauline Letters," *JBL* 87 (1968) 27-41.

Baillie, John. *Our Knowledge of God.* New York: Scribner's, 1939; repr. 1959.

Baker, Murray. "Paul and the Salvation of Israel: Paul's Ministry, the Motif of Jealousy, and Israel's Yes," *CBQ* 67 (2005) 469-84.

Balz, Horst R. *Heilsvertrauen und Welterfahrung. Strukturen der Paulinischen Eschatologie nach Römer 8.18-39.* BEvT 59; Munich: Kaiser, 1971.

Barclay, William. "Great Themes of the New Testament III: Romans 5:12-21," *ExpT* 70 (1958-59) 132-35, 172-75.

Barr, James. *The Semantics of Biblical Language.* London: Oxford University Press, 1961.

Barrett, C. Kingsley. *From First Adam to Last: A Study in Pauline Theology.* London: Black; New York: Scribner's, 1962.

————. "The New Testament Doctrine of Church and State," in his *New Testament Essays.* London: SPCK, 1972, 1-19.

Bartchy, S. Scott. "Slavery (Greco-Roman)," *ABD* 6 (1992) 68-78.

Barth, Karl. *Christ and Adam: Man and Humanity in Romans 5,* trans. T. A. Smail. Edinburgh: Oliver & Boyd, 1956; New York: Harper, 1957.

Barth, Markus. "Speaking of Sin: Some Interpretative Notes on Romans 1.18–3.20," *SJT* 8 (1955) 288-96.

————. *Was Christ's Death a Sacrifice?* Edinburgh: Oliver & Boyd, 1961.

————. "The Faith of the Messiah," *HeyJ* 10 (1969) 363-70.

————. *Justification: Pauline Texts Interpreted in the Light of the Old and New Testaments,* trans. A. M. Woodruff. Grand Rapids: Eerdmans, 1971.

————. "Theologie — ein Gebet (Röm 11,33-36)," *TZ* 41 (1985) 330-48.

Bartlett, David L. "A Biblical Perspective on Homosexuality," *Foundations* 20 (1977) 133-47.

Bartsch, Hans. "The Concept of Faith in Romans," *BibR* 13 (1968) 41-53.

Bassler, Jouette M. *Divine Impartiality: Paul and a Theological Axiom.* SBL.DS 59; Chico: Scholars, 1982.

————. "Divine Impartiality in Paul's Letter to the Romans," *NovT* 26 (1984) 43-58.

Batey, Richard. "'So All Israel Will Be Saved': An Interpretation of Romans 11:25-32," *Int* 20 (1966) 218-28.

Baxter, A. G., and J. A. Ziesler, "Paul and Arboriculture: Romans 11.17-24," *JSNT* 24 (1985) 25-32.

Beasley-Murray, Paul. "Romans 1:3f: An Early Confession of Faith in the Lordship of Jesus," *TB* 31 (1980) 147-54.

Behm, Johannes. "διαθήκη," *TDNT* 2.106-34.

Beker, J. Christiaan. *Paul the Apostle: The Triumph of God in Life and Thought*. Philadelphia: Fortress, 1980.

———. "The Jewish Character of the Argument in 1:16–4:25," in his *Paul the Apostle*, 78-83 and 94-104.

———. "The Meaning of 'Body,'" in his *Paul the Apostle*, 287-89.

———. "The Faithfulness of God and the Priority of Israel in Paul's Letter to the Romans," *HTR* 79 (1986) 10-16; repr. in *Christians among Jews and Gentiles*, ed. G. W. E. Nickelsburg and G. W. MacRae. Philadelphia: Fortress, 1986, 10-16; also repr. in Donfried, ed., *Romans Debate* 1991, 327-32.

———. "Vision of Hope for a Suffering World: Romans 8:17-30," *PSBSup* 3 (1994) 26-32.

Bell, Richard H. *No One Seeks for God: An Exegetical and Theological Study of Romans 1:18–3:20*. Tübingen: Mohr Siebeck, 1998.

———. *Provoked to Jealousy: The Origin and Purpose of the Jealousy Motif in Romans 9–11*. WUNT 63; Tübingen: Mohr Siebeck, 1994.

Berger, Klaus. "Abraham in den paulinischen Hauptbriefen," *MTZ* 17 (1966) 47-89.

———. "'Gnade' im frühen Christentum," *NTT* 27 (1973) 1-25.

———. "Apostelbrief und apostolische Rede. Zum Formular frühchristlicher Briefe," *ZNW* 65 (1974) 190-231.

———. *Formgeschichte des Neuen Testament*. Heidelberg: Quelle & Meyer, 1984.

———. "Hellenistische Gattungen im Neuen Testament," *ANRW* 2.25.2 (1984) 1031-1432, 1831-85.

Berkley, Timothy W. *From a Broken Covenant to Circumcision of the Heart: Pauline Intertextual Exegesis in Romans 2:17-29*. SBL.DS 175; Atlanta: Society of Biblical Literature, 2000.

Betz, Hans Dieter. *Galatians: A Commentary on Paul's Letter to the Church in Galatia*. Hermeneia; Philadelphia: Fortress, 1979.

———. "Das Problem der Grundlagen der paulinischen Ethik (Röm 12.1-2)," *ZTK* 85 (1988) 199-218.

———. "The Foundation of Christian Ethics according to Romans 12:1-2," in *Witness and Existence: Essays in Honor of Schubert M. Ogden*, ed. P. E. Devenish and G. L. Goodwin. Chicago: University of Chicago Press, 1989, 55-72.

Betz, Otto. "The Qumran Halakhah Text *Miqsat Ma'ase Ha-Torah* (4QMMT) and Sadducean, Essene, and Early Pharisaic Tradition," in *The Aramaic Bible: Targums in Their Historical Context*, ed. D. R. G. Beattie and M. J. McNamara. Sheffield: JSOT, 1994.

Biedermann, Hermenegild M. *Die Erlösung der Schöpfung beim Apostel Paulus. Ein Beitrag zur Klärung der religionsgeschichtlichen Stellung der paulinischen Erlösungslehre*. Würzburg: St. Rita, 1940.

Bjerkelung, Carl J. *PARAKALŌ. Form, Function und Sinn der parakolō-Sätze in den paulinischen Briefen*. Oslo: Universitetsworlaget, 1967.

Black, Matthew. "The Pauline Doctrine of the Second Adam," *SJT* 7 (1954) 170-79.

Blackman, Cyril. "Romans 3.26b: A Question of Translation," *JBL* 87 (1968) 203-4.

Blank, Josef. "Warum sagt Paulus: 'Aus den Werken des Gesetzes wird niemand Gerecht'?" EKKNT *Vorarbeiten* 1 (1969) 79-107.

———. "Kirche und Staat im Urchristentum," *Kirche und Staat auf Distanz,* ed. G. Denzler. Munich: Kösel, 1977, 9-28.

Bläser, P. Peter. *Das Gesetz bei Paulus.* Münster: Aschendorfische Verlagsbuchhandlung, 1941.

Bloesch, Donald G. "'All Israel Will Be Saved': Supersessionism and the Biblical Witness," *Int* 43 (1989) 130-42.

Boer, Martinus C. de. *Galatians: A Commentary.* Louisville: Westminster John Knox, 2011.

Boers, Hendrikus. *Theology Out of the Ghetto: A New Testament Exegetical Study Concerning Exclusiveness.* Leiden: Brill, 1970, esp. 82-104.

———. *The Justification of the Gentiles: Paul's Letters to the Galatians and Romans.* Peabody: Hendrickson, 1994.

Boismard, M.-É. "Constitué fils de Dieu (Rom 1.4)," *RB* 60 (1953) 5-17.

Borg, Marcus J. "A New Context for Romans xiii," *NTS* 19 (1972-73) 205-18.

Bornkamm, Günther. "Faith and Reason in Paul's Epistles," *NTS* 4 (1958) 93-100.

———. "Gesetz und Natur. Röm. 2,14-16," in *Studien zu Antike und Urchristentum.* BEvT 28; Munich: Kaiser, 1959, 93-118.

———. "The Revelation of God's Wrath: Romans 1-3," in his *Early Christian Experience,* trans. P. L. Hammer. London: SCM, 1969, 47-70.

———. "The Praise of God: Romans 11.33-36," in his *Early Christian Experience,* trans. P. L. Hammer. London: SCM, 1969, 105-11.

———. "Theologie als Teufelskunst. Römer 3,1-9," in *Geschichte und Glaube* II: *Gesammelte Aufsätze,* vol. 4. BEvT 53; Munich: Kaiser, 1971, 140-48.

———. "Christology and Justification (on Romans 1:3f. and 1:16f.)," Appendix III in his *Paul,* trans. D. M. G. Stalker. New York: Harper & Row, 1971, 248-49.

Bousset, Wilhelm. *Kyrios Christos.* Göttingen: Vandenhoeck & Ruprecht, 1913.

Bowers, Paul. "Fulfilling the Gospel: The Scope of the Pauline Mission," *JETS* 30 (1987) 185-98.

Brauch, Manfred T. "Perspectives on 'God's Righteousness' in Recent German Discussion," in E. P. Sanders, *Paul and Palestinian Judaism: A Comparison of Patterns of Religion.* Philadelphia: Fortress, 1977, "Appendix," 523-42.

Brockmeyer, Norbert. *Antike Sklaverei.* Ertrage der Forschung 116; Darmstadt: Wissenschaftliche Buchgesellschaft, 1979.

Brown, Michael Joseph. "Paul's Use of ΔΟΥΛΟΣ ΧΡΙΣΤΟΥ ΙΗΣΟΥ in Romans 1:1," *JBL* 120 (2001) 723-37.

Brown, Raymond E. "The Semitic Background of the New Testament *Mysterion*," *Bib* 39 (1958) 426-48 and 40 (1959) 70-87.

———. *The Semitic Background of the Term "Mystery" in the New Testament.* FBBS 21; Philadelphia: Fortress, 1968.

———. "Not Jewish Christianity and Gentile Christianity, but Types of Jewish/Gentile Christianity," *CBQ* 45 (1983) 74-79.

———. "The Beginnings of Christianity at Rome" and "The Roman Church near the End of the First Christian Generation (A.D. 58 — Paul to the Romans)," in R. E. Brown and J. P. Meier, *Antioch and Rome: New Testament Cradles of Catholic Christianity.* New York: Paulist, 1983, 92-127.

————. "Further Reflections on the Origins of the Church of Rome," in *The Conversation Continues: Studies in Paul and John in Honor of J. L. Martyn,* ed. R. T. Fortna and B. R. Gaventa. Nashville: Abingdon, 1990, 98-115.

Brownlee, William H. "The Placarded Revelation of Habakkuk," *JBL* 82 (1963) 319-25.

Bruce, Frederick F. "Paul and the Historical Jesus," *BJRL* 56 (1974) 317-35.

————. "Paul and 'The Powers That Be,'" *BJRL* 66 (1983-84) 78-96.

Bryan, Christopher. *A Preface to Romans: Notes on the Epistle in Its Literary and Cultural Setting.* Oxford: Oxford University Press, 2000.

Büchsel, Friedrich. "ἀλλάσσω . . . καταλλάσσω, καταλλαγή," *TDNT* 1.251-59.

————, and Johannes Herrmann. "ἵλεως, ἱλάσκομαι, ἱλασμός, ἱλαστήριον," *TDNT* 3.300-23.

Bultmann, Rudolf. *Der Stil der paulinischen Predigt und die kynisch-stoische Diatribe.* FRLANT 13; Göttingen: Vandenhoeck & Ruprecht, 1910; repr. 1984.

————. "Das Problem der Ethik bei Paulus," *ZNW* 23 (1924) 123-40.

————. "Neueste Paulusforschung," *Theologische Rundschau* 8 (1936) 1-22.

————. "Anknüpfung und Widerspruch. Zur Frage nach der Anknüpfung der neutestamentlichen Verkündigung an die natürliche Theologie der Stoa, die hellenistischen Mysterienreligionen und die Gnosis," *TZ* 2 (1946) 401-18.

————. "Glossen im Römerbrief," *TLZ* 72 (1947) 197-202.

————. *Theology of the New Testament,* 2 vols., trans. K. Grobel. New York: Scribners, 1951, 1955.

————. "The Kerygma of the Earliest Church," in his *Theology of the New Testament,* esp. 1.46.

————. "Christ the End of the Law," in his *Essays Philosophical and Theological,* trans. J. C. G. Greig. London: SCM, 1955, 36-66.

————. "ΔΙΚΑΙΟΣΥΝΗ ΘΕΟΥ," *JBL* 83 (1964) 12-16.

————. *The Old and the New Man in the Letters of Paul,* trans. K. R. Crim. Richmond: John Knox, 1967 (ET of 1964 German edition).

————. "Adam and Christ according to Romans 5," in *Current Issues in New Testament Interpretation* (FS A. O. Piper), ed. W. Klassen and G. F. Snyder. London: SCM, 1962, 143-65.

————. "ἀφίημι, ἄφεσις, παρίημι, πάρεσις," *TDNT* 1.509-12.

————, "ἐλπίς, ἐλπίζω," *TDNT* 2.517-23, 529-35.

————. "δόξα," *TDNT* 2.237.

————. "καυχάομαι, καύχημα, καύχησις," *TDNT* 3.645-54.

Burke, Trevor J. *Adopted into God's Family: Exploring a Pauline Metaphor.* Downers Grove: InterVarsity, 2006.

————. "Adopted as Sons (ΥΙΟΘΕΣΙΑ): The Missing Piece in Pauline Soteriology," in *Paul: Jew, Greek, and Roman,* ed. S. E. Porter. Leiden: Brill, 2008, 259-87.

Burton, Ernest deWitt. "ΑΠΟΣΤΟΛΟΣ," in *A Critical and Exegetical Commentary on the Epistle to the Galatians.* ICC; Edinburgh: T. & T. Clark; New York: Scribner's, 1921, 363-84.

Byrne, Brendan. "Living Out the Righteousness of God: The Contribution of Rom 6:1–8:13 to an Understanding of Paul's Ethical Presuppositions," *CBQ* 43 (1981) 557-81.

————. "'The Type of the One to Come' (Rom 5:14): Fate and Responsibility in Romans 5:12-21," *ABR* 36 (1988) 19-30.

————. "'Rather Boldly' (Rom 15,15): Paul's Prophetic Bid to Win Allegiance of the Christians in Rome," *Bib* 74 (1993) 83-96.

Cadbury, Henry J. "Erastus of Corinth," *JBL* 50 (1931) 42-58.

Caird, George B. *Principalities and Powers: A Study in Pauline Theology.* Oxford: Clarendon, 1956, esp. 22ff.

Cambier, Jules M. "Le jugement de tous les hommes par Dieu seul, selon la vérité, dans Rom 2:1-3:20," *ZNW* 67 (1976) 187-213.

Campbell, Douglas A. *The Rhetoric of Righteousness in Romans 3.21-26.* JSNT.SS 65; Sheffield: Sheffield Academic, 1992.

————. "The Meaning of ΠΙΣΤΙΣ and ΝΟΜΟΣ in Paul: A Linguistic and Structural Perspective," *JBL* 111 (1992) 85-97.

————. "Rom. 1:17 — A *Crux Interpretum* for the ΠΙΣΤΙΣ ΧΡΙΣΤΟΥ Debate," *JBL* 113 (1994) 265-85.

————. "Determining the Gospel through Rhetorical Analysis in Paul's Letter to the Roman Christians," in *Gospel in Paul: Studies on Corinthians, Galatians and Romans for Richard N. Longenecker,* ed. L. A. Jervis and P. Richardson. Sheffield: Sheffield Academic, 1994, 315-36.

————. "A Rhetorical Suggestion concerning Romans 2," in *Society of Biblical Literature Seminar Papers,* ed. E. Lovering. Atlanta: Scholars, 1995, 140-64.

————. "False Presuppositions in the ΠΙΣΤΙΣ ΧΡΙΣΤΟΥ Debate: A Response to Brian Dodd," *JBL* 116 (1997) 713-19.

————. "Natural Theology in Paul? Reading Romans 1.19-20," *IJST* 1 (1999) 231-52.

————. "Towards a New, Rhetorically Assisted Reading of Romans 3.27-4.25," in *Rhetorical Criticism and the Bible: Essays from the 1998 Florence Conference,* ed. S. E. Porter and D. L. Stamps. JSNT.SS 195; Sheffield: Sheffield Academic, 2002, 355-402.

————. "The Story of Jesus in Romans and Galatians," in *Narrative Dynamics in Paul: A Critical Assessment,* ed. B. W. Longenecker. Louisville: Westminster John Knox, 2002, 97-124.

————. *The Quest for Paul's Gospel: A Suggested Strategy.* London/New York: T. & T. Clark, 2005.

————. *The Deliverance of God: An Apocalyptic Rereading of Justification in Paul.* Grand Rapids: Eerdmans, 2009.

Campbell, William S. "Romans iii as a Key to the Structure and Thought of the Letter," *NovT* 23 (1981) 22-40.

Carras, George P. "Romans 2,1-29: A Dialogue on Jewish Ideals," *Bib* 73 (1992) 183-207.

Cavallin, Hans C. C. " 'The Righteous Shall Live by Faith': A Decisive Argument for the Traditional Interpretation," *ST* 32 (1978) 33-43.

Cerfaux, Lucien. "Abraham 'père en circoncision' des Gentils (Rom IV,12)," in *Mélanges E. Podechard. Études de sciences religieuses offertes pour son emeritat au doyen honoraire de la Faculté de Théologie de Lyon.* Lyon: Facultés catholiques, 1945, 57-62.

Cervin, Richard S. "A Note regarding the Name 'Junia(s)' in Romans 16.7," *NTS* 40 (1994) 464-70.

Chilton, Bruce D., and Jacob Neusner. "Paul and Gamaliel," *BBR* 14 (2004) 1-43 (esp. 41-42 on Rom 12:1-2).

Christoffersson, Olle. *Earnest Expectation of the Creature: The Flood-Tradition as Matrix of Romans 8:18-27.* CBNT 23; Stockholm: Almqvist & Wiksell, 1990.

Clements, R. E. " 'A Remnant Chosen by Grace' (Romans 11:5)," in *Pauline Studies: FS F. F. Bruce,* ed. D. A. Hagner and M. J. Harris. Exeter: Paternoster, 1980, 106-21.

Conzelmann, Hans. "Paulus und die Weisheit," *NTS* 12 (1966) 231-44.

————. "Die Rechtfertigungslehre des Paulus. Theologie oder Anthropologie?" *EvT* 28 (1968) 389-404.

————. "Current Problems in Pauline Research," *Int* 22 (1968) 171-86.

Corrigan, Gregory M. "Paul's Shame for the Gospel," *BTB* 16 (1986) 23-27.

Corsani, B. "*Ek pisteos* in the Letters of Paul," in *The New Testament Age: Essays in Honor of Bo Reicke,* 2 vols., ed. W. C. Weinrich. Macon: Mercer University Press, 1984, 1.87-93.

Cosby, Michael R. "Paul's Persuasive Language in Romans 5," in *Persuasive Artistry: Studies in New Testament Rhetoric in Honor of George A. Kennedy,* ed. D. F. Watson. JSNT.SS 50; Sheffield: Sheffield Academic, 1991, 209-26.

Cosgrove, Charles H. "Justification in Paul: A Linguistic and Theological Reflection," *JBL* 106 (1981) 653-70.

————. "What If Some Have Not Believed? The Occasion and Thrust of Romans 3.1-8," *ZNW* 78 (1987) 90-105.

Cranfield, Charles E. B. "Some Observations on Romans 13:1-7," *NTS* 6 (1959-60) 241-49.

————. "The Christian's Political Responsibility according to the New Testament," *SJT* 15 (1962) 176-92.

————. *A Commentary on Romans 12–13.* SJT Occasional Papers; Edinburgh: Oliver & Boyd, 1965.

————. "Romans 8.28," *SJT* 19 (1966) 204-15.

————. "On Some of the Problems in the Interpretation of Rom 5:12," *SJT* 22 (1969): 324-41.

————. "Some Observations on Romans 8.19-21," in *Reconciliation and Hope: New Testament Essays on Atonement and Eschatology Presented to L. L. Morris on His 60th Birthday,* ed. R. Banks. Grand Rapids: Eerdmans, 1974, 224-30.

————. "Some Notes on Romans 9.30-33," in *Jesus und Paulus. Festschrift für Werner Georg Kümmel zum 70. Geburtstag,* ed. E. E. Ellis and E. Grässer. Göttingen: Vandenhoeck & Ruprecht, 1975, 35-43.

————. *On Romans: And Other New Testament Essays.* Edinburgh: T. & T. Clark, 1998.

————. "On the Πίστις Χριστοῦ Question," in his *On Romans and Other New Testament Essays,* 81-97.

Cremer, A. H. *Die Paulinische Rechtfertigungslehre.* Gütersloh: Bertelsmann, 1900.

Cullmann, Oscar. *The Earliest Christian Confessions,* trans. J. K. S. Reid. London: Lutterworth, 1949.

————. *Christ and Time: The Primitive Christian Conception of Time and History,* trans. F. V. Filson. Philadelphia: Westminster, 1950; London: SCM, 1951.

————. *The State in the New Testament.* New York: Scribners, 1956; London: SCM, 1957, 50-70 and 93-114.

————. *The Christology of the New Testament,* trans. S. C. Guthrie and C. A. M. Hall. Philadelphia: Westminster, 1959.

Dahl, Nils A. "Der Name Israel: Zur Auslegung von Gal 6, 16," *Judaica* 6 (1950) 161-70.

————. "Two Notes on Romans 5," *ST* 5 (1951) 37-48.

————. "The People of God," *ER* 9 (1957): 53-59.

————. "The Atonement — An Adequate Reward for the Akedah? (Ro 8:32)," in *Neotestamentica et Semitica: Studies in Honour of Matthew Black,* ed. E. E. Ellis and M. Wilcox. Edinburgh: T. & T. Clark, 1969, 15-29.

————. *Studies in Paul: Theology for the Early Christian Mission.* Minneapolis: Augsburg, 1977.

———. "The Missionary Theology in the Epistle to the Romans," Appendix II: "The Argument in Romans 5:12-21," in his *Studies in Paul,* 70-91.

———. "A Synopsis of Romans 5:1-11 and 8:1-39," in his *Studies in Paul,* Appendix I, 88-90.

———. "The Future of Israel," in his *Studies in Paul,* 137-58.

———. "The One God of Jews and Gentiles (Romans 3.29-30)," in his *Studies in Paul,* 178-91.

———. "Romans 3.9: Text and Meaning," in *Paul and Paulinism: Essays in Honour of C. K. Barrett,* ed. M. D. Hooker and S. G. Wilson. London: SPCK, 1982, 184-204.

Dalman, Gustav H. *The Words of Jesus,* trans. D. M. Kay. Edinburgh: T. & T. Clark, 1909.

Dalton, W. J. "Expiation or Propitiation? (Rom iii.25)," *ABR* 8 (1960) 3-18.

Daly, R. J. "The Soteriological Significance of the Sacrifice of Isaac," *CBQ* 39 (1977) 67.

Danker, Frederick W. "Rom 5:12: Sin under Law," *NTS* 14 (1968) 424-39.

Daube, David. *The New Testament and Rabbinic Judaism.* Jordan Lectures 1952; London: University of London / Athone, 1956.

Davies, Glenn N. *Faith and Obedience in Romans: A Study in Romans 1-4.* JSNT.SS 39; Sheffield: JSOT, 1990.

Davies, P. R., and Bruce D. Chilton. "The Aqedah: A Revised Tradition History," *CBQ* 40 (1978) 514-46.

Davies, William David. "Paul and the Dead Sea Scrolls: Flesh and Spirit," in *The Scrolls and the New Testament,* ed. K. Stendahl. New York: Harper, 1957, 157-82.

———. *Paul and Rabbinic Judaism: Some Rabbinic Elements in Pauline Theology.* London: SPCK, 1958.

———. "Paul and the People of Israel," *NTS* 16 (1969) 4-39.

———. "Abraham and the Promise," in his *The Gospel and the Land: Early Christianity and Jewish Territorial Doctrine.* Los Angeles: University of California, 1974, 168-79.

Deichgräber, Reinhard. *Gotteshymnus und Christushymnus in der frühen Christenheit.* SUNT 5; Göttingen: Vandenhoeck & Ruprecht, 1967.

Deissmann, Adolf. *Die neutestamentliche Formel "In Christo Jesu."* Marburg: Elwert, 1892.

———. *Bible Studies, Contributions Chiefly from Papyri and Inscriptions to the History of the Language, the Literature, and the Religion of Hellenistic Judaism and Primitive Christianity,* trans. A. Grieve. Edinburgh: T. & T. Clark, 1901.

———. "ΙΛΑΣΤΗΡΙΟΣ und ΙΛΑΣΤΗΡΙΟΝ. Eine lexikalische Studie," *ZNW* 4 (1903) 193-212.

———. *Paul: A Study in Social and Religious History,* trans. W. E. Wilson. New York: Harper, 1912, 2nd ed. 1927.

———. *The Religion of Jesus and the Faith of Paul,* trans. W. E. Wilson. London: Hodder & Stoughton, 1923.

———. *Light from the Ancient East: The New Testament Illustrated by Recently Discovered Texts of the Graeco-Roman World,* trans. L. R. M. Strachan. London: Hodder & Stoughton, 1927.

Delling, Gerhard. *Römer 13:1-7 innerhalb der Briefe des Neuen Testaments.* Berlin: Evangelische, 1962.

———. "ἀπαρχή," *TDNT* 1.484-86.

Denney, James. *The Christian Doctrine of Reconciliation.* London: Hodder & Stoughton, 1917.

Derrett, J. Duncan M. "'You Abominate False Gods; But Do You Rob Shrines?' (Rom 2:22b)," *NTS* 40 (1994) 558-71.

Dockery, David S. "The Use of Hab. 2:4 in Rom. 1:17: Some Hermeneutical and Theological Considerations," *WTJ* 22 (1987) 24-36.

Dodd, Brian. "Romans 1:17 — A *Crux Interpretum* for the Πίστις Χριστοῦ Debate?" *JBL* 114 (1995) 470-73.

Dodd, Charles H. "'Ιλάσκεσθαι: Its Cognates, Derivatives and Synonyms in the Septuagint," *JTS* 32 (1931) 352-60; repr. in his *The Bible and the Greeks*. London: Hodder & Stoughton, 1935, 82-95.

——. *Gospel and Law*. Cambridge: Cambridge University Press, 1951.

——. *According to the Scriptures: The Sub-Structure of New Testament Theology*. London: Nisbet, 1952.

——. "Natural Law in the New Testament," in his *New Testament Studies*. Manchester: Manchester University Press, 1953, 129-42.

Doeve, J. W. "Some Notes with Reference to τὰ λόγια τοῦ θεοῦ in Romans 3.2," in *Studia Paulina in honorem Johannis de Zwaan Septuagenarii*, ed. J. N. Sevenster and W. C. van Unnik. Haarlem: Bohn, 1953, 111-23.

Donaldson, Terence L. "Zealot and Convert: The Origin of Paul's Christ-Torah Antithesis," *CBQ* 51 (1989) 655-82.

——. "'Riches for the Gentiles' (Rom 11:12): Israel's Rejection and Paul's Gentile Mission," *JBL* 112 (1993) 81-98.

——. *Paul and the Gentiles: Remapping the Apostle's Convictional World*. Minneapolis: Fortress, 1997.

Donfried, Karl P. "A Short Note on Romans 16," *JBL* 89 (1970), 441-49; repr. in Donfried, ed., *Romans Debate* 1977, 50-60.

——. "Justification and Last Judgment in Paul," *Int* 30 (1976) 140-52.

——, ed. *The Romans Debate*. Minneapolis: Augsburg, 1977; rev. ed. *The Romans Debate: Revised and Expanded Edition*, Peabody: Hendrickson, 1991.

——. "Romans 3:21-28," *Int* 34 (1980) 59-64.

Doty, William G. *Letters in Primitive Christianity*. Philadelphia: Fortress, 1973.

Doughty, Darrell J. "The Priority of ΧΑΡΙΣ: An Investigation of the Theological Language of Paul," *NTS* 19 (1973) 163-80.

Dresner, Samuel H. "Homosexuality and the Order of Creation," *Judaism* 40 (1991) 309-21.

Driessen, E. "'Secundum evangelium meum' (Rom 2,16; 16,25; 2 Tim 2,8)," *VD* 24 (1944) 25-32.

Dunn, James D. G. "Jesus — Flesh and Spirit: An Exposition of Rom 1.3-4," *JTS* 24 (1973) 40-68.

——. "The New Perspective on Paul (Manson Memorial Lecture 1982)," *BJRL* 65 (1983) 95-122.

——. "Works of the Law and the Curse of the Law (Galatians 3:10-14)," *NTS* 31 (1985) 523-42.

——. "Romans 13:1-7 — A Charter for Political Quietism?" *Ex Auditu* 2 (1986) 55-68.

——. "Paul's Knowledge of the Jesus Tradition: The Evidence of Romans," in *Christus Bezeugen. Für Wolfgang Trilling*, ed. K. Kertelge et al. Erfurter Theologische Studien 59; Leipzig: St. Benno; Freiburg: Herder, 1990, 193-207.

——. "Once More, *Pistis Christou*," in *Society of Biblical Literature 1991 Seminar Papers* 30, ed. E. H. Lovering, Jr. Atlanta: Scholars, 1991, 730-44.

——. "Yet Once More — 'The Works of the Law,'" *JSNT* 46 (1992) 99-117.

—— "The Justice of God: A Renewed Perspective on Justification," *JTS* 43 (1992) 1-22.

—————. *The Epistle to the Galatians.* Peabody: Hendrickson, 1993.

—————. "How New Was Paul's Gospel? The Problem of Continuity and Discontinuity," in *The Road from Damascus: The Impact of Paul's Conversion on His Life, Thought, and Ministry,* ed. R. N. Longenecker. MNTS; Grand Rapids: Eerdmans, 1997, 85-101.

—————. "Spirit Speech: Reflections on Romans 8:12-27," in *Romans and the People of God: Essays in Honor of Gordon D. Fee on the Occasion of His 65th Birthday,* ed. S. K. Soderlund and N. T. Wright. Grand Rapids: Eerdmans, 1999, 82-91.

—————. *The New Perspective on Paul: Collected Essays.* WUNT 185; Tübingen: Mohr Siebeck, 2005.

Dupont, Jacques. "Syneidesis," *Studia Hellenistica* 5 (1948) 119-53.

—————. "Le problème de la structure littéraire de l'Épître aux Romains," *RB* 62 (1955) 365-97.

Eichholz, Georg. "Der Ökumenische und Missionarische Horizont der Kirche. Eine exegetische Studie zu Röm 1,8-15," *EvT* 21 (1961) 15-27; repr. in his *Tradition und Interpretation. Studien zum Neuen Testament und zur Hermeneutik.* TB-NT 29; Munich: Kaiser, 1965, 85-96.

—————. *Die Theologie des Paulus im Umriss.* Neukirchen-Vluyn: Neukirchener Verlag, 1972, 189-97.

Elliott, John K. "The Language and Style of the Concluding Doxology of the Epistle to the Romans," *ZNW* 71 (1981) 124-30.

Elliott, Neil. *The Rhetoric of Romans: Argumentative Constraint and Strategy and Paul's Dialogue with Judaism.* JSNT.SS 45; Sheffield: Sheffield Academic, 1900.

—————. "Romans 13:1-7 in the Context of Imperial Propaganda," in *Paul and Empire: Religion and Power in Roman Imperial Society,* ed. R. A. Horsley. Harrisburg: Trinity, 1997, 184-204.

Ellis, E. Earle. *Paul's Use of the Old Testament.* Grand Rapids: Eerdmans, 1957.

—————. "Paul and His Co-Workers," *NTS* 17 (1971) 437-52; repr. in his *Prophecy and Hermeneutic in Early Christianity: New Testament Essays.* Grand Rapids: Eerdmans, 1978, 2-22.

Emerton, John A. "The Textual and Linguistic Problems of Habakkuk ii.4-5," *JTS* 28 (1977) 1-18.

Englezakis, B. "Rom 5:12-15 and the Pauline Teaching on the Lord's Death: Some Observations," *Bib* 58 (1977): 231-36.

Epp, Eldon J. "Jewish-Gentile Continuity in Paul: Torah and/or Faith? Romans 9:1-5," *HTR* 79 (1986) 80-90.

—————. *Junia: The First Woman Apostle.* Minneapolis: Augsburg Fortress, 2005.

Fee, Gordon D. *God's Empowering Presence: The Holy Spirit in the Letters of Paul.* Peabody: Hendrickson, 1994.

Fisher, James A. "Pauline Literary Forms and Thought Patterns," *CBQ* 39 (1977) 209-23.

Fitzer, G. "Der Ort der Versöhnung nach Paulus," *TZ* 22 (1966) 161-83.

Fitzmyer, Joseph A. "The Use of Explicit Old Testament Quotations in Qumran Literature and in the New Testament," *NTS* 7 (1961) 297-333.

—————. *Pauline Theology: A Brief Sketch.* Englewood Cliffs: Prentice-Hall, 1967, 1989.

—————. *Essays on the Semitic Background of the New Testament.* London: Chapman; Missoula: Scholars, 1971.

—————. "Reconciliation in Pauline Theology," in *No Famine in the Land: Studies in Honor of John L. MacKenzie,* ed. J. W. Flanagan and A. W. Robinson. Chico: Scholars, 1975, 155-77; repr. in his *To Advance the Gospel.* New York: Crossroad, 1981, 162-85.

————. "The Gospel in the Theology of Paul," in his *To Advance the Gospel: New Testament Studies*. New York: Crossroad, 1981, 149-61; originally published in *Interp* 33 (1979) 339-50.

————. "Habakkuk 2:3-4 and the New Testament," in his *To Advance the Gospel: New Testament Studies*. New York: Crossroad, 1981, 236-46; originally published in *De la Loi au Messie. Le développement d'une espérance. Etudes d'exégèse et d'herméneutique biblique offertes à Henri Cazelles*, ed. J. Doré and P. Grelot. Paris: Desclée, 1981, 447-57.

————. "Paul's Jewish Background and the Deeds of the Law," in his *According to Paul: Studies in the Theology of the Apostle*. New York/Mahwah/Toronto: Paulist, 1993, 18-35.

————. "The Consecutive Meaning of ἐφ' ᾧ in Romans 5.12," *NTS* 39 (1993) 321-39.

————. *Spiritual Exercises Based on Paul's Epistle to the Romans*. New York/Mahwah: Paulist, 1995.

Flückiger, Felix. "Die Werke des Gesetzes bei den Heiden (nach Röm 2,14ff.)," *TZ* 8 (1952) 17-42.

————. "Zur Unterscheidung von Heiden und Juden in Röm 1,18–2,3," *TZ* 10 (1954) 154-58.

Flusser, David, and Shmuel Safrai. "Who Sanctified the Beloved in the Womb?" *Immanuel* 11 (1980) 46-55.

Foerster, Werner. "Romans ii. 18," *ExpT* 36 (1924-25) 285.

————. "κτίζω, κτίσις," *TDNT* 3.1000-1035.

Foerster, Werner, and Georg Fohrer. "σῴζω, σωτηρία," *TDNT* 7.965-1003.

France, Richard T. "From Romans to the Real World: Biblical Principles and Cultural Change in Relation to Homosexuality and the Ministry of Women," in *Romans and the People of God: Essays in Honor of Gordon D. Fee on the Occasion of His 65th Birthday*, ed. S. K. Soderlund and N. T. Wright. Grand Rapids: Eerdmans, 1999, 234-53.

Francis, Fred, and J. P. Sampley. *Pauline Parallels*. 2nd ed., Foundations and Facets: New Testament; Philadelphia: Fortress, 1984.

Fridrichsen, Anton. "Zur Auslegung von Röm 1,19f.," *ZNW* 17 (1916) 159-68.

————. "Der wahre Jude und sein Lob. Röm. 2.28f.," in *Symbolae Arctae* I. Christiana: Erichsen, 1922, 39-49.

————. "Quatre Conjectures sur le texte du Nouveau Testament," *RHPR* 3 (1923) 349-42.

————. "Exegetisches zu den Paulusbriefen," *TSK* 102 (1930) 291-301 (esp. 291-94).

————. "Nochmals Römer 3,7-8," *ZNW* 34 (1935) 306-8.

————. *The Apostle and His Message*. Uppsala: Landequistaka bokhandeln, 1947.

————. "Aus Glauben zum Glauben, Röm 1,17," in *Walter Bauer Gottingensi Novi Testamenti philologia optime merito sacrum*. CBNT 12; Lund: Gleerup, 1948, 54.

Friedrich, Gerhard. "Das Gesetz des Glaubens. Römer 3,27," *TZ* 10 (1954) 401-17.

————. "Muss ὑπακοὴν πίστεως (Röm 1.5) mit 'Glaubensgehorsam' übersetzt werden?" *ZNW* 72 (1981) 118-23.

————. "εὐαγγελίζομαι, εὐαγγέλιον," *TDNT* 2.707-37.

Friedrich, Johannes, Wolfgang Pöhlmann, and Peter Stuhlmacher. "Zur historischen Situation und Intention von Röm 13,1-7," *ZTK* 73 (1976) 131-66.

Fuchs, Ernst. *Die Freiheit des Glaubens. Römer 5–8 ausgelegt*. BEvT 14; Munich: Kaiser, 1949.

————. "Jesu und der Glaube," *ZTK* 55 (1958) 170-85.

———. "Die Spannung im neutestamentlichen Christusglauben," *ZTK* 59 (1962) 32-45.

Fuller, Daniel P. "Paul and 'the Works of the Law,' " *WTJ* 38 (1975) 28-42.

Funk, Robert W. "The 'Apostolic Parousia': Form and Significance," in *Christian History and Interpretation: Studies Presented to John Knox,* ed. W. R. Farmer, C. F. D. Moule, and R. R. Niebuhr. Cambridge: Cambridge University Press, 1967, 249-68.

Furnish, Victor P. "The Jesus-Paul Debate: From Baur to Bultmann," *BJRL* 47 (1965) 342-81.

———. *Theology and Ethics in Paul.* New York: Abingdon, 1968.

Gager, John G. "Functional Diversity in Paul's Use of End-Time Language," *JBL* 89 (1970) 325-37.

Gagnon, Robert A. J. "Heart of Wax and a Teaching That Stamps: ΤΥΠΟΣ ΔΙΔΑΧΗΣ (Rom 6:17b) Once More," *JBL* 112 (1994), 667-87.

———. *The Bible and Homosexual Practice: Texts and Hermeneutics.* Nashville: Abingdon, 2001.

Gale, Herbert M. "Paul's View of State: A Discussion of the Problem in Romans 13,1-7," *Int* 6 (1952) 409-14.

Gamble, Harry, Jr. *The Textual History of the Letter to the Romans: A Study in Textual and Literary Criticism.* SD 42; Grand Rapids: Eerdmans, 1977.

Garlington, Don B. "The Obedience of Faith in the Letter to the Romans, Part I: The Meaning of ὑπακοὴ πίστεως (Rom 1:5; 16:26)," *WTJ* 52 (1990) 201-24.

———. "ΙΕΡΟΣΥΛΕΙΝ and the Idolatry of Israel (Romans 2.22)," *NTS* 36 (1990) 142-51.

———. *"The Obedience of Faith": A Pauline Phrase in Historical Context.* WUNT 2.8; Tübingen: Mohr Siebeck, 1991.

———. *Faith, Obedience, and Perseverance: Aspects of Paul's Letter to the Romans.* WUNT 2.79; Tübingen: Mohr Siebeck, 1994.

Garnet, Paul. "Atonement Constructions in the Old Testament and the Qumran Scrolls," *EvQ* 46 (1974) 131-63.

Gaston, Lloyd. "Abraham and the Righteousness of God," *HBT* 2 (1980) 39-68; repr. in his *Paul and the Torah.* Vancouver: University of British Columbia Press, 1987, 45-63.

———. "Works of Law as a Subjective Genitive," *SR* 13 (1984) 39-46.

———. *Paul and the Torah.* Vancouver: University of British Columbia Press, 1987.

Gerber, Uwe. "Röm viii.18ff as exegetisches Problem der Dogmatik," *NovT* 8 (1966) 58-81.

Gibbs, John G. *Creation and Redemption: A Study in Pauline Theology.* VTSup 26; Leiden: Brill, 1971.

———. "Pauline Cosmic Christology and Ecological Crisis," *JBL* 90 (1971) 466-79.

Goodenough, Erwin R. *By Light, Light: The Mystic Gospel of Hellenistic Judaism.* New Haven: Yale University Press, 1935.

Goppelt, Leonhard. "Der Missionar des Gesetzes (zu Röm 2, 21f.)," in *Basileia. Walter Freytag (Festschrift).* Wuppertal-Barmen: Rheinische Missionsgesellschaft, 1959, 199-207; repr. in his *Christologie und Ethik: Aufsätze zum Neuen Testament.* Göttingen: Vandenhoeck & Ruprecht, 1968, 137-46.

———. "Paul and *Heilsgeschichte*: Conclusions from Romans 4 and I Corinthians 10:1-13," trans. M. Rissi, *Int* 21 (1967) 315-326; ET from "Paulus und die Heilsgeschichte. Schlussfolgerungen aus Röm 4 und 1 Kor 10:1-13," *NTS* 13 (1966) 31-42, which was repr. in his *Christologie und Ethik. Aufsätze zum Neuen Testament.* Göttingen: Vandenhoeck & Ruprecht, 1968, 220-33.

———. "Versöhnung durch Christus," in his *Christologie und Ethik. Aufsätze zum Neuen Testament.* Göttingen: Vandenhoeck & Ruprecht, 1968, 147-64.

———. "Die Freiheit zur Kaisersteuer: Zu Mk. 12,17 und Röm. 13,1-7," in his *Christologie und Ethik. Aufsätze zum Neuen Testament.* Göttingen: Vandenhoeck & Ruprecht, 1968, 208-19.

———. "Apocalypticism and Typology in Paul," in his *Typos: The Typological Interpretation of the Old Testament in the New,* trans. D. H. Madvig. Grand Rapids: Eerdmans, 1982, 209-37.

Grayston, Kenneth. " 'Not Ashamed of the Gospel': Romans 1:16a and the Structure of the Epistle," *Studia Evangelica* 2.1, ed. F. L. Cross. Berlin: Akademie Verlag, 1964, 569-73.

———. "*Hilaskesthai* and Related Words in the LXX," *NTS* 27 (1981) 640-56.

Grobel, Kendrick. "A Chiastic Retribution Formula in Romans 2," in *Zeit und Geschichte. Dankesgabe an R. Bultmann zum 80. Geburtstag,* ed. E. Dinkler. Tübingen: Mohr Siebeck, 1964, 255-61.

Grundmann, Walter. "The Teacher of Righteousness of Qumran and the Question of Justification by Faith in the Theology of the Apostle Paul," in *Paul and Qumran,* ed. J. Murphy-O'Connor. London: Chapman, 1968, 85-115.

———. "ἁμαρτάνω, ἁμάρτημα, ἁμαρτία," *TDNT* 1.308-13 (on Paul).

———. "δύναμαι, δύναμις," *TDNT* 2.284-317.

Guerra, Anthony J. *Romans and the Apologetic Tradition: The Purpose, Genre and Audience of Paul's Letter.* SNTS.MS 81; Cambridge: Cambridge University Press, 1995.

Gülzow, Henneke. *Christentum und Sklaverei in den ersten drei Jahrhunderten.* Bonn: Habelt, 1969.

Haacker, Klaus. "Das Evangelium Gottes und die Erwählung Israels. Zum Beitrag des Römerbriefs zur Erneuerung des Verhältnisses zwischen Christen und Juden," *TBei* 13 (1982) 59-72.

———. *The Theology of Paul's Letter to the Romans.* New York: Cambridge University Press, 2003.

Hahn, Ferdinand. *The Titles of Jesus in Christology: Their History in Early Christianity,* trans. H. Knight and G. Ogg. London: Lutterworth; New York: World, 1969.

———. "Genesis 15:6 im Neuen Testament," in *Probleme biblischer Theologie* (FS G. von Rad), ed. H. W. Wolff. Munich: Kaiser, 1971, 90-107.

———. " 'Siehe, jetzt ist der Tag des Heils.' Neuschöpfung und Versöhnung nach 2.Korinther 5,14–6.2," *EvT* 33 (1973) 247.

Hahne, Harry A. "The Corruption and Redemption of Creation: An Exegetical Study of Romans 8:19-22 in Light of Jewish Apocalyptic Literature." Th.D. Dissertation, Wycliffe College, Toronto School of Theology, 1997.

Hall, David R. "Romans 3.1-8 Reconsidered," *NTS* 29 (1983) 183-97.

Hanson, Anthony T. *Paul's Understanding of Jesus: Invention or Interpretation?* Hull: University of Hull Publications, 1963.

———. *Studies in Paul's Technique and Theology.* London: SPCK, 1974.

———. "Abraham the Justified Sinner," in his *Studies in Paul's Technique and Theology,* 52-66.

Harder, Günther. *Paulus und das Gebet.* Gütersloh: Bertelsmann, 1936 (esp. 51-58).

Harnack, Adolf. "Zu Röm 1,7," *ZNW* 3 (1902) 83-86.

———. *Marcion. Das Evangelium vom fremden Gott.* TU 45; Leipzig: Hinrichs, 1921.

Harrelson, Walter. *Interpreting the Old Testament.* New York: Holt, Rinehart & Winston, 1964.

Harris, B. F. "Συνείδησις (Conscience) in the Pauline Writings," *WTJ* 24 (1962) 173-86.

Harris, Murray J. *Jesus as God: The New Testament Use of Theos in Reference to Jesus*. Grand Rapids: Baker, 1992, esp. 143-72.

Harrisville, Roy A. *The Figure of Abraham in the Epistles of St. Paul: In the Footsteps of Abraham*. San Francisco: Mellen, 1992.

———. "ΠΙΣΤΙΣ ΧΡΙΣΤΟΥ: Witness of the Fathers," *NovT* 36 (1994) 233-41.

Hatch, W. H. P. "A Recently Discovered Fragment of the Epistle to the Romans," *HTR* 45 (1952) 81-85.

Hauck, Friedrich. "ὀφείλω," *TDNT* 5.559-64.

Haussleiter, Johannes. "Der Glaube Jesu Christi und der christliche Glaube. Ein Beitrag zur Eklärung des Römerbriefes," *NKZ* 2 (1891) 109-45, 205-30.

———. *Der Glaube Jesu Christi und der christliche Glaube. Ein Beitrag zur Erklärung des Römerbriefes*. Erlangen/Leipzig: Deichert, 1891 (monograph form of 1891 article).

———. "Eine theologische Disputation unter den Glauben Jesu," *NKZ* 3 (1892) 507-20.

———. "Was versteht Paulus unter christlichen Glauben?" *NKZ* 6 (1895) 159-81; repr. in *Theologische Abhandlungen Hermann Cremer dargebracht*. Gütersloh: Bertelsmann, 1895, 159-81.

Hay, David M. "*Pistis* as 'Ground for Faith' in Hellenized Judaism and Paul," *JBL* 108 (1989) 461-76.

Hays, Richard B. "The Role of Scripture in Paul's Ethics," in *Theology and Ethics in Paul and His Interpreters: Essays in Honor of Victor Paul Furnish*, ed. E. H. Lovering, Jr., and J. L. Sumney. Nashville: Abingdon, 1966, 30-47.

———. "Psalm 143 and the Logic of Romans 3," *JBL* 99 (1980) 107-15.

———. *The Faith of Jesus Christ: An Investigation of the Narrative Substructure of Galatians 3:1–4:11*. SBL.DS 56; Chico: Scholars, 1983.

———. " 'Have We Found Abraham to Be Our Forefather according to the Flesh?' A Reconsideration of Rom 4:1," *NovT* 27 (1985) 76-98.

———. "Relations Natural and Unnatural: A Response to John Boswell's Exegesis of Romans 1," *JRE* 14 (1986) 184-215.

———. " 'The Righteous One' as Eschatological Deliverer: A Case Study in Paul's Apocalyptic Hermeneutics," in *Apocalyptic and the New Testament: Essays in Honor of J. Louis Martyn,* ed. J. Marcus and M. L. Soards. JSNT.SS 24; Sheffield: JSOT, 1989, 191-215.

———. *Echoes of Scripture in the Letters of Paul*. New Haven/London: Yale University Press, 1989.

———. *The Moral Vision of the New Testament*. San Francisco: Harper, 1996.

———. "ΠΙΣΤΙΣ and the Pauline Christology: What Is at Stake?" in *Pauline Theology* vol. 4: *Looking Back, Pressing On,* ed. E. E. Johnson and D. Hay. Atlanta: Scholars, 1997, 35-60.

Hebert, A. Gabriel. " 'Faithfulness' and 'Faith,' " *Theology* 58 (1955) 373-79.

Heiligenthal, Roman. *Werke als Zeichen. Untersuchungen zur Bedeutung der menschlichen Taten im Frühjudentum, Neuen Testament und Frühchristentum*. WUNT 2; Tübingen: Mohr Siebeck, 1983, 165-97.

Hengel, Martin. "Der Kreuzestod Jesu Christi als Gottes souveräne Erlösungstate. Exegese über 2.Korinther 5,11-21," in *Theologie und Kirche. Reichenau-Gespräch der Evangelischen Landessynode Würtenburg*. Stuttgart: Calver, 1967.

———. *The Son of God: The Origin of Christology and the History of Jewish-Hellenistic Religion,* trans. J. Bowden. London: SCM; Philadelphia: Fortress, 1976.

———. "Erwägungen zum Sprachgebrauch von Χριστός bei Paulus und in der 'vorpaulinischen' Überlieferung," in *Paul and Paulinism: Essays in Honour of C. K. Barrett,* ed. M. D. Hooker and S. G. Wilson. London: SPCK, 1982, 135-59.

Herold, Gerhart. *Zorn und Gerechtigkeit Gottes bei Paulus. Eine Untersuchung zu Röm. 1,16-18.* Bern: Lang, 1973.

Hill, David. *Greek Words and Hebrew Meanings: Studies in the Semantics of Soteriological Terms.* Cambridge: Cambridge University Press, 1967.

———. "The Interpretation of ἱλάσκεσθαι and Related Words in the Septuagint and in the New Testament," in his *Greek Words and Hebrew Meanings,* 23-48.

———. "The Background and Usage of λύτρον and Cognate Words in Biblical Greek," in his *Greek Words and Hebrew Meanings,* 49-81.

———. "The Background and Meaning of δικαιοσύνη and Cognate Words," in his *Greek Words and Hebrew Meanings,* 82-162.

———. "The Background and Biblical Usage of ζωή and ζωή αἰώνιος," in his *Greek Words and Hebrew Meanings,* 163-201.

———. "Liberation through God's Righteousness," *IBS* 4 (1982) 31-44.

Hirzel, Rudolf. *Agraphos Nomos.* Stuttgart: Teubner, 1900; repr. Hildesheim: Gerstenberg, 1979.

Holmberg, Bengt. *Paul and Power: The Structure of Authority in the Primitive Church as Reflected in the Pauline Epistles.* Lund: Gleerup, 1978; Philadelphia: Fortress, 1980.

Hommel, Hildebrecht. "Das Harren der Kreatur," in *Schöpfer und Erhalter. Studien zum Problem Christentum und Antike,* ed. H. Hommel. Berlin: Lettner, 1956, 7-23.

———. "Das 7 Kapitel des Römerbriefs im Licht Antiker Überlieferung," *TV* 8 (1961) 90-116; repr. with additions in his *Sebasmata. Studien zur antiken Religionsgeschichte und zum frühen Christentum,* 2 vols. Tübingen: Mohr Siebeck (1983-84), 2.141-73.

Hooke, Sidney H. "The Translation of Romans 1.4," *NTS* 9 (1963) 370-71.

Hooker, Morna D. "Adam in Romans 1," *NTS* 6 (1960) 297-306.

———. "A Further Note on Romans 1," *NTS* 13 (1967) 181-83.

———. "ΠΙΣΤΙΣ ΧΡΙΣΤΟΥ," *NTS* 35 (1989) 321-42.

———. *From Adam to Christ: Essays on Paul.* Cambridge: Cambridge University Press, 1990.

Hort, Fenton J. A. "On the End of the Epistle to the Romans," *JP* 3 (1871) 51-80; repr. in J. B. Lightfoot, *Biblical Essays.* London: Macmillan, 1893; Grand Rapids: Baker, 1979, 321-51.

Howard, George E. "On the 'Faith of Christ,'" *HTR* 60 (1967) 459-65.

———. "Rom 3:21-31 and the Inclusion of the Gentiles," *HTR* 63 (1970) 223-33.

———. "The 'Faith of Christ,'" *ExpT* 85 (1974) 212-15.

———. *Paul: Crisis in Galatia. A Study in Early Christian Theology.* SNTS.MS 35; Cambridge: Cambridge University Press, 1979, 57-59 and 95, n. 191.

Hübner, Hans. *Law in Paul's Thought,* trans. J. C. G. Grieg. Edinburgh: T. & T. Clark, 1984, esp. 51-57, 79-80, 118-23.

———. "Was heisst bei Paulus 'Werke des Gesetzes'?" in *Glaube und Eschatologie. Festschrift für Werner George Kümmel,* ed. E. Grässer and O. Merk. Tübingen: Mohr Siebeck, 1985, 123-33.

Huggins, Ronald V. "Alleged Classical Parallels to Paul's 'What I Want to Do I Do Not Do, but What I Hate, That I Do' (Rom 7:15)," *WTJ* 54 (1992) 153-61.

Hultgren, Arland J. "Reflections on Romans 13:1-7: Submission to Governing Authorities," *Dialog* 15 (1976) 263-69.

———. "The Πίστις Χριστου Formulation in Paul," *NovT* 22 (1980) 248-63.

————. *Paul's Gospel and Mission: The Outlook from His Letter to the Romans.* Philadelphia: Fortress, 1985.

Hurtado, Larry W. "The Doxology at the End of Romans," in *New Testament Textual Criticism: Its Significance for Exegesis (Essays in Honour of Bruce M. Metzger),* ed. E. J. Epp and G. D. Fee. Oxford: Clarendon, 1981, 185-99.

————. "Jesus' Divine Sonship in Paul's Epistle to the Romans," in *Romans and the People of God: Essays in Honor of Gordon D. Fee on the Occasion of His 65th Birthday,* ed. S. K. Soderlund and N. T. Wright. Grand Rapids: Eerdmans, 1999, 217-33.

————. *Lord Jesus Christ: Devotion to Jesus in Earliest Christianity.* Grand Rapids: Eerdmans, 2003.

Hvalvik, R. "A 'Sonderweg' for Israel: A Critical Examination of a Current Interpretation of Romans 11:25-27," *JSNT* 38 (1990) 87-107.

Ito, A., "Romans 2: A Deuteronomist Reading," *JSNT* 59 (1995) 33-34.

Jeremias, Joachim. "Zur Gedankenführung in den paulinischen Briefen," in *Studia Paulina in honorem Johannis de Zwaan Septuagenarii,* ed. J. N. Sevenster and W. C. van Unnik. Haarlem: Bohn, 1953, 146-53 (esp. 146-49).

————. "Chiasmus in den Paulusbriefen," *ZNW* 49 (1958) 145-56 (esp. 154-55).

————. *The Central Message of the New Testament.* London: SCM; New York: Scribner's, 1965.

————. *Abba. Studien zur neutestamentlichen Theologie und Zeitgeschichte.* Göttingen: Vandenhoeck & Ruprecht, 1966 (esp. 15-67 and 290-92).

————. "λίθος," *TDNT* 4.268-83 (esp. his section on "Christ as λίθος," 271-79).

————. *Jerusalem in the Time of Jesus.* London: SCM; Philadelphia: Fortress, 1969.

————. "Die Gedankenführung in Röm 4. Zum paulinischen Glaubensverständnis," in his *Foi et Salut selon S. Paul.* AnBib 42; Rome: Biblical Institute, 1970, 51-58.

Jervis, L. Ann. *The Purpose of Romans: A Comparative Letter Structure Investigation.* Sheffield: Sheffield Academic, 1991.

————. " 'The Commandment Which Is for Life' (Romans 7,10): Sin's Use of the Obedience of Faith," *JSNT* 27 (2004) 193-216.

Jewett, Robert. *Paul's Anthropological Terms: A Study of Their Use in Conflict Settings.* Leiden: Brill, 1971.

————. "Romans as an Ambassadorial Letter," *Int* 36 (1982) 5-20.

————. "The Redaction and Use of an Early Christian Confession in Romans 1:3-4," in *The Living Bible Text: Essays in Honor of Ernest W. Saunders,* ed. R. Jewett and D. E. Groh. Washington: University Press of America, 1985, 99-122.

————. "The Law and the Coexistence of Jews and Gentiles in Romans," *Int* 39 (1985) 341-56.

————. "Ecumenical Theology for the Sake of Mission: Romans 1:1-7 — 15:14–16:24," in *Pauline Theology* vol. 3: *Romans,* ed. D. M. Hay and E. E. Johnson. Minneapolis: Fortress, 1995, 89-108.

Johnson, Alan F. "Is There a Biblical Warrant for Natural-Law Theories?" *JETS* 25 (1982) 185-99.

Johnson, Luke Timothy. "Romans 3:21-26 and the Faith of Jesus," *CBQ* 44 (1982) 77-90.

————. "Transformation of the Mind and Moral Discernment in Paul," in *Early Christianity and Classical Culture: Comparative Studies in Honor of Abraham J. Malherbe,* ed. J. T. Fitzgerald, T. H. Olbricht, and L. M. White. NovTSup 110; Leiden: Brill, 2003, 215-36.

Johnson, S. Lewis. "Romans 5:12 — An Exercise in Exegesis and Theology," in *New Di-*

mensions in New Testament Study, ed. R. N. Longenecker and M. C. Tenney. Grand Rapids: Zondervan, 1974, 298-316.

Judge, Edwin A. "Paul's Boasting in Relation to Contemporary Professional Practice," *ABR* 16 (1968) 37-50.

Kähler, Martin. "Auslegung von Kap. 2,14-16 im Römerbrief," *TSK* 47 (1874) 261-306.

Kampen, John, and Moshe J. Bernstein, eds. *Reading 4QMMT: New Perspectives on Qumran Law and History.* Atlanta: Scholars, 1996.

Käsemann, Ernst. "Zum Verständnis von Röm 3,24-26," *ZNW* 43 (1950-51) 150-54; repr. in his *Exegetische Versuche und Besinnungen,* 2 vols. Göttingen: Vandenhoeck & Ruprecht, 1960, 1.96-100.

———. "Römer 13,1-7 in unserer Generation," *ZTK* (1959) 316-76.

———. *New Testament Questions of Today,* trans. W. J. Montague. London: SCM; Philadelphia: Fortress, 1969.

———. "'The Righteousness of God' in Paul," in his *New Testament Questions of Today,* 168-82.

———. "Paul and Israel," in his *New Testament Questions for Today,* 183-87.

———. "Worship in Everyday Life: A Note on Romans 12," in his *New Testament Questions for Today,* 188-95.

———. "Principles for the Interpretation of Romans 13," in his *New Testament Questions for Today,* 196-216.

———. "Some Thoughts on the Theme 'The Doctrine of Reconciliation in the New Testament,'" in *The Future of Our Religious Past: Essays in Honour of Rudolf Bultmann,* ed. J. M. Robinson. London: SCM; New York: Harper & Row, 1971, 49-64.

———. *Perspectives on Paul,* trans. M. Kohl. London: SCM; Philadelphia: Fortress, 1971.

———. "Justification and Salvation History in the Epistle to the Romans," in his *Perspectives on Paul,* 60-78.

———. "The Faith of Abraham in Romans 4," in his *Perspectives on Paul,* 79-101.

———. "The Cry for Liberty in the Worship of the Church," in his *Perspectives on Paul,* 122-37.

Kaylor, R. David. *Paul's Covenant Community: Jew and Gentile in Romans.* Atlanta: John Knox, 1988.

Keck, Leander E. "The Poor among the Saints in the New Testament," *ZNW* 56 (1965), 100-29.

———. "'The Poor among the Saints' in Jewish Christianity and Qumran," *ZNW* 57 (1966), 54-78.

———. "The Function of Romans 3.10-18: Observations and Suggestions," in *God's Christ and His People: Studies in Honour of Nils Alstrup Dahl,* ed. J. Jervell and W. A. Meeks. Oslo: Universitetsforlaget, 1977, 141-57.

———. "The Post-Pauline Interpretation of Jesus' Death in Romans 5:6-7," in *Theologia Crucis — Signum Crucis. Festschrift für Erich E. Dinkler zum 70. Geburtstag,* ed. C. Andresen and G. Klein. Tübingen: Mohr Siebeck, 1979, 237-48.

———. "The Law and 'the Law of Sin and Death' (Rom 8:1-4): Reflections on the Spirit and Ethics in Paul," in *The Divine Helmsman: Studies on God's Control of Human Events, Presented to Lou H. Silberman,* ed. J. L. Crenshaw and S. Sandmel. New York: Ktav, 1980, 41-57.

———. "Romans 1:18-23," *Int* 40 (1986) 402-6.

Kertelge, Karl. *"Rechtfertigung" bei Paulus. Studien zur Struktur und zum Bedeutungsgehalt des paulinischen Rechtfertigungsbegriffs.* Münster: Aschendorff, 1967.

———. "Die 'Anrechnung des Glaubens zur Gerechtigheit,' " in his *"Rechtfertigung" bei Paulus*, 185-95.

———. "Das Verständnis des Todes Jesu bei Paulus," in his *Der Tod Jesu. Deutungen im Neuen Testament*. Freiburg: Herder, 1976, 114-36.

———. " 'Natürliche Theologie' und Rechtfertigung aus dem Glauben bei Paulus," in *Weisheit Gottes — Weisheit der Welt. Festschrift für Joseph Kardinal Ratzinger*, 2 vols., ed. W. Baier et al. St. Ottilien: EOS, 1987, 83-95.

———. "The Sin of Adam in the Light of Christ's Redemptive Act according to Romans 5:12-21," *Communio: International Catholic Review* 18 (1991) 502-13.

Kim, Chan-Hie. *Form and Structure of the Familiar Greek Letter of Recommendation*. SBL.DS 4; Missoula: University of Montana Press, 1972.

Kim, Seyoon. *The Origin of Paul's Gospel*. WUNT 2.4; Tübingen: Mohr Siebeck, 1981; Grand Rapids: Eerdmans, 1982.

———. *Paul and the New Perspective: Second Thoughts on the Origin of Paul's Gospel*. Grand Rapids: Eerdmans, 2002.

Kittel, Gerhard. "*Pistis Iesou Christou* bei Paulus," *TSK* 79 (1906) 419-36.

———. "Zur Erklärung von Röm 3, 21-26," *TSK* 80 (1907) 217-33.

———. "δοκέω, δόξα, δοξάζω," *TDNT* 2.232-55.

Klassen, William. "Coals of Fire: Sign of Repentance or Revenge?" *NTS* (1963) 337-50.

———. "Love Your Enemy: A Study of New Testament Teaching on Coping with an Enemy" (1975) 147-71 (esp. 161-63).

Klein, William W. "Paul's Use of *KALEIN*: A Proposal," *JETS* 27 (1984) 53-64.

Klostermann, Erich. "Die adäquate Vergeltung in Rm 1,22-31," *ZNW* 32 (1933) 1-6.

Koch, Dietrich-Alex. "Der Text von Hab 2:4b in der Septuaginta und im Neuen Testament," *ZNW* 76 (1985) 68-85.

———. *Die Schrift als Zeuge des Evangeliums. Untersuchungen zur Verwendung und zum Verständnis der Schrift bei Paulus*. Tübingen: Mohr Siebeck, 1986.

Koch, Herbert. *Römer 3,21-31 in der Paulusinterpretation der letzten 150 Jahre*. Dissertation Theologischen Fakultät, George-August-Universität zu Göttingen; Göttingen: Funke, 1971.

König, Adrio. "Gentiles or Gentile Christians? On the Meaning of Romans 2:12-16," *JTSA* 15 (1976) 53-60.

Kramer, Werner. *Christ, Lord, Son of God*, trans. B. Hardy. SBT 50; London: SCM, 1966.

Kranz, W. *"Das Gesetz des Herzens," Rheinisches Museum für Philologie* n.s. 94 (1951) 222-41.

Kruger, M. A. "TINA KARPON: 'Some Fruit' in Romans 1:13," *WTJ* 49 (1987) 167-73.

Kümmel, Werner G. *Römer 7 und die Bekehrung des Paulus*. Leipzig: Hinrichs, 1929.

———. "Πάρεσις und ἔνδειξις. Ein Beitrag zum Verständnis der paulinischen Rechtfertigungslehre," *ZTK* (1952) 154-67.

Kuss, Otto. "Die Heiden und die Werke des Gesetzes (nach Röm 2,14-16)," *MTZ* 5 (1954) 77-98; repr. in his *Auslegung und Verkündigung*, 3 vols. Regensburg: Pustet, 1963-71, 1.213-45.

———. "Die Formel 'durch Christus' in den paulinischen Hauptbriefen," *TTZ* 62 (1956) 193-201.

Lake, Kirsopp. *The Earlier Epistles of St. Paul*. London: Christophers, 1934.

Lambrecht, Jan. "Why Is Boasting Excluded? A Note on Romans 3,27 and 4,2," *ETL* 61 (1985) 365-69.

———. "Righteousness in the Bible and Justice in the World," *TEvan* 27 (1988) 6-13.

————. "Paul's Logic in Rom 3.29-30," *JBL* 119 (2000) 526-28.

Lambrecht, Jan, and Richard W. Thompson. *Justification by Faith: The Implications of Romans 3:27-31.* Wilmington: Glazier, 1989.

Lampe, Peter. "Zur Textgeschichte des Römerbriefes," *NovT* 27 (1985) 273-77.

le Déaut, R. "La présentation targumique du sacrifice d'Isaac et la soteriologie pauliniene," in *Studiorum Paulinorum congressus internationalis catholicus,* 2 vols. AnBib 17-18; Rome: Biblical Institute, 1963, 2.563-74.

Levinson, N. *"Lutron," SJT* 12 (1959) 277-85.

Levison, John R. *Portraits of Adam in Early Judaism: From Sirach to 2 Baruch.* Sheffield: JOTS, 1988.

Lewis, Edwin. "A Christian Theodicy: An Exposition of Romans 8:18-30," *Int* 11 (1957) 405-20.

Lightfoot, Joseph B. "The Name and Office of an Apostle," in his *Saint Paul's Epistle to the Galatians.* London: Macmillan, 1865; 10th ed. 1890, 92-101.

Lillie, W. "Natural Law and the New Testament," in his *Studies in New Testament Ethics.* Edinburgh/London: Oliver & Boyd, 1961, 12-23.

Lohmeyer, Ernst. "Probleme paulinischer Theologie I. Briefliche Grussüberschriften," *ZNW* 26 (1927) 158-73.

————. "Probleme paulinischer Theologie II. 'Gesetzwerke,' " *ZNW* 28 (1929) 177-207.

Lohse, Eduard. "Ursprung und Prägung des christlichen Apostolates," *TZ* 9 (1953) 259-75.

————. *Märtyrer und Gottesknecht. Untersuchungen zur urchristlichen Verkündigung vom Sühntod Jesu Christi.* 2nd ed., FRLANT 64; Göttingen: Vandenhoeck & Ruprecht, 1963, esp. 149-54.

Loisy, Alfred. "The Christian Mystery," *HibJ* 10 (1911) 50-64.

Longenecker, Bruce W. *Eschatology and the Covenant: A Comparison of 4 Ezra and Romans 1–11.* JSNT.SS 57; Sheffield: JSOT, 1991.

————. "Πίστις in Romans 3.25: Neglected Evidence for the 'Faithfulness of Christ'?" *NTS* 39 (1993) 478-80.

————. *The Triumph of Abraham's God: The Transformation of Identity in Galatians.* Edinburgh: T. & T. Clark, 1998, esp. 95-107.

————, ed. *Narrative Dynamics in Paul: A Critical Assessment.* Louisville: Westminster John Knox, 2002.

————. *Remember the Poor: Paul, Poverty, and the Greco-Roman World.* Grand Rapids: Eerdmans, 2010.

Longenecker, Richard N. *Paul, Apostle of Liberty.* New York: Harper & Row, 1964; repr. Grand Rapids: Baker, 1976; Vancouver: Regent, 2003.

————. *The Christology of Early Jewish Christianity.* SBT second series 17; London: SCM, 1970; repr. Grand Rapids: Baker, 1981; Vancouver: Regent, 2001.

————. "The Righteous One," in his *The Christology of Early Jewish Christianity,* 46-47.

————. "Ancient Amanuenses and the Pauline Epistles," in *New Dimensions in New Testament Study,* ed. R. N. Longenecker and M. C. Tenney. Grand Rapids: Zondervan, 1974, 281-97.

————. *Biblical Exegesis in the Apostolic Period.* Grand Rapids: Eerdmans, 1975; repr. Vancouver: Regent, 1981; 2nd rev. ed., Grand Rapids: Eerdmans, 1999.

————. "The 'Faith of Abraham' Theme in Paul, James, and Hebrews: A Study in the Circumstantial Nature of New Testament Teaching," *JETS* 20 (1977) 203-12.

————. *New Testament Social Ethics for Today.* Grand Rapids: Eerdmans, 1984; repr. Vancouver: Regent, 1997.

———. "Antioch of Syria," in *Major Cities of the Biblical World,* ed. R. K. Harrison. Nashville: Nelson, 1985, 8-21.

———. "Three Ways of Understanding Relations between the Testaments — Historically and Today," in *Tradition and Interpretation in the New Testament: Essays in Honor of E. Earle Ellis for His 60th Birthday,* ed. G. F. Hawthorne with O. Betz. Tübingen: Mohr; Grand Rapids: Eerdmans, 1987, 22-32; repr. in his *Studies in Hermeneutics,* 2-18.

———. *Galatians.* WBC; Dallas: Word, 1990.

———. "The Foundational Conviction of New Testament Christology: The Obedience / Faithfulness / Sonship of Christ," in *Jesus of Nazareth: Lord and Christ* (FS I. Howard Marshall), ed. J. B. Green and M. Turner. Grand Rapids: Eerdmans, 1994, 473-88; repr. in his *Studies in Hermeneutics,* 122-44.

———. "Prolegomena to Paul's Use of Scripture in Romans," *BBR* 7 (1997) 145-68.

———. *New Wine into Fresh Wineskins: Contextualizing the Early Christian Confessions.* Peabody: Hendrickson, 1999; Grand Rapids: Baker, 2010.

———. "The Focus of Romans: The Central Role of 5:1–8:39 in the Argument of the Letter," in *Romans and the People of God: Essays in Honor of Gordon D. Fee on the Occasion of His 65th Birthday,* ed. S. K. Soderlund and N. T. Wright. Grand Rapids: Eerdmans, 1999, 49-69; repr. in his *Studies in Paul: Exegetical and Theological.* Sheffield: Phoenix, 2004, 96-121.

———. "'What Does It Matter?' Priorities and the *Adiaphora* in Paul's Dealing with Opponents during His Mission," in *The Gospel to the Nations: Perspectives on Paul's Mission in Honour of Peter T. O'Brien,* ed. P. G. Bolt and M. D. Thompson. Leicester: Apollos; Downers Grove: InterVarsity, 2000, 147-60; repr. in his *Studies in Paul: Exegetical and Theological.* Sheffield: Phoenix, 2004, 163-78.

———. "Prayer in the Pauline Letters," in *Into God's Presence: Prayer in the New Testament,* ed. R. N. Longenecker. MNTS; Grand Rapids: Eerdmans, 2001, 203-27; repr. in his *Studies in Paul: Exegetical and Theological.* Sheffield: Phoenix, 2004, 28-52.

———. *Studies in Hermeneutics, Christology and Discipleship.* Sheffield: Phoenix, 2004.

———. "A Developmental Hermeneutic: New Treasures as Well as Old," in his *New Testament Social Ethics for Today,* 16-28; repr. in his *Studies in Hermeneutics,* 19-33.

———. "Major Tasks of an Evangelical Hermeneutic: Some Observations on Commonalities, Interrelations and Differences," *Bulletin for Biblical Research* 14 (2004) 45-58; repr. in his *Studies in Hermeneutics, Christology, and Discipleship.* Sheffield: Phoenix, 2004, 72-88.

———. "Christological Materials within the Early Christian Communities," in *Contours of Christology in the New Testament,* ed. R. N. Longenecker. MNTS; Grand Rapids: Eerdmans, 2005, 47-76; also in his *Studies in Hermeneutics, Christology, and Discipleship.* Sheffield: Phoenix, 2004, 90-121.

———. "On the Writing of Biblical Commentaries, with Particular Reference to Commentaries on Romans," in *From Criticism to Biblical Faith: Essays in Honor of Lee Martin McDonald,* ed. W. H. Brackney and C. A. Evans. Macon: Mercer University Press, 2007, 74-92.

———. "Hans Dieter Betz's Galatians Commentary: A Retrospective Word of Commendation, with Some Criticisms, Thirty Years after the Commentary's Publication," *Biblical Research: Journal of the Chicago Society of Biblical Research* 54 (2009) 11-23.

————. *Introducing Romans: Critical Issues in Paul's Most Famous Letter.* Grand Rapids: Eerdmans, 2011.

Lüdemann, Gerd. *Opposition to Paul in Jewish Christianity,* trans. M. E. Boring. Minneapolis: Fortress, 1989.

Lührmann, Dieter. "Rechtfertigung und Versöhnung. Zur Geschichte der paulinischen Tradition," *ZTK* 67 (1970) 437-52.

————. *Glaube im frühen Christentum.* Gütersloh: Gütersloher Verlagshaus, 1976.

Luther, Martin. "A Treatise on Christian Liberty," in *Works of Martin Luther,* vol. 2, trans. W. A. Lambert. Philadelphia: Holman, 1916.

Luz, Ulrich. *Das Geschichtsverständnis des Paul.* BEvT 49; Munich: Kaiser, 1968, 113-16, 168-86.

————. "Zum Aufbau von Röm 1–8." *TZ* 25 (1969) 161-81.

Lyonnet, Stanislaus. "De 'iustitia Dei' in Epistola ad Romanos i,17 et iii.21, 22," *VD* 25 (1947) 23-34, 118-21, 129-44, 193-203, 257-63.

————. "De Rom 3,30 et 4,3-5 in Concilio Tridentino et apud S. Robertum Bellarminum," *VD* 29 (1951) 88-97.

————. "De doctrina praedestinationis et reprobationis in Rom 9," *VD* (1956) 193-201, 257-71.

————. "Notes sur l'exégèse de l'Epître aux Romains. II. Le Sens de *paresis* en Rom 3,25," *Bib* 38 (1957) 35-61.

————. "De notione expiationis," *VD* 37 (1959) 336-52 and 38 (1960) 65-75, 241-61; ET in L. Sabourin and S. Lyonnet. *Sin, Redemption and Sacrifice: A Biblical and Patristic Study.* AnBib 48; Rome: Biblical Institute Press, 1970, 127-36.

————. "Rom IV,12 chez Saint Augustin. Note sur l'élaboration de la doctrine Augustinienne du péché originel," in *L'Homme devant Dieu, Mélanges Henri De Lubac,* I. Théologie 56; Paris: Aubier, 1963, 327-39.

————. "'Deus cui servio in spiritu meo' (Rom 1,9)," *VD* 41 (1963) 52-59.

————. "Lex naturalis et iustificatio Gentilium," *VD* 41 (1963) 238-42.

————. "'Lex naturalis' quid praecipiat secundum S. Paulum et antiquam Patrum traditionem," *VD* 45 (1967) 150-61.

————. "'La Circoncision du coeur, celle qui relève de l'Esprit et non de la lettre' (Rom. 2:29)," in *L'Evangile, hier et aujourd'hui. Mélanges offerts au Professeur Franz-J. Leenhardt.* Geneva: Labor et Fides, 1968, 87-97.

————. "La Connaissance naturelle de Dieu," in his *Études sur l'épître aux Romains.* Rome: Biblical Institute Press, 1989, 43-70.

McDonald, J. I. H. "Was Romans 16 a Separate Letter?" *NTS* 16 (1969-70) 369-72.

————. "Romans 13:1-7 and Christian Social Ethics Today," *Modern Churchman* 29 (1987) 19-25.

————. "Romans 13:1-7: A Test Case for New Testament Interpretation," *NTS* 35 (1989) 540-49.

McDonald, Patricia M. "Romans 5:1-11 as a Rhetorical Bridge," *JSNT* 40 (1990) 81-96.

McGrath, Alister E. "The Righteousness of God from Augustine to Luther," *ST* 36 (1982) 63-78.

————. *Iustitia Dei: A History of the Christian Doctrine of Justification,* 2 vols. Cambridge: Cambridge University Press, 1986.

McNamara, Martin. *The New Testament and the Palestinian Targum to the Pentateuch.* AnBib 27; Rome: Pontifical Biblical Institute, 1966.

Malherbe, Abraham J. "MH ΓΕΝΟΙΤΟ in the Diatribe and Paul," *HTR* 73 (1980) 231-40; repr. in his *Paul and the Popular Philosophers*. Minneapolis: Fortress, 1989, 25-33.

Malina, Bruce J. "Some Observations on the Origin of Sin in Judaism and St. Paul," *CBQ* 31 (1969) 18-34.

Manson, Thomas W. "The Argument from Prophecy," *JTS* 46 (1945) 129-36.

———. "ΙΛΑΣΤΗΡΙΟΝ," *JTS* 46 (1945) 1-10.

———. *On Paul and John*. London: SCM, 1963.

Manson, William. "Notes on the Argument of Romans (ch. 1-8)," in *New Testament Essays: Studies in Memory of Thomas Walter Manson,* ed. A. J. B. Higgins. Manchester: Manchester University Press, 1959, 150-64.

Marcus, Joel. "The Circumcision and the Uncircumcision in Rome," *NTS* 35 (1989) 67-81.

Marmorstein, A. "Paulus und die Rabbinen," *ZNW* 30 (1931) 271-85.

Marshall, I. Howard. "The Development of the Concept of Redemption in the New Testament," in *Reconciliation and Hope* (FS L. L. Morris), ed. R. J. Banks. Exeter: Paternoster, 1974, 153-69.

———. "The Meaning of 'Reconciliation,'" in *Unity and Diversity in New Testament Theology: Essays in Honor of G. E. Ladd,* ed. R. Guelich. Grand Rapids: Eerdmans, 1978, 117-32.

———. "Romans 16:25-27 — Apt Conclusion," in *Romans and the People of God: Essays in Honor of Gordon C. Fee on the Occasion of His 65th Birthday,* ed. S. K. Soderlund and N. T. Wright. Grand Rapids: Eerdmans, 1999, 170-84.

Martin, Ralph P. "New Testament Theology: A Proposal; The Theme of Reconciliation," *ExpT* 91 (1980) 364-68.

———. *Reconciliation: A Study of Paul's Theology*. London: Marshall, Morgan & Scott; Atlanta: John Knox, 1981, 135-54.

———. "Reconciliation: Romans 5:1-11," in *Romans and the People of God: Essays in Honor of Gordon D. Fee on the Occasion of His 65th Birthday,* ed. S. K. Soderlund and N. T. Wright. Grand Rapids: Eerdmans, 1999, 36-48.

Mason, Steve. "'For I Am Not Ashamed of the Gospel' (Rom. 1.16): The Gospel and the First Readers of Romans," in *Gospel in Paul: Studies on Corinthians, Galatians and Romans for Richard N. Longenecker,* ed. L. A. Jervis and P. Richardson. Sheffield: Sheffield Academic, 1994, 254-87.

Maurer, Christian. "προέχομαι," *TDNT* 6.692-93.

Metzger, Bruce M. "The Punctuation of Rom 9:5," in *Christ and Spirit in the New Testament: In Honour of C. F. D. Moule,* ed. B. Lindars and S. S. Smalley. Cambridge: Cambridge University Press, 1973, 95-112.

Meyer, Ben F. "The Pre-Pauline Formula in Rom 3.25-26a," *NTS* 29 (1983) 198-208.

Meyer, Rudolf. "περιτέμνω, περιτομή," *TDNT* 6.72-84.

Michaels, J. Ramsey. "The Redemption of Our Body: The Riddle of Romans 8:19-22," in *Romans and the People of God: Essays in Honor of Gordon D. Fee on the Occasion of His 65th Birthday,* ed. S. K. Soderlund and N. T. Wright. Grand Rapids: Eerdmans, 1999, 92-114.

Minear, Paul S. "Gratitude and Mission in the Epistle to the Romans," in *Basileia. Walter Freytag zum 60. Geburtstag,* ed. J. Hermelink and H. J. Margull. Stuttgart: Evangelische, 1959, 42-48; repr. in his *The Obedience of Faith: The Purposes of Paul in the Epistle to the Romans*. SBT 19; London: SCM, 1971, "Appendix 2," 102-10.

———. *The Obedience of Faith: The Purposes of Paul in the Epistle to the Romans*. London: SCM, 1971.

Mitton, C. L. "Romans vii. Reconsidered — III," *ExpT* 65 (1954) 132-35.

Moffatt, James. "The Interpretation of Romans 6:17-18," *JBL* 48 (1929) 237.

Moir, Ian A. "Orthography and Theology: The Omicron-Omega Interchange in Romans 5:1 and Elsewhere," in *New Testament Textual Criticism: Its Significance for Exegesis (Essays in Honour of Bruce M. Metzger)*. Oxford: Clarendon, 1981, 179-83.

Moo, Douglas J. " 'Law,' 'Works of Law' and 'Legalism' in Paul," *WTJ* 45 (1983) 73-100.

———. "Paul and the Law in the Last Ten Years," *SJT* 40 (1987) 287-307.

———. "Excursus: Paul, 'Works of the Law,' and First-Century Judaism," in his *The Epistle to the Romans*. NICNT; Grand Rapids: Eerdmans, 1996, 211-17.

———. "The Christology of the Early Pauline Letters," in *Contours of Christology in the New Testament*, ed. R. N. Longenecker. MNTS; Grand Rapids: Eerdmans, 2005, 169-92.

Moody, R. M. "The Habakkuk Quotation in Romans 1:17," *ExpT* 92 (1980-81) 205-8.

Moore, George Foote. *Judaism in the First Centuries of the Christian Era,* 3 vols. Cambridge: Harvard University Press, 1927-30.

Morenz, Siegfried. "Feurige Kohlen auf dem Haupt," *TLZ* 78 (1953) 187-92; also in *Religion und Geschichte der alten Agypten. Gesammelte Aufsatze*. Weimar: Böhlaus, 1975, 433-44.

Morris, Leon L. "The Use of ἱλάσκεσθαι etc. in Biblical Greek," *ExpT* 62 (1951-52) 227-33.

———. "The Meaning of ἱλαστήριον in Romans 3:25," *NTS* 2 (1955) 33-43.

———. *The Apostolic Preaching of the Cross*. London: Tyndale, 1955.

Morrison, C. D. *The Powers That Be: Earthly Rulers and Demonic Powers in Romans 13:1-7*. SBT 29; London: SCM, 1960.

Moule, Charles F. D. "The Biblical Conception of 'Faith,' " *ExpT* 68 (1956) 157, 221-22.

Moxnes, Halvor. *Theology in Conflict: Studies in Paul's Understanding of God in Romans*. NovTSup 53; Leiden: Brill, 1980.

———. "Honor, Shame, and the Outside World in Paul's Letter to the Romans," in *The Social World of Formative Christianity and Judaism: Essays in Tribute to Howard Clark Kee,* ed. J. Neusner, P. Borgen, E. S. Frerichs, and R. Horsley. Philadelphia: Fortress, 1988, 207-18.

Müller, Friedrich. "Zwei Marginalien im Brief Paulus an die Römer," *ZNW* 40 (1941) 249-54.

Mullins, Terence Y. "Petition as a Literary Form," *NovT* 5 (1962) 46-54.

———. "Disclosure: A Literary Form in the New Testament," *NovT* 7 (1964) 44-50.

———. "Greeting as a New Testament Form," *JBL* 87 (1968) 418-26.

Mundle, Wilhelm. "Zur Auslegung von Röm 2.13ff.," *TBlä* 13 (1934) 248-56.

Murray, John. *The Imputation of Adam's Sin*. Grand Rapids: Eerdmans, 1959.

———. "Justification," in his *Romans*, "Appendix A," 1.336-62.

———. "From Faith to Faith," in his *Romans*, "Appendix B," 1.363-74.

———. "Karl Barth on Romans 5," in his *Romans*, "Appendix D," 1.384-90.

———. "The Authorities of Romans 13:1," in his *Romans*, "Appendix C," 2.252-56.

Mussner, Franz. "Christus, des Gesetzes Ende zur Gerechtigkeit für Jeden, der glaubt (Rom 10.4)," in *Paulus — Apostat oder Apostel? Jüdische und christliche Antworten,* ed. M. Barth et al. Regensburg: Pustet, 1977, 31-44.

———. "Gesetz-Abraham-Israel," *Kairos* 25 (1983) 200-222.

Nanos, Mark D. *The Mystery of Romans: The Jewish Context of Paul's Letter*. Minneapolis: Fortress, 1996.

Nebe, Gottfried. *"Hoffnung" bei Paulus. Elpis und ihre Synonyme im Zusammenhang der Eschatologie.* SUNT 16; Göttingen: Vandenhoeck & Ruprecht, 1983.

Neill, William. "Paul's Certainties I: God's Promises Are Sure — Romans iv.21," *ExpT* (1957-58) 146-48.

Nickle, Keith P. *The Collection: A Study in Paul's Strategy.* London: SCM, 1966.

Nicole, Roger R. "C. H. Dodd and the Doctrine of Propitiation," *WTJ* 17 (1954-55) 117-57.

Noack, Bent. "Current and Backwater in the Epistle to the Romans," *ST* 19 (1955) 155-66.

Nolland, John. "Romans 1:26-27 and the Homosexuality Debate," *HBT* 22 (2000) 32-57.

Norden, Eduard. *Agnostos Theos. Untersuchungen zur Formgeschichte religiöser Rede.* Leipzig: Teubner, 1929 (esp. 240-50).

O'Brien, Peter T. "Thanksgiving and the Gospel in Paul," *NTS* 21 (1974) 144-55.

————. *Introductory Thanksgivings in the Letters of Paul.* NovTSup 49; Leiden: Brill, 1977.

————. "Thanksgiving within the Structure of Pauline Theology," in *Pauline Studies: Essays Presented to Professor F. F. Bruce on His 70th Birthday,* ed. D. A. Hagner and M. J. Harris. Grand Rapids: Eerdmans, 1980, 50-66.

Olson, Stanley N. "Pauline Expressions of Confidence in His Addressees," *CBQ* 47 (1985) 282-95.

O'Rourke, John J. "Romans 1,20 and Natural Revelation," *CBQ* 23 (1961) 301-6.

————. "*Pistis* in Romans," *CBQ* 35 (1973) 188-94.

Owen, H. P. "The Scope of Natural Revelation in Rom. I and Acts XVII," *NTS* 5 (1958) 133-43.

Parke-Taylor, Geoffrey H. "A Note on εἰς ὑπακοὴν πίστεως in Romans i.5 and xvi.26," *ExpT* 55 (1943-44) 205-6.

Parsons, Michael. "Being Precedes Act: Indicative and Imperative in Paul's Writing," *EvQ* 88 (1988) 99-127.

Patte, Daniel. *Paul's Faith and the Power of the Gospel: A Structural Introduction to the Pauline Letters.* Philadelphia: Fortress, 1983, esp. 214-22.

Paulsen, Henning. *Überlieferung und Auslegung in Römer 8.* WMANT 43; Neukirchen-Vluyn: Neukirchener Verlag, 1974.

Perkins, Pheme. "Paul and Ethics," *Int* 38 (1984) 268-80.

Piper, John. *The Justification of God: An Exegetical Study of Romans 9:1-23.* Grand Rapids: Baker, 1983.

Pluta, Alfons. *Gottes Bundestreue. Ein Schlüsselbegriff in Röm 3.25a.* SBS 34; Stuttgart: Katholisches Bibelwerk, 1969.

Pohlenz, Max. "Paulus und die Stoa," *ZNW* 42 (1949) 69-104.

Porter, C. L. "Romans 1:18-32: Its Role in the Developing Argument," *NTS* 40 (1994) 210-28.

Porter, Stanley E. "The Pauline Concept of Original Sin, in Light of Rabbinic Background," *TB* 41 (1990) 3-30.

————. "The Argument of Romans 5: Can a Rhetorical Question Make a Difference?" *JBL* 110 (1991) 655-77.

Poythress, Vern S. "Is Romans 1.3-4 a *Pauline* Confession After All?" *ExpT* 87 (1976) 180-83.

Qimron, Elisha, and John Strugnell, eds. *Qumran Cave 4, V: Miqsat Ma'ase Ha-Torah.* DJD 10; Oxford: Clarendon, 1994.

Räisänen, Heikki. *Paul and the Law.* WUNT 29; Tübingen: Mohr, 1983.

————. "Zum Verständnis von Röm 3,1-8," in *The Torah and Christ: Essays in German and English on the Problem of the Law in Early Christianity.* PFES 45; Helsinki: Finnish Exegetical Society, 1986.

———. *Jesus, Paul, and Torah: Collected Essays,* trans. D. E. Orton. JSNT.SS 43; Sheffield: JSOT, 1992.

Ramsay, William M. "The Olive-Tree and the Wild Olive," in his *Paul and Other Studies in Early Christian History.* London: Hodder & Stoughton, 1908, 219-50.

Rapa, Robert Keith. *The Meaning of "Works of the Law" in Galatians and Romans.* StudBL 31; New York: Lang, 2001.

Reasoner, Mark. *The Strong and the Weak: Romans 14.1–15.13 in Context.* Cambridge: Cambridge University Press, 1999.

———. "The Theology of Romans 12:1–15:13," in *Pauline Theology* vol. 3: *Romans,* ed. D. M. Hay and E. E. Johnson. Minneapolis: Fortress, 287-99.

———. *Romans in Full Circle: A History of Interpretation.* Louisville: Westminster John Knox, 2005; esp. "Locus 12: Let Every *Psyche* Be Subject to the Authorities (13:1-7)," 129-42.

Reicke, Bo Ivar. "The Law and This World according to Paul," *JBL* 70 (1951) 259-76.

——— "Συνείδησις in Röm 2,15," *TZ* 12 (1956) 157-61.

———. "Natürliche Theologie nach Paulus," *SEÅ* 22 (1957) 154-67.

———. "Paul's Understanding of Righteousness," in *Soli Deo Gloria* (FS W. C. Robinson), ed. J. M. Richards. Richmond: John Knox, 1968, 37-49.

Reid, Marty L. "A Rhetorical Analysis of Romans 1:1–5:21, with Attention Given to the Rhetorical Function of 5:1-21," *PRS* 19 (1992) 255-72.

Reitzenstein, Richard. *Hellenistic Mystery-Religions: Their Basic Ideas and Significance.* Pittsburgh: Pickwick, 1978.

Rengstorf, Karl H. "ἀπόστολος," *TDNT* 1.407-47.

———. "ἐλπίς, ἐλπίζω," *TDNT* 2.523-29.

———. *Apostolate and Ministry: The New Testament Doctrine of the Office of the Ministry,* trans. P. D. Pahl. St. Louis: Concordia, 1969.

Reumann, John. "The Gospel of the Righteousness of God: Pauline Reinterpretation in Romans 3:21-31," *Int* 20 (1966) 432-52.

———. *Creation and New Creation.* Minneapolis: Augsburg, 1973.

Reventlow, H. Graf. *Rechtfertigung im Horizont des Alten Testaments.* Munich: Kaiser, 1971.

Rhyne, C. Thomas. *Faith Establishes the Law.* SBL.DS 55; Chico: Scholars, 1981.

Richardson, Peter. *Israel in the Apostolic Church.* SNTS.MS 10; Cambridge: Cambridge University Press, 1969.

Ridderbos, Herman. *Paul: An Outline of His Theology,* trans. J. R. DeWitt. Grand Rapids: Eerdmans, 1975.

Robinson, D. W. B. " 'Faith of Jesus Christ' — a New Testament Debate," *RTR* 29 (1970) 71-81.

Robinson, James M. "Die Hodajot-Formel in Gebet und Hymnus des Frühchristentums," in *Apophoreta. Festschrift für Ernst Haenchen.* BZNW 30; Berlin: de Gruyter, 1964, 194-235.

Roetzel, Calvin J. "Sacrifice in Romans 12–15," *WW* 6 (1986) 410-19.

Sampley, J. Paul. "Romans and Galatians: Comparison and Contrast," in *Understanding the Word,* ed. J. T. Butler, E. W. Conrad, and B. C. Ollenburger. Sheffield: JSOT, 1985, esp. 325 and 327.

Sanders, Ed P. *Paul and Palestinian Judaism: A Comparison of Patterns of Religion.* Philadelphia: Fortress, 1977.

―――. *Paul, the Law, and the Jewish People.* Philadelphia: Fortress, 1983.

―――. "Appendix: Romans 2," in his *Paul, the Law, and the Jewish People,* 123-35.

Sanders, Jack T. "The Transition from Opening Epistolary Thanksgiving to Body in the Letters of the Pauline Corpus," *JBL* 81 (1962) 348-62.

Sandmel, Samuel. "Abraham's Knowledge of the Existence of God," *HTR* 44 (1951) 55-60.

―――. *Philo's Place in Judaism: A Study of Conceptions of Abraham in Jewish Literature.* New York: Ktav, 1971.

Sandnes, Karl Olav. *Paul — One of the Prophets? A Contribution to the Apostle's Self-Understanding.* WUNT 43; Tübingen: Mohr Siebeck, 1990, esp. 146-53.

Schelkle, Karl Hermann. "Staat und Kirchen in der patristischen Auslegung von Röm 13:1-7," *ZNW* 44 (1952-53): 223-36.

―――. *Paulus — Lehre der Väter.* Düsseldorf: Patmos, 1956.

Schettler, A. *Die paulinische Formel "Durch Christus" untersucht.* Tübingen: Mohr Siebeck, 1907.

Schlier, Heinrich. "Die Erkenntnis Gottes nach den Briefen des Apostels Paulus," in his *Besinnung auf das Neue Testament.* Freiburg: Herder, 1964, 319-39.

―――. "Über die Erkenntnis Gottes bei den Heiden (nach dem Neuen Testament)," *EvT* 2 (1935) 9-26; repr. as "Von den Heiden: Römerbrief 1, 18-31," in his *Die Zeit der Kirche.* Freiburg: Herder, 1956, 29-37.

―――. "Von den Juden. Röm 2:1-29," in his *Die Zeit der Kirche.* Freiburg: Herder, 1956, 38-47.

―――. "ἀμήν," *TDNT* 1.335-38.

―――. "Eine Christologische Credo-Formel der römischen Gemeinde. Zu Röm 1:3f.," in *Neues Testament und Geschichte. Historisches Geschehen und Deutung im Neuen Testament. Oscar Cullmann zum 70. Geburtstag,* ed. H. Baltensweiler and B. Reicke. Zurich: Theologischer; Tübingen: Mohr Siebeck, 1972, 207-18.

―――. "Εὐαγγέλιον im Römerbrief," in *Wort Gottes in der Zeit. Festschrift Karl Hermann Schelke zum 65. Geburtstag,* ed. H. Feld and J. Nolte. Düsseldorf: Patmos, 1973, 127-42.

Schmidt, Karl Ludwig. "ἀγωγή . . . προσάγω, προσαγωγή," *TDNT* 1.128-34.

―――. "ἀφορίζω," *TDNT* 1.454-55.

Schmithals, Walter. *The Office of Apostle in the Early Church,* trans. J. E. Steely. Nashville: Abingdon, 1969.

―――. *Der Römerbrief als historisches Problem.* SNT 9; Gütersloh: Mohn, 1975.

Schoeps, Hans Joachim. "The Sacrifice of Isaac in Paul's Theology," *JBL* 65 (1946) 385-92.

―――. *Paul: The Theology of the Apostle in the Light of Jewish Religious History,* trans. H. Knight. Philadelphia: Westminster, 1961.

―――. "The Expiatory Character of the *Aqedath Isaac,*" in his *Paul: The Theology of the Apostle in the Light of Jewish Religious History,* trans. H. Knight. Philadelphia: Westminster, 1961 (from 1959 German original), 141-49.

Schreiner, Thomas R. " 'Works of Law' in Paul," *NovT* 33 (1991) 217-44.

―――. "Did Paul Believe in Justification by Works? Another Look at Romans 2," *BBR* 3 (1993) 131-55.

Schrenk, Gottlob. "δίκη, δίκαιος, δικαιοσύνη, δικαιόω," *TDNT* 2.174-225.

―――. "θέλημα," *TDNT* 3.52-62.

―――. "ἱεροσυλέω," *TDNT* 3.255-56.

————. "πατήρ," *TDNT* 5.976-78 (on "The Fathers in Judaism").

Schubert, Paul. *Form and Function of the Pauline Thanksgivings.* BZNW 20; Berlin: Töpelmann, 1939.

Schulz, Ray R. "Romans 16.7: Junia or Junias?" *ExpT* 98 (1986-87), 109-10.

Schulz, Siegfried. "Die Anklage in Röm. 1, 18-32," *TZ* 14 (1958) 161-73.

————. "Zur Rechtfertigung aus Gnaden in Qumran und bei Paulus," *ZTK* 61 (1959) 155-85.

Schweitzer, Albert. *The Mysticism of Paul the Apostle,* trans. W. Montgomery. London: Black, 1931.

Schweizer, Eduard. "Römer 1,3f. und der Gegensatz von Fleisch und Geist vor und bei Paulus," in his *Neotestamentica.* Zurich: Zwingli, 1963, 180-89; repr. of "Der vorpaulinische Gegensatz von Fleisch und Geist in Rom 1,3f," *EvT* 15 (1955) 563-71.

————. "Zum religionsgeschichtlichen Hintergrund der 'Sendungsformel' Gal 4,4f.; Röm 8,3f.; Joh. 3,16f.; 1Joh. 4,9," in his *Beiträge zur Theologie des Neuen Testament. Neutestamentliche Aufsätze (1955-70).* Zurich: Zwingli, 1970, 83-95; repr. of his article by the same title, *ZNW* 57 (1966) 199-210.

————. " 'Der Jude im Verborgenen . . . , dessen Lob nicht von Menschen, sondern von Gott kommt': Zu Röm 2,28f. und Matt 6,1-18," in *Neues Testament und Kirche. Für Rudolf Schnackenburg (z. 60. Geburtsag am 5. Jan. 1974 von Freunden u. Kollegen gewidmet),* ed. J. Gnilka. Freiburg im Breisgau: Herder, 1974, 115-24.

————. "πνεῦμα," *TDNT* 6.389-455.

————. "σάρξ," *TDNT* 7.119-51.

Scott, C. A. Anderson. *Christianity according to St. Paul.* Cambridge: Cambridge University Press, 1927, repr. 1961.

Scroggs, Robin. *The Last Adam: A Study in Pauline Anthropology.* Oxford: Blackwell, 1966.

————. "Paul as Rhetorician: Two Homilies in Romans 1–11," in *Jews, Greeks, and Christians (Festschrift* for W. D. Davies), ed. R. Hammerton-Kelly and R. Scroggs. Leiden: Brill, 1976, 271-98.

————. "New Being: Renewed Mind: New Perception. Paul's View of the Source of Ethical Insight," *Chicago Theological Seminary Register* 72 (1982) 1-12.

————. *The New Testament and Homosexuality: Contextual Background for Contemporary Debate.* Philadelphia: Fortress, 1983.

Segal, Alan F. " 'He Who Did Not Spare His Own Son . . .': Jesus, Paul and the Akedah," in *From Jesus to Paul: Studies in Honour of Francis Wright Beare,* ed. P. Richardson and J. C. Hurd, Jr. Waterloo: Wilfrid Laurier University Press, 1984, 169-84.

Sekki, Arthur E. *The Meaning of Ruah at Qumran.* SBL.DS 110; Atlanta: Scholars, 1989.

Shum, Shiu-Lun. *Paul's Use of Isaiah in Romans: A Comparative Study of Paul's Letter to the Romans and the Sibylline and Qumran Sectarian Texts.* WUNT 156; Tübingen: Mohr Siebeck, 2002.

Snodgrass, Klyne R. "Justification by Grace — to the Doers: An Analysis of the Place of Romans 2 in the Theology of Paul," *NTS* 32 (1986) 72-93.

Snyman, Andreas H. "Style and Meaning in Romans 8:31-9," *Neot* 18 (1984) 94-103.

————. "Style and Rhetorical Situation of Romans 8:31-39," *NTS* 34 (1998) 218-31.

Soards, Marion L. "Käsemann's 'Righteousness' Reexamined," *CBQ* 49 (1987) 264-67.

————. *Scripture and Homosexuality: Biblical Authority and the Church Today.* Louisville: Westminster John Knox, 1995.

Stanley, Christopher D. *Paul and the Language of Scripture: Citation Technique in the*

Pauline Epistles and Contemporary Literature. SNTS.MS 74; Cambridge: Cambridge University Press, 1992.

Stanley, David M. "Pauline Allusions to the Sayings of Jesus," *CBQ* 23 (1961) 26-39.

—————. *Boasting in the Lord: The Phenomenon of Prayer in Saint Paul.* New York/Toronto: Paulist, 1973.

Stauffer, Ethelbert. "εἰς," *TDNT* 2.420-42.

Stein, Robert H. "The Argument of Romans 13:1-7," *NovT* 31 (1989) 325-43.

Steinmetz, David C. "Calvin and Melanchthon on Romans 13:1-7," *Ex Auditu* 2 (1986) 74-81.

Stendahl, Krister. "The Apostle Paul and the Introspective Conscience of the West," *HTR* 56 (1963) 199-215.

Stevens, R. Paul. "'The Full Blessing of Christ' (Romans 15:29): A Sermon," in *Romans and the People of God: Essays in Honor of Gordon D. Fee on the Occasion of His 65th Birthday,* ed. S. K. Soderlund and N. T. Wright. Grand Rapids: Eerdmans, 1999, 295-303.

Stirewalt, M. Luther, Jr. "The Form and Function of the Greek Letter-Essay," in Donfried, ed., *Romans Debate* 1977, 175-206; 1991, 147-71.

Stowers, Stanley K. *The Diatribe and Paul's Letter to the Romans.* SBL.DS 57; Chico: Scholars, 1981.

—————. "Dialogical Exchange and *Exemplum* in 3:27–4:25," in his *Diatribe and Paul's Letter to the Romans,* 155-74.

—————. "Paul's Dialogue with a Fellow Jew in Romans 3:1-9," *CBQ* 46 (1984) 707-22; repr. as "Paul's Dialogue with a Fellow Jew," in his *A Rereading of Romans,* 159-75.

—————. *Letter Writing in Greco-Roman Antiquity.* Philadelphia: Westminster, 1986.

—————. "Ἐκ πίστεως and διὰ τῆς πίστεως in Romans 3:30," *JBL* 108 (1989) 665-74.

—————. *A Rereading of Romans: Justice, Jews, and Gentiles.* New Haven: Yale University Press, 1994.

—————. "Gentile Culture and God's Impartial Justice (1:18–2:16)," in his *A Rereading of Romans,* 83-125.

—————. "Warning a Greek and Debating a Fellow Jew," in his *A Rereading of Romans,* 126-58.

—————. "Paul on Sin and Works of the Law," in his *A Rereading of Romans,* 176-93.

—————. "God's Merciful Justice in Christ's Faithfulness (3:21-33)," in his *A Rereading of Romans,* 194-226. (Note: The reference in the title should be 3:21-31.)

—————. "One God & One Father Abraham (3:27–5:11)," in his *A Rereading of Romans,* 227-50.

Strathmann, Hermann. "λατρεύω, λατρεία," *TDNT* 4.58-65.

Stuhlmacher, Peter. *Gerechtigkeit Gottes bei Paulus.* FRLANT 87; Göttingen: Vandenhoeck & Ruprecht, 1965.

—————. "Theologische Probleme des Römerbriefpräskripts," *EvT* 27 (1967) 374-89.

—————. *Das paulinische Evangelium* I: *Vorgeschichte.* FRLANT 95; Göttingen: Vandenhoeck & Ruprecht, 1968.

—————. "Das Ende des Gesetzes: Über Ursprung und Ansatz der paulinischen Theologie," *ZTK* 67 (1970) 14-39.

—————. "Das paulinische Evangelium," in *Das Evangelium und die Evangelien,* ed. P. Stuhlmacher. WUNT 28; Tübingen: Mohr Siebeck, 1983, 157-82.

—————. "Jesustradition im Römerbrief? Eine Skizze," *TBei* 14 (1983) 140-50.

————. "Paul's Understanding of the Law in the Letter to the Romans," *SEÅ* 50 (1985) 87-104.

————. *Reconciliation, Law, and Righteousness: Essays in Biblical Theology,* trans. E. R. Kalin. Philadelphia: Fortress, 1986.

————. "Jesus' Resurrection and the View of Righteousness in the Pre-Pauline Mission Congregations," in his *Reconciliation, Law, and Righteousness,* 50-67 (esp. 60-63).

————. "The Apostle Paul's View of Righteousness," in his *Reconciliation, Law, and Righteousness,* 68-93.

————. "Recent Exegesis on Romans 3:24-26," in his *Reconciliation, Law, and Righteousness,* 94-109.

————. "The Purpose of Romans," trans. R. H. and I. Fuller, in Donfried, ed., *Romans Debate,* 1991, 231-42; from "Der Abfassungszweck des Römerbriefes," *ZNW* 77 (1986) 180-93.

————. "Excursus 13: Christian Life under the Power of the State," in his *Paul's Letter to the Romans: A Commentary,* trans. S. J. Hafemann. Louisville: Westminster John Knox, 1994, 205-8.

Synge, Francis C. "The Meaning of προεχόμεθα in Romans 3.9," *ExpT* 81 (1969-70) 351.

Synofzik, Ernst. *Die Gerichts- und Vergeltungsaussagen bei Paulus. Eine traditionsgeschichtliche Untersuchung.* Göttingen: Vandenhoeck & Ruprecht, 1977.

Talbert, Charles H. "A Non-Pauline Fragment at Romans 3:24-26?" *JBL* 85 (1966) 287-96.

————. "Tradition and Redaction in Romans 12:9-21," *NTS* 16 (1969) 83-93.

Taylor, Vincent. "Great Texts Reconsidered: Romans 3,25f.," *ExpT* 50 (1938-1939) 295-300; repr. in his *New Testament Essays.* London: Epworth, 1970, 127-39.

————. *Forgiveness and Reconciliation.* London: Macmillan, 1941.

————. "Does the New Testament Call Jesus 'God'?" *ExpT* 73 (1962) 116-18.

Thackeray, Henry St. John. *The Relation of St. Paul to Contemporary Jewish Thought.* London: Macmillan, 1900, 30ff., 40ff.

Theissen, Gerd. *Psychological Aspects of Pauline Theology,* trans. J. P. Galvin. Philadelphia: Fortress, 1987.

Thielman, Frank. *From Plight to Solution: A Jewish Framework for Understanding Paul's View of the Law in Galatians and Romans.* Leiden: Brill, 1989.

————. *Paul and the Law: A Contextual Approach.* Downers Grove: InterVarsity, 1994.

Thompson, Marianne Meye. " 'Mercy upon All': God as Father in the Epistle to the Romans," in *Romans and the People of God: Essays in Honor of Gordon D. Fee on the Occasion of His 65th Birthday,* ed. S. K. Soderlund and N. T. Wright. Grand Rapids: Eerdmans, 1999, 203-16.

Thompson, Michael B. *Clothed with Christ: The Example and Teaching of Jesus in Romans 12.1–15.13.* JSNT.SS 59; Sheffield: Sheffield Academic, 1991.

Thompson, Richard W. " 'We Uphold the Law': A Study of Rom 3,31 and Its Context." Ph.D. dissertation directed by Jan Lambrecht, Catholic University, Louvain, 1985.

————. "Paul's Double Critique of Jewish Boasting: A Study of Rom 3,27 in Its Context," *Bib* 67 (1986) 520-31.

————. "The Alleged Rabbinic Background of Rom 3,31," *ETL* 63 (1987) 136-48.

————. "The Inclusion of the Gentiles in Rom 3,27-30," *Bib* 69 (1988) 543-46.

Toit, Andries B. du. "Gesetzesgerechtigkeit und Glaubensgerechtigkeit in Rom 4:13-25. In Gespräch mit E. P. Sanders," *HTS* 44 (1988) 71-80.

————. "Persuasion in Romans 1:1-17," *BZ* 33 (1989) 192-209.

Torrance, Thomas F. "One Aspect of the Biblical Conception of Faith," *ExpT* 68 (1956-57) 111-14 and 221-22.

Towner, Philip H. "Romans 13:1-7 and Paul's Missiological Perspective: A Call to Political Quietism or Transformation?" in *Romans and the People of God: Essays in Honor of Gordon D. Fee on the Occasion of His 65th Birthday,* ed. S. K. Soderlund and N. T. Wright. Grand Rapids: Eerdmans, 1999, 149-69.

Vallotton, Pierre. *Le Christ et la Foi. Étude de théologie biblique.* Geneva: Labor et Fides, 1960.

van Daalen, D. H. "The Revelation of God's Righteousness in Romans 1:17," *Studia Biblica 1978: Sixth International Congress on Biblical Studies, Oxford, 3-7 April 1978,* 3 vols., ed. E. A. Livingstone. JSNT.SS 2-3, 11; Sheffield: JSOT, 1980, 3.383-89.

Vandermarck, William. "Natural Knowledge of God in Romans: Patristic and Medieval Interpretation," *TS* 34 (1973) 36-52.

Vawter, Bruce. "The Biblical Idea of Faith," *Worship* 34 (1960) 443-50.

Vielhauer, Philipp. "Paulus und das Alte Testament," in *Studien zur Geschichte und Theologie der Reformation. Festschrift für Ernst Bizer,* ed. L. Abramowski and J. F. G. Goeters. Neukirchen-Vluyn: Neukirchener Verlag, 1969, 33-62.

Vis, A. *The Messianic Psalm Quotations in the New Testament: A Critical Study on the Christian 'Testimonies' in the Old Testament.* Amsterdam: von Soest, 1936.

Vogelstein, Hermann, "The Development of the Apostolate in Judaism and Its Transformation in Christianity," *HUCA* 2 (1925) 99-123.

Vögtle, Anton. *Das Neue Testament und die Zukunft des Kosmos.* Düsseldorf: Patmos, 1970.

———. "Röm 8,19-22. Eine Schopfungs-Theologische oder Anthropologische-Soteriologische Aussage?" in *Mélanges Bibliques en Hommage au R. P. Béda Rigaux,* ed. A. Descamps and A. Halleux. Belgium: Duculot, 1970, 351-66.

Völter, D. "Die Verse Röm 3,22b-26 und ihre Stellung innerhalb der ersten Kapital des Römerbriefs," *ZNW* (1909) 180-83.

von der Osten-Sacken, Peter. *Römer 8 als Beispiel Paulinischer Soteriologie.* Göttingen: Vandenhoeck & Ruprecht, 1975.

———. "Paulinische Evangelium und Homosexualität," *BTZ* 3 (1986) 28-49; repr. in *Evangelium und Tora. Aufsätze zu Paulus.* Munich: Kaiser, 1987, 210-36.

von Rad, Gerhard. "Faith Reckoned as Righteousness," in his *The Problem of the Hexateuch and Other Essays,* trans. E. W. T. Dicken. Edinburgh: Oliver & Boyd; New York: McGraw-Hill, 1966, 125-30 (ET from *TLZ* 76 [1951] 129-32).

———, Karl Georg Kuhn, and Walter Gutbrod. "Ἰσραήλ, κτλ," *TDNT* 3 (1991) 256-91.

Wagner, Günter. *Pauline Baptism and the Pagan Mysteries: The Problem of the Pauline Doctrine of Baptism in Romans VI.1-11, in the Light of Its Religio-Historical "Parallels,"* trans. J. P. Smith. Edinburgh: Oliver & Boyd, 1967.

Warfield, Benjamin B. "The New Testament Terminology of Redemption," *PTR* 15 (1917) 201-49.

Watson, Francis P. *Paul, Judaism, and the Gentiles.* Cambridge: Cambridge University Press, 1986.

Watts, Rikki E. " 'For I Am Not Ashamed of the Gospel': Romans 1:16-17 and Habakkuk 2:4," in *Romans and the People of God: Essays in Honor of Gordon D. Fee on the Occasion of His 65th Birthday,* ed. S. K. Soderlund and N. T. Wright. Grand Rapids: Eerdmans, 1999, 3-25.

Weber, H. Emil. *Die Beziehungen von Röm 1–3 zur Missionspraxis des Paulus.* BFCT 9/2; Gütersloh: Bertelsmann, 1905.

Wedderburn, Alexander J. M. "The Theological Structure of Romans 5:12," *NTS* 19 (1973) 339-54.

———. "Philo's 'Heavenly Man,' " *NovT* 15 (1973) 301-26.

———. "Adam in Paul's Letter to the Romans," in *Studia Biblica 1978: Sixth International Congress on Biblical Studies, Oxford,* 3 vols., ed. E. A. Livingstone. JSNT.SS 2-3, 11; Sheffield: JSOT, 1980, 3.413-30.

———. "Hellenistic Christian Traditions in Romans 6?" *NTS* 29 (1983) 337-55.

———. "The Soteriology of the Mysteries and Pauline Baptismal Theology," *NovT* 29 (1987) 53-72.

———. *Baptism and Resurrection: Studies in Pauline Theology against Its Graeco-Roman Background.* WUNT 44; Tübingen: Mohr Siebeck, 1987.

———. *The Reasons for Romans.* Edinburgh: T. & T. Clark, 1988; Minneapolis: Fortress, 1991.

Weima, Jeffrey A. D., *Neglected Endings: The Significance of the Pauline Letter Closings.* JSNT.SS 101; Sheffield: Sheffield Academic, 1994, esp. 135-44, 229-30.

———. "Preaching the Gospel in Rome: A Study of the Epistolary Framework of Romans," in *Gospel in Paul: Studies on Corinthians, Galatians and Romans for Richard N. Longenecker,* ed. L. A. Jervis and P. Richardson. Sheffield: Sheffield Academic, 1994, 337-66 (esp. 353-58).

Weiss, Johannes. "Beiträge zur paulinischen Rhetorik," in *Theologische Studien. Festschrift für Professor D. Bernhard Weiss zu seinem 70. Geburtstage dargebracht,* ed. C. R. Gregory et al. Göttingen: Vandenhoeck & Ruprecht, 1897, 165-247.

Wengst, Klaus. *Christologische Formeln und Lieder des Urchristentums.* SNT 7; Gütersloh: Gütersloher Verlagshaus, 1972.

———. *Pax Romana and the Peace of Jesus Christ,* trans. J. Bowden. London: SCM; Philadelphia: Fortress, 1987, esp. 79-84, 137-40.

———. "Paulus und die Homosexualität: Überlegungen zu Röm 1,26f.," *ZEE* 31 (1987) 72-81.

Wenham, David. "Paul's Use of the Jesus Tradition: Three Samples," in *The Jesus Tradition outside the Gospels,* ed. D. Wenham. Gospel Perspectives 5; Sheffield: JSOT, 1985, 7-37.

Westerholm, Stephen. *Israel's Law and the Church's Faith: Paul and His Recent Interpreters.* Grand Rapids: Eerdmans, 1988.

———. *Preface to the Study of Paul.* Grand Rapids: Eerdmans, 1997.

———. *Understanding Paul: The Early Christian Worldview of the Letter to the Romans.* 2nd ed., Grand Rapids: Baker, 1997.

———. *Perspectives Old and New on Paul: The "Lutheran" Paul and His Critics.* Grand Rapids: Eerdmans, 2004.

White, John L. "Introductory Formulae in the Body of the Pauline Letter," *JBL* 90 (1971) 91-97.

———. *The Form and Function of the Body of the Greek Letter: A Study of the Letter-Body in the Non-Literary Papyri and in Paul the Apostle.* 2nd ed., Missoula: Scholars, 1972.

Wilckens, Ulrich. *Rechtfertigung als Freiheit. Paulusstudien.* Neukirchen-Vluyn: Neukirchener Verlag, 1974.

————. "Zu Römer 3,21–4,25. Antwort an G. Klein," *EvT* 24 (1964) 586-601; repr. in his *Rechtfertigung als Freiheit,* 50-76.

————. "Die Rechtfertigung Abrahams nach Römer 4," in his *Rechtfertigung als Freiheit,* 33-49.

————. "Was heisst bei Paulus 'Aus Werken des Gesetzes wird kein Mensch gerecht'?" in his *Rechtfertigung als Freiheit,* 77-109.

————. "Römer 13.1-7," in his *Rechtfertigung als Freiheit,* 226-30.

Wilcox, Max. " 'Upon the Tree' — Deut. 21:22-23 in the New Testament," *JBL* 96 (1977) 67.

Wiles, Gordon P. *Paul's Intercessory Prayers: The Significance of the Intercessory Prayer Passages in the Letters of St Paul.* SNTS.MS 24; Cambridge: Cambridge University Press, 1974, 186-94.

Wiles, Maurice F. *The Divine Apostle: The Interpretation of St. Paul's Epistles in the Early Church.* Cambridge: Cambridge University Press, 1967.

Williams, Sam K. "The 'Righteousness of God' in Romans," *JBL* 99 (1980) 241-90.

————. "Again Πίστις Χριστοῦ," *CBQ* 49 (1987) 431-47.

Windisch, Hans. "βάρβαρος," *TDNT* 1.546-53.

————. "Ἕλλην," *TDNT* 2.504-16.

Wisse, Frederik. "The Righteous Man and the Good Man in Romans V.7," *NTS* 19 (1972) 91-93.

Wolter, Michael. *Rechtfertigung und zukünftiges Heil. Untersuchungen zu Röm 5,1-11.* BZNW 43; Berlin/New York: de Gruyter, 1978.

Wonneberger, Reinhard. "Römer 3,21-26," in his *Syntax und Exegese. Eine generative Theorie der griechischen Syntax und ihr Beitrag zur Auslegung des Neuen Testaments, dargestellt an 2. Korinther 5,2f und Römer 3,21-26.* BBET 13; Frankfurt-am-Main: Lang, 1979, 202-307.

Wood, J. E. "The Isaac Typology in the New Testament," *NTS* 14 (1968) 583-89.

Woodward, Stephen. "The Provenance of the Term 'Saints': A *Religionsgeschichtliche* Study," *JETS* 24 (1981) 107-16.

Wright, David F. "Homosexuals or Prostitutes? The Meaning of APΣENOKOITAI (1 Cor 6:9, 1 Tim 1:10)," *VC* 38 (1984) 125-53.

Wright, N. Thomas. "The Messiah and the People of God: A Study in Pauline Theology with Particular Reference to the Argument in the Epistle to the Romans." D.Phil. diss. Oxford University, 1980.

————. "Romans and the Theology of Paul," in *Pauline Theology* vol. 3: *Romans,* ed. D. M. Hay and E. E. Johnson. Minneapolis: Fortress, 1995, 30-67.

————. "New Exodus, New Inheritance: The Narrative Structure of Romans 3–8," in *Romans and the People of God: Essays in Honor of Gordon D. Fee on the Occasion of His 65th Birthday,* ed. S. K. Soderlund and N. T. Wright. Grand Rapids: Eerdmans, 1999, 26-35.

————. *Paul: In Fresh Perspective.* Minneapolis: Fortress, 2005.

Yinger, Kent L. *Paul, Judaism, and Judgment according to Deeds.* SNTS.MS 105; Cambridge: Cambridge University Press, 1999.

Young, Frances M. "Romans xvi: A Suggestion," *ExpT* 47 (1935-36) 27-41.

Young, N. H. "Did St. Paul Compose Romans iii.24f ?" *ABR* 22 (1974) 23-32.

————. "C. H. Dodd, 'Hilaskethai' and His Critics," *EvQ* 48 (1976) 67-78.

————. "*Hilaskesthai*' and Related Words in the New Testament," *EvQ* 55 (1983) 169-76.

Zeller, Dieter. "Sühne und Langmut. Zur Traditionsgeschichte von Röm 3,24-26," *TP* 43 (1968) 51-75.

———. *Juden und Heiden in der Mission des Paulus. Studien zum Römerbrief.* Stuttgart: Katholisches Bibelwerk, 1976.

Ziesler, John A. *The Meaning of Righteousness in Paul: A Linguistic and Theological Enquiry.* SNTS.MS 20; Cambridge: Cambridge University Press, 1972.

———. "Salvation Proclaimed IX: Romans 3:21-26," *ExpT* 93 (1981-82) 356-59.

Introduction to the Commentary

The writing of biblical commentaries has always been, and will always be, an important datum of Christian experience, arising as it does from the interaction of heart and mind, of piety and inquiry. But it is also fair to say that whenever the church has felt itself (1) to have in hand a body of more "critically established" biblical texts, (2) blessed by better translations of those texts, (3) rejuvenated by new approaches to Christian understanding, (4) threatened by teaching that differs from the norm, and/or (5) confused by differing methodologies or competing ideologies — as has occurred at various times in its history and is taking place today — it has turned back to its foundational documents and produced an outburst of biblical commentaries beyond what might normally be expected. At such times the writing of biblical commentaries has been undertaken not only with a desire of achieving a better explication of what the biblical writers originally said and meant, but also with hopes of effecting within the contemporary Christian community something of a consensus regarding (1) the import of their message, (2) how that message should impact the thought and actions of people today, and (3) in what ways the Christian gospel can be more effectively contextualized in our present day. And all these factors and desires are what motivate the author of this present commentary on Romans.

1. ROMANS VIS-À-VIS PAUL'S OTHER LETTERS

Paul's letter to the Christians at Rome is in some ways very much like the other Pauline writings of the NT. It is also, however, in many ways quite different — particularly with respect to its character, its structures, and its various forms of argumentation.

A. The Character of Romans

Differing opinions regarding the character of Romans were almost entirely unknown from the second through the eighteenth centuries of Christian history,

1

for Christians in earlier times usually viewed Romans as a "compendium of Christian doctrine" (as Philipp Melanchthon called it) — or at least as a fairly complete summary of Paul's teaching and so commonly as something like an early systematic theology of the Christian church. When Romans was understood in this fashion, the question was often asked: "Why are Paul's other letters (with the possible exception of Ephesians) not like Romans?" During the past two centuries, however, emphasis has increasingly been placed (1) on the historical circumstances in Paul's writing to believers in Jesus at Rome and (2) on Romans as a letter rather than a theological compendium or treatise — with the result that the writing of Romans has come to be understood, at least in scholarly circles, in more situational manner and circumstantial terms. And when understood as a true letter, the question asked has often become reversed: "Why, then, is Romans not like Paul's other letters?"

Many earnest Christians today, of course, still think of Romans as a compendium of Christian doctrine, especially those who read it only in a devotional, theological, homiletical, or some "reader response" fashion. Likewise, a number of contemporary scholars continue to view Romans as being, in some sense, a summary of Paul's teaching, though without wanting to deny its historical circumstances or the particularity of its presentation. A few of those who view it as a summary of Paul's teaching think of it as having been originally written as a circular letter sent to various churches established by the apostle in order to remind them of his essential message and then delivered (with an appropriate change of address and perhaps a few editorial alterations) to the Christians at Rome. Others who understand Romans as a summary of the apostle's teaching propose that its basic content was first drawn up before Paul's final journey to Jerusalem, and so it was originally intended as something like Paul's "last will and testament" before that crucial (and rather disastrous) visit to Israel's capital city — and then given epistolary form and sent as a letter to believers in Jesus at Rome. Still others tend to see large portions of the main body of Romans as collections of various Pauline materials — whether sermons, addresses, and/or tractates; whether abstracted or retained relatively whole — that had previously been used by Paul in various contexts during his missionary outreach to Gentiles in eastern regions of the Roman Empire and then sent to the Christians at Rome in the form of a letter to inform them of the nature of his message, thereby bringing them into the orbit of his mission to the Gentile world and seeking support from them for a further extension of his mission to Gentiles into the western regions of the empire.

The majority of scholarly interpreters today, however, prefer not to speak of Romans as a compendium of Paul's theology or teaching. A major problem with understanding Romans in this way is that, though it is the longest of all the apostle's extant writings, Romans lacks a number of topics or expositions that seem from his other letters to have been absolutely essential to his thought and his proclamation — most obviously, (1) discussion of the resurrection of believers in Jesus, which was a subject of very great importance in his earlier

2

letters (cf. esp. 1 Thessalonians 4–5; 2 Thessalonians 2; and 1 Corinthians 15), and (2) treatment of the Lord's Supper, which was a matter of great concern when Paul wrote to his converts at Corinth (cf. 1 Cor 11:17-34). Rather, most contemporary interpreters understand Romans as a letter written in the context of a real historical situation that therefore must be read as reflecting the occasional character of a real letter and the dialogical nature of its circumstances. So most modern treatments of Romans have attempted first to spell out the nature of the problem or problems that must have existed within the Christian congregations at Rome — whether theological, ethical, or cultural; whether brought about by outside factors or arising from within — and then to explicate what Paul has written in a manner that highlights its apologetic and polemical nature, and not just to deal with the letter as though it contained exposition alone.

B. The Structure and Argument of Romans

Questions regarding the structure and argument of Romans are increasingly directed to matters having to do with what has been called the letter's "dual" or "double character" — that is, (1) it is addressed to a specific group of people and yet (2) many of its arguments are presented in the form of a more general treatise or tractate. Thus the question is frequently asked: Why are the beginning sections in 1:1-15 and the concluding sections in 15:14–16:27 so much like a letter, using many of the epistolary conventions of the day, whereas the large central section of 1:16–15:13 in its four major parts reads more like a treatise or tractate (or a collection of treatises or tractates), with few of the epistolary conventions of antiquity appearing — or appearing, at best, in such a random fashion as to be considered almost incidental? Others have phrased the question in the following fashion: Why do the beginning and concluding sections of Romans speak so directly about Paul's purposes in writing and his immediate travel plans, as though the letter is to be understood in an entirely circumstantial manner, whereas the large central portion of the letter, in both its doctrinal and its hortatory features, echoes a number of themes and expressions that appear in Paul's other letters and so seems to suggest that at least the central portion should be understood in a more general manner? Further, at other times the question has been asked: Why do the beginning sections in 1:1-15 and the concluding sections in 15:14–16:27, as well as the specific address of 11:13 ("I am talking to you Gentiles"), speak so expressly about the apostle writing to Gentiles, whereas the two theological sections of 1:16–4:24 and 9:1–11:36, as well as some of what appears in the ethical section of 12:1–15:13, set out arguments that are couched in Jewish or Jewish Christian ways and nuanced in a distinctly Jewish manner?

Likewise, the question must be asked when considering the form and structure of Paul's letter to Rome: Where is the focus or central thrust of the letter? Is it to be found in its proclamations of "the righteousness of God" and "justification by faith" in the thesis statement of 1:16-17 and then more fully in the development, elucidation, and illustration of that thesis statement in 3:21–4:25? Or is the letter's focus to be seen in the second section of the body middle of the letter, that is, in 5:1–8:39, wherein is presented a message of "peace" and "reconciliation" with God, a treatment of "death" because of Adam and the gift of "eternal life" through Jesus Christ, and a depiction of relationships that culminate with being "in Christ," being "in the Spirit," and Christ by his Spirit being "in the Christian," who is "adopted" by God into his family? Or is the letter's central thrust contained in its setting out of relations between Israel and the Christian church in 9:6–11:36? — or, perhaps, in its ethical exhortations that deal with "the obedience of faith" (cf. 1:5 for the expression) in 12:1–15:13? Or in its body closing or "apostolic parousia" section, 15:14-32, which draws together Paul's desires and requests? And if we take any of the above sections to represent the letter's central thrust and so to contain the major concern or concerns of Paul when he wrote, we must then ask: How do the other sections of the letter relate to that major section? Or to state the question in another way: How should the presentations in the central "body middle" of the letter — which extends from 1:16 through 15:13 and contains a number of subsections that appear to be almost self-contained units of material — be correlated with what may be determined to be the letter's focus or central thrust?

Such questions as expressed above deal with highly significant matters. We have attempted to sketch out the issues involved and our own resolutions of these concerns in our recently published monograph *Introducing Romans: Critical Issues in Paul's Most Famous Letter.*[1] Suffice it here to say that what is presented in this brief introduction is given much more extensive treatment in that earlier publication, and that many of the issues raised here also receive treatment in the exegetical expositions that appear later in this commentary.

2. MAJOR CRITICAL ISSUES IN THE STUDY OF ROMANS

Every serious reader of Romans is faced with a number of critical issues in his or her study of the letter. Here we will only highlight the most significant of these issues, organizing them under the three headings of "matters largely uncontested," "matters recently resolved," and "matters extensively debated today" — noting in the process our own proposals, which will guide the exegetical treatments that follow in the commentary proper.

A. Matters Largely Uncontested

Questions regarding authorship, addressees, occasion, and the relative date of Romans have often seemed fairly easy to answer — for the letter's author (Paul)

---

1. Cf. R. N. Longenecker, *Introducing Romans,* chs. 10 and 11, pp. 353-466.

and its addressees (the Christians at Rome) seem quite clearly identified in 1:1-15, and its occasion (a letter in lieu of, but in preparation for, a visit) and time of writing (at the end of Paul's missionary endeavors in the eastern part of the Roman Empire, just before his final visit to Jerusalem) appear to be fairly clearly stated in 15:23-29. There have, of course, been a number of opposing views on such matters during the past couple centuries of NT scholarship. But there is today a fairly firm consensus among scholars regarding these rather elementary concerns.

Nonetheless, many of these basic matters regarding provenance have been honed to a finer edge during the past century and so need to be understood today in a somewhat more nuanced fashion. For example, in our considerations of authorship we need also to take into account the parts that Tertius (cf. 16:22) and Phoebe (cf. 16:1-2) played in the composition, delivery, and possible personal elucidation of Paul's letter — as well as the possible involvement of other believers in Jesus in the Christian congregations at Corinth and its port-city Cenchrea. Likewise, such questions as the following regarding the addressees are being increasingly asked today: (1) Were the letter's addressees Gentile or Jewish believers in Jesus, or was the church at Rome made up of both Gentile and Jewish believers — and if ethnically mixed, in what proportions? (2) How and when was the church at Rome founded? (3) What was the situation of the Jews at Rome at the time, not only legally and socially but also religiously? (4) What was the situation of the Christians at Rome at the time, not only ethnically but also organizationally, socially, and theologically? (5) What relationship did Paul see himself as having with believers in Jesus at Rome, almost all of whom he had never met? And (6) what relationship did the Christians at Rome see themselves as having with Paul, almost all of whom had never met him?

Further, a number of questions may be asked regarding the occasion and relative date for Paul's writing to Christians at Rome. Most of these questions have to do with matters pertaining to (1) Pauline chronology, which involves a working out of relationships between what Paul says about the course of his ministry in his letters and what Luke writes about Paul's missionary outreach in his second volume, the so-called "Acts of the Apostles," and (2) what can be determined from Romans itself with respect to the time when Paul wrote to the Christians at Rome and his purpose or purposes in writing them.

Much of what can be said with respect to these questions has been set out in our book *Introducing Romans,* and more will be said in our exegetical commentary that follows. Suffice it here to affirm that (1) we are convinced that Paul was the author of Romans, (2) we are fairly sure that Tertius and Phoebe were also involved, in various ways and to various extents, in its composition, delivery, and elucidation, and (3) we entertain favorably the possibility that some of the leaders of the Christian congregations at Corinth and Cenchrea had some input in the letter's composition, particularly as they heard and responded to at least portions of it as those portions were given a preliminary reading in their presence. And while an exact date for Paul's writing of his letter to the Christians at Rome has proven to be somewhat elusive, ranging from A.D. 47 to A.D. 59, we believe that the winter of 57-58 best fits all the data available from the letter itself, from Acts, and from such external sources as are available, and so will assume the general correctness of that date in the exegetical commentary that follows.

B. Matters Recently Resolved

A great amount of scholarly endeavor during the past century and a half has been focused on matters regarding the integrity of Romans, asking questions about (1) whether our present Greek text contains later scribal glosses or interpolations, which need to be pruned from the letter, and whether certain other notations need to be inserted, and (2) whether our present canonical letter is in the form in which it was originally written or needs to be reconstructed in some other manner. All the questions and their proposed answers with respect to integrity are dependent on comparative and evaluative studies of the existing textual tradition of Romans. Happily, there has been a considerable development of understanding during the past 150 years or so with respect to the textual history of the NT (including that of Romans), and so many of the past critical issues regarding the integrity of the letter have been essentially resolved.

Glosses and Interpolations. Individual words, phrases, or statements that appear in the margins or between the lines of MSS are referred to as glosses; foreign or extraneous materials incorporated into the texts are called interpolations. At times, however, glosses were written into texts by copyists and so became interpolations. The expressions "glosses" and "interpolations," therefore, have often been used somewhat interchangeably.

Based on the facts (1) that interpolations by later authors into earlier writings was a fairly common phenomenon in antiquity, (2) that scribal glosses are rather common in our extant biblical MSS, and (3) that a number of passages in Romans are not only difficult to interpret but also seem obscure or contradictory, some scholars during the past century and a half have argued for a rather large number of glosses or interpolations in the text of Romans — and, further, have claimed to be able to distinguish what Paul originally wrote from such later recensions.

Sadly, some commentators of the past, when faced with a difficulty of interpretation, all-too-often either (1) dispensed with the problem simply by identifying the word, phrase, or passage in question as a gloss or interpolation, and so excised it from the text, or (2) inserted into the text some existing marginal reading, thereby justifying their own interpretation. And remnants of such practices continue in various quarters today. Nonetheless, arguments against any large scale incorporation of glosses or interpolations into the text of Romans based on supposed "improved understandings" of the NT's textual tradition have proven to be far more convincing to most scholars today than suppositions in their favor. And scholars today are far more prepared to entertain the possibility of difficulties and obscurities — even of contradictions — in the interpretation of Romans than were scholars in previous generations, crediting such matters either to Paul's own somewhat convoluted logic, to the interpreter's misconceived perceptions of what Paul ought to be saying, or to both, but not first of all to textual glosses or interpolations.

It is always possible, of course, that minor glosses or extraneous interpolations have somehow become incorporated into a particular biblical text, and every possible instance of such an occurrence needs to be checked by the canons of textual criticism. This constant checking is what we will endeavor to do in the "Textual Notes" and "Exegetical Comments" of the commentary proper. Suffice it here to say that NT textual criticism has come a long way during the past few decades, with the result that a great many of the textual issues with respect to every portion of the NT generally — and of Romans in particular — have been resolved. And it is this understanding of matters that we will attempt to demonstrate and explicate in the present commentary.

The Original Form of the Letter. Questions regarding the original form of Paul's letter to Rome have also been repeatedly asked during the past 150 years or so. Working backward from those matters of most concern — that is, starting from the most crucial issues that congregate mostly at the end of the letter and moving back to the letter's beginning — such questions as the following have been asked:

1. Since Marcion and Tertullian seem not to have known chs. 15 and 16, and since the Latin Vulgate and some minor manuscripts do not include them, did Romans originally end at 14:23 — with, perhaps, a doxology like that of 15:33 or 16:25-27 (or, less likely, the weakly attested doxology of 16:24) included to round off that shorter, original composition? Or should the evidence from the major manuscripts be accepted and chs. 15–16 be viewed as integral to the letter?

2. Since the long list of greetings in 16:1-23 includes names of people associated in some manner with the city of Ephesus, was this portion originally a separate letter (either in whole or in part) that was first addressed to believers at Ephesus and only later became somehow attached to the first fifteen chapters of Romans? Or were the greetings in ch. 16 always an integral part of Paul's letter to Rome?

3. Do the manuscript evidence, the theology, and/or the tone of 16:25-27 suggest that this doxological material was a post-Pauline addition to Romans? Or should it, too, be seen as part of Paul's original letter?

4. Does the absence of the expression ἐν Ῥώμῃ ("at Rome") from 1:7 and 15 in Codex G and some texts quoted by Origen and Ambrosiaster indicate that Romans was originally written without a specific Roman address? Or was the designation "at Rome" omitted at a later time when Romans came to be viewed as a theological tractate rather than a letter and was used in the churches in a more universalistic fashion?

Many of these matters were dealt with effectively by Harry Gamble in his 1977 monograph on *The Textual History of the Letter to the Romans*[2] — particularly in justification of "the long form" of sixteen chapters for the original letter and in support of the designation "at Rome" in 1:7 and 15. The presence of one or more "grace benedictions" at 16:20b and/or 24 is still somewhat debated. And the integrity of the doxology at the end of the letter at 16:25-27 is frequently held in question. But articles by Larry Hurtado and Howard Marshall have gone far in alleviating the criticisms usually raised against the integrity of the concluding doxology,[3] and Jeffrey Weima's study of the Pauline letter closings has also gone a long way toward positing a positive understanding of what Paul was doing in that doxology.[4] All of these critical issues have been discussed in greater detail in our book on *Introducing Romans* and will be treated in the "Textual Notes" and "Exegetical Comments" where they are relevant in the present commentary — as will also many other matters of this nature that have arisen of late.

C. Matters Extensively Debated Today

There are, however, a number of other critical issues in the study of Romans that are quite extensively debated today. Many of these have also been discussed at length in our volume on *Introducing Romans,* but because of their importance some of them need to be highlighted here as well. Much of what appears in the exegetical materials of this present commentary will, in fact, depend largely on the validity and explication of these particular matters.

The Identity, Character, Circumstances, and Concerns of the Letter's Addressees. Discussions regarding the addressees of Paul's letter to Rome have been, as noted above, mostly concerned with such questions of identity as: "Were the letter's addressees Gentile believers in Jesus or Jewish believers in Jesus?" or "Were the congregations of Christians at Rome made up of both Gentile and Jewish believers?" And if the church at Rome was ethnically mixed, "What were the proportions of Gentile believers and Jewish believers in it?"

Raymond Brown in 1983, however, proposed that the most basic issue with respect to Paul's addressees at Rome — and thus a matter of vital importance for a proper understanding of Romans — is not that of the addressees' ethnicity, but rather "the crucial issue is the theological outlook of this mixed Jewish/Gentile Christianity."[5] For, as Brown argued, if we take seriously the witness of Acts 2:10 and 28:21, together with certain statements by the Roman

---

2. Gamble, *Textual History.*

3. Hurtado, "Doxology at the End of Romans," 185-99; Marshall, "Romans 16:25-27."

4. Weima, *Neglected Endings,* esp. 135-44, 229-30.

5. See R. E. Brown, "Not Jewish Christianity and Gentile Christianity," 74-79; *idem,* "Beginnings of Christianity at Rome" and "The Roman Church near the End of the First Christian Generation" in *Antioch and Rome,* 92-127, quotation from *Antioch and Rome,* 109 n. 227.

historian Tacitus (c. AD 56-120) and the fourth-century Christian commentator "Ambrosiaster," we must give attention to the axis that runs from Roman Christianity back to the Jerusalem church as being of major importance.[6]

Brown's conclusions were that (1) for both Jews and Christians "the Jerusalem-Rome axis was strong," (2) "Roman Christianity came from Jerusalem, and indeed represented the Jewish/Gentile Christianity associated with such Jerusalem figures as Peter and James," and (3) both in the earliest days of the Roman church and at the time when Paul wrote to them, believers in Jesus at Rome could be characterized as "Christians who kept up some Jewish observances and remained faithful to part of the heritage of the Jewish Law and cult, without insisting on circumcision."[7] Or as Joseph Fitzmyer has described the character of Paul's addressees at Rome (applauding Brown's thesis, though without using it as a hermeneutical tool): "Roman Christians seem to have been in continual contact with the Christians of Jerusalem," with the result that their form of the Christian faith "seems to have been influenced especially by those associated with Peter and James of Jerusalem, in other words, by Christians who retained some Jewish observances and remained faithful to the Jewish legal and cultic heritage without insisting on circumcision for Gentile converts."[8]

In what follows, it is this understanding of Paul's Roman addressees that will be postulated: (1) ethnically, the Christian community at Rome included both Jewish and Gentile believers in Jesus, though with Gentile Christians in the majority, and (2) theologically, all of the Roman Christians — not only Jewish believers in Jesus but also Gentile believers — looked to the Jerusalem church as the mother church of Christianity, followed Jewish Christian liturgical rites and ethical practices, and reverenced the Mosaic law. They were not, however, "Judaizers" — that is, not like those who infiltrated the churches of Galatia with what Paul called "a different gospel, which is no gospel at all" (Gal 1:6-7). Rather, Paul considered them true believers in Jesus, "who thought," as Charles Talbert has concisely characterized their theology, "in Jewish categories."[9]

Paul's Purpose or Purposes in Writing the Letter. Two seemingly quite diverse viewpoints have dominated much of current scholarly discussion about the purpose or purposes of Romans: (1) Paul's motivation for writing Romans originated from within his own ministry and consciousness — whether to introduce himself to an unknown audience, to seek support for a forthcoming mission to the western part of the Roman Empire, to defend himself against criticism and/or misunderstanding, to assert his apostolic authority over a church he considered within the orbit of his Gentile ministry, or to set out his own understanding of the Christian gospel as something of a summary of his message or a "last will and testament." Or (2) the letter was written to counter

---

6. Cf. R. E. Brown, "Further Reflections on the Origins of the Church of Rome," 98-115.

7. R. E. Brown, "Beginnings of Christianity at Rome," 104.

8. Fitzmyer, *Romans*, 33.

9. Talbert, *Romans*, 16.

some particular problem or set of problems, that is, to deal with some identi-fiable circumstance or set of circumstances that existed among Christians at Rome — whether doctrinal or ethical, and whether arising from outside the church or from within.[10] To frame these two stances in a somewhat different manner, it may be asked: (1) Was Paul's purpose in writing Romans *missionary* in nature, motivated by his own consciousness of being an apostle to the Gentiles, his own sense of mission, and/or his own desire to present to the Christians at Rome something of a summation or testament of his message throughout the Greco-Roman world, perhaps incorporating into that tractate or letter some of the issues that had previously arisen in his ministry and that he wanted to pre-sent to believers at Rome for his own reasons? Or (2) was his purpose *pastoral,* motivated by a desire to correct problems, whether doctrinal or ethical, that he knew existed among the Christians at Rome?

These two viewpoints, stances, or sets of questions, while seemingly in opposition to one another, should probably not, however, be understood as mu-tually exclusive. A number of interpretive possibilities may be seen as existing both between them and within them. Nonetheless, in asking whether Paul's pur-pose in writing Romans was motivated principally (1) by factors that arose from within his own ministry or (2) by conditions that were then existing within the Christian congregations at Rome, scholars seem to have come to something of a watershed in their sorting out of issues, determining of priorities, and proposing of solutions. And it is probably not extreme to claim that from this watershed has flowed almost everything that has been said and can be claimed about the character, form, and content of Paul's letter to believers in Jesus at Rome.

It is the thesis of this commentary that Paul sets out in the epistolary frame of his letter two primary purposes for his writing to the Christians at Rome, with these two primary purposes explicated throughout the letter's rather large "body middle" (1:16–15:13). These purposes are related to the occasion for his writing and must be seen to have stemmed from his own missionary conscious-ness and his plans for his future ministry. They are as follows:

1. To give to the Christians at Rome what he calls in 1:11 a "spiritual gift" (χάρισμα πνευματικόν), which he thought of as something that was uniquely his (cf. his references to "my gospel" in 2:16 and 16:25), that he felt his addressees needed if they were to "mutually encourage" one another (1:11-12) and that he evidently wanted them to know in order that they might understand accurately and more appreciatively what he was proclaiming in his mission to Gentiles.

2. To seek the assistance of the Christians at Rome for the extension of his Gentile mission to Spain (cf. 1:13; 15:24), which assistance should probably be understood as including their financial support and their willingness

---

10. For a variety of answers to these issues, with some pertinent interaction between them, see Donfried, *Romans Debate,* and Donfried, *Romans Debate: Revised and Expanded Edition.*

to be used as a base for his outreach to the western regions of the empire, just as the Christians at Antioch of Syria had assisted him and served as the base for his outreach to the eastern regions of the empire.

Also important, however, is a purpose that can be discerned by a close mirror-reading of various comments, veiled allusions, and rhetorical expressions of Paul that appear in the explication of his message in the central sections of the letter, as well as a mirror-reading of some of his statements in the epistolary frame surrounding that central portion of 1:16–15:13. But since this purpose is somewhat muted and more implied than directly stated, it seems best to call it not a primary purpose for writing Romans but a subsidiary purpose:

3. To defend against certain criticisms of his person and misrepresentations of his message, with the intent that the Christians at Rome would properly understand his person, ministry, and message and be willing to assist him in his Gentile mission.

Yet two further purposes must also be included in any listing of Paul's reasons for writing Romans. Both are discernible by a process of mirror-reading, though, admittedly, they carry somewhat different degrees of probability. The first is most probable and can be distilled by mirror-reading the exhortations regarding "the Strong" and "the Weak" in 14:1–15:13, with that situation probably recalled in the additional admonitions of 16:17-20a. The second, while somewhat more inferential, can be ascertained by mirror-reading the exhortations regarding the relation of Christians to civil authorities in 13:1-5 and the quite specific directives to his Roman addressees regarding their responsibility to pay taxes and revenues in 13:6-7, which appear in the midst of the general exhortations on Christian love in 12:9-21 and 13:8-14 and seem to break the continuity of those two sections of ethical maxims. These two purposes we list here as Paul's fourth and fifth reasons for the writing of Romans, listing them in the order of their greatest probability:

4. To counsel regarding a dispute that had arisen among believers in Jesus who called themselves "the Strong" and other believers who were designated "the Weak," either within or between the various Christian house congregations at Rome, as he does in 14:1–15:13 and as he seems to recall in the further admonitions given in 16:17-20a.
5. To give directives regarding the relation of Christians at Rome to the city's government authorities and their responsibilities in paying legitimate taxes and revenues, as he does in 13:1-7.

These, however, should probably be seen as somewhat subsidiary purposes of Paul for writing the letter since, while they reflect certain circumstances of the Christians at Rome, they are not included in those sections of the letter where the primary purposes and major concerns of a letter writer of Paul's day would be expected — that is, in the epistolary "salutation" (1:1-7), "thanksgiving" (1:8-12), or "body-opening" (1:13-15) sections at the letter's beginning, nor in the epistolary "body-closing" or "apostolic parousia" section (15:14-32) at its end.

The Epistolary Genre of Romans. Romans is far longer than a typical non-literary letter of antiquity. Further, it is longer than all of the other NT letters, including those of the Pauline corpus. More significantly, however, it differs from Paul's other letters with respect to its epistolary genre. For Romans is not, as is Galatians, a "rebuke and request" letter. Nor is it a strictly "paraenetic" or "hortatory" letter, as is 1 Thessalonians; nor a mixed letter of "response, exhortation, and advice," as is 1 Corinthians; nor a letter of "friendship and advice," as is Philippians; nor simply a letter of "recommendation," as is Philemon.

Frequently Romans has been classified as a "literary epistle" or *Lehrbrief* — that is, a letter written to instruct its readers.[11] But that is a designation far too general, for it could also be applied to most of Paul's other letters, as well as to a number of other NT epistolary writings. Some have viewed Romans as a "letter of introduction" — perhaps even an "ambassadorial letter of self-introduction."[12] Chan-Hie Kim has ably discussed the provenance and epistolary features of an ancient letter of introduction (or, as he calls it, "letter of recommendation") and has reproduced the Greek and Latin texts of eighty-three such letters — most of them, of course, being Greek nonliterary papyrus letters from Egypt.[13] Stanley Stowers has dealt with a large number of Greco-Roman and Christian letters of introduction, which were written from the time of the Roman orator, philosopher, and statesman Cicero (106-43 B.C.), who, as Stowers points out, "wrote numerous letters of introduction and intercession of varying length and intensity"), to the time of Augustine, the great fifth-century Church Father (A.D. 354-430).[14] And letters of introduction, as many have noted, are referred to in both the Jewish and the Christian Scriptures.[15]

But letters of introduction in antiquity, as far as we know, were always written by others on behalf of the person or persons being introduced or accredited, and not by someone presenting his own credentials. Further, they usually included expressions of high praise for the person or people addressed, with those words of praise constituting an important part of the letter. So while Paul in Romans certainly introduces himself and his message to Christians at Rome — and while, more particularly, he undoubtedly considered himself "an apostle of Christ" (cf. Rom 1:1 and *passim*) and therefore as "Christ's ambassador" (cf. 2 Cor 5:20) — it may be questioned whether his letter to the Christians at Rome should be classified as merely a letter of introduction or is any more ambassadorial than any of his other NT letters.

11. So, e.g., Michel, *An die Römer,* 5; Black, *Romans,* 18.
12. So Jewett, "Romans as an Ambassadorial Letter," 5-22; *idem, Romans,* 44-46.
13. C.-H. Kim, *Familiar Greek Letter of Recommendation,* 150-238.
14. Stowers, *Letter Writing in Greco-Roman Antiquity,* 159.
15. Cf. 2 Kgs 5:5-6; Acts 9:1b-2; 18:27; 1 Cor 16:3; 2 Cor 3:1; see also 2 Macc 9:19-27.

A more likely hypothesis was suggested in 1977 by Martin Stirewalt, who argued that among extant letters of Paul's day there can be found evidence for a distinctive type of instructional letter — that is, an epistolary genre for which the label "literary epistle" is misleading and *Lehrbrief* is too general, but for which the term "letter essay" would be appropriate.[16] Stirewalt acknowledged that a "letter essay" cannot be shown to have been recognized as a discrete epistolary category by any author of the ancient world. Nonetheless, it is just this type of material, he argued, that appears in letters written by the Greek philosopher Epicurus (342/341-271/270 B.C.) and by the Greek rhetorician and historian Dionysius of Halicarnassus (died 8 B.C.) and can also be found in certain writings of the Greek essayist and Pythian priest Plutarch (c. A.D. 46-120) — as well as, to an extent, in the Hellenistic Jewish composition known as 2 Maccabees (which was probably written at the end of the second century B.C.) and in the Christian *Martyrdom of Polycarp* (which was written sometime toward the end of the second century A.D.).

Stirewalt characterizes these writings as "written communications with epistolary characteristics, sent between identifiable parties, on particular subjects."[17] Or, as Stirewalt defines further the ancient letter essays that he has brought together for analysis — with, of course, his underlying thesis being that they offer close parallels to Paul's letter to the Romans:

> The pieces collected here were written out of a genuine letter-setting and they retain the formal and structural epistolary characteristics [of genuine letters]. . . . On the other hand, they are losing some of the form, phraseology, and structure of the letter and are incorporating the more impersonal, objective style of the monograph. In fact, the writers themselves refer to them most often as logoi [i.e., literally "words," but here connoting "instruction"].[18]

Somewhat similar to Stirewalt's thesis is that of Klaus Berger, who in 1984 drew analogies between Paul's letter to the Romans and Greco-Roman letters in which a teacher writes to his pupils, to a community of pupils, or even to certain cities and gives them instruction.[19] Yet Berger also recognized differences between Romans and ancient Greco-Roman didactic letters, principally in that (1) Paul does not write as a teacher who lords it over his pupils, since he was not the one who founded the church at Rome, and (2) the tone of Romans is more that of a general treatise, since Paul did not really know his addressees and so could not speak more personally.[20]

---

16. See Stirewalt, "Form and Function of the Greek Letter-Essay," in *Romans Debate,* 175-206; in *Romans Debate: Revised and Expanded Edition,* 147-71.

17. Stirewalt, "Form and Function of the Greek Letter-Essay," in *Romans Debate,* 176; in *Romans Debate: Revised and Expanded Edition,* 147.

18. Stirewalt, "Form and Function of the Greek Letter-Essay," in *Romans Debate,* 176; in *Romans Debate: Revised and Expanded Edition,* 148.

19. Berger, "Hellenistische Gattungen im Neuen Testament," 1338-39.

20. Berger, "Hellenistische Gattungen im Neuen Testament," 1334-35.

These theses of Stirewalt and Berger, taken together, offer important contributions for an understanding of the epistolary genre of Romans. They do not, of course, explain why the Christians at Rome were singled out by Paul to be the recipients of such an instructional letter essay. One might have expected, in fact, that Paul would have favored his own converts and his own churches with such a document, rather than writing to believers in Jesus who had not been brought to Christ through his ministry and the great majority of whom he did not know personally. Nor do the theses of Stirewalt and Berger offer any reason that Paul would have chosen the particular time he did to write such an instructional letter. Yet when combined with our theses above regarding (1) the addressees of Romans and (2) Paul's purposes in writing to them, as well as our thesis below regarding (3) the letter's basic rhetorical genres and its incorporated rhetorical conventions, an understanding of the epistolary genre of Romans as an ancient "letter essay" — that is, as instructional material set out within an epistolary frame — provides, we believe, the most likely life setting and cultural context for a proper interpretation of the letter. And it is such a view that will be espoused and worked out in the commentary materials that follow. Over the centuries, many manuscripts, editions, and translations of the NT books between Acts and Revelation have titled each as "Epistle" or "Letter" to its named or implied recipients. Titles in the commentary series follow that convention.

The Rhetorical Genres of Romans. It has often been argued during the past few decades that Paul's argument in Romans — particularly in the long, four-part central section of his letter (1:16–15:13) — is best understood in terms of one or the other of the following ancient rhetorical models: (1) a *forensic* rhetorical model (assuming that the argument of Romans is comparable to that of Galatians), (2) a *deliberative* model (highlighting the hortatory features of the letter), or (3) an *epideictic* model (highlighting the letter's persuasive features, often with an accompanying emphasis on what is to be viewed as honorable and what as shameful). Several scholars, however, building on earlier studies of protreptic ("hortatory") speeches in antiquity, have argued that the course of the argument in the letter's first, second, and fourth central sections, that is, in 1:16–4:25; 5:1–8:39; and 12:1–15:13, is far better understood rhetorically as expressing a *protreptic* rhetorical model — that is, as a λόγος προτρεπτικός or "speech ['word' or 'message'] of exhortation" model, which was a type of address intended to win converts and attract people to a particular way of life. Those who have proposed such an understanding of these three central sections of Romans include Klaus Berger,[21] Stanley Stowers,[22] David Aune,[23] Anthony Guerra,[24] and Christopher Bryan.[25]

21. Berger, *Formgeschichte des Neuen Testament,* esp. 217.

22. Stowers, *Letter Writing in Greco-Roman Antiquity,* 112-14, 128.

23. Aune, "Romans as a *Logos Protreptikos,*" 91-124; abbreviated version: "Romans as a *Logos Protrepikos,*" in *Romans Debate,* 278-96; *idem, Westminster Dictionary,* 383-86, 430-31.

24. Guerra, *Romans and the Apologetic Tradition,* 1-22.

25. Bryan, *Preface to Romans,* 18-28.

The rhetoric of Romans, as these scholars have pointed out, is different from all the usually proposed categories of ancient "forensic," "deliberative," or "epideictic" rhetoric and cannot be made to fit easily within any of them. The letter is not an apology in which Paul defends his apostleship or message; nor is it a polemic that counters false teaching. Further, it lacks some of the important rhetorical sections that usually appear, in one order or another, in forensic, deliberative, and epideictic rhetoric — principally an *exordium,* but also a *narratio* and a *propositio.* Rather, as Stanley Stowers argues: "In both form and function, Paul's letter to the Romans is a protreptic letter."[26] Or as Anthony Guerra enunciates the thesis: "Romans is a protreptic writing seeking to affirm Paul's ministry and the gospel which he preached."[27]

Ancient "words ['speeches' or 'messages'] of exhortation" (προτρεπτικοὶ λόγοι) were characteristically structured in terms of three sections: (1) a negative section, which dissuaded and censured an opposing view, (2) a positive section, which set forth and defended the author's position, and (3) a hortatory section, which appealed to the hearers or addressees to invite them to accept what was presented in the two previous sections.[28] To each of these customary sections of protreptic discourse, however, Paul adds in his letter to the Christians at Rome his own distinctive emphases and gives his own spin to the data he presents — often, as well, speaking to his addressees on their own grounds and interjecting material of particular relevance to them. Notable in this regard is the fact that Paul restructures the first section of his protreptic discourse (1:16–4:25) to include not just negative statements about what he opposes but also positive affirmations about what he holds in common with his Christian addressees.

But the thesis that three of the central sections of Romans are developed along the lines of Hellenistic "protreptic speech" does not explain everything about the rhetoric of the letter. In 9:1–11:36 Paul inserts a further section of material between his first two theological sections (1:16–4:25 and 5:1–8:39) and his fourth, hortatory, section (12:1–15:13). The intervening material is, we believe, best understood in terms of then-current Jewish "remnant theology" rhetoric. And it is this material that would have been of particular interest to believers at Rome who understood and expressed their commitment to Jesus in ways that had been largely transmitted to them by Jewish Christians from the mother church at Jerusalem.

The study of Hellenistic protreptic speech and its relevance for the analysis of Romans is very much in its infancy, and so, as would be expected with any new discipline, differing analyses of some of its details have been proposed. Likewise, Jewish remnant rhetoric has often been neglected in many of the past analyses of chs. 9–11. Nonetheless, viewing three of the central sections of Romans as structured along the lines of an ancient λόγος προτρεπτικός offers,

---

26. Stowers, *Letter Writing in Greco-Roman Antiquity,* 114.
27. Guerra, *Romans and the Apologetic Tradition,* preface, ix.
28. Cf. Aune, *Westminster Dictionary,* 383-85.

we believe, a better way of understanding the materials contained in 1:16–4:25; 5:1–8:39; and 12:1–15:13. Certainly such an understanding provides interpreters with a far better diachronic rhetorical model than does a forensic model, a deliberative model, or an epideictic model. And understanding 9:1–11:36 in terms of then-current Jewish remnant theology gives us an important key for unlocking Paul's argument in what has often been viewed as an extremely difficult set of three chapters.

These two diachronic models of rhetorical argumentation, that is, the Greco-Roman protreptic model and the Jewish remnant model, will be spelled out in the commentary proper. And in spelling them out, we will attempt to show not only (1) how Paul made use of the basic structures of Greco-Roman protreptic discourse and the basic motifs of Jewish remnant thought in writing to the Christians at Rome (whether with deliberate intent, so as to make the greatest rhetorical impact on his addressees, or somewhat unconsciously, simply because these forms and motifs were well known to both him and his addressees, and so provided appropriate rhetorical forms for the communication of what he wanted to say in this particular letter), but also (2) how he filled these ancient rhetorical conventions with Christian theology in order to accomplish his own particular purposes in writing his letter to Rome.

The Focus or Central Thrust of Paul's Presentation in Romans. Contrary to what has traditionally been argued, it is the thesis of this commentary that the focus or central thrust of Paul's presentation in Romans is not to be found in the first section of the body middle of the letter, that is, not in 1:16–4:25 — and not even in 1:16-17 combined with 3:21–4:25 — but, rather, (1) that Paul's focus or central thrust is set forth in the second section of the body middle of the letter, that is, in 5:1–8:39,[29] and (2) that the corollary of this focal theological exposition in 5:1–8:39 is expressed in the rather general — though also, it needs always to be recognized, the much more expressly christocentric — ethical exhortations of the fourth section of the letter's body middle, that is, in 12:1-21 and 13:8-14. So we will argue that it is in 5:1–8:39 that the theological portion of Paul's "spiritual gift," which he said in 1:11 he wanted to give to the Christians at Rome and which he calls in 2:16 and 16:25 "my gospel," comes explicitly to the fore — with the more general, but decidedly christocentric, exhortations of 12:1-21 and 13:8-14 comprising the relevant ethical materials that function as corollaries to the theological materials in 5:1–8:39.

This is not to discredit what Paul writes in 1:16–4:25, for that is what he held in common with his Christian addressees at Rome. Indeed, it was probably on the basis of the truths of 1:16–4:25 that both he and his Roman addressees originally became believers in Jesus. Certainly he believed that what he wrote there was true and highly significant, both in what he argued against and in what he affirmed. In all likelihood, Paul himself had proclaimed in other contexts much of what he argues there, particularly when presenting the Christian

---

29. Cf. R. N. Longenecker, "Focus of Romans," 49-69.

gospel to Jews in the synagogues of the Jewish Diaspora (as represented in Acts) as well as when writing to Gentile Christians who had been influenced by Jewish Christian thought for the better, as had his addressees at Rome (or when writing to his Gentile converts in the province of Galatia who had been influenced by Jewish Christian thought for the worse, as he did earlier in his missionary career).

But what Paul wanted the believers in Jesus at Rome to know, and therefore what he had a particular desire to present to them in 5:1–8:39 (together with the ethical implications of that exposition as expressed in 12:1-21 and 13:8-14), was the message of the Christian gospel as he had contextualized it in his preaching to those who were ethnically Gentiles and without any preparatory religious knowledge gained from either Judaism or Jewish Christianity — that is, to those who had for all their lives existed apart from any understanding of the Jewish (OT) Scriptures. For the Christians at Rome were dominantly Gentile believers in Jesus, and so, however they had originally come to Christ, Paul viewed them as included within his God-given mandate to Gentiles and therefore within the orbit of his Gentile mission. Thus he desired to strengthen these Gentile believers in Jesus by proclaiming to them his own distinctive form of Christian proclamation. Further, he wanted these Christians at Rome to become partners with him in his further missionary outreach to Gentiles in the western regions of the Roman Empire, just as the Christians at Antioch of Syria had supported him in his missionary outreach to Gentiles in the empire's eastern regions.

The Christians at Rome, whether ethnically Jews or Gentiles, were all, it seems, very familiar with the biblical accounts of God's redemptive working within the nation Israel. Likewise, it may be presumed that they were knowledgeable about the theological and ethical teachings of the OT Scriptures. It may, therefore, be postulated that the foundational salvific story of Israel's exodus from Egypt — as well as the Jewish soteriological themes of "justification," "redemption," and "sacrifice of atonement" ("propitiation" or "expiation") — would have been important to them. But what Paul seems to have discovered in his missionary outreach to Gentiles of the Greco-Roman world was that the story of the exodus and such forensic religious expressions as justification, redemption, and propitiation/expiation — while of great importance in Jewish and Jewish Christian contexts — were largely unknown, without significance, and probably not particularly appreciated by Gentiles who had no Jewish or Jewish Christian background. So in his preaching to Gentiles, Paul, it may be postulated, would have felt it necessary to contextualize the message of the Christian gospel in a manner that he believed would be more intelligible, personal, and significant to them — that is, (1) by speaking of "peace" and "reconciliation" with God "through our Lord Jesus Christ" (5:1-11), (2) by explicating the more universal, foundational story of how sin, death, and condemnation entered the world by "one man," but how grace, life, and righteousness have been brought about "through Jesus Christ our Lord" (5:12-21), (3) by spelling out relations between sin, death, and the law, on the one hand, and grace, life, and righteousness, on the other (6:1–7:13), (4) by expressing the plight of all people in their attempts to live by their own insights and strength by the use of a familiar tragic soliloquy drawn from Greek literature and by reference to humanity's common experience (7:14-25), (5) by highlighting the new relationships that come about when one is "in Christ" and "in the Spirit" (8:1-30), and (6) by closing with a triumphal declaration of God's love and care for his own "in Christ Jesus our Lord" (8:31-39). And it is this same type of contextualization, with the highlighting of many of these same features and themes, that appears also in a number of his other NT letters where Gentile believers in Jesus are addressed directly — as, for example, in 2 Cor 5:11-21 and Eph 2:1-22.

Further, it is in this second section of the body middle (chs. 5–8) of Paul's letter to Christians at Rome that the three basic modes of persuasion of classical synchronic rhetoric come most fully to expression: *logos* (the content of the argument), *ethos* (the character of the speaker or writer), and *pathos* (the power of the presentation to stir the emotions). It is also in this section that the themes usually considered most distinctly Pauline appear most prevalently — that is, (1) "peace" and "reconciliation" with God, and (2) the believer being "in Christ" and "in the Spirit." Likewise, it also needs to be noted that it is in Romans 8 that "the heights of the epistle are reached" and that there occurs "a sustained climax which takes the argument across the watershed" — using here J. A. T. Robinson's language drawn from his characterization of Romans as "a journey by canal across an isthmus" with its "series of locks" rising to and then falling away from "a central ridge."[30]

3. DISTINCTIVE EXEGETICAL TREATMENTS
OF THE PRESENT COMMENTARY

Many of the more distinctive exegetical treatments of the present commentary are to be found in its expositions of material that we have identified as expressing the focus or central thrust of Romans — that is, in its theological statements of 5:1–8:39, as well as in its corollary ethical exhortations of 12:1-21 and 13:8-14. These include exegetical treatments of (1) the relational themes of "peace" and "reconciliation" with God in 5:1-11, (2) the universal themes regarding relations between sin, death, and the law, on the one hand, and grace, life and righteousness, on the other hand in 5:12-21, (3) the discussions regarding the significance of Christ's death for Christian living, the function of the Mosaic law, and believers in Jesus being "alive to God in Christ" and "dead to the law" in 6:1–7:6, (4) depictions of the inability of believers in Jesus to live by means of their own insights and strength in 7:7-25, (5) the participationist themes of being "in Christ" and "in the Spirit" in 8:1-17, (6) the apocalyptic themes of "suffering" and "final consummation" in 8:18-25, (7) teachings on prayer, God's working

---

30. See J. A. T. Robinson, *Wrestling with Romans*, 9.

out of his purposes in a person's life, and the resultant confidence of Christians in 8:26-30, and (8) the triumphant confession of all true believers in Jesus expressed in 8:31-39. Likewise, such distinctive exegetical treatments are also found in the ethical exhortations in 12:1-21 and 13:8-14, where we will argue that Paul sets out a christocentric basis for Christian ethics, with the details of that ethic being (1) derived from the proclamation of the Christian gospel, (2) supported by the example and teaching of the historical Jesus, and (3) in line with certain basic passages of the OT Scriptures. Further, it will be argued that Paul's presentations in these second and fourth sections of the letter (the doctrinal section of 5:1–8:39 and the moral general ethical exhortations in 12:1–15:13) are based on and come to fullest expression in his teaching about being ἐν Χριστῷ ("in Christ"), together with its cognates (6:11, 23; 8:1, 39; 9:1; 14:14; 15:17; 16:11, 13), and being ἐν πνεύματι ("in the Spirit," 8:9).

In addition to these fairly distinctive treatments in our exegesis of the second and fourth sections of the body middle of the letter, there will also appear a number of other rather unique exegetical treatments in the present commentary. Most significant among this latter lot are our proposals that Paul makes use of distinctly Jewish and/or Jewish Christian forms of argument throughout the other two major sections of the central portion of Romans — that is, (1) in the first section of his letter's body middle, that is, in 1:16–4:25, both in presenting his negative statements of 1:18–3:20 and in setting out his positive statements of 3:21–4:25, and (2) in the third section of his letter's body middle, that is, in 9:1–11:36, where he makes use of the basic features of a then-current Jewish "remnant theology," reconstituting the central features of that theology into a Christianized "remnant rhetoric" in support of his arguments regarding the relationship of the Christian gospel to Israel's national hopes. Much of Paul's negative argument in the first part (1:18–3:20) of the first section will come to a climax in his negative comments regarding the phrase ἔργα νόμου ("works of the law") in 3:20 and 28 (cf. Gal 2:16; 3:2, 5, 10). And much of what he writes positively about "righteousness" and "faith" in the second part (3:21–4:25) of the first section, as well as throughout the third section of the central portion of the letter in 9:1–11:36, will be based on his understanding of the formula πίστις Ἰησοῦ Χριστοῦ ("faith in Jesus Christ" or "the faith/faithfulness of Jesus Christ") in 3:22 and 26b (cf. Gal 2:16 [twice]; 3:22 [possibly also 3:26, as in P[46]]; Eph 3:12; and Phil 3:9).

Particularly significant for an understanding of the course of Paul's argument — as well as for an appreciation of the structure of his presentation in the first two major theological sections of the body middle (1:16–4:25 and 5:1–8:39) — will be our textual and exegetical treatments of the main verb of the sentence in 5:1. The question that has always perplexed commentators is whether it should be read as ἔχωμεν ("let us have"), that is, as subjunctive, which would suggest some kind of exhortation to move forward, or as ἔχομεν ("we have"), that is, as an indicative verb, which would signal something of an inference or consequence to follow. There can be no doubt that the textual evidence is overwhelmingly in favor of the subjunctive ἔχωμεν, "let us have" (see "Textual Notes" on 5:1). Nonetheless, the great majority of interpreters (at least, among most Protestant commentators) have asserted that the context of the passage requires that the verb be read as the indicative ἔχομεν ("we have"), despite the preponderance of external support for ἔχωμεν, and so have usually credited the appearance of the subjunctive to some early scribal error or marginal gloss. Our argument, however, is that (1) the textual history of the passage so strongly supports the subjunctive verb ἔχωμεν that it cannot easily be set aside, (2) a proper understanding of the course of Paul's argument suggests the appropriateness of the subjunctive, and (3) the subjunctive verb, while it may not demand that 5:1 be viewed as a "hinge verse" that begins a new section — that is, a verse based on what Paul has written earlier in 1:16–4:25, but also a verse that calls on both Paul's original addressees and his present readers to move forward in their thinking on the basis of what follows in chs. 5–8) — it certainly fits into such a structural understanding. Thus rather than being viewed as something of a textual conundrum, as has so often been the stance taken by commentators, we will argue that this verb in 5:1 should be seen as (1) an important textual clue as to how to interpret the passage and (2) a significant key to the understanding of what Paul presents throughout the whole second section of the body middle of his letter, that is, in 5:1–8:39.

4. PROMINENT THEMATIC FEATURES
OF THE PRESENT COMMENTARY

Also to be noted in this brief introduction are some prominent thematic features that will appear in the exegetical commentary proper that follows. Probably the most distinctive of these have to do with the following matters.

A. The Importance of Formal Patterning and
Compositional Structures for Interpretation

Past interpreters of Romans (as well as of many of the other biblical writings) have all too often paid relatively little attention to the formal patterning and compositional structures of NT writings — and even less to questions regarding the value of such patterning and structures for interpretation. The result has been that commentary writing on Paul's letter to Rome has often been something of a "fishing expedition" guided largely by (1) a particular commentator's own interests and exegetical abilities, (2) the respective lengths of the material allotted by the author to particular topics, or (3) certain themes of Christian theology. It is our thesis, however, that features of formal patterning and compositional structure — as have become apparent from comparative epistolary and rhetorical studies of Paul's letter to the Christians at Rome vis-à-vis other ancient letters of Paul's day (i.e., what may be called "diachronic epistolary and rhetorical analyses") — not only (1) provide insights into how Paul constructed his letters, but also (2) suggest something regarding the function or functions that the apostle himself wanted his various letters, as well as particular sections within each of his letters, to serve, (3) highlight the importance that he himself placed on various materials in his letters — and, therefore, (4) provide important guidance for the interpreter as to how to understand the course of Paul's argument in each of his letters. So in the introductory section on "Form/ Structure/Setting" at the beginning of our treatment of each passage of Romans, matters having to do with formal patterning and compositional structure will be set out in abbreviated fashion — with what follows in the "Exegetical Comments" being extensively impacted by such explications, whether epistolary or rhetorical in form and whether exegetical or theological in nature.

B. Use of Old Testament Quotations and Allusions

A number of perplexing questions arise when one considers Paul's use of the Jewish (OT) Scriptures in Romans. For example, one may legitimately ask: Why did Paul quote and allude to so many biblical passages in Romans, when elsewhere in his letters he is more reserved in his use of Scripture? Of the approximately 83 places in the Pauline corpus where biblical quotations are to be found (which total approximately 100 OT passages, if one disengages the conflated texts and separates the possible dual sources), well over half appear in this letter: 45 of the 83 (or 55 to 60 biblical passages of the total of 100 passages). Likewise, Romans contains a rather large number of allusions to OT passages. Yet in the Pauline letters other than Romans there are far fewer quotations of or allusions to Scripture: to count the explicit quotations alone, only 15 appear in 1 Corinthians, 7 in 2 Corinthians, 10 in Galatians, 4 in Ephesians, 1 in 1 Timothy, 1 in 2 Timothy, and none in 1 Thessalonians, 2 Thessalonians, Philippians, Colossians, Philemon, or Titus.

Also to be asked is why the distribution of biblical quotations in Romans — as well as that of recognizable allusions to Scripture in the letter — is so uneven. To take the more observable and demonstrable case of explicit biblical quotations: about 18 appear in eight or nine places in 1:16–4:25 and about 30 more in twenty-five or so places in 9:1–11:36 — with an additional 10 to be found in the exhortations of 12:1–15:13 and one more in the body-closing or "apostolic parousia" of 15:14-32 — whereas explicit biblical quotations only twice, and then somewhat tangentially, in what has seemed to many interpreters to be the apex of Paul's argument, in 5:1–8:39 (7:7's illustrative citation of "Do not covet" and 8:36's quotation of an early Christian confessional portion that makes use of Ps 44:22).

One might, in fact, well ask: Why did Paul use biblical quotations and allusions at all in writing to the Christians at Rome, particularly when he identifies his addressees as those within the orbit of his Gentile ministry (1:5-6; 13-15; 15:15-16), explicitly calls them Gentiles (11:13), and distinguishes their ancestry from his Jewish ancestry (9:3; 11:14)? One could understand why he quoted Scripture and alluded to it so often when writing Gentile Christians in the province of Galatia and the city of Corinth — particularly if, as seems likely, (1) the problems at Galatia stemmed from certain "Judaizers" who were themselves using the OT for their own purposes, and (2) the "Peter party" at Corinth was proposing some form of Jewish Christian propaganda. The use of Scripture in the letter to Ephesus and the two letters to Timothy, though much more infrequent, might even be justified on the bases of "Ephesians" being something of a circular letter written to mixed congregations in western Asia Minor and the letters to Timothy having been written to one who had been trained in the Scriptures by his grandmother and mother. But Romans cannot easily be "mirror read" so as to identify any Jewish opponents or Jewish Christian protagonists. And Paul's usual practice when writing to Gentile Christians — especially when writing Gentile Christians who were not affected by a problem of Jewish origin or Jewish Christian influence — was not to quote or allude to OT passages in support of his arguments at all (though, of course, his language was always informed by biblical idioms and expressions), as witness his letters to his Gentile converts at Thessalonica, Philippi, and Colossae and to two Gentile Christians named Philemon and Titus.

Further, when considering Paul's use of Scripture in Romans it is also incumbent on us to ask: How do Paul's exegetical practices and procedures in the letter compare with those of Second Temple Judaism and early Rabbinic Judaism, and what effect does an understanding of such cognate exegetical practices have on our understanding of Paul's treatment of the OT? Likewise when making comparisons we must ask: How does Paul's use of the OT in Romans compare to his use of Scripture in his other writings, particularly Galatians, where there are an overlap of topics and similar expositions?

And when dealing with the actual quotations themselves and Paul's use of them, another series of questions arises, such as: Why do the text forms of Paul's explicit biblical quotations differ from those attributed to Jesus in the four canonical Gospels and those credited to the earliest preachers in the Book of Acts? Paul's quotations in Romans and his other letters use a rather peculiar mix of textual readings. Over half are either absolute or virtual reproductions of the LXX, with about half of these at variance with the MT. Yet almost another half vary from both the LXX and the MT to a greater or lesser extent. Once in Romans (11:35, citing Job 41:11 in a traditional theocentric doxology), in fact, as well as three times elsewhere in the Pauline corpus (1 Cor 3:19, citing Job 5:13; 2 Cor 9:9, citing Ps 112:9; and 2 Tim 2:19, citing Num 16:5), the text of Paul's biblical quotation is in agreement with the MT against the LXX. By contrast, however, the texts used by Jesus, the earliest Christian preachers, and most of the NT writers seem to be almost exclusively Septuagintal in form.

Likewise, particularly in dealing with the interpretation of these explicitly quoted texts, it must be asked: How can the wide scope of Paul's interpretation of Scripture be understood, ranging, as it does, from his quite literal "pearl-stringing" approach in Rom 3:10-18 to his seeming disregard of the original text and context in Rom 10:6-8 (where Deut 30:12-14 is cited in an inexact and possibly proverbial manner to the advantage of his argument; cf. also Eph 4:8, where Ps 68:18 is cited in a similar fashion)? Further, when attempting to understand Paul's use of Scripture, it may legitimately be asked: Why does Paul use Scripture in the two theological sections of 1:16–4:25 and 9:1–11:33 of the body middle of his letter as the bases for his various arguments, whereas in the third, ethical section of 12:1–15:13 he uses OT passages more in support of his arguments that he asserts are principally based in the proclamation of the Christian gospel itself? And, finally, it needs to be asked: What does it mean to speak of Paul's "christocentric exegesis," and how did that orientation affect his actual interpretation of Scripture?

C. Use of Christian Confessions, Traditional Religious Aphorisms, and Jewish or Jewish Christian Devotional and Catechetical Materials

A further matter of importance with regard to Romans has to do with Paul's use of early Christian confessions, traditional religious aphorisms, and devotional or catechetical materials that presumably originated in the contexts of Jewish and/or Jewish Christian worship, instruction, and piety. Form criticism is the necessary tool for identifying these pre-Pauline materials. And content analysis of them serves to highlight their central features and their use in early Christian thought and practice. Most important for a commentary on Romans, however, is the spelling out of how Paul used these materials to structure, support, and summarize the main points of his various arguments in his letter to Christians at Rome.

There are a number of indications that Romans contains a "mother lode" of early Christian confessional material, as well as various aphoristic, devotional, and catechetical formulations — which have yet to be sufficiently mined out and whose nuggets of information can aid in understanding the nature of Paul's message and appreciating the methods that he used in its proclamation. A rather large number of early Christian confessions, as well as some of the more identifiable pre-Pauline aphoristic, devotional, and catechetical formulations, will be highlighted in this commentary. Many of these confessional materials have, of course, been identified as being somewhat distinctive by previous NT commentators, but have usually been explained in other ways than will be here proposed.

The identification and study of early Christian confessional materials in the NT has been particularly prominent among scholars during the twentieth century.[31] What has, to date, been most commonly identified as early Christian

---

31. For a brief history of such identification and study, see R. N. Longenecker, *New Wine into Fresh Wineskins,* 5-44.

confessional materials in Romans are (1) the hymn of praise to God in 11:33-36, (2) the christological formulaic passages in 1:3-4; 3:24-26 (or perhaps 3:25-26); and 4:25, and (3) the single-statement affirmation of the Lordship of Christ in 10:9. Portions of the lyrical and almost defiant affirmation of 8:33-39 should probably also be seen as confessional in nature. Perhaps there are also echoes of such material in 9:5b ("who is God over all, forever praised! Amen") and 14:9 ("Christ died and returned to life so that he might be the Lord of both the dead and the living").

Each of these portions has a strategic place in the overall argument of Romans. 1:3-4 appears in the salutation of the letter, which Paul uses to highlight a number of the themes that he intends to develop later in the letter. Similarly, 3:24-26 is included in what most commentators have viewed as a major thesis statement of the letter, that is, the broader paragraph of 3:21-26 — whether that paragraph sets out (or, probably better, "reiterates" from 1:16-17) the thesis of the whole letter or, more narrowly, the thesis of the first eight chapters — or, as we will argue later, the thesis statement of only the first major section of the letter's body middle, that is, of 1:16–4:25. And 10:9 appears at the heart of Paul's discussion of the Christian gospel and the hope of Israel in chs. 9–11, while 14:9 appears at the heart of his exhortations regarding the weak and the strong.

Further, some of these confessional portions appear as the final items of their respective sections in the letter and so serve to summarize and conclude what was said in those sections. 4:25 ("Who was delivered over to death for our sins, and was raised to life for our justification") seems to function in this manner, summarizing, as it does, the central statements of 3:21-31 and bringing to a climax the whole presentation of 1:16–4:24. Likewise, the forceful affirmations of 8:31-39, which probably include a number of early confessional statements, summarize and bring to a dramatic conclusion all that is said in chs. 5–8. And while it may be debated whether chs. 9–11 begin with a portion that includes a confessional doxology at 9:5b, certainly the majestic hymn of praise to God in 11:33-36 is confessional in nature and provides a fitting climax to those three chapters.

In addressing Christians at Rome, Paul seems to have used a number of early Christian confessional materials — as well as, it needs always to be recognized, certain Jewish or Jewish Christian aphorisms and various portions of available Jewish or Jewish Christian devotional and catechetical material. And he does so in at least two ways: (1) to support and focus his arguments, as he does in 1:3-4; 3:24-26; 10:9; and 14:9, and (2) to summarize and bring to a climax his presentations in the three main theological sections of his letter, as he does in 4:25; 8:33-39; and 11:33-36. These confessional and traditional materials, it may be assumed, were also known (whether in whole or in part) to believers in Jesus at Rome, and Paul appears to have used them to build bridges of commonality with his Roman addressees and to teach them in ways that they would readily appreciate and understand. It is important in our present commentary on Romans, therefore, to identify and spell out Paul's use of such early Christian confessional materials. Likewise, we believe it also important to attempt to identify and spell out his use of certain traditional Jewish or Jewish Christian aphorisms and various pre-existing Jewish or Jewish Christian devotional and catechetical materials, even though the latter may be less commonly recognized or discussed.

D. Narrative Substructure

Underlying all of Paul's statements in Romans, however, is the foundational narrative or story about (1) the redemptive plans and purposes of God the Father, (2) the actualization of divine redemption on behalf of humanity through the work of Jesus the Son, and (3) the bringing about of that redemption in history and people's lives through the ministry of the Holy Spirit. It is this underlying redemptive narrative that Paul builds on, argues from, interprets (or reinterprets), and uses for his own purposes. And it is this same narrative substructure of all early Christian proclamation that Paul assumes his addressees know, at least in the main, whether they have understood it as one connected narrative of divine redemption or as a cluster of redemptive episodes in history.

This narrative substructure is especially evident in (1) Paul's use of Abraham as the preeminent example of a person of faith in 4:1-24, (2) his contrast between what Adam brought into human experience and what Christ effected on behalf of humanity in 5:12-21, and (3) his analysis of relations between Israel and the church and his sketching out of "salvation history" in chs. 9–11. But it can also be seen throughout the rest of the letter, particularly in the early Christian confessional materials that Paul quotes and his use of those materials.

The recognition that a narrative substructure or underlying story of redemption is presented in the NT is not new. Christians have always believed that the "good news" of the gospel proclamation is about what God decreed in his eternal counsels and has brought about historically on behalf of humanity — primarily what he brought about at a particular time in the course of human history through the person and work of Jesus Christ. Only recently, however, have scholars come to realize that not only were the principal features of that redemptive story generative for early Christian proclamation and theology, but also such a foundational redemptive story (or, such a cluster of redemptive episodes in history) was instructional in the composition of the NT Gospels and the writing of the NT letters. So a "narrative approach" to the study of the writings of the NT, and particularly to the study of Paul's letters, has begun to take shape within biblical scholarship during the past few decades.[32] And it is this approach that needs to be taken into account at every point when interpreting Romans — both as an exegetical tool and as an interpretive control in analyzing what Paul presents in this particular letter.

32. For a survey and evaluation of scholarly proposals, see B. W. Longenecker, *Narrative Dynamics in Paul.*

E. Phenomenological Historiography

In any scholarly treatment of a NT letter (or, for that matter, any treatment of any portion of Scripture) it is also necessary, we believe, to be attuned to and involved with what has been called "phenomenological historiography" — that is, the identification and tracing out of similar themes and parallel ways of looking at things in roughly cognate and contemporary materials, with the hope of spawning fresh interpretive insights. In every type of biblical study it is necessary for the interpreter to be a "comparative religionist." This means, in particular, that in the scholarly study of the NT one must be as familiar as possible with such matters as (1) the piety and religious practices of the Jewish people during the period of Second Temple Judaism, (2) the use of the Torah by the Jewish teachers of that time, (3) Israel's Wisdom literature, (4) Greek religious philosophies and practices, (5) Jewish apocalyptic writings, (6) the Dead Sea Scrolls, (7) Philo of Alexandria, (8) Josephus, (9) Stoicism, (10) the Talmud and its associated compilations, and (11) the Nag Hammadi texts.

Admittedly, the quest for parallels between roughly cognate phenomena and contemporary writings can be a highly selective process. Often it eventuates in what has pejoratively been called "parallelomania." But when properly done, with appropriate care, perception, and caution, such a tracing out of similar themes, concepts, expressions, and approaches in cognate materials can prove to be highly significant for one's interpretation — particularly for the interpretation of Paul's letter to the Christians at Rome.

F. Developments of Thought and Expression

It is also vitally important in a scholarly reading of Romans that one be involved in observing and tracing out, at least as far as possible, the various developments of thought and expression that appear both within the letter itself and between Romans and the other writings of the NT. For a NT letter is neither an isolated nor a static piece of Christian composition. Within Romans an argument is developed, and between Romans and its neighboring canonical writings there are developments. So just as there is the need for NT scholars to give attention to matters having to do with the provenance of a letter, its historical circumstances, and such chronological relations as can be found to exist between it and other writings, there is also the need to observe and trace out the conceptual, thematic, and expressional developments that exist (1) within Romans itself, that is, within each of the four major sections of the body middle of the letter (1:15–4:25; 5:1–8:39; 9:1–11:33; and 12:1–15:13), (2) between each of these four major sections of the central portion of the letter, and (3) between Paul's presentation in Romans vis-à-vis his other letters and the other writings of the NT. This endeavor is particularly important in a study of Paul's letter to Rome because it enables the present-day reader to understand better (1) how the message of Paul functioned in that day, (2) how it related to the broader scope of early Christian proclamation, and (3) how its message can be contextualized today.

G. Varied Contextualizations of the Christian Gospel

A central concern throughout the present commentary is the highlighting of how Paul contextualizes the Christian gospel in Romans — both (1) as expressed in a context that had been extensively influenced by Jewish Christianity (which we will argue occurs principally in sections one and three of the letter's body middle; i.e., in 1:16–4:25 and 9:1–11:36) and (2) as proclaimed in a strictly Gentile context (which we will argue is portrayed in the second section of the letter's body middle, i.e., in 5:1–8:39, as well as in the more general portions of the fourth, hortatory section, i.e., in 12:1-21 and 13:8-14). This recognition of Paul's varied contextualizations of the Christian gospel, which occur in Romans more than in any of his other letters, is vitally important, we believe, not only (1) for an understanding of the letter itself, but also (2) for providing a template or paradigmatic pattern for an understanding of the nature of Christian proclamation and ministry today. And it is the highlighting of this factor in Paul's letter to the Christians at Rome that is a prominent feature in everything that follows in our exegetical commentary.

5. THE GREEK TEXTUAL TRADITION OF ROMANS

Before dealing with matters of exegesis, biblical theology, and contextualization in the commentary proper, attention must be directed to matters of text criticism — that is, to the textual tradition that underlies the Greek text of Romans and to "establishing" the text in those many places where variant readings appear. The textual basis for our exegesis will be the fourth edition of the United Bible Societies' *Greek New Testament* (GNT[4]) and the twenty-seventh edition of the Nestle-Aland *Novum Testamentum Graece* (NA[27]), which were both published in 1993 and set out the same Greek text. GNT[4] offers in its apparatus, however, a more limited selection of variant readings than does NA[27], since its purpose was to present only the most significant textual variations for translators. So in the "Textual Notes" and "Exegetical Comments" of the commentary proper we will discuss every variant in the Greek text of Romans that is cited in GNT[4], but will also need to deal with other variants noted in NA[27] and some other textual issues that have been discussed by various commentators.

A. Families of Manuscripts in the Greek Textual Tradition

The genius of Brooke F. Westcott and Fenton J. A. Hort in the area of NT text criticism was expressed in their new understanding of "family" relations between the numerous Greek manuscripts of the NT — both those previously known and those that were then being discovered. Building on the work of Karl Lachmann (1831), Constantin von Tischendorf (1841-72), and Samuel Tregelles (1857-79), Westcott and Hort set out in 1863 to establish the text of the Greek NT on a more critically assured basis. Hort seems to have been the one who was principally responsible for originating the theory of family relations between the ancient Greek NT textual materials, whereas Westcott took the lead in applying that theory in practice. On all points, however, they worked in close collaboration. And in 1881-82 they published the results of their labors in *The New Testament in the Original Greek, Introduction and Appendix,* with that book having a profound effect on all NT study thereafter.

Based on Westcott and Hort's thesis of family relationships, most scholars today recognize three basic types or "families" of Greek texts in the textual tradition of the NT, with various combinations of these families often also identified as subtypes. The earliest and probably the primary family of texts is the "Alexandrian" text, or what Westcott and Hort called the "Neutral" text because it seems relatively uncontaminated by later scribal alterations. It was prominent in the region of Alexandria, and so its name. But it was also used in various churches throughout the eastern part of the Roman Empire. A second type is a bilingual Greek-Latin text often called the "Western" text, which may have had its roots among some Christians as early as the mid-second century and was used dominantly in western portions of the empire. A third is the "Byzantine" text, which is also called the "Syrian" or "Antiochene" text because it is thought to have originated in Antioch of Syria during the late third century. This third family of texts has also been called the "Koine" ("common") text — or often today the "Majority Text" simply because, being represented by a few later uncial manuscripts and the great bulk of minuscule manuscripts from the ninth through the fifteenth centuries, it is numerically the most prevalent. It is frequently also called the "Received Text" since it is generally comparable to the text proposed in the early sixteenth century by the Dutch religious humanist Desiderius Erasmus (1469-1536), with that text then developed in the seventeenth century and called the "Textus Receptus."

The Alexandrian or Neutral text is represented most directly by two fourth-century uncial manuscripts: Codex Vaticanus (B 03) and Codex Siniaticus (א 01), which are usually in agreement — though Westcott and Hort argued that on the few occasions where they differ Codex Vaticanus is most often to be preferred. It also appears in the fifth-century uncial manuscript Codex Alexandrinus (A 02), whose text is Byzantine in the Gospels but Alexandrian in Acts and the letters of Paul, as well as in the fifth-century uncial manuscript Codex Ephraemi Rescriptus (C 04) — which, as its name suggests, is a palimpsest that was erased in the twelfth century and reused for a Greek translation of thirty-eight tractates by Ephraem — whose text is generally Alexandrian but contains other mixed readings.

Of even greater importance is the fact that the Alexandrian or Neutral type of text is dominant in the biblical papyrus manuscripts of the third and fourth centuries. It appears most extensively in P[46] ("Chester Beatty II"), which contains eight of Paul's letters and the Epistle to the Hebrews (though with numerous lacunae because of many broken edges in the folios of this papyrus codex and the omission of 2 Thessalonians, Philemon, and the Pastorals) and which dates from about A.D. 200 (with some leeway on either side). It is also to be found to a large extent in P[45] ("Chester Beatty I"), which contains the Gospels and Acts (beginning at Matt 20:24 and ending at Acts 17:17) and dates from the mid-third century. Further, it is dominant in those other manuscripts, whether papyrus, uncial, or minuscule, included by Kurt and Barbara Aland in Category I below — and, though with "alien influences" usually derived from the Byzantine text, in those manuscripts that the Alands have included in Category II.

The so-called Western text appears in the bilingual manuscripts Codex Bezae Cantabrigiensis (D 05) of the fifth century, which contains the Gospels and Acts, and Codex Claromontanus (D 06) of the sixth century, which contains the Pauline letters — with both manuscripts often identified simply as Codex Beza, since they were at one time both possessed by Theodore Beza (1519-1605), who was an important text critic and Latin translator of his day as well as John Calvin's successor at Geneva. This type of text, however, seems to have had roots in a much earlier period, for certain rather distinctive expressions, phrases, deletions, and additions in the two manuscripts also appear earlier at various places in the Greek texts of the biblical papyri and the Latin biblical quotations of such Church Fathers as Tertullian (c. 145-220), Cyprian (died c. 258), and Augustine (354-430).

The Byzantine text is found in some of the uncial Greek manuscripts, principally in codices H, L, and P — that is, in H (013), which contains the Gospels and dates from the ninth century; in H (015), which contains the Pauline letters and dates from the sixth century; in L (019), which contains the Gospels and dates from the eighth century; in L (020), which contains Acts, the Catholic or General Epistles, and the Pauline letters and dates from the ninth century; in P (024), which contains the Gospels and dates from the sixth century; and in P (025), which contains Acts, the Catholic or General Epistles, the Pauline letters, and Revelation and dates from the ninth century. But it appears far more commonly in the very large number of minuscule manuscripts that date from the ninth to the fifteenth centuries.

B. A Contemporary Reevaluation of the Greek Textual Tradition

A thorough reevaluation of the Greek textual tradition of the NT, however, has been undertaken by Kurt and Barbara Aland and their associates at the Institute for New Testament Textual Research, Münster, Germany. Their results, together with a proposed new method of analysis, were published in monograph form in 1983,[33] and have been the subject of continued study and revision ever since.

---

33. Aland and Aland, *Text des Neuen Testaments,* 1983, with a second revised German edition

The critical apparatuses and the text of GNT[4] and NA[27], both published in 1993, have been thoroughly revised to reflect this reevaluation of the textual data and history that lie behind our present text of the NT. As a result of the work of Kurt and Barbara Aland and their colleagues, the textual variants of every NT passage in both GNT[4] and NA[27] have undergone a complete review, with different significances often seen in the data from what had been previously accepted, different arrangements of the evidence available made, and different conclusions drawn with respect to particular variants.

So, for example, the Introduction to GNT[4] states:

> The selection of passages for the apparatus has undergone considerable revision since the Third Edition (corrected). . . . Accordingly the Committee selected 284 new passages for inclusion in the apparatus. Meanwhile 273 passages previously included were removed, because the variants were of less significance for translators and other readers.[34]

Likewise, each of the previously assigned letter evaluations of "A" ("certain") to "D" ("great difficulty in arriving at a decision") in GNT[4] — which represent the degree of certainty among the five editors of the Fourth Revised Edition (i.e., Barbara Aland, Kurt Aland, Johannes Karavidopoulos, Carlo M. Martini, and Bruce M. Metzger) with respect to the readings chosen — have been reconsidered and, where felt necessary, have been revised.[35] Further, the "Preface to the Fourth Edition" of GNT[4] declares that "very careful consideration was given to the selection of representatives for each group of witnesses in order to reflect faithfully the character of the textual tradition and exclude elements of uncertainty."[36] Thus the text-critical analysis of every NT passage must now take into account this most recent reevaluation of the NT's textual history.

C. Proposed Categories of Texts in the Greek Textual Tradition

The Alands and their associates have grouped the extant papyrus, uncial (or majuscule), and minuscule Greek NT manuscripts into five categories, with that fivefold classification based on the quality of the respective texts and their importance for establishing the original readings of the NT writings.[37] These five categories may be characterized as follows:[38]

---

in 1989; ET: *The Text of the New Testament: An Introduction to the Critical Editions and to the Theory and Practice of Modern Textual Criticism,* 1987; 2nd rev. ed. 1989.

34. *GNT*[4], introduction, p. 2*.
35. Cf. *ibid.,* introduction, p. 3*.
36. *Ibid.,* preface, v.
37. See Aland and Aland, *Text of the New Testament,* 2nd ed. (1989), 106, 159, 332-37.
38. As abstracted from *ibid.,* 335-36.

Category I: Manuscripts of a "very special quality," corresponding to the Alexandrian or so-called Neutral text. These manuscripts must always be given primary consideration in attempting to establish the text. To this category belong all the papyri and uncial manuscripts of the third and fourth centuries, and so it represents what the Alands have called the "early text."

Category II: Manuscripts of a "special quality." These are manuscripts that, while similar to those of Category I, must be distinguished from the manuscripts of Category I because of the presence of "alien influences," which have usually been derived from the Byzantine text. To this category belongs the "Egyptian" text, which was evidently developed from the Alexandrian tradition.

Category III: Manuscripts of a "distinctive character" with an "independent text." These are manuscripts that often exhibit a strong Byzantine influence and so are not to be used as primary evidence for establishing the text. Yet they are important for understanding the history of the textual tradition.

Category IV: Manuscripts of the so-called "Western" text (a designation no longer favored by the Alands but which continued to be used by Bruce Metzger) — that is, principally and perhaps exclusively, D (Codex Beza) in both of its two volumes (05, which contains the Gospels and Acts, and 06, which contains the Pauline letters).

Category V: Manuscripts that exhibit a purely or dominantly Byzantine text.

It is this categorization that has been used in both GNT^4 and NA^{27} as the basis for including or excluding a manuscript in the textual apparatus with respect to a given variant reading.[39]

Thus in its textual apparatus the GNT^4 includes (1) all papyrus manuscripts, most of which are from Categories I and II, though a few are from Categories III and IV, (2) all uncial manuscripts from Categories I, II, III, and V, and (3) a relatively small group of minuscule manuscripts from Categories I and II, plus some ten manuscripts from Category III that have been selected as representative for the various parts of the NT (i.e., Gospels, Acts, Paul, Catholic or General Epistles, and Revelation). Not included, however, are the minuscule manuscripts in Category IV, which represent the text type of the so-called "Western" text of Codex D, either 05 (the Gospels and Acts) or 06 (the Pauline letters). The major minuscule manuscripts that the Alands have identified as bearing "constant witness" to the Byzantine family of texts are listed in Category V. There are, of course, many hundreds of other minuscule

---

39. As the introduction to *GNT*^{4} comments: "The Committee made use of these categories in selecting manuscripts because they provide the only tool presently available for classifying the whole manuscript tradition of the New Testament on an objective statistical basis" (p. 4*).

manuscripts that belong to the more developed Byzantine text. But all of the Byzantine manuscripts included in Category V, as well as the hundreds more of Byzantine manuscripts not listed elsewhere in this catalogue of texts, have been judged by the Alands and their associates as being inferior to the Greek manuscripts of Categories I, II, and III.[40] So these latter textual materials will never be cited in the "Textual Notes" or "Exegetical Comments" of our present commentary.

D. Tabulated Manuscript Evidence for Establishing the Greek Text of Romans

The charts below set out the most important of the Greek manuscripts for Paul's letter to the Romans according to the five categories cited above. The materials in each category are grouped roughly in terms of the quality of their texts — not in the order of their discovery (as with the papyri), nor according to their dates or some letter or number designation (as with the uncials) or some assigned number (as with the minuscules). These charts may be used for reference when evaluating the textual tradition of any given reading discussed in the "Textual Notes" and/or the "Exegetical Comments" that follow in this present commentary.

PAPYRUS MANUSCRIPTS		
Category I		
P^{46}	c. AD 200	5:17–6:3; 6:5-14; 8:15-25; 8:27-35; 8:37–9:32; 10:1–11:22; 11:24-33; 11:35–12:9; 12:11–15:9; 15:11-33; 16:1-23; 16:25-27
P^{27}	third century	8:12-22, 24-27, 33-39; 9:1-3, 5-9
P^{40}	third century	1:24-27, 31–2:3; 3:21–4:8; 6:4-5, 16; 9:17, 27
P^{10}	fourth century	1:1-7
P^{26}	c. AD 600	1:1-16
P^{31}	seventh century	12:3-8
Category II		
P^{94}	fifth-sixth centuries	6:10-13, 19-22
P^{61}	c. AD 700	16:23, 25-27

40. Cf. Aland and Aland, *Text of the New Testament*, 138-42.

UNCIAL MANUSCRIPTS	
Category I	
ℵ (01)	fourth century
B (03)	fourth century
A (02)	fifth century
0220	third century
Category II	
C (04)	fifth century
D^p (06)	sixth century
F^p (010)	ninth century
048	fifth century
0172	fifth century
Category III	
D^p (06)	sixth century
G^p (012)	ninth century
H^p (015)	sixth century
P^{acpr} (025)	ninth century
Ψ (044)	eighth-ninth centuries
075	tenth century
0150	ninth century
0209	seventh century
0219	fourth-fifth centuries
0221	fourth century
Category V	
K^{ap} (018)	ninth century
L^{ap} (020)	ninth century
049	ninth century
056	ninth century
0142	tenth century
0151	ninth century

MINUSCULE MANUSCRIPTS	
Category I	
33	ninth century
1175	eleventh century
1739	tenth century
Category II	
81	eleventh century
256	eleventh-twelfth centuries
442	thirteenth century
1506	fourteenth century
1881	fourteenth century
1962	eleventh century
2127	twelfth century
2464	ninth century
Category III	
5, 6, 61, 69, 88, 104, 181, 218, 263, 322, 323, 326, 330, 365, 424ᶜ, 436, 441, 451, 459, 467, 614, 621, 623, 629, 630, 915, 917, 1241, 1243, 1319, 1398, 1505, 1563 (?), 1573, 1611, 1678 (?), 1718, 1735, 1751, 1838, 1845, 1846, 1852, 1874, 1875, 1877, 1908, 1912, 1942, 1959, 2110, 2138, 2197, 2200, 2344, 2412, 2492, 2495, 2516, 2523, 2544, 2596 (?), 2718	
Category V	
f¹ (= 1, 118, 131, 209, 1582, etc.), 94, 103, 180, 189, 205, 206, 209, 254, 378, 398, 424*, 429, 431, 522, 642, 720, 911, 918, 945, 1067, 1251, 1292, 1359, 1409, 1424, 1523, 1524, 1642, 1704, 1841, 1854, 1891, 2147, 2298, 2374, 2400, 2541, 2652	

E. A Summation with Respect to the Greek Manuscripts of Romans

Of the approximately 3,200 manuscripts that make up the Greek textual tradition of the NT, the most important for establishing the text of Romans are the following:

Among the *papyrus manuscripts* and leaves of manuscripts, eight are of primary importance for establishing the text of Paul's letter to the Romans. None contains the full text of the letter. Most, however, either date from or reflect a time earlier than the uncial manuscripts that preserve the text in its entirety and so must be considered of great significance in any evaluation of the text of Romans.

The most important of these eight, because of both its early date and the uncontaminated nature of its readings, is P^{46} in the Chester Beatty collection ("Chester Beatty II"), which can be dated about A.D. 200 and contains eight of Paul's letters and the so-called Epistle to the Hebrews (though with numerous lacunae because of damaged leaves and the omission of 2 Thessalonians, Philemon, and the Pastorals). It exhibits what the Alands have called a "free" text — that is, a text that does not clearly or consistently correlate with any of the families of texts that developed at a later period.[41] Unfortunately, the first seven folios of P^{46}, which evidently contained Rom 1:1–5:16, are missing. Further, a number of the remaining folios of Romans in P^{46} — particularly those containing 5:17–6:14; 8:15–15:9; and 15:11–16:27 — are somewhat defective because of their damaged edges. Nevertheless, because of its date and uncontaminated or "free" text, P^{46} is "a valuable witness to the unrevised Pauline text of the second century and hence to the early component parts of all later textual forms."[42]

The other biblical papyri that include Category I or Category II texts of Romans contain even smaller portions of the letter. All of these biblical papyri have writing on both sides of the page, on both the "recto" and the "verso," and so seem to stem from codices (i.e., from a book form that contained folios with pages or leaves) and not from scrolls — as do most other papyri of other parts of the NT. And this suggests that the early Christians used the codex or book form for their sacred writings from the very beginning.

Greek *uncial* (or "majuscule") *manuscripts* of the fourth to the ninth centuries have played a dominant role in NT textual criticism well into the twentieth century, being superseded only in the latter part of the century by the witness of the earlier third- and fourth-century papyri. For Constantin von Tischendorf, who published his two-volume *Novum Testamentum Graece* in 1869-72, Codex Sinaiticus (א 01) was the critical standard for the establishment of the text of the NT. On the other hand, for Brooke F. Westcott and Fenton J. A. Hort, who published their two-volume *The New Testament in the Original Greek* in 1881-82, the touchstone for all NT text criticism was Codex Vaticanus (B 03), especially where it agrees with Codex Sinaiticus, but also in those relatively few cases where B and א differed. And this B–א textual approach (i.e., basing primary textual dependence on the two fourth-century uncial manuscripts and favoring B over א where they differ) gained almost universal acceptance among NT scholars through its incorporation by Eberhard Nestle in his *Novum Testamentum Graece,* which was published in 1898.

But as Kurt and Barbara Aland have pointed out in comparing the texts of Codex Vaticanus and Codex Sinaiticus: "The textual quality of Codex Vaticanus is inferior in the Pauline corpus: in the Gospels and elsewhere it is far superior to Codex Sinaiticus (and the other uncials), but not in the letters of Paul."[43] Thus

---

41. Cf. Aland and Aland, *Text of the New Testament, esp. 95.*
42. W. G. Kümmel, "History of the Text," 363.
43. Aland and Aland, *Text of the New Testament,* 14.

even when dealing with these two primary fourth-century uncial witnesses, which together support an Alexandrian or Neutral family of texts, a "reasoned eclecticism" must be invoked — that is, an establishing of the text that takes into consideration for each particular passage not only the external data of the respective manuscripts but also the internal data of the author's argument and usage (which is, in effect, much the same methodology as that used in establishing the text of the canonical Gospels by the use of both source criticism and redaction criticism).

The *minuscule manuscripts* have long played an important role in NT textual studies — even a dominant role up through the mid-nineteenth century. For while Desiderius Erasmus knew of Codex Basilensis, the eighth-century Byzantine uncial manuscript that was brought to the Council of Basel in 1431 and is now designated E (07), he depended almost entirely on later Byzantine minuscule texts and seems to have made no use of that well-known Basel uncial in constructing his "received text." And while Theodore Beza published critical editions of the NT text, he never referred to what is now called Codex Beza and whose two volumes are now designated D (05) on the Gospels and Acts and D (06) on the Pauline letters — even though both of these bilingual volumes were in his possession and are today called by his name. But with new discoveries of many NT manuscripts, new finds of papyri containing Greek biblical materials, and new studies of relationships between the various families of Greek texts — all of which began in the mid-nineteenth century and have continued unabated since — that dominance of the minuscule tradition has been reduced dramatically.

Of the over 2,800 minuscule manuscripts that have been identified, numbered, and studied to date, all stem from the ninth through the fifteenth or sixteenth centuries, and more than eighty percent represent the Byzantine or so-called "majority" text almost exclusively. Only a few of the miniscule manuscripts of Romans "offer a valuable early text which can compete with . . . the best of the uncials."[44] Chief among these is the ninth-century minuscule manuscript 33, which has often been called the "Queen of the Minuscules," and portions of the tenth-century minuscule manuscript 1739 and the eleventh-century minuscule manuscript 1175.

In the "Minuscules" chart above, Category I (i.e., manuscripts of a "very special quality") and Category II (i.e., manuscripts of a "special quality") include only a few manuscripts that reflect, to some extent, the Alexandrian or Neutral family of texts — with most of these evidencing, as well, various "alien influences," which usually means that they represent Byzantine readings. Category III (i.e., manuscripts of a "distinctive character" with an "independent text") lists a number of textual materials that also often exhibit a strong Byzantine influence, and so, though they may be of some importance for understanding the history of the textual tradition of Romans, cannot be used as primary evi-

---

44. Aland and Aland, *Text of the New Testament,* 128.

dence for establishing the letter's text. There are no Category IV or "Western" text minuscule manuscripts for Romans. And the minuscule manuscripts of Category V (i.e., manuscripts that exhibit a purely or predominantly Byzantine text) are inferior to those of Categories I, II, and III and so will not be taken into account in either the "Textual Notes" or the "Exegetical Comments" of our commentary proper.

Nonetheless, even though only a small group of minuscule manuscripts can be included in Categories I and II, some attention must also, at times, be paid to the Byzantine family of texts when exegeting Romans. And so with respect to certain passages in Romans a "reasoned eclecticism" must also take into consideration certain Byzantine variants when attempting to establish the original text of the letter.

F. Other Textual Witnesses and Their Importance

In addition to the Greek papyrus, uncial, and minuscule manuscripts, which reflect, in whole or in part, a continuous text for Romans, there are also other textual materials that have a bearing on attempts to establish the original biblical text. These include early versions of the NT, patristic citations, and church lectionaries.

The *earliest versions of the NT* are the Old Latin (Itala or it), the Old Syriac (the Vetus Syra, and as represented by surviving materials derived from Tatian's Diatessaron), and a presumed Coptic prototype of the many extant Coptic translations, which can be dated sometime toward the end of the second Christian century (probably about AD 180-90). The Latin versions are usually referred to as the Old Latin (it), a translation that was produced at the end of the second century or first part of the third century, and the Vulgate (vg) of the fourth and fifth centuries — with both of these versions represented by a large number of manuscripts that present a great variety of textual phenomena. The Syriac versions are (1) the early Old Syriac, which is represented by the Sinaitic (syr^s) and/or the Curetonian (syr^c), as well as by the fifth-century Peshitta (syr^p), (2) the Philoxeniana (syr^{ph}), which was commissioned by bishop Philoxenus of Mabbug and translated by Polycarp in the year 507-08 (but is now as a manuscript extinct), (3) the Harklensis (syr^h), which was translated in 616 by the monk Thomas of Harkel, who was also at some time bishop of Mabbug, and (4) the Palestinian (syr^{pal}) of the sixth century, which is a partially preserved translation written in an Aramaic dialect with a Syriac script and so can only rather indirectly be called a Syriac version. The Coptic versions of the New Testament are very numerous, with the most commonly cited being the Sahidic (cop^{sa}), the Bohairic (cop^{bo}), and the fragmentary Fayyumic (cop^{fay}), all of which stem from some time in the third century or beginning of the fourth century.

All these versions were either translated directly from the Greek text or give evidence that they were thoroughly revised from a Greek base if originally dependent on another version. And all these translations, as the Introduction of GNT⁴ expresses matters, "are important witnesses for the Greek text of the New Testament because they derive from a relatively early stage of the tradition. They witness to the early form of the text as it was used at the time and place of their origin and development."[45]

A number of other ancient versions, however, were either only partially dependent on the Greek text or give evidence of having been only influenced by the Greek text at various later stages in the revision of their texts. These derived versions include the Armenian version and the Georgian version, both of which appear to be based on an Old Syriac type of text. Likewise, the Ethiopic version is probably to be viewed as something of a derived translation. For while the Ethiopic translations of Acts, the General Epistles, and the Apocalypse of John seem to be based on the Greek text, though with subsequent influences from various Coptic and Arabic translations, the character of the readings and their textual sources in many of the other portions of the Ethiopic versions are highly controversial. So like the United Bible Societies' fourth edition of The Greek New Testament (GNT⁴) and Nestle-Aland's twenty-seventh edition of Novum Testamentum Graece (NA²⁷) — which both limit the citation of versions in their apparatuses to instances where there is a clear witness to the original Greek text — our policy in all the textual discussions that follow in the commentary proper will be to refer to the early versions "only in instances where their underlying Greek text may be determined with certainty or with a high degree of probability."[46]

Quotations of the NT by the Church Fathers generally, as well as their quotations of Paul's letter to Rome in particular, pose numerous problems in any attempt to establish the biblical text. And this is true even when a Church Father writes a commentary on a NT book, where, obviously, the greatest number of patristic citations are to be found. For there was always the temptation, both for the patristic authors themselves and for later copyists of their writings, to rephrase the quoted biblical materials in terms of familiar forms of the text, rather than to give attention to how that text was actually worded in the passage under consideration. Further, there are always problems as to whether a particular Church Father was (1) alluding in a paraphrastic manner to a text or actually quoting a NT passage and (2) quoting from memory or copying from a biblical manuscript. And, of course, when Latin- or Syriac-speaking Fathers wrote in their own language, there is always the additional problem of determining how the text of the translation they quoted relates to the original Greek text.

Nonetheless, as Kurt and Barbara Aland have rightly pointed out: "Establishing the New Testament text of the Church Fathers has a strategic importance for textual history and criticism. It shows us how the text appeared at particular

45. *GNT⁴*, introduction, p. 22*.
46. *Ibid.*

times and in particular places: this is information we can find nowhere else."[47] So while a great deal still remains to be done by way of evaluating the use of Scripture by the Church Fathers and identifying the text forms they used, there will be a number of times in our textual analysis in the commentary proper when such patristic citations will be of some importance for establishing the Greek text.

Church lectionaries, of which there are about 2,300 whole or partial manuscripts in existence, are collections of biblical texts divided into separate pericopes and arranged according to their sequence as lessons appointed for the church year. These ecclesiastical lectionaries, however, are not to be related principally to the history of the NT text, but are to be understood more with respect to the history of church liturgy. For they are the products of particular liturgical needs, with the result that their form and wording are to be seen as having been heavily influenced by certain liturgical necessities.

Nonetheless, while only a few may be of any help in establishing the text of a NT passage, the ancient church lectionaries are important for the study of the later history of particular biblical texts. For since scribes, in copying a biblical text, would have been familiar with the constant repetition of that text in their worship services — and so, either consciously or inadvertently, would have incorporated portions of their worship expressions into that text — the lectionaries may be presumed to have exercised some influence on the biblical texts themselves and therefore on the textual traditions that are represented in the later manuscripts. Yet as the Alands have rightly insisted: "We can only conclude that for New Testament textual criticism, so far as the original text and its early history are concerned, nearly all of the approximately 2,300 lectionary manuscripts can be of significance only in exceptional cases."[48]

---

47. Aland and Aland, *Text of the New Testament,* 172.
48. *Ibid.,* 169.

COMMENTARY PROPER

Romans is neither a "theological tractate" nor a "compendium of Christian theology." It is, rather, a letter from the Christian apostle Paul written to believers in Jesus at Rome. When viewed rhetorically, it is best to call it a "protreptic message" of instruction and exhortation, which can be compared to an ancient "word ('speech' or 'message') of exhortation"; when analyzed in epistolary terms, it should be understood as a "letter essay" of instruction and appeal, comparable to various Greco-Roman letters of instruction.[1]

---

1. See pp. 12-16 above, and for more extensive discussions R. N. Longenecker, *Introducing Romans,* 169-235.

THE OPENING SECTIONS OF THE LETTER

As a letter, Romans begins with a "salutation" and a "thanksgiving." These two opening sections can be fairly well delineated — though it may be questioned as to where exactly the thanksgiving section ends and the body section (or "body opening") of the letter begins. Both of these opening sections evidence a number of epistolary conventions that were common in Paul's day. And each in its own way expresses something of (1) Paul's purposes and concerns when writing and (2) what he wanted to develop more fully in the rest of his letter.

I. Salutation (1:1-7)

TRANSLATION

¹:¹*Paul, a servant of Christ Jesus, called by God as an apostle, and set apart for the gospel that is from God, ²which he promised beforehand through his prophets in the Holy Scriptures — ³the gospel concerning his Son,*

> *who was descended from David*
> *with respect to his human descent;*
> ⁴*who was designated the Son of God with power*
> *with respect to his spirit [or 'the Spirit'] of holiness,*
> *by his resurrection from the dead:*
> *Jesus Christ our Lord.*

⁵*Through him we received God's special grace of apostleship in order to bring about obedience that comes from faith among all the Gentiles for the sake of his name, ⁶among whom you also are those called by God to belong to Jesus Christ.*

⁷*To all those at Rome, who are loved by God and called his holy people: Grace to you and peace from God our Father and the Lord Jesus Christ.*

TEXTUAL NOTES

1:1 The sequence Χριστοῦ Ἰησοῦ ("Christ Jesus") is supported by P[10] and uncial B, as well as by minuscule 81 (Category II), versions it[ar,mon] vg[ww, st], and Irenaeus and Origen[2/3]. The sequence Ἰησοῦ Χριστοῦ ("Jesus Christ"), however, appears in P[26] and uncials ℵ A D[absl] G P Ψ, as well as in minuscules 33 1175 1739 (Category I) and 256 1506 1881 1962 2127 2464 (Category II), versions it[b, d, g, o] vg[cl] syr[p, h, pal], and Irenaeus[lat mss] Origen[1/3] Chrysostom Theodoret Ambrosiaster Jerome Augustine[5/14]. Similar occurrences of the name Χριστοῦ Ἰησοῦ with the designation ἀπόστολος ("apostle") are found in 1 Cor 1:1; 2 Cor 1:1; Eph 1:1; Col 1:1; 1 Tim 1:1; and 2 Tim 1:1 (cf. also Phlm 1, though with δέσμιος, "prisoner," and Phil 1:1, though with δοῦλοι, "servants" or "slaves"); whereas Ἰησοῦ Χριστοῦ appears with ἀπόστολος in Gal 1:1 and Tit 1:1 (cf. also 1 Thess 1:1 and

2 Thess 1:1, though in these salutations "Jesus Christ" appears in addressing "the church of the Thessalonians" as being "in God the Father and the Lord Jesus Christ"). In Rom 1:1 the textual evidence for each of these two readings is fairly balanced, though on the basis of P[10] and B, both of which are fourth-century readings, the name Χριστοῦ Ἰησοῦ is to be preferred.

3 The reading τοῦ γενομένου ("the one born" or "descended") is overwhelmingly dominant in the Greek textual tradition. Uncial 61 of the fifth century (also reflected in syp), however, reads τοῦ γεννωμένου ("the one of the family" or "the one begotten"), but that reading probably stems from an error in hearing or from later christological speculation.

4 The Old Latin, Jerome's Vulgate, and some Latin writers translated the Greek participle ὁρισθέντος by the Latin praedestinatus, and so read "the one who was predestined." This may suggest that the Greek text they used read τοῦ προορισθέντος. More likely, however, the translation praedestinatus, rather than destinatus or definitus, should be understood as an attempt to soften any perceived "adoptionistic" tone in the Greek ὁρισθέντος at a time when that became a theological issue.

7a The phrase ἐν Ῥώμῃ ("in [or, 'at'] Rome") is well supported by P[10, 26vid] and by uncials ℵ A B C D[absl] P Ψ, as well as by minuscules 33 1175 1739 (Category I) and 81 256 1506 1881 1962 2127 2464 (Category II). It is also reflected in versions it[ar, b, d, o] vg syr[p, h, pal] cop[sa, bo], and is supported by Origen[gr, lat] Chrysostom Theodoret Ambrosiaster. A few witnesses (G 1739[mg] 1908[mg] it[g] Origen), however, omit ἐν Ῥώμῃ, "either as the result of an accident in transcription, or, more probably as a deliberate excision, made in order to show that the letter is of general, not local, application."[2]

7b The expression ἀγαπητοῖς θεοῦ ("loved of [or, 'by'] God") is widely supported by P[10, 26] and by uncials ℵ A B C P Ψ, as well as by minuscules 1739 (Category I) and 81 1962 2127 (Category II). It is also reflected in versions it[dem, x, z] vg syr[p, h, pal] and by Origen[gr, lat] Ambrosiaster Augustine. The variant ἐν ἀγάπῃ θεοῦ ("in the love of God") has inferior attestation (uncial G, versions it[ar, d*, g], and Ambrosiaster Pelagius), with some Latin witnesses combining ἐν ἀγάπῃ θεοῦ with ἐν Ῥώμῃ and so reading "to all who are at Rome [qui sunt Romae] in the love of God [dilectis / in caritate Dei]." The omission of ἀγαπητοῖς θεοῦ in the Greek text of Codex Beza (D 06) and minuscule 1915 was probably accidental.

7c The amply attested order χάρις ὑμῖν καὶ εἰρήνη ("grace to you and peace") is reversed in syp to εἰρήνη καὶ χάρις ὑμῖν ("peace and grace to you"). For Paul's usual order and usage, see "Exegetical Comments" below on v. 7.

FORM/STRUCTURE/SETTING

Greek letters began with a formulaic prescript or salutation: "A (the sender) to B (the recipient)," or at times "To B from A," with the greeting χαίρειν (literally: "to rejoice" or "be glad"; colloquially: "welcome," "good day" or

---

2. Metzger, Textual Commentary, 446.

"hello"; epistolary use: "greetings"). Sometimes a health wish such as ὑγιαίνειν (literally: "to be in good health"; colloquial and epistolary use: "good health") was connected with the greeting: χαίρειν καὶ ὑγιαίνειν ("greetings and good health").

In line with the conventions of his day, Paul also begins his letter to the Christians at Rome with an identification of himself as the sender (v. 1), an identification of the Christians at Rome as the recipients (v. 7a), and a greeting (v. 7b) — all of which are considerably expanded and filled with distinctive theological nuances. This basic threefold structure, together with the fact that a εὐχαριστῶ formula ("I give thanks") appears at the beginning of 1:8 and so signals the start of the "thanksgiving" section at that point, indicates quite clearly that the salutation of Romans is to be identified as 1:1-7.

The salutation of Romans is in the "running" (εἰρομένη) style of the unsophisticated prose of vernacular *koine* Greek, not in the "periodic" (ἐν περιόδοις) or "compact" (κατεστραμμένη) style of artistically developed prose that appears in the writings of the classical Greek authors.[3] In Greek the salutation of 1:1-7 is only one sentence, with its statements joined together by a number of relative clauses and by the juxtaposition of phrases. Further, it is longer than the prescript of any extant Greek letter — as well as the salutation of all of Paul's other letters. The most obvious reason for its length is that Paul has incorporated additional material into each of the usual salutatory units of an ancient letter. More importantly, however, the salutation of Romans is longer because in it the apostle sets out in condensed and rather cryptic form a number of highly important matters that he will later take up in his letter — thereby expressing something of his major concerns when writing, anticipating features of his primary purposes for writing, and highlighting certain themes that he wants to develop more fully in the rest of the letter.

In effect, the salutation of Romans, while appearing to be fairly simple in construction and rather straightforward in expression, is one of the most closely packed sections containing some of the weightiest theological statements in all of Paul's letters — and therefore one of the most extensively debated portions. Not only can it be said that "in recent years, more has been written about this [passage, particularly 1:3-4] than about any other New Testament text,"[4] but also that in recent years more (or at least, as much) has been written about the salutation of 1:1-7 than about any other section in Paul's letters. Therefore, without attempting to enter into every debate or marshal all of the data used in support of every proposed thesis, we need (1) to deal carefully with each item that appears in the salutation, (2) to indicate in a sufficient manner the main theses that have been proposed by way of explanation, and (3) to set out what can be validated with respect to the main points that Paul is making in such a long and highly significant salutation.

3. See Aristotle's nomenclature in *Rhetoric* 3.9.
4. Quoting Hengel, *Son of God*, 59 (with respect to 1:3-4).

EXEGETICAL COMMENTS

1:1a Παῦλος, "Paul," is a Greek name that literally means "little" or "small." As a Jew of the tribe of Benjamin (cf. Phil 3:5), the writer of this letter to Christians at Rome bore proudly the name of Israel's first king, the Benjamite Saul. As a Roman citizen (cf. Acts 16:37-38; 25:10-12), however, he would have had three names: (1) a clan or family *nomen,* which was preceded by (2) a personal *praenomen* and was followed by (3) a more commonly used *cognomen.* Greeks and other provincials who had gained in some manner Roman citizenship usually kept their Greek names as cognomens, to which they added Roman praenomens and nomens — the latter being usually that of the one to whom they owed their citizenship. Neither Paul's *praenomen* nor his *nomen* appears in the NT. As a Christian missionary to Gentiles, he seems to have used only his Greek name Paul, which, as a Roman *cognomen,* would have been acceptable to both Greeks and Romans without any nuances regarding ethnicity, nationality, family, or status.

The Church Fathers, as Gerald Bray has noted, "were especially fascinated by the name Paul itself and sought to discern why it had been changed from Saul."[5] Sometimes it was suggested that his name was changed when he was confronted by Christ on the way to Damascus as portrayed in Acts 9:1-30. But that opinion was usually viewed as unlikely since the name "Paul" is not introduced in Luke's second volume until Acts 13:9. Chrysostom proposed, on analogy with Simon Peter in Mark 3:16 par. (cf. also Matt 16:16-18a), that God changed his name at the time of his "ordination" as depicted in Acts 13:2-3.[6] Pelagius understood Paul himself as taking on a new name when he "advanced in virtues," arguing:

> We should suppose that he did this after the manner of the saints. When they advanced in virtues, they were addressed with a different name so that even in very name they might be new, as, for example, Abraham and Sarah and Cephas.[7]

Frequently the Latin Fathers suggested that he was called Paul because at the beginning of his missionary journeys he converted Sergius Paulus, the proconsul or governor of Cyprus, and so took the name "Paulus" as his own — much in the same way that rulers were in the habit of adding the names of conquered peoples to their titles.[8] To all such proposals, however, Adolf Deissmann has pertinently argued: (1) that ὁ καί ("who was also") in the statement of Acts 13:9 ("Saul, who was also called Paul") "admits of no other supposition than that he

---

5. G. Bray, ed., *Ancient Christian Commentary,* VI: *Romans,* 2.

6. Chrysostom, *Homilies of S. John Chrysostom, PG* 60.209, on Acts 13:9.

7. Pelagius, *Ad Romanos, PL* 30.645, alluding to Gen 17:5 and John 1:42.

8. So, e.g., Jerome, *De viris illustribus* 5, *PL* 23.646; cf. also Augustine, *Confessions* 8.4, though see his *De spiritu et littera* 7.12 and *Sermons* 279.5; 315-17.

was called *Saulos Paulos* before he came to Cyprus"; (2) that Luke "uses the one or the other name according to the field of his hero's labours"; and (3) that in his Gentile mission Paul thought of himself as "Παῦλος ὁ καὶ Σαῦλος — a man who laboured for the future and for humanity, though as a son of Benjamin and a contemporary of the Caesars."[9]

Most often the Church Fathers simply noted that in Scripture several people were renamed by God or became known by ascriptive surnames,[10] and that many others actually possessed two or even three names.[11] So they concluded that it was customary for Jews to have two or three names — whether given by their parents, by God, or by others; whether given affectionately, honorifically, or pejoratively. Thus Origen in the preface to his Romans commentary writes concerning the name Paul:

> It was the custom of the Hebrews to have two or three names; they gave different names to one and the same man. It seems to us that it is in accordance with this custom that Paul appears to have a second name, and that as long as he was ministering to his own people he was called Saul, which was probably the name his parents gave him, but that when he was writing laws and commandments for the Greeks and other Gentiles, he was called Paul. Scripture makes it clear when it says "Saul, who is also called Paul" [Acts 13:9] that the name Paul was not then being given to him for the first time but was already habitual.[12]

Acts 22:28 tells us that Paul claimed to have been born a Roman citizen, which implies that his family had been granted Roman citizenship in Tarsus at some time before his birth — perhaps during one of the Seleucid constitutional settlements with Rome, which would probably have included the incorporation of some prominent Jews as Roman citizens.[13] In all likelihood, therefore, his parents gave him the *cognomen* Paulus at his birth, which was a common Greek name of the day. It was probably meant to be his ordinary name in the Gentile world, just as Saul was the name they gave him for use among Jews. The NT never refers to Paul's personal name *(praenomen)* or his family name *(nomen)* — which names, it may be assumed, were also given him at birth by his parents since he was born a Roman citizen — just as it never refers to the personal or family names of such Roman officials as Agrippa, Felix, Festus, and Gallio, or

9. A. Deissmann, "SAULUS PAULUS," in *Bible Studies*, 313-17.

10. E.g., Abram was renamed Abraham, Sarai renamed Sarah, Jacob renamed Israel, Simon became Peter, and the sons of Zebedee became known as "the sons of thunder."

11. E.g., Solomon who is also called Jedidiah in 2 Sam 12:25, Zedekiah who is called Mattaniah in 2 Kgs 24:17, Uzziah who is called Azariah in 2 Kgs 15:1, Matthew who is called Levi in Luke 5:27, and Thaddeus who is called Lebbaeus in Matt 10:3, as well as others in the books of Judges, Samuel, and Kings who are referred to by double or triple names.

12. Origen, *Ad Romanos*, PG 14.837-38.

13. Cf. W. M. Ramsay, *Cities and Bishoprics of Phrygia*, 169-86.

the personal or family names of such Jewish Christians as Crispus, Justus, Rufus, and Silvanus, all of whom probably also had not only a *cognomen* but also a *praenomen* and a *nomen.*

Immediately after referring to himself by his cognomen, Paul describes himself in this salutation of Romans more expansively than in that of any of his other letters — first as δοῦλος Χριστοῦ Ἰησοῦ ("a servant of Christ Jesus"); then as κλητὸς ἀπόστολος ("one called an apostle"); and finally as ἀφωρισμένος εἰς εὐαγγέλιον θεοῦ. ("one set apart for the gospel of God"). These three self-identifications must not be read as mere effusive embellishments that only reflect something of Paul's exuberance when introducing himself to a church he had not founded and to Christians he did not (at least in the main) know personally. Rather, since in the salutations of his other NT letters he gives only rather brief descriptions of himself — and, more importantly, since those descriptions seem to be particularly relevant to the situations he faced when writing each of those other letters (cf. his identification of himself as an ἀπόστολος Χριστοῦ Ἰησοῦ in 1 Cor 1:1, 2 Cor 1:1, Gal 1:1, Eph 1:1, Col 1:1; 1 Tim 1:1; 2 Tim 1:1; and Titus 1:1; his reference to himself and Timothy as δοῦλοι Χριστοῦ Ἰησοῦ in Phil 1:1; his self-identifications δοῦλος θεοῦ and ἀπόστολος Χριστοῦ Ἰησοῦ in Titus 1:1, and his use of δέσμιος Χριστοῦ Ἰησοῦ in Phlm 1, though with no such descriptive characterizations appearing in the salutations of 1 or 2 Thessalonians) — it seems likely that here in these self-identifications of Rom 1:1 Paul is tailoring his speech to his addressees' appreciations and speaking to certain concerns among them regarding his person and status.[14]

1:1b Δοῦλος Χριστοῦ Ἰησοῦ, a "slave" or "servant of Christ Jesus," may be understood as simply an expression of humility. Origen long ago argued that understanding the phrase in this manner "would not be wrong," for,

> while Paul proclaims in Rom 8:15: "You did not receive the spirit of slavery to fall back into fear, but you received the Spirit of sonship, by which we cry Abba, Father!," he also says in 1 Cor 9:19: "Though I am free from all men, I have made myself a slave to all" — thereby indicating that he serves Christ not in the spirit of slavery but in the spirit of adoption, for Christ's service is more noble than any freedom.[15]

Others have proposed that since later in Romans Paul also speaks of Christians generally as being "slaves of God" (cf. 6:22: δουλωθέντες τῷ θεῷ), the phrase δοῦλος Χριστοῦ Ἰησοῦ may be interpreted as Paul putting himself on a par with other Christians.[16] Or the expression may be taken as connoting Paul's

---

14. As he does elsewhere in Romans at such obvious places as 1:16 and 2:16; cf. also the autobiographical references in Gal 1:1, 10, 11-12; 1 Cor 15:8-10; and Phil 3:4-7.

15. Origen, *Ad Romanos, PG* 14.837-38.

16. So, e.g., Zahn, *An die Römer,* 28-29; Lagrange, *Aux Romains,* 1-2; cf. also Barrett, *Romans,* 16: "Paul begins by describing himself as a Christian before he goes on to mention his special status and vocation."

total submission and complete commitment to Christ Jesus, who as his Lord had absolute ownership over his life — for that is how he uses the language of slavery in 6:16-22.[17] Or, more particularly, it may be a phrase that Paul himself coined for inclusion in this salutation of Rom 1:1 (also that of Phil 1:1) in contrast to the Roman appellative "Slaves of the Family of Caesar *(Familia Caesaris)*" by which slaves and freedpersons of the imperial household were known, thereby giving voice to a higher commitment, a greater Lord, and a more important family as Christians than could be true of any political allegiance — especially when addressing believers in Jesus at Rome (perhaps also at Philippi), some of whom may have been members of the imperial household (or who, at least, were aware of such an imperial appellative).[18]

But δοῦλος Χριστοῦ Ἰησοῦ in the salutation of Romans (and Philippians) should not be viewed as simply an expression of humility, an identification with his addressees, a declaration of personal commitment to Christ, or a phrase coined by Paul to counter some current Roman imperial appellation — as worthy and defensible as each of these proposals may be. More likely it is to be understood as signaling Paul's own prophetic consciousness.[19] And here in Rom 1:1 it is used in writing to Christians who would have been able to appreciate its biblical rootage and significance.[20] For while "Servant of Yahweh" (עבד יהוה) appears frequently in the OT in an honorific fashion with respect to (1) the nation of Israel,[21] (2) various leaders of the nation, such as Moses, Joshua and David,[22] and (3) God's people generally,[23] it is also used as a designation for God's prophets who spoke and enacted his message[24] and for the promised "Servant of the Lord" in the Isaian Servant Songs.[25]

Paul's use of δοῦλος Χριστοῦ Ἰησοῦ here in Rom 1:1 is probably best illuminated by the imagery and wording that he used in Gal 1:15-16a when speaking about Christ having encountered him on the way to Damascus: God "set me apart from birth," "called me by his grace," and "was pleased to reveal his Son in me so that I might preach him among the Gentiles." Paul's use of these terms and language reflects the call of certain OT prophets (cf. Jer 1:5) and that of the Servant of Yahweh (cf. Isa 49:1-6). It is a prophetic self-identification, which would probably not have been understood by Gentile Christians generally and therefore does not appear in most of Paul's other NT letters for circumstantial reasons. But it would certainly have been understood and appreciated by the

17. Cf., e.g., Fitzmyer, *Romans*, 231.

18. So M. J. Brown, "Paul's Use of ΔΟΥΛΟΣ ΧΡΙΣΤΟΥ ΙΗΣΟΥ."

19. Cf. Sandnes, *Paul — One of the Prophets?* esp. 146-53.

20. See further R. N. Longenecker, *Introducing Romans*, 55-91.

21. Cf., e.g., Ps 136:22; Isa 41:8-9; 43:10; 44:1-2, 21; 45:4; 48:20; 49:3.

22. Cf., e.g., Josh 1:2; 14:7; 24:29; Judg 2:8; 2 Sam 7:5; 2 Kgs 18:12; Ps 89:3 (MT 89:4); Isa 37:35; note also the title of Psalm 18.

23. Cf., e.g., Pss 34:22 (MT 34:23); 113:1; Isa 54:17; 56:6; 65:8-9, 13-15; 66:14.

24. E.g., 2 Kgs 9:7; 17:23; Ezra 9:11; Isa 20:3; 44:26; 50:10; 63:17; Jer 7:25; 25:4; 26:5; 29:19; 35:15; 44:4; Amos 3:7; cf. also the laments in the prayers of Ezra 9:11 and Dan 9:6.

25. Cf. Isa 42:1-4; 49:5-7; 52:13–53:12.

Christians at Rome, both Jews and Gentiles ethnically, who were steeped in OT teachings — and, presumably, would also have been understood, at least to some extent, by Paul's Gentile converts in the province of Galatia, who had been adversely affected by certain "Judaizers" who were disparaging Paul and his prophetic mission.

The prophetic self-identification "servant of Christ Jesus," therefore, is found most clearly in Paul's letters in the salutation of Romans at 1:1 and the autobiographical reference of Galatians at 1:10 (cf. also the imagery of Gal 1:15-16a and the plural use of δοῦλοι in Phil 1:1). It also appears in the salutations of Jas 1:1; 2 Pet 1:1; and Jude 1, which NT letters are probably to be identified as distinctly Jewish Christian writings. The only really different — as well as quite remarkable — thing to note in the use of this prophetic designation by Paul in Romans and Galatians (perhaps also Philippians), as well as by the authors of the afore-mentioned Jewish Christian writings, is the substitution of the name "Christ Jesus," "Jesus Christ," or simply "Christ" in the place usually reserved for Yahweh alone.

Many interpreters have viewed the diversity in the order of the names Χριστοῦ Ἰησοῦ or Ἰησοῦ Χριστοῦ in Paul's letters as being of no particular significance, for both formulations are found throughout his letters, together with the singular name Χριστός.[26] The manuscript evidence for these two readings, as noted above (see "Textual Notes"), is fairly balanced, though most scholars on the basis of P[10] and Codex Vaticanus (uncial B 03) prefer here Χριστοῦ Ἰησοῦ. Other NT authors prefer to use the double name "Jesus Christ" (about forty-seven times) more than "Christ Jesus" (about seven times). Paul, however, seems to prefer "Christ Jesus" (about eighty times) over "Jesus Christ" (about twenty-five times) — with, of course, the exact tabulations being highly dependent on such matters as (1) the authenticity of the various Pauline letters, (2) the proper textual reading in each case, and (3) whether the formulation stems from an early Christian confessional portion quoted by Paul or appears in material written by the apostle himself. Further, the pattern in Paul seems to be that (1) when he speaks of his God-given mandate to minister to Gentiles, he usually speaks of it as being on behalf of "Christ Jesus" (as here in 1:1) or "Christ" (as in Gal 1:10) and (2) when he refers to believers being incorporated either "into" (εἰς) or "in" (ἐν) Christ, the referent is always "Christ Jesus" or "Christ." All this suggests that while "Christ Jesus," "Jesus Christ," and "Christ" were often used interchangeably by him as proper names, Χριστός for Paul still carried with it nuances of the title "Messiah."[27] And this seems to be particularly evident in his letter to Rome — as witness especially (1) his use of "the Christ" (ὁ Χριστός) in 9:5, which appears in a context where the articular form of the name certainly

26. Cf., e.g., Lietzmann, *An die Römer*, 23; Murray, *Romans*, 1.2 n. 1; Hengel, "Erwägungen zum Sprachgebrauch von Χριστός bei Paulus," 137.

27. Cf., e.g., Sanday and Headlam, *Romans*, 3-4; Käsemann, *Romans*, 5; Cranfield, *Romans*, 1.51; N. T. Wright, "The Messiah and the People of God," 19-32; Moo, *Romans*, 41 n. 9.

signifies "the Messiah of Israel," and (2) his use of that same articular form in 15:3 and 7, with "the Christ" (ὁ Χριστός) appearing in the closing portion of a set of exhortations regarding "the strong" and "the weak" in 14:1–15:13.

1:1c Κλητὸς ἀπόστολος (literally "the one called an apostle") is the second self-identification of Paul here in 1:1. The substantival adjective κλητός, "the one called" (from the verb καλεῖν, "to call" or "designate"), as William Sanday and Arthur Headlam have pointed out, is:

> another idea which has its roots in the Old Testament. Eminent servants of God become so by an express summons. The typical examples would be Abraham (Gen. xii.1-3), Moses (Ex. iii.10), the prophets (Isa. vi.8, 9; Jer i.4,5, &c.). The verb καλεῖν occurs in a highly typical passage, Hos. xi.1 [LXX], ἐξ Αἰγύπτου μετεκάλεσα τὰ τέκνα μου. For the particular form κλητός we cannot come nearer than the "guests" (κλητοί) of Adonijah (I Kings i.41, 49 [LXX]).[28]

And Sanday and Headlam have gone on quite rightly to assert:

> By his use of the term St. Paul places himself on a level at once with the great Old Testament saints and with the Twelve who had been "called" expressly by Christ (Mark i.17; ii.14//). The same combination κλητὸς ἀπόστ. occurs in 1 Cor. i.1 [though here, evidently, with Paul needing to spell out for his Gentile converts at Corinth the biblical nuance of κλητός by the addition of διὰ θελήματος θεοῦ, "through the will of God"], but is not used elsewhere by St. Paul or any of the other Apostles. In these two Epistles St. Paul has to vindicate the parity of his own call (on the way to Damascus, cf. also Acts xxvi.17) with that of the elder Apostles.[29]

The Hebrew verb קרא and the Greek verb καλέω are frequently used in OT Scripture in a mundane sense to signify the naming or identification of someone or something. But throughout both the OT and the NT, one who is given a divine mandate, called to a special responsibility or office, and/or called to salvation is always "called by God."[30]

The term ἀπόστολος, "apostle," which Paul uses in association with his name in most of the salutations of his letters (except those of Philippians, 1 and 2 Thessalonians, and Philemon) to epitomize his consciousness of having been commissioned by God to proclaim with authority the message of salvation in Christ, occurs in Romans only here and at 11:13 as a self-identification — also, of course, in 16:7 in the identification of Andronicus and Junia (or Junias).

---

28. Sanday and Headlam, *Romans*, 4.

29. *Ibid.*

30. E.g., Isa 42:6; 48:15; 49:1; 51:2, passim; Rom 4:17; Gal 1:6; 5:8; 1 Thess 5:24; 1 Tim 6:12; Heb 5:4; 1 Pet 5:10, passim.

Ἀπόστολος in the NT connotes personal, delegated authority. It speaks of being commissioned to represent another. It is used broadly of anyone sent by another (cf. John 13:16, "an ἀπόστολος is not greater than the one who sent him"), of Christian brothers sent from Ephesus to Corinth (cf. 2 Cor 8:23, "they are ἀπόστολοι of the churches"), of Epaphroditus sent by the Philippian church to Paul (cf. Phil 2:25, "he is your ἀπόστολον"), and even of Jesus sent by God (cf. Heb 3:1, "the ἀπόστολον and high priest whom we confess"). More narrowly, it is used of a group of believers in Jesus who had some special function,[31] with particular reference to the twelve disciples.[32] This narrower usage is how the term is most often used in its approximately seventy-six occurrences in the NT. And that is how Paul uses it of himself in his letters — that is, as one with personal, delegated authority from God to proclaim accurately the Christian gospel.

This is not, however, how ἀπόστολος was commonly understood by Gentiles or Hellenistic Jews of the day. Classical Greek writers usually used the term in an impersonal way, most often to refer to a naval expedition for military purposes[33] or a "colony to be sent out"[34] — even, at times, of a boat used to transport such a naval expedition or colony.[35] Josephus's one clear use of ἀπόστολον carries the verbal sense of "to send out," with the noun πρεσβεία, not ἀπόστολος, used in the passage for "delegation."[36] In fact, there are only a few references in all of the extant Greek and Jewish Greek writings from the fifth century B.C. through the second century A.D. where the term means, or even could be taken to mean, something like "envoy," "delegate," or "messenger," and thus to connote the idea of a personal and delegated authority.[37]

Karl Rengstorf has pointed out that although the NT's use of ἀπόστολος cannot readily be paralleled in the Greek and Hellenistic Jewish writings of the day, it is comparable to the Jewish institution of the *shaliach* in the Talmud.[38] For in rabbinic writings the noun שליח has an assured place as a term that means "envoy" or "messenger" and carries the nuances of personal and delegated authority — as, for example, in the oft-repeated dictum: "A man's *shaliach* is as the man himself."[39] According to the rabbis, a man could appoint a *shaliach* to enter into an engagement of marriage for him,[40] to serve a notice of divorce for him,[41]

---

31. In addition to Rom 16:7, see also Luke 11:49; Acts 14:4, 14; Gal 1:19; Eph 3:5; Rev. 18:20.

32. Cf. Matt 10:2; Mark 3:14 [א B, etc.]; Luke 6:13; 9:10; 17:5; 22:14; and Acts 1:2, 26.

33. So Lysias, *Oracles* 19.21; Demosthenes, *Oracles* 3.5; 18.80, 107.

34. So Dionysius of Halicarnassus, *Antiquitates Romanae* 9.59.2.

35. So Plato, *Epistolae* 346a.

36. See Josephus, *Antiquities* 17.300.

37. See Herodotus, *History* 1.21; 5.38; *Corpus Hermeticum* 6.11-12; *POxy* 1259.10; *SbGU* 7241.48; 3 Kgdms 14:6 (LXX^A); Isa 18:2 (Symmachus).

38. Rengstorf, "ἀπόστολος," 1.414-20.

39. As expressed, e.g., in *m. Ber.* 5:5; *b. Ned.* 72b; *b. Naz.* 12b; *b. Qidd.* 43a; *b. Baba Qam.* 113b; and *b. Baba Mes.* 96a.

40. Cf., e.g., *m. Qidd.* 2:1; *b. Qidd.* 43a.

41. Cf., e.g., *m. Git.* 3:6; 4:1; *b. Git.* 21a-23b.

to perform ceremonial rituals on his behalf,[42] to act as his agent in economic matters,[43] and so on. In fact, the authority of the sender was thought of as so tied up with the *shaliach* that even if the *shaliach* committed a sacrilege, so long as he did not exceed the bounds of his commission, it was the sender and not the *shaliach* who was held responsible.[44]

Rengstorf has further argued (1) that the Jewish institution of the *shaliach* served as the model for Jesus in calling his disciples and sending them out on his behalf[45] and (2) that it was on the basis of Jesus' usage that the early Christian church used this concept for its own purposes and translated שליח by the relatively rare Greek term ἀπόστολος, probably first at Syrian Antioch.[46] And despite a great deal of further investigation and extensive debate, Rengstorf has largely continued to carry the day — not only in (1) establishing an early date for the origin of the *shaliach* institution in Judaism and (2) spelling out a connection between the sending motif of the OT and rabbinic writings and the sending motif of Jesus and the NT writers, but also in (3) correlating linguistically ἀπόστολος as used in the NT with the Jewish term שליח.[47]

There are, however, certain significant differences between the rabbinic idea of a *shaliach* and the Christian concept of an apostle. In the first place, the appointment of an agent in Judaism was always a temporary matter. When the task of the *shaliach* was completed, his commission was over. The rabbis did not think of a *shaliach* as having a lifelong calling, as is taken for granted of an apostle in the narrower sense of that term in the NT. More importantly, the *shaliach* was not viewed in a religious context or as a religious office — except, of course, in the sense that law and religion in Judaism were always inseparably intertwined. The term *shaliach,* however, was never used of prophets, missionaries, or proselytizers. So while the concept of a *shaliach* in Second Temple Judaism provides, to some extent, a reasonable background for the use of ἀπόστολος in the NT, it falls short of fully explicating that background or adequately highlighting some of the most important features of an apostle in early Christianity. For such matters, we must look as well to ideas that developed within Israel's religion having to do with the function of a prophet and to Jesus' reconstruction of both the *shaliach* concept and traditional prophetology.

Playing on the inadequacy of the Jewish *shaliach* concept to explain fully the NT's use of ἀπόστολος, Walter Schmithals argued for a gnostic origin of the term.[48] In support, he cited various references from the Church Fathers that

---

42. E.g., the heave offering, cf. *m. Ter.* 4:4.

43. Cf., e.g., *b. Baba Qam.* 102a, b.

44. Cf. e.g., *m. Meg.* 6:1-2; *b. Ketub.* 98b.

45. Rengstorf, "ἀπόστολος," 1.424-37.

46. *Ibid.*, 1.420-24, 437-45.

47. Cf. 3 Kgdms 14:6 (LXX^A), where the passive participle of שליח is treated as a noun and translated ἀπόστολος.

48. See Schmithals, *Office of Apostle in the Early Church.*

speak of so-called "Christian" gnostics as "false apostles,"[49] and he argued from these references that it was gnostic teachers who first used the title ἀπόστολος of themselves. In none of these texts, however, is it explicitly said that the gnostics ever used the term of themselves. Rather, every patristic reference cited by Schmithals is better understood as a Christian characterization of the gnostics as being "false apostles" (also "false prophets" and "false Christs") — which, of course, hardly proves that the title ἀπόστολος itself stemmed from a gnostic self-identity or arose from gnostic nomenclature.

1:1d The clause ἀφωρισμένος εἰς εὐαγγέλιον θεοῦ, "set apart [or, 'separated'] for the gospel that is from God," is best understood as the third self-identification given by Paul in 1:1 and should be read as parallel with δοῦλος Χριστοῦ Ἰησοῦ and κλητὸς ἀπόστολος. As Charles Cranfield has pointed out (contra the omission of a comma between κλητὸς ἀπόστολος and ἀφωρισμένος εἰς εὐαγγέλιον θεοῦ in UBS and Nestle-Aland, which suggests that the latter phrase is in apposition to the former): "To take the phrase as in apposition to κλητὸς ἀπόστολος, which is itself in apposition to Παῦλος, would be very clumsy."[50]

By the use of the nominative, singular, masculine, perfect, passive, substantival participle ἀφωρισμένος, Paul speaks of himself as "the one who has been set apart," just as he did by the use of the nouns δοῦλος and κλητός. The participle derives from the verb ἀφορίζειν ("to separate," "set apart," "appoint"), which is used in the LXX in the sense of being "set apart" or "separated" to God with respect to (1) every firstborn son of a family and every firstborn male of a family's livestock (Exod 13:12), (2) every first portion of one's baked goods and every first portion of one's harvest (Num 15:20), (3) the Levites in their divine service on behalf of Israel (Num 8:11), and (4) the nation Israel, which is set apart or separated from all other nations as God's special possession (Lev. 20:26). Ἀφορίζειν is often used in association with the noun ἅγιος ("holy") and the verb ἁγιάζειν ("to sanctify" or "consecrate") — as, for example, in Lev. 20:26, "You are to be *my holy people,* because I, the Lord, am *holy,* the one who *set you apart* from the nations to be my own" — and so it frequently connotes ideas of being "holy" unto God or "consecrated" by God (cf. also Ezek 45:4, where the verb appears with reference to an area of land consecrated by God for the use of the Levites and the building of the Jerusalem temple).

The fourth-century commentary writer whom Erasmus dubbed "Ambrosiaster"[51] understood Paul to be saying in his use of ἀφωρισμένος that "he has

---

49. As, e.g., Origen, *Commentary on John* 2.8; Eusebius, *Ecclesiae historia* 4.22 and 23.12; Tertullian, *De praescriptione haereticorum* 30; Ps.-Clement, *Homilies* 11.35.

50. Cranfield, *Romans,* 53; so also Michel, *An die Römer,* 35; contra Moo, *Romans,* 42.

51. Many have argued that "Ambrosiaster" was actually Hilary (c. 315-67), who was an energetic defender of orthodox Christianity, a major author of his day, and the bishop of Poitiers during 350-56. Others have suggested he may have been Evagrius of Antioch; and still others believe he was probably Isaac, a prominent convert from Judaism, in large part because his commentaries on Paul's letters (including Hebrews) evidence a great deal of interest in the relation of Christianity to Judaism and the Mosaic law (which identification I personally think is most probable).

been set apart [or, 'separated'] from the preaching of Judaism for the gospel of God, so that abandoning the law, he might preach Christ who justifies those who believe in him, which the law could not do."[52] Likewise, Augustine said much the same in distinguishing between Paul being "called" and Paul being "set apart," with the former understood to refer positively to his call to "the church, which is acceptable to God," and the latter to refer negatively to "the synagogue, whose glory had faded away."[53]

This understanding of what Paul meant by being "set apart" has been advocated, as well, by a number of twentieth-century Pauline interpreters, many of whom have also viewed Paul here as not only saying that he was "separated from the law" but also that he was separated by God from his Pharisaic past — sometimes, in fact, proposing that this distinction between law and gospel is the main theme of Paul's entire letter to the Romans.[54] And some have attempted to demonstrate a wordplay between the Greek verb ἀφορίζειν ("to set apart") and the Hebrew verb פרשׁ ("to separate"), which has often been claimed as the root of the name "Pharisee"[55] — much as Kingsley Barrett has explicitly argued:

> The Greek word is not only similar in meaning to, but also has the same consonants as the Hebrew root *p-r-sh*, which underlies the word Pharisee. Paul had been a Pharisee (Phil. iii.5), supposing himself to be set apart from other men for the service of God; he now truly was what he had supposed himself to be — separated, not, however, by human exclusiveness but by God's grace and election.[56]

While such an interpretation is possible, it is not the most probable. For in setting out in coordinate fashion his three self-identifications of (1) "a servant of Christ Jesus," (2) "called [by God] an apostle," and (3) "set apart for the gospel of God," Paul suggests that what is understood about one of them must also be understood about all of them — which, in effect, means that all three are speaking primarily in positive terms, without attempting to set up contrasts.

All three, we believe, are to be seen as rooted in Paul's prophetic consciousness, with that prophetic consciousness based biblically on Jer 1:5, "Before I formed you in the womb I knew you, before you were born I set you apart; I appointed you as a prophet to the nations (προφήτην εἰς ἔθνη)," and as expressed by him earlier in Gal 1:15-16a, "God, who set me apart from birth

52. Ambrosiaster, *Ad Romanos, PL* 17.48.

53. Augustine, *Ad Romanos inchoata expositio, PL* 35.2089.

54. Cf., e.g., Zahn, *An die Römer*, 31-33; Schlatter, *Romans*, 7; Nygren, *Romans*, 45-46; Michel, *An die Römer*, 36, 68 n. 16; though see Käsemann, *Romans*, 6, who simply states that ἀφωρισμένος "does not . . . refer to the contrast with Paul's Pharisaic past."

55. Cf., e.g., Zahn, *An die Römer*, 31; Nygren, *Romans*; K. L. Schmidt, "ἀφορίζω," 5.454; Black, *Romans*, 34; and, somewhat tentatively, Fitzmyer, *Romans*, 232.

56. Barrett, *Romans*, 17.

and called me by his grace, was pleased to reveal his Son in me so that I might preach him among the Gentiles." It is not that Paul viewed himself as having been at his birth appointed by God "a servant" and "an apostle," and then later "set apart for the gospel of God" — whether in contrast to his earlier adherence to the law or his Pharisaic past, or at his "consecration" to a Gentile ministry at Syrian Antioch as represented in Acts 13:2.[57] As the third of his three coordinate self-identifications, this affirmation of having been "set apart" must also be seen as rooted in Paul's prophetic consciousness and expressed in an entirely positive fashion.

The noun εὐαγγέλιον ("gospel") appears here without an article, but koine Greek phrases that have both a preposition and a genitive do not usually have an article in order to signify the definiteness of their subjects. Εὐαγγέλιον in the Greco-Roman world originally meant "a reward for good news," and then, in both its singular and plural forms, the content of that "good news" itself.[58] The verb εὐαγγελίζειν in the LXX means "to announce good news,"[59] especially regarding a military victory.[60] More particularly, however, when used in a religious sense, εὐαγγελίζειν (or its aorist middle form εὐαγγελίσασθαι) and its substantival participle εὐαγγελιζόμενος have to do with the in-breaking of God's reign, whether in vengeance or vindication, and the proclamation of God's salvation.[61] And it is most likely on the basis of this OT usage (1) that Jesus identified the content of his preaching as τὸ εὐαγγέλιον, that is, "the good news" or "gospel,"[62] and (2) that early believers in Jesus continued to speak of their distinctive message, evidently on the basis of Jesus' usage, as τὸ εὐαγγέλιον τοῦ θεοῦ, "the good news [or, 'gospel'] of God,"[63] and, it may be added, (3) that at some time after Paul's ministry the canonical Evangelists began to call their writings about the story of Jesus τὸ εὐαγγέλιον Ἰησοῦ Χριστοῦ, that is, "a literary Gospel about Jesus Christ."[64]

Scholars have often tried to relate the NT's use of εὐαγγέλιον to language used in the imperial cult of Rome. It was Adolf Deissmann who was most influential in arguing (1) that "gospel" was an important sacred word in the Greco-Roman world of emperor worship, and (2) that the writers of the NT not only knew that it was so used but were also responding to that pagan usage when

57. Cf. Sanday and Headlam, *Romans* 5, who mention Paul's "consecration" at Antioch as a possible interpretation.

58. See Plutarch, *Sertorius* 11.8; 26.6; *Phocion* 16.8; 23.6; Josephus, *War* 2.420; 4.618, 656.

59. See Jer 20:15.

60. See 1 Sam 31:9; note also 1 Kgs 1:42.

61. Cf. Pss 40:9 (LXX 39:10; MT 40:10); 96:2 (LXX 95:2); Isa 40:9; 52:7; 60:6; 61:1; Nah 1:15 (LXX and MT 2:1).

62. Cf. Mark 8:35; 10:29; 13:10; 14:9 par. Matt 26:13.

63. As the wording of the traditional material incorporated into Mark 1:14-15 suggests; see also τὸ εὐαγγέλιον τῆς βασιλείας, "the good news [or 'gospel'] of the kingdom" in Matt 4:23; 9:35; 24:14.

64. As appears in the caption to Mark's portrayals of Jesus in Mark 1:1, with the genitive construction of the name "Jesus Christ" understood as an objective genitive.

they used the term for the much greater "good news" that comes from God and is focused in the work and person of Christ Jesus.[65] Deissmann based his thesis principally on (1) the celebrated *Calendar Inscription from Priene,* which was inscribed about 9 B.C. and refers to the εὐαγγελία ("good news") of the birth of Augustus "the most divine Caesar,"[66] (2) another Greek inscription of the time that uses the same plural expression "good news" with reference to the emperor Septimius Geta,[67] and (3) a letter by an Egyptian high-ranking official that speaks in both articular and singular fashion of τοῦ εὐαγγελίου ("of the good news") regarding the proclamation of Gaius Julius Verus Maximus Augustus as emperor.[68] And many interpreters have accepted this understanding.[69]

Ernst Käsemann, however, has appropriately argued that "the antithesis between the worship of Christ and emperor worship does not play in the primitive Church the role presupposed for such a derivation," and so has concluded that "it is not satisfactory to derive the NT term in its absolute and technical use from this source."[70] Likewise, Peter Stuhlmacher — after a full-length study of the pre-Pauline use of εὐαγγέλιον in Jewish and Greco-Roman writings, as well as its use by Jesus, the early Jewish Christian communities of Palestine, and the Hellenistic Jewish Christian communities of the Jewish Diaspora[71] — has concluded (as expressed concisely in the 1994 English translation of his 1989 German commentary on Romans):

> The use of the word "gospel" in the Greek royal inscriptions to refer to the good news concerning the birth, inauguration, victories, or good deeds of the emperor may have been known to Jesus, the apostles, and to Paul. But it had no influence on the meaning of the language they used to describe their preaching. Moreover, the influence that it exerted on the understanding of the message of Christ in the churches is not significant enough to be mentioned.[72]

Nor can it be said that Paul picked up the term "gospel" from his rabbinic background. For while the verb בשׂר ("to proclaim good tidings") and its participle מבשׂר ("messenger of good tidings") appear occasionally in later talmudic writings, they occur only at those few places where Isa 40:9; 52:7; 60:6; and 61:1 are actually quoted — that is, where the term is retained within a quotation from Isaiah, but without any comment or theological reflection

---

65. Deissmann, *Light from the Ancient East,* 366-67.

66. Citing *Inschriften von Priene* 105.

67. Citing *Inscriptiones Graecae* 3.1081.

68. Citing G. Parthey, *Memorie dell' Instituo di Corrispondenze Archeologica* (Lipsia, 1965), 2.440.

69. Cf. G. Friedrich, "εὐαγγέλιον." *TDNT* 2.724-25; W. Schneemelcher, *NTA,* 1.71-73.

70. Käsemann, *Romans,* 7.

71. See Stuhlmacher, *Das paulinische Evangelium,* esp. 1.11ff. and 199ff.

72. Stuhlmacher, *Romans,* 25.

on this verb or participle on the part of the rabbis who are cited as quoting these passages.

"Good tidings" ("good news" or "gospel") as the content of a message does, however, appear in two places in the Dead Sea Scrolls: (1) in 1QH 18.14, where the substantival participle המבשר ("the one who brings good tidings") seems to be equated with the Teacher of Righteousness, and (2) in 11QMelch 18, where the same participle המבשר is identified as the eschatological archangel warrior Melchizedek, who is also "the one anointed by the Spirit." But these instances, while analogically interesting, must be judged as being too rare, too sociologically and culturally remote, and too ideologically distant to have had any direct bearing on the use of "gospel" in the NT.

It is "the gospel that is from God" (τὸ εὐαγγέλιον θεοῦ) that was at the heart of all of Paul's concerns. As Paul speaks about that "good news" in his letters, he refers to it as a message (1) that has God himself as its source (understanding θεοῦ here in Rom 1:1 as a genitive of source); (2) that has the person and work of God's Son, "Jesus Christ our Lord," as its content (cf. vv. 3-4 below; also v. 9: "the gospel of his Son"); (3) that was "announced in advance to Abraham" (as stated in Gal 3:8; cf. esp. Rom 4:1-24); and (4) that was "promised beforehand through his [God's] prophets in the Holy Scriptures" (cf. v. 2 below). Further, he insists (5) that this gospel is the only message he proclaimed (cf. 1 Cor 1:17-25; 2:1-16; 15:1-11); (6) that it is what God by his Spirit is calling people to accept (cf. Gal 1:6a; 3:1-5); (7) that it is what some of his converts in Galatia were deserting by accepting "a different gospel, which is in reality no truth of the gospel" (cf. Gal 2:5, 14) or not "the word of truth" (cf. Col 1:5); and (8) that it is greater and more important than any of his own personal circumstances (cf. 1 Cor 9:12-23; Phil 1:12-18). And it is commitment to this gospel and the focus of its message, which is "Jesus Christ our Lord," on which everything else in Paul's theology and ethics is based.

While an unbroken line of continuity cannot be traced back from the noun εὐαγγέλιον in the NT to the verb εὐαγγελίζειν (together with its aorist middle form εὐαγγελίσασθαι and the participle εὐαγγελιζόμενος) in the OT,[73] it may legitimately be argued (1) that it was Jesus who reached back to his Jewish (OT) Scriptures and identified the content of his preaching as τὸ εὐαγγέλιον, that is, "the good news" or "gospel,"[74] and (2) that the earliest Christians, on the basis of Jesus' usage, began to speak of their distinctive message as τὸ εὐαγγέλιον τοῦ θεοῦ, "the good news [or 'gospel'] of God,"[75] or as τὸ εὐαγγέλιον τῆς βασιλείας, "the good news [or 'gospel'] of the kingdom."[76] And it was evidently from the earliest Jewish Christian reports about Jesus' preaching and from the early Jewish Christians' own use of εὐαγγέλιον that Paul picked up this term to represent

73. Cf. Pss 40:9; 96:2; Isa 40:9; 52:7; 60:6; 61:1; Nah 1:15.
74. As in Mark 8:35; 10:29; 13:10; 14:9 par. Matt 26:13.
75. As in Mark 1:14-15.
76. As in Matt 4:23; 9:35; 24:14.

the content of what he was called to proclaim — that is, as Peter Stuhlmacher has aptly expressed matters, Paul "took over his language concerning the 'gospel' from the apostles before and beside him."[77]

The noun εὐαγγέλιον, however, appears more frequently in Paul's letters (some sixty times out of its total seventy-six NT occurrences), and with a greater degree of nuancing, than it does elsewhere in the NT — as does also the verb εὐαγγελίζειν and its cognates. The earliest use of "gospel" among Jewish believers in Jesus seems to have been in the context of the formulation "the gospel of God," with its stress not only on its content, that is, "good news," but also on its source, that is, as being "from God" (taking τοῦ θεοῦ as a genitive of source) — thereby understanding the term in this context to mean "the 'good news' from God" (cf. the traditional material of Mark 1:14-15; see also 1 Pet 4:17). Paul uses that form of expression as well — and certainly agrees with its emphases — not only here in Rom 1:1 but also elsewhere in his letters.[78] Usually, however, Paul simply speaks of "the gospel,"[79] as did undoubtedly many other Jewish believers in Jesus before him.

Yet Paul also gives εὐαγγέλιον his own particular emphasis in his highlighting of its distinctive Christian content (understanding the genitive constructions in each case as objective genitives), and so speaks of "the gospel of his [God's] Son,"[80] "the gospel of Christ,"[81] "the glorious gospel of Christ,"[82] or "the gospel of our Lord Jesus."[83] Further, he speaks in a more personal manner of this "gospel" as "my gospel,"[84] "our gospel,"[85] or "the gospel that I proclaimed"[86] (understanding the genitive contructions as possessive genitives, and with each of these expressions being related to the particular situation addressed). And at times he connects one of the gospel's intended results — such as "reconciliation,"[87] "salvation,"[88] or "peace"[89] — with the term itself (or a close cognate).

1:2 Having identified in 1:1 the gospel's source as being "from God," Paul goes further in 1:2 to highlight a point of great importance for both himself and his addressees: that this gospel is that ὃ προεπηγγείλατο διὰ τῶν προφητῶν αὐτοῦ ἐν γραφαῖς ἁγίαις ("which he [God] promised beforehand through his prophets in the Holy Scriptures"). This statement is hardly "a digression," as

77. Stuhlmacher, *Romans*, 24-25.
78. Cf. Rom 15:16; 2 Cor 11:7; Gal 1:11; 1 Thess 2:2, 8-9; 1 Tim 1:11.
79. Cf., e.g., Rom 1:16; 10:16; 11:28; 1 Cor 4:15; 9:14, 18, 23; 15:1; 2 Cor 8:18.
80. Cf. Rom 1:9, picking up from 1:3.
81. Cf. Rom 15:19; 1 Cor 9:12; 2 Cor 2:12; 9:13; 10:14; Gal 1:7; 1 Thess 3:2.
82. 2 Cor 4:4.
83. 2 Thess 1:8.
84. Cf. Rom 2:16; 16:25; 2 Tim 2:8.
85. Cf. 1 Thess 1:5; 2 Thess 2:14.
86. Gal 1:11.
87. Cf. 2 Cor 5:19.
88. Cf. Eph 1:13.
89. Cf. Eph 6:15.

Ernst Käsemann called it.[90] Rather, it makes a highly significant point that Paul will emphasize throughout the entire letter: that the Christian gospel is integrally related to what God has done redemptively throughout the course of salvation history at earlier times. This point is made abundantly evident in such ways as (1) Paul's direct characterization of the gospel as proclaiming "a righteousness from God . . . to which the law and the prophets testify" (3:21), (2) his frequent use of OT quotations, with more than half of the biblical quotations in all his extant letters appearing in Rom 1:16–4:25; 9:1–11:36; and 12:1–15:13, and (3) his repeated use of such OT themes and illustrations as "the faith of Abraham" (4:1-24), "the sin of Adam and its results" (5:11-21), the illustration regarding marriage (7:1-3, with its statement "for I am speaking to those who know the law"), and Jewish and/or Jewish Christian remnant theology (on which much of 9:6–11:32 is based).

The verb προεπηγγείλατο ("he promised beforehand"), however, appears in the NT only here in the first aorist middle and as an adjectival participle at 2 Cor 9:5 (i.e., "your 'previously promised' generous gift"). The phrase διὰ τῶν προφητῶν αὐτοῦ ("through his prophets") is a generic expression that includes all of the inspired people who are called "prophets" in the OT, including such men as Moses (cf. Acts 3:22) and David (cf. Acts 2:30-31) and not just those included in "the prophets," the second division of the Hebrew Scriptures. Here Paul speaks of the gospel as having been promised διὰ τῶν προφητῶν αὐτοῦ, "through his prophets," but without the adjectives "holy" or "sacred." Usually Paul does not use "holy," "sacred," or "dedicated" with respect to the prophets, but only with reference to "the law"[91] and when speaking of Christians[92] or their children (cf. 1 Cor 7:14). The expression "his [God's] holy prophets," however, appears in Zechariah's Song of praise in Luke 1:70 and Peter's sermon at the temple gate in Acts 3:21 and so must have been common among both Jews and Jewish Christians.

Also to be noted is the fact that the adjective ἅγιος ("holy") in connection with "Scripture" or "Scriptures" is not found in the LXX nor anywhere else in Paul's letters, even though, as noted above, Paul uses the adjective ἅγιος ("holy") with reference to ὁ νόμος ("the law") in 7:12 — and even though he repeatedly uses the articular singular ἡ γραφή ("the Scripture") without that adjective (4:3; 9:17; 10:11; 11:2)[93] and the anarthrous plural γραφαί ("[the] Scriptures," 15:4).[94] Philo, however, spoke of αἱ ἱεραὶ γραφαί, "the Sacred Scriptures,"[95] as did also Josephus.[96] So it may be presumed (1) that Jewish Christians would have referred to what we now call the OT as "the Sacred Scriptures" or "the Holy

90. Käsemann, *Romans*, 10.
91. E.g., Rom 7:12.
92. E.g., Rom 12:1; 1 Cor 3:17; Eph 2:21; 2 Tim 1:9.
93. Cf. also Gal 3:8, 22; 4:30; passim.
94. Cf. also 1 Cor 15:3, 4; passim.
95. Cf. Philo, *De Abrahamo* 61; *De congressu* 34, 90.
96. Josephus, *Contra Apion* 2.45.

Scriptures," (2) that Paul's addressees at Rome, who were dominantly Gentile Christians ethnically but also indebted to Jewish Christianity theologically and for their central religious expressions,[97] would have used such phraseology as well, and (3) that Paul, while he may not have commonly used the adjective "holy" with reference to "Scripture" or "the Scriptures" when evangelizing or writing to Gentiles elsewhere in the eastern part of the Roman Empire, was happy here in 1:2 to condition his words to the forms of expression and sensibilities of his addressees at Rome.

1:3a Previously Paul defined the Christian gospel in 1:1 by its origin and source ("from God") and in 1:2 by its having been divinely promised ("promised beforehand through his prophets in the Holy Scriptures"). Now at the beginning of 1:3 he defines that gospel further by its content — that is, περὶ τοῦ υἱοῦ αὐτοῦ ("concerning his [God's] Son"). Because of the essential repetition of the phraseology τὸ εὐαγγέλιον τοῦ υἱοῦ αὐτοῦ ("the gospel concerning his Son") just a few verses later in 1:9, it seems best to conclude that "concerning his Son" here in 1:3a is to be taken not as part of the quoted material of 1:3b-4, but, rather, as Paul's introduction of the quotation that immediately follows.

The ascription "his Son" or "God's Son" is ultimately derived from the coronation decree of God in Ps 2:7, "You are my Son; today I have begotten you." For early Christians this ascription came to dramatic expression in the acclamations from heaven of Jesus as God's Son at his baptism[98] and at his transfiguration.[99] It seems, in fact, to have been one of the earliest titles ascribed to Jesus by Jewish Christians — as witness, for example, (1) the caption of Heb 1:2 ("in these last days he has spoken to us by his Son [literally 'a son'], whom he appointed heir of all things and through whom he created the ages"), (2) the confessional portion of Heb 1:3-4 ("The Son [literally 'who'] is the radiance of God's glory and the exact representation of his being"), and (3) the first passage from Scripture cited in support of the title in Heb 1:5a ("You are my Son; today I have begotten you"). So while the proclamation of "the gospel" was always at the heart of Paul's mission, the focus of that proclamation, both among the earliest believers in Jesus and in Paul's proclamation, was on the work and person of "God's Son" — that is, on "Jesus Christ our Lord," as stated explicitly at the end of Rom 1:4.

1:3b-4 What follows in 1:3b-4 has often been understood as an early Christian confessional portion, perhaps even part of an early Christian hymn that is quoted by Paul here. One reason for such a judgment is that these verses contain some words, expressions, and motifs that appear somewhat unusual for Paul and could more readily be understood as the language of early Jewish Christianity — such as (1) the association of Jesus with "seed of David" or "son of David" imagery (cf. also 2 Tim 2:8); (2) use of the verb ὁρίζειν ("to appoint"

---

97. See pp. 8-9 above and further R. N. Longenecker, *Introducing Romans*, 55-91.
98. Cf. Mark 1:11; Matt 3:17; Luke 3:22.
99. Cf. Mark 9:7; Matt 17:5; Luke 9:35.

or "designate"), which appears nowhere else in Paul's letters but is found a number of times in Jewish Christian contexts elsewhere in the NT; (3) the phrase πνεῦμα ἁγιωσύνης ("spirit of holiness"), which seems to have a Semitic base and not to be part of the vocabulary of Paul (who usually speaks of "God's Spirit" or "the Holy Spirit"); (4) the contrast of σάρξ ("flesh") and πνεῦμα ("spirit") in a somewhat unusual Pauline manner; and (5) the association of Sonship with resurrection (found in early preaching, as in Acts 13:33, where Ps 2:7 is quoted). Further reasons for viewing this material as part of an early Christian confession or hymn are the articular substantival participles introducing each of the two major parts of 1:3b-4, which is characteristic of traditional material, and the fairly balanced structure, which can be set out as follows:

τοῦ γενομένου ἐκ σπέρματος Δαυὶδ
   κατὰ σάρκα,
τοῦ ὁρισθέντος υἱοῦ θεοῦ ἐν δυνάμει
   κατὰ πνεῦμα ἁγιωσύνης
   ἐξ ἀναστάσεως νεκρῶν,
Ἰησοῦ Χριστοῦ τοῦ κυρίου ἡμῶν.

Further, it needs also to be observed that the flow of thought beginning with "concerning his Son" (v. 3a) and concluding with "through whom we have received grace and apostleship" (vv. 5-6) would run quite smoothly as a sentence if vv. 3b-4 were omitted, as is often the case with material incorporated by an author into his own prose, and that the strophe with its two parts concludes with the naming of "God's Son" in a somewhat non-Pauline fashion: "Jesus Christ our Lord."[100] What appears here in 1:3b-4, therefore, is probably to be understood as early Christian confessional material that Paul cites in order to highlight the content of the gospel, to affirm his own acceptance of what his addressees held regarding God's Son, and to establish rapport with his Roman addressees.

The statement τοῦ γενομένου ἐκ σπέρματος Δαυὶδ κατὰ σάρκα (literally "the one born of the seed of David with respect to the flesh") is the first part of this early Christian confessional couplet. The noun σπέρμα ("seed") in Jewish thought, and particularly in the Greek OT (LXX) and NT, usually means simply "a human descendant"[101] — though in messianic contexts "seed of David" also conjures up ideas about Israel's Messiah.[102] The preposition κατά followed by a noun in the accusative case means "with respect to" or "in relation to."[103] And the noun σάρξ ("flesh") in non-ethical contexts elsewhere in Romans and Paul's other letters means simply "human" or "human descent"[104] — though in ethical

100. See our earlier discussion on the formulation "Christ Jesus" or "Jesus Christ" in 1:1.

101. Cf., e.g., Josephus, *Antiquities* 8.200; Gen 15:13; 21:12; 22:17; Job 5:25; Isa 58:7; Luke 1:55; John 8:33, 37; Acts 7:5-6; Rom 4:13; 11:1; 2 Cor 11:22; and Heb 2:16; 11:18.

102. Cf. 2 Sam 7:12; Ps 89:3-4; John 7:42; Acts 13:23; 2 Tim 2:8.

103. Cf. *Moule,* 59.

104. Cf., e.g., Rom 4:1; 9:5, 8; 11:14; 1 Cor 10:18; Gal 4:23, 29.

contexts, where σάρξ is used in contrast with πνεῦμα ("spirit" or "the Spirit"), it denotes that which is in opposition to God and to all that is "spiritual."[105] Here, however, the expression "with respect to the flesh" (κατὰ σάρκα) seems to connote no pejorative nuance.[106] Thus this first part of the couplet can be translated "the one who was descended from David with respect to his human descent (or 'according to his humanity')."

Establishing a connection between Christ and the lineage of David, however, is not a usual feature in Paul's letters, being found only here in 1:3 (quoting, it seems, part of an early Christian confession or hymn), in Rom 15:12 (quoting Isa 11:10), and in 2 Tim 2:8 (writing to a colleague who was trained in the OT Scriptures). But it is common in the Synoptic Gospels[107] and seems to come to expression in the NT particularly where an understanding that is typically Jewish Christian is to the fore.[108] Further, it needs always to be recognized that for the earliest Jewish believers in Jesus the ascription σπέρματος Δαυίδ — whether understood as a title ("Seed of David") or simply as signaling lineage ("descended from David") — would have carried with it ideas about Israel's promised Messiah. For the expectation that the Messiah would be the true descendant of David and thus the "Seed of David" as well as the "Son of David" was firmly rooted in Jewish thought.[109]

The affirmation of 1:4a, τοῦ ὁρισθέντος υἱοῦ θεοῦ ἐν δυνάμει κατὰ πνεῦμα ἁγιωσύνης ἐξ ἀναστάσεως νεκρῶν ("who was designated the Son of God with power with respect to his spirit [or 'the Spirit'] of holiness, by his resurrection from the dead"), is the second part of the couplet of 1:3b and 4. The articular, substantival, passive participle τοῦ ὁρισθέντος is derived from the verb ὁρίζειν, which when used of persons means "to appoint" or "designate." Neither ὁρίζειν nor its participle appears anywhere else in Paul's letters. It is used, however, in Acts 2:23 with reference to Christ's "appointment" to death and in Acts 10:42 and 17:31 with reference to his "appointment" or "designation" by God as the eschatological judge. And it is with that sense of "appointment" or "designation" that the participle is used here.

The Old Latin, Jerome's Vulgate, and a number of Latin writers translated ὁρισθέντος by the Latin *praedestinatus,* and so read "the one who was predestined" (as though the text read τοῦ προορισθέντος). And that understanding of Christ as having been "predestined" to be God's Son dominated the understanding of many of the Church Fathers (particularly Cyril of Alexandria and Augustine), and has been a continued feature in various segments of the theological tradition of the western church (both Roman Catholic and Protestant).

---

105. Cf. Rom 8:4-9, 12-13; 1 Cor 5:5; Gal 3:2-3; 5:16-19; Phil 3:3.
106. So, e.g., W. D. Davies, "Paul and the Dead Sea Scrolls," 163; Schweizer, "σάρξ," 7.125-29; contra Dunn, "Jesus — Flesh and Spirit," 44-49.
107. Cf., e.g., Mark 10:47-48 par.; 12:35-37 par.; passim.
108. Cf., e.g., Matt 1:1; Acts 2:30; Rev 5:5; 22:16.
109. Cf., e.g., 2 Sam 7:16; Ps 89:3-4; Isa 11:1, 10; Jer 23:5-6; 30:9; 33:14-18; Ezek 34:23-24; 37:24-25; see also *Pss Sol* 17:23 (also 21).

As early as the first half of the third century, however, Origen opposed such an understanding and quite rightly insisted:

> Although in Latin translations one normally finds the word "predestined" [*praedestinatus*] here, the true reading is "designated" [*destinatus*] and not "predestined" [*praedestinatus*]. For "designate" [*destinatur*] applies to someone who already exists, whereas "predestine" [*praedestinatur*] is only applicable to someone who does not yet exist, like those of whom the apostle said: "For those whom he foreknew he also predestined" [Rom 8:29]. . . . Those who do not yet exist may be foreknown and predestined, but he who is and who always exists is not predestined but designated. . . . He was never predestined to be the Son, because he always was and is the Son, just as the Father has always been the Father.[110]

Likewise, John Chrysostom in the latter part of the fourth century understood τοῦ ὁρισθέντος in a similar fashion — that is, as synonymous with δειχθέντος ("displayed"), ἀποφθέντος ("manifested"), κριθέντος ("judged"), and ὁμολογηθέντος ("acknowledged"), but not with προορισθέντος ("predestined").[111]

While neither ὁρίζειν nor its participle is found anywhere else in Paul's letters, both the verb and its participle appear in Luke 22:22; Acts 2:23; 10:42; 11:29; 17:26; and Heb 4:7 in the sense of "to appoint," "designate," or "determine." So here in Rom 1:4 the articular, substantival, passive participle should most likely be translated by some such wording as "the one who was appointed" or "designated" — with, of course, God himself being that one who appointed or designated Jesus as his Son.

Since the flat denial by Gustav Dalman and Wilhelm Bousset, many scholars have asserted that υἱὸς θεοῦ ("Son of God") had no messianic associations in pre-Christian Judaism.[112] Joseph Fitzmyer reflects such a stance when he writes: "The title 'Son of God' is not being used in a messianic sense . . . ; nothing is intimated in the text about Jesus' anointed status or agency, and no OT background relates 'son of God' to 'Messiah.' "[113] However in 4QFlorilegium, which is a collection of selected OT passages and interpretive comments dateable to the end of the first century B.C. or the beginning of the first A.D., the words of 2 Sam 7:14, "I will be to him a father, and he will be to me a son," are given explicit messianic import in the comment "The 'he' in question is 'the Branch of David' who will appear in Zion in the Last Days, alongside 'the Expounder of the Law.' "[114] Likewise in *4 Ezra* 7:28-29; 13:32, 37, 52; and 14:9 — which are

---

110. Origen, *Ad Romanos*, PG 14.849.
111. See Chrysostom, *Homilia XXXII ad Romanos*, PG 60.397.
112. Cf. Dalman, *The Words of Jesus*, 271-72; Bousset, *Kyrios Christos*, 53-54.
113. Fitzmyer, *Romans*, 235.
114. 4QFlor 1.12-13. For "the Branch of David" as a messianic title, see Jer 23:5; 33:15; Zech 3:8; 6:12.

passages written by a pious Jewish author only a few years after the apostolic period of early Christianity, probably about 100-120 A.D. — God is represented as speaking repeatedly of the Messiah as "my Son." So also *1 En* 105:2 in portraying God as speaking in a messianic context of "I and my Son" (though this verse has often for this very reason been viewed as a Jewish Christian interpolation into earlier Enochian material).

It should, therefore, not seem strange that "Messiah" and "Son of God" are explicitly brought together as christological titles at a number of places in the NT. Most obvious among NT instances are the following:

1. Peter's confession in Matt 16:16 (cf. also Mark 8:29 ℵ): "You are the Christ ['the Messiah'], the Son of (the living) God."
2. Caiaphas's question in Matt 26:63 (cf. also Mark 14:61, where there is a locution for God): "Are you the Christ ['the Messiah'], the Son of God?"
3. The demonic recognition of Jesus as "the Son of God" in Luke 4:41, which is said by the Evangelist to have been based on a knowledge that he was "the Christ ['the Messiah']."
4. Martha's affirmation in John 11:27: "You are the Christ ['the Messiah'], the Son of God, the One coming into the world."
5. The Fourth Evangelist's statement in John 20:31 that his purpose in writing was that his readers "may come to believe that Jesus is the Christ ['the Messiah'], the Son of God," and that by believing they "may have life in his name."
6. Paul's early preaching in the synagogues of Damascus, as represented in Acts 9:20-22, which focused on Jesus as "the Son of God" and as "the Christ ['the Messiah']."

It should, therefore, not be thought surprising that in the early Christian confessional portion cited by Paul here in 1:3b-4 "seed of David," with its messianic connotations, and the christological title "Son of God" are juxtaposed.

Actually, apart from its use here in Rom 1:4, "Son of God" as a title for Jesus appears in only two other passages in Paul's letters — that is, in 2 Cor 1:19 and Gal 2:20. Further, its cognates "the Son" and "his Son" are to be found in his letters only twelve times more — that is, in his introduction of 1:3a to the confessional couplet here in 1:3b-4, and elsewhere in his letters in Rom 1:9; 5:10; 8:3, 29, 32; 1 Cor 1:9; 15:28; Gal 1:16; 4:4, 6; and 1 Thess 1:10. As Werner Kramer has observed with regard to Paul's use of "Son of God," "the Son," and "his Son" with respect to Jesus: "In comparison with the passages in which the titles *Christ Jesus* or *Lord* occur, this is an infinitesimally small figure."[115] And as Kramer has further noted: "Paul's use of the title *Son of God* depends primarily on external factors, in that it is prompted by what has gone before."[116] Rather,

115. Kramer, *Christ, Lord, Son of God*, 183.
116. *Ibid.*, 185.

it is Matthew among the Synoptic Evangelists who gives increased prominence to the Sonship of Jesus,[117] the Fourth Evangelist who makes this theme the high point of his Christology,[118] and the writer of Hebrews who highlights in his homily the theme of the superiority of Jesus as God's Son.[119]

Thus it may reasonably be concluded (1) that early Jewish believers in Jesus used "Son of God" as a title for their acclaimed Messiah, (2) that they used it in association with the whole complex of messianic ideas and expressions with which they were familiar, (3) that Christians at Rome, being heavily indebted to the theology and religious language of Jewish Christianity, were probably also in the habit of using "Son of God" as a title for Jesus, and (4) that Paul in addressing believers in Jesus at Rome used an early Christian confessional portion — or, at least, part of such a confessional portion — which contained certain christological themes and ascriptions that were familiar to his addressees. It may be assumed that Paul agreed with what the Christians at Rome believed and confessed in the material that he quoted in 1:3b-4. Otherwise he would not have included it in the salutation of his letter. Nor would he have introduced it with the expression περὶ τοῦ υἱοῦ αὐτοῦ ("concerning his Son," 1:3a). But the pattern that Paul exhibits in all his extant pastoral correspondence (likewise, presumably, in all his evangelistic preaching) seems to have been to write (and, presumably, to speak) in ways that could be called "circumstantial" — that is, in ways that were suited to the understanding and appreciation of those whom he was addressing. And this is what he seems to have done here, as well, in writing to the Christians at Rome.

The phrase ἐν δυνάμει ("in" or "with power," 1:4a) has always been difficult for commentators to interpret. Is it part of the early Christian confessional material that Paul quotes,[120] or should it be considered a "supplement" inserted by Paul into an earlier church formulation?[121] Further, is it to be understood adverbially, thereby modifying the participle ὁρισθέντος,[122] or adjectivally, thereby qualifying υἱοῦ θεοῦ?[123] Read adverbially, "appointed in power" would emphasize the fact that Jesus was appointed or designated "Son of God" by God's mighty act of raising him from the dead. Read adjectivally, "Son of God with power" would lay stress not only on the status of Jesus as the Son of God, which was established by God at his resurrection, but also the power that Jesus possesses because of his resurrection and the power by which he is able to

---

117. Cf., e.g., Matt 2:15; 3:17; 4:3, 6; 8:29; 11:27; 14:33; 16:16; 17:5; 21:37-38; 26:63; 27:40, 43, 54; 28:19.

118. Cf., e.g., John 1:18, 34; 3:16-18, 35-36; 5:19-23, 25-26; 6:40; 8:36; 9:35; 10:36; 11:4, 27; 14:13; 17:1; 19:7; 20:31.

119. Cf. esp. Heb 1:2, 3-4, 5-6, 8-9; 4:14; 5:5, 8; 6:6; 7:28; 10:29.

120. So, e.g., Käsemann, *Romans*, 12.

121. So, e.g., Barrett, *Romans*, 18-20.

122. So, e.g., Sanday and Headlam, *Romans*, 9; cf. NEB: "declared Son of God by a mighty act"; NIV: "declared with power to be the Son of God."

123. So, e.g., Cranfield, *Romans*, 1.62; Dunn, *Romans*, 1.14; Fitzmyer, *Romans*, 235; Moo, *Romans*, 48-49; cf. KJV and NRSV: "Son of God with power."

energize all who turn to him as their risen Lord. Both readings have been persuasively argued, and each is linguistically possible. Yet it seems far better — if we (1) assume that ἐν δυνάμει was part of the confessional material quoted, and not words injected by Paul, (2) emphasize the parallelism between τοῦ γενομένου ἐκ σπέρματος Δαυίδ in 1:3b and τοῦ ὁρισθέντος υἱοῦ θεοῦ ἐν δυνάμει in 1:4a, with the first speaking of his status as "Seed of David" and the second of his status as "Son of God," and (3) note that both expressions are immediately followed by a further antithetical parallelism that begins in each case with the preposition κατά ("with respect to" or "in relation to") — to understand "with power" as being adjectivally connected with the noun phrase "Son of God." On such a reading, the movement from "Seed of David" to "Son of God" is not a transition from a purely human Messiah to a divine Son of God (as in an "adoptionist" Christology) but, rather, two affirmations of an early and inclusive christological declaration, which speaks first of Jesus' right to be considered Israel's promised Messiah because of his birth as the true descendant of David and then of his designation by God as God's true Son because of his "spirit of holiness" — all of which was decisively authenticated by his resurrection from the dead.

The most difficult question regarding the exegesis of 1:3b-4a, however, has to do with the meaning of κατὰ πνεῦμα ἁγιωσύνης in 1:4a. A somewhat bewildering array of interpretations have been proposed throughout the course of Christian history. All of them, however, fall into one of the following categories:

1. *The Divine Nature of Christ.* This first category of interpretation views κατὰ πνεῦμα ἁγιωσύνης as referring to the divine nature of Christ, that is, to his divinity. For just as κατὰ σάρκα in 1:3b has reference to his human nature, so κατὰ πνεῦμα ἁγιωσύνης here in 1:4 must be understood in antithetical fashion as referring to his divine nature. This was a common understanding among the Church Fathers.

The fourth-century commentator whom Erasmus dubbed "Ambrosiaster," for example, wrote:

> When Paul speaks about the Son of God he is pointing out that God is Father, and by adding the Spirit of holiness he indicates the mystery of the Trinity. For he who was incarnate, who obscured what he really was [i.e., during his earthly life and ministry], was then predestined according to the Spirit of holiness to be manifested in power as the Son of God by rising from the dead, as it is written in Psalm 84, "Truth is risen from the earth" [Ps 85:11 (LXX 84:11)]. For every ambiguity and hesitation was made firm and sure by his resurrection, just as the centurion, when he saw the wonders, confessed that the man placed on the cross was the Son of God [Matt 27:54].[124]

Likewise, Augustine expressed this understanding when he said:

124. Ambrosiaster, *Ad Romanos, PL* 17.50.

Christ is the son of David in weakness according to the flesh, but he is the Son of God in power according to the Spirit of sanctification. . . . Weakness relates to David, but life eternal to the power of God.[125]

And this interpretation has been carried on by such important interpreters as the sixteenth-century reformer Philipp Melanchthon,[126] the eighteenth-century Lutheran pietist Johann Bengel,[127] and such nineteenth-century commentators as Charles Hodge,[128] Robert Haldane,[129] William G. T. Shedd,[130] Edward H. Gifford,[131] and Henry P. Liddon.[132]

2. *The Person and Sanctifying Work of the Holy Spirit.* A second category of interpretation understands πνεῦμα ἁγιωσύνης as a reference to the Holy Spirit, who indwelled and energized Christ Jesus during his earthly life — and who after Jesus' resurrection was the source of power that raised Christ up to an altogether higher type of life. In particular, when in the early church the major theological issues had to do not only with Christ but also with the nature and work of the Holy Spirit in relation to Christ, the salutation of 1:1-7 was understood by many Church Fathers to contain a number of proofs by which Christ was demonstrated to be the Son of God. So πνεῦμα ἁγιωσύνης was taken to be speaking not directly about Christ's divine nature but about the Holy Spirit, whose sanctifying work stands, along with the resurrection, as evidence of Christ's Sonship.

John Chrysostom, for example, in the first of his thirty-two homilies on Romans preached at Antioch of Syria, declared with respect to the salutation of 1:1-7:

What is being said here has been made obscure by the complex syntax, and so it is necessary to expound it. What is he actually saying? "We preach," says Paul, "him who was made of David. But this is obvious. How then is it obvious that this incarnate person was also the Son of God? First of all, it is obvious from the prophets [cf. v. 2], and this source of evidence is no weak one. And then there is the way in which he was born [cf. v. 3, understanding the virgin birth as implied here], which overruled the rules of nature. Third, there are the miracles that he did, which were a demonstration of much power, for the words "in power" [v. 4a] mean this. Fourth, there is the Spirit which he gave to those who believe in him, through whom he made them all holy, which is why he adds "according to the Spirit of holiness" (κατὰ

125. Augustine, *Ad Romanos inchoata expositio, PL* 35.2091.
126. P. Melanchthon, *Loci communes theologici.*
127. Bengel, *Gnomon Novi Testamenti.*
128. Hodge, *Romans.*
129. Haldane, *Romans.*
130. Shedd, *Romans.*
131. Gifford, *Romans.*
132. Liddon, *Romans.*

πνεῦμα ἁγιωσύνης) [v. 4a]. For only God could grant such gifts. Fifth, there was the resurrection [v. 4b], for he first and he only raised himself, and he also said that this was a miracle which would stop the mouths even of those who believed arrogantly, for he said: "Destroy this temple and in three days I will raise it up" [John 2:19].[133]

Likewise, Erasmus in his paraphrase of Paul's letter to the Romans, which was finally published in 1517, read 1:3-4 as follows:

> This is the gospel concerning his Son who was born in time of the lineage of David according to the infirmity of the flesh, but was also revealed to be the eternal Son of the eternal God according to the *Spirit which sanctifies all things*.[134]

And Martin Luther in his lectures on Romans, which he delivered at the University of Wittenberg from November 3, 1515 to September 7, 1516, viewed matters in much the same way:

> When the passage reads "the spirit of sanctification" rather than the "Holy Spirit," this does not matter much, for it is the same spirit who in terms of his effect is called either holy or sanctifying.[135]

This understanding of πνεῦμα ἁγιωσύνης as "the Spirit who sanctifies" was carried on in all the early English versions from John Wycliffe's New Testament, which was produced sometime around 1380, through to (and including) William Tyndale's New Testament of 1534, the Great Bible of 1539, the Geneva Bible of 1557, and the Bishops' Bible of 1568 (as well as Theodore Beza's Latin translation of the NT of 1556 and the many vernacular German, Dutch, French, Polish, Hungarian, Icelandic, Finnish, Danish, and Slovakian translations that were produced during the sixteenth century). The translators of the King James Version of 1611, however, were evidently attempting to be somewhat conciliatory by their more literal translation "according to the spirit of holiness" — though, in all probability, their insertion of the definite article "the" was done not merely for literary purposes but also to suggest that the referent should be understood as "the Holy Spirit."

Likewise, it is this understanding that appears in most commentaries today — as, for example, those written by Franz Leenhardt,[136] F. F. Bruce,[137]

---

133. Chrysostom, *Homilia XXXII ad Romanos*, PG 60.397.
134. Erasmus, *Collected Works of Erasmus*, vol. 42: *Paraphrases on Romans and Galatians*, 15 (italics added).
135. Luther, *Lectures on Romans*, 14.
136. Leenhardt, *Romans*, 37.
137. Bruce, *Romans*, 73.

Charles Cranfield,[138] and Joseph Fitzmyer.[139] And this understanding appears, in various ways, in many modern translations — most expressly in the NIV, which reads in its text "through the Spirit of holiness" (though a footnote in the 1984 edition has "as to his spirit"), and in the NEB, which reads "on the level of the spirit — the Holy Spirit — he was declared Son of God," thereby making such an understanding quite explicit. NRSV also has this reading in a footnote, where it capitalizes "spirit" to read "according to the Spirit of holiness" (though in its text the lower case of "spirit" implies something other than the Holy Spirit).

3. *Jesus' Own Spirit of Holiness.* A third category of interpretation views πνεῦμα ἁγιωσύνης as pointing not to Christ's divine nature but to his own "spirit of holiness" — that is, his complete obedience and unswerving faithfulness to his heavenly Father, which he manifested throughout his earthly life. At times this understanding is extended by interpreters to include the "extraordinary supernatural holiness" of Christ's own human life that "from the time of the resurrection now informs a body to which it communicates a supernatural glorified spiritual existence."[140]

It was John Locke, the English philosopher (1632-1704), who seems to have been the first to propose this latter understanding of the expression. Locke devoted the final years of his life to a study of Paul's letters, with his *Paraphrase and Notes* on Galatians, 1 and 2 Corinthians, Romans, and Ephesians published posthumously in 1705-07. Appended to this work was Locke's essay entitled "Essay for the Understanding of St. Paul's Epistles by Consulting St. Paul Himself," which, as William Sanday and Arthur Headlam characterized it, "is full of acute ideas and thoughts, and would amply vindicate the claim of the author to be classed as an 'historical' interpreter."[141] In the *Paraphrase and Notes* Locke argued that the parallelism of κατὰ σάρκα in 1:3b and κατὰ πνεῦμα in 1:4a was not only highly significant, but also that both expressions must be understood as referring to Christ's human existence. Or as Locke himself expressed matters: since "according to the flesh" has reference to "the body which he took in the womb of the blessed virgin his mother [which] was of the posterity and lineage of David," the expression "according to the spirit of holyness" must be seen as having reference to "that more pure and spiritual part, which in him over ruled all and kept even his frail flesh holy and spotless from the least taint of sin."[142]

This thesis was also proposed by such nineteenth-century commentators as Frédéric Godet[143] and Joseph Lightfoot.[144] It was, however, developed by Sanday and Headlam, who argued that κατὰ πνεῦμα ἁγιωσύνης does not refer to

138. Cranfield, *Romans*, 1.62-64.
139. Fitzmyer, *Romans*, 236.
140. So B. Schneider, "Κατὰ Πνεῦμα Ἁγιωσύνης," 369.
141. Sanday and Headlam, *Romans*, cv.
142. J. Locke, *A Paraphrase and Notes on the Epistles of St. Paul*, ed. A. W. Wainwright (Oxford: Clarendon, 1987), 487.
143. Godet, *Romans*, 1.130-31.
144. Lightfoot, *Notes on Epistles of St. Paul*, 245.

either (1) the Holy Spirit, "the Third Person in the Trinity (as the Patristic writers generally and some moderns), because the antithesis of σάρξ and πνεῦμα requires that they shall be in the same person," or (2) "the Divine Nature in Christ as if the Human Nature were coextensive with the σάρξ and the Divine Nature were coextensive with the πνεῦμα, which would be very like the error of Apollinaris." It refers rather, they say, to the human πνεῦμα, like the human σάρξ, distinguished however from that of ordinary humanity by an exceptional and transcendent Holiness.[145] A number of twentieth-century commentators have also espoused this understanding, such as Marie-Joseph Lagrange,[146] Joseph Huby,[147] A. T. Robertson,[148] Eduard Schweizer,[149] Kingsley Barrett,[150] James Dunn,[151] and Douglas Moo.[152] And the phrase has been translated in this manner by Edgar Goodspeed in his *The American Translation* of 1948 ("in his holiness of spirit"), Robert Bratcher in his *Good News for Modern Man* (or, "Today's English Version") of 1966 and 1971 ("as to his divine holiness," which reading was "reviewed and approved" by the American Bible Society), and the Swedish translation of 1981 ("according to the holiness of his spirit"). Likewise, as noted above, it appears as a footnote in the 1984 edition of the NIV.

In evaluating the evidence for these three categories of interpretation, it needs to be noted, first of all, that the phrase πνεῦμα ἁγιωσύνης does not appear anywhere else in Paul's letters. Nor does it appear in the Greek translation (LXX) of the Hebrew Bible (OT). For although the Greek πνεῦμα ἁγιωσύνης is a literal translation of the Hebrew phrase רוח קדש ("spirit of holiness"), when this wording appears in Isa 63:10-11 and Ps 51:11 (LXX 50:13) it is rendered in the LXX as τὸ πνεῦμα τὸ ἅγιον ("the Holy Spirit") and not πνεῦμα ἁγιωσύνης ("spirit of holiness"). In *T Levi* 18:7, however, a passage that has often been seen as an early Christian interpolation (whether in whole or in part) into an earlier Jewish writing, the phrase πνεῦμα ἁγιωσύνης certainly signifies the Holy Spirit in the statement "the spirit of sanctification [or, 'holiness'] shall rest upon him [in the water]" — evidently alluding to the Spirit coming upon Jesus at his baptism. And in at least seventeen instances in the Dead Sea Scrolls the phrase רוח קדש refers expressly to the Holy Spirit.[153]

Also to be taken into consideration when attempting to discern the mean-

145. Sanday and Headlam, *Romans*, 9; citing in support Heb 2:17 and 4:15, "it behoved him in all things to be made like unto his brethren . . . yet without sin."

146. Lagrange, *Aux Romains*, 7-8.

147. Huby, *Aux Romains*, 45.

148. Robertson, "Epistle to the Romans," 324.

149. Schweizer, "Römer 1,3f.," 187-89.

150. Barrett, *Romans*, 19.

151. Dunn, "Jesus — Flesh and Spirit," 51-59; though see his *Romans*, 1.15, where Dunn states that the phrase "would almost certainly be understood by Paul and the first Christians as denoting the Holy Spirit, the Spirit which is characterized by holiness, partaker of God's holiness."

152. Moo, *Romans*, 50.

153. Cf. Sekki, *The Meaning of Ruah at Qumran*, esp. 71-93 and 185-91, citing such passages as 1QS 4.21; 8.16; 9.3; 1QH 7.6-7; 9.32; 12.12; 14.13; 16.7, 12.

ing of πνεῦμα ἁγιωσύνης in Rom 1:4 is the importance the NT places on the full obedience and entire faithfulness of Jesus to God the Father, both throughout his ministry (his "active obedience") and at his crucifixion (his "passive obedience") — particularly as expressed in the Christ-hymn of Phil 2:6-11 (note esp. v. 8) and other early Christian confessional portions, but also as found at other places in Paul's letters, the Gospels, and the Epistle to the Hebrews. In an earlier article I have argued that all the titles ascribed to Jesus in the NT, as well as all the metaphors used in description of the nature and effects of his work, are to be seen as founded ultimately on the early conviction of believers in Jesus regarding his obedience, faithfulness, and/or Sonship par excellence.[154] And such a basic conviction needs to be kept in mind here.

Likewise, it needs always to be taken into account when dealing with Rom 1:3b-4 (1) that these verses incorporate (at least to some extent) various confessional materials that have been drawn (in some manner) from the early church, (2) that confessional materials probably originated in the corporate worship and devotions of the early Christians, and (3) that the language of worship and devotion is often difficult to analyze with regard to what is exactly meant. As I have argued elsewhere:

> Devotional material, while having a central focus and expressing essential convictions, is frequently rather imprecise. It attempts to inspire adoration, not to explicate doctrinal nuances. It uses the language of the heart more than that of the mind. It is, therefore, not always philosophically precise, philologically exact, or theologically correct — perhaps, at times, not even logically coherent.[155]

And it is this fact, I suggest, that must be appreciated not only when attempting to exegete some of the other expressions and features of these two verses, but also, and particularly, when trying to understand this phrase πνεῦμα ἁγιωσύνης.

Taking all these matters into account — that is, (1) the linguistic parallels and differences, (2) the early christological motifs of obedience, faithfulness, and Sonship, and (3) the worship and devotional matrices of early Christian confessional material — we are compelled to conclude (1) that the phrase πνεῦμα ἁγιωσύνης probably came to expression among the earliest believers in Jesus in contexts of worship and devotion that were more functional than speculative in nature, and (2) that it probably originally referred to Jesus' own "spirit of holiness," that is, to the complete obedience and unswerving faithfulness to his heavenly Father that he manifested throughout his earthly life. What the phrase came to mean among some Christians when speculative concerns about the person of Jesus later became more prominent (i.e., speculations about

154. See R. N. Longenecker, "The Foundational Conviction of New Testament Christology," passim.

155. R. N. Longenecker, *New Wine into Fresh Wineskins,* 28-29.

the divine nature of Christ) should not, it seems, be read back into an earlier time. And what רוח קדש ("spirit of holiness") meant in the Qumran texts (i.e., the Holy Spirit) would not necessarily be how the earliest Christians used the term, for the doctrinal contents of these two groups were decidedly different and the Teacher of Righteousness of the Dead Sea sectarians was not thought of in the same way as was Jesus by the early Christians.

It may be that some early believers in Jesus understood πνεῦμα ἁγιωσύνης in one manner and other believers in Jesus in another — just as some formulations of the church's creeds, some statements of its theology, and some phrases in its hymnody are understood by some Christians today in one way and by other Christians in another. And it may be that the dilemma of modern-day NT scholars regarding whether πνεῦμα ἁγιωσύνης is to be read "his spirit of holiness" or "the Spirit of holiness" corresponds, at least in some measure, to a similar dilemma in the early church — with, perhaps, differing degrees of articulation, but probably with a somewhat similar division of opinion.

Thus we believe (1) that πνεῦμα ἁγιωσύνης was most likely understood among the earliest believers in Jesus to refer to Jesus' own obedience and faithfulness to God his Father, that is, "his spirit of holiness," which he manifested throughout his earthly life and ministry, (2) that the expressions ἐκ σπέρματος Δαυὶδ κατὰ σάρκα in 1:3b and υἱοῦ θεοῦ ἐν δυνάμει κατὰ πνεῦμα ἁγιωσύνης in 1:4a were viewed by them as expressions that aptly signaled the two most significant factors of Jesus' human existence — and so were set out in one of their early confessional formulations in parallel form, not in antithetical fashion, and (3) that at some time later these expressions were understood by at least some Christians as referring to the Holy Spirit and his sanctifying work. The phraseology of this confessional portion is somewhat ambiguous (as are many statements born in a context of worship and devotion) and therefore allows for a broader range of interpretations than may have originally been understood. Yet though the expression may be somewhat ambiguous, that is how it was transmitted to the Christians at Rome and how it came to be accepted by them. And that is how Paul quotes it in seeking to gain rapport with his Roman addressees and to proclaim his own convictions in terms of their understanding and their appreciation.

Likewise, the expression ἐξ ἀναστάσεως νεκρῶν in 1:4b, which literally may be translated "out of resurrection of dead persons," has been variously understood by various translators and commentators. Is it to be viewed as a temporal expression and therefore read "designated the Son of God with power *from the time of his resurrection from the dead*"? Or should it be understood as a causal expression, and so read "designated the Son of God with power *because of* [or 'on the basis of'] *his resurrection from the dead*"? Probably both are true, though it is difficult to incorporate both nuances into one English sentence.

The lack of an article with ἀναστάσεως has often been taken to mean that "resurrection" here means only resurrection generally, without any specific designation. But ἀνάστασις ("resurrection") appears in the NT both with and without an article "without appreciable difference in meaning"[156] — and, further, "as a rule" the article is omitted with the genitive ἀναστάσεως.[157] Likewise, the plural νεκρῶν ("of the dead") has frequently been seen as signaling primarily the idea of an eschatological, general resurrection, which, of course, Jesus' resurrection served to initiate.[158] But the plural is also used by Paul with reference to Jesus' resurrection (cf. Rom 4:24), with the genitive understood as a partitive genitive that signifies "from among the dead" (cf. Eph 5:14).

Thus, while many have translated ἐξ ἀναστάσεως νεκρῶν literally — that is, reading "out of [the] resurrection of dead persons," and so understanding the expression as having only a general resurrection in mind, we believe it best to agree with Martin Luther, who said regarding the phraseology here: "We think it better to translate according to the meaning rather than literally."[159] So along with such major English translations today as RSV, NEB, JB, and NIV, we would understand the phrase to have as its referent the resurrection of Jesus. And as with the immediately preceding phrase πνεῦμα ἁγιωσύνης, we believe it necessary to take into account here also the fact that, while it has a central focus and expresses basic convictions, the language of worship and devotion has usually framed its words in rather general terms and is often difficult to analyze with precision.

It was God's resurrection and exaltation of Jesus that validated Jesus' messiahship, as well as his Lordship (cf. Acts 2:36: "Therefore let all Israel be assured of this: God has made [ἐποίησεν] this Jesus, whom you crucified, both Lord and Christ"). And it was God's resurrection of Jesus that validated his designation as "Son of God with power." According to the Synoptic Gospels, Jesus at times during his earthly ministry had been acclaimed "Messiah" and "God's Son" (cf. esp. Mark 8:29 par. for "Messiah"; see also Mark 1:11 par. and Mark 9:7 par. for "God's Son"). But it was "his resurrection from the dead" that decisively validated the legitimacy of these titles — and it was both *after* and *because of* this validation that distinctive Christian thought came into being.

The aorist verb ἐποίησεν of Acts 2:36 ("he made" or "appointed"; cf. 1 Sam 12:6; 1 Kgs 12:31; Mark 3:14; Heb 3:2) and the articular, substantival, passive participle τοῦ ὁρισθέντος of Rom 1:4 ("the one designated" or "appointed") are functional expressions. And ἐξ ἀναστάσεως νεκρῶν, we believe, should be understood in the same manner — that is, as not suggesting that Jesus was at some later time "made" or "designated" something that he was not before (as in an "adoptionist" Christology), but as validating what he had been acclaimed at times to be during his earthly ministry (as in a "functional" Christology). Kingsley Barrett has aptly characterized the situation as follows:

156. So *BAG*, 537, col. 1.
157. *Ibid.*
158. So, e.g., Hooke, "Translation of Romans 1.4," 371.
159. M. Luther, *Lectures on Romans,* trans. and ed. W. Pauck, 15.

Undoubtedly the earliest Christology has superficially an adoptionist tinge; but this is not to say that it was 'Adoptionist' in the technical sense. The first attempts at Christological thought were made not in essential but in functional terms.[160]

The expression Ἰησοῦ Χριστοῦ τοῦ κυρίου ἡμῶν ("Jesus Christ our Lord") at the close of 1:4b is often viewed as Paul's own addition to the confessional couplet that he quotes in 1:3b-4 — usually because of the title "Lord," which is frequently assumed to be not representative of the consciousness of the earliest believers in Jesus. But "Lord" as a christological title was also used by early Jewish believers in Jesus, as witness such passages as Acts 2:36 (Peter's sermon: "God has made [or 'appointed'] this Jesus, whom you crucified, both Lord and Christ"); 1 Cor 16:22 (the Aramaic prayer addressed to Jesus: "Come, O Lord"); and Phil 2:11 (at the conclusion of an early Christ-hymn: "Jesus Christ is Lord").[161] So while many scholars prefer not to include this identification within the confessional material quoted by Paul, I believe it best to include it within the quotation — not just because the name "Jesus Christ" appears frequently in various early Christian confessional materials of the NT and because the title "Lord" was used by Christians before Paul, but also because such a statement nicely rounds off the couplet and the possessive pronoun "our" seems to continue the ring of an early Christian confession.

1:5 After quoting the theologically loaded confessional material in 1:3b-4, which focuses on the christological content of the gospel to which he has been "called" and "set apart," Paul returns in 1:5 to highlight the nature and purpose of his apostleship. The prepositional phrase δι᾽ οὗ ("through whom") at the head of 1:5 signifies the agent, who as the confession of 1:3b-4 has proclaimed is now risen from the dead, through whom Paul's apostleship came — that is, that Paul's apostleship came through "his [God's] Son." Paul is probably not here "going off at a word" from the explicit identification "Jesus Christ our Lord" at the end of 1:4, which we have proposed should be seen as the concluding phrase of the confessional portion quoted. Rather, he is reaching back to his introduction of that quoted confessional portion to speak further about "his [God's] Son" — that is, that "his [God's] Son" is not only the content of the gospel (as in 1:3b-4), he is also the agent of Paul's apostleship (as here in 1:5). It should be noted that he does not say ἀφ᾽ οὗ ("from whom"), for the source of Paul's apostleship has already been implied in the prophetically charged words of 1:1 as being God the Father (though see 1:7, where both "God our Father" and "the Lord Jesus Christ" are cited as the source of "grace and peace"). Nor does Paul say δι᾽ ὅν ("on account of whom"), as though his apostleship was for the sake of a great person now

---

160. Barrett, *Romans*, 20.

161. For a more extended discussion, see R. N. Longenecker, *Christology of Early Jewish Christianity*, 120-36.

dead, for Jesus' resurrection not only validated his earthly life and ministry but also signaled his post-resurrection life.

In 1:5a Paul uses the plural verb ἐλάβομεν ("we received"), which has sometimes been viewed as Paul acknowledging that all Christians have received "grace" (distinguishing between "grace" and "apostleship" in the following phrase) — as he does in 12:6a[162] or as he does in associating himself with other apostles as recipients of grace and apostleship.[163] More likely, however, this should be understood as a "literary plural"[164] or an "epistolary plural" "idiomatically used for the singular."[165] The mixture of first person plural verbs and participles with first person singular verbs and participles, with both having Paul himself as the referent, appears frequently in Paul's letters.[166] Here in the salutation of Romans, however, which begins with the singular name "Paul" and highlights Paul's own call as an apostle in 1:1 — and then is followed in 1:8 by the first person singular verb εὐχαριστῶ ("I give thanks") — there is no contextual reason for understanding "we received" as anything other than a literary or epistolary plural used by Paul with reference to himself.[167]

The phrase χάριν καὶ ἀποστολήν ("grace and apostleship") has frequently been read as connoting two things: (1) "grace" or unmerited favor, which all Christians have received from God and which Paul shares with all other believers, and (2) "apostleship," which Paul received as a special commission from God.[168] Probably, however, these two Greek nouns connected by the conjunction καί should be understood as a hendiadys (from the transliterated Greek words *hen-dia-dysin,* literally "one [idea] through two [words], in which the one word specifies the other"), and so read as "God's special grace of apostleship" or "the grace of being commissioned an apostle."[169] For as Charles Cranfield has pointed out,

> A statement that Paul has received grace through Christ is scarcely necessary here. What is apposite is simply a statement of his authority in respect to the Gentile world. That he should indicate, however, that he had not received this authority because of any merit of his own would be thoroughly appropriate.[170]

---

162. Cf., e.g., Augustine, *Ad Romanos inchoata expositio, PL* 35.2092; Barrett, *Romans,* 21.
163. Cf., e.g., Sanday and Headlam, *Romans,* 10; Schlatter, *Romans,* 10; Dunn, *Romans,* 1.17.
164. Cf. *ATRob,* 407.
165. Cf. *Moule,* 118-19, citing J. H. Moulton, G. Milligan, H. Lietzmann, and O. Roller.
166. Cf. 1 Cor 9:11-23; 2 Cor 1:12-14; 2:14–7:16; 10:1–11:6; 1 Thess 2:18 [probably]; 3:1-5, passim, though, where the context requires, they must be distinguished (cf., e.g., 2 Cor 1:15-24; perhaps also 1 Thess 2:18 and 3:8-9).
167. So, e.g., Lagrange, *Aux Romains,* 10; Leenhardt, *Romans,* 38-39; Cranfield, *Romans,* 1.65.
168. So, e.g., Origen, *Ad Romanos, PG* 14.852-53; Augustine, *Ad Romanos inchoata expositio, PL* 35.2092; Pelagius, *Ad Romanos, PL* 30.647; Sanday and Headlam, *Romans,* 10-11; Zahn, *An die Römer,* 42-44; Lagrange, *Aux Romains,* 10; Barrett, *Romans,* 21.
169. Cf. NEB: "the privilege of a commission"; TEV: "the privilege of being an apostle."
170. Cranfield, *Romans,* 1.66.

Many interpreters have, in fact, expressly stated that the expression "grace and apostleship" is a hendiadys.[171] And we are in agreement, believing the phrase is best read as "God's special grace of apostleship" — though most translators, both ancient and modern, have simply rendered it literally (i.e., "grace and apostleship") and left it for the commentators to interpret.

The clause εἰς ὑπακοὴν πίστεως (literally "unto the obedience of faith"), which appears here in 1:5 and again in 16:26, has proven to be difficult to interpret. Its difficulty arises first of all from the fact that ὑπακοὴ πίστεως ("obedience of faith") is not found anywhere else in any of Paul's other letters — nor anywhere else in the whole of extant Greek literature. There are, of course, other places in Romans where "faith" and "obedience" appear in similar contexts and in roughly parallel statements,[172] for faith and obedience are inseparable in Paul's theology. But this specific phrase appears only in the two places in Romans.

Second, the phrase has been difficult to interpret because of uncertainties regarding the nature and impact of the genitive πίστεως ("of faith"). A number of interpretations have been proposed, with the noun's genitive form understood in the following ways:

1. As an objective genitive: "obedience to the faith," "obedience to the message of faith," or "obedience to God's faithfulness as attested in the gospel."[173]
2. As a subjective genitive: "obedience that faith brings about faith" or "obedience that is required by faith."[174]
3. As a genitive of source: "obedience that comes from faith" or "obedience that springs from faith."[175]

171. So, e.g., Chrysostom, *Homilia XXXII ad Romanos*, PG 60.398; J. Calvin, *Romans*, in *Calvin's New Testament Commentaries*, 8.17 (with Calvin understanding it as either "apostleship freely bestowed" or "the grace of apostleship"); Bruce, *Romans*, 17; Dunn, *Romans*, 1.17; Fitzmyer, *Romans*, 237; and Moo, *Romans*, 51.

172. Cf. Rom 1:8, "your faith is reported all over the world," vis-à-vis Rom 16:19, "everyone has heard about your obedience"; see also the paralleling of "unbelief" in 11:23 and of "disobedience" in 11:30-31 in the same context.

173. Cf., e.g., the following translations: "obedience to the faith" (KJV, Moffatt), "to forward obedience to the faith" (Phillips), "obedience to the message of faith" (BV). See also such commentators as Kuss, *Römerbrief*, vol. 1, who suggested that πίστεως refers to "a body of doctrine that is to be obeyed," and G. Friedrich, "Muss ὑπακοὴν πίστεως," who argued that it should be translated "for the preaching of faith."

174. Cf., e.g., JB, which translates the phrase literally in the text, but says in a footnote that the genitive is a "subjective genitive" and therefore should be understood as "the obedience implicit in the virtue of faith."

175. Cf., e.g., the following: "obedience that comes from faith" (NIV), "obedience inspired by faith" (Williams), "obedience which springs from faith" (Lightfoot, *Notes on Epistles of St. Paul*, 246). See also Lagrange, *Aux Romains*, 10; Robertson, "Epistle to the Romans," 324, though he calls it a "subjective genitive," which he translates as "the obedience which springs from faith (the act of assent or surrender)"; Taylor, *Romans*, 21; Bruce, *Romans*, 70.

4. As an adjectival genitive: "believing obedience" or "faithful obedience."[176]
5. As a genitive of apposition or definition (an epexegetical genitive): "faith that consists of obedience" or "faith that manifests itself in obedience."[177]

Understanding πίστεως as an objective genitive has failed to carry conviction with most commentators today, simply because in the present context — as well as throughout the rest of Romans — "faith" is presented as "the lively act or impulse of adhesion to Christ" and not "a body of formulated doctrine."[178] In fact, as Adolf Schlatter has rightly observed: "A gap between faith and obedience occurs . . . when the message of God is replaced with a doctrine about God"[179] — that is, when the righteousness "of one who works" is not countered by God's unmerited favor, which is responded to by faith and obedience, but is replaced by the righteousness "of one who knows, one 'who believes all the articles of the faith.' "[180] Further, understanding πίστεως as either a subjective genitive or an adjectival genitive tends to put the emphasis on "obedience" as a human virtue and to view "faith" as simply a means for accomplishing that virtue — which is hardly in accord with Paul's central theological convictions, whether Christian or Jewish.

Most likely, therefore, πίστεως here should be understood as a genitive of source, with the phrase read as "obedience that comes [or 'springs'] from faith" — though, possibly, as a genitive of apposition or definition, with the phrase understood as "faith that consists of [or 'manifests itself in'] obedience." Either is linguistically possible and theologically defensible. Yet Paul's emphasis in Romans, as well as throughout his other letters, is on a lively faith that results in a life of obedience, and not particularly on obedience as the content of faith. As Glenn Davies has pointed out, even when Paul in Romans speaks of obedience without any explicit reference to faith, "there is an underlying assumption that it is faith which is the seedbed of all obedience which is acceptable to God."[181] Thus a genitive of source seems most probable here, understanding that Paul has received God's special grace of apostleship in order to bring about "obedience that comes [or 'springs'] from faith."

The expression εἰς ὑπακοὴν πίστεως is also difficult to interpret because of uncertainties regarding Paul's purpose in using it in his letter to Christians at Rome — and, indeed, using it only in this letter among all of his NT letters. The question regarding his usage here is this: Did Paul use the phrase here (1) to counter a lurking legalistic understanding of "obedience" among his addressees, in opposition to certain Jews and Jewish Christians who were influencing

---

176. Cf. Barrett, *Romans*, 21: "believing obedience."
177. Cf., e.g., Cranfield, *Romans*, 66-67: "faith that consists of obedience"; Fitzmyer, *Romans*, 237-38: "faith that manifests itself in obedience."
178. To quote Sanday and Headlam, *Romans*, 11.
179. Schlatter, *Romans*, 11.
180. *Ibid.*, 22.
181. G. N. Davies, *Faith and Obedience in Romans*, 29 n. 2, citing Rom 2:6-9; 6:12-23.

them?¹⁸² (2) to redefine the nature of "covenant fidelity" in opposition to ideas that were then current among Jews and certain Jewish Christians regarding the identity of God's chosen people and their required boundary markers?¹⁸³ (3) to set out in programmatic fashion "the main purpose of the Epistle to the Romans"?¹⁸⁴ or (4) to conform his language and contextualize his message to the understanding and appreciation of his addressees, who because of their familiarity with the OT quite properly wanted to connect the subjects of "faith" and "obedience" and who may have had somewhat differing understandings among them of that relationship?¹⁸⁵

A case could be made for all four of these proposals — or perhaps for some combination of them. Yet if Paul was attempting to counter some type of lurking legalism by the use of this expression (proposal 1), the question can legitimately be asked: Why, then, didn't he use ὑπακοὴ πίστεως when countering the Judaizers in Galatians? And if ὑπακοὴ πίστεως was only used to set out in programmatic fashion the main purpose of his letter to Christians at Rome (proposal 3), why did he not characterize his message by that same phrase elsewhere in his NT letters? It seems, therefore, that Paul's use of ὑπακοὴ πίστεως here, as well as later in 16:26, should be viewed along the lines of some combination of (1) a polemical rationale, wherein Paul is seen as attempting to redefine in some manner the nature of covenant theology (as in proposal 2, though without accepting all that is argued by advocates of that position), and (2) a contextualization rationale, wherein Paul was conforming his language and contextualizing his message to the understanding and appreciation of his addressees (as in proposal 4).

A polemical purpose in the use of ὑπακοὴ πίστεως in both 1:5 and 16:26 — that is, at both the beginning and the end of the letter — seems highly probable, for this particular phrase does not appear anywhere else in his other letters. Indeed, as Don Garlington has observed, "against the backdrop of faith's obedience in Jewish literature, these words assume a decidedly polemical thrust: the covenant fidelity of God's ancient people (Israel) is now a possibility apart from assuming the identity of that people."¹⁸⁶ Or as expressed by James Dunn (Garlington's "Doktorvater" at Durham) regarding Paul's polemical purpose in the use of this phrase:

> The faith which Paul's apostleship seeks to bring about is not something different from obedience, from the response God expected from his covenant people, but is rather the way in which that obedience must be expressed [i.e., understanding πίστεως as a genitive of apposition] or the (only) ef-

182. So, e.g., Michel, *An die Römer*, 76, passim.
183. So Dunn, *Romans*, 1.18, 24, passim; Garlington, "Obedience of Faith" (1990), 201, passim; see also *idem*, "*The Obedience of Faith*" (1991); *idem, Faith, Obedience, and Perseverance.*
184. So Black, *Romans*, 175; also N. T. Wright, "The Messiah and the People of God," iii.
185. As suggested by my theses regarding Paul's addressees and his purposes in writing them.
186. Garlington, "Obedience of Faith," 201.

81

fective source of that obedience [i.e., understanding πίστεως as a genitive of source].[187]

Further, I propose that by his use of ὑπακοὴ πίστεως in the salutation and the final doxology of the letter Paul is not only setting up a rhetorical *inclusio* for all that he presents in the letter, but also conforming his language to the appreciation and understanding of his addressees at Rome, who because of their familiarity with the OT were always interested in the relationship of "faith" and "obedience." In so doing, Paul may, here and in 16:26 as well as at a number of other places in Romans, be seen as both (1) contextualizing his proclamation of the Christian gospel in a way that would speak to the particular interests of his addressees and in phraseology they would understand and appreciate, and (2) seeking to begin where his addressees were in their thinking in order to lead them into a better understanding of what they professed.

The phrase ἐν πᾶσιν τοῖς ἔθνεσιν ("among all the Gentiles") specifies the arena of Paul's apostolic endeavors. The expression has sometimes here been understood in its more inclusive sense to mean "among all the nations," believing that such a more comprehensive term is better suited to the opening of the letter.[188] But ἔθνη in Paul's usage in Romans, as well as throughout his other letters, refers to non-Jews, that is, to Gentiles, with Paul viewing himself as having been called by God to be "an apostle to the Gentiles."[189] And that meant, as Douglas Moo has rightly pointed out, "not so much to minister to many different nations as it was to minister to Gentiles in distinction from Jews."[190]

Paul certainly felt free to preach also to Jews.[191] And there were early Christian outreaches to Gentiles that were not at all part of his mission.[192] But Paul's statement here, as well as his elaborations of this statement in 1:13-15 (the letter's body-opening) and 15:14-32 (the letter's body-closing), leave no doubt that Paul felt that his specific mandate in the context of God's overall plan of salvation history was to bring the "good news" regarding the person and work of "Jesus Christ our Lord" to Gentiles.

The expression ὑπὲρ τοῦ ὀνόματος αὐτοῦ ("for the sake of his name") reflects Paul's ultimate motivation for his preaching of the gospel to Gentiles — that is, not for his own benefit or aggrandizement, nor even for the benefit of his converts, but primarily for the glory of God's Son (cf. 15:7, where a Christian's welcoming of another is also εἰς δόξαν τοῦ θεοῦ, "in order to bring glory to God"). A person's name in the ancient world connoted his or her true character and significance. In all likelihood, therefore, when Paul refers to Jesus' name he

---

187. Dunn, *Romans*, 1.24.

188. Cf., e.g., Zahn, *An die Römer*, 48; Michel, *An die Römer*, 42.

189. Cf. Rom 11:13; 15:16, 18; see also Gal 1:15-16.

190. Moo, *Romans*, 53; cf. also Cranfield, *Romans*, 67; Fitzmyer, *Romans*, 238.

191. Cf. Acts 13:14-52; 15:1-7; 17:1-4, 10-12; 18:4, 19-21; 19:8-9; 28:17-28.

192. Cf. Acts 10:1-48; perhaps 11:19-21; probably also in Egypt, Syria, and Cilicia — and certainly at Rome — as Paul's letter to the Christians at Rome certainly recognizes.

has in mind what the early Christians confessed in the latter half of the Christ-hymn of Phil 2:6-11: the name "Lord," which became rightfully his when "God exalted him to the highest place and gave him the name that is above every name, so that at the name of Jesus every knee should bow, in heaven and on earth and under the earth, and every tongue confess that Jesus Christ is 'Lord', to the glory of God the Father" (as in vv. 9-11).

1:6 The statement ἐν οἷς ἐστε καὶ ὑμεῖς κλητοὶ Ἰησοῦ Χριστοῦ ("among whom you also are those called by God to belong to Jesus Christ") relates grammatically to the phrase ἐν πᾶσιν τοῖς ἔθνεσιν ("among all the Gentiles") of 1:5. But this statement has seemed somewhat parenthetical to some in-terpreters because it characterizes the Christians at Rome by the substanti-val noun κλητοί ("those called [by God]") before actually addressing them, whereas in 1:7 they are identified again by the substantival nouns ἀγαπητοί ("those loved") and κλητοὶ ἅγιοι ("those called holy ones") — and thus, it has been argued, this characterization of the addressees as "those called by God" is best associated with the later two characterizations in v. 7.[193] But to under-stand these three substantival nouns as merely three characterizations of the Christians at Rome, which for the sake of the passage's flow of thought might better be grouped together, misses Paul's point here in 1:6. For in this verse the apostle seems to be taking pains to associate his addressees' "call . . . to belong to Jesus Christ" with his own "call . . . as an apostle to the Gentiles" — thereby, in effect, signaling that they were, as predominantly Gentile believers in Jesus, within the sphere of his apostolic mandate to Gentiles[194] — and so he has the right to be in contact with them and write to them in the manner that he does in this letter.

The verb καλεῖν ("to call"), which may mean simply "to call someone," "name someone or something," "address," "designate," "invite," or "summon," is used by Paul as a technical term for God's call of someone for a particular goal or purpose.[195] The genitive Ἰησοῦ Χριστοῦ is a possessive genitive with predicate force (i.e., a "predicate genitive" that signals possession), and so to be translated as "Jesus Christ's possession" or "belonging to Jesus Christ."[196] It is not a subjective genitive, that is, "called by Jesus Christ,"[197] for in Paul's theology God the Father is always the agent of a divine call.[198]

Paul's primary emphases in 1:6, therefore, are (1) that the Christians at Rome should consider themselves as being within the sphere of his God-given,

193. So, e.g., Cranfield, *Romans*, 1.67.
194. So, e.g., Sanday and Headlam, *Romans*, 12; Barrett, *Romans*, 22; Moo, *Romans*, 54; Fitzmyer, *Romans*, 238; contra Cranfield, *Romans*, 1.68.
195. Cf. Klein, "Paul's Use of *KALEIN*," 53-64.
196. Cf., e.g., Sanday and Headlam, *Romans*, 12; Lagrange, *Aux Romains*, 11; Barrett, *Romans*, 22.
197. Contra Cranfield, *Romans*, 1.68.
198. Cf. Rom 4:17; 8:28, 30; 9:24; 1 Cor 1:9; 7:17-18, 20-22, 24; Gal 1:6, 15; 5:8; 1 Thess 5:24; 1 Tim 6:12; 2 Tim 1:9-10; see also 1 Pet 5:10.

apostolic mandate to Gentiles, and (2) that they should understand that they have been called by God "to belong to Jesus Christ" just as he was called by God "as an apostle" to the Gentiles. Implied as well in Paul's identification of his addressees in this verse are (1) the dependence of their relationship to God through Christ not on their own desires or actions, but on God's will and call,[199] and (2) the fact that as recipients of God's call they have experienced what Israel long ago experienced[200] and so have been brought into association with God's people of old.[201]

1:7 The words πᾶσιν τοῖς οὖσιν ἐν Ῥώμῃ ("to all those at Rome") constitute the "recipient unit" of Paul's salutation. They also initiate a series of relative clauses that "go off at a word" from the word πᾶς ("all") by way of elaborating on several theologically significant matters that had previously appeared in the "sender unit." One might see in the apostle's use of πᾶς "an allusion perhaps to the extensive and straggling character of the Church of the metropolis; or an endeavour to bind together the two sections of that Church."[202] But that seems to be an overly suspicious reading of a single word, which, on the face of it, has every appearance of having been included simply to greet in an inclusive fashion all of the letter's addressees.

The designation "at Rome" (ἐν Ῥώμῃ) is well supported by the manuscript tradition, with the phrase omitted only in the ninth-century bilingual Codex Boernerianus (G 012, both Greek and Latin) and the eleventh-century minuscules 1739 (Category I) and 1908 (Category III) — with its omission being explicitly noted in the margins of these two later minuscule MSS. It is also omitted in it[g], which is a ninth-century recension of the Old Latin. More important, however, is the fact that "at Rome" is not referred to at all by some of the early commentary writers when dealing with 1:7 and 1:15 — particularly not by Origen (per Rufinus's Latin translation), nor by Ambrosiaster or Pelagius. So it may be inferred that "at Rome" was not included in the texts used by these commentators.[203] But given its extensive support in the manuscript tradition, the omission of "at Rome" here in 1:7 (as well as in 1:15) likely occurred either (1) as the result of an accident in transcription, or, more probably, (2) as a deliberate excision to give the letter a more general application.[204]

The descriptive phrases ἀγαπητοῖς θεοῦ and κλητοῖς ἁγίοις ("to those loved by God" and "called his holy ones") are attributive in nature, not restrictive — that is, they characterize all the Christians at Rome, not just some smaller group of more spiritual believers within the Roman congregations nor just the leaders or people greeted in 16:3-16. Neither do these two phrases refer to two

---

199. See further 8:28-29; 9:24; 1 Cor 1:9; 2 Tim 1:9-10.

200. Cf. Isa 43:1; 48:12-15.

201. See further our treatment of Paul's remnant theology and rhetoric in 9:6–11:36.

202. So Lightfoot, *Notes on Epistles of St. Paul*, 246; see also B. Witherington and F. Watson cited in the following paragraph.

203. Cf. our earlier discussion in *Introducing Romans*, 30-32.

204. Metzger, *Textual Commentary*, 446.

separate groups of Christians at Rome: Gentile believers, who are identified as being "loved by God," and Jewish believers, who are identified as "God's holy ones" or "saints."[205] The position of the dative substantival adjective πᾶσιν ("to all") at the beginning of this verse marks "all" as emphatic, with no suggestion that Paul then went on to divide Christians at Rome "into two different categories."[206] And that inclusive emphasis is repeated in 1:8 by the phrase πάντων ὑμῶν ("all of you"; cf. also 15:33).

The substantival noun ἀγαπητοῖς ("to those loved") is probably drawn from the Hebrew noun חסד ("steadfast love," "loving kindness"), which is an attribute of God in the OT.[207] In Paul's letters the present, active, adjectival participle ἀγαπητός ("loved") and perfect, passive, substantival participle ἠγαπημένος ("those loved") appear repeatedly with respect to (1) the people of faith who are loved by God,[208] (2) unbelieving Jews, whom God loves "because of the patriarchs,"[209] and (3) those whom Paul himself loves as believers in Christ and his coworkers.[210] So common are these expressions for those loved by God that Christians are addressed in many of Paul's letters simply by the vocative plural ἀγαπητοί ("loved ones" or "dearly beloved").[211] It is also noteworthy that here in 1:7 "Paul mentions not their love for God but that which is fundamental — God's love for them, God's choice of them."[212]

The attributive phrase κλητοῖς ἁγίοις ("called holy ones" or "holy people") seems to have been drawn from a combination of two Hebrew expressions: (1) מקרא קדש ("solemn [or 'holy'] assembly"), which the LXX translated κλητὴ ἁγία,[213] and (2) עם קדוש ("people of holiness"), which the LXX translated λαὸς ἅγιος.[214]

The term ἅγιοι ("holy ones") appears frequently in the OT with reference to celestial beings[215] and sometimes to God's people in the eschatological future[216] — though it is not very often used with reference to God's redeemed people in the present.[217] In the post-biblical Greek writings of the Jewish world, ἅγιοι

205. Contra Witherington, *Romans,* 37 n. 26, building on the thesis of F. Watson that there were two groups of Christians at Rome, a dominant group of Gentile Christians and a minority group of Jewish Christians, who were not meeting together (cf. Watson, *Paul, Judaism, and the Gentiles*), and so needed to be addressed separately.
206. As Witherington argues "is very possible," *idem, Romans,* 37.
207. Cf. Pss 61:7 (MT 61:8, LXX 60:7) and 108:4 (MT 108:5, LXX 107:4).
208. E.g., Rom 9:25; Col. 3:12; 1 Thess 1:4; 2 Thess 2:13.
209. Rom 11:28.
210. E.g., Rom 16:5, 8, 9, 12.
211. Cf., e.g., Rom 12:19; 1 Cor 15:58; 2 Cor 7:1; 12:19.
212. Cranfield, *Romans,* 1.69.
213. Cf. Exod 12:16 and Lev. 23:2, 4, 7.
214. Cf. Deut 7:6; 14:2, passim.
215. Cf. Deut 33:2; Job 5:1; 15:15; Ps 89:5, 7; Dan 4:13, 17, 23; 8:13 (twice); Zech 14:5.
216. Cf. Dan 7:27: "Then the sovereignty, power and greatness of the kingdoms under the whole heaven will be handed over to 'the holy ones,' the people of the Most High."
217. One particularly significant occurrence appears in Ps 34:9: "Fear [God], you his 'holy ones'; for those who fear him lack nothing."

continues to be used most often with respect to celestial beings[218] — though, at times, also of redeemed humans.[219] Philo and Josephus, however, seem not to have used the designation at all, either for angels or for humans. Rabbinic writers appear to have used קדש ("holy") or עם קדוש ("people of holiness") with respect to God's people only three times.[220] On the other hand, ἅγιοι ("holy ones") is found sixty-one times in the NT and is always employed — or, at least, almost always used (the only possible exceptions being 1 Thess 3:13 and 2 Thess 1:10) — with respect to God's holy people, whether translated as "saints," "his holy ones," or "God's holy people." And this change of usage serves to highlight, as Stephen Woodward has pointed out, the facts that "in Christ" people "have been thrust into the final kingdom, ushered into the room of the Holiest, and graced with the unprecedented privilege of the companionship of the Celestial."[221]

Paul's emphasis in his use of κλητοῖς ἁγίοις here in 1:7 is on both (1) his addressees as being "holy people" in the sight of God[222] and (2) their having been "called" by God to this status as believers in Jesus.[223] Further, in that his use of the verb καλεῖν ("to call") always includes the concept of God as the agent in "calling" people to some purpose or responsibility (see our comments above on 1:1 and 1:6), there is an implied parallel with the emphasis in the OT on God's will and action as being the basis for the lives of God's people.[224] Thus those "called holy ones" in Paul's letters are those who have been called by God to respond in faith to the person and work of Christ, and so have been given "in Christ" the status of God's "holy people."

Paul concludes his salutation of 1:1-7 to the Christians at Rome with the words χάρις ὑμῖν καὶ εἰρήνη ("grace to you and peace"). The prescripts of Greek letters normally included the greeting χαίρειν, which is the present, active, infinitive of the verb χαίρω ("rejoice," "be glad"). As a colloquial greeting χαίρειν meant "welcome," "hello," or "good day"; at the beginning of a letter it meant "greetings." At times Greek letters also included in their prescripts a health wish, such as the infinitive ὑγιαίνειν (literally "to be in good health"; colloquial and epistolary uses: "good health"), and so would read χαίρειν καὶ ὑγιαίνειν ("greetings and good health"). Jewish letters usually included in their prescripts some form of the noun "peace," either שלום in a letter written in Hebrew or εἰρήνη in a letter written in Greek,[225] coupled with the noun "mercy" (or "cov-

218. Cf., e.g., Tob 8:15; Sir 42:17; 45:2; Wis 5:5; 10:10; *Jub* 17:11; 31:14; 33:12; *Pss Sol* 17:49; *1 En* 1:9; 9:3; 12:2; 14:23, 25; 3 Macc 2:2.

219. Cf., e.g., Tob 12:15 (B); *Jub* 2:24; Wis 18:9; 1 Macc 1:46; *1 En* 93:6; 99:16; 100:5; 3 Macc 6:9 (A).

220. Cf. *Mek. Exod.* 14:15; *Num. Rab.* 5:12; *Pesiq. R.* 104a.

221. Woodward, "Provenance of the Term 'Saints,'" 115-16.

222. Cf. 1 Cor 1:2; Phil 1:1.

223. Cf. 1:6 above; also 1 Cor 1:24; Eph 1:18.

224. Cf., e.g., Isa 49:1; 50:2; 65:12; 66:4; Jer 7:13.

225. Cf., e.g., Dan 4:1 (MT 3:31; LXX [Th] 3:98) and 4:34 (LXX [OG]): εἰρήνη ὑμῖν πληθυνθείη; "Peace to you be multiplied"; see also 2 Macc 1:1 and *2 Bar* 78:2.

enant faithfulness," "loving kindness"), either חסד (or, less frequently, רתמים, "compassion") in a letter written in Hebrew or ἔλεος in a letter written in Greek — and so would begin with the traditional Jewish greeting "mercy and peace."

Some letters in the NT have in their salutations the normal Greek greeting χαίρειν, "greetings";[226] others have the prayer wish χάρις ὑμῖν καὶ εἰρήνη πληθυνθείη, "grace to you and peace be multiplied";[227] and one has ἔλεος ὑμῖν καὶ εἰρήνη καὶ ἀγάπη πληθυνθείη, "mercy to you and peace and love be multiplied."[228] In Paul's letters, however, the greeting is expressed in terms of χάρις ("grace") and εἰρήνη ("peace").[229] Thus the typical Pauline greeting is, in reality, a prayer wish: "May you have grace and peace from God our Father and the Lord Jesus Christ" — though in wishes expressed in the secular Greek of Paul's day the optative εἴη ("may you," a second person singular, present, optative of the verb εἰμί, "I am") seems to have been omitted often.

Exactly why Paul departed from the usual Greek χαίρειν ("greetings") and substituted in its place the prayer wish χάρις ὑμῖν ("grace to you") — and, further, why he omitted the term ἔλεος ("mercy," a Greek translation of חסד) from the traditional Jewish greeting but retained εἰρήνη ("peace," a Greek translation of שׁלום) — are questions that have been frequently asked. Tertullian in 208, for example, observed that Paul's letters do not include the usual "health wish" of a normal Greek letter, but, rather, that he speaks in every prescript *(titulo)* of "grace and peace" — but as to why the apostle departed from normal Greek epistolary practice, Tertullian simply says "I cannot say."[230] Nevertheless, Tertullian goes on to mount an argument against Marcion on the basis of Paul's inclusion of the word "peace" in all of his salutations. And he does so by first noting that Paul uses the Jewish greeting "peace" in all his salutations:

> What had he, the destroyer of Judaism, to do with Jewish custom? For even today the Jews address each other in the name of peace, and earlier, in the Scriptures, they used to use that greeting.[231]

Then he makes the point that by the inclusion of this Jewish greeting in all of his letters, Paul "spoke plainly enough to make the Creator known":

> But [contrary to his statement "I cannot say" as to why Paul departed from normal Greek epistolary practice] I do understand that by his service *(officio)* he [Paul] spoke plainly enough to make the Creator known: "How beautiful are the feet of those who proclaim good news, who preach the

226. Acts 15:23; 23:26; Jas 1:1.
227. 1 Pet 1:2; 2 Pet 1:2.
228. Jude 2.
229. Not only here, but also 1 Cor 1:3; 2 Cor 1:2; Gal 1:3; Eph 1:2; Phil 1:2; Col 1:2; 1 Thess 1:1; 2 Thess 1:2; Titus 1:4; Phlm 3; with the addition of ἔλεος, "mercy," in 1 Tim 1:2 and 2 Tim 1:2.
230. Tertullian, *Adversus Marcionem* 5.5.
231. *Ibid.*

gospel of peace" [Isa 52:7]. For he who proclaimed the good news, that is the grace of God, was well aware that along with it peace was also to be proclaimed.[232]

It may be that the expression "grace to you and peace" became common in early Jewish Christian liturgical usage and that its use as an epistolary greeting was derived from that practice.[233] It may also have been that early Jewish believers in Jesus were echoing in their liturgy, whether consciously or unconsciously, the blessing that God told Moses to tell Aaron and his sons to pronounce over the Israelites, as given in Num 6:24-26: "The Lord bless you and keep you; the Lord make his face shine upon you and be gracious to you; the Lord turn his face toward you and give you peace."[234] Further, it may have been Paul who was the one who turned that early Christian liturgical blessing "grace to you and peace" into an epistolary greeting, for that wording seems not to have been used in the salutations of other early Christian letters.[235]

But however the wording of this epistolary greeting came about, Paul in all his letters constantly turns the traditional greetings of both Greek and Jewish letters into a profound theological statement that highlights the two major themes of the Christian gospel: "grace," which signals God's undeserved love and favor as revealed in Christ Jesus, and "peace," which speaks of what God has effected through the work of Christ in reconciling people to himself and to one another and reclaiming his creation. And these two themes come to expression most explicitly in his letter to Rome, where Paul (1) begins by greeting his addressees with the prayer wish "grace to you and peace,"[236] (2) uses the word "grace" some twenty-one times throughout the body of the letter,[237] (3) speaks of "peace" at least seven times elsewhere in the body of the letter,[238] and (4) closes with first a "peace benediction" in 15:33, then a peace statement in 16:20a, and finally (excluding the textually dubious second "grace benediction" that would have comprised 16:24) a "grace benediction" in 16:20b. In effect, the term χάρις (that is, God's "grace" as manifested in the work of Christ on behalf of all people) expresses for Paul the basis for all that those "in Christ" have experienced, while the term εἰρήνη (that is, "peace," with its cognate term "reconciliation") represents the sum of all the blessings of the gospel — as Paul will highlight later in 5:1-21.

---

232. Tertullian, *Adversus Marcionem* 5.5.

233. So Lohmeyer, "Probleme paulinischer Theologie," 161-62.

234. So Fitzmyer, *Romans*, 228.

235. At least not as represented by Acts 15:23; 23:26; Jas 1:1; and Jude 2; though 1 Pet 1:2 and 2 Pet 1:2 have a close parallel.

236. I.e., here in 1:7.

237. I.e., in 3:24; 4:4, 16; 5:2, 15 (twice), 17, 20, 21; 6:1, 14, 15, 17; 7:25; 11:5, 6 (three times); 12:3, 6; 15:15.

238. E.g., 2:10; 3:17; 5:1; 8:6; 14:17, 19; 15:13; cf. also the synonym "reconciliation" in 5:10-11 and 11:15.

The genitive clause ἀπὸ θεοῦ πατρὸς ἡμῶν καὶ κυρίου Ἰησοῦ Χριστοῦ ("from God our Father and the Lord Jesus Christ") identifies the source of "grace" and "peace," which here in 1:7, as well as elsewhere in Romans (cf. esp. 5:1-21), are highlighted as the two main blessings of the Christian gospel. No distinction is made here between God the Father as the source and the Lord Jesus Christ as the means or agent of the blessings of the gospel, though these ideas have been suggested earlier throughout the salutation.[239] The juxtaposition of "God our Father" and "the Lord Jesus Christ" is clearly of great significance for any consideration of early Christian attitudes toward Jewish monotheism and regarding the Christian veneration of Jesus. It is not, by itself, proof of the divinity of Jesus. But it certainly sets out in a functional manner the close relationship between the two, the Father and the Son — not only with regard to the Father being the source and the Son being the agent, but here as both being the source of all Christian blessings. The expression θεοῦ πατρὸς ἡμῶν ("God our Father") anticipates Paul's teaching in 8:15 (see the comments there). On the title κύριος as ascribed to Jesus, see the comments above on 1:4 and those below on 10:9.

BIBLICAL THEOLOGY

A number of highly significant matters immediately strike every reader of the salutation in Rom 1:1-7. The first is how Paul has taken the usual conventions of an epistolary prescript of his day and turned them into a prospectus for what he wants to say in the body of the letter that follows. His additions to the usual Greek epistolary prescript constitute, in fact, no mere literary embellishments, but have every appearance of deliberate forecasts of the major points that he wants to present later in his letter.

A second impression one gets when reading the salutation of Romans is what Sanday and Headlam have aptly called "the definiteness and maturity of the theological teaching" contained in these verses:[240]

> It is remarkable enough, and characteristic of this primitive Christian literature, especially of the Epistle of St. Paul, that a mere salutation should contain so much weighty teaching of any kind; but it is still more remarkable when we think what that teaching is and the early date at which it was penned.[241]

And a third feature that stands out in reading this salutation is how Paul has contextualized his message when writing to the Christians at Rome —

239. Cf., e.g., the implied "by God" in the divine "call" of 1:1 and 6; also the expression δι᾽ οὗ, "through whom" (i.e., "Jesus Christ our Lord") in 1:5.
240. Sanday and Headlam, *Romans*, 17.
241. *Ibid.*

even at the very beginning of his letter — in (1) speaking to their interests and concerns, (2) using early Christian confessional material that was presumably known and appreciated by them, and (3) couching his presentation in terms and language that would have resonated with them. There are many other places in his letter to Rome where it may be observed that Paul has taken pains to contextualize his proclamation vis-à-vis the interests and concerns of his addressees, as will be noted in our comments on those portions that follow. But it still remains rather striking that such contextualizations should occur in the letter as early as its salutation.

The fact that Paul begins this salutation with three self-identifications that go far beyond any of those in his other NT letters — particularly with respect to his prophetic consciousness, his apostolic ministry, and his relationship to Christ Jesus, God the Father, and the Christian gospel — suggests that these statements were meant not just as positive affirmations, but should be seen as carrying with them a polemical thrust as well. Jewish Christian opponents had, it seems, often disputed the legitimacy of Paul's apostolic claims and the validity of his Gentile mission — probably on the basis of such well-known facts as (1) that he had not been one of the original disciples who had been with Jesus during his earthly ministry but a persecutor of early believers in Jesus,[242] (2) that his conversion and commission had been mediated to him through Ananias at Damascus,[243] (3) that his early Christian ministries were in Tarsus of Cilicia and Antioch of Syria,[244] (4) that the base for his Christian outreach to Gentiles was not the church at Jerusalem but the church at Antioch of Syria, which had sent him out with Barnabas as a missionary and which he represented, together with Barnabas, as a delegate at the Jerusalem Council,[245] and (5) that his missionary activities among Gentiles in the eastern part of the Roman Empire had caused a great deal of opposition from both Jews and the Greco-Roman Gentile population.[246] And it seems highly likely that both Gentile and Jewish believers in Jesus at Rome also thought of Paul, when compared to the apostles at Jerusalem, as something of a second-class apostle — perhaps an apostle authorized only "by men," whether by Ananias of Damascus and/or by the "pillar" apostles of the Jerusalem church, Peter, James, and John. Further, it seems probable that the Christians at Rome thought of Paul as one who preached "the gospel" as taught in the church at Antioch of Syria rather than "the true Christian gospel" as proclaimed by the original apostles in the "mother church" at Jerusalem, and therefore as one whose preaching must be scrutinized, complemented, and perhaps even corrected so as to conform to the one authoritative gospel message of Jewish Christianity at Jerusalem.[247]

---

242. Cf. 1 Cor 15:9; Acts 9:1-2.

243. Cf. Acts 9:10-19; 22:12-16.

244. Cf. Acts 9:30; 13:1.

245. Cf. Acts 13:2-3; 15:1-4.

246. Cf., e.g., Acts 28:22, "people everywhere are talking against this sect."

247. On this matter, see Stuhlmacher, *Das paulinische Evangelium,* 67; *idem, Romans,* 21-22; also Holmberg, *Paul and Power,* 52-54.

More important for our purposes here, however, are the theological themes that are set out in introductory fashion in the salutation of Romans and that then resonate throughout the rest of the letter. "In the course of this formal epistolary introduction," as Joseph Fitzmyer has noted, "Paul enunciates some of the fundamental teachings which he will develop in the course of the epistle."[248] In fact, as A. T. Robertson long ago observed, "Paul's theology is clearly seen in the terms used in verses 1 to 7."[249]

Of primary importance in any list of biblical theology themes in the salutation of Romans, as well as throughout the rest of the letter, is what Paul calls τὸ εὐαγγέλιον, that is, "the gospel" or "good news" to which he has been "set apart," which is "from God," which God "promised beforehand through his prophets in the Holy Scriptures, and whose content is focused on "his [God's] Son."[250] Earlier in his letter to Gentile Christians in the Roman province of Galatia, Paul spoke of (1) his converts as turning to "a different gospel (εἰς ἕτερον εὐαγγέλιον), which was not the same gospel (ὃ οὐκ ἔστιν ἄλλο)" as they had originally received,[251] (2) that gospel that they originally received as having as its content the person and work of Christ, and so being "the gospel of Christ" (τὸ εὐαγγέλιον τοῦ Χριστοῦ),[252] (3) the Judaizers who had infiltrated the Galatian churches as "trying to pervert the gospel of Christ" (θέλοντες μεταστρέψαι τὸ εὐαγγέλιον τοῦ Χριστοῦ),[253] (4) his distinctive form of the gospel (τὸ εὐαγγέλιον τὸ εὐαγγελισθὲν ὑπ' ἐμοῦ, "the gospel that was proclaimed by me") as having been received "by a revelation from Jesus Christ" (δι' ἀποκαλύψεως Ἰησοῦ Χριστοῦ),[254] (5) the gospel message that he received as being specifically "the gospel for the uncircumcised [i.e., 'the Gentiles']" (τὸ εὐαγγέλιον τῆς ἀκροβυστίας),[255] and (6) his desire and efforts, contra those of the Judaizers, to defend "the truth of the gospel" (ἡ ἀλήθεια τοῦ εὐαγγελίου).[256]

Likewise at a number of places in his correspondence with his converts at Corinth, which letters were written prior to his letter to Christians at Rome, Paul highlights "the gospel" and its central themes as being foremost in his ministry.[257] And he will do so throughout the rest of his letter to the Christians at Rome.[258]

---

248. Fitzmyer, *Spiritual Exercises,* 18.

249. Robertson, "Epistle to the Romans," 325.

250. Rom 1:1-4.

251. Gal 1:6b-7a.

252. Gal 1:7b, understanding τοῦ Χριστοῦ here as an objective genitive.

253. Gal 1:7b.

254. Gal 1:11-12, understanding Ἰησοῦ Χριστοῦ here as a subjective genitive: "through a revelation of which Jesus Christ was the agent"; cf. also Gal 2:2.

255. Gal 2:7.

256. Gal 2:5, 14.

257. Cf. esp. 1 Cor 1:23-25; 2:1-5; 4:15; 9:12-14, 18, 23; 15:1; 2 Cor 2:12; 4:3-4; 8:18; 9:13; 10:14; 11:4, 7.

258. Cf. esp. Rom 1:9, 16; 2:16; 10:16; 11:28; 15:16, 19; 16:25, where the expression τὸ εὐαγγέλιον is actually used.

Characterizing Paul's thought in this regard, Joseph Fitzmyer has aptly formulated the following definition of the term "gospel" in Paul's usage:

> "Gospel" is Paul's one-word summary of the Christ-event, the significance and meaning that the person and lordship of Jesus have for our existence and that of all human beings. It is the concrete formulation of God's will for the disposition of human life.[259]

Directly associated with "the gospel," as we have noted above, is a further important emphasis in Paul's theology as set out in the salutation of Romans, namely, that this gospel is "from God" — that is, that its source is the will of God and its message based on the actions of God (1:1). Likewise, Paul emphasizes that this gospel is that "which he [God] promised beforehand through his prophets in the Holy Scriptures" (1:2). In no way did Paul anticipate or lay a foundation for the perverse misunderstanding of the second-century Christian teacher Marcion of Pontus. Rather, as Joseph Fitzmyer has written: "Paul sees the prophetic utterances of Israel's prophets as a *praeparatio evangelica,* a mode of preparing Israel and all humanity for the gospel, the good news of Christ Jesus."[260] So throughout the Pauline letters there are repeated emphases on (1) the one true God, whose redemptive will and actions are depicted in the OT, as the One who preeminently expressed his redemptive will and actions in the person and work of Jesus of Nazareth, as portrayed in the NT, and (2) the gospel proclamation of the NT as based on and the fulfillment of the promises of God as given in the OT through God's prophets. Indeed, as A. T. Robertson has concisely stated matters: "Paul definitely finds God's gospel in the Holy Scriptures."[261]

A further feature that appears prominently among the theological themes in the salutation of Romans is what may be called the focus of the Christian gospel, namely, that "the gospel" has at its heart a salvific message about "his [God's] Son" who is "Jesus Christ our Lord." While the gospel in its entirety was what was of major importance in Paul's thought as a Christian and his outreach to Gentiles as a missionary, the focus of that message of "good news" — and therefore the most important and pivotal feature in his Christian proclamation — is what Christ effected through his ministry, passion, death, resurrection, and exaltation. Paul highlights this revolutionary new development in God's plan of salvation by quoting an early Christian confessional portion in 1:3b-4, which was presumably known and appreciated by his Roman addressees. Then later in 5:1–8:39, which is where we believe the major theological thrust of his argument in the letter appears, he develops more fully this christological component of his Christian proclamation. It is a message that builds on the story of Jesus that was remembered and accepted by all early believers in Jesus and that the four

259. Fitzmyer, *Spiritual Exercises,* 19.
260. *Ibid.*
261. Robertson, "Epistle to the Romans," 323.

canonical Evangelists would later reproduce with their own distinctive "spins" for their own respective audiences. And it is this basic, constitutive narrative of the Christian religion that Paul spells out theologically and contextualizes pastorally for his Roman addressees.

Vv. 5 and 6 of this letter's salutation also contain a number of statements concerning Paul's consciousness of himself, his understanding of his ministry, and his recognition of his addressees' situation — and when these statements are connected with the three self-identifications in v. 1, they provide us with revealing insights into the man himself, his understanding of his Gentile mission, and his rationale for writing to the Christians at Rome. For not only does Paul declare in 1:1 that he is "a servant of Christ Jesus, called by God as an apostle, and set apart for the gospel that is from God," he also asserts in 1:5 (1) that he is the recipient of "God's special grace of apostleship," (2) that his mandate is "to bring about obedience that comes from faith among all the Gentiles," and (3) that his ultimate purpose in carrying out his mission is "for the sake of his name" — that is, for the sake of the exalted Jesus, God's Son and humanity's Lord, through whom God the Father is praised (cf. Rom 15:7) and glorified (cf. Phil 2:11). And in 1:6 he identifies his addressees as being within his God-given mandate to evangelize Gentiles, since they are predominantly Gentiles ethnically and "those called by God to belong to Jesus Christ."

After having considerably expanded the usual sender unit of a Greek letter in 1:1-6 — not only by the addition of a number of statements about himself and his mission, but also by the inclusion of certain highly significant theological affirmations about the Christian gospel, its source, its relation to the OT Scriptures, and its focus in "Jesus Christ our Lord" — Paul then goes on to expand, as well, the usual recipient unit of 1:7a and the greeting unit of 1:7b with theologically relevant comments that are also of great significance. For in 1:7a he not only identifies his addressees, but speaks of them as "loved by God" and "called [by God] his holy people." Both of these attributions carry OT connotations that highlight the close relationship of God's people to himself, and so lay the basis for a new self-understanding on the part of believers in Jesus. And in 1:7b he reconstitutes the usual Greek and Jewish epistolary greetings to highlight the basis for such a new relationship of Christians with God: "the grace of God," as expressed in the person and work of Christ Jesus, which has brought about "peace with God" and "reconciliation with God and with others" — with such "grace" and "peace" being brought about by "God our Father and the Lord Jesus Christ."

All the theological themes introduced in the seven verses of the salutation are highly significant. In fact, these themes constitute the very essence of Christian theology and Christian living, and Paul will unpack them and contextualize them in what follows in the rest of the letter — particularly in the central section of 5:1–8:39. Even the language used to express these themes is highly significant. For as Sanday and Headlam have pointed out in a highly perceptive paragraph regarding "The Theological Terminology of Rom. i.1-7":

When we come to examine particular expressions we find that a large proportion of them are drawn from the O.T. In some cases an idea which has been hitherto fluid is sharply formulated (κλητός, ἀφωρισμένος); in other cases an old phrase has been adopted with comparatively little modification (ὑπὲρ τοῦ ὀνόματος αὐτοῦ, and perhaps εἰρήνη); in others the transference involves a larger modification (δοῦλος Ἰησοῦ Χριστοῦ, χάρις, κλητοὶ ἅγιοι, Κύριος, θεὸς πατήρ); in others again we have a term which has acquired a significance since the close of the O.T. which Christianity appropriates (ἐπαγγελία [προεπηγγείλατο], γραφαὶ ἅγιαι, ἀνάστασις νεκρῶν, ἅγιοι); in yet others we have a new coinage (ἀπόστολος, εὐαγγέλιον), which however in these instances is due, not to St. Paul or the other Apostles, but to Christ Himself.[262]

CONTEXTUALIZATION FOR TODAY

Paul's salutation in Romans is so chock-full of foundational Christian teaching that it provides the reader with a veritable précis or summary of early Christian theology and thus an almost unlimited body of material for contextualizing the Christian message today. But while as Christians we are committed to the Christian message as set out in the salutation, we cannot just repeat that message in the exact forms of that day — whether in the forms used by the Christians at Rome, which seem to have been inherited from Jewish Christianity at Jerusalem, or those forms into which Paul cast the Christian message in his ministry to Gentiles, which, as we will propose, he sets out specifically in the second section of the body middle of his letter, that is, in 5:1–8:39. For just as Paul contextualized the Christian gospel for his addressees at Rome, so we as Christians today are called to contextualize that same message for people today in their different localities, diverse cultural situations, and somewhat differing perspectives and modes of thought.

There are a number of matters in the salutation of Romans that have important theological significance, and so could be developed in any contemporary Christian contextualization. The following six themes, however, seem to be set out in bold relief and therefore call for comment here:

The Basis of the Christian Message. Running throughout the Romans salutation is Paul's lively realization that the Christian message of "good news" is based not only on the ministry and work of "Jesus Christ our Lord" but also, both ultimately and effectively, on the will and salvific concerns of "God our Father." In 1:1 Paul speaks of himself as "a servant of Christ Jesus," but also recognizes that he has been "called an apostle" and "set apart for the gospel" by God. In 1:5 he speaks of having received "God's special grace of apostleship"

---

262. Sanday and Headlam, *Romans*, 18.

through "Jesus Christ our Lord," thereby highlighting both the source of his apostleship, that is, God the Father, and the agent through whom he received that apostleship, that is, Jesus Christ his Son. In 1:6-7a he refers to Christians as having been "called by God to belong to Jesus Christ," "loved by God," and "called by God his holy people." And in the reconstituted greetings unit of 1:7b, he brings the salutation to a climax by proclaiming that this new message of "grace and peace" is "from God our Father and the Lord Jesus Christ."

In our modern emphases on results and consequences, we must never forget matters having to do with source and agency. So in any contemporary contextualization of the Christian gospel, we must always keep to the forefront of our consciousness and proclamation the fact that all of our blessings as Christians stem from both (1) God's will and redemptive concerns for all humanity and the world and (2) Jesus' ministry and work in effecting God's will and salvific plans.

Apostleship and Ministry. Paul had a deep and lasting conviction of having been called by God to proclaim the good news of the Christian message to Gentiles in the Greco-Roman world. And like the prophet Jeremiah of old, whose prophetic mandate Paul seems to have understood as having been repeated in his own experience,[263] he could affirm: "His [God's] word is in my heart like a burning fire, shut up in my bones. I am weary of holding it in; indeed, I cannot."[264]

No Christian today, however, has the precise apostolic role in God's salvific plan that Paul had. Nonetheless, all Christians are called by God not only into relationship with him through the work and person of Christ Jesus, but also to minister on his behalf to people "for the sake of his name" — that is, for the sake of Jesus' exalted name "Lord."[265] Thus as Joseph Fitzmyer rightly points out: "As Paul was aware that his apostolic commission was a 'grace,' so he invites his readers to realize the 'grace' involved in the call that each of them has received from God."[266] Further, just as Paul's motivation for ministry was not his own benefit or aggrandizement, nor even the benefit of his converts, but the glorification of God's Son — and, through that honoring of his Son, the praise and glory of God the Father — so, as Charles Cranfield has stated, "the true end of the preaching of the gospel and of winning of men [and women] to faith is not just the good of those to whom the preaching is directed, but also — and above all — the glorification of Christ, of God."[267]

The Centrality of the Gospel. Of great importance to Paul was the centrality of the gospel message in all of Christian proclamation and Christian living. For the gospel is "from God" (v. 1) and is what was "promised beforehand through his prophets in the Holy Scriptures" (v. 2). It is a message that is revela-

263. Cf. Gal 1:15-16a vis-à-vis Jer 1:5.
264. Jer 20:9.
265. Cf. Phil 2:9-11.
266. Fitzmyer, *Spiritual Exercises,* 17-18.
267. Cranfield, *Romans,* 67.

tory in nature, for it was first revealed to Paul in highly dramatic fashion on his way to Damascus, being then confirmed and spelled out more fully at various times in just as significant ways throughout his Christian life and missionary activities. It is a message that is proclamatory in nature, for Paul was "set apart" by God to proclaim it to Gentiles. But it is also a message that is normative for all Christian thought and living, and so Paul felt compelled to stoutly defend it whenever necessary[268] — though, it needs also to be noted, without allowing his own circumstances or his own prestige to take precedence over "the advance of the gospel" or its proclamation by others.[269]

In days when many of the cultural, societal, psychological, and ecological ramifications and benefits of the gospel have taken center stage in Christian preaching and counseling, it is well to remind ourselves of the centrality of the gospel message itself. For though the Christian gospel has implications for all of life — and though as God's people we are called by God to work out these implications in our own lives, in the lives of people individually, and in society corporately — it yet remains true, as Paul says only a few verses later in this same letter to Rome, that it is "the gospel" that is "the power of God for the salvation of everyone who believes" (1:16). All-too-often contemporary Christian preaching and counseling have turned the gospel into some form of "religious humanism," which only uses Christian imagery and Christian jargon in a humanistic fashion for motivational purposes. But it is the gospel message of what God has done "in Christ" in "reconciling the world to himself" (cf. 2 Cor 5:19), as illumined and applied by God's Spirit, that changes our sinful human condition and that alters our confused human circumstances.

The Focus of the Gospel. Further, when highlighting the centrality of the gospel in the salutation of Romans, it is important to note that when Paul speaks about "the gospel that is from God, which he promised beforehand through his prophets in the Holy Scriptures" (vv. 1b-2), he immediately defines the content of that gospel as "concerning his [God's] Son" (v. 3a).

Earlier in writing to his converts at Corinth, who evidently had become confused as to what was really at the heart of their new Christian commitment — whether Greek wisdom, Jewish ritualism, or some type of Christian charismatic experience — Paul says such things as the following:

> Christ did not send me to baptize, but to preach the gospel — not with words of human wisdom, lest the cross of Christ be emptied of its power. (1 Cor 1:17)

> We preach Christ crucified: a stumbling block to Jews and foolishness to Gentiles, but to those whom God has called, both Jews and Greeks, Christ is the power of God and the wisdom of God. (1 Cor 1:23-24)

---

268. Cf. Gal 2:5, 14: "the truth of the gospel."
269. Cf. Phil 1:12-18; see also R. N. Longenecker, "What Does It Matter?" 163-78.

I resolved to know nothing while I was with you except Jesus Christ and him crucified. (1 Cor 2:2)

This is what we speak, not in words taught us by human wisdom but in words taught by the Spirit, expressing spiritual truths in spiritual words. (1 Cor 2:13)

It was not that Paul was against human wisdom or human rituals per se, or even against God's grace being expressed in a person's life in particular or dramatic ways. Rather, what he wanted his converts to realize was that central to his preaching and their response was "the gospel," and that the focus of that gospel had to do with the person and work of Christ. And in the salutation of Romans he telescopes that same sentiment by saying that the gospel is "concerning his Son" (1:3a) and then sets out an early christological confessional portion that serves to define what the early church meant by "his Son" (1:3b-4).

Such a focus in the Christian message has been seen by many people today, just as in Paul's day, as a "stumbling block" and "foolishness" — even by some Christian leaders. But as Paul insisted: (1) it is the gospel that is "the power of God for the salvation of everyone who believes" (Rom 1:16), and (2) it is Christ who is "the power of God and the wisdom of God" (1 Cor 1:24). It is, in fact, these two features — the centrality of the gospel and the focus of the gospel in the person and work of Jesus Christ — that epitomized the proclamation of the apostles and the early church. And these are the emphases that need to be reclaimed today as the "evangel" in our contemporary contextualizations of the Christian proclamation.

Faith and Obedience. Also of great importance for Paul are the themes of "faith" and "obedience." The expression ὑπακοὴν πίστεως, "the obedience that comes from faith," in 1:5 (understanding πίστεως as a genitive of source), may have been somewhat conditioned by certain concerns among the Christians at Rome (as we have suggested above). But certainly the relationship between faith and obedience, as well as what is to be understood by each of these terms, were issues of immense significance for both Paul and his churches.[270] These issues, of course, have been matters of intense debate at various times in the history of the Christian church (as witness, for example, Martin Luther and the Protestant Reformation). And they continue to be highly important for every Christian today.

Understanding πίστεως in 1:5 as a genitive of source, with the phrase translated as "obedience that comes from [or 'springs from'] faith," means that we are not talking about "a faith that consists of obedience" (a genitive of apposition interpretation) or "obedience to a body of formulated doctrine" (an

---

270. As witness, e.g., Paul's discussions in Rom 2–4 and 9–11 (as discussed later in this commentary), his polemical and hortatory expositions throughout Galatians, and such biographical comments as appear in Phil 3:1-11; see also Jas 2:14-26.

objective genitive interpretation) — and certainly not "obedience as a human virtue, with faith being the means for accomplishing that virtue" (an adjectival genitive interpretation, as well as some forms of a subjective genitive interpretation). Nor are we defining either obedience or faith as human virtues that God graciously allows us — or, perhaps, empowers us — to accomplish. Rather, accepting a genitive of source interpretation, we understand Paul to be speaking about an intellectual and volitional positive response to Christ, that is, a response to Christ's person and work as portrayed in the writings of the NT, which stems from the very depths of one's being and involves the engagement of one's whole person — with that positive response and total engagement resulting in attitudes and actions of obedience to God and his will. In so doing, as Paul frequently says in his letters, we are not "doing" certain prescriptions set out in God's law in order to gain a right standing before God, but "fulfilling" all that God's righteous law requires by our being people of faith, who are guided by the Spirit and act in love (cf. Rom 9:30-10:4; see also Gal 5:13-26).

Intimate Relationship with God. In the recipient unit of his Romans salutation, Paul characterizes all the Christians at Rome as those "loved by God and called his holy people" (1:7a). The people of Israel are frequently characterized in the OT as "loved by God"[271] and sometimes as God's "holy people"[272] — though more commonly the substantive "holy ones" appears in the OT with reference to celestial beings, not redeemed humans.[273] And these attributions and the patterns of their distribution are generally carried on in the post-biblical writings of Second Temple Judaism.

Paul, however, in concert with other NT writers, repeatedly uses the present, active, adjectival participle ἀγαπητός ("loved," "beloved") and perfect, passive, substantival participle ἠγαπημένος ("those loved," "beloved") with respect to believers in Jesus.[274] And he uses the substantival noun ἅγιοι ("holy ones") some forty times in his letters, with almost all the occurrences having Christians as the referent.[275] Thus these usual OT characterizations of God's people Israel as "those loved by God" and of angels as "his holy ones" have been shifted to apply now to the newly constituted people of God who believe in Jesus, the Christian church, composed of both Jews and Gentiles.

Such a shift signals a new self-consciousness among Paul and the early Christians: that because they have been "called by God to belong to Jesus Christ," believers in Jesus experience an intimate relationship with God — one in which they are "loved by God and called his holy people." And it is this consciousness that needs to be highlighted in any contextualization of the Christian gospel for God's people today.

---

271. Cf., e.g., Deut 4:37; 7:8, 13; 33:3; 1 Kgs 10:9; 2 Chr 2:11; 9:8; Isa 43:4; Jer 31:3.
272. Cf. Ps 34:9 and Dan 7:18-27.
273. Cf., e.g., Deut 33:2; Job 5:1; 15:15; Ps 89:5, 7; Dan 4:13, 17, 23; 8:13; Zech 14:5.
274. In addition to Rom 1:7, see, e.g., Rom 9:25; Col. 3:12; 1 Thess 1:4; 2 Thess 2:13.
275. In addition to Rom 1:7, see, e.g., Rom 8:27; 12:13; 15:25, 26, 31; 16:2, 15; 1 Cor 1:2; 6:1, 2; 14:33; 16:1, 15 (the only possible exceptions being 1 Thess 3:13 and 2 Thess 1:10).

II. Thanksgiving (1:8-12)

TRANSLATION

1:8First of all, in truth, I thank my God through Jesus Christ for all of you, because your faith is being reported all over the world. 9For God is my witness, whom I serve with my whole heart in the gospel of his Son, how I constantly remember you 10at all times in my prayers. And I pray that somehow, now at last, I may succeed by God's will to come to you.

11For I am longing to see you in order that I may share with you some spiritual gift so as to make you strong — 12that is, so that we may be mutually encouraged by each other's faith, both yours and mine.

TEXTUAL NOTES

1:8a The strongly supported phrase διὰ Ἰησοῦ Χριστοῦ ("through Jesus Christ") is absent in uncorrected Codex Vaticanus (ℵ* 01), which is probably due to a scribal error.

8b The preposition περί ("concerning," "with reference to," "for") has early and widespread support in uncials ℵ A B C D*, as well as in minuscules 33 1739 (Category I) and 81 1506 1881 (Category II), whereas ὑπέρ ("on behalf of"), which may be understood as being generally equivalent ("about," "concerning"), is supported by D^c G P Ψ and the later *Byz* textual tradition.

9 The possessive personal pronoun μου ("my") is widely attested by uncials ℵ A B C D^2 P and minuscules 33 1175 1739 (Category I), 1881 2464 (Category II), and 6 69 88 104 323 330 614 1241 1243 1735 1874 2344 (Category III). The dative pronoun μοι ("for me"), however, appears in uncials D* G Ψ and a number of *Byz* minuscules, probably reflecting a desire to avoid using the possessive personal pronoun in connection with God.

FORM/STRUCTURE/SETTING

Immediately following the prescript (Latin *praescriptio*) in a Greco-Roman letter, there often appeared a section that (1) sought to establish a favorable contact with the writer's addressees, (2) affirmed the addressees in some manner, (3) expressed some type of prayer for them, either a "health wish" (using the verb ὑγιαίνειν, "to be in good health") or an actual prayer (using the noun προσκύνημα, "worshipful prayer"), and (4) set out the writer's primary purposes and major concerns in writing. And Paul followed much the same pattern, not only here in his letter to the Christians at Rome but also in most of his other letters[1] — usually with the verb εὐχαριστῶ ("I give thanks") included at the beginning of these sections, though twice with the adjective εὐλογητός ("blessed," "praised") used equivalently. Therefore these opening sections in Paul's letters are today often referred to as "thanksgiving" or "eulogy" sections rather than merely "introduction" sections — particularly since the work of Paul Schubert in his 1939 monograph *The Form and Function of the Pauline Thanksgivings*.

The major exception to this pattern in the Pauline corpus is, of course, Paul's letter to his converts in the province of Galatia, which I have argued is a "rebuke and appeal" letter.[2] For while Gal 1:6-10 functions in a similar fashion as the thanksgiving or eulogy sections of Paul's other letters, it is in many respects quite different — being introduced by the verb θαυμάζω ("I am amazed" or "astonished"), devoid of any statement of affirmation or praise and without any report of prayer on behalf of those being addressed.[3]

Schubert set out an entirely new course for the study of these opening sections. He showed how the Pauline thanksgiving or eulogistic sections are distinguishable units of material and spelled out how they function in certain specific ways. The primary form of a Pauline thanksgiving Schubert identified as beginning with the phrase εὐχαριστῶ τῷ θεῷ ("I give thanks to God"), followed by one, two, or three participles, which are then followed by another clause that is subordinate to the participles. A secondary form he identified as beginning with the verb εὐχαριστῶ ("I give thanks"), which is followed by another clause introduced by ὅτι ("that") and then by a further clause subordinate to the ὅτι clause and introduced by ὥστε ("therefore," "so that"). Schubert also noted that these two forms are sometimes mixed. Further, he argued that the phrase εὐλογητὸς ὁ θεός ("Blessed be God" or "Praise be to God") is a similar phrase, which in two instances replaces εὐχαριστῶ τῷ θεῷ ("I give thanks to God").[4]

Two points highlighted by Schubert in his study of these Pauline thanksgivings are that in these distinctive units of material there appear (1) a rudimentary agenda for what will be dealt with in the body of each letter, and (2) some of the major concerns of the author as he was writing. Schubert was, in fact, the first to observe these features in the Pauline thanksgiving sections, and his seminal observations have been spelled out more fully by others in a number of

1. Cf. 1 Cor 1:4-9; 2 Cor 1:3-11; Eph 1:15-23; Phil 1:3-11; Col 1:3-8; 1 Thess 1:2-5; 2 Thess 1:3-10; Phlm 4-7.

2. See R. N. Longenecker, *Galatians*, c-cxix, passim.

3. A thanksgiving section is also omitted in 1 Timothy and Titus, though a modified form appears in 2 Tim 1:3-7.

4. Cf. 2 Cor 1:3 and Eph 1:3; see also 1 Pet 1:3.

monographs since.[5] Most commentators today, however, while making use of his terminology, have failed to appreciate Schubert's two major theses regarding the presence of Paul's "agenda" and "concerns" in his thanksgiving sections, and so, sadly, have continued to treat what Paul says in these thanksgiving sections as being merely introductory in some fashion.

But while Schubert definitively identified the beginning of a Pauline thanksgiving and cogently set out its major functions, he was less clear and less convincing with regard to the closing of these sections in their respective letters. Based on data drawn from the thanksgiving sections of 1 Cor 1:4-9; Phil 1:3-11; and 2 Thess 1:3-10, Schubert argued that the most marked feature signaling the end of a Pauline thanksgiving was its "eschatological climax." Yet not every Pauline thanksgiving section concludes with an obvious eschatological climax. So failing such a climax in all of Paul's letters, Schubert went on to argue that a thanksgiving section can also be seen to come to an end when one suddenly finds oneself at the beginning of the body of the letter itself. Yet where the body of a particular Pauline letter begins is sometimes difficult to determine. Thus while Schubert is to be applauded for his highly significant study of the linguistic features, structural forms, and major purposes of Paul's opening thanksgiving sections in his letters, his understanding of how Paul moves from a thanksgiving section to the body of his letters has required greater clarification.[6]

We must deal more directly with where the "body opening" of Romans begins, and thus where its thanksgiving ends, in the following section of our commentary proper. Suffice it here to point out that if Romans is to be treated as a letter, then all its epistolary features and their functions must be taken seriously into account. Schubert proposed that the thanksgiving of Romans ended at 1:17 and that the body of the letter began at 1:18 — but he also admitted that it is difficult to determine the extent of Paul's thanksgiving section after 1:9. We will argue later in dealing with 1:13-15, however, that the disclosure formula οὐ θέλω δὲ ὑμᾶς ἀγνοεῖν ("I do not want you to be unaware") at the beginning of 1:13, coupled with the vocative ἀδελφοί (inclusively understood as "brothers and sisters"), should be seen as signaling the start of a new section — that is, as the beginning of the "body opening" of the letter — as do similar disclosure formulas in many letters of antiquity, as well as in 2 Cor 1:8 and Phil 1:12 (perhaps also Gal 1:11).[7] And we will agree with Terence Y. Mullins that "when the Thanksgiving is followed by any recognizable element of another form (such as a 'disclosure formula'), the termination of the Thanksgiving is thereby marked."[8] For these reasons, therefore, combined with other reasons to be spelled out later, we believe that the thanksgiving of Romans should be seen as ending at the close of 1:12.

---

5. See esp. O'Brien, *Introductory Thanksgivings;* Jervis, *The Purpose of Romans,* 48-52, 86-109.
6. See esp. J. T. Sanders, "Transition from Opening Epistolary Thanksgiving to Body."
7. Cf. White, *Form and Function of the Body of the Greek Letter,* 76, 84-85.
8. Mullins, "Disclosure," 49.

Included within this thanksgiving section of 1:8-12 are (1) an acknowledgment by Paul of the Christian faith of his addressees (in 1:8), (2) a report by the apostle of the nature of his prayers for the Christians at Rome (in 1:9-10a), and (3) references to his desire to visit his addressees at Rome (in 1:10b and 11a; cf. also v. 13). Likewise, three of the themes highlighted in the salutation of 1:1-7 appear also in this thanksgiving: (1) that Paul serves God with his whole heart "in preaching *the gospel*" (1:9a), (2) that the Christian gospel is "the gospel of *his* [God's] *Son*" (1:9a), and (3) that Paul's addressees are within the scope of his Gentile mission (1:12). But it needs also to be noted that there are within this thanksgiving section two statements that reveal a great deal about Paul's primary purposes and major concerns when writing to the believers in Jesus at Rome. The first of these matters is in v. 11b: "in order that (ἵνα) I may share with you (μεταδῶ ὑμῖν) some spiritual gift (τι χάρισμα πνευματικόν) to make you strong"; and the second is in v. 12: "so that (τοῦτο δέ ἐστιν) we may be mutually encouraged (συμπαρακληθῆναι) by each others' faith, both yours and mine (ὑμῶν τε καὶ ἐμοῦ)." Thus we need to begin our reading of Romans not only by noting what Paul says about his addressees, what he reports about the content of his prayers for them, and what he says about wanting to visit them, but also by giving careful attention to what he states about his primary purpose and major concern in writing them — not only as expressed in the letter's salutation but also here in its thanksgiving.

EXEGETICAL COMMENTS

1:8 Paul's thanksgiving section begins with the neuter adverb πρῶτον ("first") and the affirmative particle μέν ("indeed"). Some Church Fathers noted that "there is no 'second' that corresponds to 'first' " and explained this as being (1) because "Paul's phrases are not always complete" or (2) because the material of 1:13-15 comprises Paul's second point, though he did not explicitly so designate it.[9] A number of more contemporary commentators have observed the same phenomenon and drawn similar conclusions, sometimes even proposing that "the second idea the apostle had in view is really to be found in ver. 10, in the prayer which he offers to God that he may be allowed soon to go to Rome."[10] Others have concluded that since "first" is not followed by "second" Paul is "carried away by his train of thought"[11] — or that "quite probably Paul meant to make a further point in continuation, and then omitted to do so."[12] Still others are prepared to leave matters somewhat unresolved and say only something along the lines of Douglas Moo's comment: "The opening word, 'first,' implies

9. Cf., e.g., Origen, *Ad Romanos*, PG 14.854-855.
10. So Godet, *Romans*, 1.142; cf. B. Weiss, *An die Römer*, 58; Zahn, *An die Römer*, 55-56.
11. So Barrett, *Romans*, 24.
12. So Cranfield, *Romans*, 1.74.

a series, but Paul never comes to a 'second' or 'next.' It is hard to know whether Paul simply forgets to maintain the sequence he begins or whether the phrase functions here simply to highlight what he considers of primary importance."[13] In all likelihood, however, πρῶτον should here be understood as an adverb of time, and so translated "to begin with" or "first of all" — or, perhaps, as an adverb of degree, which would signify some such idea as "in the first place," "above all," or "especially."[14]

The particle μέν, while generally affirmative, is used variously in koine Greek and throughout the NT (principally in Matthew, Acts, Romans, 1 Corinthians, and Hebrews), with its precise significance being always dependent on the particular author's mood and purpose in the immediate context. Here at the beginning of the thanksgiving section of Romans this particle μέν should probably be viewed as connoting the idea of an emphatic affirmation, that is, "in truth" or "indeed," with the phrase πρῶτον μέν understood as "first of all, in truth" — in concert with Paul's insistence at the beginning of 1:9 that "God is my witness" (μάρτυς γάρ μού ἐστιν ὁ θεός, with the emphatic Greek positioning of μάρτυς, "witness," suggesting the need for such an affirmation) and comparable to his use of the phrase in Rom 3:2 ("first of all, in truth") or 1 Cor 11:18 ("in the first place, indeed").

Paul's opening statement of his thanksgiving section, εὐχαριστῶ τῷ θεῷ μου διὰ Ἰησοῦ Χριστοῦ περὶ πάντων ὑμῶν ("I thank my God through Jesus Christ for all of you"), assures his addressees of his high regard for them. Christians at Rome may very well have heard from others — and, perhaps, had themselves come to believe — that Paul's "failure" to visit them was an indication of his aloofness from them, possibly even his dissatisfaction with their type of Christianity. They may even have reciprocated in kind with doubts about his Gentile mission and message. Paul, however, seeks to bridge whatever gap may have been created between them and him by asserting his thankfulness for all of the believers in Jesus at Rome, whatever their particular ethnicities and whatever their possible differences from him in their theological understandings — with that expression of thankfulness prefaced, as noted above, by the rather unusual (at least when compared with the thanksgivings in his other letters) affirmation: "first of all, in truth."

To the object of his thanksgiving, that is, to "God" (τῷ θεῷ), Paul adds the personal pronoun "my" (μου), and so speaks of his thankfulness as being directed "to my God" (τῷ θεῷ μου) — as he does also in some of the epistolary thanksgivings in his other letters.[15] What he reports to his addressees at Rome, therefore, is a prayer of praise to God for them, with the phrase "my God"

13. So Moo, *Romans,* 57.

14. So *ATRob,* 1152; *BAG,* 733-34; cf. Fitzmyer, *Romans,* 243: "first of all" or "at the outset"; see also the translations of Moffatt: "first of all"; Weymouth: "first of all"; Phillips: "I must begin"; NEB: "let me begin."

15. Cf. 1 Cor 1:4 (as attested in the better MSS); Phil 1:3, and Phlm 4.

striking a note of personal piety that stems from the language of devotion in the Psalms.[16]

The apostle's thanksgiving to God is "through Jesus Christ" (διὰ Ἰησοῦ Χριστοῦ), which phraseology is not found in any of Paul's other thanksgivings — though it occurs elsewhere in Romans in various forms,[17] as well as in Paul's other letters and at other places in the NT. The Church Fathers understood "through Jesus Christ" here in 1:8 as referring to Christ's intermediary role as intercessor in heaven. So, for example, Origen commented:

> To give thanks to God is to offer him a sacrifice of praise, and therefore he [Paul] adds "through Jesus Christ," as through a high priest. Anyone who wants to offer a sacrifice to God ought to know that he should offer it through the hands of a priest.[18]

Some scholars, however, have played down any mediatorial or priestly activity on the part of the exalted Christ in Paul's use of the preposition διά here, preferring rather (1) to highlight his use of διά in 12:1, where he speaks of Christian ethics as being in response to the mercies of God,[19] and (2) to spell out ideas that they see as underlying the early Christian use of that preposition, and so have suggested that διά here should be translated "in virtue of" or "on the basis of" — thereby arguing that it is more appropriate to understand Paul here as saying that Christ's work provides "the basis and validation of prayer,"[20] or, as more expansively stated, that "Christ is the one who has created the access to God for such thanks to be offered."[21] But though Paul was always profoundly conscious of Christ's work as the basis for a person's access before God and as what validates one's prayer to God, it yet remains true, as Joseph Fitzmyer has aptly pointed out, that Paul was also "supremely aware of Christ's actual and current intermediary role in heaven."[22] This is what is explicitly stated in 8:34, in words probably drawn from an early Christian confession: "It is Christ Jesus — the one who died; more than that, who was raised to life — who is also at the right hand of God, and who, indeed, intercedes for us." Such a mediatorial role is suggested by Paul's use of this same formula "through Jesus Christ" in such passages in Romans as 2:16; 5:1, 11, 21; 7:25a; 15:30; and 16:27.[23] Thus it seems fully appropriate to speak of Paul's proclamation of Christ as including Christ's

---

16. Cf., e.g., Pss 3:8 (LXX 3:7): ὁ θεός μου; 5:3 (LXX 5:2): ὁ βασιλεύς μου καὶ ὁ θεός μου; and 7:2 (LXX 7:1): κύριε ὁ θεός μου.

17. Cf. Rom 2:16; 5:1, 9, 11, 21; 7:25a; 8:37; 11:36; 15:30; 16:27.

18. Origen, *Ad Romanos, PG* 14.854.

19. NIV: "by the mercies of God"; NRSV: "in view of God's mercies."

20. Käsemann, *Romans,* 17; cf. Kramer, *Christ, Lord, Son of God,* 84-90.

21. Moo, *Romans,* 57.

22. Fitzmyer, *Romans,* 244.

23. Cf. A. Schettler, *Die paulinische Formel "Durch Christus"* (Tübingen: Mohr, 1907); Kuss, "Die Formel 'durch Christus.'"

office as God's appointed Mediator, as well as to epitomize the convictions of the earliest believers in Jesus in this manner — and so to affirm, along with Charles Cranfield, that "Christ is Mediator not only of God's approach to men (as, e.g., in v. 5), but also, as the risen and exalted Lord, of their responding approach to God in worship."[24]

Further, Paul says here in 1:8 that his thanksgiving to God was "for all of you" (περὶ πάντων ὑμῶν), which continues the inclusive emphasis of the recipient unit of his salutation in 1:7 ("to all those at Rome, who are loved by God and called his holy people"). It seems highly likely that Paul knew of differences and difficulties among his addressees at Rome — as witness particularly 14:1–15:13 and 16:17-20a, perhaps also 13:1-7. Here in 1:8, however, he expresses only thankfulness for all of the believers in Jesus at Rome.

The reason that Paul gives for his thankfulness is not any personal or spiritual qualities he knew existed among his Romans addressees — as cited, for example, in his thanksgiving for his converts at Philippi, who constituted one of his best churches,[25] or even in his thanksgiving for his converts at Corinth, who comprised one of his most troublesome churches.[26] Nor is anything said about the faith of the Christians at Rome as being especially great, deep, or strong or in any other way superior to that of other believers in Jesus. Paul did not know most of the Christians at Rome personally, and it would have been disingenuous for him to suggest that he did by attempting to identify any such characteristics in them or by simply flattering them. Rather, he is thankful "because your faith is being reported all over the world" (ὅτι ἡ πίστις ὑμῶν καταγγέλλεται ἐν ὅλῳ τῷ κόσμῳ).

The use of the articular expression ἡ πίστις ("the faith") to mean "the content of what is believed" is not common in Paul's letters. "The faith" as signifying "a content to be believed" does appear, however, in Gal 1:23 ("They ['the churches of Judea'] only kept hearing, 'The one who formerly persecuted us is now preaching *the faith* he once tried to destroy'"). Yet what Paul calls ἡ πίστις ὑμῶν ("your faith") here in 1:8 he will later call ἡ ὑμῶν ὑπακοή ("your obedience") in 16:19. So his emphasis is not so much on the content of what they believed as on their act of "faith" and their actions of "obedience" in response to God and his salvation as provided "in Christ."

Kingsley Barrett has drawn attention to Paul's use of the possessive pronoun "your" (ὑμῶν) in speaking of "the faith" (ἡ πίστις) of the Christians at Rome and has argued: "'Your faith' does not mean 'the Christian faith *which* you, in common with all other Christians, 'hold,' for this would be pointless in a thanksgiving; but 'the faith *as* you hold it,' that is, the understanding, constancy, and charity with which you hold it."[27] Barrett does not attempt to spell out any

---

24. Cranfield, *Romans,* 1.74.
25. Cf. Phil 1:3-11.
26. Cf. 1 Cor 1:4-9; cf. 2 Cor 1:3-7.
27. Barrett, *Romans,* 24 (italics his).

of the possible implications of his observation. But he does suggest that Paul's use of the personal pronoun "your" with respect to "the faith" of Christians at Rome reflects something of his consciousness regarding somewhat different forms of the Christian message being held by them and by him — citing as his main evidence Acts 28:21-22, "where the Roman Jews appear to have no direct acquaintance with Christianity."[28]

Nonetheless, though there may have been some differences between the theology and practices of the believers in Jesus at Rome and Paul's understanding and proclamation of the Christian gospel (as we too believe) — and though Paul's desire, both by his present letter and by a forthcoming visit, was to present what he calls "my gospel" to the Christians at Rome, since he considered them within the scope of his God-given mandate to the Gentile world and wanted them to share in the continuation of his Christian mission to Gentiles — it is probably somewhat extreme to read into the possessive pronoun "your" any sinister implications regarding something other than the Christian faith that was held in common with all other Christians. Probably all that Paul meant by "your faith" here in 1:8 is what he meant when characterizing the faith of his converts at Thessalonica as "your faith in God" in 1 Thess 1:8, that is, "your own personal response of faith toward God."

Paul's reference to his addressees' faith as being proclaimed "all over the world" (ἐν ὅλῳ τῷ κόσμῳ) is, without doubt, an "amiable hyperbole."[29] It is similar to what he says in 1 Thess 1:8 about the faith of his converts at Thessalonica as being known "not only in Macedonia and Achaia, but everywhere" (ἐν παντὶ τόπῳ) and in Col 1:6 about the gospel as "producing fruit and growing everywhere in the world" (ἐν παντὶ τῷ κόσμῳ) — also to what he says in 2 Cor 2:14 about his own ministry as having "spread the fragrance of knowing him [i.e., Christ] everywhere" (ἐν παντὶ τόπῳ). Luke uses this same type of hyperbolic expression when he speaks of "all the world" (πᾶσαν τὴν οἰκουμένην) taxed by an order of the emperor Augustus, when Quirinius was governor of Syria (Luke 2:1), and of a severe famine "over the whole world" (ἐφ’ ὅλην τὴν οἰκουμένην) during the reign of the emperor Claudius (Acts 11:28). As parallels, Adolf Deissmann has drawn attention to (1) "a heathen epitaph (now in Braunsberg) of an otherwise unknown Egyptian lady, Seratus, and her relations," which "speaks of their modesty as 'known in all the world' " and (2) "a Christian letter of later date," which "says of a (Bishop) John that his fame goes throughout 'the whole world.' "[30]

Although the gospel has universal significance,[31] Paul's reference to the

---

28. Barrett, *Romans*, 24.

29. So Deissmann, *Paul*, 56; cf. also Godet, *Romans*, 1.142; B. Weiss, *An die Römer*, 58; Lietzmann, *An die Römer*, 27; Leenhardt, *Romans*, 42; Bruce, *Romans*, 56; Cranfield, *Romans*, 1.75; Fitzmyer, *Romans*, 244.

30. Deissmann, *Paul*, 56, note 5, citing *Archiv für Papyrusforschung*, 5, p. 169 for the first parallel; *Archiv für Papyrusforschung*, 4, p. 558 for the second.

31. Cf. Rom 10:18, quoting Ps 19:4.

faith of Christians at Rome as being known "all over the world" should not be understood distributively, as though their faith was known in every area and by every person on earth. Likewise, though devotionally true, it should not be read universally — that is, as including both heaven and earth — as though Paul was here teaching that even the angels of heaven rejoiced in the faith of Gentile believers in Jesus, as some of the Church Fathers devotionally proposed.[32] Rather, what Paul means here is that the Christian faith of believers at Rome had been proclaimed "far and wide,"[33] particularly in "the microcosmos of the Christian 'world.'"[34] Certainly reports of a Christian presence at Rome, the capital city of the Roman Empire, would have been newsworthy for Christians throughout the empire. And Paul was no doubt thankful to hear such reports — just as he was thankful for the spread of the gospel elsewhere in the empire, however it came about, through whomever it was proclaimed, and in whatever form it took.[35]

1:9-10 "The verb of thanksgiving (εὐχαριστέω)," as Peter O'Brien has pointed out, "does not dominate the entire paragraph as in most other [Pauline] introductory passages. The apostle passes from thanksgiving to petitionary prayer, and on to personal details about his concern for the Christians at Rome and his desire to visit them. . . . Strictly speaking, the first sentence of the period ends with the words 'in all the world' of v. 8."[36] Thus in 1:9-10 Paul goes on to speak of his prayers on behalf of all the Christians at Rome.

The prayer materials of Paul's letters are not liturgical texts in which God is addressed directly — though such a prayer may be reflected in 1 Cor 16:22, Μαρανα θα, "O Lord Come!" (understood as an imperative request, not an indicative statement "Our Lord comes"). Rather, they are his reports to his addressees of what he has prayed for on their behalf. In Paul's direct prayers to God, he undoubtedly addressed God in the second person and people were spoken about in the third person, whereas in his prayer reports his addressees are referred to in the second person and God is spoken about in the third person. Thus prayers of adoration and prayers of thanksgiving that were originally addressed to God are recast in Paul's letters to provide a précis of what has been prayed but do not address God directly or provide an exact wording of the prayers themselves. Likewise, prayers of petition have been recast so that, while they express the central concerns of Paul in praying for his addressees, they refer to God in the third person and only set out the essence of what was prayed for.

Further, it often becomes difficult to delineate the exact boundaries of the prayer materials in Paul's letters. For (1) reports about what Paul prayed for are often merged with descriptions about his addressees' situations, and (2) prayer wishes expressed on behalf of his addressees are often combined with

32. Cf., e.g., Origen, *Ad Romanos, PG* 14.855.

33. Cf. O'Brien, *Introductory Thanksgivings,* 207; Cranfield, *Romans,* 75.

34. Deissmann, *Paul,* 56.

35. Cf. Phil 1:12-18, which expresses Paul's reaction to a different situation, though with a somewhat similar response of thankfulness.

36. O'Brien, *Introductory Thanksgivings,* 202.

exhortations to work out in their lives what has been prayed for. And all this is particularly true in the opening thanksgiving sections of Paul's letters, where praise, prayer, and exhortations are frequently intermingled.

The statement μάρτυς γάρ μού ἐστιν ὁ θεός ("for God is my witness") represents a significant beginning for the prayer materials of 1:9-10. For the fact that Paul calls on God as his witness suggests something of the great importance he attaches to his addressees' knowing that he prays for them. Evidently in the "court of public opinion" among the believers in Jesus at Rome, Paul was not held in highest regard and his interest in them was denigrated. It would, of course, have been impossible for anyone at Rome — as well as anyone anywhere else — to know Paul's real intentions and concerns. Only God knows such matters! So Paul calls on God as his witness regarding his attitudes toward and prayers for his addressees, the Roman Christians.

In some of his other letters Paul invokes God's "witness" about his work and his activities using these same words,[37] while elsewhere in his writings he uses only similar phraseology.[38] In all these affirmations Paul echoes OT usage.[39] But what he wants his addressees at Rome to know is that he is really concerned for them, as he has always been.

ᾧ λατρεύω ἐν τῷ πνεύματί μου ἐν τῷ εὐαγγελίῳ τοῦ υἱοῦ αὐτοῦ ("whom I serve with my whole heart in the gospel of his Son") is a subordinate relative clause that spells out something further with respect to Paul's relationship to the clause's immediate antecedent ὁ θεός ("God"). Further, it highlights a number of matters of great importance in Paul's understanding of his own Christian mission to Gentiles, which matters he evidently wanted his addressees to recognize were at the heart of all of his endeavors — including both his present letter to them and his anticipated future visit with them.

A first matter of great importance in this subordinate relative clause has to do with the characterization of Paul's mission to Gentiles as his service for God, using the verb λατρεύειν ("to serve worshipfully") that appears in the LXX for both the worship and the religious service of the people of God.[40] By his use of λατρεύειν Paul would inevitably have raised in his addressees' minds the highly significant cognate nouns λατρεία ("service" or "worship") and λατρία ("adoration" or "worship"), the former being used nine times in the LXX and the latter even more frequently in the Greek OT with reference to the people's response to God. Thus Paul seems to want his addressees to know, in effect, that he considers all his missionary activities as both worship and service to God — that is, as his "worshipful service" or "service of worship" given to God. So it may be said, as Joseph Fitzmyer has quite rightly pointed

37. Cf. 1 Thess 2:5: θεὸς μάρτυς, "God is witness"; 2:10: ὑμεῖς μάρτυρες καὶ ὁ θεός, "you are witnesses, and so is God"; Phil 1:8: μάρτυς γάρ μου ὁ θεός, "for God is my witness"; 2 Cor 1:23: ἐγὼ δὲ μάρτυρα τὸν θεὸν ἐπικαλοῦμαι, "but I call on God as witness."
38. Cf. Rom 9:1; 2 Cor 2:17.
39. Cf. Gen 31:50; Deut. 4:26; 30:19; 31:28; Judg 11:10; 1 Sam 12:5; also 1 Macc 2:37.
40. Cf., e.g., Exod 3:12; 10:7, 8, 26; 12:31; Deut 6:13; 10:12-13.

out: "Paul's very prayer for the Christians of Rome is an integral part of his worship of God."[41]

A second matter of importance that Paul highlights here in this subordinate relative clause has to do with his speaking of his "worshipful service" to God as being ἐν τῷ πνεύματί μου (literally "in" or "by my spirit"), which is an expression that has been variously interpreted. Some of the more prominent interpretations are as follows:

1. It refers to the Spirit of God who dwells within Paul and so should be translated "through the Spirit of God imparted to me."[42]
2. It refers to one's spiritual (i.e., Christian) service on behalf of God, as contrasted to a carnal (i.e., pagan or Jewish) service.[43]
3. It refers to "wholehearted" service to God.[44]
4. It refers to worship and service done "sincerely."[45]
5. It refers to "the organ of service," that is, "the sphere in which the service is rendered."[46]
6. It refers to one's whole person, which is sometimes designated as "one's spirit," by which one serves God completely.[47]
7. It refers to "the spiritual side of his nature," as contrasted to the material aspects of his life.[48]
8. It refers to "the inward side of his apostolic service contrasted with the outward side consisting of his preaching, etc."[49]

41. Fitzmyer, *Romans*, 244.

42. So Kümmel, *Römer 7 und die Bekehrung des Paulus*, 33; cf. Schlatter, *Romans*, 13: "'His Spirit' is the Spirit given him, that indwells and is at work in him"; E. Schweizer, "πνεῦμα, πνευματικός," *TDNT*, 6.435: "the Spirit of God individually imparted to the apostle"; Jewett, *Paul's Anthropological Terms*, 197-98: "the divine spirit which was apportioned to the apostle."

43. So Chrysostom, *Homilia XXXII ad Romanos*, PG 60.403; cf. Dunn, *Romans*, 1.29: "The phrase here clearly implies that Paul is deliberately contrasting the worship appropriate in relation to the gospel with the typically cult-oriented worship of his fellow Jews"; see also Weymouth's translation: "[Paul's] spiritual service."

44. So Pelagius, *Ad Romanos*, PL 30.648: *"Hoc est, in toto corde meo, et prompta devotione mea deservio";* see also the translations by Phillips and TEV: "with all my heart"; NIV: "with my whole heart."

45. So John Calvin, *Romans*, in *Calvin's New Testament Commentaries*, 8.22: "from the heart . . . with sincere devotion of heart," in contrast to "an external appearance of religion"; cf. Murray, *Romans*, 1.20: "the depth and sincerity of his service of God is indicated by the phrase 'in my spirit'."

46. So Sanday and Headlam, *Romans*, 20; cf. Fitzmyer, *Romans*, 244-45: "Paul does not mean that he worships God only inwardly" but that his worship is expressed in service "by that aspect of me that is open to God's Spirit."

47. So Michel, *An die Römer*, 46-47: "damit den ganzen Menschen, sein Denken, Wollen und Handeln"; cf. Käsemann, *Romans*, 18: "with his whole being Paul serves the gospel."

48. So Barrett, *Romans*, 24; cf. Godet, *Romans*, 1.143: "the most intimate part of his being, where is the organ by which his soul communicates with the divine world"; see also JB's translation: "spiritually" — that is, as stated in footnote "G": "the highest element in a human being" as distinguished from "the flesh, the lowest element."

49. So Cranfield, *Romans*, 1.77; cf. Althaus, *An die Römer*, 10.

9. It refers to "his prayer life, the chief concern of which is, of course, the progress of his missionary work," and so should be understood as his inward intercession "for the churches and for the progress of the Gospel."[50]

It may be that a number of these interpretations should be combined in some fashion,[51] for all of them can be supported, to some extent, by parallels found elsewhere in Paul's letters. A few of them, however, seem less likely — in particular, that Paul is here referring to his Christian "spiritual" service to God in contrast to that of pagans and Jews, or that he has in mind the inward, spiritual side of his being in contrast to the material aspects of his life. Likewise, some other interpretations, while defensible in terms of Paul's thought generally, seem not to be to the fore here. For while Paul always proclaimed that God has given believers "in Christ" his Holy Spirit, Paul's emphasis in this verse is on his own human spirit ("my spirit"). And while Paul was always a person of prayer and while he speaks of his prayers on behalf of his addressees in what immediately follows in 1:9b-10, his point here in 1:9a has to do not with his prayers for Christians at Rome but with his own service to God.

It is probably best, therefore, to view the expression "by my spirit" (understanding an instrumental use of the preposition ἐν) as set in the immediate context of *how* Paul serves God. An instrumental use of ἐν may signal either means or manner. Here, however, it seems to signal not so much the means by which Paul serves (i.e., "by means of my spirit") as it does the manner in which he serves — and so, most likely, should be understood as signifying some idea such as "wholeheartedly," "sincerely," or "with my whole being" (so our translation "with my whole heart").

A third matter signaled in the subordinate relative clause of 1:9a is that at the heart of all of Paul's missionary endeavors — that is, at the heart of all of his "worshipful service" to God, which he did "wholeheartedly," "sincerely" and "with [his] whole being" — is "the gospel of his [God's] Son." While the first preposition ἐν functions instrumentally, the second ἐν functions locally to indicate the focus and sphere of Paul's service to God. As Paul said earlier in the salutation, it is "the gospel of God" to which he had been "set apart" (1:1), which was "promised beforehand through his prophets in the Holy Scriptures" (1:2), which has as its content "his [God's] Son" (1:3a), and whose christological emphasis has been confessed by the church generally (1:3b-4). It is this gospel that gripped Paul in his Christian conversion, that resided at the heart of all his Christian thought, and that was the central thrust of all of his Christian ministry.[52] Further, it seems that it was with respect to an understanding of this gospel, with both its indicative assurances and its imperative implications, that Paul and the Christians at Rome

---

50. So H. Strathmann, "λατρεύω, λατρεία," 4.64; cf. *Str-Bil,* 3.26, where it is noted that "serving in the heart" is used by the rabbis with reference to prayer; cf. Zahn, *An die Römer,* 57: "das inwendige Gebetsleben des Pl."

51. So Moo, *Romans,* 58.

52. Cf. our "exegetical comments" on "the gospel" in 1:1.

somewhat differed. So here in the thanksgiving section of his letter, as he did earlier in the salutation section, Paul cannot restrain himself — even in the midst of a subordinate relative clause — from speaking about the focus and sphere of his entire Christian ministry as being "the gospel of his [God's] Son."

Paul Schubert observed that a major function of a Pauline thanksgiving was "to indicate the occasion for and the contents of the letters which they introduce."[53] Thus the Pauline thanksgiving sections serve both epistolary and didactic purposes — that is, (1) in their epistolary function they establish contact with the recipients, reminding them of previously given instructions and setting the tone for each of the letters, and (2) in their didactic function they highlight the main themes or topics to be dealt with in their respective letters.

But while the Pauline thanksgivings have, indeed, epistolary and didactic functions, they also express the apostle's deep pastoral concerns for those he addresses. Paul does this by reporting, in summary fashion, on (1) his prayers of thanksgiving to God for his addressees and (2) his prayers of petition on their behalf. So in the thanksgiving sections of his letters he tells his addressees that his prayers are directed "to God"[54] or "to my God,"[55] who is known to Paul as "the Father of Jesus Christ,"[56] and that they have been offered "always,"[57] "unceasingly,"[58] or "constantly"[59] on behalf of the addressees — which means not that he was continuously in a state of prayer but that he always included references to his addressees in his regular times of prayer.[60]

In 1:9b Paul reports to the believers in Jesus at Rome regarding the earnestness of his prayers on their behalf, expressing himself in the following words: ὡς ἀδιαλείπτως μνείαν ὑμῶν ποιοῦμαι πάντοτε ἐπὶ τῶν προσευχῶν μου ("how I constantly remember you at all times in my prayers"). Hans Lietzmann has suggested that what Paul really meant to say was not ὡς ("how") but ὅτι ("that"), and so his statement should be read "*that* I constantly remember you at all times in my prayers."[61] Yet while "that" may read nicely, "how" connects well with the adverb ἀδιαλείπτως ("constantly") that immediately follows it and therefore should not be too readily displaced.[62] The middle voice of the verb ποιοῦμαι, which derives from the present, active ποιέω ("I make," "form," "do," "accomplish"), together with the noun μνείαν ("remembrance"), is used elsewhere in Paul's letters in the sense of remembering someone in prayer.[63]

53. Schubert, *Form and Function of the Pauline Thanksgivings,* 26.

54. 1 Cor 1:4; 1 Thess 1:2; 2:13; 3:9; 2 Thess 1:3; 2:13.

55. Rom 1:8; Phil 1:3; Phlm 4.

56. Col 1:3.

57. 1 Cor 1:4; Phil 1:4; Col 1:3; 1 Thess 1:2; 2 Thess 1:3; 2:13; Phlm 4.

58. 1 Thess 1:2.

59. Rom 1:9b.

60. Cf. Harder, *Paulus und das Gebet,* 8-19.

61. Lietzmann, *An die Römer,* 28.

62. Cf. Cranfield, *Romans,* 1.77 n. 1.

63. Cf. Eph 1:16; 1 Thess 1:2; Phlm 4; see also Plato, *Phaedrus* 254a; *idem, Protagoras* 317c; *1 Clement* 56:1.

Of greater importance, however, is the perennially vexing question about how the phrases of 1:9b (about Paul's earnestness) and 1:10 (about the content of his prayers) are to be related. Are they to be joined, thereby closing off the sentence that began with "God is my witness" in 1:9a with the words "how I constantly remember you at all times in my prayers"? Or does the phrase of 1:10a begin a new sentence and thus relate to what immediately follows in 1:10b, thereby reading: "At all times in my prayers I pray that somehow, now at last, I will succeed by God's will to come to you." These phrases have frequently been separated by the versification that has become traditional during the past three centuries, with a period, semicolon, or comma inserted after "how I constantly remember you" at the end of 1:9 — and with, then, "at all times in my prayers" viewed as the beginning of all that follows in 1:10. Justification for such a division was evidently based on the opinion that the presence of two such nearly synonymous adverbs as ἀδιαλείπτως ("constantly") and πάντοτε ("always," "at all times") was a bit much for one sentence or clause and so required their distribution into two sentences.

But rather than view "constantly" and "at all times" as awkwardly repetitious when combined in one sentence, it is just as possible to understand these two adverbial expressions as included in one sentence for emphasis. Even more telling against separating the adverbs by allocating them to two separate sentences — and more significant in support of their original appearance together in one sentence — is the fact that, as Charles Cranfield has aptly expressed matters,

> While it is perfectly understandable that Paul should say that he always mentions the Roman Christians when he prays, it seems questionable whether he would be so likely to say that whenever he prays he always asks that he may be allowed to visit them (did this particular desire really occupy quite so prominent a place in his thoughts?).[64]

The content of Paul's prayers on behalf of the Christians at Rome is given very briefly in the statement of 1:10: δεόμενος εἴ πως ἤδη ποτὲ εὐοδωθήσομαι ἐν τῷ θελήματι τοῦ θεοῦ ἐλθεῖν πρὸς ὑμᾶς ("and I pray that somehow, now at last, I may succeed by God's will to come to you"). The first person singular, present, indicative, middle participle δεόμενος is probably best understood as a complementary adverbial participle, which completes the action of the immediately previous verb ποιοῦμαι in 1:9b. It should, therefore, be translated "and I am praying," with the conjunction "and" and the pronoun "I" having to be supplied (as is required for every complementary adverbial participle). The use of the conditional particle εἰ ("if") with the enclitic particle πώς ("somehow," "in some way," "perhaps") is certainly unusual after a direct statement that one is praying. In all likelihood, such an expression as "somehow," "if in some way"

64. Cranfield, *Romans*, 1.77.

or "if perhaps" is to be understood as signaling some uncertainty on Paul's part regarding what he is praying for. It may also, as Marie-Joseph Lagrange has suggested, reflect Paul's desire to be in submission to the will of God.[65] The adverb ἤδη ("now") coupled with the enclitic particle of time ποτέ ("once," "some time," "at length") also suggests some uncertainty on Paul's part regarding the fulfillment of his request and some impatience about its delay.

It needs particularly to be observed that the content of Paul's prayer here in 1:10 has more to do with his own desire to visit the Christians at Rome than it does with any specific request on their behalf: that "somehow, now at last," he would succeed "by God's will" to come to them. The first person singular, future passive verb εὐοδωθήσομαι, which stems from εὐοδόειν (literally "walk a good road" or "have a successful journey"), usually appears in the LXX and the Jewish Greek writings of Second Temple Judaism in the metaphorical sense of "prosper," "get along well," or "succeed."[66] Often, as well, the passive voice of this future verb was treated as a subjunctive. So Paul's prayer of 1:10b should most likely be read: "that I may succeed, by God's will, to come to you."

The expression ἐν τῷ θελήματι τοῦ θεοῦ ("by the will of God" or "by God's will") appears frequently in Paul's letters,[67] as it did also in the Semitic and ancient worlds generally. Adolf Deissmann has shown "how widespread its use must have been, even in the lower strata of society," by reference to its frequent appearance in the common papyrus letters found in the Fayyum district of Egypt.[68] With Paul, however, as both a Jew and a Christian, the expression was particularly meaningful, highlighting, as it does, his submission to the will of God in all of the events of his life.

1:11-12 Vv. 11-12 have frequently been treated rather lightly by commentators of both the past and today, who usually deal only in very general terms with the meaning of words and phrases in the passage. We would argue, however, that these two verses are actually highly significant for a proper understanding of the letter. For what is stated in 1:11 and then explicated in 1:12 provides us, in compact form, with two very important statements regarding Paul's primary purpose and his major concern in writing to the Christians at Rome. And further, when combined with statements in the salutation of 1:1-7, commentators are in possession of extremely important interpretive keys for (1) all that Paul will write throughout the theological and ethical sections of the letter's body-middle in 1:16–15:13 and (2) all that he will say with respect to his purposes in the body closing (or "apostolic parousia") section of 15:14-32 and in the concluding sections of 15:33–16:27.[69]

The statements in 1:11-12 are introduced by ἐπιποθῶ γὰρ ἰδεῖν ὑμᾶς ἵνα ("for I am longing to see you in order that"). The postpositive γάρ ("for") is

---

65. Lagrange, *Aux Romains,* 14; cf. Fitzmyer, *Romans,* 247; Moo, *Romans,* 59.
66. Cf., e.g., Josh 1:8; Prov 28:13; 2 Chr 18:11; 1 Macc 3:6; *1 En* 104:6; *T Gad* 7:1; *4 Ezra* 5:8.
67. Cf. Rom 12:2; 15:32; 1 Cor 1:1; 2 Cor 8:5; Gal 1:4; Eph 1:1; 6:6; Col 1:1; 1 Thess 4:3.
68. See A. Deissmann, "τοῦ θεοῦ θέλοντος," in *Bible Studies,* 252.
69. Cf. Kettungen, *Abfassungszweck des Römerbriefes.*

often used in koine Greek and Paul's letters without any explanatory or causal force, serving simply to indicate a continuation or connection with what has preceded.[70] The first person singular, present, indicative, active, contract verb ἐπιποθῶ, by the addition of the prefix ἐπί, functions as an intensified form of ποθέω ("I desire," "wish"), and so should be read as "I am longing." Paul's desire "to see" (ἰδεῖν) the Christians at Rome is to be understood in much the same way as his desire "to see" (ἱστορῆσαι) Peter at Jerusalem (Gal 1:18) — that is, to visit and be with them for the mutual benefit of both them and himself. Until that could take place, however, the apostle views his present letter as accomplishing something of the same purpose. The conjunction ἵνα functions with the subjunctive to denote "purpose," "aim" or "goal," and thus is best translated here as "in order that" (v. 11b).

Paul expresses quite explicitly his purpose in writing the Christians at Rome in 1:11b: ἵνα τι μεταδῶ χάρισμα ὑμῖν πνευματικὸν εἰς τὸ στηριχθῆναι ὑμᾶς ("in order that I may share with you some spiritual gift so as to make you strong." The verb μεταδίδωμι ("give," "impart," "share"), from which the first person singular, second aorist, subjunctive μεταδῶ ("I may give," "impart," "share") is derived, appears elsewhere in Paul's letters in the sense of sharing with someone.[71] The aorist passive infinitive στηριχθῆναι (with or without the article), when preceded by the preposition εἰς, expresses purpose, and so may be translated "so as to make you strong." Thus as Alexander Wedderburn, in agreement with Marku Kettunen, has expressed matters: *"It is clear from 1.11 that Paul feels himself responsible to further the Romans' faith, whether by a personal visit or by letter, and that is evidence of his conviction that he was their apostle too and pastorally responsible for them."*[72] And as Wedderburn goes on to conclude regarding Paul's words in 1:11: "This much is clear from this verse and that is a valuable clue to Paul's frame of mind in writing the letter."[73]

The expression τι χάρισμα πνευματικὸν ("some spiritual gift"), however, undoubtedly is the most significant exegetical feature of this statement. Yet it is also the most difficult and so needs to be considered here more intensely and at greater length. The noun χάρισμα ("gift," "favor bestowed") is used by Paul in Romans and his other letters in a number of ways: (1) of God's gifts of righteousness and eternal life through Christ Jesus,[74] (2) of God's special gifts given to his people, both individually and corporately, for the building up of his church,[75] (3) of God's gifts of celibacy and marriage,[76] and (4) of the gift of an

---

70. Cf. the use of γάρ in the following verses in Romans: 1:18; 2:25; 4:3, 9; 5:7; 12:3; 14:5.

71. Cf. 1 Thess 2:8: "we were delighted to share (second aorist infinitive μεταδοῦναι) with you not only the gospel of God but also our own lives"; Eph 4:28: "so as to be able to share (present infinitive μεταδιδόναι) with those in need"; see also Rom 12:8; Luke 3:11.

72. Wedderburn, *Reasons for Romans*, 98 (italics throughout the quote are his).

73. *Ibid.*; see also Jervis, *The Purpose of Romans*, 103.

74. Cf. Rom 5:15-16; 6:23.

75. Cf. Rom 12:6; 1 Cor 12:4, 9, 28, 30-31.

76. Cf. 1 Cor 7:7.

office in the church, which is mediated by the laying on of hands.[77] Likewise, the adjective πνευματικός ("spiritual," "pertaining to the spirit") is used by Paul in several diverse ways: (1) of the Mosaic law given by God at Mount Sinai,[78] (2) of the blessings given by God to Israel,[79] (3) of the food and water that God supplied to the Israelites in the wilderness,[80] (4) of the "rock" that followed the Israelites in the wilderness, "which rock was Christ,"[81] (5) of Jesus, "the second man from heaven,"[82] (6) of songs sung to the Lord / God,[83] (7) of the "wisdom and understanding" given by God's Holy Spirit,[84] (8) of Christians who live by the guidance of the Holy Spirit, and not by their own "fleshly" desires or legal understandings,[85] (9) of special gifts given to God's people by the Spirit for the building up of the church,[86] and even (10) of "spiritual forces of evil in the heavenly realms" that are in constant warfare against the people of God.[87] So close in meaning are the noun χάρισμα ("gracious gift" or "favor") and the substantival use of the adjective πνευματικός ("spiritual blessing" or "gift") that they are, in fact, sometimes used by Paul interchangeably.[88] Yet Rom 1:11 is the only place in Paul's letters where the noun χάρισμα and the adjective πνευματικόν are brought together into the one expression "spiritual gift." And this quite unique collocation of terms, combined with the neuter indefinite pronoun τι ("some," "a certain"), has been variously interpreted.

What was this "some [or 'a certain'] spiritual gift" that Paul wanted to share with his addressees? At the end of the nineteenth century William Sanday and Arthur Headlam declared:

> St. Paul has in his mind the kind of gifts — partly what we should call natural and partly transcending the ordinary workings of nature — described in I Cor. xii-xiv; Rom. xii.6ff. Some, probably most, of these gifts he possessed in an eminent degree himself (I Cor. xiv.18), and he was assured that when he came to Rome he would be able to give the Christians there the fullest benefit of them (Rom. xv.29).[89]

Otto Michel argued that here in Rom 1:11 Paul speaks of "some spiritual gift" in order to legitimize himself in the eyes of certain πνευματικοί in the Christian

---

77. Cf. 1 Tim 4:14; 2 Tim 1:6.
78. Rom 7:14.
79. Rom 15:27.
80. 1 Cor 10:3-4a.
81. 1 Cor 10:4b.
82. 1 Cor 15:46-47.
83. Eph 5:19; Col 3:16.
84. Col 1:9.
85. 1 Cor 2:15; 3:1; Gal 6:1.
86. 1 Cor 12:1; 14:1, 37.
87. Eph 6:12.
88. Esp. in 1 Cor 12:1–14:40.
89. Sanday and Headlam, *Romans*, 21.

congregations at Rome, though without acknowledging the validity of their claims.[90] While J. K. Parratt, expressing what is certainly a minority view, has proposed that Paul's reference to a "spiritual gift" that he wanted to share with the Christians in Rome probably refers to an office in the church that was mediated by the laying on of hands, which he as an authorized apostle wanted to do in appointing some Christians at Rome to.[91]

Most commentators today, however, understand the expression "spiritual gift" in a more general sense, and so argue that it connotes either (or perhaps both): (1) one of the gifts mentioned in Rom 12:6-8 and 1 Cor 12:8-10, though "since elsewhere Paul lays stress on the variety of such gifts it is hardly profitable here to inquire what precise gift he may have had in mind,"[92] or (2) "a blessing or benefit to be bestowed on the Christians in Rome by God through Paul's presence."[93] And some have understood the indefinite pronoun τι ("some," "a certain") as suggesting that "what gift Paul may want to share with the Romans cannot be specified until he sees what their needs may be."[94]

Yet there is also a growing realization of another understanding of what Paul meant by "some spiritual gift" here in Rom 1:11. That other understanding seems to have been first proposed by James Denney in 1900:

No doubt, in substance, Paul imparts his spiritual gift through this epistle: what he wished to do for the Romans was to further their comprehension of the purpose of God in Jesus Christ — a purpose the breadth and bearings of which were yet but imperfectly understood.[95]

And that interpretation has been partially accepted, though somewhat tentatively, by Joseph Fitzmyer in his Anchor Bible commentary of 1993, who — after saying that Paul probably had in mind (1) some of the *charisms* of 1 Corinthians 12 and (2) his own presence among the Christians at Rome — offers a further possibility:

It may be, however, that Paul also intends his very writing of Romans to be a way of passing on to the Christians of Rome some spiritual gift. That is, his plan to visit Rome also supplies a motivation for his writing of Romans. This is then a way of discharging his apostolic and missionary obligation, as he writes this letter. He is sharing the gospel, as he says in 1 Thess 2:8, and in due time he will share himself.[96]

90. Michel, *An die Römer*, 82.
91. J. K. Parratt, "Romans i.11 and Galatians iii.5 — Pauline Evidence for the Laying On of Hands?" *ExpT* 79 (1967-68) (arguing from his reading of the use of χάρισμα in 1 Tim 4:14 and 2 Tim 1:6).
92. So, e.g., Barrett, *Romans*, 25.
93. So, e.g., Cranfield, *Romans*, 1.79.
94. So Moo, *Romans*, 60.
95. Denney, *Romans* (EGT), 2.588.
96. Fitzmyer, *Romans*, 248.

James Denney's understanding of Paul's "spiritual gift" here in Rom 1:11 has been fully espoused by Gordon Fee, who argues that Paul is not talking here about some "gifting" by the Spirit, as in Rom 12:6-8 and 1 Cor 12:8-10, but about the present letter as a "Spirit gift" sent to believers at Rome in lieu of a personal visit.[97] Or as Gordon Fee has set out his position in more explicit terms:

> In its present context, and especially in light of the letter as a whole, the "Spirit gift" that he most likely wishes to share with them is his understanding of the gospel that in Christ Jesus God has created from among Jews and Gentiles one people for himself, apart from Torah. This is the way they are to be "strengthened" by Paul's coming, and this surely is the "fruit" he wants to have among them when he comes (v. 13). If so, then in effect our present letter functions as his "Spirit gifting" for them. This is what he would impart if he were there in person: this is what he now "shares" since he cannot presently come to Rome.[98]

I agree with Denney and Fee in their understanding of "some spiritual gift" as having reference to Paul's letter to the Roman Christians, either in its entirety or with particular reference to its central thrust. Likewise, I agree with Denney that "what he [Paul] wished to do for the Romans was to further their comprehension of the purpose of God in Jesus Christ — a purpose the breadth and bearings of which were yet but imperfectly understood."[99] And I agree with Fee that what Paul "most likely wishes to share with them is his understanding of the gospel"[100] — that is, as I understand Paul's desire as expressed in this verse, to share with the Christians at Rome the Christian message as he had proclaimed it in his mission to Gentiles, which form of the gospel message he calls "my gospel" in 2:16 and 16:25.

I demur, however, with respect to Fee's traditional understanding of the focus of Paul's message in Romans. For rather than understand the letter's focus or central thrust to be set out in 1:16–4:25, which can be characterized as a declaration that "in Christ Jesus God has created from among Jews and Gentiles one people for himself, apart from Torah,"[101] I propose that the focus of Romans is to be found in the theological exposition of 5:1–8:39, which highlights the themes of "peace" and "reconciliation" with God, the antithesis of "death" and "life," and the relationships of being "in Christ" and "in the Spirit" — together with the corollary ethical exhortations of 12:1-21 and 13:8-14, which set out a Christian love ethic that is integrally related to the theological exposition of chs. 5–8. Further, I suggest that the neuter indefinite pronoun τι ("some," "a certain") does not express uncertainty about what Paul wants to say. Rather, it

---

97. Fee, *God's Empowering Presence,* 486-89.
98. *Ibid.,* 488-89.
99. Quoting again Denney, *Romans* (EGT), 2.588.
100. Quoting again Fee, *God's Empowering Presence,* 488.
101. *Ibid.*

should be seen as stemming from the apostle's natural reticence to spell out with any greater explicitness in this thanksgiving section of his letter (vv. 8-12) what he wants to say until he has had the opportunity (1) to build the case negatively against any reliance on "works of the law" (as in 1:16–3:20), (2) to clarify and develop certain basic Jewish Christian convictions regarding "righteousness," "faith," and "faithfulness" (as in his positive statements of 3:21–4:25), and (3) to explicate his own form of Christian proclamation to the Gentile world (as in 5:1–8:39). And it is on the foundation of these proposals that all the "exegetical comments" that follow in this commentary will be based.

The second statement of 1:11-12 begins with the expression τοῦτο ἔστιν ("that is") and the postpositive connective δέ (a mildly adversative "but," though here probably best translated simply "and"), which together signal an explication. So this second statement is meant to clarify and expand on the immediately preceding statement.

But what did Paul have in mind when he spoke of being "mutually encouraged by each other's faith" and then emphasizing the reciprocal nature of that encouragement by the addition of the phrase "both yours and mine"? The language, while suggestive, is considerably compressed. Later in the body closing (or, "apostolic parousia") section of 15:14-32 it will be unpacked to mean (1) Paul's sharing with his Christian addressees at Rome the gospel message that he proclaimed in his Gentile mission (15:14-22), which he believed they needed to understand and accept since they were predominantly Gentile believers in Jesus themselves, and (2) their readiness to assist him in his proposed missionary outreach to Gentiles in Spain and its environs in the western portion of the Roman Empire (15:23-24, 32b), which would include both their prayers and their financial support, much as the church at Antioch of Syria had prayed for and assisted him throughout his ministry in the eastern part of the empire.

It is these two statements at the end of his thanksgiving section that provided Christians at Rome with a compact form of Paul's primary agenda and his major concerns for what he will write in the large central portion, that is, the body middle, of his letter. And though the apostle's statements in 1:11-12 have often been treated rather superficially by both past and present commentators, we argue that these two verses are, in fact, of very great importance if we are ever to gain a proper understanding of the apostle's purpose (or purposes) in writing to the Christians at Rome and of the course and development of his argument in his letter.

BIBLICAL THEOLOGY

While often treated hesitantly with respect to its extent, uncertainly with respect to its nature, and superficially with respect to its content, the thanksgiving of 1:8-12 actually contains a number of statements of importance having to do with (1) the situation of the believers in Jesus at Rome, (2) Paul's attitude toward them, (3) what the apostle considered most important in his own ministry, (4) his prayers for his addressees, and (5) his primary purpose and major concern in writing to them. Some of these matters have significance for the construction of a biblical theology and some give guidance for the contextualization of the Christian gospel today, whereas others provide a context for a better understanding of what Paul writes later in his letter.

The fact that Paul begins this thanksgiving section of Romans with the affirmations "First of all, in truth, I thank my God through Jesus Christ for all of you" (1:8) and "For God is my witness . . . how I constantly remember you at all times in my prayers" (1:9-10a) suggests that he was conscious of some suspicions and a certain degree of alienation directed against him on the part of the Christians at Rome. Both he and they appear to have been well aware of differences between the content and form of the Christian faith as expressed in the Christian congregations of Rome, which had been influenced by the theology and religious language of Jewish Christianity at Jerusalem, and the Christian message as Paul proclaimed it in his Gentile mission, which he seems to have consciously attempted to contextualize for his Gentile audiences. It may also have been that some of these differences were referred to in the reports that the Christians of Rome had received about Paul and his ministry, as well as in those that Paul received about them with respect to their theological perspectives, liturgical practices, religious language, and ethical lifestyle.

Paul, however, had no doubt about the authenticity of his Roman addressees' Christian faith — that is, their basic Christian convictions and their vital Christian experience. While the Christians at Rome had probably been extensively influenced by Jewish Christian theology, language, and practices, they were not, it seems, like the Judaizers who had infiltrated the churches of Galatia and attempted to divert Gentile believers in Jesus "into a different gospel (εἰς ἕτερον εὐαγγέλιον), which is not at all the same gospel (ὅ οὐκ ἔστιν ἄλλο)" as they had earlier accepted (Gal 1:6-7a). Paul and the Christians at Rome may have differed with respect to certain matters of theology, liturgy, language, and ethics. But whatever the nature of those matters, Paul was convinced regarding the allegiance of the Roman Christians to Jesus as Messiah and Lord. So he begins his letter by attempting to bridge whatever gap may have existed between them and him, first by asserting his thankfulness for them and then by assuring them of his repeated prayers on their behalf. It is not that "Paul flatters them by acknowledging their Christian commitment," as Joseph Fitzmyer has suggested somewhat in passing.[102] Rather, (1) Paul truly commends them for their allegiance to Christ, for which he is truly happy, and (2) he wants to begin his letter to them on the basis of what he and they have in common — that is, on their oneness as true believers in Jesus, whatever their differences.

102. Cf. Fitzmyer, *Spiritual Exercises,* 20.

As in the salutation of Romans,[103] so in the letter's thanksgiving: what Paul considered most important for the early Christian movement was "the gospel of his [God's] Son" (1:9). Paul's whole service for God, in fact, had as its focus "the gospel," with the content of that proclamation being "God's Son." So in the construction of any true Christian theology and in the expression of all real Christian service for God, it is of great importance that our historical investigations, critical insights, exegetical endeavors, theological formulations, sermonic statements, and pastoral counsel as Christians keep constantly to the fore "the good news" of "the gospel of God's Son." For that is what the Christian religion is all about. And while that primary focus has a great many legitimate implications for both the Christian church corporately and Christians personally — which implications need to be explicated and enacted for the "good news" of the Christian gospel to be adequately realized and appropriately contextualized — we as Christians must always keep to the fore and evaluate everything by "the gospel of God's Son."

But Paul was not just a theologian. Nor was he just a missionary evangelist. He was also a "pray-er" who earnestly sought God's will in his life and ministry and who asked for God's blessings for his converts, for believers in Jesus everywhere, and for all people in their various situations and circumstances.[104] He may not have had "prayer lists," as Archibald Robertson once ventured to propose.[105] He did, however, tell the Christians at Rome that he never omitted them in his prayers, and, further, that he was presently praying that "now at last by God's will the way may be opened for me to come to you" (1:9-10).

It is this aspect of Paul as a person of prayer, while often overlooked in our studies of the apostle and his writings, that needs always to be highlighted. For in the recognition that Paul was a man of prayer, there comes about also the growing realizations (1) that his dependence was on God, not on himself, and (2) that his strength and accomplishments came about because of the enablement and working of God's Spirit, and not just because of his own abilities or endeavors. And such a recognition is highly significant for the construction of a true Christian theology and for the transformational task of every biblical commentator in presenting the message of Scripture in a manner that is pertinent for the theology and life of the Christian church corporately and relevant for the understanding and living of Christians personally.

Yet every biblical theology must be rooted in the specific context in which its affirmations and statements have come to expression. That means for affirmations and statements drawn from Romans, due consideration must be given to the apostle's concerns and purposes when writing. And so what he writes in 1:11-12 — which verses, we have argued, set out in condensed fashion Paul's pri-

---

103. See our "Exegetical Comments" on 1:1 and 3-4; also our "Biblical Theology" section on 1:1-7.

104. Cf. R. N. Longenecker, "Prayer in the Pauline Letters."

105. Robertson, "Epistle to the Romans," 4.325.

mary purpose and major concern in wanting to visit the Christians at Rome, but also in writing to them in lieu of and in preparation for that visit — provides the context for what Paul writes later in his letter: "that I may share with you some spiritual gift to make you strong, that is, so that we may be mutually encouraged by each other's faith, both yours and mine."

CONTEXTUALIZATION FOR TODAY

In his thanksgiving of 1:8-12 Paul teaches Christians today a number of things about contextualizing the Christian message. Of prime importance is his emphasis on "the gospel," which has as its content "his [God's] Son," as being at the heart of all Christian proclamation and service. All too often we become so involved with the legitimate implications of the gospel that we tend to forget or minimize what lies at the heart of Christian conviction: the "good news" of what God has done historically though the person and work of his Son, Jesus Christ, and what he is doing today by way of application, illumination, and empowerment through the ministry of his Spirit.

Further, it is of great importance to note that Paul situates his own service for God in the context of worship (i.e., "worshipful service" or "service of worship") and that he speaks of that worshipful service as being done "wholeheartedly," "sincerely," or "with [his] whole being." Paul was not driven by personal ambition or aggrandizement. Rather, he viewed his preaching of the gospel and his missionary outreach to Gentiles as expressions of his worship of God. For consumed by the wonder of the gospel message, awed and empowered by a personal relationship with Christ, and humbled by the experience of reconciliation to God — all of which came about in response to the "good news" about the redemptive work of God's Son, who is rightly acclaimed as Israel's Messiah and humanity's Lord — he could not help but serve God wholeheartedly, sincerely, and with his whole being.

John Calvin has wisely said with respect to the contextualization of these emphases on "the gospel of his Son" and Paul's "wholehearted" service of worship:

> We deduce from this some useful teaching which ought to add no small encouragement to ministers of the Gospel when they hear that in preaching the Gospel they are rendering an acceptable and valuable service to God. Is there anything that should prevent them from doing so, when they know that their labors are so pleasing to God and approved by Him as to be considered an act of the highest worship?[106]

In many ways, Paul seems to have felt about his preaching much as the prophet Jeremiah did about his. For having been confronted by Christ on the

---

106. J. Calvin, *Romans*, in *Calvin's New Testament Commentaries*, 8.23.

Damascus Road and overwhelmed by the greatness of the "good news" that he was commissioned to proclaim — and despite all sorts of difficulties, afflictions, and dangers[107] — Paul, like Jeremiah of old, could say: "His word is in my heart like a burning fire, shut up in my bones, and I am weary of holding it in; indeed, I cannot."[108] And in comparable measure, though not the same circumstances, Christians today are to be encouraged by that same prophetic consciousness and motivated by that same wholehearted response in our worshipful service to God.

We can also, however, learn a number of lessons from the thanksgiving section of 1:8-12 about how our Christian service to God is to be carried out in our day and circumstances — with particular relevance for our own proclamation of the gospel and our contemporary attempts to express more adequately the implications of that gospel. One lesson is suggested by the very first sentence of Paul's epistolary thanksgiving: "I thank my God through Jesus Christ for all of you" (v. 8). It is a statement that expresses thankfulness for the Christians at Rome, commends them for what they and he hold in common, and indicates a desire to begin his discussions with them on that basis. There may have been, as we have proposed, a number of differences between the Roman Christians and Paul. But Paul, it seems evident, wanted to begin on the basis of common ground with his addressees, giving thanks for whatever he could give thanks for. And that is a lesson of great importance for all of us who possess a common humanity and profess a common Christian faith, whatever our differences.

It is true that at times Paul responded somewhat differently to those who opposed him — sometimes castigating them in caustic and virulent language,[109] at other times pleading with them in a self-deprecating and humble manner,[110] and at still other times taking a rather relaxed attitude toward them and their preaching.[111] In writing to the Christians at Rome, however, he recognized that he was speaking to true and earnest believers in Jesus with whom he was in basic agreement on the primary tenets of the Christian faith. Paul and his addressees may have differed with respect to their backgrounds, theological emphases, liturgical forms, lifestyles, and interests. For his addressees were dominantly Gentile Christians who, it seems, had been extensively influenced in their understanding and practice of the Christian religion by the Jewish Christianity of the "mother church" at Jerusalem, whereas he was a Jewish Christian who sought to contextualize "the truth of the gospel" in ways appropriate to Gentiles. Nonetheless, though different, they were united in commitment to Jesus and on the fundamental matters of the Christian faith. So Paul expresses his thankfulness for his addressees at Rome, acknowledging that their Christian faith has

107. Cf. 2 Cor 11:23-29.
108. Jer 20:9.
109. Cf. Gal 1:6-9; 5:12.
110. Cf. 2 Cor 10–13.
111. Cf. Phil 1:15-18; see R. N. Longenecker, "What Does It Matter?"

been widely reported — thereby beginning his letter to them on the basis of their mutual relationship to Jesus Christ and the gospel truths that they shared.

Further, it needs to be noted that Paul did not just (1) focus in his preaching on "the gospel," which has as its central theme the person and work of "his [God's] Son," (2) recognize his ministry as "worshipful service" to God, and so serve God "wholeheartedly," "sincerely," and "with his whole being," and (3) begin on the basis of common ground with his addressees, giving thanks for whatever he could give thanks for — all of which are vitally important matters for any Christian contextualization of the gospel today. He also (4) bathed all of his ministry in the context of prayer, (5) earnestly desired to have personal contact with those to whom he had been called by God to minister, by both a letter and a visit, (6) longed to share with them "some spiritual gift" that would strengthen them, and (7) wanted both himself and those to whom he ministered to be "mutually encouraged by each other's faith."

Paul well knew from his Jewish background, as well as from his Christian experience, that prayer is the lifeblood of religion, the indispensable factor in every form of piety and faith — that it (1) lies at the heart of all religious experience, (2) expresses in essence a person's deepest convictions about God, this world, human life, and all human relationships, and (3) reflects the vitality of a person's central convictions and controlling spirituality. Further, he was well aware that Christian ministry is all about "personal contact" with those to whom one is called by God to minister and desiring to share "some spiritual gift" that will strengthen them. And with respect to being "mutually encouraged by each other's faith," William Sanday and Arthur C. Headlam have aptly observed:

> We note of course the delicacy with which the Apostle suddenly checks himself in the expression of his desire to impart from his own fulness to the Roman Christians: he will not assume any airs of superiority, but meets them frankly upon their own level; if he has anything to confer upon them they in turn will confer an equivalent upon him.[112]

All these latter "more practical" matters are, in fact, just as important as the previous "more theoretical" matters for any truly valid contextualization of the Christian gospel today.

112. Sanday and Headlam, *Romans*, 21.

THE BODY SECTIONS OF THE LETTER

The body of Romans consists of three main parts: (1) a brief "body opening" (1:13-15), (2) an extensive "body middle" (1:16–15:13), which can be subdivided into four rather large sections (1:16–4:25; 5:1–8:39; 9:1–11:36; and 12:1–15:13), and (3) a "body closing" (15:14-32), which of late has been called an "apostolic parousia." The "body opening" of 1:13-15 and the "body closing" of 15:14-32 reflect a number of the usual conventions of ancient letter writing — as did also the "salutation" (1:1-7) and "thanksgiving" (1:8-12) at the beginning of Romans and as will the two "concluding" sections (15:33–16:16 and 16:17-27). The large "body middle" of 1:16–15:13 — except for a few vocatives of direct address, a few verbs of saying, and some disclosure formulas, which appear at certain strategic places in the presentation — contains very few of the usual epistolary features of the day. Rather, it is more amenable to rhetorical analysis, both diachronic and synchronic.

It may therefore be said with respect to its structure that Romans is a "concentrated theological and ethical argument" (1:16–15:13) that is enclosed in a "letter envelope" (1:1-15; 15:14–16:27).[1] This theological and ethical argument should most likely be understood rhetorically as a type of "protreptic message" of instruction and exhortation (λόγος προτρεπτικός), that is, a presentation intended to win someone over to a particular enterprise, way of understanding, or lifestyle by exposing the errors of an alternate view and demonstrating the truth claims of the author's position, with that protreptic message set within what may be called a "letter essay."[2]

---

1. So Talbert, *Romans*, 25, who rightly begins his commentary proper with this sentence — though wrongly, we believe, assigning 1:16-17 to the "letter envelope" rather than understanding these two verses as an important portion of the beginning of the "theological and ethical argument."

2. Cf. Introduction to the Commentary, 12-18 (on the epistolary and rhetorical features of Romans).

A. Body Opening

Commentators have often had difficulty in identifying the beginnings and endings of the various sections in certain NT letters and in understanding how one section relates to another. This has been true with respect to Paul's letter to the Christians at Rome — and particularly here in the identification of where the letter's "thanksgiving" ends and its "body opening" begins. Three positions with respect to the body opening of Romans have been taken. The most dominant view, which may be called "the traditional view," is that the thanksgiving of Romans ends at 1:15 and its body, thesis, or theme begins at 1:16.

This understanding is based primarily on a scanning of the contents of 1:1-17, attempting to observe where one topic ends and the next topic begins. There can be no doubt that a scan of the contents of Romans — or, for that matter, of any written material — is always of great importance for interpretation. But simply scanning a letter in order to note its changes of topic, apart from any more precise epistolary or rhetorical controls, all too often results in a rather high degree of subjectivity. And the fact that various commentators, on the basis of their scanning of the first seventeen verses of Romans, have proposed a number of differing positions regarding relations between the materials of 1:1-7, 8-9, 10-12, 13-15, and 16-17 suggests that there has been a rather large measure of subjectivity in many of their views.

Most interpretations of 1:1-17 have been structured along the lines of (1) a "Prescript" or "Salutation" in 1:1-7, (2) an "Introduction" or "Thanksgiving" in 1:8-15, and (3) a "Theme" or "Thesis Statement" in 1:16-17. Among the more prominent proponents of this view, both in earlier days and today, are such commentators as Frédéric Godet,[3] William Sanday and Arthur Headlam,[4] Theodor Zahn,[5] Kingsley Barrett,[6] John Murray,[7] James Dunn,[8] Douglas

---

3. Godet, *Romans*, vol. 1 (1880).
4. Sanday and Headlam, *Romans* (1895).
5. Zahn, *An die Römer* (1910).
6. Barrett, *Romans* (1957).
7. Murray, *Romans*, vol. 1 (1959).
8. Dunn, *Romans*, vol. 1 (1988).

Moo,[9] and Ben Witherington.[10] Variations within such a traditional understanding have also occurred both in the identification of the various units and with respect to how the contents of those respective units have been captioned. Charles Cranfield, for example, has captioned the first section of 1:1-7 as "Superscription, Address and Salutation," identified the second section as appearing in 1:8-16a and captioned it "Paul and the Roman Church," and identified the third section, 1:16b-17, as "The Theme of the Epistle."[11] Ernst Käsemann spoke of a "Prescript" in 1:1-7, a "Proem" in 1:8-15, and the letter's "Theme" in 1:16-17.[12] Joseph Fitzmyer analyzed 1:1-17 in terms of four units of material and captioned them: "Address and Greeting" in 1:1-7, "Thanksgiving" in 1:8-9, "Proem" in 1:10-15, and "Theme Announced" in 1:16-17.[13] All these proposals, however, are only variations of a traditional understanding of the structure of 1:1-17, and each of them is similarly based on a particular commentator's scanning of its contents. Further, and most important for our purposes here, all these proposals have also understood 1:13-15 as being closely connected with what immediately precedes it and so view these three verses as part of the Introduction or Thanksgiving of 1:8-15 — or, as Joseph Fitzmyer has suggested, part of the Proem that expresses "Paul's desire to come to Rome" in 1:10-15.

An "alternative view" is that the thanksgiving section of Romans ends at 1:17 and the body begins at 1:18. This understanding is based, in large measure, on analyses of the thanksgiving sections found elsewhere in the Pauline corpus, with those analyses then applied to the opening sections of Romans.

It was Paul Schubert who in 1939 first pointed out that the thanksgiving sections of Paul's letters evidence a rather distinct epistolary form that was used in antiquity to set out particular literary functions, and so should be viewed not as merely introductory materials of a rather general sort but as reflecting fairly well established epistolary conventions of the day, which Paul used in expressing his own purposes and concerns.[14] But while Schubert noted that a typical Pauline thanksgiving usually came to a close with what he called an "eschatological climax," he conceded that such a climax was "wanting" in the thanksgiving of Romans.[15] So he proposed that the material of 1:16-17 should be seen as an appropriate substitute — for the terms εὐαγγέλιον ("gospel") and σωτηρία ("salvation"), as well as the phrase δικαιοσύνη θεοῦ . . . ἀποκαλύπτεται ("the righteousness of God . . . is revealed"), which appear in these two verses (as well as elsewhere in Paul's letters), have "eschatological

9. Moo, *Romans* (1996).
10. Witherington, *Romans* (2004).
11. Cranfield, *Romans*, vol. 1 (1975).
12. Käsemann, *Romans* (1980).
13. Fitzmyer, *Romans* (1993).
14. Cf. our earlier treatment of Schubert's thesis in the thanksgiving section of this commentary.
15. Schubert, *Pauline Thanksgivings*, 5.

significance."[16] And many have generally agreed with him, though they have often also expressed some hesitation.[17]

Another "alternative understanding" of matters with respect to the structure of this early portion of Romans is that the thanksgiving section of the letter ends at 1:12 and its body opening begins at 1:13. This position is based mainly on studies of epistolary conventions in the Hellenistic world generally and in other NT letters in particular. It is founded, in the main, on the phrase οὐ θέλω δὲ ὑμᾶς ἀγνοεῖν . . . ὅτι ("I do not want you to be unaware . . . that"), which was a standard "disclosure formula" often used to begin new sections of ancient Greek letters, including other NT letters, and which appears at the beginning of 1:13 in Romans. In addition, it notes that the vocative ἀδελφοί ("brothers and sisters"), which is found frequently in Paul's letters at the start of various new sections of material, is included within this disclosure formula in 1:13.

Terence Mullins in 1964, based on his analyses of nineteen epistolary papyri and a number of NT letters, showed how the typical Greek disclosure formula consisted of four features: (1) the verb θέλω ("I wish," "want," or "desire"), (2) a noetic verb used in the infinitive (e.g., the present infinitive γινώσκειν, the perfect infinitive εἰδέναι, or the present negative infinitive ἀγνοεῖν, all of which have reference to one's knowledge or lack of knowledge), (3) the person or persons addressed cast in the accusative case (as here in 1:13 by the use of the second person plural accusative pronoun ὑμᾶς, "you"), and (4) the information being given frequently, though not invariably, by means of a ὅτι clause — with, sometimes, the recipient(s) of the letter addressed also in the vocative case (as here in 1:13 by the use of the vocative ἀδελφοί, "brothers and sisters").[18] And since all four of these features appear at the beginning of 1:13, it has been argued that we have here a disclosure formula (1) that functions as a transition from Paul's earlier epistolary salutation and thanksgiving to a body opening section and (2) thus serves to introduce the four body middle subsections of the letter.[19]

It is somewhat difficult to make a definitive decision with respect to the limits, function, and significance of the material in 1:13-15, for all three of the positions above are to some extent supportable. The "traditional" understanding (i.e., view 1 above), which is based primarily on a scanning of contents, understands all of the eight verses of 1:8-15 as comprising the letter's epistolary "Introduction" or "Thanksgiving." Important among the reasons usually cited in support of this view are (1) that there is an obvious beginning of a new section at 1:8, and (2) that it is necessary to view 1:16-17 as separate from what precedes it,

---

16. Schubert, *Pauline Thanksgivings*, 33.

17. Cf., e.g., O'Brien, *Introductory Thanksgivings*, 200-202; Gamble, *Textual History*, 90; see also the second edition of F. O. Francis and J. P. Sampley, eds., *Pauline Parallels* (Philadelphia: Fortress, 1984), 326.

18. Cf. Mullins, "Disclosure."

19. Cf., e.g., J. T. Sanders, "Transition from Opening Epistolary Thanksgiving to Body," 360; White, *Form and Function of the Body of the Greek Letter*, 95; Jewett, "Ambassadorial Letter," 12-14; and Toit, "Persuasion in Romans 1:1-17."

for the phrase "first for the Jew, then for the Gentile," which appears in 1:16 and twice in 2:9-10, sets up an *inclusio* that frames the textual unit of 1:16–2:10 and therefore requires that 1:16-17 be firmly associated with what follows and not with what precedes.[20] Yet the legitimacy of some of the arguments usually given in support of this position (as discussed more fully below) may be disputed — such as (1) that 1:13-15 is so closely "conjoined with the preceding" material of 1:8-12 and so obviously "follows on directly from vv. 11 and 12" that it cannot be separated from what precedes it,[21] or (2) that 1:13-15 "is functionally inappropriate as the opening of a letter-body, for it does not introduce matters with which the body-middle is concerned."[22] Further, and much more structurally important, such an understanding fails to take seriously into consideration the disclosure formula at the beginning of 1:13.

The first of the "alternative" understandings of the opening sections of Romans (i.e., view 2 above), which is based, in the main, on analyses of the thanksgiving sections in many of the apostle's other letters, also considers 1:13-15 as inseparably bound to what precedes it in 1:8-12 — and in some cases, as in Schubert's original proposal, to what follows it in 1:16-17. But that view is seriously deficient in its failure to appreciate Paul's use of a disclosure formula at the beginning of 1:13.

The third understanding of these matters (as cited above), which views the thanksgiving of Romans as ending at the close of 1:12 and the letter's body opening as beginning at 1:13, builds principally on the disclosure formula at the beginning of 1:13, οὐ θέλω (δὲ) ὑμᾶς ἀγνοεῖν, ἀδελφοί ("I do not want you to be unaware, brothers and sisters"). This same formula signals the start of a body opening in 2 Cor 1:8 and indicates the beginning of distinctive units of material in Rom 11:25; 1 Cor 10:1; 12:1; and 1 Thess 4:13. Likewise, similar disclosure formulas appear elsewhere in Paul's letters: γνωρίζω / γνωρίζομεν (γάρ/δέ) ὑμῖν, ἀδελφοί ("I [or 'we'] want you to know, brothers and sisters"), which signals the start of a body opening in Gal 1:11 and indicates the beginning of distinctive units of material in 1 Cor 12:3; 15:1; and 2 Cor 8:1, and the formula γινώσκειν [δὲ] ὑμᾶς, ἀδελφοί ("[I want you] to know, brothers and sisters"), which signals the start of a body opening in Phil 1:12.

Prima facie evidence, therefore, unless proven otherwise by other data, suggests that the disclosure formula of 1:13 is to be understood as signaling the start of the body opening of Romans. And it is this understanding of the body opening as beginning at 1:13 that is proposed in this commentary and will be more fully explicated in what follows. That the body opening comes to a close at the end of 1:15 will be defended later in our comments on 1:15 and 1:16-17.

---

20. See our later discussion on "Form/Structure/Setting" in the commentary proper with respect to 1:13-15 and 1:16-17; cf. esp. Bassler, *Divine Impartiality*, 123-28.

21. So, e.g., O'Brien, *Introductory Thanksgivings*, 202 n. 17b.

22. So, e.g., Jervis, *The Purpose of Romans*, 106; see also 105.

III. A Brief Introduction to Paul's Protreptic Message (1:13-15)

TRANSLATION

1:13I do not want you to be unaware, brothers and sisters, that I have many times planned to come to you (but have been prevented from doing so until now) in order that I might have a harvest among you, just as I have had among other Gentiles. 14I am obligated both to Greeks and to barbarians, both to the wise and to the foolish. 15That is why I am eager to preach the gospel also to you who are at Rome.

TEXTUAL NOTES

1:13 The expression οὐ θέλω ("I do not want") is attested by the vast majority of MSS: by P²⁶ᵛⁱᵈ and uncials ℵ A B C Dᶜ P Ψ, as well as by minuscules 1175 1739 (Category I), 256 1506 1881 2127 2464 (Category II), and 6 104 1241 (Category III). It is also reflected in versions it^ar, mon vg syr^(p), h cop^(sa), bo and supported by Origen^lat Chrysostom. It is to be preferred to οὐκ οἴομαι ("I do not think," "suppose," or "expect"), which appears only in the Western textual witnesses (uncials D* G, versions it^d, e, g, and Ambrosiaster Pelagius) with the corruption οὐκ οἴσμαι being even more limited (D^d D^absl). The plural οὐ θέλομεν ("we do not want") appears only in minuscule 81 (Category II).

15 The phrase τοῖς ἐν Ῥώμῃ ("those at Rome") is attested by P²⁶ᵛⁱᵈ and uncials ℵ A B C D P Ψ, as well as by minuscules 33 1175 1739 (Category I) and 81 1506 1881 1962 2127 (Category II). It is also reflected in versions it^ar, b, d, mon, o vg syr^p, h, pal cop^sa, bo, and in Origen^lat 1/2 Chrysostom. It is, therefore, to be accepted. Its omission by ninth-century uncial G (012), also reflected in it^g and the Latin translation of Origen^lat 1/2, was in all likelihood in order to give the letter a more general application (see comments on ἐν Ῥώμῃ at 1:7).

FORM/STRUCTURE/SETTING

There are certainly some connections between the material of 1:13-15 and the thanksgiving in 1:8-12 — principally in that (1) 1:13 picks up from an earnestly desired visit to Christians at Rome that was mentioned earlier in 1:10, and (2) 1:15 clarifies somewhat what was referred to earlier in 1:11-12. Most commentators, therefore, have understood 1:13-15 to be a continuation of the thanksgiving section. Our thesis, however, is that here in 1:13-15 Paul moves beyond his prayers and desires as set out in the thanksgiving section and provides a brief "body opening" or "introduction" to what he wants to present throughout the central "body middle" of his letter — particularly as will be set out in the second section of the body middle (5:1–8:39) but also as will be presented in the first section (1:16–4:25) and in all that follows in the third and fourth sections (9:1–11:33; 12:1–15:13).

A common objection against identifying 1:13-15 as the body opening of Romans is that the material of these verses is so closely "conjoined with the preceding" material of 1:8-12 and so obviously "follows on directly from vv. 11 and 12" that it cannot be separated from what precedes it.[23] But as Peter Stuhlmacher has noted, the joining of 1:8-12 and 1:13-15 as a single unit of material sets up an unwarranted contradiction between what Paul writes at the close of the body in 15:14-32 and what he writes here in 1:13-15.[24] For in the body closing (or "apostolic parousia") of 15:14-32 "he declares with much pride that he has always considered it his honor to preach the gospel only in those places where no other missionary before him has yet been; in his mission he does not want to build on a foundation laid by others (15:20f.)," whereas in 1:13-15 he speaks of his desire "to have a harvest among you, just as I have had among the other Gentiles" and "to preach the gospel also to you who are at Rome."[25]

As Stuhlmacher has set out the problem:

> If one sees Rom. 1:13-15 merely to be the continuation of 1:10-12, and then (with Wilckens, among others) translates v. 15 to read, "So I am ready, as far as it concerns me, also to preach the gospel to you in Rome," a serious contradiction then exists with 15:20ff. While Paul boasts there of a missionary practice which excludes building further upon a foundation laid by others, he declares in 1:15 that his intention in Rome is exactly this very practice.[26]

But "the contradiction is resolved," Stuhlmacher declares, when one understands that different concerns are at work in Paul's words of 1:11-12 and his words of 1:13-15. In the former, "Paul is merely speaking of his desire to come to an agreement concerning the faith during his visit with the Christians in Rome," which hope he will express again in 15:24. In 1:13-15, however, Paul states that he

> does not desire to visit the Roman Christians in order to preach the gospel to them anew. Rather, he desires with his letter and his personal visit to cre-

---

23. As noted above, quoting O'Brien, *Introductory Thanksgivings*, 202 n. 17b.
24. Stuhlmacher, *Romans*, 26-27.
25. *Ibid.*, 26.
26. *Ibid.*

ate clarity concerning his gospel (disputed all the way to Rome) and in this way to secure the support of the Roman church for his mission plans, with their goal of reaching Spain (cf. Rom. 15:22-24). Verses 16 and 17 indicate that the Pauline gospel is disputed, but Paul is determined to stand by the message with which he was commissioned.[27]

There may be some lack of clarity in Stuhlmacher's statements about Paul's purposes and concerns in 1:13-15 vis-à-vis the thanksgiving section that precedes it. But Stuhlmacher certainly must be credited as perceptive in (1) noting that a contradiction is created when one views "Rom. 1:13-15 merely to be the continuation of 1:10-12,"[28] (2) identifying a difference between Paul's concerns in 1:13-15 vis-à-vis what he prays for in 1:10 and wants to accomplish in 1:11-12, and (3) understanding Paul's major purpose "with his letter and his personal visit" as being "to create clarity concerning his gospel (disputed all the way to Rome) and in this way to secure the support of the Roman church for his mission plans, with their goal of reaching Spain."[29]

It is simply not true, however, as many have claimed, that 1:13-15 "is functionally inappropriate as the opening of a letter-body, for it does not introduce matters with which the body-middle is concerned."[30] Rather, in these verses Paul speaks (1) of God's purposes as being fulfilled in his Gentile mission and his relations with the Christians at Rome (v. 13b, with the first person singular, aorist passive formulation "I have been prevented from doing so" understood as "God hindered me from it," as is often the case in Paul's letters), and (2) of his own desire — even, in fact, his obligation — to minister to Christians at Rome, in order, as he says, "that I might have a harvest among you, just as I have had among other Gentiles" (vv. 13c-14). Even more important, however, by way of introducing what follows, Paul announces his great desire to proclaim the gospel to his addressees, which by his use of the aorist infinitive middle form εὐαγγελίσασθαι should undoubtedly be understood to mean his own contextualization of the gospel message among Gentiles (v. 15).

What, in effect, Paul is announcing here at the climax of his letter's body opening, which serves to introduce the central feature of what he writes in the letter's body middle, is his own distinctive contextualization of the Christian gospel as contained in 5:1–8:39, with its ethical corollary in the christological exhortations of 12:1–15:13 — which is what he proclaimed to pagan Gentiles in his evangelistic endeavors throughout the eastern part of the Roman Empire. It is this contextualization of the gospel to the Gentiles that he wants to share with his predominantly Gentile Christian addressees at Rome. He has no doubt that what he calls "my gospel" (2:16; 16:25) will strengthen them. More specifically,

---

27. Stuhlmacher, *Romans*, 26.
28. *Ibid.*
29. *Ibid.*, 27.
30. As noted above, quoting Jervis, *The Purpose of Romans*, 106; see also p. 105.

his hope is that the Christians at Rome will acknowledge the legitimacy of his contextualization of the gospel message, and on the basis of that acceptance will support him in his outreach to Gentiles in the western part of the empire.

EXEGETICAL COMMENTS

Having spoken of his prayers for the Roman Christians (1:9b-10a) and of his desire to visit them (1:10b), Paul now goes further to address the question: Why had he never come to Rome in his Christian mission to Gentiles, for Rome was the capital of the empire and the center of the world? Perhaps some of his friends and relatives living at Rome (as later identified in 16:3-15) had written to tell him that this question was being asked by some of the Christians of that city. They may even have reported that certain damning implications with respect to his person and his ministry were being drawn from his having never come to Rome — such as, (1) that he was a loner who chose to remain personally aloof from the Jerusalem apostles and from the believers in Jesus at Rome, (2) that he was disinterested in the state of the Christian faith in the capital city, (3) that he was negligent in carrying out his Gentile mission — or, even more damaging to his reputation, (4) that he was ashamed to proclaim his version of the Christian message in a city where there lived those who really knew the Christian gospel because of their relations with the mother church at Jerusalem. So Paul begins the body opening of his letter to Rome with his answer to the question as to why he had not earlier come to Rome.

1:13 The body opening of Paul's letter to Rome begins with the statement οὐ θέλω δὲ ὑμᾶς ἀγνοεῖν . . . ὅτι ("I do not want you to be unaware . . . that"), which is a typical "disclosure formula" of ancient Greek letters. Because of its negative οὐ and its alpha-privative ἀγνοεῖν (with such a double negative being proper in Greek but not in English), Paul's words here are probably best expressed in English positively as "I want you to know that."[31] Included within this disclosure formula is the vocative of address ἀδελφοί (inclusively understood as "brothers and sisters"), as it is also in all of the other ten disclosure formulas of Paul's letters. This is the first appearance of ἀδελφοί in Romans. It is used again in Romans at 11:25 as part of another disclosure formula and in 7:1; 12:1; 15:14; and 16:17 at the start of various sections, thereby suggesting that it may only reflect an epistolary convention of the day. But Paul also uses ἀδελφοί in Romans at 7:4; 8:12; 10:1; 14:10, 13, 15, 21; 15:30; and 16:14, 23 to highlight "the closeness experienced by those who were followers of the risen Christ and a sense of the intimate relations that Paul has with those he so addresses."[32]

---

31. Cf. the cases of a similar double negative in Rom 11:25; 1 Cor 10:1; 12:1; 2 Cor 1:8, and 1 Thess 4:13; see also cognate formulations in Gal 1:11; 1 Cor 12:3; 15:1; 2 Cor 8:1; and Phil 1:12.

32. Fitzmyer, *Romans*, 249.

Jews spoke of other Jews as "brothers."[33] Likewise, members of Greek religious communities designated one another as "brothers."[34] The practice in the early church of calling other believers in Jesus "brothers" (or inclusively, "brothers and sisters") may have derived, in part, from both Jewish and Greek usages. More particularly, however, it stemmed from Jesus having called his disciples "brothers" because of their relationship to him and their doing the Father's will.[35]

Paul, too, views believers in Jesus as ἀδελφοί, "brothers and sisters," because of their common relationship to Christ.[36] And on the basis of this shared relationship, he goes on in his use of ἀδελφοί to stress the affectionate and mutually helpful attitude of Christians to one another in the family of God.[37] Even in his letter to confused and wayward converts in the province of Galatia, amidst tones of sternness and severity, Paul addresses them as "brothers and sisters"[38] — thereby reminding them of his and their shared relationship in the family of God, even though some of his addressees were beginning to forget it.

The explanation that Paul gives of why he had not come to Rome before is expressed in the words πολλάκις προεθέμην ἐλθεῖν πρὸς ὑμᾶς, καὶ ἐκωλύθην ἄχρι τοῦ δεῦρο ("I have many times planned to come to you, but I have been prevented from doing so until now"). The first statement contains the first person, aorist, indicative, middle verb προεθέμην (from προτίθημι, "plan," "purpose," "intend"), which is stronger than the verbs βούλειν or θέλειν (which both meant simply "wish," "want," or "desire") — thereby suggesting that Paul had on a number of occasions actually planned to come to Rome and visit the Christians there. And the adverb πολλάκις ("many times," "frequently," "often"), which is in the emphatic position at the beginning of the statement, strengthens the supposition that he had, indeed, often made plans to visit them.

The conjunction καί at the beginning of the second statement is to be understood not as a mere connective, nor as explicative or ascensive in nature, but as adversative ("but," "and yet," "yet for all that") — most likely reflecting Semitic influence from the Hebrew copula w.[39] The first person, aorist, indicative, passive verb ἐκωλύθην (from κωλύειν, "to hinder," "prevent," "forbid") implies that it was not any disinterest or reluctance on the apostle's part that prevented him from coming to Rome earlier, but that something else (or perhaps someone else) kept him from such a visit.

Paul speaks in 1 Thess 2:18 of Satan (ὁ Σατανᾶς) as having hindered him from returning to Thessalonica, and Luke recounts in Acts 16:6-7 how the Holy

33. Cf. Lev 19:17; Deut 1:16; 15:2-3, 7-11; 2 Macc 1:1; Tob 5:5, 9, 11; 6:7, 14; Josephus, *War* 2.122; Acts 2:29; 3:17; 7:2, 26; Rom 9:3.
34. See *M-M*, 9.
35. Cf. Mark 3:31-35; see also Matt 23:8.
36. Cf. Rom 8:29; see also 8:16-17.
37. Cf. Rom 14:10, 13, 15; 1 Cor 5:11; 6:5-8; 8:11-13; 15:58; 2 Cor 1:1; 2:13.
38. See Gal 1:11; 3:15; 4:12, 28, 31; 5:11, 13; 6:1, 18.
39. Cf. *Moule*, 178; see also Luke 7:35; 18:7.

Spirit (τὸ ἅγιον πνεῦμα) or "the Spirit of Jesus" (τὸ πνεῦμα Ἰησοῦ) prevented Paul from preaching the gospel in the Roman province of Asia. Here, however, Paul seems to have had in mind his missionary activities in the eastern part of the Roman Empire that kept him from going to Rome any earlier.[40] But what had previously prevented him ἄχρι τοῦ δεῦρο ("until now"), using the improper preposition ἄχρι ("until") with the articular adverb τοῦ δεῦρο as a substantive in the genitive case ("the present"), was no longer a factor — and so he now wants to visit the Christians at Rome on his way to Spain.

The purpose statement ἵνα τινὰ καρπὸν σχῶ καὶ ἐν ὑμῖν καθὼς καὶ ἐν τοῖς λοιποῖς ἔθνεσιν ("in order that I might have a harvest among you, just as I have had among other Gentiles as well") expresses what was always Paul's reason for wanting to visit the Christians at Rome. The noun καρπός ("fruit") is an agricultural term used among Jews (1) as a euphemism for "offspring" or "children"[41] and (2) as a locution for the praise-offering.[42] It was also used widely in antiquity, however, as a metaphor for any "result," "outcome," "product," "gain," or "profit."[43]

Paul's use of "fruit" later in Romans as a locution for the money he was collecting from his Gentile churches for the impoverished Jewish believers in Jesus at Jerusalem (cf. 15:28) — as well as his use of this same term in Philippians for the money he had received from the Philippian church (cf. Phil 4:17) — has led some interpreters to think that he had principally in mind here the financial support that he wanted to receive from the Christians at Rome for his intended mission to Spain.[44] But the expression τινὰ καρπόν ("some fruit") is scarcely so specific as to mean only money. Rather, it should probably be understood, in conjunction with the agricultural imagery of 1 Cor 3:6-9 and Phil 1:22, as a "spiritual harvest" that would result from his ministry among the Christians at Rome — that is, as Charles Cranfield has expressed the matter: "the return to be hoped for from apostolic labours, whether new converts gained or the strengthening of the faith and obedience of those already believing."[45]

The idiomatic expression καί . . . καθὼς καί ("even as also," "just as also") appears frequently in various forms in the NT,[46] usually with the comparative particle ὡς ("as," "like") but sometimes with the adverb καθώς used as a comparative ("just as"). Here καθώς expresses a causal sense, as it does later in 1:28. The phrase καὶ ἐν τοῖς λοιποῖς ἔθνεσιν ("among the other Gentiles as well")

---

40. Cf. Pelagius, *Ad Romanos*, *PL* 30.648: " 'Prevented' here means 'busy', because he was preaching in other provinces."

41. Cf. Gen 30:2; Ps 131 (132):11; Lam 2:20; Mic 6:7; Luke 1:42; Acts 2:30.

42. Cf. Hos 14:2; Heb 13:15.

43. Cf. *BAG*, 495-96; see also Matt 7:16, 20; 21:43; Luke 3:8; Rom 6:21-22; Phil 1:11; Heb 12:11; Jas 3:17-18.

44. So, e.g., Nickle, *The Collection*, 70; see also Kruger, "TINA KARPON."

45. Cranfield, *Romans*, 1.82.

46. Cf., e.g., 2 Cor 8:6; Col 3:13.

picks up from Paul's God-given mandate to Gentiles that he referred to in 1:5 — with that Gentile mission, as in 1:6, also including his Roman addressees.

1:14 The phrases Ἕλλησίν τε καὶ βαρβάροις, σοφοῖς τε καὶ ἀνοήτοις ("both to Greeks and to barbarians, both to the wise and to the foolish"), which begin this verse, have seemed in their structures somewhat strange to many interpreters. For the sentence begins with two couplets, each consisting of two nouns ("Greeks" and "barbarians") or two substantival adjectives ("the wise" and "the foolish"), all in the dative case. But this positioning of these predicate expressions at the beginning of the sentence was evidently done by Paul in order to emphasize them. And by the inclusion of the personal pronoun εἰμί ("I am") at the end of the sentence, he has also intensified the subject of the verbal idea in ὀφειλέτης ("obligated," "a debtor"), thereby highlighting as well his own sense of obligation.

Further, there is no connecting particle between 1:13 and 1:14, and so the logical relation of this sentence to what precedes it and with what follows it in 1:15 may be debated. Ever since Origen, therefore, it has commonly been claimed that "this sentence contains a rhetorical aside *(hyperbaton)* and its construction is defective [i.e., an *asyndeton*]."[47] Yet 1:15 begins with the adverb οὕτως ("so," "hence," "that is why"), which indicates that an inference is drawn from what precedes. It therefore seems that 1:14 and 1:15 must be viewed as not only grammatically but also logically connected.

The more difficult determination for commentators, however, has been with respect to what or whom Paul had in mind by the use of these couplets and how his argument flows from 1:14 to 1:15. Charles Cranfield has concisely set out the options regarding what or whom Paul had in mind by the nouns "Greeks" and "barbarians" and by the substantival adjectives "the wise" and "the foolish":

> At least the following possibilities need to be considered: (i) Each pair of contrasted terms denotes the whole of mankind, and the two groupings are identical; (ii) Each pair denotes the whole of mankind, but the two pairs represent different groupings; (iii) The first pair denotes the whole of Gentile humanity, but the second the whole of mankind; (iv) Both pairs denote the whole of Gentile humanity, and both groupings are identical; (v) Both pairs denote the whole of Gentile humanity, but they represent different groupings of the same totality.[48]

Since Paul concludes 1:13 with a reference to his Gentile ministry, any understanding that views both couplets as referring to "the whole of mankind" (as in options i and ii) is probably too broad in its classification and so not to be envisioned here. Rather, with Paul's focus being on his Gentile ministry, as seen not only at the end of 1:13 but also in 1:5 in his salutation, it seems that the theme of

47. Origen, *Ad Romanos, PG* 14.858.
48. Cranfield, *Romans,* 1.83.

"Gentile humanity" must be carried on in some manner into the interpretation of the couplets of 1:14 (as in the first couplet in option iii or in both couplets in options iv and v). And since 1:15 begins with the adverb οὕτως ("so," "hence," "that is why"), it is probably best to view 1:14 as setting out the major divisions of people within the Gentile world, as they were popularly identified in that day, and to understand 1:15 as Paul's allusion to what was for him an obvious conclusion — that is, that Gentile Christians at Rome are to be included within his God-given mandate.

The term Ἕλληνες in the first couplet originally denoted Greek tribes and Greek city-states that were united by a common language, culture, and religion. After the military conquests of Alexander "the Great" of Macedonia (356-323 B.C.), however, with their resultant Hellenization of conquered peoples, the term became widely used for any group of people, whatever their ethnicity, who spoke Greek and who shared Greek culture and education. Romans adopted much of Greek culture and so would have been included within the designation by others — even appropriating the term for themselves in this latter sense. Most Jews, however, did not so identify themselves, but, like Paul, used Ἕλληνες to designate "Gentiles" as contrasted to Jews.[49]

Βάρβαροι ("barbarians," "stammerers," "stutterers," "those with unintelligible speech and inferior culture") is an onomatopoeic word (i.e., a word that sounds like what it means) that plays on the repetition of the sounds *bar . . . bar . . . bar,* which was all that Greek-speaking people could comprehend when first coming into contact with foreigners. This concocted and highly pejorative term both mocked the way that foreign languages sounded to those who spoke Greek and denigrated the supposedly uncouth and inferior cultures of those who uttered such unintelligible sounds. It was used in the Greco-Roman world both for enemies, such as the Persians and Egyptians, and for those who lived at the extremes of the Roman Empire, such as the Spaniards, Gauls, and Germans.[50] It is a term that, however, appears only a few times in the NT: in Acts 28:2 and 4 with reference to the "natives" (NRSV) or "islanders" (NIV) of Malta, and in Paul's letters here at 1:14 and in 1 Cor 14:11 and Col 3:11. "The new thing" in Paul's use of the term, as Hans Windisch has rightly highlighted, is "his desire to lead the βάρβαροι to the εὐαγγέλιον θεοῦ, and the doctrine that Greeks, Jews, Scythians and barbarians are all fashioned into a totality in Christ."[51]

The substantival adjectives "the wise" and "the foolish" in the second couplet may (1) go beyond the more restricted designations "Greeks" and "barbarians" to include the much larger category of "the whole of humanity,"[52] (2) be used as rough equivalents of the nouns in the first couplet in order to emphasize the apostle's point of inclusiveness,[53] or (3) embrace the same people as the

---

49. Cf. in Romans such passages as 1:16; 2:9-10; 3:9; 10:12.

50. Cf. Windisch, "βάρβαρος," 1.546-53.

51. *Ibid.,* 1.553.

52. So, e.g., J. Huby, J. A. Fitzmyer, and D. J. Moo, explicating option #3 above.

53. So, e.g., Pelagius, J. Calvin, O. Kuss, and H. Schlier, explicating option #4 above.

nouns of the first couplet but do so from a different perspective, with the nouns signaling a difference of language and the adjectives a difference of culture and education.[54] It is somewhat difficult to decide which of these possibilities is most probable, and a precise identification or differentiation may not be too important. It seems most likely, however, that a fourth option, which views the couplets as being roughly equivalent, is to be preferred. For Paul appears here to be only attempting to characterize "the whole of Gentile humanity" by the use of these popular categories of the day, setting them out only for rhetorical effect in order to highlight the inclusiveness of his ministry to Gentiles in the Greco-Roman world, without any effort at specificity.

Paul's very brief statement ὀφειλέτης εἰμί ("I am obligated") expresses his feeling of responsibility to "the whole of Gentile humanity." Origen asked, "In what sense was the apostle under obligation to Greeks and to barbarians, to the wise and to the foolish?" — and he answered that question by citing (1) Paul's obligation to the Greeks in that he "spoke in tongues more than all of you" (1 Cor 14:18), (2) the apostle's obligation to the wise in that "he has received the wisdom hidden in the mystery, which he is to speak to the perfect and to the wise" (1 Cor 2:7-10), and (3) his obligation to the foolish "in that he has received the grace of patience and long-suffering, for it is the height of patience to be able to endure the furor of the foolish."[55] Commentators have sometimes played with ideas about what Paul may have learned from various people and how he would have felt obligated to them because of what he had received from them.[56] But without denying his indebtedness to others in many ways, certainly the indebtedness that Paul felt most keenly was (1) to God himself, who had called him to a prophetic ministry as an apostle to the Gentiles (cf. 1:1a, 5), and (2) to the proclamation of the Christian gospel, for which he had been set apart by God (cf. 1:1b, 9).

1:15 What Paul said generally in 1:14 about his mission to "the whole of Gentile humanity" he now relates specifically in 1:15 to the situation of the Christians at Rome, who were predominantly Gentile believers in Jesus — saying quite expressly: οὕτως τὸ κατ᾽ ἐμὲ πρόθυμον καὶ ὑμῖν τοῖς ἐν Ῥωμη εὐαγγελίσασθαι ("that is why I am eager to preach the gospel to you also who are at Rome"). It may be tempting to equate his addressees at Rome with one or more of the categories set out in 1:14, as some have tried to do. But "Paul does not indicate," as James Denney once pointed out, "where they would stand in the broad classification of ver. 14."[57] Any such identification seems to have been far from his purpose. Rather, all that Paul says in 1:14-15 is that just as he had

54. So, e.g., Erasmus, W. Sanday and A. C. Headlam, and C. E. B. Cranfield, explicating option #5.
55. Origen, *Ad Romanos, PG* 14.860.
56. Cf., e.g., Barclay, *Romans*, 8; also, to an extent, Dunn, *Romans*, 1:33: "It is possible that he also includes the sense of how much he owed to all sorts and conditions of people, uncultured as well as sophisticated."
57. Denney, *Romans*, 2.589.

earlier felt compelled to proclaim the Christian gospel to all sorts of people in his Gentile mission in the eastern part of the Roman empire, always conditioning his presentation to their respective circumstances, he now feels compelled to proclaim that same message to the Christians at Rome, suiting his presentation to their specific situation and appreciation.

The adverb οὕτως functions (as noted above) by way of drawing an inference from what precedes, and therefore is to be translated "so," "hence," or "that is why." The phrase τὸ κατ᾽ ἐμὲ πρόθυμον can be variously explained. The simplest way is (1) to take τὸ κατ᾽ ἐμὲ ("that which depends on me") as the subject, (2) to view πρόθυμον ("eager") as a predicate nominative, and (3) to supply the verb ἐστιν ("it is"), thereby reading "that which depends on me is eager" — or in more idiomatic English, "for my part, I am eager."[58] It is also possible, however, to take τὸ κατ᾽ ἐμὲ ("so far as it depends on me") as "a self-contained adverbial phrase" with the subject ἐγώ ("I") being understood, and so read "as far as I am concerned."[59] Or perhaps we should take all four words of the phrase together as the subject, insert the understood verb ἐστιν, and view the infinitive εὐαγγελίσασθαι at the end of the sentence as the predicate, thereby reading "my desire is to preach the gospel."[60] Each of these readings can be defended linguistically. But however the syntax is understood, "the contrast implied," as James Denney has pointed out, "is that between *willing* (which Paul for his part is equal to) and *carrying out* the will (which depends on God, ver. 10)."[61]

The climax of this body opening of Romans comes at its close with the words καὶ ὑμῖν τοῖς ἐν Ῥώμῃ εὐαγγελίσασθαι ("to preach the gospel also to you who are at Rome"). The phrase τοῖς ἐν Ῥώμῃ ("those at Rome") is well-supported.[62] More importantly, however, its inclusion here is of great importance for understanding what Paul writes in his letter to Christians at Rome. For while the aorist, infinitive, middle verb εὐαγγελίσασθαι means literally just "to proclaim" or "preach" (the middle appearing in the NT more commonly than the active, though with both having the same meaning), the term (1) always connotes "a divine message," "the messianic proclamation," "the good news," or "the gospel,"[63] and, further, (2) must always be understood in the context of what a particular writer wants to convey by its usage.

The full intent of any writer, however, is hardly ever conveyed by his or her simple thesis statement or by any opening words of introduction. Rather, introductory statements are usually expressed quite allusively, with a writer's purpose becoming more fully understood by unpacking what follows. And this,

---

58. So, e.g., Sanday and Headlam, *Romans*, 21-22; cf. τὰ κατ᾽ ἐμέ, "my affairs," in Eph 6:21; Phil 1:12; Col 4:7.

59. So, e.g., *Moule*, 58.

60. So, e.g., Cranfield, *Romans*, 1.85.

61. Denney, *Romans*, 2.589, italics his.

62. Cf. "Textual Notes" on v. 15 above; see also "Textual Notes" and "Exegetical Comments" on v. 7.

63. Cf., e.g., Ps 68:11 (LXX 67:12); Isa 60:6; *Pss Sol* 11:2; Luke 4:43; Acts 8:35; Gal 1:8b.

we believe, is how we should read Paul when he says in this body opening of Romans that he is eager "to preach the gospel also to you who are at Rome" (1:15) — that is, as expressing very generally his purpose in writing, which purpose he will then elucidate further in what follows.

Our reading of what follows in the body middle of Romans is that Paul principally wanted to convey to the Christians at Rome what he had proclaimed as the Christian message to Gentiles in the eastern part of the Roman Empire, which contextualization of the gospel he calls "my gospel" in 2:16 and 16:25. They were, after all, predominantly Gentile believers in Jesus, and so legitimately came within the scope of his Gentile ministry. But evidently they also (1) had accepted the Christian gospel through the witness of Jewish believers in Jesus, and (2) were attempting to be guided in the expression of their new Christian faith by what they understood to be the theology, liturgy, language, and ethics of the mother church at Jerusalem. So they needed to understand and come to appreciate the Christian gospel as Paul had been commissioned by God to proclaim it to Gentiles — and, further, in understanding and agreeing with him, to join him in a more extensive Christian outreach to the Gentiles in Spain and its environs.

This attempt to bring the Christians of Rome "onside" with respect to his mission and message is what is set out throughout Paul's letter to them. It is done in a fourfold manner: (1) by reiterating in 1:16–4:25 those matters that he and his addressees held in common, refuting in the process any possible misunderstanding about that message, his presentation of it, or himself, (2) by going beyond those matters of agreement to spell out in 5:1–8:39 the main features of his own contextualization of the Christian gospel, (3) by inserting his own Christianized form of Jewish "remnant theology" rhetorical discussion in 9:1–11:33 of how his contextualization of the gospel proclamation relates to God's promises to Israel, and (4) by concluding with an extended hortatory section in 12:1–15:13 on how such a contextualization of the Christian gospel is to be expressed ethically, both generally in its major features and specifically with respect to certain matters of concern among the Christians at Rome. And all of this, I suggest, is what Paul had in mind when he spoke of his desire "to preach the gospel also to you who are at Rome."

So I propose that 1:13-15 should be understood as the body opening of Paul's letter to the Christians at Rome, with that body opening introducing the apostle's message as set out throughout the letter's body middle of 1:16–15:13. Further, as will be developed later, I propose (1) that the first section (1:16–4:25), second section (5:1–8:39), and fourth section (12:1–15:13) of that body middle should be understood as conforming fairly closely to the formal structures of ancient Greek "protreptic" rhetoric, but (2) that the third section (9:1–11:33) breaks the usual pattern of a protreptic message by including material that parallels in many ways Jewish "remnant" theology and rhetoric, which would have been particularly meaningful to the Christians at Rome who looked to the Jerusalem church, the mother church of the early Christian movement, as the principal source for their theology, liturgy, and ethics.

BIBLICAL THEOLOGY

One might not expect to find much of theological significance in a letter's body opening. Nonetheless, there are some matters of great theological and personal importance in these few verses. First of all, it needs to be noted that Paul always expected to minister for Christ and to reap a harvest ("fruit") wherever he was, whether among those who were sophisticated or those more uncultured, whether among the learned or the unlearned. His mission was not just to certain people in certain situations, but to all people whatever their circumstances. For all people are loved by God and all people are those for whom Christ died.

Further, it needs to be recognized that Paul's contacts with people, whatever their particular situation or circumstances, were always based on the principle he stated earlier in 1 Cor 9:19-23:

> Though I am free and belong to no one, I have made myself a slave to everyone, so that I may win as many as possible. To the Jews I became like a Jew, in order to win Jews. To those under the law I became like one under the law (though I myself am not under the law), so that I might win those under the law. To those not having the law I became like one not having the law (though I am not free from God's law but am under Christ's law), so as to win those not having the law. To the weak I became weak, so that I might win the weak. I have become all things to all people, so that by all possible means I might save some. I do all of this for the sake of the gospel, so that I may share in its blessings.

Thus as Origen long ago observed: "He gathers fruit from the Greeks, fruit from the barbarians, fruit from the wise, fruit even from the foolish. . . . Some he teaches from the law and the prophets; others he persuades with signs and wonders."[64]

Also of importance for any Christian biblical theology are the following two realizations: (1) that Paul always kept to the fore in his own consciousness and dealings with people the centrality of the Christian gospel, to which he had been set apart by God, and (2) that he always attempted to contextualize that message in ways that would be meaningful to his hearers and addressees. And it is just such a dual focus on the centrality of the Christian gospel and the need for contextualization of that good news to all people in their various situations and circumstances that is necessary for Christian thought and action today.

CONTEXTUALIZATION FOR TODAY

Little more need be said regarding the contextualization of the Christian gospel today, as based on the body opening of 1:13-15, than what has just been said. Suf-

---

64. Origen, *Ad Romanos, PG* 14.859.

fice it here to repeat the exhortations of three commentators, each of whom is known among somewhat different Christian groups and represents a different theological position — yet all of whom, though very different in many ways, are at this point in basic agreement and have something of significance to say to us all.

John Calvin: "All teachers also have here a rule to follow, viz. to accommodate themselves in a modest, courteous way to the ignorant and unlearned. By doing so they will more patiently endure much stupidity of conduct and bear with innumerable instances of pride, which might otherwise overcome them. It is, however, their duty to remember that their obligations to the foolish mean that they are not to indulge their folly beyond moderation."[65]

Gerald R. Cragg: "The constraint of the gospel overrides all artificial divisions. Differences of language, degrees of culture — such things are immaterial when a man feels the irresistible constraint of a task which has been laid upon him by God. Elsewhere in his letters Paul has set forth in greater detail the way in which the gift of God breaks down the barriers by which we separate ourselves from others (Col. 3:11; I Cor. 12:13); not often has he so explicitly related the unity created by the gospel to the specific task of making that gospel universally known. He has preached his message wherever the open door of opportunity allowed; he will preach it at Rome too."[66]

Floyd E. Hamilton: "Paul recognized that his obligation was to preach the gospel to all nations, to all classes and to all types of individuals. It is not his task to select his hearers according to their innate capacity to understand the message. He owes them the gospel because his obligation is God-given. Uneducated, unintelligent, and ignorant people are just as precious in God's sight as the 'intelligentsia,' the rich, or the scientifically trained. God's elect are to be found in all ranks of society, even among the most unprepossessing. Our duty is to see that all have an intelligent presentation of the gospel message with all the power, persuasion, and winsomeness of which Christians are capable. No class or nation or group is to be ignored."[67]

65. J. Calvin, *Romans*, in *Calvin's New Testament Commentaries*, 8.26.
66. G. R. Cragg, "Romans" (Exposition), in *Interpreter's Bible*, 9.389.
67. Hamilton, *Romans*, 27.

B. Body Middle

Ancient "words ['speeches' or 'messages'] of exhortation" (λόγοι προτρεπτικοί) were usually composed of two sections, with a third section also frequently included: (1) a negative section, which dissuaded and censured an opposing position, (2) a positive section, which set forth and defended the position of the speaker or author, and often (3) a hortatory section, which appealed to the hearers or addressees by way of inviting them to accept what was presented in the two previous sections.[1] For each of these usual sections of protreptic discourse, however, Paul in his letter to Christians at Rome incorporates his own emphases and gives his own spin to what he presents — often, as well, speaking to his addressees on their own grounds and interjecting material of particular relevance for them. Notable in these latter regards are at least three important features that need to be particularly observed in Paul's use of the form of a traditional protreptic "speech" or "message" of exhortation: (1) he restructures the first section of his protreptic message (1:16–4:25) to include not just negative words of censure but also positive statements about what he affirms, (2) his manner of presentation in this first section suggests — both in his negative words of 1:18–3:20 and his positive statements of 1:16-17 and 3:21–4:25 — that he believed he held these convictions in common with his addressees and that he wanted to build on their agreement with respect to these basic matters, and (3) he adds a further major section in 9:1–11:36 — after the first two theological sections of 1:16–4:25 and 5:1–8:39 and before the final hortatory section of 12:1–15:13 — that would have been of particular interest to the Christians at Rome, who understood and expressed their commitment to Jesus in ways that had been largely transmitted to them by Jewish believers in Jesus who were in some way in contact with the mother church at Jerusalem.

---

1. Cf. Aune, "Romans as a *Logos Protrepikos*," in *Romans Debate* (1991), 278-96; see also his *Westminster Dictionary*, 383-85.

IV. Section I: Righteousness, Faithfulness, and Faith (1:16–4:25)

In the first section of the body middle of Romans, that is, in 1:16–4:25, four rather obvious features need to be immediately highlighted:

1. The word chain of δικαιοσύνη ("righteousness," "uprightness"), πίστις ("faith," "faithfulness"), and πιστεύειν ("to believe") dominates the discussion, both in the thesis statement of 1:16-17 and repeatedly throughout the rest of the section, thereby suggesting the essential unity of all the material within 1:16–4:25.

2. Paul's argument in 1:16–4:25, especially at its start in 1:16-17 and in building to a climax in 3:1–4:25, is chock-full of biblical quotations, with some fifteen to eighteen quotations appearing at eight or nine places in these four chapters — which, particularly in comparison with the lack of explicit biblical quotations in the following section, 5:1–8:39, also suggests something about the unity of the material within this first section of the letter's body middle.

3. While there are relatively fewer explicit biblical quotations in 1:18–2:16, there appear throughout this subsection of the material a number of allusive references to Scripture, a few biblically based aphorisms, and some traditional formulations that seem to stem from Jewish and/or Jewish Christian devotional and catechetical materials.

4. The illustration of Abraham in 4:1-24, together with a Christian confessional portion in 4:25, aptly concludes the section.

Further, it needs to be observed that the material of this first section of the body middle of Romans, that is, 1:16–4:25, is thoroughly Jewish and/or Jewish Christian in character, not only in its contents but also in its type of argumentation. Throughout this section, in fact, Paul sounds very much like a righteous Jew or an authentic Jewish Christian in (1) denouncing humanity's godlessness and evil, (2) rebutting the false concept of religious legalism, and (3) arguing for faith as the only proper response to God, who has acted redemptively on behalf of his people and his creation.

Scanning the Contents. This first section of the body middle begins with a thesis statement in 1:16-17 that (1) speaks of the universality of the gospel ("both for the Jew first and for the Gentile"), (2) emphasizes that the gospel is based on "the righteousness of God" and appropriated only "by faith," and (3) supports that conjunction of "righteousness" and "faith" by quoting Hab 2:4. Immediately following the thesis statement is an extended negative presentation in 1:18–3:20 that argues that all people, both Gentiles and Jews, are sinful and without excuse before a righteous God. This argument proceeds in four movements, the first in 1:18-32 paralleling the depiction in Wis 13–14 of the wickedness of the Gentile world, the second in 2:1-16 dramatically turning the self-aggrandizing Jewish propaganda of Wis 15:1-6 on its head and proclaiming God's judgment on all who sin, without partiality and whatever a person's ethnicity, the third in 2:17-29 denouncing any form of Jewish legalism, and the fourth in 3:1-20 presenting the situation of the Jews before God, setting out a series of rhetorical questions (3:1-9) and a catena of biblical quotations (3:10-20) that are all to the effect that "Jews and Gentiles alike are all under sin" (3:9) and that Jewish privileges and prerogatives bestowed by God serve to make Jews even more accountable before God and not morally superior to Gentiles (3:19-20).

In the latter half of this opening section, that is, in 3:21–4:25, Paul speaks much more positively in (1) arguing in 3:21 that the righteousness of God, while witnessed to by the Law and the Prophets, is now made known in the gospel apart from the Mosaic law (χωρὶς νόμου), (2) repeating in 3:22-23 in an expanded and more developed manner his original thesis statement of 1:16-17, (3) supporting in 3:24-26 that expanded thesis statement with an early Christian confessional portion, (4) elaborating in 3:27-31 on the "divine impartiality" feature of that thesis, and (5) illustrating in 4:1-24 the important factor of faith that is contained in the thesis statements of 1:16-17 and 3:21-23 by the example of Abraham. Paul then concludes in 4:25 with a Christian confessional portion that speaks of Christ's work in humanity's redemption and justification and provides a fitting conclusion not only to the exposition of Abraham as the example of faith in 4:1-24 but also to all that was said in 1:16–4:24 regarding (1) God's "righteousness," (2) Christ's "faithfulness," (3) the inadequacy of "works of the law," and (4) the necessity of "faith."

Use of Scripture. The first explicit quotation of Scripture in this section is in 1:17b, quoting Hab 2:4b: "The righteous [or possibly 'My Righteous One'] will live by faith." The second is in 2:24, where Paul reverses the self-congratulatory characterization of Jews in Wis 15:1-6 with a prophetic denunciation of Israel drawn from a conflation of Isa 52:5b and Ezek 36:22b: "God's name is blasphemed among the Gentiles because of you." A third quotation appears in 3:4b, quoting Ps 51:4: "So that you may be proved right in your words and prevail in your judging." Each of these quotations of Scripture is introduced by the formulaic phrase "just as it is written" (καθὼς γέγραπται). In addition there appear in this section, particularly in 1:18–2:29, a number of allusive references to Scripture, a few biblically based aphorisms, and some traditional formulations that stem from Jewish and/or Jewish Christian confessional, devotional, or catechetical materials.

The eight to ten passages strung together in 3:10-18, which are also introduced by "just as it is written" (καθὼς γέγραπται), deserve special comment, for this catena of passages has often been seen as an early set piece or *testimonia* collection that Paul used to emphasize the fact that no one is righteous before God. The selection of passages in this catena is not quite Pauline. For unpacking all of the possible conflated texts, the quotations are from Qoheleth (Eccl 7:20), Proverbs (1:16), Isaiah (59:7, 8), and the Psalms (14:1-3; 53:1-3; 5:9; 140:3; 10:7; 36:1), which is a collection of passages common to Judaism generally, but not as a collected series of passages found elsewhere in Paul's writings. Further, the text-forms of these passages evidence a variety of LXX and MT readings, with the wording sometimes not exactly either. And the structure of the material in 3:10-18, while probably not strophic, evidences great care in its composition, with its sixfold repetition of "there is none" (οὐκ ἔστιν) and its cataloging of various parts of the body ("throats," "tongues," "lips," "mouths," "feet," and "eyes") to make the point that all human beings are sinful in their totality. All these factors, taken together, suggest that this catena of passages was constructed by some earlier Jewish teacher and had some sort of history in Judaism and/or early Jewish Christianity.

Paul's point in quoting these texts is that Scripture refers not just to the plight of the pagan world, but, and more particularly, to the condition of those who claim to be God's people, the Jews — for, as he argues in 3:19, "whatever the law says, it says to those who are under the law, so that every mouth might be silenced and the whole world held accountable to God." It need not be supposed, however, that such a collection of biblical texts was unique to Paul or that the conclusion he drew from them was new to his addressees. Rather, he introduces his statement of 3:19 with the words "Now we know" (οἴδαμεν δέ), which suggests that he believed this catena of passages was not only known to his addressees, who we have posited had been extensively influenced by the theology, ways of thinking, language, and practices of Jerusalem Christianity,[2] but also that there was a large measure of agreement between his Christian addressees at Rome and himself on these matters.

The final group of quotations in Paul's discussion of "righteousness" and "faith" appears in 4:1-24 where Abraham is presented as the example par excellence of faith. Four texts are quoted: (1) Gen 15:6 ("Abraham believed God, and it was credited to him as righteousness"), which appears in 4:3 and 4:22, with the first instance introduced by the rhetorical question, "For what does the Scripture say?" (τί γὰρ ἡ γραφὴ λέγει) and the second by the inferential conjunction "for this reason" (διό); (2) Ps 32:1-2 ("Blessed are those whose offenses have been forgiven and whose sins have been covered; blessed are those whose sin the Lord will never count against them"), which appears in 4:7-8 and

---

2. See "Introduction to the Commentary," 8-9.

is introduced by "David says" (Δαυὶδ λέγει); (3) Gen 17:5 ("I have made you a father of many nations") as found in 4:17 (and alluded to in 4:18), which is introduced by "as it is written" (καθὼς γέγραπται); and (4) Gen 15:5 ("So shall your seed be") in 4:18b, which is introduced by "according to what was said" (κατὰ τὸ εἰρημένον). Gen 15:5-6 and 17:5 are the main passages that speak of God's blessing and promise to Abraham. To these standard passages is added Ps 32:1-2, which is cited in midrashic fashion to support Gen 15:6 and to highlight God's action in both "crediting righteousness" (ἐλογίσθη εἰς δικαιοσύνην) and "not reckoning/counting sin" (οὐ μὴ λογίσηται ἁμαρτίαν) — using in both cases the verb λογίζομαι, which signifies "to reckon" or "credit" something to someone.

Approach and Purpose. Paul begins this first section of the body middle of his letter to Christians at Rome in quite a traditional manner — not only (1) censuring what he opposed (as in the first section of a typical protreptic speech or writing), but also (2) agreeing with his addressees where possible (as was his usual practice in gaining a hearing) and (3) using materials and methods that they and he held in common (as he often did in his other letters so as to be convincing). He firmly believed, just as he wrote earlier in the *propositio* of his letter to his own converts in Galatia (cf. Gal 2:15-21), that all true believers in Jesus know that a person is not justified by "the works of the law" but, rather, by what Christ has effected and by a person's faith in him (vv. 15-16). So Paul writes with that same confidence to his Roman addressees, expressing in this first major section of the body middle of his letter what he believed both they and he held in common — that is, the futility of legalism and acceptance before God as being only by faith — before then going on in the second major section of the letter's body middle in 5:1-8:39 to speak of matters that pertain to the distinctive nature of his proclamation of the Christian gospel in his Gentile mission, that is, what he calls "my gospel" in 2:16 and 16:25, concerning which there seems to have been some uncertainties, disputes, and even criticisms among the Christians at Rome.

Paul's purpose in this first section of 1:16-4:25, as in the first part of any ancient protreptic "word ['speech' or 'message'] of exhortation" (λόγος προτρεπτικός), was to dissuade and censure — that is, to dissuade any believer in Jesus, whether ethnically Jewish or ethnically Gentile, from being enticed by any form of religious legalism and to censure any such legalistic attitude with respect to relations with God. But he goes beyond dissuasion and censure to enunciate, as well, the basic principles of "righteousness," "faithfulness," and "faith," which were at the heart of matters for both (1) the religion of Israel, as set forth in the Jewish Scriptures (which Christians accepted as their OT), and (2) authentic Jewish Christianity, as founded on the apostolic preaching about the person, teaching, and work of Jesus of Nazareth (which Christians insisted was not only in line with but also the fulfillment of the prophetic message of the OT). So he writes throughout this first major section of the body middle of his letter as one who is confident that he and his addressees, though different in their respective emphases and strategies, were in basic agreement regarding "the righteousness of God" and "justification by faith." And he does so believing that his addressees' recognition of this agreement was an important first step by way of preparation for what he wants to tell them later in his letter about his own proclamation of the Christian gospel to Gentiles in his God-ordained Gentile mission.

PART ONE OF SECTION I (1:16–3:20)

The interpretation of this first part of the first major section of the body middle of Romans, that is, 1:16–3:20, has been notoriously difficult for almost every commentator. Luke Timothy Johnson has given voice to the commentator's recurrent complaint: "The question of how to read this section is one of the most difficult in the interpretation of Romans."[3]

The Jewish Character, Perspective, and Ethos of Paul's Argument. A number of recent treatments of Paul's argument in this first section of the body middle of Romans, that is in 1:16–3:20, refer to its "Jewish character," its "Jewish perspective," and/or its "Jewish ethos."[4] But opinions differ widely as to how to understand the "Jewishness" of this material.

At times this first part of Section I of the letter's body middle, especially 2:1–3:9, is characterized as "Paul's dialogue with a fellow Jew."[5] At other times, it is referred to as "homiletical material" drawn by Paul from "a synagogue sermon" of Diaspora Judaism[6] or as "a dialogue on Jewish ideals."[7] It has even been argued that what appears in 1:16–3:20 (as well as throughout 1:16–4:25) is not to be viewed as representative of Paul's own commitments at all, but, rather, should be understood as a portrayal of "the Jewish position of his opponents that Paul opposes."[8] It is necessary, therefore, even before engaging in any direct exegesis, to identify some of the major problems of interpretation in the first part of this section and to suggest a way of resolving them.

Major Problems of Interpretation. Most interpreters believe that there is little difficulty in understanding the function and general thrust of Paul's statements regarding "righteousness" and "faith" in 1:16-17. Nor do most com-

---

3. L. T. Johnson, *Reading Romans,* 31.

4. Cf., e.g., Beker, *Paul the Apostle,* 78-83, 94-104; E. P. Sanders, "Appendix: Romans 2," 123-35; Nanos, *The Mystery of Romans,* 8-16, passim; see also from a previous generation W. Manson, "Notes on the Argument of Romans," 150-64.

5. So Stowers, *Diatribe and Paul's Letter to the Romans,* 93-98, 110-13; idem, "Paul's Dialogue with a Fellow Jew," 707-22; idem, *Rereading of Romans,* 159-75.

6. So E. P. Sanders, *Paul, the Law, and the Jewish People,* 123, 129.

7. So Carras, "Romans 2,1-29," 183-207.

8. So D. A. Campbell, *Quest for Paul's Gospel,* 233-61. See also his *Deliverance of God: An Apocalyptic Reading of Justification in Paul* (2009), which is a *tour de force* (i.e., a feat of skill, perception, and ingenuity) with which I agree both (1) in its highlighting of the problems that appear in Rom 1:16–4:25 and (2) in its focusing on the "in Christ" theme of Rom 8 as being central in Paul's proclamation — but with which I disagree in its setting aside of the message of justification in the understanding of Paul (as well as discounting the other forensic salvific expressions associated with justification in 1:16–4:25). My thesis on what Paul is doing in the first section of the body middle of Romans is set out in fairly extensive detail in my exposition that follows.

mentators doubt that Paul repeats, expands, and supports in 3:21-4:25 what he has written in 1:16-17. Problems arise, however, when one attempts to explain why Paul, after so positive a proclamation as expressed in 1:16-17 — and then repeating, expanding, and developing that proclamation in 3:21-23, supporting it in 3:24-26, elucidating it further in 3:27-31, and illustrating it in 3:21–4:25 — inserts such negative and condemnatory statements as found in 1:18-32 and such judgmental evaluations as appear in 2:1–3:20. And problems multiply when one attempts to identify exactly who is being talked about and/or addressed in the various portions of 1:18–3:30.

The first problem, that of a rationale for the materials of 1:18–3:20, is of somewhat recent vintage, and will be discussed later in direct fashion when we deal with 1:18-32 (as well as more indirectly in dealing with the materials of 2:1–3:20). The second, however, regarding who is being talked about and/or addressed in 1:18–3:20, was of great concern to many early interpreters, such as Origen, Jerome, Augustine, and Erasmus, and it continues to plague commentators today. Are Gentiles talked about or addressed in 1:18-32, Jews in 2:1-5, Gentiles in 2:6-16, then Jews again in 2:17–3:19, with a conclusion in 3:20? Or is it Gentiles in 1:18-32 and Jews in 2:1–3:19, with a conclusion pertaining to both in 3:20? Or is it humanity generally in 1:18–2:16 and Jews (or a particular type of Jew) in 2:17–3:19, with a conclusion in 3:20?

Likewise, problems arise when one tries to evaluate the structures incorporated within 1:18–3:20. In the first part of this section, that is, in 1:18-32, there appears a denunciation of idolatry and immorality that parallels quite closely the characterizations of Gentile idolatry and immorality in Wis 13:1–14:31. Thus many scholars have argued that Paul must have drawn, in some fashion, on the portrayals and language of Wis 13 and 14, and perhaps also from some of the statements about the pagan world in Wis 11 and 12, for his denunciations of godlessness and wickedness in Rom 1:18-32. Further, that he may also have known and wanted to counter the Jewish self-aggrandizing statements of Wis 15:1-6 when he wrote Rom 2:1-15 — or that, perhaps, he and the writer of Wisdom of Solomon drew from similar traditions.

The second portion of this subsection of material, especially 2:1–3:8, abounds with characteristic features and stylistic traits of both Greek diatribal dialogues and Jewish or Jewish Christian traditional materials. And 3:10-18, which contains the longest catena of biblical passages in the Pauline corpus, has been viewed by many as a collection of *testimonium* passages most likely first brought together by Jews or Jewish Christians and then used by Paul in support of his thesis that "Jews and Gentiles alike are all under sin" (3:9; cf. 3:19, 23).

More importantly, however, problems of interpretation multiply when one asks: How does what Paul says about Gentiles and Jews in ch. 2 correspond to what he says about humanity generally and Jews in particular in the rest of his letter? For while his conclusions regarding God's impartiality (2:11), Jews and Gentiles being alike under sin (3:9-19, 23), and no one being able to be declared righteous by observing the law (3:20) are clear, four passages in Romans 2 seem to set forth a theology of salvation by "good works" and by doing "works of the law" — that is, by "obedience" to the Mosaic law. And only once in this chapter, that is, in 2:16, does explicit Christian language come to the fore.

The first problem passage appears in 2:7, 10, where it is said that God will give "eternal life" — or, "glory, honor, and peace" — to those who persist in doing "good work" (v. 7: ἔργου ἀγαθοῦ) and "the good" (v. 10: τὸ ἀγαθόν), which seems to conflict with what is said about being justified solely by faith in 3:21-30; 4:1-25; and throughout 9:1–11:36. The second problem passage is 2:13, where it is said that "those who obey the law [are the ones] who will be declared righteous," which has every appearance of being in conflict with (1) Paul's statement in 3:20 that no one is declared righteous by observing the law, (2) his references in 7:14-25 to people being unable to obey the law, and (3) his denunciations of Israel in 9:30–11:12 for attempting to gain righteousness by means of the Mosaic law. The third passage is 2:14-15, where there is the statement that some Gentiles who "do by nature the things required by the law (φύσει τὰ τοῦ νόμου ποιῶσιν)" actually show that "the requirements of the law (τὸ ἔργον τοῦ νόμου) are written on their hearts" — with the inference being that in so doing they are justified before God. Assuming that Paul is using the term νόμος ("law") in much the same way throughout this passage to mean the Mosaic law, such an inference seems to contradict his earlier depiction of the pagan world in 1:18-32 and his conclusion about the impossibility of being righteous before God by observing the law in 3:20. And the fourth problem passage is 2:25-27, which appears to be built on the assumption that righteousness is associated with the observance of the Mosaic law. But, again, this seems to fly in the face of (1) Paul's express conclusion to this section in 3:20, (2) his statement that the "righteousness of God" is "apart from the law" in 3:21, (3) his use of Abraham as the exemplar of faith in 4:1-25, and (4) all of his statements regarding the relation of the Christian gospel to the hope of Israel in 9:1–11:36 — as well as, of course, his arguments of Gal 2:15-16; 3:6-14 and his exhortations in Gal 4:12–5:12, which can be found also elsewhere at various places in his other letters.

How can these major problems of interpretation with respect to 1:18–3:20 be understood? For pedagogical purposes (as well as space limitations), it is necessary to hold our explicit treatments of these matters — as well as our proposals to that very perplexing question regarding how these problems should be understood — for the comments on each of the passages in question. Suffice it here only to raise the questions with the promise of further consideration later.

1. Thesis Statement on Righteousness, Faithfulness, and Faith (1:16-17)

TRANSLATION

^{1:16}*I am not ashamed of the gospel, because it is the power of God with respect to the salvation of everyone who believes: both for the Jew first and for the Gentile.* ¹⁷*For in it the righteousness of God is being revealed — a righteousness that is based on divine faithfulness and leads to [or 'results in'] a human response of faith, just as it is written: "The righteous will live by faith."*

TEXTUAL NOTES

1:16a The appearance of τὸ εὐαγγέλιον ("the gospel") without the addition of the phrase τοῦ Χριστοῦ ("of Christ") is supported by P²⁶ and uncials ℵ A B C D* G, as well as by minuscules 33 1739 (Category I) and 81 1506 1881 (Category II). It is also reflected in all of the Latin, Syriac, and Coptic versions. The addition τοῦ Χριστοῦ ("of Christ"), however, appears repeatedly in the Byzantine textual tradition, as represented by the ninth-century *Byz* uncials K (018) L (020) and P (025), as well as by the great bulk of ninth- to fifteenth-century *Byz* minuscules. The addition is also included in a corrected copy of the Western Text, that is in Codex Dᶜ. It is far easier, however, to understand the addition of the phrase than to explain its omission in the course of the text's transmission, and so τὸ εὐαγγέλιον minus the possessive phrase τοῦ Χριστοῦ should be accepted.

16b The phrase εἰς σωτηρίαν ("for salvation") is omitted in the ninth-century uncial G (012), but included in all other textual witnesses. Its omission must be viewed as a scribal omission, which may have been due to an inability of a scribe to appreciate the term "salvation" in Paul's vocabulary (see the exegetical comments below).

16c The neuter adverb πρῶτον ("first") is omitted in uncials B G, with that omission reflected, as well, in itᵍ copˢᵃ, Tertullian (reporting on Marcion's text), and Ephraem. It is included, however, in all other textual witnesses. Its omission is undoubtedly due to the influence of Marcion, for whom any Jewish priority or privilege was unacceptable.

17a Marcion probably also omitted the introductory formula καθὼς γέγραπται ("just as it is written") and the quotation of Hab 2:4b (ὁ δὲ δίκαιος ἐκ πίστεως ζήσεται), for they are not mentioned in Tertullian's discussion of Marcion's treatment of Romans.

17b The addition of the personal possessive pronoun μου ("my") in uncorrected Codex Ephraemi Rescriptus (C* 04), thereby reading ἐκ πίστεως μου ζήσεται ("he will live by my faith/faithfulness"), is probably a scribal assimilation to the LXX version of this Habakkuk quotation.

FORM/STRUCTURE/SETTING

The thesis statement of 1:16-17 is comparatively brief. Its interpretation, how-ever, has often been difficult. Two matters regarding the passage's form, struc-ture, and setting need to be clarified before any progress can be made in exegesis and biblical theology: (1) its rhetorical features, and (2) the place and function of this short passage in the immediate and overall structure of Paul's letter.

Rhetorical Features (Both Probable and Less Likely). One rhetorical con-vention that finds its inception in this opening thesis statement of the first major section of the body middle is what has been called anaphora, which is the repeti-tion of a word or expression at the beginning of a series of successive statements — or, as in an extended anaphora, the repetition of a word or expression at the resumption of a discussion that has been interrupted by another section of ma-terial. The first part of this rhetorical convention appears in this thesis statement of 1:16-17, which speaks of "righteousness" and "faith." When coupled with the restatement, expansion, and development of that same thesis in 3:21-23, these two occurrences are probably best viewed as forming an extended anaphora.

Jouette Bassler has also identified the expression "both for the Jew first and for the Gentile" ('Ιουδαίῳ τε πρῶτον καὶ ῞Ελληνι) as the first part of another rhetorical convention, given the name *inclusio* by later rhetoricians, which is completed by the repetition of the same words twice in 2:9-10. And on the ba-sis of this proposed *inclusio,* together with the repetition of several words and phrases that appear first in 1:18-20 and then again in 2:1-9, she has argued for the structural unity of 1:16–2:10 — even proposing that not only must 1:16–2:10 be viewed in terms of a "ring-structure," which she sees as coming close to being worked out in terms of an epistolary *chiasmus,* but also that the axiom of "divine impartiality" enunciated at the section's conclusion in 2:11 must be understood as the theme of all that Paul writes in 1:16–2:29.[9]

Bassler's principal claim is that the statement of 1:16, "for the salvation of everyone who believes, 'both for the Jew first and for the Gentile' ('Ιουδαίῳ τε πρῶτον καὶ ῞Ελληνι)," forms a deliberate structural *inclusio* with the statement "glory, honor, and peace for everyone who does good, 'both for the Jew first and for the Gentile' ('Ιουδαίῳ τε πρῶτον καὶ ῞Ελληνι)" found in 2:10.[10] In addition, however, she points out (1) that the expression "the wrath of God is revealed" (ἀποκαλύπτεται ὀργὴ θεοῦ) of 1:18a is repeated in the words "wrath" (ὀργή) and "is revealed" (ἀποκάλυψις) of 2:5, (2) that the phraseology "against all the godlessness . . . of men who suppress the truth by their wickedness" (ἐπὶ πᾶσαν ἀσέβειαν . . . ἀνθρώπων τῶν τὴν ἀλήθειαν ἐν ἀδικίᾳ κατεχόντων) of 1:18b forms something of a parallel with the phraseology "against every human being who does evil" (ἐπὶ πᾶσαν ψυχὴν ἀνθρώπου τοῦ κατεργαζομένου τὸ κακόν) in 2:9,

---

9. Cf. Bassler, *Divine Impartiality,* esp. 121-70; building on the work of M. Pohlenz, "Paulus und die Stoa" (1949), and J. A. Fisher, "Pauline Literary Forms and Thought Patterns" (1977).

10. Bassler, *Divine Impartiality,* 124-25.

(3) that the triple-word formulation of "wrath" (ὀργή), "wickedness" (ἀδικία), and "truth" (ἀλήθεια) in 1:18 appears again in the words "truth" (ἀλήθεια), "wickedness/evil" (ἀδικία), and "wrath" (ὀργή) in 2:8; and (4) that the damning expression "without excuse" (ἀναπολόγητος) of 1:20 is also to be found in the phrase "therefore you are without excuse" (διὸ ἀναπολόγητος εἶ) in 2:1.[11] Further, she observes that the theme of "measure-for-measure retribution" *(ius talionis)* appears in both 1:18-32 and 2:1-10.

But Bassler's thesis, together with her working out of that thesis, have failed to convince most scholars today. Its major problems are (1) that it does not sufficiently take into account the shift from the third person plural in 1:18-32 to the second person singular that begins at 2:1, which suggests that a new focus begins or a new group of people comes into view at 2:1 and that thus a new section (or subsection) of Paul's overall argument begins there, (2) that it does not take seriously enough the vocative expression "O man" (ὦ ἄνθρωπε), which heads up all of what follows in 2:1-16 and seems to provide the reader with an epistolary clue for the identification of a new section (or subsection) in the apostle's argument, and (3) that it fails to account for the dramatic shift of style between 1:18-32 and 2:1-10, with a diatribe form of argumentation, which was not evident in 1:18-32, being prominent in 2:1-5 and then continuing in the sections (or subsections) of Paul's argument that follow (cf. 2:17-29 and 3:1-9). Thus though Bassler has argued that 1:16–2:10 must be understood in terms of its "ring-structure," which, she argues, comes close to being an epistolary *chiasmus,*[12] most scholars believe that she has not worked out her thesis with sufficient perception or stringency. For the presence of common themes, similar phrases, parallel expressions, and the repetition of words, while significant in the development of an overall argument, need not imply some form of rhetorical or structural ring composition — and certainly not the presence of an epistolary *chiasmus.*

Rather, as most commentators today believe, what Bassler has observed is simply that several expressions, phrases, and words in 1:16-18 are repeated in 2:5-9 — but she has not taken sufficiently into account such other important features in these two sections as (1) the change of focus or group that is discussed, (2) the change of personal pronouns, and (3) the change of literary style. So while, for example, the word ἀναπολόγητος ("without excuse") appears in 1:20 and then reappears in 2:1, this is probably not to be viewed as a parallel usage in the same context, but, rather, a means of charging somewhat different groups of people with the same judgment — that is, both pagan Gentiles and "whoever you are who passes judgment" (πᾶς ὁ κρίνων) as being "without excuse."

Further, as James Dunn has rightly observed, Bassler's understanding of 1:16–2:11 as an identifiable single literary unit "makes too much of a break in the developing indictment of chap. 2 itself."[13] Or as Joseph Fitzmyer has com-

11. Bassler, *Divine Impartiality,* 125-31.
12. *Ibid.,* "Appendix D," page 199.
13. Dunn, *Romans,* 79.

mented regarding Bassler's thesis, even while acknowledging that "she is right in stressing divine impartiality" as a prominent theme in 2:1-11: "Her suggestion that 2:11 closes a unit that begins at 1:16 is unconvincing. Her ring construction cuts across an obvious division in the structure of this part of the letter."[14] And both Dunn and Fitzmyer are undoubtedly correct in arguing that it is "better to see 2:1-11 as an overlapping section" that binds the more specific indictments of what precedes and what follows together.[15]

The Place and Function of 1:16-17 in the Structure of the Letter. What, then, can be said about the place and function of 1:16-17 in the structure of this first major section of the body middle of Paul's letter to Christians at Rome (i.e., Section I, 1:16–4:25) and in the overall structure of the letter, particularly in its second and third major theological sections (i.e., Section II, 5:1–8:39, and Section III, 9:1–11:36)? In the first place, it needs to be noted that an extended anaphora of a thesis statement in 1:16-17 and its repetition, expansion, and development in 3:21-23 suggests that the first major section of the letter's body middle (Section I) is to be understood as set out in two parts: the first part in 1:16–3:20, which is introduced by the thesis statement of 1:16-17, and the second part in 3:21–4:25, which is introduced by the repetition, expansion, and development of that first statement in 3:21-23. Also, it needs to be observed (1) that certain words, word chains, phrases, expressions, and emphases that appear in these two thesis statements of 1:16-17 and 3:21-23 reappear frequently throughout the whole of 1:16–4:25 (particularly in its latter half), but also (2) that they tend to be replaced in the second section of the letter's body middle, that is, in 5:1–8:39, by other word chains, expressions, and emphases (as will be discussed later when dealing with that second section). So, on the basis of these two rather elementary observations, it may be proposed here (and developed later) that 1:16-17 — while an important thesis statement and so to be highlighted by being set off by itself (as should also its repetition and expansion in 3:21-23) — is probably not to be understood as the overall thesis statement for the whole letter (as most interpreters have assumed), but, rather, should be viewed as the thesis statement for the first major section of the letter's body middle, that is, for 1:16–4:25, with the basic themes of that thesis statement later picked up again, defended, and clarified in the inserted third major section of the expanded protreptic discourse, that is, in 9:1–11:36.

EXEGETICAL COMMENTS

1:16a Paul begins this first section of the body middle of Romans, just as he began the letter's salutation (cf. 1:1-4), with an emphasis on τὸ εὐαγγέλιον ("the gospel") — stating: οὐ γὰρ ἐπαισχύνομαι τὸ εὐαγγέλιον ("I am not ashamed

---

14. Fitzmyer, *Romans*, 298.
15. Quoting Dunn, *Romans*, 79; see also Fitzmyer, *Romans*, 298.

of the gospel"). The postpositive γάρ ("for," "because"), which has frequently been understood by interpreters to connect 1:16a in a causal or explanatory fashion with what precedes it in 1:13-15 (as it does in 1:16b and 1:17a), probably appears here simply as a transitional conjunction to indicate the continuation of Paul's writing, as it seems also to function in 1:18a (so also 2:25; 3:3). The noun εὐαγγέλιον ("gospel," "good news"), whether with or without the article, appears more frequently in the letters of Paul (some sixty times out of a total seventy-six NT occurrences), and with a greater degree of nuancing, than it does anywhere else in the NT — as does also the verb εὐαγγελίζειν ("to proclaim the gospel") and its cognates. It was, in fact, "the gospel" that was at the heart of all of Paul's thoughts and concerns, the content of all that he proclaimed, and the substratum for all that he taught.[16]

It has often seemed strange to commentators, however, that the apostle begins the body middle portion of his letter to Rome with the statement "I am not ashamed of the gospel" (οὐ γάρ ἐπαισχύνομαι τὸ εὐαγγέλιον) — particularly in view of his bold proclamations and forthright defenses of the Christian gospel in his earlier letters, without any evident sense of shame or embarrassment for what he said or how he defended it. Certainly there is no shame expressed in Galatians or the Corinthian correspondence — neither in Philippians, whether written earlier or later than Romans. Nor do Luke's portrayals of Paul's Gentile ministry in Acts suggest any such shame or embarrassment.[17] What, therefore, could Paul possibly have been ashamed of in writing to the Christians at Rome? What would have occasioned such a remark? What did he have in mind?

One opinion is that Paul is here using a figure of speech called litotes — that is, an understatement in which one speaks affirmatively by means of a negation (as, for example, "I am not unhappy" or "he is not a bad singer"). So it has been suggested that we should understand Paul here as really saying "I am proud of the gospel." Chrysostom in the fourth century provided some impetus for this understanding in one of his homilies on Romans when he said: "Paul *understates* that he is not ashamed in order to teach them [the Christians at Rome] not to be ashamed of Christ either."[18] And a number of commentators and translators of the immediately past generation have also espoused this view.[19]

But Paul does not commonly use litotes in his letters. The closest parallels are to be found in 2 Cor 2:11 ("We are not unaware of his [i.e., 'Satan's']

16. Cf. our "Exegetical Comments" on Paul's use of εὐαγγέλιον θεοῦ in 1:1.
17. Cf. esp. Acts 28:31, the closing sentence of Luke's second volume, which states in its final two words that during his two years of house arrest at Rome Paul preached "boldly" (μετὰ πάσης παρρησίας) and "without hindrance" (ἀκωλύπως) — with that preaching having taken place in the very city to which the apostle's present letter was addressed.
18. Chrysostom, "Homilies of St. John Chrysostom on the Epistle of St. Paul the Apostle to the Romans," in *Nicene and Post-Nicene Fathers of the Christian Church*, 11.348 (italics mine).
19. Cf., e.g., C. H. Dodd, *Romans*, 9; Taylor, *Romans*, 25; Bruce, *Romans*, 74, with that understanding coming to explicit expression in some of the NT translations of their day (cf. Moffatt: "I am proud of the gospel"; TEV: "I have complete confidence in the gospel").

schemes") and 2 Cor 11:15 ("It is no great thing, then, if his [i.e., 'Satan's'] servants masquerade as servants of righteousness"); perhaps also in 1 Cor 10:5 and 1 Thess 2:15. It appears, as well, in the narrative of Acts, particularly with the use of the expression οὐκ ὀλίγος ("not a few").[20] Yet while such an understanding is possible, more cogent explanations can be given.

Another way of understanding Paul's statement here in 1:16a that he was "not ashamed of the gospel" is to view his remark in the context of criticisms against the Christian message by non-believing Jews and pagan Gentiles of his day — that is, as the apostle's defiant response to the common reactions to the gospel expressed by both Jews and Gentiles throughout the Greco-Roman world: (1) that of revulsion to the simplicity and lowliness of the gospel, which was a matter of extreme embarrassment to those who considered themselves more worldly-wise and religiously sophisticated, and (2) that of hostility to the proclamation of a crucified Messiah, Lord and Savior, which seemed to some a political threat and to others a religious absurdity. And in support of such an understanding, Paul's statement of 1 Cor 1:23, where he provides a brief characterization of the reactions of both non-believing Jews and non-believing Gentiles to the Christian gospel ("A stumbling block to Jews and foolishness to Gentiles"), has often been cited.[21]

John Chrysostom in the fourth century, for example, in positing a rationale for Paul's "not ashamed" statement, said:

> The Romans were most anxious about the things of the world, because of their riches, their empire, their victories, and they thought that their emperors were equal to the gods. . . . While they were so puffed up, Paul was going to preach Jesus, the carpenter's son who was brought up in Judea, in the house of a lower-class woman, who had no bodyguards, who was not surrounded by wealth, but who died as a criminal among thieves and endured many other inglorious afflictions.[22]

Pelagius, the British monk and theologian, writing in the first decade of the fifth century, interpreted Paul's remark as follows:

> This is subtly intended to censure the pagans who, although they do not blush to believe that for the sake of monstrous lust their god Jove [Jupiter] turned himself into irrational animals and inanimate gold, suppose that we [Christians] should be ashamed to believe that for the salvation of his image [created humanity] our Lord was crucified in the flesh he assumed, though in the one case the disgrace is shocking, in the other a mark of fidelity and power.[23]

---

20. Cf. Acts 12:18; 14:28; 17:4, 12; 19:23, 24; 27:20; see also 19:11; 20:12; 21:39; 28:2.
21. Cf., e.g., Lightfoot, *Notes on Epistles of St. Paul,* 250; Sanday and Headlam, *Romans,* 22.
22. Chrysostom, "Homilies," in *Nicene and Post-Nicene Fathers,* 11.348.
23. Pelagius, in *Pelagius's Commentary on St. Paul's Epistle to the Romans,* 62 (PL 30.649).

And John Calvin in 1540, understanding Paul as having "the taunts of the un-godly" in mind, said of this statement:

> He hints indeed that it [i.e., the gospel] was contemptible in the eyes of the world, when he says that he is not ashamed of it himself. Thus he prepares them for bearing the reproach of the cross of Christ, that they might not undervalue the Gospel when they saw it exposed to the fears and taunts of the ungodly.[24]

These are but a few examples of how most Christian commentators down through the centuries have understood Paul in saying that he was "not ashamed of the gospel." And such an understanding has been most aptly expressed in our day by Charles Cranfield:

> Paul knows full well the inevitability of the temptation to be ashamed of the gospel in view of the continuing hostility of the world to God, on the one hand, and, on the other, the nature of the gospel itself, its unimpressiveness over against the impressiveness of the world, the fact that God (because He desires to leave men room to make a free personal decision of faith rather than to compel them) has intervened in history for the salvation of men not in obvious might and majesty but in a veiled way which was bound to look to the world like abject weakness and foolishness.[25]

On the other hand, Otto Michel has voiced a somewhat different under-standing of the apostle's "not ashamed" remark in proposing that in Paul's mind there was a firm connection between Jesus' teaching about not being ashamed of the gospel, as later recorded in Mark 8:38 and Luke 9:26 ("If anyone is ashamed of me and my words, the Son of Man will be ashamed of him when he comes in his glory and in the glory of the Father and of the holy angels"), and the church's forthright confession of Jesus, as admonished and declared in 2 Tim 1:8 and 12 ("Do not be ashamed to testify about our Lord. . . . I am not ashamed, because I know whom I have believed, and am convinced that he is able to guard what I have entrusted to him for that day"). Thus Michel argued that "I am not ashamed" (οὐκ ἐπαισχύνομαι) should be taken in the sense of "I confess" or "I bear witness to" the gospel.[26] Kingsley Barrett, however, has suggested that Paul, "an obscure provincial," may have been embarrassed to come to Rome, "the centre of the world," and so as "a self-styled apostle, lacking the self-evident authorization of the Twelve, he approaches a Church where his authority and even his credentials may well be questioned."[27]

24. J. Calvin, *Romans*, in *Calvin's New Testament Commentaries*, 8.26.
25. Cranfield, *Romans*, 1.86-87.
26. Michel, *An die Römer*, 51.
27. Barrett, *Romans*, 27.

Another explanation of 1:16a is that of Gerhart Herold, who argued that Paul's statement should be understood in the context of an eschatological lawsuit or trial in the divine courts, and so the present tense of the verb ἐπαισχύνομαι ("I am ashamed") should be read proleptically in a future sense: "I will not be put to shame by the gospel."[28] In a somewhat similar vein, though with an emphasis on the "new temporal framework defined by God's already efficacious act of eschatological deliverance in Christ," Richard Hays interprets Paul as "echoing" Isa 50:7-8 — though with the transformation of Isaiah's future tense to a present tense — in declaring that he is "not ashamed of the gospel," since in a very real present sense "the gospel is God's eschatological vindication of those who trust in him."[29] And a number of others have drawn attention to the fact that "shame" in the OT is attributed to those who have acted on a false assumption or with misplaced confidence,[30] and therefore suggest that what Paul is doing here at the beginning of the body middle of his letter is assuring his addressees that what he will present in the following theological and ethical sections is firmly based.

There are, of course, a number of features in some of the views cited above that may be acclaimed as highly laudable. Nonetheless, the very variety of interpretations (1) suggests something of the widespread distribution and diverse use of the expression throughout both the OT and the NT and (2) alerts interpreters to the need of rooting each appearance of the expression in its own particular context. And in the context of his letter to believers in Jesus at Rome, we propose that Paul's "I am not ashamed of the gospel" should be viewed primarily as highly apologetic or polemical in nature and as responding to certain criticisms of his person, mission, and/or message being voiced by at least some of the Christians at Rome — with those criticisms evidently having been relayed to him by some of his coworkers, friends, and/or relatives who were residing in Rome (in all likelihood, some of those listed in 16:1-15).

The thesis that Paul wrote Romans for a number of reasons, which included the polemical reasons of (1) to counter some criticisms of his person and Gentile ministry and (2) to correct certain misunderstandings of his message that had arisen among the Christians at Rome, has been argued, in various ways and with differing nuances, by a number of scholars during the past half century or so — not only focusing on the apostle's statement in 1:16a, but also highlighting various passing comments, veiled allusions, rhetorical questions, and one rather pithy exhortation at the end of the letter in support.[31] Most significant among the advocates of this understanding has been Peter Stuhlmacher, who in 1986 set out a catalog of such passing comments, veiled allusions, and rhetorical questions that appear in Romans, and drew from that data such a conclusion.[32] Also important in this regard is the work of Alexander Wedderburn, who in 1988

---

28. Herold, *Zorn und Gerechtigkeit Gottes,* 229.
29. Hays, *Echoes of Scripture,* 38-39, 59-60.
30. Cf., e.g., Pss 35:26; 40:14-15; 69:19; 71:13; 119:6.
31. See further R. N. Longenecker, *Introducing Romans,* 123-26.
32. Cf. Stuhlmacher, "Purpose of Romans" (ET, 1991).

devoted a sizeable concluding portion of his book to a defense of this polemical understanding and his own explication of it.[33] Prominent in this final portion of his book is the assertion that, beginning with 1:16a, *"the argument of the rest of Romans from this point to the end of chapter 11 is a defence of Paul's message and ministry against charges which claimed that it was indeed shameful."*[34] And near the end of his discussion Wedderburn provides the following summary statement of his position:

> This chapter has attempted to show that the seemingly very general argument of Romans 1–11 is by no means written without any reference to the situation of the Roman Christians. Rather its main purpose is to answer those criticisms of Paul's gospel and ministry which would prevent the Christians in Rome who had espoused a Judaizing form of Christianity from offering their support, their endorsement and their prayers for the success of his visit to Jerusalem with the collection; the same criticisms and suspicions, if not allayed, would in turn have presented him with considerable difficulties when eventually he reached Rome and sought to exercise his ministry amongst them as their apostle.[35]

Further, during the recent past there have arisen within biblical scholarship important discussions regarding the impact of "shame" and "honor" motifs in the Mediterranean world on a number of matters in the writings of the NT. It is probably somewhat extreme to declare, as does Robert Jewett, that Paul in his letter to the Christians at Rome "employs honor categories from beginning to end."[36] But, accepting the theses of Stuhlmacher and Wedderburn regarding why Paul speaks in 1:16a of being "not ashamed" (though, it need also be stated, not their views regarding the nature of Christianity at Rome or some of their nuancing of the issues involved), I would also applaud Halvor Moxnes's comment on this passage in his highlighting of the motifs of "honor" and "shame" in the Mediterranean world and in the NT:

> Although the ground for Paul's confidence is found in the gospel, the fact that he is not ashamed expresses his relations to his environment. Even in their most theological use, "shame" and "not to be ashamed" do not relinquish their everyday meaning, in which a person stands within a relationship not only to God but [also] to other people within a community.[37]

---

33. Cf. Wedderburn, *Reasons for Romans,* 104-42.

34. *Ibid.,* 104 (italics his).

35. *Ibid.,* 139.

36. Jewett, *Romans,* 49; see also his treatments at many other places in his commentary.

37. Moxnes, "Honor, Shame, and the Outside World," 207. Probably such "honor" and "shame" motifs also come into play later in Paul's letter to Rome in 13:1-7, where he urges "respect," "honor," and "submission" to those in governmental authority, and in 14:1–15:13, where he speaks against dishonoring and shaming a weaker believer in Jesus.

It is impossible, of course, to know exactly what was being said by the Christians at Rome in criticism of Paul, his mission, and/or his message. Possibly they were asserting that Paul's preaching of the gospel was (1) deficient in not properly interpreting or not laying sufficient emphasis on "the righteousness of God" in an attributive sense, (2) defective in not highlighting the covenant that God made with Israel, (3) errant in speaking of pagan Gentile believers in Jesus, who had no previous relationship with or appreciation for Israel, as being now as believers in Jesus "the elect of God," (4) quite wrong in not focusing more directly or not speaking more clearly on such forensic matters as "justification," "redemption," and "expiation/propitiation" — perhaps also in not bringing to the fore more expressly such an important biblical term as "salvation" — all of which expressions they seem to have viewed as being absolutely necessary for any authentic Christian proclamation, or perhaps (5) tending toward antinomianism in its ethical thrust. They may also have denigrated Paul's apostleship, simply because he was not one of the original disciples of Jesus — or perhaps they disparaged his person because they thought of him as something of a "local yokel" from the hinterland of Palestine who would only embarrass himself should he ever come to the sophisticated capital city of the empire. They may even have cast aspersions on his direct outreach to pagan Gentiles, since all the prophecies in the Scriptures spoke of God's blessings to the Gentiles as mediated through a redeemed Israel — as was the case with most if not all of the Gentile believers in Jesus at Rome, who had been, in one way or another, evangelized and taught by Jewish Christians and so had become extensively influenced by the theology, ways of thinking, and religious vocabulary of Jewish Christianity and the mother church at Jerusalem.

Such possible criticisms need to be more fully considered in the course of our exegetical comments on specific statements in this first major section of the letter (i.e., 1:16–4:25) and in the letter's third major section (i.e., 9:1–11:36). Here in 1:16a, however, as he begins the first major section of his protreptic discourse, Paul proclaims his vital concern for "the gospel" and declares that he is "not ashamed" of speaking about that message of "good news" to his Christian addressees at Rome — whatever they might have thought about him, his Gentile ministry, or his proclamation of the Christian gospel to Gentiles in the Greco-Roman world.

1:16b Two rather obvious features need to be noted in Paul's statement regarding the nature of "the gospel" that he proclaims — that is, δύναμις γὰρ θεοῦ ἐστιν εἰς σωτηρίαν ("for [or, 'because'] it is the power of God with respect to salvation"). First, the antecedent of the verb ἐστιν ("it is") is τὸ εὐαγγέλιον ("the gospel"), and so the gospel continues to be the subject discussed here. Second, the postpositive γάρ ("for," "because") connects this clause with the first statement of the verse by way of explanation, and so what Paul says here should be understood as his explanation for why he is "not ashamed of the gospel."

In the LXX δύναμις ("power") usually translates חיל, which denotes "power," "ability," or "competence" — though it also, at times, translates גבורה,

כֹּחַ, or עֹז, which connote more the ideas of "strength," "might," and "mighty act." But it is not used in the LXX of the forces of nature, which in the Gentile world were associated with a plethora of impersonal gods, but with respect to the creative, redemptive, and sustaining manifestations of the one truly personal divine being.[38] It is practically synonymous with the noun ἐνέργεια ("manifestation," "action," "operation," "way of working"), which also appears in the Pauline letters in connection with God's activity.[39] But ἐνέργεια often had to do more with the idea of *process,* whereas δύναμις speaks of *factuality* and *source.* So Paul in referring to "the gospel" (τὸ εὐαγγέλιον) as "the power of God" (δύναμις θεοῦ) should be understood as saying that the Christian gospel is the mighty redemptive and sustaining manifestation of the will of the one truly personal God, thereby highlighting both its divine source and its highly significant function (as he did earlier in 1:1-5). "As used here," as Joseph Fitzmyer has aptly pointed out, "the phrase formulates the dynamic character of God's gospel; the word [i.e., 'the word of the cross'] may announce the death and resurrection of Jesus Christ, but the emphasis is on that word as a force or power unleashed in human history."[40]

The telic use of the preposition εἰς ("with respect to," "in connection with") indicates that the purpose and final goal of God's redemptive power as expressed in the gospel is "with respect to (or 'in connection with') the salvation of everyone who believes."[41] The abstract idea of "salvation" is present in the writings of all of the world's major religions, for that is what every religion worthy of the name — however it defines humanity's primary problem — desires to effect in some manner in the lives of its devotees. The term σωτηρία ("salvation," "deliverance," "preservation"), however, is particularly prominent in the LXX[42] and in the writings of early Judaism.[43] It is frequently found, as well, in parts of the NT that reflect the religious vocabulary of early Jewish Christianity.[44] But, while it is present in the Pauline corpus,[45] the term "salvation" does not appear as often in Paul's letters as it does in those materials that reflect the religious

38. Cf., e.g., Exod 15:6, 13; 32:11; Deut 4:37; 9:26, 29; 26:8.

39. Cf., e.g., Eph 1:19; 3:7; Phil 3:21; Col 1:29; 2:12; 2 Thess 2:11.

40. Fitzmyer, *Romans,* 256; citing the association of δύναμις with "the gospel" and "Jesus Christ" in such passages as Rom 1:4; 1 Cor 2:4-5; 6:14; 2 Cor 13:4; Phil 3:10.

41. Cf. Stauffer, "εἰς," 2.429, where Stauffer discusses what he calls a "consecutive and final εἰς" — that is, where "the preposition denotes the direction of an action to a specific end." See also three other uses of such a "consecutive and final εἰς" later in Paul's letter to Rome at 9:31; 10:1; and 10:10; cf. also other possible similar uses of the preposition εἰς in Paul's letters in Rom 9:17; 14:9; 2 Cor 2:9; Eph 6:22; and Col 4:8.

42. Cf., e.g., Gen 49:18; Exod 14:13; 15:2; Deut 32:15; Judg 15:18; 1 Sam 2:1; 11:9; 14:45; also used extensively throughout the Psalms and Isaiah.

43. Cf., e.g., *Jub* 31:19; *T Dan* 5:10; *T Naph* 8:3; *T Gad* 8:1, *T Jos* 19:11; also often in the Dead Sea Scrolls, as in 1QH 7.18-19; CD 20.20, 34.

44. Cf. Luke 1:69-71, 77; 2:30; 3:6; 19:9; John 4:22; Acts 4:12; 13:26, 47; 16:17; Heb 1:14; 2:3, 10; 5:9; 6:9; 9:28; 1 Pet 1:5, 9-10; 2 Pet 3:15; Jude 3; Rev 7:10; 12:10; 19:1.

45. In addition to its appearances in Romans (as cited below), see 2 Cor 1:6; 6:2; 7:10; Eph 1:13; Phil 1:28; 2:12; 1 Thess 5:8-9; 2 Thess 2:13; cf. also 2 Tim 2:10; 3:15; Titus 2:11.

vocabulary of the religion of Israel, of early Judaism, and of Jewish Christianity — and so it may be presumed to represent more the language of Jews and Jewish Christians than specifically that of Paul in writing to his Gentile converts. Nonetheless, Paul here uses that term when writing to the Christians at Rome, who had been, it seems, extensively influenced by the theology and language of the mother church at Jerusalem.

Paul frequently uses the verbs σῴζειν ("to save," "rescue," "deliver," "preserve") and ῥύομαι (which also means "save," "rescue," "deliver," "preserve"), but he does not make use of the noun σωτηρία ("salvation") as often as the other NT writers do. Once, in fact, he even uses σωτηρία in a mundane fashion to refer to his hoped-for release from Roman imprisonment.[46] In Romans, while Paul uses σωτηρία in a distinctly religious sense in Sections I, III, and IV of the letter's body middle[47] — where, as I argue, he writes more in ways that the Christians at Rome, who had been extensively influenced by the theology and language of Jewish Christians, would understand — he does not use the term at all in Section II, 5:1–8:39, where, as I propose, he sets out the essence of his gospel proclamation to Gentiles in the Roman Empire who had not been so influenced by either Judaism or Jewish Christianity.

1:16c παντὶ τῷ πιστεύοντι ("to all the believing ones"). Paul's emphasis on πιστεύειν ("to believe," "trust in") and πίστις ("faith," "trust") throughout this first section of his protreptic message, that is, in 1:16–4:25, as well as throughout the third section, that is, in 9:1–11:36, is obvious. Here in 1:16c (as well as throughout 1:17), in setting out the thesis statement for this first section he speaks of "believing" and "faith" four times — making use of the substantival participle of the verb once in 1:16 and the noun three times in 1:17.

"Believing" and "faith" have to do with a positive response to and an acceptance of the gospel proclamation — and therefore a trust in the one who is the content of that message, that is, in Jesus Christ, as well as a reliance on the one who has provided that message and its content, that is, on God. Believing and faith are the necessary human responses to what God has provided for all people in the work and person of Jesus. They are not, however, qualities that certain people already have, which would make them eligible to receive God's love and benefits. Nor are they contributions that people bring to God in order to fulfill a condition imposed by him for the reception of his love and benefits. Such understandings would make "believing" and "faith" simply another set of meritorious works by which people may establish a claim on God and of which they can be proud. Rather, believing and faith, as Paul proclaims them, are opposed to all human deserving and every human credit.

It is God who has brought about the message of the gospel through the person and work of his Son, Jesus Christ. But it is also God who, by his Spirit, brings that message to the consciousness of every individual and lays people's

46. See Phil 1:19.
47. I.e., here in 1:16b; also later in 10:1, 10; 11:11; 13:11.

hearts open to respond positively. One of the amazing paradoxes of God's working in a person's heart and consciousness is that, while faith in the gospel, in Christ Jesus, and in God is always a gift from God, it is also in a very real sense more fully and more truly a person's own decision than anything he or she could decide or do by themselves. For it is the freedom that God, by his Spirit, restores to finite, sinful, and unable creatures that is primarily involved in the salvation and restoration of sinful and undeserving people — that is, the freedom that God gives to human beings, which they lost in their sin and rebellion, to respond in love and obedience to his love, mercy, and grace.

The adjective παντί ("all," "everyone") with the substantival participle τῷ πιστεύοντι ("the one who believes") highlights the fact that the gospel is "the power of God" that is effective "for salvation" to everyone, without exception or distinction, who will respond to it positively. This inclusiveness of the gospel (1) has been proclaimed earlier in 1:5 ("for the obedience of faith among all the Gentiles"), (2) is expressed in the statement that immediately follows in 1:16 and is found again in 2:9-10 ('Ιουδαίῳ τε πρῶτον καὶ "Ελληνι, "both for the Jew first and for the Gentile"), and (3) will appear repeatedly throughout Romans in such places as 3:22-24; 4:16; 5:18; 8:32; 10:4, 11-13; 11:32; and 15:10-11.

1:16d The phrase 'Ιουδαίῳ τε πρῶτον καὶ "Ελληνι ("both for the Jew first and for the Gentile") is extremely difficult to translate, simply because it contains both (1) an inclusive emphasis in the use of the enclitic particle τε ("both") with the dative nouns 'Ιουδαίῳ καὶ "Ελληνι ("for the Jew and for the Gentile"), which speaks of God's salvation as being universal in nature, *and* (2) a particularistic thrust in the use of the substantival adjective πρῶτον ("first"), which signals an ethnic priority and advantage for Jews within that universal outlook. It is probably best to translate it exactly (though, admittedly, somewhat awkwardly): "both for the Jew first and for the Gentile." The inclusive emphasis appears repeatedly throughout Romans (see the passages cited above), though the particle τε ("both") of this statement is hardly ever translated in any contemporary translations. The particularistic, prioritizing thrust signaled by πρῶτον ("first") has been variously explained.

Marcion, of course, simply deleted πρῶτον (see the textual notes above). Popular expositors often understand πρῶτον as referring merely to the historical fact that the gospel was preached to the Jews before it was preached to the Gentiles. Theodor Zahn, however, believed that πρῶτον should be taken not just with 'Ιουδαίῳ but with the whole statement 'Ιουδαίῳ τε . . . καὶ "Ελληνι, and so he understood Paul here as contrasting the Jews and Gentiles who first believed in Jesus with the "barbarians" and "foolish" of 1:14 who would follow later.[48] Anders Nygren argued that while Paul here indicates that he once recognized the special position of Jews in the divine *Heilsgeschichte,* it must be said — particularly in view of his words in Gal 3:28 and Eph 2:14-15 — that he did not as a follower of Jesus continue to advocate such an understanding,

48. Zahn, *An die Römer,* 73-77.

but rather saw any special position for Jews as now abolished.[49] Yet in light of Paul's fuller discussions of relations between Jews and Gentiles in Sections I and III of the body middle of Romans, where emphases on both inclusiveness and priority are not only sustained but also intertwined, it must be said (1) that Paul always saw both features as continuing throughout the course of salvation history and (2) that the mention of these features here comprises not only an introduction to what else he will write in this first major section of the letter, that is, in 1:16–4:25, but also to what he will write later in the third major section of the letter, 9:1–11:36.

It may be that Ἰουδαίῳ τε πρῶτον καὶ Ἕλληνι was an adage or tersely formulated aphorism that originated among the Christians of Rome in explanation of their own particular situation — that is, an adage stemming from (1) their recognition of the inclusive relation that existed among believing Jews and believing Gentiles in the Christian congregations at Rome, yet also (2) their awareness of the special place that Jews and Jewish Christians had, and continue to have, in God's overall plan of salvation history. Or it may have been that the saying originated among Jewish believers in Jesus at Jerusalem and was picked up from them by the Christians at Rome.[50] Or perhaps it was an expression that Paul himself coined to explain what he and other believers in Christ Jesus understood to be the course of salvation history, not only in the past but also in his own day. But however it came about, the inclusion of the particle τε ("both") highlights the equality of Jews and Gentiles before God, both as recipients of God's grace (as here in 1:16b) and as recipients of God's judgment (as later in 2:9-10), while the inclusion of the adjective πρῶτον ("first") speaks to the fact that God has ordained a certain priority and certain privileges for Jews and Jewish Christians.

1:17a δικαιοσύνη γὰρ θεοῦ ἐν αὐτῷ ἀποκαλύπτεται ("for in it the righteousness of God is being revealed"). Having given one important reason in 1:16b for not being ashamed of the gospel — "because it is the power of God for the salvation of everyone who believes" — Paul now sets out another highly significant reason: "for in it the righteousness of God is being revealed." The postpositive γάρ ("for," "because") functions as an explanatory conjunction (as it did earlier in 1:16b) and so introduces a statement that explains what preceded it. The locative pronoun αὐτῷ ("it") has as its antecedent the articular noun τὸ εὐαγγέλιον ("the gospel") of 1:16a, which was the unexpressed subject of 1:16b and continues to be so here in 1:17a. The third person singular, present, indicative, passive verb ἀποκαλύπτεται ("it is being revealed") suggests the ongoing proclamation of the "good news" of the Christian message as it was preached throughout the Greco-Roman world — not only by the Jerusalem church to Jews in the Jewish homeland, but also (1) by certain Jewish believers in Jesus to those at Rome, both Jews and Gentiles, and (2) by Paul in his outreach directly to Gentiles.

49. Nygren, *Romans*, 73.
50. Further, see our suggestion regarding the expression in the "Exegetical Comments" on 2:9-10, where it appears twice.

EXCURSUS: "THE RIGHTEOUSNESS OF GOD" AND "RIGHTEOUSNESS" IN PAUL

Discussions regarding the expression δικαιοσύνη θεοῦ ("the righteousness of God") and the abstract noun δικαιοσύνη ("righteousness") have been extensive, with whole volumes dedicated to the exposition of their respective meanings. We have dealt with this matter in *Introducing Romans*.[51] Here, however, because of the subject's great importance, it is necessary to set out again the major issues and repeat our suggestions in order to understand better what Paul is saying in his thesis statement of 1:16-17 — as well as to understand how he develops, supports, elucidates, and illustrates the central features of that thesis statement when he takes it up again in extended anaphoric fashion in 3:21–4:25.

1. The Occurrences of δικαιοσύνη θεοῦ and δικαιοσύνη in Paul and the NT. The expression δικαιοσύνη θεοῦ ("the righteousness of God") is most prominent in Paul's letters in the first section of the body middle of Romans, appearing (1) here in 1:17a in the thesis statement of 1:16-17, (2) in the rhetorical question of 3:5 (εἰ δὲ ἡ ἀδικία ἡμῶν θεοῦ δικαιοσύνην συνίστησιν, τί ἐροῦμεν; "But if our unrighteousness brings out God's righteousness more clearly, what shall we say?"), (3) in 3:21a and 3:22a in the repetition, expansion, and development of that first thesis statement of 1:16-17, and (4) in 3:25 and 3:26 ("He did this in order to show/demonstrate/prove 'his righteousness/justice,'" τῆς δικαιοσύνης αὐτοῦ), where it appears in the confessional material that is quoted in 3:24-26 in support of the repeated thesis of 3:21-23. It also appears once in the third section of the body middle of Romans at 10:3 (τὴν τοῦ θεοῦ δικαιοσύνην, "They did not know 'the righteousness that comes from God' and sought to establish their own"). The occurrences of the abstract noun δικαιοσύνη ("righteousness") in Romans are in 5:17 ("the gift of 'righteousness'"), in 5:21 ("so that grace might reign through 'righteousness' to bring eternal life through Jesus Christ our Lord"), and in 9:30 ("What then shall we say? That the Gentiles, who did not pursue 'righteousness,' have obtained it, a 'righteousness' that is by faith?"), while in 2 Corinthians the noun appears alone in 3:9 ("the ministry that brings 'righteousness'") — with all four of these verses using the term to refer to the righteousness that is bestowed by God.

Elsewhere in Paul's letters "the righteousness of God" appears only in 2 Cor 5:21 ("so that in him [Christ] we might become 'the righteousness of God'") and in Phil 3:9 ("'the righteousness of God' that is based on faith"). And in both of these verses it also quite clearly refers to a righteousness bestowed by God — that is, it is used in a *communicative* or *objective sense* (with the genitive τοῦ θεοῦ signifying that God is the source or originating agent of the righteousness that is communicated), and therefore to be understood as "the gift of righteousness" given by God (as expressed in Rom 5:17) to those who have responded "by faith" (to anticipate the discussion and definitions below).

Δικαιοσύνη θεοῦ appears, as well, in Matt 6:33, where the Evangelist seems to have expanded a "Q" saying by inserting the phrase (cf. its omission in the better texts of Luke 12:31) — though with the use of the personal pronoun αὐτοῦ, which, of course, refers back to the antecedent noun θεοῦ ("Seek first the kingdom of God and 'his righteousness,' and all these things will be given to you as well"). It appears also in the warning given in Jas 1:20 ("A person's anger does not bring about 'the righteousness of God'"),

---

51. R. N. Longenecker, *Introducing Romans,* esp. 388-400.

which is reminiscent of Sir 1:22. And it is found in a slightly varied form (i.e., with the article τοῦ and personal pronoun ἡμῶν) in the salutation of 2 Pet 1:1 ("To those who 'through the righteousness of our God' and Savior Jesus Christ have received a faith as precious as ours").

The abstract noun δικαιοσύνη ("righteousness," "uprightness," "justice") is frequently used in a religious sense throughout the LXX, the writings of early Judaism, and the NT — as also the adjective δίκαιος ("righteous," "upright," "just"), the verb δικαιόω ("justify," "vindicate," "acquit," "make free"), and the adverb δικαίως ("uprightly," "justly," "in a just manner"). Yet NT occurrences of the explicit expression δικαιοσύνη θεοῦ ("the righteousness of God"), as noted above, are somewhat limited. And most NT appearances of the abstract noun δικαιοσύνη, especially where used in attributive or subjective senses (to anticipate our later definitions and discussion below), are in contexts that seem to reflect the vocabulary and usage of the OT, early Judaism, and Jewish Christianity.

2. The Meaning of δικαιοσύνη θεοῦ and δικαιοσύνη in the Earliest Writings, Both Classical and Christian. What, then, does Paul mean in Romans by the expression δικαιοσύνη θεοῦ ("the righteousness of God") — particularly as he uses it in 1:17 and then again in 3:21-22? It is not enough, however, to deal only with the explicit expression δικαιοσύνη θεοῦ. Paul's use of δικαιοσύνη without the possessive noun θεοῦ or pronoun αὐτοῦ — as well as his use of the adjective δίκαιος, the verb δικαιόω, and the adverb δικαίως — must also be taken into account. Likewise, it must always be asked how this complex of δικαι-words was used by authors before Paul and by other writers and translators of his day — not only as can be determined from a study of its use in classical Greek literature, but more particularly by its use in the LXX translation of the OT, the writings of early Judaism, and other NT authors.

In the Greek classical period the noun δικαιοσύνη had to do with the observance of law and the fulfillment of duty,[52] and so in legal contexts was almost invariably used where a person was punished by being given what was deserved according to the law.[53] In the Greco-Roman world of earliest Christianity, in fact, the term was closely associated with judicial justice and most often connoted the idea of retributive punishment. Thus the common Latin translation of δικαιοσύνη θεοῦ in the NT came to be *iustitia Dei* ("the justice of God"), both in the Old Latin, which was produced at the end of the second century or first part of the third, and in Jerome's Vulgate, which was translated during the latter part of the fourth century and first part of the fifth. So most Latin theologians came to understand "the righteousness/justice of God" in primarily an *attributive sense* — that is, as an attribute of God, with an emphasis on his character as being absolutely just and his actions as always expressed justly and in terms of justice.

This sense was buttressed by the writings of Tertullian of Carthage, who was trained as a lawyer and philosopher but excelled as a Christian apologist and theologian after his conversion to Christ. Tertullian was extremely prolific, writing literally scores of apologetic and theological tractates (both orthodox and sectarian) — many of which were kept and cherished, though others lost and forgotten. It was Tertullian who took away the reproach of theological and literary barrenness that was commonly leveled in his day against Latin Christianity. For he developed a system of juridical and forensic Christian doctrine that instructed such contemporary Roman Christian thinkers and

52. Cf. Plato, *Republic* 4.433a.
53. Cf. Aristotle, *Rhetoric* 1.9.

writers as Cyprian, Minucius Felix, Arnobius, and Lactantius — and which continued to inspire many later Christian worthies, such as Jerome and Augustine.

Such an attributive or subjective understanding of "the righteousness of God" was expressed in the fourth century by a Latin commentator, whose commentary on the Pauline letters was thought to have been written by Ambrose but who was later dubbed "Ambrosiaster" by Erasmus. For in his treatment of the phrase *iustitia Dei* in Rom 1:17, Ambrosiaster writes:

> It is the justice of God, because he has given what he has promised; hence the one who believes that he has acquired that which God had promised through his prophets shows that God is just and becomes a witness to his justice.[54]

Further, connecting "justice," "mercy," and "promise," Ambrosiaster says of the phrase as it appears in Rom 3:21:

> That is said to be God's justice which seems to be his mercy, because it is rooted in his promise. . . . And when he welcomes those who take refuge in him, it is said to be justice, because not to welcome those who seek refuge is iniquity.[55]

Augustine, however, during the final decade of the fourth century and the first three decades of the fifth (i.e., from 391 until his death in 430), came more and more to interpret the expression *iustitia Dei* in his Latin Bible not only in a *subjective sense* but also in an *objective sense* — that is, not only as an attribute of God and his actions, but also with reference to God's justification of repentant sinners, his bestowal on them of a status of righteousness, and his endowment of them with his own quality of righteousness.[56] For after returning to North Africa in 391 (some four years after his conversion to Christ in Milan), and shortly following his ordination as a presbyter in the diocese of Hippo, Augustine, in response to questions asked him at a conference in Carthage, wrote a series of expository comments on selected passages from Rom 5–9 that he grouped into 84 sections and published in 394 as *Expositio quarundam propositionum ex epistula ad Romanos*.[57] It was sometime during this period that Augustine seems to have first begun to think seriously about the nature of God's grace — though his understanding of unmerited grace developed considerably over the next few years, as appears evident from what he wrote later to his friend Simplicianus on the subject in 396-98.[58] And it was this topic of God's grace that dominated all of Augustine's thought during the last thirty years of his life, that is, from the beginning of the fifth century until his death in 430, and that redirected much of Christian theology thereafter. Further, it may be assumed that it was this deep-seated conviction regarding the nature of God's grace that caused Augustine to understand the phrase *iustitia Dei* not only as an attribute of God (i.e., the attributive or subjective sense of the phrase) but also as that which God gives to repentant sinners in redeeming them by his grace (i.e., the communicative or objective sense).

3. *The Meaning of* δικαιοσύνη θεοῦ *and* δικαιοσύνη *in the Middle Ages.* In the Middle Ages (i.e., from the fifth to fifteenth centuries of European history) two interpretations

---

54. Ambrosiaster, *Ad Romanos* on 1:17; *CSEL* 81.1.36-37.

55. Ambrosiaster, *Ad Romanos* on 3:21; *CSEL* 81.1.116-17.

56. Cf. Augustine, *De Trinitate* 14.12.15 (*CCLat* 50A.443); *De spiritu et littera* 9.15 (*CSEL* 60.167); 11.18 (*CSEL* 60.171); *Ep* 140.72 (*CSEL* 44.220); *In Johannis evangelium* 26.1 (*CCLat* 36.260).

57. Augustine, *Expositio quarundam propositionum ex epistula ad Romanos*, *PL* 35.2063-88.

58. Augustine, *De diversis Quaestionibus ad Simplicianum*, *PL* 40.102-47.

of "the righteousness of God" (δικαιοσύνη θεοῦ, *iustitia Dei*) vied for acceptance. The first, which was understood at that time as the classical view, viewed the phrase as having reference to the righteous and just nature of God, his fidelity to his promises, and the justice of his actions in dealing with humanity (i.e., the *attributive* or *subjective sense*). The other, influenced by Augustine and Paul's use of the expression in 2 Cor 5:21 and Phil 3:9, viewed δικαιοσύνη θεοῦ and *iustitia Dei* more in the context of God's salvific activity in human history (i.e., the *communicative* or *objective sense*), though understood it also as referring to God's righteous and just nature. So in speaking about "God's righteousness/ justice," theologians during the fifth through the fifteenth centuries frequently combined, in various ways, both (1) what is true about God's character and actions *and* (2) what God gives to those who believe the gospel and commit themselves to him.

This collation of nuances seems to have been expressed by some of the major Roman Catholic commentators during the Middle Ages. Thomas Aquinas, for example, spoke of "the justice of God" in Rom 1:17 as that "by which God is just and by which he justifies human beings" *(iustitia qua Deus iustus est et qua Deus homines justificat),* thereby joining Augustine's understanding of God's grace in justifying people with Anselm's understanding of God's mercy as being the fullness of his justice.[59] Likewise, this same union of views appears in the commentary writings of Thomas de Vio, who was surnamed Cajetan. For Cajetan, a scholastic theologian of immense stature and great influence (who had in 1518 presided as the papal legate in the examination of Luther at Augsburg), devoted himself during the final decade of his life, 1525 to 1534, entirely to the writing of biblical commentaries — first on the Psalms, then on the Gospels, the Acts, and the letters of the NT (including Romans), and finally on the Pentateuch, Joshua, Proverbs, Ecclesiastes, and Isaiah 1–3. But though Cajetan was considered the most eminent Thomist theologian of his day, he got into trouble with his ecclesiastical superiors during his declining days when his NT commentaries were published — not only because he had departed from the Vulgate text, using instead the critical editions of the Greek text prepared by Erasmus and Faber, but also, and much more seriously in the eyes of his distractors, because he often sounded too much like Luther in the interpretation of Paul's statements regarding "God's justice/righteousness" and "faith." And although Augustine was widely revered during the Middle Ages as one of the church's greatest theologians, he was also rather diversely understood — with the result that his broader understanding of the expression "God's righteousness/justice" was often interpreted along the lines of the more strictly *attributive, subjective* and "classical" view of such writers as Anselm and Ambrosiaster.

4. Luther's Understanding of δικαιοσύνη θεοῦ and δικαιοσύνη. It was Martin Luther, however, who most effectively highlighted the *communicative* or *objective sense* of "the justice/righteousness of God" and the vital importance of "faith" in Paul's letters and so brought about a new appreciation in western Christianity of Augustine's emphasis on God's unmerited grace. In his earlier experience as a monk Luther had pondered deeply, with considerable consternation and great sorrow, the meaning of the phrase *iustitia Dei* ("the justice of God") in his Latin Bible. In 1515, however, Luther came to what was for him an entirely new discovery regarding Paul's teaching on "the justice/righteousness of God" and "justification by faith" in Rom 1:17, which new discovery became the catalyst for his own spiritual rebirth, an open door into "paradise," and "a gateway to heaven," and so the start of a thoroughgoing religious revolution in his life — and which, of course,

---

59. Cf. T. Aquinas, "Epistola ad Romanos," in *Opera Omnia,* 13.3-156, on 1:17.

eventuated in the Protestant Reformation. Later in 1545, recalling the resolution of his spiritual struggles when he came to a proper understanding of this phrase, Luther wrote (with the translation of the Latin *iustitia Dei,* "the justice of God," in the text, and that of the Greek δικαιοσύνη θεοῦ, "the righteousness of God," in brackets):

> I greatly longed to understand Paul's Epistle to the Romans, and nothing stood in the way but that one expression, "the justice ['righteousness'] of God," because I took it to mean that justice ["righteousness"] whereby God is just ["righteous"] and deals justly ["righteously"] in punishing the unjust ["unrighteous"]. My situation was that, although an impeccable monk, I stood before God as a sinner troubled in conscience, and I had no confidence that my merit would assuage him. Therefore I did not love a just ["righteous"] and angry God, but rather hated and murmured against him. Yet I clung to the dear Paul and had a great yearning to know what he meant.
>
> Night and day I pondered until I saw the connection between the justice ["righteousness"] of God and the statement that "the just ['righteous'] will live by his faith." Then I grasped the truth that the justice ["righteousness"] of God is that righteousness whereby, through grace and sheer mercy, he justifies us by faith. Thereupon I felt myself to be reborn and to have gone through open doors into paradise. The whole of Scripture took on a new meaning, and whereas before "the justice ['righteousness'] of God" had filled me with hate, now it became to me inexpressibly sweet in greater love. This passage of Paul became to me a gateway to heaven.[60]

Luther's discovery was in line with Augustine's emphasis on the unmerited nature of God's grace. Luther was not opposed to understanding "just" and "justice" (in Latin), or "righteous" and "righteousness" (in Greek), as attributes of God and his actions (i.e., the *attributive* or *subjective sense*). But his emphasis was on "God's righteousness as a divine gift" (i.e., the *communicative* or *objective sense*), which puts the person who receives God's gift "by faith" in an entirely new relationship with the one true, righteous Divine Being (i.e., forensic justness or rightness) and causes that person to live in an entirely new way both personally and in society (i.e., ethical justice or righteousness).

5. A New Focus on the OT and the Writings of Early Judaism. A new focus in modern biblical scholarship with regard to the understanding of "righteousness" and "the righteousness of God," however, was begun by Hermann Cremer at the beginning of the twentieth century.[61] For Cremer argued that NT interpreters should not treat these expressions in terms of the use of δικαιοσύνη in Greek classical writings, nor deal with them just theologically, but must first understand them with reference to their rootage in the OT. So he argued that Paul's use of the abstract noun δικαιοσύνη and the expression δικαιοσύνη θεοῦ must be viewed primarily vis-à-vis the OT masculine noun צדק and its feminine counterpart צדקה, which in both genders denoted a broad range of concepts having to do with "justness," "justice," "rightness," and "righteousness" — and so were used in the religion of Israel to connote both (1) an attribute of God and the quality of his actions[62] *and* (2) what God accomplishes redemptively on behalf of his people, often in

---

60. M. Luther, "Preface to Latin Writings," in *Luther's Works,* 34.336-37; see also *idem,* "Table Talk," *ibid.,* 54.193, 309, 442.

61. Cf. A. H. Cremer, *Die Paulinische Rechtfertigungslehre* (1900).

62. Cf., e.g., Ps 36:6 (MT 36:7): "Your 'righteousness' is like the mighty mountains, your justice like the great deep"; Ps 71:19: "Your 'righteousness' reaches to the skies, O God."

conjunction with the concept of "salvation."[63] And this understanding of "righteousness" and "the righteousness of God" as rooted in the OT Scriptures, with both *attributive* and *communicative* nuances present, has been seen to be supported by a number of other OT passages that (1) speak of the character and actions of God in terms of "rightness" and "righteousness"[64] *and* (2) refer to God's deliverance and salvation of his people as "his acts of righteousness."[65] Further, such a joining of nuances is supported by passages in the LXX and the Dead Sea Scrolls where God's righteousness is depicted as both his granting of a new status to people as a result of his removal of their sins[66] *and* his transformation of people by his enablement.[67]

In addition to these passages, "the best perception of God's righteousness" in writings that may be claimed to represent the better Jewish spiritual milieu of Paul's day is probably, as Peter Stuhlmacher has argued, "offered by the Old Testament and early Jewish prayers of repentance" — particularly those of Dan 9:4-19; *4 Ezra* 8:20-36; and 1QS 10-11.[68] The prayer of repentance in Dan 9:4-19 incorporates toward its close the following words:

> O Lord, in keeping with all your righteous acts, turn away your anger and your wrath from Jerusalem, your city, your holy hill. . . . We do not make requests of you because we are righteous, but because of your great mercy.[69]

Ezra's prayer of repentance in *4 Ezra* 8:20-36 concludes with the following statement:

> For in this, O Lord, your righteousness and goodness will be declared, when you are merciful to those who have no store of good works.[70]

And the Qumran covenantors' hymn of repentance in 1QS 10-11 includes the following words of confidence, which reflect not only an attributive but also a communicative understanding of God's righteousness:

> If I should waver, God's mercies will be my salvation; if I stumble in the wayward-ness of flesh, I shall be set aright through God's righteousness ever-enduring. . . . In His righteousness He will cleanse me from all the pollution of man and from the sin of humanity, that I may acknowledge to God His righteousness, and to the Most High His majestic splendor.[71]

When Paul's use of δικαιοσύνη θεοῦ ("the righteousness of God") is understood in terms of this background, its range of meaning and comprehensive nature can be more fully appreciated. No longer can such past alternatives be proposed as (1) whether the possessive τοῦ θεοῦ ("of God") or αὐτοῦ ("of him") is to be interpreted as a subjective or

---

63. Cf., e.g., Isa 46:13: "I am bringing my 'righteousness' near, it is not far away; and my salvation will not be delayed. I will grant salvation to Zion, my splendor to Israel"; Isa 56:1: "Maintain 'justice' and do what is right, for my salvation is close at hand and my 'righteousness' will soon be revealed."

64. Cf. Deut 33:21; Judg 5:11; Pss 89:16; 96:13; 98:9; 111:3; 143:1, 11; Mic 6:5.

65. Cf. 1 Sam 12:7; Isa 45:8, 24-25; 51:4-8; Dan 9:16.

66. Cf., e.g., LXX Ps 50:1-14; 1QS 11.3; 1QH 12.37.

67. Cf., e.g., LXX Ps 71:1-2; 1QS 11.14; 1QH 13.37.

68. Stuhlmacher, *Romans* 30.

69. Dan 9:16, 18.

70. *4 Ezra* 8:36.

71. 1QS 11.12, 14-15.

an objective genitive, (2) whether the expression should be understood in an attributive or a communicative fashion, (3) whether it is best viewed soteriologically or eschatologically, or (4) whether its thrust has to do primarily with theology or anthropology. In light of Paul's Jewish background, all of these dichotomies, as Graf Reventlow has long ago observed, "quickly show themselves to be much too narrow."[72] It is not whether one or the other of these alternative views is correct for an understanding of Paul's use of δικαιοσύνη θεοῦ (or δικαιοσύνη αὐτοῦ) in Rom 1:17; 3:5, 21-22 (twice), 25-26 (twice); 10:3; 2 Cor 5:21; and Phil 3:9. Rather, the more comprehensive range of meaning found in the OT and the writings of early Judaism must be credited, as well, to Paul's use of the expression — particularly in his thesis statements of 1:16-17 (at v. 17a) and 3:21-23 (at vv. 21a and 22a). For "the righteousness of God" that Paul speaks of in these passages is both (1) an attribute of God and a quality that characterizes all of his actions (the *attributive sense*) *and* (2) a gift that God gives to people who come to him "by faith" (the *communicative sense*). It is a type of righteousness that enables God to be both δίκαιον ("just") and δικαιοῦντα ("justifier" or "the one who justifies"), as the confessional material of 3:24-26 affirms at its close in v. 26b.

        6. *Righteousness as a Forensic Status or an Ethical Quality.* But even when a communicative sense of "the righteousness of God" and "righteousness" is included within the range of meaning of these expressions, there has continued to exist in the minds of many the question as to whether in speaking of the gift of "God's righteousness" and/or "righteousness" Paul is referring primarily to (1) a status of righteousness that God confers (i.e., a forensic or declaratory understanding) or (2) an ethical quality of life (i.e., an effective or ethical understanding) that God empowers. Roman Catholic interpreters have laid stress on the noun δικαιοσύνη ("righteousness," "uprightness," "justice") and the adjective δίκαιος ("righteous," "upright," "just"), interpreting the verb δικαιόω ("to justify," "vindicate," "acquit," "make free") in terms of the noun and the adjective, and so have concluded that δικαιοσύνη means primarily an acquittal from past sins and a "making righteous" in an ethical sense — but that a final declaration of righteousness awaits the last judgment. Protestants, on the other hand, have emphasized that the verb δικαιόω must be viewed in the sense of "to account as righteous" or "declare righteous," and so have interpreted the entire cluster of δικαι-words in terms of a "right relationship" established by God (i.e., forensic, declaratory, or sometimes called "imputed" righteousness) rather than as first of all "ethical uprightness" (i.e., effective, ethical, or sometimes called "real" righteousness). Or to put the question in a more modern form: Is Paul's use of δικαι-words to be viewed as "transfer terminology"[73] or as applicable to "the day-to-day conduct of those who had already believed"?[74]

        Based on his study of "about 481 cases" of the use of צדק as a noun, an adjective, or a verb in the OT, John Ziesler has, we believe, largely resolved this dilemma in demonstrating how Paul used (1) the Greek verb δικαιόω in a forensic or declaratory fashion to mean "to justify," "vindicate," or "acquit," but also used (2) the Greek noun δικαιοσύνη in a more comprehensive manner to signify not just a status or standing before God but also a person's ethical "uprightness," "righteousness," or "justice" and (3) the Greek adjective

72. Reventlow, *Rechtfertigung im Horizont des Alten Testaments*, 113 (my translation).

73. So E. P. Sanders, *Paul and Palestinian Judaism*, 470-72; idem, *Paul, the Law, and the Jewish People*, passim.

74. So Dunn, "New Perspective on Paul," 121.

δίκαιος to include being ethically "upright," "righteous," or "just."[75] In so doing, Ziesler has shown how Paul joined both forensic and ethical categories in his understanding of righteousness, with the one always involving the other.

7. The Distribution and Varied Nuances of δικαιοσύνη θεοῦ in Paul's Letters and the Rest of the New Testament. There yet remains, however, one rather nagging difficulty for many interpreters of Paul. This has to do with (1) the distribution of the expression δικαιοσύνη θεοῦ ("the righteousness of God") in Paul's letters and its three other NT appearances and (2) the varied nuances that this expression evidences in those passages where it appears. As Peter Stuhlmacher has stated the difficulty:

> It has long been a matter of debate in Pauline exegesis whether one should under-stand the righteousness of God in Paul's thought above all, on the basis of Phil. 3:9, as the gift of God, the righteousness of faith, or "the righteousness which is valid before God" (Luther); or whether the accent is to be placed, with Schlatter among others, on God's own juridical and salvific activity (in and through Christ).[76]

Stuhlmacher himself seeks to settle this debate with the following comment, which, as far as it goes, is certainly correct:

> One should not establish a false alternative between the two [understandings]. The expression incorporates both, and it must be determined from passage to passage where Paul places the accent.[77]

Likewise, Joseph Fitzmyer, while acknowledging the probable presence of both an *attributive sense* and a *communicative sense* in Paul's understanding of the expression, highlights the dilemma faced by some Pauline interpreters — particularly with respect to the apostle's use of "the righteousness/justice of God" in Romans: "What is debatable, however, is whether the gift idea of *dikaiosunē theou* is suitable anywhere in Romans."[78] For while Fitzmyer seems to have little doubt about the *communicative sense* of the ex-pression being present in 2 Cor 5:21 and Phil 3:9, he has difficulty seeing anything but the *attributive sense* in its more numerous appearances in Romans.

Such a dilemma for interpreters, however, may be somewhat mitigated if we un-derstand, as I have proposed, (1) that Romans was written to believers in Jesus who had been extensively influenced by Jewish Christian theology and vocabulary, whatever their particular ethnic backgrounds, and (2) that in writing to the Christians at Rome Paul often used certain theological expressions and religious vocabulary that he believed his addressees cherished, particularly in the first and third sections (1:16–4:25; 9:1–11:36) of the body middle of his letter. And on such a thesis, the following fourfold scenario may be proposed as present in Romans:

1. In his thesis statements of 1:16-17 and 3:21-23 Paul uses the expression "the righ-teousness of God" in a comprehensive fashion, including in its range of meaning both an *attributive* or *subjective sense* and a *communicative* or *objective sense.*
2. In support of his thesis, he cites in 3:24-26 a portion of an early Christian con-fession that was then current within Jewish Christianity, which spoke of God's

---

75. Cf. Ziesler, *Meaning of Righteousness in Paul,* passim.
76. Stuhlmacher, *Romans,* 31.
77. *Ibid.,* 32.
78. Fitzmyer, *Romans,* 262.

"justice" (vv. 25b and 26a) and suggested the motif of God's "justification" (v. 26b; note esp.: "to demonstrate *his justice* [twice], . . . so as to be *just* and *the one who justifies*") — thereby highlighting the *attributive sense* of the expression in speaking of God's "justice" and of God as "just," but also including something of the *communicative sense* in its reference to God as "the one who justifies."

3. In 3:5 the *attributive sense* is certainly to the fore ("If our injustice/unrighteousness serves to confirm the justice/righteousness of God, what shall we say?").

4. In 10:3 the expression is clearly used in the first part of the verse in a *communicative sense* — though with, perhaps, both *communicative* and *attributive* nuances present in the last part of the verse ("They did not know the righteousness that comes from God. . . . They did not submit to God's righteousness").

An *attributive sense* of "the righteousness of God" is dominant in the three NT uses of the expression outside the Pauline corpus, that is, in Matt 6:33; Jas 1:20; and 2 Pet 1:1. That may have been how the Christians at Rome, as well, understood the expression. But Paul's emphasis in his Gentile mission was on God's righteousness as a gift given by God to those whom he reconciles to himself through the work of Christ, the ministry of his Holy Spirit, and their response of faith — as is evident in all of his letters to his own converts, but highlighted explicitly in his use of δικαιοσύνη alone (cf. esp. Rom 5:17) and his use of δικαιοσύνη θεοῦ when writing to his own converts at Corinth and Philippi (cf. 2 Cor 5:21; Phil 3:9) and not just responding to the terminological nuancing of others (as in Rom 10:3). So while always acknowledging the "justness," "justice," and "righteousness" of God in an *attributive sense,* Paul's emphasis in his Gentile mission was primarily on "the righteousness of God" in a *communicative sense,* as can be seen most clearly in 2 Cor 5:21 ("God made him who had no sin to be sin for us, so that in him we might become the righteousness of God") and Phil 3:9 ("that I may gain Christ and be found in him, not having a righteousness of my own that comes from the law, but that which is through faith in Christ — the righteousness that comes from God and is by faith").

It may have been that the Christians at Rome objected to what they perceived to be an imbalance in Paul's theology and proclamation — that is, that he preached very well "the righteousness of God" in a *communicative sense,* but was less vocal about God's righteousness in an *attributive sense.* But in writing to them he begins by affirming the broad range of meaning that the expression "the righteousness of God" incorporates. In effect, he agrees with them in their attributive understanding — which, however, may have been conceptualized by them in a somewhat static manner with respect to the character and actions of God. But he also wants them to think in revelatory, historical, and redemptive terms — and so, it may be presumed, in a more dynamic fashion. Thus he emphasizes the fact that God's righteousness "is now being revealed" by God himself (using the present indicative passive verb ἀποκαλύπτεται) in the Christian gospel — which is a truth that he believed both they and he confessed and so held in common.

1:17b Ἐκ πίστεως εἰς πίστιν (literally "out of faith unto faith") has also been extensively debated, both in earlier times and during the past one hundred and fifty years of NT scholarship. Most patristic interpreters understood the expression to mean "from faith in the law to faith in the gospel," and so to signify the movement in redemptive history as "from faith" as expressed in the OT "to faith" as proclaimed in the NT. Tertullian, for example, commenting directly on this expression in 1:17b, said, "He [God] removes people from faith in the law to faith in the gospel — that is to say, His own law and His own gospel."[79] Likewise, Origen argued, "The first people were in the faith because they believed God and Moses his servant, from which faith they have now gone over to the faith of the gospel."[80] In the sixteenth century John Calvin referred to most interpreters of his day as understanding "from faith to faith" as "an implied comparison between the Old and New Testaments."[81] And in the eighteenth century John Wesley proposed that the expression has to do with "a gradual series of still clearer and clearer promises" as first "revealed by the law" and now "revealed by the gospel."[82]

The fourth-century commentator Ambrosiaster seems to have been the first to have understood the first mention of "faith" in the expression as referring, in some manner, to God and the second as referring to the one who responds to God, though without spelling out how he visualized "the faith of God" — and so he wrote, "What does this mean, except that 'the faith of God' is in him because he promises, and 'the faith of man' is in him because he believes the one who promises."[83] And Augustine in the fifth century interpreted the expression to mean "from the faith of those who preached the gospel [particularly, Paul's own faith and his preaching of faith] to the faith of those who heard the gospel preached"[84] — or, more expansively, "from the faith of words (whereby we now believe what we do not see) to the faith of the things, that is, realities (whereby we shall hereafter possess what we now believe in)."[85]

Most commentators today, however, have carried on Calvin's understanding that the expression "marks the daily progress of every believer,"[86] and so have understood ἐκ πίστεως εἰς πίστιν as signaling some type of progression of faith in the Christian life. Joseph Lightfoot, for example, interpreted the phrase to mean "faith the starting point and faith the goal."[87] James Denney read Paul as saying that God's righteousness in a person's life "presupposes faith" and "leads to faith."[88] And William Sanday and Arthur Headlam understood the phrase

79. Tertullian, *Adversus Marcionem* 5.13.

80. Origen, *Ad Romanos, PG* 14.861; see also 14.858.

81. J. Calvin, *Romans,* in *Calvin's New Testament Commentaries,* 8.28 (though, as noted below, Calvin himself believed these words are better understood as referring to "the daily progress of every believer").

82. J. Wesley, *Explanatory Notes,* 520.

83. Ambrosiaster, *Ad Romanos, PL* 17.56; *CSEL* 81.3.

84. Augustine, *De spiritu et littera* 11.18.

85. Augustine, *Quaestionum evangelicarum* 2.39.

86. J. Calvin, *Romans,* in *Calvin's New Testament Commentaries,* 8.28.

87. Lightfoot, "Romans," in *Notes on Epistles of St. Paul;* so also Robertson, "Romans," 4.327; cf. NEB: "starts from faith and ends in faith."

88. J. Denney, "Romans," in *Expositor's Greek Testament,* 2.591; cf. Weymouth: "depending on faith and leading to faith"; Phillips: "a process begun and continued by faith."

along similar lines and so translated it "starting from a smaller quantity of faith to produce a larger quantity."[89]

Others have viewed Paul's second reference to faith (εἰς πίστιν) as an "emphatic equivalent" of his first reference (ἐκ πίστεως), and have read the expression as emphasizing that the Christian life is "altogether by faith."[90] Still others have understood the phrase as being simply rhetorical, and so have read Paul as declaring that a person's response to the Christian gospel, as well as to God's righteousness revealed in that gospel, is "by faith from start to finish."[91] And many have attempted to combine all these understandings, as does Joseph Fitzmyer in saying that (1) possibly the expression means "from a beginning faith to a more perfect or culminating faith," or (2) possibly " 'through faith' would express the means by which a person shares in salvation; 'for faith' would express the purpose of the divine plan,' " or (3) more likely the phrase means that "salvation is a matter of faith from start to finish, whole and entire."[92]

Admittedly, ἐκ πίστεως εἰς πίστιν is notoriously difficult to interpret. But when πίστις is understood in terms of the Hebrew word אמונה, which means both "faith" and "faithfulness," it is not too difficult to view Paul as having in mind here both (1) *divine faithfulness* in his use of the genitive phrase ἐκ πίστεως (whether the reference is to the faithfulness of God or the faith/faithfulness of Jesus Christ, or both), and (2) *human faith* in his use of the accusative phrase εἰς πίστιν. Viewed in this manner, Paul can be seen here as setting out, in rather cryptic and somewhat perplexing brevity, both of the primary factors involved in God's salvation and reconciliation of humanity: (1) *divine faithfulness,* which is the source and basis for all that the gospel proclaims, and (2) *human faith,* which is necessary for its reception.

The most common way of interpreting ἐκ πίστεως and εἰς πίστιν has been, until recently, to understand them both as referring to a person's faith in God, faith in Christ Jesus, and/or trust in the proclamation of the Christian gospel — not only the second phrase εἰς πίστιν, which is clearly an accusative of direct object and therefore must be understood to signify human faith, but also the first phrase ἐκ πίστεως, which has usually been read as an objective genitive (i.e., the noun in the genitive functions as the object of the verbal idea). So both ἐκ πίστεως and εἰς πίστιν have been usually understood as referring to *human faith* — that is, to a person's faith in God, in Christ Jesus, and/or in the gospel.

From the early 1890s to the present, however, there has been a rising tide of scholarly opinion that πίστεως is a subjective genitive functioning as the subject of the verbal idea, thereby signaling that the source and basis for the

89. Sanday and Headlam, *Romans,* 28; so also Lagrange, *Aux Romains,* 20; cf. JB: "faith leads to faith"; Williams: "faith that leads to greater faith."

90. So, e.g., Cranfield, *Romans,* 1.100; cf. Knox: "faith first and last"; TEV: "through faith from beginning to end."

91. So, e.g., C. H. Dodd, *Romans,* 13-14; Barrett, *Romans,* 31; cf. NIV: "by faith from first to last."

92. Fitzmyer, *Romans,* 263.

salvation of any person is the faithfulness of God and/or of Christ Jesus. On such an understanding the phrase ἐκ πίστεως εἰς πίστιν is understood not as referring twice to human faith but first to "divine faithfulness" as the basis for all that is proclaimed in the Christian gospel and then to "human faith" as the necessary response for the reception of that "good news" in a person's life.

This thesis was first proposed in the late nineteenth century by Johannes Haussleiter.[93] It was popularized in the English-speaking world during the 1950s by Gabriele Hebert[94] and Thomas Torrance.[95] Karl Barth was the first commentator on Romans to espouse this position in his *Römerbrief* of 1919, translating ἐκ πίστεως εἰς πίστιν as "from faithfulness unto faith *(aus Treue dem Glauben)*."[96] It was then advocated by T. W. Manson in his Romans commentary of 1962.[97] And during the past fifty or sixty years this understanding of the conjunction of "divine faithfulness" and "human faith" in Paul's theological language — both here in 1:17b and in 3:22a (probably also 3:26 and perhaps 3:30), as well as elsewhere in his letters — has been developed by a number of scholars in various articles and monographs.[98]

As an indication of the growing acceptance of this thesis, it may be noted that such an understanding has been accepted as an alternative footnote reading for the expression διὰ πίστεως Ἰησοῦ Χριστοῦ in 3:22 by both the NRSV ("through the faith of Jesus Christ") and the TNIV ("through the faithfulness of Jesus Christ"). Further, this interpretation has begun to be proposed by some recent commentators on Romans — principally by Charles Talbert, who in his commentary of 2002 translated (1) ἐκ πίστεως εἰς πίστιν here in 1:17 as "through/out of either God's or Jesus' *faithfulness* for the faith of humans,"[99] (2) διὰ πίστεως Ἰησοῦ Χριστοῦ in 3:22 as "through the *faithfulness* of Jesus Christ,"[100] (3) διὰ τῆς πίστεως ἐν τῷ αὐτοῦ αἵματι in 3:25 as "through his/Jesus' *faithfulness* in his blood,"[101] and (4) τὸν ἐκ πίστεως Ἰησοῦ in 3:26 as "the one who lives out of the *faithfulness* of Jesus."[102] I, too, argued for this understanding in my *Paul, Apostle of Liberty* of 1964, my Galatians commentary of 1990, and my article "The Foundational Conviction of New Testament Christology: The Obedience/Faithfulness/Sonship of Christ" of 2004.[103] And I continue to believe that these features of "divine faithfulness" and "human faith" are what

93. See Haussleiter, *Der Glaube Jesu Christi; idem,* "Was versteht Paulus unter christlichen Glauben," 159-81.

94. Hebert, " 'Faithfulness' and 'Faith,' " 373-79.

95. Torrance, "One Aspect of the Biblical Conception of Faith," 111-14, 221-22.

96. K. Barth, *Römerbrief,* 17-18 (ET = *Romans,* 41); *idem, Shorter Commentary,* 22-23.

97. T. W. Manson, "Romans," 942.

98. For a bibliography of such commentators, see our "Exegetical Comments" on 3:22.

99. Talbert, *Romans,* 41-47 (italics mine, as also in the following three cases).

100. *Ibid.,* 41-47, 107-10.

101. *Ibid.,* 41-47, 107, 110.

102. *Ibid.,* 41-47, 108.

103. Cf. R. N. Longenecker, *Paul, Apostle of Liberty,* 149-52; *idem, Galatians,* 87-88; *idem,* "The Foundational Conviction of New Testament Christology," esp. 132-37.

Paul had in mind when he used this rather cryptic expression ἐκ πίστεως εἰς πίστιν here in 1:17b — which expression he will (1) develop further in 3:22 in the context of his expanded thesis statement of 3:21-23, (2) cite in 3:25 and 26 as prominent in the early Christian confessional material that he quotes in 3:24-26, and (3) highlight in his responses of 3:27b-29 and of 3:30 in elucidating his expanded thesis statement of 3:21-23, which repeats and builds on his original thesis statement of 1:16-17.

There is, of course, much more that could be said — and, indeed, that needs to be said further — about Paul's understanding of "divine faithfulness" and "human faith" in Romans and his other letters. And a great deal more could be highlighted regarding contemporary scholarly treatments of ἐκ πίστεως εἰς πίστιν here in 1:17b and its cognates elsewhere in Romans and Paul's other letters. But since Paul's understanding of these vitally important matters is set out in only very abbreviated fashion in this opening thesis statement of 1:16-17 and since these same features appear again in 3:21-23, 24-26, and 27-31, it is best to reserve a more extensive discussion for our comments on these later passages.

1:17c Paul's quotation of Hab 2:4 is introduced by the expression καθὼς γέγραπται ("just as it is written"), which combines the comparative adverb καθώς ("just as") and the perfect verb γέγραπται ("it has been/is written"). The great majority of Paul's biblical quotations are introduced by some sort of introductory formula. Most often he uses, particularly in Romans, καθὼς γέγραπται, though a number of times he also introduces biblical passages by only the perfect verb γέγραπται ("it has been/is written"), sometimes by references to "God," "Moses," "David," "Isaiah," "Hosea," "the Scriptures," or "the law" as speaking, and a few times just by the conjunction γάρ ("for") used as a brief quasi-introductory formula. The expression καθὼς γέγραπται appears in the LXX in 2 Kgs (4 Kgdms) 14:6 as the translation of Hebrew ככתוב ("what is written"). More exactly, however, καθὼς γέγραπται appears in Theodotion's translation of כאשר כתוב ("as it is written") in Dan 9:13,[104] which introduces biblical warnings and teachings drawn from a number of OT passages. It is also used repeatedly in the Dead Sea Scrolls to introduce citations of various biblical passages.[105] All this suggests that the introductory formula "just as it is written," which stems generally from 2 Kgs 14:6 but more specifically from Dan 9:13, was a common way among pious Jews of Paul's day to introduce and show respect for passages quoted from Scripture — and may be postulated to have been current, as well, among first-century Jewish believers in Jesus.

Καθὼς γέγραπται ("just as it is written") is used here and another twelve times in Romans (3:4, 10; 4:17; 8:36; 9:13, 33; 10:15; 11:8, 26; 15:3, 9, 21) to introduce immediately following biblical quotations. Outside Romans, however,

---

104. Theodotion's translation was done in the late second century A.D., probably sometime during 180-190; its history, however, particularly with respect to the translation of the book of Daniel, seems to have had much earlier roots.

105. Cf., e.g., 1QS 5.17; 8.14; CD 7.19; 4Q178 3.2.

καθὼς γέγραπται is found in Paul's letters only three times in 1 Corinthians (1:31; 2:9; 10:7) and twice in 2 Corinthians (8:15; 9:9). Its usage is in line with the distribution of biblical quotations in his letters. Of the approximately 83 quotations of Scripture in Paul's letters — or about 100 biblical citations if one disengages conflated texts and separates possible dual sources — well over half appear in Romans (45 of 83 citations or some 55 to 60 OT passages of a total of about 100), whereas elsewhere in the Pauline corpus there are only 15 quotations of biblical passages in 1 Corinthians, 7 in 2 Corinthians, 10 in Galatians, 4 in Ephesians, 1 in 1 Timothy, 1 in 2 Timothy, and none in 1 Thessalonians, 2 Thessalonians, Philippians, Colossians, Philemon, or Titus. So it is understandable that most of the occurrences of what seems to be a rather distinctive type of introductory formula used by pious Jews and (presumably) by Jewish Christians — whether understood in its Hebrew form as כאשר כתוב ("just as it is written") or as expressed in Greek translation as καθὼς γέγραπται — appear in Romans, where over half of Paul's biblical quotations are found.

Nonetheless, it still needs to be recognized that most of the places where this Jewish type of introductory formula appears most prominently in Paul's letters are in Romans, with the occurrences of this formula being much less frequent in the other Pauline letters that contain OT quotations. This has some importance for an understanding of what Paul writes in Romans (even though, admittedly, at this point only of rather minor importance) — particularly if the Christians at Rome, both Jewish and Gentile believers in Jesus, had been extensively influenced by the theology, ways of thinking, and religious language of the mother church at Jerusalem. Further, and possibly more significant for our present purposes, this particular introductory formula καθὼς γέγραπται appears principally in those sections of the letter where Paul is arguing in a distinctly Jewish and/or Jewish Christian manner with his addressees: four times in the first section of the letter's body middle (1:16–4:25) and seven times in the third section (9:1–11:36). It is also found once in the letter's body closing (15:14-32) when Paul explains to his Roman addressees why he has not come to them earlier and uses this introductory formula at 15:21 to introduce his quotation of Isa 52:15 in support.

The appearance of καθὼς γέγραπται at 8:36, which is embedded in material at the end of the second section of the letter's body middle (i.e., 5:1–8:39) and introduces the quotation of Ps 44:22, may seem to be opposed to Paul's pattern of usage in Romans as proposed above. But the final part of Romans 8, particularly 8:33-39, is probably to be seen as incorporating various early Christian confessional materials — perhaps even a full early Christian confession — which Paul seems to have drawn from the worship of the earliest Jewish believers in Jesus. So the appearance of this distinctively Jewish and Jewish Christian introductory formula — appearing as it does in the second section of the body middle of Paul's letter to Rome, where Paul sets out the substance of his contextualized proclamation of the Christian gospel to Gentiles in the Greco-Roman world, may also be seen as having rootage in materials that Paul's

Christian addressees at Rome would appreciate. So even with respect to this relatively minor matter of the apostle's pattern of use of καθὼς γέγραπται, Paul's circumstantial use of traditional Jewish and Jewish Christian religious language — which, it may be assumed, was familiar to and used by his addressees — can be observed and appreciated.

1:17d Paul's quotation of the latter part of Hab 2:4, ὁ δὲ δίκαιος ἐκ πίστεως ζήσεται ("the righteous [or 'the Righteous One'] will live by faith"), has presented commentators with a number of difficulties. One major problem has to do with how this text was read in Paul's day. The MT and 1QpHab 7.17 have וצדיק באמונתו יחיה, "but the righteous/just person by his faith/faithfulness/ fidelity shall live." The preposition ב ("by") and the third person pronominal suffix ו ("his") joined with אמונה make it clear that the verse is talking about the "faith," "faithfulness," or "fidelity" of a "righteous" or "just" person. But what is signified by "faith," "faithfulness," or "fidelity" (אמונה)? Who is this "righteous" or "just" person (צדיק)? And what is meant by "he shall live" (יחיה)?

The Greek translations of Hab 2:4b, however, set up a number of other textual and interpretive problems. One family of LXX texts represented by MSS א, B, Q, and W* reads ὁ δὲ δίκαιος ἐκ πίστεως μου ζήσεται ("but the righteous/ just one by my faith/faithfulness/fidelity shall live"), thereby making it clear by the use of the Greek first person pronoun μου ("my") for the Hebrew third person pronominal suffix ו ("his") that the πίστις ("faith," "faithfulness," or "fi-delity") in view is God's faithfulness. Another family of LXX texts represented by MSS A and C reads ὁ δὲ δίκαιος μου ἐκ πίστεως ζήσεται ("but my righteous one by faith/faithfulness/fidelity shall live"), suggesting by its positioning of the Greek first person pronoun μου ("my") a close connection between "the righteous one" and God himself. Further, the article ὁ ("the") in both Greek versions suggests that δίκαιος ("righteous") is to be understood not just generically as "anyone who is just or righteous" but more specifically in a substantive sense as "the just or righteous one."

There is also a fragmentary Greek reading of this final portion of Hab 2:4 in a scroll of the Minor Prophets found in cave 8 of Wadi Habra that seems to read as follows: [δίκ]αιος ἐν πίστει αὐτοῦ ζήσετ[αι] ("the righteous by his faith/ faithfulness/fidelity shall live").[106] And three other Greek translations of the OT, all dating from the second century A.D., present somewhat different versions of this final phrase of Hab 2:4: (1) that of Aquila of Pontus (early second century) reads καὶ δίκαιος ἐν πίστει αὐτοῦ ζήσεται ("and the righteous by his faith/faith-fulness/fidelity shall live"); (2) that of Symmachus "the Ebionite" (mid or late second century) reads ὁ δὲ δίκαιος τῇ ἑαυτοῦ πίστει ζήσεται ("but the righteous one, based on his own faith/faithfulness/fidelity, shall live"); and (3) that of Theodotion (c. 180-90) reads: ὁ δὲ δίκαιος ἐν πίστει αὐτοῦ ζήσεται ("but the righteous one by his faith/faithfulness/fidelity shall live").

The Dead Sea covenantors applied Hab 2:3-4 to their own situation, un-

106. 8HevXIIgr., col. 12.

derstanding these verses as exhorting a strict observance of the Mosaic law and an absolute fidelity to the sect's founding teacher. Thus their comment on וצדיק באמונתו יחיה ("but the righteous/just one by his faith/faithfulness/fidelity shall live") is as follows:

> The interpretation of this concerns all those who observe the law in the house of Judah, whom God will deliver from the House of Judgment because of their suffering and because of their fidelity to the Teacher of Righteousness.[107]

The rabbis of the Talmud seem to have coupled Hab 2:4b with Gen 15:6 as two important *testimonia* passages having to do with the nation's inheritance of Abraham's meritorious faith[108] and thus viewed Hab 2:4b as presenting a summation of the whole Mosaic law in one principle: "faithfulness rewarded by faith."[109]

In the NT the author of Hebrews gives an interpretive rendering of Hab 2:3-4 (Heb 10:37-38) in support of his exhortation to his addressees not to draw back from their faith in and faithfulness to "the One who will soon come and not delay." But the purpose of that anonymous Jewish Christian author was different from that of Paul in Romans. Likewise, the Greek text on which that author based his exhortation seems to have been different from Paul's, being evidently drawn from the LXX reading found in MSS A and C (ὁ δὲ δίκαιος μου ἐκ πίστεως ζήσεται, "but my righteous one on the basis of faith/faithfulness/ fidelity shall live"). Paul in Gal 3:11, however, quotes Hab 2:4b in arguing for the supremacy of faith, using, it seems, some type of conflation of the Hebrew text and one of the then existing Greek translations — though without including "his" from the Hebrew or either "my" or "his" from the Greek.

C. H. Dodd argued that Hab 2:4b should probably be understood as an early Christian *testimonium* passage that drew its text-form from various translations that were then current and was used for a variety of purposes by the earliest believers in Jesus.[110] Likewise, Ernst Käsemann proposed that Paul should not be viewed as the originator of the version of Hab 2:4b that appears in Rom 1:17b — for, in all likelihood, the situation was that "he took it over from the Jewish-Christian mission, which found in Hab 2:4 a prophecy of salvation by faith in the Messiah just as Qumran found salvation in commitment to the Teacher of Righteousness."[111]

A good case could also be made for a *testimonium* use of Hab 2:4b by

---

107. 1QpHab 8.1-3, commenting on this immediately preceding phrase in 7.17.

108. Cf. *Exod. Rab.* 23:5.

109. Cf. *Midr. Ps.* 17A.25 and *b. Mak.* 24a, where David is said to have summed up the entire law in eleven principles (in Ps 15), Isaiah in six (in Isa 33:14-16), Micah in three (in Mic 6:8), Isaiah again in two (in Isa 56:1), Amos in one (in Amos 5:4), and Habakkuk in one (in Hab 2:4b).

110. Cf. C. H. Dodd, *According to the Scriptures,* 50-51.

111. Käsemann, *Romans,* 31.

Jewish teachers generally, whether orthodox or sectarian (as noted above with respect to its use by the Essene covenantors at Qumran and the later rabbis in preserving an earlier tradition). And it may also be surmised that not only did Paul know of such a use and apply the passage in various ways to his own life and ministry, but that believers in Jesus at Rome accepted Hab 2:4b as a basic *testimonium* passage as well.

Further, it needs to be noted that at a number of places in the Jewish writings of Paul's day the expression "the Righteous One" (ὁ δίκαιος) is used as a messianic title. In the *Parables* or *Similitudes of Enoch* there is a reference to "the Righteous One" who will "appear before the eyes of the righteous, those elect ones whose works are wrought in dependence on the Lord of the Spirits"[112] — and later the following statement appears: "After this [i.e., God's final judgment on earth], the Righteous and Elect One will reveal the house of his congregation. And from that time, they shall not be hindered in the name of the Lord of the Spirits."[113] Such a messianic title seems presupposed, as well, in portrayals of this same person found in *1 En* 39:6 ("the Elect One of Righteousness") and 46:3 ("the Son of Man to whom belongs righteousness and with whom righteousness dwells"). All these references and allusions to the Messiah as "the Righteous One" were evidently based on Isa 53:11, where "my righteous servant" is used in a messianic sense.

Likewise, the reading of Isa 51:5 in one of the major Isaiah scrolls found at Qumran seems to suggest — both in its parallelism of "my Righteousness" and "my Salvation" and in its substitution of the third person singular suffix "his" for the expected first person singular suffix "my" — that the Essene covenantors understood "my righteousness" more as a messianic title than a divine attribute:

Near is my Righteousness (צדקי).
My Salvation (ישעי) has gone forth,
 and *his* arm (הרועו) will rule the peoples;
in *him* (אליו) the coastlands trust,
 and for *his* arm (זרועו) they wait.[114]

The *Psalms of Solomon* also lay emphasis on the anointed Son of David as a righteous king who will establish righteousness and direct people in deeds of righteousness.[115] And the Talmud contains reflections of an earlier period when the rabbis spoke of "the righteous Messiah," using "the righteous branch" of Jer 23:5-6; 33:15 and the description in Zech 9:9 in support.[116] It may be postulated, therefore, that the LXX's substantival translation ὁ δίκαιος ("the righteous one") was understood by the earliest believers in Jesus not just generically (i.e., "any-

112. *1 En* 38:2.
113. *1 En* 53:6.
114. 1QIs^a on 51:5 (italics mine).
115. Cf. *Pss Sol* 17:23-51; perhaps also Wis 2:18.
116. For a listing of talmudic passages, see G. Schrenk, "δίκαιος," *TDNT* 2.186-87.

one who is upright/righteous/just") — nor even as an attribute of Jesus[117] — but, more particularly, as a prophetic christological title.

In Acts, Jesus is explicitly identified as "the Righteous One" (ὁ δίκαιος) by (1) Peter before the Sanhedrin (3:14), (2) Stephen before the Council (7:52), and (3) Paul in addressing a Jerusalem crowd from the steps of the Antonia fortress (22:14). James speaks of the rich who condemned and killed "the Righteous One" (Jas 5:6). And probably δίκαιος, even without the article ὁ ("the"), should be understood as something of a quasi-title in 1 Pet 3:18 ("Christ suffered once for sins, 'the righteous [one]' for the unrighteous") and 1 John 2:1 ("We have an advocate with the Father, Jesus Christ 'the righteous [one]'").

This is how, it may be assumed, the LXX translation ὁ δίκαιος in Hab 2:4b was understood by the Christians at Rome — who, though dominantly Gentiles ethnically, had been extensively influenced by the theology, ways of thinking, and religious language of the mother church at Jerusalem. And it may also be that this is how Paul used this expression both in Gal 3:11 and here at Rom 1:17b, as has been proposed at various times during the past century by a variety of scholars.[118]

So Paul's quotation of Hab 2:4b here in Rom 1:17b may be viewed as containing a further and somewhat more subtle nuance than is immediately obvious. And in partial support of such a suggestion, it should be noted that when Paul restates his thesis statement of 1:16-17 in expanded and developed form in 3:21-23, he does so not only by speaking further regarding δικαιοσύνη θεοῦ ("the righteousness of God") and πίστις ("faith/faithfulness/fidelity") but also by incorporating into that later version of his thesis the expression διὰ πίστεως Ἰησοῦ Χριστοῦ — which, as we will argue in our exegetical comments on 3:22, is probably best translated as a subjective genitive that signifies "through the faith" and/or "the faithfulness of Jesus Christ."

How, then, did Paul use Hab 2:4b here in Rom 1:17b? First of all, as Ernst Käsemann has rightly insisted, it must be recognized that "Paul's interpretation of Hab 2:4 neither does justice to the OT text nor finds any support in Jewish exegesis."[119] He did not quote the text according to either the MT or the best MSS of the LXX. Likewise, he did not have in mind in his use of the Greek verb ζήσεται ("he will live") simply deliverance from a military invasion and death, as did the prophet Habakkuk in his use of the Hebrew יחי. Nor did he understand the Hebrew אמונה or the Greek πίστις to mean primarily a person's own "integrity" or "faithfulness" to God and his law, as did most Jews of his day. Rather, Paul interpreted this OT *testimonium* passage from a Christian perspective, us-

---

117. Cf. δίκαιός ἐστιν of 1 John 1:9; 2:29; 3:7; δίκαιος εἶ of Rev 16:5.

118. Cf. e.g., Haussleiter, *Der Glaube Jesu Christi*, 212-13; *idem*, "Was versteht Paulus unter christlichen Glauben," 159-81; T. W. Manson, "The Argument from Prophecy," 133-34; Hanson, *Paul's Understanding of Jesus*, 6-9; *idem*, *Studies in Paul's Technique and Theology*, 42-45; Hays, *The Faith of Jesus Christ*, 151-54; *idem*, "'The Righteous One' as Eschatological Deliverer," 191-215.

119. Käsemann, *Romans*, 32, citing P. Billerbeck, *Str-Bil*, vol. 3, *loc. cit.*; Moore, *Judaism*, 2.23/-38.

ing it, it seems evident, in support of a Christian understanding of "faith" and "life" — perhaps even viewing the subject of the sentence, "the righteous one" (Hebrew צַדִּיק, Greek ὁ δίκαιος), as having messianic significance.

Principally, however, Paul used this Habakkuk *testimonium* in support of his emphasis on "faith" as the only proper response to God's gift of "righteousness," which is "now being revealed in the gospel," just as he did in Gal 3:11. For "the righteousness of God" is not only "based on the divine faithfulness" (ἐκ πίστεως), it also calls for "a response of human faith" (εἰς πίστιν). It is, Paul insists, only on the basis of "divine faithfulness" and a response of "human faith" that a person can "live" (Hebrew יִחְיֶה, Greek ζήσεται) — with "life" used here as equivalent to the experience of "salvation" (σωτηρία) and a positive response to the gift of "God's righteousness" (δικαιοσύνη θεοῦ), which were highlighted earlier in this thesis paragraph of 1:16-17. And it is this insistence on "divine faithfulness" and a "human response of faith" for the experience of "salvation" that Paul elaborates on and develops further throughout Romans, particularly in Section I (1:16–4:25) and Section III (9:1–11:36) of the body middle of his letter to the Christians at Rome.

BIBLICAL THEOLOGY

No set of concepts and terms was more important among the earliest believers in Jesus than (1) "the gospel," as effected by and focused on the work and person of Jesus, (2) "the power of God," (3) "the righteousness of God," (4) the universality of God's provision of "salvation," even while favoring Jews with his presence and provisions, (5) "divine faithfulness," (6) human "faith," and (7) the witness of the OT Scriptures. These are the themes that Paul highlights in his thesis statement of 1:16-17, that govern the entire first section of the body middle of his letter to the believers in Jesus at Rome (1:16–4:25), and that are picked up and elaborated on further in the third section of the letter's body middle (9:1–11:36). And these are the basic tenets that reside at the heart of the Christian faith.

Yet it needs also to be noted that these themes, both here and throughout what follows in 1:18–4:25, are set out in ways that are dominantly forensic in nature — that is, with emphases on (1) the gospel as "the power of God," (2) "righteousness" as primarily an attribute of God's person and actions, (3) the work of Christ as a faithful response to God's judicial requirements, and (4) human faith as necessary for both acceptance by God and status before God.[120] There are, of course, a number of relational implications and participationistic inferences that can be drawn from these more forensic concepts and judicial terms. But such overtly relational concepts as "peace" and "reconciliation" with God,

---

120. On the forensic nature of the religious language in 1:16-17, cf. Ziesler, *Meaning of Righteousness in Paul,* esp. 212; see also Fitzmyer, *Romans,* 262-66.

such universal dimensions as "sin," "judgment," and "death" as countered by "grace," "obedience," "righteousness," "love," and "life," and such participation-istic themes as being "in Christ" and "in the Spirit" do not come to the fore in this thesis statement of 1:16-17 or in its explications of 3:21–4:25. Rather, these more relational, universal, and participationistic themes are largely reserved for what follows in 5:1–8:39.

Many have proposed that this difference between the sections is because 1:16–4:25 (or 1:16–5:11) deals with "justification" whereas 5:1–8:39 (or 5:12–8:39) deals with "sanctification."[121] Others have argued that 5:1–8:39 (or 5:12–8:39) is simply a repetition of the argument of 1:16–4:25 (or 1:16–5:11), though with other terms used by way of explanation — either "without any reference whatever to the previous exposition"[122] or with an implied correlation in order to clarify and emphasize what has been earlier presented.[123] And still others argue that these two sections of Romans serve to highlight "the peculiar double character of sal-vation" presented by the apostle, first (in 1:16–4:25 or 1:16–5:11) its "future" char-acter, then (in 5:1–8:39 or 5:12–8:39) its "already present" character.[124] Almost all proponents of these various proposals, however, have openly acknowledged that the relations between these two main sections of the first eight chapters of Romans have often left a "confusing impression" on any serious reader of the letter, and so they have focused on one or the other of the above solutions.

Our thesis, however, is that (1) what Paul presents in the first section (1:16–4:25) of his protreptic message to the Christians at Rome is what he believes both he and his addressees agree on, both negatively (1:18–3:20) and positively (3:21–4:25), whereas (2) what he sets out in the second section (5:1–8:39) of the body middle of his letter is the essence of what he has proclaimed — and intends to continue to proclaim — to Gentiles in the Greco-Roman world as his own con-textualized version of the Christian gospel. The believers in Jesus at Rome seem to have feared that this so-called "apostle to the Gentiles," in his more relational, personal, and participationistic preaching, was ignoring — or at least minimizing — many of the forensic, judicial, and legal features of the Christian gospel and so diluting or distorting the Christian message. They may even have accused him of being ashamed of such a forensic message. Paul, however, begins the body middle of his letter by assuring his addressees (1) that he is "not ashamed" of these basic features of the gospel, as they might have thought, and (2) that on these matters he is fully in line with the gospel proclamation as they accepted it from the mother church at Jerusalem and were proclaiming it in their congregations at Rome. And on the basis of this thesis statement he goes on throughout the rest of the first section of the body middle of his letter to spell out these matters of agreement, both negatively and positively — denouncing in the process any false ideas about

121. So, e.g., traditional Roman Catholic and many pietistic Protestant interpreters.
122. So, e.g., Schweitzer, *Mysticism of Paul the Apostle*, 225-26.
123. So many Protestant interpreters.
124. So, e.g., Bultmann, *Theology of the New Testament*, 1.279.

righteousness being attainable by human deeds or "works" (1:18–3:20) and affirming the importance of justification by faith (3:21–4:25).

CONTEXTUALIZATION FOR TODAY

Paul's letter to the Christians at Rome is an excellent example of contextualizing the Christian gospel, for it (1) acknowledges the legitimate interests and concerns of a body of Christians who had been, it seems, extensively influenced by the theology, ways of thinking, and religious language of Jewish Christianity in their understanding and proclamation of the Christian message, (2) reflects the apostle's desire to remain in vital contact with those believers in Jesus at Rome, even though they and he may have differed somewhat in their respective emphases, (3) represents what he had been proclaiming as his version of the Christian message to pagan Gentiles in the Greco-Roman world, and (4) gives some paradigmatic direction, primarily by way of illustration and example, of how to contextualize that same gospel message in various other situations today. Historically, each of the important centers of early Christianity — that is, Jerusalem, Antioch of Syria, Alexandria in Egypt, Ephesus, and Rome, as well as various other cities in the eastern portion of the Roman Empire where Paul established churches — seems to have possessed a common body of doctrinal materials — not only the OT Scriptures, but also certain traditions regarding the work and person of Jesus and certain early confessional materials. But Christians at those early centers of the Christian faith also seem to have expressed that common body of Christian doctrine in ways that were contextualized for their own time and locality. And it is a reflection of such a scenario of common conviction *and* circumstantial contextualization that is to be found in this letter.

The Christian faith is not "kept alive" or "advanced" by mere repetition of normative doctrines or use of standard expressions — important as these may have been in the past and significant as they may continue to be in certain localities and situations and/or among certain people today. There is in the proclamation of the Christian gospel the need to be (1) constantly in continuity with the biblical revelation, both OT and NT, (2) continually in conversation with all the various presentations of that biblical revelation of both the past and the present — especially where a "sense of center" is retained, and (3) always endeavoring to contextualize that biblical revelation and its Christian message today in different localities, within differing cultural situations, and among people of diverse ideological perspectives. Thus Paul's letter to Rome should be read not only as providing basic doctrine for the Christian church — whether that doctrine is drawn principally from the first section (1:16–4:25) or the second section (5:1–8:39) of its body middle, or both — but also as giving us (1) a portrait of how Paul contextualized the message of the Christian gospel in his own missionary outreach to Gentiles in the Greco-Roman world and (2) a paradigm for the contextualization of that same message in our own situations today.

2. God's Wrath against Human Rebellion, Idolatry, and Debauchery (1:18-32)

TRANSLATION

1:18 *The wrath of God is being revealed from heaven against all the godlessness and wickedness of those who suppress the truth by their wickedness.*

19 *Because what can be known about God is plain to them, for God has shown it to them.* 20 *For ever since the creation of the world God's invisible attributes — his eternal power and divine nature — have been clearly seen, being understood by what has been made, so people are without excuse.*

21 *Because although they knew God, they did not glorify him as God or give him thanks, but their thinking became futile and their foolish hearts were darkened.* 22 *While claiming to be wise, they became fools.* 23 *And they exchanged the glory of the immortal God for the likeness of an image made to look like a mortal human being — or like birds or animals or reptiles.*

24 *Therefore God gave them over in the sinful desires of their hearts to sexual impurity for the degrading of their bodies with one another,* 25 *since they exchanged the truth of God for a lie and worshiped and served created things rather than the Creator, who is forever to be praised. Amen.*

26 *For this reason, God gave them over to disgraceful passions. Their women exchanged natural sexual intercourse for unnatural relations.* 27 *Likewise, their men also abandoned intercourse with women and were inflamed with lust for one another — men committing indecent acts with one another and receiving in their own persons the due penalty for their perversion.*

28 *And since they did not think it worthwhile to retain the knowledge of God, God gave them over to a depraved mind and to do the things that ought not to be done.* 29 *They became filled with every kind of wickedness, evil, greed, and depravity. They are full of envy, murder, strife, deceit, and malice. They are gossips,* 30 *slanderers, God-haters, insolent, arrogant, and boastful. They invent ways of doing evil; they disobey their parents.* 31 *They are senseless, faithless, heartless, and ruthless.*

32 *Although they know God's decree that those who do these things deserve death, they not only continue to do these very things but also applaud those who practice them.*

TEXTUAL NOTES

1:18a It has often been said that Marcion deleted the possessives θεοῦ ("of God") in 1:18 and τοῦ θεοῦ ("of God") in 2:2, reading only "wrath is revealed against all the godlessness and wickedness of people who suppress the truth by their wickedness"

189

(1:18) and "we know that judgment against those who do such things is based on truth" (2:2) — thereby expunging "wrath" and "judgment" as attributable to the God of the Christian gospel.[1] But while such deletions would have been entirely consistent with Marcion's theology, it appears on a closer reading of what Tertullian actually said that the heretic Marcion retained — indeed, quite inconsistently — these two references to *God's* wrath and *God's* judgment. For Tertullian appears to have had Marcion's retention of θεοῦ and τοῦ θεοῦ in these two verses particularly in mind when he wrote regarding "what he [Marcion] has seen fit to leave unerased, strange instances as they are also of his negligence and blindness."[2]

18b Tertullian (in *Adversus Marcionem* 5.13.3), Hippolytus (in *Treatise on Christ and Antichrist* 64), and Ambrosiaster (on Rom 1:18), together with a number of Latin and Syriac versions of the text, reflect the addition of the possessive τοῦ θεοῦ ("of God") after τὴν ἀλήθειαν ("the truth"). But that probably reflects a scribal harmonization with the expression "the truth *of God*" that appears later in 1:25.

20 The omission of the adjective ἀΐδιος ("eternal") in the ninth-century uncial L (020) and the fourteenth-century minuscule 1506 (Category II) seems to be simply a scribal error.

23 The active form of the verb ἤλλαξαν ("they exchanged") is strongly supported in the textual history of this verse. The middle form ἠλλάξαντο ("they gave in exchange," "exchanged for themselves") appears in the ninth-century uncial K (018) and such minuscules as 6 88 630 (Category III). This reading evidently came about by assimilation with the LXX reading of Ps 105:20.

24 The preposition ἐν with the intensive pronoun αὐτοῖς ("among themselves," "with one another") is well supported by P[40vid] and uncials ℵ A B C D*, as well as by minuscules 81 1881 (Category II) and 88 104 323 1735 (Category III). The reflexive pronoun ἑαυτοῖς ("to themselves," "with one another") is more weakly attested in uncials D[1] G Ψ (also *Byz* K L), minuscules 33 1175 1739 (Category I), 1506 1881 2464 (Category II), and 6 69 326 330 365 424[c] 614 1241 1243 1319 1505 1573 1874 2344 2495 (Category III). This variant reading was evidently intended to bring 1:24 into alignment with the use of ἑαυτοῖς at the end of 1:27 — though the unaccented pronoun αυτοις (when understood with a rough breathing, which understanding can be supported only contextually) could also be read as a reflexive pronoun.

26 The particle τε ("both," "but," "likewise"), which is a virtually untranslatable connective, is fairly well supported by uncials ℵ B D[c], as well as by minuscules 1175 (Category I), 81 2464 (Category II), and 69 88 323 326 365 614 1241 1243 1319 1735 (Category III). The variant δέ ("but"), however, is attested by uncials A D* G P Ψ, minuscules 33 1739 (Category I), 1881 (Category II), and 104 330 424[c] 630 1505 1573 2344 2495 (Category III), and versions lat sy[h]. The use of the variant δέ is certainly possible and even understandable, but it ruins the balance of the repetition of τε and τε that appears in the last part of 1:26 and the first part of 1:27.

---

1. So Harnack, *Marcion*, 103, based on his reading of Tertullian's comments in *Adversus Marcionem* 5.13.2-3; see also, e.g., Michel, *An die Römer* 97; Dunn, *Romans*, 53; Fitzmyer, *Romans*, 278.

2. Tertullian, *Adversus Marcionem* 5.13.3.

27a At the end of this verse, a number of MSS, including fourth-century Codex Vaticanus (B 03) and ninth-century *Byz* uncial K (018), read the intensive pronoun αὐτοῖς ("among themselves") rather than the much more widely supported reflexive pronoun ἑαυτοῖς ("with one another") — evidently in order to bring 1:27 into alignment with αὐτοῖς at the end of 1:24. This is the reverse of the situation noted above in 1:24, though both αυτοῖς (when understood with a rough breathing) and ἑαυτοῖς could be read as reflexive pronouns.

27b The ninth-century uncial G (012) increases the reciprocal force of the final verb by reading the prepositional prefix as ἀντι (i.e., ἀντιλαμβάνοντες, "receiving back") rather than ἀπό (i.e., ἀπολαμβάνοντες, "receiving") — attempting, it seems, to effect a stylistic improvement that conforms to the prefix ἀντι in ἀντιμισθίαν ("penalty") that appeared earlier in the sentence.

28 The omission of ὁ θεός ("God") by uncials ℵ* A and minuscule 1735 (Category III) was probably intended as a stylistic improvement that would avoid the repeated use of "God" in a single sentence.

29 The word πορνεία ("fornication") is included in this list of vices in some MSS, sometimes before πονηρία ("wickedness"), as in the TR, and sometimes after πονηρία, as reflected in the Vulgate. Probably, however, πορνεία was not originally in the text, as witness its omission in uncials ℵ A B and Origen and Basil. It likely came about, as Bruce Metzger has suggested, by a conflation of πονηρία and πορνεία.[3] Πονηρία ("wickedness") and κακία ("wickedness," "depravity") are interchanged in some MSS.

31 The word ἀσπόνδους ("implacable," "irreconcilable") is also included in this list of vices in a number of MSS, most often after ἀστόργους ("heartless," "unloving"), as it does in a corrected edition of ℵ, a secondary edition of C, the ninth-century uncial Ψ, and minuscules 81 (Category II) and 104 (Category III) — with all of these variants evidently reflecting later *Byz* influence. A few times ἀσπόνδους appears before ἀστόργους, as in ninth-century minuscule 33 (Category I). Its inclusion, however, is not supported by the better MSS of the Greek textual tradition. Probably it was inserted, as Bruce Metzger has suggested, from a remembrance of the similar catalog of vices in 2 Tim 3:2-5, where ἄστοργοι is followed by ἄσπόνδοι.[4]

32a The additions γάρ ("for") in uncial D* and δέ ("but," "and") in minuscules 1175 (Category I) and 1241 1874 (Category III) should probably be considered only scribal insertions intended to improve the syntax of the sentence by the use of some introductory explanatory, adversative, or connective particle.

32b The nominative, plural, masculine, second aorist active participle ἐπιγνόντες ("knowing," "they know") is amply attested in the Greek textual tradition, though the participial form ἐπιγνώσκοντες ("knowing," "they know") appears in Codex Vaticanus (B 03) and minuscule 1506 (Category II). The variant form is probably a scribal redaction intended to bring the verbal idea into correspondence with the present tense verbs elsewhere in this verse.

32c Codex Vaticanus (B 03) substitutes the present tense participles ποιοῦντες

---

3. Cf. Metzger, *Textual Commentary*, 447.
4. *Ibid.*, 448.

("doing") and συνευδοκοῦντες ("applauding") for the present tense finite verbs ποιοῦσιν ("they are doing") and συνευδοκοῦσιν ("they are applauding") that are amply attested elsewhere in the early textual tradition. This substitution of participles for finite verbs was likely influenced by the presence of participles instead of finite verbs earlier in this verse.

FORM/STRUCTURE/SETTING

The form, structure, and setting of 1:18-32 have been extensively discussed by scholars, but there have been frequent disagreements about these matters among them. It is necessary, therefore, to deal here in an introductory fashion with a number of these features and concerns — particularly those that have a bearing on the interpretation of the passage at hand.

Rhetorical Features. Two rhetorical conventions embedded in this passage are immediately evident. Most obvious is the thrice-repeated phrase "God gave them over" (παρέδωκεν αὐτοὺς ὁ θεός) in vv. 24, 26, and 28, all used, it seems, to hold together the structure of 1:24-31 and to drive home the impact of what is being said in that part of the passage. Likewise in vv. 23, 25, and 26 the verb "they exchanged" appears three times, first as a simple aorist (ἤλλαξαν) and then twice more as a compound aorist (μετήλλαξαν), with the compound form evidently meant to intensify the significance of the verb's action and the ominous sound of the final Greek syllable of the word (-ξαν), which would ring in the minds of the hearers and resonate in their memories.

Both repetitions of "God gave them over" and of "they exchanged" may be classified rhetorically as anaphora (i.e., the repetition of a phrase or word at the beginning of a series of successive statements) — though they could also be viewed as instances of paronomasia (i.e., the play on two or more words in a relatively brief context that are similar in form, that sound alike, or that make use of different meanings of the same word). Jean-Noël Aletti has proposed a number of other possible rhetorical features in 1:18-32 (as well as in 2:1–3:20).[5] But these two instances of anaphora (or paronomasia) are the most obvious rhetorical conventions in the passage.

Two observations about these two sets of anaphora (or paronomasia) in 1:18-32 need, however, to be highlighted: (1) such rhetorical conventions, whether in oral or written communication, were always intended to function as aids for the understanding and remembrance of what was said or written, and (2) their inclusion in whatever written material they appear suggests something of an original oral setting for that material. Thus when Paul includes these two instances of anaphora, it may be presumed that he does so (1) with the hope that his addressees will better understand and remember what he writes, but also (2) with the suggestion that what he writes has a history in some type of past

---

5. Aletti, "Rm 1,18–3,20," passim.

oral communication — whether drawn from his own past preaching or from an earlier writing that incorporated such oral communication, or both.

Wisdom of Solomon and Romans 1:18-32. Also of importance when considering the form and structure of Rom 1:18-32 is to observe that what Paul writes in 1:19-32 about humanity's basic knowledge of God, their subsequent idolatries, and their resultant immoralities and injustices — with that material used to support and elaborate on the theme statement of 1:18, which declares that "the wrath of God" is directed "against all the godlessness and wickedness of people who suppress the truth by their wickedness" — parallels, in large measure, what appears in Wis 13:1–14:31, as well as certain statements contained in chs. 11 and 12 of that Jewish apocryphal writing.

Wisdom of Solomon was probably written by a Hellenistic Jewish author (or authors) sometime between 50 B.C. and A.D. 10. It divides quite easily into three major sections: (1) "The Book of Eschatology" (1:1–6:8), which contrasts the different destinies that await the righteous and the ungodly who oppress them; (2) "An Oration on Wisdom" (6:9–11:1), which in poetic form eulogizes wisdom as a heavenly being and urges its readers to respond positively; and (3) "A Glorification of the Jews" (11:2–19:22), which in a self-aggrandizing manner lauds the Jewish people and expresses hatred toward Gentiles. The second section, the "Oration on Wisdom," gives the book its name and is by far the most lofty and edifying. The book's first section, "The Book of Eschatology," sets out a doctrine of soulish immortality occurring immediately after death and argues that suffering, childlessness, and/or an early death do not signify God's displeasure. The third section of the book, that is, its "Glorification of the Jews," is largely a self-congratulatory piece of nationalistic propaganda (especially in chs. 13–15), which is expressed in language that sounds biblical (thus a "midrash" in glorification of the Jews). Some scholars have argued that chs. 13–15, which contain the bulk of the material of concern for study of Rom 1:18-32 (and perhaps of Rom 2:1ff.), are to be understood as having been inserted by someone later.

Wisdom of Solomon, whether in whole or in part, seems to have been widely read by Jews and Jewish Christians of Paul's day. Scholars have often viewed this Hellenistic Jewish writing as having had some impact on the concepts, imagery, and language of such Jewish Christian canonical writings as the Fourth Gospel, the Epistle of James, the Epistle (or "Sermon") to the Hebrews, and the Apocalypse of John. It was, however, Johann Gottfried Eichhorn (1752-1827), often considered "the father of Old Testament criticism," who first highlighted resemblances between Wisdom and Romans in his study of the OT apocrypha — especially the resemblances between Wis 13–15 and Rom 1–2, but also between Wis 12:12-18 and the treatment of predestination in Rom 9 (as well as in Eph 1). And the parallels between Wis 13:1–14:31 and Rom 1:19-32 have been seen by many NT scholars since to be particularly close.

Sanday and Headlam, for example, in their classic commentary on Romans of 1895 — after noting rather close similarities to Rom 1:19-32 in seventeen of the verses of Wis 13–14 and in another four verses in three of the other chapters of Wisdom — declared:

> It will be seen that while on the one hand there can be no question of direct quotation, on the other hand the resemblance is so strong both as to the main lines of the argument (i. Natural religion discarded; ii. idolatry; iii. catalogue of immorality) and in the details of thought and to some extent of expression as to make it clear that at some time in his life St. Paul must have bestowed upon the Book of Wisdom a considerable amount of study.[6]

Likewise, C. H. Dodd in 1932, referring to the impact of Wis 13–14 on Jewish and Christian thought of the day, said of the parallels between this material and Rom 1:19-32: "Paul follows its line of thought so closely that our present passage might be taken for a brief summary of it."[7] More lately, James Dunn in 1988 has insisted: "The parallel between Wisd Sol 12–15 and vv. 19-32 is too close to be accidental."[8] And Joseph Fitzmyer in 1993, after referring to Wis 11:15-16, which speaks of God's punishment of the "foolish, wicked thoughts" and idolatries of pagan humanity, argued with respect to Rom 1:19-32: "Paul's argument about the inexcusable situation of pagan humanity has to be understood against the background of such pre-Christian Jewish thinking [i.e., Wis 11:15-16], especially that in *Wisd* 13:1-19 and 14:22-31."[9]

Indeed, Paul's denunciations of humanity's idolatries, immoralities, and injustices in 1:19-32 parallel quite closely — sometimes almost verbatim — the denunciations of Gentile idolatry and immorality in Wis 13:1–14:31, together with some earlier statements in Wis 11–12. Many scholars, therefore, have viewed Paul when writing Rom 1:19-32 to have drawn, in some manner, on this apocryphal Jewish writing. Perhaps some of the material from Wisdom of Solomon — not only from the book's loftier portions, but also from chs. 13–14 (as well as ch. 15) — was used in some of the sermons delivered in some of the Jewish synagogues of that day.[10] It may also have been that Paul had heard Wisdom, including chs. 13–15, read and expounded in the synagogue of his youth at Tarsus.[11] He may even have preached from it as a Jewish teacher before his confrontation by Christ when traveling to Damascus. And it may even be that, on occasion, Paul used such language and characterizations as found in these

---

6. Sanday and Headlam, *Romans* (1902[5]), 52.

7. C. H. Dodd, *Romans,* 27.

8. Dunn, *Romans,* 56-57.

9. Fitzmyer, *Romans,* 272; see also *idem, Spiritual Exercises,* 35, with respect to "Paul's picture of pagan humanity" in Rom 1:19-32: "It depends much on *Wisdom* 13 and 14."

10. So E. P. Sanders, *Paul, the Law, and the Jewish People,* 123 and 129.

11. So R. E. Brown, "Letter to the Romans," in his *Introduction to the New Testament,* 566, with particular reference to Wis 13–14: "In much of the portrayal of Gentiles that opens Rom[ans] Paul may be drawing on a standard Hellenistic synagogue depiction with which he was reared."

chapters of Wisdom in his evangelistic ministry to Gentiles in the Greco-Roman world.[12]

But whatever might be hypothesized regarding the original provenance of what now appears in Rom 1:19-32, or whatever might be thought about the content of these verses, it needs always to be recognized that Paul drew for his theme statement of 1:18 from a much broader biblical, Jewish, and Christian tradition than merely Wisdom of Solomon. For discussions of "the wrath of God" directed "against all the godlessness and wickedness of people who suppress the truth by their wickedness" were common in (1) the Jewish (OT) Scriptures,[13] (2) the writings of early Judaism,[14] (3) the message of John the Baptist,[15] and (4) the teachings of Jesus.[16]

So it may be assumed that such expressions as "the wrath of God," "the wrath of the Lord God Almighty," or "the wrath of Almighty God" — or "the wrath of the Lamb," as that expression appears in more distinctly Christian contexts — would have been fairly common in the preaching of the earliest Jewish believers in Jesus as well.[17] And so it may reasonably be argued that Paul believed that (1) what he wrote as his theme statement of 1:18 and (2) how he supported it by the portrayals and language of 1:19-32 would strike responsive chords among his addressees at Rome — the first, 1:18, being rooted in Scripture and in both Jewish and Jewish Christian theology, and the second, 1:19-32, closely paralleled by portrayals of the pagan Gentile world in a widely read apocryphal Jewish writing which circulated within various Jewish and Jewish Christian circles of the day and may have served as the basis for some of the sermons preached in those circles.

When, therefore, Paul began his proclamation of the Christian message in his letter to Christians at Rome, he began in a way that he believed would be familiar to and appreciated by his addressees — that is, in a manner that reflected a rather distinctive type of Jewish presentation and ethos. Christians at Rome, whatever their ethnicity, seem to have been extensively influenced by Jewish Christianity and so would probably have readily understood such an approach and accepted it. Further, it was a type of approach and form of argumentation that would have been very well known and appreciated by Paul as a Jewish Christian — even though, as one who declared himself to be "all things to all people, so that by all possible means I might save some" (1 Cor 9:22), he may not have usually used this type of approach or form of argumentation in his own evangelistic ministry to Gentiles.

---

12. So Michel, *An die Römer,* 96.

13. Cf., e.g., Num 16:46; 18:5; Josh 9:20; 22:20; Pss 38:1; 102:10; Isa 60:10; Jer 10:10; 21:5; 32:37; 50:13; Zech 7:12.

14. Cf., e.g., *1 En* 106:15; *Let Aris* 254; *T Reub* 4:4; Philo, *De somniis* 2.179; *De vita Mosis* 1.6; Josephus, *Antiquities* 3.321; 11.127; *Sib Or* 4:162; 5:75-76.

15. Cf. Matt 3:7//Luke 3:7.

16. Cf. Luke 21:23; John 3:36.

17. Cf., e.g., Heb 3.11, 4.3; Rev 6:16, 17; 11:18; 16:19; 19:15.

Who Is Discussed in 1:18-32? As for who is being discussed in 1:18-32, it must be acknowledged that Wis 13:1–14:31 presents a number of vehement, even rather vitriolic, denunciations of Gentiles and conditions in the Gentile world, which are then followed by self-congratulatory statements about Jews and the Jewish world. So Paul's use of material drawn from Wis 13–14 could also be understood as his denunciation of the godlessness and wickedness of non-Jews in the Gentile world. Some commentators, in fact, have argued that Paul in 1:18-32 is speaking *exclusively* regarding "the situation of the Gentile world."[18]

But though Paul uses material drawn from Wis 13–14 in speaking about idolatries, immoralities, and injustices, it needs also to be recognized that he never once in 1:18-32 uses the term ἔθνος ("heathen," "pagan," "Gentile," or "nation"). Rather, in his theme statement of 1:18 he uses the more generic expression ἄνθρωποι ("men," "persons"), and thus should be understood as speaking not only about Gentiles but about all humanity. As Bruce Longenecker has rightly argued: "It is not the gentile condition alone that Paul is describing here but a more fundamental *anthropological* condition which includes in itself no ethnic differentiation."[19]

Later in 2:1-16 the apostle will speak in rather broad fashion to "whoever you are who passes judgment on someone else" about God's judgment as being without impartiality against all who sin, whatever their ethnicity. Then in 2:17-29 he will narrow his focus to speak specifically to Jews about any form of Jewish legalism. And finally in 3:1-20 he will narrow his focus yet further to speak about the situation of the Jews before God. Here in 1:18-32, however, Paul's focus is best understood as being on humanity generally — even though he uses material that originally had to do only with the idolatries, immoralities, and injustices of non-Jews, that is, with the "godlessness" and "wickedness" of the Gentile world.

From "Plight to Solution" or "Solution to Plight"? Our highlighting of the "Jewishness" of the material underlying Paul's words in 1:18-32 may not only provide an explanation for certain features of form, structure, and language in the passage, it might also give some insight into the setting of the passage — that is, as to why Paul argues in the manner that he does at the very beginning of the formal content of his letter. For one question that has nagged interpreters for centuries but appears only of late to have found its voice is this: Why does Paul — after having set out in positive fashion his thesis regarding the gospel in 1:16-17 (and before restating that thesis in expanded fashion in 3:21-23, and then going on to support, explicate, and illustrate it in 3:24–4:25) — begin this first section of the body middle of his letter with such an emphasis on God's wrath and judgment and such a damning portrayal of humanity's godlessness

18. Cf., e.g., Gaston, *Paul and the Torah*, 140; Räisänen, *Paul and the Law*, 97; Ziesler, *Romans*, 78.

19. B. W. Longenecker, "Paul's Description of the Anthropological Condition," in his *Eschatology and the Covenant*, 173.

and wickedness as appears in 1:18-32 (and as continued in more focused fashion in 2:1–3:20), whereas in his other NT letters he seems to suggest that he usually began his missionary preaching and pastoral counseling with positive presentations of God's solution to humanity's plight as provided in the work of Jesus Christ and through the ministry of God's Holy Spirit?

The first two chapters of Galatians, particularly Gal 1:6-10 and 2:11-21, may be seen to parallel, at least to some extent, what appears in Rom 1:18–3:20 — if not in content, at least in tone. But even in the very bombastic Galatian letter, when Paul sets out his theological argumentation *(probatio)* in 3:1–4:11, which constitutes an exposition of his immediately preceding thesis paragraph *(propositio)* of 2:15-21, he does so by first recalling for his converts his earlier proclamation of Christ's redemptive work on their behalf and their initial reception of that message — that is, his preaching of "Jesus Christ" as "clearly portrayed as crucified" (3:1), their reception of that "good news" (3:2), their experience of the working of the Holy Spirit in their midst (3:3-5), and the example of Abraham as the man of faith par excellence, whom they are to emulate (3:6-9). Likewise, many of Paul's other letters seem to indicate that throughout his mission to Gentiles in the Greco-Roman world he usually, if not always, began his proclamation of the Christian gospel on a "christological" basis, rather than on an "anthropological" basis. And in this respect (as well as with regard to other matters that will be identified later), the question to be asked is not "Why are Paul's other letters not like Romans?" (as has been frequently asked by many down through the course of Christian history), but "Why is Romans so different from Paul's other letters?"

It was Ed Sanders who brought this issue to the attention of scholars in a rather graphic manner, characterizing Paul in his Gentile mission as follows: "He did not *start* from man's need, but from God's deed."[20] Further, Ed Sanders has suggested that "Romans may not reflect Paul's actual missionary preaching"[21] — starting, as it does, with "humanity's plight" (1:18–3:20) before setting out "God's solution" (3:21–4:25), whereas in many of his other letters the pattern seems to be reversed. On the other hand, Frank Thielman, in opposition to Sanders, has shown how "both canonical and non-canonical Jewish literature from the era in which Paul lived demonstrate familiarity with a pattern of thinking about God's dealings with Israel which runs from plight to solution."[22] Further, Thielman has attempted to demonstrate that this pattern of "plight to solution" is ingrained throughout the course of Paul's argumentation in both Galatians and Romans[23] — and so, presumably, in all of Paul's thought as a Jew-

---

20. E. P. Sanders, *Paul and Palestinian Judaism*, 444; see his fuller discussions of "the solution as preceding the problem" as argued in pp. 442-47, 474-75.

21. *Ibid.,* 444.

22. Thielman, *From Plight to Solution*, 45; see also pp. 28-45 for the pertinent passages and Thielman's comments.

23. For F. Thielman's treatment of the passages in Galatians, see his *From Plight to Solution*, ch. 3, pp. 46-86, for his treatment of the passages in Romans, see *ibid.,* ch. 4, pp. 87-116.

ish Christian and in all of his proclamation of the Christian gospel. Thus while Paul's preaching and teaching were always christocentric in their conclusions, the pattern of his ministry, according to Thielman, should be understood as having usually, if not always, begun with a depiction of humanity's plight — particularly as judged by God's eternal ethical laws — moving on then to a portrayal of God's solution as provided by the work of Christ and the ministry of God's Spirit, rather than the reverse.

My own evaluation of this debate and the issues involved is that (1) both Sanders and Thielman are generally correct with regard to their observations of the data, but (2) both have somewhat skewed the data in the interests of their particular theses: Sanders may be somewhat too rigid in reading Paul as always, with the exception of only Romans, moving from God's solution (Christology) to humanity's plight (anthropology), and Thielman seems to have misread Galatians and some of Paul's other letters in an attempt to make those writings more like Romans in order to establish a consistent pattern of humanity's plight (anthropology) to God's solution (Christology). So the observations and conclusions of both need to be adjusted and corrected.

With respect to the data in question, we believe it necessary to acknowledge

(1) that Paul in Rom 1:18-32 (and continuing in 2:1–3:20) starts with damning depictions of humanity's plight apart from the work of Christ and the ministry of God's Spirit and then moves on to a proclamation of God's solution in 3:21–4:25 (and continuing through the rest of Romans) — as both Sanders and Thielman have observed,

(2) that Paul in his other letters — including Galatians[24] — reflects the fact that he usually began his evangelistic preaching and pastoral counseling with a proclamation of God's solution through the work of Christ and the ministry of the Holy Spirit and only then spoke about how that message of "good news" provides the solution to humanity's plight — as Sanders has claimed was Paul's usual pattern in his ministry, but Thielman has denied, and

(3) that the OT and the literature of Second Temple Judaism indeed evidence "a pattern of thinking about God's dealings with Israel which runs from plight to solution," as Thielman has demonstrated.

For a proper understanding of Romans we must recognize the basic "Jewishness" of Paul's argument in this first section of the body middle, that is, in 1:16–4:25. For Paul was writing to believers in Jesus at Rome who, while ethnically both Gentiles and Jews, had been extensively influenced by the theology, ways of thinking, and manner of expression of Jewish Christianity and so would likely have conceived matters in Jewish Christian ways, expressed themselves in

24. See R. N. Longenecker, *Galatians*, passim.

a Jewish Christian manner of argumentation, and used the vocabulary of Jewish Christianity. Therefore it may be postulated that Paul began his presentation of the Christian gospel to his addressees at Rome in a manner that would have been both familiar to and accepted by them — whereas in letters to his own Gentile converts, who were largely devoid of such a Jewish background, he usually began with a christological proclamation of God's solution to humanity's plight rather than a portrayal of humanity's plight as the background and rationale for God's solution. It is this recognition of the "Jewishness" of Paul's Romans addressees, whatever their ethnicity (together with that of the "statesmanship" of Paul in being "all things to all people," as he declares in 1 Cor 9:22), that we believe provides interpreters a better understanding of this first section of the body middle of Romans (1:16–4:25) and particularly of the passage here in question (1:18-32).

The Structure of the Passage. Numerous attempts have been made to structure 1:18-32 according to some particular linguistic feature or rhetorical convention that appears in the passage. Such attempts have often been worked out in terms of (1) the verb παρέδωκεν ("he gave/delivered over") in vv. 24, 26, and 28, (2) the verb ἤλλαξαν and its intensified form μετήλλαξαν ("they exchanged") in vv. 23, 25, and 26, and/or (3) the inferential conjunctions διότι ("because," "therefore") in v. 21 and διό ("therefore") in v. 24, together with the preposition διά with the neuter accusative pronoun τοῦτο ("because of this") in v. 26.[25] There is, however, little agreement among the commentators who propose such a structuring on these bases.

Rather, it seems best to structure the passage topically, following generally the analyses proposed by James Dunn[26] and Joseph Fitzmyer,[27] as follows:

1. a theme statement on the wrath of God (1:18), which pronounces God's wrath "against all the godlessness and wickedness of those who suppress the truth by their wickedness";
2. depictions of humanity's idolatries (1:19-23), which set out humanity's rebellion against God, independence from God, and lack of praise and thanks to God — and thus the inauguration of various forms of idolatry;
3. portrayals of humanity's immoralities and injustices (1:24-31), which set out a direct link between idolatry and immorality and characterize the resultant moral sins and ethical injustices of people; and
4. consequent judgment proclaimed: death (1:32), which expresses God's verdict on those who do and approve such things.

In our "exegetical comments" these four headings will be used to structure the presentation.

25. Cf., e.g., Klostermann, "Die adäquat Vergeltung in Rm 1,22-31"; Jeremias, "Zu Röm 1,22-32," *ZNW* 45 (1954); S. Schulz, "Die Anklage in Röm. 1,18-32"; W. Popkes, "Zum Aufbau und Charakter von Römer 1.18-32," *NTS* 28 (1982).

26. Dunn, *Romans,* 1.53.

27. Fitzmyer, *Romans,* 276.

EXEGETICAL COMMENTS

I. Theme Statement on the Wrath of God (1:18)

1:18 The passage on "the wrath of God" begins in 1:18 with the postpositive γάρ ("for," "because"), which was earlier used three times in the thesis statement of 1:16-17: first at its beginning in 1:16a as a transitional particle to signal the continuation of what Paul writes as he moves from the "body opening" of the letter (1:13-15) to his thesis statement (1:16-17), which heads up the whole first section of the letter's "body middle" (1:16–4:25), then twice more in 1:16b and 17a as an explanatory conjunction, both instances introducing explanations of why Paul was "not ashamed of the gospel." Many, therefore, in line with these latter two instances, have viewed γάρ at the beginning of 1:18 as also an explanatory conjunction and so see it as introducing elucidations regarding "the gospel" in 1:16 and "the righteousness of God" in 1:17. Their argument is based linguistically on the fact that the same verb ἀποκαλύπτω ("reveal") appears in the same form (third person singular, present, indicative, passive ἀποκαλύπτεται, "is being revealed") with respect to both "God's righteousness" (1:17) and "God's wrath" (1:18) — and therefore, they argue, God's righteousness and God's wrath must be seen as two essential features of the one Christian gospel. Or, as Matthew Black has expressed this position, "Verse 18 goes clearly with verse 17 and at the same time serves as a transition to verses 19ff. The same verb is used of the 'revelation' of God's anger as in connection with the 'revelation' of his 'righteousness.' God's wrath is the manifestation of his 'righteousness.'"[28]

Others, however, have proposed that γάρ here in 1:18 should be understood as an adversative conjunction. Their argument is that (1) linguistically "the wrath of God" in this verse is referred to as revealed "from heaven" (ἀπ' οὐρανοῦ), whereas "the righteousness of God" is spoken of in 1:17 as revealed "in the gospel" (ἐν αὐτῷ), and (2) contextually "the wrath of God" is not to be identified as a feature of either "the gospel" or "the righteousness of God," which are highlighted in 1:16-17, but as contrasted to them.[29]

Indeed, "righteousness" and "wrath" are both attributes of God and may be considered, in some ways, as parallel features in God's redemptive activities (so the truth of the first position). Likewise, it is quite right to highlight the contrast involved in moving from 1:16-17 to 1:18-32 (so the truth of the second position). Yet all that γάρ necessarily connotes here at the beginning of 1:18 is that, having set out his thesis statement of 1:16-17, Paul now moves on in 1:18-32 (and as continued in more focused fashion throughout 2:1–3:20) to speak of humanity's plight apart from what God has provided in the gospel and people's

---

28. Black, *Romans,* 48; cf. also Barrett, *Romans,* 33; Cranfield, *Romans,* 103-8, 111.

29. So, e.g., C. H. Dodd, *Romans,* 18; Huby, *Romains,* 79; Stuhlmacher, *Gerechtigkeit,* 80; Kertelge, "'Rechtfertigung' bei Paulus," 88; Wilckens, *An die Römer,* 1.101; Dunn, *Romans,* 54; Fitzmyer, *Romans,* 277.

acceptance of that "good news" by faith. So this γάρ should probably be viewed as simply another transitional particle — like that at the beginning of 1:16, which functions to connect, in some manner, what follows with what was said before — without, of itself, intending to introduce either an elucidation of or a contrast to what has appeared immediately before.[30] And such a transitional particle would be particularly suitable if (as we believe is most likely) what appears in the theme statement of 1:18 and the following portrayals of 1:19-32 regarding humanity's idolatries and immoralities has been drawn by Paul from earlier sermonic materials (either his earlier sermons or those of others), which were themselves based on traditional Jewish theology (for the theme statement of 1:18) and on Wis 13–14 (for the characterizations and language of 1:19-32).

The phrase ὀργὴ θεοῦ ("the wrath of God") provides the subject of the theme statement. The prophets of the Jewish (OT) Scriptures often used the expression "the wrath of God" to speak of God's righteous judgment against sin and sinners in the future,[31] but they also used it with respect to God's past and present judgments.[32] And that is how Paul and the other writers of the NT employ the expression as well — that is, in an eschatological sense to refer to God's future judgment,[33] but also with respect to both God's past judgments on sin and sinners[34] and his present judgments on human rebellion and evil, as well as on those who espouse such stances and actions.[35]

The "wrath of God," as Vincent Taylor has aptly defined it, is "not angry passion, but the condemnation which falls upon sin and sinners in conscious rebellion against God."[36] It is, as William Barclay spoke of it, God's "annihilating reaction" against sin and all those who have turned away from God and gone their own way.[37] Or as Luke Timothy Johnson points out regarding God's wrath, "It is a retribution that results, not at the whim of an angry despot but as the necessary consequence of a self-distorted existence."[38]

"The wrath of God" is an anthropomorphism (i.e., an ascription to God of human feelings), which expresses a more intensive response to sin and those who sin than mere human words can articulate. It speaks of (1) God's horror, which exceeds all human understanding, with respect to the idolatries and immoralities of humanity, and (2) God's rightful judgment, which goes beyond human comprehension, on all such rebellious thoughts and actions. Like "the love of God" — which is also an anthropomorphism that speaks in human fash-

30. So, e.g., Lietzmann, *An die Römer,* 31; Kuss, *Römerbrief,* 1.35.

31. Cf., e.g., Isa 13:13; 26:20; Ezek 7:19; Zeph 3:8.

32. E.g., Ps 78:31; Isa 9:19, 21; 13:9.

33. Cf., e.g., Rom 2:5, 8-9; 5:9; Col 3:6; 1 Thess 1:10; 5:9; see also Rev 6:16-17; 11:18; 14:10; 16:19; 19:15.

34. Cf., e.g., 1 Thess 2:16; see also Heb 3:11; 4:3.

35. As here at 1:18; see in Romans also 12:19 and 13:4-5.

36. Taylor, *Romans,* 28.

37. Barclay, *Romans,* 25.

38. L. T. Johnson, *Reading Romans,* 33.

ion of God's inexpressible concern for the welfare of all people and his unfathomable redemptive actions on their behalf — "the wrath of God" enunciates in stammering human language God's horror with respect to humanity's rebellion, self-centeredness, and lawlessness, all of which result in people's self-imposed separation from God and their inhumane injustices toward each other.

God's wrath against sin and those who sin is a concept that derives from the OT prophetic warnings against idolatry.[39] In the prophecy of Joel it is related to "the day of the Lord," which is a term for both a time of God's judgment in the near future (as in Joel 1:15; 2:1, 11) and a time at the end of the ages when God will bring about final judgment (as in 2:31; 3:14). And that is how the phrase "the wrath of God" is used in the NT generally and Paul's letters in particular: with regard to both a future final judgment and God's present judgments — at times explicitly associating "the wrath of God" with "the day of the Lord,"[40] though at other times using some such synonymous phraseology as "the day of God,"[41] "the day of judgment,"[42] or simply "that day."[43]

In Paul's letter to the Christians at Rome "the wrath of God" plays a thematic role, not only here at 1:18 but also theologically at 2:5, 8; 5:9; 9:22[44] and ethically at 12:19; 13:4.[45] Many of the Church Fathers, such as John Chrysostom, Theodore of Mopsuestia, and Gennadius of Constantinople, understood God's wrath in 1:18 as simply his eschatological wrath in the future, in line with Paul's references in 2:5, 8-9 to "the day of wrath, when God's righteous judgment will be revealed."[46] Paul, however, also speaks in Romans of God's wrath as a present reality, which is expressed not only against the rebellion and lawlessness of those outside Christ but also against the sinfulness of God's own people.[47] Thus just as "righteousness" and "life" are positive realities bestowed by God in both the present and the future, so "wrath" and "death" are negative factors brought about by God in both the present and the future — in the present, in an inaugurated and developing manner; in the future, finally and fully.

The verb ἀποκαλύπτειν ("to reveal," "disclose," "bring to light") that appears here in 1:18 in connection with God's wrath was used in 1:17 in connection with God's righteousness. Further, it appears here in 1:18 in the same grammatical form as it did in v. 17 (i.e., ἀποκαλύπτεται, in the third person, present tense, indicative mode, and passive voice). All of this has led some commentators to understand "God's wrath" as an aspect of divine righteousness and so, in some

39. See Isa 51:7; Jer 6:11; Hos 13:11; Zeph 1:15.
40. Cf. Acts 2:20 (quoting Joel 2:31); 1 Thess 5:2; and 2 Pet 3:10.
41. 2 Pet 3:12.
42. Matt 11:22, 24.
43. 2 Tim 1:12, 18; 4:8.
44. Cf. also Eph 2:3; 1 Thess 1:10; 2:16; 5:9.
45. Cf. Eph 5:6; Col 3:6.
46. Cf. H.-J. Eckstein, " 'Denn Gottes Zorn wird vom Himmel her offenbar werden'. Exegetische Erwägungen zu Röm 1,18," *ZNW* 78 (1987) passim.
47. Cf. Rom 3:5; 4:15; 9:22; see also Eph 2:3; 1 Thess 2:16.

way, as an important part of the content of the Christian gospel — as if what has been called "condemning righteousness" and "justifying righteousness" are to be understood as the two essential features of the Christian proclamation, which in some manner run parallel to each other and so are to be proclaimed together.[48]

But Paul does not say that God's wrath is revealed "in the gospel," as he did of God's righteousness in 1:17, but that "the wrath of God" is revealed "from heaven" (ἀπ' οὐρανοῦ), thereby laying stress on the cosmic nature of God's judgment on all the rebellion and lawlessness of humanity — and, in the process, suggesting that the declaration of divine wrath, which in certain cases may be justified as a preparatory feature for the Christian proclamation, is not to be equated with "the good news" of the Christian message, which focuses on what God has done in and through the work and person of Jesus Christ. "Righteousness" and "wrath" are both attributes of the one true God, but God's righteousness is uniquely revealed "in the gospel," whereas his wrath is revealed "from heaven" (ἀπ' οὐρανοῦ) — and, therefore, the two are not to be equated or considered simply two features of the same proclamation.[49]

The object of God's wrath is stated in the words ἐπὶ πᾶσαν ἀσέβειαν καὶ ἀδικίαν ἀνθρώπων τῶν τὴν ἀλήθειαν ἐν ἀδικίᾳ κατεχόντων ("against all the godlessness and wickedness of people who suppress the truth by their wickedness"). The noun ἀσέβεια ("godlessness") is used in Deut 9:5 (LXX) with respect to the wickedness of "the nations" in opposition to Israel and is found elsewhere in ancient Jewish Greek writings in the sense of "wickedness" or "violence."[50] It is an expression, however, that is seldom used by Paul, appearing in Romans only here and at 11:26.[51] The noun ἀδικία ("unrighteousness," "lawlessness," "evil," "wickedness," "injustice"), however, is found frequently in Jewish and Christian writings for all sorts of lawlessness, injustice, and deception,[52] and it appears fairly often in Paul's letters.[53] This same pair of terms is found in the LXX translations of Ps 73:6 (LXX 72:6) and Prov 11:5, though not in similar fashion or the same order.

Paul sets out these two nouns in parallel fashion as apparent synonyms and introduces them by the one adjective πᾶσαν ("all"), which suggests that he thought of them as expressing something of a *hendiadys* (i.e., one idea expressed

48. So, e.g., with varying emphases, such significant commentators as M. Black, K. Barth, C. K. Barrett, and C. E. B. Cranfield, as cited above.

49. So, rightly, Nygren, *Romans,* 106; Michel, *An die Römer,* 97; Käsemann, *Romans,* 35; Wilckens, *An die Römer,* 1.103; Fitzmyer, *Romans,* 277.

50. Cf. Ps 73:6 (LXX 72:6); Philo, *De confusione linguarum* 21; *De migratione Abrahami* 60; Josephus, *War* 7.260.

51. Cf. also 2 Tim 2:16; Titus 2:12.

52. Cf., e.g., Ps 73:6 (LXX 72:6); Jer 31:34 (LXX 38:34); Sir 17:20; Bar 3:8; Tob 13:5; Philo, *De confusione linguarum* 21; *De migratione Abrahami* 60; Josephus, *War* 7.260; Heb 8:12, quoting Jer 31:34 (LXX 38:34).

53. Not only here in Romans but also at 1:29; 2:8; 3:5; 6:13; 9:14; see also 1 Cor 13:6; 2 Cor 12:13; 2 Thess 2:10, 12; 2 Tim 2:19.

in more forceful manner by the use of two roughly synonymous expressions). We should probably, therefore, not view Paul's use of these terms as referring to two types or dimensions of human wickedness: the first, ἀσέβεια ("godlessness"), as directed against God; the second, ἀδικία ("unrighteousness," "lawlessness," "evil," "wickedness," "injustice"), as having in mind people's relations with one another.

The fifth-century Church Father Gennadius of Constantinople understood Paul's use of ἀσέβεια and ἀδικία in this twofold fashion, writing as follows:

> Generally speaking, there are two types of sin — discord with God and discord with one's neighbor. Paul mentions them both, putting discord with God first because it is the greater sin, and calling it "ungodliness." Then he mentions the second kind of discord, the one with one's neighbor, calling it "wickedness."[54]

And such an understanding has been often proposed — as, for example, by more recent commentators such as Otto Michel, who viewed ἀσέβεια as referring to violations of the first commandment of the Decalogue and ἀδικία as having in mind violations of all the commandments that follow,[55] and Paul Billerbeck, who viewed ἀσέβεια as referring to irreligion before God and ἀδικία to immorality among people.[56] Nonetheless, the combination of these two rather synonymous nouns is probably best understood as a *hendiadys* that functions in a forceful manner to signal the whole gamut of human rebellion, lawlessness, and sin[57] — all of which, however defined, is under God's rightful judgment.

Further, it needs to be noted that πᾶσαν ("all") in this passage has a decidedly polemical thrust. For in setting out his theme statement of 1:18 — which functions as the caption not only for what immediately follows in 1:19-32 but also for all that is said regarding ἀσέβεια ("godlessness") and ἀδικία ("wickedness") in 2:1–3:20 — Paul clearly has in mind not only "the rebellion, idolatry, and debauchery" of Gentiles but also "the irreligion and injustice" of Jews who considered themselves God's δίκαιοι ("righteous ones") and therefore as immune to and separated from the sinful practices of Gentiles. In opposition to such Jewish self-congratulatory statements as found in Wis 15:1-6 ("But Thou, our God, art gracious and true, longsuffering, and in mercy ordering all things. For even if we sin, we are thine, knowing thy dominion. But we shall not sin, knowing that we are accounted thine"), Paul argues in 2:8-9 that for those who are ἀσεβής ("godless") and do ἀδικία ("unrighteousness," "wickedness," "injustice") there will be "trouble and distress, both for the Jew first and for the Gentile" — and, further, he declares in 3:5 that such Jewish acts of ἀδικία cannot be justified by

---

54. Gennadius of Constantinople, in *Pauluskommentare aus der griechischen Kirche*, 15.356.
55. Michel, *An die Römer*, 98-99.
56. P. Billerbeck, *Str-Bil* 3.31.
57. So Fitzmyer, *Romans*, 278.

the specious claim that "our unrighteousness brings out God's righteousness more clearly."

Paul's reference to "the truth" (ἡ ἀλήθεια) in speaking of "people who suppress the truth by their wickedness" (ἀνθρώπων τῶν τὴν ἀλήθειαν ἐν ἀδικίᾳ κατεχόντων) may seem, at first glance, somewhat vague. For "truth" has a variety of connotations in Paul's letters. Yet Paul uses the term here, as he does almost always, with an article — which suggests a particular meaning in mind, with that meaning always dependent on the particular context.

As a Jewish Christian, Paul in referring to "the truth" could very well have had in mind God's faithfulness to his covenant people. Or as a Christian apostle and evangelist, he may have been thinking of the content of the Christian message, "the truth of the gospel," which he sought always to defend and proclaim.[58] But because of what follows immediately in 1:19-23, which speaks of what can be known about God from creation and humanity's suppression of that knowledge by its idolatries, it seems most likely that "the truth" that Paul has principally in mind here, that which has been (and is being) suppressed by human godlessness and wickedness, is to be understood in a theistic sense as being God's "eternal power and divine nature" (as in 1:20). So Paul should probably be read here as saying that the godless thoughts and wicked actions of people have prevented them from acknowledging even the basic truth of the existence, nature, and power of God — let alone all that the OT Scriptures declare about God's desired covenantal relations with his people and all that the Christian message proclaims about what God has done in and through Jesus for the salvation of all people.

II. Depictions of Humanity's Idolatries (1:19-23)

In the five verses that follow the theme statement of 1:18, Paul presents two reasons why God's wrath is now being expressed against humanity: (1) because (διότι, understanding the conjunction in a causal sense) God has revealed to all people through his creation some of the basic matters regarding his existence and person, thereby leaving them without any excuse for ignoring him (vv. 19-20), and (2) because (διότι, again understood causally) people, while in possession of this universal and elemental knowledge about God, have not responded by glorifying God or thanking him, but have turned to the worship of idols of their own invention (vv. 21-23).

1:19 The phrase τὸ γνωστὸν τοῦ θεοῦ, which appears at the start of 1:19 and controls all of the presentation of 1:19-23, may be read as either (1) "what is known about God," suggesting a rather full knowledge of God,[59] or (2) "what can be known (or 'is knowable') about God," suggesting certain basic matters

---

58. Cf. Gal 2:5, 14; see also Rom 2:8; Eph 1:13; 4:21; Col 1:5; 2 Thess 2:12; 2 Tim 2:15.
59. Which is how it is used in the LXX and in Acts 1:19; 2:14; 4:10, 16; 9:42; 13:38; 15:18; 19:17; 28:22, 28.

that can be known about God.[60] The articular noun τὸ γνωστόν does not appear elsewhere in Paul's letters. Here, however, the context calls for it to be understood in the latter sense of "what can be known" or "is knowable." As John Calvin insisted, it is a knowledge "that God exists and is powerful, that he is humanity's creator, and that therefore all people are to glorify God."[61] Further, as Calvin goes on to say, it is a knowledge that is "too forceful to allow men to escape from it" — but also that it "avails only to prevent men from making excuses," and so "differs greatly from the knowledge which brings salvation."[62]

In the statement φανερόν ἐστιν ἐν αὐτοῖς ("it is plain to them"), the neuter adjective φανερόν ("plain," "clear," "evident") used with the third person singular copula ἐστιν ("it is") states quite simply that certain significant matters regarding God are evident to all people — picking up the πᾶσαν ("all") of 1:18. The following statement ὁ θεὸς γὰρ αὐτοῖς ἐφανέρωσεν ("for God has made it plain to them") states the reason such a basic knowledge of God is plain to all: because God has made it plain to everyone.

The preposition ἐν with the dative plural personal pronoun αὐτοῖς in the first sentence of the verse could be translated "in them,"[63] or "in their midst,"[64] or "among them"[65] — thereby suggesting, perhaps, an emphasis on how divine revelation must enter a person's consciousness and be personally appropriated in order to be effective. All these translations are appropriate and need to be more fully developed on the basis of other exegetical data. But Paul, together with many other NT writers, uses ἐν in a great variety of ways — even, at times, to signify the indirect object of a sentence's verb and so to identify the recipient of a stated action.[66] Likewise, the LXX frequently uses ἐν in this functional and directional manner, as in Hab 2:1 ("I will keep watch to see what he will say *to me*") and Zech 1:9 ("The angel who talked with me said *to me*").[67] Thus here with the αὐτοῖς ("to them") in the second sentence of this verse, which functions as a simple dative of indirect object, the phrase ἐν αὐτοῖς in the verse's first sentence probably should be understood as only a variant construction of the same point: that God has made the basic matters of what may be known about him evident *to all people*.

1:20 The postpositive γάρ in this verse is evidently meant to be explanatory in nature. Yet almost every statement in the explanation has been a matter of dispute among exegetes and theologians. What are τὰ ἀόρατα αὐτοῦ ("the

---

60. As found in the Greek classical writings and as appears in Sir 21:7 ("The able person can be known from a distance by his speaking") and Philo, *Legum allegoriae* 1.60-61.

61. J. Calvin, *Romans*, in *Calvin's New Testament Commentaries*, 8.30-31.

62. *Ibid.*, 8.31-32.

63. So, e.g., Lietzmann, *An die Römer*, 31; Huby, *Romains*, 82.

64. So, e.g., Michel, *An die Römer*, 99; Cranfield, *Romans*, 113-14.

65. So, e.g., Barrett, *Romans*, 35.

66. Gal 1:16, "to reveal his Son *to me*"; 1 Cor 14:11, "he is a foreigner *to me*"; see also Luke 2:14; Acts 4:12.

67. See also Zech 1:13, 14, 19; 2:3; 4:4, 5; 5:5, 10; 6:4.

invisible things of him [God]")? What is meant by ἀπὸ κτίσεως κόσμου ("from the creation of the world")? What is signified by τοῖς ποιήμασιν νοούμενα καθορᾶται ("they have been clearly seen, being understood by what has been made")? What is to be understood by ἥ τε ἀΐδιος αὐτοῦ δύναμις καὶ θειότης ("his eternal power and divine nature")? And how does the final statement of this verse function: εἰς τὸ εἶναι αὐτοὺς ἀναπολογήτους ("so people are without excuse")?

Further, it needs to be noted that much of the language in 1:20 reflects more the religious language of the Greek world and Hellenistic Judaism during the first Christian century than it does the language of Paul himself. For example, certain key terms are either absent from or extremely rare in Paul and the rest of the NT, such as the noun θειότης ("divine nature"), which appears only here in the NT, and the adjective ἀΐδιος ("eternal"), which can be found only here and in Jude 6. Both of these terms, however, seem to have been fairly common in the Greek and Jewish Greek writings of the day[68] — which, of course, raises questions about how Paul understood these terms when he used them here in 1:20.

Clarifying "what can be known about God," Paul speaks first in this verse of τὰ ἀόρατα αὐτοῦ (literally "the invisible things of him," that is, "God's invisible attributes") and goes on to identify those attributes generally as "his eternal power and divine nature" (ἡ ἀΐδιος αὐτοῦ δύναμις καὶ θειότης). In so saying, the apostle sets out the basis for the distinction that Origen later enunciated between (1) "something about God that can be known," which is revealed to all people by the fabric of God's created world, and (2) "something about him that is unknown," which becomes known only by God's further revelations of himself — that is, his further revelations of himself first in his dealings with the primal families of history, with the Jewish patriarchs, with the lawgiver Moses, with the Jewish prophets, and with the entire nation of Israel, as recorded in the Jewish (OT) Scriptures, and then through the ministry, teachings, and redemptive work of his Son, Jesus Christ, together with the activities of his Holy Spirit, as portrayed in the Christian (NT) Scriptures and as experienced in the personal and corporate lives of Christian believers.[69]

By τὰ ἀόρατα αὐτοῦ Paul undoubtedly had in mind God's attributes or essential qualities, which, according to the OT, the Talmud, and such NT passages as Col 1:15; 1 Tim 1:17; and Heb 11:27, are "invisible" to humans.[70] The clarification of this expression by the phrases ἡ ἀΐδιος αὐτοῦ δύναμις ("his eternal power") and [αὐτοῦ] θειότης ("[his] divine nature") is, admittedly, rather general. But these phrases speak, at least, of the existence of a divine being who is powerful, and they imply that humanity is in some significant sense both dependent on and responsible to that being.

68. See, e.g., the materials cited in *BAG*, 21, col 2 and 354, col 2.
69. Origen, *Ad Romanos*, *CER* 1.136.
70. For passages from these various materials, see those cited in *Str Bil*, 3.31-32.

The expression ἀπὸ κτίσεως κόσμου ("from the creation of the world") could be read in a number of ways, for the preposition ἀπό ("from") is used in the NT to signify a number of things — most commonly (1) separation, (2) source or origin, or (3) means or cause, but also (4) the temporal idea of duration. And since a number of parallel NT constructions use ἀπό in this *temporal* sense,[71] it seems best to view the preposition in this first part of 1:20 as signifying the temporal idea of "since" and to understand that what is said here is that "ever since the creation of the world" all people have had some knowledge of "God's invisible attributes" — that is, "his eternal power and divine nature." This is not to deny that a general knowledge of God can be derived from the fabric of the created universe, for that is what is declared in the very next statement of this verse ("they have been seen, being understood by what has been made"). But it is to say that to view ἀπό here as having reference to *source* is to set up a redundancy with the statement that immediately follows, and therefore it seems best, for both lexical and logical reasons, to understand the preposition in this statement of 1:20a in a temporal sense.[72]

The statement τοῖς ποιήμασιν νοούμενα καθορᾶται ("they have been clearly seen, being understood by what has been made") raises a number of questions regarding what exactly is being signified. The intensive verb καθοράω ("see clearly," "observe closely"), which appears here in its third person plural present passive form ("they have been clearly seen"),[73] is found only here in the whole NT. It frequently appears, however, in classical and koine writings — though in these secular materials it usually denotes an external observation, not necessarily with any mental apprehension or understanding. On the other hand, the verb νοέω ("apprehend," "understand," "perceive," "gain insight into"), which appears here as a nominative plural neuter present passive participle ("being understood"), is found a further thirteen times in the NT and always connotes some type of apprehension or understanding.[74] Thus it seems that both of the ideas of (1) external observation of data and (2) inner apprehension or understanding of that data are present in this statement — similar to the use of the simple verbs ὁράω ("see") and νοέω ("understand") in Matt 24:15; Mark 13:14; and John 12:40 (quoting Isa 6:10). So we may conclude that Paul is not merely speaking of people having observed certain data having to do with God's eternal power and divine nature — or, more minimally, that such data is available for people to see — but that "all people" have also had, and continue

---

71. Cf. Matt 24:21, "*from* ('since') the beginning of the world"; Matt 25:34; Luke 11:50; Rev 13:8; 17:8, "*from* ('since') the foundation of the world"; Mark 10:6; 13:19; 2 Pet 3:4, "*from* ('since') the beginning of creation"; Matt 11:12, "from ('since') the days of John the Baptist until now"; and 2 Cor 8:10; 9:2, "from ('since') last year."

72. So, e.g., Sanday and Headlam, *Romans,* 42-43; Cranfield, *Romans,* 1.114; Fitzmyer, *Romans,* 280; Moo, *Romans,* 105 n. 64.

73. I.e., the present tense understood as a "historic present."

74. See Matt 15:17; 16:9, 11; 24:15; Mark 7:18; 8:17; 13:14; John 12:40; Eph 3:4, 20; 1 Tim 1:7; 2 Tim 2:7; Heb 11:3.

to have (unless they have suppressed or perverted what has been seen), some appreciation or understanding of the significance of that data for their own lives.

Greek and Roman philosophers argued that while the "ultimate reality" that stands behind everything that exists cannot be seen, the human mind can reason inductively from the pattern and functions of what exists ("the cosmological argument"), as well as from the nature and qualities of human beings themselves ("the ontological argument"), and thus, by means of a succession of observable effects and their postulated causes, draw certain conclusions regarding a "first principle," "first cause," or original "unmoved mover."[75] Jews also thought somewhat along these lines.

Yet however much Jewish thinkers might evidence agreement with such quasi-theistic speculations, they could never accept the metaphysical tenets of the ancient philosophers regarding indirect causation, a non-personal first principle or final cause, or the innate ability of the human mind to reason back to that first unmoved mover. For God's actions in creating and preserving the world were understood by Jewish thinkers to be both personal and direct, and so theistic deduction was considered possible only because God himself had implanted a revelation of himself in the warp and woof of his created universe.

It was for Jews a matter of God's revelation of the basic features regarding himself that he consciously built into in his creation, and not that of people's ability to ferret out such features by their own intellect or reasoning. That is, for Jews even an elemental knowledge of God did not constitute some sort of "natural theology" that bases itself on human reason and works its way back inductively by means of a succession of observable effects and postulated causes to some non-personal "first cause" or "unmoved mover." Instead, a "revelation in creation" has been implanted and maintained by God himself in the fabric of the universe that he himself created — a revelation that calls on all of God's creation, both personal and non-personal, to respond to God, the creator, appropriately. Such a "general revelation" in creation, together with the relation of that revelation to God's "special revelation" in the written Torah, is eloquently portrayed in Ps 19, with the "general revelation" in creation spoken of in vv. 1-6 (which begin with the affirmation "the heavens declare the glory of God; the skies proclaim the work of his hands") and God's "special revelation" highlighted in vv. 7-13 (which begins with the declaration "the Law of the Lord is perfect, reviving the soul; the statutes of the Lord are trustworthy, making wise the simple"). To such a divine revelation in two forms, the only truly appropriate human response is that set out in v. 14: "May the words of my mouth and the meditation of my heart be pleasing in your sight, O Lord, my Rock and my Redeemer."

God's revelation in creation is also referred to in a number of Jewish writings composed during the period of Second Temple Judaism, and so during a time roughly contemporary with Paul — most prominently Wis 13:1-9 (cited ear-

75. Cf., e.g., Plato, *Timaeus* 28A-30C, 32A-35A; Aristotle, *Metaphysics,* bk. 2; *De Mundo* 6.397b-399b; Cicero, *Laws* 1.8.4; *Tusculan Disputations* 1.29.70.

lier) and *Sib Or* 3:8-45. Most often the references to God's revelation in creation in these materials of Second Temple Judaism are to be found in discussions of how Abraham came to recognize the existence of God.[76] Likewise, there appear in the Talmud similar statements about how the patriarch Abraham came to discover the existence of God by reasoning back from what exists in creation to a first cause, as in *Genesis Rabbah* 38:13 and 39:1.[77]

Paul was hardly original in arguing that although God is invisible, his basic attributes — that is, "his eternal power and divine nature" (ἥ τε ἀΐδιος αὐτοῦ δύναμις καὶ θειότης) — (1) can be discerned from his creation and so to some extent (2) can be "understood by what has been made" (τοῖς ποιήμασιν νοούμενα). Further, it appears evident from his statements here in 1:19-20 that Paul believed that every person, in whatever time, place, or circumstance, knew the basic truths about God because of God's revelation of himself in his creation. And while such a basic knowledge of God as revealed in God's creation is hardly ever alluded to in his letters to his own Christian converts (i.e., other than here in his letter to Rome), it comes to the fore in two contextualized forms in Luke's portrayals of Paul's evangelistic preaching to Gentiles: first in Acts 14:15-17 to a group of Gentile country people, then in Acts 17:24-27 to a group of Gentile philosophers who viewed themselves as knowledgeable and sophisticated.

The first reason set out in 1:19 as to why God's wrath is now being expressed against humanity — because God has made "plain" to everyone by means of his creation a basic knowledge of "his eternal power and divine nature," but they have failed to respond appropriately — is concluded here in 1:20 by the statement "so people are without excuse" (εἰς τὸ εἶναι αὐτοὺς ἀναπολογήτους). The preposition εἰς with the articular infinitive τὸ εἶναι is a common construction in koine Greek for signaling *result*. Yet it frequently also carries the nuance of *purposeful result*. So while the phrase is most naturally translated "so people are without excuse," it may also suggest purpose: "so that people would be without excuse."

Linguistically, "they are without excuse" (αὐτοὺς ἀναπολογήτους, literally "the inexcusability of them") may be paralleled by what is said about Gentiles in the penultimate sentence of Wis 13:1-9 — which, as we have argued earlier, Paul probably knew and may have drawn on when writing Rom 1:19-32: "Further, they are not to be pardoned (πάλιν δὲ οὐδ' αὐτοὶ συγγνωστοί)." A parallel may also be found in *Assumption of Moses* 1:13, where God's purpose in creation is said to be "in order that the Gentiles might thereby be convicted; indeed, to their own humiliation, that they might by their arguments convict one another." Yet theologically, in the context of Paul's broader teaching, and particularly as expressed elsewhere in Romans, Chrysostom's words about humanity's lack of

---

76. See esp. *Jub* 12:16-24; Philo, *De Abrahamo* 17.77-79; 33.185; 72-74; *De migratione Abrahami* 32; *De gigantibus* 62-64 (though Philo usually uses a form of the ontological argument rather than the cosmological argument); Josephus, *Antiquities* 1.154-56; and *Apoc Ab* 1-7.

77. Cf. Sandmel, "Abraham's Knowledge of the Existence of God," 55-60.

response to God's revelation of himself in creation remains true: "God did not set so great a system of teaching before the heathen in order to deprive them of any excuse but so that they might come to know him. It was by their failure to recognize him that they deprived themselves of every excuse."[78]

1:21 The second reason that God's wrath is now being expressed against humanity is set out in 1:21-23. These three verses begin with "because although they knew God, they did not glorify him as God or give him thanks" (διότι γνόντες τὸν θεὸν οὐχ ὡς θεὸν ἐδόξασαν ἢ ηὐχαρίστησαν). The conjunction διότι, which as in 1:19 is used in a causal manner, introduces all the features of this second explanation in these verses — which cumulatively argue that people, while in possession of a basic knowledge of God as provided by him in his creation, have not responded to him by glorifying him or thanking him, but, rather, have turned to the worship of images and idols of their own invention. "The root of the matter," as Kingsley Barrett has pointed out, is expressed in the words "although they knew God, they did not glorify him as God or give thanks to him."[79] And as Barrett aptly goes on to say:

> As God's creature, man [humanity] was bound to render glory and thanksgiving to his Creator; this means not merely to acknowledge his existence, and to employ the words and rites of religion, but to recognize his lordship and live in grateful obedience — in fact (in the Pauline sense) to believe, to have faith. This men [people] failed to do; instead they rebelled against God, and their fault lay not in lack of knowledge but in their rebellion.[80]

In declaring "but their thinking became futile and their foolish hearts were darkened" (ἀλλ' ἐματαιώθησαν ἐν τοῖς διαλογισμοῖς αὐτῶν καὶ ἐσκοτίσθη ἡ ἀσύνετος αὐτῶν καρδία), Paul identifies the starting point for humanity's awful descent, both spiritually and morally. Here in 1:21a are encapsulated the two primary factors that gave (and continue to give) rise to the awful condition of all human beings: "they did not glorify him as God" and "they did not give him thanks." Rebellious people have always been unwilling to glorify or praise God; rather, they seek praise only for themselves. Nor can they bring themselves to give thanks to God, either for their creation or for what he has brought about redemptively on their behalf; rather, they laud their own wisdom and flaunt their own efforts. But (notice the use of the strong adversative ἀλλά) such egoistic pretensions and defiant stances result in thoroughly disastrous consequences. For as Paul describes the plight of such people here at the close of 1:21: "their thinking became futile and their foolish hearts were darkened."

1:22 James Dunn has argued that Paul's statement "while claiming to be wise, they became fools" (φάσκοντες εἶναι σοφοὶ ἐμωράνθησαν) of 1:22 is an

78. Chrysostom, "Homilies," in *Nicene and Post-Nicene Fathers*, 11.352.
79. Barrett, *Romans*, 36.
80. *Ibid.*

"obviously deliberate echo of the Adam narratives"[81] and "obviously modeled on the account of man's fall in Gen 3."[82] This thesis was first proposed by Morna Hooker,[83] and has been lauded and developed by Alexander Wedderburn.[84] It rests largely on the observations (1) that the verbs ἐξαπέστειλεν ("he sent forth/ banished") and ἐξέβαλε ("he cast/drove out") of Gen 3:24-25 (LXX) are similar to the verb παρέδωκεν ("he gave/delivered over") of Rom 1:24, 26, and 28, (2) that there is an emphasis in both the narrative of Genesis 3 and Paul's statement here on the human desire for greater knowledge apart from that given by God, which results in a decline into a position of disadvantage and decidedly lower regard, and (3) that the Genesis account of the fall of Adam appears widely in the writings of Second Temple Judaism, often as a paradigm for humanity's sinful condition.[85]

Other scholars, however, have found such an intended parallel between what Paul says in Romans 1 and the story of Adam's fall in Genesis 3 quite difficult to accept. Joseph Fitzmyer, for example, observing that (1) the verbs of Gen 3:24-25 (LXX) and Rom 1:24, 26, and 28 are, though close in meaning, still somewhat different in form (as Hooker herself acknowledged), and arguing that (2) "the alleged echoes of the Adam stories in Genesis are simply nonexistent," has concluded that "this interpretation reads too much of Genesis into the text" and therefore is to be rejected.[86] And Stanley Stowers, building on the work of John Levison in his *Portraits of Adam in Early Judaism,* has pronounced the parallels drawn between Romans 1 and the story of Adam's fall in Genesis 3 to be "profoundly unconvincing," largely because "the reading of Genesis that interpreters assume is transparent did not yet exist in Paul's time" — for, as Levison has demonstrated, "Jewish literature before 70 C.E. shows little interest in the effects of Adam's transgression."[87]

The best that it seems possible to say is (1) that Paul *may* have been thinking of Adam's fall in Genesis 3 when he wrote Rom 1:21-22, and so echoes of that Genesis account are to be found in his language of these verses, or (2) that his Christian addressees *might* have thought of such a background and connection when they read this portion of his letter. But whatever the merits of such a possibility or possibilities (which I personally think to be tenuous), Paul's words here are certainly in line with what he wrote earlier in 1 Cor 1:18–2:10 about human wisdom, with its feigned stance of superiority and its vaunted assertions of independence from God vis-à-vis the wisdom given by God.

Whom did Paul have in mind in speaking of those who claimed to be wise but became fools? Origen speculated that "while these things apply to all

81. Dunn, *Romans*, 1.53.
82. *Ibid.,* 1.60.
83. Hooker, "Adam in Romans 1," 297-306; *idem,* "A Further Note on Romans 1," 181-83.
84. Wedderburn, "Adam in Paul's Letter to the Romans," 3.413-30.
85. See esp. Wis 2:23-24; *Jub* 3:28-32; *Adam and Eve; 4 Ezra* 4:30; and *2 Bar* 54:17-19.
86. Fitzmyer, *Romans*, 274.
87. Stowers, "Gentile Culture and God's Impartial Justice," 86-87.

human beings who possess natural reason, they more specifically apply to those called philosophers who are wise in the things of this world — whose job it is to ponder the creatures of this world and everything which is made in it, and from the things which are seen, to perceive in their minds the things which are invisible."[88] It was, therefore, commonly asserted by both patristic and medieval commentators that Paul had in mind principally the Greek philosophers — particularly, as often identified, such ancient philosophers as Pythagoras, Socrates, Plato, Aristotle, Democritus, and Epicurus. Yet as John Calvin rightly insisted:

> All men have sought to form some conception of the majesty of God, and to make Him such a God as their reason could conceive Him to be. This presumptuous attitude to God is not, I maintain, learned in the philosophical schools, but is innate, and accompanies us, so to speak, from the womb. . . . The error of forming an image of God did not originate with the philosophers, but was received from others, and also stamped by their own approval.[89]

1:23 In writing καὶ ἤλλαξαν τὴν δόξαν τοῦ ἀφθάρτου θεοῦ ἐν ὁμοιώματι εἰκόνος φθαρτοῦ ἀνθρώπου καὶ πετεινῶν καὶ τετραπόδων καὶ ἑρπετῶν ("and they exchanged the glory of the immortal God for the likeness of an image made to look like a mortal human being — or like birds or animals or reptiles"), Paul expresses an even more disastrous consequence of humanity's rebellion against God and people's failure to give God thanks. This statement echoes the damning language used of Israel in LXX Ps 105:20 (MT 106:20): "They exchanged (ἠλλάξαντο) their Glory (τὴν δόξαν) for the likeness/similitude (ἐν ὁμοιώματι) of a bull which eats grass" — which is, of course, a reference to the people of Israel constructing the idolatrous golden calf in Exod 32. Likewise, it echoes the description of Israel in Jer 2:11: "My people have exchanged (ἠλλάξατο) their Glory (τὴν δόξαν, i.e., their God) for something that does not profit."

To be immediately noted in this verse is the first occurrence of the thrice-repeated expression "they exchanged" (ἤλλαξαν here in 1:23; μετήλλαξαν in 1:25 and 26). While the repetition of this expression does not seem intended to mark out any distinct stages in the development of Paul's presentation, as a rhetorical anaphora (i.e., the repetition of a phrase or word at the beginning of a series of successive statements) it was evidently used — first as a simple aorist in 1:23, then in heightened fashion as a compound aorist in 1:25 and 26 — to intensify the significance of the verb's action, with the ominous sound of the final Greek syllable (-ξαν) probably meant to ring in the ears of the hearers and resonate in their memories.

Another rather obvious feature to be noted in Rom 1:23 is the addition of the genitive singular εἰκόνος ("of an image") to the expression ἐν ὁμοιώματι

---

88. Origen, *Ad Romano, CER* 1.142.
89. J. Calvin, *Romans,* in *Calvin's New Testament Commentaries,* 8.33.

("for the likeness"). Such a combination of similar terms probably stems from the wording of Gen 1:26, "And God said, 'Let us make man according to our image and likeness (κατ' εἰκόνα ἡμετέραν καὶ καθ' ὁμοίωσιν)'" — which suggests, since in what immediately follows in Gen 1:27a only the one term εἰκών appears ("So God made man; in the image of God [κατ' εἰκόνα θεοῦ] he made him"), that the bringing together of κατ' εἰκόνα and καθ' ὁμοιωσιν in 1:26 should be understood as something of a *hendiadys.* Many translators, therefore, have viewed the combination of "likeness" and "image" in Rom 1:23 as an unnecessary redundancy — or have combined them, since both refer to an "image," into the one plural term "images."[90] It may be, however, that Paul was also influenced in his wording here by Wis 13–14 (which we have argued both he and his addressees probably knew), where εἰκών ("image") appears four times (13:13, 16; 14:15, 17), in close proximity to the verb ὁμοιόω ("make [something] like," in 13:14) and the noun ὁμοίωμα ("likeness," 14:19) in depictions of the idolatries and immoralities of pagan Gentiles.

The word δόξα in secular Greek literature meant "opinion" or "estimation." It was, however, used by the translators of the LXX for the Hebrew word כבוד, which denotes an external appearance of "glory," "majesty," or "splendor." So it came to connote the presence of God himself in all his "glory," "majesty," and "splendor."[91] In John 1:14 the Evangelist proclaims that the eschatological manifestation of God's "glory" has taken place in "the Word made flesh," God's one and only Son. The term ἄφθαρτος ("immortal") is used by Paul only with respect to God — here in 1:23 in contrast to "mortal (φθαρτός) humans," and later in 1 Tim 1:17 in doxological praise "to the immortal (ἀφθάρτῳ) King eternal."

Understanding this passage of 1:19-23 as a distinct unit of material that sets out the descent of the pagan world into idolatry, John Chrysostom enumerated Paul's charges against humanity with respect to its idolatries as follows:

> Paul's first charge against the heathen was that they failed to find God [vv. 19-20]. His second was that, although they had great and clear means of doing it they did not [v. 21]. The third is that they nevertheless claimed to be wise [v. 22]. And the fourth was that not only did they not find the Supreme Being, they lowered him to the level of devils, stones and wood [v. 23].[92]

It is this awful descent into various forms of idolatry — based, as it is, on humanity's rebellion against God, vaunted independence from God, and therefore failure to respond in praise and thankfulness to God — that lies at the heart of "the human predicament," both in humanity's past history and in its experience today. And it is this problem of idolatry that is under "the wrath of God," as

90. So, e.g., NIV and NRSV.
91. Cf., e.g., LXX Ps 96:6 (MT 97:6); Exod 40:35; Isa 6:3; 40:5.
92. Chrysostom, "Homilies," in *Nicene and Post-Nicene Fathers,* 11.352-53.

announced in 1:18 — and that expresses itself in disastrous ways in human lives, as will be portrayed in what follows in 1:24-31.

III. Portrayals of Humanity's Immoralities and Injustices (1:24-31)

This section relates idolatry, immorality, and injustice directly, arguing (1) that humanity's idolatries and its immoralities and injustices are inseparably linked, with the former being the fundamental reason for the latter, and (2) that the consequences of idolatry, which stems from humanity's rebellion against God, independence from God, and failure to respond in praise and thankfulness to God, work themselves out in the lives of people in ways that are morally perverse and ethically disastrous. The section is introduced by the inferential conjunction διό ("therefore"). It is held together by the thrice-repeated expression παρέδωκεν αὐτοὺς ὁ θεός ("God gave them over") in 1:24, 26, and 28. It is also held together, to a certain extent, by the final two instances of the verb ἤλλαξαν ("they exchanged"), which first appeared as a simple verb in 1:23 but now appears in intensified form in 1:25 and 26 — with these instances of rhetorical anaphora being used to drive home the impact of what is said in this passage to the minds and hearts of the addressees.

The first part of this section, 1:24-27, has to do with sensual or sexual perversions, (1) in 1:24-25 dealing with matters pertaining to ἀκαθαρσία ("filth," "impurity"), which is the word that Jesus is recorded as having used quite literally for the contents of "whitewashed tombs" in Matt 23:27, but which appears throughout Paul's letters in a moral sense for immorality generally and sexual immorality in particular,[93] and (2) in 1:26-27 dealing with "disgraceful passions" (πάθη ἀτιμίας) and "unnatural sexual intercourse" (τὴν φυσικὴν χρῆσιν εἰς τὴν παρὰ φὺσιν, literally they exchanged "natural sexual intercourse for that which is against nature"), which are locutions for homosexual thoughts and actions. The second part of the section, 1:28-31, sets out a list of vices that certainly have to do with antisocial behavior. More than that, however, this second part has to do with depraved thoughts and totally evil actions — that is, with thinking and doing τὰ μὴ καθήκοντα ("the things that ought not to be done").

1:24-25 In this first part of 1:24-27, Paul begins his presentation with "therefore God gave them over" (διὸ παρέδωκεν αὐτοὺς ὁ θεός), which highlights the part that God plays — both in the past and today — in the judgment of people who rebel against him, who live independent of him, and who set up their own forms of idolatry. That "giving over" people by God was explained by various fourth- and fifth-century Church Fathers as follows: "God left them to their own concoctions,"[94] "God abandoned them to the desires of their own

---

93. Cf. Rom 6:19; 2 Cor 12:21; Gal 5:19; Eph 4:19; 5:3; Col 3:5; 1 Thess 4:7; see also Prov 6:16; 24:9; Wis 2:16; 3 Macc 2:17; 1 Esd 1:40; *Let Aris* 166; Philo, *Legum allegoriae* 2.29.

94. So Chrysostom, "Homilies," in *Nicene and Post-Nicene Fathers*, 11.354.

hearts,"[95] or "God simply abandoned them."[96] Paul goes on to say in 1:24b-25a "in the sinful desires of their hearts to sexual impurity for the degrading of their bodies with one another" (ἐν ταῖς ἐπιθυμίαις τῶν καρδιῶν εἰς ἀκαθαρσίαν τοῦ ἀτιμάζεσθαι τὰ σώματα αὐτῶν ἐν αὐτοῖς) — thereby declaring that it is not because God seeks retribution that he has ordained judgment for certain people, but God has abandoned rebellious and evil people to their own desires "because (οἵτινες) they exchanged (μετήλλαξαν) the truth of God for a lie and worshiped and served created things rather than the creator (τὴν ἀλήθειαν τοῦ θεοῦ ἐν τῷ ψεύδει καὶ ἐσεβάσθησαν καὶ ἐλάτρευσαν τῇ κτίσει παρὰ τὸν κτίσαντα)." And that rationale is then restated at the beginning of 1:26 in encapsulated form by the expression διὰ τοῦτο ("for this reason").

The attributive clause with the affirming expression at its close, "Who is forever to be praised. Amen" (ὅς ἐστιν εὐλογητὸς εἰς τοὺς αἰῶνας. Ἀμήν), which affirms that praise is due to God, stems from the Jewish acclamation of God that is used whenever his name or one of his titles is mentioned. And while Paul usually uses ἀμήν ("so let it be") to signal the close of a doxology, a peace or grace benediction, or a section or subsection of material,[97] here he uses that attributive statement with its affirming expression in a strictly Jewish manner and so expresses a typical Jewish and Jewish Christian attribution of God.[98]

In contemplating God's dealing with humanity, the following factors must always be taken into account: (1) God's will for people, (2) God's establishment of a moral order in his creation on behalf of created humanity, (3) God's ordaining of human freedom so that loving relationships may be established, (4) people's failure to respond in praise and thankfulness to God, and (5) the inevitable personal and moral consequences of people's rebellion against God, independence from God, and failure to respond positively to God. In a real sense, as John Robinson has observed with respect to the expression "God gave them over,"

> He [God] leaves pagan society to stew in its own juice. The retribution which overtakes it, resulting in automatic moral degradation, is what "comes on" almost like a thermostat when, as it were, the moral temperature drops below a certain point.[99]

This is certainly in line with the Jewish sentiment found in Wis 11:15-16: "In return for their [the Gentiles'] foolish devices and wicked thoughts, which led them astray to worship irrational serpents and worthless animals, you sent upon

95. So Augustine, *Expositio quarundam propositionum ex epistola ad Romanos,* Prop. V, *PL* 35.2064. See also *Augustine on Romans,* 3.
96. So Theodoret of Cyrrhus, *Interpretatio in Epistulam ad Romanos, PG* 82.64.
97. Cf. Rom 11:36; 15:33; (16:24?); 16:27; Gal 6:18; Eph 3:21; Phil 4:20, ([23?]); 1 Tim 1:17; 6:16; 2 Tim 4:18.
98. Cf. also Rom 9:5; Gal 1:5.
99. J. A. T. Robinson, *Wrestling with Romans,* 18.

them a multitude of irrational creatures to punish them, that they might learn that a person is punished by the very things by which he sins." And it is also in line with such rabbinic statements as "Every fulfillment of duty is rewarded by another, and every transgression is punished by another"[100] and "Whoever attempts to keep himself pure receives the power to do so; whoever will be impure, to him is it [the door of vice] thrown open."[101] Nonetheless, behind all the retributions experienced by people because of their rebellions, apostasies, and sins — which, indeed, they have brought on themselves — there stands the sovereign God, who is ultimately responsible for their creation, their freedom, and their judgment, even though he is never responsible for their sins of thought and deed. For God is the one who "gave them over" to the inevitable results of their own sinning.

1:26-27 Paul speaks in these verses by way of clarifying what he said more generally in 1:24 about ἀκαθαρσία ("sexual impurity"). And in these two verses he speaks quite explicitly and damagingly about homosexual conduct — both on the part of women in 1:26b (i.e., "female homoeroticism" or "lesbian" behavior) and on the part of men in 1:27 (i.e., "male homoeroticism" or "gay" behavior). These two verses are filled with a number of extremely unpleasant expressions in the description of homosexuality: πάθη ἀτιμίας ("disgraceful passions"), τὴν παρὰ φύσιν ("unnatural relations"), ἐξεκαύθησαν ἐν τῇ ὀρέξει αὐτῶν εἰς ἀλλήλους ("they were inflamed in their lust for one another"), τὴν ἀσχημοσύνην κατεργαζόμενοι ("committing indecent acts"), and τὴν ἀντιμισθίαν . . . τῆς πλάνης ("the penalty . . . of their [idolatrous] perversion"). Paul's attitude toward homosexual behavior could hardly be more adversely expressed. For he condemns it totally — as did also all Jews and all Jewish Christians of his day.

While there can be no question about Paul's attitude toward homosexuality, the question may legitimately be asked: Why does he list homosexuality first and speak about it so extensively when drawing the connection between humanity's idolatries and humanity's immoralities? One reason, of course, is that it was so prevalent in the Greco-Roman world and so often justified as being normal.[102] A more important reason, however, is that male homoeroticism is explicitly denounced in the Jewish (OT) Scriptures[103] and in a number of the writings of Second Temple Judaism[104] — with female homoeroticism, while not

---

100. *M. Abot* 4:2.

101. *B. Shabb.* 104a.

102. Cf. H. Licht, *Sexual Life in Ancient Greece* (London: Routledge & Kegan Paul, 1932), esp. 411-98; D. M. Robinson and E. Fluck, *A Study of Greek Love-Names, Including a Discussion of Paederasty and Prosopographia* (Baltimore: Johns Hopkins University Press, 1937; repr. New York: Arno, 1979); K. J. Dover, *Greek Homosexuality* (Cambridge, MA: Harvard University Press, 1978).

103. See Lev 18:22, "Do not lie with a man as one lies with a woman; that is detestable"; Lev 20:13, "If a man lies with a man as one lies with a woman, both of them have done what is detestable. They must be put to death; their blood will be on their own heads."

104. See *Let Aris* 152; Philo, *De Abrahamo* 26.135-36; *De specialibus legibus* 2.14.50; Josephus, *Contra Apion* 2.25, 199; *Sib Or* 2:73; 3:185-87, 594-600, 763; 5:386-433; *2 En* 10:4; *T Levi* 14:6; 17:11; *T Naph* 4:1.

mentioned in the Jewish (OT) Scriptures or in the writings of Second Temple Judaism, being also condemned in the Talmud.[105]

Likewise important for understanding Paul's rationale in highlighting homosexuality when explicating the connection between idolatry and immorality is the fact that Paul viewed homosexuality as the most obvious result of humanity's failure to respond appropriately to God's revelation in creation. For though it was often asserted by those who practiced it that homosexuality was "natural" — even, as argued both then and today, a legitimate feature of divine creation — Paul viewed such a claim as in direct opposition to the moral order established by God in creation, where only in marriage do a man and a woman "become one flesh" (Gen 2:24).

Further, it needs to be noted that the connection between homosexuality and idolatry was commonly made by both Jews and Jewish Christians of Paul's day. For example, in *T Naph* 3:2-4, which is probably a Jewish writing that was later redacted by first-century Jewish Christians, there is the statement:

> The sun, moon, and stars do not change their order, so you must not change the law of God by the disorder of your deeds. Gentiles, in going astray and forsaking the Lord, have changed their order and gone after stones and wooden objects, led away by spirits of error. But not so you, my children. You have recognized in heaven's vault, in the earth, in the sea, and in all created things the Lord who made them all, so you should not become like Sodom, which changed the order of its nature.

And that is how Paul viewed matters as well.

Some have argued that what Paul had in mind by his use of the phrase ἄρσενες ἐν ἄρσεσιν ("male with male") in 1:27 was not homosexuality in general but only "male prostitution" or "pederasty" (i.e., anal intercourse with a man, or especially with a young boy). For, it is claimed, those were the only forms of homoeroticism practiced in the Greco-Roman world. Such an understanding has been proposed by John Boswell in *Christianity, Social Tolerance, and Homosexuality* (1980) and by Robin Scroggs in *New Testament and Homosexuality* (1983). But the arguments of Boswell and Scroggs for such an understanding have been devastatingly demolished by David Wright in his article "Homosexuals or Prostitutes?" (1984), by Richard Hays in his article on "Relations Natural and Unnatural" (1986), and by Marion L. Soards in his monograph on *Scripture and Homosexuality* (1995).

We can deal here only with the principal exegetical argument of Boswell and Scroggs, which is that the noun ἀρσενοκοίτης in the first Christian century — which term appears explicitly in the Pauline corpus only in 1 Cor 6:9 and 1 Tim 1:10 but is certainly also to be understood with respect to the phrase ἄρσενες ἐν ἄρσεσιν ("male with male") in Rom 1:27 — meant only "male pros-

---

105. See, e.g., *Sifra Lev.* 18:3; *b. Sabb.* 65a; *b. Yebam.* 76a.

titution" or "pederastic sexual activity" and does not include the whole range of homosexual practices. One important point in rebuttal of such a claim is the fact that the noun ἄρσην ("male") and the verb κοιμάσθαι ("to have intercourse") appear in the LXX of both Lev. 18:22 and 20:13, which are the biblical passages that explicitly forbid a man lying with another man "as with a woman." And Paul, knowing not only the Hebrew text of his Jewish (OT) Scriptures but also the Greek translation (LXX), could hardly have viewed these prohibitions of Leviticus as having reference only to "male prostitution" and/or "pederasty" and not to the whole range of homosexual practices — explicitly all forms of male homoeroticism (i.e., "gay" activities), but also inferentially all forms of female homoeroticism (i.e., "lesbian" activities).

1:28-31 A gruesome list of the thoughts and actions of people at their worst is presented in these verses. Similar "vice lists" can be found in Greek classical literature[106] and in the writings of Second Temple Judaism.[107] Parallels are also to be found in the Dead Sea Scrolls, as, for example, in 1QS 4.9-11:

> To the spirit of perversity belong cupidity and slackness in the service of righteousness, impiety and falsehood, pride and haughtiness, falsity and deceit, cruelty and abundant wickedness, impatience and much folly; burning insolence and abominable deeds committed in the spirit of lust, and the ways of defilement in the service of impurity; a blaspheming tongue, blindness of eye and hardness of ear, stiffness of neck and heaviness of heart causing one to walk in all the ways of darkness and malignant cunning.

And parallels appear elsewhere at a number of places in Christian writings as well — not only in Rom 13:13 and some of the other writings in the Pauline corpus,[108] but also elsewhere in the NT[109] and other early Christian writings.[110]

The total list of vices set out in 1:28-31 need not be repeated here. In its totality it speaks directly to the perversions of rebellion, lawlessness, and sin — and its individual items hardly merit linguistic analysis. Suffice it to say that all the vices listed in these verses have come about (1) because of people's rebellion against God in refusing to retain the knowledge of him (οὐκ ἐδοκίμασαν τὸν θεὸν ἔχειν ἐν ἐπιγνώσει) and (2) because God, in his wisdom, has allowed people to cherish their own desires, to express their own wills, to be independent of him, and to go their own way (παρέδωκεν αὐτοὺς ὁ θεός). Thus human history has been replete with antisocial and unjust behavior, for which the "depraved mind" of humans themselves must be held totally responsible.

---

106. Cf., e.g., Plato, *Gorgias* 525; *idem, Republic* 4.441c.

107. Cf., e.g., Wis 14:23-26; Philo, *De sacrificiis Abelis et Caini* 32; 4 Macc 1:26-27; 2:15; *T Levi* 14:5-8; CD 4.17-18.

108. See Gal 5:19-21a; 1 Cor 5:9-11; 6:9b-10; 2 Tim 3:2-5a.

109. See Mark 7:21-22; Rev 21:8.

110. See *1 Clement* 5:9-11; *Barn* 20:1; *Didache* 5:1.

IV. Consequent Judgment Proclaimed: Death (1:32)

The final verse of this passage brings the ghastly depictions of humanity's idolatries and the portrayals of humanity's immoralities and injustices to a close with the proclamation of consequent judgment — that is, God's decree of death! Just as in the account of the fall of humanity in Genesis 3, so in this recapitulation of that experience in people's lives: the failure to respond positively to God's revelation of himself and to his will results in death — in this life separation from God and being given over by God to one's own desires; in what transpires after this life, final judgment. All people, Paul declares, well know God's decree that rebellion against God, independence from him, and the failure to praise and thank him brings death. Yet the sad story of human history and the universal experience of us all is that people "not only continue to do these very things but also approve of those who practice them" (οὐ μόνον αὐτὰ ποιοῦσιν ἀλλὰ συνευδοκοῦσιν τοῖς πράσσουσιν). And it is this disastrous human story, as we must all confess, that each of us as humans has inherited and each of us has lived out as well.

BIBLICAL THEOLOGY

Rom 1:18-32 is an important passage for Christian theology, not just because it is where Paul begins in writing the four major sections of the body middle of his letter to the believers in Jesus at Rome, but principally because it presents material that is challenging for the Christian church and Christians today. What it sets out regarding God's reaction to human rebellion, lawlessness, and sin is sobering; what it states regarding God's revelation in creation is informative; what it depicts regarding humanity's idolatries and actions is sorrowful; and what it portrays regarding the resultant immoralities and injustices of people is totally gruesome.

The Wrath of God Revealed. Divine wrath is a subject that Christians do not like to think or talk about. But "wrath" and "love" are both attributes of the one true God, as proclaimed by both Judaism and Christianity. Nor do Christians easily identify "the godlessness and wickedness of people who suppress the truth by their wickedness" with their own thoughts and actions, but more commonly with the attitudes and actions of others or with persons and events of past times. Nonetheless, as John Chrysostom observed in commenting on this passage:

> There are various kinds of unrighteousness. One is in financial affairs, as when someone deals unrighteously with his neighbor in these; another in regard to women, when a man leaves his own wife and intrudes upon the marriage of another. . . . Others do not injure wife or property but the reputation of their neighbor, and this too is unrighteousness.[111]

111. Chrysostom, "Homilies," in *Nicene and Post-Nicene Fathers,* 11.351.

Likewise, Christians have no difficulty in speaking of a final judgment by God, but are somewhat hesitant to think about divine judgment on sin as being expressed today — particularly, in God giving over people to their own "sinful desires" (1:24), their own "disgraceful passions" (1:26), and their own "depraved minds" (1:28), with all the personal and societal disasters that inevitably result.

But the verses that bracket this passage, which function as something of a literary *inclusio* for all that is presented, announce (1) that "the wrath of God *is being revealed* against *all* the godlessness and wickedness of people who suppress the truth by their wickedness" (1:18), which highlights the present expression of God's wrath and the fact that divine judgment is directed against every type of godlessness and wickedness of whatever time or type, and (2) that God has decreed that "people who do (as well as 'approve of') such things deserve death" (1:32), which speaks not only of personal disasters, dysfunctions, and alienation but also of separation from God and so of living apart from God's love, purpose, and direction in life.

The Revelation of God in Creation. Paul's statements in 1:19-20 about a "revelation in creation" — a revelation that (1) has been implanted and maintained by God in the warp and woof of the fabric of the universe he created, (2) has been "clearly seen" and "understood" by all people of whatever time, place, or circumstance, at least with respect to the basic truths regarding "his [God's] eternal power and divine nature," and (3) calls on all people to respond to the God of creation and renders them "without excuse" for not doing so — have been the subject of a great deal of controversy in contemporary NT scholarship and Christian theology.

One major problem is that such a basic knowledge of God as revealed in creation is hardly ever alluded to in Paul's extant letters to his own Christian converts, that is, other than in his letter to Christians at Rome, the great majority of whom were not his converts. There are, of course, important links made by Paul in his other letters between "general revelation" and "special revelation" — as, for example, in 1 Cor 8:6 ("for us there is one God, the Father, from whom are all things and for whom we exist, and one Lord, Jesus Christ, through whom are all things and through whom we exist"; cf. also Col 1:15-20). Further, there are significant features of continuity drawn by Paul between what God has done by way of creation and what he has done redemptively through Jesus Christ, as in 2 Cor 4:6 ("It is the God who said 'Let light shine out of darkness' who has shone in our hearts to give the light of the knowledge of the glory of God in the face of Jesus Christ"). And in Rom 8:19-25 Paul continues such a linking when he speaks of both "the creation" and all redeemed people "in Christ" longing for and finally being involved in the full manifestation of God's salvation. Yet direct Pauline statements about a revelation of God in creation, other than what appears here in Rom 1:19-20, come to the fore only in two contextualized forms in Luke's portrayals of Paul's preaching to Gentiles at Lystra in Acts 14:15-17 and at Athens in Acts 17:24-27a.

More important as an explanation for the widespread aversion to Paul's statements in Rom 1:19-20 is the fact that, as Joseph Fitzmyer has expressed the situation:

> Ever since the Enlightenment, when thinkers tried to extol human reason and to substitute for Christian revelation a natural religion or a religion of reason, some commentators have subconsciously reacted by denying the capability of the human mind to attain some knowledge of God. As a result, they have taken refuge in a form of fideism. In doing so, they have been reluctant to admit what Paul himself actually says about natural theology; they deny that God makes himself known in any other manner than in Christ. Preoccupation with the problem that the Enlightenment introduced has thus obscured for them what Paul is actually teaching in this passage. From this problem has come a connotation of "natural theology" that is not Pauline and that does not reckon sufficiently with what Paul, who wrote centuries before the Enlightenment, was really saying.[112]

There is also, however, much that appears in the first part of Romans, particularly in 1:18–3:20, that does not appear in Paul's other letters — for circumstantial reasons, we would argue, not only in writing to the Christians at Rome but also in writing to his own converts in the other cities and regions of the Roman Empire. Further, it needs always to be recognized that what Paul writes about in 1:19-20, that is, God's "revelation in creation," is not the same as what has been called "natural theology."

It is, therefore, important for Christian theology today that we hear again the teaching of Paul as set out here in 1:19-20 (and as depicted in Acts 14:15-17 and 17:24-27) about the knowledge that has been given by God to all people through his creation, which has to do with "his eternal power and divine nature" and which calls for a positive human response. That "general revelation" given by God in creation must never be understood as sufficient of itself for a personal relationship with God, and so take the place of "special revelation." Nor should it be viewed as a "natural theology" — a theology of nature that parallels God's revelation of himself and his salvation for all humanity as set out in the Jewish (OT) and Christian (NT) Scriptures, and as preeminently expressed in the person and work of Jesus Christ. Nonetheless, what creation does proclaim needs always to be recognized as (1) God's ordained prolegomena to all else in a theistic understanding and (2) God's intended backdrop for all else that he has given by way of "special revelation" for a fuller appreciation and personal appropriation of the story of his redemptive actions on behalf of all humanity and of all his non-human creation.

Humanity's Idolatries. Paul's statement about idolatry in Rom 1:21 highlights the basic problem of humanity — that is, the main issue with respect to what has rightly been called "the human predicament" or the central spiritual

---

112. Fitzmyer, *Romans*, 274.

and moral problem of all people. For the basic human problem is not (1) some unending cycle of time in which people are trapped or (2) certain limitations of finitude that condition and constrain us all, and from which we must be extricated (as in some forms of ancient thought). Nor is it the material aspects of the world and our own material existence from which we must seek to be free (as in Greek religious philosophy). Nor is it postulated personhood or creatureliness from which we must seek release by means of an ethical life, certain prescribed rituals, and a resultant series of upward reincarnations, which will bring us eventually to a state of non-personal utopia or nirvana (as in many forms of Eastern religion). And certainly it is not just human ignorance from which we must endeavor to free ourselves through the advances of scientific research and human reason (as in much of Western thinking). Rather, the basic spiritual and moral problem of all people is that we have failed to respond positively to God — that is, to glorify God by our praise and thankfulness to him ("they did not glorify God as God or give him thanks").

At the heart of the matter is the human assertion of independence, which results in people rebelling against any thing or person they see as an impediment to their vaunted independence — and thus, their rebellion against God. As Kingsley Barrett has rightly observed, "A vicious circle operates: denying the knowledge of God they have, men [people] plunge further and further into unbelief. The result is that they are ignorant of God, and of themselves cannot know him; yet their ignorance is culpable ignorance, for it is rooted in rebellion."[113] And underlying all of humanity's self-aggrandizing assertions of independence, and thus people's rebellion against God, lies the fact that people cannot bring themselves to praise or give thanks to God — for to praise and thank God would signal something of dependence and therefore be a denial of humanity's self-assured claim to independence (as, sadly, we have all had a tendency to think in our own warped minds).

The essence of sin is the desire to have something we can call our own *apart from God*. So throughout human history people have not been averse to worshiping one form or another of an idol — whether such an idol is made to resemble a person or figure that would be recognizable within their known world or constructed as a concept or idea that resides in their own minds. For idols, whether material or immaterial, are people's own human productions, which they are able to feel comfortable with because they can call them their own. So we as human beings are prepared to give praise to and thanks for what we have produced. We are even quite happy to express praise and thanks to others who exist beyond the boundaries of our own persons, including some nebulous being called "God" — but usually, it seems, only using such expressions as societal conventions, cultural niceties, or expedient tools that we calculate will enhance our own pretensions or self-interests.

The verdict that Paul levels against all such self-centered and self-assertive

113. Barrett, *Romans*, 37.

"independence" is given in Rom 1:22: "While claiming to be wise, they became fools." And the height of humanity's resultant rebellion and sin is set out in v. 23: "They exchanged the glory of the immortal God for the likeness of an image made to look like a mortal human being — or like birds or animals or reptiles."

Such an exchange from "the glory of the immortal God" to the mere fabricated image of a mortal human being, bird, animal, or reptile is — when we really think about it — almost beyond comprehension. But that is what each of us does when we become self-centered and self-assertive — that is, when we become so enraptured with what we are and what is ours that we begin to claim it to be ours *apart from God.* So the message of Rom 1:21-23 to God's people is that we should be people who glorify God by expressing true praise and thankfulness to him for all that he is and all that he has done, both in creation and in redemption.

Humanity's Immoralities and Injustices. Paul's cataloging of the immoralities and injustices of humanity here in 1:24-31 is not a wholesale condemnation of all people — nor, for that matter, of all non-Jews. Later in 2:14-15 he will speak of Gentiles "doing by nature (φύσει ποιῶσιν) the things required by the law (τὰ τοῦ νόμου)," even though they do not know "the contents of the law (τὰ μὴ νόμον ἔχοντα)." And much later in this same letter, in such passages as 9:24-26, 30 and 10:19-20, he will speak of Gentiles who have responded to God "by faith" without having any knowledge of the Jewish (OT) Scriptures or any contact with God's own people Israel. Such passages as these in Romans certainly suggest a recognition on Paul's part that some people, even though they have no knowledge of God's "special revelation," live lives that are moral and just.

What Paul does do in these verses, however, as we have noted above, is to make two highly significant points: (1) that humanity's idolatries and humanity's immoralities and injustices are inseparably linked, with the former being the fundamental reason for the latter, and (2) that the consequences of idolatry — which stems from humanity's rebellion against God, independence from God, and failure to respond in praise and thankfulness to God — work themselves out in the lives of people in ways that are morally perverse and ethically disastrous.

Almost everyone today would join with Paul in condemning the ethical and societal injustices listed in 1:28-31, though without always assigning them the same fateful judgment as he did. In our contemporary Western culture, however, many people are troubled by Paul's devastating critique of homosexuality in 1:24-27 and by his placing homosexuality at the head of the list of moral perversions that he sets.

But with homosexuality so prevalent in the Greco-Roman world, Paul viewed that particular sexual practice as the most obvious result of humanity's failure to respond appropriately to God's revelation in creation. In fact, he seems to have viewed homosexuality as flagrantly in opposition to the moral order established by God in both his "general revelation" and his "special revelation," where only the sexual joining of a man and a woman in marriage is ordained by God. Other human injustices and other ethical perversions are certainly to be understood as opposed to God's will and therefore deserving divine judgment. But homosexuality, with its claim to be "natural" — even, as often argued, to be in accord with God's creation — was for Paul particularly opposed to God's moral order and so especially to be condemned.

Raymond E. Brown has rightly noted with respect to Paul's view of homosexuality vis-à-vis the moral order of God's creation that "an outlook based on the revelation of God's will in creation itself would not be easily changed."[114] And Brown's conclusion to this important matter can hardly be improved on:

> Scholarly discussion of the issue will continue, challenging Paul's outlook on the "unnatural." Nevertheless, in insisting on the sexual limits imposed by the divinely commanded state of marriage between a man and a woman, Paul and, indeed, Jesus himself, walking among us in our times, would not be frightened by being considered sexually and politically "incorrect," any more than they minded being considered overly demanding in the Greco-Roman and Jewish world of their times.[115]

CONTEXTUALIZATION FOR TODAY

In the study of Paul's letters, as of all the NT writings, what needs always to be noted is how Paul contextualized his proclamation of the Christian message to the understanding and appreciation of his addressees — thereby evidencing, it may be postulated, how he attempted to speak meaningfully to their situations and so in the process to set out something of the fullness of the Christian gospel. The question is not "Why are Paul's other letters not like Romans?" as was asked in earlier days, or even "Why is Romans so different from Paul's other letters?" as is frequently asked today. Rather, a major question to be asked of every Pauline letter is this: How did Paul contextualize the message of the Christian gospel in this particular letter to these particular people? And an ensuing question must also always be asked: "What do the patterns and features of Paul's contextualization in this letter suggest about how the Christian gospel can be contextualized in circumstances and cultures of today?"

Paul's letter to the Christians at Rome provides an excellent case study for the pursuit of these questions, for Romans (1) explicates matters that are at the very heart of the Christian gospel, and yet (2) presents the reader with a number of rather distinct features. And one place in the letter where such distinctive features are clearly to be found is in Paul's teaching on "the wrath of God" in 1:18-32. Seven matters stemming from Paul's contextualization of the gospel in this passage may here be profitably highlighted.

On Preaching God's Wrath as a Prolegomenon to the Proclamation of

---

114. R. E. Brown, *Introduction to the New Testament,* 530.
115. *Ibid.*

the Gospel. It has often been argued by earnest Christians, who desire to be "biblical" in both their message and their methods, that the proclamation of the Christian gospel must first of all attempt to convince people that they are sinners and in need of salvation — as Paul did in this first part of the first section of the body middle of Romans, that is, in 1:18-32 (and as continued in 2:1–3:20) — before there can be any positive presentation of what "God in Christ" has done by way of reconciling people and the world to himself and before people can be called upon to respond "by faith" so as to receive that reconciliation for themselves. But such an understanding, while often pious and laudable, fails to take seriously into account the diverse ways in which Paul himself contextualized the Christian message in the various situations and circumstances that he encountered — particularly, with respect to how he presented the Christian gospel to Gentiles who had not been influenced by the teachings of Judaism, and so were without any background in the Jewish Scriptures (as seems was the case for most of his pastoral letters), and how he presented the gospel to Jews and Gentiles who had been so influenced, and so had such a Jewish or Jewish-Christian background (as we have argued was the case with respect to Romans).

This is not to say that issues regarding "the wrath of God," God's "revelation in creation," idolatry, homosexuality, and/or injustices of both a personal and a societal nature are to be ignored or excluded in Christian ministry, for the gospel of Christ has a great deal to say about every one of these matters. But it is to point out that Paul's usual practice in his Gentile ministry was to focus positively on the salvation that had been brought about by God through the person and work of his Son Jesus Christ — with the expectation that many of the more negative matters enumerated above would be (1) dealt with in an effective manner by the ministry of God's Holy Spirit (i.e., as Jesus is reported in John 14:26 to have promised: "The Counselor, the Holy Spirit, whom the Father will send in my name, will teach you all things and remind you of everything I have said to you") and/or (2) treated by Paul himself or one of the other church leaders in a pastoral fashion on the basis of believers in Jesus being "new creations in Christ."

On the Use of Other, Somewhat Tangential Material. Also to be noted in this passage is the use of other, somewhat tangential material that came to birth in different settings and may have been used by others for other purposes in other contexts, but was used by Paul in 1:18-32 for his own purpose and given his own interpretive "spin" — that is, material drawn, either directly or indirectly, from Wis 13–14 (as well as from various other verses in the latter section of this Hellenistic Jewish writing) and that seems to have been used widely by others for their own purposes. It is not that Paul felt free to use and reinterpret just any writing that he came across to his own advantage. For the overall message of Wis 13–14 is generally in line with Paul's understanding. So while he seems to have borrowed some of the structure, terms, and language of Wis 13–14 for his own use, Paul broadened the focus of those chapters to include humanity and not just Gentiles — and with such a revision, he made use of this material to present his own teaching.

Evidently, as we have argued, this was material (1) that had a wide currency among Jews and Jewish Christians of Paul's day and (2) that Paul was confident was known and appreciated by his addressees. The basic content, flow, and form of what he wrote in 1:19-32, therefore, was probably not composed originally by him, but, rather, appears to have been drawn, in some manner, from the Wisdom of Solomon. But Paul used this material, evidently, because (1) he accepted the general thrust of its presentation, (2) his addressees at Rome also knew it and accepted what it said as being true and important, and (3) he could make significant contact with those Roman Christian addressees with only a minimal adjustment of that material at hand, by beginning the first central section of his letter with such a presentation of matters on which both he and they agreed.

Just why Paul began his exposition of the Christian gospel as he did in 1:18-32, and why in this passage he used material drawn ultimately from the Wisdom of Solomon (particularly in vv. 19-32), are matters having to do with circumstantial contextualization. But they suggest a practice that we need not only to understand but also to assimilate into our own Christian ministries and proclamation of the gospel today.

On God's Revelation in Creation and Humanity's Knowledge of God. Paul's declaration of God's "revelation in creation" and humanity's basic knowledge of him is concisely set forth in 1:19-20: "What can be known about God is plain to them, for God has shown it to them. For ever since the creation of the world God's invisible attributes — that is, his eternal power and divine nature — have been clearly seen, being understood by what has been made, so that people are without excuse." Many thinkers during the Renaissance of the fourteenth through seventeenth centuries and the Enlightenment of the eighteenth century, together with a great many people since, have denied any such revelation of God in creation.

Yet for most Christians today — as well as for the great majority of people of whatever time or place — the reminiscence of John Baillie, the eminent Edinburgh theologian, regarding the earliest beginnings of his own consciousness strikes a positive chord of remembrance in them as well:

> No matter how far back I go, no matter by what effort of memory I attempt to reach the virgin soil of childish innocence, I cannot get back to an atheistic mentality. As little can I reach a day when I was conscious of myself but not of God as can I reach a day when I was conscious of myself but not of other human beings. My earliest memories have a definitely religious atmosphere. They are already heavy with "the numinous." They contain as part of their substance a recognition, as vague and inarticulate as you will, yet quite unmistakable for anything else, of what I have now learned to call the divine as a factor in my environment. I cannot remember a time when I did not feel, in some dim way, that I was "not my own."[116]

116. Baillie, *Our Knowledge of God,* 4; see also 182-83.

And such primal consciousness is of great significance not only for every person in the world today but also for the Christian church in carrying out its mandate to be a witness to all people of God's salvation as has been effected by the person and work of Jesus Christ. For the church in its witness goes forth with the conviction that it is not entering into alien territory, but that God's revelation of himself is already present throughout the whole world and that he has prepared all people through his "general revelation" in creation for the reception of his "special revelation" in the proclamation of the gospel.

On the Basic Reason for People's Rejection of God. In 1:21, as we have noted above, Paul highlights the essential problem of humanity and the basic reason for people's rejection of God: that they have asserted their own independence from God, and so are in a state of rebellion against God. Thus they cannot bring themselves to glorify him or express thanks to him.

John Baillie's own religious experience, as he spoke about it quite freely in lectures and private conversation, included at one time a profession of atheism — particularly during the heady willfulness of his university days. But in recalling that period of "atheism" in his life, he always added: "I never was, however, really an atheist. In fact, there were a number of things that I wanted to hear from God. And I wondered why he did not speak more plainly. But there were also a number of other things that I did not want to hear from God. And my deafness in the one area extended over into the other area, and so I proclaimed that I was an atheist" (as remembered almost verbatim from Baillie's lectures and private conversations). And such an understanding of the human condition, in both its claimed independence and vaunted rebellion, also strikes a responsive chord in the hearts of most thoughtful and sensitive people, for it resonates with our own human attitudes and desires as expressed at various times in our lives.

On Humanity's Idolatries. The statements about humanity's idolatries in 1:23 and 25 are shocking: "They exchanged the glory of the immortal God for the likeness of an image made to look like a mortal human being — or like birds or animals or reptiles" (v. 23); and "They exchanged the truth of God for a lie and worshiped and served created things rather than the Creator, who is forever to be praised" (v. 25). It is fairly easy to be repelled by such religious crudities and to observe how disastrous are the results of such idolatries when worked out in the lives of primitive people in foreign lands. Yet as Douglas Moo has pertinently observed: "This tragic process of human 'god-making' continues apace in our own day, and Paul's words have as much relevance for people who have made money or sex or fame their gods as for those who carved idols out of wood or stone."[117]

In contemporary Western society it is not too hard to be repelled by "pagan" forms of idolatry. Such idolatry often appears to us in our "civilized" and "cultured" environments to be gross and uninformed. But any contextualization

117. Moo, *Romans,* 110.

228

of Paul's teaching in this passage must also recognize that his words have relevance, as well, for all of the various forms of idolatrous attitudes and actions today — including all those more idolatrous attitudes and actions of our own as Christians.

On Humanity's Immoralities and Injustices. The lists of vices that appear rather frequently in various writings of the ancient world suggest that there existed among the ancient teachers and writers no standard catalog of ethical evils to which moralists commonly referred. Nor does Paul seem to have had before him any such list from which he worked in his ethical statements of 1:24-31.

Writing to his converts in the churches of Galatia, Paul lists as "works of the flesh" the following: "sexual immorality, impurity, debauchery, idolatry, witchcraft, hatred, discord, jealousy, rage, selfish ambition, dissensions, factions, envy, drunkenness, carousing, and things like these" (Gal 5:19-21). Writing to converts at Corinth he warns against associating with anyone who claimed to be "a brother or sister" (i.e., a Christian or fellow believer "in Christ") but was actually "sexually immoral, greedy, an idolater, a slanderer, a drunkard, or a swindler" (1 Cor 5:9-11). Then later in that same letter he identifies "the wicked" (i.e., "those who will not inherit the kingdom of God") as those who are "sexually immoral, idolaters, adulterers, male prostitutes, homosexual offenders, thieves, greedy, drunkards, slanderers, and swindlers" (1 Cor 6:9b-10). In 2 Tim 3:2-5a there is a somewhat similar listing that describes people "in the last days" as being "lovers of themselves, lovers of money, boastful, proud, abusive, disobedient to their parents, ungrateful, unholy, without love, unforgiving, slanderous, without self-control, brutal, not lovers of the good, treacherous, rash, conceited, lovers of pleasure rather than lovers of God, having a form of godliness but denying its power." And in the fourth major didactic section of his present letter to Rome (the ethical section in 12:1–15:13), Paul urges the Christians at Rome to "behave decently, as in the daytime" — "not in orgies and drunkenness, not in sexual immorality and debauchery, not in dissensions and jealousy" (Rom 13:13).

Frequently matters having to do with sexual immorality appear at or near the top of the Jewish and Christian vice lists. That is, it seems, because both Jews and Christians viewed personal relationships — not only relations between God and humans, but also relations among people — as being supremely important. Therefore whatever challenged the moral order established by God or perverted relations among people was considered especially heinous (as both Rom 1:24-27 and Wis 14:24-26 emphasize).

In particular, homosexuality is often highlighted in the Jewish and Christian vice lists as an especially heinous social sin and abominable personal offense against both the person of God and the personhood of others. The Christian church today is increasingly faced with many questions about how to maintain God's ethical standards and yet deal responsibly and helpfully with people who defy them. And in regard to the question of homosexuality, Charles Talbert's counsel can hardly be improved on:

Modern Christians who seek to adhere to the biblical values expressed by Paul will neither celebrate homosexual practice nor single it out as the only sin expressing human fallenness. Furthermore, if homosexual acts are wrong, those committing them are sinners, like the rest of us, who are in need of a Savior. So Christians are called to show Christ's love to them, not a radical intolerance. While acknowledging that the Bible regards all sexual activity outside of a permanent heterosexual marriage as sin, Christians must also confess that we are all sinners being saved by grace. Whereas Christians should love and welcome all sinners, we cannot, however, affirm and condone all actions and ways of life. The church is a place of transformation, discipline, and learning, not merely a place to be indulged.[118]

The fact that most of the vices in the extant vice lists of antiquity (including those of Jews and Christians) are simply set out *ad seriatim* (i.e., in a series without any necessary order) — with certain vices often interchanged with others — seems to indicate that we are not today to try to arrange human immoralities and injustices in any necessary order or to group them under any such labels as "mortal sins" (those of serious consequence and committed deliberately) and "venial sins" (those that are relatively slight or committed without full reflection or consent). So in any present-day contextualization of Paul's list of human vices in 1:24-31 we should undoubtedly treat those items listed as only representative human evils, without attempting to weigh one against another as to their respective sinfulness. For all of them stem from the much greater evils of rebellion against God and asserted independence from God, which have been, sadly, dominant factors throughout the course of human history — and which, in often secret and insidious ways, are repeated in the experiences of even Christians today.

The Antidote to Humanity's Idolatries, Immortalities, and Injustices. We cannot, however, conclude our discussion of contextualizing today what is said in Rom 1:18-32 without also observing that throughout the passage there implicitly appears the antidote to all of humanity's idolatries, immortalities, and injustices. This is so because every one of Paul's negative statements about idolatry, immorality, and injustice can be reversed and made to suggest something positive — as is true, of course, for everything ever said or written of a negative character on whatever topic. And all this is especially true with respect to what Paul writes in 1:21: "Although they knew God, they did not glorify him as God or give him thanks."

Implicitly, Paul declares here in 1:21 that the antidote to idolatry, immortality, and injustice is a heart that glorifies God by praising him and giving him thanks — both for who he is *and* for what he has done (and continues to do) in his works of creation and redemption. That antidote appears in many ways throughout Paul's letters. But it is most clearly expressed in his closing exhor-

118. Talbert, *Romans*, 76.

tation of Phil 3:1: "Finally, my brothers and sisters, rejoice in the Lord! It is no trouble for me to write this to you, and for you it is a safeguard" — which Paul then repeats some twenty-five verses later in Phil 4:4: "Rejoice in the Lord always. Again I will say it: Rejoice!"[119] It is praise and thanksgiving to God, therefore, that counter the disastrous litany of vices set out in Rom 1:19-32. And it is praise and thanksgiving to God, together with their resultant actions, that comprise "a safeguard" for Christians today.

119. Cf. similar closing exhortations in Rom 15:5-11 and 1 Thess 5:16-18.

3. God's Condemnation of All Who Sin Is Just and Impartial (2:1-16)

TRANSLATION

²:¹*You, therefore, O man or woman, whoever you are who passes judgment on someone else, are without excuse. For at whatever point you judge the other, you are condemning yourself, because you who pass judgment do the same things. ²Now we know that "God's condemnation of those who do such things is based on truth." ³Do you really think, O man or woman, you who pass judgment on those who do such things and yet do them yourself, that you will escape the condemnation of God? ⁴Or do you show contempt for the riches of his goodness, forbearance, and long-suffering, not realizing that God's goodness leads you to repentance? ⁵Because of your stubborn and unrepentant heart, you are storing up wrath for yourself on the day of wrath, when God's righteous judgment will be revealed.*

⁶*God will give to everyone according to what they have done:*

⁷*To those, indeed, who by steadfast endurance in doing good*
    seek glory, honor, and immortality,
    he will give eternal life.
⁸*But for those who, out of selfish ambition, disbelieve the truth*
    and follow evil,
    there will be wrath and anger.
⁹*There will be distress and anguish for every person*
    who does evil,
    both for the Jew first and for the Gentile;
¹⁰*but glory, honor, and peace for everyone who does good,*
    both for the Jew first and for the Gentile.
¹¹*For, "There is no favoritism with God."*

¹²*All who sin without having the law will also perish without the law, and all who sin while possessing the law will be condemned by the law. ¹³Because it is not those who hear the law who are righteous in God's sight, but those who obey the law who will be declared righteous. ¹⁴For,*

Whenever Gentiles, who do not have the law, do by nature the things required by the law, even though they do not have the law, they are a law for themselves, ¹⁵since they show that the work of the law is written in their hearts, their consciences joining in bearing witness and their thoughts within them now accusing, now even excusing them.

¹⁶*This will take place on the day when God will judge everyone's secrets through Christ Jesus, as my gospel declares.*

TEXTUAL NOTES

2:1 The presence of διό ("therefore"), whether understood as an inferential or a transitional conjunction (see "Exegetical Comments"), is solidly supported by the external textual evidence. Anton Fridrichsen, however, has proposed that the internal argument of 2:1-29 requires that διό be viewed as simply a mistake by some early scribe who erred in attempting to write the adverb δίς, which means "twice" or "again."[1] Fridrichsen's argument, however, rests on the mistaken assumption that the argument of 2:1-16, as well as that of 2:17-29, is directed only to Jews.

2 The postpositive δέ ("but," "now") following οἴδαμεν ("we know") is supported by uncials A B D^gr G P Ψ, as well as by minuscules 1175 1739 (Category I), 81 1881 1506 2464 (Category II), and 6 88 104 181 323 326 330 365 614 629 630 1241 1243 1505 1735 1874 1877 2495 (Category III). It is also reflected in versions it^ar (vid) sy^(p) g, and by Marcion Tertullian Ambrosiaster Theodoret. The variant γάρ ("for") is somewhat less supported by uncials ℵ C, minuscules 33 (Category I), 1962 2127 (Category II), and 436 2492 (Category III), versions it^d vg cop^sa, bo, and Chrysostom. The reading δέ is not only supported somewhat more strongly in the textual tradition, it also makes better sense of the passage since v. 2 presents a further consideration in line with v. 1 (so the appropriateness of δέ) and not a reason for or explanation of that previous verse (as with γάρ).

5 The addition of the conjunction καί ("and") following ἀποκαλύψεως ("revelation") is supported by uncials ℵ^2 D^c P Ψ, by minuscules 33 1175 1739 1881 (Category I), 1881 2464 (Category II), and 88 104 326 330 365 424^c 614 1241 1243 1319 1505 1735 1874 2344 2495 (Category III), and by version sy^h, thereby reading "the day of wrath and of revelation and of the righteous judgment of God." The omission of καί, however, is somewhat better supported by uncials ℵ* A B D* G, as well as by minuscule 81 (Category II). It is also reflected in versions it vg syr^p cop^sa, bo. The omission of καί presents a slightly more difficult reading — and therefore, presumably, a more original reading — in which there is a piling up of genitives: "the day *of* wrath and *of* the revelation *of* the righteous judgment *of* God."

13a The definite article τῷ ("the") before θεῷ ("God") is strongly supported by uncials ℵ A D^c G Ψ, as well as by minuscules 33 1175 1739 (Category I), 1506 1881 2464 (Category II), and 6 69 88 104 323 326 424 614 1241 1243 1319 1505 1573 1735 1874 2344 2495 (Category III). The article, however, is not included in uncials B D* and minuscule 1874 (Category III). Its omission was probably the result of some scribes considering it unnecessary, since θεός is sufficiently definite by itself without an article.

13b The ninth-century codex G (012) adds after the verb δικαιωθήσονται ("they will be declared righteous") the phrase παρὰ θεῷ ("before God"), which is probably a dittography generated by the expression δίκαιοι παρὰ τῷ θεῷ ("righteous before God" or "righteous in the sight of God") in the first part of the verse — but it is totally unnecessary here.

14 Codex G also replaces οὗτοι νόμον ("those [who do not have] the law"), which is amply attested elsewhere throughout the textual tradition, with the synonymous ex-

---

1. Fridrichsen, "Der wahre Jude," 40; *idem*, "Quatre Conjectures," 440.

pression οἱ τοιοῦτοι νόμον ("such ones [who do not have] the law"), which is evidently an attempt to improve the text stylistically.

15 Codex G likewise replaces λογισμῶν ("thoughts"), which is amply attested, with the intensified form διαλογισμῶν ("arguments"), which evidently some scribe thought was an improvement.

16a The phrase ἐν ἡμέρᾳ ὅτε ("on a day when") is widely supported by uncials ℵ D G Ψ, as well as by minuscules 33 1175 1739 (Category I), 1881 2464 (Category II) and 6 69 104 323 326 330 365 424^c 614 1241 1243 1319 1505 1573 1735 1874 (Category III). It is also reflected in versions it vg syr^h. Codex Vaticanus (B 03), however, reads ἐν ᾗ ἡμέρᾳ ("in the day"), while Codex Alexandrinus (A 02) and minuscules 1506 (Category II) and 88 (Category III) reverse that order to read ἐν ἡμέρᾳ ᾗ ("on a day in which"). The more amply attested first option now appears in *GNT*$^{3, 4}$, which is a change from the earlier *GNT*^{2}, where the reading of codex B was chosen. Evidently the reading of B was earlier chosen because it expresses by the use of the article a more explicit eschatological reference — although an eschatological reference may also be seen in the more widely supported phrase ἐν ἡμέρᾳ ὅτε, understanding the noun ἡμέρα to be definite.

16b Determination as to whether κρινει should be read as present tense (κρίνει, "he judges") or future tense (κρινεῖ, "he will judge") is complicated by the fact that in codices ℵ A B* D*, which are the earlier uncial MSS, this verb has no accent at all. It is read as present tense by uncials B^2 Ψ and minuscules 6 1241 1243 (Category III), but it is read as future tense by uncial D^2, minuscules 33 1175 1739 (Category I), 1506 1881 (Category II), and 69 88 104 323 326 365 614 1241 1319 1505 1573 1735 1874 2495 (Category III), and most Latin and Coptic versions. It is impossible to decide the matter based on external evidence alone. *NA*$^{26/27}$ opts for present tense κρίνει ("he judges"), evidently because it is the more difficult reading and therefore would explain the possible later corrections. Contextually, however, the future tense κρινεῖ ("he will judge") fits the passage better, and so is preferred in our translation above and our comments below (cf. the same question regarding the tense of κρινει in 3:6b).

16c The sequence Χριστοῦ Ἰησοῦ ("Christ Jesus") appears in uncials ℵ*^{vid} B, as well as in minuscules 81 1506 (Category II) and Origen. The sequence Ἰησοῦ Χριστοῦ ("Jesus Christ"), however, is found in uncials ℵ^c A D Ψ (also *Byz* uncials K L), minuscules 33 1175 1739 (Category I), 1881 1962 2127 2464 (Category II), and 6 104 365 424^c 1241 (Category III), and versions it vg syr$^{p, h}$ cop$^{sa, bo}$. Probably the former, Χριστοῦ Ἰησοῦ, is to be preferred, mainly because of its earlier attestation — though, as Bruce Metzger has noted, there is "considerable doubt as to which sequence is original."[2] *GNT*$^{3, 4}$ accepts Χριστοῦ Ἰησοῦ, thereby reversing the earlier position of *GNT*^{2}.

16d The possessive pronoun μου ("my") is omitted only by minuscule 69 (Category III) and versions it^d cop^{sa}, and therefore its early and widespread attestation in the Greek textual tradition cannot be set aside.

---

2. Metzger, *Textual Commentary*, 448.

FORM/STRUCTURE/SETTING

Almost all of the material contained in 1:18–3:20 parallels, in large measure, the Jewish and Jewish Christian teaching of Paul's day, both in form and in content. Throughout this section Paul portrays the sinfulness of all people and their deserved condemnation by God — that is, the sin and condemnation of both Gentiles and Jews — from a dominantly Jewish and Jewish Christian point of view. The only place where distinctive Christian language explicitly breaks through is in 2:16.

This is particularly true for the passage at hand, that is, for 2:1-16. For, as George Carras has pointed out, this first portion of Rom 2, together with the second portion of the chapter in vv. 17-29, constitutes an "inner Jewish debate," where what is written "is best understood as a diatribe whereby two Jewish attitudes on the nature of Jewish religion are being debated."[3] And such an understanding has been extensively argued, as well, by Stanley Stowers in his studies of Paul's use of the Greek diatribe in a Jewish context.[4] Yet the Jewish character and the Greek diatribe styling of the materials in these two sections of Rom 2 have seldom been recognized as important interpretive keys for a proper understanding of Paul's argument. Nor have the traditional Jewish and Jewish Christian materials of this section been adequately identified or interpreted. We will attempt to rectify both interpretive omissions in the treatments of 2:1-16 and 2:17-29 that follow.

Epistolary and Rhetorical Features. Two epistolary conventions of antiquity have been frequently identified in the first major section of the letter's body-middle, that is, in 1:16–4:25. The first is the vocative "O man or woman" (ὦ ἄνθρωπε; cf. also 2:3) at the beginning of 2:1, which a number of translators have viewed, for one reason or another, as impossible to translate,[5] while some commentators have rendered it in ways considered either more refined or less offensive.[6] The second of these conventions comes at the start of 4:1, where a verb of "saying" is included in the question "What then shall we say?" (τί οὖν ἐροῦμεν; cf. also 4:3, "What does the Scripture say?" [τί ἡ γραφὴ λέγει]). These instances of what have usually been viewed as epistolary conventions are, however, probably better related to the particular rhetorical modes of expression in which they are embedded (as noted above) — that is, (1) the vocative "O man or woman" as the opening gambit of a rhetorical diatribe in 2:1-5, and (2) the question "What then shall we say" as introducing the paradigmatic illustration of Abraham in 4:1-24. Nonetheless, whether epistolary or rhetorical in nature, these particular textual features provide the reader with some understanding of how the larger presentation of material in 2:1–4:25 is to be delineated — with

---

3. Carras, "Romans 2,1-29," 185.

4. Cf. Stowers, *Diatribe and Paul's Letter to the Romans,* 93-98, 112-13; *idem,* "Gentile Culture and God's Impartial Justice," 83-125; *idem,* "Warning a Greek and Debating a Fellow Jew," 126-58.

5. So, e.g., NIV, NRSV, TNIV.

6. So, e.g., Barrett: "my good man" or "my man"; Dunn: "you sir"; Moo: "O person"; Fitzmyer and L. T. Johnson: "human being."

the vocative here in 2:1 evidently meant to signal the start of a new subsection in Paul's overall presentation and the "verb of saying" doing the same in 4:1.

Of greater importance, however, are the more explicit rhetorical conventions in this first major section of Paul's letter to Rome, which function by way of identifying some of the structures and highlighting some of the developments in Paul's argument. Particularly important for a study of 2:1-16 are the following:

1. *Apostrophe* (i.e., the interruption of a discourse in order to address a person or personified thing), which phenomenon occurs both at the start of this passage as the first words of 2:1 ("You, therefore, O man or woman, whoever you are," etc.) and immediately after this passage as the first words of 2:17 ("Now if you, who call yourself a Jew," etc.). These two occurrences of apostrophe suggest that the material enclosed by them, that is, 2:1-16, should be viewed as a discrete unit of material in the development of Paul's argument.

2. *Diatribe* (i.e., a lively dialogical style that makes use of direct address to an imaginary interlocutor, hypothetical objections, and false conclusions). The clearest and most sustained instances of diatribe in the NT are in Romans, particularly in 2:1-5 and 2:17-24, where, as Stanley Stowers observes, "Paul seems to stop speaking directly to the recipients of the letter and begins to speak as if he were addressing an individual."[7] Diatribe styling has also been seen in such passages as 3:1-8 (perhaps including v. 9), 27-31 (perhaps including 4:1-2); 9:19-21; 11:17-24; and 14:4-11, though with varying degrees of certainty. 2:1-5 and 17-24 are, however, clearly and most demonstrably in the style and form of a Greek diatribe, with each of these two diatribe passages beginning a fairly discrete subsection in Paul's presentation.[8]

3. *Chiasmus* (i.e., an inverted relationship between syntactical elements of parallel phrases). The passages in "Part One" of the first major section of Romans that have been claimed to be chiastic in nature are:

   2:7-10 (or perhaps 2:6-11), which has been most often identified as a chiasmus,
   3:4-8, which has sometimes been so identified, and
   2:12-29, which has been seen by some as reflecting certain chiastic features, though probably erroneously so.

There is in any identification of a chiastic construction, however, whether real or supposed, always the highly important matter of intentionality.

---

7. Stowers, *Diatribe and Paul's Letter to the Romans*, 79.

8. These two passages of 2:1-5 and 2:17-24 could also, of course, be understood as reflecting a rhetorical *prosopopoeia* — that is, the introduction of a specific character, whether person or thing, who or which is allowed to speak.

Two questions, in fact, must always be asked of every proposed chiastic identification. The first is this: Is what appears as a chiasmus to be credited to the literary ability of the author or to the ingenuity of the reader? And if it is credited to the author, then a second question arises: Was this chiasmus intentionally or unintentionally created by its author? So, with respect to the passage at hand, the presence of what appear to be chiastic features in 2:7-10 (or perhaps more extensively in 2:6-11) needs to be noted, but the significance of those features with respect to the author's intention and the passage's interpretation can be debated.

4. *Inclusio* (i.e., similar verbal phenomena, including similar sentences, statements, phrases, clauses or words, that appear at the beginning and end of a relatively short unit of text and serve to frame the material presented). It is beyond doubt that the phenomenon of a rhetorical *inclusio* appears later in Romans, in chs. 5-8 with the use of the expression "through/by our Lord Jesus Christ" (διά / ἐν τοῦ κυρίου ἡμῶν Ἰησοῦ Χριστοῦ), which is repeated six times with only slight variation in 5:1, 11, 21; 6:23; 7:25; and 8:39. And it may be that an *inclusio* was intended by Paul when writing the phrase "both for the Jew first and for the Gentile" (Ἰουδαίῳ τε πρῶτον καὶ Ἕλληνι) in 1:16 and then twice more in 2:9-10, as Jouette Bassler has argued — though that seems far less likely (for an evaluation of Bassler's thesis, see my comments on 1:16-17 above; for a proposal regarding the phrase itself, see my comments on 2:9-10 below).

Use of Scripture and Traditional Materials. Paul's indictment of all humanity, Gentiles and Jews alike, runs from 1:18 to 3:20 — building, as Richard Hays has aptly characterized Paul's argument, "like a fireworks display toward a climactic explosion of scriptural condemnations in Rom. 3:10-18."[9] Further, as Hays goes on point out, while this "explosion of scriptural condemnations" comes to full expression in ch. 3 with a catena of biblical passages, in Rom 2 Paul "weaves together themes and language reminiscent of Old Testament wisdom and prophecy as well as of several intertestamental Jewish writings" — with "the texture of Paul's language here" in 2:1-16 being quite "densely allusive."[10]

Many examples of Paul's allusive use of Scripture will be cited in the "exegetical comments" that follow. One example of his allusive use of Jewish nonbiblical materials from the Second Temple period, which continues on from his allusive use of Wis 13:1–14:31 in depicting humanity's idolatries, immoralities, and injustices in 1:19-32, is what seems to be his similar use of Wis 15:1-5 in the first five verses of Rom 2. For in 2:1-5 Paul appears to have had in mind — and seems to have wanted to counter — the self-congratulatory boast at the beginning of Wis 15, which in quite a self-aggrandizing manner (and in obvious contrast to the portrayal of the Gentiles in Wis 13–14) reads:

9. Hays, *Echoes of Scripture*, 41.
10. *Ibid.*

But you, our God, are good and true, long-suffering and in mercy ordering all things. If we sin, we are yours, knowing your power. But we will not sin, knowing that we are yours. For to know you is perfect righteousness; indeed, to know your power is the root of immortality. For neither did the mischievous invention of people deceive us, nor an image spotted with diverse colors, the painter's fruitless labor; the sight whereof entices fools to lust after it, and so they desire to form a dead image that has no breath.[11]

Thus here in Rom 2:1 Paul writes: "You, therefore, O man or woman, whoever you are who passes judgment on someone else, are without excuse. For at whatever point you judge the other, you are condemning yourself, because you who pass judgment do the same things."

Paul also appears to have incorporated into 2:1-16 two Jewish or Jewish Christian aphorisms drawn from Jewish (OT) Scripture and two more extended quotations of Jewish or Jewish Christian devotional or catechetical materials. These traditional portions come to the fore in the following verses:

1. In 2:2: "God's condemnation of those who do such things is based on truth." This has every appearance of being a Jewish aphorism drawn from Scripture — and which is introduced by the phrase "now we know that" (οἴδαμεν δὲ ὅτι), which brings together an epistolary disclosure formula ("now we know") and an epistolary *hoti recitativum* ("that") that serve together as something of an introductory formulation, just as that same formulation is used to introduce the biblically-based aphorisms of 3:19; 8:28 (cf. also 1 Tim 1:8).

2. In 2:6-10: "God will give to everyone according to what they have done, etc." This passage begins with the relative pronoun "who" (ὅς), sets out its material in parallel structures of thought *(parallelismus membrorum)*, uses words and phrases not found elsewhere in Paul's letters (i.e., *hapax legomena*), and conflates in quite an allusive fashion a number of OT passages — all of which signals elsewhere in Paul's letters, as well as at various places throughout the rest of the NT, the use of early Christian confessional, devotional, and/or catechetical materials.

3. In 2:11: "There is no favoritism with God." This, too, has every appearance of being a Jewish or (perhaps) Jewish Christian aphorism drawn from biblical and (possibly) apocryphal sources. The conjunction "for" (γάρ) seems to be used here to introduce the biblically-based aphorism, just as it introduces Paul's more identifiable quotations of Scripture in 2:24; 10:13; 11:34-35 and 1 Cor 2:16; 10:26; 15:27.

4. In 2:14-15: "When Gentiles, who do not have the law, etc." Because of its content and style, this passage should probably also be viewed as a portion of traditional catechetical material originally composed in a Jewish or

---

11. Wis 15:1-5.

Jewish Christian milieu. It features another introductory use of the conjunction "for" (γάρ), incorporates some fairly significant *hapax legomena* of wording and usage, and reflects an awkwardness of syntax not usual for Paul.

The identification of these verses as containing traditional materials stemming from a Jewish and/or Jewish Christian milieu can be justified by (1) their confessional, devotional, or catechetical contents, which, it may be presumed, would have been recognized by those immersed in Jewish and Jewish Christian traditions, (2) their literary styling and vocabulary, which appear somewhat different from Paul's usual style and wording, (3) "now we know that" (οἴδαμεν δὲ ὅτι), which appears as an introductory formula for the citation of other biblically-based aphorisms in Rom 3:19; 8:28; and 1 Tim 1:8, and (4) introductory use of the conjunction "for" (γάρ), which serves to introduce quotations of Scripture in Rom 2:24; 10:13; 11:34-35 and 1 Cor 2:16; 10:26; 15:27.

Most readers today have difficulty in identifying such traditional materials within the writings of the NT, principally because they have become almost entirely dependent on quotation marks and indentations to mark off this type of material. Further, they seem unable to identify them because they are not accustomed — as were the Jews and the early Christians — to confess these materials in their corporate worship, to hear them in their times of catechetical instruction, or to ponder them in their more private devotional experiences. But a number of confessional, devotional, and catechetical materials were undoubtedly circulating among the early believers in Jesus and in their various congregations, and the content of some of these materials would have been known to both Paul and his Roman addressees. So it may be proposed (1) that vv. 2, 6-10, 11, and 14-15 (as cited above) incorporate some of those confessional, devotional, or catechetical materials used by the early believers in Jesus in their worship, instruction, and evangelistic witness, (2) that Paul allusively used some of those biblically-based materials here in 2:1-16 in the development of his argument, and (3) that these materials appear here for much the same reasons and same purposes as the more explicit confessional materials that appear elsewhere in Romans and Paul's other letters, as well as at a number of other places throughout the NT.[12]

All these matters will be considered more fully in the exegetical comments that follow. Suffice it here to say that what Paul writes in 2:1-16 should probably be viewed (1) as rooted in Jewish and Jewish Christian theology, literature, and language, (2) as known and appreciated by Paul's Christian addressees at Rome, (3) as used by Paul because he believed there was a basic agreement between him and his addressees regarding these materials and what they taught, and (4) as having been given Paul's own interpretive "spin" at certain crucial points.

Who Is Addressed and/or Described in 2:1-16? A particularly difficult mat-

---

12. For more extended treatments of such confessional materials in the NT, see R. N. Longenecker, *New Wine into Fresh Wineskins*, passim.

ter, however, arises when one attempts to identify who is being addressed or described in 2:1-16. It is fairly easy to identify Jews as addressed and described in 2:17-29 and 3:1-20, for in those sections the name "Jew" is explicitly used and the situation of the Jews is clearly discussed. Further, it has seemed fairly obvious to many commentators that Gentiles are described in 1:18-32, even though the term ἔθνη ("heathen," "pagans," "Gentiles") never appears in that passage. For there are a number of parallels of both content and language between 1:19-32 and Wis 13:1–14:31 — in particular, parallels in their respective portrayals of idolatry, immorality, and injustice — which can easily be accredited to the pagan Gentile world. So it has usually been assumed that throughout 1:18-32 Paul is speaking principally, if not exclusively, about Gentiles (though see our treatment above for our understanding of this passage).

But whom is Paul addressing or talking about in 2:1-16? Does he have in mind humanity generally, both Gentiles and Jews? Or perhaps only Gentiles, in continuity with the previous passage? Or only Jews, in continuity with the passages that follow? Or is he in some manner addressing both and/or speaking about both? This was an exceedingly difficult matter for such earlier interpreters as Origen, Jerome, Augustine, and Erasmus to determine, and it continues to plague commentators today.

Most commentators today have agreed with William Sanday and Arthur Headlam that 2:1 marks the "transition from Gentile to Jew" in Romans,[13] and with James Denney, who stated that "it is the Jew who is really addressed in this chapter [i.e., chapter 2] from the beginning, though he is not named till ver. 9."[14] Charles Cranfield has mounted the most extensive and cogent defense of this position, arguing that "there are weighty reasons for thinking that Paul had the Jews in mind right from 2.1."[15] Yet a number of commentators, of late, have understood 2:1-16 in more general terms as referring to all people, both Gentiles and Jews — as, for example, Kingsley Barrett: "It is not till v. 17 that he [Paul] turns specifically to the problem of the Jews; here, as vv. 9ff., 12-16 show, his thought applies to both Gentiles and Jews."[16]

Who is addressed and/or described in 2:1-16 is, indeed, a difficult matter to determine, which may never be conclusively resolved. But (1) the passage is distinguishable from what precedes it by its use of the second person singular pronoun of direct address "you" as the passage begins in 2:1-5, whereas the third person plural pronoun "they" appears throughout 1:18-32, (2) the passage seems distinct from what follows it by its lack of any direct address of Jews (the phrase "both to the Jew first and to the Gentile" of vv. 9-10 being used in a different manner), whereas the direct address of Jews is a feature found a number of times throughout 2:17–3:20, (3) the passage is bracketed by the expressions

13. Sanday and Headlam, *Romans* (1895), 53-62.
14. Denney, *Romans* (1900), 595.
15. Cranfield, *Romans,* 1.138; see his extensive discussion in 1.137b-40.
16. Barrett, *Romans,* 43.

"you, O man or woman" (εἶ, ὦ ἄνθρωπε) of 2:1 (cf. also 2:3) and "now if you" (εἰ δὲ σύ) of 2:17, which suggests that the intervening material is a distinguishable unit of material, and (4) what is said in the passage is addressed to some imaginary interlocutor who is described in fairly general fashion as "whoever you are who passes judgment" (πᾶς with the nominative, singular, masculine, present, active, substantival participle ὁ κρίνων) — all of which suggests, despite the obvious associations with what precedes and what follows, that 2:1-16 is best understood as a discrete unit of material.

When analyzed on the basis of its general content, the passage seems to function as a literary hinge between Paul's treatment of "God's wrath against humanity's godlessness and wickedness" in 1:18-32 and his "denunciation of any form of Jewish legalism" in 2:17-29. And when analyzed according to its theological theme or themes, the passage certainly serves as a significant hinge between 1:18-32 and 2:17-29, for its message of God's impartiality in judgment — that is, as 2:11 states by way of epitomizing the whole presentation: "There is no favoritism with God!" — is of great significance in the development of Paul's argument from humanity generally to Jews in particular.

The Major Theological Problem of the Passage. There is, however, a major theological problem in Rom 2, which appears first rather generally in vv. 7 and 10 but then erupts into what most interpreters have viewed as a very serious problem in the final words at the end of v. 13 and immediately afterward in the supporting statements of vv. 14-15 (also later, somewhat parenthetically, in vv. 25-27 of the same chapter). It is a problem that has caused most contemporary commentators to agree with the bewilderment expressed in 2 Pet 3:16 — that there are in Paul's letters "some things that are hard to understand."[17] That major theological problem is this: How can what Paul says about Gentiles and Jews in Rom 2 be reconciled with what he says about humanity generally and Jews in particular throughout the rest of Romans? For while his conclusions elsewhere in Romans regarding God's impartiality (2:11), Jews and Gentiles being alike under sin (3:9-19, 23), and no one being able to be declared righteous by observing the law (3:20) are clear, there are verses in ch. 2 that seem to espouse a theology of salvation by good works for Gentiles and by obedience to the Mosaic law for Jews. Indeed, as many have pointed out, Paul appears to allow in ch. 2 what in chs. 1 and 3 of the same letter he categorically denies.

The first place where this problem appears is in 2:7, 10, where it is said that God will give "eternal life" (v. 7) or "glory, honor, and peace" (v. 10) to those who persevere in doing "good work" (v. 7: ἔργου ἀγαθοῦ) or "good" (v. 10: τὸ ἀγαθόν), which seems to conflict with what is said about justification solely by faith in 3:21-30; 4:1-25; and throughout 9:1–11:36. The second is in 2:13, where it is said that "those who do ['obey,' 'observe'] the law (οἱ ποιηταὶ νόμου) [are the ones who] will be declared righteous," which seems to conflict with Paul's

---

17. Cf., e.g., P. Achtemeier's 1984 article, "'Some Things in Them Hard to Understand,'" which begins by focusing on "Paul's use of language" in Rom 2:14.

statement about no one being declared righteous by observing the law in 3:20, his references to humans being unable to obey the law in 7:14-25, and his denunciation of Israel for attempting to gain righteousness by means of the Mosaic law in 9:30–11:12. The third is the parenthetical reference in 2:14-15 to some Gentiles who "do by nature things required by the law (τὰ τοῦ νόμου)" and so "show that the requirements of the law (τὸ ἔργον τοῦ νόμου) are written on their hearts," with the inference being that by these actions they are justified before God. But assuming that Paul is using the word "law" throughout this passage in much the same way, such an inference seems to contradict his earlier picture of the Gentiles in 1:18-32 and his conclusion about the impossibility of righteousness before God by observing the law in 3:20.

The fourth place where this problem is found is in the argument of 2:25-27 — which, of course, is in the following section, which deals with Jews and the Mosaic law but is still relevant to the discussion at hand, which seems to be built on the assumption that righteousness is associated with observing the Mosaic law. But this seems to fly in the face of Paul's express conclusion to this section in 3:19-20, his thesis statement regarding the "righteousness of God" being "apart from the law" in 3:21-23, his use of Abraham as the exemplar of faith in 4:1-25, and his entire depiction of the relation of the gospel to the hope of Israel in 9:1–11:36 — as well as his arguments in Gal 2:15-16; 3:6-14 and his exhortations in Gal 4:12–5:12, as repeated here and there in some of his other letters.

This is a theological problem, however, that is just too large, too complicated, and with too many diverse ways of treatment to be discussed in any cursory fashion here in our introductory comments. It can only be effectively considered in the context of detailed exegesis. So it is necessary to delay any further treatment of this matter until it can be discussed in the "exegetical comments" below.

The Setting and Structure of the Passage. The direct association of 2:1-16 with 1:18-32 has often been made, with 1:18-32 understood as comprising the first half of a larger passage and 2:1-16 the second half. Such a connection has also been made on a literary basis, with the phrase "both for the Jew first and for the Gentile" (Ἰουδαίῳ τε πρῶτον καὶ Ἕλληνι), which appears first in 1:16 and then twice more in 2:9-10, understood as a rhetorical *inclusio* that brackets all of the material in 1:16 through 2:11 — with, of course, what is enclosed viewed as being a single unit of material on the subject of humanity's sin and God's judgment, both of Gentiles and of Jews.[18] On the other hand, 2:1-16 has more commonly been joined with what follows in 2:17–3:20, understanding 1:18-32 as God's indictment against Gentiles and all of 2:1–3:20 as expressing God's indictment against Jews.

There are, however, certain features in 2:1-16 which suggest that this passage is best understood as a discrete unit of material — that is, while beginning on an inferential basis from what is presented in 1:18-32 and concluding by

---

18. As, again, has been argued by J. M. Bassler. For an evaluation of Bassler's thesis, see our introductory and exegetical comments on 1:16-17 above; on her treatment of the phrase itself, see our exegetical comments on 2:9-10 below.

pointing forward to what will be said in 1:17–3:20, the passage is probably best not to be connected directly with or considered only a subsection of either of these other passages. Its distinction from what precedes is signaled by its use of the second person pronoun of direct address "you" in 2:1-5, whereas the third person pronoun "they" dominates throughout 1:18-32. Its distinction from what follows is signaled by its lack of any explicit direct address to Jews (though, of course, the twice-repeated phrase "both to the Jew first and to the Gentile" of 2:9-10 explicitly mentions Jews, but not in direct address), whereas Jews are directly addressed in 2:17-29 and 3:1-20. Further, "you, O man or woman" in 2:1 (cf. 2:3) and "now if you" in 2:17 bracket the material between them and thus seem to set off this passage as a discrete or distinguishable unit of material.

Therefore, while relating 2:1-16 both to what precedes and to what follows, it seems best to conclude that this passage should not be viewed as merely a continuation of what precedes or as the first part of what follows. Rather, it should be understood — both literarily and with respect to content — as a hinge between 1:18-32 and 2:17–3:20. It moves the discussion forward from the condemning statements about humanity generally in 1:18-32 to the more focused statements about the responsibilities of and God's judgment on the Jews in 2:17–3:20. But also, and of far greater importance theologically, it highlights both the inexcusability of all people ("You are without excuse!"), however their willful rebellion against and vaunted independence from God is expressed, *and* the impartiality of God's judgment in matters of righteousness and sin ("God does not show favoritism!"), regardless of a person's ethnicity.

The structure of Paul's argument on human inexcusability and divine impartiality in 2:1-16 develops as follows:

1. All who do evil, whatever their claims of moral superiority and accusations of others, are without excuse and condemned by God (2:1-5).
2. God's righteous judgment is impartial and based on what people have done (vv. 6-11).
3. All who sin without having the Mosaic law and all who sin while possessing the Mosaic law will be judged equally and impartially by God (vv. 12-16).

EXEGETICAL COMMENTS

I. All Who Do Evil, Whatever Their Claims of Moral Superiority and Accusations against Others, Are without Excuse and Condemned by God (2:1-5)

In 2:1-5 Paul uses the form of a Greek diatribe and shifts from the third person plural pronoun "they" (as in 1:18-32) to the second person singular pronoun "you" in the fashion of a rhetorical apostrophe. In a typical Greek diatribe a speaker or writer digresses from his usual style of argumentation to address an imaginary interlocutor, raising in the process various objections or arguments in keeping with that person's perspective in order to censure or encourage certain kinds of thought or behavior.

Rudolf Bultmann claimed that the diatribe style of argument was used by ancient Cynic and Stoic philosophers as a rhetorical technique of mass propaganda to persuade the common man on the street.[19] Abraham Malherbe and Stanley Stowers, however, have persuasively argued that the diatribe was a pedagogical form of oral rhetorical discourse that originated in the ancient schools of philosophy, though its style was often imitated in literary documents.[20] The person addressed in a Greek diatribe was viewed not as an opponent but as someone under the instruction of a teacher. Further, the teacher was not motivated by contempt for his student, but by concern to lead his student into a more mature understanding of the issue at hand. Thus through a diatribal question-and-answer dialogue the teacher endeavored to lead the student to (1) a realization of his error, (2) a deeper understanding of what was being taught, and (3) a commitment to the instruction presented.

Paul's dialogical style in Romans, therefore, should be viewed not in terms of his subconscious preaching style (contra Bultmann) but as an intentional means of presenting himself to the Christians at Rome as their *teacher* (as per Malherbe and Stowers). In this regard, it is particularly important to note that while 2:1-5 and 2:17-24 are quite clearly set out in a Greek dialogical style — and while features of a Greek diatribe certainly appear later in 9:19-21 and 11:17-24 and perhaps also in 14:4-11 (though probably not, as sometimes argued, in 3:1-8[-9] or 3:27-31 [-4:2]) — outside Romans Paul seems to have used a diatribal form of argument only (at best) a very few times. Perhaps a diatribal form of argument can be found in 1 Cor 6:12-13; 15:30-34 and Gal 2:17; 3:21. But even if present, it does not appear in those passages outside Romans in any extended or fully articulated fashion. So it may be argued that Paul's use of diatribal styling in Rom 2:1-5, 17-24; 9:19-21; 11:17-24 (perhaps also 14:4-11), should be understood (1) as something fairly unique in Paul's letters and (2) as reflecting something of his own self-consciousness and the nature of his presentation when writing to the Christians at Rome — that is, that he was writing to them as an accredited Christian teacher, whose mandate as a missioner to the Gentile world included them as his pupils, but not as their spiritual father to whom they owed allegiance, as he expressed himself when writing to his own converts.

2:1 It has been extensively debated whether the conjunction διό ("therefore") at the beginning of this section is (1) inferential in nature, presenting material whose statements follow from what was argued earlier in 1:18-32,[21] or

---

19. Bultmann, *Der Stil der paulinischen Predigt.*

20. Malherbe, "MH ΓΕΝΟΙΤΟ in the Diatribe and Paul," esp. 239; Stowers, *Diatribe and Paul's Letter to the Romans,* esp. 76-77.

21. So, e.g., Cranfield, *Romans,* 1.298-99; Dunn, *Romans,* 1.79; Fitzmyer, *Romans,* 298-99.

(2) transitional, presenting material that moves on from what was argued earlier[22] — or perhaps, as Anton Fridrichsen has argued (see the textual notes above), it should be considered a mistake by some early scribe who was attempting to write the adverb δίς, which here should be read as simply "again."[23] In all likelihood, however, διό here is not merely transitional, but carries an inferential force. For it echoes the inferential use of the same particle in the phrase διὸ παρέδωκεν αὐτοὺς ὁ θεός ("therefore God gave them over") in 1:24 and resonates with many of the terms and expressions used in 1:18-32 (see our comments below). Further, as Stanley Stowers has observed, it was not at all unusual in a Greek diatribe to begin with διό.[24]

The predicate nominative accusation ἀναπολόγητος εἶ ("you are without excuse / inexcusable") picks up on the concluding accusation of 1:20, "so people are without excuse" (εἰς τὸ εἶναι αὐτοὺς ἀναπολογήτους). The appearance of "without excuse" at the beginning of the first sentence of 2:1 gives it emphasis. In an English translation, however, where an emphasis is normally achieved by building toward a climax, "without excuse" is best placed at the end of the sentence.

The vocative ὦ ἄνωρωπε ("O man or woman"), which appears later again in resumptive fashion in 2:3 after the intervening aphorism of 2:2, is the opening gambit of the rhetorical diatribe that appears in 2:1-5. Here Paul speaks directly to an imaginary interlocutor, whom he sets up in this verse and describes as πᾶς ὁ κρίνων ("whoever you are who passes judgment"). The use of the vocative ὦ ἄνωρωπε to address an imaginary interlocutor was a common convention of the Greek diatribe. But the generalization of that address by the further use of πᾶς ("all," "everyone," "whoever"), together with the substantival participle ὁ κρίνων ("the one who passes judgment"), was not, as Stanley Stowers has pointed out, a usual feature in a Greek diatribe; rather, this use of "everyone who passes judgment" should be understood as "clearly Paul's attempt to emphasize that everyone, both Jews and Greeks, who sin are equally accountable."[25]

Such an imaginary interlocutor, however, was hardly "imaginary" for Paul in the sense of "fictitious" or "lacking factual reality." In his missionary journeys he must have frequently encountered Gentiles who claimed to follow the enlightened teaching of the philosophers, but who also practiced some of their well-known vices. The Greek satirist Lucian of Samosata (c. A.D. 120-200) was famous for mocking the philosophers of various schools for the wide gap between their lofty teachings and their vile practices[26] — that is, for being models of sobriety and wisdom by day but given to drink and debauchery at night.[27] Likewise, Paul probably knew Jews who claimed to be religiously and morally

---

22. So, e.g., Lietzmann, *An die Römer,* 37-39; Michel, *An die Römer,* 73; Murray, *Romans,* 1.56.
23. Cf. Fridrichsen, "Der wahre Jude," 40; *idem,* "Quatre Conjectures," 440.
24. Cf. Stowers, *Diatribe and Paul's Letter to the Romans,* 213.
25. *Ibid.,* 93.
26. See esp. Lucian's *Auction of Philosophers.*
27. Cf. Lucian, *Timon* 54.

superior to Gentiles — but in feigned piety applauded the prayer of Asaph to God in Ps 79:6 with respect to all such outcast Gentiles: "Pour out your wrath on the nations that do not acknowledge you, and on the kingdoms that do not call on your name." So Paul's interlocutor represents everyone — not just Jews but both Jews and Gentiles — who agrees with all that is written in 1:18-32 about God's wrath as rightfully coming on all the idolatries, immoralities, and injustices of humanity, but who, while knowing God's truth and moral principles, fails to act in accordance with them — and so, under the guise of other expediencies and definitions, continues to practice the same vices.

Paul's accusation against people who simply disapprove mentally of idolatry, immorality, and injustice — even those who condemn others who espouse such ideologies and actually practice them — is that such attitudes are far from sufficient. For, as he writes in the latter part of 2:1: ἐν ᾧ γὰρ κρίνεις τὸν ἕτερον, σεαυτὸν κατακρίνεις, τὰ γὰρ αὐτὰ πράσσεις ὁ κρίνων ("for at whatever point you judge the other, you are condemning yourself, because you who pass judgment do the same things"). Sadly, all people, in their own ways and as condoned by their own prejudices and societies, do much the same things — and therefore also deserve God's righteous judgment.

Rudolf Bultmann and Ernst Käsemann, in denying that διό at the beginning of 2:1 has any inferential force, have argued (1) that 2:1 is really "an early marginal gloss which originally drew the conclusion from v. 3 and was then put at the beginning," (2) that 2:2 should be connected with 1:32 and considered the conclusion of ch. 1, (3) that 2:3 is best understood as the first verse of ch. 2, and (4) that, as Käsemann expressed it: "To be sure, ἀναπολόγητος εἶ ["you are without excuse"] cannot then be ascribed to Paul, even though it points back to 1:20 and is appropriate to the situation."[28] But such a proposed deletion, rearrangement, and reinterpretation is entirely uncalled for — especially if (1) the conjunction διό of 2:1a carries with it an inferential nuance, (2) the material of 2:1 is viewed as the topic statement for all that follows in 2:1-5, (3) 2:2 relates an aphorism drawn from the Jewish (OT) Scriptures, and (4) the material of 2:3 is understood as a reaffirmation of the topic statement of 2:1, with both topic statement and reaffirmation expressing a dire warning of God's rightful judgment as was pronounced throughout 1:18-32 — all of which I argue is the case here.

2:2 The phrase οἴδαμεν δὲ ὅτι ("but/now we know that"), which begins this verse, is a typical "disclosure formula" of ancient epistolary writing. Such an opening expression, as Stowers has pointed out, "is not a feature of the diatribe"; rather, "Paul uses οἴδαμεν when he wants to emphasize that a statement is a matter of common ground between himself and the addressee(s)."[29] This same phrase also begins two other portions of material later in Romans, in 3:19 and 8:28 (cf. also οἴδαμεν γὰρ ὅτι, "for we know that," in 7:14), as well as in 1 Tim 1:8. And in all these places it appears to be used as a quasi-introductory formula

---

28. Käsemann, *Romans,* 54; echoing Bultmann, "Glossen im Römerbrief," 200.
29. Stowers, *Diatribe and Paul's Letter to the Romans,* 94.

to highlight the quotation of a traditional aphorism (i.e., a condensed form of truth) that had at some time earlier than Paul been drawn generally from the Jewish (OT) Scriptures.

The aphorism drawn by Paul from the OT Scriptures and introduced by the conventional disclosure formula "but/now we know that" is as follows: τὸ κρίμα τοῦ θεοῦ ἐστιν κατὰ ἀλήθειαν ἐπὶ τοὺς τὰ τοιαῦτα πράσσοντας ("God's condemnation of those who do such things is based on truth"). Drawn from the general teaching of the Scriptures, it was evidently used as a traditional bit of instruction not only among Jews but also among Jewish believers in Jesus.

The noun κρίμα ("condemnation") picks up from the immediately previous uses in 2:1 of the substantival participle ὁ κρίνων ("the one who passes judgment," twice), the verb κρίνεις ("you are judging"), and the intensified verb κατακρίνεις ("you are condemning"). It can mean a "lawsuit" (as in 1 Cor 6:7) or a "decision" or "judgment made" about certain matters (as in Rom 11:33). More frequently, however, it connotes the idea of "condemnation" or an "adverse judicial sentence" (as in Rom 3:8; 13:2; cf. also Gal 5:10), which is how it should be understood here. The phrase ἐστιν κατὰ ἀλήθειαν ("is based on truth," literally "is according to truth") when first used in the aphorism probably referred to "God's truth as revealed in the Holy Scriptures." So it would have connoted to most Jews the standard that God set for his people in the law of Moses. But Paul's use of ἀλήθεια ("truth"), while including such a Jewish nuancing, was undoubtedly meant to suggest all of what God has revealed by both "general revelation" and "special revelation" — as appears evident from his references to "truth" in 1:18b and 2:2b in the context of his emphases on God's "revelation in creation" in 1:19-20 and God's "law written on the heart" in 2:14-15, as well as his emphasis on the Mosaic law in 2:12-13.

The primary reason for Paul's quotation of this aphorism was, evidently, its stress on God's condemnation of people who are actually *doing* evil things (ἐπὶ τοὺς τὰ τοιαῦτα πράσσοντας, literally "on those who are *doing* such [evil] things"), despite their assertions of religious and moral superiority and their applauding of God's condemnatory justice on others. For that is the point that Paul emphasizes in 2:3 when he tells his imaginary interlocutor that, while passing judgment on others, he or she "does the same things" (ποιῶν αὐτά).

C. H. Dodd, however, proposed a quite different interpretation of 2:2, understanding it as expressing the words of a representative Jewish interlocutor who "complacently" argues that "the doom of God falls justly upon those who practice such vices" — and to whom Paul retorts in 2:3: "Very well, and do you imagine you will escape God's doom, O man, you who judge those who practice such vices and do the same yourself?"[30] Kingsley Barrett has followed Dodd in so understanding the verse: "At this point the objector speaks. *Now we know* introduces his complaint."[31] And the translators of the NRSV have

30. Dodd, *Romans,* 32.
31. Barrett, *Romans,* 44.

incorporated this view of matters into their translation by adding "You say," before "We know that. . . ."

It is, however, far better to understand 2:2 as Paul still speaking[32] — with the additional point, as we are proposing, that he is using a traditional aphorism drawn from Scripture to highlight the fact that God's condemnation comes "on those who *do* such [evil] things." And this "doing the same things" (ποιῶν αὐτά) he attributes to both Gentiles and Jews — despite whatever mental agreements they might have in common with respect to divine judgment on the evil practices of others.

2:3 After the intervening aphorism in 2:2, Paul returns to address his imaginary interlocutor directly, as signaled by his resumptive use of the vocative ὦ ἄνωρωπε ("O man or woman"). Here the apostle asks the first of two rhetorical questions, which (1) highlight the delusion of such a supposedly superior interlocutor, (2) point out the damnable consequences of his or her judgment of others while doing the same things, and (3) speak of the interlocutor's contempt for the "goodness, forbearance, and long-suffering" of God.

The first question picks up from the rhetoric of the topic statement of 2:1 and asks quite directly of those who pass judgment on others and yet do the same things themselves: λογίζῃ δὲ τοῦτο . . . ὁ κρίνων τοὺς τὰ τοιαῦτα πράσσοντας καὶ ποιῶν αὐτά, ὅτι σὺ ἐκφεύξῃ τὸ κρίμα τοῦ θεοῦ; ("Do you really think, . . . you who pass judgment on those who do such things and yet do them yourself, that you will escape the condemnation of God?"). The question repeats in condensed fashion the accusatory style and judgments of Isa 57:3-13 against a people who judge others but continue to do the same evil things themselves. For the prophet begins in Isa 57:3-4 as follows: "But you — come here, you sons of a sorceress, offspring of adulterers and prostitutes! Whom are you mocking? At whom do you sneer and stick out your tongue?" — and then the prophet goes on throughout 57:5-13 to set out a litany of practices of God's people just as evil as those being done by the people they were judging. Thus Paul's first question here in Rom 2:3 probably echoes the prophet's denunciatory statements of Isa 57:3-13 — as well, it seems, the sentiment of the writer of *Pss Sol* 15:8, which was presumably well-known to pious Jews and earnest Jewish Christians: "Those who commit lawlessness will not escape the condemnation of the Lord" (τὸ κρίμα κυριοῦ).

2:4 The second rhetorical question is: ἢ τοῦ πλούτου τῆς χρηστότητος αὐτοῦ καὶ τῆς ἀνοχῆς καὶ τῆς μακροθυμίας καταφρονεῖς, ἀγνοῶν ὅτι τὸ χρηστὸν τοῦ θεοῦ εἰς μετάνοιάν σε ἄγει; ("Or do you show contempt for the riches of his goodness, forbearance and long-suffering, not realizing that God's goodness leads you to repentance?"). Three attributes of God are expressed here in three genitive nouns: τῆς χρηστότητος αὐτοῦ ("of his goodness," "kindness," "generosity"), τῆς ἀνοχῆς [αὐτοῦ] ("of his forbearance," "clemency," "tolerance"), and τῆς μακροθυμίας [αὐτοῦ] ("of his long-suffering," "pa-

---

32. So Cranfield, *Romans,* 143; Fitzmyer, *Romans,* 300, and many others.

tience," "endurance"). It is not too difficult to postulate that these three attributes were commonly mentioned among Jews and so became an integral part of the vocabulary of the early Jewish believers in Jesus. The first, χρηστότης ("goodness," "kindness"), together with its adjective χρηστός ("good," "kind"), appears frequently in conjunction with ἔλεός ("mercy") in praise to God for his "goodness" and "mercy," as found in LXX Pss 24:7; 68:16; 85:5; 99:5; 105:1; 108:21; 144:7-9. Likewise, it appears separately as a primary attribute of God in LXX Pss 30:19; 118:65-68; Philo, *Migration of Abraham* 122, and Josephus, *Antiquities* 1.96; 11.144. The third, μακροθυμία ("patience"), is attributed to God in Jer 15:15 and Sir 5:4.[33] Probably more important for our purpose here, however, is that the opening sentence of Wis 15:1-5 — which both Paul and his addressees probably knew well, and whose self-congratulatory statements Paul seems to have had in mind and sought to counter throughout 2:1-16 — reads: "But thou, our God, art good (χρηστός) and true (ἀληθής), long-suffering (μακρόθυμος), and in mercy (ἐν ἐλέει) ordering all things."[34] This direct parallel suggests that Paul was not simply using in rather general fashion some OT, Jewish, and Jewish-Christian terms with respect to God, but was quite intentionally using the same attributes of God that his envisioned interlocutor would have used.

While the first question has to do with the delusion of self-assured, supposedly superior, and critical interlocutors who judge others but do the same evil things themselves, this second question depicts the contempt of such a person for God's gracious dealings. For, as Joseph Fitzmyer has pointed out, "to make light of the delay on God's part to punish sin, which should lead to repentance, is to manifest one's culpable negligence."[35] In effect, Paul portrays such a misguided interlocutor as being so blind and callous as actually to be proclaiming by his or her attitude and speech: "If I were God, I would do things differently! I would judge the heathen much more quickly for all their apostasy, immorality, and injustice!" But Paul's comment on such a self-confident and self-aggrandizing assertion is that it evidences contempt "for the riches of his [God's] goodness, forbearance, and long-suffering, not realizing that God's goodness leads you to repentance."

The word "repentance" (μετάνοια) literally means a "change of mind," but in a religious sense it came to mean "remorse" or "turning away from" evil and to connote "the beginning of a new religious and moral life" or "conversion." The expression εἰς μετάνοιάν σε ἄγει ("leads you to repentance") suggests more the idea of giving someone the opportunity to repent.[36] The use of the second person singular accusative pronoun σέ ("you") continues the diatribe form of

33. On God's "patience" in Jewish thought, see *Str-Bil* 3.77-78.
34. Wis 15:1.
35. Fitzmyer, *Romans*, 301.
36. As in Wis 11:23: εἰς μετάνοιάν, "an opportunity for repentance"; 12:10: τόπον μετανοίας, "a place for repentance"; rather than giving assurance to someone that "he [God] gives repentance for sins," as in Wis 12:19: ἐπὶ ἁμαρτήμασι μετάνοιαν.

direct address, as do the second person singular nominative pronoun σύ in 2:3 and the repetition of σέ in 2:27. It is used in these instances for emphasis, as also in 11:22 (though there perhaps not in the context of a diatribe).

2:5 The judgment that Paul levels against any such self-assured interlocutor is this: κατὰ δὲ τὴν σκληρότητά σου καὶ ἀμετανόητον καρδίαν θησαυρίζεις σεαυτῷ ὀργὴν ἐν ἡμέρα ὀργῆς καὶ ἀποκαλύψεως δικαιοκρισίας τοῦ θεοῦ ("Because of your stubborn and unrepentant heart, you are storing up wrath for yourself on the day of wrath, when God's righteous judgment will be revealed"). Instead of being led "to repentance" (εἰς μετάνοιάν), such a self-assured and critical interlocutor is characterized as having a "stubborn and unrepentant heart" (τὴν σκληρότητά σου καὶ ἀμετανόητον καρδίαν). The articular noun ἡ καρδία ("the heart") is used here, as often in the NT, in an all-inclusive sense to mean not only the human faculty of thought ("the mind"), but also the full scope of a person's will, emotions, desires, and general disposition.

Rather than adding the conjunction καί ("and") after the genitive noun ἀποκαλύψεως ("of revelation"), thereby reading "the day of wrath and of revelation and of the righteous judgment of God," the better textual evidence supports its omission. So the line is best read literally as "the day of wrath and of revelation of the righteous judgment of God" — or, in more colloquial English, "the day of wrath, when God's righteous judgment will be revealed." Paul's reference to "the day of [God's] wrath" picks up from the wording of 1:18 ("the wrath of God"), his language in 2:1 ("you are condemning yourself"), and the aphorism quoted in 2:2 ("God's condemnation on those who do such things is based on truth"). It also echoes the denunciations in the writings of the OT prophets.[37] And it functions as a warning of dire consequences not only to Paul's immediate addressees and humanity generally, but also to us today.

II. God's Righteous Judgment Is Impartial and Based on What People Have Done (2:6-11)

The structure of 2:6-11 has been frequently discussed and analyzed. In 1958 Joachim Jeremias proposed that a chiasmus can be seen in 2:7-10, which he laid out as follows: *reward* (ζωὴν αἰώνιον, "eternal life") in v. 7 and *punishment* (ὀργὴ καὶ θυμός, "wrath and anger") in v. 8, which are balanced in chiastic fashion in reverse order by *punishment* (θλῖψις καὶ στενοχωρία, "trouble and distress") in v. 9 and *reward* (δόξα δὲ καὶ τιμὴ καὶ εἰρήνη, "glory, honor and peace") in v. 10. In addition, he noted that in 2:7-8 *reward* and *punishment* are proclaimed at the end of their respective clauses, whereas in 2:9-10 *punishment* and *reward* appear at the beginning of their clauses.[38]

In 1964 Kendrick Grobel set out another chiastic construction for this

---

37. Cf., e.g., Isa 13:9; 37:3; Lam 1:12; Zeph 1:14-15, 18; 2:3.
38. See Jeremias, "Chiasmus in den Paulusbriefen," 149.

passage, which built on Jeremias's more elemental proposal (though without referring to Jeremias) but included all of 2:6-11 and was much more complex.[39] Grobel's chiastic analysis is as follows (with my own translation, as given above):

A 6. [θεὸς]
(God)

  B ἀποδώσει ἑκάστῳ κατὰ τὰ ἔργα αὐτοῦ
(will give to everyone according to what they have done [literally "his works"])

    C 7. τοῖς μὲν < > δόξαν καὶ τιμὴν καὶ ἀφθαρσίαν
(to those indeed < > glory, honor, and immortality)

      D ζητοῦσιν
(who seek)

        E ζωὴν αἰώνιον
(eternal life)

          F 8. τοῖς δὲ < > πειθομένοις < > τῇ ἀδικίᾳ,
(but those < > who follow < > evil)

            G ὀργὴ καὶ θυμός.
(wrath and anger)

            G' 9. θλῖψις καὶ στενοχωρία
(distress and anguish)

          F' ἐπὶ πᾶσαν ψυχὴν ἀνθρώπου τοῦ κατεργαζομένου τὸ κακόν
(on every person who does evil)

        E' 10. δόξα δὲ καὶ τιμὴ [καὶ εἰρήνη]
(but glory, honor, and peace)

      D' τῷ ἐργαζομένῳ
(for everyone who does)

    C' τὸ ἀγαθόν < >
(good)

  B' 11. οὐ γάρ ἐστιν προσωπολημψία παρὰ
(for there is no favoritism)

A' τῷ θεῷ
(with God).

That some sort of chiastic arrangement is present in 2:6-11 is recognized by many commentators today, whether in the elemental form proposed by Jeremias (as has been most commonly favored) or in the more extended and complex form argued by Grobel (which has often been criticized). One major criticism of Grobel's more extensive and more involved chiastic proposal, as Douglas Moo has pointed out, is that "Unlike some chiastically structured paragraphs, the main point of vv. 6-11 occurs not at the center but at the beginning and the end

---

39. See Grobel, "Chiastic Retribution Formula," 255-61.

(vv. 6, 11): God will judge every person impartially, assessing each according to the same standard — works."[40] This quite valid observation suggests that, while 2:7 and 2:8 share an antithetic parallelism and a similar structure — and while the material of 2:9-10 does the same, only in reverse fashion — the materials of 2:6 (at the beginning) and 2:11 (at the end) should be seen as structured in other ways and as functioning for other purposes than simply to begin and end a rhetorical chiasmus. Further, with respect to a number of its details, Grobel's schematic construction can be criticized (1) for not clearly expressing the antithetic parallelism and similar structures of 2:7-8 and their reverse parallels in 2:9-10 and (2) for not keeping together, evidently for the sake of symmetry, the article τοῖς with its participle ζητοῦσιν in C and D, but keeping together the article τῷ and its participle ἐργαζομένῳ in D'. James Dunn has voiced the reservation of a number of scholars in saying: "Grobel's suggestion of a larger chiasm, vv. 6-11, becomes less persuasive with its greater complexity."[41]

Ernst Käsemann, agreeing to an extent with Grobel, has argued that "by no means accidentally are vv. 7-10 hymnic and highly stylized rhetorically."[42] Further, Käsemann has noted with respect to certain features in the passage that (1) "verses 9f. repeat vv. 7f. chiastically," (2) "verse 11 is a conclusion which formally parallels v. 6, but which also gives the reason for its content," (3) "the verbs are completely absent in vv. 7-10," (4) "to speak of an anacoluthon [i.e., a syntactical inconsistency or incoherence in any of these four verses] is to miss its [i.e., that verse's] character as acclamation," and (5) "in the style of holy law, which rules out any hypothetical interpretation of what precedes, the criterion of the last judgment is unveiled in its universal scope and in its present validity, as in the acclamations of Revelation."[43]

In arguing that 2:6-11 should be seen as "a chiastic retribution formula," Grobel has also proposed that Paul has taken over "a pre-Pauline piece of Jewish tradition": "It is almost as if he were quoting some familiar and authoritative document of the very point of view which Romans was written to refute."[44] According to Grobel, the best indication that this unit of material was not originally written by Paul is the presence in 2:9 and 10 of "footnotes," namely, the two uses of the Pauline phrase Ἰουδαίῳ τε πρῶτον καὶ ῞Ελληνι, which "ruins the chiastic pattern of the unit."[45] And some NT scholars have generally agreed with Grobel.[46] Further, Grobel has argued that if the material of 2:6-11 does, indeed, reflect a Jewish piece of traditional material, it probably was originally composed in Hebrew or Aramaic, and that in crossing the language boundary from Hebrew or Aramaic into Greek the symmetry of that original piece of

40. Moo, *Romans*, 136.
41. Dunn, *Romans*, 1.78.
42. Käsemann, *Romans*, 59.
43. *Ibid.*
44. Grobel, "Chiastic Retribution Formula," 256.
45. *Ibid.*
46. So, e.g., Bassler, *Divine Impartiality*, 124, 130-31.

tradition likely suffered damage before Paul used it. So Grobel suggested various emendations in an endeavor to show how the original pre-Pauline piece of Jewish tradition might have looked.[47]

Most commentators, however, have not considered the possibility that Paul incorporated within 2:6-11 a piece of Jewish or Jewish Christian traditional material. And few, if any, would argue (nor would I) that these verses were originally composed in Hebrew or Aramaic. Yet it needs to be noted that 2:7-10 has a hymnic quality and stylized character and that because of their lack of verbs the possibility arises that these verses were originally meant to be something of an acclamation. Further, it also should be noted that the material in 2:6-11 reflects a Jewish and/or Jewish Christian understanding of the Jewish (OT) Scriptures and seem to incorporate Jewish and/or Jewish Christian patterns of thought and expression. So I would here propose — taking seriously into account all these observations, together with the insights and criticisms of Jeremias, Käsemann, Moo, and Dunn cited earlier — the following understanding of 2:6-11:

1. While a chiastic arrangement may underlie, at least to some extent, the antithetic parallelism, similarity of construction, and inversion of order in 2:7-10, the structure of these verses as they now appear in Paul's letter to the Christians at Rome is better understood as antithetic Hebrew parallelism rather than Greek chiasmus.

2. While 2:6 and 2:11 are certainly related to the material in 2:7-10, they should be viewed not as simply the beginning and ending elements of a chiastic construction but as a topic sentence (2:6) that introduces the antithetic statements of 2:7-10 and that was from the first an integral part of that traditional unit of material, and then a conclusion (2:11), wherein Paul sums up by the use of a traditional Jewish and/or Jewish Christian aphorism one vitally important teaching of what has been set out in vv. 6-10.

3. While the material of 2:7-10 can be seen as being "hymnic and highly stylized rhetorically" (to repeat Käsemann's descriptive phrase), one can go further to suggest that the topic sentence of 2:6 and the stylized material 2:7-10 are best understood together as comprising a single unit of Jewish Christian devotional or catechetical material — which, in turn, was rooted in Jewish piety — that both Paul and the Christians at Rome knew and that Paul quotes here.

4. Paul adds in 2:11 his own concluding comment to that single unit of Jewish Christian devotional or catechetical material, which he gives in the form of a recognizable Jewish and/or Jewish Christian aphorism.

Thus I suggest that a better schematic understanding of 2:6-11 is as follows (using my own translation of the passage):

47. Cf. Grobel, "Chiastic Retribution Formula," 256.

Topic Sentence (the caption for the material quoted in vv. 7-10):
6. [θεὸς] ἀποδώσει ἑκάστῳ κατὰ τὰ ἔργα αὐτοῦ,
   (God will give to everyone according to what they have done:)
Antithetical Hebrew Parallelism (the material captioned by v. 6):
7. τοῖς μὲν καθ᾽ ὑπομονὴν ἔργου ἀγαθοῦ
   (To those who, indeed, by steadfast endurance in doing good
        δόξαν καὶ τιμὴν καὶ ἀφθαρσίαν ζητοῦσιν
        seek glory, honor, and immortality)
   ζωὴν αἰώνιον
   ([he will give] eternal life)
8. τοῖς δὲ ἐξ ἐριθείας καὶ ἀπειθοῦσι τῇ ἀληθείᾳ
   (But for those who, out of selfish ambition, disbelieve the truth
        πειθομένοις δὲ τῇ ἀδικίᾳ
        and follow evil)
   ὀργὴ καὶ θυμός.
   ([there will be] wrath and anger.)
9. θλῖψις καὶ στενοχωρία ἐπὶ πᾶσαν ψυχὴν ἀνθρώπου
   ([There will be] distress and anguish for every person
        τοῦ κατεργαζομένου τὸ κακόν,
        who does evil,)
   Ἰουδαίου τε πρῶτον καὶ Ἕλληνος·
   (both for the Jew first and for the Gentile;)
10. δόξα δὲ καὶ τιμὴ καὶ εἰρήνη παντὶ τῷ ἐργαζομένῳ τὸ ἀγαθόν,
    (but glory, honor, and peace for everyone who does good,)
    Ἰουδαίῳ τε πρῶτον καὶ Ἕλληνι·
    (both for the Jew first and for the Gentile.)
Conclusion (an aphorism used by Paul to conclude the quotation of vv. 6-10):
11. οὐ γάρ ἐστιν προσωπολημψία παρὰ τῷ θεῷ.
    (For "There is no favoritism with God.")

And it is this understanding of the passage that will be developed more fully in the comments that follow.

2:6 The relative pronoun ὅς ("who," understood here as "God") signals in this verse, as it does also elsewhere in Paul's letters and in some of the other writings of the NT, the incorporation of a traditional portion of confessional material.[48] It should, therefore, probably be viewed as introducing all of what follows in 2:6-10 as a unit of early Jewish Christian confessional, devotional, or catechetical material. As such, Paul uses this traditional unit of material to support his argument in 2:1-5 that God's judgment of people is "based on truth" and to focus not merely on what people know but on "what they have done."

The topic sentence, ἀποδώσει ἑκάστῳ κατὰ τά ἔργα αὐτοῦ ("He will give to everyone [literally 'to each one'] according to what they have done [literally

---

48. Cf., e.g., Phil 2:6-11; Col 1:15-20; 1 Tim 3:16b; Heb 1:3-4; 1 Pet 2:22-23.

'his or her works'])" employs almost verbatim the words of Ps 62:12 (LXX 61:13) and Prov 24:12:

Ps 62:12: σὺ ἀποδώσεις ἑκάστῳ κατὰ τὰ ἔργα αὐτοῦ.
("You will give to each one according to his or her works.")
Prov 24:12: ὃς ἀποδίδωσιν ἑκάστῳ κατὰ τὰ ἔργα αὐτοῦ.
("Who [God] gives to each one according to his or her works.")
Rom 2:6: ὃς ἀποδώσει ἑκάστῳ κατὰ τὰ ἔργα αὐτοῦ.
("Who [God] will give to each one according to his or her works.")

This maxim expresses a basic principle of all Jewish religion.[49] It was central, as well, in the teaching of Jesus,[50] and of great importance in the understanding of believers in Jesus.[51]

2:7-10 A series of four statements begins in 2:7 and continues through v. 10, with each statement lacking an express verb, which suggests that they should be viewed as four parts of a single affirmation that began at 2:6 and so as a single unit of traditional material — that is, a portion of some earlier confessional, devotional, or catechetical material. The first two statements in 2:7-8 share an antithetic parallelism and similar structure, with the descriptions of their respective persons being given first and the results of their actions stated last. In the two statements of 2:9-10 the antithetic parallelism and similarity of structure are set out in reverse fashion, with the results stated first and the descriptions of the persons given last. Further, not only is there a reversal in the descriptions of the people and the results of their actions between 2:7-8 and 2:9-10, there is also an inversion of those descriptions and results, with the good descriptions and results set out in the first and fourth statements (vv. 7 and 10) and the bad descriptions and results set out in the second and third statements (vv. 8 and 9).

All of this, of course, suggests something of a chiastic arrangement — though it is hardly a true chiasmus, since the main point of the passage occurs not at its center (2:8-9) but in the topic sentence at the beginning (2:6) and in the conclusion (2:11). It is better, therefore, to postulate that, while some type of chiastic arrangement, whether intentional or unintentional, may very well lie in some fashion behind 2:7-10, the material of these verses should be understood, at least as it now appear in Romans, as primarily reflecting the thought patterns of an antithetic type of Hebrew parallelism. Such an antithetic parallelism, as based on Jewish patterns of thought, was undoubtedly a common feature among Jewish Christians of the day. It may be presumed, as well, to have been well

---

49. See not only Ps 62:12 and Prov 24:12, but also Jer 17:10: ἐγὼ κύριος . . . τοῦ δοῦναι ἑκάστῳ κατὰ τὰς ὁδοὺς αὐτοῦ, "I the Lord . . . give to every one according to his or her ways."

50. Cf. Matt 16:27: "The Son of Man . . . will reward each person according to what he or she has done."

51. Cf. 2 Cor 5:10; Col 3:25; 2 Tim 4:14; 1 Pet 1:17; Rev 2:23; 20:12; 22:12; see further Heiligenthal, *Werke als Zeichen*, 1/2-/5.

known to both Paul and his Christian addressees at Rome. In addition, there is added to the descriptions of the people in view at the end of both 2:9 and 2:10 the same phrase: "both for the Jew first and for the Gentile."

2:7 In the statement that appears at the beginning of 2:7, τοῖς μὲν καθ' ὑπομονὴν ἔργου ἀγαθοῦ δόξαν καὶ τιμὴν καὶ ἀφθαρσίαν ζητοῦσιν ("to those, indeed, who by steadfast endurance in doing good seek glory, honor, and immortality"), there is an echo of what God desires for his people as portrayed in Job 40:10 (LXX 40:5): "Adorn yourself with a lofty bearing (ὕψος) and power (δύναμιν), and clothe yourself with glory (δόξαν) and honor (τιμήν)." Likewise, this statement of 2:7 reflects what the psalmist declares God to have bestowed on humanity at creation in Ps 8:5: "You made him a little lower than the heavenly beings (ἀγγέλους) and crowned him with glory (δόξῃ) and honor (τιμῇ)."[52]

The noun ὑπομονή connotes ideas of "patience," "endurance," "fortitude," "steadfastness," and "perseverance." It is probably best translated here as "steadfast endurance" — which is how it is also probably best translated later in 5:3-4; 8:25; and 15:4-5, as well as elsewhere in the Pauline corpus and throughout the rest of the NT.[53] The phrase καθ' ὑπομονὴν ἔργου ἀγαθοῦ (literally "by the patient endurance of good work") may seem somewhat strange to some vis-à-vis other expressions of Paul's theology in Romans and his other letters, though its sense is repeated again in 2:10 (παντὶ τῷ ἐργαζομένῳ τὸ ἀγαθόν, literally "to everyone who is doing/working the good"). This appreciative reference to "doing/working the good" here in 2:7 — as well as the commendatory comments regarding "doing/working the good" in 2:10 and regarding "the things/work of the law" in 2:14-15 — may seem somewhat surprising from Paul's pen, perhaps even viewed as Pauline *hapax legomena*. For earlier in Gal 2:16 (three times); 3:2, 5, 10 and later in Rom 3:20-28 the expression "the works of the law" is used disparagingly. Yet as Kingsley Barrett has pointed out, "The answer to this serious and important question must inevitably begin, 'It depends on what you mean by works.'"[54] For in the context, Paul certainly seems to approve of these apparently strange expressions (which is a matter that must be discussed more appropriately below in dealing with 2:13 and then again with 2:14-15). Also to be noted in 2:7 is the use of the affirmative particle μέν ("indeed"), which is frequently not represented in modern translations — but which, while difficult to translate, suggests that Paul is stating something here that he believed his addressees already knew.

The expression ζωὴν αἰώνιον ("eternal life") is used at the end of 2:7 for the first time in Romans, though it is found earlier in Paul's letters in Gal 6:8 and

---

52. That same language regarding God's creation of and desire for humanity is also fairly closely paralleled in Wis 2:23 and 4 Macc 17:12.

53. On ὑπομονή as "steadfast endurance," see F. Hauck, *TDNT* 4.586-88. In addition to its other uses in Romans at 5:3-4; 8:25; and 15:4-5, see also 2 Cor 6:4; 1 Thess 1:3; 2 Thess 1:4; 1 Tim 6:11; 2 Tim 3:10; Titus 2:2; similarly Heb 10:36; Jas 1:3-4; 2 Pet 1:6; Rev 2:2-3, 19.

54. Barrett, *Romans*, 46.

later in Rom 5:21; 6:22-23.[55] It does not, however, appear in the Jewish (OT) Scriptures until LXX Dan 12:2 ("Many of them that sleep in the dust of the earth shall awake, some to eternal/everlasting life (εἰς ζωὴν αἰώνιον) and some to reproach and eternal/everlasting shame"). Based on Dan 12:2, the expression evidently came to be used by Jews during the period of Second Temple Judaism for the final destination of the righteous.[56] In the non-Pauline writings of the NT it is used for what God gives to believers in Jesus — that is, "eternal/everlasting life," which is defined as a divine gift for both the present and the future.[57]

2:8 Two fairly difficult words to translate appear in the opening clauses of 2:8, τοῖς δὲ ἐξ ἐριθείας καὶ ἀπειθοῦσι τῇ ἀληθείᾳ πειθομένοις δὲ τῇ ἀδικίᾳ ("but for those who, out of selfish ambition, disbelieve the truth and follow evil"). The first is the noun ἐριθείας (here in the genitive), which is derived from the noun ἔρις ("strife," "discord," "contention"); the second, the participle ἀπειθοῦσι (dative plural masculine present), which may connote either being "disobedient" or "disbelieving."

To understand ἐριθεία in terms of its etymology, that is, as derived from the noun ἔρις, "strife," "discord," or "contention," is to define it as "contentious," "factious," or "factious ambition."[58] But to understand it in terms of its two extant uses in antiquity, Aristotle, *Politics* 1302b:4 and 1303a:14, where it signifies the pursuit of public office by intrigue, is to define it more in the terms of "self-seeking" or "selfish ambition."[59] And it is that definition by contextual usage, rather than by etymology, that we believe to be the best in this passage, and which also suits far better its other NT uses in 2 Cor 12:20; Gal 5:20; Phil 1:17; 2:3; and Jas 3:14, 16[60] — though, of course, translators and commentators have also struggled over how to define the term in each of these other passages.

The verb ἀπειθέω, on which the participle ἀπειθοῦσι is built, was used widely in antiquity to mean "disobey" or "be disobedient." And that is how it is used by Paul with respect to the Jews in Rom 10:21 (quoting Isa 65:2) and 11:31 — as well as, in all likelihood, in Rom 15:31. For Jewish believers in Jesus, however, the supreme disobedience was refusal to believe the proclamation of the Christian gospel, and so the verb ἀπειθέω and its participle ἀπειθῶν came to connote among those early Jewish believers the meanings "disbelieve" and "an unbeliever."[61] It may, therefore, be proposed that here in 2:8 — in what we have suggested is probably an early Jewish Christian confessional portion — the early Christian connotation of "disbelieve" is most prominent, rather than Paul's usual use of the verb and its participle in the sense of "disobey" or "be disobedient."

---

55. Cf. also 1 Tim 1:16; 6:12; and Titus 1:2; 3:7.

56. Cf. 2 Macc 7:9; 1QS 4.7; and 4 Macc 15:3.

57. Cf., e.g., Mark 10:17 par.; 10:30 par.; Luke 10:25; John 3:15-16, 36, passim; Acts 13:46, 48; 1 John 1:2; 2:25, passim; Jude 21.

58. So, e.g., RSV: "them that are factious."

59. So NIV and NRSV: "self-seeking."

60. Cf. also Ignatius, *To the Philadelphians* 8:2.

61. Cf. John 3:36; Acts 14:2; 19:9; 1 Pet 2:8; 3:1, 20; 4:17.

Likewise, the articular noun τῇ ἀληθείᾳ ("the truth"), which is in the dative here, could have been used with quite different nuancing by Jews (i.e., truth as expressed in the Mosaic law) and early Christians (i.e., truth as uniquely expressed in Jesus Christ and the Christian gospel) — even with a somewhat different nuancing by early Jewish Christians and by Paul (depending on how each nuanced some of the details of the early Christian proclamation).

The terms ὀργή ("wrath") and θυμός ("anger") are often joined together in the LXX with reference to God's judgment,[62] particularly in association with the expression "the day of the Lord"[63] and with reference to God's final judgment.[64] As an intensified couplet, "wrath and anger" would certainly have been understood by Jews, Jewish Christians, and Paul as signaling the awfulness and anguish of divine judgment, however the details of that judgment might be conceptualized and spelled out.

2:9 The material of 2:9-10 repeats the antithetic statements of 2:7-8, but (1) in reverse and inverted order, (2) with synonyms used in the second set of statements for some of the earlier expressions used in the first set, and (3) with the addition of the phrase "both for the Jew first and for the Gentile" after each of the final two statements. Such a reversal and inversion of these two sets of antithetic statements may represent a chiastic arrangement, whether intentional or unintentional. The structure of these verses, however, could just as easily be understood — and probably better — as a case of antithetic Hebrew parallelism, with the features of reversal and inversion being also involved (see above on 2:6-11).[65]

Θλῖψις καὶ στενοχωρία ("distress and anguish") is the couplet used to express God's displeasure with wicked people in Isa 8:22 and 30:6,[66] and it parallels in synonymous fashion the couplet ὀργὴ καὶ θυμός ("wrath and anger") at the end of Rom 2:8. The phrase ἐπὶ πᾶσαν ψυχὴν ἀνθρώπου (literally "on every soul of man") makes use of the Hebrew word for "soul" (נֶפֶשׁ) as a locution for "human being" or "person,"[67] and so is best translated "for every person (who does evil)."

2:10 Δόξα καὶ τιμὴ καὶ εἰρήνη, "glory and honor and peace," parallels the trilogy δόξαν καὶ τιμὴν καὶ ἀφθαρσίαν ("glory and honor and immortality") in 2:7, only with "peace" in place of "immortality." And the phrase παντὶ τῷ ἐργαζομένῳ τὸ ἀγαθόν, "to/for everyone who does good," parallels the expression τοῖς καθ' ὑπομονὴν ἔργου ἀγαθοῦ ("to those who by patient endurance in

---

62. Cf., e.g., Deut 29:27; Ps 78(77):49; Jer 7:20; 21:5; Sir 45:18.

63. Cf. Isa 13:9.

64. Cf. Isa 30:30.

65. So we have proposed that the material of 2:6-10 is best viewed as (1) a topic sentence in 2:6, (2) two sets of antithetic statements, the first in 2:7-8 and the second in reversed and inverted order in 2:9-10, and (3) two uses of the phrase "both for the Jew first and for the Gentile," which appear at the end of each of the final two statements of 2:9-10 and together function as a fitting climax to the presentation of 2:6-10 — thereby highlighting the theme of the impartiality of God in his judgment of sin and sinners.

66. Cf. also Deut 28:55, 57.

67. Cf. Lev 24:17; Num 19:20.

doing good") in 2:7. The "good" referred to in 2:7 and "working/doing good" in 2:10 are not denounced, as are "works of the law" later in 3:20 and 28.[68] Rather, they are commended. For as Kingsley Barrett has rightly observed: "The 'good' which God will reward does not consist in 'works of law,' but in patient seeking, in looking beyond human activity to its divine complement."[69]

Ἰουδαίῳ τε πρῶτον καὶ Ἕλληνος ("both for the Jew first and for the Gentile"), which appears at the end of both 2:9 and 2:10, was, of course, the phrase used in a highly significant manner in the thesis statement of 1:16-17. But this phrase is not used in Paul's restatement of his thesis in 3:21-23 or anywhere else in any of his other NT letters. So it may reasonably be conjectured (1) that the phrase was included in the traditional material that Paul quoted in 2:6-10, (2) that it was used by him in 1:16 by way of anticipating the confessional material he would later incorporate, and (3) that while he fully agreed with the statement "both for the Jew first and for the Gentile" and strategically used it in 1:16-17 in writing to the Christians at Rome, it was neither coined by him nor represented how he usually expressed himself to Gentiles in his Gentile mission.

2:11 The statement appended as a conclusion to the quoted material of 2:6-10, οὐ γάρ ἐστιν προσωπολημψία παρὰ τῷ θεῷ ("For 'there is no favoritism with God' "), should in all likelihood be understood as a further traditional aphorism quoted by Paul. It begins with what appears to be an introductory use of the conjunction γάρ ("for"), which Paul used to introduce quotations of Scripture in Rom 2:24; 10:13; 11:34-35 and 1 Cor 2:16; 10:26; 15:27. Further, its content is abundantly represented throughout the Jewish (OT) Scriptures[70] and the Jewish apocryphal writings.[71]

James Dunn speculates that the term προσωπολημψία "may well be a Christian formulation," since it first appears in the NT here in Rom 2:11 and then in Eph 6:9; Col 3:25; and Jas 2:1. Cognate expressions, however, as Dunn also notes, are to be found at a few other places in the NT: (1) the noun προσωπολήμπτης ("one who shows favoritism") in Acts 10:34, where Peter is represented as beginning his message to the Roman centurion Cornelius with the words "I now realize how true it is that God does not show favoritism," (2) the verb προσωπολημπτέω ("show favoritism") in Jas 2:9, (3) the adverb ἀπροσωπολήμπτως ("without respect of persons," "without favoritism," "impartially") in 1 Pet 1:17, and (4) the idiom πρόσωπον ὁ θεὸς ἀνθρώπου οὐ λαμβάνει ("God does not judge by external appearance," literally "God does not take [into account] the face of a man") in Gal 2:6.[72] Interestingly, and I believe of some significance, is the fact that most of these instances of cognate expressions

---

68. Cf. also a denunciatory use of "works of the law" in Gal 2:16 (three times); 3:2, 5, 10.

69. Barrett, *Romans*, 48.

70. Cf. esp. Deut 10:17: God "does not accept persons nor take a bribe"; 2 Chr 19:7: "with the Lord our God there is no injustice or favoritism or bribery"; Job 34:19: God "shows no partiality to princes and does not favor the rich over the poor, for they are all the work of his hands."

71. Cf. esp. *Jub* 5:15; Sir 35:12-13; Wis 6:7; *Pss Sol* 2:18.

72. Cf. Dunn, *Romans*, 1.88.

in the NT appear in materials that can be, in one way or another, attributed to a Jewish and/or Jewish Christian context — which suggests that προσωπολημψία ("favoritism," "partiality") is probably best understood as having arisen and been used in such a milieu. But without pressing that point, it needs at least to be recognized that the Greek noun προσωπολημψία used here in Rom 2:11 stems from the Hebrew expression פנים נשׂא ("receiving the face"), which is a Jewish locution for an unwarranted act of favoritism. And in the Jewish (OT) Scriptures, judges are particularly warned against partiality and favoritism.[73]

All these parallels cited above suggest that here in 2:11 Paul cites what appears to be a Jewish and/or Jewish Christian aphorism that (1) was solidly based in the Jewish (OT) Scriptures and the literature of Second Temple Judaism, (2) was well known to the Christians at Rome, and (3) used by Paul to conclude his quotation of Jewish Christian confessional material in 2:6-10 — which message he evidently wanted to resonate strongly in the minds and hearts of his Roman addressees: that "there is no favoritism with God."

III. All Who Sin without Having the Mosaic Law and All Who Sin While Possessing the Law Will Be Judged Equally and Impartially by God (2:12-16)

The third and final subsection of 2:1-16 has a number of structural, syntactical, and interpretive problems, especially in vv. 14-16. The most difficult problem with respect to all of Romans 2, however, erupts most explicitly in this subsection of the chapter, that is, in vv. 13-15. For while the statements of 2:7 and 10 — that God will give "eternal life" (v. 7) and "glory, honor, and peace" (v. 10) to those who persevere in doing "good work" (v. 7, ἔργου ἀγαθοῦ) and doing "the good" (v. 10, τὸ ἀγαθόν) — have presented to many a problem of interpretation when compared with what Paul says in 3:21-30; 4:1-25; and 9:1–11:36 about being justified solely by faith (see the exegetical comments on 2:7 and 10 above), the statements here in 2:13-15 — that "those who obey/do the law (οἱ ποιηταὶ νόμου) [are the ones who] will be declared righteous" (v. 13), that some Gentiles "do by nature (φύσει) things required by the law (τὰ τοῦ νόμου)" (v. 14) and so "show that the requirements of the law (τὸ ἔργον τοῦ νόμου) are written on their hearts (γραπτὸν ἐν ταῖς καρδίαις αὐτῶν)" (v. 15), with the inference being in all three verses that by such actions Gentiles are justified before God — have presented far greater difficulties. What can be made of these seemingly non-Pauline statements in Romans 2? A number of ways of reconciling these statements with what Paul says elsewhere in Romans and his other letters have been proposed.[74]

---

73. Cf. Lev 19:15: "Do not pervert justice; do not show 'partiality to the poor' (LXX: πρόσωπον πτωχοῦ) or 'favoritism to the great' (LXX: πρόσωπον δυνάστου), but judge your neighbor fairly"; see also Deut 1:17; 16:19.

74. Cranfield lists and evaluates ten such ways in his *Romans*, 1.151-53.

One popular way of understanding these statements vis-à-vis the apostle's teaching elsewhere in Romans and his other letters is to propose that here in Romans 2 Paul has in mind *Christian* Gentiles, not pagan Gentiles — that is, that he is referring to Gentiles who obey the Jewish law through faith in Christ and life in the Spirit.[75] Another way is to argue that Paul in Romans 2 is speaking about *pre-Christian* Gentiles who have faith in God or about godly Jews *before* the coming of the gospel — or, perhaps, in some blended fashion, speaking about (1) pre-Christian Gentiles who possessed a God-given faith, together with (2) faithful Jews who before the coming of Christ expressed their trust in God through the forms of the Mosaic law, *and* (3) Christian believers in Jesus.[76] Evaluating this latter position, Klyne Snodgrass says in agreement: "Those people who have seen Romans 2 as a description of circumstances prior to the coming of the gospel are correct."[77]

Still other ways of viewing these statements have been proposed, mostly by some rearrangement of the above two approaches. Ernst Käsemann, for example, interprets Romans 2 in terms of (1) pagan Gentiles in 2:12-16, (2) a "purely fictional" Gentile soteriology in 2:24-27, and (3) the "true Jew" as a Gentile Christian in 2:28-29 — that is, in terms of "three distinct moments in the chapter."[78] Joseph Fitzmyer argues that in 2:7 and 10 Paul is referring to Christians "whose conduct (good deeds) is to be understood as the fruit of their faith"[79] but that in 2:14-15 and 2:26 he is referring to pagan Gentiles and not Christian Gentiles.[80] James Dunn and Thomas Schreiner have argued that in 2:7, 10, 26-29 Paul is thinking of Christian Gentiles, whereas in 2:14-15 he is referring to pagan Gentiles.[81] Somewhat similarly, Heinrich Schlier held that pagan Gentiles are designated in 2:14-15 while in 2:27 Paul passes almost unconsciously into describing Christian Gentiles.[82]

Another approach has been to see Paul in Romans 2 as referring to a *hypothetical or theoretical possibility* of being justified by good works or obedience to the law, but then going on to deny that possibility in order to highlight the real-

---

75. Cf., e.g., Mundle, "Zur Auslegung von Röm 2,13ff.," 249-56; Bultmann, *Theology of the New Testament,* 261; Flückiger, "Die Werke des Gesetzes bei den Heiden," 17-42; K. Barth, *Shorter Commentary on Romans,* 36-39; Black, *Romans,* 55-56; Cranfield, *Romans,* 1.152-62, 173-76; König, "Gentiles or Gentile Christians?" 53-60; Ito, "Romans 2," 33-34.

76. Cf., e.g., Schlatter, *Gottes Gerechtigkeit,* 74-112; Bläser, *Das Gesetz bei Paulus,* 195-97; Barrett, *Romans,* 42-51; Cambier, "Le jugement," 210; G. N. Davies, *Faith and Obedience in Romans,* 55-56.

77. Snodgrass, "Justification by Grace," 81.

78. Käsemann, *Romans,* 59, 65, and 73 (using E. P. Sanders's characterization of Käsemann's understanding as "three distinct moments in the chapter," which Sanders calls an example of "tortured exegesis" in his *Paul, the Law, and the Jewish People,* 127).

79. Fitzmyer, *Romans,* 297; see also 302.

80. *Ibid.,* 310, 322.

81. See Dunn, *Romans,* 1.86, 98, 100, 106-7, 122-25; Schreiner, "Did Paul Believe in Justification by Works?" 131-55.

82. Schlier, *Der Römerbrief,* 77-79, 88.

ity of righteousness before God as being only by faith — that is, arguing that *if people could obey the law they would be justified,* but *no one can.* Such a view was established in modern NT critical scholarship by Hans Lietzmann, who argued that here in this chapter Paul is viewing matters "from a pre-gospel standpoint *(vom vorevangelischen Standpunkt)*" and setting out what would have been the case "if (1) there was no gospel *(das Evangelium nicht da wäre),* and (2) it were possible to fulfill the Law *(die Erfüllung des Gesetzes möglich wäre)."*[83] And this understanding has been espoused by a number of recent scholars, though in various ways and with somewhat different definitions given to the adjectives "hypothetical" and "theoretical."[84]

On the other hand, there are a few scholars who have argued that many, if not all, of the problem passages in Romans 2 are flatly contradictory to Paul's teaching elsewhere in Romans — though they have offered diverse explanations for the texts in question. John C. O'Neill, for example, as might be expected from his similar treatment of what he identified as "contradictory" passages in Galatians, believed that all of what appears in 1:18–2:29 is both in opposition to Paul's teaching and irrelevant for his purpose and so declared that 1:18–2:29 must be viewed as an interpolation by a later glossator who drew on material from a Hellenistic Jewish missionary tractate.[85] Heikki Räisänen, rejecting any such recourse to an interpolation theory, has argued that 2:14-15 and 26-27 are blatantly in conflict with Paul's main thesis in 1:18–3:20 that all are under sin and so evidence quite clearly that "Paul's mind is divided" with respect to humanity's ability to keep the Mosaic law.[86] And Ed Sanders has proposed that in 1:18–2:29 "Paul takes over to an unusual degree homiletical material from Diaspora Judaism, that he alters it in only insubstantial ways, and that consequently the treatment of the law in chapter 2 cannot be harmonized with any of the diverse things which Paul says about the law elsewhere."[87]

Douglas Campbell has set out a more rhetorically-based argument that, while decidedly different from the theses of O'Neill, Räisänen, and Sanders, comes to similar conclusions about the non-Pauline nature of 1:18–3:20. Building on the legitimate insights that in exercising his rhetorical skills (1) "Paul at times displays great argumentative sophistication" and (2) "seems to be something of a master at taking the terminology and/or basic position of some rival

---

83. Lietzmann, *An die Römer,* 39-40; see also 13 and 44.

84. Cf., e.g., Fridrichsen, "Der wahre Jude," 43-44; J. Knox, "Romans" (Introduction and Exegesis), in *Interpreter's Bible,* 9.409, 418-19; Kuss, *Römerbrief,* 1.64-68, 70-71, 90-92; Bornkamm, "Gesetz und Natur," 110; Kähler, "Auslegung von Kap. 2,14-16," 274, 277; Wilckens, *An der Römer,* 1.132-33, 145; Barrett, *Romans,* 50; Harrisville, *Romans,* 43-50; Bruce, *Romans,* 90; Thielman, *From Plight to Solution,* 94-96; and Moo, *Romans,* 155-57, 171-72; see also Fitzmyer, *Spiritual Exercises,* 43, who, with respect to the statement "Jews have had a mode of achieving the status of uprightness or rectitude in God's sight," says "Paul admits this theoretically."

85. See O'Neill, *Romans,* 41-42, 49, 53-54, 264-65.

86. See Räisänen, *Paul and the Law,* 100-107; for a critique of Räisänen, see Cranfield, "Giving a Dog a Bad Name," in his *On Romans,* 99-107.

87. E. P. Sanders, *Paul, the Law, and the Jewish People,* 123.

and turning it inside-out and using it to his own advantage,"[88] Campbell has argued that in 1:18–3:20 Paul uses "an *ad hominem* strategy" in ironic fashion "as a critique of 'another Gospel.'"[89] That ad hominem strategy, as Campbell understands it, "begins by mimicking its opponent" — that is, "by recapitulating the probable *elenchic* [syllogistic refutations] or condemnatory opening of the position that it intends ultimately to undermine" — and then "flushes out" the presuppositions of its opponents by means of "a series of devastating reductions" to demonstrate their impossible conclusions, with "the result of these moves" being "the discrediting of the entire programme, in its own terms."[90] Thus as Campbell understands Paul's purpose in the rhetorical movements of his argument in 1:18–3:20: "The end result of this process of exposure and extrapolation is consequently a thorough discrediting of the entire position. It is a useless and contradictory 'gospel,' on several counts."[91]

By way of introducing his understanding of Paul's rhetorical strategy in 1:18–3:20, Campbell says, "My alternative reading shifts Paul's own commitments within the argument as it unfolds. Essentially, it places him on the other side of the argumentative tensions as they are developed from 1.18 through to 3.20, so the initial voice of the text is not, in my view, Paul's."[92] And in concluding his treatment of Paul's rhetorical strategy, Campbell says with regard to all the statements in 1:18–3:20 (with, of course, the exception of what Paul writes in 2:16, though even that must be read in the context of irony): "They would belong to the gospel of Paul's opponents, the Teachers, hence the attribution of those premises to Paul himself through much of Romans' interpretive history is an unintended irony that, as we have said, he would greatly resent."[93]

Most attempts to understand Romans 2 — other than those of O'Neill, Räisänen, Sanders, and Campbell — have begun with the assumption, whether stated or simply assumed, that everything in Romans 2 represents Paul's teaching, however derived, and therefore try to reconcile what is presented in the chapter with what Paul says elsewhere. For most of those who begin on such a assumption, it has always seemed incredible that Paul would speak about justification without also having the idea of faith in mind. So scholars have usually found it necessary in commenting on Romans 2 either (1) to clarify the nature of the referents beyond what the apostle himself has done or (2) to understand what is said as a hypothetical presentation, which functions rhetorically to prepare for a later discussion.

How, then, should the seemingly non-Pauline statements of Roman 2 —

---

88. D. A. Campbell, *Quest for Paul's Gospel*, 259.

89. *Ibid.*, 246.

90. *Ibid.*

91. *Ibid.*

92. *Ibid.*, 233.

93. *Ibid.*, 261. For a far more extensive exposition of Campbell's thesis, see his later *magnum opus* that is entitled *Deliverance of God: An Apocalyptic Rereading of Justification in Paul* (2009), passim.

and particularly those in vv. 12-16, which constitute our present concern — be understood? It is certainly a question of great concern to every commentator. Yet for pedagogical reasons, it seems best to reserve any detailed discussion of this matter for the exegetical comments on vv. 12-16 that follow.

2:12-13 What Paul writes here builds on the principles that are (1) proclaimed in the aphorism of 2:2 ("God's condemnation of those who do such things is based on truth"), (2) announced in the topic sentence of 2:6 ("God will give to everyone according to what they have done"), (3) set out in antithetic parallel fashion in the confessional material of 2:7-10, which comes to explicit expression in vv. 9-10 ("Both for the Jew first and for the Gentile"), and then are (4) stated in the aphorism of 2:11 ("There is no favoritism with God"). Here in 2:12-13, however, he introduces for the first time in Romans a new feature — that is, a reference to the Mosaic law. And the issue regarding the centrality of the Mosaic law in Paul's discussion from this point on in Romans 2, as well as throughout the rest of the letter, is clearly evident by the fact that in 2:12 the adverb ἀνόμως ("without the law," which obviously refers to the Mosaic law) occurs twice, with the noun νόμος ("law," which also refers to the Mosaic law) appearing throughout 2:12-29 no less than nineteen times.

Commenting on what appears before and what follows 2:12, Kingsley Barrett has aptly observed:

> In the preceding paragraph Paul has reached the conclusion that Jew and Gentile are equal before God. To this statement there is one evident objection. The difference between Jew and Gentile is not simply a matter of race, but of religion, or rather, of revelation. God through Moses gave the law to Israel; this was an advantage the Gentiles never had.[94]

And Barrett goes on to summarize Paul's message in 2:12-13 — first with respect to the Gentiles: "Lack of a revealed law is now seen not to open a way of escape from judgment,"[95] then with respect to the Jews: "The law is not a talisman calculated to preserve those who possess it. It is an instrument of judgement, and sin is not less sin, but more, when it is wrought within the sphere of the law."[96]

Paul here in 2:12-13 seems to be anticipating an objection by the imaginary interlocutor he introduced in 2:1 and spoke against throughout 2:1-5: "But Paul, you have forgotten the advantage of Jews in their possession of the law of Moses, which was given directly by God himself." To this Paul responds that God's impartial judgment applies to all people, whether they possess the Mosaic law or not. For the mere possession of the law counts for nothing, and Jews must realize that the Mosaic law was not given to protect them from God's judgment. So in a rather neat parallelism of structure Paul states:

94. Barrett, *Romans*, 49.
95. *Ibid.*
96. *Ibid.*

12. ὅσοι γὰρ ἀνόμως ἥμαρτον, ἀνόμως καὶ ἀπολοῦται,

All who sin without having the law will also perish without the law,

καὶ ὅσοι ἐν νόμῳ ἥμαρτον, διὰ νόμου κριθήσονται.

and all who sin while possessing the law will be condemned by the law.

13. Οὐ γὰρ οἱ ἀκροαταὶ νόμου δίκαιοι παρὰ τῷ θεῷ,

Because it is not those who hear the law who are righteous in God's sight,

ἀλλ᾽ οἱ ποιηταὶ νόμου δικαιωθήσονται.

but those who obey the law who will be declared righteous.

This structure has sometimes been viewed as chiastic, either alone as a discrete unit of material or in conjunction with the parallel statements of 2:14-15. But while a parallelism of structure appears in 2:12-13 — and can be seen, though less obviously, in the combination of 2:12-13 with 2:14-15 — no movement of thought to a central focus or primary truth can be identified either in 2:12-13 by itself or in the conjunction of 2:12-13 with 2:14-15. So it must be concluded that though there is a discernible pattern of parallel thought in both sets of passages, neither 2:12-13 alone nor in tandem with 2:14-15 can be truly identified as a chiasmus.

The conjunction γάρ ("for," "because") begins each of the two sentences of 2:12 and 2:13. It cannot, however, be claimed that in either sentence it introduces a traditional aphorism or some other quoted material, as it does at the start of 2:11. Rather, in 2:12 it seems to serve as only a transitional particle, moving the argument from one stage to the next (so it is not usually translated), while in 2:13 it functions in an explanatory manner ("because"). These two statements, therefore, have every appearance of being Paul's own statements that (1) repeat his emphasis earlier in the passage on the necessity of actually doing "the good" rather than just knowing what is good, (2) reiterate his insistence regarding God's impartiality in judging sin and sinners, and (3) advance those arguments by bringing into the discussion the question of the Mosaic law — that is, by speaking of the responsibilities of and judgments on both those who are "without the [Mosaic] law" and those who "possess the [Mosaic] law."

The adverb ἀνόμως ("without law," "apart from the law"), which has a history in the Jewish writings of Paul's day,[97] appears twice in 2:12, but these are the only occurrences in the NT. The adjective ἄνομος ("lawless") and its substantival form ὁ ἄνομος ("the lawless"), however, appear rather frequently, not only in the Greek writings of the day and the non-Pauline materials of the NT, but also in Paul's letters[98] — and the cognate phrase χωρὶς νόμου ("without/

97. Cf. 2 Macc 8:17; Philo, *Legum allegoriae* 1.35; Josephus, *Contra Apion* 1.147; 2.151; *Antiquities* 15.59.

98. Cf. 1 Cor 9:21: "to those without the law (τοῖς ἀνόμοις) I became like one without law (ὡς ἄνομος), though not without God's law (μὴ ὢν ἄνομος θεοῦ)"; see also 1 Tim 1:9.

apart from the law") appears in Rom 3:21 (cf. also χωρὶς ἔργων νόμου, "without/apart from the works of the law" in 3:28). The third person plural future indicative passive verb κριθήσονται (from κρίνω) at the close of 2:12, together with the instrumental phrase διὰ νόμου that precedes it, surely connotes "they will be condemned [by God] in accordance with the dictates of the law," as does the first person singular present indicative passive verb κρίνομαι, "I will be condemned," that appears a number of verses later in 3:7.

The third person plural future indicative passive verb δικαιωθήσονται ("they will be declared/made righteous"), which derives from the verb δικαιόω ("to be righteous"), appears here for the first time in Romans and is found thereafter another fourteen times in Romans. Questions regarding the significance of the verb's future tense (Does "they will be" signify a present reality, a future reality, or both?) and its passive mood (Should the verb be understood in the forensic sense "to be declared righteous," in an ethical sense "to be made righteous," or both?) ask too much of Paul's statement here — though they are matters that will certainly be open for discussion later in the letter.[99] Here all that Paul wants to do is to challenge any comfortable understanding, such as was proposed by his imaginary interlocutor of 2:1-5, regarding who is accepted by God and on what basis that reconciliation takes place — hearing God's law, knowing its contents, and approving of its judgments, or obeying and doing God's will.

Theologically the most troubling matter is Paul's statement at the end of 2:13: "those who obey the law will be declared righteous (οἱ ποιηταὶ νόμου δικαιωθήσονται)." Here Paul alludes to traditional Jewish teaching, which contrasts mere knowledge of the law with observance,[100] in order to undermine the smugness of his postulated interlocutor, who assumes that a Jew's mere possession of God's law — without also being obedient to God's law and doing it — guarantees acceptance by God. Further, he echoes Lev 18:5, "You shall keep my decrees and my laws, for the one who obeys them will live" — which is a central verse in the Jewish religion, but one Paul quotes in quite a disparaging manner in Gal 3:12.

What Paul says here, including his favorable echoing of Lev 18:5, seems very different from what he writes elsewhere in Romans and Galatians on the topics of "righteousness," "the Mosaic law," and "doing the law" — and certainly from what he says about Lev 18:5 in Gal 3:12. A number of important factors, however, need always to be taken into account when attempting to understand what Paul says explicitly and by way of allusion here, which material has every appearance of being a direct statement by Paul himself that echoes a number of central OT passages — likewise in trying to understand some of the statements in 2:6-10, 14-15; and 3:25-27, which, as we propose, are best understood as tradi-

---

99. Esp. in the fourth major section of the letter's body middle, i.e., in the hortatory section of 12:1–15:13.

100. Cf. *Str-Bil*, 3.84-88.

tional Jewish and/or Jewish Christian materials that Paul quotes with approval in support of his arguments. At least the following five important considerations need to be taken into account.

First, it is important to note that there is much in Romans 2 that parallels the teaching of James, who was the leader of the Jerusalem Church when Paul wrote Romans, as recorded in the so-called "Epistle of James." This is true with respect to Paul's emphasis on not only knowing what is right and good but also doing what is right and good, which is a prominent theme throughout the confessional material he quotes in 2:6-10 and is stated concisely in the topic sentence of that material in 2:6: "God will give to everyone according to what they have done," vis-à-vis the exhortations of Jas 1:22-27, which begin with "Do not merely listen to the word, and so deceive yourself. Do what it says." It is also true with regard to Paul's emphasis on the impartiality of God's judgment on sin and sinners, which is expressed concisely in the aphorism he quotes in Rom 2:11: "There is no favoritism (προσωπολημψία) with God," vis-à-vis the denunciation of favoritism in Jas 2:1-9, which begins with προσωπολημψία in 2:1 and concludes with the cognate verb προσωπολημπτέω ("show favoritism") in 2:9.

More significant for our purpose in comparing Paul with James, however, is the fact that a close parallel exists between (1) Paul's explicit statement at the end of Rom 2:13, "it is not those who hear the law who are righteous in God's sight, but those who obey the law who will be declared righteous," together with the commendations in v. 7 of doing "good work" (ἔργου ἀγαθοῦ) and in v. 10 of "the good" (τὸ ἀγαθόν) that are drawn from early confessional materials, and (2) James's teaching on the importance of good works in Jas 2:14-26, which reverberates with the Jewish or Jewish Christian aphorism of 2:26: "Faith without works is dead" (ἡ πίστις χωρὶς ἔργων νεκρά ἐστιν; cf. also 2:17: ἡ πίστις, ἐὰν μὴ ἔχῃ ἔργα, νεκρά ἐστιν καθ᾽ ἑαυτήν).

A second important consideration to be taken into account is that the Christians at Rome, having been extensively influenced by the theology, ways of thinking, and religious language of the Jerusalem church, were probably happier with the theology, concerns, and teachings of James as expressed in the "Epistle of James," than they were with those of Paul — at least as they understood Paul's theology, concerns, and teachings from reports they had received about him and his Gentile mission from others. And it is for such a reason, at least in part, that Paul uses their terms and language, as well as their traditional aphorisms and their confessional, devotional, and/or catechetical materials, when writing to them in this first major section of his letter — attempting not only to gain a measure of rapport with his addressees but also to speak meaningfully to them as he seeks to correct them (where necessary) and to highlight areas of agreement between himself and them (where able), and so to lead them further into his own more distinctive presentation of what he calls "my gospel" (cf. 2:16; 16:25) later in his letter, that is, in the theological section of 5:1–8:39 and its corollary ethical section of 12:1–15:13.

A third factor to take into account when seeking to understand Paul's statement and allusions in 2:13 is this: while Paul's emphasis as an evangelist was always on the positive proclamation of the Christian gospel, which has as its content what God has brought about on behalf of all people through the person and work of Christ, he also as a pastor felt quite keenly about the importance of believers in Jesus doing "good works" and "the good." Further, he expected that in the final judgment both he and all those who are God's own people would not only be received into God's heavenly bliss because of Christ's work, as appropriated "by faith," but that they also would be evaluated by God the Father and their Savior Christ Jesus on the basis of their "works" — as he says quite clearly with respect to all Christians in 14:10-12: "For we will all stand before God's judgment seat . . . So then, each of us will give an account of himself or herself to God."[101]

Indeed, Paul was decidedly opposed to either diluting or confusing "the truth of the gospel" by any mixture of "good works" or "works of the law," as his bombastic letter to his own Christian converts in the province of Galatia clearly demonstrates. But he was also just as certainly in favor of his converts doing "good works" and "the good," as his exhortation at the close of the body of that same Galatian letter says quite clearly: "Let us do [ἐργαζώμεθα, a present subjunctive deponent verb] good [the articular τὸ ἀγαθὸν, which in association with the verb ἐργαζώμεθα suggests 'good works'] to all people (πρὸς πάντας), especially to those who belong to the household of faith (πρὸς τοὺς οἰκείους τῆς πίστεως)."[102] And with respect to God's final, eschatological judgment, he declares elsewhere in his letters: "We must all appear before the judgment seat of Christ, that each one may receive what is due him or her for the things done while in the body, whether good or bad,"[103] and "Anyone who does wrong will be repaid for his or her wrong, and there is no favoritism"[104] — just as Jesus taught[105] and as the early Jewish Christians also believed.[106]

A fourth highly significant consideration to keep in mind when seeking to understand what Paul writes at the end of 2:13 and quotes in support throughout Romans 2 is the argument Paul is building in the first half of Romans and the place of ch. 2 in that argument. First Paul establishes the universal guilt of all people, both Jews and Gentiles (1:18–3:20); then he argues for the God-ordained universal solution for the redemption of all people, which is justification by faith in Christ (3:21–4:25); and finally he sets out the nature of the Christian life as being life "in Christ" and "by the Spirit" (5:1–8:38). Paul's purpose in ch. 2 is not to expound on the human criterion for salvation. That he will do later in 3:21ff., where that criterion is clearly spelled out as faith in Christ. Here in 2:12-13 Paul's aim is simply to demonstrate to his Christian addressees that God's impartiality (so the aphorism quoted in 2:11, "There is no favoritism with

---

101. See also 1 Cor 3:12-15; 4:4-5; 2 Cor 5:10; Gal 6:7-9; Eph 6:8; 1 Tim 5:24-25.
102. Gal 6:10.
103. 2 Cor 5:10.
104. Col 3:25.
105. Cf. Matt 16:27.
106. Cf. esp. 1 Pet 1:17; Rev 2:23; 20:12; 22:12.

God") rules out any claim on the part of Jews or Jewish Christians that they are privileged and protected by God simply because they possess and know God's law as given through Moses.

The "problem passages" of Romans 2 must be understood in the context of the entire argument in 1:18–3:20. Clearly universal guilt and divine impartiality are Paul's central concerns in ch. 2. He seems, in fact, not even to have considered the difficulty that these passages might create when taken out of their immediate context, dealt with abstractly, and compared with other Christian teachings (as well as with the teachings of the better rabbis of Judaism) on the topic of justification by faith. Further, he appears not to have had any desire to bring into his presentation the topics of faith and salvation from a Christian perspective, evidently desiring to reserve these discussions until he moves from this section on "the wrath of God revealed" (1:18–3:20) to the following section on "the righteousness of God revealed" (3:21–4:25). He speaks as he does in ch. 2 (1) in order to gain rapport with his Christian addressees at Rome, who themselves evidently used such teaching, as drawn from Jewish and Jewish Christian sources, in their own worship, proclamation, and instruction, and (2) because these passages served, when rightly understood, to support and enforce the points he wanted to make in this section of his letter: that God judges people on the basis of what they do, not just what they possess and know, and that God judges people impartially, not according to any special privilege of race, religion, or circumstance.

A further question remains to be asked, and so a fifth factor remains to be taken into consideration when attempting to understand Paul's statement that "those who do the law will be declared righteous" and his favorable allusions to various OT passages (particularly Lev 18:5) about "doing" the law in Rom 2:13. The question is: Did Paul himself view the Mosaic law as, in any sense, a means of becoming righteous or being justified by God? Douglas Moo has set the question in its proper context and stated it appropriately in general terms as follows:

> The view that God gave the law to Israel as a means of justification is now generally discredited, and rightly so. The OT presents the law as a means of regulating the covenant relationship that had already been established through God's grace. But, granted that the law was not given for the purpose of securing one's relationship before God, it may still be questioned whether it sets forth *in theory* a means of justification.[107]

And Moo answers that question regarding "whether in theory" with the following brief response: "We would argue that it does."[108]

---

107. Moo, *Romans,* 155 (italics mine).

108. *Ibid.,* citing Westerholm, *Israel's Law and the Church's Faith,* 145-46, and R. T. Beckwith, "The Unity and Diversity of God's Covenant," *TB* 38 (1987) 112-13, as two recent interpreters with whom he agrees.

In large measure, that is the question I have attempted to answer in many of my own writings, particularly my 1964 monograph *Paul, Apostle of Liberty* (second edition, 2015) and my 1990 commentary on *Galatians*. In those works I proposed that in order to understand Paul's teaching properly a distinction needs to be made between (1) the term *legalism* — that is, the endeavor to "keep," "be obedient to," or "do" the Mosaic law in order to gain righteousness or status before God, and (2) what I called *nomism* — that is, to "keep," "be obedient to," or "do" the Mosaic law as a response to God's loving-kindness, mercy, and grace in bringing people to himself and establishing a covenant relationship with them. These two terms, "legalism" and "nomism," while seemingly similar in many respects, actually connote two quite different understandings of the religious life of people as expressed within both Judaism and Christianity. Much could be said in explication and defense of this thesis (as I attempted to do in my earlier writings). Suffice it only to highlight in what follows the various ways of interpreting God's command to Israel in Lev 18:5, "You shall keep my decrees and my laws, for the one who obeys them will live" — which is a command of God, with a stated promise, that comprises the central teaching of Judaism, and one that Paul echoes with seeming approval here in Rom 2:13 but quotes in quite a disparaging manner in Gal 3:12.

Lev 18:5 was interpreted by Jews and by Christians in a variety of ways. The Hebrew word חיה ("live") was translated by the translators of the Greek LXX as ζήσεται ἐν αὐτοῖς ("he shall live by them"), which suggests living life in the present time under the guidance of God's decrees and laws. But the translators of the Aramaic Targums, which arose out of the readings of Holy Scripture in the early synagogues of Palestine, seem to have understood this passage as having reference to life in "the age to come" and so as being the reward of obedience to the Torah: "You shall keep my decrees and my laws, which if a man does he shall live by them an everlasting life" *(Targum Onqelos)*, or "You shall keep my decrees and my laws, and the order of my judgments, which if a man does he shall live by them in the life of eternity, and his position shall be with the just" *(Targum Ps-Jonathan)*.

But more important for our purposes here is the concept of "doing the law" (LXX: ποιήσετε αὐτά, "you shall do them"). For among Jewish "legalists" it was viewed as obedience to the requirements of the Mosaic law "in order to" become righteous and gain status before God, whereas among Jewish "nomists" it was understood as obeying the law's requirements "because of" having experienced God's loving-kindness, mercy, and grace and "in response to" God having established a covenant relationship with them.

The Judaizers who came to Paul's churches in Galatia, whom Paul saw as proclaiming an entirely different gospel than the Christian gospel, were probably, at least in their own eyes, pious nomistic Jewish believers in Jesus — but in their insistence on the theological necessity of a nomistic lifestyle for Gentile Christians, they were, at least in Paul's eyes, actually preaching a legalistic religion with only a facade of Christian teaching. And the Christians at Rome, both Gentile and Jewish believers in Jesus, may very well have been advocates of a form of nomistic Christianity, simply because of their background in and admiration for a Jewish Christian understanding of the Christian faith, as had been mediated to them through efforts from the mother church at Jerusalem.

For Paul, however, the promise of Lev 18:5 of gaining life by "obeying" or "doing" the requirements of the law has been nullified — not because of the inability of the law itself, but because of the inability of sinful people to "obey" or "do" it. So Paul declares in Rom 8:3-4:

> For what the law was powerless to do in that it was weakened by the sinful nature (διὰ τῆς σαρκός), God did by sending his own Son in the likeness of sinful humanity (ἐν ὁμοιώματι σαρκὸς ἁμαρτίας), and as a sin offering (περὶ ἁμαρτίας) he condemned sin in sinful humanity (ἐν τῇ σαρκί), in order that the righteous requirements of the law might be fulfilled in us, who do not live according to the sinful nature (κατὰ σάρκα) but according to the Spirit (κατὰ πνεῦμα).

Thus in Gal 3:10-14, when lining up passages that speak of "promise" and "life" vis-à-vis passages that speak of "curse" and "death," Paul lists Lev 18:5 not among the passages that speak of promise and life but among those that have to do with judgment, curse, and death.

It was not because the promise of life contained in the law was given only as a hypothetical possibility, but because the law's promise could not be attained because of humanity's sinfulness and inability. The Mosaic law was, in one important respect, a "system of righteousness." But that system never came to fruition because of the inability of sinful people to obey and do it. So Paul proclaims in Rom 10:4 that "Christ is the end (τέλος) of the law with respect to righteousness (εἰς δικαιοσύνην) for everyone who believes (παντὶ τῷ πιστεύοντι)."

Yet while the Mosaic law as a religious system was ineffective because of people's inability and sin, God's law as the "standard of righteousness and judgment" — or as C. H. Dodd has aptly called it, God's "standard of repentance"[109] — continues in full effect. So Paul speaks of God's law, as given preeminently in the law of Moses, as God's standard of righteousness and judgment — and so humanity's standard of repentance — that reveals sin and judges all who sin. For the law in this primary sense of "standard" has never been abrogated, but continues as God's standard for all human attitudes and actions — including all the attitudes and actions of believers in Jesus.

In his own inimitable, yet perceptive, fashion, Martin Luther best captured Paul's intent in Romans 2: "All the Scriptures of God are divided into two parts: commands and promises — the former being 'God's strange work' to bring us down; the latter 'God's proper work' to raise us up."[110] The contrast

109. Cf. C. H. Dodd, *Gospel and Law,* passim.
110. M. Luther, "A Treatise on Christian Liberty," in *Works of Martin Luther,* 2.317.

between what Paul says and alludes to here in 2:13 (as well as what he quotes by way of support in 2:6-10, 11, 14-15 and 25-27), on the one hand, and what he proclaims in 3:21–4:25 (as well as elsewhere throughout the rest of the letter), on the other hand, represents what Luther identified as the "two parts" of God's redemptive dealing with his people: "commands and promises."

Somewhat similarly, though much more colloquially, commentators have sometimes distinguished between "the work of God's left hand" (the *opus alienum*) and "the work of God's right hand" (the *opus proprium*). Thus, in line with Luther's rubric, it needs to be noted that (1) when Paul speaks of the teachings of God's law (as in 1:18–3:20), and especially when he speaks about "the commands" of the law to those who have been extensively influenced by the theology and language of Jewish Christianity (as he does here in 2:1–3:20), he does so in terms of what the Mosaic law itself says and of how his addressees needed to understand it — that is, in terms of the requirement to "do" the law and the universal reality of coming under the law's condemnation because of people's sin and inabilities. But (2) when he speaks of the Christian gospel (as he does in 3:21ff.), he begins by announcing that it is "apart from the law," yet a gospel "to which the law and the prophets testify" — with his proclamation, both theologically and ethically, being primarily in terms of the content of the gospel itself (as in 5:1–8:39 and 12:1–15:13).

2:14-15 Because of their content and style, these two verses, as we have suggested above, are probably to be understood as a portion of traditional Jewish and/or Jewish Christian teaching that Paul used in support of his statements and allusions in 2:12-13, along with all that he incorporated into his argument from traditional sources in 2:1-11. These verses are introduced by the introductory use of the conjunction γάρ ("for"), as was the aphorism quoted in 2:11. And they incorporate some fairly significant *hapax legomena* (i.e., once-spoken or differently used words) and some rather different syntax, as did the confessional material quoted in 2:6-10.

The material of these verses, however, is hardly hymnic. Nor are there any strophes evident. Further, the language, syntax, and structure of these verses are somewhat strange and a bit awkward. Nevertheless, what is presented in 2:14-15 can be set out in the form of a very rough parallelism, as follows:

14. ὅταν [γὰρ] ἔθνη τὰ μὴ νόμον ἔχοντα,
Whenever Gentiles, who do not have the law,
φύσει τὰ τοῦ νόμου ποιῶσιν
do by nature the things required by the law,
οὗτοι νόμον μή ἔχοντες
even though they do not have the law,
ἑαυτοῖς εἰσιν νόμος
they are a law for themselves,
15. οἵτινες ἐνδείκνυνται τὸ ἔργον τοῦ νόμου
since they show that the work of the law

γραπτὸν ἐν ταῖς καρδίαις αὐτῶν,
is written in their hearts,
συμμαρτυρούσης αὐτῶν τῆς συνειδήσεως
their consciences joining in bearing witness
καὶ μεταξὺ ἀλλήλων τῶν λογισμῶν κατηγορούντων ἢ καὶ
ἀπολογουμένων.
and their thoughts within them now accusing, now even
excusing them.

The initial temporal particle ὅταν ("whenever") serves to highlight the conditional nature of what follows — that is, that what follows is to be taken as an illustrative possibility, perhaps only for the sake of argument.[111] It then speaks of ἔθνη ("Gentiles") and refers to them in a sustained fashion throughout vv. 14-15. Here at the beginning of 2:14, however, ἔθνη appears without an article, which suggests that "Gentiles" is to be understood in a generic, non-specific sense.

Such a non-articular, generic reference to Gentiles can be paralleled by a Jewish tradition recorded in the Talmud stemming from the Tannaitic period of rabbinic Judaism, that (1) highlights the fact that the generic Hebrew word "man" (אדם), rather than the more usual articular form "the man" (האדם), appears in Lev 18:5 ("You shall keep my decrees and my laws, for 'a man' [MT אדם, LXX ἄνθρωπος] who obeys them will live"), and (2) draws from this observation the conclusion that even a Gentile — since a generic use of "man" would include all humanity — may be regarded in God's sight as a high priest if he observes the law. Thus Rabbi Meir (a second-generation Tanna) is credited in b. Sanhedrin 59a as saying:

> Whence do we know that even a Gentile who studies the Torah is as a High Priest? From the verse "[You shall, therefore, keep my statutes and my judgments,] which if a man does, he shall live in them" [Lev 18:5]. Priests, Levites, and Israelites are not mentioned, but "men"; hence you may learn that even a Gentile who studies the Torah is as a High Priest.[112]

Paul's phrase τὰ μὴ νόμον ἔξοντα ("those not having the law") makes explicit the status of the Gentiles as being without the Mosaic law, as stated earlier in 2:12a — with that same phrase repeated, evidently for emphasis, in the midst of what follows in 2:14b: οὗτοι νόμον μὴ ἔχοντες ("those not having the law"). The somewhat broken statement in 2:14b, that whenever the Gentiles φύσει τὰ τοῦ νόμου ποιῶσιν . . . ἑαυτοῖς εἰσιν νόμος ("do by nature the things

---

111. Cf. 4 Ezra 3:36 with reference to non-Jewish people and other nations: "You may, indeed, find individual men who have kept your commandments, but nations you will not find."

112. Cf. also b. Baba Qam. 38a; Midr. Ps. 1:18; Num. Rab. 13:15-16, where the same tradition appears.

of [or 'required by'] the law . . . they are a law for themselves"), serves, as Paul Achtemeier has rightly noted,

> not to commend the Gentiles but to censure the Jews. The point is not that the Gentiles are superior because they know naturally what the Jews could know only by revelation. The point is that the Jews cannot boast simply because they *possess* the law.[113]

Similarly, Joseph Fitzmyer says of Paul's use of this statement:

> Paul does not want to speak of the pagan's fulfillment of the law as such; he uses such pagan fulfillment to show that the Jew's trust in the law is not well based. . . . To counteract the confidence of the Jew who has the law, Paul uses the pagan who does not have it, yet who sometimes does by nature what the law requires. Thus Paul's argument depends on the contrast of the knowledge of the law and the observance of it.[114]

A rather serious interpretive problem, however, arises in 2:14a with respect to the use of the dative singular noun φύσει ("by nature"). Some view it as modifying what precedes it, the noun "Gentiles," yielding "Gentiles by nature," thereby understanding the expression to mean that Gentiles lack the law by virtue of their birth.[115] The major exegetical support for the former view is that in the nine other places where the noun φύσις ("nature") is used in the Pauline corpus in the dative or the nominative or with a preposition, it "is used in the overwhelming number of cases in an adjectival rather than an adverbial sense"[116] — as in Rom 1:26-27; 2:27; 11:21, 24; 1 Cor 11:14; Gal 2:15; 4:8; and Eph 2:3. Others understand φύσει ("by nature") as modifying what follows, that is, as an adverb modifying the verb "do," and so read "whenever Gentiles, who do not have the law, do by nature the things of the law."[117]

This latter adverbial understanding is most likely correct. For if Paul had meant φύσει to be understood adjectivally, he could better have placed it within the participial phrase τὰ μὴ νόμον ἔχοντα (probably best between νόμον and ἔχοντα). Further, it needs to be noted that an adjectival understanding of φύσει here makes for a rather odd sentence, since to add that it was "by birth" that Gentiles do not have the law sets up another redundancy in a verse that is already encumbered by the redundant use of τὰ μὴ νόμον ἔξοντα ("the ones not having the law") and οὗτοι νόμον μὴ ἔχοντες ("those not having the law") —

---

113. Achtemeier, "'Some Things in Them Hard to Understand,'" 258.

114. Fitzmyer, *Romans*, 307.

115. So, e.g., Achtemeier, "'Some Things in Them Hard to Understand,'" 255-59; idem, *Romans*, 45; Cranfield, *Romans* 1.156-57.

116. Achtemeier, "'Some Things in Them Hard to Understand,'" 258.

117. So, e.g., Leenhardt, *Romans*, 81; Bassler, *Divine Impartiality*, 142-43; Dunn, *Romans*, 98; Fitzmyer, *Romans*, 310.

which may be understood as being for the sake of emphasis, but one redundancy does not require or validate a second. The syntax and balance of the sentence, therefore, suggest that φύσει ("by nature") should be understood as an adverb and taken with what follows. In addition, it may also be observed that if Paul is quoting earlier Jewish and/or Jewish Christian material in 2:14-15 (as we have proposed), the use of φύσει in that quoted material need not necessarily conform to his own use of the word elsewhere.

Many have viewed the appearance of the noun φύσις here in 2:14a, along with statements about God's revelation of himself in creation in 1:19-20, as indicating that Paul accepted some type of "natural theology," and so have argued for "natural law" and "natural morality" as being basic components of Paul's thought. It is impossible to deal here with the subject in detail. Suffice it to say that the natural theology that was posited during the "Enlightenment" of the eighteenth century, which substituted a religion of human reason for Christian revelation, is certainly not what Paul was espousing. But neither does Paul say that God can be known only from the Scriptures or only by an encounter with the risen Christ. In 1:19-20 he states that the material creation "makes evident (φανερόν) what can be known about God." And in 2:14 the sense is that some Gentiles, "even though they do not have the Mosaic law," still respond in obedience to certain precepts of God's law *instinctively,* that is, by the natural order of things, without being in possession of any special revelation. "What Paul may say in these passages about natural theology or natural morality," as Joseph Fitzmyer rightly points out, "is certainly not a complete treatise on these matters; yet one has to respect the snippets of such teaching that are really there."[118]

The words τὰ τοῦ νόμου ποιῶσιν ("they do the things of [or 'required by'] the law") are, in their context, to be understood in terms of Gentiles "doing" *some* of the law's commands, not all that the Mosaic law prescribes. Those interpreters who identify ἔθνη here in 2:14 as *Christian* Gentiles speak of the statement "they do the things of [or 'required by'] the law" as referring to a complete obedience to the whole Mosaic law that only a Spirit-filled believer in Jesus is able to achieve — as did, for example, Augustine in the fifth century[119] and Martin Luther in the sixteenth century.[120] Others have suggested that νόμος here probably refers not to the Mosaic law, but to a Stoic understanding of "natural law."[121] Both of these interpretations, however, are impossible to hold, since they nullify the essence of Paul's argument that obedient Gentiles shame disobedient Jews. That argument requires that the same premise and the same

118. Fitzmyer, *Romans,* 274; cf. also Lillie, "Natural Law and the New Testament," 12-23; A. F. Johnson, "Is There a Biblical Warrant for Natural-Law Theories?" 185-99.

119. See Augustine, *De spiritu et littera* 26.43–28.49 (*CSEL* 60.196-204); *Contra Iulianum* 4.3.25 (*PL* 44.750).

120. See M. Luther, "Lectures on Romans: Glosses and Scholia," in *Luther's Works* 25.185; also K. Barth, *Romans,* on 2:14, and Cranfield, *Romans,* 1.156 in the twentieth century.

121. So, e.g., Black, *Romans* 57.

type of response be in view — that is, (1) the premise of a pre-Christian revelation of God, however given (whether by "revelation in creation" alone or by "revelation in creation" and "the law of Moses"), and (2) the same type of response to God and his will, based respectively on a "revelation in creation" that all humans have been given and the further revelation in the Mosaic law that Jews have received.

The statement ἑαυτοῖς εἰσιν νόμος ("they are a law for themselves") is a statement that has deep roots in the religious philosophies of Paul's day. Fitzmyer cites some of the more prominent Greek, Roman, and Jewish religious philosophers of that day and their statements:

> The Stoic Chrysippus [c. 280-207 BC] in Plutarch, *De stoicorum repugnantiis* 9.1035C: "It is not possible to find any other beginning or source of justice *(dikaiosynē)* than from Zeus and universal nature *(ek tēs koinēs physeōs)*." Cicero [106-43 BC], *De legibus* 1.6.18: "Law is the highest reason implanted in Nature, which commands what ought to be done and forbids the contrary. This reason, when firmly fixed and perfected in the human mind, is Law." Cf. Philo [c. 30 BC-AD 45], who also attests such philosophical thinking, *De Abr.* 46.276: *nomos autos ōn kai thesmos agraphos,* "[the Sage], being himself a law and an unwritten statute"; *Quod omnis probus liber* 7.46: "Right reason is an infallible law engraved not by this mortal or that, and thus perishable, nor on lifeless scrolls or stelae, and thus lifeless, but by immortal nature on the immortal mind"; *De Josepho* 6.29: "This world, the Megalopolis, has one polity and one law, and this is the word of nature, dictating what must be done and forbidding what must not be done." Cf. *1 Enoch* 2:1-5.[122]

The dative plural reflexive pronoun ἑαυτοῖς in the phrase ἑαυτοῖς εἰσιν νόμος ("they are a law for themselves") is not to be taken as "to themselves," as though whatever Gentiles may do becomes the norm for their lives. Rather, it should be understood as "for themselves" in the sense that, as Ernst Käsemann has expressed it, Gentiles "experience the transcendental claim of the divine will," which comes to them "from outside" — and yet, "paradoxically," which they experience "in their inner beings."[123]

2:15 Οἵτινες ἐνδείκνυνται τὸ ἔργον τοῦ νόμου γραπτὸν ἐν ταῖς καρδίαις αὐτῶν ("since they show that the work of the law is written in their hearts"). The statement of 2:15 concludes the portion of traditional Jewish and/or Jewish Christian teaching that Paul quotes in 2:14-15. It is given in support of the statements and allusions in 2:12-13 (as well as in support of all that Paul has incorporated into his argument from traditional sources in 2:1-11). More immediately, it supports and clarifies the final statement of 2:14b, which speaks of Gentiles being "a law for themselves." It does this by proposing that the actions

122. Fitzmyer, *Romans,* 310-11.
123. Käsemann, *Romans,* 64.

of some Gentiles provide evidence that the "work [or 'requirements'] of the law" (τὸ ἔργον τοῦ νόμου) is/are "written on their hearts" (γραπτὸν ἐν ταῖς καρδίαις αὐτῶν).

This first part of Rom 2:15 is similar to the words directed to God in *4 Ezra* 3:36, which, while acknowledging that there are no Gentile nations that keep God's commandments, yet state: "You [God] may, indeed, find individual men [Gentiles] who have kept your commandments." Such statements about Gentiles are quite different from the litany of indictments leveled in Rom 1:18-32, which seem to have been drawn by Paul from the language of Wis 13–14. But neither 1:18-32 nor 2:14-15 speak about all people — certainly not about all Jews, and just as certainly not about all Gentiles. Further, it should be acknowledged that if Paul depends extensively in 1:18-32 on Wis 13–14, which denounces the pagan Gentile world, and then quotes in 2:14-15 a portion of traditional Jewish or Jewish Christian material that speaks favorably about some Gentiles, we need not try to reconcile these two source materials that he uses. All we need to recognize is that Paul considers each of these materials, in its own way and for its own purpose, to contain some truth that he wants to highlight — and, further, that he selects from each of them what suits his purpose in making his respective points, first in 1:18-32 and then in 2:12-16.

Additional support and clarification of the statement "they are a law for themselves," which appears at the end of 2:14, is expressed in two comments in the latter part of 2:15: (1) "their consciences joining in bearing witness" (συμμαρτυρούσης αὐτῶν τῆς συνειδήσεως) and (2) "their thoughts within themselves now accusing, now even excusing them" (μεταξὺ ἀλλήλων τῶν λογισμῶν κατηγορούντων ἢ καὶ ἀπολογουμένων). The first comment highlights the existence of the human συνείδησις ("conscience"), which it assumes is a part of every person's "inner being" and proposes that this functional feature in the lives of all people has a part to play in what they know in their hearts to be right or wrong. The second comment, though expressed in somewhat tortuous Greek syntax, argues that this witness of the human conscience is evident by the fact that people struggle "within themselves," that is, in their "inner being," regarding what is right and wrong, and so evidence by that struggle that their consciences are at work in either accusing or excusing their actions.

A number of lexical and exegetical matters need to be at least noticed in 2:15, though each of them would require a monograph to explicate fully. First, it should be observed that the phrase τὸ ἔργον τοῦ νόμου ("the work ['requirements'] of the law"), appears in the singular and is used positively, whereas Paul usually uses the plural τὰ ἔργα τοῦ νόμου ("the works of the law"), in a pejorative sense.[124] Second, the law is spoken of 2:15a is γραπτὸν ἐν ταῖς καρδίαις αὐτῶν ("written on their hearts"). Many commentators have drawn attention to God's promise of a new covenant with his people in Jer

---

124. Cf. the plural, pejorative use of the phrase just a chapter later in 3:20 and 28; see also Gal 2:16 (three times), 3:2, 5, 10.

31:31-34 ("I will put my law within them, and I will write it on their hearts")[125] and have suggested that these words of Jer 31:33 are what Paul has in mind here — thereby supporting the view that the Gentiles of 2:14-15 are *Christian* Gentiles. Ernst Käsemann, however, is undoubtedly right to question such a collation of passages, for what the Gentiles share with the Jews is not a written law that becomes an internal law; rather, "They [the Gentiles] have an analogue to the γραφή [the Scriptures] and are accountable to this as the Jews are to the Torah received by them."[126]

Third, it needs to be noted that there appears in 2:15b the Greek philosophical notion of a συνείδησις ("conscience"), which term was used in the ancient world as the designation for the capacity of the human mind to judge, usually in retrospect, one's own actions whether right or wrong — sometimes even to judge the rightness or wrongness of one's own future actions, though that nuance of the human conscience as a positive guide never appears in the NT. A fourth matter to note is that the prepositional phrase μεταξὺ ἀλλήλων (literally "between one another") is extremely difficult to interpret. Some have quite literally translated it "in their dealings with one another," and so have understood it as referring to the criticism or defense of the actions of others.[127] It is probably best, however, to understand the phrase as referring to the inner debate that goes on within the conscience of a person — that is, "within themselves," especially here within Gentiles — regarding right and wrong in their own conduct. Also to be noted in 2:14-15 is the fact that the structure, language, and syntax of these two verses (as pointed out at various places in the discussion above) seem rather convoluted — and increasingly so as the passage develops — with at least one redundancy, two or three *hapax legomena* of expression and usage, and rather difficult syntax, especially in the latter half of 2:15.

All these lexical and exegetical features could be dealt with more extensively, but they are of such a nature that each treatment would take much more space than is available here. Suffice it here to say that all these matters together tend to suggest that what appears here in 2:14-15 is material that Paul quotes from traditional Jewish and/or Jewish Christian sources in support of his own statements in 2:12-13.

2:16 The textual history of 2:16 suggests that this verse is best viewed as beginning with the words ἐν ἡμέρᾳ ὅτε, "in/on the day when" (see the "Textual Notes" above). Thus this verse is best understood as directly connected with what comes before, either (1) with what has been said in 2:15b, (2) with what has been said in 2:14-15, or, perhaps, reaching even further back, (3) with all that has been said in 2:12-15. Yet there is a real problem in connecting 2:16 with what is said in the verse or verses before it — a problem with which every commentator since Origen has struggled. Jouette Bassler states the problem concisely: "Since

---

125. Cf. also Isa 51:1, "You people who have my law in your hearts."
126. Käsemann, *Romans,* 64.
127. So, e.g., Sanday and Headlam, *Romans,* 61; Lyonnet, *Romains,* 74.

the eschatological tenor of this verse [i.e., 2:16] is unmistakable, a problem arises concerning the logical connection between this reference to the final judgment and the participial phrases of v. 15b, which seem to describe instead the present ongoing activity of the inner conscience."[128]

A myriad of solutions have been proposed.

> One is that God's judgment referred to in 2:16 should probably not be understood as his final, eschatological day of judgment, but rather as a present, earthly day of encounter with the word of God[129] or as the day of one's conversion.[130]
>
> A second proposal is that the material of 2:14-15 was originally a marginal gloss in some ancient manuscript that a later scribe incorporated into the text.[131]
>
> A third view is that when Paul addressed Jewish audiences, he likely used the bulk of the material that now appears in Rom 2 — which original sermonic material probably had his final statement of v. 16 following immediately after his statements of vv. 12-13 — but that when he wrote to the Christians at Rome and used that earlier material he "inserted verses 14-15 parenthetically" in a letter "meant for Gentile as well as Jewish readers."[132]
>
> A fourth position is that, while 2:14-15 may be considered too long for a parenthesis by Paul, 2:15b, which speaks about the human conscience and conflicting human thoughts, should probably be seen as parenthetical material inserted by Paul, with the primary flow of the apostle's logic moving from 2:15a to 2:16.[133]
>
> A fifth understanding is that 2:16 is a marginal gloss that has somehow found its way into the text.[134]
>
> A sixth proposal is to delete the noun ἡμέρᾳ ("day") and connect the phrase ἐν ᾗ ("in the") preceding it in 2:16 with the noun συνείδησις ("conscience") in 2:15b, thereby reading "their consciences bearing witness when God judges everyone's secrets."[135]
>
> A seventh suggestion is that 2:14-16 is best understood as "a polemic against Jewish claims of an eschatological advantage" in God's judgment of people, with 2:14-15a speaking about the impartiality of God's

---

128. Bassler, *Divine Impartiality*, 147.

129. So Weber, *Beziehungen von Röm 1-3*, 142ff.

130. So Reicke, "Natürliche Theologie nach Paulus," 161.

131. So J. Weiss, "Beitrage zur Paulinischen Rhetorik," 218.

132. So C. H. Dodd, *Romans*, 35.

133. So Mundle, "Zur Auslegung von Röm 2,13ff.," 255.

134. So Bultmann, "Glossen im Römerbrief," 200-201, 282-84; also Käsemann, *Romans*, 67, though with some reservations.

135. So H. Sahlin, "Einige Testemendationen zum Römerbrief," 93, building on the reading of Codex B (see "Textual Notes").

present judgment and 2:15b-16 speaking about the impartiality of God's future judgment.[136]

And an eighth view is that the third person plural present indicative active verb ἐνδείκνυνται ("they show") of 2:15a, like the third person singular future indicative active verb κρινεῖ ("he will judge," whose final syllable is best accented with a circumflex accent) of 2:16, should be understood futuristically ("they will show"), so that both 2:15 and 2:16 refer to a future judgment of God through Christ Jesus.[137]

Theories that propose an emendation of the text have, indeed, been rampant (as noted above). Yet "the MS tradition," as Joseph Fitzmyer points out, "is constant, save for the order of the words *hê hêmera* (MS B) or *hêmera hê* (MS A)."[138] Likewise, there have been a number of proposed interpretive solutions that, while not emending the text, have often been seen as forcing the text to read in an unnatural manner (as also noted above). So most commentators have tended (1) to treat 2:14-15 as simply a Pauline parenthesis between 2:13 and 2:16, (2) to take the logical flow of Paul's argument as being from the end of 2:13 ("they will be declared righteous") to the beginning of 2:16 ("on the day when God will judge"), and sometimes (3) to suggest that some sort of transitional phrase needs to be supplied at the start of 2:16, such as "and they will be justified," "all this will be made plain," or "this will take place."[139]

A better solution to the logical dislocation within 2:12-16 is, we believe (and have argued above), to understand 2:14-15 as catechetical material brought together earlier in a Jewish and/or Jewish Christian milieu and used by Paul here to support his statements in 2:12-13. The presence of different terms and usages, awkward syntax, and varied nuances (as noted above) seems to suggest that Paul was not the author of the material in 2:14-15. But he evidently (1) approved of the content of the material, at least its major theological thrusts if not all of its wording, and (2) used it to his own advantage in speaking to his Christian addressees at Rome — introducing it with the conjunction γάρ ("for"), as he did in 2:11 when citing a traditional aphorism that seems to have had a similar conceptual and compositional background.

The statement κρίνει ὁ θεὸς τὰ κρυπτὰ τῶν ἀνθρώπων κατὰ τὸ εὐαγγέλλιόν μου διὰ Χριστοῦ Ἰησοῦ ("God will judge everyone's secrets through Christ Jesus, as my gospel declares") is logically connected with what Paul has declared in 2:12-13. Further, it completes his final statement of 2:13, thereby stating in the logical connection of these two verses that "those who obey the law (are the ones) who will be declared righteous. . . on the day when God will judge everyone's secrets through Christ Jesus." But with the interjection of the

---

136. So Bassler, *Divine Impartiality,* 148, citing in support N. A. Dahl, "Paulus som föresprackare," *STK* 18 (1942) 174.

137. So such various scholars as H. Lietzmann, H. W. Schmidt, and H. N. Ridderbos.

138. Fitzmyer, *Romans,* 312 (see "Textual Notes").

139. So, e.g., NIV: "This will take place."

traditional material in 2:14-15, which speaks of righteous Gentiles "who do not have the law" doing "by nature the things required by the law" and so being included among "those who obey the law," the connection between 2:13 and 2:16 became linguistically somewhat obscured. Nonetheless, the flow of Paul's argument, apart from this interjected material, is still evident. So it is probably best in any English translation to signal that logical continuity of 2:16 with the statements of 2:12-13 by the use of some such expression as "this will take place" at the beginning of 2:16 (as does the NIV).

Going beyond, however, these rather formal matters of structural and linguistic connections, three significant matters pertaining to Paul's own theology stand out in 2:16 — two stated quite explicitly, the third rather obviously implied. First, although the high point of his proclamation of the Christian gospel is reached in ch. 8 (esp. in 8:1-17, where he speaks of the Christian as being "in Christ," "in the Spirit," and "led by the Spirit," but also throughout the whole of the chapter building to his triumphant outburst of defiant praise in 8:31-39), Paul still retains an emphasis on a future, universal judgment of all people. His message as a Christian evangelist is no longer that of "futuristic eschatology," as it was formerly as an adherent of Judaism; but neither is it simply "realized eschatology," with everything now fulfilled in a spiritual fashion in the Christian life. Rather, as Oscar Cullmann has rightly argued, Paul's proclamation of the gospel is best characterized as "inaugurated eschatology," which (1) begins with what Christ has effected on behalf of the salvation of all people, with the believer's present experience described as that of being "in Christ" and "in the Spirit," (2) culminates with Christ's return and judgment of all people, with the believer's future experience depicted as being forever "with Christ," and (3) visualizes the Christian life as lived between these two realities of what Christ has effected and what Christ will yet bring about.[140] In such a scenario, both being now "in Christ" and awaiting a future time of judgment are kept in constant tension as the two focuses of a Christian understanding of God's "salvation history" — with, then, the mandate for every Christian being to live out progressively that understanding in one's own life and society.

A second matter highlighted in 2:16 is that this final judgment of all people will be carried out not just by God, as was the standard Jewish understanding, but specifically by Christ Jesus. Various nonconformist Jews of Paul's day had speculated about God's use of some heavenly representative to serve as the eschatological judge of all humanity — as, for example, the "elect one,"[141] Melchizedek,[142] or Abel.[143] The earliest Jewish believers in Jesus, however, proclaimed that "he ('Jesus of Nazareth') is the one ordained by God as judge of the

---

140. Or, to use O. Cullmann's terminology in his *Christ and Time,* between the decisive event of "D Day" and the final victory of "V Day."

141. Cf. *1 En* 37–71, esp 45:3-6; perhaps Enoch himself.

142. Cf. the eighteen lines of 11QMelch.

143. Cf. *T Ab* 13:5.

living and the dead."[144] And that is what Paul also stated in 2 Cor 5:10 when he spoke of "the judgment seat of Christ" — as well as what Jesus taught[145] and the early Jewish Christians affirmed in what they wrote.[146] Specifically Christian language breaks through in this first major section of the body middle of Romans in 2:16 for the first time since 1:16-17 — though Paul does not elaborate here on his reference to Christ Jesus, but reserves all further christological discussion for later in his letter.

A third matter is implicitly highlighted in 2:16 by the reference to "the day when God will judge everyone's secrets": for Paul there was no contradiction between (1) being justified "by faith" through the work of Christ, and (2) being judged by God "through Christ Jesus" on the final day of judgment. In Pauline terminology, this final judgment will be based on "the things done while in the body, whether good or bad"[147] — though Jewish Christians seem to have preferred to speak of this final judgment using the expressions "by works" or "by what a person has done,"[148] which terminology Paul uses as well here when interacting with the Christians of Rome, who have been extensively influenced by Jewish Christianity.[149] As Paul proclaims here in Rom 2, this final, eschatological judgment of all people will be a judgment (1) "based on truth" (so v. 2), (2) that takes into account what people have done and not done, and not just on what they have affirmed (so vv. 3-10), (3) expressed without favoritism or partiality (so vv. 11-15), and (4) that will deal not only with actions and inactivity, but also with the intentions and secrets of the human heart (so v. 16).

The material of 2:16 also includes the phrase κατὰ τὸ εὐαγγέλιόν μου ("according to my gospel" or "as my gospel declares"). The expression appears to be parenthetical in nature, for it modifies neither "on the day when God will judge everyone's secrets" (as though only Paul's message proclaimed such a judgment) nor "through Christ Jesus" (as though only Paul's message announced who would be the judge in that final day of judgment). Most translations, therefore, have either tucked this phrase into the text itself as something of a parenthetical comment, setting it off by commas,[150] or tacked it onto the end of the verse as a closing parenthetical comment, distinguishing it from the rest of the verse by a comma.[151]

---

144. Cf. Acts 10:42, which is a portion of Peter's sermon at the home of Cornelius.

145. Cf. Matt 16:27.

146. Cf. John 5:27; Rev 2:23; 22:12.

147. 2 Cor 5:10.

148. Cf. Jas 2:14-26.

149. For significant and contemporary discussions of this final, eschatological day of God's judgment in Paul's understanding as being important, all inclusive, and based on what Christians as well as non-Christians have done, see Donfried, "Justification and Last Judgment in Paul"; Synofzik, *Gerichts- und Vergeltungsaussagen bei Paulus;* N. M. Watson, "Justified by Faith, Judged by Works — an Antinomy?" *NTS* 29 (1983); Snodgrass, "Justification by Grace"; and Yinger, *Paul, Judaism, and Judgment according to Deeds.*

150. As NRSV.

151. As NIV.

Eusebius of Caesarea (c. A.D. 260-339), who was a prominent Christian theologian and historian of the early fourth century, believed that Paul's reference to "my gospel" at the end of 2:16 and at the beginning of 16:25 was an allusion to the canonical Gospel of Luke, which Paul dictated to his friend Luke. But that suggestion is hardly compatible with the nature of the Third Gospel itself. Almost all commentators today hold "that by 'my gospel' Paul did not mean a peculiarly Pauline form of the gospel but simply the gospel which he preached together with other Christian preachers"[152] — though some would go a bit further to personalize "my gospel" somewhat more expressly by defining it as "the gospel, common to all Christians, which has been entrusted by God to Paul for his preservation and proclamation."[153] Joseph Fitzmyer goes even further in his brief statement: "In using 'my,' he [Paul] refers to his personal way of announcing the good news."[154]

I have argued that one of Paul's major purposes in Romans was to give to the Christians at Rome what he calls in 1:11 a "spiritual gift" (χάρισμα πνευματικόν), which he (1) thought of as being uniquely his, (2) proclaimed throughout the Greco-Roman world in his mission to Gentiles, (3) summed up theologically in 5:1–8:39, and (4) referred to as "my gospel" in 2:16 and 16:25. Paul evidently felt that the Christians at Rome needed to know what he was proclaiming in order (1) that he and they might be able to "mutually encourage" one another (cf. 1:11-12) — that is, on his part, by presenting the content of what he was proclaiming in his mission to Gentiles — and (2) that they might, having come to understand more accurately and more appreciatively his proclamation to the Gentiles, willingly come to his assistance in the extension of his Gentile mission to Spain (cf. 1:13; 15:24).

Further, I have agreed with Peter Stuhlmacher and Alexander Wedderburn, as well as at a number of points with such a diverse group of other scholars as Kenneth Grayston, Walter Schmithals, Neil Elliott, and Douglas Campbell, that there are a number of passing comments, veiled allusions, and rhetorical questions in the didactic materials of 1:16–11:36 and the exhortations of 12:1–15:13 and 16:17-19 that carry something of an apologetic tone and so should probably be understood as instances where Paul is defending himself against certain criticisms and misrepresentations by at least some of the Christians at Rome. These include in this first major section of the body middle of Romans the comment "for I am not ashamed of the gospel" in 1:16 (as noted earlier); likewise, the allusion to those who "slanderously report" and "claim" that Paul's message boils down to the axiom "Let us do evil that good may result" in 3:8 (as will be treated later).

This phenomenon of an implicit Pauline defense, as I have proposed (in

---

152. So, e.g., Cranfield, *Romans,* 1.163.

153. So, e.g., Moo, *Romans,* 155.

154. Fitzmyer, *Romans,* 754; commenting on 16:25, to which the readers are directed in his comments on 2:16.

concert with Stuhlmacher and Wedderburn, together with most of the other scholars mentioned above), should also be seen as reflected in the parenthetical remark at the end of 2:16: "as my gospel declares." What Paul is saying here, in effect, is that despite certain criticisms and misrepresentations regarding his message and mission to Gentiles, all of what he has written in 2:1-16a is what he personally believes and has proclaimed as part of the Christian gospel — although later in this same letter to Rome, especially in its theological section of 5:1–8:39 and its hortatory section of 12:1–15:13, Paul will evidence that, while he agrees with his addressees on the matters set out in 2:1-16a, as well as throughout the letter's first major section of 1:16–4:25, his own contextualization of the gospel should be understood in terms that Gentiles would better understand and in ways they would more appreciatively respond to.

BIBLICAL THEOLOGY

Rom 2:1-16, as Richard Hays has observed, is "strewn with exegetical stumbling-blocks for interpreters who presuppose that Paul must always and everywhere preach only justification by faith apart from works."[155] Its form and content are dominantly Jewish and/or Jewish Christian, with Paul's distinctive Christian language breaking through only in 2:16. It has been characterized as an "inner Jewish debate." [156] Yet a number of matters of great importance for Christian theology appear in 2:1-16.

Doing, Not Just Knowing. The first matter of importance for Christian theology is the emphasis in Rom 2 on the fact that God judges people not just on the basis of what they know, believe, or affirm about him and his will, but on the basis of their doing what they know to be the will of God — that is, on the basis of how they act and respond to what they know, believe, and affirm. Throughout 2:1-16 there reverberates this central theme of the importance of actually doing God's will, not just claiming to know God's will. This is the central point of the diatribal material of 2:1-5 ("You are without excuse . . . because you who pass judgment do the same things"). It is also prominent in the material that Paul quotes in 2:6-10, with the topic sentence of v. 6 stating explicitly that "God will give to everyone according to what they have done" and vv. 7-10 spelling out that point in two sets of antithetic parallel statements. And it comes to the fore in Paul's statements regarding God's judgments vis-à-vis the Mosaic law in 2:12-13, which close with the words: "It is not those who hear the law who are righteous in God's sight, but those who obey (οἱ ποιηταί, literally 'those who do') the law who will be declared righteous."

This emphasis on doing the will of God in no way disparages — either in Paul's writings or elsewhere in the NT — the importance of knowledge, com-

---

155. Hays, *Echoes of Scripture*, 41.
156. So, as noted earlier, Carras, "Romans 2,1-29," 185.

mitment, or faith. It is, rather, a call to take seriously the importance of actually doing God's will. In this matter Paul would thoroughly agree with James in his pastoral counsel:

> Do not merely listen to the word, and so deceive yourselves. Do what it says (γίνεσθε ποιηταὶ λόγου, literally "be doers of the word"). (Jas 1:22)
> What good is it, my brothers and sisters, if a person claims to have faith but has no works (ἔργα)? Can faith save such a person? (Jas 2:14)
> As the body without the spirit is dead, so faith without works (χωρὶς ἔργων) is dead. (Jas 2:26)

Divine Impartiality. A second matter of theological importance in this passage, which feature runs parallel to the first throughout the material, is that of God's impartiality in his judgment of people. This theme is stated in the aphorism quoted by Paul in 2:11, "There is no favoritism with God." And it permeates Paul's own statements in 2:12-13, which begin with "All who sin without having the law will also perish without the law, and all who sin while possessing the law will be condemned by the law."

This theme of divine impartiality, which carries with it significant implications not only for our appreciation of God but also for our understanding of the people of God in their relations with one another, seems to have been foundational in early Jewish Christian thought. It was also, we may assume, a principle of great importance to the Christians at Rome, influenced as they were by the theology of the mother church at Jerusalem. In the Epistle of James, which represents the teaching of the pastor of the Jerusalem church, the exhortations are given: "Don't show partiality/favoritism!" (Jas 2:1) and "Love your neighbor as yourself . . . without showing partiality/favoritism" (Jas 2:8-9).

God's Judgments Based on Truth. A third matter highlighted in Rom 2:1-16 is this: God's judgments are based on truth. It is an axiom that Paul believed was basic not only for his own understanding about God but also for his addressees' theological understanding. For in 2:2 he introduces what appears to have been a traditional Jewish aphorism with the words "now we know that" and then quotes that aphorism: "God's condemnation of those who do such things is based on truth."

It was such a conviction, even in the midst of an extremely troubling situation of great personal importance, that motivated the rhetorical question that Abraham asked of God: "Will not the judge of all the earth do right?" (Gen 18:25). And it is just such a conviction that must underlie all Christian thought and understanding — whether with respect to judgment, salvation, the purposes and plans of God, the guidance and direction of God's people, or whatever else might arise in any given situation or circumstance.

God's Goodness, Forbearance, and Long-Suffering. Evident also in Rom 2:1-16, and a fourth matter of importance to be emphasized here, is Paul's reference to the "goodness, forbearance, and long-suffering" of God. "Rebellious human beings," as Joseph Fitzmyer has observed, "might be tempted to think that God does not care, or that he is always merciful, forbearing, and not judgmental. Yet Paul's words draw us up short, implicitly summoning us to repentance and penitence."[157]

As people who are "in Christ," we must always be thankful to God for his goodness, forbearance, and long-suffering in bringing us to himself in our conversion — but we need also to always bask in his goodness, forbearance, and long-suffering as we grow in our Christian lives. Likewise, it is these qualities that need to be constantly reflected in our relationships with others, both with those who have not yet responded to God "by faith" and with "those who belong to the family of believers."[158] Just as important, as well, is the need for all Christian theological thought and expression to be permeated with God's goodness, forbearance, and long-suffering.

Pagan Gentiles. A fifth theological feature of this passage has to do with the spiritual nature and status before God of pagan Gentiles — particularly those who, though not possessing or knowing any "special revelation" from God, experience in their "inner being" something of the "transcendental claim of the divine will" in their lives, and so "do by nature the things required by the law (φύσει τὰ τοῦ νόμου ποιῶσιν, literally 'do by nature the things of the law')." What appears to be a traditional Jewish and/or Jewish Christian passage quoted in 2:14-15 speaks of pagan Gentiles as "a law for themselves (ἑαυτοῖς εἰσιν νόμος)," possessing an active conscience (συνείδησις), and having conflicting thoughts regarding right and wrong. It is a matter that theologians and lay people have always wanted to know much more about. But such teaching as appears in this passage is not given so that we might speculate further about how God deals with people other than ourselves. Rather, it is given so that those of us who know God by means of his "special revelation," however that revelation has been given, might be shamed into doing God's will when compared to those who have been given and know far less and yet do far more.

Judged according to Works. Also of great importance theologically in this passage, and a sixth feature that needs to be highlighted, is the teaching that in the final judgment even God's own people will be judged "according to what they have done" (v. 6: κατὰ τὰ ἔργα αὐτοῦ, literally "according to his or her works") — that is, they will be judged on the basis of their "doing/working good" (v. 7: ἔργου ἀγαθοῦ, literally "good work") and "doing/working the good" (v. 10: παντὶ τῷ ἐργαζομένῳ τὸ ἀγαθόν, literally "for everyone who does the good"). Or as Paul says in 2:13: "those who obey/do the law [are the ones] who will be declared righteous (οἱ ποιηταὶ νόμου δικαιωθήσονται)."

That the law was fulfilled by Jesus in his earthly ministry (his "active obedience") and by his death on the cross (his "passive obedience"), in order that all people might come to God "by faith" and so be declared righteous, is a truth

---

157. Fitzmyer, *Spiritual Exercises,* 42.
158. Gal 6:10, πρὸς τοὺς οἰκείους τῆς πίστεως; literally "those of the household of faith."

that must never be diminished or perverted in any way by stray thoughts regarding justification by works — that is, by "works of the law (ἔργα νόμου)." But the law of God still exists as God's standard for all of his created universe and for the lives of all his people. So while believers in Jesus are justified "by faith" and enabled now to live their lives "in Christ," they will also be judged "on the day when God will judge everyone's secrets through Christ" (v. 16) on the basis of what they have done as Christians in response to the known will of God — that is, in response to God's holy and righteous standards ("the law of God") as expressed in the teachings and example of Jesus ("the law of Christ") — with Christ himself being their final judge ("through Christ").

CONTEXTUALIZATION FOR TODAY

All that Paul says and quotes in 2:1-16 is expressed in a highly circumstantial manner and set out in ways that (1) would be understood and appreciated by the Christians at Rome, (2) would allay their fears, criticisms, and misunderstandings about him personally and the nature of his ministry and message to Gentiles, and (3) would clear a path for him to bring his addressees to his central theological focus in 5:1–8:39, his understanding of relations between the Christian gospel and God's promises to Israel in 9:1–11:33, and his ethical exhortations in 12:1–15:13. Nonetheless, what Paul writes in this section of his letter to believers in Jesus at Rome is highly significant for Christians and the Christian church today, with respect to both its content and how he has contextualized the Christian message to a particular people and their concerns in that day — which in a number of ways provides a pattern for the contextualization of that same message in our day and in our own particular circumstances.

The situation that Paul faced at Rome was undoubtedly well-known to him personally as a believer in Jesus who (1) had been deeply influenced by his own Jewish background and (2) was knowledgeable about the ways of thinking and religious language of Jewish Christianity. It was, however, somewhat different from what he had encountered during his Gentile mission or when writing any of his other NT letters. For in writing to the Christians at Rome he was writing to believers in Jesus (1) who had been evangelized by Jewish Christians, and so had experienced an entirely different history than had his converts, and (2) who were evidently continuing to be influenced by the theology, ways of thinking, and religious language of the mother church at Jerusalem. In fact, it seems that the Christians at Rome, both Gentile and Jewish believers in Jesus, were more enamored with what was proclaimed, honored, and practiced by James and the Jewish believers at Jerusalem than they were appreciative of Paul and his ministry and message to Gentiles in the Greco-Roman world.

Paul, as himself a Jewish believer in Jesus, well knew the substance, contours, and variations of a Jewish Christian proclamation of the gospel. He was certainly aware of differences between himself and his Jewish Christian colleagues in their ministries. Yet he also rejoiced in their oneness as believers in Jesus, and he seems to have applauded their missionary outreach to their own people the Jews. The leaders of the Jerusalem church and Paul had earlier faced many of the issues regarding an outreach to Gentiles vis-à-vis an outreach to Jews, and they had agreed to respect each other's differences of ministry while acknowledging each other as true believers in Jesus (cf. Gal 2:6-10).

The Christians of Rome at the time when Paul wrote them, however, were dominantly Gentiles ethnically. So as a basically Gentile community of believers in Jesus, Paul considered them within his God-given mandate of ministry. Yet even though the various Christian congregations in the capital city were largely composed of Gentile Christians, the outlook and sympathies of the city's believers in Jesus, whatever their ethnicity, had been captivated by one branch of the early Christian mission, that is, by Jewish Christianity — and it seems that, at least in Paul's view, they had become somewhat overly enamored with that particular form of Christian proclamation, theology and experience. As Gentile Christians who had been recently brought into the whole complex of Jewish history and Jewish Christian experience, the old adage was probably true: "There is no zealot quite like a new convert." So Paul, while recognizing the oneness he had with his addressees in the central matters of the Christian faith and while often agreeing with them, evidently wanted to dampen some of their extremes, to correct some of their errors, and to lead them into what he believed was a fuller understanding of the Christian gospel — that is, to lead them into such an understanding of the Christian message as he sets out for them theologically in 5:1–8:39 and that passage's ethical corollary in 12:1–15:13. And he does this in order that they might join with him in the extension of his own particular way of contextualizing that gospel proclamation to Gentiles, which contextualization he calls "my gospel," into the western part of the Roman Empire.

All of what Paul writes in 2:1-16 evidences a side of Paul that is not always apparent in his other NT letters. It is not that in writing 2:1-16 Paul was inconsistent or confused. Nor, as is sometimes suggested, that what appears in this portion of Romans 2 was added by some later writer or editor, or that it evidences some contradictions in Paul's thought, or that it should be understood rhetorically as an attempt to decimate a position that he rejected. Rather, what Paul writes in this passage is far better understood as his basic agreement with his Christian addressees at Rome — though also, it appears, his debate with certain of them — on matters regarding (1) the need to actually do what God's law requires, and not just know and approve that law and judge others according to it, (2) the realization that Jews and Gentiles alike have broken God's law, and so are under God's condemnation, and (3) the fact of the impartiality of God in judging sin and sinners. Further, it needs always to be recognized that his arguments in this passage are set out as positively as possible in a manner that his Christian addressees at Rome will understand them. (Though in the passage that immediately follows, 2:17-29, it also needs to be noted that Paul ceases any further positive argumentation of this sort and simply denounces (1) those who, while knowing the requirements of God's law, do not obey or do God's law, (2) those who, while claiming to possess God's covenant, have broken it, and (3) those who, while claiming that their fleshly circumcision protects them from harm, demonstrate that they have uncircumcised hearts, which is a spiritually disastrous situation.)

Romans evidences in many of its passages Paul's contextualization of the Christian gospel in a particular circumstance. We will argue later that 5:1–8:39 is a particularly good example of Paul's theological contextualization of the Christian gospel in a non-Jewish and strictly Gentile context. But though 2:1-16 is in many respects different from what follows in 5:1–8:39, it is also a good example of Paul's contextualization of the Christian gospel — even though the whole of the first part of the body middle of Romans, that is, 1:16–4:25, reflects quite different addressees and quite different circumstances than are usually apparent in Paul's other letters. From such examples of Pauline contextualization, and as here set out in Rom 2:1-16, modern interpreters can learn a great deal — not only with respect to what Paul was doing in his ministry, but also with regard to the template or pattern he provides for contextualizing the gospel for Christian ministry and proclamation today.

4. Denunciations of Jews and Jewish Failures (2:17-29)

TRANSLATION

²:¹⁷*Now you, if you call yourself a Jew; if you rely on the law and boast about your relationship to God;* ¹⁸*if you know God's will and are able to discern the things that are superior because you are instructed by the law;* ¹⁹*if you are convinced that you are a guide for the blind, a light for those in the dark;* ²⁰*if you consider yourself an instructor of the foolish, a teacher of infants, because you have in the law the embodiment of knowledge and truth —* ²¹*You, then, who teach others, do you not teach yourself? You who preach against stealing, do you steal?* ²²*You who say that people should not commit adultery, do you commit adultery? You who abhor idols, do you rob temples?* ²³*You who boast about the law, do you dishonor God by breaking the law?* ²⁴*For "God's name is blasphemed among the Gentiles because of you," just as it is written.*

²⁵*Circumcision, indeed, has value if you observe the law, but if you are a transgressor of the law, your circumcision has become uncircumcision.* ²⁶*If then a man who is not circumcised should keep the law's requirements, will he not be regarded as though he were circumcised?* ²⁷*The one who is not circumcised physically, and yet who satisfies the requirements of the law, will condemn you who, even though you have the written code and circumcision, are a lawbreaker.*

²⁸*A person is not a Jew who is only one outwardly, nor is circumcision merely external and physical.* ²⁹*Rather, a person is a Jew who is one inwardly, and real circumcision is a matter of the heart — by the Spirit, not by the written code. Such a person's praise is not from other people but comes from God.*

TEXTUAL NOTES

2:17a The reading εἰ δέ — that is, the conditional particle εἰ ("if") and the conjunction δέ, which may signal a mild contrast ("but") though was frequently used as only a connecting particle ("now") and so is often omitted in translations — is well supported by uncials ℵ A B D* Ψ, as well as by minuscules 81 1506 (Category II) and 88 104 630 (Category III). It is also reflected in versions it[d, g] vg syr[p] cop[sa, bo] arm eth. The particle ἴδε, which is properly the imperfect form of the verb εἶδον ("see," "perceive") but was often used in koine Greek to introduce something or someone ("here is," "you see," "behold"), appears later in the *Byz* textual tradition in uncials D[c] L, most minuscules, and syr[h] — therefore in the TR and so translated "Behold" by the KJV. Bruce Metzger has commented: "This reading arose either as an itacism (ει and ι were pronounced alike) or as a deliberate amelioration of an otherwise extremely long and drawn out sentence (with the apodosis in ver. 21)."[1]

---

1. Metzger, *Textual Commentary*, 448.

17b The use of νόμῳ ("law") without the definite article is well supported by ℵ A B D*, which are the earliest uncial MSS. Many later MSS, however, add the article, thereby making explicit the reference to the Mosaic law (also in vv. 18, 20, 23b, 26 and 27a) — though νόμος is also without the article in vv. 23a, 25a, 25b, and 27b. The referent in all of these instances is the same: "the Mosaic law."

25 The verb πράσσῃς ("you do," "accomplish") is so amply attested in the MSS that it certainly must be considered the original reading. Codex Bezae Claromontanus (D 06), however, reads φυλάσσῃς ("you keep," "observe"), which is a somewhat more technical term that makes abundantly clear the meaning of "you do" in this context, and so is an appropriate understanding of what Paul originally wrote.

26 The negative οὐχ ("not") is strongly attested since it appears in the fourth-century uncials ℵ and B (also uncial Ψ), as well as in minuscules 1506 (Category II) and 1735 (Category III). The more emphatic negative οὐχί ("not"), however, appears more widely in uncials D G (also *Byz* uncials K L) and minuscules 33 1175 1739 (Category I), 1881 2464 (Category II), 6 69 88 104 323 326 330 365 424ᶜ 614 1241 1243 1319 1505 1573 1874 2344 2495 (Category III). Probably the simple negative οὐχ is to be preferred.

27 The ninth-century uncial G omits the phrase τὸν νόμον τελοῦσα ("the one who keeps/completes/satisfies the requirements of the law"), but that omission is clearly a scribal error.

FORM/STRUCTURE/SETTING

There is probably no more ignored passage in the NT than Rom 2:17-29. It seems to have little, if anything, to say about justification by faith, about the gospel of Christ, or about any of the other distinctive teachings of Paul. Further, it has contributed little to the development of Christian doctrine, and most commentators have considered it to contain little, if any, historical significance. It deals primarily with Jewish identity and failures, accusing the Jews of having broken God's covenant (vv. 17-24) and being uncircumcised in their hearts (vv. 25-29). Only the references in 2:26-27 to (1) the possibility of some Gentiles "keeping" and "obeying" the law and (2) God's possible acceptance of such people can be viewed as having any positive thrust. Yet those statements are given not to say something positive about Gentiles but only to shame the Jews. Otherwise, the passage is devoted entirely to denunciations of Jews and Jewish failures to keep the Mosaic law.

Nonetheless, 2:17-29 is an essential part of Paul's overall argument in this first half (1:16-3:20) of Section I (1:16-4:25) of the "body middle" (1:16-15:13) of his letter to the Christians at Rome. After the thesis statement of 1:16-17, Paul castigates the godlessness and wickedness of humanity generally in 1:18-2:16 and the unfaithfulness and injustices of Jews in 2:17-3:20 — with all this polemic set out in order to provide a backdrop for the Christian message of righteousness "by faith in Jesus Christ to all who believe" in 3:21-4:25 and for Paul's distinctive contextualization of that gospel message to the Gentile world in 5:1 8:39.

In tone, this passage's denunciations of Jewish failures is very much like Paul's bitter denunciation of humanity's godlessness, which has resulted in rampant idolatry, immorality, and injustice — with both Gentiles and Jews coming under "the wrath of God." And in its depiction of the Jews, it is similar to the adverse characterization of Jews that appears in 1 Thess 2:15-16.

While in 2:17-29 Paul quotes in conflated fashion the accusations of Isa 52:5 and Ezek 36:22 and echoes some of the rebuking language of the OT prophets (which also appears in some statements of the sages of Second Temple Judaism), the questions raised and accusations made in this passage do not argue a case from Scripture or from any Jewish or Jewish Christian traditional material, as was done in 2:1-16. Rather, in 2:17-29 Paul simply denounces the Jews in their failures to "obey," "keep," or "do" the Mosaic law, which they "possess," "affirm," and "claim" to rely on. And most of what is said in these denunciations consists simply of explications of what was already said and quoted earlier in 2:1-16 — that is, explications about passing judgment on others but doing the same things oneself (as in vv. 1-5), about knowing the law but not doing or keeping the law (as in vv. 12-13), and about Gentiles "doing by nature the things of the law" and so being "a law for themselves" (as in vv. 14-15).

Who Is Addressed and/or Described in 2:17-29? The referent throughout this second part of Rom 2, as it will be in 3:1-20, is certainly the Jews of Paul's day. It is probably not, however, to be understood in terms of Jews generally or Judaism per se. Rather, the referent is most likely some type of proud and censorious, but entirely inconsistent, Jew who viewed himself as a moral teacher of pagan Gentiles, but who caused the name of God to be dishonored among those same Gentiles because he himself failed to live up to the moral standards of the Mosaic law. Further, Paul's referent in this passage seems to have been a Jew who was conscious of his people's privilege in having been given the Mosaic law, yet also one who believed that that privilege of possessing God's law would somehow shield him from God's judgment, despite his own transgressions of God's law.

Two Prominent Rhetorical Conventions in the Passage. Two rhetorical conventions of Paul's day appear prominently in 2:17-29. The first is apostrophe (i.e., the interruption of a discourse in order to address a person or personified thing). This rhetorical convention occurred earlier in 2:1-5 with the use of the vocative of direct address "O man or woman" in 2:1 and 2:3 — and then with that mode of direct address continued throughout 2:4-5 by the use of the second person singular pronouns in vv. 4-5, the use of the second person singular reflexive pronoun σεαυτῷ in v. 5, and repeated appearances of second person singular verbal suffixes. And here in 2:17-29, while the vocative "O man or woman" is not used, this feature of direct address to some postulated individual (i.e., some "imaginary interlocutor"), rather than to the Christians at Rome as a group, comes to the fore with Paul's use of the second person singular pronouns σύ, σοῦ, and σέ ("you") in vv. 17, 25, and 27, his use of the second person singular reflexive pronoun σεαυτόν ("yourself") in vv. 19 and 21, and his use of a number of second person singular verbal suffixes throughout the passage.

Even more prominent in this subsection of material is the appearance of Paul's statements and questions set out in the form of a Greek diatribe. The material of 2:1-5 has been properly viewed as styled in the form of a diatribe. And that is what appears as well here in 2:17-24 — with this second diatribe passage being the longest, most explicit, and most intense of all Paul's diatribes. In these two passages, as Stanley Stowers has noted earlier with regard to 2:1-5, "Paul seems to stop speaking directly to the recipients of the letter and begins to speak as if he were addressing an individual."[2] Further, as Stowers has also observed, whereas "in 2:1-5 Paul paints the picture of the pretentious person and indicts him by exposing his moral inconsistency and basic falsehood," here in 2:17-24 "the characterization takes on more concreteness, since the person is the member of a specific group, a Jew."[3]

Is There a Ring Composition and/or Chiasmus in the Passage? A further matter with regard to rhetorical conventions is whether there is a "ring composition" or chiasmus in the passage. For while Jouette Bassler has shown that the theme of "divine impartiality" functions as a major motif throughout Rom 2 (though, of course, she extends the boundaries of that theme considerably and identifies its subsections quite differently), she has also argued that the materials of 2:12-29 form a structural unity, as did those of 1:16–2:11, along the lines of a "ring composition," which reflects, as well, certain features of a Greek chiasmus.[4]

The structure of this proposed ring composition, which she believes verges on being a chiasmus, Bassler sets out as follows:[5]

General statement (οὐκ . . . ἀλλά)	vv. 12-13
Conditional case A (ὅταν)	vv. 14-16
Conditional case B (εἰ δέ)	vv. 17-24
Conditional case B (ἐάν)	v. 25
Conditional case A (ἐάν)	vv. 26-27
General statement (οὐκ . . . ἀλλά)	vv. 28-29

In support, Bassler cites some interesting word repetitions and verbal echoes that she believes serve to create a unity of thought within the passage. For example, she cites the verb ἐπονομάζῃ ("you call/name yourself") in 2:17, which is echoed by the noun ὄνομα and its possessive τοῦ θεοῦ ("the name of God") in 2:24; — also the statements ἐπαναπαύῃ νόμῳ ("you rely on the law") and καυχᾶσαι ἐν θεῷ ("you boast in God") in 2:17, which are paralleled in ἐν νόμῳ καυχᾶσαι ("you boast in the law") in the summary statement of 2:23, and the final epithet of 2:19-20, διδάσκαλον νηπίων ("a teacher of infants"), which forms

---

2. Stowers, *Diatribe and Paul's Letter to the Romans,* 79.
3. *Ibid.,* 113.
4. Cf. Bassler, *Divine Impartiality,* 137-54.
5. *Ibid.,* 139 52.

the topic for the first question of 2:21-22, ὁ οὖν διδάσκων ἕτερον σεαυτὸν οὐ διδάσκεις; ("You, then, who teach others, do you not teach yourself?").

But while Bassler's analysis of 2:12-29 can be applauded for having identified a number of interesting word repetitions and verbal echoes in the passage, she may be legitimately accused of not having established this portion as a discrete literary unit whose structure can be described as a ring composition with certain chiastic features. It is more accurate, we believe (as has been argued above), to view 2:1-16 as a discrete unit of material that functions as a hinge passage, both literarily and thematically, between 1:18-32 and 2:17-29 (and then further into 3:1-20). And if this be so, it may not then be thought too surprising to find (1) some word repetitions and verbal echoes within that hinge passage itself, and (2) some expressional correspondences between 1:18-32 and 2:1-16, on the one hand, and 2:1-16 and 2:17-29, on the other.

What Bassler has done has been to impose too specific a compositional structure on the materials of 1:18-3:20, basing that proposed structure on certain word repetitions and expressional resemblances — but without paying sufficient attention to other epistolary, rhetorical, and contextual indicators. And this appears particularly evident in 2:12-29, which she treats as a chiasmus — or as including, particularly in vv. 14-27, certain chiastic features. But instead of viewing these latter verses as dealing in chiastic fashion first with Gentiles, then with Jews, then with Jews, and finally again with Gentiles on an equal and impartial basis, it seems far better to understand Paul in these verses as speaking of the situation of the Gentiles only illustratively as a means of supporting his arguments against the disobedience of the Jews. Nonetheless, while Bassler may be accused of not having made her case with respect to the structures of 1:16–2:11 and 2:12-29 — and, further, of having run somewhat roughshod over the more obvious features that demarcate distinguishable and fairly discrete units of material in 2:1-16 and 2:17-27 — she is certainly correct to highlight the theme of "divine impartiality" as a major feature in Rom 2 (though, of course, she would extend the parameters of that theme beyond the limits of ch. 2 itself).

Use of Scripture and Traditional Materials. As in 2:1-16, here also in 2:17-29 a number of Paul's questions, statements, and denunciations echo OT prophetic accusations — particularly from Deuteronomy, Isaiah, Jeremiah, and Ezekiel. Further, a number of parallels can be drawn between Paul's questions, statements, and phraseology in this passage and similar features found in the writings of Second Temple Judaism and in the Talmud. And once, in 2:24, he quotes a conflation of the indicting words of Isa 52:5 and Ezek 36:22, introducing it with the conjunction γάρ ("for") and concluding it with the familiar formula καθὼς γέγραπται ("just as it is written") — which formula, however, is not used here to introduce the quotation, but seems to be appended in order to heighten the impact of Paul's accusations by pointing out that what he has said is directly in line with the accusations of the prophets Isaiah and Jeremiah (see our exegetical comments on 2:24).

But while there are similarities between 2:1-16 and 2:17-27 in the fact that there are a number of allusions to biblical and non-biblical materials in both passages, they differ somewhat in that while in 2:1-16 there appear quotations of Jewish and/or Jewish Christian aphorisms (2:2, 11) and catechetical materials (2:6-10, 14-15) here in 2:17-29 there is a direct quotation of Scripture (in 2:24). More importantly, however, these two blocks of material differ in their respective uses of Scripture and traditional materials. For while allusions to Scripture and quotations of traditional Jewish and/or Jewish Christian materials are used in 2:1-16 to carry forward Paul's arguments, the echoing of the language of Scripture in 2:17-29, as well as wording that is similar to some of what is said in the writings of Second Temple Judaism, seem only to suggest that there are prophetic parallels to Paul's denunciations of the Jews of his day — and, in the case of the conflated quotation of Isa 52:5 and Ezek 36:22 in 2:24, to provide biblical evidence that Paul's denunciations are in line with the prophetic denunciations of Israel, God's own people, by the ancient prophets.

The Setting and Structure of the Passage. In 2:17-29 Paul mounts a withering attack against any Jew who believes that his status in God's covenant, his possession of the Mosaic law, and his physical circumcision will give him an advantage with respect to God's judgment — but who fails to respond positively to God from his heart, and so actually breaks God's law. Here Paul spells out in detail his earlier rather general arguments against the disobedience of all people, both Jews and Gentiles, that appeared in 2:1-16 — particularly those that appeared in 2:1-3 ("You do the same things," i.e., you disobey God's righteous decree) and 2:12-13 ("all who sin under the law will be judged by the law" and "it is not the hearers of the law who are righteous before God, but the doers of the law who will be declared righteous"). And here in 2:17-29 he applies those general accusing statements directly to Jews and to Jewish failures to obey the law.

The material of 2:17-29 functions as the missing link in Paul's argument of 2:1-16. For whereas in that first part of ch. 2 Paul spoke somewhat generally about people not being obedient to the law, here in the second part of the chapter he focuses his attack on Jews and makes his indictment against them crystal-clear.

The passage is organized structurally into two sub-units of material. The first, vv. 17-24, which Ernst Käsemann has called "a masterpiece of rhetoric,"[6] denounces in diatribal fashion the Jews for having broken God's covenant. It consists of (1) a protasis (i.e., an opening part) of five descriptive statements in vv. 17-20 that characterize the self-identity and self-consciousness of a typical Jew of Paul's day, (2) an unexpected breaking off of that protasis without an apodosis (i.e., a closing part), and so presenting the reader with an anacoluthon (i.e., a shift from one syntactical construction to another, and therefore an unfinished sentence that can only be represented by a dash in English translation), (3) a series of five accusatory rhetorical questions in vv. 21-23, which counter the overall impression given by the five descriptive statements of the

6. Käsemann, *Romans,* 69.

previous verses, and (4) a scriptural quotation in 2:24 conflating Isa 52:5 and Ezek 36:22.

The second part of this first portion of the passage, that is, the five sentences in 2:21-23 that can be read either as further descriptive statements or as accusatory rhetorical questions, are all similar in structure. The first, however, includes the negative particle οὐ ("not"), which calls for it to be read as a rhetorical question. And that rhetorical question seems to set the pattern for all of the following four sentences to be read as rhetorical questions as well.

Stanley Stowers has pointed out with respect to this pattern of (1) direct address, (2) descriptive statements, and (3) accusing rhetorical questions in 2:17-23 vis-à-vis a typical Greek diatribe: "Although the exact form with the anacoluthon may be unique, the statement-question pattern is not."[7] In support, Stowers cites Epictetus's address to an imaginary interlocutor in *Dissertations* 2.8.11-12:

> But you are a being of primary importance; you are a fragment of God; you have within you a part of Him. Why, then, are you ignorant of your own kinship? Why do you not know the source from which you have sprung?

Likewise, Seneca's accusations against the one who loves luxury in *Epistles* 77.17:

> You are a connoisseur in the flavor of the oyster and of the mullet; your luxury has not left you anything untasted for the years that are to come; and yet these are the things from which you are torn away unwillingly. What else is there which you would regret to have taken from you? Friends? But who can be a friend to you? Country? What? Do you think enough of your country to be late to dinner?

Also noted by Stowers is a typical question-statement construction by Epictetus in *Dissertations* 2.1.28:

> You, for example, who are able to turn others about (σὺ ὁ ἄλλους στρέφειν), have you no master?

Closing off the diatribe of 2:17-24, Paul quotes in conflated fashion the words of Isa 52:5 ("all day long my name is constantly blasphemed") and Ezek 36:22 ("for the sake of my holy name, which you have profaned among the nations where you have gone"). The wording of the quotation, of course, stems from Paul's Jewish background. Yet Stowers's point with regard to the use of quotations in a Greek diatribe remains pertinent: "Quotations can be used in addressing the opponent in the diatribe."[8] Here in 2:24, it needs to be noted,

7. Stowers, *Diatribe and Paul's Letter to the Romans*, 96.
8. *Ibid.*, 97.

Paul is not only aligning himself with the Jewish prophetic tradition, he is also claiming by this alignment that what he has written in 2:17-23 is to be understood as a contemporary prophetic denunciation against the descendants of God's ancient people Israel. It is a very serious charge he is making. For he is in effect asserting that the Jews of his day have broken God's covenant and therefore are not to be considered any better than the Gentiles whom they despise.

In the second subsection of 2:17-29, vv. 25-29, "Paul adopts," as Joseph Fitzmyer has observed, "a didactic tone and seeks to forestall an objection" on the part of his Jewish interlocutor, whom he identified in 2:17 ("if you call yourself a Jew") and to whom he has been speaking directly from that verse on — which objection Fitzmyer words as follows:

> Perhaps we Jews do not observe the law as we should, but at least we are circumcised. In this regard at least we have carried out God's command. Did not God himself set up the covenant with Israel and make circumcision the seal of that covenant, the very shield against God's wrath?[9]

But Paul rejects such a claim, denouncing in these final five verses of the section those who claim the spiritual advantages of physical circumcision but have experienced no inward, spiritual "circumcision of the heart."

Five issues are highlighted in the latter portion of this section, in vv. 25-29: (1) the value of circumcision (v. 25a), (2) the central requirement of obedience to the law (vv. 25b-27), (3) the prospect of judgment (throughout the context, but specifically alluded to in v. 27), (4) the contrast between Jews and Gentiles, that is, the circumcised and the uncircumcised, with respect to their keeping of the law (vv. 26-27), and (5) a definition of the "true" Jew in relation to circumcision and obeying the law (vv. 28-29). At the end of this latter sub-unit of material, in 2:29b, Paul includes what appears to be a Jewish aphorism that reflects a subtle word-play on the Hebrew words for "Jew," "Judah," and "praise," thereby reinforcing his insistence that it is the circumcised heart that is praised in God's sight (see our exegetical comments on 2:29b).

The passage in addressing such a Jewish interlocutor evidences the following two major topics contained in these two major sub-sections of material:

1. Jews as Having Broken God's Covenant (in 2:17-24), which appears in three parts: descriptive statements (vv. 17-20); accusatory questions (vv. 21-23); and a conclusion (in 2:24).
2. The Uncircumcised Hearts of Jews (2:25-29).

And our "exegetical comments" that follow will be organized in terms of these two major topics and subsections of material.

Theological Issues. The major theological problems that arise in 2:17-29

9. Fitzmyer, *Romans*, 320.

may be expressed in the following questions: (1) How can Paul so severely criticize Jewish spiritual and moral failures (as he does throughout the entire thirteen verses of this passage) when it was the moral caliber of the Jewish religion, as well as the ethical lives of many of its adherents, that made Judaism so attractive to a number of Gentiles, especially to "proselytes" and the so-called "God-fearers"? (2) Does Paul teach that Gentiles will be accepted by God by obeying the law as they knew it and in their own fashion (as in vv. 26-27)? (3) Does Paul hold that the "true" Jew is, in fact, a Christian who has been circumcised in the heart by the Holy Spirit (as in vv. 28-29), and so by the Spirit can obey the law?

EXEGETICAL COMMENTS

I. Jews as Having Broken God's Covenant (2:17-24)

As in the first part of the previous section, 2:1-5, so here in the first part of 2:17-29, vv. 17-24, Paul makes use of a Greek diatribe style of teaching, which has been allowed to fade away since it first appeared in vv. 1-5. And here in vv. 17-24 the apostle's point is that by their failure to do what the law requires, Jews have, despite their self-assertive claims, actually broken God's covenant.

A. The Self-Identity and Self-Consciousness of Jews (2:17-20)

Paul begins his diatribe of 2:17-24 with five statements in vv. 17-20 regarding the self-identity and self-consciousness of Jews in his day. The first of these statements in 2:17a, "You call yourself a Jew," is followed by four further statements, all in direct address, all affirming the claimed status of a Jew, and all conditioned by the particle εἰ ("if"), the first word of 2:17a. Further, it is important to note that this particle εἰ, which signals the start of a first class conditional sentence, suggests that all of what is said in these five statements is to be affirmed, that is, understood not as a caricature of Jews or hypothetical portrayal of a Jewish self-understanding but as what Paul really believes does, in fact, characterize the self-identity and self-consciousness of many Jews of his day:

> "If you call yourself a Jew" (v. 17a);
> "if you rely on the law and boast about your relationship to God" (v. 17b);
> "if you know his will and are able to discern the things that are superior because you are instructed by the law" (v. 18);
> "if you are convinced that you are a guide for the blind, a light for those who are in the dark" (v. 19); and
> "if you consider yourself an instructor of the foolish, a teacher of infants, because you have in the law the embodiment of knowledge and truth" (v. 20).

2:17 Paul begins these five statements regarding Jewish self-identity and self-consciousness by characterizing his imaginary interlocutor in the words: εἰ δὲ σὺ Ἰουδαῖος ἐπονομάζῃ ("now you, if you call yourself a Jew"). The verb ἐπονομάζῃ is either middle voice ("you call yourself") or passive voice ("you are called [by others]"). The context, however, requires that it be understood as in the middle voice and therefore that the expression be translated: "Now you, if you call yourself a Jew."

The name "Israel" (Hebrew יִשְׂרָאֵל, Greek Ἰσραήλ) literally means "the one who persisted (or 'persevered') with God." It was derived from the coupling of the substantival use of the verb שׂרה, "to persist" or "persevere," and the divine name אֵל, and it was the name given by God himself to Jacob when Jacob "would not let God go" until God blessed him.[10] It is a highly honorable name that all of Jacob's descendants gladly accepted and that Paul will later use in this same letter in honorific fashion in 9:4 and 11:2, 25.[11]

The name "Hebrew" (Hebrew עִבְרִי, Greek Ἑβραῖος) is the designation that Israelites used for themselves and which those who were not Israelites sometimes also called them — in contradistinction to those who were "Greek" (Ἕλλην or Ἑλληνίς) by birth, language, and culture, or were identified as Grecian because of either language, culture, or both.[12]

The name "Jew" (Hebrew יְהוּדִי, Greek Ἰουδαῖος), which was derived from the patriarchal name Judah (יְהוּדָה), became prominent during the Maccabean period to designate the people of the province of Judea, who were largely from the tribe of Judah. It came to be commonly used by the people of Israel themselves, as well as by most non-Jews of the Greco-Roman world, to identify those who (1) adhered to the monotheism of the OT, (2) had a particular history and national identity, (3) accepted a Levitical form of cultic religion, and/or (4) attempted to live their lives governed by the law of Moses. It was used by Jews as synonymous with the older names "Israelite" and "Hebrew," for it carried with it — both for those of the homeland and for those dispersed throughout the Greco-Roman world (the Jewish "Diaspora") — all the honorific connotations of "Israelite" and "Hebrew." For non-Jews in the Greco-Roman world, however, it signified simply a group of people who by birth, religion, and/or culture constituted a distinctive group of people who originated in a particular geographic locality and who endeavored to keep their distinctiveness.

Origen, writing near the close of his life in the middle of the third century, said of Paul's form of direct address here in 2:17:

> The first thing to notice here is that Paul does not say that the person he is rhetorically addressing is a Jew; only that he calls himself one, which is not at all the same thing. For Paul goes on to teach that the true Jew is the one

---

10. Gen 32:28.
11. Cf. also Phil 3:5.
12. Cf. Phil 3:5; see also Acts 6:1.

who is circumcised in secret, that is, in the heart, who keeps the law in spirit and not according to the letter, whose praise is not from men but from God. But the man who is circumcised visibly in the flesh, observing the law in order to be seen by men, is not a real Jew; such a man only appears to be one.[13]

Undoubtedly even when writing these opening words of 2:17 Paul was anticipating his later discussion about true circumcision in 2:25-29, particularly about what it means to be a true Jew in 2:28-29. So it may be that here Paul was hinting that it is not enough simply to call oneself a Jew — that there is much more to being a Jew than merely calling oneself a Jew and the physical act of circumcision. Yet Paul's point here in 2:17-20 (as well as throughout the entire passage) is to show that: (1) while status as a Jew is a valid claim and possession of the Mosaic law is a God-given privilege, yet (2) without a positive response to God and actually keeping God's law, Jews have no advantage over Gentiles with respect to divine judgment. Thus this opening address to the imaginary interlocutor of the passage need not be read as irony or mere casuistry on Paul's part; it is better understood as affirming a rightful claim — though a claim that has failed, as Paul will spell out in what follows, to be demonstrated or validated in action.

The second statement of Paul in 2:17 that characterizes the Jews begins by speaking of them as relying on the Mosaic law: καὶ ἐπαναπαύῃ νόμῳ ("and you rely on the law"). The verb ἐπαναπαύῃ is also best read as in the middle voice and so translated "you rely on (or 'find rest in') the law." The verb ἐπαναπαύομαι ("rest," "find rest," "rely on") is used in the NT only here and in Luke 10:6 ("your peace will rest on him"). It appears, however, a number of times in the LXX to denote the idea of "to lean on" someone or something for support,[14] but also "to lean on" or "rely on" God.[15]

Paul then goes on to characterize his Jewish interlocutor with καὶ καυχᾶσαι ἐν θεῷ ("and you boast in God") — that is, "you boast about your relationship to God." The verb καυχᾶσθαι ("to boast"), in both transitive and intransitive uses, together with the nouns καύχημα ("boast") and καύχησις ("boasting"), appear a number of times in the NT — most in Paul's letters.[16] In the OT there are proverbs that speak against boasting of oneself in a self-glorying manner[17] and passages where boasting is viewed as the expression of a foolish and ungodly person.[18] Yet there are also texts where the justifiable pride of a person is commended[19] and where true boasting in God is praised.[20] The LXX uses

---

13. Origen, *Ad Romanos, CER* 1.238.

14. 2 Kgs 5:18; 7:2; Ezek 29:7; 1 Macc 8:12.

15. Mic 3:11, though in this Micah passage it is a false claim.

16. The verb καυχᾶσθαι appears 35 times in Paul, twice in James; the neuter noun καύχημα 10 times in Paul, once in Hebrews; and the feminine noun καύχησις 10 times in Paul, once in James.

17. Cf., e.g., 1 Kgs 20:11; Prov 25:14; 27:1.

18. Cf., e.g., Pss 52:1; 75:4; 94:3.

19. Cf., e.g., Prov 16:31; 17:6.

20. Cf. esp. Jer 9:23-24.

καυχᾶσθαι, καύχημα, and καύχησις for a number of Hebrew words that speak of "confidence," "joy," and "thanksgiving" expressed to God. Paradoxically, as Rudolf Bultmann has aptly observed, in the biblical and Pauline uses of the expression the one who boasts in God "looks away from himself, so that his glorying [or 'boasting'] is a confession of God."[21]

Paul carries over from the OT this multiform understanding of human boasting and even uses it in its laudatory sense for his own apostolic confidence, joy, and thanksgiving before God — which he expects will be experienced, as well, in the lives of his converts.[22] And such a multiform use of the expression appears a number of times in Romans — not only here in 2:17 but also in this same section at the end of 2:23.[23]

2:18 Paul then sets out a third statement by which he characterizes certain Jews of his day: γινώσκεις τὸ θέλημα καὶ δοκιμάζεις τὰ διαφέροντα κατηχούμενος ἐκ τοῦ νόμου ("you know God's will and are able to discern the things that are superior because you are instructed by the law"). The article with θέλημα signals the possessive phrase "God's will,"[24] though even without the article θέλημα seems to have been used by Jews and Jewish Christians to designate "the divine will," as it is probably best translated in 1 Cor 16:12 ("it was not God's will to come now"). And by the singular use of θέλημα, with or without the article, the idea is suggested that God's will is one unified entity that coheres in all its parts. Further, as Gottlob Schrenk has appropriately argued, "God's will is expressed in the singular because the concept is shaped not by individual legal directions, but by the conviction that this θέλημα of God is a powerful unity."[25]

A common liturgical formula in the Jewish synagogues of Paul's day was "to do his will" or "to do the will of the Father in heaven."[26] And though the apostle will later reprove Jews for not "doing" God's will as expressed in the law, here in 2:18 he acknowledges that Jews "know" God's will. Likewise, while he will later speak of their failure, Paul also acknowledges in this third statement that God has given Jews an ability to "discern (or 'determine') the things that matter most" because of their having been "instructed by the law." The verb δοκιμάζω ("test," "examine," "discern," "determine," "approve") appears often in Paul's letters with a variety of meanings.[27] But his use of δοκιμάζω in Rom 12:2 ("then you will be able *to test and approve* [i.e., 'discern' or 'determine'] what God's will is") and Phil 1:10 ("so that you may be able *to discern* what is

21. Bultmann, "καυχάομαι, καύχημα, καύχησις," 3.647.
22. Cf. Bultmann, "καυχάομαι, καύχημα, καύχησις," 3.648-52; see also Judge, "Paul's Boasting," 37-50; D. M. Stanley, *Boasting in the Lord*, passim.
23. Note also its use in Rom 3:27; 4:2; 5:2, 3, 11; 15:17; likewise its compound form κατακαυχᾶσθαι, which appears twice in Rom 11:18.
24. Cf. Rom 12:2.
25. Schrenk, "θέλημα," 3.54.
26. See Schrenk, "θέλημα," 3.54, who cites such rabbinic patriarchs as Johanan ben Zakkai and Gamaliel III.
27. Cf., in addition to here, Rom 1:28; 12:2; 14:22; 1 Cor 3:13; 11:28; 16:3; 2 Cor 8:22; 13:5; Gal 6:4; Eph 5:10; Phil 1:10; 1 Thess 2:4; 5:21; 1 Tim 3:10.

best") — together with his use of the plural neuter substantival participle τὰ διαφέροντα ("the things that matter most," "the things that are superior") — suggests that his words here are best translated "and you are able to discern the things that are superior."

2:19 Paul's fourth characterization of certain Jews of his day is this: πέποιθάς τε σεαυτὸν ὁδηγὸν εἶναι τυφλῶν, φῶς τῶν ἐν σκότει ("and you are convinced that you are a guide for the blind, a light for those in the dark"). The second person singular perfect indicative verb πέποιθας (from πείθω, "convince," "persuade"), coupled with the accusative singular masculine reflective pronoun σεαυτόν ("yourself"), was in all likelihood meant to be understood as "you have convinced yourself" — though, since the perfect tense of the verb signals not only a past conviction but also a continuing persuasion, πέποιθάς σεαυτόν is probably best translated simply as "you are convinced." The post-positive enclitic particle τέ, which appears more than twenty times in Romans to connect two features or two parts of sentences closely related to each other, alerts readers to the fact that two matters will be highlighted in what follows with respect to this self-consciousness of Jews in Paul's day: (1) that they are ordained by God to be ὁδηγὸν τυφλῶν ("a guide for the blind") and (2) that this divine mandate includes being φῶς τῶν ἐν σκότει ("a light for those in the dark"). Both of these features of a Jewish self-consciousness are rooted in the promises of God to the people of Israel, particularly in Isa 42:6-7 — which verses of a well-known "Servant of Yahweh" passage were understood by Jews of Paul's day to refer to the nation of Israel corporately:

> I, the Lord, have called you in righteousness; I will take hold of your hand. I will keep you and will make you to be a covenant for the people and *a light for the Gentiles, to open eyes that are blind,* to free captives from prison and to release from the dungeon *those who sit in darkness.*

And such a Jewish self-consciousness appears in a number of writings of Second Temple Judaism — as, for example, in *1 En* 105:1: "In those days, he says, 'The Lord will be patient and cause the children of the earth to hear. Reveal it to them with your wisdom, for you are their guides.'"[28] It is also echoed, though in quite an adverse manner, in the characterization of Jews in Matt 15:14; 23:16, 24.

2:20 Paul's fifth and final statement regarding the self-identity and self-consciousness of Jews in his day is: [πέποιθάς σεαυτὸν] παιδευτὴν ἀφρόνων, διδάσκαλον νηπίων, ἔχοντα τὴν μόρφωσιν τῆς γνώσεως καὶ τῆς ἀληθείας ἐν τῷ νόμῳ ("[you consider yourself] an instructor of the foolish, a teacher of infants, because you have in the law the embodiment of knowledge and truth"). This may be viewed as a continuation of the statement in 2:19. And in all likelihood, because of the styling and clipped nature of both statements, the subject of

---

28. Cf. also Wis 18:4; *T Levi* 18:9; 1QS[b] 4.27-28; Josephus, *Contra Apion* 2.291-95; *Sib Or* 3:194-95.

that fourth statement ("you have convinced yourself" or "are convinced") is probably to be understood as also the subject of this additional statement in 2:20 — though for variety of the English expression, it is probably best here translated "you consider yourself."

The emphasis in the word παιδευτής ("instructor," "teacher") may at times be on correcting and disciplining[29] — as is true for the cognate noun παιδεία and verb παιδεύω. But the close association of παιδευτής and διδάσκαλος ("teacher") in this statement suggests quite clearly that what Paul is speaking about is a Jewish self-identity and self-consciousness that considers oneself an instructor and a teacher of others. Non-Jews and Samaritans were generally considered by Jews as ἄφρων ("foolish people") who were without morals. And νηπίων ("infants," "minors") is the word commonly used for young children who need basic instruction.[30] So Paul speaks here in 2:20a of his imaginary interlocutor, whom he earlier identified in 2:17 as a Jew, as confident that he is "an instructor of the foolish" — that is, probably of Gentiles — and "a teacher of infants" — that is, of young children who need basic instruction in God's law. And this confidence was based on the conviction that as a Jew he possessed "in the law the embodiment of knowledge and truth," as is said in 2:20b.

It is not that Paul disputes these Jewish privileges and advantages. Nor does he speak ironically of such Jewish claims, as many Christian commentators have suggested — and as Origen seems to have been the first to argue:

> What Paul says about the Jews is meant to be taken ironically, since anyone who genuinely relies on the law, glories in God and proves the things which are most useful would be doing the things which are listed here.[31]

Rather, what is implied throughout 2:17-20 is that the mere *possession* of the Mosaic law, merely *knowing* the will of God, only *approving* what is superior, and just *being instructed* in the requirements of the law — which are certainly causes for legitimate boasting — can only result in God's judgment when not matched by *obeying, practicing,* and *doing* God's law.

B. An Anacoluthon

After the protasis (the introductory "if"-clauses) of five statements given in 2:17-20 regarding the self-identity and self-consciousness of the Jews in Paul's day, there does not appear, as might be expected, a corresponding apodosis (a main "then"-clause) that sets out the apostle's evaluation of his people's lofty claims. Rhetorically, the implied answer to each of the five statements is "Yes."

---

29. I.e., "a corrector who disciplines," as in LXX Hos 5:2; *Pss Sol* 8:29; as well as in Heb 12:9, which is the only other appearance of this noun in the NT.

30. Cf. 1 Cor 3:1; Eph 4:14; Heb 5:13.

31. Origen, *Ad Romanos, CER* 1.238.

But instead the reader is left with an anacoluthon (a blank in the grammatical structure). Paul will do something similar at the end of 5:12 (see the comments there). Here his purpose has been to state what Jews of his day claimed for themselves. And evidently because of their repeated failures of practice, he has no desire to give an affirmative "yes" to what they claimed. So he breaks off his statements about these quite legitimate features of Jewish self-identity and self-consciousness, shifting from one form of syntactical construction to another, in order to set out — despite their claims and lofty principles — the failure of the Jews in their practice, which he does by means of the following five indicting rhetorical questions.

C. Accusatory Rhetorical Questions (2:21-23)

The second portion of this first part of the passage, that is, 2:21-23, consists of five sentences that can be read either as further descriptive statements or as accusatory rhetorical questions. All the sentences are similar in structure. The first, however, includes the negative particle οὐ ("not"), which calls for it to be read as a question and sets the pattern for all of the following sentences to be read interrogatively as well. Thus located within the structure of a Greek diatribe, five rhetorical questions are thus asked — with the implied answer "No" for the first but "Yes" for the following four:

> "You who teach others, do you not teach yourself?" (v. 21a);
> "you who preach against stealing, do you steal?" (v. 21b);
> "you who say that people should not commit adultery, do you commit adultery?" (v. 22a);
> "you who abhor idols, do you rob temples?" (v. 22b); and
> "you who boast about the law, do you dishonor God by breaking the law?" (v. 23).

2:21a The first of these five rhetorical questions, with its implied negative answer, is as follows: ὁ οὖν διδάσκων ἕτερον, σεαυτὸν οὐ διδάσκεις; ("you, then, who teach others, do you not teach yourself?"). The second person singular verb διδάσκεις ("you teach") and the reflexive pronoun σεαυτόν ("yourself") indicate that this verse is to be understood as a continuation of the diatribe form of argument begun with the direct address in 2:17, "now you, if you call yourself a Jew." So though Paul uses the substantival articular participle ὁ διδάσκων with the accusative noun ἕτερον (which is literally translated "the one who teaches another"), he is addressing that same imaginary interlocutor of 2:17 here in 2:21, and thus the Greek syntactical construction of a substantival articular participle and accusative noun here in 2:21 is to be understood and translated as "you who teach others" (as is also the case with respect to the comparable syntax in the second, third, and fourth questions). Likewise, the appearance of second person singular verbs in all of the four questions that follow in 2:21b-23 indicates that these questions are also included as parts of that diatribe. Further, the postpositive inferential particle οὖν ("then") associates the rhetorical questions of 2:21-23 with the earlier statements of 2:17-20 and so suggests that these latter rhetorical questions are to be understood as the five real answers to the five former statements.

In form, Paul's first accusatory question "Do you not teach yourself?" picks up from his fifth conditional statement, "If you consider yourself an instructor of the foolish. . . ." More important, however, this first question parallels in its content (though in abbreviated fashion) God's ancient indictment in Ps 50 of "the wicked ones" who existed among his people of a much earlier day:

> What right have you to recite my laws or take my covenant on your lips? You hate my instruction and cast my words behind you. When you see a thief, you join with him. You throw in your lot with adulterers. You use your mouth for evil and harness your tongue to deceit. You speak continually against your brother and slander your own mother's son. These things you have done and I kept silent. You thought I was altogether like you. But I will rebuke you and accuse you to your face.[32]

It also finds something of an unintended echo in the words of Rabbi Nathan, a prominent Jewish rabbi of the latter part of the second century A.D., who expressed his complaint to God as follows:

> You have many a man who teaches himself, but does not teach others; many a man who teaches others, but does not teach himself; many a man who teaches himself and others; and many a man who teaches neither himself nor others.[33]

2:21b-22a Here Paul asks two accusatory rhetorical questions that are explicitly dealt with in the Decalogue as found in Exod 20:2-17 and Deut 5:6-21:

> ὁ κηρύσσων μὴ κλέπτειν, κλέπτεις; "You who preach against stealing, do you steal?" (cf. Exod 20:15; Deut 5:19: "You shall not steal").
> ὁ λέγων μὴ μοιχεύειν, μοιχεύεις; "You who say that people should not commit adultery, do you commit adultery?" (cf. Exod 20:14; Deut 5:18: "You shall not commit adultery").

Paul Billerbeck brought together a considerable amount of material from the Talmud in demonstration of the fact that Jewish leaders during the first five centuries A.D. were often extremely concerned about Jewish rabbis who (1) proclaimed "You shall not steal" yet stole from others and (2) affirmed the

---

32. Ps 50:16-21.
33. *Abot de R. Nathan*, 29:8a.

commandment "You shall not commit adultery" yet were sexual offenders themselves.[34] And Anton Fridrichsen has called attention to denunciations by Epictetus, the Stoic philosopher of Hierapolis who was active sometime around A.D. 100, against those who called themselves Stoics and espoused high morals but stole from others and committed various sexual offenses.[35] But the exposure of such actions vis-à-vis such lofty teachings can hardly be reserved for Jewish teachers or Greek philosophers. Sadly, disparities between principles and practice are all too common in the lives of all too many people, both historically and today — whatever their status or situations in life, whatever their lofty affirmations, and whatever their self-justifying defenses.

2:22b ὁ βδελυσσόμενος τὰ εἴδωλα, ἱεροσυλεῖς; ("you who abhor idols, do you rob temples?") is Paul's fourth rhetorical question and has often been difficult for translators and commentators to understand. The verb ἱεροσυλέω appears only here in the NT. It is, however, used a number of times in Greek and Jewish Greek writings of Paul's day to mean quite literally "commit temple robbery."[36] Yet the Jewish world of Paul's day seems to have been entirely devoid of heathen idolatry and did not countenance heathen temples. At least that is the testimony of Judith 8:18 regarding the Jews prior to Paul's day: "There arose none in our age, neither is there any now in these days — neither tribe, nor family, nor people, nor city among us — that worship gods made with hands, as had been before." And Billerbeck brought together a number of statements from the rabbis after Paul's day to this same effect.[37] So it may be asked: How could Paul have spoken about Jews "who abhor idols" and who rob heathen temples? What temples did Paul have in mind as being robbed by Jews, who would have nothing to do with heathen idols or idolatry? Was he referring to Jews robbing the Jerusalem temple? And what action or actions does his statement envision by the term "robbing"?

"The robbery of temples, [which was] originally the removal of sacred property from a sacred site," was, as Gottlob Schrenk has pointed out, "in Greek, Roman and Egyptian eyes one of the most serious of offences. . . . Temple robbery [in extant Greek, Roman, and Egyptian texts] is generally classified with treason and murder."[38] And in the Jewish world the Deuteronomic prohibition against the Israelites taking anything from any heathen temple in their conquest of Canaan was considered by all Jews of Paul's day as the primary biblical text dealing with idols and idolatry:

The images of their gods you are to burn in the fire. Do not covet the silver and gold on them, and do not take it for yourselves, or you will be ensnared

---

34. Billerbeck, *Str-Bil*, 3.105-111.

35. Fridrichsen, "Der wahre Jude," 45; citing Epictetus, *Dissertations* 2.19.19-28; 3.7.17; 3.24.40.

36. Cf. esp. 2 Macc 9:2; Philo, *De confusione linguarum* 163; Josephus, *Antiquities* 17.163; *Contra Apion* 1.249.

37. Billerbeck, *Str-Bil*, 3.111-12.

38. Schrenk, "ἱεροσυλέω," 3.255.

by it, for it is detestable to the Lord your God. Do not bring a detestable thing into your house or you, like it, will be set apart for destruction. Utterly abhor and detest it, for it is set apart for destruction.[39]

It was a lesson that Israel learned to its sorrow in the sad episode of Achan's confiscating for himself "the devoted things" of those whom Joshua and his army had conquered.[40]

Later in Israel's history, however, Jewish merchants seem to have been permitted certain degrees of latitude in matters pertaining to the buying and selling of heathen idols and the buying and selling of gold, clothing, and property that had been previously associated with heathen temples. As Schrenk has further pointed out, drawing from statements in the Talmud — particularly from halakic rulings in the Mishnah tractate *Abodah Zarah* ("Idolatry"), its gemarah (*b. Abodah Zarah*), *b. Sanhedrin* ("Legislation of the Sanhedrin"), all of which record earlier rabbinic understandings of the Mosaic law:

> The attitude of the Rabbis is much laxer than one would expect from Dt. 7. They have no legal term for intentional temple robbery. Whipping is an adequate punishment. According to b Sanh. 84a it is only the violation of a prohibition. It is thus judged more leniently than murder. Capital punishment by God, but not by human courts, may also be the punishment. The softening of Dt. 7:25f. is astonishing. . . . R. Samuel says in [*b. Abodah Zarah*] 52a that an idol may be accepted if it is deconsecrated. But the Mishnah AZ [*m. Abodah Zarah*] has the qualification that only a Gentile and not a Jew may deconsecrate it. In [*m. Abodah Zarah*] 4,2 the gold, clothing or vessels found on the head of an idol may be put to positive use. [Further, *m. Abodah Zarah*] 4,5 mentions the case of a Gentile selling or pledging [to a Jewish merchant] his idol.[41]

And Billerbeck also collected a number of statements in the Talmud having to do with Jewish merchants buying and selling heathen idols and/or the property of pagan temples.[42]

Paul's association of "temple robbery" (here in the fourth question) with "stealing" (in the second question) and "adultery" (in the third question) indicates that he was accusing the Jews of quite literally robbing temples — that is, not, in some redefined sense of the verb ἱεροσυλέω, of refusing to pay the Jerusalem temple tax,[43] "misappropriating temple funds,"[44] being "dishonest

---

39. Deut 7:25-26.

40. Cf. Josh 7:1-26.

41. Schrenk, "ἱεροσυλέω," 3.255-56.

42. Billerbeck, *Str-Bil*, 3.114-15.

43. So J. C. K. von Hofmann in his 1868 Romans commentary, as cited by Schrenk, "ἱεροσυλέω," 3.256.

44. So Michel, *An die Römer*, 89.

towards heathen temples,"[45] or simply "committing sacrilege."[46] And while Jewish sectarians of the day often accused their nation's religious leaders of having "stolen from" and "desecrated" the Jerusalem temple,[47] it seems far better to understand Paul here as referring to Jews who stole from heathen temples — as John Chrysostom understood him at the end of the fourth century in preaching on Paul's letter to the Romans: "It was strictly forbidden for Jews to touch any of the treasures deposited in heathen temples, because they would be defiled. But Paul claims here that the tyranny of greed had persuaded them to disregard the law at this point."[48]

But did Paul view Jews as actually looting heathen temples — that is, physically taking their idols, carting away their artifacts, ripping out inlaid jewels, and scraping goldleaf from architectural features, confiscating furnishings and vestments, or absconding with money deposited in temple treasuries? Probably not. For all these direct acts of looting were explicitly condemned by Jewish law and Jewish history.

Nonetheless, as Duncan Derrett has pointed out, Jewish merchants seem to have often felt free to "handle" for purely commercial purposes such merchandise as came their way from heathen temples, whether directly or indirectly, since halakah (Jewish case law regarding human conduct) — when read with "casuistical skill" — did not specifically deal with such commercial transactions.[49] "The Jewish antique dealer," as Duncan Derrett suggested, "might not take the 'abomination' aspect [of the prohibition of Deut 7:25-26] too seriously; and he could protest that nothing of any 'devoted thing' actually 'cleaved to his hand' within the meaning of Deut 13.17(18)."[50]

But Paul, as Derrett concludes, viewed such commercial profiting "from assets irrevocably dedicated to an idolatrous purpose" as (1) "a crime against the Torah as properly interpreted," (2) if not explicitly a crime in Roman and Greek law, "certainly contrary to pagan *mores*," (3) hostile to "the reputation of the Jewish community" and "the attractiveness of the Hebrew religion," and (4) an offense to "the 'repute' of its deity."[51] And it is evidently along the lines of such a scenario that Paul's rhetorical question "Do you rob temples?" should be understood.

2:23 Paul's statement ὃς ἐν νόμῳ καυχᾶσαι, διὰ τῆς παραβάσεως τοῦ νόμου τὸν θεὸν ἀτιμάζεις can be read either (1) as an accusatory summary statement, "You who boast in the law, you dishonor God by breaking the law,"[52] or (2) as a further accusing question, "You who boast in the law, do you dishonor

---

45. So J. B. Phillips's translation.
46. So Cranfield, *Romans*, 1.169-70.
47. Cf., e.g., *T Levi* 14:5; *Pss Sol* 8:11-13; CD 6.15.
48. Chrysostom, "Homilies," in *Nicene and Post-Nicene Fathers*, 11.369.
49. Cf. Derrett, " 'You Abominate False Gods; But Do You Rob Shrines?' " 565.
50. *Ibid.*, 567.
51. *Ibid.*, 571.
52. NEB, JB, NJB.

God by breaking the law?"[53] Many significant exegetical commentators of the past century have taken it as a statement summing up the preceding four rhetorical questions rather than as a further accusing question.[54] Charles Cranfield has probably best stated the rationale for understanding this view in his argument that the verse "is more naturally read as a statement than as a question, in view of the fact that the following verse is a confirmation of its truth (γάρ)."[55] Further, "The change of construction (the use of ὅς and the indicative after the series of four participles with the article) also suggests that this is not a further question. It sums up vv. 21 and 22."[56]

But, if in 2:24 (1) the postpositive γάρ does not signal the appearance of supporting or explanatory material, but rather introduces the conflated quotation of Isa 52:5 and Ezek 36:22 — as it introduces quotations of Scripture in Rom 10:13; 11:34-35: 1 Cor 2:16; 10:26; 15:27 and introduces, as earlier in ch. 2, what appear to be a Jewish aphorism in 2:11 and Jewish Christian catechetical material in 2:14-15, (2) the phrase καθὼς γέγραπται after the quotation — and not, it needs to be noted, in its usual place before a quotation — serves not to introduce a biblical quotation, as it usually does, but is used here for some other purpose, and (3) the conflated quotation itself is not used to "confirm," "clinch," or "support" from the OT what has been said but appears for some other purpose or purposes — all of which will be argued and explicated below — then the structure of 2:23 is probably better understood in line with the pattern of rhetorical questions that precedes it in 2:21-22 rather than in terms of what may be understood as the purpose and structure of what follows it in 2:24. So in all likelihood the apostle's words in 2:23 are probably best read as comprising the final accusatory rhetorical question in a series of five such questions: "You who boast about the law, do you dishonor God by breaking the law?"

That Jews boasted about their possession and knowledge of the Mosaic law is abundantly clear from their writings. Sir 24:23, for example, speaks of "the book of the covenant of God Most High (βίβλος διαθήκης θεοῦ ὑψίστου)" as "the law which Moses commanded as a heritage for the congregations [i.e., 'synagogues'] of Jacob (νόμον ὅν ἐνετείλατο Μωυσῆς κληρονομίαν συναγωγαῖς Ἰακώβ)" — and Sir 39 refers to one who gives "all of his attention to the law of the Most High (ὑψίστου) and is occupied in meditating on it" (v. 1) as one who "will boast in the law of the covenant of the Lord (ἐν νόμῳ διαθήκης Κυρίου καυχήσεται)" (v. 8). And Paul Billerbeck has drawn attention to a number of other Jewish passages that speak to this same effect.[57]

53. KJV, RSV, TEV, NIV, NRSV, NASB.
54. So, e.g., Sanday and Headlam, *Romans,* 66; Lietzmann, *An die Römer,* 66; Lagrange, *Romains,* 54; Cranfield, *Romans,* 1.170; Dunn, *Romans,* 113; Fitzmyer, *Romans,* 318; Moo, *Romans,* 165-66.
55. Cranfield, *Romans,* 1.170.
56. Cranfield, *Romans,* 1.170.
57. See Billerbeck, *Str-Bil,* 3.115-18.

The rightness or wrongness of boasting, of course, depends on the nature of that boasting — that is, whether as an expression of self-confidence and self-glorification or an expression of confidence, joy, and thanksgiving to God in response to who he is and what he has done.[58] Even boasting about God's law is, of itself, not only legitimate but can also be laudatory. But boasting about one's supremacy over others because of one's possession or knowledge of God's law — or speaking of others as inferior because they do not have or know God's law — is a perversion of biblical religion, and so to be denounced. In particular to be denounced is the self-assertiveness reflected in 2 Bar 48:22, which suggests that because a person possesses God's law he or she is better than others in God's sight and will be protected by God (which, sadly, is a tenet that all-too-frequently lurks beneath the surface in many religions, Christianity included):

> In you we have put our trust, because your Law is with us, and we know that we will not fall as long as we keep your statutes. We will always be blessed. At least, we will not mingle with the nations. For we are all a people of the Name — that is, we who received the Law from the One [i.e., God]. And that Law that is among us will help us, and that excellent wisdom which is in us will support us.[59]

And boasting about one's relationship with God, and yet not keeping or doing God's law, is a breaking of God's covenant, and therefore similarly to be denounced.

It cannot be assumed, however, that what Paul writes in Rom 2:17-23 is a blanket condemnation of all Jews. Many writings of both Second Temple Judaism and Rabbinic Judaism also recognize such inconsistencies and perversions in the Jewish experience.[60] But it is to say that Paul evidently intended his statements and rhetorical questions in 2:17-23 to be understood as characterizing much of the Jewish experience of his day — to epitomize, in fact, his understanding of what a religion of law inevitably perpetuates — and so to prepare for his proclamation of the Christian gospel later in his letter.

D. A Conclusion (2:24)

Closing off the diatribe of 2:17-24, Paul quotes in conflated fashion the words of Isa 52:5 and Ezek 36:22. A number of features need to be observed with regard to this conflated quotation. In the first place, it should be noted that Paul introduces this quotation with the introductory γάρ ("for"), as he does sometimes elsewhere in his letters[61] — and as he did in the previous section of this chapter

---

58. See our exegetical comments above on 2:17.
59. 2 Bar 48:22-24.
60. Cf. R. N. Longenecker, "The Piety of Hebraic Judaism," in Paul, Apostle of Liberty, 65-85.
61. Cf., e.g., Rom 10:13; 11:34-35; 1 Cor 2:16; 10:26; 15:27.

when introducing a traditional aphorism in 2:11 and earlier catechetical material in 2:14 — rather than by the introductory formulaic phrase καθὼς γέγραπται ("just as it is written"), as he usually does.

Second, while καθὼς γέγραπται does not appear prior to the quotation by way of introducing it, the phrase does appear at the end of the quotation in appended fashion, which it never does with any of Paul's other quotations of Scripture. Third, Isa 52:5 in its own context, as Richard Hays has rightly insisted, "is part of Yahweh's *reassurance* of Israel in exile: precisely because Israel's oppressed condition allows the nations to despise the power of Israel's God, the people can trust more surely that God will reveal himself and act to vindicate his own name."[62] Further, it needs to be observed that when the words of Isa 52:5 ("all day long my name is constantly being blasphemed") are conflated with those of Ezek 36:22 ("for the sake of my holy name, which you have profaned among the nations where you have gone"), the resultant wording becomes a message not of consolation or reassurance but of accusation and denunciation.

These four features have sometimes been noted by commentators, but have never been viewed as having any particular relevance for interpretation. We propose, however, that when these features are viewed together they become highly significant for an understanding of what Paul is doing and saying here. For while they may not demonstrably "prove" any particular thesis, we suggest: (1) that the conflation of these words drawn from Isa 52:5 and Ezek 36:22 and the adjustment of nuancing that has thus taken place were probably done by Jewish Christians before Paul, known by his Christian addressees at Rome, and used by Paul to speak to his addressees in a manner that they would understand and appreciate; (2) that by his introductory use of the conjunction γάρ ("for") Paul indicates that he is treating what he quotes more along the lines of traditional material than strictly Scripture, much as he does in the previous section of this same chapter at 2:11 and 2:14; and (3) that by placing καθὼς γέγραπται ("just as it is written") not in its usual place before a quotation but — and only this one time in his letters — after the quotation, Paul is probably using the phrase not to introduce what follows but only to suggest that his denunciations of the Jews of his day, as set out previously in 2:17-23, are in line with the prophetic denunciations of God's own people Israel. In effect, therefore, Paul is most likely saying that his denunciations of certain Jews and their practices in his day are to be seen as being in line with Isaiah's and Ezekiel's denunciations in their day.

It seems best, therefore, *not* to understand Paul in 2:24 as using an OT quotation to support or confirm what he said previously in the diatribal statements and questions of 2:17-23. Rather, he is probably using this conflated quotation (1) to align himself with the Jewish prophetic tradition in a manner that would have been known, understood, and appreciated by his addressees and

---

62. Hays, *Echoes of Scripture,* 45.

(2) to claim by this alignment that what he has written in 2:17-23 is to be viewed as a contemporary prophetic accusation directed against a number of the descendants of God's ancient people Israel.

But however these features of the passage and Paul's purpose(s) in citing this conflated quotation are understood, it is a very serious charge he is making. For, in effect, he is asserting that the Jews of his day have broken God's covenant and therefore are not to be considered any better than the Gentiles whom they despise.

II. The Uncircumcised Hearts of Jews (2:25-29)

Just as the statements and rhetorical questions of 2:17-24 attempted to highlight the fact that the Jews' possession of the law will not shield them from God's judgment, because it is the "keeping" and "doing" of the law and not merely possession or knowledge of it that matters, so here in 2:25-29 Paul asserts that physical circumcision is of no benefit unless the law is obeyed and there is a "circumcision of the heart" effected "by the Spirit." Later rabbinic writings, which sought to codify earlier Jewish teaching, claimed that "no person who is circumcised will go down to Gehenna."[63] Paul, however, rejects this argument because obedience to God's instruction is the central criterion for relationship with God — not physical circumcision, which is only an outward sign of the covenant. Thus just as he declared in 2:17-24 that if the law is not observed the covenant is broken, and having broken God's covenant Jews cannot expect to be spared from God's wrath, so here in 2:25-29 Paul insists that uncircumcised hearts can never be compensated for by mere circumcision of the flesh, for essential to true biblical religion is an inward "circumcision of the heart" that is brought about "by the Spirit."

2:25a Paul begins this second subsection of his argument by insisting that physical circumcision has spiritual value only if one observes the law — that is, by stating that περιτομὴ μὲν γὰρ ὠφελεῖ ἐὰν νόμον πράσσῃς ("circumcision, indeed, has value if you observe the law"). The postpositive conjunction γάρ is used here in a transitory manner to connect what will be said in 2:25-29 to what has been said in the diatribe of 2:17-24 above. The affirming particle μέν ("to be sure," "indeed"), which appears about 182 times throughout the NT, is used here by Paul to state quite expressly what he is about to say — both in opposition to what others might think he believes and to support what he truly believes. The verb ὠφελέω means "help," "aid," "value," and is further defined by its cognate adjective ὠφέλιμος, which signifies "useful," "beneficial," "advantageous," or "valuable" for someone or something. The use of the conditional ἐάν ("if") with the second person singular present subjunctive verb πράσσῃς (literally "if you should observe," "keep," or "do") suggests

---

63. *Exod. Rab.* 19:81c; cf. *Gen. Rab.* 48:30a; *b. Tanch.* 60b.

"what will possibly occur" — or perhaps "what is expected to occur" — with respect to "obeying," "keeping," or "doing" νόμον, that is, the Mosaic law, but which, as Paul has previously asserted (and will continue to assert), was not being done.

Three reasons are given in Jewish writings for circumcision, that is, the removal of the male foreskin. The first and undoubtedly most important reason for any pious Jew was simply because God had commanded it,[64] and so every act of circumcision was done in obedience to the divine precept.[65] A second reason often given in Paul's day, but one without express biblical support, was in order to identify Jewish males and keep them "from mixing with others."[66] A third rationale for circumcision, which was proposed during the Maccabean period, was that it was a sign of fidelity to the covenant and therefore an indispensable identity marker for Jewish males.[67]

Philo of Alexandria, the Hellenized Jewish philosopher-theologian who was a contemporary of Paul, explains circumcision in an allegorical fashion to himself and his readers, but also insists that Jews wherever they lived should practice it literally.[68] He mentions some Hellenized Jews who did not circumcise their infant sons,[69] and Josephus refers in his account of the conversion of Izates to some Jews who may have exempted adult Gentile male converts from the rite.[70] The overwhelming dominant opinion, however, not only in the homeland but also throughout the Diaspora, was that all male Jewish infants and all male adult proselytes were to be circumcised.

Rabbinic literature also views circumcision as a highly important rite for every male Jew. *M. Nedarim* 3, for example, closes with a number of quotations from second-century A.D. rabbis:

> "Great is circumcision, whereby the covenant was made thirteen times" (the word "covenant" appears thirteen times in Genesis 17).
> "Great is circumcision which overrides even the rigor of the Sabbath" (circumcision takes precedence over even the Sabbath).
> "Great is circumcision which even for the sake of Moses, the righteous, was not suspended so much as an hour" (cf. Exod 4:24-26).

64. Gen 17:10-11; cf. *Jub* 15:28.

65. Cf., e.g., Josephus, *Antiquities* 20.44-45, who reports this as the reason given Izates by Eleazar, who was the king's spiritual counselor.

66. So Josephus, *Antiquities* 1.192, who speaks of God's intention in the command of Gen 17:10-11 to Abraham and his male descendants to be circumcised as being "that his posterity should be kept from mixing with others."

67. Cf. 1 Macc 1:48 on the Seleucid attitude toward Jewish circumcision and 1 Macc 2:46 on the Jewish attitude; see also 1 Macc 1:60-61 and 2 Macc 6:10, where the case is related of two women who were gruesomely killed by the Seleucids because they had circumcised their baby boys; cf. R. Meyer, "περιτέμνω," 6.74-78.

68. Cf. Philo, *De migratione Abrahami* 89-94.

69. Cf. Philo. *De specialibus legibus* 1.1-11; 304-6; *De Abrahamo* 92.

70. Josephus, *Antiquities* 20.17-48.

"Great is circumcision, which overrides the laws of leprosy-signs" [cf. m *Negaim* 7:5: "If leprosy appears on the tip of the foreskin, a man may nevertheless be circumcised").

"Great is circumcision, for despite all the religious duties which Abraham our father fulfilled, he was not called 'perfect' until he was circumcised, as it is written, 'Walk before me and be thou perfect' [Gen 17:1]."

"Great is circumcision; except for it the Holy One, blessed is he, had not created his world, as it is written, 'Thus saith the Lord, "but for my covenant day and night, I had not set forth the ordinances of heaven and earth"' [Jer 33:25]."

Paul had no desire to say anything against the Jewish rite of circumcision. Indeed, as he highlights by use of the affirmative particle μέν ("indeed"), the physical act and religious rite of circumcision "has value" for the Jewish world.[71] And Paul would undoubtedly have affirmed that its value lay in the fact that it is the human response of obedience ordained by God in his covenant with Abraham and his posterity, that is, the God-ordained response for all Jewish males who claimed to be in covenant relationship with God[72] — though not, as Paul's letter to his Gentile converts in Galatia insists, a God-ordained response for Gentile Christians, who by their faith in Jesus the Christ ("Messiah") have Abraham as their spiritual father and so have become legitimate recipients of the promises given to Abraham and his "seed."[73]

But Paul's point here, as throughout Rom 2, is that circumcision has spiritual value for Jews only ἐὰν νόμον πράσσῃς ("if you should 'obey'/'do' the law"). He does not deny the value of physical circumcision, but he insists that circumcision per se means nothing without actually "obeying," "keeping," and "doing" the law, as Lev. 18:5 explicitly requires: "Keep my decrees and laws, for the one who obeys them will live by them. I am the Lord."[74]

2:25b Paul goes on, however, to express an indictment against professing but not practicing Jews: ἐὰν δὲ παραβάτης νόμου ᾖς, ἡ περιτομή σου ἀκροβυστία γέγονεν ("but if you are a transgressor of the law, your circumcision has become uncircumcision"). Again the apostle's use of the conditional ἐάν ("if") with the second person singular present subjunctive verb ᾖς (literally "if you should be" or simply "if you are"), coupled here with the noun παραβάτης ("transgressor," "one who breaks") and the genitive νόμου ("the law," see the textual notes above on νόμος and ὁ νόμος as synonymous) is probably best understood as "if you should be a transgressor of the law" — that is, "one who breaks the Mosaic law." Such a statement would have been absolutely shocking to a Jew of Paul's day, just as it would be to Jews today. It is, however, entirely

---

71. Cf. Rom 2:25: περιτομὴ μὲν γὰρ ὠφελεῖ ("for indeed circumcision has value").
72. Cf. Gen 17:9-14.
73. Cf. esp. Gal 3:6-9, 15-18.
74. See also Deut 30:16.

consistent with Paul's attitude toward circumcision as expressed earlier in 1 Cor 7:19: "Circumcision is nothing and uncircumcision is nothing. Keeping God's commands is what counts."[75] The perfect tense of the verb γέγονεν signals a past reality ("has become") that continues to be a present reality ("is now a continuing reality"). Thus because of their transgressions of the law, Jews "have become uncircumcised," and so are no better than Gentiles — who were designated by Jews as ἡ ἀκροβυστία ("the uncircumcised"), which may have been a taunt or term of derision used against Gentiles by Jews, perhaps also by some Jewish Christians, and possibly even some of the Gentile Christians at Rome who had been influenced by the theology and language of Jewish Christians.

2:26-27 Paul's words here in 2:26-27 are very much like those that appear earlier in 2:14-15. For in both passages he speaks of the possibility of a Gentile observing God's standards of righteousness and conduct as expressed in the Mosaic law even without possessing or knowing the law of Moses (2:14-15) or being circumcised (2:26-27). Likewise, the two passages are alike in that they both only contemplate the possibility that Gentiles might keep the law, but never actually say that they have, that they could, or that they would want to. The first passage signals such a contingent possibility by the use of the temporal particle ὅταν ("whenever," "when") in 2:14; the second, by the use of a "third class condition" syntactical construction that uses the conditional particle ἐάν ("if") with the third person singular present subjunctive verb φυλάσσῃ ("he should keep") in the protasis in 2:26. Further, the two passages are similar in their respective purposes. For while 2:14-15 speaks about the situation of the Gentiles before God, it does so in the context of rebuking Jews for believing that God will favor them over Gentiles in the final judgment, and 2:26-27 uses the possibility of an uncircumcised Gentile keeping God's laws only as something to shame Jews.

The scenario set out in 2:26 is in terms of some postulated Gentile man (ἡ ἀκροβυστία, "the uncircumcised") possibly keeping (ἐάν ... φυλάσσῃ, "if he should keep") the requirements of the Mosaic law (τὰ δικαιώματα τοῦ νόμου, "the regulations/commandments of the law"). And it asks the question οὐχ ἡ ἀκροβυστία αὐτοῦ εἰς περιτομὴν λογισθήσεται; (literally "Will not his uncircumcision be credited unto circumcision?" or more idiomatically expressed in English: "Will he not be regarded as though he were circumcised?") — with the implied answer to that question being "Yes."

Paul does not, however, elaborate further on the state of his postulated Gentile. Rather, he turns this possible scenario of God's acceptance of a Gentile who obeys the law against Jews who possess and affirm God's law but do not obey or keep it — saying only: καὶ κρινεῖ ἡ ἐκ φύσεως ἀκροβυστία τὸν νόμον τελοῦσα σὲ τὸν διὰ γράμματος καὶ περιτομῆς παραβάτην νόμου ("the one who is not circumcised physically, and yet who satisfies the requirements of the law, will condemn you who, even though you have the written code and circumci-

75. See also Gal 5:6; 6:15.

315

sion, are a lawbreaker"). In order to satisfy our own inbred curiosity, we would like Paul to speak further about the spiritual situation of such a Gentile. But all he really says, as Joseph Fitzmyer has paraphrased his words, is that "the uncircumcised pagan who follows his conscience and obeys thereby some of the prescriptions of the law will stand in judgment over the circumcised Jew who violates the law."[76]

Paul's words here are very much like those of Jesus regarding the repentance of non-Jews at Nineveh vis-à-vis the callousness of heart of God's own people: "The men of Nineveh will stand up at the judgment with this generation and condemn it, for they repented at the preaching of Jonah, and now one greater than Jonah is here."[77] For neither Jesus' comment on the biblical story nor Paul's statement regarding Gentiles tells us anything about how God views non-Jews who respond to him positively on the basis of what they know about him — whether from his revelation of himself in creation (as in Rom 1:19-20), from "the law written on their hearts" (as in 2:15a), or from the actions of their own consciences in either accusing or excusing them (as in 2:15b). Rather, the purpose of both the comment of Jesus recorded in Luke 11:32 and the statement of Paul here in Rom 2:27 is to declare God's rightful judgment of Jews who profess to know God's will but do not do it.

The emphasis on "judgment" is heightened by the appearance of the third person singular future indicative active verb κρινεῖ ("he will judge," "condemn") at the very beginning of this sentence in 2:27. Further, the significance of such a judgment is clearly suggested by the context as an "indicting judgment" or "justifiable condemnation," while the time when such a condemnation will take place may be assumed to be at the final eschatological judgment of all people by God. The noun φύσις ("nature") when used of a person signifies one's "natural endowment" or "physical condition," and so the prepositional phrase ἐκ φύσεως is probably best translated "with respect to one's physical condition" or "physically."

Paul uses the genitive singular γράμματος ("letter") here in 2:27 (also the dative singular of the noun in 2:29) with reference to the commandments of Scripture, which, in parallelism to the genitive singular noun περιτομῆς ("circumcision"), which here signifies "the practice of circumcision," is probably best translated "the written code." The expression τὰ ἱερὰ γράμματα ("the holy writings") — with or without the article τὰ and with or without the adjective ἱερὰ — was commonly used among Greek-speaking Jews with reference to their Scriptures.[78] Philo, however, used the singular γράμμα, with or without the article, to refer to the whole of the Jewish Scriptures, to the Decalogue expressed in Exodus and Deuteronomy, or to a single verse within those Scriptures.[79] Else-

---

76. Fitzmyer, *Romans*, 322.
77. Luke 11:32.
78. Cf. Josephus, *Antiquities* 10.10.4; 13.5.8; 20.12.1.
79. Cf. Philo, *De migratione Abrahami* 15.85; 25.139; *De congressu eruditionis gratia* 12.58.

where in his letters Paul uses singular γράμμα ("letter"), in contrast to πνεῦμα ("spirit" or "Spirit"), to refer to the Mosaic law — particularly to the regulations of the Decalogue.[80]

2:28-29a Paul concludes his denunciation of Jews and Jewish legalism by declaring in a twofold fashion, first negatively, οὐ γὰρ ὁ ἐν τῷ φανερῷ Ἰουδαῖός ἐστιν οὐδὲ ἡ ἐν τῷ φανερῷ ἐν σαρκὶ περιτομή ("for a person is not a Jew who is one only outwardly, nor is true circumcision merely external and physical"), then positively, ἀλλ' ὁ ἐν τῷ κρυπτῷ Ἰουδαῖος, καὶ περιτομὴ καρδίας ἐν πνεύματι οὐ γράμματι ("rather, a person is a Jew who is one inwardly, and real circumcision is a matter of the heart — by the Spirit, not by the written code").

The postpositive γάρ in 2:28 is used in an explanatory and concluding manner, but the question remains whether it does so in relation to 2:25-27 (which deals with circumcision) or 2:17-27 (which says far more about Jewish practices). Because the passage is a unified whole, starting at 2:17 with a question about Jewish identity and ending in 2:28-29 with much the same type of question ("Is a Jew one who has been 'outwardly and physically' circumcised, or is he also one who has experienced an 'inward' circumcision 'of the heart'?"), the γάρ at the beginning of 2:28 is probably best viewed as introducing the conclusion of the entire passage — and so can be represented in English by simply indenting the passage's final two-verse paragraph.

In this final paragraph Paul contrasts external, physical circumcision vis-à-vis inward, spiritual circumcision — or what he calls in 2:29 the "circumcision of the heart," which comes about "by the Spirit" and "not by the written code." Three antitheses are thus set out: (1) ἐν τῷ φανερῷ ("outwardly," "external") contrasted with ἐν τῷ κρυπτῷ ("secretly," "inward"), (2) ἐν σαρκί ("in the flesh," "physical") contrasted with καρδίας ("of the heart"), and (3) [ἐν] γράμματι ("by the letter," "written code") contrasted with ἐν πνεύματι ("by the Spirit"). The Jewish (OT) Scriptures, as well as various writings from the period of Second Temple Judaism, also made such distinctions, arguing that the external sign of circumcision be accompanied by inward circumcision of the heart, as for example:

> Lev 26:40-42: "If they [the people of Israel] will confess their sins and the sins of their fathers — their treachery against me and their hostility toward me, which made me hostile toward them so that I sent them into the land of their enemies — then when their uncircumcised hearts are humbled and they pay for their sin, I will remember my covenant with Jacob and my covenant with Isaac and my covenant with Abraham, and I will remember the land."
>
> Deut 10:16: "Circumcise, therefore, the foreskin of your hearts, and do not be stiff-necked any longer."

80. Cf. Rom 7:6; 2 Cor 3:6-8.

Deut 30:6: "The Lord your God will circumcise your hearts and the hearts
of your descendants, so that you will love the Lord your God with all
your heart and with all your soul, and live."

Jer 4:4: "Circumcise yourselves to the Lord, remove the foreskin of your
hearts, O people of Judah and inhabitants of Jerusalem."

Jer 9:25-26: "'The days are surely coming,' says the Lord, 'when I will punish all who are circumcised only in the flesh — Egypt, Judah, Edom,
Ammon, Moab, and all who live in the desert in distant places. For all
these nations are really uncircumcised, and even the whole house of
Israel is uncircumcised in heart.'"

Jub 1:23: "After this [Israel's repentance and confession of sin] they will
turn to me in all uprightness and with all their heart and with all their
soul, and I will circumcise the foreskin of their hearts and the foreskin
of the hearts of their descendants, and I will create in them a holy
spirit, and I will cleanse them so that they shall not turn away from me
from that day unto eternity."

1QpHab 11.13 (on Hab 2:16): "Its interpretation concerns the Priest whose
shame has exceeded his glory because he did not circumcise the foreskin of his heart."

Thus in speaking of the necessity of an "inward" circumcision "of the
heart" brought about "by the Spirit," Paul is in full accord with the OT as well
as with many pious Jewish teachers of his day — both within what may be called
mainline Pharisaic Judaism and among various forms of sectarian Judaism. It
is a feature of importance that Paul's addressees at Rome undoubtedly also
accepted, since, whatever their respective ethnic backgrounds, they had all
been extensively influenced by Jewish Christian teaching, which was rooted in
the concepts, themes, and language of the OT. And it is an emphasis that Paul
wanted to build on in his depiction of the common Christian proclamation in
3:21-4:25, in the presentation of his own distinctive message in 5:1-8:39, and
then in his development of a "remnant theology" understanding of relationships
between the Christian gospel and the hope of Israel in 9:1-11:36.

2:29b Paul concludes his description of a true Jew with the statement:
οὗ ὁ ἔπαινος οὐκ ἐξ ἀνθρώπων ἀλλ᾽ ἐκ τοῦ θεοῦ ("such a person's praise is
not from other people but comes from God"). The adverb οὗ, which is really
the genitive of the relative pronoun ὅς ("who," "which," "what"), is used here
in a figurative sense to suggest the circumstance or situation of something or
someone, and so is probably best translated as "such a one" or "such a person."
It may be questioned how this statement is relevant to its immediate context.
Further, it may be observed that the statement has every appearance of being
a Jewish aphorism, such as appeared in 2:2 and 2:11. There has been, therefore,
some uncertainty among commentators regarding the purpose and function of
this final statement of the passage.

It needs to be recognized, however, as has been observed by a number of scholars, that the Greek word ἔπαινος ("praise," "approval") probably reflects a Jewish wordplay on the name Ἰουδαῖος ("Jew"). For while the name "Jew" (Hebrew יהודי) was derived from the patriarchal name "Judah" (יהודה), in Jewish popular theology יהודה seems to have been etymologically associated with the hiphil or passive form of the verb ידה ("to be praised") — with that association stemming from statements by Judah's mother Leah at his birth in Gen 29:35 and his father Jacob in his final words to his sons in Gen 49:8.[81] And if, indeed, such a wordplay is reflected in Rom 2:29b, then Paul should be seen here as concluding his treatment of circumcision in 2:25-29 — as well as closing off his entire discussion of Jews and Jewish failures in 2:17-29 — with a telling reminder that it is only the circumcised heart that is praised by God, as is implied in the very name "Jew" when nuanced by its association with the patriarchal name "Judah" and the Hebrew verb "praise" in its hiphil or passive form.

Such an association and play on words — as well as such a conclusion to a passage that deals with circumcision (and, more broadly, a passage that also deals with the self-identity of Jews vis-à-vis their failures of practice) — may appear somewhat strange to Christian commentators. Paul, however, evidently thought that this concluding statement of 2:29b would be meaningful to his Christian addressees at Rome — who, it seems (as we have argued), had been extensively influenced by Jewish Christian concepts, themes, and expressions. Further, if the statement had originally been a Jewish aphorism that was later carried over into Jewish Christianity and so became known to the Christians at Rome (as we are here suggesting was likely the case), it may be assumed that Paul used it with every expectation that it would have a telling impact on his Christian addressees at Rome and aid in establishing his thesis among them regarding circumcision in 2:25-29a, as well as supporting all that he had said earlier about Jews and their failures in 2:17-24. For what is said in this aphoristic saying highlights something of very great importance about every true Jew — and, consequently, about every true Jewish or Gentile believer in Jesus — that "such a person's praise is not from other people but comes from God."

BIBLICAL THEOLOGY

There is, admittedly, not much that can be derived positively from a passage that is devoted almost entirely to the denouncing of spiritual and ethical failures. Nonetheless, there are truths to be learned from such indicting statements, questions, and expositions, and therefore features of importance that merit every Christian's reflection and meditation — likewise, statements that need to be taken seriously into consideration in any Christian biblical theology.

81. Cf. Sanday and Headlam, *Romans,* 68, who credited E. H. Gifford in his 1881 *Romans* commentary as "the first to point out that there is here an evident play on the name 'Jew': Judah = 'Praise.'" More likely, however, R. Haldane in his 1839 Romans commentary should be so credited.

Jewish Spiritual and Moral Failures vis-à-vis the Moral Caliber of Judaism.
A problem for most commentators has been how to understand Paul's extremely
severe criticisms of Jewish spiritual and moral failures in 2:17-29 when it was the
moral caliber of the Jewish religion, as well as the ethical lives of many of its adherents, that made Judaism so attractive to a number of Gentiles of that day — not
only to Gentiles who became Jewish "proselytes" but also to pagan Gentile "God-
fearers." Was Paul exaggerating or generalizing from a few isolated cases? Was he
disqualifying all Jews because of the failures of a few? Or should what is written in
this passage be viewed as being flatly contradictory to Paul's teaching elsewhere in
Romans, and therefore understood as (1) an interpolation by a later glossator who
drew on material from some Hellenistic Jewish missionary tractate,[82] (2) a portion
of homiletical material that was drawn from one or more of the synagogues of
Diaspora Judaism, which Paul incorporated into Romans without any substantial
editing,[83] or (3) a product of Paul's "divided mind" with respect to the ability of
Jews to keep the Mosaic law, which resulted here in a highly polemical "piece of
propagandist denigration" that condemns the Jewish nation *in toto*?[84]

But Paul's statements and questions here need to be understood in the
context of similar accusatory rhetorical flourishes of his day. As Anton Fridrichsen pointed out in 1927,[85] the Stoic philosopher Epictetus, who was active
during the last part of the first century A.D., denounced in comparable fashion
those who called themselves Stoics but whose practices fell far short of their
lofty ideals.[86] More importantly, the Jewish (OT) Scriptures roundly denounced
the spiritual and moral failures of God's people in their day,[87] as did also a number of other Jewish writers during the period of Second Temple Judaism.[88] Jesus, too, is portrayed as having denounced the whole body of Pharisees of his
day.[89] And there are a number of places in the Talmud and other rabbinic literature where various rabbis are reported to have criticized in such an inclusive
fashion all whom they viewed as having fallen short in their practice of what they
professed.[90] So Paul's sweeping indictments of Jews and their failures here in
2:17-29 should not be viewed as some form of idiosyncratic rant from an apos-
tate Jew who wanted to denounce all Jews and renounce everything connected
with the Jewish religion — and certainly not as justification for any form of anti-
Semitism. Rather, Paul's accusatory statements, questions, and expositions in
this passage must be viewed as set within the context of a rhetorical style that
was common in his day to express with conviction and vigor the rebukes and

82. So O'Neill, *Romans*, 41-42, 49, 53-54, 264-65.
83. So E. P. Sanders, *Paul, the Law, and the Jewish People*, 123, 129.
84. So Räisänen, *Paul and the Law*, 100-107.
85. A. Fridrichsen, "Der wahre Jude," 45.
86. See Epictetus, *Dissertations* 2.19.19-28; 3.7.17; 3.24-40.
87. Cf., Isa 3:14-15; Jer 7:8-11; Ezek 22:6-12; Mal 3:5; see also Asaph in Ps 50:16-21.
88. Cf. *Pss Sol* 8:8-14; *T Levi* 14:4-8; CD 6.16-17; see also Philo, *De confusione linguarum* 163.
89. Cf. Matt 23:1-36//Luke 11:39-52.
90. Cf. Billerbeck, *Str-Bil*, 3.105-111.

exhortations of a speaker or author. What Paul evidently wanted to convey to his Christian addressees at Rome was that he was writing to them as a prophet — and there would probably have been very little doubt among his addressees about either his intention or his meaning.

"Paul's target," as James Dunn has aptly observed, "is not any or all Jews as individuals, but Jewish assurance of standing in a position of ethical privilege by virtue of the law."[91] And Paul's point, as Dunn has rightly gone on to elaborate, is that "the very fact that there are Jews who do what their law clearly forbids should be enough to undermine the confidence that the Jew *per se* stands in a position of superiority or advantage over the non-Jew by virtue of being a member of the people of the law."[92] It is, therefore, important in every Christian biblical theology to note with clarity (1) that God is no respecter of a person's background, privileges, status, or even affirmations of belief about God and his will, but (2) that God looks for a person's positive response to him of love, which includes the actual doing of God's will.

The Gentiles and Their Acceptance by God. A further constantly recurring question that arises from this passage, that is, from Paul's statements in 2:26-27 — as it did also with respect to his statements in 2:14-15 — is this: Does Paul teach that Gentiles will be accepted by God by obeying the law as they know it and in their own fashion? The question, of course, has profound implications. Yet it must immediately be pointed out here, as it was in our "exegetical comments" on 2:14-15 and 2:26-27, that neither there (in speaking about Gentiles generally) nor here in 2:26-27 (in speaking about some postulated Gentiles who might possibly keep the basic tenets of God's law) does Paul say that any Gentile has actually kept — or could keep — God's will as expressed in the Mosaic law sufficiently so as to stand acquitted before God. Rather, earlier Paul spoke rhetorically in the service of his main point that both Jew and Gentile stand in need of the righteousness of God, while here he speaks using such a scenario only to shame Jews for their spiritual and moral failures.

We may as Christians today be troubled by what has been called "the problem of the heathen." As rationalists we may attempt to work out our own set of speculative answers. Or as fatalists we may simply condemn all people other than ourselves to perdition. But Paul's view of the matter seems to have been twofold: (1) with respect to God's judgments, he was convinced, as was the patriarch Abraham, that "the Judge of all the earth will do right!"[93] and (2) with respect to his own mandate, he was also convinced that he had been appointed by God as a Christian apostle to proclaim the gospel of God, which has as its focus the work and person of Jesus Christ, in order "to call people from among all the Gentiles to the obedience that comes from faith."[94] Just how these two

---

91. Dunn, *Romans,* 1.114; citing "particularly Wilckens."
92. Dunn, *Romans,* 1.114.
93. Gen 18:25.
94. Cf. Rom 1:1-5; see also 1 Cor 1:17–2:5.

convictions interacted and played out in Paul's own mind we are never told. Certainly the first did not nullify the second; nor did the second abrogate the first. And in any Christian biblical theology both convictions need always to be considered basic features of both thought and action.

Physical Circumcision and Circumcision of the Heart by the Spirit. A great deal of discussion has gone on among Christian interpreters regarding what Paul meant in 2:25-29 by physical "circumcision" and "circumcision of the heart by the Spirit." Was he proclaiming that the "true" Jew is a Christian who has been circumcised in heart by the Holy Spirit and so by the Spirit's enablement can obey the law? Or was he speaking solely about Jews who had been physically circumcised but needed also to be circumcised in their hearts — with, then, what he says about Jews applied in principle also to Christians? It is a matter that resides at the very heart of a Christian understanding and has been discussed down through the centuries by all sorts of Christian theologians. Thus it is a matter of great importance for Christian biblical theology.

The issues involved in the debate, while not always clearly defined, were prominent among the early Church Fathers. Origen, for example, who influenced most profoundly the exegesis of Alexandrian Christianity, understood Paul in 2:25-29 to be speaking about Christians, and so interpreted circumcision allegorically as "the cleansing of the soul and the rejection of all vices" — which takes place by "the grace of baptism."[95] Further, he viewed Paul in his use of γράμμα ("letter") as referring to the literal sense of Scripture and πνεῦμα ("spirit") as referring to Scripture's spiritual, allegorical sense.[96]

On the other hand, John Chrysostom, who was the leading expositor of Antiochean Christianity and stood in opposition to the allegorical interpretations of Alexandrian Christianity, understood circumcision as a literal and physical religious rite of the Jews and so says of what Paul writes in 2:25-29 such things as:

> Paul accepts the value of circumcision in theory but abolishes it in practice. For circumcision is only useful if the one circumcised keeps the law. . . . But a circumcised person who breaks the law is really uncircumcised, and Paul condemns him without hesitation.[97]

> Having moved the uncircumcised who does good deeds over to the category of the circumcised and having pushed the circumcised man who leads a corrupt life into the ranks of the uncircumcised, Paul states his preference for being physically uncircumcised.[98]

---

95. Origen, *Ad Romanos* (*PG* 14.899; *CER* 1.248-58).

96. *Ibid.;* see also *idem, Contra Celsum* 6.70 (*GCS* 3.140.16); cf. Athanasius, *Ep 1 ad Serapionem* 8 (*PG* 26.549).

97. Chrysostom, *Homilia XXXII ad Romanos*, *PG* 60.435; "Homilies," in *Nicene and Post-Nicene Fathers*, 11.370.

98. Chrysostom, *Homilia XXXII ad Romanos*, *PG* 60.436; "Homilies," in *Nicene and Post-Nicene Fathers*, 11.370-71.

By saying this [that "real circumcision is the circumcision of the heart"] Paul sets aside everything that is merely of the body. For circumcision is external, and so are the sabbaths, the sacrifices and the purification. . . . The circumcision of the flesh must be set aside, and the need for a good life is everywhere demonstrated.[99]

And Ambrosiaster, that mysterious commentator of the fourth century, seems to have tried to hone out something of a middle position between the allegorical exegesis of Alexandria and the historical exegesis of Antioch — particularly in holding to the external physical nature of the Jewish rite of circumcision, but also understanding "circumcision of the heart" and "keeping the law" as equivalent to "believing in Christ":

Why did Paul prohibit what he shows to be of value if the law is observed? Paul answers by saying that if the law is not kept, the Jew effectively becomes a Gentile. . . . But to keep the law is to believe in Christ, who was promised to Abraham. . . . For every mention of salvation in the law refers to Christ. Thus the one who believes in Christ is the one who keeps the law. But if he does not believe, then he is a transgressor of the law because he has not accepted Christ.[100]

These various views have been formulated and repeated down through the centuries by all sorts of Christian theologians and commentators. Yet it still needs to be insisted that what Paul writes in 2:17-29 is only a part of his overall argument in 1:18–3:20, which sets out the universal sinfulness of all people in order to provide the backdrop for (1) the universal Christian message of righteousness "by faith in Jesus Christ to all who believe" in 3:21–4:25 and (2) his own distinctive contextualization of that gospel proclamation to the Gentile world in 5:1–8:39. What he says is not a veiled or allegorized message about Christians. Rather, what Paul writes in this passage is about Jews and their spiritual and moral failures. Nonetheless, underlying that specific message regarding Jews and their failures is a vitally important principle that applies to Christians as well: those who profess to be Christians must not rely on only external forms or outward appearances, important as these factors might be both historically and culturally, but must be truly followers of the Lord Jesus Christ both inwardly and from the heart, directed by God's Spirit and not by written codes — with the realization that "such a person's praise is not from other people but comes from God." And it is this principle that is vital in the construction and living out of any truly Christian biblical theology.

---

99. Chrysostom, *Homilia XXXII ad Romanos,* PG 60.436-37; "Homilies," in *Nicene and Post-Nicene Fathers,* 11.371.

100. Ambrosiaster, *Ad Romanos, CSEL* 81.84.

CONTEXTUALIZATION FOR TODAY

All that Paul says in denouncing Jews in 2:17-29 is, by extension, applicable to every form of human conviction — and, in particular, applicable to distinctively Christian convictions and Christian living. For it is not just possessing, knowing, and believing the message of the Christian gospel that make one a true Christian. It is also in responding to God through Christ Jesus with a heartfelt and positive response, doing God's will as expressed in "the gospel of Christ," and being open to God's Spirit for direction and enablement.

As Christians, we can all too easily identify the perversions and failures of Judaism — and, for that matter, of any other religion. Paul teaches us, by analogy, that as those who are committed to "God in Christ" we need constantly to be aware of the disparities in our lives between profession and practice, and to bring these matters before God in repentance and confession. Further, we need always to recognize that it is not only the major disparities between affirmation and action that disgrace the Christian message and shame the Christian, it is also "the little foxes that spoil the vine."

5. The Situation of the Jews before God (3:1-20)

TRANSLATION

³:¹*What advantage, then, is there in being a Jew? Or what is the value of circumcision?* ²*Much in every way! First of all, indeed, they [the Jews] were entrusted with the words of God.*

³*What if some of them were unfaithful? Will their unfaithfulness nullify the faithfulness of God?* ⁴*Certainly not! "Let God be true but every human being a liar." Just as it is written:*

> *"So that you may be justified when you speak*
> *and will prevail when you are judged."*

⁵*But if our unrighteousness serves to demonstrate more clearly God's righteous justice, what shall we say? Shall we say that God is unjust to pronounce his wrath on his people? (I am speaking in a human manner.)* ⁶*Certainly not! If that were so, how will God judge the world?* ⁷*And if the truth of God is enhanced unto his glory by my falsehood, why am I also still condemned as a sinner?* ⁸*Why not say — just as we are being slanderously reported as saying, and just as some claim we are saying — "Let us do evil that good might result"? Their condemnation is deserved.*

⁹*What then shall we conclude? Are we [Jews] any better? Not at all! For we have already charged that both Jews and Gentiles are all under sin.* ¹⁰*Just as it is written:*

> *"There is no one righteous, not even one;*
> ¹¹*there is no one who understands,*
> *there is no one who seeks God.*
> ¹²*All have turned away,*
> *they have together become worthless;*
> *there is no one who does good,*
> *there is not even one."*
> ¹³*"Their throats are open graves;*
> *their tongues practice deceit."*
> *"The poison of vipers is on their lips."*
> ¹⁴*"Their mouths are full of cursing and bitterness."*
> ¹⁵*"Their feet are swift to shed blood;*
> ¹⁶*ruin and misery mark their ways,*
> ¹⁷*and the way of peace they do not know."*
> ¹⁸*"There is no fear of God before their eyes."*

¹⁹*Now we know that whatever the law says, it says to those who are under the law, so that every mouth may be silenced and the whole world held accountable before God.*

²⁰*Therefore "no one will be declared righteous in his [God's] sight" on the basis of "works of the law," for through the law is the consciousness of sin.*

TEXTUAL NOTES

3:1 The inclusion of the article ἡ ("the") with the noun ὠφέλεια ("use," "gain," "value") is widely supported by uncials אᶜ A B D Ψ, as well as by minuscles 33 (Category I), 1506 1881 2464 (Category II), and 6 69 88 104 326 330 365 614 1319 1573 1735 1874 2344 (Category III). The article is omitted in uncials א* G and minuscules 323 1241 1505 2495 (Category III), probably as the result of a scribal error due to haplography that אᶜ evidently sought to correct.

2a The expression πρῶτον μέν (literally "first indeed"), which is difficult to translate, is very widely supported by the Greek textual tradition. It is, however, omitted by tenth-century minuscule 1739 (Category I) and thirteenth-century minuscule 6 (Category III), which read instead πρῶτοι γὰρ ἐπιστεύθησαν ("for they were the first ones entrusted"). This variant reading was probably not just an attempted literary or stylistic improvement of the difficult πρῶτον μέν reading. In all likelihood it was also theologically motivated (see "Exegetical Comments" below).

2b The postpositive γάρ ("for") appears in uncials א A D² (also *Byz* K L), as well as in minuscules 33 1175 (Category I), 1506 2464 (Category II), and 69 88 104 323 326 330 365 614 1319 1735 1874 2495 (Category III). It is also reflected in versions syʰ and cop. It is, however, omitted in B D* G Ψ and most *Byz* minuscules and is not translated by syᵖ and boᵐˢˢ. The textual evidence, therefore, is almost equally divided. But since the second part of the verse is given as an explanation of the emphatic response πολὺ κατὰ πάντα τρόπον ("Much in every way!"), one would expect such an explanatory conjunction as γάρ ("for") at the beginning of this sentence. So it should probably be retained in the Greek text, even though it may not be translated in more colloquial English versions.

4a The adverb καθώς ("just as") is widely supported by uncials A D G (also *Byz* K L), as well as by minuscules 33 1175 1739 (Category I) and 1881 2464 (Category II). The adverb καθάπερ ("just as"), however, appears in uncials א and B, which are the most highly respected Alexandrian (or "Neutral") uncials of the fourth century, which most earlier text critics followed here in v. 4a (but καθώς in v. 8 [twice] and v. 10) — though text critics today favor καθώς in all four instances in vv. 4, 8 (twice), and 10. The choice remains difficult, but the difference in meaning is inconsequential since the adverbs are synonymous.

4b The future indicative verb νικήσεις ("you will be victorious" or "prevail") is supported by uncials א A D, as well as minuscules 81 2464 (Category II) and 6 88 104 326 424ᶜ 1319 (Category III). The aorist subjunctive verb νικήσῃς ("you may be victorious" or "prevail"), however, is attested by uncials B G Ψ (also *Byz* L), as well as minuscules 1175 1739 (Category I), 1881 (Category II), and 69 323 330 365 614 1241 1243 1505 1573 1735 1874 2344 2495 (Category III). The reading of minuscules 33 (Category I) and 1506 (Category II) is uncertain.

This variation in the tense and mood of the verb probably originated from an early confusion in dictation, since the pronunciations of the future indicative and the aorist subjunctive forms of the verb would have been similar. The external textual evidence for originality is almost equally divided. The aorist subjunctive form of the verb seems to be somewhat better attested and is in line with the Septuagint reading (cf. LXX Ps 50:6b). Yet the future indicative form is the "more difficult reading" and could be read with much the same sense as the aorist subjunctive. Ultimately, however, the decision between the two readings must be made on a contextual basis rather than a strictly textual basis (see "Exegetical Comments" below).

5 The expression κατὰ ἄνθρωπον λέγων ("I am speaking as a human" or "in a human manner") is amply attested in the Greek MSS. The plural phrase κατὰ ἄνθρωπων ("according to humans" or "according to people") appears in minuscule 1739 (Category I), cop[sa], and Origen[lat, gr], but is too weakly supported to be accepted.

6 The present verb κρίνει ("he judges") is supported by uncials B² D², as well as by minuscules 1506 (Category II) and 365 629 1243 (Category III). The future verb κρινεῖ ("he will judge"), however, is attested by uncial Ψ, as well as by minuscules 1175 1739 (Category I), 1881 (Category II), and 6 69 88 104 323 326 330 365 424[q] 614 1241 1319 1505 1735 1874 2344 2495 (Category III). It is also reflected in the Latin and Coptic versions. Determination as to whether the tense of this verb here (also in 2:16b) should be read as present or future is complicated by the fact that κρινει is without any accent in ℵ A B* D*, which are our earliest uncial MSS dating from the fourth and fifth centuries — for accents did not become extensively used in the NT textual tradition until the sixth and seventh centuries. The decision, therefore, must ultimately be made on the basis of context, and most commentators today believe that the context of this verse (as also that of 2:16b) suggests that the future tense κρινεῖ ("he will judge") is more appropriate.

7 The reading εἰ δέ ("but if," "and if") appears in uncials ℵ A, as well as in minuscules 81 256 1506 2127 (Category II) and 263 365 1319 1573 1852 (Category III). It is also reflected in versions it[x, z] cop[bo] arm. The reading εἰ γάρ ("for if"), however, appears in uncials B D G P Ψ (also *Byz* K L), minuscules 33 1175 1739 (Category I), 1962 2464 (Category II), and 6 69 88 104 323 326 330 424[c] 436 451 459 614 629 1241 1243 1319 1505 1962 1735 1836 1874 1881 2200 2344 2492 2495 (Catgory III), and is reflected in versions it[ar, d, dem, e, g] vulg syr[p, h] cop[sa] and such early commentators as Origen[lat] Ambrosiaster Chrysostom Theodoret. The external textual evidence, therefore, is slightly in favor of εἰ γάρ ("for if").

*GNT*⁴ and *NA*²⁷, however, have preferred εἰ δέ, and therefore "but if" appears in the NRSV. Bruce Metzger explained the rationale of the translation committee of the NRSV (many of whom also served on the editorial committees of *GNT*⁴ and *NA*²⁷) as follows: "A majority of the Committee, feeling that Paul's argument requires a parallel between verses 5 and 7, preferred the reading εἰ δέ and regarded εἰ γάρ as a rather inept scribal substitution, perhaps of Western origin."[1] And it is this understanding that we have accepted in our translation (above) and in the "Exegetical Comments" (below). Thus we read εἰ δέ as beginning both v. 5 and v. 7, and so will highlight the parallels that exist between 3:5-6 and 3:7-8.

8a The conjunction καί ("and") before the second καθώς ("just as") is absent in

---

1. Metzger, *Textual Commentary*, 448.

uncial B (also *Byz* K), as well as in minuscules 326 629 (Category III). The omission is probably a scribal error that came about because of the similar opening sounds of καὶ and καθώς.

8b The definite article τά ("the") before κακά ("evil") is omitted in uncial D*, evidently for stylistic reasons. It is, however, corrected in D^c, in line with the witness of the other early uncial MSS.

9a The present indicative middle verb προεχόμεθα — which, as will be argued below, is best understood interrogatively as "Are we superior?" "Do we surpass/excel?" "Do we have an advantage?" or, more colloquially, "Are we [Jews] any better?" — is attested by the fourth-century uncials א and B (also the later uncials D^c and K), as well as by minuscules 33 1175 1739 (Category I), 81 1881 1962 2464 (Category II), and 6 69 88 181 323 326 365 424^c 436 451 614 629 630 1241 1243 1319 1573 1877 2344 2492 (Category III). It is also reflected in the Latin, Syriac, and Coptic versions. The ninth-century uncial P (025) has the present indicative middle verb προεχόμεθα, but omits the phrase that follows: οὐ πάντως (which we will argue later should be understood to mean "Not in every respect!" or, more colloquially, "Not at all!"). The subjunctive προεχώμεθα ("Might we have an advantage?") appears in uncial A of the fifth century and uncial L (020) of the ninth century, whereas the present indicative phrase προκατέχομεν περισσόν ("Do we have excessive possession?") is found in uncials D* (06) G (012) and Ψ (044), as well as in minuscules 104 1505 1735 2495 (Category III). It is also reflected in versions it sy$^{p, h}$ cop^{bo} and Ambrosiaster. The reading προεχόμεθα οὐ πάντως of both Codex Sinaiticus (א 01) and Codex Vaticanus (B 03), however, is most likely original, with the difficulty of understanding how to interpret that reading evidently generating all the ancient scribal variants (as noted above) and all the modern interpretations (see "Exegetical Comments" below).

9b The absence of γάρ ("for") in uncial D* and minuscule 1611 (Category III), and as reflected in sy^p, is very likely a scribal error, which was later corrected in D^c.

9c The first person plural aorist middle verb προῃτιασάμεθα ("we have before/already charged") is widely supported throughout the textual tradition and so to be accepted. The verb ᾐτιασάμεθα ("we have charged") without the prepositional prefix πρό ("before") appears in uncials D* G, minuscules 104 1505 2495 (Category III), and the Latin versions. C. E. B. Cranfield suggests: "The reading ᾐτιασάμεθα may well be simply due to Latin influence, there not being an equivalent verb to προαιτιᾶσθαι."[2]

9d Codex Alexandrinus (A 02) adds πρῶτον ("first") after Ἰουδαίους τε, thereby reading "both Jews first and Gentiles," probably as influenced by Paul's language in 1:16 and 2:9,10. But the inclusion of πρῶτον here in v. 9 is not supported elsewhere in the Greek textual tradition.

11 Codex Vaticanus (B 03) has the masculine participle ζητῶν ("seeking"). But the substantival prepositional participle ὁ ἐκζητῶν ("who seeks out," understood with the addition of the preposition as "intensively seeks"), which is widely supported in the Greek textual tradition, was probably the original reading.

12a As in v. 11, the masculine participle ποιῶν ("doing") appears without the article in uncials A B G Ψ (also *Byz* K L), as well as in minuscules 33 1175 1739 (Category I),

---

2. Cranfield, *Romans*, 1.191.

1881 2464 (Category II), and 6 69 88 104 323 330 365 424^c 614 1241 1243 1319 1505 1573 1735 1874 2344 2495 (Category III). The substantival participle ὁ ποιῶν ("who does good"), however, is somewhat better supported by uncials ℵ and D, as well as by minuscules 81 (Category II) and 326 (Category III), and so is probably to be considered the original reading.

12b The second instance of οὐκ ἔστιν ("there is not") in this verse does not appear in uncial B, minuscule 1739 (Category I), syr^p, or Origen^{gr}. It is, however, included by uncials ℵ A D G P Ψ (also *Byz* K L), as well as by minuscules 33 1175 (Category I), 81 256 1506 1881 1962 2127 2464 (Category II), and almost all of the minuscules of Category III. It is also reflected in versions it$^{ar, d, dem, e, g, x, a}$ vulg syr^h cop$^{sa, bo}$ arm and Origen^{lat} Ambrosiaster.

The phrase was perhaps deleted by B, 1739, sy^p and Origen^{gr} simply because it was considered superfluous. Its inclusion by the greater mass of textual witnesses, however, suggests that it should be retained, even though it adds nothing to the sense of the verse. Further, viewed rhetorically as an anaphoric feature that begins each of six lines in vv. 10, 11 (twice), 12 (twice), and 18, there seems to be good reason to include it in the final line of v. 12.

14 The possessive pronoun αὐτῶν ("their") after the articular noun τό στόμα ("the mouths") appears only in uncial B and minuscules 33 (Category I) and 88 (Category III), evidently so as to balance the two sets of couplets that begin in v. 13 and continue on into v. 14. It must, therefore, be concluded that the textual evidence for αὐτῶν after τό στόμα is fairly weak. Further, it needs to be recognized that the articular τό στόμα may by itself incorporate the possessive idea. On the other hand, it also needs to be noted that the inclusion of a medial αὐτῶν in v. 14 is matched by two other uses of a medial αὐτῶν in vv. 13b and 15, as well as by three uses of this same possessive pronoun at the ends of their respective lines in vv. 13a, 13c, and 18. So the inclusion of αὐτῶν in this verse, while not linguistically necessary, aptly highlights the two sets of couplets that are present in vv. 13-14, and therefore may be understood as not only balancing these verses but also as appropriately expressing their meaning.

FORM/STRUCTURE/SETTING

Rom 3:1-20 has frequently been viewed as an extremely difficult passage to interpret. Difficulties arise with regard to what exactly 3:1-8 is saying. They also arise with respect to how these first eight verses relate to the "conclusion" given in 3:9, to the catena of OT passages set out in support of that conclusion in 3:10-18, and to the application of the message of that catena of biblical passages in 3:19. Further, they arise with respect to what exactly Paul meant by (1) the use of the middle-passive verb προεχόμεθα, which has the general sense of "advantage" but here in 3:9 can be variously understood, (2) by the expression ἔργα νόμου ("works of the law") in 3:20, and (3) by the future passive verb δικαιωθήσεται ("will be declared righteous") that also appears in 3:20.

With respect to the interpretation of 3:1-8, Frédéric Godet referred to this passage as "one of the most difficult, perhaps, in the Epistle."[3] Hans Lietzmann viewed these verses as drifting away from the main theme of the apostle's letter.[4] And C. H. Dodd wrote:

> The fact is that the whole argument of iii. 1-8 is obscure and feeble. When Paul, who is normally a clear as well as a forcible thinker, becomes feeble and obscure, it usually means that he is defending a poor case. His case here is inevitably a poor one, since he is trying to show that, although "there is no partiality about God," yet "the Jew's superiority" is, somehow, "much in every way." It is no wonder that he becomes embarrassed, and in the end dismisses the subject awkwardly. The argument of the epistle would go much better if this whole section were omitted.[5]

More recently, David Hall began his discussion of these first eight verses of ch. 3 with the following statement: "Romans 3.1-8 is one of the most puzzling passages in the epistle."[6] And Heikki Räisänen has gone so far as to assert that Paul here in 3:1-8, because of his excessive zeal, simply loses track of his argument.[7]

The reasons for interpreters' difficulties in understanding 3:1-8 and how these verses relate to (1) the conclusion in 3:9, (2) the catena of biblical passages in 3:10-18, (3) the application of these OT passages in 3:19, and (4) the closing statement that speaks of human inability before God, "righteousness," "works of the law," and the purpose of the law in 3:20 seem to have arisen principally from the following factors:

1. The rapid-fire succession of fairly long questions and brief answers in 3:1-8 is different from Paul's usual style of brief questions and more extensively developed answers.
2. It is uncertain whether Paul is using a diatribe style of argumentation in the questions and answers of 3:1-8 (perhaps also including 3:9) — that is, putting objections into the mouth of some postulated external opponent or imaginary interlocutor, which are then answered in the form of a dialogue — or simply expressing objections that he felt might arise from what he has said in chs. 1-2 and believed needed to be dealt with at least briefly here.
3. There is also uncertainty regarding the relation between the questions of 3:1-8 and the questions of 3:9: Are the questions different? Or are they, while expressed differently, to be understood as similar or complementary in nature? Further, do the questions of 3:9 really introduce a "conclusion" to the issues raised by the questions asked in 3:1-8?

---

3. Godet, *Romans* (ET 1880-81), 1.220.
4. Lietzmann, *An die Römer* (1906, 1928²), 45.
5. C. H. Dodd, *Romans* (1932), 46.
6. Hall, "Romans 3.1-8 Reconsidered," 183.
7. Räisänen, "Zum Verständnis von Röm 3,1-8," 185.

4. The relation between the answers in 3:2 and 3:9 is unclear: Are "Much in every way!" and "Not at all!" opposed to one another, thereby setting up a contradiction in the passage? Or are they to be understood as compatible in some way?

5. It has been difficult to establish the original texts of the passage (see "Textual Notes") and to interpret a number of words and expressions that are used, particularly πρῶτον μέν in 3:2a, προεχόμεθα in 3:9a, and δικαιωθήσεται in 3:20a, but also at many other places.

6. There is the seeming anomaly of Paul's mixed rhetorical styling, wherein what has appeared to many as a Greek diatribe in 3:1-8 (or perhaps 3:1-9) is followed by a Jewish or Jewish Christian catena of biblical passages in 3:10-18.

7. And it is unclear who is addressed and/or referred to in the passage, especially in the "conclusion" in 3:9, the application in 3:19, and the closing statement in 3:20. Are the addressees — and particularly the referent — to be understood as Jews, Jewish Christians, or Gentile Christians?

Further, determination of what Paul had in mind and was opposing in 3:20 by his use of the phrase ἔργα νόμου ("works of the law") has always been a problem for NT interpreters — and recently it has become an even more difficult problem. The primary question today is this: By ἔργα νόμου ("works of the law") was Paul referring to the Mosaic law understood in a religious sense as a legal system, whose observance was thought to gain a right standing before God? Or did the apostle have in mind the Mosaic law understood in a nationalistic and cultural sense as connoting certain "ethnic identity markers" for the people of Israel — particularly circumcision, Sabbath observance, and certain dietary laws, which Jews believed should be observed not only as a means of self-identification (i.e., as particularistic "identity markers") but also as divinely ordained legislation meant to separate them from all other nations and people (i.e., as nationalistic "boundary markers")?

Rhetorical Conventions. A number of rhetorical conventions have frequently been seen in 3:1-20, principally: (1) an *inclusio* marked by use of τί οὖν ("what then?") in 3:1 and 3:9, (2) a diatribe in 3:1-8 (perhaps also 3:9), (3) a chiasmus in 3:4-8, and (4) a lengthy catena of biblical passages in 3:10-18. There is, however, a rather high degree of uncertainty with regard to the presence of some of these features, and so a brief introductory discussion about these matters is here required.

1. Those who have seen a rhetorical *inclusio* marked by use of the elliptical phrase τί οὖν ("what then?") in 3:1 and 3:9 have understood 3:1-8 not as followed by another unit beginning at 3:9, but as a discrete unit of material.[8] But in this same letter to Christians at Rome, Paul frequently uses τί οὖν ("what then?"),

---

8. So, e.g., Bornkamm, "Theologie als Teufelskunst," 140-48; Stowers, "Paul's Dialogue with a Fellow Jew," 707-22; Fitzmyer, *Romans,* 326.

with or without the verb ἐροῦμεν ("shall we say"), to raise questions about what he has taught and so to further his argument (4:1; 6:1, 15; 7:7; 8:31; 9:14, 30; 11:7).[9] And in these cases, as Douglas Moo has rightly observed, "Paul is not so much reproducing for his readers an argument between himself and another person [i.e., a diatribe] as he is posing questions and objections to himself in order to make his views clear to the Romans," that is, questions that he realizes will arise from what he has said earlier.[10]

Therefore, we conclude that no conscious or unconscious *inclusio* is seen in 3:1-9. Rather, with τί οὖν Paul simply (1) introduces in 3:1a his own four sets of rhetorical questions and four responses, which are set out in 3:1-8, and then (2) introduces in 3:9a his own conclusion to these matters, which he presents in his response of 3:9b — as well as, it needs also to be noted, in his inclusion of a catena of biblical passages in 3:10-18 and his application of these verses in 3:19.

2. Frequently seen in the questions and answers of 3:1-8 (perhaps 3:1-9) is a diatribe style of argumentation — that is, a lively form of argument that makes use of direct address to an imaginary interlocutor, hypothetical objections, and false conclusions. Earlier instances of diatribe have appeared in 2:1-5 and 2:17-24, and such diatribal styling will appear again in 9:19-21 and 11:17-24 (possibly, though less likely, also in 3:27-31 [perhaps including 4:1-2] and 14:4-11). Fairly representative of an earlier position is that of William Sanday and Arthur Headlam, who in their 1895 commentary marked out a number of "casuistical objections" in 3:1-8 and spoke of some "external objector" whom Paul was refuting in these verses[11] — but who also argued that in 3:9-20 "St. Paul is there rather following out his own thought than contending with an adversary."[12] Thus in their translation of 3:1-8 they inserted such phrases as "an objector may urge" (3:1), "you say" (3:3 and 7), "a new objection arises" (3:5), "any such objection" (3:6), "so the objector" (3:8a), and "these sophistical reasoners" (3:8b), whereas in their translation of 3:9a they translated the elliptical question "What then?" as "What inference are *we* to draw?" and interpreted the first person plural verbs of 3:9b and 3:19 as referring to Paul himself.[13] And this seems to have been a fairly common way of understanding the course of the argument of the passage in their day — as it does also rather often in our day, in both academic and popular circles.

Since Rudolf Bultmann's 1910 study of the Greek diatribe,[14] however, the postulated "external objector" of Sanday and Headlam has more commonly been referred to as a "diatribal interlocutor" and the influence of the Greek diatribe on Paul has been highlighted both here and at a number of other places in Romans. It is this understanding of 3:1-8 (or 3:1-9, as usually proposed by the

---

9. As observed by Moo, *Romans*, 180.
10. *Ibid.*, 181.
11. Sanday and Headlam, *Romans*, 68-69.
12. *Ibid.*, 70.
13. *Ibid.*, 68-70.
14. See Bultmann, *Der Stil der paulinischen Predigt*.

more ardent proponents of such a diatribal understanding of the passage) that has been most ably argued, though with a number of important refinements to Bultmann's thesis, by Stanley K. Stowers[15] and is generally accepted by most commentators today.[16]

Nonetheless, though interpreters today generally agree with Stowers, Fitzmyer, and others that here at the beginning of ch. 3 "Paul returns to his diatribe and indulges further in his dialogic discussion with the imaginary Jewish interlocutor,"[17] questions may still legitimately be raised as to whether the material of 3:1-8 (or 3:1-9, as Stowers, Fitzmyer, and others would hold) truly represents the form of a Greek diatribe. For normally in a diatribe the interlocutor's questions are stated briefly and the author's replies are set out in greater detail, whereas in 3:1-8 the questions are given in somewhat greater detail and Paul's replies are expressed very briefly.

More significantly, however, it should be noted that in Paul's normal use of diatribe styling, objections from an imaginary interlocutor are cast in the form of a challenge from someone who is identified by the second personal singular pronoun "you" or the verbal singular suffix "you" — as throughout the diatribes of Rom 2:1-5 and 2:17-24, as well as those found later in 9:19-21 and 11:17-24. Further, a diatribe styling in Paul's letters is usually introduced by some such diatribal introductory formulas of the day as "you will say then" (ἐρεῖς οὖν), as in Rom 9:19 and 11:19, or "but someone will say" (ἀλλ' ἐρεῖ τις), as in 1 Cor 15:35. At times the apostle even addresses a postulated interlocutor using the vocative "O man or woman" (ὦ ἄνθρωπε), as in Rom 2:1, 3; 9:20. Here in 3:5a, however, he uses the first person plural future indicative of the verb εἴρω ("to say") with the interrogative particle τί ("what") to ask rhetorically "What shall *we* say (τί ἐροῦμεν)?" — with the argument that follows this interrogative question "What shall *we* say?" suggesting that 3:5b should be understood as beginning with the unspoken but obvious question "Should *we* say that .. ?" And this absence of the typical diatribal second person singular "you" (either as a pronoun or a verbal suffix), together with the absence of the vocative "O man or woman" (both of which would highlight the presence of a postulated interlocutor) and the appearance of the first person plural, which serves to introduce questions that Paul himself expresses in a more usual rhetorical fashion, seem to require, as David Hall has argued, that we understand 3:1-8 (perhaps extending also to 3:9) as "an internal debate rather than an external objection."[18]

In 9:19 and 11:19 Paul uses the formula "you will say then" (ἐρεῖς οὖν) to introduce the two further cases of diatribe styling that can be found in 9:19-21 and 11:17-24, but he introduces his own questions to his addressees with "what

15. See Stowers, *Diatribe and Paul's Letter to the Romans*, 119-20; *idem*, "Paul's Dialogue with a Fellow Jew," 710-14.

16. Cf., e.g., Käsemann, *Romans*, 78-85; Dunn, *Romans*, 1.129-30, 146, passim; Fitzmyer, *Romans*, 325, passim; Talbert, *Romans*, 89; Jewett, *Romans*, 239-40, passim.

17. Quoting the first sentence of Fitzmyer's comments on this passage in his *Romans*, 325.

18. Hall, "Romans 3.1-8 Reconsidered," 183.

then shall we say" (τί οὖν ἐροῦμεν, 9:14, 30) or "what then" (τί οὖν, 11:7). It is this pattern of interweaving the formula "you will say then," which appears in conjunction with diatribe styling, and the expressions "what then shall we say" (τί οὖν ἐροῦμεν) or simply "what then" (τί οὖν), which are used to introduce rhetorical questions posed by Paul himself, that seems applicable to the four sets of questions that appear in 3:1-8 (as well as the two elliptical questions of 3:9) vis-à-vis the diatribal styling of questions that appeared earlier in 2:1-5 and 2:17-24.

Frédéric Godet long ago seems to have best captured the style and nature of Paul's argument in 3:1-8 when he said: "There is no need of expressly introducing an opponent, as many commentators have done. Paul does not here make use of the formula: *But some one will say.* The objections arise of themselves from the affirmations, and Paul puts them in a manner to his own account."[19] This is not to deny Paul's use of diatribe styling elsewhere in his letters — particularly in Romans, where it appears earlier in 2:1-5 and 2:17-24 and then later in 9:19-21 and 11:17-24 (though less likely in 3:27–4:2 and 14:4-11). It is only to say that what is set out in 3:1-8, as well as throughout 3:9-19, is probably best understood in terms of an internal debate that Paul knew could very well arise from what he had written earlier, especially from 2:17-29.

3. Joachim Jeremias in 1958 proposed that there appears in 3:4-8 a chiasmus, that is, an arrangement of paired words, statements, or texts in inverted symmetry around a focal word, statement, or text. Such a chiastic construction he found signaled in the use of the adjective ἀληθής ("true," "truthful," "righteous") and the second person singular aorist subjunctive passive verb δικαιωθῇς ("you may be proved right," "declared righteous") in 3:4, which are taken up in reverse order in the rhetorical questions of 3:5 and 3:7-8.[20]

However, as we noted earlier with respect to the identification of a chiasmus in 2:7-10 (or perhaps 2:6-11), there is in the identification of any proposed chiastic arrangement of words, statements, or texts always the highly important matter of intentionality: Is what appears as a chiasmus to be credited to the literary ability of the author, or to the ingenuity of the reader? And was this chiasmus, if it is credited to the author, created intentionally or somewhat unintentionally? And while these questions have been somewhat difficult to answer with respect to the chiastic features of 2:7-10 (or 2:6-11), they are even more difficult to answer with respect to 3:4-8. It may, in fact, be legitimately doubted that a chiasmus truly exists in this passage — or, if present, was intended by Paul. And because of such doubts, the material of 3:4-8 will not be treated as such in our exegetical comments that follow.

4. In 3:10-18 there appears a catena of biblical passages, which is the most extensive grouping of OT quotations in the entire Pauline corpus. The verses quoted are stitched together by a sixfold repetition of "there is no one" (οὐκ

19. Godet, *Romans* (ET 1880), 1.220.
20. See Jeremias, "Chiasmus in den Paulusbriefen," 154-55.

ἔστιν), and they set out an enumeration of various parts of the body ("throats," "tongues," "lips," "mouths," "feet," and "eyes") to make the point that all human beings are in their totality sinful. This catena of passages has, in fact, every appearance of being very carefully structured. Further, it appears to have been originally brought together within the Jewish world (see the exegetical comments below), and so may be postulated to have been traditional within Judaism and among the earliest Jewish believers in Jesus and known by Paul's Christian addressees at Rome. And as a traditional collection of OT passages that was probably known to his addressees, it was used by Paul in support of his insistence that "both Jews and Gentiles are all under sin."[21]

Paul's argument throughout 3:1-20, as it was in 1:16-2:29, seems to be thoroughly Jewish and/or Jewish Christian in both its content and its manner of presentation. So it is not surprising to find such an extensive collection of biblical verses here at the conclusion of the first half of the first major section of his letter's protreptic body middle — even though the passages quoted in this catena differ in selection and presentation quite noticeably from Paul's usual ways of quoting Scripture (as we will attempt to demonstrate immediately below and in the exegetical comments that follow).

Use of Scripture and Traditional Materials. Paul's use of Scripture in 3:1-20 is somewhat strange when compared with his use of Scripture elsewhere in his letters. When Paul quotes or alludes to Scripture in support of his teaching elsewhere he usually selects (or at least seems to have in mind) passages from the Prophets and the Pentateuch — whereas the quotations of the OT here in 3:4b and 3:10b-18 are drawn principally from the Psalms, which was the hymnal and prayer book of Judaism and early Jewish Christianity, with only one passage from the prophet Isaiah quoted and two rather traditional echoes from Proverbs and Ecclesiastes perhaps also alluded to:

3:4b	quoting Ps 51:4b (MT 51:6b, LXX 50:6b)
3:10b-12	paraphrasing and quoting Ps 14:1-3 (LXX 13:1-3), perhaps also echoing Ps 53:1-3 (LXX 52:1-3) and Eccl 7:20
3:13a	quoting Ps 5:9b (MT and LXX 5:10b)
3:13b	quoting Ps 140:3b (MT 140:4b, LXX 139:4b)
3:14	quoting Ps 10:7a (LXX 9:28a)
3:15-17	quoting Isa 59:7-8, perhaps echoing also Prov 1:16
3:18	quoting Ps 36:1b (MT 36:2b, LXX 35:2b)

Further, it needs to be noted that the structure of the group of passages in 3:10b-18, while not poetic in nature, evidences a great deal of compositional care, what with its sixfold repetition of "there is none" (οὐκ ἔστιν) and its cataloging of various parts of the human body ("throats," "tongues," "lips," "mouths," "feet," and "eyes") to make the point that all human beings are in their totality sinful.

---

21. Rom 3:9; cf. also 3:19, 23.

All these features of selection, structure, and usage, which seem to be not quite in line with Paul's usual ways of quoting Scripture, suggest (1) that this catena of passages in 3:10b-18 should be understood as something of a pre-Pauline *testimonia* collection that was brought together earlier by some Jewish teacher in support of the doctrine that no one is righteous before God, and (2) that the apostle used this catena of biblical passages, which he evidently believed the Christians at Rome also knew and accepted, to reinforce his own teaching in a manner that his Roman addressees would readily accept. Likewise, it may be postulated that (1) the statement "Let God be true, and every human being a liar" just before Paul's quotation of Ps 51:4b in 3:4b in support of his emphatic response μὴ γένοιτο ("Let it not be!" colloquially "Certainly not!"), (2) the words "no one will be declared righteous in [God's] sight" in 3:20a, which are based ultimately on the lament of Ps 143:2, and (3) the phrase "works of the law," which appears most significantly also in 3:20a, should all be understood as traditional Jewish religious aphorisms, much like the aphoristic materials quoted earlier in 2:2, 6-10, 11, 14-15, which Paul used to support his teaching in a manner that his Christian addressees at Rome would understand and accept.

The biblical passages quoted and the traditional materials used in 3:1-20 should therefore most likely be viewed as (1) rooted in a milieu of Jewish and/or Jewish Christian piety and theology, (2) known and appreciated by Paul's addressees at Rome, (3) used by Paul because he believed there was a basic agreement between him and his addressees regarding these materials and what they taught, and (4) given the apostle's own interpretive "spin" at certain crucial points.

Who Is Addressed or Referred to in 3:1-20? The referent throughout 2:17-29 is certainly Jewish. And all the questions asked, answers given, and statements made in 3:1-20 continue this focus on Jews — specifically dealing with matters regarding the situation of the Jews before God. The materials of 2:17-29 and 3:1-20, therefore, must always be kept together in (1) their denunciations of Jews and Jewish failures (2:17-29), which can be paralleled in both Jewish and other Christian sources, and (2) their depictions of the situation of the Jews before God (3:1-20), which reflect both mainline Jewish and Jewish Christian perspectives.

The specific referent of the previous denunciations in 2:17-29, however, is probably not to be understood in terms of Jews generally or Judaism per se. Rather, it is more likely a proud and censorious, but entirely inconsistent, Jew who viewed himself as a moral teacher of pagan Gentiles, but in his own lifestyle and practice caused the name of God to be dishonored among those same Gentiles because he himself failed to live up to the moral standards of the Mosaic law. The depictions of the situation of the Jews before God in 3:1-20, on the other hand, include all Jews — speaking pointedly with respect to their true, God-given advantages and their presumed, but falsely claimed, superiority.

The Structure of the Passage. Four sets of two rhetorical questions each appear in 3:1-8, with each of these four sets of questions immediately answered in a brief, emphatically stated reply. The implied premises for each of these four sets of questions are rooted in what Paul wrote earlier in 1:18–2:29 (with these premises being later spelled out much more fully in 9:1–11:36). Likewise, the four answers given in 3:1-8 repeat in very brief and emphatic form what Paul wrote earlier in 1:18–2:29 (and they, too, will be nuanced in much greater detail in 9:1–11:36).

These four sets of rhetorical questions in 3:1-8, together with their implied premises and brief answers, may be set out as follows:

Set I (3:1-2)

Implied Premise: Both Gentiles and Jews will be judged impartially by God, without favoritism and without consideration given to ethnicity, in accordance with the revelation they have received — for (1) " 'There is no favoritism with God.' All who sin without having the law will also perish without the law, and all who sin while possessing the law will be condemned by the law" (2:11-12, which epitomizes all that Paul has written in 1:18–2:16); and (2) "A person is a Jew who is one inwardly, and real circumcision is a matter of the heart — by the Spirit, not by the written code" (2:29, which epitomizes all that Paul wrote in 2:17-29).

Questions: "What advantage, then, is there in being a Jew?" and "What value is there in circumcision?" (3:1).

Answer: "Much in every way!" Primarily because "they ['the Jews'] have been entrusted with the words of God" (3:2).

Set II (in 3:3-4):

Implied Premise: Jewish possession of the words of God did not result in the end that it was intended to serve — that is, in Israel's faith in the Messiah.

Questions: "What if some of them did not have faith?" and "Will their unfaithfulness nullify God's faithfulness?" (3:3).

Answer: "Certainly not! Let God be true, and every human being a liar" (3:4).

Set III (in 3:5-6):

Implied Premise: Israel's rejection of Jesus, the Messiah, was used by God for the greater extension and expression of God's righteousness — in particular, for the salvation of the Gentiles.

Questions: "If human unrighteousness [or 'injustice'] serves to demonstrate more clearly God's righteousness [or 'righteous justice'], what shall we say?" and "Should we conclude that God is unjust in bringing his wrath on his people?" (3:5).

Answer: "Certainly not! If that were so, how will God judge the world?" (3:6).

Set IV (in 3:7-8):

Implied Premise: God has made use of his people's rejection and unfaithfulness for his own purposes and to glorify himself.

Questions: "If my falsehood enhances God's truthfulness and so increases his glory, why am I still condemned as a sinner?" and "Why not say, 'Let us do evil that good may result'?" (3:7-8a).

Answer: "Their condemnation is deserved" (3:8b).

The second part of the passage begins in 3:9a with the expression "What then?" (τί οὖν;), which is an elliptical question. That question is immediately followed by a second elliptically stated question: "Are we any better?" (προεχόμεθα;). These two questions are then answered by the emphatic negative statement "Not at all!" (οὐ πάντως). And that brief rebuttal is supported (1) by a reminder of what Paul believes he has already established throughout 1:18–2:29, that is, that "both Jews and Gentiles are all under sin" (3:9b), (2) by a catena ("chain") of biblical passages that speaks in carefully constructed fashion to the point that "there is no one righteous, not even one; there is no one who understands, no one who seeks God" (3:10b-18), and (3) by an application of that catena of passages meant to highlight its significance for the letter's addressees (3:19).

In the closing statement of 3:20 Paul sets out in very brief form a fitting conclusion to all he has said about human sin and inability, about God's righteousness and judgment, and about the purpose and function of the Mosaic law. He does this (1) by alluding, in a rather aphoristic fashion, to the psalmist's lament in Ps 143:2, (2) by the use of the phrase "works of the law," which seems to have been a significant current expression within Judaism and Jewish Christianity, and (3) by declaring that the law was never intended to be a means whereby people might be "declared righteous in his [God's] sight," but was intended, rather, to bring about "the consciousness of sin." In addition, 3:20 prepares for Paul's fuller presentation of "righteousness" and the Christian message in 3:21–4:25.

Paul's discussion of the situation of the Jews before God in 3:1-20, therefore, may be set out in terms of

1. four sets of rhetorical questions and the apostle's emphatic responses (in 3:1-8),
2. a conclusion supported by a catena of passages and an application (in 3:9-19), and
3. a closing statement (3:20), which brings to a conclusion all the negative argumentation of 1:18–3:19 but also provides a transition to the positive presentation of righteousness that was announced in 1:16-17 and will be developed in 3:21–4:25.

This three-point outline of the passage will structure our comments below.

EXEGETICAL COMMENTS

I. Four Sets of Rhetorical Questions and Paul's Emphatic Responses (3:1-8)

Paul's proclamation (1) that "there is no favoritism with God" (as epitomized by the aphorism quoted in 2:11), and (2) that "a person is a Jew who is one inwardly, and real circumcision is a matter of the heart" (as stated in 2:29) are basic tenets not only of the Christian gospel and Jewish Christianity, but also of the religion of Israel and of the better rabbis of Judaism. It is possible, however, that such teachings could be understood by some unthinking person "to imply that the specificity of Jewishness is meaningless, that its particularity is subsumed and negated by a nebulous universal spirituality."[22] Or it could be argued that, because of what God has done redemptively through the work and person of Jesus Christ, (1) Israel's election has been abrogated, (2) the promises made to Israel have been negated, and (3) the righteousness of God, on which Israel's hope is based, has been discounted or set aside. "The question raised," as Charles Cranfield has rightly observed, "is nothing less than the question of the credibility of God"[23] — or as Richard Hays expresses matters: "The issue is, at bottom, the question of God's integrity."[24]

It is this issue of God's "faithfulness," "righteousness," "righteous justice," "credibility," and "integrity" that lies at the heart of Paul's first set of rhetorical questions about "the advantage of being a Jew" and "the value of circumcision" in 3:1 and his emphatic response in 3:2. It is also this issue that Paul repeats throughout all the contrasts that he sets out in the four sets of questions and responses in 3:3-8 — that is, (1) "human unfaithfulness" (ἡ ἀπιστία αὐτῶν) vis-à-vis "God's faithfulness" (τὴν πίστιν τοῦ θεοῦ) in 3:3, (2) "humans as liars" (πᾶς ἄνθρωπος ψεύστης) vis-à-vis "God as true" (ὁ θεός ἀληθής) in 3:4, (3) "our unrighteousness" or "injustice" (ἡ ἀδικία ἡμῶν) vis-à-vis "God's righteousness" or "righteous justice" (θεοῦ δικαιοσύνη) in 3:5, and (4) "my falsehood" (τῷ ἐμῷ ψεύσματι) vis-à-vis "God's truthfulness" (ἡ ἀλήθεια τοῦ θεοῦ) in 3:7.[25] Further, it is this issue that will be explicated in much greater detail in the third major portion of the body middle of Paul's letter to Rome, particularly in 9:6–11:32.

3:1 The first question of the first of the four sets of questions, τί οὖν τὸ περισσὸν τοῦ Ἰουδαίου; ("What advantage, then, is there in being a Jew?"), begins with the interrogative particle τί ("what?" "why?"). The second question, τίς ἡ ὠφέλεια τῆς περιτομῆς; ("Or what is the value of circumcision?") begins with the particle ἤ ("or"), which is often used by itself elsewhere in Paul's letters to introduce a question (as, e.g., in 3:29), and the interrogative pronoun τίς

---

22. Hays, "Psalm 143 and the Logic of Romans 3," 109.
23. Cranfield, *Romans,* 1.177.
24. Hays, "Psalm 143 and the Logic of Romans 3," 109.
25. See Hays's schematic layout in his "Psalm 143 and the Logic of Romans 3," 110.

("who?" "which?" "what?" "why?"). These same particles and pronoun are used both alone and combined in extant papyrus letters of the day and elsewhere in the NT to introduce direct, indirect, and rhetorical questions.

In Romans Paul seems particularly fond of using τί and τίς interrogatively with other particles or words — as is evident in his use of such conflated expressions as τί οὖν ("what then"),[26] τί γάρ ("for what [if]"),[27] τί ἐροῦμεν ("what shall we say"),[28] τί ἔτι ("why yet/still"),[29] ἀλλὰ τί ("but what"),[30] ἢ τί ("or what"),[31] and ἢ τίς ("or what").[32] Luke, to an extent, does this as well, as can be seen in his use of the expressions τί ἄρα ("what then")[33] and τίς ἄρα ("which then").[34] This conflation of particles should probably be viewed as only a stylistic trait used by certain authors, whether consciously or unconsciously, to express an element of "dialectical liveliness and perspicuity" in their writings.[35]

The articular neuter noun τὸ περισσόν means "that which exceeds the usual" or "is beyond the ordinary," and so is probably best translated "advantage" here in 3:1. The articular feminine noun ἡ ὠφέλια signifies "a benefit bestowed," "a profit received," or what could be called "the good," and so is best read in this verse as "the value of" male circumcision. The two questions "What *advantage* is there in being a Jew?" and "What is the *value* of circumcision?" are far from inconsequential or frivolous. For, as Charles Cranfield has pointed out,

> What has just been said in chapter 2, and particularly in vv. 25-29, might indeed seem to imply that there is no advantage of the Jew over the Gentile and no profit in circumcision. But if this really were the implication of Paul's argument, then it would have called in question the truthfulness of the OT or the faithfulness of God; for, according to the testimony of the OT, God chose this nation out of all mankind to be His special people and gave them circumcision as a token of the covenant which He had made with them.[36]

3:2a The noun πολύ ("much") is neuter, corresponding to the articular neuter noun τὸ περισσόν ("the advantage") in 3:1. The prepositional phrase κατὰ πάντα τρόπον ("according to every respect" or "in every way") suggests that the advantage of the Jews has to do with a number of matters.[37] Paul's response

---

26. As here in 3:1; also 3:9; 4:1, passim.

27. As in 3:3; also 4:3, passim.

28. As in 3:5; also 4:1; 7:7; 8:31; 9:14, 30, passim.

29. As in 3:7; also 9:19, passim.

30. As in 11:4.

31. As in 11:2.

32. As here in 3:1.

33. Cf. Luke 1:66; Acts 12:18.

34. Cf. Luke 22:23.

35. So *ATRob*, 1198, citing *BDF* from the 1913 German 4th ed., 304.

36. Cranfield, *Romans*, 1.176.

37. Cf. Num 18:7 (LXX); see also Ignatius, *To the Ephesians* 2:2; *To the Trallians* 2:3; and *To the Smyrnaeans* 10:1.

"Much in every way!" has been criticized as being opposed to both (1) his earlier denunciations of Jews and their dependence on circumcision in 2:17-29, and (2) his later response "Not at all!" in 3:9. Pelagius, the British monk and theologian who at some time during 406-409 wrote commentaries on all thirteen of the canonical Pauline letters, found it difficult to accept "Much in every way!" as an affirmation by Paul, and so attributed all of what is said in 3:1-4 to a Jewish objector — with Paul's own view of matters only being expressed afterwards in 3:5-20.[38] Likewise, C. H. Dodd argued that "the logical answer" to the questions of 3:1 should have been "None whatever!" — in line with the negative response "Not at all!" of 3:9 — and that here in 3:2 Paul has simply become confused.[39] And Heikki Räisänen has expressed similar opinions about what he considers to have been Paul's frequent states of mental confusion, attributing what he views as Paul's contradictory statements here in 3:1-8 to his excessive zeal in attempting to win over his addressees to his own views.[40]

Paul's purpose in 2:17-29 and 3:1-20, however, is not to deny that God granted the Jews certain privileges, which were not given to the Gentiles. Rather, it was to point out that these privileges did not give the Jews any favored status or advantage over Gentiles in matters of divine judgment. For, as Paul declares here in 3:2, it is because "they ['the Jews'] were entrusted with the words of God" that they will be judged by God by a higher standard — that is, not just on the basis of (1) their response to God's general revelation in creation, (2) their possession of God's special revelation as given in the Mosaic law, or (3) their acceptance of the rite of male circumcision as a sign of God's covenant, but on the basis of how they have responded in obedience to God's words of instruction (i.e., Torah), which has been entrusted to them in the Jewish (OT) Scriptures, and thus how they have responded to God in matters of personal relationship.

No contradiction, therefore, should be read into Paul's response "Much in every way!" here in 3:2a. It is the appropriate response of both Jews and Christians to the two questions of 3:1, affirming, as it does, (1) that there is, indeed, a real advantage in being a Jew, and (2) that religious value exists in Jewish male circumcision as a sign of God's covenant — though, as Paul has made clear earlier throughout ch. 2 and will insist later in 3:9-20, such God-given privileges do not include any favored status or advantage when judged by God, but, rather, involve a greater degree of responsibility, as well as greater accountability, in matters having to do with a person's standing before God.

3:2b The phrase πρῶτον μέν (literally "first indeed" or "first of all, indeed") implies that Paul had in mind many other benefits as well when he spoke of the advantage of the Jews, that is, other God-given privileges that he could have listed here — just as he does later in 9:4-5 when speaking more extensively

---

38. Cf. Pelagius, *Ad Romanos, PL* 30.658.
39. C. H. Dodd, *Romans,* 47.
40. Cf. Räisänen, "Zum Verständnis von Röm 3,1-8," 185.

about the privileges that God has given the Jews: "the adoption, the divine glory, the covenants, the receiving of the law, the temple worship, the promises, [and] the patriarchs, and from them is traced the human ancestry of the Messiah."

Here in 3:2b, however, Paul narrows his list of Jewish advantages to only one matter: that the Jews had been "entrusted with the words of God," that is, with the Holy Scriptures.[41] He does so because the Jews' reception of God's law and their failure to keep it was the topic of discussion implicitly in 2:1-16 and explicitly in 2:17-29. Thus he speaks of this Jewish privilege in terms of it being the major matter on his present agenda and so what he wanted to list πρῶτον ("first of all") in his present discussion. Further, he seems to have included the affirmative particle μέν ("indeed") to acknowledge that this advantage was, as both Jews and Jewish believers in Jesus acknowledged, a vitally important factor throughout all that he wrote earlier in ch. 2.

Two late but relatively important minuscule MSS, that is, 1739 (tenth century, Category I) and 6 (thirteenth century, Category III), have substituted for πρῶτον μέν ("first indeed") the phrase πρῶτοι γὰρ ἐπιστεύθησαν ("for they were the first ones entrusted with [the words of God]").[42] This variant is probably not simply some scribe's attempt to improve the text stylistically. Rather, it was likely theologically motivated in order to support a later Christian view of relations between Judaism and Christianity that held that all the God-given privileges originally accorded to "national Israel" have been transferred by God to "spiritual Israel," that is, the Christian church, whereas all of God's curses on his people Israel as expressed in the OT are still to be assigned to the Jews. On such an understanding, whereas the Jews were "the first ones entrusted with the words of God," that privilege has now been given to the Christian church. During the course of church history that understanding of Christian-Jewish relations has frequently been attributed to Paul's statements in 9:6–11:12. That view of the relationship is, however, deficient on other grounds and is only weakly supported by the textual tradition here at 3:2.

3:3 The first question of the second set of questions, τί γὰρ εἰ ἠπίστησάν τινες; ("What if some of them were unfaithful?"), is introduced by the interrogative particle τί ("what," "why"), as was also the first question of the first set in 3:1. The second, μὴ ἡ ἀπιστία αὐτῶν τὴν πίστιν τοῦ θεοῦ καταργήσει; ("Will their unfaithfulness nullify the faithfulness of God?"), has no interrogative particle or pronoun introducing it. Such a particle, however, is assumed, being carried over from the first question of the set. The postpositive conjunction γάρ, which most often expresses nuances of cause, inference, or explanation, is used here simply in a transitional manner to signal the continuation of what has been previously stated in 3:1-2 — just as it was used earlier in 1:16; 1:18; and 2:25 (see also the

41. On the identification of "the words of God" with "the Holy Scriptures," see Doeve, "Some Notes with Reference to τὰ λόγια τοῦ θεοῦ in Romans 3.2," 111-23.
42. See "Textual Notes."

comments on 3:1-2 above). So while γάρ is probably best not translated here in 3:3, it needs to be recognized that it signals in some sense a continuation of what has just previously been said in 3:1-2.

This connection between 3:1-2 and 3:3-4 is further highlighted by the presence of four "faith/faithful" expressions, all built on the πιστ- stem and appearing prominently in the answer in 3:2 and the questions of 3:3: ἐπιστεύθησαν ("they were entrusted"), ἠπίστησαν ("they were unfaithful"), ἡ ἀπιστία ("their unfaithfulness"), and τήν πίστιν τοῦ θεοῦ ("the faithfulness of God") in 3:3c. This series of cognate expressions is not just a semantic play on words. Rather, it incorporates the essence of Paul's argument in this passage: that being *entrusted* with the words of God does not guarantee a person's *faith* in God or *faithfulness* to God; nor does such a great privilege provide exemption from divine judgment — and, conversely, nor does a person's *unfaithfulness* discredit or bring to an end God's *faithfulness.*

This first question of the second set, "What if some of them were unfaithful?" is a rhetorical question posed by Paul himself. He evidently realized that this question could come to someone's mind when talking about "the advantage" of Jews being that they were "entrusted with the words of God," and about "the value of circumcision" as a sign of God's covenant. The nominative, plural, masculine, indefinite pronoun τινες ("some of them") could be understood rhetorically as a meiosis (i.e., an understatement used to attain greater effect). It is, however, in line with Paul's later statement in 11:17 that God "broke off *some* [i.e., not 'all'] of the branches" (τινες τῶν κλάδων ἐξεκλάσθησαν) of the original olive tree. So by his use of τινες ("some of them"), it is evident that Paul is not here in 3:3 (or later in chs. 9–11) arguing that all Jews have been unfaithful to God. He may have been thinking of "the remnant" within Israel, as he will later throughout 9:6–11:24 (cf. esp. 9:27 and 11:5), who were faithful to God in their Jewish experience and became "fulfilled Jews" in their acceptance of Jesus of Nazareth as God's Messiah. He does not, however, excuse the "some of them" who "were unfaithful," highlighting rather God's continued faithfulness and abundant bounty toward them. And later in 11:25-32 he will argue that the "some" will become "all."

The second question of this second set asks rhetorically "Will their unfaithfulness nullify the faithfulness of God?" This question, as Paul undoubtedly realized, could arise from his argument in 2:17-29 that those Jews who did not obey the law — even though they possessed and knew the law and were physically circumcised — were unfaithful in their response to God who gave them the law.

It may be argued, of course, as some interpreters have done (taking the question out of context), that the question could be answered in the affirmative. But Paul uses here the negative μή ("not"), which is "the negative of will, wish, doubt,"[43] and not the more common negative οὐ ("not"). Admittedly,

---

43. So *ATRob*, 1167.

the "border-line between οὐ and μή," as A. T. Robertson observed, "is very narrow at times," and often an author's "mood and tone have much to do with the choice of οὐ or μή."[44] Yet as Robertson has taken pains to point out, there exists between these two negatives an important distinction: "If οὐ denies the fact, μή denies the idea."[45] Thus Paul, by the use of μή at the beginning of this question, prepares his addressees for his very emphatic negative response at the beginning of 3:4: μὴ γένοιτο ("Certainly not!") — which he will then support by citing what appears to be a traditional Jewish or Jewish Christian aphorism and quoting from Psalm 51.

3:4a The negative expression μὴ γένοιτο ("Let it not be!" more colloquially "By no means!" or "Certainly not!"), which combines the negative particle μή with the optative verb γένοιτο (from γίνομαι, "to be," "become," "happen"), appears in an absolute sense (i.e., by itself without a modifying substantive) and after questions almost exclusively in the NT in Paul's letters — ten times in Romans (3:4, 6, 31; 6:2, 15; 7:7, 13; 9:14; 11:1, 11), once in 1 Corinthians (6:15), and two or three times in Galatians (2:17; 3:21; perhaps also 6:14). It is to be found in this manner elsewhere in the NT only once, in the response of "the people" reported in Luke 20:16. Outside the NT, only Epictetus, the Stoic philosopher of the early second century A.D., can be shown to have used μή γένοιτο in an absolute sense in his writings[46] — though the expression was also used with other linguistic components in sentences expressing prohibitions by such Greek classical writers as Aeschylus,[47] Euripides,[48] and Herodotus,[49] by a number of Greek authors during the koine period, and by the translators of the LXX.[50]

In every instance of its NT absolute use, μὴ γένοιτο should be understood as an emotionally charged and highly negative response. It can literally be translated "Let it not be!" or "May it not be!" But while such a translation is linguistically accurate, it fails to represent the religious ethos or emotional anguish expressed in its use by Paul (as well as by "the people" in Luke 20:16). So contemporary NT translations — attempting to stay as close as possible to its actual words, yet wanting also to include something of its pathos — have rendered the expression here in 3:4a (also, usually, its other nine instances in Romans) by some such phraseology as "By no means!"[51] "Certainly not!"[52] "Never!"[53]

---

44. *ATRob*, 1167.

45. *Ibid.*

46. Cf. Malherbe, "Μή γένοιτο in the Diatribe and Paul," 26, who cites a number of such instances in Epictetus, *Dissertations* (esp. 1.1.13; 1.2.35; 1.5.10; 1.8.15; 1.29.1-8).

47. Aeschylus, *Agamemnon* 1249.

48. Euripides, *Ion* 731; *Heracles* 714.

49. Herodotus, *Historiae* 5.111.

50. Cf. Gen 44:7 (LXX): "*Be it far from* (μὴ γένοιτο) *your servants to do anything like that!*"; Gen 44:17 (LXX): "*Be it far from* (μὴ γένοιτο) *me to do such a thing!*"; see also Josh 22:29.

51. Goodspeed, RSV, NRSV.

52. NEB, TEV, NIV, TNIV.

53. Moffatt.

"Not at all!"[54] "Of course not!"[55] "May it never be!"[56] "Absolutely not!"[57] or the freer locution "That would be absurd!"[58] Probably, however, the KJV long ago captured best the religious context and emotional anguish of μή γένοιτο by its translation "God forbid!" — even though that expression does not correspond in any literal fashion to either of the two words involved.

3:4b The statement γινέσθω δὲ ὁ Θεὸς ἀληθής, πᾶς δὲ ἄνθρωπος ψεύστης ("let God be true, but every human being a liar") has been extremely difficult for commentators to understand in its context, and so has generated a great variety of translations. Heinrich Meyer, Frédéric Godet, and others translated the first phrase as "Let God's theodicy come to pass."[59] Theodor Zahn, Charles Hodge, and others translated it "Let God be recognized as true."[60] William Sanday and Arthur Headlam, Heinrich Schlier, and others understood the statement as referring to God as *becoming* the truthful being that he already is, in contradistinction to the existing character of all human beings, and so translated it with some such wording as "God must be seen to be [or, 'demonstrated to be' or 'proved to be'] true, though all mankind are convicted of falsehood."[61] Charles Cranfield and Douglas Moo take the first phrase as a human confessional statement and so read: "We confess rather that God is true."[62] John O'Neill also viewed the first phrase of the statement as relating to a human response rather than speaking of God's nature and therefore translated it "You must recognize that God remains true."[63] Adolf Schlatter, Ernst Käsemann, and others understood the phrase in an eschatological sense to mean "from the perspective of the end of history" and so translated the first part of the statement "May it become true and attest itself so."[64] And Robert Jewett basically agrees with Schlatter and Käsemann and therefore translates the statement as "Let God show himself to be true but every person [show himself to be] a liar!"[65]

Four problems for any interpretation of this statement in 3:4b are the following: (1) the imperative verb γινέσθω seems to suggest the thought of God *becoming* true, whereas elsewhere in his letters Paul expresses no doubt that he believed God to have been always "true," to be in the present always "true," and to continue in the future to be always "true"; (2) the noun ἀλήθεια incorporates both meanings of being "true" or "honest" (in speaking of one's character) and "faithful" or "loyal" (in speaking of one's actions); (3) the declarations "God is

54. Williams.
55. Phillips, NLT.
56. NASB.
57. NET.
58. JB.
59. Cf. H. A. W. Meyer, *Romans*, 1.143; Godet, *Romans*, 1.134.
60. Cf. Zahn, *An die Römer*, 151; Hodge, *Romans, ad loc.*
61. Cf. Sanday and Headlam, *Romans*, 71; Schlier, *Römerbrief*, 93.
62. Cf. Cranfield, *Romans*, 1.181; Moo, *Romans*, 186.
63. O'Neill, *Romans*, 61.
64. Cf. Schlatter, *Romans*, 77; Käsemann, *Romans*, 80.
65. Jewett, *Romans*, 245.

true" and "every human being is a liar," which are statements regarding character, are meant to support the affirmation in v. 3 that God is always "faithful," which is a statement regarding actions; and (4) the wording of the statement depends heavily on both allusions to and a verbatim quotation of statements made by the canonical psalmists (see below in our continued exegesis of this verse), whereas Paul seems usually not to have derived biblical support for what he taught from the Psalms (see below on the catena of passages in 3:10-18). The words used in this statement of support here in 3:4a are, of course, analogically equivalent. But they are not the same πιστ-stem words that Paul used in his affirmation in 3:2b or his questions in 3:3, which would have seemed more likely to have been the case. Thus the vocabulary and nuancing of this statement in 3:4a — particularly its selection of the words ἀληθής ("true") and ψεύστης ("liar"), its use of the imperative verb γινέσθω ("Let him be," or perhaps "Let him become"), and its dependence on the canonical Psalms — seem somewhat different from the vocabulary of 3:3, which it is intended to support, and somewhat different from the usual practice of Paul in quoting Scripture.

A possible solution to all the above difficulties — and the one that we here propose — is that this statement of 3:4b should be viewed as another Jewish aphorism, based on the teachings of the Jewish (OT) Scriptures and circulated within various circles of Early Judaism and early Jewish Christianity. As such, it may reasonably be assumed that Paul viewed this aphorism as well-known to his Christian addressees at Rome and therefore used it in support of his argument that God is always faithful, even though "some of them [i.e., Jews] did not have faith." Much like the materials we have earlier identified as aphoristic in nature in 2:2 ("God's condemnation of those who do such things is based on truth") and 2:11 ("There is no favoritism with God"), this statement here ("Let God be true, but every human being a liar") evidences by its confessional and/or catechetical nature, its somewhat different vocabulary, its dependence on the Psalms, and its literary styling many of the characteristics of a traditional aphorism.

An aphorism, of course, is a terse formulation of a truth or principle that uses rather specific terms and imagery, yet is applicable by analogy to a whole host of situations. People have often used, for example, such rather homespun aphoristic sayings as "A stitch in time saves nine," "You can't teach an old dog new tricks," "A barking dog never bites," and "Out of the frying pan into the fire" for a number of human situations and circumstances — all the while, however, insisting not that the words of the saying match exactly the situation to which they are applied but only that they bear some analogical relation to the matter at hand. So Paul should probably here be understood as using a Jewish and/or Jewish Christian aphorism, which was based on some general teaching or particular passage of Jewish (OT) Scripture, in support of his argument that God is always "faithful" (that is, always "true" to himself and to the covenant he made with his people), even though "some of them did not have faith" and so were "unfaithful" — or, in the words of the supporting statement itself, that

346

"some of them" by their "lack of faith" and "unfaithfulness" demonstrated the dismal truth that "every human being is a liar."

The adjective ἀληθής ("true," "truthful," "righteous"), together with the noun ἀλήθεια ("truth," "truthfulness," "uprightness"), appears frequently in the LXX translation of the Psalms with reference to God in his covenantal faithfulness.[66] The statement "every human being is a liar" (πᾶς ἄνθρωπος ψεύστης) in the second part of the aphorism reproduces verbatim the psalmist's words in Ps 116:11 (LXX 115:11), which were expressed in "anguish" and "sorrowful dismay," that "every human being is a liar" (πᾶς ἄνθρωπος ψεύστης). Paul's purpose in citing this seemingly Jewish and/or Jewish Christian aphorism was to support the biblical conviction — which, of course, he thoroughly agreed with — that God remains "true" (i.e., "faithful") to the covenant that he has established with his people, even though his people are "liars" (i.e., "lack faith" and are "unfaithful").

3:4c Here Paul quotes Ps 51:4b (MT 51:6b, LXX 50:6b): Ὅπως ἂν δικαιωθῇς ἐν τοῖς λόγοις σου καὶ νικήσεις ἐν τῷ κρίνεσθαί σε ("So that you may be justified when you speak and will prevail when you are judged"). He introduces the quotation by the formulaic expression καθὼς γέγραπται ("just as it is written") — that is, the conjunction of the conflated adverb καθώς ("just as"), which stems from the joining of the preposition κατά, "according to," and the relative adverb ὡς, "as," with the third person singular perfect indicative passive verb γέγραπται ("it has been written," and so "is written"). Καθὼς γέγραπται is the formula that the apostle uses most often in his letters to introduce biblical quotations[67] — though he also introduces biblical quotations with γέγραπται alone or γάρ alone, as well as by such statements as "he [God] says [or 'said']," "Scripture says [or 'said']," "Moses writes [or 'wrote']," "David says," "Isaiah says," or "Hosea cried out."

Psalm 51 is a penitential psalm ascribed to David "when the prophet Nathan came to him because he had been with Bathsheba." The Hebrew text of v. 4b (MT 51:6b) may be translated either (1) as a declarative statement regarding God's person in his judgment of the penitent psalmist: "You are righteous when you pass sentence on me and blameless in your judgment," or (2) as a result clause that expresses an important feature with respect to God in his purification of the psalmist from his sin: "So that you may be justified when you speak and blameless when you give judgment." Combining both ideas, acknowledgment and result, William Sanday and Arthur Headlam have argued: "The sense of the original is that the Psalmist acknowledges the justice of God's judgement upon him. The result of his sin is that God is pronounced righteous in His sentence, free from blame in His judging."[68]

---

66. Cf., e.g., Ps 89 (LXX 88):2, 5, 8, 14, 24, 33.

67. In Romans, not only here at 3:4 but also at 1:17; 2:24 (perhaps, though see our exegetical comment on this verse); 3:10; 4:17; 8:36; 9:13, 33; 10:15; 11:8, 26; 15:3, 9, 21; cf. also 1 Cor 1:31; 2:9; 2 Cor 8:15; 9:9; Gal 3:10, 13.

68. Sanday and Headlam, *Romans*, 72.

The Greek translators of the LXX, however, used the aorist tense and subjunctive mood for the two verbs δικαιωθῇς ("you may be righteous [or 'justified']") and νικήσῃς ("you may be victorious [or 'prevail']"), thereby making it a result clause, perhaps even turning it into something of a prayer: "So that (ὅπως ἄν) you may be justified (δικαιωθῇς) in your words (ἐν τοῖς λόγοις σου) and may be victorious (νικήσῃς) when you are judged (ἐν τῷ κρίνεσθαί σε)." Paul's quotation of the passage is generally in line with the LXX in its wording and thrust — though, while he retains the LXX's aorist tense and subjunctive mood for the first verb δικαιωθῇς ("you may be righteous [or 'justified']"), he changes the second verb to future indicative νικήσεις: "you will be victorious [or 'will prevail']." Thus the quotation as it appears here in 3:4b is probably best translated: "So that you may be justified [or 'shown to be righteous'] when you speak [literally 'in your words'] and will prevail [or 'be victorious'] when you are judged."

It is impossible to determine with any degree of certainty which of the forms of this second verb of Paul's quotation in 3:4c should be viewed as original — though we have accepted, somewhat tentatively, the future indicative "you will prevail (or, 'be victorious') in our translation, simply because it is "the more difficult reading" and seems to fit better the context of Paul's argument.[69] Neither is it possible to identify with any conviction the stages in the transmission of the text from the MT to the LXX and then from the LXX to Paul's quotation, nor set out possible reasons for such changes.[70] Paul may even have been quoting, as we believe was in this case likely, neither from the MT nor the LXX but from a version of the text that was then circulating within early Jewish Christianity — probably because he thought that such a version would be more familiar to the Christians at Rome and so more acceptable to them.

Nonetheless, Paul's purposes in quoting this portion from Psalm 51, as well as his quoting it in the fashion that he does, seem abundantly clear: (1) to give a biblical answer to the questions he posed in 3:3 ("What if some of them did not have faith?" "Will their lack of faith nullify the faithfulness of God?") and (2) to provide that biblical answer in a form that his Christian addressees at Rome would appreciate and readily accept. His first reaction to the two questions in 3:3 was to utter from the depths of his heart the highly emotional response "Certainly not!" (μή γένοιτο). He then followed that emotive response by citing what appears to have been a traditional Jewish and/or Jewish Christian aphorism, "Let God be true but every human being a liar" — which equated in aphoristic fashion "true" with "faithful" on God's part and "liar" with "unfaithful" on the Jews' part. Now here in the latter part of 3:4 he quotes material from Psalm 51 that implies, as Joseph Fitzmyer has aptly characterized its message,

<hr>

69. See "Textual Notes."

70. For a summary of these changes and their possible rationale, see Moo, *Romans*, 186-88, esp. nn. 49, 50, and 51.

that "though human sin is a rebellion against God's will, it serves to magnify divine fidelity and uprightness."[71]

Such an understanding of the relation of "human sin" and "rebellion" vis-à-vis "divine fidelity" and "uprightness" may not have been prominent in the Hebrew version of the passage. Nor can it be claimed to have been to the fore in the consciousness of the religion of Israel as expressed throughout the OT. But it is highlighted in the LXX translation of Psalm 51 (LXX Psalm 50), so it may reasonably be presumed that it had some importance in certain circles of early Judaism and among at least some of the earliest Jewish believers in Jesus. And though Paul seems not to have nuanced his proclamation of the Christian gospel in this manner in his evangelistic outreach to Gentiles, and while it cannot be found in his explications of "Israel's lack of faith" and "God's faithfulness" in Romans 9–11, he does set out such an understanding here in 3:4b by quoting Ps 51:4b in line with the wording and intent of the LXX.

Paul's wording and application of this statement from Psalm 51 may be credited, at least to some extent, to his circumstantial use of Scripture — that is, to his use of a passage that in its wording and application arose within a Jewish and/or a Jewish Christian context, and therefore would have been particularly suitable for the Christians at Rome. For, as we have argued earlier, the Christians at Rome seem to have been extensively influenced by the thought, forms, and practices of Jewish Christianity, as expressed and transmitted to them by the mother church at Jerusalem. Nevertheless, though Paul may not have considered it either opportune or appropriate to include such a nuanced feature of the Christian message in his proclamation to Gentiles, it may be posited that as a Jewish believer in Jesus he would have himself accepted such an explanation of human unfaithfulness vis-à-vis God's faithfulness. So with no qualms or reservations, he quotes a passage from Psalm 51 that in its LXX wording and evident intent implies that human "lack of faith" and "unfaithfulness" actually functions in some way to magnify and extol God's "faithfulness" and "righteousness."

3:5-8 What is implied in the quotation of 3:4c Paul goes on in 3:5-8 to state explicitly, applying that message first to Christians generally in 3:5-6, both Jewish and Gentile believers alike, and then to himself personally in 3:7-8. The structure of 3:5-8 parallels that of 3:1-4 — that is, two sets of rhetorical questions in 3:5-8, each followed by a brief, emphatic response, which parallels the pattern of two sets of rhetorical questions in 3:1-4, with each set followed by a brief, emphatic response. Paul evidently realized that false conclusions could be drawn from what he had just presented in 3:3-4, and so he seeks here in 3:5-8 to guard against any possible misunderstandings.

3:5a The first question of this third set of questions, εἰ δὲ ἡ ἀδικία ἡμῶν θεοῦ δικαιοσύνην συνίστησιν, τί ἐροῦμεν; ("But if our unrighteousness [or 'injustice'] serves to demonstrate more clearly God's righteousness [or 'righteous justice'], what shall we say?") ends with τί ἐροῦμεν ("what shall we say"), which

71. Fitzmyer, *Romans*, 328.

otherwise in Romans he uses, with the postpositive particle οὖν ("then"), to introduce questions.[72] The question concerns what can be said "if our unrighteousness" or "injustice" (ἡ ἀδικία) should serve in some way to "demonstrate," "show," "bring out," or "make more clear" (συνίστησιν) "God's righteousness" or "righteous justice" (θεοῦ δικαιοσύνην).

3:5b The question set out in 3:5a is, however, very quickly and dramatically sharpened by a second question: μὴ ἄδικος ὁ θεὸς ὁ ἐπιφέρων τὴν ὀργήν; (Shall we say that) "God is unjust to pronounce his wrath on his people?" The question could be answered affirmatively if nothing more were indicated in the question itself. But Paul introduces this second question with the negative particle μή ("not"), just as he did the second question of 3:3, which, here as there, signals that the only proper response must be an emphatic "No!" Further, he acknowledges by his parenthetical comment "I am speaking in a human manner" (κατὰ ἄνθρωπον λέγω, literally "I am speaking according to a man") that such a question is so far removed from reality that even asking it could be considered blasphemous — at least by Jews, Jewish Christians, and those who have been extensively influenced by Jewish Christianity, as were his Christian addressees at Rome. And he had no desire even to appear blasphemous.

3:6 Here Paul repeats his highly emotional negative response of 3:4a: μὴ γένοιτο ("Certainly not!"). Then he sets out a logical impossibility: ἐπεὶ πῶς κρινεῖ ὁ θεὸς τὸν κόσμον; ("If that were so, how will God judge the world?"). That is, if God cannot "pronounce [or 'inflict,' 'bring'] his wrath on his people," how can he be a just God and in the future be able to "judge the world"? This answer to the question in v. 5b is extremely brief. There is, however, nothing more that needs to be said — whether emotionally from the heart or logically from the mind — by anyone who truly knows God and has come to understand anything about God's character and will.

3:7-8 Paul's two rhetorical questions and one brief response in 3:7-8 are directly tied to the two rhetorical questions and one brief response in 3:5-6 by the expression εἰ δέ ("but if," "and if") appearing at the beginning of both 3:5 and 3:7.[73] Thus while he asks and responds to matters regarding God's judgment of his people in 3:5-6, here in 3:7-8 he deals with those same matters but applies them more directly to himself. Further, in these latter two verses he takes the occasion to respond to certain criticisms and accusations that he evidently knew were being leveled against him. So he asks: (1) "If the truth of God is enhanced unto his glory by my falsehood, why am I also still condemned as a sinner?" and (2) "Why not say — just as we are being slanderously reported as saying, and just as some claim we are saying — 'Let us do evil that good might result'?"

Exactly what was being said about Paul by the Christians at Rome we simply do not know. But it seems fairly apparent that he is responding here to certain criticisms that had been leveled against him and certain accusations that

---

72. Cf. also 4:1; 6:1; 7:7; 8:31; 9:14, 30.
73. See "Textual Notes."

had been mounted against his Gentile mission by some of his Jewish Christian opponents — which criticisms and accusations, in all likelihood, had "taken on a life of their own" in their spread from Asia Minor and Greece to Rome. So it may be hypothesized that criticisms and accusations of this type against Paul and his Gentile mission were known — perhaps even repeated with approval — by some of the Christians at Rome.

Paul's response to such criticisms and accusations as expressed in 3:8b is the briefest and most bombastic of all his four responses in this passage. He says simply: "Their condemnation is deserved" (ὧν τὸ κρίμα ἔνδικόν ἐστιν). These are, Paul implies, simply libelous charges based on sophistic reasoning, which show that those who mount them know nothing regarding the nature of God, the message of the Christian gospel, or the character of those who are Christ's people — and thus they deserve the κρίμα ("condemnation") with which God will judge such people. Or as Origen long ago said with respect to this verse:

> This is an argument raised by unjust people against the Christian faith. They blaspheme us even more by suggesting that because we believe that God's truthfulness abounds in the falsehood of men and that his justice is confirmed by our unrighteousness, we also believe that we should do evil so that good may come of it and that we should tell lies so that God's truthfulness will shine out even more clearly because of it. But in claiming that this is what we think, they are blaspheming us, as if these things were somehow the logical conclusion of our beliefs. But in fact the logic of our beliefs does not accept this line of reasoning, because we understand that God is a just and true judge.[74]

II. Conclusion Supported by a Catena of Passages and Application (3:9-19)

3:9 The clause τί οὖν ("what then") is elliptical and therefore somewhat difficult to understand in the context of the flow of Paul's argument. Many interpreters have viewed it as signaling the end of a rhetorical *inclusio* begun in 3:1. I have, however, argued that it serves to introduce a further question that brings matters to a conclusion.[75] The expression is likely best translated here "What then [shall we conclude]?" For 3:9 sets out the conclusion of what Paul has been arguing, not only in the preceding section of 3:1-8 but also earlier in 2:17-29: that although God has brought the people of Israel into covenant relationship with himself and given them particular advantages and blessings, (1) all Jews will be judged impartially, as will also all Gentiles, by a just, faithful, and righteous God, and (2) all Jews have come under God's wrath, as have also all Gentiles, because

74. Origen, *Ad Romanos, CER* 2.48, 50.
75. See comments above on "Rhetorical Conventions."

of their failure to respond to God by faith, as expressed by their unrighteous attitudes and their unjust actions.

There can be little doubt that the question προεχόμεθα; ("Are we any better?") — together with the negative response οὐ πάντως ("Not at all!") — should be accepted as original, for they are both strongly attested in the textual tradition.[76] Further, it can hardly be doubted that the context calls for the verb to be understood as a question and the negative expression as an exclamation. But προεχόμεθα (from προέχω, which means "jut out," "excel," "have an advantage") is in form both middle and passive. It has, therefore, been interpreted in three quite different ways: (1) as a proper middle verb, which should be understood in terms of some such translation as "What then do we hold before us as a defense?" "What then do we plead in defense?" "Can we then excuse [or 'defend'] ourselves?" or "Have we a shelter under which we can regard ourselves as delivered from wrath?";[77] (2) as a middle verb that carries an active meaning, which is probably best expressed as "Are we superior to [or 'better off than'] them?" "Do we surpass [or 'excel'] them?" "Do we have an advantage?" or, more colloquially, "Are we any better?";[78] or (3) as a passive verb and so read "Are we surpassed ['equaled' or 'excelled'] by them?" or "Are we at a disadvantage to [or 'worse off than'] them?"[79] Each of these readings has its own linguistic and conceptual problems, and Luke Timothy Johnson may be right in saying that "a final resolution appears impossible."[80] Particularly is this the case if the verb is understood as middle in form but active in meaning, for the question then may be asked: If Paul wanted to express an active meaning, why did he not simply use the active form προέχομεν?

The context of the passage, however, seems to demand an active sense for the middle form of the verb here. It has often been observed that there is no other instance of προέχω in the extant Greek literature of antiquity that is middle in form but active in meaning. Yet a number of other koine Greek verbs were sometimes used in just such a manner.[81] And it is this understanding of a middle Greek verb that expresses an active meaning that is reflected in the Latin translation *praecellimus eos* in Jerome's Vulgate. Thus, as Christian Maurer declared in 1968, "The absence of examples does not count so heavily when one remembers that this change of mood occurs elsewhere in the NT."[82] Or as

---

76. See "Textual Notes."

77. So, e.g., Godet, *Romans,* 1.234-35; Dahl, "Romans 3.9," 184-204; Dunn, *Romans,* 1.147-48; Stuhlmacher, *Romans,* 54-55.

78. So, e.g., Lagrange, *Aux Romains,* 67-68; C. H. Dodd, *Romans,* 46-47; Michel, *An die Römer,* 140-41; Barrett, *Romans,* 67-69; Maurer, "προέχομαι," 6.692-93; Synge, "The Meaning of προεχόμεθα in Romans 3.9," 351; Cranfield, *Romans,* 1.189-90.

79. So, e.g., Sanday and Headlam, *Romans,* 75-76; Fitzmyer, *Romans,* 330-31; Stowers, "Paul's Dialogue with a Fellow Jew," 173-74; L. T. Johnson, *Reading Romans,* 45-46; Jewett, *Romans,* 257.

80. L. T. Johnson, *Reading Romans,* 45.

81. See the examples in *BDF* 316.1 and in N. Turner, *Syntax* (vol. 3 of *M-T*), 106-7.

82. Maurer, "προέχομαι," 6.693.

Charles Cranfield noted, "It would not be the only case of the use of a middle form, where an active is to be expected."[83]

It is difficult linguistically to argue with certainty regarding the meaning of προεχόμεθα here. All three options are linguistically possible. Contextually, however, προεχόμεθα is probably best understood as a middle verb that carries an active meaning and therefore translated "Do we have an advantage?" or "Are we any better?" — that is, "Do we [Jews] have an advantage over" [or 'Are we any better than'] Gentiles in our standing or acceptance before a faithful and righteous God because of these privileges and blessings?" And the answer that Paul immediately gives to this question is a resounding "Not at all!" (οὐ πάντως).

As for the difference between Paul's response "Not at all!" here in 3:9 and his earlier response "Much in every way!" in 3:2, which has often raised such questions as whether these answers are contradictory or can be understood as compatible in some way, John Calvin's exposition is significant and offers a reasonable explanation. Calvin acknowledged a difference between these two responses, but credited that difference to different issues being addressed:

> His [Paul's] answer seems to be slightly different from what he had said above, since he now deprives of all dignity those on whom he previously had bestowed so much. There is, however, no disagreement, for those privileges in which he had admitted their [the Jews'] preeminence were external to themselves, and dependent on the goodness of God and not on their own merit. [But] Paul inquires [here in v. 9] whether they had any worthiness in which they could glory in themselves. The two answers, therefore, which he gives agree with one another in such a way that one follows from the other. [For] when he extolled their privileges, including them among the benefits of God alone, he showed that they had nothing of their own. The answer which he now gives could have been inferred at once from this, for if their chief excellence lies in the fact that the oracles of God are deposited with them, and if they possess this preeminence by no merit of their own, then they have no cause for boasting in the sight of God.[84]

Some interpreters have trouble validating Paul's claim in 3:9b that προῃτιασάμεθα γὰρ 'Ιουδαίους τε καὶ ''Ελληνας πάντας ὑφ' ἁμαρτίαν εἶναι ("for we have already charged that both Jews and Gentiles are all under sin"). Dieter Zeller and Heikki Räisänen, for example, have argued that it is difficult to identify where the apostle in Romans has made such an inclusive assertion and such a damning accusation.[85] Admittedly here in 3:9 is the first time that he

---

83. Cranfield, *Romans*, 1.189.

84. J. Calvin, *Epistles of Paul the Apostle to the Romans and to the Thessalonians*, in *Calvin's New Testament Commentaries*, 8.65.

85. See Zeller, *An die Römer*, 99-100; Räisänen, "Zum Verstandnis von Röm 3,1-8," 99.

uses the word ἁμαρτία ("sin"). But surely he has enunciated, at least in essence, such an all-inclusive assertion ("both Jews and Gentiles") and such a damning accusation ("are all under sin") in what he wrote earlier in 1:18–2:29 — that is, in speaking so extensively and pointedly about (1) "God's wrath" as "directed against humanity's godlessness and wickedness" in 1:18-32, (2) "God's condemning judgment" on all "unrighteousness" and "injustice" as being "just and impartial" in 2:1-16, and (3) "Jewish unfaithfulness and failures" in 2:17-29. As James Dunn has aptly said: "The force of 1:18–2:29 here becomes fully clear."[86] And it is this accusation that Paul seeks to support by the catena of biblical passages that he sets out afterward in 3:10b-18.

The phrase "both Jews and Gentiles" (Ἰουδαίους τε καὶ Ἕλληνας) is obviously influenced by Paul's entire inclusive argument in 1:16–3:20. In particular, however, it is influenced by the wording he used in 1:16 and 2:9-10: "both for the Jew first and for the Gentile" (Ἰουδαίῳ τε πρῶτον καὶ Ἕλληνι). Yet the phrase "both Jews and Gentiles" here in 3:9 does not possess exactly the same nuancing as that earlier wording in 1:16 and 2:9-10. For while "both Jews and Gentiles" here incorporates the inclusive emphasis signaled by the enclitic particle τε ("both") found in both 1:16 and 2:9-10, which emphasis is repeated in other ways at many other places in Paul's letter to Rome,[87] it does not include the particularistic thrust signaled by the substantival adjective πρῶτον ("first") in 1:16 and 2:9-10 — despite the inclusion of πρῶτον in 3:9 by the fifth-century Codex Alexandrinus (A 02), which is not supported elsewhere in the Greek textual tradition.[88]

The phrase "under sin" (ὑφ' ἁμαρτίαν, "under sin") means here in 3:9 a state of being under God's righteous condemnation of sin, which is the dire situation of "both/all Jews and Gentiles." The similar expression "having been sold into slavery under sin" (πεπραμένος ὑπὸ τὴν ἁμαρτίαν) is used later in this letter at 7:14 to describe the personal experience of Paul and all people and suggests subjection to the rule, power, or authority of sin. This use of ἁμαρτία ("sin") for a state of existence, and not just an act of defiance, is somewhat surprising, since the teachers of Judaism, Paul, and most other early Christian writers usually spoke of "sin" as a transgression of God's law. But as Walter Grundmann has rightly observed: "For Paul sin does not consist only in the individual act. Sin is for him a state which embraces all humanity."[89]

3:10-18 The catena ("chain") of biblical passages in 3:10b-18 constitutes an important feature in support of the conclusion that the apostle has set out in 3:9. Paul evidently believed that this group of passages would be of particular significance to his Christian addressees at Rome, and so he used it to clinch all that he had argued earlier with respect to these matters. The catena of passages

---

86. Dunn, *Romans*, 1.156.
87. Cf. also Rom 3:22-24; 4:16; 5:18; 8:32; 10:4, 11-13; 11:32; and 15:10-11.
88. See "Textual Note."
89. W. Grundmann, "ἁμαρτάνω," *TDNT* 1.309; see also 308-13 elaborating the point.

(1) draws principally on the Psalms, (2) ties these OT passages together by a sixfold repetition of the expression οὐκ ἔστιν ("there is no one"), and (3) itemizes in the process six parts of the human body ("throats," "tongues," "lips," "mouths," "feet," and "eyes") as a rhetorical means of highlighting the totality of humanity's lack of understanding, the extent of its unrighteousness, and the nature of its injustice. Further, it is a collection of passages that Paul introduces by his usual introductory formula when citing Scripture, καθὼς γέγραπται ("just as it is written") — thereby laying stress on the fact that this conclusion of 3:9 is backed by the authority of Scripture.

A number of considerations, however, need to be taken into account when dealing with this catena of OT passages. The first has to do with the provenance of this collection of passages. For it is often assumed that it was Paul himself who brought this catena of biblical passages together, either spontaneously when writing to the Christians at Rome or at some time during his Gentile mission before he wrote the letter.[90]

I have pointed out in my *Biblical Exegesis in the Apostolic Period* that "a recurring feature in Paul's biblical quotations is his practice of 'pearl stringing' — that is, of bringing to bear on one point of an argument passages from various parts of the Bible in support of the argument."[91] Likewise, I noted that "pearl stringing" is found prominently in Paul's letters[92] and that intrinsic to such pearl stringing is the practice of highlighting analogous words or expressions in the passages brought together, with those words or expressions, in turn, serving as the basis for their union.[93] So I am certainly not prepared to declare it at all impossible for Paul himself to have brought together such a collection of OT texts as appears here in Rom 3:10b-18.

Yet the collecting of biblical passages that contain the same word or expression — or that, more generally, have similar themes or corollary ideas — was a rather common practice among the Jewish teachers of antiquity.[94] Thus every instance of a collection of texts must be investigated not only as to its use by a particular author but also with respect to its possible earlier provenance. And this is what, we believe, is required with regard to the catena of passages here in 3:10b-18.

A number of factors — principally, (1) the complex nature of the biblical quotations in this collection of passages, (2) the rather exact correspondences

90. Cf., e.g., D.-A. Koch, *Schrift als Zeuge des Evangeliums,* 181-83; C. D. Stanley, *Paul and the Language of Scripture,* 88-89; and Shum, *Paul's Use of Isaiah in Romans,* 181-84.

91. Cf. R. N. Longenecker, *Biblical Exegesis,* 2nd ed., 99-100.

92. As appears not only here in 3:10b-18, but also in Rom 9:12-29; 11:8-10; 15:9-12; and Gal 3:10-13 — as well as, though to a more limited extent, in Rom 4:1-8; 9:33; 1 Cor 3:19-20; 15:54-55; and 2 Cor 6:16-18.

93. As found in Paul's writings not only here in 3:10b-18, but also in the use of οὐ λαός μου in Rom 9:25-26, λίθος in Rom 9:32-33, σοφοί in 1 Cor 3:19-20, θάνατος in 1 Cor 15:54-55, ἐπικατάρατος in Gal 3:10, 13, and ζήσεται in Gal 3:11-12.

94. See, e.g., the examples drawn from the Babylonian Talmud in R. N. Longenecker, *Biblical Exegesis,* 2nd ed., 99-100 n. 27.

between the wording of these quotations and the wording of these same verses in the oldest versions of the LXX, (3) the obvious compositional care that has been taken in bringing these passages together into one unified catena of texts, (4) the striking coherence of the unit's overall presentation, and (5) the absence in this catena of passages of any distinctively Christian teaching or traits — have alerted a number of NT interpreters to the probability that this group of biblical texts should be understood as an early *testimonia* collection or traditional set piece of texts. Further, it has also been postulated by some NT scholars that such factors as indicated above suggest the possibility that this grouping of passages was formed originally by some Jewish or (perhaps) Jewish Christian teacher prior to Paul, who in all likelihood wanted to highlight the fact of a definite biblical basis for his teaching that no one can claim to be righteous (δίκαιος) before God on the basis of one's own efforts.[95]

Possibly of even greater significance in support of this thesis of a pre-Pauline, Jewish (or perhaps Jewish Christian) provenance for this collection of texts are the facts (1) that the passages quoted are drawn principally from the Psalms, which was the hymnal and prayer book of Judaism (as well as, of course, of early Jewish Christianity), with only one passage from the prophet Isaiah and two rather traditional echoes of material in Proverbs and Ecclesiastes, and (2) that such a pattern of selection varies from Paul's usual habit in his selection of biblical passages to quote. For when Paul quotes Scripture elsewhere in Romans and his other letters, the great majority of passages are drawn from the Prophets and the Pentateuch — that is, more than seventy from the Prophets and the Pentateuch (as occurs in Romans, 1 and 2 Corinthians, Galatians, but also a few times in Ephesians and the Pastoral Epistles) — with only twelve or thirteen quotations, in addition to those here in 3:4 and 3:10b-18 (perhaps also 3:20; see below), drawn from the Psalms.[96]

A parallel that draws attention to such a differing pattern of selection — and one that I believe to be highly significant for the question at hand — is that between Paul and the writer of the "Letter (or 'Homily') to the Hebrews" in their different selections of quotable biblical materials. For whereas Paul usually quotes from the Prophets and the Pentateuch in support of his teaching, the writer to the Hebrews, a Jewish Christian pastor writing to Jewish believers who were confused with respect to their formerly professed Christian commitments, builds his presentations of Jesus principally on *testimonia* passages drawn from the Psalms that he evidently believed would be particularly meaningful and convincing to his Jewish Christian addressees.[97] And it may be argued that Paul's quotations from the Psalms in Rom 3:4, 10b-18 (and perhaps also 3:20), together with the form of those quotations, served much the same purpose: to

95. Cf. the treatments of these issues by Käsemann, *Romans,* 86; Albl, *"Scripture Cannot Be Broken,"* 172-77; and Jewett, *Romans,* 254-55.

96. Cf. the list of Paul's OT quotations in R. N. Longenecker, *Biblical Exegesis,* 2nd ed., 92-95.

97. Cf. esp. Vis, *Messianic Psalm Quotations in the New Testament;* S. Kistemaker, *The Psalm Citations in the Epistle to the Hebrews* (Eugene, Ore.: Wipf and Stock, 2010).

support his teaching in a manner that would be both meaningful and convincing to his Christian addressees at Rome, who were all, it seems, whatever their various ethnic backgrounds, extensively influenced by the theology, outlook, and practices of the mother church at Jerusalem.

The closeness in wording of the passages Paul quotes here to that of the oldest versions of the LXX, with only a few rather slight variations reflecting Hebraic influence, can readily be seen in the following scanning of the passage:

3:10b-12 abbreviates the first two verses and quotes the third verse of Psalm 14 (LXX Psalm 13) (perhaps also echoing Ps 53:1-3 [LXX 52:1-3] and Eccl 7:20 [LXX 7:21]), altering the Greek version of the psalm only by omitting the first part of the passage, "The fool says in his heart, 'There is no God!'" which could allow these verses to be read as referring primarily to Gentiles, and inserting in its place the operative word δίκαιος ("righteous").

3:13 quotes Ps 5:9b (MT and LXX 5:10b) literally and Ps 140:3b (MT 140:4b, LXX 139:4b).

3:14 alters Ps 10:7a (LXX 9:28a) only slightly.

3:15-17 abbreviates Isa 59:7-8, perhaps also echoing Prov 1:16.

3:18 quotes Ps 36:1b (MT 36:2b, LXX 35:2b) word for word.

Further, the first five and the last statements in this catena of passages (vv. 10b-12 and v. 18) are held together by a sixfold repetition of the phrase "there is none" (οὐκ ἔστιν). In addition, there appears in the last six verses of the passage (vv. 13-18) a catalog of various parts of the human body ("throats," "tongues," "lips," "mouths," "feet," and "eyes").

Beyond these rather obvious literary features, however, it is extremely difficult, if not impossible, to structure this group of verses any further. Yet the drawing together of these biblical passages — which was probably done in some pre-Pauline Jewish milieu and may be presumed to have been known to Paul's Christian addressees at Rome — certainly highlights in a quite dramatic fashion Paul's central point in his conclusion of 3:9: all human beings, whatever their ethnicity, are totally sinful and so stand under God's righteous judgment of sin and sinners!

3:19a The expression οἴδαμεν δὲ ὅτι ("now we know that") was a rather common epistolary "disclosure formula" of the day. And as with its appearances earlier in 2:2 and later in 8:28,[98] it may be assumed that Paul used this introductory formula here, as Stanley Stowers has aptly pointed out, "to emphasize that a statement [that follows] is a matter of common ground between himself and the addressee(s)."[99] This suggests that Paul believed that what he was about to say

---

98. Cf. 1 Tim 1:8; see also οἴδαμεν γάρ ὅτι, "for we know," which introduces the statement of Rom 7:14.

99. So Stowers, *Diatribe and Paul's Letter to the Romans,* 94.

in concluding his quotation of the catena of passages in 3:10b-18 was accepted in Jewish and Jewish Christian circles and therefore would be accepted as true by all the Christians at Rome — since, it seems, all of them, whatever their ethnic backgrounds, had been extensively influenced by the theology, ways of thinking, and religious language of the mother church at Jerusalem.

3:19b Contrary to what might have been thought by some Jews — particularly if the beginning of Ps 14:1-3 (LXX 13:1-3, quoted in Rom 3:10b-12), "The fool has said in his heart 'There is no God!'" were remembered, and all of Psalm 14, together with the other verses quoted in the catena of passages in Rom 3:10b-18, were understood as referring primarily to Gentiles — Paul insists here in 3:19b that ὅσα ὁ νόμος λέγει τοῖς ἐν τῷ νόμῳ λαλεῖ, ἵνα πᾶν στόμα φραγῇ καὶ ὑπόδικος γένηται πᾶς ὁ κόσμος τῷ θεῷ ("Whatever the law says, it says to those who are under the law, so that every mouth may be silenced and the whole world held accountable before God"). This statement, like all the other statements prefaced by the introductory formula οἴδαμεν δὲ ὅτι ("now we know that"), is probably to be viewed as a traditional Jewish aphorism that would have been widely accepted by both Jews and Jewish Christians and therefore known and accepted by most, if not all, of the believers in Jesus at Rome, whatever their ethnic backgrounds. And by its use Paul proclaims once again that though God gave the Jews ὁ νόμος ("the law," a term that here refers specifically to the Mosaic law but also generically to the whole of the OT Scriptures) — which he identified in 3:1-2 as their primary "advantage" — they have not lived up to the standard of that law, and so will be condemned by it. For, as Ernst Käsemann has aptly summarized Paul's message, "Gifts granted to the Jew in salvation history do not protect him against universal judgment."[100]

The ἵνα clause of 3:19b, "*so that* every mouth may be silenced and the whole world held accountable before God," is most likely to be understood as purposive in function (indicating that what precedes is intended to fulfill a conscious purpose or design), not simply consecutive (indicating what follows in course after what has just been said) or even resultative (indicating what results as a consequence). The expression πᾶν στόμα φραγῇ ("every mouth may be silenced") is a biblical idiom that refers to God stopping or "silencing the mouths of" all those who are unrighteous and practice injustice.[101] The term ὑπόδικος, which etymologically came about by bringing together the preposition ὑπό ("under") and the noun δίκη ("penalty," "punishment"), is never used in the LXX and appears only this once in the NT. It was, however, a term used widely in Greco-Roman jurisprudence to mean "liable to judgment" or "punishment" (i.e., "under legal indictment"), and therefore "legally answerable" or "legally accountable."[102] Πᾶς ὁ κόσμος ("all the world," "the whole world") echoes the

---

100. Käsemann, *Romans*, 61.

101. Cf. esp. Ps 63:11 (LXX 62:11): ὅτι ἐνεφράγη στόμα λαλούντων ἄδικα, "For the mouth of those who speak unjust things has been silenced"; Ps 107:42 (LXX 106:42): πᾶσα ἀνομία ἐμφράξει τὸ στόμα αὐτῆς "all wickedness shall stop its mouth."

102. Cf. *BAG*, 852; see also the numerous examples given in *LSJM*, 1880 and *M-M*, 657.

reference to τὸν κόσμον in 3:6, with both uses of the expression signaling in the most inclusive fashion possible the full extent of God's judgment.

Thus in responding to Jews who might have thought they were exempt from God's judgment because they possessed God's law, Paul first repeats what appears to have been a Jewish aphorism: "Whatever the law says, it says to those who are under the law." Then he adds, whether continuing that aphoristic statement or providing his own rationale: "so that every mouth may be silenced and the whole world held legally accountable before God." Gentiles are obviously accountable before God. But Jews as well must "silence their mouths" in the realization that they have not met the standards of God's law. So "the whole world," both Gentiles *and* Jews, are "under sin" and "legally accountable" before God. For the very Scriptures that God gave his people Israel have, as James Dunn has colloquially expressed matters, placed the Jews "firmly 'in the dock' along with everyone else."[103]

III. Closing and Transitional Statement (3:20)

3:20 has usually been understood as simply the second sentence of 3:19-20, with these two verses containing Paul's application of the catena of biblical passages in vv. 10b-18, and so as the final statement in the conclusion of 3:9-20. Our thesis, however, is that 3:20 is far more significant than that. For in reality it is Paul's closing statement for the whole first part (1:16–3:20) of the first protreptic section of his letter to the Christians at Rome (1:16–4:25) — a statement that (1) brings to a conclusion the negative argumentation of 1:18–3:19, but also (2) provides a transition to the positive presentation of righteousness that was announced in 1:16-17 and will be developed in 3:21–4:25. Joseph Fitzmyer has suggested such an understanding in noting at the beginning of his exegetical comments on 3:20 that in this verse (1) "Paul sums up the argument that he began in 1:18," and (2) "[t]he mention of 'justification,' however, serves as a transition to the main positive explanation of the theme announced in 1:16-17."[104]

The first half of our thesis, that 3:20 concludes the argument in 1:18–3:19, has been, at times, somewhat tentatively acknowledged by various commentators — though usually in a rather veiled manner. William Sanday and Arthur Headlam, however, explicitly recognized the statement of 3:20 along these lines, as indicated by their separation of it from the rest of the passage and their translation of the conjunction διότι rather expansively as "This is the conclusion of the whole argument."[105] On the other hand, the latter half of our thesis, that 3:20 provides the transition to the presentation of righteousness in 3:21–4:25,

103. Dunn, *Galatians*, 1.152.
104. Fitzmyer, *Romans*, 337.
105. Sanday and Headlam, *Romans*, 76.

has more recently been argued by Richard Hays in dealing with Paul's use of Ps 143:2 (LXX 142:2) in the first part of 3:20 as follows:

> It is almost universally held by commentators [which, however, is a bit of an overstatement] that this citation summarizes and brings to a close a major section of the discussion. Virtually no one, however, has ever noticed that Psalm 143 also provides the point of departure for what *follows*. In addition to the dictum that "no living being will be justified in his sight," Ps 143 contains several references to God's *righteousness*.[106]

Both of these functions of this closing statement of 3:20, however, need to be recognized and highlighted.

3:20a The conjunction διότι ("because," "therefore," "for") could be understood in four ways here: (1) in a causal sense, as a contraction of διὰ τοῦτο ὅτι, and so translated "because," (2) in an inferential sense, as a contraction of διὰ τοῦτο, and so translated "therefore," (3) as equivalent to the causal use of ὅτι and so translated as "for" in a causal sense, or (4) as equivalent to the ὅτι *recitativum,* which often signals direct discourse and may also be used to introduce biblical quotations, and so translated as "for" in an introductory sense. Commentators have varied considerably as to how to nuance διότι in its various occurrences in Paul's letters and thus how to translate it in each case. Earlier we argued that Paul used διότι in a causal sense at the beginning of 1:19 and 21 and so translated it in those verses as "because." Here in 3:20, however, particularly at the beginning of this closing statement of the first part (i.e., 1:16–3:20) of the first protreptic section (i.e., 1:16–4:25) of his letter to Rome, it is probably best to understand the conjunction in an inferential sense, that is, as signaling a conclusion deduced by inference, and so translate it "therefore."

3:20b The preposition ἐκ often denotes separation, and so frequently suggests the idea of being "from," "out of," or "away from." Here, however, it signals the thought of "origin," "source," "cause," or "reason" and therefore may be translated "on the basis of [the law]" or "that have their source in [the law]." The phrase ἔργα νόμου ("works of the law") appears at the beginning of 3:20, with its location at the beginning of its Greek sentence suggesting something of its importance (though in our translation it has been moved to the end of the sentence, where emphasis is usually to be found in an English sentence).

This phrase ἔργα νόμου ("works of the law") appears eight times in Paul's letters: six times in Galatians, most significantly in 2:16 (three times) and then in 3:2, 5, and 10; twice in Romans, most significantly here in 3:20 and then a few verses later in 3:28.[107] In Paul's earlier letter to his own converts in the

---

106. Hays, "Psalm 143 and the Logic of Romans 3," 113 (italics his).

107. Analogous expressions appear in Gal 2:21; 3:11; Rom 3:21; 3:27; 4:2, 5-6, 13-15; 9:32; and Eph 2:9 (perhaps also Rom 2:15, though see our earlier comments on that verse's singular wording τὸ ἔργον τοῦ νόμου, "the work of the law").

province of Galatia, who were struggling with issues regarding commitment to Jesus vis-à-vis observance of the Mosaic law, the expression "works of the law" appears at a strategic point in the development of his argument, in 2:15-16, which constitutes the opening statement of Paul's *propositio* or thesis statement (vv. 15-21), which, as Hans Dieter Betz has rightly pointed out, both "sums up the *narratio*'s material content" that precedes it and "sets up the arguments to be discussed later in the *probatio*" that follows.[108] And here in Rom 3:20 Paul uses that same phrase "works of the law" in the closing sentence of the first part (1:16–3:20) of the first section (1:16–4:25) of the body middle (1:16–15:13) of his letter.

Three additional introductory observations need also to be highlighted with respect to Paul's use of "works of the law" in these strategically significant passages in Galatians and Romans. First, in both letters Paul attaches "works of the law" to the words drawn from Ps 143:2, which suggests that he viewed both "works of the law" and the words drawn from the psalmist's lament as aphoristic in nature. Second, in both places Paul introduces these aphorisms with epistolary "disclosure formulas" commonly used in that day, (1) by an explicit use of εἰδότες ὅτι ("knowing that") in Gal 2:15-16, and (2) by an inferential use of οἴδαμεν δὲ ὅτι ("now we know that") in Rom 3:19, which suggests that the aphoristic expressions introduced by these disclosure formulas were not only known to him and to his addressees in the province of Galatia and at Rome, but also that they were generally accepted by Jews and Jewish Christians of his day. And third, whereas in Gal 2:15-16 "by works of the law" *follows* the expression "no person will be justified," in the Greek text of Rom 3:20a it *precedes* "no person will be declared righteous in his [God's] sight," which suggests, because of its positioning before the words drawn from Ps 143:2, that some type of emphasis should be seen in Paul's use of "works of the law" here in Rom 3:20.

All these observations and their implications, taken together, serve to support the following conclusions:

1. Rom 3:20 should be seen as a significant closing statement to a subsection of Paul's argument in his letter to Rome, and not just as an additional sentence tacked onto the conclusion of the catena of biblical passages in 3:10b-18 or the application of those OT passages that runs from 3:9 through 3:19.
2. The words drawn from Ps 143:2 and the phrase "works of the law" were viewed by Paul as being similar in nature, that is, as traditional religious aphorisms (whatever may have been their difference of origin and dissimilarity of content).
3. These words from Ps 143:2 and the phrase "works of the law" were also viewed by at least some, if not many, Jews and Jewish Christians of Paul's day as religious aphorisms.

108. H. D. Betz, *Galatians*, 114; see also R. N. Longenecker, *Galatians*, 80-83.

4. Paul may have been the first to bring these two aphorisms together and use them strategically, initially in Galatians and then in Romans.

5. Paul was evidently convinced that the addressees of both letters would understand his use of these aphorisms and respond accordingly, since both had been extensively influenced by Jewish believers in Jesus who had some type of contact with the mother church at Jerusalem — negatively in the churches of Galatia but positively among the various congregations at Rome.

EXCURSUS: "THE LAW," "WORKS OF THE LAW," AND "THE NEW PERSPECTIVE"

During the past two millennia of the church's history, attention has been focused principally on what Paul meant by "the law" when he spoke pejoratively about "the law" and "works of the law" in Galatians and Romans. The questions usually asked were: "Was Paul in his use of νόμος speaking about the whole Mosaic law, both ceremonial and moral?" or "Did he have in mind only the ceremonial law, which came to an end with Christ?"[109]

1. The Whole Law or Only One Part of It? John Calvin's opening comments on "by the works of the law shall no flesh be justified" in Rom 3:20a are fairly representative of this perplexity on the part of many biblical interpreters during the past two millennia:

> Even among learned scholars there is some doubt about what is meant by "the works of the law." While some extend them to include the observance of the whole law, others restrict them to ceremonies alone.[110]

And Calvin's resolution of this matter represents the conclusion of most interpreters of Paul today:

> We contend, however, not without reason, that Paul is here speaking of the whole law. We are abundantly supported by the thread of reasoning which he has followed up to this point, and continues to follow. There are [also] many other passages which do not allow us to think otherwise. It is, therefore, a memorable truth of the first importance that no one can obtain righteousness by keeping the law.[111]

A number of other interpreters throughout Christian history have understood Paul's pejorative use of "law" — and particularly his reference to "works of the law" — as speaking not of the Mosaic law itself, whether in whole or in part, but rather about a legalistic misunderstanding on the part of people regarding the law. This definition has often been expressed in popular Christian writings and sermons of both the past and the present. And it is still argued by a few scholars today.[112] Nonetheless, with Calvin and the vast host of scholarly commentators, we believe that "Paul is here speaking of the whole law" and arguing forthrightly that "no one can obtain righteousness by keeping the law."

---

109. Cf., e.g., M. F. Wiles, *The Divine Apostle,* 67-69.
110. J. Calvin, *Romans,* in *Calvin's New Testament Commentaries,* 8.69.
111. *Ibid.,* 8.70.
112. See esp. Fuller, "Paul and 'the Works of the Law,'" 28-42; note also K. R. Snodgrass's translation of ἔργα νόμου as "works done in the flesh" in his "Justification by Grace," 84.

2. "The New Perspective" on "Works of the Law." During the last two decades of the twentieth century, however, and continuing on into the twenty-first, there has arisen a "new perspective" on Paul and what he meant by the phrase "works of the law." It views (1) Paul's pejorative use of "works" as not having in mind legalistic observances that were thought to gain acceptance before God and (2) his pejorative use of "the law" as not referring to a legal system by which Jews thought they could gain righteousness. Instead it interprets "works of the law" in a national and cultural sense as connoting certain religio-societal legislation that had been given by God to the people of Israel — particularly legislation having to do with circumcision, the Sabbath, and certain dietary matters, which Jews took pride in as identifying them a distinct people and nation (i.e., "identity markers") and as separating them from all other people and nations (i.e., "boundary markers").

This new perspective on Paul grew out of Ed Sanders's important thesis regarding Palestinian Judaism in Paul's day, which he proposed in Part One of his *Paul and Palestinian Judaism* in 1977 and then developed further in his *Paul, the Law, and the Jewish People* in 1983. Sanders argued that (1) Palestianian Judaism was not a legalistic religion; that is, it did not require Jews to observe the Mosaic law in order to "get in" or be accepted by God into his covenant, and so become God's people — for Jews always considered themselves to be, by God's grace and mercy, already in God's covenant, and so in a right relationship with God; yet (2) Palestinian Judaism also taught that, having been received into God's covenant by God's grace and mercy, the Jewish relationship with God within his covenant was to be maintained and expressed by obedience to the Mosaic law, that is, that Jews must obey the precepts of the Mosaic law in order to "stay in" or remain within that covenantal relationship with God, and so be, in truth, God's people. Sanders called this type of religious orientation "covenantal nomism,"[113] distinguishing it from any form of " 'works-righteousness' concern, as commonly conceived."[114] And he delineated the "pattern" or "structure" of Jewish "covenantal nomism," as depicted by the earliest portions of the Talmud and other early rabbinic writings, as follows:

> The "pattern" or "structure" of covenantal nomism is this: (1) God has chosen Israel and (2) given the law. The law implies both (3) God's promise to maintain the election and (4) the requirement to obey. (5) God rewards obedience and punishes transgression. (6) The law provides for means of atonement, and atonement results in (7) maintenance or re-establishment of the covenantal relationship. (8) All those who are maintained in the covenant by obedience, atonement and God's mercy belong to the group which will be saved. An important interpretation of the first and last points is that election and ultimately salvation are considered to be by God's mercy rather than human achievement.[115]

Such a description of Judaism, of course, raises questions about Paul's statements about the Jews and Judaism in his letters, and particularly about his pejorative use of the phrase "works of the law" in Galatians and Romans. So in Part Two of *Paul and Palestinian Judaism* Sanders set out what he understood as the "pattern" or "structure" of Paul's theology, focusing particularly on Paul's differences with the mainline Judaism of his day. Sanders argued that Paul's Christian proclamation was not rooted in first-century

---

113. Cf. E. P. Sanders, *Paul and Palestinian Judaism*, 75, 236, 422-23.
114. *Ibid.*, 74-75.
115. *Ibid.*, 422.

Jewish "patterns" or theological constructs of thought but on his conviction that Jesus of Nazareth was the Jewish Messiah and the Savior of the whole world. Thus "Paul's type of religion is basically different from anything known from Palestinian Judaism," for whereas "there was a generally prevailing religious type in Palestinian Judaism," that of "covenantal nomism," "Paul's pattern of religious thought" was that of "participationist eschatology."[116]

Sanders argued, therefore, that Paul must not be seen as faulting Judaism as a "legalistic, self-righteousing, self-aggrandizing" religion of works; rather, Paul faults Judaism simply because, as Sanders put it, *it is not Christianity.*"[117] Traditional interpreters, Sanders insisted, have misunderstood Paul. And because of their failure to understand Paul, they have failed also to understand Palestinian Judaism. Thus with respect to Paul's use of the phrase "works of the law," interpreters today must understand that Paul was "not against a supposed Jewish position that enough good works earn righteousness"; rather, he was simply expressing his own view, which had been drawn from his own convictions about Jesus Christ and his own type of participationist-eschatological soteriology, that "one need not be Jewish to be 'righteous.'"[118]

Some of the ethos for Sanders's argument had been provided by Krister Stendahl in his 1963 article "The Apostle Paul and the Introspective Conscience of the West." Stendahl argued that Christians of the Western world have misread Paul as anti-Jewish and anti-Judaistic, and so of speaking pejoratively about Jewish "works of the law," largely because they have been overly influenced by Martin Luther's anxieties about his guilty conscience, his struggles to gain personal justification, and his polemic against the "Papists" of his day — whom Luther viewed as essentially the same as the "Judaizers" of Paul's day, and vice versa.[119] And much of Sanders's depiction of Palestinian Judaism was accepted by James Dunn, who then attempted to describe Paul in a manner that affirmed the apostle's basic Christian convictions and yet was compatible with Sanders's understanding of the Judaism of Paul's day. Dunn first argued his understanding of Paul's proclamation of the Christian gospel vis-à-vis Sanders's views of first-century Judaism in his Manson Memorial Lecture of 1982, in which he coined the expression "The New Perspective on Paul."[120] Thereafter Dunn has written and lectured extensively on this "new perspective"[121] — all the while influencing a number of other scholars, perhaps most obviously Tom Wright in his book *Paul: In Fresh Perspective.*[122]

A number of features in Sanders's analysis of Palestinian Judaism are both noteworthy and important. In my 1964 monograph *Paul, Apostle of Liberty,* I also argued that the theology of mainline Judaism in Paul's day was not — at least as taught by the better Jewish rabbis — an "acting legalism," holding that one must observe the Mosaic law in order to gain acceptance and righteousness before God. Judaism's teaching on the neces-

---

116. E. P. Sanders, *Paul and Palestinian Judaism,* 552.

117. E. P. Sanders, *Paul and Palestinian Judaism,* 552 (italics his); see also *idem, Paul, the Law, and the Jewish People,* 45-48 and 154-62.

118. E. P. Sanders, *Paul, the Law, and the Jewish People,* 46.

119. Cf. Stendahl, "Apostle Paul and the Introspective Conscience," 199-215.

120. Cf. Dunn, "New Perspective on Paul," 95-122.

121. For a collection of Dunn's articles on the subject, together with a further article in response to his critics, see Dunn, *The New Perspective on Paul.*

122. N. T. Wright, *Paul.*

sity for Jews to observe the law must, rather, be understood in terms of a "responding" or "reacting nomism": because one has been brought into God's covenant by his grace and mercy, one must respond to God by a life of faithful obedience to his will, as expressed in the Mosaic law.[123] Where my analysis of first-century Judaism differed from Sanders's portrayals in *Paul and Palestinian Judaism,* and where I continue to differ with him, is principally with respect to his confidence that "covenantal nomism" dominated the totality of mainline Jewish thought and practice in Paul's day. The same rabbinic writings that Sanders cites for his understanding of early Judaism (i.e., from about 200 B.C. to A.D. 200) also contain some Jewish teachings, refer to some Jewish teachers, and report some Jewish situations that reflect an outlook that can only be called "legalistic" and not "nomistic" — and which, at times, some of the leading rabbis of the period denounced. Further, it needs always to be recognized that even lofty principles can be viewed and practiced in legalistic ways — which is, sadly, true with respect to every religious philosophy, both Judaism and Christianity included.

Likewise, I have agreed with Sanders earlier in this present commentary in my treatment of 1:18-32 that Paul's usual approach in his evangelistic preaching to Gentiles, as well as in his pastoral counseling with his own converts, was to start not from human need but from God's deed.[124] But I also added an important caveat to such an understanding, that it was, it appears, quite the reverse when he proclaimed the Christian gospel to Jews and when he wrote to Gentile Christians who have been extensively influenced by Judaism and/or Jewish Christianity — as I argued was the case when he wrote the Christians at Rome.

There are, of course, many other matters in the analyses of Paul proposed by Ed Sanders and James Dunn that may rightly be acclaimed as laudatory. It would, however, be extraneous, as well as nearly impossible, to attempt an enumeration of such positive matters here. Suffice it only to say by way of criticism of Sanders and Dunn that I believe their respective views on the expression "works of the law" in Rom 3:20, as well as in its appearances elsewhere in Galatians and Romans, is faulty. For to argue (1) that Paul's use of "works of the law" has been misunderstood by past interpreters, or that he may have been under some type of foreign (perhaps Hellenistic) influence when he wrote those words (as does Sanders), or (2) that Paul was using "works of the law" with reference only to Jewish legislation on circumcision, Sabbath, and certain dietary matters, which some Jews of that day were using in a nationalistic fashion as their "identity markers" and "boundary markers," and not to any form of Jewish "legalism" as usually understood (as does Dunn), is to twist the evidence in support of an alien thesis.

Sanders and Dunn seem to be attempting, each in his own way, to exonerate Paul from the charge of being anti-Jewish, anti-Judaistic, or anti-Semitic, and that is, to some extent, certainly laudatory. More importantly, Sanders and Dunn want to highlight the emphases in the teachings of mainline Judaism in Paul's day on (1) God's election of Israel, (2) divine grace and mercy, (3) human faith in response to God, and (4) a doctrine of forgiveness — which are features of great importance that need to be highlighted, particularly in response to the bleak picture of Jewish theology that was painted by many Christian interpreters during the nineteenth and early twentieth centuries. But as important as their motivations and these emphases may be, it still must be said that

123. See R. N. Longenecker, "The Piety of Hebraic Judaism," in *Paul, Apostle of Liberty,* ch. 3, pp. 65-85.
124. Quoting E. P. Sanders, *Paul and Palestinian Judaism,* 444.

the treatments of Sanders and Dunn of Paul's phrase "works of the law" in Rom 3:20a (and elsewhere in Galatians and Romans) and of his pejorative statements about Jews and the Mosaic law in Rom 2:17–3:19 (and elsewhere in his letters), misconstrue Paul's teaching — and so fall short of understanding properly what he said about the Jews and what his attitude was regarding mainline Judaism in his day.

3. Interpretations of "Works of the Law" Based Principally on Contextual Consider-ations and Circumstantial Historical Data. The interpretation of the phrase "works of the law" has been seriously complicated by the following factors: (1) apart from Paul's usage elsewhere in his letters (as cited above), there are no close verbal parallels to this expression in the rest of the NT or in the LXX, (2) there are only a few places in the writings of Early Judaism (i.e., about 200 B.C. to A.D. 200) where analogous terminology exists, and (3) the infrequent phrases that are corollary to the expression ἔργα νόμου occur only in a few writings of the Dead Sea Scrolls and in *2 Baruch*. So scholars have had to base their understanding about what Paul meant by "works of the law" principally on contextual considerations and circumstantial historical data, with very little parallel linguistic evidence available — though, of late, that linguistic database has been somewhat improved by six reconstructed Qumran texts identified as 4QMMT and published as 4Q394-99, as will be discussed below.

That Gentiles were required to observe the Mosaic law in order to become converts to Judaism, and so be included within God's covenant as God's people, is clear in the writings of Second Temple Judaism — as well as in later rabbinic materials codified in the Mishnah and the Babylonian Gemaras (i.e., the Talmud) and in such other rabbinic collections as the Palestinian Gemaras, the Tosephta ("Additions"), and the "Sayings" of various early "Abot" ("Fathers"), "Soferim" ("Scribes"), and "Tannaim" (literally "repeaters," i.e., the early "Teachers of the Law"). Even more significant for our purposes, however, are certain statements and reports by the Jewish historian Josephus with regard to these matters. For though Josephus was not a theologian, he sought to explain Jewish theology in a popular fashion to his "more sophisticated" Gentile readers. And, though he desired to present the basic facts of first-century Jewish life and Jewish thought in a manner that would be appealing to non-Jews, he did not hesitate to speak of the distinctive principles and practices of his people.

Thus by way of highlighting some of the most significant passages in Josephus's writings regarding the requirement for Gentiles to observe the Mosaic law in order to convert to Judaism and so be accepted by God, it should be noted first that he spoke of many Greeks in his day who "have agreed to adopt our laws, of whom some have remained faithful, while others, lacking the necessary endurance, have again seceded."[125] Further with respect to Moses, the Mosaic law, and Gentiles who desired to convert to Judaism, after a long detailing of what he considered to be the main "precepts and prohibitions of our Law,"[126] Josephus wrote:

> The consideration given by our legislator to the equitable treatment of foreigners also merits attention. For it will be seen that he took the best of all possible measures at once to secure our own customs from corruption, and to throw them open ungrudgingly to any who elect to share them. To all who desire to come and live under the same laws with us, he gives a gracious welcome, holding that it is not

125. Josephus, *Contra Apion* 2.123.
126. *Ibid.,* 2.190-208.

family ties alone which constitute relationship, but agreement in the principles of conduct.[127]

Likewise in his account of Helena, queen mother of Adiabene, and her son King Izates in *Antiquities* 20.17-53, Josephus highlights a specific instance of the necessity of keeping even the most onerous provision of the Mosaic law in order to become a convert to Judaism and so be accepted by God. Helena and Izates desired to convert to Judaism, but feared the repercussions that might follow in their kingdom if Izates was circumcised. A traveling Jewish merchant named Ananias, however, told Izates that "God Himself would pardon him if, constrained by necessity and by fear of his subjects, he failed to perform this rite" — with Ananias even arguing that Izates' desire to be "a devoted adherent of Judaism" was "counted [by God] more than circumcision."[128] But another Jew from Galilee spoke quite plainly to Izates, rebuking and instructing him as follows:

> In your ignorance, O king, you are guilty of the greatest offence against the law and thereby against God. For you ought not merely read the law but also, and even more, do what is commanded in it. How long will you continue to be uncircumcised? If you have not read the law concerning this matter, read it now, so that you may know what an impiety it is that you commit.[129]

And Josephus goes on to tell his readers that "upon hearing these words, the king postponed the deed (τὴν πρᾶξιν: 'act,' 'action,' 'deed') no longer"[130] and that, though his mother and other officials in the court of Adiabene feared that Izates might lose his throne because of his being circumcised, God protected him and so "demonstrated that those who fix their eyes on Him and trust in Him alone do not lose the reward of their piety."[131]

There is, of course, no explicit use of the phrase "works of the law" in any of these three passages in Josephus. Nonetheless, as Charles Talbert has aptly pointed out: "What seems clear from Josephus's statements is that a Gentile 'got in' [using Sanders's expression] the people of God by works of the law."[132]

There are also passages in the writings of Second Temple Judaism that speak of Abraham, the father of all Jews, as being accepted by God because of his obedience to God's commands. For example, the writer of *Jubilees* (which was probably written sometime in the middle of the second century B.C.) speaks of God telling Abraham to be pleasing before him and that as a consequence God would make a covenant with Abraham and multiply his descendants: "And the Lord appeared to Abram and he said to him: 'I am God Shaddai. Be pleasing before me and be perfect. And I will make my covenant between me and you, and I will make you increase very much.'"[133] And the *Cairo Damascus Covenant* (which was originally called by that title because it was found in Cairo and speaks of a community of sectarian Jews in Damascus, but has also been identified among the scrolls found at Qumran and called the *Zadokite Fragments*) asserts that Abraham was counted as "the Friend of God" because "he kept the commandments

---

127. Josephus, *Contra Apion* 2.209-10.
128. Josephus, *Antiquities* 20.41.
129. *Ibid.*, 20.44-45.
130. *Ibid.*, 20.46.
131. *Ibid.*, 20.47-48.
132. Talbert, *Romans*, 93.
133. *Jub* 15:3-4.

of God and did not prefer the desires of his own spirit."[134] In neither of these statements about Abraham, however, does the phrase "works of the law" appear.

   4. Recent Linguistic Data Provided by 4QMMT. Prior to fairly recent studies of the Dead Sea Scrolls, scholars have been able to identify similar phraseology in Jewish writings, though with some variations, only in 4QFlor 1.7 (מעשי תורה, "works of [the] law"), 1QS 5.21 and 6.18 (מעשיו בתורה, "his works in [the] law"), 1QS 5.32 (מעשיו, "his works"), and 2 Bar 57:2 (Latin: *opera praeceptorum,* "works of the precepts" or "law"). The Latin expression in 2 *Baruch,* however, stems from the late first or early second century A.D. and probably refers to precepts that were understood to be in force at an earlier time before the giving of the Mosaic law — that is, to primeval "unwritten laws" of creation and conscience, which the earlier mid-second century B.C. author of *Jubilees* evidently understood were what Abraham kept and God rewarded, when he declared: "For Abraham was perfect in all of his actions with the Lord and was pleasing through righteousness all of the days of his life."[135]

   But in 1984 material from what has been designated 4QMMT was presented to the scholarly world at the International Conference on Biblical Archaeology in Jerusalem. Then in 1994 these six reconstructed manuscripts, which contain a total of approximately 130 extant lines (probably representing only about 40% of an original document that had at some time early in the experience of the Dead Sea covenanters somehow found its way into their community at Wadi Qumran), were officially published as 4Q394-99.[136] And with that presentation in 1984 and resultant publication in 1994, attention has been focused on a number of topics and issues arising from the data in these six reconstructed manuscripts.

   Most important for our purpose here is the Hebrew phrase מעשי התורה ("works" or "deeds of the law") that appears in 4QMMT manuscript C (4Q396), line 27 — with that line most likely to be read: "We have written to you some of the 'works of the law.'" This sentence, elliptical as it may now seem, evidently introduced in the original document a conclusion to a list of practices or "works of the law" that had been previously set out in the writing but is no longer extant. Further, the observance of these "works of the law" was probably considered necessary in order to be accepted and rewarded by God. For the final extant line of manuscript C tells its readers — evidently in hortatory fashion — that by observing these "works of the law" "You will be doing 'righteousness' (צדקה) before Him." And it is likely that the expression מקצת מעשי התרה ("some works of the law"), which appears in manuscript C, line 29, as well as the word מעשים ("works" or "deeds"), which appears in manuscript B (4Q395), line 2 and manuscript C, line 23, are to be related to this phrase as well.

   The dating of 4QMMT is largely conjectural. There is little doubt that it was written at some time prior to Paul, but exactly when is uncertain. Scholarly speculation is that it was written before the establishment of the sectarian encampment on the plateau area immediately north of Wadi Qumran, at the northwest tip of the Dead Sea, and that the document somehow became part of the group of scrolls that were retained and studied by the covenanters who resided there. But whatever the exact provenance of these reconstructed six manuscripts, the presence of the phrase "works of the law" in the context

---

134. CD 3.2; i.e., the Cairo Genizah text of the *Damascus Document,* or the *Zadokite Fragments* 6QD and 4QD^b from Qumran.

135. *Jub* 23:10.

136. See *Qumran Cave 4, V: Miqsat Ma'ase Ha-Torah* (in DJD 10).

of a list of prescribed practices and followed by an exhortation that speaks of doing acts of righteousness before God suggests, as Joseph Fitzmyer has rightly pointed out, "that Paul is tributary to a genuine pre-Christian Palestinian Jewish tradition."[137]

Based, therefore, not only on contextual considerations (which are always of great importance for an understanding of any author's use of any particular word or phrase) and on circumstantial historical data (which may be considered supportive), but also now on an expanded linguistic database (as drawn from the Dead Sea Scrolls, and principally from 4QMMT), it seems highly likely that the expression ἔργα νόμου ("works of the law") was used by Paul to refer to "deeds done in obedience to the Mosaic law" that were viewed in a legalistic manner as gaining "righteousness" before God and so acceptance by him. Paul's anarthrous use of νόμος in the phrase ἔργα νόμου, when compared with the generally articular use of התורה in 4QMMT, may be thought to pose a problem.[138] But the context of the use of νόμος or ὁ νόμος in each passage where the word appears is far more important than the presence or absence of an article.[139] Further, the genitive form of νόμου may be interpreted as being either objective, that is, "works that fulfill the law," or subjective, that is, "works that the law requires." But while the subjective genitive is perhaps more likely, either reading suggests that Paul used the phrase in a pejorative manner.

5. Summation. We must, therefore, conclude that "the new perspective on Paul" — despite its laudatory motivations, some very significant observations, and a fairly wide acceptance of that view today — actually misconstrues Paul's use of the phrase "works of the law" and somewhat distorts his attitudes toward compatriot Jews and first-century Palestinian Judaism. For in its endeavors to highlight certain positive features within the "nomism" of ancient Judaism, it is somewhat blind to the "legalism" that was also present (as it is, sadly, in every religion, both ancient and modern). And in its attempt to restrict the definition of "works of the law" only to matters regarding prideful nationalism and cultural prejudice and thereby to minimize any connotation of "legalism," it has run a bit roughshod over Paul's argument in Rom 2:17–3:20.

Rather, we argue, in agreement with the great majority of Christian commentators of the past, that here in 3:20 — as well as in the phrase's other appearances in Galatians and Romans (see above) — Paul was using "works of the law" pejoratively in an effort to deny the legalism that the phrase connoted in certain Jewish and/or Jewish Christian circles. Further, we believe it likely (1) that Paul viewed "works of the law" as a religious aphorism, which came into the religious parlance of at least some Jews during the period of Early Judaism (i.e., c. 200 B.C. to A.D. 200), (2) that he believed his Christian addressees at Rome also knew this aphorism and its use by others, but (3) that he was fairly confident that his addressees agreed with him in his usage, and not with those who used it in a legalistic fashion. Thus Paul uses the expression "works of the law" in his closing statement of Rom 3:20 to summarize his teaching in 1:18–3:19: while in principle "those who obey the law will be declared righteous" (2:13), in practice no one is able to obey the law well enough to gain righteousness and be accepted by God — with

---

137. Fitzmyer, *Romans,* 338.

138. Though תורה appears without an article in the phrase מעשי תורה of 4QFlor 1.7 (i.e., in 4Q174.1-2); cf. also the displacement of the article ה ("the") by the preposition ב ["in"] in the phrase מעשיו בתורה of 1QS 5.21 and 6.18.

139. C. F. D. Moule's dictum: "The context is a surer guide to the meaning than is the use of the article" (*Moule,* 113).

the result that both Jews and Gentiles are under the dominance of sin and under God's condemnation. And therefore all endeavors to be "declared righteous in his [God's] sight *by works of the law*" are futile.

3:20c The sentence οὐ δικαιωθήσεται πᾶσα σὰρξ ἐνώπιον αὐτοῦ ("no one will be declared righteous in his [God's] sight") is drawn from Ps 143:2 (LXX Ps 142:2), which in the LXX reads οὐ δικαιωθήσεται ἐνώπιόν σου πᾶς ζῶν ("no living being will be justified in your sight") — with that Greek translation reproducing almost exactly the Hebrew of the MT. These words express the sad lament of the psalmist regarding his and humanity's spiritual condition apart from God's redemptive intervention. And it is this same understanding of the fundamental problem of all human beings, though voiced in various ways by the use of various equivalent expressions, that appears at a number of places in the Dead Sea Scrolls — as expressed most graphically in 1QS 11.9-10: "I belong to wicked humanity and to the assembly of perverse flesh. My iniquities, my transgression, my sin, together with the perversities of my heart, belong to the assembly of worms and of things that move in darkness."[140] So it may legitimately be argued that such an evaluation of humanity's basic spiritual problem was foundational for all true piety in the OT religion of Israel and among many pious Jews of Paul's day. Further, it may be assumed that Paul's use of these words from Ps 143 would find resonance in the hearts and minds of his Christian addressees at Rome.

In his use of these words Paul recasts ἐνώπιόν σου ("before your eyes") to ἐνώπιον αὐτοῦ ("before his [God's] eyes"), as would be necessary in changing direct address to indirect reference, and he alters the phrase πᾶς ζῶν ("all those living" or "all living persons") to πᾶσα σάρξ ("all flesh"), evidently in conformity to his own use of σάρξ as signifying humanity living apart from God and operating only by means of its own finite energy. He does not, however, introduce these words drawn from Ps 143:2 by the introductory formula καθὼς γέγραπται ("just as it is written"), as was his usual practice when quoting a biblical passage. Nor did he do so earlier in Gal 2:16, it needs also to be observed, when using the same wording of Ps 143:2 to declare that "no person will be justified" (οὐ δικαιοῦται ἄνθρωπος). Further, it should be noted that these words drawn from Ps 143:2 in Gal 2:16 are also attached to the phrase ἐξ ἔργων νόμου ("by works of the law"), just as they are here in Rom 3:20.

All this suggests that in both Gal 2:16 and Rom 3:20a Paul is not quoting these words from Ps 143 but alluding to them. Or probably it would be more accurate to say that he was using a traditional Jewish religious aphorism that was based generally on the teachings of the Jewish (OT) Scriptures but came to expression most explicitly in those Scriptures in the psalmist's personal lament of Ps 143:2.

---

140. Cf. 1QH 4.29-31: "I know that uprightness belongs to no human being, or rectitude to any son of man"; see also 1QH 7.16; 12.19; 13.16-17.

3:20d Ernst Käsemann rightly observed that the statement διὰ γὰρ νόμου ἐπίγνωσις ἁμαρτίας ("for through the law is the consciousness of sin") is "oracular in its brevity"[141] — that is, it is pithy and wise, perhaps comparable to utterances expressed by an ancient Greek oracle, and meant, therefore, to be accepted as true. Nonetheless, as Käsemann went on to argue, this final statement of the verse should not, simply because of its form, be understood as "a general truth"[142] or even as a traditional aphoristic maxim (as we have proposed may be found in 2:2, 11; 3:4a, 20a). Rather, it is probably best understood as Paul's own Christian understanding of the purpose and function of the Mosaic law, with which he believed his addressees at Rome would agree and in support of which he has just written in 3:20a (note the explanatory use of γάρ, "for").

Paul dealt with this same issue of the purpose and function of the law in Gal 3:19-25, beginning there in v. 19a by asking "Why, then, the law?" Then after stating in vv. 19-21a a number of factors to be taken into account with respect to God's giving of the Mosaic law, he set out in vv. 21b-25 three propositions regarding the purposes and functions of the law:

1. The law was never intended by God to provide "life" or "righteousness" by means of any human observance, "for if a law had been given that could give life, then righteousness would certainly have been on the basis of law" (v. 21b). This is Paul's basic argument against "legalism."

2. The law was given by God as a "supervisory guardian" (παιδαγωγός) for God's people Israel, but this supervisory function was only meant to be in effect "until this coming faith (τοῦ ἐλθεῖν τὴν πίστιν [i.e., 'faith in Jesus'] should be revealed" — and "now that this faith has come (ἐλθούσης δὲ τῆς πίστεως), we are no longer under a supervisory guardian" (vv. 23-25). This is Paul's argument against the continued existence of "nomism" (as I called it in 1964) or "covenantal nomism" (as Ed Sanders called it in 1977 and as that expression has been commonly used since).

3. In God's redemptive purposes the law has always had — and will always have — the function of "confining everyone without distinction under sin, so that the promise that is based on the faith [or 'the faithfulness'] of Jesus Christ might be given to those who believe." This is what Paul asserts is the primary purpose of the law in any Christian understanding and its continuing function in every Christian life.[143]

This function of "confining everyone without distinction under sin" spoken of in Gal 3:22, especially when understood in conjunction with Paul's statement that "it [the Mosaic law] was added because of transgressions" in v. 19, should most likely be interpreted in a *cognitive* fashion to mean that the law

---

141. Käsemann, *Romans,* 89.
142. *Ibid.,* 89-90.
143. See R. N. Longenecker, *Galatians,* 136-50.

was given so as to bring about a consciousness of sin in sin-hardened humanity, and not in a *causative* fashion to suggest that the law was given to bring about more sin or to increase human sinfulness.[144] Further, it may legitimately be assumed that what Paul wrote in his earlier letter to his converts in Galatia is what he also had in mind here in this closing statement of Rom 3:20: (1) God did not give the Mosaic law to be interpreted legalistically, for "no one will be declared righteous by works of the law"; (2) the law had a legitimate role to play as a supervisory guardian over God's people Israel, but this supervisory function came to an end with the coming of Christ — and so believers in Jesus are not now to take on themselves the law's past nomistic function; and (3) God's purpose in giving the law was always, and continues to be, to bring about "the consciousness of sin" in all people — particularly among those who claim to be followers of Jesus Christ.

This concluding statement about the purpose and function of the Mosaic law in Rom 3:20 brings to an end the entire negative argumentation of Rom 1:18–3:20. But the themes contained here in v. 20 regarding (1) "righteousness" (δικαιοσύνη), (2) the inability of humanity apart from God (i.e., πᾶσα σάρξ, "all flesh") to "be declared righteous in his [God's] sight," (3) the futility of "works of the law" (ἔργα νόμου), and (4) the purpose of the law to bring about "the consciousness of sin" (ἐπίγνωσις ἁμαρτίας) — all these themes will continue to resonate and be explicated further in what appears later in Paul's letter, especially in the positive part of Section 1 of his protreptic presentation, which immediately follows (3:21–4:25) and in his portrayal of his own contextualized proclamation to Gentiles in Section 2 (5:1–8:39).

BIBLICAL THEOLOGY

In the development of his argument in Rom 1:18–3:20, Paul spoke first in broad terms about: (1) "God's wrath against humanity's godlessness and wickedness" in 1:18-32 and (2) "God's condemnation of all who sin as just and impartial" in 2:1-16. In 2:17–3:20, however, he narrowed his focus to the Jews and set out material that highlighted: (3) "denunciations of Jews and Jewish failures" in 2:17-29 and (4) "the situation of the Jews before God" in 3:1-20. The rationale for Paul's focus on the Jews in these latter two sections of 2:17-29 and 3:1-20 is well expressed by Douglas Moo:

> The Jews become, as it were, representative of human beings generally. If the Jews, with the best law that one could have, could not find salvation through it, then *any* system of works is revealed as unable to conquer the power of sin. The "bottom line" in Paul's argument, then, is his conviction that sin creates for every person a situation of utterly helpless bondage.

144. R. N. Longenecker, *Galatians*, 138-39.

"Works of the law" are inadequate not because they are "works of *the law*," but, ultimately, because they are "works." This clearly removes the matter from the purely salvation-historical realm to the broader realm of anthropology. No person can gain a standing with God through works because no one is able to perform works to the degree needed to secure such a standing. This human inability to meet the demands of God is what lies at the heart of Rom. 3.[145]

Three highly significant theological themes underlie all that Paul writes throughout 1:18–3:20, with these themes coming quite explicitly to expression in the densely packed and somewhat difficult materials of 3:1-20 — and particularly in the conclusion of 3:9 and the closing statement of 3:20: (1) sin as a state of bondage, (2) the inability of any person to attain righteousness and acceptance before God, and (3) the futility of a person's "works" in gaining righteousness or status with God. And it is these three theological themes that need to be spelled out somewhat more fully in what follows.

Toward an Understanding of Sin. The word "sin" (ἁμαρτία) first appears in Romans in the final sentence of Paul's conclusion in 3:9: "both Jews and Gentiles are all under sin" (Ἰουδαίους τε καὶ Ἕλληνας πάντας ὑφ' ἁμαρτίαν εἶναι). It appears the second time as the final word of the closing statement in 3:20: "for through the law is the consciousness of sin" (διὰ γὰρ νόμου ἐπίγνωσις ἁμαρτίας). Yet though the word "sin" itself appears first in these two verses, sin underlay all of what Paul denounced earlier in 1:18–3:8 — that is, humanity's "godlessness and wickedness" in 1:18-32, "unrighteousness" and "injustice" in 2:1-16, "unfaithfulness and failures" in 2:17-29, and "lack of faith," "unrighteousness," "falsehood," and "evil" in 3:1-8. All these expressions function interchangeably throughout these passages and so serve to interpret one another. And all of them are encapsulated in the single word "sin."

What, then, is to be understood by "sin" in Paul's preaching and teaching? "For most people," as Charles Talbert has pointed out, " 'sin' means actions that violate some social norm, usually associated with a church body's view."[146] But, as Talbert goes on to insist, "Paul's views are different."[147] For Paul, as Luke Timothy Johnson (who is as also cited by Talbert) has rightly observed:

> Sin is not a moral category but a religious one. The distinction is of fundamental importance. He [Paul] does not suggest that every pagan was lost in vice or that every Jew is incapable of virtue. But Jews and Greeks can be virtuous — they can do good deeds. Immorality may be a result and sign of sin, but it is not itself sin.[148]

---

145. Moo, *Romans,* 217 (italics his).
146. Talbert, *Romans,* 102.
147. *Ibid.*
148. L. T. Johnson, *Reading Romans,* 47-48.

Further:

> Sin has to do with the human relationship with God — or, better, with the breaking of the human relationship with God. In this sense, the opposite of sin is not virtue but faith. Sin and faith are, for Paul, the two basic options available to human freedom vis-à-vis the power and presence of God. Paul makes the disjunction explicit in 14:23 — "Whatever is not out of faith *(ek pisteos)* is sin *(hamartia)*" — but it is presumed throughout. Paul uses the singular *hamartia* for the same reason. It is a matter not of "sinful acts" but of a fundamental disposition of human freedom, a basic rebellion of the will against God.[149]

Paul also, of course, speaks of "sins" in moral terms when speaking of matters regarding sensuality, social injustice, and personal evil. But in Paul's view, as well as that of all the biblical writers, such sins are ultimately sins against God. For, as Charles Talbert has emphasized, "In each case, the behavior runs contrary to God's will for the creation and the creature. Hence it is against God."[150] And in a day when atheism, humanism, and relativism seem to reign supreme in contemporary Western society, such an understanding of "sin" and "sins" needs to be brought to the forefront in our Christian consciousness and understanding.

The Inability of Any Person to Attain Righteousness and Acceptance before God. In his use of the aphorism drawn from Ps 143:2 in the closing statement of 3:20, Paul altered the phrase πᾶς ζῶν ("all those living" or "all living persons") to read πᾶσα σάρξ ("all flesh"). At first glance such a change might seem rather trivial. But "flesh" (σάρξ) is of great importance in Paul's vocabulary, for it represents a highly significant concept in his theology. He used it earlier in Galatians to contrast "the works of the flesh" and "the fruit of the Spirit."[151] And later in Romans he will use it as a locution for a life lived according to one's sinful nature, which is diametrically opposed to a life lived in terms of the guidance and empowerment of the Spirit.[152]

For Paul, "flesh" is shorthand for "humanity living apart from God and operating only by means of its own finite energy" (quoting our definition above in the exegetical comments on 3:20). Or as Luke Timothy Johnson has more extensively, and undoubtedly more adequately, represented what Paul meant: "He means by flesh the measurement of life apart from spirit, and specifically apart from the Holy Spirit of God. It is life in denial of transcendence; a life lived on the basis of perceived reality, taken as a closed system."[153]

It is a gruesome existence to live apart from God and to operate only by

---

149. L. T. Johnson, *Reading Romans,* 48.
150. Talbert, *Romans,* 102.
151. See Gal 5:19-26.
152. Cf. Rom 7:5, 18, 25; 8:3-7.
153. L. T. Johnson, *Reading Romans,* 48.

means of one's own limited strength and sinful proclivities. Such an existence has terrible results for one's outlook on life, and so for one's person. It also has disastrous implications for one's relations with others, and so for one's family, society, and culture. But more than all of that, important as those matters are, is the fact that the dominance of "sin" and "flesh" in the experience of every human being makes it impossible for any person, by means of his or her own abilities, to attain righteousness and acceptance before God.

The Futility of "Works" to Gain Righteousness or Status with God. Paul's conclusion in 3:9 and his closing statement in 3:20 — particularly as he encapsulates what he says by use of the terms "sin" and "flesh" — drive home the point of the utter futility of any human attainment to gain righteousness or status with God. Thus he brings to a close his whole discussion in 1:18–3:19 with a statement that includes the expression "by works of the law" (ἐξ ἔργα νόμου).

"Works of the law" is a phrase that was evidently being used affirmatively in certain Jewish and Jewish Christian circles of Paul's day. Here in 3:20, however, Paul uses it pejoratively to encapsulate everything he has been arguing against. Yet we need to recognize that Paul was not opposed to "works" because they are "works *of the law*." The words of 1 Tim 1:8, whatever may be thought regarding the authorship of that letter, are certainly Pauline in declaring that "the law is good if one uses it properly." Rather, Paul opposed "works of the law" and considered them futile in any attempt to gain righteousness or status with God simply because they are human "works" based ultimately on "sin" and "flesh." Righteousness and status with God are, in Paul's understanding, always matters of God's grace and mercy — with human faith and thankfulness being the only requisites for the reception of these divine gifts.

CONTEXTUALIZATION FOR TODAY

The material of 1:16–3:20 represents the first part of Section I in Paul's protreptic presentation (i.e., 1:16–4:25) in the body middle (1:16–15:13) of his letter to the Christians at Rome. After the thesis statement of 1:16-17 (which will be declared again, developed more fully, and then defended in 3:21-26), the argument of 1:18–3:20 is almost entirely negative. That is, it argues (1) that all people, both Gentiles *and* Jews, are sinful, (2) that God will judge all people justly, impartially, and without ethnic preference, and (3) that no one can be declared righteous before God on the basis of his or her own works or personal attainments. Further, I have suggested that in arguing these points Paul (1) used what he considered rather standard Jewish and/or Jewish Christian sources and arguments, (2) believed these materials and such a mode of argumentation were used in similar ways by his addressees, and (3) was confident that the Christians at Rome would agree with him. In effect, what Paul did in this first negative part (1:16–3:20) of his first protreptic section (1:16–4:25) of the body middle of Romans was to contextualize the Christian gospel in a manner that he believed would be understood and appreciated by his addressees at Rome — as he will continue to do in the second positive part (3:21–4:25) of the first protreptic section and in various ways throughout the rest of the letter. This he has done and will do in preparation for what he wants to make central and focus on in the second protreptic section of the letter, that is, in 5:1–8:39.

Throughout 1:16–3:20 Paul has written in a manner that spoke to the interests, understanding, and appreciation of his Christian addressees at Rome. And that fact might be taken to mean that his letter to them is only of antiquarian interest for us today. But in noting how Paul in 1:16–3:20 began to contextualize the Christian gospel when writing to Christians at Rome we also become sensitized to the need (1) to contextualize that same gospel message in various situations today and (2) to learn something of how to do so in our own circumstances. And though what Paul says in 1:18–3:20 is dominantly negative, such a message needs to be contextualized in a new way for our own lives, for the Christian church, and for Western society and culture today.

Thus, for example, when Paul speaks about "sin" and uses that term to encapsulate all the unrighteous, unjust, and evil actions of people, we can learn a great deal about how to understand our own actions and the situations that occur all around us in society today. Charles Talbert is quite right when he speaks of contemporary society vis-à-vis Paul's understanding of the human condition:

> Modern culture . . . has all but lost any sense of personal responsibility. Individuals are viewed as victims of their collectives. Hence, when society encounters something that is truly bad (e.g., two high school students on a rampage, shooting a host of other students and teachers), it finds it almost impossible to talk about it except in banalities. It was symptomatic of our culture's social or psychological causes. It was symptomatic of our culture's Male Identity Crisis; it was because the individuals were poor, fatherless, abused; it was because they were not part of the in-crowd at school; it was because society made guns available to them. Always personal responsibility is forgotten in the assignment of social and psychological blame.[154]

And Talbert is also right when he says of Paul's understanding of "sin" and "sins":

> To label the acts as sin or sins implies two things: first, the acts are against the Creator, and second, the actors are personally responsible for their deeds. Pauline thought lends a corrective to the practical atheism and the avoidance of personal responsibility that dominate our culture.[155]

Likewise, we can learn much from Paul's understanding of "flesh," which we have defined as living apart from God and attempting to operate only by

154. Talbert, *Romans*, 102.
155. *Ibid.*, 103.

means of one's own finite energy. Luke Timothy Johnson has aptly characterized life lived on such a basis as follows:

> Seeking to establish one's own life and worth within such a framework requires boasting and arrogance. It demands competition and hostility toward others. The reason is simple. Since life as a *gift* is rejected, then life on one's own terms must be by means of having or possessing. Insofar as I have and own, I can claim "this is mine." And since I view the world as a closed system, there is only so much "having" available. I am inevitably in competition with other humans for life and worth. My self-aggrandizement must be at another's expense. Rivalry, envy, hatred, and murder are the logical expressions of the idolatrous impulse, for the "need to be" that derives from the refusal of the first gift is an endless hunger, an unslakable thirst.[156]

But as Johnson goes on to point out: "What appears under the form of boasting and haughtiness and arrogance as 'strength' . . . is what Paul rightly calls the 'weakness of the flesh.' "[157]

Examples could be multiplied, and much more could be written, in spelling out many other contemporary contextualizations comparable to those expressed by Johnson and Talbert above. Suffice it to say, by way of conclusion, that — while it may be fairly easy to agree with all that Paul says in 3:1-20, for he was a Christian apostle and his words are directed against the errors and shortcomings of the Jews — we as Christians need always to realize, as Joseph Fitzmyer has pointed out, that

> Paul's comments concern the Christian reader too, because what he levels against his fellow Jews, he can also level against fellow Christians. For they too have the advantage of knowing what God desires of them; they have their Christian Bible, given to the church, as a guide for their living and conduct. Therein they too find "oracles of God." But do they always follow its counsels in the conduct of their lives? Paul's conclusion is applicable to the Christian as well: "It is not those who listen to the law who are upright before God; rather, those who observe the law will be justified before him" (2:13).[158]

---

156. L. T. Johnson, *Reading Romans,* 48.
157. *Ibid.*
158. Fitzmyer, *Spiritual Exercises,* 43-44.

The second part of Section I of the body middle of Romans, that is, 3:21–4:25, is a highly significant portion of the letter and deserves close scrutiny and careful consideration. Yet, while the material of 3:21–4:25 is of great importance, it has often been misunderstood and distorted.

The Present State of the Question. Since the Protestant Reformation of the sixteenth century, 3:21–4:25 has usually been viewed by Protestant scholars as containing the primary thrust of Paul's teaching in Romans — with, in particular, the first portion of this material, 3:21-31 (or, more narrowly, 3:21-26), understood as setting out in definitive fashion the central message of the Christian proclamation. John Reumann, for example, began his 1966 article on "the righteousness of God" with the following statement: "Romans 3:21-31 takes us to the heart of the earliest Christian Gospel as do few other New Testament passages" — which assertion he emphasized further in his following sentence: "Within Romans, the section 3:21-31 is the most significant passage."[1] More narrowly, Charles Cranfield has stated: "3.21-26 is, I believe, the heart of the whole epistle";[2] Thomas Schreiner has asserted with respect to 3:21-26: "Most scholars rightly acknowledge this paragraph as the heart of the epistle."[3]

Almost all Protestant interpreters have understood Martin Luther's emphasis on "justification by faith" to express the central theme of Paul's Christian proclamation. That is what, it is commonly claimed, Paul highlighted earlier in Rom 1:17 in (1) bringing together the two prepositional phrases ἐκ πίστεως and εἰς πίστιν (literally "out of faith . . . unto faith") and (2) quoting Hab 2:4b in support — however those phrases and their accompanying biblical quotation are understood.[4] And that is what, it is insisted, Paul developed more fully in (1) his use of the prepositional expressions διὰ πίστεως Ἰησοῦ Χριστοῦ and εἰς πάντας τοὺς πιστεύοντας in 3:22, (2) his employment of the prepositional phrases διὰ τῆς πίστεως and ἐκ πίστεως Ἰησοῦ in 3:25-26, and (3) his illustration of Abraham as the example par excellence of a "person of faith" in 4:1-25.

Some Protestant interpreters have focused more on Paul's proclamation of δικαιοσύνη θεοῦ ("the righteousness of God") as the primary theme of Romans — understanding that expression to refer not only to a vitally important attribute of God himself, that is, his righteous nature, character, and actions,

---

1. Reumann, "The Gospel of the Righteousness of God," 432.

2. Cranfield, "Preaching on Romans," in his *On Romans,* 73; cf. also *idem, Romans,* 1.199: "It [3:21-26] is the centre and heart of the whole of Rom 1.16b-15.13."

3. Schreiner, *Romans,* 178.

4. See our exegetical comments on 1:17 above.

but also to incorporate nuances regarding God's gift of righteousness, which he gives to all who respond positively to him by faith. That this theme of "the righteousness of God" was highly significant in Paul's understanding is supported by the fact that δικαιοσύνη θεοῦ appears prominently in the thesis statement of 1:16-17 and then twice more in the developed version of that thesis statement in 3:21-23 — with two further instances of the synonymous expression δικαιοσύνη αὐτοῦ appearing in 3:25-26 (though used somewhat differently in that latter context), followed by nine appearances of the noun δικαιοσύνη in ch. 4 alone.

Other interpreters have focused most of their attention on one or another of such soteriological terms as (1) the noun σωτηρία ("salvation") in 1:16, (2) the noun ἀπολύτρωσις ("redemption") in 3:24, (3) the noun ἱλαστήριον ("sacrifice of atonement," "propitiation," or "expiation") in 3:25, or even (4) the verb λογίζομαι ("credit," "reckon," "account," or "impute") in 4:4-10 and 22-24 — with these terms, taken separately or in concert, often understood as representing the heart of Paul's Christian proclamation. And still others, while acknowledging the importance of the themes of "justification by faith" and "the righteousness of God" — as well as the significance of much that is said in Romans by the use of such forensic soteriological expressions as cited above — have tended to expend most of their energies on questions regarding the relation of the Christian gospel to the Mosaic law.

With such a concurrence of opinion among interpreters — albeit with varying emphases — most Protestant Christians have felt fairly secure in understanding the statement of 1:16-17, together with what is proclaimed in 3:21-31 and the illustration of Abraham given in 4:1-25, as representing the primary message of Paul in his letter to believers in Jesus at Rome. Thus they have frequently understood Romans as containing, in the main, only two principal features: (1) an extensive polemic against both Gentile godlessness and Jewish legalism, which appears throughout 1:18–3:20, and (2) a fervent proclamation of the Christian gospel that has to do with righteousness and faith, which is set out first in 1:16-17 and then developed, elucidated, and illustrated in 3:21–4:25 (or, some would argue, 3:21–5:11) — and so have viewed all else in Romans as essentially an elaboration of these two major themes.

Frédéric Godet, for example, in his two-volume commentary of 1880-81 (which had a widespread impact on many Christians of an earlier day), epitomized such an understanding when he captioned the central sections of the letter as follows (with the substance of his outline and titles, though not always their exact wording, embedded in the psyches of many readers of Romans today):

1. "The Statement of the Subject" (1:16-17)
2. "The Fundamental Part" (1:18–5:21)
3. "The Supplementary Parts" (6:1–8:39 and 9:1–11:36)
4. "The General Part" (12:1–15:13)

But viewing 2:17–3:20 (or 2:1–3:20) as a Christian polemic directed against the Jewish religion — coupled with an understanding of 3:21–4:25 (or 3:21–5:11) as the Christian answer to everything Paul said about Jews and Judaism in that previous passage — has often resulted in a caricature of Judaism in the apostle's day as "a casuistic religion of works righteousness" and has engendered anti-Semitic feelings toward Jews and Judaism. Further, and more importantly for a commentary on Romans, it has failed to appreciate the true focus of Paul's presentation in his letter to Rome and muddled the course and development of his argument in that letter.

Two Recent Significant Advances and Challenging Perspectives. During the latter half of the nineteenth century and throughout the twentieth century, a number of significant advances and challenging perspectives have been proposed — along with, of course, some "dead ends" — in the scholarly study of the NT. Two of these proposed advances or perspectives need to be highlighted here, for an acceptance or rejection of either or both of them has immense importance on how one approaches what Paul has written in 3:21–4:25.

The first proposal was set out in 1892 by Adolf Deissmann in response to the question: "What, exactly, stood at the heart of Paul's Christian theology?" On the basis of a survey of the expression "in Christ Jesus" and its cognates "in Christ," "in the Lord," and "in him" in the apostle's letters, Deissmann argued that at the heart of all that Paul proclaimed and taught was an all-consuming consciousness of an intensely personal relationship between the exalted Christ and himself, with that consciousness also present in all those who were truly committed followers of Jesus Christ — that is, a consciousness of a relationship between Christ and believers in Christ that was so close, lively, and personal that it could properly be called a type of "Christian mysticism."[5]

Building on Deissmann's thesis (though without proper acknowledgment), Albert Schweitzer in 1910 asserted that central to the "developed" thought of Paul, and therefore the main theme in Romans, was not "justification by faith" — which Schweitzer called "a subsidiary crater" in the Pauline landscape "formed from the rim of the main crater" — but "the mystical doctrine of redemption through being-in-Christ."[6] And ever since Deissmann's original thesis, as well as its somewhat aberrant employment by Schweitzer, NT interpreters have frequently spoken of Paul's theology as essentially "participationist," "personal," "relational," or even "mystical" — at times (1) setting out his "participationist," "personal," "relational," or "mystical" language in contrast to his "forensic" soteriological statements; at other times (2) viewing his "in Christ," "in the Lord," or "in him" expressions as simply extensions or elaborations of his forensic statements; or, usually, (3) just allowing the "participationist," "personal," "relational," or "mystical" features to reside side by side with the "forensic" features of his message, without attempting resolution.

5. See Deissmann, *Die neutestamentliche Formel "In Christo Jesu."*
6. Cf. Schweitzer, *Mysticism of Paul the Apostle,* esp. 225.

Likewise, there has come to the fore during the latter decades of the twentieth century another challenging proposal of great significance for an understanding of 3:21–4:25. This perspective has to do, first of all, with what Paul wrote regarding the Jews in 2:17–3:20. But it also affects how one understands what he wrote about the Christian message here in 3:21–4:25. In effect, this more recent proposal offers an important corrective to the imbalance in biblical scholarship that arose during the past centuries with regard to (1) a proper understanding of mainline Palestinian Judaism in Paul's day (as well as of early rabbinic Judaism, as represented by the Tannaitic rabbis whose teachings are codified in the Talmud), and so a "new perspective" on what Paul wrote in 2:17–3:20 — and, therefore, (2) a more accurate appreciation of the Jewish background of Paul's teaching, which has resulted, in particular, in a "new perspective" on what he wrote in 3:21–4:25. It is a challenging "new" understanding of 2:17–3:20 and 3:21–4:25 that is rightly credited, in large part, to Ed Sanders in his *Paul and Palestinian Judaism* and his *Paul, the Law, and the Jewish People.*[7]

It may be that scholarship has swung too far, in pendulum-like fashion, from one extreme position to another, exchanging blind condemnation for an almost equally blind approbation. Such approbation of Judaism seems to go, at times, even beyond some of the adverse evaluations by the better Jewish teachers, as represented in the Talmud and the other rabbinic writings that claim to represent an earlier period, regarding some of the deviant teachers of the Jewish religion and some of their aberrant teachings. Nonetheless, though scholars have expressed varying opinions regarding how one should understand the Palestinian Judaism of Paul's day, one matter seems fairly well established in the consciousness of most NT scholars today — that is, that no longer can the Jewish religion of Paul's day be simply written off as a legalistic religion of "works righteousness." Interpreters of Paul today have been alerted that (1) there is much in the apostle's writings that he took over from Judaism, though with all his earlier thought and piety "baptized" into his Christian experience, and (2) the basic structures of Jewish thought and the underlying ethos of Jewish piety continued to play a large part in Paul's life as a follower of the exalted Jesus of Nazareth, whom he accepted as Israel's Messiah and humanity's Lord.

The Relation between 3:21–4:25 and the Earlier Materials of 1:16–3:20. This relation has frequently been a matter of concern and uncertainty among NT scholars. For while there is a high degree of agreement between Paul's thesis statement of 1:16-17 and his repetition and development of that statement in 3:21-31, there is an obvious contrast between the positive presentation of the Christian message in 3:21–4:25 and the earlier negative depictions of godless Gentiles and faithless Jews in 1:18–3:20. Further, the joining of the adverb νυνί ("now," "at the present time") and the adversative conjunction δέ ("but"), with the resultant expression "but now" at the beginning of 3:21, alerts the reader of

---

7. See also, however, my 1964 chapter "The Piety of Hebraic Judaism," in R. N. Longenecker, *Paul, Apostle of Liberty,* 65-85.

Romans to a change of stance and content in what Paul writes in 3:21-4:25 —
whether that change should be viewed as "logical," "chronological," or both.
Thus commentators have often highlighted the antithetical relations that exist
between these two sets of passages.[8]

Yet a number of features appear prominently in both 1:16-3:20 and 3:21-
4:25, tying together the materials of these two parts of this first section of the
body middle of Paul's letter. Most obvious are (1) the word chain πιστεύειν
("to believe") / πίστις ("faith") and (2) the focus on the forensic expression
δικαιοσύνη ("righteousness," "justification," "uprightness"), suggesting that
a basic unity underlies all of 1:16-4:25. Further, Paul's argument throughout
1:16-4:25 is full of explicit biblical quotations, with some fifteen to eighteen
quotations appearing at eight or nine places in these four chapters — which,
compared to the rarity of biblical quotations in the immediately following section of 5:1-8:39, also implies something about the unity of the material in this
first section of the letter's body middle. And while in 1:18-2:16 (which is concerned with humanity generally) there may be fewer explicit biblical quotations
than there are elsewhere in this first part of the first section, there can be found
throughout 1:16-4:25 — both in its negative materials of 1:18-3:20 and in its
positive materials of 1:16-17 and 3:21-4:25 — a number of allusive references
to Scripture, a few biblically based Jewish and/or Jewish Christian aphorisms,
and some traditional formulations that seem to stem from Jewish Christian devotional, confessional, and/or catechetical materials.

In his study of "the internal logic of the argument in Romans 3," Richard
Hays put forward the thesis that Paul's "allusion" in 3:20 (as Hays understood
it) to Ps 143:2 (LXX 142:2), "no one will be declared righteous in his [God's]
sight," indicates that there was in Paul's mind an "intended continuity" between (1) his treatment of "the righteousness of God" (θεοῦ δικαιοσύνην) in
3:5, together with his inclusion of "apparently synonymous expressions" in 3:3-
7, and (2) his two references to "the righteousness of God" (δικαιοσύνη θεοῦ)
in 3:21-22 (see also the two uses of τῆς δικαιοσύνη αὐτοῦ in 3:25-26), together
with what appear to be synonymous expressions throughout all that follows
in 3:21-4:25.[9] For Ps 143 "contains several references of God's *righteousness*"[10]
— principally in Ps 143:1, which immediately precedes the words alluded to by
Paul, then again in Ps 143:11b, which is near the end of the psalmist's prayer.
Thus, while it cannot be proven that Paul had in mind all of Ps 143 when he
used these words of the psalmist — or, as Hays would have it, when Paul was
constructing a midrash on Ps 143 in Rom 3 — it seems highly likely that he
was conscious of the same pattern of thought and expression in writing to his
Christian addressees at Rome.

8. Cf., e.g., Barrett, *Romans*, 72, commenting on the phrase νυνὶ δέ that appears at the
beginning of 3:21a: "At this critical stage we find one of the great turning points of the epistle"; see
also Schreiner, *Romans*, 178: "Romans 3:21-26 turns the corner in the argument."

9. Hays, "Psalm 143 and the Logic of Romans 3," 107-15.

10. *Ibid.*, 113 (italics his).

The argument of Hays is that while "it is universally held by commentators that this citation summarizes and brings to a close a major section of the discussion," it needs to be recognized "that Psalm 143 also provides the point of departure for what *follows*."[11] So Hays's conclusion is as follows:

> Our evidence converges on a single conclusion. The major structural break which commentators usually posit between Rom 3:20 and 3:21 has no "justification" in the text, and Paul's continuing use of terminology from Psalm 143 (δικαιοσύνη) shows clearly the intended continuity. Rom 3:21 carries on the discussion from the earlier part of chapt. 3.[12]

It is, of course, difficult to prove (as Hays himself acknowledges) that Paul had all of Ps 143 in mind when he used the words of 143:2 in his closing statement of Rom 3:20 — especially if those words had become something of an aphorism in Paul's day (as I have proposed above) and so may not have been intended to be understood as a conscious biblical allusion (as Hays assumes). Yet, it seems reasonable to postulate that Paul — simply because of his Jewish heritage and training — was conscious of the same pattern of thought as expressed in Ps 143:2 and therefore incorporated that pattern (whether consciously or unconsciously) into what he wrote in Rom 3. Or as Hays has more aptly expressed his rationale for such a thesis: "Even if Paul was not consciously constructing a midrash on Psalm 143, he *was* operating out of a background of theological categories and assumptions into which Psalm 143 provides a very helpful insight."[13] Thus this first section of the body middle of Romans, 1:16–4:25, can be viewed as a unified body of material, even though the central thrusts and foci of its two parts differ in both tone and content.

Various reasons in support of the unity of 1:16–3:20 and 3:21–4:25 can be given. That of Richard Hays, while difficult to prove, is certainly possible. My own rationale for the unified nature of these two parts is based principally on the exegetical and thematic similarities that appear prominently in both sets of passages (as cited above) — that is, (1) the word chain πιστεύειν — πίστις that appears in both parts, (2) the term δικαιοσύνη that appears in 1:17 and 3:5 of the first part and then twelve times more in the second part (i.e., 3:21, 22, 25, 26; 4:3, 5, 6, 9, 11 [twice], 13, 22), and (3) the explicit biblical quotations, allusive biblical references, traditional biblically based aphorisms, and devotional, confessional, and/or catechetical materials incorporated within both parts of this first section of the letter's body middle. Further, the unified nature of these two parts is highlighted by (4) Paul's repetition and development in 3:21-23 of his earlier thesis statement in 1:16-17 (as has been frequently pointed out by commentators), and (5) his elucidation in 3:27-31 of the repeated and developed thesis statement of

---

11. Hays, "Psalm 143 and the Logic of Romans 3," 113 (italics his).
12. *Ibid.*, 115.
13. *Ibid.*, 115 n. 33b (italics his).

3:21-23, which takes up again, though from a distinctly Christian stance, the basic issues inherent in his previous discussion of Jews and their status before God in 2:17-3:30 (as has been seldom noted).

Toward a Proper Understanding of 3:21-4:25. Much of what Paul has written in 3:21-4:25 about "righteousness," "justification," "redemption," "sacrifice of atonement/propitiation/expiation," and "faith," as NT scholars have come to recognize today, rests solidly on Jewish theological foundations.[14] Likewise, a number of scholars have shown that early Christian devotional, confessional, and/or catechetical materials that presumably circulated within the early Christian communities were used by Paul in his letters and reflect the convictions of at least a number of Jewish Christians of his day.[15] Further, what Paul writes in this section of Romans regarding "righteousness" and "faith" not only was based on (1) the teachings of the Jewish (OT) Scriptures, but also was founded on (2) the basic tenets of what is today called "early Judaism" and (3) the formative convictions of the earliest Jewish believers in Jesus.

The material of 3:21-4:25, in both structure and argument, is extensively Jewish and/or Jewish Christian in character, with roots in the religion of Israel as expressed in the OT. We have argued that this is true for what appears in 1:16-3:20. And it will continue to be seen as true throughout 3:21-4:25 — though always now with a more decidedly Christian "spin" and a more distinctive Christian content.

Some Parallels in Paul's Other Letters and Luke's Acts to the Apostle's Diversified Approach and Contextualized Content in Romans. In 1 Cor 9:19-23 Paul speaks of a self-imposed missionary principle, which he says conditioned all his preaching, teaching, and pastoral endeavors, that of being "all things to all people, so that by all possible means I might save some" (v. 22). In Acts Luke also represents Paul as both (1) speaking to his hearers in a way that would be relevant to the background and interests of each hearer, and (2) contextualizing his message in a manner that each would understand and appreciate. Portrayals of Paul's diversified approach and contextualized content appear in (1) Paul's description of important episodes in Israel's history as he preaches to Jews (Acts 13:14-41), (2) his proclaiming that God "has shown kindness by giving you rain from heaven and crops in their seasons; he provides you with plenty of food and fills your hearts with joy" as he proclaims the gospel to a pagan, agriculturally based populace (Acts 14:14-18), and (3) his using an inscription "To an Unknown God" as his text in his presentation to government administrators, who were probably also somewhat philosophically oriented (Acts 17:22-31). Such portrayals are also found in the accounts of Paul's five

---

14. See esp. Dunn, "How New Was Paul's Gospel?" (1994), and *idem*, "Paul and Justification by Faith" (1997); both articles, together with many of Dunn's other writings on closely related topics, are brought together in his *The New Perspective on Paul.*

15. Cf. R. N. Longenecker, *Christology of Early Jewish Christianity,* passim; also *idem,* "Christological Materials within the Early Christian Communities," 47-76; and *idem, New Wine into Fresh Wineskins,* 48-65.

defenses in Acts 22–26, each with its own distinctive approach and special manner of treatment.[16]

More significant, however, is the way Paul approaches certain issues and deals with certain concerns in 1 Corinthians — particularly those matters that he treats in chs. 7–14, where he expressly indicates that he is responding to questions that his converts at Corinth have asked him in an earlier letter.[17] In most if not all of these matters Paul begins on common ground with his addressees — even acknowledging that there are elements of truth in the positions that they somewhat erroneously hold. But then in each instance he goes on to correct their failure to understand correctly, often using a line of argument that he evidently believed would be appreciated by them and convincing to them.[18]

Even more important for our purposes here, however, is the parallel that can be drawn between Paul's approach and contextualized argument in Galatians vis-à-vis his approach and line of argumentation in Romans. In the first part of the *propositio* of Gal 2:15-21, Paul argues, on the basis of what he believes to be common ground with his addressees, that all true believers in Jesus — particularly Jewish believers, but also, by extension, Gentile believers who have been influenced by Jewish thought in some way — know that a person is not justified by "works of the law" (ἐξ ἔργων νόμου) but by (1) what Christ has objectively effected (διά / ἐκ πίστεως Ἰησοῦ Χριστοῦ, which I have argued should be viewed as a subjective genitive construction and so understood as "by the faith [or 'faithfulness'] of Jesus Christ"), and (2) one's own response of faith (or "trust") in Christ and what he has done (ἐπιστεύσαμεν εἰς Χριστὸν Ἰησοῦν).[19] It may legitimately be postulated that Paul does something similar in writing to the Christians at Rome, first in Section I of the body middle of the letter, that is, in the two parts of 1:16–4:25, presenting both negatively (1:18–3:20) and positively (1:16-17 and 3:21–4:25) what he believes he holds in common with his addressees, then going on in Section II, 5:1–8:39, setting out his own distinctive way of contextualizing the Christian message to Gentiles.[20]

Summation. 1:16–4:25 is therefore best understood as a unified section of material presented in two parts: the first, the negative part, 1:18–3:20; the second, the positive part, 1:16-17 and 3:21–4:25. Paul, it appears, wanted to speak about "the gospel," "salvation," "the righteousness of God," and "faith" — which topics he set out in his initial thesis statement of 1:16-17 and then repeated and developed in 3:21-23 — in a way that would be understood and appreciated by his Christian addressees at Rome. So after the thesis statement of 1:16-17, he presents (1) a polemic against humanity's godlessness and wickedness in 1:18–2:16, (2) a polemic against Jewish faithlessness and injustice in 2:17–3:20, and

16. For discussions of Paul's defenses in these portrayals in Luke's Acts, see R. N. Longenecker, "Acts," in EBC, 1981 ed., 9.524-56; 2007 rev. ed., 10.1043-80.

17. Cf. 1 Cor 7:1, "now concerning the matters about which you wrote."

18. Cf. R. N. Longenecker, "All Things to All Men," in *Paul, Apostle of Liberty*, 230-44.

19. Cf. R. N. Longenecker, *Galatians*, 80-96.

20. Cf. Paul's references to "my gospel" in Rom 2:16 and 16:25.

(3) a proclamation of the Christian message, which closes with the example of Abraham and an early Christian confessional statement in 3:21-4:25. In all that he presents in 1:16-4:25 Paul speaks in a distinctly Jewish Christian manner, for his addressees at Rome had evidently been extensively influenced by the theology, ways of thinking, and religious language of the mother church at Jerusalem. And throughout these two parts of this first section of the body middle of his letter, he uses language and materials that not only would be understood by his addressees but also would resonate favorably with them — especially in the passage at hand, 3:21-4:25, where he uses (1) forensic Jewish and Jewish Christian soteriological terms; (2) explicit biblical quotations, allusive references to Scripture, and biblically based aphorisms; (3) Jewish and/or Jewish Christian devotional, confessional, and/or catechetical materials; and (4) the illustration of Abraham, the father of the Jewish nation and the man of faith par excellence.

Paul evidently wrote 1:16-4:25 in this fashion because he wanted to begin speaking to his addressees at Rome in a manner that he believed they would understand, appreciate, and accept. For though they were largely (with only a few exceptions) unknown to him personally, he evidently knew a great deal about them generally — and so presumably knew that they had a Jewish Christian background, even though they were dominantly non-Jewish ethnically. As a Jewish believer in Jesus, Paul would certainly have understood this Jewish Christian way of conceptualizing and proclaiming the "good news" of the Christian message. In all likelihood he himself first came to appreciate his own conversion to Jesus, the Jewish Messiah, along these lines, using such Jewish and Jewish Christian forensic terms to understand and express that new experience. Doubtless, as well, he reveled in the realities of which these forensic terms spoke. So when he addressed Jews or Jewish Christians — as well as when he wrote to those who had been extensively influenced by such categories of thought (as had his Christian addressees at Rome) — he had no reticence or difficulty in speaking to them about Jesus Christ and the Christian gospel in this manner.

But Paul had been called by God as a Christian apostle to proclaim the "good news" of the Christian message to Gentiles in the Greco-Roman world. His mandate was to people who had no knowledge of the Jewish (OT) Scriptures and no background in the Jewish religion. Thus, as may reasonably be conjectured, he found it necessary to contextualize the Christian message in his Gentile mission in a manner that would be readily understood and accepted by his Gentile hearers. That required, it seems, a ministry that spoke of the "good news" of the Christian proclamation in more "personal," "relational," and "participationist" terms, speaking of relationships Paul himself had known in his own commitment to Christ and therefore desired to present to non-Jewish pagans in his ministry to Gentiles — and not just the forensic soteriological language of Judaism and early Jewish Christianity.

Paul wanted the believers in Jesus at Rome to understand and appreciate this contextualization of the Christian gospel to Gentiles (1) because they were dominantly Gentile believers and therefore within his God-given mandate to proclaim the gospel to Gentiles, and (2) because he desired their prayers and financial support for the extension of this form of Christian proclamation to the Gentiles in Spain. And it is this form of Christian proclamation, which he calls "my gospel" in 2:16 and 16:25, that he presents in Section II of the body middle of Romans, 5:1–8:39 (and which he applies in his ethical exhortations of Section IV of the letter's body middle, 12:1–15:13) — a form of Christian contextualization of the gospel message that he prepares his Roman addressees for by what he writes here in Section I, that is, in 1:16–4:25.

6. The Thesis Statement Developed, Supported, and Elucidated (3:21-31)

TRANSLATION

³:²¹*But now, apart from the law, the righteousness of God has been revealed, being attested by the law and the prophets.* ²²*This righteousness of God is through the faithfulness of Jesus Christ and given to all those who believe. There is no difference.* ²³*For all have sinned and fall short of the glory of God.*

²⁴*We are justified freely by his grace through the redemption that is in Christ Jesus,* ²⁵*whom God presented publicly as a sacrifice of atonement, through his [Jesus'] faithfulness, by his blood. God did this in order to demonstrate his righteous justice, because in his divine forbearance he had left unpunished the sins previously committed.* ²⁶*He did this in order to demonstrate his righteous justice at this present time, so as to be both just and the One who justifies the one who is based on the faithfulness of Jesus.*

²⁷*Where, then, is boasting? It is eliminated! By what kind of law? Of works? Never! Rather, [it is eliminated] by the law of faith!* ²⁸*For we maintain that a person is justified by faith apart from "works of the law."*

²⁹*Is God the God of the Jews only? Is he not also the God of the Gentiles? Yes, also of the Gentiles,* ³⁰*since "God is one," who will justify "the circumcised" based on the divine faithfulness [of Jesus] and "the uncircumcised" through that same faithfulness.*

³¹*Do we, then, nullify the law by this [message of] faith/faithfulness? Certainly not! Rather, we establish the law.*

TEXTUAL NOTES

3:22a The expression διὰ πίστεως Ἰησοῦ Χριστοῦ ("through faith in Jesus Christ," reading it as objective genitive, *or* "through the faith/faithfulness of Jesus Christ," reading it as subjective genitive) is strongly attested in the Greek textual tradition. Codex Alexandrinus (A 02), however, reads διὰ πίστεως ἐν Χριστῷ Ἰησοῦ ("through faith in Christ Jesus") — inserting the preposition ἐν ("in"), changing the order of "Jesus Christ" to "Christ Jesus," and altering the case of "Christ" to conform to the preposition. This variant reading appears to be a deliberate change, probably made to forestall any possible subjective genitive interpretation of Ἰησοῦ Χριστοῦ.

Codex Vaticanus (B 03), and apparently Marcion (as quoted by Tertullian), omit Ἰησοῦ (so too *W-H* mg.) from the much more widely supported Ἰησοῦ Χριστοῦ (cf. P⁴⁰, etc.), probably in conformity to Paul's usual practice of using only the name Χριστός.

22b The reading εἰς πάντας ("unto all") is amply attested by P⁴⁰, uncials ℵ* A B

C P Ψ, and minuscules 1739 (Category I), 81 1881 (Category II), 104 424^c 2200 (Category III). It is also reflected in syr^{pal} cop$^{sa,\ bo,\ arm}$ and by Origen$^{lat5/6}$ Apollinarius Cyril Augustine. Some Latin witnesses reflect the use of the prepositional phrase ἐπὶ πάντας ("upon all"), principally versions it$^{z\ vid}$ vg$^{ww,\ st}$ and the Church Fathers Ambrosiaster and Pelagius. A third reading, which conflates the above two readings to read εἰς πάντας καὶ ἐπὶ πάντας ("unto all and upon all"), appears in uncials ℵ^2 D G (also *Byz* K L) and minuscules 33 1175 (Category I), 256 1962 2127 2464 (Category II), and 365 424^c 1241 1319 1573 1852 1912 (Category III). This third reading is reflected in vg^{cl} syr$^{p,\ h}$ and by Origen$^{latl/6}$ Chrysostom, thereby "producing an essentially redundant and tautological expression."[21]

25a The presence of the article τῆς before the noun πίστεως ("through *the* faith[-fullness]") is attested by P^{40vid}, uncials B C^3 D^2 P Ψ (also *Byz* K L), and minuscules 33 1175 (Category I), 81 2464 (Category II), 263 424* 1241 1912 2200 (Category III), and Chrysostom. It is omitted in uncials ℵ C* D* F G, minuscules 1739 (Category I), 256 1881 1962 (Category II), 6 104 365 424^c 436 1852 (Category III), and Origen Eusebius Didymus Cyril. External MS evidence is stronger for the inclusion of τῆς, principally because it is attested by P^{40vid} and Codex Vaticanus (B 03). Internally, however, the matter could be argued either way. As Bruce Metzger has observed: "On the one hand, the article may have been added by copyists who wished to point back to διὰ πίστεως Ἰησοῦ Χριστοῦ in v. 22. On the other hand, later in the chapter when Paul uses πίστις absolutely (i.e. without a modifier), διά is followed by the article (cf. verses 30 and 31)."[22] Thus, as Metzger reports, to indicate authenticity and yet express some doubt, the editors of *GNT*^{4} "preferred to include τῆς in the text, but to enclose it within square brackets."[23]

With regard to the omission of the whole clause διὰ [τῆς] πίστεως in Codex Alexandrinus (A 02) and minuscule 2127 (Category II), Metzger concludes that it "must be accidental."[24]

25b The phrase διὰ τὴν πάρεσιν ("because of the remission," "passing over," "letting go unpunished") is strongly attested in the Greek textual tradition. The expression is, however, difficult to translate, and so some late minuscule MSS have attempted to clarify it. Minuscule 1908 (Category III), for example, adds *after* διὰ τὴν πάρεσιν the phrase ἐν τῷ νῦν αἰῶνι, thereby reading "because of the remission *in the present aeon*"; whereas minuscule 1875 (also Category III) adds *before* διὰ τὴν πάρεσιν the phrase ἐν τῷ νῦν καιρῷ, thereby reading "*in the present time* because of the remission (or 'hardening')."

26a The inclusion of the conjunction καί ("and") between the noun δίκαιον and the participle δικαιοῦντα in 3:26a is very well attested in the Greek textual tradition. Its omission in ninth-century uncials F (010) and G (012), as well as its earlier reflection in the Old Latin version and Ambrosiaster's commentary, probably represents an attempted syntactical improvement — that is, changing the participle δικαιοῦντα from a compound predicate adjective to a circumstantial participle of means, which would then

21. Metzger, *Textual Commentary*, 449.
22. *Ibid.*
23. *Ibid.*
24. *Ibid.*

explain how God is righteous: "so that he is righteous in setting right 'a person who has faith in Jesus' (or 'a person on the basis of the faith/faithfulness of Jesus')."

26b The name Ἰησοῦ ("Jesus") at the end of 3:26 is well attested by uncials ℵ A B C K P and minuscules 1739 (Category I), 81 1881 1962 (Category II), and 88 104 630 1241 2495 (Category III). It is expanded to read Ἰησοῦ Χριστοῦ ("Jesus Christ") in minuscule 629 (Category III), which variant is also reflected in versions it[ar, c, (d*), dem, gig, z] vg[cl] syr[pal] cop[bo] and by Origen[lat] Ambrosiaster Theodoret. Bruce Metzger calls this variant reading "a natural scribal accretion."[25] Metzger further comments on the following minor variants: "The reading of syr[P] (κυρίου ἡμῶν Ἰησοῦ Χριστοῦ) corresponds to Syriac ecclesiastical idiom. The omission of Ἰησοῦ by F G 336 it[g] and the reading Ἰησοῦν [in the accusative case] in D[gr] Ψ 33 614 Lect al are probably results of copyists' blunders."[26]

27 The addition of the possessive pronoun σου ("your") after ἡ καύχησις ("boasting") in ninth-century uncial G, and as reflected in it vg[ww], is too weakly attested to be accepted. It may be an attempt to parallel the second-person pronominal verbal suffixes and reflexive pronouns that appear throughout 2:1-5, as well as the explicit use of second-person pronouns in 2:4-5.

28a The postpositive γάρ ("for") is fairly well supported by uncials ℵ A D* G Ψ and minuscules 1739 (Category I), 81 256 1506 1881 1962 2127 (Category II), 263 365 1852 2200 (Category III). It is also reflected in it[ar, b, d, f, g, o] vg syr[pal] cop[sa, bo] and by Origen[lat] Ambrosiaster. The reading οὖν ("therefore," "consequently," "then") has somewhat less textual support, being found in uncials B C D² P [also *Byz* K L] and minuscules 33 1175 (Category I), 2464 (Category II), 6 104 424 459 1241 1912 (Category III), as well as reflected in versions it[mon] syr[p, h] and by Chrysostom Theodore. In addition to external textual support, the context favors γάρ since 3:28 gives a reason for the content in 3:27 rather than a conclusion derived from it. Probably the presence of οὖν here in 3:28 should be judged a needless scribal repetition of the οὖν of the previous verse.

28b The indicative verb λογιζόμεθα ("we reckon," "maintain") is very well attested in the textual tradition, though the subjunctive verb λογιζώμεθα ("let us reckon," "maintain") appears in ninth-century uncials K P, tenth-century uncial 049, and minuscules 1175 (Category I) and 2464 (Category II). The subjunctive form, however, is probably the result of a dictation error, since the vowels o and ω would have sounded the same (see something of the same textual problem regarding an indicative verb or a subjunctive verb in 5:1, though the weight of the external MS evidence is decidedly different).

28c The dative singular πίστει ("by faith"), which is widely attested in the textual tradition, is replaced by the prepositional phrase διὰ πίστεως ("through faith") in ninth-century uncial G. This change is also reflected in *it* and *vg*. It was apparently made in order to conform to the prepositional phrase διὰ πίστεως that appears in 3:21-22, which is in contrast with χωρὶς νόμου.

29 The adverb μόνον ("only") is widely attested throughout the Greek textual tradition. Codex Vaticanus (B 03), however, as well as minuscules 1739[c] (Category I) and 88 323 330 (Category III), change it to the genitive plural μόνων, thereby bringing

25. Metzger, *Textual Commentary,* 449.
26. *Ibid.*

390

it into line with the plural Ἰουδαίων and so more expressly to read "Jews only." And Codex Beza (D 06) changes the adverb to the nominative singular μόνος, thereby bringing it into line with the nominative ὁ θεός and so to read "God alone." But the presence of the adverb μόνον ("only") is too firmly attested in the textual tradition to be easily set aside.

30 The reading εἴπερ ("if indeed," "if after all," "since") is well attested by uncials ℵ* A B C D¹ and minuscules 1739 (Category I), 1506 (Category II), and 6 365 1319 1573 (Category III). A variant reading ἐπείπερ ("since indeed") is supported by uncials ℵ² D* F G P Ψ [also *Byz* K L] and minuscules 33 1175 (Category I), 1881 2464 (Category II), and 69 88 104 323 326 330 424ᶜ 614 1241 1243 1505 1735 1874 2344 2495 (Category III). This latter reading, however, is not only less strongly supported by the better uncial MSS, it also appears to be only an attempted stylistic improvement.

FORM/STRUCTURE/SETTING

A note that appears in the margin of Luther's Bible alongside 3:21-26 reads: "The chief point, and the very central place of the Epistle, and of the whole Bible." Many commentators today have expressed a similar understanding in lauding this section of Paul's letter, stating it almost as enthusiastically. Charles Cranfield, for example, declared at the beginning of his discussion of 3:21-26 that "this short section" is not only "the centre and heart of the main division to which it belongs" but also "the centre and heart of the whole of Rom 1:16b–15:13."[27] Likewise, Ernst Käsemann began his discussion of this passage with the conviction that "the doctrine of justification forms the center of his [Paul's] theology and of the present epistle."[28]

Such statements, however, may be somewhat overly enthusiastic. They may even, I believe, misrepresent what Paul is actually doing in this letter. Yet 3:21-26 is certainly a highly important passage in Romans — whether it is considered, because of its large number of exegetical difficulties, the most obscure and difficult passage in Paul's letter,[29] or viewed as "the most theologically profound and crucially important pericope in the letter."[30] "Few Pauline passages," as John Ziesler stated in the opening sentence of his article on Rom 3:21-26, "are more pregnant, or more controversial, than this."[31] Further, as David Hill insists about the passage at hand (which he speaks of as 3:21-28): "Every phrase, indeed every single word, carries weight and bears investigation and exposition."[32] Thus the passage must be treated with precision, perception, and understanding.

27. Cranfield, *Romans*, 1.199.
28. Käsemann, *Romans*, 92.
29. So, e.g., J. Weiss, "Beiträge zur paulinischen Rhetorik," 222.
30. So, e.g., Hill, "Liberation through God's Righteousness," 31.
31. Ziesler, "Salvation Proclaimed," 356.
32. Hill, "Liberation through God's Righteousness," 31.

Rhetorical Conventions. Two rhetorical conventions current in Paul's day have often been identified in 3:21-31. The first is the *extended anaphora,* which has to do with the repetition of a word or an expression — or of words or expressions — at the resumption of a discussion that has been interrupted by another section of material. The latter part of such an *extended anaphora* has frequently been seen in 3:21-23, where Paul repeats and develops the thesis he had earlier enunciated in 1:16-17 about "the gospel," "salvation," "God's righteousness," and "faith." Such a rhetorical convention appears here in 1:16-17 and 3:21-23: first in stating the thesis for the entire first section of the body middle of the letter in 1:16-17, which is followed by a long negative polemic against the godlessness and wickedness of humanity generally *and* against the faithlessness and injustice of Jews in particular in 1:18–3:20; then, lest his original thesis be somehow lost in the discussion — and, more importantly, to highlight its highly significant Christological features — in repeating that thesis in developed form in 3:21-23.

A second rhetorical convention often identified in this passage is a *diatribe* in 3:27-31, where a series of questions and responses is set out (and sometimes seen as continuing on in the question of 4:1 and the response of 4:2). Stanley Stowers, for example, has argued that "individual features of 3:27–4:2 are quite similar to what one finds in the diatribe, particularly in the 'dialogues' of Epictetus."[33] It is probably better, however, to understand these questions and responses of 3:27-31 (also of 4:1-2) as not set out in the form of a diatribe — although Paul may legitimately be seen as having used such a diatribal styling earlier in Romans in 2:1-5 and 2:17-24 (as we believe), and will use it again in 9:19-21 and 11:17-24 (perhaps also in 14:4-11). Rather, the questions and responses in 3:27-31 (as well as in 4:1-2) are probably best viewed as comparable to his questions and responses in 3:1-8 — which questions evidently arose from what he had written immediately prior in 2:17-29 and which he knew needed an immediate answer. So I propose that the questions and responses of 3:27-31 should be understood much like those of 3:1-8 — and for many of the same reasons, both negative and positive, as those given for the material of 3:1-8 — that is, as concerns ("questions") that Paul knew would inevitably arise from what he had written earlier about the Jews in 2:17–3:20 and as clarifying explanations ("answers") that he viewed as being inherent in the expanded thesis statement of 3:21-23 and the supporting statements of 3:24-26.

Some Prominent Exegetical Difficulties. A number of exegetical difficulties are present in 3:21-31, and will be dealt with in greater detail in the "Exegetical Comments" that follow. Some of them, however, at least the most obvious and problematic, need to be identified here. We take them in the order they appear in the text:

1. The significance of the phrase νυνὶ δέ ("but now") in 3:21, asking in particular (a) whether it is to be understood as signaling some type of logical

---

33. Stowers, *Diatribe and Paul's Letter to the Romans,* 165; see his full discussion in 164-67.

development in Paul's argument or some type of temporal development, or both; (b) why it appears at the very beginning of this important section, when the beginning of a Greek sentence is often reserved for a matter the author wants to highlight; and (c) what the combination of these two very brief words suggests regarding the unfolding nature of God's program of salvation history.

2. The meaning of the immediately following phrase χωρὶς νόμου ("apart from the law") in 3:21, asking (a) what is here signified by the term "law" and (b) in what way are believers in Jesus to respond to God and to express their new lives as Christians (i.e., Χριστιανοί, "followers of Christ") "apart from the law."

3. The relation between the expression δικαιοσύνη θεοῦ ("the righteousness of God"), which appears twice in 3:21-22, and its twin expression δικαιοσύνη αὐτοῦ ("his [God's] righteousness" / "justice" / "justness"), which appears twice in 3:25-26. The first two occurrences in 3:21-22 highlight, in their context, the communicative or objective sense of the expression (i.e., "God's righteousness," which he gives as a gift to those who believe the gospel and commit themselves to God through Christ), whereas the latter two occurrences in 3:25-26 speak primarily, in their context, regarding the attributive or subject sense of the expression (i.e., "God's righteousness" / "justice" / "justness," which is an attribute of his person and character).

4. The meaning of the statement μαρτυρουμένη ὑπὸ ποῦ νόμου καὶ τῶν προφητῶν ("being attested by the law and the prophets") in 3:21, asking particularly regarding (a) what is signified by the terms "the law" and "the prophets," (b) how the law and the prophets attest the Christian proclamation of "the righteousness of God," and (c) how this statement is to be related to Paul's closing statement in 3:31, which declares that by the Christian message of faith/faithfulness "we establish" (ἱστάνομεν) the law (νόμον).

5. The phrase διὰ πίστεως Ἰησοῦ Χριστοῦ in 3:22, for the genitive Ἰησοῦ Χριστοῦ may be understood either as an objective genitive (i.e., "through faith in Jesus Christ to all who believe," thereby, possibly, setting up in its two clauses something of a redundancy), or as a subjective genitive (i.e., "through the faith/faithfulness of Jesus Christ, to all who believe").

6. The form and function of the participle δικαιούμενοι ("being justified") at the beginning of 3:24, for linguistically it seems not to be connected with what was presented immediately prior in 3:21-23 and functionally its relation to what follows in 3:25-26 has been extensively debated.

7. The use of ἀπολύτρωσις ("redemption") in 3:24 in the sense of a salvation already attained, for this noun appears in this manner elsewhere in Paul's major missionary letters only in Rom 8:23 and 1 Cor 1:30 (and then in the so-called Prison Epistles in Eph 1:7 and Col 1:14).

8. The use of the verb προτίθημι ("put forward," "present") with reference

to God's action in 3:25 (i.e., the third-person, singular, aorist, indicative, middle προέθετο, "he put forward," "presented"), which is only somewhat paralleled by Paul's use of προεθέμην ("I planned," "purposed") with respect to his own plans.

9. The use of ἱλαστήριον ("sacrifice of atonement," "propitiation," or "expiation") in 3:25 to describe Christ's work on the cross, for this noun does not appear anywhere else in Paul's letters.

10. The use of the expression διὰ τῆς πίστεως ἐν τῷ αὐτοῦ αἵματι, which may be translated either "through [the] faith in his blood" or "through [the] faithfulness in his blood." The first, with or without the article, seems rather strange on Paul's lips, for while he often speaks of having faith in a person, that is, "in God" and/or "in Jesus Christ," he never speaks elsewhere in his letters of "faith in Christ's blood." The second, with or without the article, possibly points back to διὰ πίστεως Ἰησοῦ Χριστοῦ ("through the faith/faithfulness of Jesus Christ") in 3:22, and so having in mind Jesus' "faithfulness" even to the extent of shedding his blood.

11. The noun πάρεσις ("pass over," "let go unpunished") in 3:25, which does not appear elsewhere in Paul's letters or throughout the rest of the NT (i.e., it is a *hapax legomenon,* or "once spoken" NT word).

12. The verb προγίνομαι ("happen before," "done before," "previously committed," or "commit beforehand"), which appears as προγεγονότων (a genitive, plural, neuter, perfect participle) in 3:25, is also a Pauline and NT *hapax legomenon.*

13. The plural of ἁμαρτία ("sin") that appears in the genitival phrase τῶν προγεγονότων ἁμαρτημάτων ("of the previously done sins") in 3:25, which is an expression not normally used by Paul in characterizing humanity; rather, he usually speaks of people who live apart from God as being in the state of "sin" (cf. our discussion above on the closing statement of 3:20).

14. The significance of the expression ἐν τῷ νῦν καιρῷ ("at this present time") in 3:26 and how it relates to the phrase νυνὶ δέ ("but now") at the beginning of 3:21.

15. The meaning of τὸν ἐκ πίστεως Ἰησοῦ at the end of 3:26, which may be read either as an objective genitive ("the one who has faith in Jesus") or as a subjective genitive ("the one who is based on the faith/faithfulness of Jesus"). Questions also need to be asked about how ἐκ πίστεως Ἰησοῦ here in 3:26 relates (a) to the previously used cognate expressions διὰ πίστεως Ἰησοῦ Χριστοῦ in 3:22 and διὰ τῆς πίστεως in 3:25, and (b) to the similar phrases ἐκ πίστεως and διὰ τῆς πίστεως that follow in the second part of 3:30 and to διὰ τῆς πίστεως that appears at the close of this entire passage in 3:31.

Early Christian Confessional Material in 3:24-26. In his article of 1936 on scholarly research on Paul during the early twentieth century, Rudolf Bultmann made the then rather novel suggestion that traditional Christian material had been incorporated by Paul into 3:24-26a[34] — and in 1948 he repeated that proposal more explicitly and fully in his chapter "The Kerygma of the Earliest Church" in his *Theologie des Neuen Testaments*.[35] Since Bultmann's original proposal, extensive study has been directed to matters concerning (1) the identification of traditional Christian material in 3:24-26, (2) the provenance of this material, and (3) the relation of 3:24-26 to its immediate context.

The primary reasons for understanding 3:24-26 as incorporating, in some way and to some extent, early Christian tradition have to do with (1) the presence in these verses of words and concepts that seem not typical of Paul's usual presentation of the Christian gospel or that are used somewhat differently than elsewhere in his letters, and (2) the fact that these seemingly "non-Pauline" features are rather closely clustered together in these verses. Other reasons often proposed are (3) the awkward syntactical transition that exists between 3:23 and 3:24, with the participle δικαιούμενοι ("being justified") continuing neither the thought nor the construction of 3:23, but rather, being inserted as an "unconnected" first linguistic item of "intrusive" material that follows; (4) the presence of the accusative, singular, masculine, relative pronoun ὅν ("who," "he") at the beginning of 3:25, which in its nominative form (ὅς) often signals the start of some early Christian confessional material in Paul's letters; (5) the generally balanced structure of the presentation throughout 3:24-26 (or, at least, throughout 3:25-26); and (6) the specifically parallel structure of the two ἔνδειξις ("proof," "demonstration") clauses in 3:25b-26.

As Bultmann understood 3:24-26, everything from the participle δικαιούμενοι ("being justified") at the beginning of 3:24 to the description of God as δίκαιον ("just") toward the end of 3:26 should be viewed as traditional Christian material quoted by Paul — with the exception of what Bultmann viewed as three typically Pauline phrases that Paul himself inserted: (1) δωρεὰν τῇ αὐτοῦ χάριτι ("freely by his grace") in 3:24; (2) διὰ [τῆς] πίστεως ("through faith") in 3:25; and (3) καὶ δικαιοῦντα τὸν ἐκ πίστεως Ἰησοῦ ("and the justifier of the one who believes in Jesus") in 3:26. Käsemann, who studied under Bultmann, agreed, spelling out Bultmann's thesis in greater detail and presenting additional evidence for it; further, Käsemann went on to postulate that Paul in his editing of this material corrected the statement πρὸς τὴν ἔνδειξιν τῆς δικαιοσύνης αὐτοῦ ("to demonstrate his [God's] righteousness/justice/justness") by adding the words ἐν τῷ νῦν καιρῷ ("at the present time") in 3:26.[36] A number of NT scholars have essentially agreed with Bultmann and Käsemann in understanding 3:24-26a as incorporating Christian traditional material that Paul edited to bring into line with his own theology and for his own purpose (or purposes) — for ex-

34. Cf. Bultmann, "Neueste Paulusforschung," 11-12.
35. Cf. Bultmann, *Theology of the New Testament,* 1.46-47.
36. Cf. Käsemann, "Zum Verständnis von Rom 3,24-26," 150-54; *idem, Romans,* 100-101.

ample, Klaus Wegenast, John Reumann, Alfons Pluta, Georg Eichholz, and Ralph Martin.[37]

In the early 1960s, however, Eduard Lohse, while accepting the presence of early Christian traditional material in the passage, challenged a number of features in this growing Bultmann-Käsemann consensus. He insisted that all the expressions in 3:24 are essentially Pauline in nature; argued that the traditional material begins not with the participle δικαιούμενοι at the beginning of 3:24a but with the accusative singular masculine relative pronoun ὄν ("who") at the start of 3:25a; and demonstrated that the non-Pauline words and concepts are clustered within 3:25a-26a, and therefore that the traditional material should be delineated as from 3:25a to 3:26a.[38] Further, Lohse argued that because of its references to ἱλαστήριον ("expiation"), αἷμα ("blood"), ἡ ἀνοχή τοῦ θεοῦ ("the forbearance of God"), and τὰ προγεγονότα ἁμαρτήματα ("the previously committed sins"), the material of this passage must have originated within early Jewish Christian celebrations of the Eucharist.[39] A number of NT scholars have agreed with Lohse — including, for example, his doctoral student Herbert Koch, who in 1971 published his doctoral dissertation as *Römer 3,21-31 in der Paulus-interpretation der letzten 150 Jahre,* as well as such significant scholars as Klaus Wengst, Peter Stuhlmacher, Ben Meyer, and Robert Jewett.[40]

In addition to these widely held, somewhat alternative analyses of 3:24/25-26a, Dieter Zeller argued in 1968 that the traditional material of these verses begins at 3:25a with the relative pronoun ὄν ("who," "he"), in agreement with Eduard Lohse, but that it concludes at the end of 3:26b with the name Ἰησοῦ ("Jesus"), going beyond the theses of both Bultmann and Lohse.[41] On the other hand, in opposition to any hypothesis of earlier Christian materials having been incorporated by Paul in 3:24/25-26a, Charles Talbert asserted in 1966 that the so-called traditional features of the passage suggest, rather, a post-Pauline interpolation[42] — though in his 2002 commentary on Romans, Talbert posits that everything in these verses is probably best understood as Paul's own composition, since, as he has attempted to demonstrate, most of the disputed words and concepts (with only three exceptions) can be paralleled, at least to some extent, elsewhere in Paul's letters.[43] And Douglas Moo, while acknowl-

37. K. Wegenast, *Verständnis der Tradition bei Paulus* (Neukirchen-Vluyn: Neukirchener Verlag, 1962); J. Reumann, "The Gospel of the Righteousness of God," *Int* 20 (1966); Pluta, *Gottes Bundestreue;* G. Eichholz, *Die Theologie des Paulus im Umriss* (Neukirchen-Vluyn: Neukirchener Verlag, 1972), 189-97; and Martin, *Reconciliation,* 81-89.

38. Cf. Lohse, *Märtyrer und Gottesknecht,* 149-54.

39. Lohse, *Märtyrer und Gottesknecht,* 149-54.

40. Wengst, *Christologische Formeln und Lieder,* 87-90; Stuhlmacher, "Recent Exegesis on Romans 3:24-26" (1986; ET of his 1975 German article); B. F. Meyer, "The Pre-Pauline Formula in Rom 3.25-26a"; and Jewett, *Romans,* 270-71.

41. Cf. Zeller, "Sühne und Langmut," 51-75; see also *idem, An die Römer, ad loc.*

42. Cf. Talbert, "A Non-Pauline Fragment at Romans 3:24-26?" 287-96; so also Fitzer, "Der Ort der Versöhnung nach Paulus," 161-83.

43. Cf. Talbert, *Romans,* 106-10; so also Wonneberger, *Syntax und Exegese,* 202-77; N. H.

edging the "possibility" that "Paul is quoting an early Christian tradition," has attempted something of a middle-of-the-road stance in proposing that "it is more likely that Paul has himself written these verses in dependence on a certain Jewish-Christian interpretation of Jesus' death."[44]

Toward an Understanding of the Structure of 3:21-31. It is impossible here to interact exegetically with all the proposals sketched out above, and so to evaluate them in any proper manner. That is what will be attempted in the "Exegetical Comments" below. Suffice it here to say that I believe the following:

1. The evidence cited above suggests the high probability that Paul has incorporated early Christian traditional material within 3:24-26.

2. This traditional material is probably best understood as beginning at 3:24a with the nominative, plural, masculine, present, passive participle δικαιούμενοι, which may be understood as a circumstantial adverbial participle — that is, a participle that (1) expresses an attendant thought or circumstance, or an additional idea or fact, (2) is best translated into English by the conjunction "and" (whether expressed or understood) followed by a finite construction, and (3) can be translated "[and] we are justified" — though, since Paul did not include in his quotation the verbal clause or statement that such an adverbial circumstantial participle would have followed, there exists a rather awkward linguistic transition between 3:23 and 3:24.

3. This traditional material ends at the close of 3:26 with the name Ἰησοῦ ("Jesus"), for Paul himself does not commonly use the single name "Jesus" in his prose — though that single name "Jesus" often appears in early Christian traditional material he quotes.[45]

4. This traditional material quoted by Paul probably originated within the corporate worship of early Jewish believers in Jesus and may have been used in their observance of the Eucharist or Lord's Supper (though not necessarily confined to such occasions), and so may be presumed to express something important in the theology and religious language of early Jewish Christianity, which was centered in the mother church at Jerusalem.

5. As traditional Christian material springing from the very heart of pre-Pauline Jewish Christian worship, what Paul quotes in 3:24-26 can prop-

---

Young, "Did St. Paul Compose Romans iii.24f?" 23-32; J. Piper, "The Demonstration of the Righteousness of God in Romans 3:25, 26," *JSNT* 7 (1980) 7-9; and D. A. Campbell, *Rhetoric of Righteousness in Romans 3.21-26*, 45-57.

44. Moo, *Romans*, 220.

45. Cf., e.g., Phil 2:10, "that at the name of *Jesus* every knee should bow, in heaven and on earth and under the earth"; 1 Thess 4:14a, "that '*Jesus* died and rose again'"; Rom 10:9, "that if you confess with your mouth '*Jesus* is Lord'"; 1 Cor 12:3, "no one can say by the Spirit of God '*Jesus* is cursed,' and no one can say '*Jesus* is Lord' except by the Holy Spirit"; see also 1 Cor 11:23, 2 Cor 4:8-11, 14; 11:4; and 1 Thess 1:10.

erly be called a portion of early Christian confessional material, whether quoted in whole or in part.

6. This portion of early Christian confessional material was evidently well known and respected by both Paul and his Christian addressees at Rome, and so was used by Paul in a circumstantial manner to create another point of contact between himself and his Roman addressees.

7. Paul used this early Christian confessional material, whether in whole or in part, not only to gain rapport with his Christian addressees at Rome but also — and primarily — to support his thesis of 3:21-23 (which repeats and develops the first statement of that thesis in 1:16-17) in a manner they would appreciate.

Understanding 3:24-26 in this fashion allows us to consider what precedes this body of quoted traditional material and what follows it as distinguishable units of Paul's own prose. So I propose that the structure of 3:21-31, with captions characterizing the contents of each of these units of material, should be understood as follows:

1. The original thesis statement repeated and developed in 3:21-23.
2. The developed thesis statement supported by early Christian confessional material in 3:24-26.
3. The developed thesis statement elucidated in 3:27-31.

This threefold structure will organize and guide our "Exegetical Comments" on the passage below.

EXEGETICAL COMMENTS

I. The Original Thesis Statement Repeated and Developed (3:21-23)

Rom 3:21-23 is dominated linguistically by the subject δικαιοσύνη θεοῦ ("the righteousness of God") and its predicate πεφανέρωται ("it has been revealed"), which appear in 3:21. This subject and predicate function as the semantic spine of the passage, with δικαιοσύνη θεοῦ being repeated at the beginning of 3:22. This centrality of δικαιοσύνη θεοῦ πεφανέρωται ("the righteousness of God has been revealed") in 3:21-23 is in line with the centrality of the subject δικαιοσύνη θεοῦ ("the righteousness of God") and its synonymous predicate ἀποκαλύπτεται ("is being revealed") that appeared at the heart of Paul's original thesis statement in 1:16-17.

The four prepositional phrases — (1) χωρὶς νόμου ("apart from the law") in 3:21a, (2) ὑπὸ τοῦ νόμου καὶ τῶν προφητῶν ("by the law and the prophets") in 3:21b, (3) διὰ πίστεως Ἰησοῦ Χριστοῦ ("through faith in Jesus Christ"; or, as we will argue below, "through the faithfulness of Jesus Christ") in 3:22, and

(4) εἰς πάντας τοὺς πιστεύοντας ("to all who believe") in 3:22 — are all dependent, as well, on this central affirmation that "the righteousness of God has been revealed," which appears in 3:21. Also dependent on this central affirmation are the two statements introduced by the postpositive conjunction γάρ ("for"): οὐ γάρ ἐστιν διαστολή ("for there is no difference") in 3:22c, and πάντες γὰρ ἥμαρτον καὶ ὑστεροῦνται τῆς δόξης τοῦ θεοῦ ("for all have sinned and fall short of the glory of God") in 3:23. Each of these six phrases or statements of 3:21-23 represents both a linguistic development and a conceptual advance with respect to the thesis statement of 1:16-17. Yet each of them is rooted in what Paul wrote earlier in Romans, either in his original thesis statement of 1:16-17 or in his negative comments of 1:18–3:20 — or, as in at least a couple of these cases, in both.

3:21a Νυνὶ δέ, "but now," is an expression that frequently appears in Paul's letters. It sometimes connotes a logical contrast, and can be understood along the lines of the expression "but now here is the situation."[46] Usually, however, Paul uses it when speaking about the temporal contrast that has been brought about by God through the work of Christ and the ministry of the Holy Spirit — either in the course of salvation history or in the life of a believer in Jesus in passing from a former experience apart from Christ to his or her present experience as a Christian — and understood as connoting "but now in the transition from one epoch or status to another."[47] Or as Charles Cranfield has aptly summarized Paul's use of νυνὶ δέ here in 3:21: " 'But now' points to the decisiveness of what was accomplished in the gospel events, emphasizing the contrast between the situation before and the situation after those events."[48]

The early Church Fathers had great difficulty understanding relations between God's redemptive activities in the OT and God's redemptive activities in the NT. Marcion and his followers viewed the religion of the OT and the gospel proclaimed by Paul as being quite different — in fact, diametrically opposed to one another, with entirely different "gods" or "Gods" being envisioned. The Alexandrian Fathers, on the other hand, in their attempts to counter Marcion, did everything they could to ensure that Paul's negative statements about the Mosaic law were kept to a minimum, and so tended to view relations between the testaments in a somewhat static fashion — that is, viewing God's revelations of himself and his redemptive actions in the two testaments as being essentially the same, though under different guises and with different historical particulars. The Antiochean Fathers, however, while affirming continuity between the testaments, had a much livelier sense of historical development and redemptive fulfillment than did their Alexandrian counterparts. Thus they expressed in their exegesis a much more dynamic approach to Scripture, which emphasized not only theological and logical connections between the two testaments but also

46. As in Rom 7:17; 1 Cor 12:18; 13:13.
47. As in Rom 5:9; 6:19, 22; 7:6; cf. the nontheological, temporal uses of νῦν later in 15:23, 25; see also 2 Cor 8:22; Eph 2:13; Phlm 9, 11.
48. Cranfield, "Preaching on Romans," in his *On Romans,* 73.

historical and theological differences between them because of God's own advances in his unfolding drama of redemptive history — with their understanding regarding the course of salvation history in the NT being focused on the new eschatological experience, which was promised in the OT and brought about by God through the work of Christ and the ministry of his Spirit.[49]

Here at the beginning of 3:21 the phrase νυνὶ δέ ("but now"), understood along Antiochean lines of interpretation, signals an important distinction between God's salvific activity within the religion of Israel, as depicted in the Jewish (OT) Scriptures, and his salvation that has "now been revealed" through the work of Christ and the ministry of the Holy Spirit, as proclaimed in the Christian gospel — that is, the contrast effected by God, through Christ and his Spirit, in transforming the circumstances that previously pertained in the course of salvation history. It is, in fact, the eschatological "now" of which Paul speaks in 2 Cor 6:2: "Behold, now (ἰδοὺ νῦν) is the time of God's favor; behold, now (ἰδοὺ νῦν) is the day of salvation."

3:21b The phrase χωρὶς νόμου, "without" or "apart from the law," has no explicit roots in the thesis statement of 1:16-17. Rather, it is one of the new features of 3:21-23 that is included in the repetition and development of that original thesis statement. Nonetheless, it is not an entirely new feature in Paul's letter to the Christians at Rome, for (1) it is rooted in what he wrote regarding the Jews and their relation to the Mosaic law in 2:17–3:20, which came to a climax in his pejorative use of the phrase "works of the law" in 3:20a, and (2) it expresses an important matter associated with the temporal contrast signaled by the phrase νυνὶ δέ ("but now"), which he used immediately before this statement in 3:21a.

The early Church Fathers frequently debated what Paul meant by the term νόμος ("law"). Origen, for example, argued that Paul used νόμος in two ways in Rom 3: "natural law" and "the Mosaic law"; and he proposed, as a general rule (though not an inflexible rubric), that "When the law of Moses is intended, the article is used; but when the natural law is meant, the article is omitted."[50] Yet coming on the heels of (1) Paul's insistence in 3:2 that the chief advantage of being Jews was that "they were entrusted with the words of God (τὰ λόγια τοῦ θεοῦ)," (2) his statement in 3:19 that "whatever the law (ὁ νόμος) says," it says to those who are under the law (τοῖς ἐν τῷ νόμῳ), and (3) his pejorative reference in 3:20 to "works of the law" (ἔργα νόμου) — followed in 3:28 by the phrase "apart from works of the law (χωρὶς ἔργων νόμου)" — there can hardly be any doubt that what Paul had in mind here in 3:21 by χωρὶς νόμου was "apart from *the Mosaic law.*"

But what did Paul mean in declaring that "God's righteousness," which "has been revealed" in this time of the eschatological "now," is "apart from the Mosaic law"? It has frequently been assumed because of the close association of νυνὶ δέ ("but now") and χωρίς νόμου ("apart from the law") that Paul was

---

49. Cf. R. N. Longenecker, "Three Ways of Understanding," 2-18.
50. Origen, *Ad Romanos,* on Rom 3:21; *PG* 14.959.

contrasting (1) the Christian proclamation of God's unmerited love, mercy, and grace, as expressed in the work of Christ and proclaimed in the message of the NT, with (2) a legalistic "works righteousness" based on the regulations of the OT and developed by Jews into a system of legalistic casuistry. Yet God's covenantal relations with his people in the religion of Israel, as represented in the OT and as understood by the better rabbis of early Judaism, were never (except when perverted) predicated on a legal basis. Rather, the relation was always understood by the OT prophets and the better Jewish rabbis of Paul's day as having been established by God himself on the basis of his own love, mercy, and grace — and it was always viewed as implemented in the contexts of God's redemptive acts on behalf of his people and his readiness to forgive those who had sinned against him.

For a Jew, it would have been — and continues to be — shocking to separate "God's righteousness" and "the Mosaic law." For God, whose person is righteous and whose actions are just, had given his holy instructions to his people through the law of Moses. And while the OT prophets and better Jewish rabbis proclaimed that covenantal relationship with God was based on God's love, mercy, grace, and forgiveness, and not on a legalistic observance of God's laws, the people of Israel always understood that the covenant God established with them was to be expressed in ways prescribed by the Mosaic law — as well as, particularly in situations that developed beyond those of the time of Moses, in ways spelled out by the accredited teachers of Judaism, in accordance with the spirit and express statements of the Mosaic law.

Thus Judaism became a "religion of the book." For in their endeavors to express their faith in God, Jewish prophets and teachers (whether of antiquity, medieval times, or today) have always insisted that those who had been brought into covenant relationship with God must express their response to God and his redemptive actions on their behalf in terms of what may be called "nomism" (or, in today's parlance, "covenantal nomism") — that is, not in some type of "acting legalism," which seeks to gain acceptance and status before God by what a person can do, but by a "reacting" or "responding nomism" that (1) bases itself on what God has done redemptively for his people and (2) responds in love and obedience to God's love, mercy, and grace by keeping his words of instruction (i.e., Torah), as expressed in the Mosaic law (i.e., "Written Torah"), interpreted by the early accredited Jewish teachers (i.e., "Oral Torah," which was later codified in the Talmud and associated rabbinic collections), and constantly reinterpreted by accredited teachers today.

The OT prophets denounced "legalism," but they never wanted to loosen the responsive constraints of a true "nomism." The Dead Sea covenanters likewise opposed legalism. Yet they also expected that God's people in the coming messianic age would observe the Mosaic law more conscientiously and in a manner that expressed more appropriately their response to God and his actions on their behalf — and they wanted their community, even in its extremes, to be a prototype of such a nomistic observance.

Paul, however, understood that with God's provision for humanity in the work of Christ, coupled with the more intensive ministry of the Holy Spirit, a new age in the course of God's salvation history had dawned — that is, that the promised eschatological "now" had been inaugurated and was being experienced. So he proclaimed (1) that a nomistic faith (or "covenantal nomism"), which had served its God-given purpose effectively in the days of the old covenant, had come to an end,[51] and (2) that a "new covenant piety" was now by God's ordination in effect, which was opposed, as always, to any form of "legalism," but also brought to an end the requirement of necessarily expressing one's response to God's love, mercy, grace, and forgiveness in terms of "covenantal nomism."

By Christ's direct encounter of him on his journey to Damascus, Paul came to understand that Jesus of Nazareth, who had been exalted by God, was Israel's Messiah and humanity's Lord. He also learned in that "Damascus Road" experience, coupled with the continued ministry of God's Spirit, a great deal more about the unfolding nature of God's salvation for all humanity (including, as he will later insist in 8:19-23, the redemption of "the whole creation"). Further, by understanding his ministry and proclamation in terms of an Antiochean perspective (see above), it can legitimately be said that Paul came to appreciate — both because of his commitment to Jesus and because of his continued growth by means of the Spirit's ministry — something of great importance regarding the developing nature of God's redemptive program (i.e., salvation history): that God has been moving forward throughout all of his redemptive activity, bringing that activity to a focus in the work and person of Christ Jesus and explicating that focus through the ministry of the Holy Spirit. Thus God's people, he believed, needed also to move forward (1) in their understanding of God's redemptive working, (2) in the focus of their faith, and (3) in the manner in which they respond to God's love, mercy, grace, and forgiveness.

It was on the basis of such an understanding of God's unfolding "redemptive program" that Paul in Gal 3:21–4:7 rebuked his Gentile converts in the province of Galatia for even thinking about accepting certain "minimal requirements" of the Mosaic law so as to express their Christian faith "better" through what some Jewish believers in Jesus from the mother church at Jerusalem were arguing was the "God-ordained," and therefore the "required" and "proper," nomistic course of action. Likewise, it will be from this perspective that he will write his Christian addressees at Rome later in 10:4: "For Christ is the end of the law (τέλος γὰρ νόμου Χριστός) in connection with righteousness (εἰς δικαιοσύνην) for everyone who believes (παντὶ τῷ πιστεύοντι)." And it is from this perspective that we need to understand Paul here in Rom 3:21 when he says: "But now (νυνὶ δέ), apart from the law (χωρὶς νόμου), the righteousness of God has been revealed."

3:21c Matters having to do with the meaning of the noun δικαιοσύνη

---

51. Cf. R. N. Longenecker, "The End of Nomism," in *Paul, Apostle of Liberty*, 128-55.

("righteousness") and the use of the expression δικαιοσύνη θεοῦ ("the righteousness of God") in Romans, as well as elsewhere in the NT, are of great importance — not only for an understanding of Paul's letter to Christians at Rome, but also for Christian theology generally. We have already said much about Paul's use of δικαιοσύνη and δικαιοσύνη θεοῦ, as well as the slightly differently worded phrases δικαιοσύνη αὐτοῦ ("his [God's] righteousness") and θεοῦ δικαιοσύνη ("God's righteousness"), in our exegetical comments on 1:17. Yet certain features of a circumstantial nature that were there noted, as well as certain proposals regarding development there suggested, need to be highlighted here with respect to Paul's use of δικαιοσύνη θεοῦ in his expanded thesis statement of 3:21-23 — particularly because in this passage the apostle (1) lays emphasis on the expression by using it twice as the subject of 3:21-22 and (2) nuances it more fully by the four prepositional phrases and two explanatory clauses that he associates with it.

Generally speaking, Vincent Taylor has quite ably expressed in popular language the growing consensus of scholarly opinion in his day regarding Paul's understanding of δικαιοσύνη θεοῦ: "The 'righteousness of God' is not simply a quality possessed by Him, but is also, and at the same time, His saving activity amongst men; it is both what He is and what He gives."[52] Yet more, I believe, needs to be taken into account with respect to (1) the occurrences of δικαιοσύνη θεοῦ in the letters of Paul and the rest of the NT, (2) the varying nuances of this expression in Paul's letters, particularly in Romans, as well as elsewhere in the NT, and (3) a rationale for the somewhat different nuances incorporated within the expression in its somewhat diverse contexts. So I think it necessary to highlight briefly here what I have written earlier regarding these matters in commenting on 1:17, as follows:

1. *On the Occurrences of δικαιοσύνη θεοῦ in Paul and the Rest of the NT.* Paul uses the expression δικαιοσύνη θεοῦ in only two verses outside of Romans, in 2 Cor 5:21 ("so that in him [Christ] we might become 'the righteousness of God'") and in Phil 3:9 ("'the righteousness of God' that is based on faith"). 2 Cor 5:21 was certainly written before Paul wrote his letter to the Christians at Rome; Phil 3:9 probably was also written before, although it may have been written after, he wrote Romans.

The expression δικαιοσύνη θεοῦ, however, is most prominent among Paul's letters in Romans, particularly in the first section of the body middle of the letter. In Romans it appears (1) once in 1:17a, which is at the heart of the thesis statement of 1:16-17; (2) once in the rhetorical question of 3:5 (εἰ δὲ ἡ ἀδικία ἡμῶν θεοῦ δικαιοσύνην συνίστησιν, τί ἐροῦμεν; "But if our unrighteousness serves to demonstrate more clearly God's righteousness, what shall we say?"); (3) twice in 3:21a and 3:22a as the subject of the repeated and expanded thesis statement of 3:21-23; and (4) twice more in a slightly different form as τῆς δικαιοσύνης αὐτοῦ ("his [God's] justice/righteousness") in 3:25 and 3:26, which is part of the

---

52. Taylor, "Great Texts Reconsidered," 297.

confessional material of 3:24-26 that Paul quotes (as we will argue) in support of his thesis statement of 3:21-23. It also appears once in the third section of the body middle of Romans at 10:3: "They did not know 'the righteousness of God' (τὴν τοῦ θεοῦ δικαιοσύνην), and so sought to establish their own."

The phrase δικαιοσύνη θεοῦ appears at only three places elsewhere in the NT: (1) Matt 6:33, "Seek first the kingdom of God and 'his righteousness' (τὴν δικαιοσύνην αὐτοῦ), and all these things will be given to you as well"; (2) Jas 1:20, "A person's anger does not bring about 'the righteousness of God' (δικαιοσύνην θεοῦ)"; and (3) 2 Pet 1:1, "to those who 'through the righteousness of our God' (ἐν δικαιοσύνη τοῦ θεοῦ ἡμῶν) and Savior Jesus Christ have received a faith as precious as ours."

2. *On the Varying Nuances of δικαιοσύνη θεοῦ in Paul and Elsewhere in the NT.* The nuancing of δικαιοσύνη θεοῦ in Paul's letters and the three instances where it appears elsewhere in the NT is somewhat varied. In both 2 Cor 5:21 and Phil 3:9 the expression is clearly used in a *communicative* or *objective sense* (i.e., the genitive τοῦ θεοῦ used as an objective genitive, which signifies that God is the source or originating agent of the righteousness that is communicated), and therefore to be understood as "the gift of righteousness" that is given by God to those who respond "by faith."

In Romans, a fourfold scenario may be proposed as to how Paul nuances δικαιοσύνη θεοῦ (including its slightly varied wording δικαιοσύνη αὐτοῦ and θεοῦ δικαιοσύνη):

1. In his thesis statements of 1:16-17 and 3:21-23, where both *attributive* and *communicative* nuances seem to be present.

2. In support for his thesis in 3:24-26 by the quotation of a portion of early Christian confessional material, where the *attributive sense* of the expression is certainly highlighted in referring to God's "justice" and his nature as being "just" — but where the *communicative sense* is also present in referring to God as "the one who justifies."

3. In speaking of "God's righteousness" or "righteous justice" (θεοῦ δικαιοσύνην) in 3:5, where the *attributive sense* is clearly to the fore ("If our 'unrighteousness/injustice' demonstrates more clearly God's 'righteousness/faithfulness/justice', what shall we say?").

4. In his statement of 10:3, where the expression is obviously used in the first part of the verse in a *communicative sense* ("They did not know the righteousness of God") — though with, it seems, both *communicative* and *attributive* nuances being present in the last part of the verse ("They did not submit to God's righteousness").

The *attributive sense* of "the righteousness of God," however, is dominant in its three NT uses outside of the Pauline corpus, that is, in Matt 6:33, Jas 1:20, and 2 Pet 1:1. That seems to have been how the earliest Jewish believers in Jesus, as represented by the writers of our canonical Matthew, James, and 2 Peter, understood the expression — and it is probably how the Christians at Rome most often used it as well.

But Paul's emphasis in his Gentile mission was on God's righteousness as a gift given by God to those he reconciles to himself through the work of Christ, the ministry of his Holy Spirit, and their response of faith — as is evident in many ways throughout all his letters to his own converts, but especially highlighted in his uses of the noun δικαιοσύνη alone[53] and the expression δικαιοσύνη θεοῦ when writing to his own converts at Corinth and Philippi.[54] Thus, while acknowledging the "justness," "justice," and "righteousness" of God in an *attributive sense,* Paul's emphasis in his Gentile mission was primarily on "the righteousness of God" in a *communicative sense,* as can be seen most clearly in 2 Cor 5:21: "God made him who had no sin to be sin for us, so that in him we might become 'the righteousness of God,'" and in Phil 3:9: that I may gain Christ "and be found in him, not having a righteousness of my own that comes from the law, but that which is through faith in Christ — 'the righteousness of God' that is by faith."

3. *On a Rationale for These Somewhat Differing Nuances in Diverse Contexts.* It may be postulated (as I believe) that the Christians at Rome believed Paul's Christian proclamation was out of balance — that is, he preached well regarding "the righteousness of God" in a *communicative sense,* but he was less vocal about "God's righteousness" or "justice" in an *attributive sense.* So in writing them, Paul begins by affirming the broad range of meaning that the expression "the righteousness of God" incorporates. In effect, he agrees with them in their attributive understanding — which, however, may have been understood by them in a rather static manner with respect to the character and actions of God. But he also wants them to think in revelatory, historical, and redemptive terms — and so to conceptualize what God has done through the work of Jesus Christ and is now doing by the ministry of the Holy Spirit in a more dynamic fashion. Thus he emphasizes that God's righteousness "is now being revealed" by God himself (using the present indicative passive verb ἀποκαλύπτεται) in the Christian gospel — which truth he believed both they and he confessed, and so held in common.

3:21d The verb πεφανέρωται ("it has been revealed") parallels the verb ἀποκαλύπτεται ("it is being revealed"), which appeared in the central thematic assertion of 1:17 that lies at the heart of the thesis statement of 1:16-17. The two verbs are synonyms, and so, apparently, first the one and then the other was used to avoid monotony (i.e., a tedious sameness) in using the same expression in the predicates of two sentences that speak about the same subject (i.e., "the righteousness of God"). However, the verb φανερόω ("reveal," "make known," "show") is expressed in the perfect tense, that is, as translated "it [the righteousness of God] has been revealed," whereas ἀποκαλύπτεται in 1:17 is in the present

53. Cf. esp. Rom 5:17.
54. 2 Cor 5:21; Phil 3:9.

tense, that is, as translated "it is being revealed" — which highlights the facts that by his use of the perfect tense in 3:21, Paul is speaking about (1) a decisive act that has already taken place and (2) the effects of that past act that continue on into the present.

This change of tense from the present ἀποκαλύπτεται ("it is being revealed") to the perfect πεφανέρωται ("it has been revealed") is one of the new developments that appears in this thesis statement of 3:21-23 vis-à-vis the original thesis statement of 1:16-17. It is a change of tense that is conditioned by the expression νυνὶ δέ ("but now") at the beginning of v. 21, which signals the temporal contrast that has been effected by God through the work of Christ and the ministry of the Holy Spirit in the course of salvation history (see above, ad loc.). And it is in line with the eschatological "now" that reverberates throughout this developed thesis statement of 3:21-23, its confessional support in 3:24-26, and its elucidation in 3:27-31. Further, (1) this same emphasis on the eschatological "now" is to the fore in the concluding doxology of Romans in 16:25-27, which functions to summarize some of the most important matters that Paul wanted his Roman addressees especially to remember of all that he was writing them in his letter — that is, in speaking about "the revelation of the mystery that was hidden for long ages past *but is now being revealed* (φανερωθέντος δὲ νῦν)" in Rom 16:25b-26a, and (2) it is highlighted, as well, in a significant autobiographical statement in Col 1:24-27, which includes a reference to Paul's God-given mandate to proclaim "the mystery that has been kept hidden for ages and generations *but is now revealed* (νῦν δὲ ἐφανερώθη)" in Col 1:26.

3:21e The present passive participle μαρτυρουμένη ("being attested") picks up on the imagery of the law court given in 3:19, where it is used to express a major function of the Mosaic law that has always existed and continues to exist today: "Whatever the law says, it says to those who are under the law, so that every mouth may be silenced and the whole world held accountable to God." But the nominative singular of that present passive participle here in 3:21b emphasizes a further important function of the Mosaic law and of the message of the OT prophets — that is, that "the righteousness of God," which "has been revealed" (and continues to be in effect) in the proclamation of the Christian gospel, is "being attested by the law and the prophets." Thus while "the righteousness of God" is "now apart from the law," the Mosaic law and the OT prophets continue to function in their primary responsibilities: (1) judging sin and condemning sinners, and (2) pointing beyond themselves to "God's righteousness," both in an *attributive sense* (i.e., his righteous nature and just actions) and in a *communicative sense* (i.e., his gift of righteousness to those who respond positively).

Paul rarely refers in an abstract manner to the OT prophets — though, of course, he did so earlier in Rom 1:2 when speaking of "the gospel of God that he [God] promised beforehand through his prophets (διὰ τῶν προφητῶν αὐτοῦ) in the Holy Scriptures." But he does not use the expression "the law and the prophets" ([ὁ] νόμος καὶ [οἱ] προφῆται) elsewhere in his letters. Yet "the law

and the prophets" was commonly used in Jewish and Jewish Christian circles
to refer to the Jewish (OT) Scriptures as a whole — as appears, for example,
(1) in the writings of early Judaism,[55] (2) on the lips of Jesus,[56] (3) in the report
of Philip's witness about Jesus to Nathaniel,[57] (4) in Paul's preaching to Jews and
to those who had some understanding of Jewish thought and expression,[58] and
(5) in statements of a number of Jewish rabbis whose words are preserved in
the Talmud and other rabbinic collections.[59] It may reasonably be postulated,
therefore, that while Paul usually referred to the OT as "Scripture" (ἡ γραφή),[60]
"the Scriptures" (αἱ γραφαί),[61] or "the Holy Scriptures" (γραφαί ἅγιαι),[62] here
he uses a locution for the OT, that is, "the law and the prophets," which seems
to have been used commonly by Jews and Jewish believers in Jesus — and so,
it may be assumed, was used by Paul's Christian addressees at Rome, who had
been influenced by the theology and religious language of the mother church
at Jerusalem.

3:22a The postpositive δέ is one of the most frequently used particles in
classical and koine Greek. It often signals some type of contrast between one
sentence or clause and another — though almost as often it functions simply as
a connective without any contrast implied. Here δέ, because of its association
with the repetition of the subject δικαιοσύνη θεοῦ ("righteousness of God") in
3:21, is best understood as introducing a fuller and more significant definition
of that subject — that is, that "this righteousness of God" is, as stated in the
immediately following two clauses, to be understood as both (1) διὰ πίστεως
Ἰησοῦ Χριστοῦ and (2) εἰς πάντας τοὺς πιστεύοντας (which two clauses will
be discussed below).

This phenomenon of the particle δέ appearing with a noun, verb, or
phrase that had been used just previously in the same context (with both instances being in the same grammatical form) — with its purpose being to signal
a fuller and more significant use of that previously used noun, verb, or phrase
— appears elsewhere in Paul's letters.[63] Here in 3:22 the repetition of δικαιοσύνη
θεοῦ should be understood as providing a closer definition of the same subject
as appeared in 3:21, which in turn repeats the subject of 1:17. Thus the two uses
of the expression "the righteousness of God" in 3:21-22 must be seen as conveying the full gamut of nuanced meanings of its earlier use in 1:17 — that is, as
suggesting both an *attributive sense* with regard to God's nature and character

55. Cf. the prologue of Sirach; 2 Macc 15:9; 4 Macc 18:10.
56. Cf. Matt 5:17; 7:12; 11:13//Luke 16:16; 24:44.
57. Cf. John 1:45.
58. Cf. Acts 13:15; 24:14; 28:23.
59. Cf. *Str-Bil,* 3.164-65.
60. Cf. Rom 4:3; 9:17; 10:11; Gal 3:8; 4:30.
61. Cf. Rom 15:4.
62. Cf. Rom 1:2.
63. Cf. 1 Cor 2:6: σοφίαν . . . σοφίαν δέ; Gal 2:1-2: ἀνέβην . . . ἀνέβην δέ; Phil 2:8: θανάτου
. . . θανάτου δέ.

407

("his righteousness," "justice," "just actions") and a *communicative sense* with respect to what God gives as a gift to those who respond positively to him by faith (i.e., "righteousness bestowed or given," which, by the working of God's Spirit, is the basis for and enables "justice" and "just actions").

This use of δέ with a repeated noun, verb, or phrase (and always in the same grammatical form) is paralleled later in Rom 9:30 where Paul (1) twice uses the accusative form of the noun δικαιοσύνην ("righteousness") in speaking about the failure of Gentiles to pursue "righteousness" and obtain "righteousness," and then (2) a third time in that same verse uses that same accusative δικαιοσύνην ("righteousness") — though this time in association with the postpositive particle δέ to signal the presence of a further defining statement: "[that is,] a 'righteousness' (δικαιοσύνην δέ) that is by faith (τὴν ἐκ πίστεως)."

There is no expressed Greek verb in this sentence of 3:22, which is begun by the subject δικαιοσύνη δὲ θεοῦ. This absence serves to highlight both the dramatic nature of his statement and the dynamic force of what he is saying. Our English translations, of course, usually require at least one verb in every sentence. But decisions regarding the nature, number, and placement of the verb (or verbs) that seem to be assumed in this sentence depend largely on (1) how the subject δικαιοσύνη θεοῦ in this verse, as well as in the preceding verse, is understood, that is, whether to be nuanced in a dominantly *attributive sense* or a dominantly *communicative sense* (or both); (2) how the prepositional phrase διὰ πίστεως Ἰησοῦ Χριστοῦ is interpreted, that is, whether "through faith in Jesus Christ" or "through the faithfulness of Jesus Christ" (see discussion below); and (3) whether the following prepositional phrase εἰς πάντας τοὺς πιστεύοντας repeats in essence the immediately preceding prepositional phrase, or should be understood as a complementary phrase that makes it own point (see discussion below). So in understanding the nuancing of δικαιοσύνη θεοῦ here as being dominantly *communicative,* and then later taking the positions that we do regarding the prepositional phrases that follow (see discussions below), the verbs "is" and "given" have been inserted in our translation above.

3:22b What Paul means by πίστεως (or πίστις in the nominative) Ἰησοῦ Χριστοῦ has been during the past century, as noted above,[64] a vigorously debated issue. The expression πίστις Ἰησοῦ Χριστοῦ (or the synonymous πίστις Χριστοῦ or πίστις αὐτοῦ; also πίστις Ἰησοῦ without Χριστοῦ) appears in Paul's letters only six, seven, or eight times in total — that is, here in Rom 3:22 (probably also expressly in 3:26, as well as more obliquely in 3:25 and 3:30, as we will argue later); earlier in Gal 2:16 (twice) and 3:22 (perhaps also 3:26, which in P[46] concludes with the phrase διὰ πίστεως Χριστοῦ); and then in Eph 3:12 and in Phil 3:9. The prepositions ἐκ ("from," "based on," "by reason of") and διά ("through," "by means of"), which variously precede and condition the genitive form πίστεως in these six, seven, or eight instances, are probably used interchangeably, as is particularly evident in their synonymous use in Gal 2:16

---

64. See our "Exegetical Comments" above on 1:17.

— though they may in some of their other contexts signal a further refinement of ideas.

The generally accepted view has been that Ἰησοῦ Χριστοῦ is syntactically an objective genitive, and so διὰ πίστεως Ἰησοῦ Χριστοῦ should be read as "through faith in Jesus Christ." The vast majority of past commentators on Romans have understood the expression in this manner.[65] Likewise, almost all contemporary English versions have translated διὰ πίστεως Ἰησοῦ Χριστοῦ in Rom 3:22 in this way — though a few, of late, have added a footnote in recognition of the possibility of a subjective genitive reading.[66] Only one modern English version to date, however, has actually incorporated the translation "through the faithfulness of Jesus Christ" into its text.[67] Further, a number of very competent scholars have written articles in defense of the traditional objective genitive interpretation "through faith in Jesus Christ."[68]

From the late nineteenth century to the present, however, there has been a rising tide of scholarly opinion that understands Ἰησοῦ Χριστοῦ as a subjective genitive, and so interprets πίστις Ἰησοῦ Χριστοῦ as "the faith/faithfulness of Jesus Christ." This reading was first proposed by Johannes Haussleiter in 1891[69] and then argued by Gerhard Kittel in 1906.[70] Karl Barth was the first commentary writer to espouse such an understanding in his *Römerbrief* of 1918, translating not only ἐκ πίστεως εἰς πίστιν in 1:17 in this fashion (i.e., *auf Treue dem Glauben,* "from faithfulness unto faith") but also all of Paul's other uses of πίστις in 3:21-31. It was largely through Barth's influence that this view was popularized in the English-speaking world during the mid-1950s by Gabriel Hebert and Thomas Torrance.[71] It was then advocated by T. W. Manson in his Romans commentary of 1962,[72] and has since begun to be accepted by a few commentators on Romans — particularly by Charles Talbert in 2002.[73]

Prominent among a growing number of scholars who have argued for a subjective genitive understanding of πίστις Ἰησοῦ Χριστοῦ — whether understood as "the *faith* of Jesus Christ," "the *faithfulness* of Jesus Christ," or "the

---

65. E.g., Sanday and Headlam, *Romans,* 83-84; Nygren, *Romans,* 150-61; Leenhardt, *Romans,* 99-101; Barrett, *Romans,* 74; Bruce, *Romans,* 102; Cranfield, *Romans,* 1.203; Schlier, *Römerbrief,* 105, 115; Käsemann, *Romans,* 94, 101; Dunn, *Romans,* 1.166-67; Moo, *Romans,* 224-26; and Jewett, *Romans,* 277-78.

66. NRSV: "through the faith of Jesus Christ"; TNIV: "through the faithfulness of Jesus Christ."

67. So NET.

68. See esp. Hultgren, "The Πίστις Χριστοῦ Formulation in Paul," 248-63; Dunn, "Once More, *Pistis Christou,*" 730-44; and Cranfield, "On the Πίστις Χριστοῦ Question," 81-97.

69. Haussleiter, *Der Glaube Jesu Christi;* see also *idem,* "Eine theologische Disputation über den Glauben Jesu," 507-20; *idem,* "Was versteht Paulus unter christlichen Glauben?" 159-81.

70. Kittel, "*Pistis Iesou Christou* bei Paulus," 419-36.

71. Hebert, " 'Faithfulness' and 'Faith,' " 373-79; Torrance, "One Aspect of the Biblical Conception of Faith," 111-14.

72. T. W. Manson, "Romans," in *Peake's Commentary on the Bible,* 2nd ed., 942.

73. Talbert, *Romans,* 41-47 (on 1:17) and 107-10 (on 3:22 and 26).

fidelity [of God] in Jesus Christ" — have been Ernst Fuchs, Pierre Vallotton, Karl Kertelge, Markus Barth, George Howard, D. W. B. Robinson, Sam Williams, Richard Hays, Luke Timothy Johnson, Morna Hooker, and Bruce Longenecker.[74] I also have argued for this understanding in my *Paul, Apostle of Liberty* of 1964, my Galatians commentary of 1990, and my article "The Foundational Conviction of New Testament Christology" of 2004.[75]

Linguistically, the phrase πίστις Ἰησοῦ Χριστοῦ has always been difficult to interpret and so to translate. But when the Greek noun πίστις is understood in terms of the Hebrew noun אמונה, *'emûnâ*, which includes the nuances of both "faith" and "faithfulness," it is not too difficult to view Paul as using πίστεως Ἰησοῦ Χριστοῦ in 3:22 in much the same way as he used the expressions (1) τὴν πίστιν τοῦ θεοῦ ("the faithfulness *of* God") earlier in 3:3, (2) τῆς πίστεως τοῦ πατρὸς ἡμῶν Ἀβραάμ ("the faith *of* our father Abraham") later in 4:12, and (3) πίστεως Ἀβραάμ ("the faith *of* Abraham") in that same later context in 4:16.

Jerome in the Vulgate translated πίστις Ἰησοῦ Χριστοῦ quite literally as *fides Iesu Christi*, as did Erasmus — though, unfortunately, such a Latin rendering is as ambiguous as the Greek expression itself. Likewise, the translators of the KJV, evidently influenced by Paul's references to "the faith *of* Abraham" in 4:12 and 16 (though, it seems, not by the expression "the faithfulness *of* God" in 3:3), translated διὰ πίστεως Ἰησοῦ Χριστοῦ here in 3:22 as "by the faith *of* Jesus Christ," thereby understanding Ἰησοῦ Χριστοῦ syntactically as a subjective genitive. Further, five other occurrences of this expression that are worded in almost exactly the same manner are also translated in the KJV in a subjective genitive fashion: twice in Gal 2:16 ("by the faith *of* Jesus Christ" and "by the faith *of* Christ"), once in Gal 3:22 ("by faith *of* Jesus Christ"), once in Eph 3:12 ("by the faith *of* him"), and once in Phil 3:9 ("through the faith *of* Christ") — though the single name Ἰησοῦ in the roughly synonymous phrase τὸν ἐκ πίστεως Ἰησοῦ of Rom 3:26 was understood by those early-seventeenth-century scholars as an objective genitive, and thus they translated it as "him which believeth *in* Jesus" (or, as reworded by the RSV: "him who has faith *in* Jesus").

Inspired by Karl Barth's treatment of πίστις Ἰησοῦ Χριστοῦ in his *Römerbrief*, and on the basis of the earlier studies of that expression by Johannes Haussleiter and Gerhard Kittel, Gabriel Hebert argued that just as אמונה meant both "faithfulness" and "faith" in Jewish writings, so Paul used "the one word *pistis*

---

74. Fuchs, "Jesu und der Glaube," 170-85; Vallotton, *Le Christ et la Foi,* 41-144; Kertelge, *"Rechtfertigung" bei Paulus,* 162-66; M. Barth, "The Faith of the Messiah," 363-70; see also *idem, Ephesians,* 2 vols., AB (New York: Doubleday, 1974), esp. 1.224, 347; Howard, "On the 'Faith of Christ,'" 459-65; see also *idem,* "The 'Faith of Christ,'" 212-15, and *idem, Paul,* 57-65; D. W. B. Robinson, "'Faith of Jesus Christ,'" 71-81; Williams, "The 'Righteousness of God' in Romans," 241-90; see also *idem,* "Again Πίστις Χριστοῦ," 431-47; Hays, *The Faith of Jesus Christ,* esp. 170-74; see also *idem,* "ΠΙΣΤΙΣ and the Pauline Christology," 35-60; L. T. Johnson, "Romans 3:21-26 and the Faith of Jesus," 77-90; Hooker, "ΠΙΣΤΙΣ ΧΡΙΣΤΟΥ," 321-42; B. W. Longenecker, *The Triumph of Abraham's God,* 98-103.

75. R. N. Longenecker, *Paul, Apostle of Liberty,* 149-52; *idem, Galatians,* 87-88; *idem,* "The Foundational Conviction of New Testament Christology," 132-37.

for the two things, Divine faithfulness and human faith."[76] Hebert went on to point out (1) that the Hebrew idea of "faithfulness" often emerges in the LXX's use of πίστις, citing in particular the LXX translation of Hab 2:4, and (2) that there is no disagreement that Paul and the other NT authors often used πίστις elsewhere in their writings in this Hebrew sense, citing Rom 3:3 ("the *faithfulness* of God"); 1 Cor 1:9, 10:13 ("God is *faithful*"); 1 Thess 5:24 ("*faithful* is the one who calls you"); 2 Thess 3:3 ("the Lord is *faithful*"); and such non-Pauline passages as Heb 2:17, 3:2, 1 John 1:9, and Rev 1:5, 3:14, 19:11. Hebert noted, as well, that in three of the passages where πίστις Ἰησοῦ Χριστοῦ appears, that is, in Rom 3:22, Gal 3:22, and Phil 3:9, the words that immediately follow it, that is, εἰς πάντας τοὺς πιστεύοντας ("to all who believe"), are, at least to some extent, redundant if the objective genitive translation "through faith *in* Jesus Christ" is accepted. Thus Hebert argued that πίστις Ἰησοῦ Χριστοῦ is best translated "the faithfulness of Jesus Christ," with that translation understood to mean "God's faithfulness revealed to him."[77]

In those early days of the *Pistis Jesu Christou* debate, therefore, the expression πίστις Ἰησοῦ Χριστοῦ was at times understood as referring in some manner to "divine faithfulness." Karl Barth, for example, translated διὰ πίστεως Ἰησοῦ Χριστοῦ here in 3:22 as "his [God's] faithfulness in Jesus Christ," giving the following explanation: "The faithfulness of God and of Jesus the Christ confirm one another. The faithfulness of God is established when we meet the Christ in Jesus."[78] Gabriel Hebert translated πίστις Ἰησοῦ Χριστοῦ as "the faithfulness of Jesus Christ," but understood the expression to refer to "God's faithfulness revealed to him [i.e., Jesus]"; while Thomas Torrance translated it as "the faithfulness of Jesus Christ." When we consider (1) Paul's Hebraic background in which the word אמונה signified both "faith" and "faithfulness," (2) his other uses of πίστις in this passage in the sense of "faithfulness" (cf. also 3:25, 26, and possibly 30), and (3) the redundant nature of the immediately following expression εἰς πάντας τοὺς πιστεύοντας in 3:22 — as well as the equivalent expressions that appear in Gal 3:22 and Phil 3:9 — an emphasis on "divine faithfulness" (whether that of God or of Jesus Christ) and the translation "through the faithfulness of Jesus Christ" seem most linguistically convincing.

Yet interpretation of a particular statement or expression in the Bible is not just a linguistic matter. Biblical exegesis is also vitally interested in (1) the context of every statement or expression in question, both its broader context and its immediate context, and (2) the overall theology of the particular author involved. Proponents of both positions in the present *Pistis Jesu Christou* debate readily acknowledge the importance of bringing together all the relevant linguistic, contextual, and theological issues that pertain to this particular exegetical determination — as do, for example, Arlan Hultgren in arguing for

---

76. Hebert, "'Faithfulness' and 'Faith,'" 376.
77. *Ibid.,* 373.
78. K. Barth, *Romans,* 96.

an objective genitive interpretation[79] and Luke Timothy Johnson in arguing for a subjective genitive understanding.[80] So it is necessary here, in addition to dealing with the relevant linguistic features, to speak regarding the contextual and theological issues involved.

Contextual Considerations. Throughout the material just prior to his use of the expression διὰ πίστεως Ἰησοῦ Χριστοῦ in 3:22, that is, throughout 2:17–3:20, Paul has been speaking extensively about the "unfaithfulness" of Jews vis-à-vis the "faithfulness of God" — with that discussion coming to explicit expression in his two rhetorical questions of 3:3: What if some of them were unfaithful (τί εἰ ἠπίστησάν τινες)? and, Will their unfaithfulness (ἡ ἀπιστία αὐτῶν) nullify the faithfulness of God (τὴν πίστιν τοῦ θεοῦ)? These questions are immediately followed by his vociferous, even vehement, response of 3:4a: "Certainly not (μὴ γένοιτο)!"

Further, the central affirmation of the early Christian confession quoted by Paul in Phil 2:6-11, which is voiced at the center of that early confessional material (i.e., at the end of v. 8), has to do with the "obedience" (ὑπακοή) of Jesus: "he became obedient (γενόμενος ὑπήκοος) to the extent (μέχρι) of death (θανάτου)" — which statement, it appears, Paul wanted to emphasize, and therefore himself added the appended words: "even death on a cross (θανάτου δὲ σταυροῦ)." Later, at the beginning of Section II of the body middle of Romans, in 5:19b, Paul picks up on this theme of Christ's "obedience" (διὰ τῆς ὑπακοῆς τοῦ ἑνός) as effecting "righteousness" for "the many" (οἱ πολλοί), and so may be seen as using the noun "obedience" (ὑπακοή) as a synonym for the noun "faithfulness" (πίστις) in connection with the work of Christ. Admittedly, apart from its appearance at the end of v. 8 in the confessional material quoted in Phil 2:6-11, only here in Rom 5:19 does Paul use in his letters the term ὑπακοή ("obedience") when speaking about the work of Christ. But theology is more than mathematics; and while the literary-historical criterion of "multiple attestation" is always important, one does not appeal only to the frequency of particular words in support of significance.

Thus with respect to context, Paul's use of διὰ πίστεως Ἰησοῦ Χριστοῦ in 3:22, as well as his use of ἐκ πίστεως Ἰησοῦ only four verses later in 3:26, appears (1) almost immediately after his extended discussion of "the unfaithfulness" of Jews vis-à-vis the "the faithfulness" of God in 2:17–3:20 (particularly as expressed in 3:3) and (2) shortly before his contrast between "the disobedience of the one man [Adam]" and "the obedience of the one man [Christ]" in 5:19 (cf. also his contrast between Adam's "one trespass" and Christ's "one righteous act" in 5:18). So it may legitimately be argued that Paul's use of πίστις in a subjective sense in 3:22 (as well as in 3:26) fits appropriately into the broader and more immediate contexts of Romans.

A Theological Consideration. Paul's "high" Christology allows him to

79. Hultgren, "The Πίστις Χριστοῦ Formulation in Paul," 263ff.
80. L. T. Johnson, "Romans 3:21-26 and the Faith of Jesus," 78ff.

make a significant association of the following three important matters: (1) the titles "Son" and "Son of God" applied to Jesus, Israel's Messiah and humanity's Lord; (2) an early Christian confessional reference and his own reference to Jesus' "obedience"; and (3) his references to Christ's "faithfulness." All of these, as I've argued elsewhere, speak in a functional manner of Jesus' fulfillment of the will of God in effecting human redemption through his earthly ministry, sacrificial death, and physical resurrection.[81] Further, it may be postulated that as a Jewish believer in Jesus, whose faith was rooted not only in the person and work of Jesus Christ but also in the Jewish (OT) Scriptures, Paul's thought was impacted formatively by the messianic prophecy of Isa 11 — particularly the words of Isa 11:5 regarding "The Branch from Jesse," which affirm: "Righteousness (MT צדק) will be his belt and faithfulness (MT אמונה) the sash around his waist."

In effect, what appears most likely is that Paul used πίστις Ἰησοῦ Χριστοῦ (and its cognate forms) to signal the historical basis for the Christian gospel — that is, to highlight the fact that the Christian proclamation of "good news" in this time of the eschatological *"now"* is founded historically on the perfect response of obedience and faithfulness that Jesus, the Son, offered to God, the Father, both actively in his life and passively in his death. Perhaps he developed the formulation διὰ πίστεως Ἰησοῦ Χριστοῦ from the phrase ἐκ πίστεως Ἰησοῦ that appears at the close of Rom 3:26, which are the final words of what we will argue later is a portion of early Christian confessional material.[82] Yet whatever the validity of such a supposition, it seems evident that Paul both explicated and developed in 3:22 the rather cryptic expression ἐκ πίστεως εἰς πίστιν that he used earlier in 1:17 in his original thesis statement of 1:16-17.[83] And in so doing, he attempted to make clear, we believe, the following important point: that God's gift of righteousness in this period of the eschatological "now" has been brought about "through the faithfulness of Jesus Christ."[84]

3:22c Paul in 3:22b prefaced the immediately previous phrase πίστεως Ἰησοῦ Χριστοῦ ("the faith/faithfulness of Jesus Christ") using the preposition διά ("through," "by"). Here in 22c he prefaces πάντας τοὺς πιστεύοντας ("all who believe") by the preposition εἰς ("unto," "to"). As Archibald Robertson

81. Cf. R. N. Longenecker, "The Foundational Conviction of New Testament Christology," 122-44.

82. See our "Exegetical Comments" below on 3:24-26.

83. See our "Exegetical Comments" above on 1:17.

84. Lloyd Gaston's assertion is something of an overstatement of the situation today: "The correctness of the translation of πίστις Ἰησοῦ Χριστοῦ as the 'faith or faithfulness *of* Jesus Christ' has by now been too well established to need any further support" (Gaston, *Paul and the Torah*, 12). For, despite its merits, very few current commentary writers on Romans have espoused this position. Karl Barth was the early exception, translating the expression in 3:22 as *"durch seine* [i.e., God's] *Treue in Jesus Christus"* and commenting on it as follows: "The faithfulness of God and Jesus the Christ confirm one another. The faithfulness of God is established when we meet the Christ in Jesus" (K. Barth, *Romans*, 96). Charles Talbert is most notable among today's commentators who have argued for "the faithfulness of Jesus Christ" as the proper understanding of Paul's meaning in 3:22 (cf. Talbert, *Romans*, 107-10).

has pointed out: "The variation of the preposition is a skilful way of condensing thought, each preposition adding a new idea."[85] Here in 3:22 the apostle's practice of "condensation by variation," as Robertson calls it, highlights two distinctive features of his gospel proclamation: that prefaced by the preposition διά, which focuses on a vitally important objective feature in the redemptive ministry of Jesus, that is, his "faithfulness"; and that prefaced by the preposition εἰς, which focuses on the central subjective matter having to do with humanity's response, that is, a person's "faith."

Paul's emphasis on "faith" as the only proper response to God's love, mercy, grace, and forgiveness is rooted in his thesis statement of 1:16-17, where it appears three times: (1) in the opening words, which speak of "the gospel" as being "the power of God for the salvation παντὶ τῷ πιστεύοντι ('of everyone who believes')," (2) in the latter portion of the statement, as expressed in the cryptic phrase ἐκ πίστεως εἰς πίστιν (literally "out of faith unto faith"), and (3) in the final phrase of the supportive quotation from Hab 2:4, ἐκ πίστεως ζήσεται ("he will live by faith"). Robert Morgenthaler counted 140 occurrences of πίστις in the NT (including all its various uses), with 39 or 40 of them appearing in Romans.[86] Most of these occurrences of πίστις speak of "faith," "trust," or "confidence" in God or in Christ — though there are also instances where it must be read in a subjective genitive sense with reference to "the faithfulness of God," "the faith of Abraham," or "the faith/faithfulness of Jesus Christ."

Further, of the 39 or 40 occurrences of πίστις in Romans, most appear in three of the four major sections of the letter's body middle, that is, 21 times in Section I (1:16-4:25), 6 times in Section III (9:1–11:36), and 7 times in Section IV (12:1–15:13). Only once does the noun πίστις appear in Section II (5:1–8:39) — that is, in 5:1a (perhaps twice, if the highly disputed variant ἡ πίστις, "the faith," of 5:2 is accepted; but that is unlikely).[87] But that one textually assured instance appears in the "hinge verse" of 5:1, which looks back to what was written previously in Section I — and so should not be included as representing the teaching of 5:1–8:39, but understood as recalling what was said in the previous section of 1:16-4:25. Nonetheless, despite this relative unevenness of the appearances of πίστις in the body middle of Romans (which is, however, always an important matter to observe in the analysis of any of Paul's letters), the vital importance of faith in God and faith in Christ Jesus is a primary conviction that underlies all of what Paul (1) writes negatively about humanity's godlessness and wickedness in 1:18-2:16 and the Jews' unfaithfulness and injustices in 2:17-3:20, (2) declares forthrightly about what he and his Christian addressees at Rome believed regarding the message of the Christian gospel in 3:21-31, (3) highlights in the illustration of Abraham as the man of faith par excellence in 4:1-25, (4) assumes as foundational in his portrayal of his own contextualized message to Gentiles

85. ATRob, 567.
86. Morgenthaler, Statistik, 132.
87. See "Textual Notes" on 5:2.

in 5:1–8:39, (5) bemoans as to its absence within unresponsive "national Israel" but applauds as to its presence among "the remnant of Israel" in chs. 9–11, and (6) draws upon in his Christocentric exhortations of 12:1–15:13.

These two redemptive factors of "divine faithfulness" and "human faith" are, in fact, to the fore not only in the thesis statement of 1:16-17, but also — even more prominently and in a more developed fashion — in the development of that thesis statement here in 3:21-23, together with its confessional support in 3:24-26, its further elucidation in 3:27-31, and its use of Abraham as the example of faith par excellence in 4:1-24. Thus the Christian "good news" in this time of the eschatological "now" (1) is based historically on the trust, faithfulness, and obedience that Jesus, the Son, offered to God, the Father, on behalf of all people, and (2) calls for a corresponding response of trust, faithfulness, and obedience to God through Christ Jesus on the part of all people who hear the Christian message and are drawn to God by his Holy Spirit. And it is this call for a positive response of faith and faithfulness, because of the work of Christ and the ministry of the Holy Spirit, that is repeatedly sounded throughout all that Paul writes in Romans.

3:22d It is the statement οὐ γάρ ἐστιν διαστολή ("for there is no difference") that Paul uses here in 3:22 in support of the substantival adjective πάντας ("all"), which is the accusative plural of πᾶς that appears in the immediately previous clause of this same verse — εἰς πάντας τοὺς πιστεύοντας ("to all those who believe"), which is also expressed in the accusative case and plural number. Further, the phrase "there is no difference" is rooted in the thesis statement of 1:16-17 and carries on its emphasis regarding the universal nature of the Christian gospel. For just as the apostle highlighted in 1:16b the substantival adjective παντί ("everyone," the dative singular of πᾶς) in the clause παντὶ τῷ πιστεύοντι ("to everyone who believes"), so by adding the phrase Ἰουδαίῳ τε πρῶτον καὶ Ἕλληνι ("both for the Jew first and for the Gentile"), which functions to reinforce the universal nature of the Christian gospel, he adds here in 3:22b after παντάς ("everyone") the supportive statement οὐ γάρ ἐστιν διαστολή ("for there is no difference"), which likewise highlights the universal nature of the gospel's message.

3:23 Paul's emphasis on the universal nature of the Christian gospel is continued in 3:23 in writing πάντες γὰρ ἥμαρτον καὶ ὑστεροῦνται τῆς δόξης τοῦ θεοῦ ("For all have sinned and fall short of the glory of God") — here on the universality of the dire situation of all people in their state of sin (summarizing much of what he wrote earlier in 1:18–3:20), but with significant implications for the universality of God's redemptive grace and the renewal of God's glory in the lives of all those who respond to him in faith, trust, and commitment. Using Hillel's first rule of biblical interpretation, that is, *qal waḥomer* (קל וחומר), which may be defined as "what applies in a less important case will certainly apply in a more important case," Paul inferentially argues that if "all people (πάντες) have sinned (the third-person plural aorist indicative verb ἥμαρτον) and fall short (the third-person plural present middle verb ὑστεροῦνται) of the glory of God," then certainly God's gift of righteousness, which is based on "the faithfulness of Jesus Christ" — and which is surely a far greater and much more significant scenario than that of the universality of people's sin — is universally available "to everyone who believes" (παντί τῷ πιστεύοντι, as stated earlier in 1:16) and given "to all those who believe" (τοὺς εἰς πάντας πιστεύοντας, as stated just prior to this verse in 3:22). In effect, Paul's argument here is that if there is a universality of human sin and inability, then, arguing from the lesser situation to the greater, the salvation provided by God through the work of Christ and the ministry of God's Spirit must be universal in nature as well.

Such an inferential type of argument, which cites something from "a less important case" in support of something having to do with "a more important case," might not resonate well with a modern audience. It may be presumed, however, that it would have been understood and appreciated by addressees who had been influenced by Jewish Christian theology, language, and methods of argumentation (as we have postulated was the situation among the believers in Jesus at Rome).

The aorist tense of ἥμαρτον ("sinned") could be understood as referring to the sin of all people "in and with Adam," as has often been understood with respect to this same verb and its tense later in Rom 5:12.[88] Clearly a climax is reached in Paul's portrayal of the disastrous effects of Adam's sin by the use of πάντες ἥμαρτον in 5:12, and undoubtedly a parallel between 3:23 and 5:12 can be postulated.[89] Nonetheless, the aorist verb ἥμαρτον here in 3:23 is probably best understood as a constative use of the aorist — or as it has been called today, a "collective historical aorist"[90] or "summary aorist"[91] — that would view all the sins of all people throughout history as gathered together into a collective whole or a single moment. And accepting the aorist verb ἥμαρτον here as a constative aorist, Joseph Fitzmyer is certainly correct to conclude: "A reference to Adam is here eisexegetical."[92]

The teaching "all have sinned" was voiced by many Jews, both before and after Paul's day.[93] While a doctrine of "original sin" (in whatever form) was not prominent in the theology of later rabbinic Judaism, an understanding of the sinfulness of all people underlies many statements in the Talmud and in a number of other early rabbinic writings. And such an understanding is particularly evident in *4 Ezra,* which is a spiritually sensitive Jewish apocalyptic writing of about A.D. 100, in such statements as the following: "For who among the living is there who has not sinned, or who among men who has not transgressed your covenant?" (*4 Ezra* 7:46) and "For in truth there is no one among those who

---

88. So, e.g., Dunn, *Romans,* 1.167-68.
89. Cf. our "Exegetical Comments" below on 5:12.
90. So, e.g., *Burton,* section 54.
91. So *Porter,* 222.
92. Fitzmyer, *Romans,* 347.
93. For a treatment of Jewish views regarding human sin and responsibility, see "Exegetical Comments" below on 5:12-14.

have been born who has not acted wickedly, and among those who have existed there is no one who has not transgressed" (8:35).

The present tense and middle voice of the verb ὑστερέω ("fail," "lack," "fall short of"), which appears in the statement ὑστεροῦνται τῆς δόξης τοῦ θεοῦ ("they fall short of the glory of God"), suggest that all people in their experience have always fallen short of God's glory — not just that *they will fall short* in the eschatological judgment, but that *they presently fall short* in their sinful human condition. It is an expression, as Matthew Black has observed, that "means virtually the same as the preceding 'all men [people] have sinned.'"[94]

The phrase ἡ δόξη τοῦ θεοῦ ("the glory of God") is a "highly poetic expression" that "has undergone a remarkable change of meaning in Biblical Greek."[95] Matthew Black has summarized the evidence:

> In classical Greek it means "opinion"; in Biblical Greek it means the divine Sinai [Exod. 24:16], in the Pillar of Cloud [Exod. 16:10], in the Tabernacle [Exod. 24:16] or Temple [1 Kg. 8:11]. According to rabbinical tradition, it also shone on the face of Adam before the Fall, but, along with the divine image, was withdrawn at the Fall. The "glory" in this sense was only to be recovered when Adam's divine attributes were restored in messianic times.[96]

The program of divine redemption, therefore, involves the restoration of "the glory of God" to God's creation, which restoration includes all that is human as well as all that is animate and inanimate. So Paul speaks of "the glory of God" as being restored in both the experience of God's own and throughout his created universe — not only with reference to the final culmination of his redemptive program in the future on behalf of his own and his world,[97] but also with reference to the Christian's present earthly experience in fellowship with Christ.[98]

II. The Developed Thesis Statement Supported by Early Christian Confessional Material (3:24-26)

There has been a great deal of discussion among NT interpreters, as well as a large measure of uncertainty, about a number of matters that appear in 3:24-26 — principally regarding the following:

1. Certain terms, expressions, and syntactical constructions that seem somewhat different from Paul's usual vocabulary and style;
2. The nature of the material in these verses, that is, whether it is a portion

94. Black, *Romans*, 67.
95. *Ibid.*, 66-67.
96. *Ibid.*
97. Cf. Rom 5:2; 8:18-21; Phil 3:21; Col 1:27; 2 Thess 2:14.
98. Cf. 2 Cor 3:18; 4:6.

of some early Christian traditional material quoted by Paul or material composed by Paul himself;

3. The relation of the nominative plural present passive participle δικαιούμενοι ("being justified"), which appears at the beginning of 3:24, to what immediately precedes it in 3:21-23;

4. The identification of where this portion of material begins and ends;

5. The possibility of various interpolations and/or editorial insertions in the passage; and,

6. How 3:24-26 functions with respect to what the apostle has just previously written in his developed thesis statement of 3:21-23.

Our proposal is that in 3:24-26 Paul quotes a portion of an early Christian confession that he viewed as vitally important in support of his developed thesis statement of 3:21-23 — that is, a portion of Jewish Christian confessional material (1) that he believed was well known to his Christian addressees at Rome, (2) that he was convinced expressed what both he and his addressees viewed as foundational for their Christian faith, and (3) that he thought was expressed in a manner that his addressees would readily understand and appreciate. It is this understanding of the passage that will be explicated in the exegetical comments that follow. Further, in our exegesis we will attempt to highlight (1) how 3:24-26 reflects early Jewish Christian teaching, which had been formative for the Christians at Rome and which they continued to espouse; (2) how Paul used this material to support his developed thesis statement of 3:21-23, which he was confident his addressees would agree with if they were shown how the significant features of that expanded thesis statement were supported by what they had already confessed in their Jewish Christian liturgy; and (3) how this material reveals to us today some of the most important convictions of the earliest Jewish believers in Jesus — as well as some of the basic convictions of those who had been evangelized by them, as had the Christians at Rome — regarding the redemptive work of their Messiah and Savior vis-à-vis Paul's contextualization of that same Christian message in his preaching to Gentiles in the Greco-Roman world.

The material of 3:24-26 is set out in two parts. The first part sets out an affirmation of basic Christian belief, which is expressed in forensic terms and cultic language (vv. 24-25a); the second part presents a Christian rationale for what has been just affirmed (vv. 25b-26). The rationale of the second part is based on the foundational convictions of (1) the biblical concept of "the righteousness of God" (ἡ δικαιοσύνη αὐτοῦ; literally "his [God's] righteousness") in 3:25b and 26a, which is here understood primarily in an attributive sense to connote the idea of "God's righteous justice," and (2) the distinctly Christian understanding of "the faithfulness of Jesus" (πίστις Ἰησοῦ, understood as a subjective genitive and so to signify "the faith/faithfulness of Jesus") in 3:26b — which, as we believe, Paul nuanced, in line with the phrase διὰ τῆς πίστεως in 3:25a, to connote the covenantal faithfulness of Jesus in both his "active obedience" (i.e., in his

418

life) and his "passive obedience" (i.e., in his death) to God the Father.[99] Our exegesis of the passage, therefore, will be organized in terms of the two headings of "affirmation" and "rationale." More importantly, it will attempt to spell out Paul's nuancing of "God's righteousness" and "Jesus' faithfulness."

A. An Affirmation of Basic Christian Belief (3:24-25a)

Accepting the theses (1) that Paul in 3:24-26 is quoting a portion of early Christian confessional material, and (2) that he believed this portion of traditional material was well known to his addressees at Rome, we must recognize how intrinsic to this passage are its forensic terms and its cultic language. Further, we must realize that what Paul quotes in these verses probably represents certain basic tenets of Jewish Christianity generally and of the mother church at Jerusalem in particular — with the most likely corollary being that these Jewish Christian terms and expressions would have resonated favorably with Paul's Christian addressees at Rome.

3:24a William Sanday and Arthur Headlam began their exegetical comments on the material of 3:24-26 with a discussion of the participle δικαιούμενοι, which is the first word of that subsection of material, as follows: "The construction and connexion of this word are difficult."[100] They then listed four ways in which this first-person plural present passive participle was understood by the "leading scholars" of their day; they evaluated three ways and gave their own preference as the fourth:[101]

1. Understanding δικαιούμενοι to "mark a detail in, or assign a proof of, the condition described by ὑστεροῦνται [i.e., 'fall short of the glory of God']," thereby laying stress on δωρεὰν τῇ αὐτοῦ χάριτι ("freely by his grace") — and so reading 3:23b-24a: "men are far from God's glory, *because* the state of righteousness has to be given them; they do nothing for it." The evaluation of Sanday and Headlam of this view, however, is: "But this is rather far-fetched. No such proof or further description of ὑστεροῦνται is needed."

2. Viewing ὑστεροῦνται ("they fall short") and δικαιούμενοι ("being justified") as coordinates that are connected in sense by the conjunction καί ("and"), which requires either changing the participle δικαιούμενοι to its verbal form δικαιοῦνται ("they are justified") or, perhaps, the verb ὑστεροῦνται to its participial form ὑστερούμενοι ("having fallen short") — and so reading 3:23-24a either "they fall short of the glory of God and are justified freely by his grace," or perhaps, "being justified and having

---

99. Cf. R. N. Longenecker, "The Foundational Conviction of New Testament Christology," 122-44.

100. Sanday and Headlam, *Romans*, 85.

101. *Ibid.*, 85-86 (the italics in the quotations that follow are theirs).

fallen short." But, as Sanday and Headlam have rightly observed, "this is dubious Greek."

3. Taking δικαιούμενοι not "with what precedes," but viewing it as beginning "a new clause," in which case we are presented with "an anacoluthon and must supply some such phrase as πῶς καυχώμεθα ("how we boast in" or "rejoice in") — and so reading 3:24 after the anacoluthon as exclaiming: "How we boast/rejoice in being justified freely by his grace." Sanday and Headlam pointed out: "But that would be harsh and a connecting particle seems wanted."

4. Understanding Paul's use of δικαιούμενοι in its nominative form as "suggested" by the nominative πάντες of 3:23, but really "in sense" to be referring to, and so associated with, the accusative τοὺς πιστεύοντας of 3:22. In this view, 3:22b and all of 3:23 should be understood as parenthetical in nature — and so 3:22a and 3:24a are to be read together as follows: "This righteousness of God is . . . to all who believe (εἰς πάντας τοὺς πιστεύοντας), who are being justified (δικαιούμενοι) freely by his grace." But while Sanday and Headlam judged this view "easier and more natural than any of these [other three] expedients seem to be," they also admitted that syntactically "such a construction would be irregular" — indeed, as we would insist, to view the accusative substantival participle τοὺς πιστεύοντας as the referent of the nominative participle δικαιούμενοι would certainly be highly irregular — though Sanday and Headlam go on to argue that "it may be questioned whether it is too irregular for St. Paul."

It is in one of these four ways that the form and function of this first-person plural present passive participle at the beginning of 3:24 continue to be understood by most interpreters today — at least by those who cannot accept, for whatever reason, the participle δικαιούμενοι as being the first word of a portion of early Christian traditional material quoted by Paul. We believe, however, that the theses (1) that Paul incorporated within 3:24-26 a portion of Christian confessional material, which he drew from the kerygma of the early Jewish Christian church, and (2) that the syntactical awkwardness of the participle δικαιούμενοι signals the beginning of this quoted material, however that participle was formed and functioned in its original context, have been sufficiently vindicated to merit acceptance.

This is, in the main, the proposal first put forward by Rudolf Bultmann in 1936, which he developed further in his *Theologie des Neuen Testaments* of 1948.[102] And that proposal has been argued in more detail by Ernst Käsemann, Klaus Wegenast, John Reumann, Georg Eichholz, and Ralph Martin.[103] Thus,

102. See the discussion under the heading "Early Christian Confessional Material in 3:24-26" in our section "Form/Structure/Setting" above.

103. Käsemann, "Zum Verständnis von Röm 3,24-26," 150-54; see also his *Romans* (ET 1980), 95-101; Wegenast, *Das Verständnis der Tradition bei Paulus* (1962); Reumann, "The Gospel of the

as Käsemann summarized this thesis with respect to 3:24-26 in his translated *Romans* commentary of 1980: "He [Paul] is building on a settled tradition. This may be seen especially in the abrupt change in sentence structure in v. 24."[104]

James Dunn has suggested that "the syntactical awkwardness of δικαιούμενοι" at the beginning of 3:24 may be "the result of Paul's adapting the beginning of a preformed formula to make it fit to his flow of thought; or, alternatively, of his adapting his own terminology to make the incorporation of the preformed formula possible"[105] — either of which may be possible. And Dunn has gone on to aptly argue with respect to the statement "he [God] presented Jesus Christ as a ἱλαστήριον διὰ πίστεως ἐν τῷ αὐτοῦ αἵματι (which may be variously translated as 'a sacrifice of atonement/propitiation/expiation through faith/faithfulness in/by his blood'"):

> The fact that Paul can put this forward as a bare assertion, without substantive supporting argument, confirms that the pre-Pauline formula expressed a fundamental element of the confession of the first Christian churches. As such the recipients of the letter would accept it without argument, as part of their shared faith.[106]

Further, Dunn has observed with respect to this pre-Pauline material as being part of "the shared faith" of Paul and his addressees: "Hence the unlikelihood of Paul's 'correcting' the earlier formula."[107]

It seems best, therefore, to understand this first-person plural present passive participle δικαιούμενοι as a circumstantial adverbial participle — which type of participle (1) expresses an attendant thought or circumstance, or an additional idea or fact; (2) is most adequately translated into English by the conjunction "and" (whether expressed or understood) followed by a finite construction; and so (3) should be understood here at the beginning of 3:24 as "and we are justified." It may reasonably be presumed that in its original confessional context, this present passive circumstantial adverbial participle followed another early Christian confessional statement. But that preceding statement was evidently not directly relevant to the points that Paul wanted to make in support of his developed thesis statement of 3:21-23. Thus since Paul did not include in his quotation that previous statement but simply incorporated the traditional material that began with the circumstantial adverbial participle δικαιούμενοι — and since he evidently believed his Christian addressees at Rome would recognize this quoted material as having been part of a more extensive portion of early Christian traditional material, and so did not feel the need to introduce it

---

Righteousness of God," 432-52; Eichholz, *Die Theologie des Paulus im Umriss,* 189-97; Martin, *Reconciliation,* 81-89.

104. Käsemann, *Romans,* 95.
105. Dunn, *Romans,* 1.164.
106. *Ibid.*
107. *Ibid.*

in any formal manner — there exists between 3:23 and 3:24 a syntactical break that results in an awkward transition from prose to quotation.

The verb δικαιόω ("justify," "vindicate," "declare righteous") appears three times earlier in Romans in Paul's extended negative polemic of 2:1–3:20 — in 2:13 ("not those who hear the law . . . but those who obey the law will 'be declared righteous'"); in 3:4, quoting Ps 51:4b ("so that you may 'be justified' when you speak and will prevail when you are judged"); and in 3:20 ("no one will 'be declared righteous' in his [God's] sight by works of the law"). However, this is the first time in the letter that Paul uses δικαιόω (and that in its first-person plural, nominative, present, passive, participial form) in a positive manner to refer to believers in Jesus as those "being justified" — though he will continue this positive usage later in Rom 3:26, 28, 30; 4:5; 5:1, 9; 8:30, 33.[108]

3:24b The accusative δωρεάν (from the nominative δωρεά, "gift" or "bounty") is used in the latter portion of this verse as an adverb to mean "as a gift," "without payment," "gratis," or "freely." The free nature of God's mercy and grace is emphasized in many ways throughout the NT.[109] The expression τῇ αὐτοῦ χάριτι ("by his grace") denotes the unmerited and unconditional character of God's redemptive action. Some interpreters who understand 3:24-26 (either whole or in part) as a portion of some early Christian tradition that is quoted by Paul have viewed "freely" and "by his grace" as Paul's own insertions into this earlier material. But Judaism also understood its covenantal relationship with God as having been brought about solely by God, who is merciful, gracious, and forgiving. And certainly Jewish Christians believed that God had acted redemptively on their behalf through the work of Christ Jesus in a manner that was "freely by his [God's] grace." One need not, therefore, restrict these expressions to Paul. For "freely" and "by God's grace" are emphases that appear in both the OT and the NT — and they have been carried on, at least to an extent, in all the various forms of both Judaism and Christianity.

3:24c The noun ἀπολύτρωσις ("redemption"), which is a relatively rare word in the NT, appears seven times in Paul's letters (in addition to here in 3:24, also in Rom 8:23; 1 Cor 1:30; Eph 1:7, 14; 4:30; Col 1:14), twice in Hebrews (9:15; 11:35), and once in Luke's Gospel (21:28). Ἀπολύτρωσις, however, is also to be associated with such cognate Greek expressions as λύτρον ("ransom," "price of release"; cf. Matt 20:28; Mark 10:45), ἀντίλυτρον ("ransom"; cf. 1 Tim 2:6), λυτροῦσθαι ("to set free by paying a ransom," "to redeem"; cf. Luke 24:21; Titus 2:14; 1 Pet 1:18), λύτρωσις ("ransoming," "releasing," "redemption"; cf. Luke 1:68; 2:38; Heb 9:12), and λυτρωτής (cf. Acts 7:35, "redeemer") — with the meaning of all these words stemming from the noun λύτρον, "ransom" or "price of release," and its verbal infinitive λύειν, "to loose," "set free," or "redeem."

In classical and koine Greek, as Benjamin Warfield long ago pointed out, the verb λύειν "has the general meaning of 'to loose,' which was applied and

---

108. Cf. also its appearance in 1 Cor 4:4; 6:11; Gal 2:16-17; 3:8, 24; and Titus 3:7.
109. Cf., e.g., Matt 10:8; 2 Cor 11:7; 2 Thess 3:8; Rev 21:6; 22:17.

extended in a great variety of ways," but "when applied to men, its common meaning is 'to loose, release, set free,' especially from bonds or prison, and so, generally from difficulty or danger."[110] In the LXX the noun λύτρον — together with many of its cognates, such as ἀντίλυτρον, λύτρωσις, λυτρωτής, λυτρωτός, ἀπολυτροῦν, ἀπολύτρωσις, and ἐκλύτρωσις — is used extensively as the translation for the Hebrew nouns כפר ("the price of a life," "ransom"), פדיון ("ransom"), and גאלה ("redemption"). In religious contexts, which, of course, abound in the Jewish (OT) Scriptures, these Hebrew and Greek words were used for (1) deliverance from bondage in Egypt,[111] (2) deliverance from Babylonian captivity,[112] (3) deliverance of a person from some present evil or from evil in general,[113] and (4) the redemption of God's people in the eschatological future.[114]

Ἀπολύτρωσις ("redemption") was a rather common "coin of the realm" in the Greco-Roman world used for "deliverance" from such civil calamities as slavery, imprisonment, and oppression of whatever sort. In the religious language of the Jews, however, it was also used as a *terminus technicus* for what God accomplished in his salvific work on behalf of his people and in speaking about their resultant relationship with God. It may, therefore, be presumed that Jewish Christians — as well as Christians of whatever ethnic background who had any understanding of the OT, and certainly Paul himself — understood ἀπολύτρωσις in the same forensic manner as did the Jews when speaking about God's salvation. The only change in their use of this term was that in this period of the "eschatological *now*" of salvation history,[115] God's redemption had been brought about ἐν Χριστῷ Ἰησοῦ ("by Christ Jesus"), that is, through the work of Christ Jesus. And this understanding of the term seems to have continued on among Christians during at least early patristic times — as attested by the following statement by Origen, writing about 250, regarding Paul's use of ἀπολύτρωσις in Rom 3:24:

> "Redemption" is the word used for what is given to enemies in order to ransom captives and restore them to their liberty. Therefore human beings were held in captivity by their enemies until the coming of the Son of God, who became for us not only the wisdom of God, and righteousness and sanctification [cf. 1 Cor 1:30], but also redemption. He gave himself as our redemption, that is, he surrendered himself to our enemies and poured out his blood on those who were thirsting for it. In this way redemption was obtained for believers.[116]

110. Warfield, "The New Testament Terminology of Redemption," 202.
111. Cf., e.g., Exod 6:6; Deut 7:8; 9:26; 13:5 (LXX 13:6); 15:15; Neh 1:10; Ps 77:15 (LXX 76:15).
112. Cf. Isa 43:14; 52:3; Jer 50:33-34 (LXX 27:33-34); passim.
113. Cf. 2 Sam 4:9; 1 Kgs 1:29; Pss 34:22 (LXX 33:22); 144:10 (LXX 143:10); passim.
114. Cf., e.g., Isa 41:14; 44:22-24; 51:11; 62:12; 63:9.
115. See "Exegetical Comments" above on 3:21.
116. Origen, *Ad Romanos, PG* 14.945.

Later, in Romans 8, Paul will highlight the expression ἐν Χριστῷ Ἰησοῦ in a way that reflects his own more personal, relational, and participationistic contextualized soteriology. This "in Christ" type of soteriology appears with increasing frequency throughout Paul's letters, from the earliest to the latest.[117] Here, however, the expression τῆς ἐν Χριστῷ Ἰησοῦ — which is conditioned by the article τῆς, and so should be understood as an adjectival phrase that functions to qualify the articular noun τῆς ἀπολυτρώσεως ("the redemption") — is used in the sense of source or agency, and therefore is best translated as "'the redemption' *that came by Christ Jesus.*"

3:25a The understanding and translation of 3:25a have varied considerably among scholars — witness, for example, the following three modern English translations: "Who was appointed by God to sacrifice his life so as to win reconciliation through faith" (JB); "God presented him as a sacrifice of atonement, through faith in his blood" (NIV); and "Whom God put forward as a sacrifice of atonement by his blood, effective through faith" (NRSV). In fact, as Kingsley Barrett has observed, "There is scarcely a word in this statement that could not give rise to long discussion."[118]

The interpretation of 3:25a has been considered particularly difficult, especially during the past century, because of uncertainties regarding the meaning of ἱλαστήριον. Should it be understood as (1) designating the "mercy seat," "place of atonement," or "atonement cover" in the Jewish sacrificial system; (2) having in mind the theological concepts of "propitiation" (of God) or "expiation" (of sin); or (3) connoting more generally the idea of "sacrifice" or "sacrifice of atonement"? In addition, the function and meaning of ἐν τῷ αὐτοῦ αἵματι ("in/by his blood") has often been questioned. Should it be viewed as (1) modifying Christ's "sacrifice of atonement" (NRSV), (2) modifying the believer's "faith" (NIV), or (3) an expression not intended to be read in any literal fashion, but rather, incorporated in some more oblique manner into the overall translation (JB)?

Most NT commentators understand this first half of 3:25 to highlight two principal features in the early proclamation of the Christian gospel: (1) the objective factor of what God has done in presenting Jesus as a "sacrifice of atonement" (ἱλαστήριον), which appears in the first part of the statement, and (2) the subjective factor of how people are to respond positively to God "by faith" (διὰ πίστεως), which appears in its second part — with the further phrase "in/by his blood" (ἐν τῷ αὐτοῦ αἵματι) understood as modifying either the first matter (Jesus' "sacrifice of atonement by his blood") or the second matter ("through faith in his blood"). Contextually, however, this statement of 3:25a is, we believe, far better understood as having only one purpose and function: to set out a more precise explanation of how one should understand the expression "through the redemption that came by Christ Jesus," which appears immediately prior in 3:24b and identifies Jesus as the source and/or agent of God's salvific action on

---

117. See "Exegetical Comments" below on the "in Christ Jesus" motif at 8:1.
118. Barrett, *Romans,* 77.

behalf of all people. For since the noun ἀπολύτρωσις ("redemption") was used quite broadly in antiquity, both in civil and religious contexts (see above), the qualifying phrase "that came by Christ Jesus" (τῆς ἐν Χριστῷ Ἰησοῦ) could be understood in a number of ways with respect to how Jesus brought about this redemption — and so required a more precise explication. Thus, as Kingsley Barrett notes (though attributing the wording of this explanation to Paul himself, rather than to some Jewish believer in Jesus who authored this confessional portion quoted by Paul): even after affirming that God's work of justification has been effected "through the redemption that is in Christ Jesus" (as stated in 3:24b), one "still has to explain how the death of Jesus was an act of redemption, capable of rectifying the relations between God and man."[119]

Our understanding regarding the purpose and function of this statement in 3:25a is fivefold: (1) that the statement was meant to offer a more precise and explicit explanation of the expression "through the redemption that came by Christ Jesus"; (2) that it does so in distinctly Jewish Christian religious terminology; (3) that its focus is on the one "whom God set forth," that is, on Christ Jesus; (4) that by reminding his Christian addressees at Rome of what they have previously confessed in this early Christian confessional portion, Paul is attempting to support his expanded thesis statement of 3:21-23; and (5) that Paul is doing so in a manner he believed would be convincing to his addressees. Thus in 3:25a there appear three rather distinctive Jewish Christian terms or phrases that function to define more precisely the nature of "the redemption" that God effected through the work of Christ: (1) the term ἱλαστήριον ("mercy seat," "place of atonement," "propitiation," "expiation," or "sacrifice of atonement"), (2) the phrase τῆς πίστεως (literally "the faithfulness"), and (3) the phrase ἐν τῷ αὐτοῦ αἵματι ("in/by his blood") — which expressions Paul evidently viewed as being generally supportive, if not also specifically affirming in at least one case (i.e., its use of πίστις with respect to Jesus), of the most important details in his developed thesis statement of 3:21-23.

EXCURSUS: THREE EXEGETICAL AND THEMATIC MATTERS IN ROM 3:25A THAT ARE OF PARTICULAR IMPORTANCE (THOUGH ALSO FREQUENTLY DISPUTED) AND THEREFORE DESERVING OF SPECIAL CONSIDERATION

A. *The Expression* ὃν προέθετο ὁ θεός *("Whom God Presented Publicly").* The third-person aorist indicative middle verb προέθετο (from προτίθημι, "set before," "offer"), which with its prefix προ and its middle form connotes "a public presentation" or "public display," speaks of God as having set forth the redemptive work of Jesus in a public manner.[120] Some have argued that προέθετο is used here in synonymous fashion with the

---

119. Barrett, *Romans,* 77.

120. So, e.g., F. Büchsel, "ἵλεως," *TDNT* 3.321; Zeller, "Sühne und Langmut," 57-58; Käsemann, *Romans,* 97.

third-person aorist indicative active verb προώρισεν ("he predestined"), which appears later in 8:29 and 30,[121] and thus should be understood as referring to God's predestination.[122] Other interpreters have suggested, based on the parallel of προέθετο with the third-person singular aorist indicative passive verb προεγράφη ("he was publicly portrayed") of Gal 3:1, "that προέθετο denotes the apostolic preaching which sets Jesus before the eyes of men."[123] And still others have viewed προέθετο as signifying God's "plan," "purpose," or "design," drawing parallels with the use of the same verb in Rom 1:13 (προεθέμην, "I planned") and Eph 1:9 (προέθετο, "he [God] purposed"), and so have translated these first words of 3:25a as "whom God purposed" or "designed."[124] Yet the presence in this verse of the term ἱλαστήριον ("sacrifice of atonement"), the expression διὰ τῆς πίστεως ("through his [Christ's] faithfulness"), and the phrase ἐν τῷ αὐτοῦ αἵματι ("in/by his blood") — all three of which will be discussed more fully below, with all three having distinct sacrificial connotations — indicates quite clearly that the cross of Christ is here primarily in view. So it seems best to understand προέθετο here in 3:25a not as referring to the divine plan of salvation, whether "predestined," "proclaimed," "planned," or "designed," but as having principally in mind the actual crucifixion of Jesus — comparable, indeed, to how Paul used the verb προγράφω ("publicly" or "clearly portray") in Gal 3:1, though not so much, as is the case with his use of προεγράφη in Gal 3:1, with an emphasis on "the apostolic preaching which sets Jesus before the eyes of men,"[125] but with a focus on Jesus' sacrificial death on the cross. Thus, as Douglas Moo has paraphrased this first line of 3:25a, expressly inserting the phrase "on the cross": "God 'displayed him publicly,' or 'set him forth as a sacrifice,' on the cross as a *hilasterion*."[126]

B. *The Noun ἱλαστήριον ("Sacrifice of Atonement").* The noun ἱλαστήριον has been the focus of considerable scholarly debate, particularly during the past century.[127] Grammatically, ἱλαστήριον is probably best understood as a substantive neuter noun that is derived from the adjective ἱλαστήριος[128] — not as (1) a masculine noun[129] nor (2) an adjective that modifies the relative pronoun ὅν ("whom") at the beginning of the verse.[130]

Throughout most of Christian history, ἱλαστήριον in 3:25a has been understood in terms of the "mercy seat" in "the Holy of Holies," which was the cover or lid of the ark of the covenant — "the place of atonement" on which the blood of the sin offerings was poured and where God's presence, grace, mercy, and forgiveness were supremely manifested. Of the twenty-seven uses of ἱλαστήριον in the LXX, twenty-one appear in Exodus, Leviticus, and Numbers[131] — translating the Hebrew noun כפרת ("mercy seat,"

---

121. Cf. also the nominative singular aorist active participle προορίσας in Eph 1:5 and the nominative plural aorist passive participle προορισθέντες in Eph 1:11.

122. Cf., e.g., Pluta, *Gottes Bundestreue,* 59-61.

123. Cf., e.g., Büchsel, "ἵλεως," 3.321.

124. Cf., e.g., Cranfield, *Romans,* 1.208-10; note NEB: "God designed him."

125. Quoting Büchsel as cited above in *TDNT* 3.321.

126. Moo, *Romans,* 231.

127. For histories of the debate, see Pluta, *Gottes Bundestreue,* 17ff., and Hultgren, *Paul's Gospel and Mission,* 47-72.

128. Cf. *ATRob,* 154; F. Büchsel, "ἱλαστήριον," *TDNT,* 3.319-20.

129. As viewed by such Latin Fathers as Ambrose, Ambrosiaster, Jerome, and Pelagius, and thus translated *propitiatorem* ("propitiator") in a number of Vulgate MSS.

130. As suggested by Sanday and Headlam, *Romans,* 88.

131. Cf. Exod 25:17-23 (LXX 25:16-21); 31:7; 35:12; 37:6-9 (LXX 38:5-8); Lev 16:2-15; and Num 7:89.

"atonement cover," or "place of atonement"), which derives from the verb כפר ("to cover over [sin]"). The other LXX uses translate the Hebrew noun עזרה in Ezek 43:14, 17 and 20, which refers to the altar in the Jerusalem temple where the blood of the sin offerings is put "on the four horns of the altar and on the four corners of the upper ledge and all around the rim" to effect purification of the altar and atonement for sin. It is, however, the sacrificial imagery and language of Exodus, Leviticus, and Numbers that is used in Heb 9:5 in speaking about the Holy of Holies of the wilderness tabernacle and the ark of the covenant within it, not that of the Jerusalem temple and its altar: "Above the ark were the cherubim of the Glory, overshadowing τὸ ἱλαστήριον (i.e., 'the mercy seat,' 'the atonement cover,' 'the place of atonement')."

The Greek Fathers Origen and Theodoret of Cyrrhus, writing commentaries on Romans in the mid–third century and the mid–fifth century, respectively, understood ἱλαστήριον in this way here in 3:25a — as stated most clearly by Theodoret:

> The mercy seat was gold-plated on top of the ark. On each side was the figure of a cherub. When the high priest approached it, the holy kindness of God was revealed.
>
> The apostle teaches us [in Rom 3:25a] that Christ is the true mercy seat, of which the one in the Old Testament was but a type. The name [i.e., "ἱλαστήριον"] applies to Christ in his humanity, not in his divinity. For as God, Christ responded to the expiation made at the mercy seat. It is as man, however, that he receives this label, just as elsewhere he is called a sheep, a lamb, sin, and a curse.
>
> Furthermore, the ancient mercy seat was bloodless because it was inanimate. It could only receive the drops of blood pouring from the sacrificial victims. But the Lord Christ is both God and the mercy seat, both the priest and the lamb, and he performed the work of our salvation by his blood, demanding only faith from us.[132]

The Latin Fathers also understood Rom 3:25a in this manner, working from one of the three translations of ἱλαστήριον in their Latin Bibles — that is, basing their views most often on the Latin *propitiatio,* but also on *propitiatorium* or *propitiator.*

All the Protestant commentators of Reformation times also understood the noun ἱλαστήριον here in 3:25a as signaling such a sacrificial context and as referring to Christ's death on the cross as prefigured by the "mercy seat" of the ark of the covenant — as, for example, such major reformers as Martin Luther and John Calvin, as well as the later Lutheran pietist Johann Bengel. And this understanding has been incorporated into many important commentaries on Romans produced during the twentieth century — for example, those by Karl Barth, Anders Nygren, C. Kingsley Barrett, Ulrich Wilckens, and Joseph A. Fitzmyer. Further, it continues to be ably defended by a number of significant biblical scholars of the past generation and to-day — most prominently by such scholars as Thomas W. Manson, Alfons Pluta, Peter Stuhlmacher, and Arland Hultgren.[133]

132. Theodoret, *Ad Romanos, PG* 82.83, 86.

133. T. W. Manson, "ΙΛΑΣΤΗΡΙΟΝ," 1-10; Pluta, *Gottes Bundestreue,* 62-70; P. Stuhlmacher, "Zur neueren Exegese von Rom 3:24-26," in *Jesus und Paulus,* ed. E. E. Ellis and E. Gräser (Göttingen: Vandenhoeck & Ruprecht, 1975), 320-30; Hultgren, *Paul's Gospel and Mission,* 47-72.

In the early twentieth century, however, Adolf Deissmann, based on his studies of OT usage (both MT and LXX), Philo's treatment, and Greek inscriptional evidence, argued that "it is not correct to take the LXX's equation of words [i.e., of ἱλαστήριον and כפרת] as being an equation of ideas."[134] Rather, Deissmann insisted, ἱλαστήριον as it appears in the LXX, Philo, and the ancient Greek inscriptions, and therefore also in Rom 3:25a (though Deissmann did not take into account the presence of τὸ ἱλαστήριον in Heb 9:5), should be understood as connoting more generally a "propitiatory sacrifice" or "means of propitiation."[135] Many NT interpreters during the first half of the twentieth century agreed with Deissmann, and so rejected a strictly cultic understanding of ἱλαστήριον in Rom 3:25a and sought to understand the term in this verse more broadly.[136]

In the early 1930s Charles H. Dodd went further, reacting strongly to the use of the noun "propitiation" as the translation of the noun ἱλαστήριον in Rom 3:25a — likewise to the uses of "to propitiate" for the verb ἱλάσκεσθαι (or ἐξιλάσκεσθαι) and of "propitiatory" for its "cognates, derivatives and synonyms" ἱλασμός, ἐξιλασμός, ἐξίλασις, and ἐξίλασμα in the LXX (as was done traditionally and continued by Deissmann).[137] With respect to the meaning of the ἱλαστήριον in the LXX vis-à-vis how it was used by pagan authors and how it appears on Greek inscriptions, Dodd argued:

> The Greek word *(hilasterion)* is derived from a verb which in pagan writers and inscriptions has two meanings: (a) "to placate" a man or a god; (b) "to expiate" a sin, i.e. to perform an act (such as the payment of a fine or the offering of a sacrifice) by which its guilt is annulled. The former meaning is overwhelmingly the more common. In the Septuagint, on the other hand, the meaning (a) [i.e., "to placate"] is practically unknown where God is the object, and the meaning (b) [i.e., "to expiate"] is found in scores of passages. Thus the biblical sense of the verb is "to perform an act whereby guilt or defilement is removed."[138]

And with respect to its use in Rom 3:25:

> In accordance with biblical usage, therefore, the substantive *(hilasterion)* would mean, not propitiation, but "a means by which guilt is annulled": if a man is the agent, the meaning would be "a means of expiation"; if God, "a means by which sin is forgiven." Biblical usage is determinative for Paul. The rendering propitiation is therefore misleading, for it suggests the placating of an angry God, and although this would be in accord with pagan usage, it is foreign to biblical usage. In the present passage it is God who puts forward the means whereby the guilt of sin is removed, by sending Christ. The sending of Christ, therefore is the divine method of forgiveness.[139]

---

134. Deissmann, *Bible Studies*, 127.

135. *Ibid.*, 129-30; note also the fuller context in pp. 124-35; see also *idem*, "ΙΛΑΣΤΗΡΙΟΣ und ΙΛΑΣΤΗΡΙΟΝ," 193-212.

136. Cf., e.g., J. Denney, *Romans* (1900), 2.611; Sanday and Headlam, *Romans* (5th ed. 1902), 87-88; Scott, *Christianity according to St. Paul*, 68; and Taylor, "Great Texts Reconsidered," 295-97.

137. Cf. C. H. Dodd, *Romans* (1932), 54-55; for Dodd's more extensive and detailed treatment, see *idem*, "Ἱλάσκεσθαι" (1931).

138. C. H. Dodd, *Romans*, 54.

139. *Ibid.*, 55.

Much can be said about each of the three positions referred to above: (1) the "traditional position," which is still very much alive in many quarters today, (2) the position of Adolf Deissmann, also still held by many, and (3) the position of C. H. Dodd, features of which need always to be taken into account. The literature is extensive, with the debate still quite lively. It can, however, be said with certainty that Dodd's negative argument — that the concepts of propitiating God and turning away his wrath are totally absent in the Bible — is largely erroneous.[140] Yet, whatever is said in the OT about God being propitiated and God's wrath turned away, it is never said with the nuance of "celestial bribery" but always in the sense of "a removal of the Divine wrath against sin by a process in which God's own holy will had the initiative."[141] Or, as Friedrich Büchsel has pointed out, ἱλαστήριον and the complex of terms associated with it (particularly ἵλεως, ἱλάσκομαι, and ἱλασμός) cannot be understood to mean " 'to propitiate,' as though God were an object. This is excluded by the fact that it is God who has made the ἱλαστήριον what it is."[142]

Just where we stand today with respect to the interpretation of ἱλαστήριον in Rom 3:25a remains somewhat confusing and a bit difficult to spell out with precision. A major question has to do with whether this neuter noun (1) is to be attributed directly to Paul himself or (2) should be understood as an expression embedded in the early Christian confessional material that he quotes. If the former, it can be pointed out that there is no other instance of ἱλαστήριον or its cognates in Romans — nor anywhere else in Paul's other NT letters. If the latter, however, such OT sacrificial symbolism and language are paralleled by numerous references to the worship of God's people in the Jewish tabernacle that appear throughout Heb 8–10, where Jesus is presented not only as the sacrificial offering but also as the officiating priest and place of atonement ("mercy seat") — and so may be attributed to the conceptual imagery and religious language prevalent among Jews and Jewish Christians of Paul's day and beyond.

Undoubtedly the symbolism of the Jewish sacrificial system continued to resonate in Jewish Christian hearts and minds. Nonetheless, even with such a background and among those who appreciated that background, the term ἱλαστήριον seems to have been used more broadly by Jewish believers in Jesus to refer to all that came about (1) διὰ τῆς πίστεως ("through the [i.e., Christ's] faithfulness") and (2) ἐν τῷ αὐτοῦ αἵματι ("by his [i.e., Christ's] blood"), which features are highlighted in the immediately following statements of 3:25b. So ἱλαστήριον here in 3:25a may be seen, in line with Adolf Deissmann's thesis, as being used in a manner not specifically restricted to analogies drawn between God's redemption through the work of Christ Jesus and God's redemption of his people through the sacrificial system set out in the religion of Israel. And therefore ἱλαστήριον here in 3:25a is probably best understood and translated as "sacrifice of atonement," which translation keeps the important sacrificial nuances of the term without highlighting the narrower cultic symbolism and language of the OT sacrificial system.[143]

---

140. Cf. esp. the rebuttals of Dodd on this matter by Büchsel and Herrmann, "ἵλεως, ἱλάσκομαι, ἱλασμός, ἱλαστήριον," 3.300-323, and by Morris, *The Apostolic Preaching of the Cross*, 136-56; see also Nicole, "C. H. Dodd and the Doctrine of Propitiation," 117-57; Hill, "The Interpretation of ἱλάσκεσθαι," 23-48; and Garnet, "Atonement Constructions in the Old Testament and the Qumran Scrolls," 131-63.

141. Quoting Morris, "The Use of ἱλάσκεσθαι etc. in Biblical Greek," 233.

142. Büchsel, "ἱλαστήριον," *TDNT*, 320.

143. So NIV; see also NRSV, where the noun "expiation" of the earlier RSV is displaced by the expression "sacrifice of atonement."

C. *The Prepositional Phrases* διὰ τῆς πίστεως *and* ἐν τῷ αὐτοῦ αἵματι (*"through His [Jesus'] Faithfulness, by His Blood"*). The two prepositional phrases διὰ τῆς πίστεως and ἐν τῷ αὐτοῦ αἵματι of 3:25b have been translated in a variety of ways; here are the translations of three of the most prominent English versions today:

1. "through faith in his blood" (NIV; as also KJV);
2. "by his blood, effective through faith" (NRSV; cf. RSV: "by his blood, to be received by faith"); and,
3. "so as to win reconciliation through faith" (JB; cf. Knox: "in virtue of faith, ransoming us with his blood").

All these translations understand the genitive πίστεως as referring to the "faith" of those who respond positively to God, who has "set forth [Christ Jesus] publicly as a sacrifice of atonement." Yet all the translators of these English versions, as well as most commentators, have had difficulty understanding (1) the article τῆς that appears after the preposition διά and before the noun πίστεως, which, being attested by P[40vid] and Codex Vaticanus (B 03), has strong textual support,[144] and (2) the phrase ἐν τῷ αὐτοῦ αἵματι ("in/by his blood") as the object of πίστις, since nowhere else in his letters does Paul use πίστις with the preposition ἐν or speak of having "faith in [or 'by'] Christ's blood." Translators and commentators, therefore, have usually (1) simply ignored the presence of the article τῆς in the expression τῆς πίστεως, and (2) interpreted ἐν τῷ αὐτοῦ αἵματι as modifying ἱλαστήριον and not πίστεως.

Further, many who have argued for traditional Christian material being quoted by Paul in 3:24-26 (wherever that material is viewed as beginning and ending) have suggested that the expression διὰ πίστεως here in 3:25 (which is usually treated without any consideration of the article) is one of possibly two, three, or even four insertions that Paul himself made in his editing of this traditional Christian material that he quotes in 3:24-26 (cf. also δωρεὰν τῇ αὐτοῦ χάριτι, "freely by his grace," in 3:24; ἐν τῷ νῦν καιρῷ, "at the present time," in 3:26a; and καὶ δικαιοῦντα τὸν ἐκ πίστεως Ἰησοῦ, "and the justifier of the one who believes in Jesus," in 3:26b). He added it to make the formulaic material that he quotes more in line with his message of salvation by faith (assuming, of course, that the message of "salvation by faith" was unique to Paul, being neither true of the Judaism of Paul's day nor prominent among Jewish believers in Jesus before Paul). Or, as Ernst Käsemann has said, giving voice to what a number of recent commentators today have assumed: the phrase διὰ πίστεως here in 3:25a is an instance of "Paul's reworking of the tradition" in the form of a "rough interpolation," which he interjected "in order to be able to relate salvation and faith to one another," and thus it "should be treated as a parenthesis."[145]

Believing Käsemann's "insertion theory" is "founded on suspicious grounds, misleading in its simplicity and ultimately unconvincing," Bruce Longenecker has quite appropriately raised the following three exegetical issues in opposition to the Bultmann-Käsemann thesis:[146]

1. "It needs to be asked why Paul would have inserted πίστις so awkwardly into the natural phrase ἱλαστήριον ἐν τῷ αὐτοῦ αἵματι. If Paul had intended to introduce

144. See "Textual Note" above on 3:25b.
145. Käsemann, *Romans,* 98.
146. B. W. Longenecker, "Πίστις in Romans 3.25," 479.

a reference to the believer's faith into the formula, would he have done it in such a clumsy manner? One would expect Paul to include a reference to the faith of the Christian in a way which would not interrupt the flow of the imagery describing Christ's death."

2. "It would seem problematic if πίστις described the faith of the Christian, for precisely the same reason as was suggested above: it would break apart the otherwise cohesive unit, ἱλαστήριον ἐν τῷ αὐτοῦ αἵματι."

3. "Similarly, it is difficult to think that πίστις should be thought of as God's own faithfulness. Such would disrupt the flow, ἱλαστήριον referring to Christ, πίστις referring to God, and ἐν τῷ αὐτοῦ αἵματι referring again to Christ."

Rather, based on "the flow of the imagery describing Christ's death," Bruce Longenecker argues that "the πίστις phrase in Rom 3:25 should be understood as an original part of the quoted formula."[147]

Spelling out his thesis, Bruce Longenecker concludes his brief article by setting out the following three significant exegetical affirmations with respect to the expression διὰ τῆς πίστεως in 3:25a:[148]

1. "Πίστις, being original to the formula, describes a characteristic of Jesus, all three terms of Rom 3:25a (ἱλαστήριον, πίστις, αἵμα) being descriptive of Jesus' death on the cross."

2. "When πίστις is identified as Jesus' own . . . the formula stands as a coherent unit, without disruption from Paul."

3. "Rom 3:25a should read something like: 'whom God put forward as an atoning sacrifice, through (Jesus') faithfulness by means of his blood.'"

Further, his comment on the purpose of Paul's quotation of this Christian traditional material in 3:24-26 — with, in particular, its use of διὰ τῆς πίστεως here in 3:25a — is both highly defensible and particularly noteworthy, and so to be applauded and reproduced here:

> Paul seems to have incorporated the early Christian formula into his letter, knowing it to speak not only of the righteousness of God, to which Paul refers in 3:21-2, but also of the faithfulness of Christ. It becomes clear from this that Paul's own πίστις Ἰησοῦ Χριστοῦ formulation in Rom 3:22 and the πίστις Ἰησοῦ formulation in Rom 3:26 both include the subjective sense.[149]

And this understanding is incorporated by Charles Talbert in his Romans commentary of 2002, where he translates διὰ τῆς πίστεως in 3:25 as "through his/Jesus' faithfulness"[150] and ἐκ πίστεως Ἰησοῦ in 3:26 as "out of the faithfulness of Jesus."[151]

The second prepositional phrase, ἐν τῷ αὐτοῦ αἵματι, which immediately follows the first (i.e., διὰ τῆς πίστεως), should also be viewed (1) as instrumental in function (not

147. B. W. Longenecker, "Πίστις in Romans 3.25," 479.
148. *Ibid.*
149. *Ibid.;* cf. also *idem, The Triumph of Abraham's God,* 98-103.
150. Talbert, *Romans,* 107, 110.
151. *Ibid.,* 108.

locative) and (2) as modifying the noun ἱλαστήριον (not πίστεως), and so translated "by his [Christ's] blood" and understood as a synonym for "by his [Christ's] death on the cross." That is how the expression is used by Paul in Rom 5:9, where ἐν τῷ αἵματι αὐτοῦ ("by his blood") is paralleled by διὰ τοῦ θανάτου τοῦ υἱοῦ αὐτοῦ ("through the death of his [God's] Son") in 5:10 — likewise, how it appears elsewhere in his letters.[152] Two corollary matters are as follows: (1) in Lev 17:11 (LXX) the verbal forms ἐξιλάσκεσθαι ("to make an atonement") and ἐξιλάσεται ("it shall make an atonement"), which represent cognates of the noun ἱλαστήριον ("sacrifice of atonement"), are directly associated with αἷμα ("blood"), since "the life of all flesh is in its blood,"[153] and (2) this association of the phrase ἐν τῷ αἵματι αὐτοῦ ("by his [Christ's] blood") with Jesus' sacrificial death on the cross, as well as its instrumental use, not only appears in the passion narratives of the Synoptic Gospels[154] and Luke's report of Paul's farewell words to the Ephesian elders at Miletus,[155] but is particularly prominent in various NT homilies, tractates, and letters that were not only written by Jewish Christian leaders but also directed to Jewish Christian addressees.[156]

These two prepositional statements of 3:25a that modify in an instrumental manner the expression "sacrifice of atonement" (ἱλαστήριον) of Christ Jesus — that is, "through his (Jesus') faithfulness" (διὰ τῆς πίστεως) and "by his (Jesus') blood" (ἐν τῷ αὐτοῦ αἵματι) — are probably best understood as paralleling the central affirmation of the early Christian hymn quoted by Paul in Phil 2:6-11, which declares that in his humanity Jesus humbled himself "by becoming obedient [to God]" (γενόμενος ὑπήκοος) "to the extent of death" (μέχρι θανάτου). In all probability, therefore, (1) the expression "his [Jesus'] faithfulness" (τῆς πίστεως) here in 3:25a should be viewed as equivalent to Christ being "obedient" (ὑπήκοος) in Phil 2:8, and (2) the phrase "by his [Jesus'] blood" (ἐν τῷ αὐτοῦ αἵματι) in 3:25a as equivalent to "death" (θανάτου) in Phil 2:8,[157] which in connection with the latter statement Paul goes on immediately to exclaim "even death on a cross!" (θανάτου δὲ σταυροῦ).

B. The Rationale for What Is Affirmed (3:25b-26)

The rationale for what has just been affirmed in 3:24-25a is structured in terms of two purpose clauses in 3:25b and 3:26a, which are then followed by a further purpose clause in 3:26b. The argument first builds on a biblical understanding of "God's righteousness" (ἡ δικαιοσύνη αὐτοῦ) — with that expression being used here primarily in an *attributive sense* to mean that God is "just" (δίκαιον), but also used to connote in a communicative sense that God is "the One who justifies" (δικαιοῦντα). And it comes to a climactic conclusion in a distinctly

---

152. Cf. 1 Cor 10:16, though in a locative manner in 11:25; also Eph 2:13, though with the substitution of the preposition διὰ in Eph 1:7 and Col 1:20.

153. Cf. also 4 Macc 6:29; 17:22.

154. Cf. Matt 26:28//Mark 14:24//Luke 22:20.

155. Cf. Acts 20:28.

156. Cf. Heb 9:12-14; 10:19, 29; 13:12, 20; 1 Pet 1:2, 19; 1 John 1:7; 5:6; Rev 1:5; 5:9; 7:14; 12:11.

157. Cf. Talbert, *Romans*, 110, who also parallels these passages, explicitly drawing attention to the equations in Paul's thought of Jesus' "faithfulness" as signifying his "obedience" and his "blood" as referring to his "death."

Christian emphasis on God, "the One who justifies," as justifying "the person who is based on the faithfulness of Jesus" (τὸν ἐκ πίστεως Ἰησοῦ).

3:25b The first purpose clause of 3:25b reads as follows: εἰς ἔνδειξιν τῆς δικαιοσύνης αὐτοῦ διὰ τὴν πάρεσιν τῶν προγεγονότων ἁμαρτημάτων ἐν τῇ ἀνοχῇ τοῦ θεοῦ (literally "unto the demonstration of his righteousness [or 'righteous justice'], because of the passing over [i.e., 'letting go unpunished'] of the previously committed sins in the forbearance [or 'clemency'] of God"). The use of the preposition εἰς with the accusative singular ἔνδειξιν may seem somewhat strange. A. T. Robertson, however, has aptly observed: "Sometimes indeed εἰς appears in an atmosphere where aim or purpose is manifestly the resultant idea," citing its use here in 3:25b as a prominent example[158] — though, as Robertson, being well aware of the various uses of εἰς in koine Greek, went on to say: "It remains a matter for the interpreter to decide."[159]

The noun ἔνδειξις ("sign," "proof," "demonstration") is a relatively rare word in the NT, appearing twice here in 3:25b-26a and only two times more, in Phil 1:28 ("a demonstration of salvation") and 2 Cor 8:24 ("the demonstration [or 'proof'] of your love"). Outside of the NT, ἔνδειξις also appears rather infrequently in the extant writings of Greek authors who were roughly contemporary with the writers of the NT, being found only occasionally in the works of Polybius, Philo, Josephus, and Plutarch.[160] Its verb, ἐνδείκνυμι ("show," "prove," "demonstrate"), is used somewhat more often in the NT,[161] and can be found a number of times in the LXX, some of the Jewish apocalyptic writings, Josephus, and various other Greek materials of the period.[162] So the verb ἐνδείκνυμι provides lexical support for an understanding of its noun ἔνδειξις in terms of "proof" or "demonstration."

The expression τῆς δικαιοσύνης αὐτοῦ, which appears here in 3:25b and then again in 3:26a, parallels the twofold use of δικαιοσύνης θεοῦ in 3:21-22. The exact form of the phrase in its two occurrences in 3:25b-26a, however, as compared with its two uses earlier in 3:21-22, is somewhat different. Two linguistic features are particularly obvious. The first is that the genitive form of the expression in both of its occurrences in 3:25b-26a is prefixed by the article τῆς ("the"), whereas it earlier appeared without the article in its two nominative uses in 3:21-22. But as A. T. Robertson has pointed out in discussing "the correlation of the article" in koine Greek: "If two substantives are united by the genitive, the article occurs with both or is absent from both."[163] The second is that the possessive pronoun αὐτοῦ ("his") appears in both references to δικαιοσύνης

158. *ATRob,* 594; see also in Paul's letters Rom 8:15; 11:36; 1 Cor 11:24; 2 Cor 2:12; Phil 1:11; cf. Matt 10:41; 26:28; Mark 1:4; Acts 2:38.

159. *ATRob,* 595.

160. Polybius, *History* 3.38.5; Philo, *De opificio mundi* 45 and 87; Josephus, *Antiquities* 19.133; Plutarch, *De Pericle* 31.1.

161. Cf. Rom 2:15; 9:17, 22; Eph 2:7; 1 Tim 1:16; 2 Tim 4:14; Titus 2:10; 3:2; Heb 6:10, 11.

162. Cf. *BAG, ad loc.*

163. *ATRob,* 780, citing remarks by W. F. Moulton.

in 3:25b-26a, whereas the possessive noun θεοῦ is used instead in connection with the two earlier references to the same term in 3:21-22. But this difference, like the former, is a purely stylistic matter. For the use by any writer of the noun θεός ("God") or the pronoun αὐτός ("his") with reference to God is always determined by the particular linguistic contexts of the respective passages.

Most interpreters who understand 3:24-26 as material composed by Paul himself, and not as a portion of Christian traditional material that he quotes, have assumed that the two uses of δικαιοσύνη here in 3:25b-26a carry the same nuance of meaning as does the same noun in 1:17a and its two further occurrences in 3:21b-22a — that is, as connoting in a *communicative sense* God's "gift of righteousness" given to those who respond to him "by faith."[164] Yet, as Charles Cranfield has commented:

> While there is an obvious neatness about ascribing to δικαιοσύνη in vv. 25 and 26 the same meaning as it had in vv. 21 and 22, the reference to God's being righteous in the last part of v. 26 would seem to tell strongly in favour of understanding δικαιοσύνη in these two verses as referring to God's own righteousness.[165]

While the *communicative sense* of δικαιοσύνη may also be understood as present in the reference to God as "the one who justifies" (δικαιοῦντα; literally "the justifier"), which appears in the final portion of 3:26b, the *attributive sense* seems more expressly to the fore in the two references to δικαιοσύνη in 3:25b-26a because of the explicit reference in this portion of material to God being "just" (δίκαιον). The use of δικαιοσύνη here in 3:25b-26a is, in fact, probably more like its use in 3:5, where the expression highlights the *attributive sense* of God's own "just nature" and "righteous justice." And here in 3:25b-26a, in line with that earlier understanding, we believe the translation of τῆς δικαιοσύνης αὐτοῦ as "his [God's] righteous justice" is even more valid.

The preposition διά with an accusative noun signals the idea of "because of," "by reason of," or "on account of."[166] Thus διά here introduces the first part of the passage's rationale for God having "publicly presented" Jesus as "a sacrifice of atonement," which was effected "through his [Jesus'] faithfulness, by his blood" (as affirmed in the first part of 3:25): "because God, in his divine forbearance, left unpunished the sins previously committed." Such a "forbearance" or "clemency" in "passing over" sins that were committed before the "redemption that is in Christ Jesus," which was effected through his "sacrifice of atonement,"

---

164. So, e.g., Lietzmann, *An die Römer* (1906), *ad loc.*; Althaus, *An die Römer* (1935), *ad loc.*; Schrenk, "δικαιοσύνη," *TDNT,* 2.205 (from his 1935 German article); Nygren, *Romans,* 160 (from his 1944 Danish commentary) — all of whom wrote prior to the development of the thesis that Paul is here quoting Christian traditional material. So also many commentators today, who often cite in support these earlier interpreters.

165. Cranfield, *Romans,* 1.211.

166. Cf. *ATRob,* 583.

is what is spoken of here in 3:25b-26a as "God's righteous justice." Implied in that divine forbearance, together with the sacrificial system that was provisionally instituted by God, was what God would do more fully and finally "through the [i.e., Jesus'] faithfulness, by his blood." In effect, God's judgment of "sins previously committed" awaited the future revelation of "the redemption that is in Christ Jesus." And God's nonjudgmental attitude toward "the sins previously committed" must be credited to his divine "forbearance" or "clemency" (i.e., ἐν τῇ ἀνοχῇ τοῦ θεοῦ), which he expressed toward not only his own people but also all the people of his creation as they awaited his full and final solution to humanity's sin through the person and work of Jesus, Israel's promised Messiah.

Luke reports that Paul gave a similar rationale during the course of his Gentile mission, when he denounced the idolatry of the Athenians in speaking to members of the city council at Athens: "In the past God overlooked (ὑπεριδὼν ὁ θεός) such ignorance (τῆς ἀγνοίας), but now (νῦν) he commands all people everywhere to repent" (Acts 17:30). It may be assumed, however, that this type of rationale was particularly prevalent among early Jewish believers in Jesus. For Jewish believers in Jesus would have been confronted at many times with the question of how God in the past dealt with the sins of people generally — and with, in particular, the sins of his own people, the Jews — before "the redemption that is in Christ Jesus," as referred to in Rom 3:24, and before Jesus' "sacrifice of atonement," as referred to in 3:25.

In the second century, Christians frequently used the "logos" portrayal of Christ in John 1:1 (i.e., ὁ λόγος, "the Word") to explain this vexing problem, arguing that the same divine λόγος who was incarnate in Jesus was also present in the pre-Christian worthies of antiquity. This latter portion of 3:25, however, suggests that the earliest Jewish believers in Jesus explained this problem of how God dealt with the sins of people in the past — both those of the vast majority of people in the non-Jewish world, and those of ancient Jewish worthies — in terms of God's "forbearance" or "clemency." They could, of course, point to the sacrificial system of the OT as having been ordained by God for the purpose of provisionally "covering over" the sins of God's own people before, and in anticipation of, the perfect and final sacrifice of Jesus on the cross. But they also, as may be inferred from this passage, spoke of God's "forbearance" or "clemency" (ἐν τῇ ἀνοχῇ τοῦ θεοῦ) in "letting go unpunished (or 'passing over') the sins previously committed" (διὰ τὴν πάρεσιν τῶν προγεγονότων ἁμαρτημάτων) as examples of God's "just" nature and his "righteous justice."

3:26a The second purpose clause of 3:26a reads πρὸς τὴν ἔνδειξιν τῆς δικαιοσύνης αὐτοῦ ἐν τῷ νῦν καιρῷ (literally "for the purpose of the demonstration of his righteous justice at the present time"). The preposition πρός with its corresponding noun in the accusative case suggests some type of movement "to" or "toward," and so connotes such ideas as "purpose," "destiny," or "result." Thus πρὸς τὴν ἔνδειξιν here is legitimately read as "for the purpose of demonstrating" or "in order to demonstrate." Likewise, when used in the sense of purpose, the preposition πρός in association with an accusative noun often suggests that what follows is to be understood as an "intensification" or "more definite conception" of what has just been said.[167] This meaning of purpose, together with the suggestion of intensification or more definite conception, seems to be present here in the phrase πρὸς τὴν ἔνδειξιν.

The noun ἔνδειξις is used here in 3:26a, as it was in 3:25b, to mean "demonstration" or "proof." And the expression τῆς δικαιοσύνης αὐτοῦ continues in this verse to be used, as in the previous verse, in an *attributive sense* to refer primarily to God's nature as being "just" and his actions as expressing his "righteous justice" — though the references that follow in this verse to "at the present time," "the one who justifies," and "the faithfulness of Jesus" seem to move what is being said from a basically *attributive sense* into an area of meaning that includes a *communicative sense* as well.

The expression ἐν τῷ νῦν καιρῷ ("at this present time") expresses the primary point, or what may be called the "more definite conception," of the second purpose clause in 3:26a. Its focus is not on any period of human calendrical time, but rather on the climactic "now" of God's redemptive program — that is, the focal point of divine salvation history. Paul had used the phrase νυνὶ δέ ("but now") at the beginning of his developed thesis statement of 3:21-23 to signal that the eschatological "now" of God's redemptive program has been inaugurated by the work of Christ and the ministry of the Holy Spirit.[168] Here, in the Christian confession material he quotes, Paul evidently sees in the expression ἐν τῷ νῦν καιρῷ support of his emphasis on the eschatological "now" with which he begins his developed thesis statement of 3:21-23.

3:26b The second purpose clause of 3:26 is completed with the words εἰς τὸ εἶναι αὐτὸν δίκαιον καὶ δικαιοῦντα (literally "so as to be just and the One who justifies"). The use of the preposition εἰς ("into," "in") with the articular infinitive τὸ εἶναι to denote purpose appears over 124 times in the LXX and some 72 times in the NT. It is used in this manner some 50 times in the Pauline corpus.[169] Here in 3:26b εἰς τὸ εἶναι draws to a close the rationale of 3:25b-26 with a statement regarding God's purpose in "publicly presenting" Jesus as "a sacrifice of atonement."

The syntax of what follows in this final portion of 3:26b, however, presents a number of difficulties for interpreters. In the first place, the intensive noun αὐτός ("self"), which in koine Greek functions by (1) laying emphasis on a person (masculine case) or thing (neuter case) already mentioned (i.e., here "God") and (2) setting off that person or thing from any other individual or thing (i.e., here "not anyone else"), is almost impossible to translate. Although it highlights the uniqueness of God, as opposed to any other so-called god or person with regard to one of his essential attributes (i.e., he is "just") and with respect to one of his important actions (i.e., he is "the One who justifies"), translators and com-

---

167. Cf. *ATRob,* 781.
168. See "Exegetical Comments" above on 3:21.
169. Cf. esp. Rom 7:4; 8:29; Eph 1:12; Phil 1:10; 1 Thess 3:5.

mentators have found it difficult to carry over such nuances, and so have simply inserted into their translations the obvious third-person singular pronoun "he" that can be drawn from the context. Likewise, the neuter singular noun δίκαιον ("upright," "just," "righteous"), which may be in its case either nominative or accusative, probably should be understood as a predicate nominative, and so to define the nature of its unique subject — that is, to declare that God is "just" in a manner that is true of no other "god" or person. Further, the masculine singular substantival participle δικαιοῦντα should probably be understood to function as a compound predicate adjective, thereby to offer a further statement regarding God's nature and his redemptive activity — that is, that he is "the One who justifies." As will be discussed in exegeting the final portion of the passage in 3:26c, the phrase τὸν ἐκ πίστεως Ἰησοῦ possesses its own set of difficulties.

Even the conjunction καί, which is amply supported in the textual tradition,[170] has been difficult for both ancient and modern commentators to understand. Does it function in this verse as a copulative, thereby saying that God is both "just" and "justifier," and therefore that these two attributes are not to be viewed as contradictory?[171] Or is it to be viewed as an intensive, ascensive, or concessive particle, thereby suggesting that God maintains his righteousness even while being the justifier of the wicked?[172] Or should it be interpreted in an instrumental fashion, thereby proclaiming that God maintains his righteousness by justifying people?[173] Or, perhaps, understood as explicative, thereby asserting that God justifies the wicked without polluting his justice *or* explaining how God is righteous because he justifies the wicked?[174]

Understanding εἰς τὸ εἶναι αὐτὸν δίκαιον καὶ δικαιοῦντα of 3:26b in the context of the discussion of God's "demonstration" (ἔνδειξιν) of "his righteous justice" (τῆς δικαιοσύνης αὐτοῦ) in 3:25b-26a, translating the intensive noun αὐτός ("self") as simply "he" or "God" (though recognizing the uniqueness of God's nature and actions), treating the conjunction καί as being copulative in function, and viewing the noun αὐτόν ("just") and the participle δικαιοῦντα ("justifier," "the One who justifies") as defining the nature and actions of God — it seems best, we believe, to translate these opening words of this third purpose statement of 3:25b-26 as follows: "God did this in order to demonstrate that he is both just and the One who justifies." While it may be impossible (at least without some type of rather cumbersome clause) to incorporate into any modern translation the nuances suggested by the intensive noun αὐτός, it still needs to be recognized that what is declared to be true of God in this portion of early Christian confessional material — that is, that he is both "just" and "the One who justifies" — cannot be said to be true of any other so-called god or person.

In providing a rationale for the affirmation of Christian belief that was

170. See "Textual Notes" above.
171. So most translators and commentators have insisted.
172. So, e.g., Blackman, "Romans 3:26b," 203-4.
173. So, e.g., Moo, *Romans*, 242.
174. So, e.g., D. A. Campbell, *Rhetoric of Righteousness in Romans 3.21-26*, 167-70.

given just prior in 3:24-25a, the essential points of this rationale of 3:25b-26 are the following:

1. That *in the past*, God's δικαιοσύνη (his "righteous justice") has been evidenced by his divine "forbearance" or "clemency" in "leaving unpunished the sins previously committed," which fact demonstrates that he is δίκαιον ("just"); and,

2. That *now* ("at this present time"; ἐν τῷ νῦν καιρῷ) God's δικαιοσύνη (here nuanced not just in an *attributive sense* to mean his "righteous justice" but also in a *communicative sense* to connote his "gift of righteousness") is expressed by his redemptive actions as δικαιοῦντα (i.e., "the One who justifies") — with the foci of this present message of "good news" being expressed in the phraseology that immediately follows in the final four words of 3:26, which speak of "the faithfulness of Jesus" (πίστεως Ἰησοῦ) and of the positive response of "the person based on the faithfulness of Jesus" (τὸν ἐκ πίστεως Ἰησοῦ).

3:26c It has often been argued, both by those who believe Paul wrote 3:24-26 himself and by those who think these verses contain a portion of earlier Christian traditional material quoted by Paul, that these final words of 3:26, καὶ δικαιοῦντα τὸν ἐκ πίστεως Ἰησοῦ (usually translated: "and the One who justifies the person who has faith in Jesus"), are uniquely Paul's own; this has also been frequently argued for such expressions in the passage as δικαιούμενοι ("being justified"), δωρεὰν τῇ αὐτοῦ χάριτι ("freely by his grace"), and διὰ τῆς πίστεως (traditionally translated "by faith").[175] While such affirmations were important to Paul, it cannot be said they were absent in the vocabulary of the earliest Jewish believers in Jesus (nor, to an extent, in the Judaism of Paul's day).

3:26 closes with the appearance of the single name "Jesus," which is well attested in the textual history of the verse.[176] Yet the name that Paul usually uses to designate his Lord differs quite consistently from the name used by many of the other writers of the NT — also, in particular, from the name that appears in the various portions of early Christian confessional materials that he quotes. This difference is obvious in comparing Paul's usage with that of the four Evangelists who authored the four canonical Gospels, who most commonly use the single name "Jesus" and usually with the article (i.e., ὁ Ἰησοῦς). In Hebrews the name "Jesus" appears ten times,[177] with the double name "Jesus Christ" appearing only three times.[178] More significant for our purposes here, however, is the name used in the early Christian confessional portions quoted by Paul in his letters. There the usual designation is simply "Jesus" — as, for example, in

175. See "Exegetical Comments" above on 3:24-25a.
176. See "Textual Notes" above.
177. Heb 2:9; 3:1; 4:14; 6:20; 7:22; 10:19; 12:2, 24; 13:12; 13:20.
178. Heb 10:10; 13:8, 21.

Phil 2:10 ("that at the name of *Jesus* every knee should bow, in heaven and on earth and under the earth"); 1 Thess 4:14a ("that '*Jesus* died and rose again'"); Rom 10:9 ("that if you confess with your mouth '*Jesus* is Lord'"); and 1 Cor 12:3 ("no one can say by the Spirit of God '*Jesus* is cursed,' and no one can say '*Jesus* is Lord' except by the Holy Spirit").[179]

In what Paul himself writes in his letters — apart from the early Christian confessional materials he quotes — the single name "Jesus" is rather consistently transposed into the name "Christ," "Christ Jesus," or "Jesus Christ." There are, of course, exceptions to this pattern. But most of them are found (1) in other early Christian traditional materials that he uses, such as the grace benedictions of Rom 16:20 ("The grace of our Lord Jesus be with you") and of 1 Cor 16:23 ("The grace of the Lord Jesus be with you"), as well as the doxology of 1 Thess 3:11 and 13 (where twice the reference is to "our Lord Jesus"); (2) in his comments on a confessional portion he has just quoted, using the same form of the name in his comments as appeared in the quoted material, as in 1 Thess 4:14b (in both cases simply "Jesus"); (3) in his references to Jesus' historical afflictions, death, and resurrection, using, as do the four canonical Gospels, the single name "Jesus," as in Rom 4:24; 2 Cor 4:10-11, 14; Gal 6:17; and 1 Thess 2:15; or (4) in setting out roughly parallel statements, with both "Jesus" and "Christ" (or "Jesus Christ") appearing in the parallelism as equivalent names, as in Rom 8:11, Eph 4:20-21, and 2 Thess 1:12. Only a handful of other possible exceptions can be found; most, if not all, of them appear in Paul's use of the expression "the Lord Jesus," as in Rom 14:14.[180]

The use of the single name "Jesus," therefore, while not scorned by Paul, is rather exceptional in what he himself writes (as distinguished from earlier confessional or traditional materials he quotes) when compared to his much more abundant use of the single name "Christ" or the compound names "Christ Jesus" and "Jesus Christ." Thus the use of the possessive genitive Ἰησοῦ as the final word in 3:24-26 suggests that the single name "Jesus" — as well as the prepositional phrase ἐκ τῆς πίστεως with which it is joined — should be understood as an essential part of the early Christian confessional material Paul is quoting here. It may, in fact, be reasonably assumed that the Jewish Christian writer (or writers) who first composed this early Christian confessional material actually intended these four final words of 3:26, τὸν ἐκ πίστεως Ἰησοῦ, to be understood as the climactic part of the rationale of 3:25b-26, which was given in support of the affirmation of basic Christian belief set out in 3:24-25a — and therefore to be understood as being of great importance for an understanding of early Christian belief and its rationale.

Our argument is (1) that διὰ τῆς πίστεως in 3:25a is best translated "through his [Jesus'] faithfulness," (2) that ἐκ πίστεως Ἰησοῦ here at the end of

179. Cf. also 1 Cor 11:23; 2 Cor 4:8-11, 14; 11:4; 1 Thess 1:10.
180. See also 1 Cor 5:4 (twice); 2 Cor 1:14; 11:31; Eph 1:15; Phil 2:19; Col 3:17; 1 Thess 4:1, 2; 2 Thess 1:7, 8; 2:8; and Phlm 5.

3:26 was meant to be in line with and to support that use of διὰ τῆς πίστεως in 3:25a, and (3) that Paul's purpose in quoting this portion of early Christian confessional material in 3:24-26, which includes both of these expressions in 3:25a and 3:26c, was to support his developed thesis statement of 3:21-23 — which has as a vitally important central feature the assertion that "the righteousness of God" (δικαιοσύνη θεοῦ), particularly in this time of the "eschatological now" (νυνὶ δέ) of salvation history, is "through the faithfulness of Jesus Christ" (διὰ πίστεως Ἰησοῦ Χριστοῦ). All this, if true (as we, of course, believe is the case), implies that these final four words τὸν ἐκ πίστεως Ἰησοῦ of 3:26 are best translated "the one who is based on the faithfulness of Jesus."[181]

Here in Romans — as Bruce Longenecker has specifically argued with respect to the phrase διὰ τῆς πίστεως in 3:25a, but has also cogently proposed for the entire portion of the early Christian traditional material that is quoted by Paul in 3:24-26 — there appears:

> a convergence of covenantal ideas, revolving around the covenant fidelity of God (δικαιοσύνη θεοῦ) in relation to the covenant fidelity of Jesus (πίστις Χριστοῦ). For Paul, the faithfulness of Christ is the basis through which covenant relationship with God is established. God's covenant of grace operates through Jesus to those who believe because Jesus embodied the kind of faithfulness which was pleasing to God, in contrast to the people of Israel who, according to Paul in Romans 2–3, had proven themselves to be anything but faithful.[182]

It may be that it was on the basis of this "convergence of covenantal ideas" in this portion of Christian confessional material in 3:24-26, which convergence of ideas was presumably widely known among Jewish believers in Jesus of the day (Paul included), that Paul came to explicate the theme of "the faithfulness of Christ" (πίστις Χηριστοῦ) as it appears in his developed thesis statement of 3:21-23[183] — and as Paul used that expression at an earlier time when writing his Galatian converts,[184] and then later twice more in writing converts at Philippi and Ephesus.[185] However that might be, we believe it proper to assert here (1) that Paul saw inherent in this Christian confessional portion of 3:24-26, and particularly in the material he quotes in 3:25a and 3:26c, what we today call the *Pistis Iesou Christou* theme — even though in the context in which he found it,

---

181. Cf. Talbert, *Romans,* 108: "the one who lives out of the faithfulness of Jesus"; see also NET: "the one who lives because of Jesus' faithfulness"; or as expressed earlier by K. Barth, *Romans,* 104: "him that is grounded upon the faithfulness which abides in Jesus."

182. B. W. Longenecker, "Πίστις in Romans 3.25," 480; *idem, The Triumph of Abraham's God,* 98-103.

183. As we have suggested in our "Exegetical Comments" above on διὰ πίστεως Ἰησοῦ Χριστοῦ in 3:22.

184. Cf. Gal 2:16 and 3:22; possibly also 3:26 as in P[46].

185. Cf. Phil 3:9 and Eph 3:12.

that theme may not have been spelled out as explicitly as he might have desired it and as he himself would express it,[186] and (2) that he used that theme as he found it in embryonic form in a portion of early Christian confessional material in support of his statement to the same effect in 3:22: "this righteousness of God is *through the faithfulness of Jesus Christ* (διὰ πίστεως Ἰησοῦ Χριστοῦ) and 'given to all those who believe' (εἰς πάντας τοὺς πιστεύοντας)."

III. The Developed Thesis Statement Elucidated (3:27-31)

The final portion of 3:21-31, that is, the material of 3:27-31, is structured in terms of two sets of rhetorical questions, first in 3:27a and then in 3:29a, with a further rhetorical question set out in 3:31a — with each of these questions, or sets of questions, followed by an emphatic response in 3:27a, 3:27b-28, 3:29b-30, and 3:31b. In asking these questions and giving his responses, Paul elucidates in a few concluding words his developed thesis statement of 3:21-23 — that is, he highlights, amplifies, and contextualizes for his Christian addressees at Rome what he has declared in 3:21-23 to be the central themes of the Christian gospel in this period of the eschatological "now" of salvation history. In so doing Paul also reaches back to the central issues that underlie his earlier presentations in 2:17–3:20 and interacts with certain important features of the early Christian confessional material he quoted in 3:24-26.

In this final paragraph of rhetorical questions and emphatic responses, Paul asserts: (1) that there is no room for boasting on the part of anyone, for God justifies people not by "the law of works" (νόμος ἔργων) but only by "the law of faith" (νόμος πίστεως) (3:27); (2) that it is an axiom of biblical religion, and particularly of the Christian gospel, that a person is justified "by faith" (πίστει) and "apart from works of the law" (χωρὶς ἔργων νόμου) (3:28); (3) that God treats Jews and Gentiles alike, for there is only one God and therefore he must be the God of both the Jews and the Gentiles (3:29-30a); and, further, (4) that since God brings people into a right relationship with himself only "through the law of faith" (διὰ νόμου πίστεως, as highlighted in 3:27b) and "by faith" (πίστει, as highlighted in 3:28), not only are Jews justified by God ἐκ πίστεως ("on the basis of the divine faithfulness") but also Gentiles are justified διὰ τῆς πίστεως ("through that same faithfulness") (3:30b). Ethnicity, therefore, is not a factor in God's justification or acceptance of people. Rather, God's righteousness is given, and his acceptance is accorded, to all who respond positively to him "on the basis of divine faithfulness" (as expressed uniquely by Jesus Christ) and "by faith" (as the only proper human response possible), whatever their ethnic heritage. Thus Paul concludes this elucidation of his developed thesis statement of 3:21-23 by insisting that this is the message that in its proclamation

186. See the "Biblical Theology" section below with regard to the nature and wording of Christian confessional materials quoted by Paul and other writers of the NT.

and reception truly fulfills God's law — that is, "we establish the law" (νόμον ἱστάνομεν), and therefore bring to completion God's ultimate purpose in his giving of the Mosaic law (3:31).

3:27 The postpositive particle οὖν ("therefore," "consequently," "then"), which appears here at the beginning of Paul's rhetorical questions and emphatic responses, reaches back (1) to all that he argued negatively in his denunciation of Jews in 2:17–3:20, (2) to all that he presented positively in his expanded thesis statement of 3:21-23, and (3) to certain features of the confessional material that he quoted in 3:24-26. Or, as Richard Thompson has more succinctly stated with respect to the function of the particle here: "Οὖν suggests that an interpreter must take the whole argument of 2,17 up to 3,26 into account when deciphering Rom 3,27."[187]

Thus the question ποῦ ἡ καύχησις; ("Where is boasting?") should be understood as recalling all the issues regarding "bragging" about the Mosaic law and "boasting" about one's relationship to God that underlie all of what Paul has written in 2:17–3:20.[188] Likewise, the following queries διὰ ποίου νόμου; τῶν ἔργων; ("By what kind of law? Of works?") echo those statements about the futility of observing the law and "works of the law" in order to gain righteousness that appear throughout 2:17–3:20.[189] Further, the assertion ἐξεκλείσθη ("it is eliminated") διὰ νόμου πίστεως ("by the law of faith!") reaches back to Paul's explicit bipartite affirmation that lies at the heart of his developed thesis statement of 3:21-23 — that is, that "the righteousness of God" is "through the faithfulness of Jesus Christ" (διὰ πίστεως Ἰησοῦ Χριστοῦ) and given "to everyone who believes" (εἰς πάντας τοὺς πιστεύοντας) in 3:22. And it also echoes two important statements in the Christian confessional material quoted by Paul in 3:24-26: (1) that God's presentation of Christ Jesus as a "sacrifice of atonement" was effected "through his [Jesus'] faithfulness" (διὰ τῆς πίστεως), as stated in 3:25b, and (2) that people "at this present time" (ἐν τῷ νῦν καιρῷ) in the course of salvation history are to respond positively to God "on the basis of the faithfulness of Jesus" (ἐκ πίστεως Ἰησοῦ), as expressed in 3:26b.

The verb καυχάομαι ("boast," "glory," "pride oneself in"), the neuter noun καύχημα ("boast"), and the feminine noun καύχησις ("boasting") were often used by Greek poets, dramatists, and philosophers in the bad sense of prideful self-glorification — that is, to connote trumpeting one's own renown — and so commonly appear in classical Greek writings in the contexts of denunciation and ridicule.[190] There are also in the Jewish (OT) Scriptures "many proverbs against self-glorying or boasting,"[191] with statements in the Psalms that speak of boasting as "not merely a casual fault" but as "the basic attitude of the foolish

---

187. R. W. Thompson, "Paul's Double Critique of Jewish Boasting," 521.

188. Recalling particularly Paul's use of the second-person singular, present, indicative verb καυχᾶσαι in 2:17 and 23.

189. As expressed particularly in the expression ἐξ ἔργων νόμου in 3:20.

190. Cf. R. Bultmann, "καυχάομαι, καύχημα, καύχησις," *TDNT* 3.645-46.

191. Cf., e.g., 1 Kgs 20:11; Prov 25:14; 27:1.

and ungodly man."¹⁹² But a number of OT passages give a place (1) for boasting in cases of "justifiable pride"¹⁹³ and (2) for "true boasting which consists in self-humbling before God."¹⁹⁴ It is this latter, bipolar, even somewhat "paradoxical" use of καυχάομαι, καύχημα, and καύχησις that appears in the letters of Paul, with this complex of expressions being used almost exclusively in his letters vis-à-vis all the rest of the NT authors.¹⁹⁵

Thus, while Paul uses καύχησις and its cognates in an unfavorable sense in Romans to mean an improper "boasting," "glorying," or "pride,"¹⁹⁶ he uses these same words elsewhere in his letters in a favorable sense to mean (1) a "justifiable pride,"¹⁹⁷ (2) a "self-humbling before God" that expresses joy, praise, and thanksgiving to God,¹⁹⁸ and (3) trust and confidence in Christ by both himself and those who are true followers of Christ.¹⁹⁹

In this first question of 3:27, "Where then is boasting?" Paul's use of the article ἡ ("the") with the noun καύχησις ("boasting") suggests that he had in mind his two previous uses of boasting in 2:17 and 23 — where in the context of 2:17-22 he denounces a perverse Jewish "boast in God" (καυχᾶσαι ἐν θεῷ) that does not obey God's instructions, and then in the context of 2:23-24 condemns a self-confident Jewish "boast in the law" (ἐν νόμῳ καυχᾶσαι) that dishonors and actually blasphemes God by breaking his law. And he immediately answers that question with the resounding one-word statement ἐξεκλείσθη: "It is excluded!" or "It is eliminated!"

The verb ἐκκλείω denotes the idea of "shutting out," "excluding," or "alienating" someone from something or from someone's company. That is how Paul used it earlier in Gal 4:17 when he said of the Judaizers who were troubling his converts: "Those who are zealous to win you over, but for no good, want to alienate (ἐκκλεῖσαι) you [from us], so that you might be zealous for them." His use here of this same verb in its third-person, singular, aorist, indicative, passive form ἐξεκλείσθη — and particularly his use of only this one word in his brief response — suggests that Paul's answer to any such self-glorification should be understood in terms of such a forceful statement as "It is entirely excluded!"; "It is eliminated once and for all!"; or "It is absolutely impossible!"

The two rhetorical questions that follow, "By what kind of law?" (διὰ ποίου νόμου;) and "Of works? (τῶν ἔργων;), first raise the question of what brings about this elimination of boasting and then ask whether the agency in-

192. Cf. Pss 52:1 (LXX 51:1); 75:4 (LXX 74:4); 94:3 (LXX 93:3).
193. Cf. Prov 16:31; 17:6.
194. Cf. Jer 9:23-24; Ps 34:2.
195. Appearing elsewhere in the NT only in Heb 3:6; Jas 1:9; 4:16.
196. As he did earlier in 1:30; 2:17, 23, as he does here in 3:27, and as he will do later in 11:8; cf. also Eph 2:9; 2 Tim 3:2.
197. 1 Cor 15:31; 2 Cor 1:14; 7:14 (twice); 8:24; 9:2-3 (twice); 10:7–12:10 (a number of times); Phil 1:26; and 1 Thess 2:19.
198. Cf. 1 Cor 1:31 (quoting Jer 9:24); 2 Cor 10:17 (also quoting Jer 9:24).
199. Cf. Phil 3:3: "we are the circumcision . . . who worship by the Spirit of God, who 'boast' in Christ Jesus, and who put no confidence in the flesh."

volved is the law "of works." There can be no doubt that in the contexts of (1) Paul's negative discussion in 2:17–3:20 of Jewish failures to keep the Mosaic law, (2) his positive presentation in 3:21-23 of God's gift of righteousness in this time of the eschatological "now" (νυνὶ δέ) as being "apart from the Mosaic law" (χωρὶς νόμου), and (3) his quotation of early Christian confessional material in 3:24-26, which concludes in 3:26 with a reference to God, "at this present time" (ἐν τῷ νῦν καιρῷ) in the course of salvation history, being "the One who justifies the person who is based on the faithfulness of Jesus" (δικαιοῦντα τὸν ἐκ πίστεως Ἰησοῦ) — and as he also evidences in his statement of 3:28, which immediately follows, where he sets out a sharp distinction between "faith" and "works of the law" — that Paul here in 3:27 is denying that the law of Moses, while it condemns all self-righteous boasting, has any power to effect its elimination.

Paul's answer to these two very brief questions is itself exceedingly brief: "Never!" "Rather, [it is eliminated] by the law of faith!" The adversative particle οὐχί is stronger than the simple negative οὐ ("no"), and so should be translated emphatically as "never." Likewise, the adversative particle ἀλλά is stronger than any adversative use of the conjunction δέ ("but"), and so is best translated "rather." The preposition διά is used to express the instrumental idea of "through" or "by"; the noun νόμος ("law," which is in the genitive case as governed by the preposition) connotes "principle" or "teaching"; and the noun πίστις ("faith," which appears here as a genitive of definition or description) signals the nature and quality of that primary biblical principle or teaching.

Paul's insistence that boasting of one's own attainments before God — which includes all forms of self-glorification and every sort of self-justifying pride — is eliminated "by the law of faith" (διὰ νόμου πίστεως) serves to summarize everything he has argued from his original thesis statement of 1:16 through to this extremely brief response here in 3:27. For it is the "law of faith" (νόμος πίστεως) that reigns supreme in biblical religion, and particularly so in the "good news" (εὐαγγέλιον) of the Christian proclamation — not any kind of "law of works" (νόμος τῶν ἔργων).

Further, it seems evident — as (1) suggested in his original thesis statement of 1:16-17 (particularly in the phrase ἐκ πίστεως εἰς πίστιν of 1:17), (2) developed in his expanded thesis statement of 3:21-23 (particularly in his joining of the two prepositional clauses διὰ πίστεως Ἰησοῦ Χριστοῦ and εἰς πάντας τοὺς πιστεύοντας in 3:22), and (3) supported by his quotation of early Christian confessional material in 3:24-26 (particularly by its use of the clause διὰ τῆς πίστεως in 3:25, as well as the appearance of ἐκ πίστεως Ἰησοῦ in 3:26) — that what Paul meant by "faith" (πίστις) in the phrase "the law of faith" (νόμος πίστεως) here in 3:27b should be understood to connote both "the faithfulness of Jesus" and "a positive response of trust and commitment on the part of people" (whether translating the Greek word πίστις or the Hebrew word אמונה). So in his speaking of πίστεως at the close of this verse, Paul should be understood as referring (admittedly, in a somewhat cryptic manner) to both (1) Jesus' own "faith" and "faithfulness," which he expressed to God throughout his life (i.e., his "active obedience") and in his death (i.e., his "passive obedience"), and (2) people's necessary response of "faith" and "trust," which is expressed to God through the work of Christ and the ministry of God's Spirit.

Paul's use of νόμος in the phrase "the law of faith" (νόμος πίστεως) here in 3:27b is probably best understood when compared to (1) his use of τὸν νόμον τοῦ Χριστοῦ in Gal 6:2, where he asks his Galatian converts not to give in to the Judaizers' insistence that they must observe the law of Moses in order to properly express their commitment to God's Messiah, Jesus "the Christ," but rather, that they should endeavor to fulfill "the law of Christ," and (2) his use of ἔννομος Χριστοῦ in 1 Cor 9:21, which may be translated "in-lawed to Christ" or "under Christ's law." In these two earlier uses of "law" Paul is not speaking of the Mosaic law nor of Jewish teaching as it was later codified in the Jewish Talmud; rather, he is speaking of the principles of the Christian gospel, which are based on the historical work and teachings of Jesus and have been explicated to his people through God's Holy Spirit. Likewise, Paul's use of "law" (νόμος) later in Rom 8:2, where he declares that "the law of the Spirit of life in Christ Jesus (ὁ νόμος τῆς πνεύματος τῆς ζωῆς ἐν Χριστῷ Ἰησοῦ) has set us free from the law of sin and death," does not speak of the Mosaic law but refers to the work of the Holy Spirit and an essential principle or teaching of the Christian gospel.

3:28 Debate has been extensive as to whether 3:28 provides a reason for the content of 3:27 or gives a conclusion derived from what is said in that previous verse. Determination of this matter hinges largely on whether one accepts as original the postpositive conjunction γάρ ("for"), which is fairly well supported in the textual tradition, or the postpositive particle οὖν ("therefore," "consequently," "then"), which has less textual support.[200] In our view, γάρ is to be accepted as original, since (1) it is better attested externally in the textual tradition, (2) it eliminates the redundancy of two appearances of the postpositive particle οὖν in the passage, the first at the beginning of 3:27 and the second at the beginning of 3:28, and (3) it seems best understood contextually as providing a reason for the content of 3:27 rather than a conclusion derived from that previous verse.

The verb λογίζομαι ("I reckon," "consider," "credit," "maintain") appears frequently in the letters of Paul, as it does in other Greek authors of his day. Only here in 3:28, however, does λογίζομαι appear in Paul's letters in its first-person plural form λογιζόμεθα ("we reckon," "maintain"). Further, this first-person plural verb is placed as the first item in its sentence, which in an ancient Greek sentence often suggests it should be given some type of emphasis. Such observations have fairly often, particularly of late, encouraged commentators to assert that λογιζόμεθα ("we maintain"), rather than being simply an editorial plural, actually introduces a "conviction" that was "common to all believers"[201] — or, as expressed somewhat differently, functions to introduce "the common opinion among all the

---

200. See "Textual Notes" on 3:28.
201. So Cranfield, *Romans*, 1.220-21.

Christian communities"[202] or "the accepted Christian teaching on justification." Douglas Moo, however, is probably more accurate in saying: "The plural form of the verb may be editorial, or it may include both Paul and other Christian teachers, but it probably embraces both Paul and his readers."[203] Viewed in this fashion, that is, as meant to signal an understanding that Paul believed was common to both himself and his readers, this first-person plural form of the verb reflects again — as we argued earlier with regard to a number of other features in the course of his argument — something of (1) Paul's desire to gain rapport with his Christian addressees at Rome, and (2) his confidence that his addressees were in basic agreement with him on what he argued earlier and now states in summary form in the remainder of this verse: that "a person is justified by faith apart from 'works of the law'" (δικαιοῦσθαι πίστει ἄνθρωπον χωρὶς ἔργων νόμου).

The Christians at Rome may have been uncertain about a number of matters regarding their Christian faith — in particular, about how their newly formed Christian convictions should be expressed in their own particular situations.[204] They may also have been unable to articulate the Christian proclamation as well as Paul and some other Christian teachers could. But on (1) the impossibility of their own "works of the law" effecting acceptance by God and (2) the importance of "faith" for any type of proper relationship with God — which teachings were foundational in their Jewish Christian heritage, being rooted in the prophetic message of the OT (and expressed by at least some of the better Jewish rabbis of their day) — Paul was convinced that he and his Christian addressees at Rome were in essential agreement. He may have had to remind them of these matters and clarify implications (as he did throughout 2:17–3:20). But he was convinced that when these foundational features of biblical religion were spelled out and clarified (as he did throughout 2:17–3:20) — and particularly when they were placed in the context of what God has done redemptively through the work of Christ in this time of the eschatological "now" (as he did in his developed thesis statement in 3:21-23 and his quotation of early Christian confessional material in 3:24-26) — there could be no difference of opinion between himself and his Christian brothers and sisters at Rome.

Thus what Paul said with confidence in the closing statement of 3:20, that is, that "no one will be declared righteous in his [God's] sight by works of the law, for through the law is the consciousness of sin" (ἐξ ἔργων νόμου οὐ δικαιωθήσεται πᾶσα σὰρξ ἐνώπιον αὐτοῦ, διὰ γάρ νόμου ἐπίγνωσις ἁμαρτίας) — quoting in the first part of his statement the authoritative words of Ps 143:2 — he here in 3:28 reaffirms with even greater confidence in declaring that "a person is justified by faith apart from 'works of the law'" (δικαιοῦσθαι πίστει ἄνθρωπον χωρὶς ἔργων νόμου). For he was convinced that such an understanding was also that of his Christian addressees at Rome. And this sharing of such

---

202. So Dunn, *Romans*, 1.187.
203. Moo, *Romans*, 250 n. 24.
204. As seems evident in such passages as 7:1-6; 13:1-5; 13:6-7; and 14:1–15:13.

a basic understanding of biblical religion was particularly important in view of their shared Christian conviction (as expressed in their commonly accepted Christian confessional material quoted by Paul in 3:25a) that God "at this present time" in the course of salvation history has "presented publicly" Christ Jesus "as a sacrifice of atonement, through his [i.e., Jesus'] faithfulness, by his blood."

3:29-30 Throughout Israel's history there always existed a tension between (1) the affirmation that God is the Creator of all people, who has demarcated their respective boundaries and ordained their various situations, and (2) the conviction that God is the Redeemer of Israel, who has chosen the people of Israel to be his own people and acted frequently on their behalf. It is this division of humanity into Israelites (Jews) and non-Israelites (Gentiles) that underlies much of the Song of Moses in Deut 32:1-43, coming to expression explicitly in Deut 32:8-9: "When the Most High gave the nations their inheritance, when he divided all mankind, he set up boundaries for the peoples. . . . [But] the Lord's portion was his people, Jacob his allotted inheritance." It is this bifurcation of the world's population that is echoed by the author of Sirach, writing sometime during the first quarter of the second century B.C. (probably about 180-175 B.C.), in declaring: "For every nation he appointed a ruler, but Israel is the Lord's portion" (Sir 17:17). And such a distinction between Jews and Gentiles was continued and developed during the period of early Judaism, as witnessed, for example, in the rewriting of OT history in the *Book of Jubilees,* which was composed sometime during the mid–second century B.C. (probably between 161 and 140) — most explicitly in the following statements:

> He [God] chose Israel that they might be a people for himself. And he sanctified them and gathered them from all the sons of man, because there are many nations and many people, and so they all belong to him. But over all of them he caused spirits to rule so that they might lead them astray from following him. Over Israel, however, he did not cause any angel or spirit to rule, because he alone is their ruler and he will protect them and he will seek for them at the hand of his angels and at the hand of his spirits and at the hand of all of his authorities, so that he might guard them and bless them and they might be his and he might be theirs henceforth and forever. (*Jub* 15:30b-32)

It also appears in the Jewish Talmud and other rabbinic writings of the second through sixth centuries A.D. — as witnessed, for example, in the statement attributed to Simeon ben Yohai, who was a prominent fourth-generation Tannaitic rabbi of about 140-165:

> God spoke to the Israelites: "I am God over all who come into the world, but my name have I associated only with you. I have not called myself the God of the nations of the world, but the God of Israel."[205]

205. *Exod. Rab.* 29:4.

It is this old ethnic distinction between Jews and Gentiles that Paul spoke strongly against when writing earlier to his own converts in Galatia, insisting that because they were "sons and daughters of God" because of their "faith in Christ Jesus," they should not continue to hold on to such a bifurcation of humanity, since for those "in Christ Jesus . . . there is neither Jew nor Greek."[206] And it is this ethnic division that he sought to undermine in his argument throughout all the first part (i.e., 1:16–3:20) of this first major section (i.e., 1:16–4:25) of the body middle of Romans — particularly in 2:1-16, where, in speaking about the equality of all people, he declares that everyone (whether Jew or Gentile) is under the judgment of God, for "There is no favoritism with God" (quoting what appears to be a traditional aphorism in 2:11) — which argument and thesis he evidently believed his Christian addressees at Rome agreed with him about.

Thus here in 3:29-30 Paul reaches back to that old ethnic distinction between Jews and Gentiles, which had dominated Israel's thinking throughout its history — and which, worst of all, had been developed during the period of early Judaism in highly particularistic, discriminatory, and adversarial ways. In 3:29 he asks in rhetorical fashion the challenging questions: "Is God the God of the Jews only (Ἰουδαίων μόνον)?"; "Is he not also the God of the Gentiles (οὐχὶ καὶ ἐθνῶν)?" And he answers that challenge to think through the issues involved with a decidedly affirmative response: "Yes, also of the Gentiles (ναὶ καὶ ἐθνῶν)!" The affirmative particle ναί ("yes"), while frequently used in Greek writings of the day and elsewhere in the NT, does not appear often in Paul's letters. But where Paul does use it, he uses it — as he does here — with a decided emphasis on the affirmative.[207]

In 3:30 Paul sets out the basis or sufficient cause for what he affirmed previously in 3:29, that is, that "God is one" (εἷς ὁ θεός) — and therefore that God must be understood not only as the God of the Jews but also as the God of the Gentiles. A number of instances of so-called philosophic monotheism among the Greeks can be cited, which affirmed the oneness of a people's deity in *an elative sense* — that is, that a certain deity in question was "unique, singular, without any denial of the existence of other gods."[208] Such an understanding of monotheism (i.e., "the oneness of God") can be traced back to the Greek philosopher Xenophanes (c. 570-480 B.C.), who was quoted by Clement of Alexandria as teaching that there is "one God, greatest among gods and humans, who is in no way similar to mortals in either body or mind."[209] In this sense, as Nils Dahl has pointed out,

philosophical monotheism was tolerant and coexisted with religious pluralism, polytheism, and the worship of images. The one God of the philos-

206. Cf. Gal 3:26-29, where Paul brings together a traditional Christian "sayings" statement in 3:26, an early Christian confessional portion in 3:27-28, and his own contextualized conclusion in 3:29.

207. Cf. esp. 2 Cor 1:17-20; see also Phil 4:3; Phlm 20.

208. Cf. Dahl, "The One God of Jews and Gentiles," 179-82.

209. Clement of Alexandria, *Stromata* 5.109; cf. also 7.22.

ophers left room for the many gods of civil religion and of cult associations. The traditional names of the gods could either be taken to refer to the one God, who had many names, or they could be interpreted as mythopoetic designations of the many powers, who were the agents of his rule.[210]

Both Philo and Josephus frequently presented Jewish monotheism to their Greek and Roman readers in such an elative fashion.[211] But for the great majority of Jews in Paul's day and today, monotheism was understood in *an exclusive sense* — that is, that there is only one God, the God proclaimed in the Jewish (OT) Scriptures, which fact excludes the reality of all other so-called gods.

Paul's statement εἷς ὁ θεός ("God is one") in 3:30a repeats the first words of the Jewish confession of faith that brings together Deut 6:4-9, 11:13-21, and Num 15:37-41 — that is, the Shema, which begins with the words of Deut 6:4, "Hear, O Israel, the Lord our God, the Lord is one!" and encapsulates the essence of Jewish monotheism. It is a doctrinal tenet that the people of Israel tenaciously affirmed with confidence, devotion, and pride — but also a statement that they came to use as a catchword or phrase to distinguish themselves from all the other peoples of the world. Paul, however, while agreeing with all that Judaism affirmed positively about the exclusive oneness and uniqueness of God, saw in this basic creedal statement not only affirmations having to do with the salvation of Jews but also implications for the salvation of all humanity. For since there is only one God, it follows, he insisted, that this monotheistic God is the God of both Jews and Gentiles.

Paul introduced his rationale for that creedal statement by using the composite particle εἴπερ ("if indeed," "if after all," "since"), which is formed by bringing together the conditional particle εἰ ("if") and the enclitic particle περ (the shortened form of the preposition περί, "about" or "concerning"). Such a joining of the conditional εἰ to the shortened form περ functions by adding force to Paul's statement.[212] Yet Paul did not leave matters at that — that is, arguing for the Lordship of God over both Jews and Gentiles, and so the equality of Jews and Gentiles before God, simply on the basis of an exclusivistic understanding of Jewish and Christian monotheism. Rather, for Paul, such a revolutionary understanding of the equality of all people before God was based primarily on what God has done in this period of the eschatological "now" (3:21) and "at this present time" (3:26) in his presentation of Christ Jesus as "a sacrifice of atonement," which was effected "through his [i.e., Jesus'] faithfulness, by his blood" (3:25; cf. also 3:22 and 3:26). Thus just as he wrote earlier to his own converts in Gal 3:23-25, arguing that "before the coming of this faith (τὴν πίστιν; i.e., 'the Christian faith') we were held prisoners by the law" (3:23) but that now "with the coming of this faith (τῆς πίστεως; again, 'the Christian faith') we are no lon-

---

210. Dahl, "The One God of Jews and Gentiles," 180.
211. Cf., e.g., Josephus, *Contra Apion* 2.167-69.
212. As it does also in Rom 8:9, 17; 1 Cor 8:5; 15:15; and 2 Thess 1:6.

ger under the supervision of the law" (3:25), so here in Rom 3:30 Paul insists that God's one provision through the redemptive work of Christ Jesus for all people means that all people, whether Jews or Gentiles, are justified and accepted by God in the very same way — that is, ἐκ πίστεως with respect to Jews and διὰ τῆς πίστεως with respect to Gentiles — with the noun πίστις, which appears here in its genitive form πίστεως (as governed by the prepositions ἐκ and διά), being the essential factor in God's justification of both "the circumcised" (i.e., "the Jews") and "the uncircumcised" (i.e., "the Gentiles").

Debate has often arisen whether Paul's use of the third-person singular, future verb δικαιώσει ("he will justify") is to be understood as "a logical future, since justification already follows," and so a present reality,[213] or whether it "looks forward also to the final judgment, and thus has in mind principally a future reality."[214] But as we have argued with respect to the third-person plural, future, passive form of the verb δικαιωθήσονται ("they will be declared righteous"), which appeared earlier in 2:13, such a question asks too much of Paul's use of the future both here and there, though that question will later be to the fore in the hortatory section of 12:1–15:13.

Also to be observed in 3:30 is Paul's use of περιτομὴν ("the circumcised") and ἀκροβυστίαν ("the uncircumcised") as locutions for Jews and Gentiles respectively, which calls to mind his similar use of these expressions earlier in 2:26-27 and then later in 4:9.[215] These identity catchwords probably reflect the rather lewd epithets that were being hurled by Gentiles against Jews, calling them "the circumcised," and by Jews in retaliation against Gentiles, calling them "the uncircumcised."[216]

More important for an understanding of Paul's message in 3:29-30, however, are the prepositional phrases ἐκ πίστεως with respect to Jews and διὰ τῆς πίστεως with respect to Gentiles. Almost all commentators insist that Paul could hardly have meant by these two phrases any sort of distinction between Jews and Gentiles, for that would have invalidated his teaching regarding the equality of all people, both Jews and Gentiles, before God — which important thesis runs throughout all of what he wrote from 1:16 to 3:30a. Therefore whatever difference there might be between ἐκ πίστεως and διὰ τῆς πίστεως here in 3:30 has usually been considered merely stylistic. Further, the article τῆς in the second phrase has usually been understood to refer back to the first phrase, and so διὰ τῆς πίστεως should probably be translated "that same faith."

Contextually, however, we believe (1) that ἐκ πίστεως in 3:30 should be understood as having in mind Paul's use of that same expression in 1:17, where (as we have argued) it most likely refers to "the divine faithfulness," and (2) that διὰ τῆς πίστεως in this same verse has in mind his similar use of διὰ πίστεως

---

213. So, e.g., Käsemann, *Romans,* 104; also Cranfield, *Romans,* 1.222: it is "probably to be understood as simply logical."

214. So, e.g., Dunn, *Romans,* 1.189.

215. Cf. also Gal 2:7 and Eph 2:11.

216. Cf. Marcus, "The Circumcision and the Uncircumcision in Rome," 72-83.

Ἰησοῦ Χριστοῦ in 3:22 and of the same phrase διὰ τῆς πίστεως that he quotes in 3:25, where (as we have also argued) "the faithfulness of Jesus Christ [or 'of Jesus']" is in view. Thus we have translated ἐκ πίστεως here in 3:30 as God's justification of Jews "based on the divine faithfulness" (as in 1:17) and διὰ τῆς πίστεως in this same verse as his justification of non-Jews "through the faithfulness of Jesus Christ" (as in 3:22) or "through Jesus' faithfulness" (as in 3:25 and 26).

3:31a It may reasonably be postulated that one of the major criticisms against Paul, as charged by at least some of the Christians at Rome, was that in his evangelistic outreach to Gentiles he had actually set aside the Mosaic law — or had, in effect, seriously diminished its importance.[217] Such a criticism probably arose from what the Christians at Rome had heard from others about Paul's Gentile mission in the eastern regions of the Roman Empire. It may even have arisen from what they believed they knew, whether directly or indirectly, about the contents of his earlier letter to his own converts in the province of Galatia — particularly about what he wrote in Gal 3:1–6:18 in countering the Judaizers' claim that all true believers in Jesus, whatever their ethnicity, must necessarily express their commitment to Jesus in a Jewish "nomistic" lifestyle governed by "the law of Moses." However such a criticism might have arisen among the Christians at Rome, Paul seems to have been aware of it. And having proclaimed in his developed thesis statement of 3:21-23 that "the gift of God's righteousness" is, in this time of the eschatological "now" in God's program of salvation history, based on "the faithfulness of Jesus Christ" and given "to all those who believe" — and, further, having (1) supported that central emphasis in his thesis statement by the quotation of a portion of early Christian confessional material, which included a fuller Christian understanding of the important term πίστις, as he did in 3:24-26, and (2) elucidated it by speaking more directly about "the law of faith," "faith," and "divine faithfulness" as the bases for the justification of both Jews and Gentiles, as he did in 3:27-30 — the apostle evidently felt compelled here in 3:31 to deny that such a proclamation of the Christian message "nullifies" the Mosaic law. Rather, he insists, this understanding of πίστις as including both "divine faithfulness" and "human faith" actually "establishes" the law.

The postpositive particle οὖν ("therefore," "consequently," "then") draws to a close all that Paul has said negatively about Jewish boasting and reliance on the Mosaic law in 2:17–3:20. Further, it introduces an inference that Paul knows will be raised by his Christian addressees with regard to what he has affirmed

217. The thesis that Paul felt it necessary to defend himself in Romans against certain criticisms of his person and certain challenges to his preaching has been made by a number of scholars — principally by Peter Stuhlmacher with respect to the presence of such criticisms here in 3:31 (cf. our discussion in *Introducing Romans*, ch. 5, "Purpose"; also note in that discussion references to a number of other scholars who have drawn attention to the presence of similar criticisms and challenges elsewhere in Paul's letter, particularly in 1:16–4:25). And it is such a criticism that we, too, believe is reflected in Paul's rhetorical question and response here in 3:31.

in his thesis statement of 3:21-23 and the first two questions and answers of his elucidation in 3:27-30. The first word and the penultimate word of 3:31 are the noun νόμος ("law"), which (1) appears in both instances in its accusative form (νόμον) and (2) functions as the predicate object of both the verb καταργοῦμεν ("we nullify") in Paul's question and the predicate object of the verb ἱστάνομεν ("we establish") in his response. However, Paul has moved the accusative νόμον forward to the beginning of the sentence in his rhetorical question, thereby highlighting the central issue of the question posed — with that central issue being understood as continuing in the answer given.

What Paul means by νόμος ("law") here in 3:31 is undoubtedly the entire body of instruction that God gave his people Israel in "the law of Moses" (i.e., the Jewish Torah). This body of instruction, together with its later clarifications and codifications, was always associated in a "nomistic" fashion in the religion of Israel with righteousness and justice — without, at least in its original gift by God, any intention of legalistic observance. That is how Paul used the term earlier in this same passage in 3:21a,[218] as well as how he usually used it elsewhere in Romans (except in such phraseology as "the law of the Spirit of life in Christ Jesus" in 8:2) and his other letters (except in such expressions as "the law of Christ" in Gal 6:2 and being "in-lawed to Christ" or "under Christ's law" in 1 Cor 9:21). However, Paul makes no distinctions in 3:31 between any particular features of that law of Moses. So it cannot be claimed that he is speaking here only about "the ritual or ceremonial laws of the Mosaic code" or only about "the moral instructions of the OT" — nor only about "the commandments of the Decalogue" — as the instruction ("Torah" or "Law") of God in the OT is often bifurcated (or even trifurcated) by many Christians today. Rather, what Paul meant by νόμος in 3:31 must be understood as "the law of Moses" in its entirety.

The verb καταργέω connotes the ideas of "set aside," "make ineffective," or "nullify" something. Paul used it earlier when telling his Galatian converts that "the law (i.e., 'the Mosaic law') that was introduced 430 years later (i.e., after Abraham) does not nullify ('make ineffective,' 'set aside') the covenant previously established by God, and thus do away with the promise" (Gal 3:17). He used it also when telling his Corinthian converts that "God chose the lowly things of this world and the despised things, even the things that are not, to nullify ('make ineffective,' 'set aside') the things that are, so that no one might boast before him" (1 Cor 1:28-29a). More particularly, Paul used καταργέω when speaking about the unfaithfulness of some Jews vis-à-vis God's faithfulness in Rom 3:3-4 (which verses appear in a passage just prior to his developed thesis statement of 3:21-23): "What if some of them were unfaithful? Will their unfaithfulness nullify ('make ineffective,' 'set aside') the faithfulness of God?" (3:3) — with that rhetorical question immediately responded to by the emphatic negative expression μὴ γένοιτο, "Certainly not!" which is then followed by the quotation of a Jewish aphorism and a portion of Ps 51:4b (MT 51:6b; LXX

---

218. See "Exegetical Comments" above on Rom 3:21.

50:6b) in support and by way of explanation (Rom 3:4). And it is this same usage and pattern of argument that Paul uses here in asking: "Do we, then, nullify the law by this [message of] faith/faithfulness?" — which he answers by using that same emphatic negative assertion "Certainly not!" and by going on from that to insist: "Rather, we establish the law."

The contrasting Greek verbs καταργέω ("abolish," "wipe out," "set aside," "nullify") and ἱστάνω (from the earlier μι verb ἵστημι that connotes "establish," "confirm," "make/consider valid"), which both appear in 3:31 in their first-person plural, present, indicative, active forms as καταργοῦμεν (in the question posed: "Do we nullify?") and ἱστάνομεν (in the response given: "We establish!"), have often been seen as equivalents to the Hebrew verb בטל and Aramaic verb בטיל ("cease," "render futile," "neglect") vis-à-vis the Hebrew verb קום and Aramaic verb קים ("establish," "confirm," "fulfill"). Such a use of these contrasting verbs can be found in 4 Maccabees, a Jewish composition written in Greek by a Diaspora Jew sometime after Pompey's conquest of Judea (after 63 B.C.) and before the fall of Jerusalem (before A.D. 70). A sharp contrast is drawn in 4 Macc 5:25 and 33 between "those who believe the law to be established by God" (πιστεύοντες θεοῦ καθεστᾶναι τὸν νόμον, v. 25) and one who would "break the law of my country" (τὸν πάτριον καταλῦσαι νόμον, v. 33). And this same contrast appears in a Jewish maxim credited to Rabbi Jonathan (probably R. Jonathan b. Joseph, a third-generation Tannaitic rabbi of the mid–second century A.D., who had been a disciple of the venerable Rabbi Akiba) in *Pirke Abot* ("Sayings of the Fathers"), which is the earliest tractate of the Mishnah: "He who *fulfills* (מקים) the Law in poverty will in the end *fulfill* (לקימה) it in wealth; he who *neglects* (מבטל) the Law in wealth shall in the end *neglect* (לבטלה) it in poverty."[219]

The expression διὰ τῆς πίστεως is notoriously difficult to interpret. That is not only because of difficulties in understanding the meaning of the noun πίστεως ("faith" or "faithfulness"), but also because of difficulties in understanding the function of the article τῆς ("the") that modifies πίστεως. A Greek noun is sufficiently definite of itself, and so does not require an article to make it definite. Rather, an article in Greek is what may be called "a pointer" that serves to distinguish one individual from other individuals, one class or situation from other classes or situations, or one quality from other qualities. That is how we have understood the article τῆς in the expression διὰ τῆς πίστεως in 3:25a — that is, as having been viewed by Paul as an important feature in support of his developed thesis statement of 3:21-23, and so used by him to point back to his statement in 3:22 that the gift of "God's righteousness" is, in this time of the eschatological "now," "through the faithfulness of Jesus Christ" (διὰ πίστεως Ἰησοῦ Χριστοῦ). Likewise, that is how we viewed τῆς in this same phrase διὰ τῆς πίστεως in 3:30b, which by the use of the conjunction καί ("and") is clearly set out as coordinate with the immediately previous prepositional phrase ἐκ

---

219. *M. Abot* 4:9.

πίστεως (which we rendered "based on the divine faithfulness"), as pointing back to that previous phrase ἐκ πίστεως, and so have translated διὰ τῆς πίστεως in 3:30b as "through that same faithfulness" (understood as "the faithfulness that was expressed by Jesus Christ"). Further, we have translated the expression τὸν ἐκ πίστεως Ἰησοῦ, which appears as the concluding statement of the Christian confessional portion quoted by Paul, that is, at the end of 3:26b, as "the one who is based on the faithfulness of Jesus."

Therefore we propose that διὰ τῆς πίστεως here in 3:31a, with its identifying article τῆς, should be understood as having in mind (i.e., as "pointing back to") the immediately previous two sets of rhetorical questions and their responses in 3:27-30: the first, in 3:27-28, where Paul asserts the supremacy of "the law of faith" (νόμος πίστεως) and the necessity for "a person to be justified by faith (πίστει) apart from the works of the law (χωρὶς ἔργων νόμου)"; the second, in 3:29-30, where he speaks of the basis for God's justification of both Jews and Gentiles as being the same — that is, for Jews as being "based on the divine faithfulness [of Jesus]" and for Gentiles as being "through that same faithfulness." Therefore we believe it proper to translate (or, at least, to understand) the phrase διὰ τῆς πίστεως in the rhetorical question of 3:31 as "by this [message of] faith/faithfulness" (even though the inclusion of the phrase "message of" may seem somewhat intrusive and the rendering of πίστις may be considered rather cumbersome) — thereby understanding Paul's statements in 3:27-30, and then again his rhetorical question here in 3:31a, to include the two most prominent biblical nuances of the Hebrew אמונה and the Greek πίστις, that is, "human faith" (as in 3:27-28; cf. also 3:22b) and "divine faithfulness" (as in 3:30; cf. also 3:22a).

3:31b For a discussion of this emotionally charged and highly negative response μὴ γένοιτο ("Certainly not!"), which in the NT is used in an absolute sense almost exclusively by Paul (ten times in Romans, once in 1 Corinthians, and two or three times in Galatians), see our "Exegetical Comments" above on 3:4a.

3:31c The adversative particle ἀλλά in Greek always signals a clear difference with, as well as a sharp contrast to, the sentence or clause that precedes it. It is stronger than any adversative connotation in the conjunction δέ ("but"), stronger than the negative adverb οὐ ("no" or "not"), stronger than the negative conjunction οὐδε ("and not," "not"), and even stronger than the negative compound adverb οὐκέτι ("no more," "no longer," "no further"). It is entirely proper, therefore, to translate this adversative particle here as "rather" or "on the contrary."

In the final words of his presentation in 3:21-31, that is, in this extremely brief two-word statement νόμον ἱστάνομεν ("we establish the law"), Paul sets out the essence of his conviction as to how his "message of faith/faithfulness" relates to the Mosaic law. Undoubtedly he meant these two words to settle that question among his Christian addressees at Rome — at least for the present. Later, in 9:1–11:36 (in "The Christian Gospel vis-à-vis God's Promises to Israel,"

Section III of the body middle of the letter), the apostle will deal more fully with this matter. Here, however, he desires to state his understanding of relations clearly, concisely, and without any equivocation. And he evidently believes that his addressees will understand him.

Yet interpreters have often found it difficult to comprehend what Paul meant in saying νόμον ἱστάνομεν ("we establish the law"). Some have insisted that what he really meant is that "we cancel the Law," since "the moral principles which underlie the precepts of the Law are, in fact, fulfilled by those who rely on divine grace"[220] — even suggesting, as did C. H. Dodd, that because his "Jewish or Jewish-Christian readers" would have found such a forthright statement "distasteful," Paul "hesitates to draw the conclusion," though "it would have made things clearer if he had boldly done so."[221] Others have understood Paul as saying that the message of the gospel brings an end not to the law itself (i.e., the OT expression of God's will) but to the law as "a principle of achievement" (i.e., "legalism")[222] — for, as Ernst Käsemann has explicated such an understanding, "the OT will of God can be manifested only when the *nomos* comes to an end as a principle of achievement," and therefore "the law does not contradict the righteousness of faith [nor, evidently, does the righteousness of faith contradict the law]; it [the law] summons us to it [the righteousness of faith]."[223] And still other interpreters have viewed Paul's use of ἱστάνομεν in 3:31 as being similar to, if not actually synonymous with, the aorist infinitive πληρῶσαι ("to fulfill") used by Jesus in speaking of his mission vis-à-vis the Mosaic law, as reported later in Matt 5:17: "Do not think that I have come to abolish (καταλῦσαι) the Law or the Prophets; I have not come to abolish (καταλῦσαι) them but to fulfill (πληρῶσαι) them."[224]

One of the more common understandings of the phrase νόμον ἱστάνομεν ("we establish the law") among Christian commentators, which carries with it the idea of "fulfillment" (though without explicitly correlating the verbs ἱστάνω and πληρόω), has been expressed by William Sanday and Arthur Headlam, who (1) in their introductory comments to 3:31b speak of the law's "deeper principles" being "fulfilled,"[225] (2) in their paraphrase of νόμον ἱστάνομεν read "Law itself (speaking through the Pentateuch) lays down principles (Faith and Promise) which find their true fulfilment in Christianity,"[226] and (3) in their exegetical comments explicate Paul's meaning to be "All these things [i.e., 'the message of Faith and Promise'] are realized in Christianity."[227] Another understanding along these same lines of what Paul meant by νόμον ἱστάνομεν is expressed

220. C. H. Dodd, *Romans,* 63-64.
221. *Ibid.,* 63.
222. So, e.g., Käsemann, *Romans,* 105.
223. *Ibid.,* citing G. Bornkamm in support.
224. So, e.g., Michel, *An die Römer,* 112; see also *Str-Bil,* 1.241.
225. Sanday and Headlam, *Romans,* 94.
226. *Ibid.,* 95.
227. *Ibid.,* 96.

by Douglas Moo, who (1) in his paraphrase reads "faith in Christ provides for the full satisfaction of the demands of the law,"[228] and (2) in his final exegetical comment on the phrase says, "the Christian faith, far from shunting aside the demands of the law, provides (and for the first time!) the complete fulfillment of God's demand in his law."[229]

Whatever is said about Paul's insistence that his message of "faith" and "faithfulness" does not nullify the Mosaic law, but that it actually establishes the law of God (the "Torah" or "instruction of God"), must, we believe, take seriously into account the following two important observations — the first by David Daube; the second by Richard Hays:

1. "One nuance of *qiyyem* [i.e., the Aramaic verb, which underlies the Greek verbs πληρόω in Matt 5:17 and ἱστάνω here in 3:31b] ... is 'to uphold Scripture' in the technical sense of 'to show that the text is in agreement with your teaching.' This is a frequent application of the verb [in rabbinic teaching], based on the idea that the test of any teaching you propound is whether, proceeding from it, you can give full effect to, 'uphold,' every word of the Law."[230]

2. "Paul's proclamation presents the righteousness of God not as some unheard-of soteriological novelty but as the manifestation of a truth attested by Scripture from the first. When he says that his message confirms the Law, he refers not to the specific commandments of the Pentateuch but to the witness of Scripture, read as a *narrative* about God's gracious election of a people" — with that narrative coming to focus in "the Abraham story," which "becomes for Paul the crucial test case."[231]

Much more needs to be said about how Paul read his OT Scriptures with respect to God's promise and human faith. Paul will deal with that more fully in his example of Abraham in 4:1-24 — and we must discuss that topic more extensively in treating that passage. Suffice it here to say that when Paul wrote "we establish the law" in 3:31b, he evidently had in mind at least two things: (1) the upholding of Scripture in the sense of showing how a specific text is in agreement with his teaching, as he will do in reaching back to the statement of Gen 15:6 (as supported by Ps 32:1-2) in 4:1-24 (à la David Daube), and (2) the witness of the entire OT narrative, which comes to focus in the story of Abraham, the father of the Jewish nation, who was the man par excellence of both promise and faith (à la Richard Hays). However, when Paul wrote "we establish the law," he was focused on the twofold message of the Christian gospel: (1) that of the crucial significance of "the faithfulness of Jesus Christ," which is the prin-

---

228. Moo, *Romans*, 254.
229. *Ibid.*, 255.
230. Daube, *New Testament and Rabbinic Judaism*, 60-61.
231. Hays, *Echoes of Scripture*, 53-54 (italics his).

cipal objective factor in a distinctly Christian proclamation, and (2) that of the vital necessity of "human faith," which is the primary subjective factor in all biblical religion, both in the OT and in the NT — with the conjoining of these two important factors serving to bring to completion God's ultimate purpose in his giving of the Mosaic law.

BIBLICAL THEOLOGY

In Rom 3:21-31 Paul presents from a Christian perspective the most important portion of material in the first major section (1:16–4:25) of the body middle (1:16–15:13) of his letter to the Christians at Rome. For in the developed thesis statement of 3:21-23, which repeats and expands on his original thesis statement of 1:16-17 — together with the support of that original thesis statement and its repeated, developed form, which he draws from a portion of an early Christian confession in 3:24-26, *and* his elucidation of that developed thesis statement in 3:27-31 — Paul sets out in a positive manner the basic features of the Christian gospel in a Jewish Christian forensic fashion. He does so with the confidence that his addressees at Rome, because they had been extensively influenced by the theological conceptualizations and religious language of Jewish Christianity, would understand and appreciate what he presents and what he quotes in support.

It is this material that has served down through the centuries as the basis for much of Christian theology, and rightly so. And it is from this material that we may draw the basics of the early "forensic" proclamation of the Christian gospel. Later, in 5:1–8:39, Paul will set out for his Christian addressees at Rome his own, more "personal," "relational," and "participationistic" understanding of that same gospel, as he contextualized it to non-Jews in his Gentile mission. Still later, in 12:1–15:13, he will highlight the Christocentric ethical and social implications of that proclamation, both generally and with attention to the specific matters the Christians at Rome were facing. It is, however, from the material here in 3:21-31 that we can begin to formulate something of an elemental biblical theology for our understanding as Christians today — grouping such basic matters for pedagogical purposes under the following headings and summarizing them as follows:

A. *"The Righteousness of God" as the Basis for the Redemptive Program of God on Behalf of All People, with That Righteousness Understood as Both an Attribute of God and a Gift from God.* The expression δικαιοσύνη θεοῦ ("the righteousness of God") dominates all of what Paul writes in his developed thesis statement of 3:21-23 (cf. its two occurrences in vv. 21-22) — just as it did in his original thesis statement of 1:16-17 (cf. v. 17) and in his rebuke of Jewish unfaithfulness in 3:1-20 (cf. v. 5), just as it does in his quotation of early Christian confessional material in 3:24-26 (cf. its two appearances in vv. 25-26), and just as it will do in 10:3. Further, the expression appears in a distinctly communicative sense in 2 Cor 5:21 and Phil 3:9.

457

The importance of this theme of "the righteousness of God" in Romans, as well as in 2 Cor 5:21 and Phil 3:9, is enhanced by the facts (1) that it is a dominant theme in the canonical Jewish (OT) Scriptures, with both attributive and communicative nuances being present,[232] (2) that it appears as a central theme in the teaching of Jesus,[233] and (3) that it is also central in the teachings attributed to James and to Peter, who were two of the earliest leaders of the Jewish Christian mother church at Jerusalem.[234]

Christian theology, therefore, needs always to emphasize "the righteousness of God," both as an essential attribute of God's person and as the primary gift given by God to repentant sinners. For all else would be impossible if it were not for the fact that God is righteous and just. Further, all else would be hopeless if it were not for the facts that God (1) declares righteous all those who come to him in repentance and ask for his forgiveness, (2) makes righteous all those who in humility depend on him, and (3) expresses justice on behalf of his own and all those in need, particularly those who in their despair turn to him for help and strength.

B. *The Three Principal Foci of the Christian Gospel: "the Righteousness of God," "the Faithfulness of Jesus Christ," and "the Faith of a Person Who Believes."* Most interpreters of Paul have understood him as proclaiming "God's righteousness" as the primary basis for the provision and effecting of human redemption and "human faith" as the necessary positive response in the reception of God's gift of salvation. These two highly significant factors have sometimes been (sadly) bifurcated into an emphasis on either one or the other. During the past century, however, there has increasingly been brought to the fore the recognition of a further significant factor in the soteriology of Paul — that is, the matter regarding "the faithfulness of Jesus Christ," which Paul, in particular, saw as the climactic factor in God's redemptive program and the objective means by which salvation has been effected on behalf of all people "at this present time" of the eschatological "now."

It is particularly in 3:21-31 that these three principal foci of the Christian gospel are brought together: (1) *God's righteousness* as the primary basis for and source of salvation; (2) *Jesus' faithfulness,* both in his life (i.e., his "active obedience") and in his death (i.e., his "passive obedience"), as the objective means for human salvation; and (3) *people's faith* as the only proper response to the provision of God and the work of Christ. And it is these three foci of the Christian message that need always to be included in any truly Christian biblical theology and any truly Christian proclamation today.

C. *Paul's* Pistis Iesou Christou *Theme More Fully Explicated.* Particular note must be given Paul's reference to "the faithfulness of Jesus Christ" — which

---

232. Cf., e.g., Deut 33:21; Judg 5:11; 1 Sam 12:7; Pss 89:16 (LXX 88:16); 96:13 (LXX 95:13); 98:9 (LXX 97:9); 111:3 (LXX 110:3); 143:1, 11 (LXX 142:1, 11); Isa 45:8; 51:4-8; Dan 9:16; and Mic 6:5.
233. Cf. Matt 6:33//Luke 12:31.
234. Cf. Jas 1:20; 2 Pet 1:1.

we have argued (1) appears in his developed thesis statement at 3:22 (διὰ πίστεως Ἰησοῦ Χριστοῦ) and explicates more fully his earlier expression ἐκ πίστεως at 1:17; (2) is incorporated somewhat more obliquely in the early Christian confessional material that he quotes at 3:25 (διὰ τῆς πίστεως) and 3:26 (ἐκ πίστεως Ἰησοῦ); and (3) is found in the penultimate portion of his elucidation at 3:30 (ἐκ πίστεως with respect to Jews and διὰ τῆς πίστεως with respect to Gentiles). For this *Pistis Iesou Christou* theme, though well argued and supported by a number of contemporary NT scholars, has all too often been neglected (sometimes even denied) by commentators of the recent past and today. Yet the Greek expression πίστις Ἰησοῦ Χριστοῦ appears not only here in Rom 3:21-31, but also in Gal 2:16 (twice) and 3:22 (perhaps also in 3:26, as in P[46]), in Eph 3:12, and in Phil 3:9 — with the theme also found, both in Paul's letters and elsewhere in the NT, in treatments of "the obedience" of Jesus and "the Sonship" of Christ.[235]

Thomas Torrance has aptly observed with respect to Paul's statement in 2 Cor 1:20 ("For no matter how many promises God has made, they are 'Yes' in Christ; and so through him the 'Amen' is spoken by us to the glory of God"), which he explicitly applies to the subjects of "the faithfulness of Jesus Christ" and "the righteousness of God":

> Jesus Christ is thus not only the incarnation of the Divine *pistis*, He is the embodiment and actualization of man's *pistis* in covenant with God. He is not only the Righteousness of God, but the embodiment and actualization of our human righteousness before God.[236]

Likewise Markus Barth, discussing Paul's teaching on justification under the caption "Jesus Christ Comes, Demonstrating Faithfulness to God and Man," has commented:

> The Son is not only sent out by the Father and Judge to be a passive tool, as it were, of God. He also renders *obedience* to his commission by *coming* to fulfill his office. With his advent, "faith came." . . . Thus faith in God (or better, faithfulness to God) and love for men are realized in Jesus Christ at the same time in the same deed.[237]

James Denney had earlier captured something of this same understanding when, in a more devotional manner, he spoke three times of the central message of the Christian gospel in his classic *The Christian Doctrine of Reconciliation*, using the first two lines of the third stanza of Charles Wesley's hymn "Jesus, Lover of My

---

235. Cf. R. N. Longenecker, "The Foundational Conviction of New Testament Christology," 122-44.

236. Torrance, "One Aspect of the Biblical Conception of Faith," 113.

237. M. Barth, *Justification,* 38-39 (italics his); cf. also *idem,* "The Faith of the Messiah," 363-70.

Soul": "It is the voice of God, no less than that of the sinner, which says, 'Thou, O Christ, art all I want; more than all in Thee I find.' "[238]

It is in "the faithfulness of Jesus Christ," as Thomas Torrance has pointed out, that we find

> the supreme difference between the Old Testament and the New Testament. Like the Old Testament, the New Testament also lays emphasis upon the faithfulness of God, and requires from man a corresponding faithfulness. But in the gospel the steadfast faithfulness of God has achieved its end in righteousness and truth in Jesus Christ, for in Him it has been actualized as Truth, and is fulfilled in our midst.[239]

Or as Bruce Longenecker has aptly noted with respect to the covenantal relations that God established first in the OT and then in the NT:

> Where Israel failed to be Israel, Christ succeeded — that is, succeeded in being Israel; whereas Israel was expected to be holy just as their God is holy (e.g., Lev. 11.44), Paul finds that Jesus has met that expectation.[240]

D. *The Use of Forensic Soteriological Terms in the Early Church and by Paul.* There appear in 3:21-31 a number of soteriology terms that connote fairly evident judicial or forensic nuances — that is, terms that seem to have belonged to, were used in, or are suitable to a court of law and/or the religious cultus. Such terms are particularly noticeable in the Christian confessional material that Paul quotes in 3:24-26. But they also appear in Paul's developed thesis statement of 3:21-23 and in his elucidation of that statement in 3:27-31. Most obvious of these expressions (listing them generally in the order in which they appear in the passage) are the following:

1. The noun δικαιοσύνη ("righteousness") in 3:21a, 22a, 25b, and 26a;
2. The verb μαρτυρέω ("bear witness," "attest," "testify") in 3:21b;
3. The verb ὑστερέω ("fail," "miss," "fall short") in 3:23;
4. The verb δικαιόω ("justify," "acquit," "vindicate"), which appears in participial form in 3:24a and 26b and in verbal form in 3:28a and 30a;
5. The noun ἀπολύτρωσις ("redemption," "buying back") in 3:24b;
6. The verb προτίθημι ("set before," "display") in 3:25a;
7. The noun ἱλαστήριον ("propitiation," "satisfaction," "expiation," "sacrifice of atonement") in 3:25a;
8. The noun ἔνδειξις ("demonstration," "proof") in 3:25b and 26a;
9. The noun πάρεσις ("passing over," "letting go unpunished") in 3:25b;

---

238. Denney, *Christian Doctrine of Reconciliation,* 162, 235, 301.
239. Torrance, "One Aspect of the Biblical Conception of Faith," 113.
240. B. W. Longenecker, "Πίστις in Romans 3.25," 479.

10. The noun ἀνοχή ("forbearance," "clemency") in 3:26a;
11. The adjective δίκαιος ("upright," "righteous," "just") in 3:26b;
12. The verb καταργέω ("make ineffective," "nullify," "abolish") in 3:31a; and
13. The verb ἱστάνω, which developed from the earlier form ἵστημι ("establish," "confirm," "consider [or 'make'] valid"), in 3:31b.

Many of these terms may have been drawn from the jurisprudence of the Roman world. More likely, however, they were taken over by the early believers in Jesus from their Jewish background and used to illustrate the various ways in which God's salvation through the work of Christ can be understood. For Jewish Christians, in particular, these forensic terms carried highly significant religious nuances, and so were honored. Likewise, in Paul's heart and mind they undoubtedly reverberated with much the same honored status and meaning. Yet not everyone in the ancient world would have understood them alike. And Paul's letters suggest that in his Gentile mission when he proclaimed the Christian gospel (i.e., the message of "good news") — which in its earliest forms was most likely replete with judicial and forensic terminology — he found it necessary to contextualize these forensic expressions into somewhat different forms for differing audiences.

In his lectures entitled *The Religion of Jesus and the Faith of Paul,* Adolf Deissmann attempted to mark out a path that he believed Christians, both scholars and laypeople, should take in dealing with the various theological terms that appear in Paul's letters. When speaking of Paul's teaching on justification, Deissmann argued:

> According to my conception, the doctrine of justification is not the quintessence of Paulinism, but one witness among others to his experience of salvation. Justification is one ancient picture-word, alongside many others. Justification is one note, which, along with many others — redemption, adoption, etc. — is harmonised in the one chord that testifies to salvation.[241]

On the variety of soteriological terms used by Paul in his letters, Deissmann wrote:

> The impression of complexity has only arisen because we have not understood the similes as similes which were synonymous with one another, though to the mind of antiquity they would easily have been so understood. The single so-called Pauline ideas have been isolated by us, and then the attempt has been made to reconstruct a chronological order of salvation, an "ordo salutis," as our ancestors called it. As a matter of fact, the religion of Paul is something quite simple. It is communion with Christ.[242]

241. Deissmann, *The Religion of Jesus and the Faith of Paul,* 271.
242. *Ibid.,* 222-23.

Deissmann's statements, of course, must be seen in the context of his own agenda: the primacy of being "in Christ" or "Christ mysticism" in Pauline thought. That understanding of Paul cannot easily be set aside. In fact, we will develop that emphasis in our exegesis of Paul's statements in Rom 8, though not exactly in the way Deissmann did. Whatever might be thought of his overall thesis, Deissmann's proposal regarding the forensic soteriological expressions that are dominant in 3:21-31 is suggestive and helpful — and needs to be taken into account in any construction of a Christian biblical theology.

E. *The Dynamic and Developmental Nature of Biblical Theology, with an Emphasis on the Eschatological "Now" of Salvation History.* Many Christians have understood biblical theology in a somewhat static fashion, tracing out the course of God's redemptive actions throughout first the OT and then the NT with an emphasis on "sameness" — which, as they would insist, exists both *within* the materials of each of the testaments and *between* the presentations of the two testaments. This was the basic hermeneutical approach of the Alexandrian Church Fathers in their opposition to Marcion (fl. c. 140-160), who claimed that the Jewish (OT) Scriptures and the Christian (NT) Scriptures were diametrically opposed to one another — that is, the basic approach of Clement of Alexandria (c. 150-214) and Origen (185-254). And it has been carried on by what may be called "mainline" Roman Catholic, Protestant Reformed, and Puritan theologians, even though the doctrinal stances of their respective confessional positions are often quite opposed to each other.

On the other hand, many other Christians have understood biblical theology in a more dynamic manner, not only focusing on matters of continuity within and between the testaments, but also highlighting features that have to do with historical contingency and doctrinal development. This was the hermeneutical approach of the Antiochean Church Fathers — most notably of (1) John Chrysostom (c. 345-407), the illustrious preacher ("John the Golden Mouth") and statesman of Syrian Antioch, who also served as archbishop of Constantinople during 398-407; (2) Theodore of Mopsuestia (c. 350-429), who was born in Tarsus but raised in Antioch, was a classmate and close friend of Chrysostom, and later became bishop of the ecclesiastical see of Mopsuestia; and (3) Theodoret (c. 393-460), a native of Antioch and a disciple of Theodore, who later became the bishop of Cyrrhus in Syria. And it has been carried on by such interpreters as Martin Luther (at least "the younger Luther") and by many biblical scholars from the modern biblical theology movement today, though in various ways and sometimes to extremes.[243]

Paul's phrase νυνὶ δέ ("but now") at the beginning of 3:21 — which functions to move forward his discussion from denunciations of Jewish unfaithfulness in living "under the Mosaic law" in 2:17–3:20 to his presentation of "life based on the faithfulness of Jesus Christ" in 3:21-31 — expresses such a dynamic and developmental understanding of God's redemptive activity throughout the

---

243. Cf. R. N. Longenecker, "Three Ways of Understanding."

course of human history. For whereas the expression νυνὶ δέ can be understood in certain Pauline contexts to connote only a *logical contrast* (i.e., "but now here is the situation"), as in Rom 7:17, 1 Cor 12:18, and 13:13, Paul usually uses νυνὶ δέ when speaking about a *temporal contrast* that has been effected by God through the work of Christ and the ministry of the Holy Spirit, either in the course of salvation history or because of a believer's new Christian experience (i.e., "but now in the transition from one epoch or status to another"), as in Rom 6:22; 7:6; 15:23, 25; 2 Cor 8:22; Eph 2:13; and Phlm 9, 11.

Further, Paul's use of the two purpose statements in Rom 3:25b-26, which appear in the latter half of the early Christian confessional portion he quotes in 3:24-26, also supports such a temporal understanding of νυνὶ δέ in 3:21a — particularly in the contrast they set up between a former time of God's dealing "in his divine forbearance" with "previously committed sins" and how God justifies people "at this present time" (ἐν τῷ νῦν καιρῷ) "on the basis of the faithfulness of Jesus" (ἐκ πίστεως Ἰησοῦ). And what seem to be Paul's readings of "Jesus' faithfulness" in the expressions διὰ τῆς πιστεως of 3:25, ἐκ πίστεως of 3:26, and ἐκ πίστεως and διὰ τῆς πίστεως of 3:30, as we have interpreted them, do so as well.

Here in Paul's "but now" (νυνὶ δέ) at the beginning of 3:21, as well as in the early Christian confessional support supplied by the expression "at this present time" (ἐν τῷ νῦν καιρῷ) in 3:26, there is signaled an important distinction between God's redemptive activity in the religion of Israel, as depicted in the Jewish (OT) Scriptures, and his salvation as "it has [now] been revealed" (πεφανέρωται) through the work of Christ and the ministry of the Holy Spirit, as proclaimed in the Christian (NT) Scriptures. It is this dynamic character and developmental understanding of salvation history that are reflected in Paul's earlier statement in Gal 4:4-5: "When the fullness of time came, God sent his Son, born of a woman, born under the law, in order that he might redeem those under the law, so that we might receive the full rights of sonship"; and, further, that Paul spoke about in 2 Cor 6:2: "Behold, now (ἰδοὺ νῦν) is the time of God's favor; behold, now (ἰδοὺ νῦν) is the day of salvation!" And it is such dynamic and developmental emphases that need always to resound in any truly Christian biblical theology.[244]

F. Acceptance by God and God's Gift of Righteousness as "Now Apart from the Law." The Jewish religion has always insisted — whether during the times of (1) the "religion of Israel," as expressed in the OT, (2) "early Judaism," as appears in the nonconformist writings of the Jewish apocrypha and the Dead Sea Scrolls, (3) "rabbinic Judaism," as codified in the Talmud and other ancient rabbinic tractates, or (4) "Orthodox, Reform, and Conservative Judaism," as practiced today — that those who have been brought by God into a covenant relationship with him must necessarily express their response to God and his

244. For a broader and more general treatment of this subject, see R. N. Longenecker, "A Developmental Hermeneutic."

redemptive actions in terms of what may be called "nomism" (or in today's parlance, "covenantal nomism"), that is, an earnest and loving obedience to the instructions God has decreed through his servant Moses ("the Mosaic law" or "Torah"), as interpreted by the people's appointed leaders regarding how a person's life should be lived both personally and societally. The OT prophets and psalmists denounced "legalism," that is, the attempt to gain status before God and righteousness from God on the basis of what one could do by his or her own efforts — even on the basis of one's obedience to the Torah ("instruction," "law") of God as given through Moses. But they never wanted to loosen the responsive constraints of a true "nomism." Nor have any Jewish rabbis of antiquity, or any Jewish teachers of today, ever wanted to set aside the necessity of a nomistic observance of the Mosaic law.

Paul, however, understood that with God's final provision for humanity in the person and work of Jesus, Israel's Messiah and humanity's Lord, coupled with the more intensive ministry of the Holy Spirit, a new age of redemption has dawned — that is, that the promised eschatological "now" of salvation history was "at this time" in effect and being experienced. Thus he proclaimed (1) that even a nomistic type of faith, which had served its God-given purpose effectively in the days of the old covenant, had come to an end,[245] and (2) that a new, more personal type of response to God was now by God's ordination in effect — which type of response has aptly been called "new covenant piety."[246] This more personal new covenant piety is opposed, as always, to any form of "legalism." But it has also brought to an end the necessity of expressing one's appreciative response to God's love, mercy, grace, and forgiveness in terms of a prescribed "nomism" or "covenantal nomism" (though Paul himself seems to have had no problem with allowing Jewish believers in Jesus to continue to express their new lives "in Christ" in such a Jewish fashion). Thus, as Paul will write later in Rom 10:4: "Christ is the end of the law (τέλος νόμου) in its connection with righteousness (εἰς δικαιοσύνην) to all who believe (παντὶ τῷ πιστεύοντι)."[247]

Such an understanding of Paul's teaching has sometimes been viewed as somewhat radical, and therefore to be shunned. Yet it is ingrained in Paul's letter to his own Gentile converts in the Roman province of Galatia, coming to expression particularly in his theological statements of Gal 3:19–4:7 and his ethical exhortations of Gal 5:1–6:10.[248] And this understanding of God's gift of righteousness as being "now apart from the law" is a vitally important matter for both truly Christian thought and truly Christian living, and so needs to be incorporated into any truly Christian biblical theology.

G. *Christian Proclamation as Attested by the Law and the Prophets.* While God's gift of righteousness is "apart from the law" in both (1) a legalistic

---

245. Cf. R. N. Longenecker, "The End of Nomism," in *Paul, Apostle of Liberty,* 128-55; see also *idem, Galatians,* passim.

246. So Talbert, *Romans,* 101.

247. See "Exegetical Comments" below on 10:4.

248. On these passages, see R. N. Longenecker, *Galatians, ad loc.*

sense (as it has always been in God's redemptive actions on behalf of people) *and* (2) a nomistic sense (as proclaimed in the Christian gospel), that does not mean that "the law and the prophets" have ceased to function in a meaningful way for believers in Jesus. Rather, the instructions given in the Mosaic code, the devotion expressed in the hymns of the canonical Psalms, and the teachings, rebukes, and promises of Israel's prophets all have an important place in the consciousness of Christians today. For together they (1) set out God's standards of righteousness and justice, (2) judge sin and condemn sinners when these divinely mandated standards are ignored or violated, (3) point beyond themselves to "God's righteousness," both in an *attributive sense* and in a *communicative sense,* and (4) promise a time beyond that of the religion of Israel when God would bring about a more effective means of redemption (i.e., through the work of Jesus, the Messiah), a more universal message of salvation (i.e., as focused on the universal Lordship of Christ), and a more intensive experience of relationship with God (i.e., through the greater ministry of God's Holy Spirit).

Paul in his understanding of the law and the prophets did nothing that would in any way lay the foundations for, or even suggest, a Marcion type of interpretation of the OT Scriptures. Rather, while he gives clear evidence of not viewing the religion of Israel and faith in Jesus Christ as *the same,* Paul was always eager and ready to trace out *lines of continuity* between them — as he did earlier in his denunciations in 2:1–3:20, will do in the immediately following section in his illustration of Abraham in 4:1-20, and will continue to do extensively in relating the message of the Christian gospel to the hope of Israel in 9:1–11:36. And Christians today need also always to relate the Christian gospel to the instructions, judgments, devotional expressions, and promises given in the OT, for each of these, in its own way, attests to the Christian proclamation in these days of the eschatological "now" of salvation history.

H. *Not Ethnicity, but All People, regardless of Heritage, as the Subjects of God's Saving Grace.* In the first major section of Romans, 1:16–4:25, Paul began by declaring in 1:16 that "the gospel" (τὸ εὐαγγέλιον) is "the power of God for the salvation of everyone who believes, both for the Jew first and for the Gentile." This focus on the universality of God's saving grace is a vitally important feature of his thesis statement of 1:16-17. Paul repeats this universalistic emphasis in his developed version of that original thesis statement in 3:21-23, particularly in his insistence in 3:22 that "God's righteousness" is at this time of the eschatological "now" to be understood as a gift that is "given to all those who believe, for there is no distinction." Further, he speaks of that same universal emphasis in his elucidation of that developed thesis statement in 3:27-31, particularly in his declaration in 3:29-30 that both Jews and Gentiles are now in this final period of salvation history justified on the same basis. Ethnicity, therefore, is no longer a factor in God's dealing with people. Rather, based on the efficacious work of Christ, God's saving grace is now available to all, both Jews and Gentiles alike, and on the same basis for all.

"Paul is not suggesting by this," Bruce Longenecker has pointed out, "that

God had abandoned his covenant relationship with Israel; Paul argues against such an understanding especially in Romans 9–11."[249] It is, rather, to insist that ethnicity has no part in a truly Christian biblical theology. For just as Paul wrote earlier to his converts in Galatia that for those "in Christ Jesus" there is "no longer Jew or Greek, no longer slave or free, no longer male and female, for you are all one in Christ Jesus,"[250] so here in 3:21-31 he declares that relationship with God on the basis of "the faithfulness of Christ" negates all such former ethnic divisions with their accompanying prejudices, suspicions, and evil practices. And this is a vitally important matter for Christians today to espouse, both in theory and in practice.

I. *Not Works of the Law, but Faith in God through Christ.* Paul prefaced his developed thesis statement of 3:21-23 by a denunciation of "works of the law" in 3:20: "No one will be declared righteous in his [God's] sight on the basis of 'works of the law,' for through the law is the consciousness of sin." He began that expanded thesis statement with the words of 3:21: "But now apart from the law." He elucidated that same thesis statement with the inclusion of the affirmation of 3:28: "We maintain that a person is justified by faith apart from 'works of the law.'" And he will declare in 4:1-8 and throughout the rest of ch. 4 the dictum that the patriarch Abraham was not justified "by works" in obedience to the Mosaic law, but by "faith . . . apart from works."

All these statements of Paul are within the context of Jewish attempts to be accepted by God and declared righteous in his sight by one's obedience to the Mosaic law. Yet while his statements here all relate to this particular context of one's observance of the Mosaic law, it may assuredly be said that Paul was opposed to any type of "works" or "deeds," however good and in whatever form, that are done with the purpose of gaining status, acceptance, or righteousness from God — though he was not opposed to proper motives and helpful actions in the expression of God's gift of righteousness. It is such an understanding of "works" in the Christian life — an understanding that denies their validity as a means of gaining status before God (i.e., done in order to gain status and righteousness before God) but affirms their importance as expressions of gratitude to God (i.e., done because of the gift of righteousness from God) — that must also be included in every truly Christian biblical theology.

CONTEXTUALIZATION FOR TODAY

Romans is a highly significant letter, not only for a knowledge of doctrine (i.e., what it teaches) but also for an appreciation of how the Christian message was

---

249. B. W. Longenecker, "Πίστις in Romans 3.25," 480.
250. Gal 3:28, where Paul evidently quotes an early Christian confessional portion that speaks of the three traditional divisions between people who have been dramatically affected by the Christian gospel — though in this context he focuses only on the first.

understood and proclaimed among various groups of early believers in Jesus (i.e., how it contextualizes the "good news" of the Christian gospel). Most of the other NT writings (not only letters, but also Gospels, Acts, and the Apocalypse) reveal to us how various important apostolic figures contextualized the message of the Christian gospel to certain people in their own particular situations. Paul in his letter to the believers in Jesus at Rome does this as well — showing us (1) something of how the Christians at Rome (who were dominantly Gentile believers in Jesus, but who had come to Christ through the witness of traveling Jewish Christians, and so had been influenced by the theological concepts and religious language of Jewish Christianity) understood and expressed their Christian faith, as those matters are reflected in much of what Paul writes in 1:16–4:25 (as well as at many places in 9:1–11:36), and (2) how he clarified some of the basic Jewish Christian teachings and concerns that he shared with his addressees in his denunciations of 1:18–3:20, and then went on to sharpen certain basic Christian "forensic" language and commitments in his positive statements of 1:16-17; 3:21-23, 27-31; and 4:1-25. But Paul's letter to Rome also shows us — as will be seen in the more personal, relational, and participationistic message he sets out in 5:1–8:39, together with his more general Christocentric ethical exhortations in 12:1–15:13 — how he contextualized the Christian gospel in his own ministry to Gentiles who had little or no knowledge of the Jewish (OT) Scriptures and had not been influenced by either Judaism or Jewish Christianity.

Yet Paul's letter to Rome does even more than all of this. For Romans also gives insight into some of the central tenets of early Jewish Christianity, which looked to the Jerusalem church as the mother church of Christianity and sought to reproduce its preaching, piety, and lifestyle — with such insight being provided particularly by the early Christian confessional material quoted in 3:24-26. Thus, while all the NT writers evidence a bipolar relationship between the orientation, circumstances, and needs of the people being addressed, and the Christian gospel as contextualized by each of them for a particular people, Paul's letter to Christians at Rome reveals four such polarities: (1) that of Paul himself, as expressed in the body opening and body closing sections of the letter — and especially in his thesis statement of 1:16-17 and his expanded thesis statement of 3:21-23, as well as in the "spin" that he gives throughout the letter; (2) that of the mixed group of Gentile and Jewish Christians at Rome, who were his addressees, as he addresses them in a manner that he believed they would understand and appreciate in 1:16–4:25 and then in 9:1–11:36; (3) that of his own Gentile converts, as he sets out before his Roman addressees a portrayal of the essential features of his Christian proclamation to them, which they had accepted apart from any Jewish understanding or Jewish Christian influence, as in 5:1–8:39 and then at various places in the Christocentric ethical exhortations of 12:1–15:13; and (4) that of early Jewish Christianity, which was centered in the mother church at Jerusalem, whose confessional material he quotes in 3:24-26.

Christian confessional materials were rooted and came to expression in the context of early Christian worship, both corporate and private — that is, in the contexts of praise to God and adoration of Christ. Such materials are essentially devotional in nature, and so — while having a central focus and giving voice to certain basic convictions — they are (1) often rather imprecise, desiring to foster conviction and inspire adoration, but not always endeavoring to explicate doctrinal nuances, (2) usually functional in their portrayals of God and Christ, without going too deeply into ontological matters, except to assert their realities, and (3) always reflective of the similes and metaphors and religious language of their day, in speaking about God, the work of Christ, and what God through his Spirit is doing redemptively on behalf of people generally and among his own people specifically.[251]

Rom 3:24-26 is, we believe, a classic example of an early Christian confessional portion. As a devotionally based composition, it (1) incorporates concepts and expressions that theologians today could wish were more precisely stated and more exactly explicated, (2) sets out its statements in forms that are basically functional, and (3) uses the similes, metaphors, and religious language of Judaism and Jewish Christianity that were current in its day — such as the forensic terms "justification," "redemption," and "propitiation" (or "expiation," "satisfaction," "sacrifice of atonement"). Nonetheless, what these Christian confessional statements express is highly important theologically and of great significance for an understanding of early Jewish Christianity.

Paul used this confessional material in support of his expanded thesis statement of 3:21-23. And he used it — despite the imprecision of its statements, the functional nature of its expressions, and the dominance of its forensic language — because he believed (1) that it provided a common bond between himself and his Christian addressees at Rome, (2) that it served in a general fashion to support his thesis statements of 1:16-17 and 3:21-23, and (3) that he could interpret this somewhat more general devotional material of 3:24-26 for his addressees by his more explicit thesis statement of 3:21-23 and his elucidation of that statement in 3:27-31.

The themes that Paul contextualized for his addressees at Rome, and which need to be contextualized in our own Christian witness today, are principally those listed above under the heading "Biblical Theology." They have to do with the following:

1. "The righteousness of God," understood in both an *attributive sense* and a *communicative sense;*
2. "New covenant righteousness," as focused on Jesus Christ and his faithfulness, obedience, and Sonship;
3. "New covenant piety," as focused on God's love, Christ's work, and the guidance of God's Spirit, rather than on any form of "nomism" or "covenantal nomism";

---

251. For a more extended discussion of the nature of the confessional materials, see R. N. Longenecker, *New Wine into Fresh Wineskins,* 28-33.

4. The dynamic and developmental nature of God's salvific program;
5. The universal outreach of God's saving grace to everyone, with ethnicity having come to an end "in Christ";
6. The gospel of Christ as "attested by the law and the prophets"; and,
7. Faith in God through Christ, without any reliance on one's own "works" in order to gain acceptance by God or righteousness from God.

In effect, such a "new covenant agenda" signals a whole new understanding in this present time of the eschatological "now" of (1) what it means to be "the people of God," (2) what "mission for God and on behalf of people" signifies, and (3) how "the people of God," who are involved in a "mission for God and on behalf of people," are to regard all other people, whether like them or somewhat dissimilar from them.

7. The Example of Abraham with Respect to Righteousness and Faith (4:1-24)

TRANSLATION

$^{4:1}$*What, then, shall we say that Abraham, our forefather according to the flesh, discovered regarding this matter?* ^{2}*For if Abraham was justified by works, he had something to boast about — but not before God.*

^{3}*What does the Scripture say? "Abraham believed God, and it was credited to him as righteousness."* ^{4}*Now to the one who works, a wage is not credited as a gift but as an obligation.* ^{5}*However, to the one who does not work but trusts in God who justifies the wicked, that person's faith is credited as righteousness.*

^{6}*Just as also David declares regarding the blessedness of the person to whom God credits righteousness apart from works:*

^{7}*"Blessed are those whose transgressions are forgiven,*
   whose sins are covered;
^{8}*Blessed is the person to whom the Lord will never credit sin."*

^{9}*Is this blessedness, then, only for the circumcised, or also for the uncircumcised? We maintain that it was Abraham's faith that was credited to him as righteousness!* ^{10}*How, then, was it credited? Was it when he was circumcised or when he was uncircumcised? Not when he was circumcised. Rather, it was when he was uncircumcised!* ^{11}*And he received the sign of circumcision, a seal of the righteousness that he had by faith while he was still uncircumcised.*

So then, he is the father of all those who believe but have not been circumcised, in order that the righteousness of which we speak might be credited to them — ^{12}*as well as the father of the circumcised who not only are circumcised but also walk in the footsteps of the faith of our father Abraham when he was uncircumcised.*

^{13}*It was not through the law that the promise was made to Abraham and to his descendants that he would be "the heir of the world"; rather, it came through the righteousness of faith.* ^{14}*For if "those of the law" are the heirs, the faith [of Abraham] has no value and the promise [of God] is worthless.* ^{15}*Because the law [of Moses] brings wrath. But where there is no law there is no transgression.*

^{16}*Therefore, the promise comes by faith, so that it may be by grace and guaranteed to all Abraham's descendants — not only to those who are of the law but also to those who are of the faith of Abraham. He is the father of us all.* ^{17}*Just as it is written, "I have made you a father of many nations." He is our father in the sight of God, in whom he believed — the God who gives life to the dead and calls things that are not as though they were.*

^{18}*Against all hope, Abraham in hope believed and so became the father of many nations, just as it had been said to him, "So shall your descendants be."* [19] *And without weakening in his faith, he faced the facts that his body was dead, since he was about a hundred years old, and that Sarah's womb was also dead.* [20] *He did not waver through unbelief regarding the promise of God, but was strengthened in his faith and gave glory to God.* [21] *He was fully persuaded that God had power to do what he had promised.* [22] *This is why "it was credited to him as righteousness."*

[23] *The words "it was credited to him" were not written for him alone,* [24] *but also for us to whom God will credit righteousness — for us who believe in him who raised Jesus our Lord from the dead.*

TEXTUAL NOTES

4:1a The perfect infinitive verb εὑρηκέναι ("to have found") appears before Ἀβραάμ ("Abraham") in uncials ℵ* [1, 2] A C*[3] D F G Ψ and minuscules 81 256 1506 2127 (Category II), 263 330 365 629 1319 1573 1852 (Category III), which placement is also reflected in versions syr[(p), pal] cop[sa, (bo)] arm and by Origen[gr/lat] Cyril Ambrosiaster Pelagius Augustine. It is, however, located after ἡμῶν ("our") in uncial P [also *Byz* K L] and minuscules 33 1175 (Category I), 1881 1962 2464 (Category II), 69 88 104 323 326 424[c] 436 459 614 1241 1243 1505 1735 1874 1912 2200 2344 2495 (Category III). And it is omitted in fourth-century Codex Vaticanus (B 03) and in minuscules 1739 (Category I) and 6 (Category II).

There would have been no reason for copyists to have inserted εὑρηκέναι either before "Abraham" or after "our" if it had not been originally in the text. Its omission in fourth-century Codex Vaticanus (B 03) and minuscules 1739 (Category I) and 6 (Category III) is probably best explained by the supposition that εὑρηκέναι, coming immediately after ἐροῦμεν, accidentally fell out of the text due to the similar beginnings of the two verbs. Assuming the legitimacy of its presence, the placement of εὑρηκέναι before Ἀβραάμ is more strongly attested in the textual tradition and makes better sense, and so to be accepted, whereas its placement after "our" (ἡμῶν) has weaker external support and is inferior in sense, and therefore to be rejected. All three of these options reflect something of the grammatical and syntactical difficulties of the sentence.[1]

1b The accusative singular προπάτορα ("forefather") is attested by uncials ℵ[2] A B C and minuscules 81 256 1506 2127 (Category II), 330 1319 (Category III); it is also reflected in sy[(p), pal] sa bo arm and supported by Origen[gr lem] Cyril. The accusative singular πατέρα ("father"), however, appears in uncials ℵ[1] C[3] D F G P Ψ (also *Byz* K L), minuscules 33 (Category I), 1881 1962 2464 (Category II), 88 104 424[c] 436 459 1175 1241 1319[c] 1573 1852 1912 2200 (Category III), and is reflected in it[mss] vg and supported by Origen[lat]. Minuscule 365 (Category III) has both προπάτορα ("forefather") and πατέρα ("father"). Προπάτορα, though a *hapax legomenon* in Paul's letters and the rest of the NT, has better textual support, and thus should be accepted. Probably πατέρα appears

---

1. See "Exegetical Comments" below, *ad loc.*

later in the Greek textual tradition because it is the usual designation for Abraham in Paul's letters and the rest of the NT.[2]

6 The textual evidence is very strong for the inclusion of the adverb καθάπερ ("just as"), whereas the roughly synonymous adverb καθώς ("just as") is more weakly supported by uncials D F and G. This is a somewhat similar situation as appeared in 3:4 (see *ad loc.*), with modern text critics preferring καθώς for internal reasons in that earlier passage. In this instance, however, καθάπερ has not only much stronger external support but also better internal probability, and thus is to be preferred.

Here in 4:6, as well as earlier in 3:4, the difference in meaning is somewhat inconsequential, since the adverbs are roughly synonymous. The use of καθώς or καθάπερ seems to have depended, in large measure, on whether (1) a biblical passage or reference to Scripture was being introduced (thus the use of καθώς, "just as," or the more common introductory formula καθώς γέγραπται, "just as it is written"), or (2) a comparison was being made (thus the use of καθάπερ, "just as," or καθάπερ καί, "just as also").

8 The genitive singular relative pronoun οὗ ("of whom"), which is grammatically awkward, is strongly attested by P[40vis], uncials ℵ* B D* G, and minuscules 1739 (Category I) and 1506 (Category II). The dative singular relative pronoun ᾧ ("to whom") is supported by ℵ[2] A C D[c] F P Ψ (also *Byz* K L) and minuscules 33 1175 (Category I), 1881 2464 (Category II), 104 323 326 365 424[c] 614 1241 1505 1573 1735 1874 2496 (Category III). The reading οὗ ("of whom") is better attested and the more difficult reading, and so to be preferred; the dative ᾧ ("to whom") was probably inserted as a grammatical correction.

9a The omission of the neuter adjective μόνον ("only"), used as an adverb, is widely attested by the Greek textual tradition — that is, throughout the Greek textual tradition other than in bilingual Codex Beza (D 06). It is included, however, before ἐπὶ τὴν περιτομήν ("for the circumcised") in both the Greek and Latin texts of sixth-century Codex Beza (D 06), as well as reflected in versions it vg[d], and by the Latin commentator Ambrosiaster, evidently to clarify what might have been considered unclear. Its omission has much better external support, though the logic of the sentence suggests that an adverbial use of "only" should be understood.

9b The omission of ὅτι ("that") is attested by such important fourth-century uncial MSS as Codex Sinaiticus (ℵ 01) and Codex Vaticanus (B 03), as well as by sixth-century, bilingual Codex Beza (D 06). The inclusion of ὅτι ("that"), which appears before the paraphrase of the latter half of Gen 15:6, is supported by uncials A C D[c] F G P Ψ (also *Byz* K L) and minuscules 33 1175 (Category I), 1506 2464 (Category II), 6 69 88 104 323 326 330 365 424[c] 614 1241 1243 1319 1505 1573 1735 1874 2344 2495 (Category III). The external textual evidence, however, attests its omission. Internal evidence likewise suggests it should be omitted, since Gen 15:6b is not quoted in 4:9b but only paraphrased[3] — and so there would be no need for a ὅτι *recitativum*.

11a The genitive noun περιτομῆς ("of circumcision") is amply attested in the Greek textual tradition, whereas the accusative περιτομήν ("circumcision") is more weakly supported by uncials A C* and by minuscules 1739 (Category I), 1506 1881 (Cat-

---

2. Cf. later in this passage at 4:12; see also Luke 16:24, 30; John 8:53; Acts 7:2.
3. See "Exegetical Comments" below, *ad loc.*

egory II), and 6 424ᶜ (Category III). To read here an accusative would result in the presence of three accusatives within two Greek clauses, which seems somewhat difficult to conceive. The genitive περιτομῆς ("of circumcision"), however, is amply attested, and thus for both external and internal reasons merits acceptance.

11b The insertion of the preposition διά ("through") in ninth-century uncial G is undoubtedly an attempted grammatical improvement, but without early support and therefore unwarranted.

11c The conjunction καί used as an adverb ("also") appears after the aorist passive infinitive λογισθῆναι ("credited") in uncials ℵ² C D F G P [also *Byz* K L] and minuscules 1175 (Category I), 256 1962 2127 (Category II), and 104 263 365 424* 436 459 1241 1319 1573 1852 1912 (Category III); it is also reflected in itᵐˢˢ vg syrᵖ, ʰ, ᵖᵃˡ copˢᵃ and supported by Origenˡᵃᵗ¹/³ Ambrosiaster — thereby giving the sense "in order that righteousness might be credited *also* to them." Λογισθῆναι, however, appears alone in uncials ℵ* A B Ψ and in minuscules 1739 (Category I), 81 1506 1881 2464 (Category II), 6 424ᶜ 630 2200 (Category III), and is reflected in itᵐˢˢ vgᵐˢˢ copˢᵃ ᵐˢ, ᵇᵒ and supported by Origenᵍʳ, ˡᵃᵗ²/³. According to Bruce Metzger, either καί was overlooked in transcription since it resembled the final syllable of λογισθῆναι or was added by some copyists to sharpen the argument,[4] and therefore καί has been placed within square brackets in *GNT*⁴. But the absence of καί is slightly better supported by the external textual evidence, and so its presence should probably be discounted.

11d The article τὴν ("the") before the final word δικαιοσύνην ("righteousness") of 4:11 is included by uncials B C* F G P Ψ (also *Byz* K L) and minuscules 33 1175 (Category I), 2464 (Category II), and 69 88 104 323 326 1241 1243 1505 1735 1874 2344 2495 (Category III). It is, however, excluded by uncials ℵ C² D* and minuscules 1739 (Category I), 1506 (Category II), 6 365 424ᶜ (Category III). The textual evidence is almost equally divided, though with a slight balance in favor of its inclusion. In all likelihood τὴν functions to point back to the previous use of δικαιοσύνη in the verse, as Greek articles commonly do, and therefore should be retained.

The wording εἰς δικαιωσύνην ("unto" or "for righteousness") that appears in uncial A and minuscules 424ᶜ 1319 1881, instead of τὴν δικαιοσύνην ("the" or "that righteousness"), is likely a scribal assimilation to εἰς δικαιωσύνην at the end of 4:5.

12 The article τοῖς ("to those") has often been viewed as being "superfluous," and so it has been suggested either that the reflexive pronoun αὐτοῖς ("themselves") should be added (thereby reading "to those who themselves walk") or that τοῖς should be deleted, as in Codex Beza (i.e., D 06). Most modern translations simply ignore it.

15 The mildly adversative postpositive conjunction δέ ("but") in the second sentence of the verse is attested by uncials ℵ* A B C and minuscules 81 1506 (Category II) and 104 436 1852 (Category III); it is also reflected in vgᵐˢˢ sa bo syʰᵐᵍ arm eth geo and supported by Origenˡᵃᵗ ⁶/⁷ Ambrosiaster Augustine. The postpositive explanatory conjunction γάρ ("for"), however, is supported by uncials ℵ² D F G P Ψ (also *Byz* K L) and minuscules 1175 1739 (Category I), 256 1881 1962 2127 2464 (Category II), and 6 69 88 263 323 326 330 365 424ᶜ 459 1241 1243 1319 1505 1573 1735 1874 1912 2200 2344 2495 (Cat-

---

4. Cf. Metzger, *Textual Commentary*, 450-51.

egory III); it is also reflected in vg sy^(p, h) and supported by Cyril Ambrosiaster Augustine Pelagius. The textual evidence for δέ is considerably stronger, primarily because of its attestation by codices ℵ and B (as well as A and C). Probably the previous series of three γάρs in 4:13-15a has influenced the later inclusion of γάρ at the beginning of 4:15b as well.

16 The inclusion of the third-person singular subjunctive verb ᾖ ("it might be") that appears in fifth-century uncial A and minuscules 1505 2495 (Category III) is, evidently, an attempted improvement of the text — though unnecessary, since the logic of the sentence could be seen to support such a subjunctive "may" or "might."

18 The ninth-century uncials F G and minuscules 205 109^c (Category V) add after the quotation of Gen 15:5 the words "as the stars of heaven and the sand of the sea," but this is clearly a later scribal addition.

19 The third-person singular aorist κατενόησεν ("he considered"), without the negative οὐ ("not"), is strongly attested by uncials ℵ A B C and minuscules 1739 (Category I), 81 256 1506 2127 (Category II), and 6 263 365 424 1319 (Category III); it is also reflected in it^(mon*) vg^(ww, st) syr^p cop^(sa, bo, fay) and supported by Origen^(gr, lat 1/3) Chrysostom^(1/4). The negative phrase οὐ κατενόησεν ("he did not consider"), however, is supported by uncials D F G P Ψ [also *Byz* K L] and minuscules 33 1175 (Category I), 1881 1962 2464 (Category II), and 104 424^c 1241 1319 1852 1912 2200 (Category III); it is also reflected in it^(ar, b, d, f, g, mon2, o) vg^(cl) syr^h and supported by Origen^(lat2/3) Chrysostom^(3/4) Ambrosiaster. The reading κατενόησεν ("he considered") without the negative οὐ ("not") is far better attested externally. It is also preferable on internal grounds, for Paul is here suggesting not that Abraham's faith was blind to the reality of his old age, but that his faith faced reality and remained undaunted by it.

The inclusion of the adverb ἤδη ("already," "by this time," "just as good as") is supported by uncials ℵ A C D P Ψ [also *Byz* K L] and minuscules 33 1175 (Category I), 81 256 1506 1962 2127 2464 (Category II), and 6 104 263 365 424^c 436 459 1241 1319 1573 1852 1912; it is also reflected in it^(mon, o) vg^(mss) syr^(h with*) cop^(bo) and supported by Origen^(gr, lat3/4). The adverb does not, however, appear in uncials B F G, minuscules 1739 1881 2200, versions it^(ar, b, d, f, g) vg syr^(p, pal), cop^(sa), or the Church Fathers Origen^(latl/2) Chrysostom Ambrosiaster. The external evidence is fairly well balanced for the two options, though because Codex Vaticanus (B 03) and other important textual witnesses omit it, we believe it best to omit it as well (the UBS committee, however, concluded that the weight of evidence favored its inclusion).

On internal grounds the presence of the adverb ἤδη gives the impression of a scribal interpolation in order to heighten or adjust the account. Perhaps since Gen 25:1-2 says that after Sarah's death "Abraham took another wife, whose name was Keturah, and she bore him six sons: Zimran, Jokshan, Medan, Midian, Ishbak and Shuah," and since Gen 25:6 speaks of other sons of Abraham's concubines, some scribe thought it necessary to insert the idea of "already" or "just as good as dead." But as Bruce Metzger has rightly asked, "Who would have omitted the word had it stood in the text originally?"[5] Probably, therefore, the adverb ἤδη should be viewed as not original.

21 The conjunction καί ("and") is absent in ninth-century uncial G, but that appears to have been a scribal attempt to improve the reading of the passage.

---

5. Metzger, *Textual Commentary,* 451.

22 An adverbial use of the conjunction καί ("also") following the inferential conjunction διό ("therefore") is attested in uncials ℵ C D¹ P Ψ [also *Byz* K L], minuscules 1175 1739 (Category I), 81 256 1506 1881 1962 2127 2464 (Category II), and 6 104 263 424ᶜ 436 459 1241 1319 1573 1852 1912 2200 (Category III), versions itᵃʳ vg syrʰ, and by Origenˡᵃᵗ. It is omitted, however, in uncials B D* G, minuscule 365 (Category III), and versions itᵇ, ᶠ, ᵍ, ᵐᵒⁿ, ᵒ vgᵐˢ syrᵖ, ᵖᵃˡ copˢᵃ, ᵇᵒ. In view of the balance of external evidence, the UBS committee placed καί in square brackets. Yet its omission in Codex Vaticanus (B 03) is highly significant. Further, the fact that the quotation of Gen 15:6 in 4:3 contains the conjunction καί leads one to suspect that καί was simply assimilated here, and therefore should probably be rejected.

23 The phrase "for righteousness" is added to the quotation "it was credited to him" (ἐλογίσθη αὐτῷ) at the end of this verse in uncial D², minuscule 1241 (Category III), and versions vgᶜˡ and syᵖ, but evidently only in an attempt to improve the text.

FORM/STRUCTURE/SETTING

Paul used the three sets of questions and their respective answers he set out in 3:27-31 (1) to elucidate his expanded thesis statement of 3:21-23 and (2) to support his understanding of certain significant statements in the early Christian confessional portion that he quotes in 3:24-26. These questions and answers also, however, prepare for the paradigmatic example of Abraham that he presents here in Rom 4. Thus the query "Where, then, is boasting?" of 3:27a, which was Paul's first question in that previous series of questions and answers in 3:27-31, is picked up in his rhetorical question of 4:1a, which begins his presentation of Abraham in Rom 4: "What, then, shall we say that Abraham, our forefather, discovered in this matter?" And his earlier very brief response "It is excluded!" of 3:27b is spelled out more fully with reference to Abraham by his statement of 4:2: "If, in fact, Abraham was justified by works, he had something to boast about, but not before God" — with that statement serving as the thesis for all the rest of what Paul says about Abraham in the remainder of this passage.

Likewise, matters regarding "righteousness" and "faith," which were spoken about in both the first and second sets of questions and their answers in 3:27-30, are illustrated throughout 4:1-24 by the example of Abraham. And even Paul's concluding rhetorical question of 3:31 about the possibility of his Christian proclamation actually setting aside the Mosaic law, together with his fervent insistence "Rather, we establish the law!," functions in such a dual fashion — that is, not only concluding his elucidation of 3:27-31 but also preparing for his illustration of the example of Abraham in 4:1-24. For as Nils Dahl has pointed out: "If Paul's contention that a person is justified by faith without works of the Law does uphold the validity of the Law, it follows *e contrario* that works of the Law do not."[6]

6. Dahl, "The One God of Jews and Gentiles," 179.

The Exemplum of Abraham. The primary and most obvious rhetorical convention used by Paul in 4:1-24 is *paradeigma* — the highlighting of an important person or the recounting of a significant story as an *exemplum* or model to be either imitated or avoided. It is a rhetorical convention widely used by speakers and writers of the Greco-Roman world, as well as by ancient Jewish teachers and authors — and, of course, has been (and will continue to be) used by all people of whatever time, location, or culture.

Paul does not, however, attempt to "christianize" Abraham by suggesting that his faith in God was based on the "obedience" or "faithfulness" of Jesus Christ — that is, as Leonhard Goppelt has expressed matters, "Abraham's justification in Romans 4 is never seen as a timeless model of justification by Christ."[7] Rather, as Goppelt goes on to say: "The faith of Abraham has the same structure, but a different content from the Christian faith."[8] Paul, therefore, does not use Abraham's faith in support of his own use of the expression διὰ πίστεως Ἰησοῦ Χριστοῦ ("through the faithfulness of Jesus Christ") in 3:22. Nor does he use it to support his understanding of the early church's phraseology διὰ τῆς πίστεως ("through [Jesus'] faithfulness") in 3:25, or to support what seems to be his understanding of ἐκ πίστεως Ἰησοῦ ("based on the faithfulness of Jesus") at the end of 3:26. Rather, he uses the example of Abraham to illustrate only those matters that have to do with "righteousness" and "faith" — which matters played a large part, though not everything, in what he proclaimed in 3:21-23, what he supported by a quotation of early Christian confessional material in 3:24-26, and what he elucidated in 3:27-31.

Abraham was highly regarded by both Jews and Jewish Christians as the father of the Jewish nation[9] and "the friend of God."[10] The esteem with which he was held and the role he played in Jewish thought are clearly reflected in Sir 44:19-21:

> Abraham, the father of a multitude of nations, tarnished not his glory. He kept the commandment of the Most High and entered into covenant with Him. In his flesh He [God] engraved him an ordinance, and in trial he [Abraham] was found faithful. Therefore with an oath He promised him "to bless the nations in his seed," to multiply him "as the dust of the earth," and to exalt his seed "as the stars"; to cause them to inherit "from sea to sea, and from the River to the ends of the earth."

Jub 23:10 says in veneration of Abraham: "For Abraham was perfect in all his deeds with the Lord, and well-pleasing in righteousness all the days of his life"; and 1 Macc 2:52 states such veneration in the form of a question: "Was

---

7. Goppelt, "Paul and *Heilsgeschichte*," 322.
8. *Ibid.*, 325.
9. Cf. Schrenk, "πατήρ," 5.976.
10. Cf. 2 Chr 20:7; Isa 41:8; *Jub* 19:9; Philo, *De Abrahamo* 273; Jas 2:23.

not Abraham found faithful in temptation, and it was reckoned unto him for righteousness?"

Abraham in rabbinic writings is often affectionately called "a bag of myrrh," for "just as myrrh is the most excellent of spices, so Abraham was the chief of all righteous men."[11] As early as Shemaiah and Abtalion, who are listed as the immediate predecessors to Hillel and Shammai in the line of rabbinical succession in *m. Abot* 1:10-12, questions as to the nature of Abraham's faith and the relation of merit to that faith were being discussed among the Pharisees.

Two emphases about Abraham are constantly made in the postbiblical literature of Judaism: (1) that Abraham was counted righteous because of his faithfulness under testing, and (2) that Abraham's faith spoken of in Gen 15:6 must be coupled with his acceptance of circumcision as referred to in the covenant of Gen 17:4-14. The tests or trials of Abraham were usually considered to have been ten in number, but there is no agreement in the various passages as to exactly what these ten were — though the tenth is always listed as the 'Aqedah Isaac, or "Binding of Isaac." Further, Abraham's faithfulness under testing is always presented in Jewish postbiblical writings as being meritorious, both for Abraham himself and for his posterity.

In *Exodus Rabbah* 44, for example, there is a long parable attributed to Rabbi Abin in the name of Rabbi Aha that well illustrates the Jewish attitude toward the merit of Abraham's faithfulness. It is a tale about a king whose friend deposited with him ten pearls and afterward died. After his friend's death the king married the man's only daughter, making her his chief lady and giving her a necklace of ten pearls. But, alas, the lady lost the pearls, and the king in his anger sought to banish her from his presence. Her best friend, however, came to plead her case before the king; and when he saw how adamant the king was, he reminded him of the ten pearls the father had left with the king and suggested that they be accepted in place of the ten that the lady had lost. The spiritual application of the story is then spelled out by Rabbi Abin:

> So when Israel sinned, God was angry with them and said: "Now, therefore, let Me alone, that My wrath may wax hot against them, and that I may consume them" [Exod 32:10]. But Moses pleaded: "Lord of the Universe! Why art Thou angry with Israel?" "Because they have broken the Decalogue," He replied. "Well, they possess a source from which they can make repayment," he urged. "What is the source?," He asked. Moses replied: "Remember that Thou didst prove Abraham with ten trials. So let those ten [trials of Abraham] serve as compensation for these ten [broken commandments]."[12]

Admittedly, the parable comes from a time later than the NT period, for both Rabbi Abin and Rabbi Aha were fourth-generation Amoraim. Nonetheless,

11. *Cant. Rab.* 1:13.
12. *Exod. Rab.* 44.4

though the story is later than Paul's day, the conviction it carries regarding the meritorious character of Abraham's faith has roots that go back to a much earlier time.[13]

Likewise, in Jewish writings there is the repeated insistence that Abraham's faith referred to in Gen 15:6 must always be coupled with Abraham's acceptance of physical circumcision in the covenant of Gen 17:4-14, so that the two matters of believing ("faith") and keeping the covenant ("nomism") are to be constantly brought together when one speaks of the righteousness of Abraham. There is in Judaism the motif of truth appearing in two forms, an elemental form and a developed form, and only when one brings the two together can one come to understand truth in its fullness.[14] Abraham, therefore, can certainly be spoken of as being righteous by faith in Gen 15:6. But that is only the elemental statement of the matter. It is in Gen 17:4-14 — with its explicit insistence by God himself that "my covenant shall be in your flesh an everlasting covenant; any uncircumcised male who is not circumcised in the flesh of his foreskin shall be cut off from his people, he has broken my covenant" — that the full nature of Abraham's righteousness is proclaimed.

For Judaism, then, trust in God and obedience to the law were inseparable. And though Abraham lived before the actual giving of the Mosaic law, he anticipated the keeping of that fuller expression of God's will (i.e., Torah) in his acceptance of circumcision and his offering of a ram in the 'Aqedah Isaac on Mount Moriah. Thus *Leviticus Rabbah* 2:10 (on Lev 1:12) argues: "Abraham fulfilled the whole of the Torah, as it is said, 'Because that Abraham hearkened to My voice and kept My charge, My commandments, My statutes, and My laws' [Gen 26:5], and 'he offered a ram as a sacrifice.'"

When Paul, however, speaks of Abraham, he lays all the emphasis on Abraham as being righteous by faith in response to the promise of God, apart from any effort on his part to keep the law. Thus in his earlier letter to his own converts in Galatia, Paul takes pains to point out (1) that the righteousness credited to Abraham in Gen 15:6 is associated solely with God's promise and the patriarch's faith (cf. Gal 3:6, "he believed God, and it was credited to him as righteousness"); (2) that the principle of righteousness by faith was expressed in Abraham's life long before the Mosaic law was given (cf. Gal 3:17: "430 years" before the law was given); (3) that the promise God gave to Abraham was indeed meant for the patriarch and his posterity, but the true "seed" of Abraham is Christ *and* all who belong to Christ (cf. Gal 3:16, 29); and (4) that since righteousness in the divine economy is based on God's promise and people's response of faith, the Judaizers' attempt to impose the requirements of the Mosaic law on Gentile believers should be treated in the same way that God told Abraham to treat his mistress Hagar and her son: "Get rid of the slave woman

---

13. Cf., e.g., Sir 44:19-21 and 1 Macc 2:52, as cited above.

14. Cf. Daube, "Public Retort and Private Explanation," in his *New Testament and Rabbinic Judaism,* 141-50.

and her son, for the slave woman's son will never share in the inheritance with the free woman's son" (Gal 4:30). And this same understanding of righteousness and faith will be spelled out more fully in Paul's letter to the Christians at Rome here in 4:1-24.

Two Midrashic Interpretive Rules or Conventions. Also important in Paul's use of Abraham as the example par excellence of righteousness and faith are two midrashic (i.e., Jewish interpretive) rules or conventions, which, it may be assumed, he learned in his early training as a Pharisee. The most obvious is his use of the second of the seven interpretive rules *(middoth)* attributed to Hillel, who was a highly revered Jewish teacher of the mid–first century B.C. to the early first century A.D. (c. 60 B.C. to A.D. 20), under whom Gamaliel I (who had been Paul's teacher) studied Torah — that is, the rule *gezerah shawah* (גזירה שוה). This rule argued that when the same word, expression, or theme appears in two or more passages of Scripture, wherever located and however diverse, the same considerations apply to all of them. This exegetical procedure, called "pearl stringing," was practiced by Jewish teachers not only (1) to demonstrate the unity of the Jewish (OT) Scriptures (i.e., the Written Torah) but also (2) to support by means of multiple attestation, as drawn from various parts of those Scriptures, a particular point of interpretation. This interpretive convention was set out earlier by Paul in Rom 3:10b-18 (whether that catena of passages is to be attributed to Paul himself or to some earlier Jewish or Jewish Christian author he quoted), with that same interpretive understanding underlying the bringing together of various biblical passages later in this same letter in 9:13-33, 11:8-10, and 15:9-12.[15]

Paul invokes this practice of "pearl stringing" in 4:3-8 when recounting the story of Abraham. He does this (1) by quoting Gen 15:6, "Abraham believed God, and it was *credited* (ἐλογίσθη) to him as righteousness";[16] and then (2) by joining to that quotation the words of the psalmist in Ps 32:1-2 (LXX 31:1-2): "Blessed are those whose transgressions are forgiven, whose sins are covered. Blessed is the person to whom the Lord will never credit (λογίσηται) sin"[17] — inferring from the presence of the same verb λογίζομαι in these two passages (though in different contexts and with differing statements) that it should be concluded that the psalmist "David" was actually speaking about "the blessedness of the person to whom God credits righteousness apart from works" (as Paul states explicitly in Rom 4:6 to introduce his quotation of Ps 32:1-2). This interpretive practice of "pearl stringing" is probably also to be seen in Paul's biblical buttressing of the quasi-confessional statement in Rom 4:16: "Abraham is the father of us all" — which, it seems, he (1) primarily based on his reading of God's promise to Abraham in Gen 15:5, "Look up at the heavens and count the stars — if, indeed, you can count them. So shall your descendants be!" (with the

---

15. Cf. also 1 Cor 3:19-20; 15:54-55; 2 Cor 6:16-18.
16. Rom 4:3.
17. Rom 4:7-8.

latter part of that promise, that is, "So shall your descendants be!" as explicitly quoted in 4:18b), but (2) supported, as well, by the statement of Gen 17:5, "I have made you a father of many nations."

Paul also uses in his example of Abraham a second midrashic convention that had been attributed to the great teacher Hillel — that is, the seventh of Hillel's interpretive rules or *middoth:* the rule *dabar halamed me- 'inyano* (דבר הלמד מעינינו). This rule argued that a passage must always be interpreted by its context. It is a hermeneutical rule that appears operative, whether consciously or unconsciously, in Paul's depiction of Abraham's situation in 4:10-22 at the time when God *promised him a son* (Gen 15:4-5) and *credited him as righteous* (Gen 15:5) — that is, in the order discussed by Paul, (1) with respect to the time when God credited Abraham as righteous, whether it was before or after he was circumcised (4:10-11a), and (2) with respect to the circumstances in Abraham's life when God promised him a son and his positive response of faith, for God's promise was given and Abraham's response of faith occurred at a time when "his body was dead" and "Sarah's womb was also dead" (4:18-22).

On the Possible Form of a Greek Diatribe in the First Part of Paul's Example of Abraham. Commentators have sometimes viewed the first part of Paul's example of Abraham — either the question and answer of 4:1-2 alone, or all four of the questions and their respective responses in 4:1-12 — as structured in the form of a Greek *diatribe.*[18] We earlier argued that a diatribe styling is clearly evident in 2:1-5 and 2:17-24, and we will later propose that echoes of a diatribe structure are to be found in 9:19-21 and 11:17-24 (possibly also in 14:4-11).[19] The question here, however, is: Should the material of 4:1-2 or that presented in 4:1-12 be viewed as set out in the form of a Greek diatribe? Some scholars have understood 4:1-2 in this manner, and so have connected the question and answer of these two verses with the questions and answers of 3:27-31.[20] Others have gone further to argue that all four of the questions and their respective responses in 4:1-12 exhibit such a diatribe styling.[21]

Much of what we said earlier regarding the identification of a diatribe in 3:1-5 — particularly regarding (1) Paul's expressional habits as drawn from elsewhere in Romans and his other letters, which also have a bearing on the issue at hand, and (2) our own view of the matter, as based on these patterns of Pauline expression — has relevance, we believe, for the question posed and answer given in 4:1-2, as well as for all four questions and their respective responses in 4:1-11. We would, therefore, ask readers to apply those observations, comments, and conclusions to the structure and contents of this first part of Paul's Abra-

18. For discussions of the Greek *diatribe* and specific treatments of Paul's use of it, see the sections "Form/Structure/Setting" and the "Exegetical Comments" above pertaining to 2:1-5, 2:17-24, and 3:1-5. Note also his use of the rhetorical question "What, then, shall we say?" in 8:31a.

19. See "Exegetical Comments" above and below on these passages.

20. Cf. esp. Stowers, "Dialogical Exchange and *Exemplum* in 3:27–4:25," 155-74; *idem,* "One God & One Father Abraham," 234-42.

21. So particularly Jewett, *Romans,* 305.

ham *exemplum* as well. Suffice it here simply to repeat Frédéric Godet's dictum, which he enunciated in the latter part of the eighteenth century with respect to the style and nature of Paul's argument in 3:1-8:

> There is no need of expressly introducing an opponent, as many commentators have done. Paul does not here make use of the formula: *But someone will say.* The objections arise of themselves from the affirmations, and Paul puts them in a manner to his own account.[22]

And these words, we believe, apply also to Paul's rhetorical questions and his responses of 4:1-12, and for the same reasons as we have enumerated earlier.

The Course and Structure of Paul's Argument in 4:1-25. There has been considerable debate among scholars regarding the course and structure of Paul's argument in 4:1-24. Further, there have been uncertainties about how 4:25 relates to the previous twenty-four verses.

There is general agreement that throughout 4:1-24 Paul presents Abraham as the example par excellence of what he has written about earlier in 3:21-31, and so all of 4:1-24 must be viewed as one connected presentation. The presence of certain key words, which appear throughout the passage, indicates such a unity of presentation — principally the nouns δικαιοσύνη ("righteousness"; seven times in vv. 3, 5, 6, 9, 11, 13, 22) and πίστις ("faith"; ten times in vv. 5, 9, 11, 12, 13, 14, 16 [twice], 19, 20), but also the verbs πιστεύω ("believe"; five times in vv. 3, 5, 17, 18, 24) and λογίζομαι ("credit," "reckon," "account"; eleven times in vv. 3, 4, 5, 6, 8, 9, 10, 11, 22, 23, 24). Yet there are thematic and structural variations in 4:1-24. And some commentators have identified certain bits and pieces of other materials that they believe have been incorporated within the passage, and so have treated those portions separately.

Three major parts of the passage can rather easily be observed: (1) the opening thesis statement and challenge of 4:1-2, (2) a first major portion of the argument that focuses on the statement and implications of Gen 15:6, "Abraham believed God, and he credited it to him as righteousness," which appears in 4:3-12, and (3) a second major portion that focuses on the promise that God gave to Abraham and its implications in 4:13-24. A fourth and final part, the material in 4:25, has also been somewhat vaguely noted, though questions about its nature and function have been largely ignored. The first part in 4:1-2 begins with a rhetorical question about "what Abraham discovered" and answers that question in a negative fashion, thereby setting the theme for all that follows: Abraham was not justified "by works," and so had nothing to boast about before God. The second part, in 4:3-12, is dominated by an exploration of the meaning of the verb ἐλογίσθη ("it was credited") in the statement of Gen 15:6: "Abraham believed God, and *it was credited* to him as righteousness." Three rhetorical questions are asked in this portion of

22. Godet, *Romans* (FT 1880), 1.220.

the passage that deal directly with the meaning and significance of the verb λογίζομαι ("credit," "reckon," or "account"). In the course of Paul's exposition in this second part there occur (1) a sharp contrast between "faith" (πίστις) and "works" (ἔργα), (2) a defining statement regarding the irrelevancy of the status of "noncircumcision" (ἀκροβυστία) vis-à-vis that of circumcision (περιτομή), and (3) a concluding statement having to do with the fatherhood of Abraham for all people of faith, whatever their status with respect to being "circumcised" or "uncircumcised."

The third part of the passage, in 4:13-24, focuses on "the promise" (ἡ ἐπαγγελία) that God gave "to Abraham and to his descendants" (τῷ Ἀβραάμ ἢ τῷ σπέρματι αὐτοῦ), arguing that it was not made on the basis of "law" (νόμος) but had to do with "faith" (πίστις) — and, further, asserts that God's promise to Abraham had to do not only with Abraham and his descendants ("his seed"), but also includes all "who believe in him [God] who raised Jesus our Lord from the dead." Prominent in this part of the passage are the words ἐπαγγελία ("promise"), κληρονόμος ("inheritance"), σπέρμα ("seed," "offspring," or "descendant"), πιστίς ("faith"), χάρις ("grace"), and πᾶς ("all").

The nature, purpose, and function of the statement in 4:25, "He was delivered over to death for our sins and was raised to life for our justification," have not always been apparent to the vast majority of commentators. The statement has usually been referred to in rather simplistic fashion as (1) a "simple formula" that "terminates a lengthy discussion of the significance of Abraham," (2) a "neat summary" of what has been said before, (3) an "epigrammatic sentence" that closes ch. 4, or (4) a "traditional formulation" that prepares for what follows in ch. 5. But such characterizations hardly provide any adequate understanding with respect to its nature, its purpose, or its function.

As I understand the course and structure of Paul's argument in 4:1-25, I propose (1) that what is presented in 4:1-24 expresses an intrinsically related argument throughout, and so its unity must be preserved, but (2) that the material of 4:1-24 is structurally and thematically set out in three parts or sections. Then at the close of the chapter, that is, in 4:25, an early Christian confessional statement is given, which draws to a conclusion not only all that appears in 4:1-24 but also all that was written throughout 1:16–4:24.

The first part of the material, in 4:1-2, which is in the form of an opening rhetorical question and a challenging response, comprises the thesis statement or caption of the passage and presents Abraham as the example par excellence of "faith apart from works." The second part, in 4:3-12, which is the first major portion of the presentation, argues that "righteousness" (δικαιοσύνη) was "credited" (ἐλογίσθη) by God to Abraham on the basis of "faith" (πίστις), and not on the basis of "works" (ἔργα). It is structured in terms of three rhetorical questions that Paul raises in 4:3, 9, and 10, with his responses to these questions being supported by (1) a use of Hillel's second interpretive rule (gezerah shawah) that joins Gen 15:6 and Ps 32:1-2 on the basis of the verb λογίζομαι ("credit," "reckon," "account"), which appears in both the Genesis passage and the Psalms passage (Rom 4:3-8), and (2) a use of Hillel's seventh interpretive rule *(dabar halamed me- 'inyano),* which insists that a passage must always be interpreted by its context (4:10-11a). This portion of Paul's argument is drawn to a close in the affirmation: "So then, he [Abraham] is the father of all who believe," whether they are "uncircumcised" or "circumcised" (4:11b-12).

The third part of the passage, in 4:13-24, which is the second major argumentative portion of the presentation, highlights God's "promise to Abraham" (ἡ ἐπαγγελία τῷ Ἀβραάμ) and "to his descendants" (τῷ σπέρματι αὐτοῦ). In this portion of the passage Paul insists that God's promise was not given "through the law" (διὰ νόμου) but "through the righteousness that comes by faith" (διὰ δικαιοσύνης πίστεως). This assertion is supported by another use of Hillel's seventh interpretive rule or convention — here by noting that in the Genesis story Abraham and Sarah were too old to conceive and give birth to a child, and so drawing the inference that God's promise of a son had nothing to do with their own circumstances or endeavors (4:18-22). This portion of Paul's argument may also involve another use of the second of Hillel's interpretive rules, the rule that notes the similarities of word, expression, or theme in various passages and seeks to interpret those passages alike.

This third part of the passage comes to a close in a twofold conclusion: (1) that God's promise to Abraham could not have come about by any natural process of generation (i.e., "works"); rather, "righteousness" and the fulfillment of God's promise could only be "credited" to Abraham on the basis of faith, and (2) that, while such a crediting of righteousness was true for Abraham, it is also true "for us, to whom God will credit righteousness" — that is, "for us who believe in him who raised Jesus our Lord from the dead" (4:23-24).

Our "Exegetical Comments" on Paul's example of Abraham, therefore, will be structured as follows:

1. A thesis statement on Abraham as the example of faith in 4:1-2.
2. Righteousness credited to Abraham on the basis of faith, not works, in 4:3-12.
3. The promise given to Abraham and his descendants, as well as to believers in Jesus, on the basis of faith in 4:13-24.

The statement in 4:25 is, we believe, an early Christian confessional statement that Paul appended as a fitting conclusion not only to his treatment of Abraham as the example par excellence of faith in 4:1-24 but also to all that he wrote in 1:16–4:24, that is, to all that he wrote in Section I of the body middle of his letter. It is comparable in provenance and purpose to the two confessional portions that appear at the close of Section II (5:1–8:39) and the close of Section III (9:1–11:36), as well as to the doxological statement that appears at the end of Section IV (12:1–15:13). It will be discussed in a brief section that follows this present section — as will the confessional portions at the close of Sections II, III, and IV be discussed following their respective sections.

EXEGETICAL COMMENTS

In his presentations in 3:21-31 about "righteousness," "faithfulness," and "faith," Paul began by insisting that "the law and the prophets" testify to what he is proclaiming (3:21) and concluded by asserting that by such a proclamation "We do not nullify the law! Not at all! Rather, we establish the law" (3:31). Later, in Section III of his letter's body middle, 9:1–11:36, he will speak more explicitly and extensively about how the Christian gospel is in line with the purposes of the Mosaic law and the promises of God. Here in 4:1-24, however, Paul focuses on Abraham as the example par excellence of "righteousness" and "faith," using the example of Abraham — or, more accurately, the points he sees as vitally important in Abraham's story — to support his theses about "righteousness" and "faith" being at the core of all biblical religion.

Before we take up the exegetical features in Paul's illustrative use of Abraham, it needs to be observed that Paul's highlighting of Abraham's experience with respect to righteousness and faith carries with it a number of highly significant implications for a Christian understanding of the course of "salvation history" (i.e., *Heilsgeschichte*) — or, as may be stated in other terms, for (1) one's understanding of relations between the Jewish (OT) Scriptures and the Christian (NT) Scriptures, (2) one's appreciation of the course of God's redemptive program as it has been enacted and worked out by God himself in humanity's history, and (3) one's attempts to take into account how that forward-moving program of divine redemption, particularly at its most important and crucial stages, has been not only understood but also developed and contextualized by the various biblical authors who wrote these two canonical bodies of scriptural writings.

We will speak later under the heading "Biblical Theology" about the implications that can be drawn from Paul's use of Abraham. Suffice it here to say, however, that Paul's highlighting of the example of Abraham in support of his Christian theses has much to teach us today about (1) relations of structure and content that exist between the OT and the NT, (2) continuities and discontinuities that appear in the course of God's redemptive program, and (3) habits of expression, patterns of development, and various forms of contextualization that seem evident in the various biblical writers' portrayals of the stages and events of salvation history.

All this, we believe, is necessary in a Christian biblical theology, for we are often faced today by two disparate extremes of interpretation — that is, (1) by "displacement" or "replacement" theories, which view the Christian gospel as having entirely displaced or replaced the proclamation of God's righteousness and human redemption in the Jewish (OT) Scriptures, and (2) by "sameness" or "identical" theories, which argue that the same salvific features of the Christian gospel (as proclaimed in the NT) are able to be identified in the religion of Israel (as portrayed in the OT), though under different guises or differing forms. It is our hope that a number of these issues will be brought to the fore in the exegetical comments below — and that, following those comments, they will then be explicated somewhat more fully in the "Biblical Theology" section that follows.

I. Thesis Statement on Abraham as the Example of Faith (4:1-2)

Romans 4 begins with a thesis statement about Abraham, the example par excellence for Jews of a faithful Jew and the example par excellence for Paul of a person of faith. It is in 4:1 that Paul sets the topic for all that follows in 4:1-24. Yet this verse, while seemingly straightforward, has presented a number of textual, grammatical, syntactical, and interpretive difficulties — not only for exegetes of the past, as seen in numerous attempts by ancient scribes and editors to improve or correct the wording of the various readings that appear in the Greek textual tradition, but also for commentators today, as seen in all sorts of contemporary endeavors by scholars to understand what the apostle is saying in this verse. And in 4:2 Paul expresses the theme of the passage in the form of a challenge.

4:1 Paul's example of Abraham begins with a question, Τί οὖν ἐροῦμεν εὑρηκέναι Ἀβραὰμ τὸν προπάτορα ἡμῶν κατὰ σάρκα; ("What then shall we say that Abraham, our forefather according to the flesh, discovered regarding this matter?"). His question appears to include an epistolary "verb of saying," ἐροῦμεν ("shall we say"). Here, however, τί ἐροῦμεν; ("What shall we say?") is best viewed not as a traditional epistolary convention, but rather as the opening feature of a rhetorical *paradeigma*. The postpositive οὖν ("therefore," "then") of this verse functions as a transitional particle that (1) looks back to the material or subject previously treated, but also (2) looks forward to something further that needs to be said or asked with respect to what has just been said or presented — whether by way of clarification, amplification, application, or illustration. It is used in these ways in a number of rhetorical questions in the NT, particularly in Paul's questions in Rom 3:9, 27, 31; 6:15; 10:14; 11:7.[23] And it is used in these ways in his rhetorical question "What, then, shall we say?" (τί οὖν ἐροῦμεν;), which appears seven times in this letter (and only in this letter of the NT Pauline corpus) — in 3:5; 4:1 (here); 6:1; 7:7; 8:31; 9:14, 30.

In asking "What, then, shall we say?" Paul repeats the form of the question he asked in 3:5. But he also uses the question to introduce what he will write in 4:2-24 about Abraham, whose example he employs to "attest" (cf. the participle μαρτυρουμένη of 3:21) and "establish" (cf. the verb ἱστάνομεν of 3:31) from the Jewish (OT) Scriptures what he has set out in 3:21-31 regarding "righteousness" and "faith."

The textual problems of 4:1 have to do with (1) whether the perfect infinitive εὑρηκέναι ("to have found," "discovered") is to be included in the text, and if included, (2) whether it is to be placed before Ἀβραάμ ("Abraham") or after ἡμῶν ("our"). The grammatical problems have to do with the incompleteness

---

23. Cf. also 1 Cor 6:15b; 10:19; 14:15, 26; Gal 3:19, 21; 4:1

of the question or questions in the verse, for the infinitive εὑρηκέναι has no express subject and no proper object, and so raises questions as to (1) whether the infinitive εὑρηκέναι functions as the subject of the sentence or (2) whether the name Ἀβραάμ, which is indeclinable, should be understood as a nominative, and therefore the subject of the sentence, or as an accusative, and therefore the object of the verbal infinitive. The syntactical problems that must be faced are (1) whether there are one or two rhetorical questions being asked in this verse, and (2) whether κατὰ σάρκα ("according to the flesh") goes with the name Ἀβραάμ or with the infinitive εὑρηκέναι. Some of the more singular interpretive questions are as follows: (1) Who is in mind in the use of the first-person plural suffix of the verb ἐροῦμεν ("what shall we say") and the first-person plural personal possessive pronoun ἡμῶν ("our")? Is it Paul himself (understood as an editorial "we" or "our"), nonbelieving Jews, Jewish believers in Jesus, Gentile believers in Jesus, or all Christians, Jews and Gentiles alike? (2) Why is the titular title ὁ προπάτωρ ("the forefather") used and what significance does it carry, for προπάτωρ is a Pauline (as well as a NT) *hapax legomenon,* which appears here in the accusative case as τὸν προπάτορα?

The presence and placement of the infinitive εὑρηκέναι ("to have found" or "discovered") have been from the earliest days of Christian history matters of dispute, as seen in the Greek textual tradition, the reflected testimony of the early versions, and the quotations of this verse by various early commentators — though both the external and the internal evidence seem sufficiently strong to warrant accepting εὑρηκέναι as included in the original text and as appearing in that text before the name "Abraham" (see "Textual Notes" above). While the presence and placement of εὑρηκέναι may seem fairly well established today, its appearance without an express subject and without a proper object — as well as a number of other grammatical and syntactical features in 4:1, as noted above — has engendered, particularly of late, a great deal of controversy.[24]

Rom 4:1 reads literally "What, then, shall we say 'to have discovered' Abraham our forefather 'according to the flesh' " — which, at best, is grammatically awkward; at worst, it presents a number of difficulties for translators and commentators. One suggested alternative reading of 4:1 is proposed by Richard Hays, who argues (1) that τί οὖν ἐροῦμεν, "what then shall we say," which phraseology occurs only in Romans, constitutes a complete sentence (as it does in 3:5; 6:1; 7:7; 9:14, 30; though, admittedly, not in 8:31), and therefore should be closed off with a question mark after the verb ἐροῦμεν; and (2) that the infinitive εὑρηκέναι, which follows this proposed first question in 4:1, is best understood as incorporating a first-person plural connotation, and so should be read "we have found" (as in a statement) or "have we found?" (as in a question) — and therefore 4:1 should be understood as setting out two rhetorical questions and translated: "What then shall we say? Have we [i.e., 'Jews,' understanding the

---

24. Cf. T. H. Tobin, "What Shall We Say That Abraham Found? The Controversy behind Romans 4," *HTR* 88, no. 4 (October 1995) 437-52.

unstated subject of the sentence to be 'the Jews'] found (on the basis of Scripture) Abraham [understanding the indeclinable name 'Abraham' as the object of the sentence] to be our forefather according to the flesh?"[25]

Another reading, which takes a similar stance regarding the presence of two questions but is different in its understanding of the second question, is put forward by Stanley Stowers: "What then will we say? Have we found Abraham to be our forefather by his own human efforts [that is, 'according to the flesh']?"[26] And Douglas Campbell's translation of this verse, while slightly different, is in line with that of Stowers: "What then shall we say? Did Abraham obtain paternity for us, the Gentiles, in relation to flesh?"[27]

Both the translation proposed by Hays and those proposed by Stowers and Campbell have been fairly well received (though with minor reservations) by a number of NT scholars today. Nonetheless, there remains one exception elsewhere in Romans where τί οὖν ἐροῦμεν ("what then shall we say") does not constitute a complete sentence, and so is not to be concluded after the verb by a question mark — that is, the question at 8:31: τί οὖν ἐροῦμεν πρὸς ταῦτα ("What then shall we say *with respect to these things?*"). It may, therefore, be held that τί οὖν ἐροῦμεν here in 4:1 is another exception.

More important, however, is that the translations suggested above require in their proposed second question the insertion of the adverb "only" (either expressly or implied) after the understood verb "is" in order to link this question with what follows in 4:3-10. For what follows in 4:3-10 has to do with the rejection of Jewish exclusiveness — particularly as expressed in the rhetorical question of 4:9, "Is this blessedness, then, *only* (as implied by the context) for the circumcised, or *also* (as expressed in the conjunction καί, which is used here adverbially) for the uncircumcised?"[28]

It seems better, therefore, to understand Paul's use of the infinitive εὑρηκέναι ("to have found," "discovered") as an echo of Gen 18:3, where Abraham finds favor (LXX εὑρίσκει χάριν) in God's sight, as Otto Michel and Ulrich Wilckens earlier suggested.[29] This is the position that James Dunn has spelled out more fully in arguing:

> Paul may well have intended to evoke the phrase which occurs quite frequently in the LXX: εὑρίσκειν χάριν (or ἔλεος), "to find grace (or mercy)."

---

25. Hays, "'Have We Found Abraham to Be Our Forefather according to the Flesh?'" following the suggestion of Zahn, *An die Römer* (1910), 212-18; cf. also N. T. Wright, who translates the verse as Hays does but varies in his understanding of the implied subject "we": "What then shall we say? Have we [i.e., 'Christians, Jews and Gentiles alike'] found Abraham to be our forefather according to the flesh?" as proposed in his "Romans and the Theology of Paul," 38-39.

26. Stowers, "One God & One Father Abraham," 234-42.

27. D. A. Campbell, "Towards a New, Rhetorically Assisted Reading of Romans 3.27–4.25," 386-90, esp. 388.

28. See the discussion below, *ad loc.*

29. See Michel, *An die Römer* (1978), 161-62; Wilckens, *An die Römer*, 1.261.

It is prominent particularly in Genesis (13 times), but also in Exod 33 (4 times), 1 Samuel (6 times), and *Sirach* (7 times). Elsewhere cf., e.g., Deut 24:1, Dan 3:38 (LXX), Bar 1:12, and 1 Macc 11:24. Note particularly Gen 18:3 — Abraham himself speaks of "finding favor in God's sight." That the phrase was still in familiar usage in the first century in Jewish circles is indicated by Luke 1:30, Acts 7:46, Heb 4:16, and *4 Ezra* 12.7.[30]

The problem usually raised with respect to this hypothesis is that such an echo of εὑρίσκειν χάριν or ἔλεος ("to find grace" or "mercy") — as the expression appears in the Jewish (OT) Scriptures and can be found in other Jewish writings, and particularly as it reverberates in Gen 18:3 — would have been unintelligible to Paul's Gentile Christian addressees at Rome.[31] But the hypothesis of εὑρηκέναι here in 4:1 as an echo of the biblically sanctioned phrase εὑρίσκειν χάριν or ἔλεος can, perhaps, be more readily appreciated if we postulate that most, if not all, of the Christians at Rome, whether ethnically Jews or ethnically Gentiles, had been extensively influenced by the outlook, thought, and language of Jewish Christianity and the mother church at Jerusalem — even, perhaps, influenced by the biblical stories of the Jewish patriarchs, and particularly by the story and example of Abraham.

It is probably best, therefore, to understand 4:1 as comprising a single question that idiomatically introduces Paul's use of the example of Abraham to his Christian addressees at Rome in a manner he believed they would appreciate and resonate with. Idiomatic expressions are always difficult to translate from one language and one culture to another, but they strike quickly to the heart of matters for those to whom they are familiar. Thus, as James Dunn has theorized:

> Paul's purpose in evoking the phrase [εὑρίσκειν χάριν] would probably be to prepare the ground for the following exposition in which χάρις features (vv. 4, 16), by implying from the outset that Abraham's standing before God was an act of divine favor.[32]

And as Dunn goes on to suggest:

> The perfect tense also is a subtle indication that what Abraham found to be the case when he first found favor with God determined his standing with God thereafter.[33]

---

30. Dunn, *Romans*, 1.198.

31. This problem of possible unintelligibility could also, of course, be raised with respect to Paul's reference to Abraham as προπάτωρ ("forefather") and his use of the possessive pronoun ἡμῶν ("our") with respect to Abraham, which are matters that will be raised in our exegetical comments below.

32. Dunn, *Romans*, 1.198.

33. *Ibid.*

"It is not necessary, however," Dunn points out in defense of his suggested rationale regarding Paul's purpose, "that Paul intended χάρις to answer the opening τί."[34] So we may simply translate this first verse of ch. 4 in the following rather prosaic, nonidiomatic fashion: "What, then, shall we say that Abraham, our forefather according to the flesh, discovered regarding this matter?" — taking the indeclinable name Abraham as the subject (not the object) of the infinitive εὑρηκέναι, linking the phrase κατὰ σάρκα ("according to the flesh") with its preceding articular noun and possessive pronoun clause τὸν προπάτορα ἡμῶν ("our forefather"), and accepting that some such implied expression as "regarding this matter" needs to be added as a general characterization of Paul's topic and of all that he will say about it in what follows.

The spelling of Abraham's name as Ἀβραάμ is taken from Gen 17:5 (LXX), where God changes the patriarch's name from אברם (LXX Ἄβραμ, "the father exalted") to אברהם (LXX Ἀβραάμ, "the father of many nations"). It is this form of the name that appears also in quotations of Gen 15:6 in Gal 3:6 and in Jas 2:23, though the record of God's change of the patriarch's name does not appear until Gen 17:5.

The physical descendants of Abraham were indeed "many nations" — that is, (1) his son Ishmael by Sarah's handmaid Hagar, and Ishmael's many descendants; (2) the promised son Isaac by Abraham's first wife Sarah, and Isaac's many descendants; and (3) the six sons of his second wife Keturah, whom Abraham married after the death of Sarah, and their many descendants.[35] Paul's argument in his earlier letter to his own Gentile converts in Galatia regarding God's promise to "Abraham and his seed" was (1) that when God gave his promise "to Abraham and to his seed," he intentionally included as Abraham's "Seed" the "one person, who is Christ" (Gal 3:16), and (2) that "if you belong to Christ, then you are Abraham's 'seed,' and heirs according to the promise" (Gal 3:29). And it is this understanding that Paul will repeat later in Romans at 4:16-17 and 4:23-24.[36]

Jews spoke of Abraham as their προπάτωρ, "forefather."[37] However, this reference to Abraham as προπάτωρ ("forefather") does not appear elsewhere in Paul's letters and the rest of the NT; it is a *hapax legomenon* (appearing only here in 4:1), with the usual designation for Abraham elsewhere being simply πατέρα, "father."[38] Nonetheless, προπάτορα is adequately attested by the textual tradition and therefore should be accepted.[39] Likewise, the first-person plural

---

34. Dunn, *Romans,* 1.198.

35. Cf. Gen 25:1-4; see also Josephus, *Antiquities* 1.238-41, regarding the sons of Abraham and Keturah, as well as some of their grandsons, of whom Josephus says, "Abraham contrived to send out to found colonies."

36. See our "Exegetical Comments" below on these passages, *ad loc.*

37. Cf. Josephus, *War* 5.380, where Sarah is referred to as τὴν μητέρα τοῦ γένους ἡμῶν, "the mother of our race," and Abraham as ὁ ταύτης ἀνὴρ Ἀβραάμ, προπάτωρ, "her husband Abraham, [our] forefather."

38. Cf. later in this passage at 4:11b-12 (twice); see also Luke 16:24, 30; John 8:53; Acts 7:2.

39. See "Textual Notes" above.

possessive pronoun ἡμῶν ("our"), whether following προπάτορα or πατέρα (which is here less externally supported), is amply attested in the external MS evidence — in fact, there is no dispute about the legitimacy of its presence in the Greek textual tradition.

The people of Israel were explicitly exhorted to refer to Abraham as "our father" in Isa 51:1-2a:

> Listen to me, you who pursue righteousness
>   and who seek the LORD;
> Look to the rock from which you were cut out,
>   and to the quarry from which you were hewn;
> Look to Abraham, your father,
>   and to Sarah, who gave you birth.

During the period of early Judaism, however, this prerogative was reserved for only those who were born Jews, and therefore "even proselytes," as W. D. Davies has pointed out, "were not allowed to call Abraham 'our father.'"[40] Yet Paul's point in the conclusion to the first major section of his argument in this passage, that is, in 4:3-12, is that Abraham is "the father of all who believe" (4:11b) — that is, the father of both those who believe "but have not been circumcised" and those who are circumcised "but who also walk in the footsteps of the faith that our father Abraham had before he was circumcised" (4:12). So, while calling Abraham "our father" or "forefather" may have been considered by Jews a special privilege reserved only for born Jews (i.e., "cradle Jews"), among the early believers in Jesus — and certainly by Paul — such a right of designation was extended to all who "walk in the footsteps of the faith that Abraham had before he was circumcised." Thus Paul had no scruples about calling Abraham "our forefather" in a manner that included not only himself and all other Jewish believers in Jesus, but also all the Christians at Rome whatever their ethnicity (as well as, undoubtedly, all the believers in Jesus elsewhere in the Roman Empire). This is what he did, in effect, in his earlier letter to his own Gentile converts in Galatia when he proclaimed: "If you belong to Christ, then you are Abraham's seed and heirs according to the promise" (Gal 3:29) — and what he did more expressly, contrary to the Judaizers' assertions, in declaring at the end of that letter that all true believers in Jesus, whatever their ethnicity, are "the Israel of God" (Gal 6:16b).

But if "Abraham our forefather" is to be understood in a spiritual sense, why then the further phrase κατὰ σάρκα ("according to the flesh") that immediately follows τὸν προπάτορα ἡμῶν ("our forefather") and concludes the question? Every translator of this passage has wrestled with this problem.[41] Likewise

---

40. W. D. Davies, "Abraham and the Promise," 177.

41. Cf., e.g., the NIV of 1978 and 1983, whose translators did not translate κατὰ σάρκα because they considered it somewhat extraneous, whereas the translation committee for the 2001 NIV re-

Stanley Stowers, arguing that the entire dialogical context from 3:27 through to 4:2 presents relationships in a spiritual context, with denunciations against mere physical descent, insists that κατὰ σάρκα "is better understood as 'by human efforts' and thus as cohering with the issue of justification" that Paul presents in *diatribe* form in this passage.[42]

The issues involved are complex and difficult to determine precisely. Nonetheless, it may be affirmed that here in 4:1, while Paul's emphasis is on the spiritual factor of Abraham as "the father of all who believe," whether circumcised or uncircumcised, he also acknowledges that Abraham was the "forefather" or "father" of the Jewish nation — which dialectic between "spiritual" and "physical" features will reverberate extensively in all his later discussions of "national Israel" and "the remnant of Israel" in 9:1–11:36.

4:2 The postpositive conjunction γάρ ("for") is not used here in the statement εἰ γὰρ Ἀβραὰμ ἐξ ἔργων ἐδικαιώθη, ἔχει καύχημα. ἀλλ' οὐ πρὸς θεόν ("For if Abraham had been justified by works, he has something to boast about — but not before God") only to signal some type of continuity between 4:1 and 4:2 (though, of course, it does that). Rather, it seems to be primarily used to highlight in an inferential fashion two vitally important negative points that Paul wants to make about God's "justification" of Abraham: (1) that it was apart from any of Abraham's "works," however good his actions might have been, and (2) that even Abraham could not "boast" about his own righteousness before God. Here Paul picks up from his question in 3:27, "Where, then, is boasting?" — which question, in its context, (1) recalls all the issues regarding "bragging" about the Mosaic law and "boasting" about one's relationship to God that underlie what he wrote in 2:17–3:20, and (2) reminds his addressees of all that he wrote about the Christian proclamation in 3:21-26. More particularly, however, Paul presents the theme of what he will write in 4:3-12 regarding the righteousness that God credited to Abraham and in 4:13-24 regarding the promise that God made to Abraham and his descendants — and he does so in the form of a challenge that contests the interpretation of Abraham widely accepted by many Jews of Paul's day.

During the period of early Judaism (c. 200 B.C.–A.D. 100), Abraham's example of faithfulness to the Mosaic law was often cited as the pattern or model for devout Jews. Sir 44:19-21, for example, in praising the ancient "men of piety," says of Abraham (alluding to incidents and phraseology in Gen 15; 17; and 22):

> Abraham, "the father of a multitude of nations,"
>   tarnished not his glory;
> he kept the commandment of the Most High,
>   and entered into a covenant with Him.

---

vision, that is, the TNIV, translated the whole expression τὸν προπάτορα ἡμῶν κατὰ σάρκα as "the forefather of us Jews"; see also JB, "the ancestor from whom we are all descended."

42. Stowers, "One God & One Father Abraham," 242.

In his [Abraham's] flesh He [God] engraved him an ordinance,
   and in trial he was found faithful.
Therefore with an oath He promised him
   "to bless the nations in his seed,"
to multiply him "as the dust of the earth,"
   and to exalt his seed "as the stars" —
to cause them to inherit "from sea to sea,
   and from the River to the ends of the earth."

In a similar vein, the last words of the Maccabean leader Mattathias on his death-bed to his sons, as reported in 1 Macc 2:50-52 (which cites Abraham as the first in a line of pious and praiseworthy Israelites, and quotes Gen 15:6 in support), are these:

> Be zealous for the Law, and give your lives for the covenant of your fathers. And call to mind the deeds of the fathers, which they did in their generations, that you may receive great glory and an everlasting name. Was not Abraham found faithful in temptation, and it was "credited to him as righteousness"?

This same embellishing of the story of Abraham and lauding of his faithfulness to the Mosaic law as the example par excellence for Jewish piety appear throughout the literature of early Judaism; witness, for example, the statements expressed in tribute to Abraham in the following passages:

Jub 6:19 — "Abraham alone [of those in his day] observed Shabuoth" (i.e., the Festival of Weeks, which later was called Pentecost and commemorated God's giving the Ten Commandments on Mount Sinai).
Jub 23:10 — "Abraham was perfect in all of his actions with the Lord and pleasing through [his] righteousness all the days of his life."
Wis 10:5 — "Wisdom knew the righteous man [Abraham] and preserved him blameless unto God, and kept him strong when his heart yearned toward his child."
2 Bar 57:2 — speaking of "Abraham and his generation": "At that time the unwritten law [i.e., the 'Oral Law,' which later was codified in the Talmud and other rabbinic writings] was in force among them, and the works of the commandments were accomplished in that time."

This lauding of Abraham because of his faithfulness to the Mosaic law was continued in later rabbinic lore; see, for example, *Leviticus Rabbah* 2:10 (on Lev 1:12): "Abraham fulfilled the whole of the Torah, as it is said, 'Because Abraham hearkened to My voice and kept My charge, My commandments, My statutes, and My laws [Gen 26:5], and he offered a ram as a sacrifice [Gen 22:13].'"

To all these Jewish claims that Abraham had a great deal to boast about because of his faithfulness to God in observing the Mosaic law, Paul answers: "If, in fact, Abraham was justified by works, he had something to boast about — but not before God." Paul does not attempt to minimize the greatness of the person of "Abraham our forefather." Nor does he endeavor in any way to discredit Abraham's status as a "friend of God" or to discount the nobility of Abraham's actions before God and on behalf of others. But Paul directly challenges much of Jewish theological propaganda in saying (1) that Abraham was credited by God as being righteous on the basis of faith, apart from "works" (as he does in 4:3-12), and (2) that God's promise was given to Abraham and his posterity on the basis of faith, apart from what they themselves could have done (as he does in 4:13-24). Paul believed, it may be assumed, that his Christian addressees at Rome — because they were extensively influenced by a Jewish Christian understanding of the story of Abraham — would agree with him.

II. Righteousness Credited to Abraham on the Basis of Faith, Not Works (4:3-12)

Following his thesis statement of 4:1-2, Paul sets out in 4:3-12 the first part of his argument regarding Abraham, focusing particularly on Gen 15:6 and supporting his interpretation of that passage by the quotation of Ps 32:1-2. His presentation is dominated by an exploration of the meaning and significance of the term ἐλογίσθη ("it was credited") in the statement of Gen 15:6: "Abraham believed God, and *it was credited* to him as righteousness." Four rhetorical questions are asked in the development of his argument: the first in 4:3a, which serves to introduce the quotations of Gen 15:6 and Ps 32:1-2; three more in 4:9a and 4:10a, which, in combination, function to highlight certain significant implications that he argues must be drawn from these verses. This first portion of Paul's argument is then concluded in 4:11b-12 with a declaration that God's crediting of righteousness, and thus the fatherhood of Abraham, is for all people of faith, whatever their status — that is, whether "circumcised" Jews or "uncircumcised" Gentiles.

4:3 Unlike the γάρ in 4:2, the postpositive conjunction γάρ here in 4:3 probably signals only the idea of continuation (not cause, purpose, inference, or explanation), and so is best understood as simply tying together this first major portion of Paul's argument in 4:3-12 with what has been said by way of introduction in 4:1-2 (and so is probably best left untranslated) — just as it will later function in 4:13 to tie together the second major portion of Paul's argument in 4:13-24 with all that has gone before in the chapter (and so is also best left untranslated). The articular ἡ γραφή (literally "the writing") as a designation for the Jewish (OT) Scriptures stems from the LXX expression κατὰ τὴν γραφήν ("according to the Scripture") in such OT passages as 1 Chr 15:15, 2 Chr 30:5, and Ezra 6:18 (cf. also παρὰ τὴν γραφήν, "contrary to the Scripture," in 2 Chr 30:18). It was used by Jews of Paul's day to refer to both (1) an individual biblical passage[43] and (2) the biblical writings collectively.[44] Paul and other NT writers also used it for both an individual OT passage[45] and the OT Scriptures collectively.[46] Paul is probably using ἡ γραφή here in 4:3a with reference only to Gen 15:6, which he then immediately quotes in 4:3b — though he may, as well, have had in mind Ps 32:1-2, which he goes on to quote in 4:7-8.

The wording of the second clause of the Hebrew text of Gen 15:6 has often raised doubt about how the passage should be interpreted. The first clause, in its context, is clear: "and he [Abraham] believed in Yahweh" (והאמן ביהוה). The second clause, however, "and he credited to him righteousness" (ויחשבה לו צדקה), has provoked questions about who was crediting righteousness to whom — whether it was God who credited righteousness to Abraham or Abraham who credited (or "acclaimed") God as righteous. Such questions arise grammatically because of (1) the active form (i.e., Qal) of the verb, (2) the subject being indicated by only a pronominal suffix, and (3) the object being indicated by only a pronoun. In its context, however, this second clause is most likely to be understood as God crediting righteousness to Abraham rather than as Abraham declaring God to be righteous. And so it may legitimately be judged that the LXX's translation of this second clause, "and it [i.e., Abraham's faith] was credited [using the third-person singular aorist passive form of the verb] to him [Abraham] as righteousness" (καὶ ἐλογίσθη αὐτῷ εἰς δικαιοσύνην), is an entirely appropriate translation — understanding, in its context, the active (Qal) form of the Hebrew verb חשׁב as implying a passive (Niph'al) nuance of meaning.

The translators of the LXX may have been influenced by the statement about Phinehas in Ps 106:31 (LXX 105:31), where — because Phinehas's zeal for the law and his intervention on its behalf "checked the plague" that had been sent by God — it is said that "it [i.e., his zealous action] was credited to him as righteousness (ותחשב לו לצדקה) for endless generations to come." This statement about Phinehas's zeal and action uses the passive (Niph'al) form of the verb חשׁב ("to think," "reckon," "account," "credit"). Thus the passage was translated by the translators of the LXX, using the third-person singular aorist passive Greek verb ἐλογίσθη ("it was credited"), as follows: καὶ ἐλογίσθη αὐτῷ εἰς δικαιοσύνην ("and it was credited to him as righteousness" — which is how the LXX translates the second clause of Gen 15:6, even though the Hebrew text of Gen 15:6 has the active [Qal] rather than the passive [Niph'al] form of the verb חשׁב). The appearance of this same translation in both texts may indicate that the LXX translators thought that these two portions of biblical material, which have similar contexts, should be translated the same — thereby clarifying the

<hr>

43. Cf. 4 Macc 18:14; Philo, *Quis rerum divinarum heres sit* 266.

44. Cf. Philo, *De fuga et inventione* 4; *De specialibus legibus* 1.214; *Quis rerum divinarum heres sit* 106, 159; Josephus, *Contra Apion* 2, 45.

45. Cf. Rom 11:2; 2 Tim 3:16; see also Mark 12:10; 15:28; Luke 4:21; John 13:18; 19:24, 36-37; Acts 1:16; Jas 2:8, 23.

46. Cf. Rom 9:17; 10:11; 11:2; 1 Cor 15:3-4; Gal 3:8; 4:30; 1 Tim 5:18; see also John 2:22; 10:35; 20:9; Acts 8:32; Jas 2:8; 2 Pet 1:20.

somewhat ambiguous wording of Gen 15:6 by the more explicit wording of Ps 106:31 (LXX 105:31).

In 1951 Gerhard von Rad attempted to elucidate the verb "to reckon" or "credit" (חשב; λογίζομαι) and the noun "righteous" or "righteousness" (צדקה; δικαιοσύνην) in the Hebrew tradition, by (1) identifying the historical situation within which these terms arose within the religion of Israel, (2) clarifying their meanings in Israel's sacrificial cultus, and (3) highlighting the difference between a cultic understanding of these terms and the way they are used in Gen 15:6.[47] As for the original context and meaning of these terms, von Rad argued that they arose in a "priestly" context as "declaratory formulae" wherein a priest, on behalf of Yahweh, pronounced judgments on individual worshipers — either accepting or rejecting (i.e., "reckoning") the worshipers as being worthy (i.e., "righteous"), and thereby either accepting or rejecting their offerings as acceptable to God (i.e., as "reckoned" by God as "righteousness"). In the process von Rad isolated a number of negative declarations that the Israelite priests were to make with respect to unworthy, inappropriate, or ill-timed sacrificial offerings — citing, in particular, such passages of rejection that used the verb חשב ("reckoned") as Lev 7:18b ("he who offers it [i.e., the peace offering after the third day of its sacrifice] shall not be accepted, neither shall it be *reckoned* to him, it shall be an abomination") and Lev 17:4 ("if anyone does not bring it [i.e., the animal he had killed] to the door of the tent of meeting . . . blood-guilt shall be *reckoned* to that man").[48]

On the other hand, von Rad also cited passages that speak of the life of a righteous man, whose sacrifices are properly offered, as being accepted by Yahweh. One particularly important passage in this latter vein is Ezek 18:5-9, which von Rad believed also stems from a priestly situation and ends in v. 9 with the statement: "He follows my decrees and faithfully keeps my law. That man is righteous (צדיק); he will surely live."[49]

Underlying all of Gerhard von Rad's work was, of course, his own form of the then-current "documentary hypothesis," which drew a sharp distinction, based on the differing provenances and purposes of the proposed documents, between priestly and prophetic materials in the OT. Indeed, distinctions between "priests" and "prophets" can certainly be made, though not necessarily on the same critical basis that informed all of von Rad's work. Nonetheless, the important thing for our purposes is what he has called the "astonishing difference" between a cultic understanding of "reckoning" and "righteousness," on the one hand, and the use of these terms in Gen 15:6, on the other.[50] For as von Rad expressed matters, "the cultic 'reckoning' depended on something done by the human worshipper, by way of sacrifice or specific obedience, and at all

47. See von Rad, "Faith Reckoned as Righteousness" (ET 1966), 125-30.
48. *Ibid.*, 126-27.
49. *Ibid.*, 127b-29a.
50. Cf. *ibid.*, 129.

events in some active manner," whereas in Gen 15:6, "in a solemn statement concerning the divine purpose, it is laid down that it is *faith* which sets men on a right footing with God."[51]

And it is such an understanding of Gen 15:6 that Paul sees clearly in the passage — in opposition to any suggestion, however current in his day, that God's "reckoning" or "crediting" of righteousness to Abraham was based on the intrinsic quality of his own righteousness, which existed either prior to or concurrently with his expression of faith in God's promise of progeny. For as Paul understood matters, God's reckoning or crediting Abraham as righteous meant that what was bestowed on Abraham was *the status of God's own righteousness* in response to Abraham's expression of faith, and not that God declared Abraham's faith as expressing *a quality of his own righteousness* that was in some manner intrinsic to him already — as seen in what he says about righteousness as "a gift, not an obligation" and as "by faith, apart from works" in 4:4-6, as well as what may be inferred from all that he argues by way of explication in 4:9-24.

God's promise to Abraham that he would be "the father of many nations" appears a number of times in Genesis — not only in 15:5, but also earlier in 12:2-3 and later in 17:4-5, 18:18, and 22:17-18. There are also two versions in Genesis of God's giving the covenant to Abraham, in 15:18 and 17:2-21. However, only in 15:6 are the three factors of (1) Abraham's "faith" in God, (2) God's "crediting" of Abraham's faith, and (3) God's gift of "righteousness" to Abraham brought together. Further, only in Gen 17:4-5 does the account appear of his name being changed from "Abram" to "Abraham." Thus it is these two biblical passages that Paul quotes in his portrayal of Abraham in Rom 4: the first and most prominent, that of Gen 15:6, as quoted in 4:3 and discussed throughout the rest of the passage (with Ps 32:1-2 brought into the presentation by way of support in 4:6-9a); the second, that of Gen 17:4-5, as quoted in 4:17.

4:4-5 Picking up from the third-person singular aorist passive ἐλογίσθη ("it was credited") that appears in Gen 15:6, Paul uses the verb λογίζομαι ("reckon," "account," "credit") twice more in 4:4-5 (as well as eight more times in Rom 4). He first denies that "righteousness" (δικαιοσύνη) is to be associated with any concept of human "works" (ἔργα) that bases itself on such false concepts as divine "obligation" (ὀφείλημα) or a deserved "payment," "wage," or "reward" (μισθός). Then he declares that God's "crediting of righteousness" is actualized only when "righteousness" is understood as a "gracious gift" (κατὰ χάριν) that is given in response to a person's "faith" (πίστις) and "trust" (πιστεύω) in him.

There is no clarifying treatment in these two verses of the meaning of "the righteousness of God" (δικαιοσύνη θεοῦ), that is, no discussion regarding whether the expression should be understood in an *attributive sense* or a *communicative sense,* or both. Righteousness as an attribute of God's person and his actions — as well as righteousness as a gift, at least in some sense, that God

51. Von Rad, "Faith Reckoned as Righteousness," 129 (italics his).

bestows on his people — seem to have been matters widely accepted without controversy, not only by Paul and his Christian addressees at Rome but also by the better Jewish teachers during the period of early Judaism and the better Christian teachers within the time of early Jewish Christianity. Nor is there any treatment in these verses regarding "the faithfulness of Jesus Christ" (πίστις Ἰησοῦ Χριστοῦ). For Paul is not using the example of Abraham as an occasion to set forth the more developed content of the Christian gospel, which focuses on the work and person of Jesus Christ. He is using the biblical statement about Abraham in Gen 15:6 simply to illustrate the basic structure of all biblical religion.

So here in 4:4-5 the apostle deals with the themes of "righteousness" as a gift of God and "faith" as the necessary response of people, arguing: (1) that Gen 15:6 speaks only about Abraham's trust in God ("Abraham believed in God"), without saying anything about Abraham's acclaimed "good works"; (2) that the verb λογίζομαι ("reckon," "account," "credit") in its biblical context has to do with God's gracious gift, without any intervening ideas about obligation, merit, or reward; (3) that the gift of righteousness that God gives to those who put their trust in him is his own "righteousness," which both changes the recipient's status before God and transforms his or her character and resultant actions; and (4) that God is "the One who justifies the wicked" (which expression must have been shocking to many of Paul's contemporaries, especially to those with a Jewish heritage) simply on the basis of their trust in him and apart from any consideration of such matters as payment, wage, or reward.

The verb ἐργάζομαι ("work," "be active," "accomplish," "carry out") was used as a substantival participle in a positive fashion earlier by Paul in Rom 2:10 when speaking about "glory, honor, and peace *for everyone who does good*" (παντὶ τῷ ἐργαζομένῳ τὸ ἀγαθόν). And that is how the verb, its participle, and its corresponding noun ἔργον ("work," "deed") also appear in such other Pauline passages as 1 Cor 16:10, Gal 6:10, and Col 3:23.

Likewise, the noun ὁ μισθός ("pay," "wage," "reward") was used positively in an earlier letter by Paul in 1 Cor 3:8: "The one who plants and the one who waters have one purpose, *and each will be rewarded* (ἕκαστος δὲ τὸν ἴδιον μισθὸν λήμψεται) according to his or her own labor." And that is how it also appears in such other places in the NT as Matt 5:12, 6:1, Mark 9:41, Luke 10:7, and Rev 11:18. Here in 4:4, however, the dative articular substantival participle τῷ ἐργαζομένῳ ("to the one who works") and the nominative articular noun ὁ μισθός ("payment," "wage," "reward") — as well as the noun ὀφείλημα ("debt," "what is owed," "obligation") — are used negatively in contradistinction to the expression κατὰ χάριν ("according to [God's] gracious gift"), which requires only a human response of "faith" or "trust." For the central point that Paul draws from the statements in Gen 15:6 about Abraham, as he says quite expressly in 4:5, is simply this: "To the one who does not work (τῷ μὴ ἐργαζομένῳ) but trusts in (πιστεύοντι δὲ ἐπί) the One [i.e., God] who justifies the wicked (τὸν δικαιοῦντα τὸ ἀσεβῆ), that person's faith (ἡ πίστις αὐτοῦ) is credited (λογίζεται) as righteousness (εἰς δικαιοσύνην)."

4:6 In this verse Paul supports his statements of 4:4-5 by citing the psalmist David in Ps 32:1-2 (LXX 31:1-2). The adverb καθάπερ ("just as") appears almost exclusively in the NT in Paul's letters — either alone, as later in Rom 12:4,[52] or with the intensive use of the conjunction καί ("also"), as here in 4:6.[53] The synonymous adverb καθώς ("just as") is frequently used with the third-person singular perfect verb γέγραπται ("it is written") to introduce a biblical quotation (or, more broadly, to refer to some teaching of the OT Scriptures), as in Rom 1:17; 2:24 (perhaps); 3:4, 10; 4:17; 8:36; 9:13, 33; 10:15; 11:8, 26; 15:3, 9, 21.[54]

Καθάπερ here in 4:6 is far better attested in the Greek textual tradition than it was in 3:4 and has stronger internal probability here than there, and so in this verse is to be preferred.[55] The adverbs καθάπερ and καθώς are largely synonymous in meaning, and so could easily have been confused in editorial transmission. Yet it seems evident from the data cited above that the use by an NT author of one or the other of these adverbs was determined, in large measure, by whether (1) a comparison was being made, in which case καθάπερ ("just as") or καθάπερ καί ("just as also") was considered most appropriate, or (2) a biblical passage was being quoted or referred to, in which case καθώς γέγραπται ("just as it is written") or, possibly, καθώς ("just as") alone was thought most appropriate. The feature of comparison is most prominent in Paul's reference to what is said about people who are blessed by God in Ps 32:1-2 vis-à-vis what is said about Abraham in Gen 15:6 (even though Paul goes on to include an exact quotation of the psalmist's words themselves), and so the adverb καθάπερ καί ("just as also") appears most properly here.

Ps 32 in the MT carries the title "Of David. A *Maskil*" (לדוד משכיל), with the title for this same psalm in the LXX (Ps 31) being "Of Instruction by David" (Συνέσεως τῷ Δαυίδ). Thus Paul, in line with all his Jewish and Jewish Christian contemporaries, spoke of Ps 32 (LXX 31) as words of instruction by David for the understanding of God's people — that is, instruction both (1) for those who held firmly to the Torah (i.e., the "instruction") that God gave in the old covenant through Moses and (2) for those who were committed to Jesus in this time of the new covenant, the "present age" of the eschatological "now."

The substantive τὸν μακαρισμόν (here in the accusative case), which stems from the adjective μακάριος ("blessed," "fortunate," "happy"), signifies "the blessedness," "fortunate state," or "happy condition" of a person "to whom God credits righteousness."[56] The reason for Paul's quotation of Ps 32:1-2 is ex-

---

52. Cf. 1 Cor 12:12; 2 Cor 3:13, 18; 8:11.

53. Cf. 1 Thess 3:6, 12; 4:5; see also Heb 4:2, where καθάπερ appears in the similar expression καθάπερ κἀκεῖνοι, "just as they did."

54. Cf. also its repeated use in this fashion throughout 1 and 2 Corinthians and Galatians; see also Matt 26:24; Mark 1:2; 9:13; 14:21; Luke 2:23; Acts 15:15.

55. See "Textual Notes" above.

56. Cf. the two other uses in the NT where such a substantive form of the adjective is found: Rom 4:9, which immediately follows the quotation of Ps 32:1-2 in this passage, and Gal 4:15; both appear in the nominative case.

pressly stated in the final words of this introductory sentence: "God credits righteousness apart from works" (ὁ θεὸς λογίζεται δικαιοσύνην χωρὶς ἔργων). It is a reason that picks up from the final four words of the quotation from Gen 15:6, ἐλογίσθη αὐτῷ εἰς δικαιοσύνην ("it was credited to him as righteousness"). More importantly, it clarifies any possible misunderstanding regarding those final four words of the biblical passage, for it declares (1) that it is *God* (ὁ θεός) who credits righteousness to a person, and (2) that God's crediting of righteousness is *apart from works* (χωρὶς ἔργων).

The generic use of "works" (ἔργα) certainly has in mind any Jewish reliance on the Mosaic law as a means of obtaining acceptance by God and in one's reception of his gift of righteousness. It also, however, includes all the "good works" traditionally attributed to Abraham by the Jews — as well as whatever "good works" might be claimed by any person of whatever ethnic background in a misguided attempt to gain status before God and be rewarded by God.

4:7-8 Here Paul supports his use of Gen 15:6 in Rom 4:3 by again quoting Ps 32:1-2 (LXX 31:1-2). In bringing together Gen 15:6 and Ps 32:1-2, Paul employs the second of the seven traditional *middoth,* or interpretive rules, attributed to the great Jewish teacher Hillel — the rule *gezerah shawah* (גזירה שוה). This hermeneutical rule argued that when the same word, expression, or theme is found in two or more passages of Scripture, wherever located and however diverse, the same considerations apply to them all. This interpretive practice appeared earlier in Romans, being most obviously set out in the catena of passages of 3:10b-18 (whether that collection of passages should be attributed to Paul himself or to some earlier Jewish or Jewish Christian author whom he quoted) — it also lay under the bringing together of various OT passages later in the letter at 9:13-33, 11:8-10, and 15:9-12.[57]

Paul invokes this same procedure of "pearl stringing" here in 4:3-8 by first quoting Gen 15:6, "Abraham believed God, and it was *credited* (ἐλογίσθη) to him as righteousness" (in 4:3), and then joining to it the words of Ps 32:1-2 (LXX 31:1-2), particularly those of v. 2: "Blessed is the person to whom the Lord will never credit (λογίσηται) sin" (in 4:7-8). He infers from the presence of the verb λογίζομαι in these two passages that both are speaking about the same thing (even though in different settings, and with the one passage speaking positively and the other negatively) — that is, that they both speak about "the blessedness of the person to whom God credits righteousness apart from works" (as he says explicitly in 4:6).

It is evident that Paul thought of all four of the major soteriological expressions that are to the fore in 4:6-8 — first in his introductory statement of 4:6; then in his quotation of Ps 32:1-2 in 4:7-8 — as being roughly synonymous: (1) "God credits righteousness" (ὁ θεὸς λογίζεται δικαιοσύνην) in 4:6; (2) "transgressions are forgiven" (ἀφέθησαν αἱ ἀνομίαι) in 4:7a; (3) "sins are covered" (ἐπεκαλύφθησαν αἱ ἁμαρτίαι) in 4:7b; and, as expressed negatively,

57. See also 1 Cor 3:19-20; 15:54-55; 2 Cor 6:16-18.

(4) "the Lord will never credit sin" (οὐ μὴ λογίσηται κύριος ἁμαρτίαν) in 4:8. The apostle does not, however, use the soteriological expressions "repentance" (μετάνοια) and "forgiveness" (ἄφεσις) very often in his own letters, and their relative absence in his writings has often caused bewilderment and concern. George Foote Moore, speaking on behalf of the Jewish world, has stated the problem as follows:

> How a Jew of Paul's antecedents could ignore, and by implication deny, the great prophetic doctrine of repentance, which, individualized and interiorized, was a cardinal doctrine of Judaism, namely, that God, out of love, freely forgives the sincerely penitent sinner and restores him to his favor — that seems from the Jewish point of view inexplicable.[58]

Further, not only are "repentance" and "forgiveness" central themes in Judaism, they are also prominent elsewhere (i.e., apart from the Pauline letters) in the NT, appearing particularly in the following instances:

1. Zechariah's prophecy about the future ministry of his infant son John, which includes the statement: "he will give knowledge of salvation to his people by the forgiveness of their sins (ἐν ἀφέσει ἁμαρτιῶν αὐτῶν)" (Luke 1:77).
2. The Synoptic Evangelists' characterization of the ministry of John the Baptist as "a baptism of repentance (μετανοίας) for the forgiveness (εἰς ἄφεσιν) of sins" (Mark 1:4//Luke 3:3; cf. Matt 3:7-8, 11).
3. Jesus' reference to his own ministry as a calling of "sinners to repentance" (εἰς μετάνοιαν).[59]
4. The prayer that Jesus taught his disciples to pray (the "Lord's Prayer"), which includes the coupling of "God's forgiveness (ἄφεσις)" of "our sins/transgressions," and "our forgiveness (ἄφεσις)" of "others who sin/transgress against us" (Luke 11:4//Matt 6:12).
5. Jesus' words at the "Last Supper": "This is my blood of the covenant, which is poured out for many for the forgiveness (εἰς ἄφεσιν) of sins."[60]
6. Jesus' final words to his disciples, as portrayed in Luke's Gospel: "This is what is written: The Messiah will suffer and rise from the dead on the third day, and repentance (μετάνοιαν) unto the forgiveness of sins (εἰς ἄφεσιν ἁμαρτιῶν) will be proclaimed in his name to all nations, beginning at Jerusalem" (Luke 24:46-47).
7. Peter's preaching on the Day of Pentecost, which concludes with an appeal and a promise: "Repent (μετανοήσατε) and be baptized, every one

58. Moore, *Judaism*, 1.151.
59. Luke 5:32; though without the phrase "to repentance" in the parallel accounts of Matt 9:13 and Mark 2:17.
60. Matt 26:28; though without the phrase "for the forgiveness of sins" in the parallel accounts of Mark 14:24 and Luke 22:20.

of you, in the name of Jesus Christ so that your sins may be forgiven (εἰς ἄφεσιν τῶν ἁμαρτιῶν ὑμῶν). And you will receive the gift of the Holy Spirit" (Acts 2:38).

8. The second defense of Peter and "the other apostles" before the Jewish Sanhedrin, which includes the following significant proclamation: "God exalted him [Jesus] to his own right hand as Prince and Savior that he might give repentance (μετάνοιαν) and forgiveness of sins (ἄφεσιν ἁμαρτιῶν) to Israel" (Acts 5:31).

9. Peter's message to Cornelius and his household, which closes with the statement: "All the prophets testify about him [Jesus] that everyone who believes in him receives forgiveness of sins (ἄφεσιν ἁμαρτιῶν) through his name" (Acts 10:43).

10. A later characterization of the early Christian message, which was given in view of the seeming delay of Christ's parousia: "The Lord is not slow in keeping his promise, as some understand slowness. He is patient with you, not wanting anyone to perish, but everyone to come to repentance (εἰς μετάνοιαν)" (2 Pet 3:9).

Paul's letters, however, in seeming contradistinction not only to the soteriological emphases of Judaism but also to the teaching of Jesus and the consciousness of his earliest Jewish followers, are almost entirely devoid of references to (1) "repentance" (μετάνοια)[61] and (2) "forgiveness" (ἄφεσις).[62] Yet in Acts where Paul's ministry is depicted, in a few places the apostle is portrayed as (1) calling for "repentance" (Acts 13:24; 17:30; 26:20), (2) proclaiming God's "forgiveness" through the work and person of Jesus (13:38; 26:18), and (3) speaking generally of his preaching of the Christian gospel as a proclamation of "repentance" (20:21).

In all likelihood, Joachim Jeremias was moving in the right direction when he declared that for Paul "justification is forgiveness; nothing but forgiveness."[63] In support of Jeremias's dictum, it may be argued that Paul viewed the Jewish and Jewish Christian δικαι-complex of soteriological terms (i.e., the noun δικαιοσύνη, "righteousness"; the adjective δίκαιος, "righteous" or "just"; the verb δικαιόω, "justify" or "vindicate"; and the adverb δικαίως, "justly" or "uprightly") as more theologically significant than the terms "repentance" (μετάνοια) and "forgiveness" (ἄφεσις), as seems evident from his discussions throughout Rom 1:16–4:25. Yet even more perceptive for an understanding of Paul's outlook with respect to these matters is the assertion of Rudolf Bultmann that "in Paul the thought [of repentance and forgiveness] is expressed in such

---

61. The noun μετάνοια appears only in Rom 2:4, "the kindness of God leads to *repentance*," and 2 Cor 7:9, "your sorrow led you to *repentance*."

62. The noun ἄφεσις appears, in addition to its use here in the quotation of Ps 32:1 in Rom 4:7, only in Eph 1:7, "in him [Christ] we have redemption through his blood, the *forgiveness* of sins," and in parallel form in Col 1:14, "in whom [Christ] we have redemption, the *forgiveness* of sins."

63. Jeremias, *Central Message of the New Testament*, 66.

terms as δικαιοσύνη ['righteousness'] and καταλλαγή ['reconciliation']."[64] For while Paul seems to agree in many ways with his Christian addressees at Rome regarding "the righteousness of God" and "righteousness" in his presentations of 1:16–4:25, his more distinctive emphases are to be found, we believe, in 5:1–8:39, and have to do with such matters as "peace with God" (εἰρήνην πρὸς τὸν θεόν), "reconciliation" (καταλλαγή), and being "in Christ Jesus" (ἐν Χριστῷ Ἰησοῦ). Paul evidently viewed these personal, relational, and participationistic soteriological expressions as not only more theologically significant, but also more personally compelling and more ethically life changing, than the ancient terms "repentance" (μετάνοια) and "forgiveness" (ἄφεσις).

Thus it may be conjectured that Paul simply preferred the more personal, relational, and participationistic soteriological language that he uses in 5:1–8:39 — together, of course, with the δικαι set of forensic terms he uses in 1:16–4:25 in seeking common ground with his Christian addressees at Rome — to the language of "repentance" and "forgiveness" that was widely prevalent in Jewish and Jewish Christian circles. Evidently he believed that his favored soteriological expressions, which are found particularly in 5:1–8:39, not only (1) expressed better what he himself had experienced through the work of Christ and the ministry of God's Spirit, but also (2) connoted certain significant features that were more theologically profound and more ethically significant, and (3) conveyed certain nuances that resonated better with his Gentile audiences in his Gentile mission. He may have had no aversion in particular situations to call for "people's repentance" and to proclaim "God's forgiveness," particularly when speaking or writing in a Jewish or Jewish Christian context.[65] But it seems evident that in his Gentile mission he preferred to speak and write in a more personal, relational, and participationistic manner.

4:9-11 At the beginning of his presentation of the example of Abraham, that is, in 4:1, Paul asked the question, "What, then, shall we say that Abraham, our forefather according to the flesh, discovered regarding this matter?" Here in 4:9-11a he asks and answers three further rhetorical questions by highlighting certain important features that he insists must be noted, and from which certain significant implications need to be drawn, in what is said about Abraham in Gen 15:6 (and supported by Ps 32:1-2). And in these three questions and answers he focuses on two matters that he sees as crucial for an understanding of the statement "it [Abraham's 'faith' or 'trust' in God] was credited to him as righteousness" (ἐλογίσθη αὐτῷ εἰς δικαιοσύνην): (1) that the passage says only that "Abraham believed in God" (ἐπίστευσεν δὲ Ἀβραὰμ τῷ θεῷ), without any

---

64. Bultmann, "ἀφίημι, ἄφεσις, παρίημι, πάρεσις," 1.512.

65. As seen (1) when Paul addressed members of a Jewish synagogue at Antioch of Pisidia (Acts 13:24, 38), (2) when he spoke to a Roman ruler who knew something about the Jewish (OT) Scriptures and had been influenced, at least to some extent, by Jewish customs and thought (Acts 26:18, 20), (3) when he denounced pagan idolatry (Acts 17:30), and of course, (4) when he here quotes Ps 32:1-2 to Gentile believers in Jesus who have been extensively influenced by the theology and language of Jewish Christianity.

reference to any religious rites or meritorious actions on Abraham's part; and (2) that the context of the passage makes it clear that God credited righteousness to Abraham before he was circumcised, not when or after he was circumcised.

4:9 The first of Paul's three questions and answers in this section of Rom 4 has to do with the recipients of God's blessing referred to in Ps 32:1-2: "Is this blessedness, then, only for the circumcised or also for the uncircumcised?" followed by the answer: "We maintain that it was Abraham's faith that was credited to him as righteousness!" The logic of Paul equating Ps 32:1-2 with Gen 15:6 may seem somewhat tortuous to the Western mind. It is, however, understandable when viewed in terms of Hillel's second interpretive rule, which argued that when the same word, expression, or theme appears in two or more passages of Scripture, wherever located and however diverse, the same considerations apply to all of the passages. Because the same verb, λογίζομαι, was used in both, Paul viewed these two biblical passages (1) as necessarily to be read together, and (2) as speaking of Abraham's faith, and nothing else, as being the sole human factor in God's crediting righteousness to him — with the implications of these two passages being, as Paul understood them: (1) that God credits righteousness to anyone who has faith, and (2) that faith is not dependent on any particular ethnic heritage. And thus the apostle concluded that "this blessedness" of God's "gift of righteousness" is available to both Jews ("the circumcised") and Gentiles ("the uncircumcised"). Further, we may presume that such an argument, together with its implications, would be both understood and appreciated by Paul's Christian addressees at Rome, who, it seems, though dominantly Gentiles ethnically, had been influenced by Jewish Christians in their theology, patterns of thought, and religious language — as well as, in all probability, their inherited exegetical procedures in their interpretation of the OT Scriptures.

The postpositive γάρ in the expression λέγομεν γάρ (literally "for we are saying") is probably best understood as a colloquial introduction to some teaching or instruction (i.e., a form of direct discourse). It certainly suggests continuity with what has just been said. It also, however, signals the idea of explanation. Yet since the literal rendering "for" could suggest to readers of an English translation the ideas of causation or purpose, neither of which are factors here, it is probably best to leave the conjunction untranslated.

The statement ἐλογίσθη τῷ Ἀβραὰμ ἡ πίστις εἰς δικαιοσύνην ("the [his] faith was credited to him as righteousness"), therefore, is not to be understood as a direct quotation of Gen 15:6 (even though it is set in italics in most modern Greek texts today). Rather, it is Paul's own summation of the first and most obvious implication that needs to be drawn from Gen 15:6 — that is, that it was Abraham's "faith" alone that God credited as righteousness. It is this emphasis on faith in the experience of Abraham, Paul asserts, that God intended to be central in the structure of the religion of Israel (i.e., the religion of the OT Scriptures). And it is this same emphasis, he insists, that has also been central in his proclamation of the Christian message, both in his Gentile mission *and* in what he is writing to his Christian addressees at Rome (cf. the expression λέγομεν γάρ, which introduces a teaching or word of instruction, and so is best translated "for we are declaring" or "we maintain").

4:10 The second and third questions and answers of this section focus on the time when God credited righteousness to Abraham, that is, whether it occurred after he was circumcised or before. In these two questions and their answers Paul invokes the seventh of Hillel's exegetical rules *(middoth),* the rule *dabar halamed me- ʿinyano* (דבר הלמד מעינינו). This interpretive rule argued that a passage must always be interpreted by its context. Paul used this type of argument when he argued for the supremacy of God's promise over the supremacy of the Mosaic law in his message to his own Christian converts in Galatia — basing his argument on the historical fact that God first gave his covenant to Abraham and then much later gave the law (his Torah or words of instruction) to Moses, as follows:

> So I maintain this (τοῦτο δὲ λέγω): That the law, which appeared 430 years later (ὁ μετὰ τετρακόσια καὶ τριάκοντα ἔτη γεγονὼς νόμος; literally "the after four hundred and thirty years having been given law"), does not annul the covenant previously established by God, to do away with the promise. For if the inheritance is based on the law, then it is no longer based on promise. But God graciously gave (κεχάρισται ὁ θεός) it to Abraham by promise. (Gal 3:17-18)

Samuel Sandmel has pointed out that here in their respective understandings of "the relationship between Abraham, the ancestor, and the descendant, Moses, and his Law," there comes to the fore "a fundamental problem" for the Jewish rabbis of the homeland, for Philo of Alexandria, and for Paul: "If Moses' Law was the divine law, how could Abraham (and the other patriarchs) have flourished without it?" "The rabbis," Sandmel noted, "solve the problem in their way by asserting that Abraham observed the Mosaic Law; in fact, Abraham observed the 'Oral' Law also." With respect to Philo, the Jewish philosopher-theologian of Alexandria, Sandmel observed:

> Philo gives his own answer, an answer possible only in Greek and not rabbinic thinking: Abraham observed the law of nature, and Abraham was himself a law; the Law of Moses is the copy of the law of nature, and the Law of Moses derives its specifications from those specific things which Abraham (and other patriarchs) did.

As for Paul, Sandmel's characterization of his position was that "his solution is to regard the Law as having only temporal validity, beginning long after Abraham, who did not observe it, and enduring until Jesus, at which time it was abrogated."[66]

---

66. All Sandmel quotations in this paragraph from Sandmel, *Philo's Place in Judaism,* 107.

One may want to nuance somewhat better the verbs "did not observe" (with respect to Abraham) and "abrogated" (with respect to Paul). Nonetheless, Samuel Sandmel has quite rightly highlighted an important difference between Paul and most (at least) of the Jewish teachers of his day with regard to relations between Abraham and God's promise, on the one hand, and Moses and God's Torah, on the other.

It is here in 4:10 that Paul raises again this important question regarding the relationship of the Abrahamic covenant and the Mosaic law, dealing in both Gal 3:17-18 and Rom 4:10 with the matter of timing. For in both passages the apostle asserts that the larger context of Gen 15:6 makes it clear that God credited righteousness to Abraham *before* he was circumcised (which account of God's crediting of righteousness is given in Gen 15:6) and *not after* he was circumcised (which account of God's call for Abraham and his descendants to be circumcised is given in Gen 17:9-14). So Paul argues, in effect, just as he did earlier in his Galatian letter, (1) that the covenantal promise God gave to Abraham, as set out in Gen 15:6, was based only on Abraham's "faith" or "trust" in God and God's crediting of that faith "as righteousness" (cf. Gal 3:6-9); and (2) that the ritual of the circumcision of Abraham and his descendants, as spoken about in Gen 17:9-14, neither altered nor annulled the paradigmatic importance of Abraham's faith in God — which example of faith is the structural core of the religion of Israel and the prototype of all true religion (cf. Gal 3:17-18).

4:11a Circumcision, which is the surgical removal of the foreskin of the male penis, was performed by various groups of people in ancient times and continues in some cultures today. It was practiced in Egypt at least as early as the Old Kingdom or "Pyramid Age" (i.e., during the Third–Sixth Dynasties; c. 2700-2190 B.C.), as evidenced by exhumed mummies from that time and by wall drawings of the operation from that period. The Assyrians, Babylonians, Philistines, and the early inhabitants of Canaan did not circumcise their male children. Among Israel's immediate neighbors, however, circumcision was practiced by Edomites, Ammonites, Moabites, and various desert peoples.[67]

The Jewish (OT) Scriptures trace the origin of circumcision as a religious rite back to God's reaffirmation of his covenant with Abraham, as recorded in Gen 17:4-14. It was normally to be performed on the eighth day of an infant boy's life, with the operation, because of its covenantal significance, taking precedence over even the prohibition against work on the Sabbath when the eighth day was a Sabbath day. During Israel's Babylonian captivity, when God's people lived among uncircumcised Babylonians, the rite became of great importance as a national identity marker. And its importance as a religious and national identity marker became even greater when many of the Jews were repatriated

---

67. Cf., e.g., Jer 9:25-26: " 'The days are coming,' declares the Lord, 'when I will punish all who are circumcised only in the flesh — Egypt, Judah, Edom, Ammon, Moab, and all who live in the desert in distant places. For all these nations are really uncircumcised, and even the whole house of Israel is uncircumcised in heart.' "

to their homeland and needed to reassert their identity as a distinct people —
as well as, for much the same reason, during all the time they lived under the
authority of Greek and Roman rulers.

Circumcision, in fact, increasingly became a metonymy (i.e., a figure of
speech that uses the name of one thing for that of another of which it is an attribute or with which it is associated), which was used by both Jews and non-Jews
to identify Jewish people and to distinguish them from all other peoples — with
approval, of course, by the Jews themselves, but pejoratively by non-Jews. In
rabbinic times circumcision was the sign of both the Abrahamic covenant and
the Mosaic covenant (i.e., both the "elemental" form of God's dealing with his
people, as with Abraham, and the "developed" form of God's dealing, as expressed through Moses). It was often considered by Jews as the epitome of
being Jewish, with uncircumcision viewed as "the impurity of all impurities . . .
the mistake of all mistakes."[68] In the future, as rabbinic lore conceptualized it:
"Abraham will sit at the entrance of Gehenna and will not permit any circumcised Israelite to descend into it."[69]

For Paul, however, circumcision was not the essence of being a Jew (cf.
Rom 2:28-29). Nor would he, in all likelihood, have called the Mosaic law "a covenant of circumcision," as Stephen is reported to have called it in Acts 7:8. Rather,
playing on the phrase used in Gen 17:11, where circumcision is referred to as "the
sign of the covenant" (MT אות ברית; LXX σημεῖον διαθήκης), Paul speaks here
in 4:11a of Abraham having "received the sign of circumcision" (σημεῖον ἔλαβεν
περιτομῆς) — which he then immediately (1) defines as "a seal (σφραγῖδα) of the
righteousness that he [Abraham] had by faith" (τῆς δικαιοσύνης τῆς πίστεως),
and (2) notes that Abraham received that righteousness from God at a time
"when he was still uncircumcised" (τῆς ἐν τῇ ἀκροβυστίᾳ).

The noun σφραγίς means literally a material seal that was placed on a
document or scroll (as with the seven seals of Rev 5–6), which usually consisted
of an impression of a ruler's signet or an official's stamp that authenticated the
contents of what was written. It was, however, often used figuratively with reference to any act, situation, or statement that confirmed, attested, or authenticated something of importance. That is how Paul used the term with reference
to the confirming of his own apostleship in 1 Cor 9:2: "For you are my seal (ἡ
γὰρ σφραγίς μου . . . ἐστε) of our apostleship (τῆς ἀποστολῆς ὑμεῖς) in the
Lord." And that is how he uses it here in 4:11a in speaking of circumcision as a
"sign" (σημεῖον) or "seal" (σφραγίς) that functioned to confirm God's previous
gift of righteousness to Abraham — a righteousness that was already present in
Abraham's life at the time when God commanded him (as well as all of his future
male descendants) to be circumcised.

68. Cf. *Pirke de Rabbi Eliezer* 29B 4:36.

69. *Gen. Rab.* 48:8; for other rabbinic statements on the importance of circumcision, see
the rabbinic passages cited in the "Exegetical Comments" above by way of introducing Paul's denunciations in 2:25-29.

4:11b-12 The first major portion of Paul's argument regarding Abraham's faith is concluded in 4:11b-12 with a declaration that God's crediting of righteousness, and thus the fatherhood of Abraham, is for all people of faith, whatever their status — that is, whether "circumcised" Jews or "uncircumcised" Gentiles. The preposition εἰς ("into," "in") with an articular infinitive (which is always in the accusative case) is used to express either purpose or result. Here in 4:11b that construction appears twice, evidently being used in both ways: first, to express result by the phrase εἰς τὸ εἶναι ("so then"); second, to express purpose by the clause εἰς τὸ λογισθῆναι καὶ αὐτοῖς τὴν δικαιοσύνην ("in order that the righteousness might be credited to them").

The textual evidence for the inclusion of the adverbial use of καί ("also") after the aorist passive infinitive λογισθῆναι ("be credited") is not as strong as it is for its omission, and therefore the presence of καί here in this verse should probably be discounted (see "Textual Notes"). Yet the idea of "also" is certainly present in the text (note the use of ἀλλὰ καί, "but also," with respect to "the circumcised" in 4:12b), and so one could legitimately read "in order that the righteousness might be credited *also* to them (i.e., 'the uncircumcised')." While the textual evidence is almost equally divided between the inclusion and the omission of the article τὴν ("the") before the final word of 4:11, that is, before the noun δικαιοσύνην ("righteousness"), there is a slight balance in the textual tradition in favor of its inclusion (see "Textual Notes"). And if it is included, as we believe most likely, the article τήν should be understood as pointing back to the previous use of δικαιοσύνη in 4:11 (as is often the function of an article in Greek), with the resultant translation of τὴν δικαιοσύνην being something like the following: "the righteousness that we have spoken about previously," or, more colloquially, "the righteousness of which we speak."

The relation of what Paul says in 4:12 to what he said immediately before in 4:11b has frequently been disputed. Ernst Käsemann, for example, viewed 4:12 as something of an afterthought on Paul's part — that is, (1) his belated endeavor to bring into the discussion the state of the circumcised Jews, for usually he spoke of "the Jew first and also the Gentile," and (2) his attempt to "to qualify" the "exaggerated" nature of that previous statement and "soften" its "roughness" — for by simply saying that Abraham is "the father of those who believe but have not been circumcised," as he does in 4:11b, "Judaism is robbed of both Abraham and circumcision," which would not have been Paul's considered intention.[70]

In response to Käsemann, it needs to be said that, indeed, Paul speaks of two groups of people in 4:11b-12: first, "those who believe but have not been circumcised"; second, "those who are not only circumcised but also walk in the faith that our father Abraham had before he was circumcised." But the order in which he speaks of these two groups should not be seen as confused, and therefore in need of correction. Rather, Paul speaks of them in the order of the

70. Cf. Käsemann, *Romans,* 116.

Genesis references — that is, as in Gen 15:6, where Abraham in his uncircumcised state trusts God and is credited by God as righteous; and then, as in Gen 17:4-14, where God reiterates his covenant with Abraham and commands him and his descendants to be circumcised. Further, what Paul is doing here in 4:11b-12 is not attempting to rob Judaism either of Abraham or of circumcision — that is, neither to discredit Abraham's fatherhood of the Jewish people nor to dismiss circumcision as a valid religious rite — but rather, to insist that without one's possession of the faith of Abraham, his patriarchal status and his circumcision are without meaning for the Jewish people.

Paul's use of the phraseology οὐ μόνον, ἀλλὰ καί ("not only, but also") in 4:12, rather than some such dismissive expression as οὐ(κ), ἀλλά ("not, but"), nicely signals the balance in his thought between (1) his acceptance of both Abraham as the father of the Israelite nation and the rite of circumcision as a "sign" or "seal" for Jews of God's covenant with them (which later became a marker of their national identity), and (2) his insistence that any righteousness before God, while obviously influenced by these factors, is primarily a matter rooted in their individual and corporate responses of "faith" or "trust" in God. This, in essence, is what Paul said earlier in 2:28-29 when he declared:

> A person is not a Jew who is only one outwardly, nor is circumcision merely external and physical. Rather, a person is a Jew who is one inwardly, and real circumcision is a matter of the heart — by the Spirit, not by the written code. Such a person's praise is not from other people but comes from God.

Only here in his conclusion of 4:11b-12, as James Dunn has observed, "Paul goes beyond this [i.e., the passage in 2:28-29] in pressing the logic of Abraham's antitype: 'if faith is more important than outward ritual, then righteousness depends primarily on faith rather than the outward ritual, and is accorded also to those who have the faith without the outward ritual.'"[71]

III. God's Promise Given to Abraham and His Posterity, as well as to Believers in Jesus, on the Basis of Faith (4:13-24)

While the first part of Paul's argument in 4:3-12 is dominated by an exploration of the meaning and significance of the term ἐλογίσθη ("it was credited"), as appears in the statement about Abraham in Gen 15:6 and the affirmation about "the blessed person" in Ps 32:1-2, the second part of his argument in 4:13-24 is largely concerned with the nature of God's promise given to Abraham, as spoken about in Gen 15:4-5 and in Gen 17:4-6. There is also throughout this second part a continuing focus on Abraham's "faith" and "trust" in God, and so there appears repeatedly, in one form or another, the insistence that "the promise comes by

---

71. Dunn, *Romans*, 1.211.

faith." In the final portion of this second part the verb λογίζομαι ("reckoned," "credited") is brought back into view, with Paul insisting that it was because of Abraham's "faith" in God "to do what he promised" that God "credited righteousness to him" — with an application to his Christian addressees at Rome that for those "who believe in him [God] who raised Jesus our Lord from the dead," God also "will credit righteousness."

4:13 Here Paul states his thesis for what follows throughout all of this second part of his argument with regard to the example of Abraham. The postpositive conjunction γάρ functions to simply tie this second major portion of Paul's argument in 4:13-24 to what he previously in the chapter — just as the conjunction γάρ functioned earlier at the beginning of 4:3 to tie the first major portion of his argument in 4:3-12 to what he said previously by way of introduction in 4:1-2.

The noun ἐπαγγελία ("the promise") first appears in Romans here in 4:13 — though, of course, the topic is implied in Paul's quotation of Gen 15:6 in 4:3 (for that verse is set in the Genesis account in the context of God's promise of progeny to Abraham; cf. Gen 15:4-5) and in Paul's comments on that verse in 4:4-12. Further, this theme of God's promise will dominate the rest of Paul's *exemplum* of Abraham in 4:14-22. The use of the article ἡ ("the") with the noun ἐπαγγελία signals that a particular promise is in mind, which in context must certainly be understood as the promise of God to Abraham about his progeny given in Gen 15:4-5 and on which the statement of Gen 15:6 about Abraham's trust in God and God's crediting of righteousness to him is founded.

During the Greek classical period the word ἐπαγγελία was used by philosophers and orators in the sense of an "announcement," as in the writings of Aristotle (384-322 B.C.), one of the greatest of the Greek philosophers,[72] and as in the orations of Demosthenes (also 384-322 B.C.), the greatest of the Greek orators. In the second century B.C., however, ἐπαγγελία began to be used by Greek and Jewish writers more in the sense of "pledge," "assurance," or "promise."[73]

There are a number of promises set out in Genesis that were given by God to Abraham: the promise of a son born of his wife Sarah, who would be his true heir (Gen 15:4; 17:16, 19); the promise that his descendants would become a "great nation" (12:2); the promise that his own name would be great (12:2); the promise that he would be the father of many nations (17:4-6); the promise that he and his descendants would be given the land of Canaan as their perpetual possession (12:7; 13:14-15, 17; 17:8); the promise that his descendants would be exceedingly numerous, too many to be counted, just like "the dust of the earth," "the stars of the heaven," and "the sand on the seashore" (13:16; 15:5; 17:2, 6; 18:18; 22:17); and the promise that "all the nations of the earth will be blessed" through him and his posterity (12:2; 18:18; 22:18). Here in Rom 4:13 (and con-

72. See esp. Aristotle, *Nicomachean Ethics* 10.1.
73. Cf., e.g., Polybius, *History* 1.43.6; 7.13.2; 18.11.1; Diodorus Siculus, *Universal History* 1.5.3; 4.16.2; 1 Macc 10:15; Philo, *De mutatione nominum* 37; Josephus, *Antiquities* 5.8.11.

tinuing on throughout 4:14-24), however, Paul speaks in a generic fashion of only the promise that God gave to Abraham about his becoming "the heir of the world" — which is a locution for both (1) the new status and life credited to him by God *and* (2) the widespread and significant presence of Abraham and his progeny in the then-known world. And Paul insists in this thesis statement of 4:13 that God's promise "to Abraham and to his descendants" (τῷ Ἀβραὰμ ἢ τῷ σπέρματι αὐτοῦ) was given "not through the law" (οὐ διὰ νόμου) but "rather through the righteousness that comes by faith" (ἀλλὰ διὰ δικαιοσύνης πίστεως).

The particle ἤ, when used in a disjunctive fashion between opposites, functions to separate those mutually exclusive components, and so is translated "or," but when used between related or similar components, ἤ is equivalent to the conjunction καί, and so is to be translated "and" — as here in the expression τῷ Ἀβραὰμ ἢ τῷ σπέρματι αὐτοῦ (literally "to Abraham and to his seed"). Further, it may be assumed that Paul's negative insistence that the promise is "not through the law" (οὐ διὰ νόμου) was given in response to a common Jewish practice of his day that viewed the promises of God in the Jewish (OT) Scriptures (whether made to Abraham or to others) as (1) subordinate to the promises of the Mosaic law and (2) able to be received only through a person's faithfulness in observing God's Torah (i.e., "instruction") as given in that law.[74] Also to be noted is that Paul's positive statement that Abraham received God's promise "through the righteousness that comes by faith" (διὰ δικαιοσύνης πίστεως) involves an epexegetical or appositional use of the genitive πίστεως, which is best understood as stating the way in which the patriarch Abraham received God's promise, that is, "by faith."

For an appreciation of Paul's understanding of God's unfolding program of salvation in human history (i.e., *Heilsgeschichte*), it is important to note the following two significant matters in his thesis statement of 4:13: (1) that in his argument for faith, Paul reaches back behind Moses and goes directly to the experience of Abraham, and (2) that in speaking about God's promise, he does not include any reference to the territorial aspect of the promise given to Abraham and to his descendants. W. D. Davies has perceptively highlighted the first point in saying:

> Paul deliberately by-passes Moses to go back to Abraham, the prototype, not of Christ, but of Christian faith, and finds the continuity between the Gospel and Judaism, at least primarily, not in a historical sequence of a salvation-history but in the promise (not the Law).[75]

In support of this statement, Davies cites evidence drawn from Paul's earlier letter to his own converts in Galatia:

74. Cf., e.g., 2 Macc 2:17-18, "as he promised through the law"; *Pss Sol* 12:6, "Let the Lord's pious ones inherit the promises of the Lord"; see also *Sib Or* 3:768-69; *2 Bar* 14:12-13.
75. W. D. Davies, "Abraham and the Promise," 173 n. 19.

The Law Paul interprets as having been an intervention between the promise to Abraham and its fulfilment in Christ. Its role had been a particularized one, that is, directed only to Israel, which had thus been set apart from other peoples, but only in order to bring Israel to Christ, and that for the sake of all peoples. But even the particular role of the Law had been purely provisional (Gal. 3:19ff). Now, in the coming of Christ, the promise had been fulfilled and the Law was no more necessary (Gal. 3:10-14, 23-26). The children of the promise had achieved maturity and entered into their inheritance (Gal. 4:7). The preparatory, particularized time of the Law had now given place to the universalism of grace manifested in the fulfilment of the promise to Abraham "in Christ" (Gal. 3:15-18; Rom. 4:16).[76]

W. D. Davies has also pertinently spoken about the second matter cited above, that is, the lack of reference to territory in Paul's reference to God's promise to Abraham here in 4:13, in pointing out that "Paul ignores completely the territorial aspect of the promise. The land is not within his purview"[77] — then repeating that evaluation: "His [Paul's] interpretation of the promise is a-territorial."[78] And lest it be thought that Paul's silence about territory here was occasioned by political reasons — because Rome was the capital city of the Roman Empire and the center of world power in that day, it would have been not only audacious but also potentially dangerous to write any addressees living at Rome regarding Jewish territorial rights — Davies cites Paul's similar silence in his letter to addressees living in the outlying province of Galatia, where such "political correctness" would, presumably, not have been necessary:

> In Galatians we can be fairly certain that Paul did not merely ignore the territorial aspect of the promise for political reasons: his silence points not merely to the absence of a conscious concern with it, but to his deliberate rejection of it. His interpretation of the promise is a-territorial.[79]

The emphasis in Paul's thesis statement of 4:13 is on the positive point that it was "through the righteousness of faith" (διὰ δικαιοσύνης πίστεως) that Abraham received God's promise — which expression had become in Paul's vocabulary a rather clipped way of speaking about "the righteousness credited by God to those who receive it by faith." Here Paul proclaims the basic structure of all truly biblical religion, which structure was exemplified in the experience of Abraham and which remains the only pattern for people today.

4:14-15 In these verses Paul sets out two arguments in the form of what the ancient rhetoricians classified as *enthymeme* — that is, an abbreviated or

---

76. W. D. Davies, "Abraham and the Promise," 179.
77. *Ibid.*, 178.
78. *Ibid.*, 179.
79. *Ibid.*, 178-79.

imperfect syllogism, whose premises may involve matters of character *(ethos),* emotion *(pathos),* or reason *(logos),* but whose conclusion must be supplied by the audience or addressees: "For if those of the law are the heirs, the faith [of Abraham] has no value and the promise [of God] is worthless. For the law [of Moses] brings wrath. But where there is no law there is no transgression." The primary purpose of these two uses of enthymeme is to support the thesis statement of 4:13, that is, that God's promise to Abraham did not come through the law but through faith, and so they both begin with an explanatory use of the conjunction γάρ ("for"). This rhetorical technique of enthymeme will be found later in Romans in the questions of 6:1 ("Shall we go on sinning so that grace may increase?"), 6:2 ("How can we who died to sin still live in it?"), 6:15 ("Shall we sin because we are not under the law but under grace?"), and 7:7 ("Is the law sin?"), as well as elsewhere in his other letters.[80]

Paul's use of enthymeme here in 4:14-15 appears in the midst of his discussion of "God's promise" and "Abraham's faith," and so the articular expressions "the promise" (ἡ ἐπαγγελία) and "the faith" (ἡ πίστις) in 4:14 must be understood as meaning "the promise of God" and "the faith of Abraham," respectively. Likewise the three uses of the term "law" (νόμος) in 4:14-15, appearing as they do in the midst of discussions where νόμος has reference to "the Mosaic law," must also be understood as having in mind the Mosaic law, and not some general principle of "law" or "legality." Further, as an abbreviated statement (which is characteristic of an enthymeme), (1) the plural noun "heirs" (κληρονόμοι) in 4:14 should be understood in terms of its usage earlier in 4:13 (i.e., "heir of the world") and (2) the terms "wrath" (ὀργή) and "transgression" (παράβασις) in 4:15 should be understood in ways congenial to Paul's usage elsewhere in Romans and his other letters.[81]

The first enthymeme of 4:14 is probably best interpreted when (1) the substantival phrase οἱ ἐκ νόμου (literally "those of the law") is understood as "those people who base their lives on the Mosaic law" and (2) the plural noun κληρονόμοι ("the heirs") is viewed as connoting "a new status and life that has been credited by God." When they are understood in such a manner, Paul is simply saying here in 4:14 that to base one's life on the Mosaic law is, in effect, to discount God's promise of righteousness and to deny the efficacy of a human response of faith. It is to live a life of legalistic observance, and so to miss the quality of life as entailed in God's promise and as expressed by Abraham's faith. Such a life, therefore, only serves to demonstrate the truthfulness of Paul's thesis statement in 4:13: that God's promise given to Abraham became (and becomes) effective "not through the law . . . but through the righteousness that is received by faith."

The second enthymeme, in 4:15, begins with a premise regarding the Mo-

---

80. Cf., e.g., Gal 2:14; 3:3; 1 Cor 6:15.
81. With respect to the use of "wrath" in Romans, see 1:18; 2:5, 8; 3:5; with respect to the use of "transgression," see 2:23.

saic law: "For the law brings wrath!" This premise is followed by an inference about the absence of any accusation with respect to one's transgressions when there is no law: "But where there is no law there is no transgression." In Gal 3:10-14 Paul set out four biblical passages in two opposing categories: two of them, Deut 27:26 and Lev. 18:5, had to do with "law" and "curse," and he argued that attempting to "do" the law only brings on oneself a curse; the other two, Hab 2:4 and Deut 21:23, had to do with "faith" and "righteousness," and he argued that they provide the true pattern for the structure of biblical religion. What Paul does here in Rom 4:15 is very similar to what he did earlier in Gal 3:10-14 when he quoted Deut 27:26 and Lev 18:5 and commented on their negative implications. For here in 4:15 he declares in a very condensed and bombastic manner: "For the law brings wrath!"

It is this understanding of the law — as highlighted in Gal 3:10-14, stated here in 4:15 in brief and bombastic fashion, and to be developed more fully in 9:1–11:36 — that makes it absolutely impossible to claim that God's promise to Abraham and God's crediting of righteousness to him were generated by the Mosaic law or resulted from Abraham's own faithfulness to that law. And Paul concludes this second rhetorical enthymeme with the inferential statement: "But where there is no law there is no transgression" — arguing not the "truism" that "a person cannot be charged as a transgressor of the law if there is no legislation regarding the matter," but rather, that because the Gentiles were not given the Mosaic law, their status of righteousness before God cannot be said to arise from God's Torah ("instruction") given through Moses but must depend solely on God's grace, God's promise, and their response of faith.

Paul is not interested in setting out in this Romans passage any comprehensive teaching about the purpose and function of "the law of Moses" in the course of God's developing program of salvation. Much of that he did already in his Galatian letter, particularly in Gal 3:19–4:7, which is introduced by the question, "Why, then, the law?"[82] A number of matters of crucial importance in that discussion he will deal with later in this letter to the Christians at Rome in 9:1–11:36. His interest here is exclusively with whether God's promise came to Abraham and his descendants — and thus to people in Paul's day (and today) — through the Mosaic law or through a person's faith. And his use of the enthymeme form of rhetorical argumentation in 4:14-15 was intended solely to support his thesis statement of 4:13: "It was not through the law that the promise was made to Abraham and to his descendants . . . but through the righteousness of God that is received by faith."

4:16 In the immediately previous passage of 4:14-15, Paul highlighted by the use of two rhetorical enthymemes the negative point he made at the beginning of his thesis statement of 4:13, that is, that God's promise to Abraham came "not through the law" (οὐ διὰ νόμου). Here in 4:16 he highlights the positive point made at the conclusion of that thesis statement: that God's promise came

---

82. See R. N. Longenecker, *Galatians*, 135-78, passim.

"through the righteousness of faith" (διὰ δικαιοσύνης πίστεως). In so doing, he begins to draw to a conclusion all he has been saying about Abraham as the example par excellence of righteousness and faith.

The material of 4:16 begins with an idiomatic use of the preposition διά with the aorist singular neuter demonstrative pronoun τοῦτο (literally "because of this fact" or "because of what has been said"), which is best translated simply "therefore." The verse also begins with an elliptical sentence (i.e., a sentence marked by an extreme economy of words) that has neither an expressed subject nor an expressed verb in its first clause (simply ἐκ πίστεως) and neither an expressed subject nor an expressed verb in its second clause (simply ἵνα κατὰ χάριν). In light of the context of the sentence, however, there can hardly be any doubt that ἡ ἐπαγγελία ("the promise") should be understood as the subject and ἐστίν ("it is") as the verb of the first clause, with that subject and verb understood as well in the second clause.

What is particularly to be noted, however, is the way Paul joins the triumvirate of "promise" (ἐπαγγελία), "faith" (πίστις), and "grace" (χάρις) in this verse, which themes constitute the three-legged platform or "stool" on which the structure of all true religion rests. The reason why these three great foundational themes must be joined together is, as Paul says, "in order that (εἰς τὸ εἶναι) the promise (τὴν ἐπαγγελίαν) might be guaranteed (βεβαίαν) to all Abraham's descendants (παντὶ τῷ σπέρματι)." The adjective βέβαιος denotes such ideas as "firm," "permanent," "reliable," "dependable," and "steadfast." Adolf Deissmann has pointed out that the adjective was also used in substantival form as a technical term in many quarters and in various situations of the ancient world to connote a "legally guaranteed security."[83] It is this nuance of the word that seems most applicable here.

Paul's reference to "all Abraham's descendants" (παντὶ τῷ σπέρματι; literally "to all the seed") appears in a decidedly different context than it was used in the Judaism of his day, where σπέρμα ("seed," "posterity," "descendant") commonly appeared with reference only to "cradle Jews."[84] For Paul's use of the expression "to all the seed" is inclusive, and so signals "not only those who are of the law but also those who are of the faith of Abraham." Further, Paul includes in this verse the adjective μόνον ("only"), which appears here as an adverb in the statement "[the promise comes] *not only* (οὐ μόνον) to those who are of the law [i.e., 'Jews'] *but also* (ἀλλὰ καί) to those [i.e., 'Gentiles'] who are of the faith of Abraham." Paul seems to have employed the expressions "not only" (οὐ μόνον) and "but also" (ἀλλὰ καί) to dispel any stray thoughts about Jews being set aside in the family of God by the inclusion of Gentiles.

But Paul's use of the phrase "to those who are of the law" (τῷ ἐκ τοῦ νόμου) raises the question: Does he mean here in 4:16, as he did in the similar

---

83. Cf. Deissmann, *Bible Studies*, 104-9.
84. Cf., e.g., 4 Macc 18:1: "O Israelites, children born of the seed of Abraham, obey this law and be righteous in all ways."

expression "those of the law" (οἱ ἐκ νόμου) only two verses earlier in 4:14, "those people who base their lives on the law" — which, in that context, certainly meant Jews committed to the Mosaic law but not to Jesus? Or does he mean, as he did four verses earlier in 4:12, Jewish believers in Jesus "who not only are circumcised but also walk in the footsteps of the faith of our father Abraham when he was uncircumcised"? Scholars have been somewhat divided on the matter. A number of commentators have argued for the former view, that is, that Paul has here in mind law-observant Jews who remain within the realm of God's promise to Abraham, even though they have not expressed faith in Jesus — usually pointing out that Paul as a Christian apostle continued to have an interest in nonbelieving Jews, simply because he believed that God continued to have a covenantal interest in them, as seen in what he writes in 9:1–11:36, particularly in 11:25-32.[85] The majority of commentators, however, have understood Paul's reference here in 4:16 to "those who are of the law" as having in mind Jewish believers in Jesus.[86]

While it may be argued that Paul here in 4:16 had in mind not only believers in Jesus but also law-observant Jews who were not believers (but to whom God had irrevocably given promises in his covenant with the nation Israel), it seems more likely from the immediate context that "those who are of the law" in this verse are Jewish believers in Jesus (even though Paul had used a similar expression in 4:14 for nonbelieving, law-observant Jews). For the phrase "by faith" (ἐκ πίστεως) that appears at the beginning of 4:16 dominates the entire verse, and so Paul's speaking of Abraham's descendants as including "not only . . . those who are of the law" in 4:16 should most likely be understood as referring to Jewish believers in Jesus (as in 4:12, though not as in 4:14).

The material of 4:16 ends with an almost confessional statement: "He is the father of us all!" (ὅς ἐστιν πατὴρ πάντων ἡμῶν). A number of interpreters have noted (1) the solemnity of the statement and (2) the fact that it begins with ὅς ἐστιν ("who is"), which is a formula Christians often used in their Christological confessions.[87] Such an inclusivistic conviction that "God is the father of us all" — meaning by "all," which is reiterated from the earlier use of "all" in this same verse, not just Jews who believe in Jesus but also Gentiles who have come to God through faith in Jesus — was evidently based on the early Christians' reading of God's promise to Abraham in Gen 15:5: "Look up at the heavens and count the stars — if, indeed, you can count them. So shall your descendants be!" The affirmation "He [God] is the father of us all!" may even have been a statement that was treasured among the Christians at Rome, where it would have functioned to designate a new group identity that transcended all their

85. So, e.g., B. Weiss, *An die Römer*, 203-5; Murray, *Romans*, 144-45; Dunn, *Romans*, 1.216; and Jewett, *Romans*, 330-31.
86. So, e.g., Sanday and Headlam, *Romans*, 112; Käsemann, *Romans*, 121; Morris, *Romans*, 207; Cranfield, *Romans*, 1.242-43; and Moo, *Romans*, 278-79.
87. Cf. esp. Michel, *An die Römer*, 170; Cranfield, *Romans*, 1.243; Jewett, *Romans*, 331-32.

previous ethnic and cultural identities. And so it may be seen as a statement that Paul quotes back to his addressees, affirming his agreement with them.

4:17 Paul begins this verse by recalling the account of God's reiterated promise to Abraham in Gen 17:5-6 and quoting from that promise the statement "I have made you a father of many nations." By the way in which he will later in the second part of 4:18 (i.e., almost immediately after 4:17) associate Abraham's hope for progeny with the final words of Gen 15:5, "so shall your descendants be," it may be assumed that the apostle, as well as his Christian addressees at Rome, understood "the promise" (ἡ ἐπαγγελία) he had been speaking about (at least since 4:13) as the promise given by God in Gen 15:5 — which promise "Abraham believed," as stated in Gen 15:6, and which belief "was credited to him as righteousness," as Paul takes pains to point out throughout his discourse on the example of Abraham.

The joining of Gen 15:5 and Gen 17:5-6 here in 4:17-18, while not as overt as the joining of Gen 15:6 and Ps 32:1-2 earlier in 4:3-8, appears to be also a case of "pearl stringing," which interpretive practice stemmed from Hillel's second of his seven exegetical rules *(middoth)*. Paul, however, seems somewhat averse to quote from Gen 17 — particularly from 17:9-14, which speaks of God's command to Abraham and his descendants to be circumcised.[88] Perhaps his reticence was because of Judaism's habit of viewing Gen 17 as a more developed, and therefore a more authoritative, understanding of Abraham's situation than the more elemental material set out in Gen 15.[89] The pattern of Paul's argumentation in Rom 4, as noted above, was to bypass Moses and Mosaic legislation in favor of founding his presentation on Abraham and the themes of "promise," "faith," and "grace."[90] Nonetheless, God's statement as recorded in Gen 17:5, "I have made you a father of many nations," was, it seems, just too significant for Paul to ignore. Thus he employs it here in 4:17a in a "pearl stringing" fashion (i.e., the same theme expressed in similar language) as an additional biblical support for the quasi-confessional affirmation "He is the father of us all!" of 4:16b — which affirmation, as suggested by 4:18b where he quotes the concluding words of Gen 15:5 ("So shall your descendants be!"), was evidently understood (probably by both Paul and the Christians at Rome) as based primarily on God's promise as given in Gen 15:5.

The first clause of the latter half of 4:17, that is, κατέναντι οὗ ἐπίστευσεν θεοῦ, is exceedingly difficult to translate and to relate to its immediate context. One major problem for interpreters is that the clause is elliptical (i.e., marked by an economy of words) — being without a subject, which must be understood from its context. In addition, it begins with the adverb κατέναντι ("in

88. On the precarious situation that Paul faced in quoting from Gen 17, see Donaldson, *Paul and the Gentiles*, 124-27.

89. See our discussion above in "Form/Structure/Setting" with respect to a Jewish understanding of Gen 15:6 as representing an "elementary form of truth" regarding "faith" and Gen 17:4-14 as declaring a "developed form of truth" with respect to the joining of "faith and circumcision."

90. See particularly our "Exegetical Comments" above on 4:13 and 16.

the sight of," "in the presence of," "before"), which has been difficult for many to interpret.

Further, there appears in the clause an idiomatic "attraction" or "assimilation" of the relative pronoun to the case of the noun θεοῦ ("of God") with which it is associated, with the result that the case of the relative pronoun is altered from its original dative case (from ᾧ) to the genitive case (to οὗ) of its associated noun; such "attractions" of a relative pronoun to a particular noun with which it is associated are fairly common in NT Greek.[91] The relative pronoun of this clause in 4:17, though assimilated to a genitive form by its association with the genitive θεοῦ or τοῦ θεοῦ, still needs, however, to be read as a dative — with the result that the present "assimilated" clause κατέναντι οὗ ἐπίστευσεν θεοῦ needs to be read in what was presumably its earlier "unassimilated" or "unattracted" form as follows: κατέναντι τοῦ θεοῦ ᾧ ἐπίστευσεν. A literal rendering of the unassimilated clause, therefore, would read: "in the sight of [or, 'before,' 'in the presence of'] God, in whom he believed."

But the question still persists with regard to the unexpressed subject of this clause in 4:17 — which, it seems, Paul thought would be obvious from the context, but which many translators and commentators have found difficult to identify. The question is this: Is the unexpressed subject of the clause "the *promise* that God made to Abraham"?[92] Or is it "the *fatherhood* of Abraham,"[93] which was highlighted at the close of 4:16 in the quasi-confessional statement "He is the father of us all"? Or should the position be taken that if Paul has not expressed a subject in this clause, it is best for translators also to leave it blank and allow the reader to insert the subject as seems best from the context?[94]

The Greek adverb κατέναντι is probably derived from the Hebrew לִפְנֵי ("at the face of," "in front of," "in the presence of," "before"), which occurs in Gen 17:1: "When Abram was ninety-nine years old, the Lord appeared to him and said, 'I am God Almighty; walk *before* (לְפָנַי; "in the presence of") me and be blameless.'" That is how it was understood by a number of Jewish writers of koine Greek who were roughly Paul's contemporaries.[95] And that is how Paul uses it in the other two instances where it appears in his letters — in 2 Cor 2:17 and 12:19, both of which read κατέναντι θεοῦ ἐν Χριστῷ λαλοῦμεν (literally "*in the sight of;* or, 'in the presence of' or 'before' God, in Christ we are speaking"). Evidently, therefore, Paul meant this clause of 4:17 to define the context in which Abraham is to be understood as "our father." And so, amidst a variety of translations proposed by translators and commentators, probably the translation of the NIV is best: "*He is our father* in the sight [or 'presence'] of God,

---

91. For a discussion of this phenomenon, citing a number of other instances of it in the NT, see *ATRob,* 715-17.

92. So, e.g., NEB and LB: "this promise"; TEV: "so the promise is good."

93. So, e.g., Weymouth: "Abraham is the father of all of us"; Knox: "we are his children"; NIV: "he is our father."

94. So, e.g., KJV, RSV, and NRSV.

95. Cf., e.g., Sir 28:26; Jdt 12:15, 19; *Sib Or* 3:499.

in whom he believed" — which subject (as italicized) picks up from the quasi-confessional statement of 4:16b that Paul seems to have thought would have been obvious to his original addressees (and, as we may assume, probably was).

Closing off this affirmation of Abraham as "our father in the sight of God, in whom he believed," Paul adds in almost doxological fashion his praise to God as "the one who gives life to the dead and calls things that are not as though they were" (τοῦ ζῳοποιοῦντος τοὺς νεκροὺς καὶ καλοῦντος τὰ μὴ ὄντα ὡς ὄντα). This ascription of God was expressed, in whole or in part, in a number of Jewish prayers of Paul's day. Most significantly for our purposes, the first part of Paul's ascription, "the one who gives life to the dead," appears in the only prayer that was commanded by the early Tannaitic rabbis to be prayed — that is, in the second prayer of the *Shemoneh Esreh*, or "Eighteen Benedictions," which prayer begins with the words: "Blessed be you, Lord, who gives life to the dead."

It may be debated when the *Shemoneh Esreh* was first formulated (the Talmud credits it to Ezra) and how it developed through history (modern Jewish scholars have posited various stages in its development).[96] All that can be said with confidence is (1) that its formulation began sometime before the first century A.D. and (2) that its full complement of eighteen benedictions, blessings, or prayers antedates the destruction of the Jerusalem temple. The first three benedictions are foundational for the following twelve petitions to God, which have to do with the nation's circumstances and the people's needs (where most of the developments in the prayer have been postulated to have taken place) — as well as foundational for the final three prayers of thanksgiving. The second benediction or prayer, being among the first three, can therefore be viewed as quite traditional and widely known to Jews and Jewish Christians in Paul's day.

The second part of Paul's statement here at the close of 4:17, "who calls things that are not as though they were," may be paralleled by the following two prayers in 2 *Baruch*:

> 2 *Bar* 21:4: "O hear me, you who created the earth, the one who fixed the firmament by his word and fastened the height of heaven by his spirit, *the one who in the beginning of the world called that which did not exist and they obeyed you.*"

> 2 *Bar* 48:8: "O Lord . . . with your word *you bring to life that which does not exist,* and with great power *you hold that which has not yet come.*"

This almost doxological praise at the end of 4:17 certainly reflects Paul's feelings of gratitude for (1) God's promise to Abraham, (2) Abraham's faith in God, and (3) the Jewish patriarch's universal fatherhood of all those who, like

---

96. On the formulation, development, and importance of the *Shemoneh Esreh* in Judaism and in Paul's own religious experience, see R. N. Longenecker, "The Background of Paul's Prayers," in *Into God's Presence*, 209-12.

Abraham, trust in God. Yet the primary reason for Paul's affirmation here was to introduce the salient points in the Genesis story about Abraham and Sarah, who had a son of their own at a time in their lives when such an occurrence seemed beyond hope — a son born to them in fulfillment of God's promise, with a great many descendants to follow.

4:18-19 As his exposition of the story of Abraham moves into its final stage, Paul focuses in 4:18-19 on the circumstances in Abraham's life when God promised him a son, and he builds on that situation to highlight certain important points with respect to Abraham's faith in God and God's promise — thus declaring: "Against all hope, Abraham in hope believed and so became the father of many nations, just as it had been said to him, 'So shall your descendants be.' And without weakening in his faith, he faced the facts that his body was dead, since he was about a hundred years old, and that Sarah's womb was also dead." Paul's statements here are much like those of 4:10-11a, where he asked about the time when God credited righteousness to Abraham, whether it was before or after he was circumcised, building on that situation in the story of Abraham to make his point. In both of these passages he uses a midrashic convention that had been attributed to Hillel — that is, the seventh of Hillel's seven exegetical rules or *middoth,* which argued that a passage must always be interpreted by its context.

In sum, Paul argues that one cannot really understand either the magnitude of God's promise or the greatness of Abraham's faith without taking into account the seeming impossibility of the situation from a human perspective. For "Abraham was about a hundred years old" and "Sarah's womb was dead." Thus, God's promise must be seen in the context of human "impossibility," and Abraham's faith must be understood in the context of his and his wife's "hopelessness." So, contrary to the seeming stability that law (particularly the Mosaic law) provides — as well as in opposition to the self-righteousness that one's keeping of law (particularly the Mosaic law) often engenders — Paul implies that it is only when one is based on the triumvirate of "promise," "faith," and "grace,"[97] whatever the situation, that "righteousness" as a gift of God can be received and that a person can live acceptably before God.

As W. D. Davies has aptly pointed out with respect to Paul's understanding of Abraham's trust in God and his faith in God's promise of a son:

> Paul recognizes in Abraham's trust in the promise the same quality of faith that he knew for himself. The centre of Abraham's faith was his trust that God "gives life from the dead and calls into existence the things that do not exist" (Rom. 4:17), and this is also the faith of those who trust in Christ, because they have believed that God raised him from the dead — that is, gave life from the dead and called into existence things that did not exist. In this way Abraham's faith is linked with the faith of Christians in the Resurrec-

---

97. See our "Exegetical Comments" above on 4.16.

tion. It was as a man of such a faith that Paul interpreted Abraham, in whose trust in God's promise Paul recognized a faith comparable to his own.[98]

4:20 Paul begins his closing statements about Abraham as the example par excellence of faith by asserting that Abraham "did not waver in unbelief regarding the promise of God, but was strengthened in his faith and gave glory to God." The verb διακρίνω ("be at odds with oneself," "doubt," "waver") seems to have had an established history in early Jewish Christian circles. For it is rooted in a "saying" of Jesus about the importance of faith that was later recorded by the Jewish Christian Evangelists Mark and Matthew (though not by the Gentile Evangelist Luke) in their respective accounts of Jesus cursing the unproductive fig tree:

> "Have faith in God (ἔχετε πίστιν θεοῦ). I tell you the truth, if anyone says to this mountain, 'Go throw yourself into the sea,' and does not waver (μὴ διακριθῇ) in his heart but believes (πιστεύῃ) that what he says will happen, it will be done for him." (Mark 11:22-23; see also Matt 21:21)

Even the third-person aorist singular passive form of the verb that appears in Mark 11:22-23 and Matt 21:21, which suggests some such translation as "no doubt should make him waver," appears here in Rom 4:20 (though not in the other NT occurrences in Acts 10:20, Jas 1:6, 2:4, and Jude 22). And Paul reinforces his conclusion about Abraham as not wavering by adding the clause "in unbelief" (τῇ ἀπιστίᾳ).

Yet Gen 17:17-18 reports that Abraham's initial reaction to God's promise of a son was one of derision: "Abraham fell facedown; he laughed and said to himself, 'Will a son be born to a man a hundred years old? Will Sarah bear a child at the age of ninety?' And Abraham said to God, 'If only Ishmael might live under your blessing!'" It may not have been, as Joseph Fitzmyer characterized Abraham's response on hearing God's promise, that "Abraham was *convulsed* in laughter at the thought that he might beget a son."[99] But the writer of the *Book of Jubilees,* probably composed sometime between 161 and 140 B.C., is undoubtedly much too generous in his interpretation of the laughter of Abraham and Sarah in writing that "both of them rejoiced very greatly" (*Jub* 16:19). But Paul — who usually bypassed the Mosaic law in reaching back to Abraham[100] and who seemed reticent to make too much of Gen 17 in retelling Abraham's story[101] — must still be judged somewhat too lenient in not even mentioning Abraham's laughter or his suggestion about God's acceptance of Ishmael. Rather, Paul preferred to highlight only Abraham's more thoughtful and settled response to God

---

98. W. D. Davies, "Abraham and the Promise," 174-75.

99. Fitzmyer, *Romans,* 387 (italics mine).

100. See our "Exegetical Comments" above on 4:13.

101. See our "Exegetical Comments" above on 4:17.

and God's promise, which he evidently felt characterized Abraham's life much more than his initial response.

In his positive statement about Abraham's faith in 4:20b-21, Paul speaks of the strengthening of Abraham's faith (ἐνεδυναμώθη τῇ πίστει) in contrast to the possible "weakness" (ἀσθενήσας) of his faith when he faced the facts of his advanced age and that of his wife as well (cf. 4:19). The expression ἐνεδυναμώθη τῇ πίστει is also included in one of Paul's more memorable autobiographical comments, written to a group of believers in Jesus who were probably his most loyal converts in the city of Philippi — that is, the affirmation of Phil 4:13: "I can do all things in him who strengthens me" (πάντα ἰσχύω ἐν τῷ ἐνδυναμοῦντί με). The use of the aorist passive ἐνεδυναμώθη here in Rom 4:20b speaks of someone or something outside of himself that he considered to be the real agent and/or factor that empowered or strengthened him, which agent and factor he understood as God and the surety of his promise. The articular dative τῇ πίστει is to be understood in a locative sense meaning "in respect to his faith," not in a causal sense signifying "by means of" or "because of his faith."

The final statement of 4:20, "and he gave glory to God" (δοὺς δόξαν τῷ θεῷ) — which begins with the nominative singular masculine aorist participle δοὺς (from the verb δίδωμι, "give") in an adverbial and complementary fashion (thereby completing the action of the verb ἐνεδυναμώθη of the clause "he was strengthened"), and so is properly translated "and he gave" — highlights the fact that there was nothing in the life of either Abraham or Sarah that could be relied on as a basis for the fulfillment of God's promise (as stated in the previous verse of 4:19), but that Abraham's only possible response was to "give glory to God." Paul often expresses in his "eulogy"-type prayers, which appear at the end of various sections of his letters or as the final words of some of his letters, this emphasis on giving glory to God — as in:

Rom 11:36: "To him ['God'] be the glory (ἡ δόξα) forever! Amen."
Rom 16:27: "To the only wise God be glory (ἡ δόξα) forever through Jesus Christ! Amen."
Gal 1:5: "To whom ['our God and Father'] be glory (ἡ δόξα) for ever and ever! Amen."
Eph 3:21: "To him ['God'] be glory (ἡ δόξα) in the church and in Christ Jesus throughout all generations, for ever and ever! Amen."
Phil 4:20: "To our God and Father be glory (ἡ δόξα) for ever and ever! Amen."

It is a response that only faith can engender. And it is the response that in closing his exhortations in the fourth major section of the body middle of his letter to Rome (i.e., in 12:1–15:13) Paul earnestly requests his Christian addressees to exhibit more fully.[102]

102. See our "Exegetical Comments" below on 15:5-12.

4:21-22 All of Paul's concluding statements in 4:16-22 come to a close in his two affirmations of 4:21-22: (1) that Abraham was "fully persuaded that God had power to do what he had promised" (καὶ πληροφορηθεὶς ὅτι ὃ ἐπήγγελται δυνατός ἐστιν καὶ ποιῆσαι) (in v. 21); and (2) that is why "it was credited to him as righteousness" (διὸ ἐλογίσθη αὐτῷ εἰς δικαιοσύνην) (in v. 22). The first affirmation makes it abundantly clear that Abraham's faith was in God himself, the One who promised, and not just in the content of what God promised. This is a highly significant point for all Christians to realize and appropriate in their lives — whether believers in Jesus at Rome to whom Paul originally wrote or believers in Jesus today. For it is all too easy to think only of promises, programs, and/or scenarios of God's working in human history and in one's own life, but to forget about God himself, to ignore basking in his faithfulness, and/or to fail to "give him glory." The second brings everything Paul has been saying about Abraham to a resounding climax by its insistence that it was Abraham's full confidence in God that "was credited to him as righteousness." It was not his "meritorious works," as Paul has made abundantly clear through his illustration of Abraham as a person of faith par excellence; but also not his understanding of how God's promise of a son would be fulfilled. And it is certainly not, as some Christians today seem to espouse, a person's understanding of God's program of salvation or some scenario of God's working in human history.

4:23-24 Here in these two verses Paul adds a postscript that applies what he has been saying about the nature and structure of Abraham's faith specifically to his Christian addressees at Rome. What Paul says in this postscript is highly significant for a Christian understanding of (1) "biblical theology" and (2) "contextualization today," which are topics that will be spelled out more fully in the sections that immediately follow.

In this postscript, Paul uses again the couplet "not only" (οὐκ μόνον) and "but also" (ἀλλὰ καί), which he used twice before in 4:12, 16 (and will use again, though in another context, in 5:3, 11). In so doing, just as he did earlier in 4:12 and 16, he is endeavoring to relate the experience of Abraham and God's people in the religion of Israel to the experience of believers in Jesus and God's "new covenant people." At the heart of biblical religion, whether that of the "old covenant" or that of the "new covenant," are two central themes that constitute the basic structure of all that is proclaimed about the relationship of people with God and about the lives of God's people: (1) that God's crediting "righteousness" is a gift to those who trust him completely, and (2) that people's "faith" is the necessary response to God's person and his salvific activity on their behalf.

For Paul, biblical interpretation involves two "situations," "contexts," or "horizons." The first has to do with God's dealing with his creation and his people in the past (i.e., here in Rom 4 with Abraham); the second has to do with the implications of God's past dealings for what he wants to do both creatively and redemptively in the present (i.e., in the Greco-Roman world of Paul's day and among God's people of that day) — and on behalf of those who will later respond to God through his people's witness. Paul does not usually attempt to "allegorize" God's actions of the past or to "christianize" God's people in Israel's history.[103] Nor does he "christianize" the content of what the pre-Christian worthies believed by reading into their experiences the message of the Christian gospel. Yet he does take pains to draw parallels of structure between the religion of Israel and the Christian proclamation of the salvific work and person of Jesus Christ.

It is this matter of parallels of structure that Paul highlights in the final clause of his postscript to the story of Abraham, laying emphasis on the fact that the structure of Abraham's experience with God and the structure of a Christian's experience with God are the same. For Abraham believed in a God who raises the dead, and Christians also believe in a God who raises the dead. In Abraham's case, he believed that God would give life to both himself and his wife when their bodies were "dead."[104] In a Christian's case, there is the firm conviction that the God "who raised Jesus our Lord from the dead" will also raise believers in Jesus who have died and bestow on them at the time of their resurrection immortality and transformed bodies.[105]

BIBLICAL THEOLOGY

In concluding his exegetical comments on Paul's example of Abraham, C. H. Dodd rather pejoratively characterized the contents of Rom 4 as Paul's "digression about Abraham."[106] In his final paragraph, he wrote:

> This discussion of the case of Abraham was, no doubt, important in Paul's apologetic against Jewish opponents within and without the Church; but for us it throws little light, except incidentally, on his main theme. It served to rebut objections which were serious to him, but have little interest and no weight for us, while the artificial method of argument from Scripture makes the whole exposition seem remote and unenlightening. Perhaps the chief positive truth which emerges is that when Paul speaks of faith he is referring to something which did not begin with Christianity, but is an original and permanent element of all genuinely religious life, even though in some forms of religions, as in the extreme legalist form of Judaism, faith is empty of meaning.[107]

---

103. Though he did so to an extent, for what appear to be polemical reasons, in Gal 4:21-31 and 1 Cor 10:1-13.

104. See "Textual Notes" on 4:19 with respect to what is evidently a scribal interpolation of the adverb ἤδη, which could be read as "just as good as dead."

105. Cf. 1 Cor 15:42-49.

106. C. H. Dodd, *Romans*, 70.

107. *Ibid.*, 70-71.

Dodd was certainly right in citing the subject of "faith" as a positive feature in Rom 4, which has important implications for "all genuinely religious life." But his caricature of Judaism as an "extreme legalist form" of religion and his evaluation of the rest of the contents of Rom 4 as having "little interest and no weight for us" today are, in both cases, at best misleading and at worst terribly wrong. Indeed, Rom 4 does not tell us everything we might like to know about Paul's theology and about the Christian life, but much in the chapter is relevant for a Christian biblical theology.

Of primary importance for Christian theology are three matters: (1) the light that Rom 4 casts on Paul's understanding of what has been called *Heils-geschichte*, that is, "salvation history," or what we prefer to call "continuity and development in the course of God's program of redemption"; (2) the light the chapter sheds on the vitally important subject of righteousness as "a gift of God"; and (3) the more developed nuances that this passage reveals with respect to Paul's understanding of "faith." The first matter has to do with the *essential structure* of biblical religion, the *unfolding content* of God's "progressive revelation," and his people's *developing understanding* of that revelation. The second and third matters have to do with highly significant doctrinal themes, that is, with "righteousness" and "faith," which appear repeatedly in the religion of Israel (as depicted in the Jewish/OT Scriptures) and in early Christian proclamation (as portrayed in the Christian/NT Scriptures) — with the explication of these themes in Judaism and Christianity both uniting (with respect to structure) and differentiating (with respect to content) these two world religions.

A. *"Continuity" and "Development" in the Course of God's Redemptive Program.* In his article "Paul and *Heilsgeschichte*," which carries the subtitle "Conclusions from Romans 4 and I Corinthians 10:1-13," Leonhard Goppelt focused on what he called "the conceptual structures" that Paul "himself advocated and employed in his theology."[108] In that article — first published in German in 1966,[109] then translated into English and republished in 1967 — Goppelt set out a number of theses regarding Paul's treatment of the example of Abraham in Rom 4. It is impossible to interact with all his theses, but the following points of his argument are of great significance in any attempt to understand the course of "salvation history" *(Heilsgeschichte),* that is, of "God's redemptive program," in the biblical accounts of both the OT and the NT:

1. "The events recorded in the *Old Testament* point *beyond themselves* according to their own intention as well as according to the insights of the recorders or witnesses."[110]
2. "Paul understands the Old Testament history as a pre-representation of

---

108. L. Goppelt, "Paul and *Heilsgeschichte:* Conclusions from Romans 4 and I Corinthians 10:1-13," trans. M. Rissi, *Int* 21 (1967) 315-26, here 315.

109. L. Goppelt, "Paulus und die Heilsgeschichte," *NTS* 13 (1966) 31-42.

110. Goppelt, "Paul and *Heilsgeschichte*," 319 (italics his), citing G. von Rad, *Old Testament Theology* (1965), 2.383-84.

the New Testament events, and . . . he accordingly makes selections and arrangements of material in the light of the New Testament situation and provides interpretations which point beyond the historical meaning of the materials — of course only under the presupposition that Jesus is really 'the One who is to come.' "[111]

3. "Abraham's justification in Romans 4 is never seen as a timeless model of justification by Christ. It is reckoned to Abraham, rather, in a specific historical situation and is since then a document of promise for history. Therefore, it does not preclude the revelation of God's justice [i.e., the δικαιοσύνη θεοῦ] through Jesus Christ (Rom. 1:17; 3:21), but is, according to Romans 4:3, its *typos,* that is to say, its promising pre-representation."[112]

4. "The relationship with God shaped by the Law is [in Paul's understanding] replaced within history by the new relationship as to all who believe."[113]

5. "It is essential for the structure of faith that behind the appearance of Christ in an historical perspective a preceding activity of God appears. This preceding activity of God, that is to say, the justification of Abraham in Romans 4, is seen here indeed as a temporally, that is, historically, preceding act."[114]

6. "The faith of Abraham has the same structure, but a different content from the Christian faith."[115]

One may want to nuance somewhat differently Goppelt's statements about "Old Testament history" being "a pre-representation of the New Testament events" (see point 2) and about the example of Abraham as a "promising pre-representation" of God's righteousness through Jesus Christ (see point 3). Nevertheless, without buying into all his distinctive *typos* theology, Goppelt's treatment of relations between the religion of Israel (as depicted in the OT) and early Christian proclamation (as portrayed in the NT) is suggestive, essentially sound, and therefore highly laudatory — especially so with respect to his understanding of (1) the continuity of structure that runs throughout the salvation history of biblical religion, vis-à-vis (2) the development of doctrine that appears both within and between the presentations of the OT and the NT.

Indeed, when Paul thinks and speaks about the nature of God, the love and mercy of God, the will of God, the redemptive purposes of God, and the structure of biblical religion, he does so in *continuity* with all that God has revealed about these matters through his creation and by his written Torah ("instruction"), which he gave in "the Law, the Prophets, and the Writings" of Holy Scripture through chosen men in the history of the nation of Israel. That continuity is clearly in evidence throughout all that Paul has written in the first major

111. Goppelt, "Paul and *Heilsgeschichte*," 319.
112. *Ibid.,* 322-23.
113. *Ibid.,* 324.
114. *Ibid.,* 325.
115. *Ibid.*

section of the body middle of his letter to the Christians at Rome (i.e., in 1:16–4:24, apart from the Christian confessional statement of 4:25) — particularly when speaking about God's person; God's righteousness; God's wrath against sin and sinners; God's love for and covenant with his people; the Mosaic law; humanity's rebellion, godlessness, and sin; Jewish unfaithfulness and injustice; the impossibility of gaining status before God or attaining righteousness from God by any form of "works righteousness"; and the importance of responding to God's love and mercy "by faith" and "trust" in him. These matters have to do with the person of God and the structure of true religion, which God himself revealed and Paul proclaimed "both to Jews first and also to Gentiles."

But when Paul writes about the *content* of how God has acted redemptively on behalf of his created humanity (and through them on behalf of all his creation), he gives evidence of understanding also features of development in the historical course of God's program of redemption. Such an understanding seems evident in his thesis statement of 3:21-23, where he (1) defines more clearly the meaning of "the righteousness of God," with an emphasis on the *communicative sense* of that expression, (2) proclaims that the present time in God's redemptive program is that of the eschatological "now," (3) speaks of the object of faith in this time of the eschatological "now" (cf. 3:26a, "at this present time") as focused expressly on "Jesus Christ," (4) identifies the new basis for faith as being "the faithfulness of Jesus Christ," (5) declares that acceptance by God and the reception of his righteousness are now "apart from the Mosaic law," and (6) announces that all who have sinned, which is everyone, whatever their ethnic background, are accepted by God on the basis of their faith in God, whether they are Jews under the Mosaic law or Gentiles who know nothing about that law. This is Paul's message not only in his thesis statement of 3:21-23, which he supports by quoting a relevant early Christian confessional portion in 3:24-26 and then elucidates further in 3:27-31, but also throughout his treatment of the example of Abraham here in 4:1-24.

In the Holy Scriptures of both the OT and the NT we have in fact a record of God's progressive revelation and unfolding redemption: first in Israel's history, then in Jesus' ministry, and finally in the apostolic church's witness. But this record is coupled with accounts of the developing endeavors of God's people in working out the theological ramifications and ethical implications of that unfolding revelation and progressive message of salvation. And in this scenario of unfolding revelation and developing understanding there is, at all times, the conjunction of the old and the new.

In the Jewish (OT) Scriptures, for example, the "latter prophets" reinterpreted the "former prophets" in order to make new applications of the words of the Mosaic law — not opposing the former, but expressing their significance more fully and applying their message to new situations. Perhaps the most obvious example of this conjunction of old and new in the OT is in Dan 9, where Jeremiah's prophecy of seventy years (Jer 25:12-14) is reinterpreted to mean "seventy heptads" and to have significance far beyond what was initially thought (cf. esp. Dan 9:1-3, 20-27). Another example is in Ps 110, where the Canaanite chieftain Melchizedek of Gen 14 is brought into the lineage of Israel as one of the nation's ancient worthies (Ps 110:4).

In the NT there appears throughout a similar conjunction of old and new. The earliest preaching of the apostles was cast almost entirely in functional categories, as, for example, in the preaching of Peter as recorded in Acts 2:14-39 — and specifically in Acts 2:22-24:

> "Jesus of Nazareth was a man accredited by God to you by miracles, wonders and signs, which God did among you through him, as you yourselves know. This man was handed over to you by God's set purpose and foreknowledge; and you, with the help of wicked men, put him to death by nailing him to the cross. But God raised him from the dead, freeing him from the agony of death, because it was impossible for death to keep its hold on him."

It was a message that stressed God's intervention in human affairs in the work and person of Jesus of Nazareth, focusing almost entirely on the fulfillment of God's redemptive purposes in what Jesus as Israel's Messiah did. Presupposed in that message, of course, were many theological nuances. But full-blown theological formulations and developed ethical stances were, at first, largely held in the substratum of the apostles' preaching and appear only in the overtones of their message.

As Jews, the earliest believers in Jesus possessed a basic theology regarding God's person and divine redemption, as well as basic instructions about how to live in response to God's actions on their behalf. As Christians, however, their distinctive theological affirmations were derived from God's self-revelation and redemptive activity in Jesus of Nazareth, and their ethical exhortations were focused on the example and teaching of Jesus as illuminated, applied, and energized by the Holy Spirit. They seem to have worked in their thinking from functional categories — that is, from what God did in and through the ministry of Jesus — to theological, ontological, and speculative categories — that is, to how all this should be understood, who Jesus was (and is), why it all came about, and what it means for everyday living. So in the NT we have a record of how these early believers began to work out the nuances of their basically functional "new covenant" stance — under, as we Christians believe, the guidance of God's Spirit — into a rudimentary system of Christian doctrine and a rudimentary style of Christian living. Thus the NT, paralleling the OT in this regard, contains both (1) a record of God's progressive revelation of himself and his unfolding redemption on behalf of humanity, and (2) accounts of his people's endeavors to work out the theological ramifications and ethical implications of that progressively revealed program of redemption that has come to fulfillment in the work and person of Jesus, Israel's Messiah and humanity's Lord.

Jesus' promise of the Spirit as recorded in John 14–16 includes the expectation that his disciples would more fully understand his teaching and ministry in the future; their understanding would not be divorced from Jesus but rooted in all that he said and did:

> "I have much more to say to you, more than you can now bear. But when he, the Spirit of truth, comes, he will guide you into all truth. He will not speak on his own; he will speak only what he hears, and he will tell you what is yet to come." (John 16:12-13)

John's Gospel has at least two references to biblical interpretation being more perceptive after Jesus' ascension, and suggestions that the ministry of the Spirit was understood by the earliest Christians to include advances in the understanding of Scripture. For in John 2 we are told that it was only after Jesus' resurrection that his disciples understood Ps 69:9 in the context of Jesus' ministry:

> His disciples remembered that it is written: "Zeal for your house will consume me." . . . After he was raised from the dead, his disciples recalled what he had said. Then they believed the Scripture and the words that Jesus had spoken. (John 2:17, 22)

And in John 12, which portrays Jesus' entry into Jerusalem and depicts the use of Ps 118:25-26 and Zech 9:9 in that connection, we are told:

> At first his disciples did not understand all this. Only after Jesus was glorified did they realize that these things had been written about him and that they had done these things to him. (John 12:16)

In these two Johannine accounts, one at the beginning of the Evangelist's "Book of Signs" (i.e., chs. 2–12) and the other at its close, the disciples are portrayed as coming to understand certain actions and sayings of Jesus in light of the OT only at a later time — along, of course, the general lines of interpretation laid out by Jesus, but without any direct word from him.

The four Gospels evidence, each in its own way, how the canonical Evangelists attempted to be both (1) true to the proclamation they had received and (2) relevant to the situations they faced. The NT Gospels are in fact recastings of the original gospel tradition to meet specific issues and particular concerns within the respective communities they addressed, as redaction criticism has so abundantly illustrated.

Likewise, Paul's letters evidence this wedding of old and new in their pastoral applications of the Christian gospel to various theological and ethical problems in the churches. One particularly obvious conjunction of what Jesus was known to have taught and Paul's application of the thrust of that teaching for a somewhat different situation can be found in 1 Cor 7. For while in 7:10-11 Paul quotes a saying of Jesus as settling one matter ("To the married I give this command; not I, but the Lord"), in the immediately following verses of 7:12-16 (and probably throughout 7:17-40) he speaks as one who authoritatively expresses the gospel's intent regarding believers and unbelievers continuing to live together as married partners — about which situation the church possessed no explicit word of Jesus.[116]

It is rather tempting, as well as fairly easy, to go on and on in speaking about the theme of "continuity and development in the course of God's redemptive program" — which includes such matters as (1) God's progressive revelation of himself and his unfolding program of redemption; (2) God's work through Christ and the Spirit in bringing to fulfillment his salvation on behalf of all people; (3) developments of understanding by God's people with regard to God's person, actions, and relations with them; (4) the joining of old and new redemptive features within each of the two testaments; and (5) relations of both structure and content between the two testaments.[117] All that needs to be said here about biblical theology, however, is that Paul's treatment of Abraham in Rom 4 presents NT interpreters with a highly significant paradigmatic passage that (1) requires them to recognize *continuities of structure* between old covenant and new covenant patterns of "righteousness" and "faith," but also (2) calls on them to respect *differences of content* that have been brought about by God's progressive revelation and unfolding program of redemption, as expressed particularly through the work of Jesus Christ and the ministry of God's Spirit.

B. *"Righteousness" as a Gift of God.* Paul uses the expression δικαιοσύνη θεοῦ ("the righteousness of God") most often in his letters in Section I of the body middle of his letter to Rome (i.e., in 1:16–4:25), where it appears (1) first in 1:17a ("in the gospel 'the righteousness of God' is revealed"), (2) then in the rhetorical question of 3:5 ("But if our unrighteousness brings out 'the righteousness of God' more clearly, what shall we say?"), (3) then again in 3:21a and 3:22a, where he speaks twice of "the righteousness of God" as the subject of two statements in his repeated and expanded thesis statement of 3:21-23, and (4) finally in this first section, in 3:25 and 3:26, where the expression appears twice in the confessional material that he quotes in 3:24-26 and is probably best translated as "God's justice." Elsewhere in Romans the expression is found only in Section III of the body middle of the letter, that is, in 10:3, where he says Jews who did not respond positively to Christ "did not know 'the righteousness of God' and so sought to establish their own righteousness." In Paul's other letters the expression appears only in 2 Cor 5:21 ("so that in him [Christ] we might become 'the righteousness of God'") and in Phil 3:9 ("'the righteousness of God' that is based on faith").

---

116. Cf. 1 Cor 7:12: "To the rest I say this; I, not the Lord"; cf. also 7:25: "I have no command from the Lord, but I give a judgment as one who by the Lord's mercy is trustworthy," and 7:40: "In my judgment, . . . and I think that I have the Spirit of God."

117. As I have tried to do on a theoretical basis in my article "A Developmental Hermeneutic: New Treasures as Well as Old," and then attempted to explicate more fully in my monograph *New Testament Social Ethics for Today* and my commentary on Galatians.

As for the abstract noun δικαιοσύνη ("righteousness"), apart from its eight explicit appearances in ch. 4, it appears in Rom 5:17 ("the gift of 'righteousness' "), 5:21 ("so that grace might reign through 'righteousness' to bring eternal life through Jesus Christ our Lord"), and 9:30 ("What then shall we say? That the Gentiles, who did not pursue 'righteousness,' have obtained it, a 'righteousness' that is by faith?"). It is also found in 2 Cor 3:9 ("the ministry that brings 'righteousness' "). In all four of these verses the term refers to the righteousness that is given or bestowed by God (as it does in all its uses in Rom 4).

The use of δικαιοσύνη θεοῦ ("the righteousness of God") in 1:17a, particularly in the context of Paul's declaration at the very beginning of his thesis statement of 1:16-17 that he was "not ashamed of the gospel," has suggested to a number of scholars that the expression should be understood as carrying something of an apologetic or polemical nuance — that is, viewed as Paul highlighting "the righteousness of God" in his thesis statement of 1:16-17 in response to certain criticisms of his person, his mission, and/or his message that were then being voiced by some of the Christians at Rome.[118] And it is likely, as we have argued, that some of his critics at Rome were asserting that while Paul proclaimed "the righteousness of God" in a *communicative sense,* he was less vocal about "the righteousness of God" in an *attributive sense.*

Further, it may be argued that while in the early Christian confessional material that Paul quotes in 3:24-26 the *communicative sense* of δικαιοσύνη is to the fore in the reference to God as "the one who justifies" (δικαιοῦντα; literally "the justifier"), which appears in the final portion of 3:26b, the *attributive sense* is more to the fore in the two uses of the expression τῆς δικαιοσύνης αὐτοῦ (literally "the righteousness" or "justice of him") in 3:25b-26a.[119] In all likelihood, in fact, the use of τῆς δικαιοσύνης αὐτοῦ in 3:25b-26a should be interpreted much like the same expression in 3:5, where δικαιοσύνης αὐτοῦ appears in the *attributive sense* of God's own "just nature" and "righteous justice." So, in line with that earlier use in 3:5, we have translated τῆς δικαιοσύνης αὐτοῦ in 3:25b-26a as "his [God's] righteous justice."

Discussions regarding the expression δικαιοσύνη θεοῦ ("the righteousness/justice of God") and the abstract noun δικαιοσύνη ("righteousness/justness") in Pauline usage have been extensive, with whole volumes dedicated to the exposition of their meanings. Our own "suggested hypothesis" in attempting to resolve the problem has been as follows:[120]

1. That the Christians at Rome probably did criticize Paul for what they perceived to be an imbalance in his proclamation — that is, that he preached well "the righteousness of God" in a *communicative sense,* but was less vocal about God's righteousness in an *attributive sense;*

---

118. See our "Exegetical Comments" above at 1:16-17.
119. See our "Exegetical Comments" above on 3:25b-26a.
120. As set out in our "Exegetical Comments" on Paul's thesis statement of 1:16-17.

2. That Paul begins Section I of his letter by affirming the broad range of meaning that the expression "the righteousness of God" incorporates, and so, in effect, agrees with them in their attributive understanding — which may have been conceptualized by them in a somewhat static manner with respect to the character and actions of God;

3. That Paul also, however, wants his addressees to think in revelatory, historical, and redemptive terms — and so, it may be presumed, in a more communicative and dynamic fashion; and therefore,

4. That Paul's message to the Christians at Rome is that they need to think more of God's righteousness in a *communicative sense* as "now being revealed" by God himself (using the present indicative passive verb ἀποκαλύπτεται) in the Christian gospel — which is a truth that he believed both they (at least on serious reflection) and he confessed, and so should be seen as being held in common.

However true such a suggested scenario might be, the fact is that in the eight explicit uses of δικαιοσύνη in Rom 4:3, 5, 6, 9, 11 (twice), 13, and 22, as well as in all that he writes in the context of these eight occurrences of the noun, Paul's emphasis is on the *communicative sense* of "righteousness" — that is, on the fact that God *credited righteousness to Abraham,* as stated in Gen 15:6 and as supported by Ps 32:2. Such an emphasis is in line with Paul's use of δικαιοσύνη θεοῦ in his thesis statement of 1:16-17 and in his development of that thesis statement in 3:21-23. Further, it is supported by his two references to δικαιοσύνη θεοῦ outside of Romans in 2 Cor 5:21 and Phil 3:9, as well as by his references to δικαιοσύνη alone in Rom 5:17, 21; 9:30; and 2 Cor 3:9. And this emphasis on the *communicative sense* of "the righteousness of God," while never neglecting the *attributive sense* of the expression, must, as Paul's presentation of the example of Abraham highlights, always be kept to the fore in a truly Christian biblical theology.

C. Paul's Understanding of "Faith." Charles Talbert observes at the close of his exegetical comments on Rom 4 that "perhaps no issue in Pauline theology is more difficult for modern Christians than his [Paul's] understanding of faith."[121] Talbert presents seven theses that arise out of his reading of Rom 4 with respect to Paul's teaching on the subject. All of Talbert's theses are stated at the start in negative fashion. Nonetheless, all of them have positive implications for a Christian biblical theology. And in their negative forms, many have a bit more bite and impact for Christian thought and life than any mere positive statements would have. Thus, because of their importance and impact, Talbert's seven theses are here reproduced as an apt summary of Paul's teaching on "faith" in Rom 4 (and elsewhere in his letters) and as a challenge to think biblically on the subject.[122]

121. Talbert, *Romans,* 125.
122. As set out in *ibid.,* 125-27.

1. "One is not saved by faith. God saves. We are saved by grace (= God's initiative). Faith is the human reception of salvation. So we are saved by grace and through faith."

2. "Faith is not a work (= something we do to cause God to respond favorably to us). Faith responds. It is not because of our faith that God justifies us but through our faith. Even justification by faith can be understood legalistically if faith is looked upon as the necessary precondition required for salvation. Faith is not the condition of our justification. It is our acceptance of it or our experience of it."

3. "Faith is not believing doctrinal propositions. The object of faith is a person: either God (Rom 4:24; 1 Thess 1:8) or Christ (Rom 10:14; Gal 2:16). . . . Romans 10:8-10 is the only passage where Paul seems to have equated saving faith with belief in a certain proposition. . . . Faith is a religious/relational term rather than an intellectual one. . . . Out of a faith-relationship with God in Christ may come intellectual conviction and clarity. . . . From a Pauline perspective, the latter arises out of the former."

4. "Faith is not a subjective feeling or attitude that is acceptable to God when our actions are not. The difference between works and faith is not that one ('works') is action and the other ('faith') is feeling or attitude. In Paul, works can be a feeling or attitude as well as actions. Likewise, faith involves action as well as feeling and attitudes."

5. "Faith is not a one-time event. It is both an act that begins the Christian life (Rom 10:9) and an orientation by which the Christian life continues (Gal 2:20). A Christian believes in Christ and then goes on believing. This means that the Christian life does not begin with faith and then passes on to something else like love or knowledge or works. The Christian life, for Paul, begins and ends with our faithful response to God in Christ. Our faith may deepen, but it is never displaced by something else."

6. "Faith is not a partial response to God. It is not a response of action only or attitude only. It involves the whole person. It is not a response of trust only or of obedience only. It is both together. Faith is one's total response to the total relation with God."

7. "Faith is not only my decision to follow Jesus. It is God's gift (Phil 1:29). Just as one cannot merely decide to fall in love with another person because the time seems right or because the person meets all the specifications, so one cannot merely decide to have faith. For a love relation to exist, something has to happen. An event has to take place that enables one to enter the relationship. Just so, for a relation with God to exist a happening has to take place. There must be an event that enables one to respond to God in Christ. That event is the grace nature of the relationship. The enabled response is the faith dimension."

CONTEXTUALIZATION FOR TODAY

W. D. Davies begins his 1974 article "Abraham and the Promise" by pointing out that — although "the apostle certainly shared in the deep veneration of the Jewish people for Abraham" — "it is only in Romans and Galatians" that Paul specifically discusses Abraham. About this rather limited use of the story of Abraham by Paul, Davies evocatively comments: "At first sight, this is surprising," and offers the following explanation — which builds on the premise that "the Pauline epistles are directed to concrete situations and are strictly occasional":

> It is, therefore, understandable that only in the two epistles where he confronts the question of the terms of salvation or of inclusion in the people of God truly descended from Abraham, a question raised by his Jewish and Jewish-Christian opponents especially, but also by Gentile Christians, does the foundation figure of Judaism directly engage Paul.[123]

This is the explanation most often proposed, both by scholars and laypeople, to resolve such a seeming anomaly in the writings of one who was trained in the Jewish traditions and so frequently evidences in his letters his Jewish background in so many other ways, yet who relatively rarely discusses the great patriarch of the Jewish nation Abraham — speaking of him by name only in Rom 4:1-22; 9:7-9; and Gal 3:6-9, 18, 29, though also alluding to him within the rubric of οἱ πατέρες, "the fathers," in Rom 11:28.

In Galatians and Romans, however, Paul is dealing with two quite different Jewish Christian mind-sets. The one in Galatians was an erroneous form of Jewish Christian theology that had somehow invaded the Gentile Christian communities of Galatia and was threatening the Christian gospel; the one in Romans was evidently a form of Jewish Christian theology that had extensively influenced the mixed Gentile-Jewish Christian congregations of Rome in essentially very good ways, but also represented an expression of the Christian religion that Paul believed needed to be developed more fully, in order that believers in Jesus at Rome (1) would more adequately understand and experience the "good news" of the Christian gospel and (2) would join and support him in his planned further outreach to Gentiles in western regions of the Roman Empire. The issues in Galatia had to do with what the "Judaizers" were asking Paul's Gentile converts to accept and do in order to become more like Jews who believed in Jesus as the Jewish Messiah — and who, as they pointed out, both honored and practiced the Jewish traditions. The crucial issue at Rome, however, was not a matter of ethnicity, but had to do with "the theological outlook of this mixed Jewish/Gentile Christianity"[124] — an outlook or mind-set that the Christians at Rome, whether ethnically Jews or ethnically Gentiles, had

---

123. W. D. Davies, "Abraham and the Promise," 168.
124. R. E. Brown, "The Beginnings of Christianity at Rome," 109 n. 227.

evidently picked up from Jewish Christianity and had largely incorporated into their understanding of the Christian gospel. So, for both the Gentile believers in Jesus in Galatia and the mixed community of Jewish and Gentile believers in Jesus at Rome — both of whom had been influenced by Jewish Christian ways of thinking and expression, but with the purposes and proposed results of that influence being quite different — Paul's dealing with Abraham, the great Jewish patriarch, would have been understood, appreciated, and highly important.

Thus there is somewhat diverse "circumstantial" use of the story of Abraham by Paul in Gal 3:6-9 (as mentioned again in 3:18 and 29) and in Rom 4:1-22 (as picked up again in 9:7-9) — that is, a use that is dependent on the circumstances of its presentation in the specific situations being addressed for its thrust and form. A circumstantial use of the Abraham story is also found in Jas 2:20-24 and Heb 11:8-19, which constitute the only two other references to Abraham in the NT. Each of these presentations deals with Abraham in a somewhat different manner and for quite different purposes. However, these four somewhat varied uses in Galatians, Romans, James, and Hebrews are all speaking to a mind-set that had been extensively impacted, in one way or another, by Jewish and/or Jewish Christian traditions and ways of looking at things. And each of them would have been highly significant and meaningful to their respective addressees.[125]

Christians can learn a great deal about contextualizing the Christian gospel in their own situations today — as well as in differing situations that exist worldwide — by taking note of how the Christian message was contextualized in different situations and in fairly diverse ways by the writers of the NT. This may be done by (1) understanding the purpose or purposes of the respective NT authors, (2) appreciating the intellectual and historical circumstances of the various addressees, (3) giving attention to how each author spoke circumstantially to his addressees' particular mind-set, interests, and ability to understand, and (4) drawing lessons from these NT portrayals — not only with regard to matters of content, but also with regard to paradigmatic patterns set out with respect to communicating the Christian message to differing mind-sets in different situations.

In particular, it is important for our purposes here (1) to note how Paul in his *exemplum* of Abraham in Rom 4 speaks to Christian addressees who had been influenced by Jewish theology, tradition, language, and ways of thinking, and so (2) to realize that he presents material to them in a form that they would understand, appreciate, and accept. Later in Romans, particularly in 5:1–8:39 and 12:1–15:13, Paul will set out what he has been proclaiming to Gentiles, who had not been influenced by the Jewish (OT) Scriptures or by Judaism itself. In these two major sections, Paul presents his material in a somewhat different manner and with somewhat differing foci than in 1:16–4:25 and 9:1–11:33 — all so that his addressees (1) will understand and appreciate his Christian proclamation, and so (2) will join with him in a further extension of his Gentile mission.

125. Cf. R. N. Longenecker, "The 'Faith of Abraham' Theme," 203-12.

8. Concluding Early Christian Confessional Statement (4:25)

TRANSLATION

[25]*He was delivered over to death for our sins and was raised to life for our justification.*

FORM/STRUCTURE/SETTING

Rom 4:25 has often been seen as Paul's quotation of an early Christian confessional statement — or, at least, his echoing of some such traditional affirmation, which he may have slightly reworded.[126] Most obvious in defense of this thesis are (1) the parallelism of structure in the verse *(parallelismus membrorum),* which may reflect some type of hymnic or poetic background, (2) the use at the beginning of the statement of the relative pronoun ὅς ("who"), which often appears elsewhere in the NT at the beginning of quoted Christian confessional material, and (3) the affirmation of a basic Christian conviction, which usually has to do with the work or person of Jesus Christ. Also, (4) the two verbs in the statements of the verse are both positioned first in their respective clauses, which seems to reflect a Semitic style (cf. the same phenomenon in the Christological confession of 1 Tim 3:16); (5) the conjunction of "the resurrection" (of Jesus) with "the justification" (of sinners) in the second statement is neither how Paul spoke earlier of "righteousness," "faithfulness," and "faith" in his thesis statement of 3:21-23 nor how he will speak immediately following of "peace" and "reconciliation" in 5:1-11 (though, of course, it would not have been impossible for Paul to have brought "resurrection" and "justification" together in such a manner); (6) the theme of "justification" in 4:25 resonates well with the theme of "being justified" that begins the confessional portion quoted by Paul in 3:24-26, which may suggest (though certainly does not require) that both portions represent similar mind-sets — perhaps even that they stem from the same pre-Pauline confessional material; and (7) 4:25 does not pick up any of the imagery, language, or specific details of Paul's treatment of the story of Abraham in 4:1-24 (as do the concluding section of 4:16-22 and the postscript of 4:23-24), but rather, appears to function more rhetorically than logically.

---

126. Cf. the commentaries by Lietzmann, *An die Römer,* 56; Michel, *An die Römer,* 174; Schlier, *Römerbrief,* 135-36; Käsemann, *Romans,* 128; Dunn, *Romans,* 1.224; and Jewett, *Romans,* 342-43; see also the monographs by K. Wegenast, *Verständnis der Tradition bei Paulus* (Neukirchen-Vluyn: Neukirchener Verlag, 1962), 80-82; Wengst, *Christologische Formeln und Lieder,* 101-3; and Stuhlmacher, *Reconciliation, Law, and Righteousness,* 55-56.

Paul's habit in Romans (and elsewhere in his letters) seems to be to close off large sections of material with a confessional statement or doxological passage, which he either quotes verbatim or paraphrases. We will argue later that he does this in (1) his "Triumphal Affirmation of God's Love in Christ" that appears in 8:31-39, which closes off Section II (i.e., 5:1–8:39) of the body middle of Romans, (2) his "Praise to God for His Wisdom and Knowledge" that appears in 11:33-36, which closes off Section III (i.e., 9:1–11:36) of the body middle of the letter, and (3) his doxological statement "May the God of hope fill you with all joy and peace in believing, so that you may abound in hope by the power of the Holy Spirit" that appears in 15:13, which closes off Section IV (i.e., 12:1–15:13). Each of these closings nicely summarizes what is written in the section preceding it, but does it in a fashion that is more rhetorical than strictly instructional. It is plausible to believe that this is how Paul intended 4:25 to function as well.

EXEGETICAL COMMENTS

Most commentators have understood the statements of 4:25, whoever originally composed them, to have been influenced by the LXX translation of the Suffering Servant Song of Isa 52:13–53:12. The passive form of the verb παραδίδωμι ("hand over," "give over," "deliver [over]") is prominent in the final two statements of LXX Isa 53:12, just as it is in the first statement of 4:25:

> Isa 53:6: "The Lord delivered him for our sins" (Κύριος παρέδωκεν αὐτὸν ταῖς ἁμαρτίαις ἡμῶν).
> Isa 53:12a: "His soul was delivered to death" (παρεδόθη εἰς θάνατον ἡ ψυχὴ αὐτοῦ).
> Isa 53:12b: "He was delivered because of their iniquities" (διὰ τὰς ἀνομίας αὐτῶν παρεδόθη).

Likewise, the preposition διά ("through" with the genitive; "because of" with the accusative) is used in the two clauses of 4:25, as it was in Isa 53:12b — not the more usual Christian use of the preposition ὑπέρ with the genitive to mean "for," "for the sake of," "on behalf of," "instead of." It may, however, be somewhat difficult to analyze in any precise manner each of the linguistic components in such a confessional statement as 4:25, for early Christian confessional materials arose within the context of Christian worship and devotion — and devotional expressions, while heartfelt, are often rather imprecise both conceptually and linguistically.

Nonetheless, these two statements of 4:25 are clear in their proclamation that it is Jesus' death and resurrection that constitute both God's remedy for human sin and God's provision for people's justification. Paul, therefore, must be seen as using here this short Christian confessional statement, which epitomizes the very heart of the Christian gospel, in order (1) to put an end to all stray thoughts about gaining acceptance before God by any form of legalistic obedience to the Mosaic law or by any so-called meritorious works, as denounced in 1:18–3:20, and (2) to draw to a conclusion all that he wrote about God's "gift of righteousness," Jesus' "faithfulness," and Abraham's "faith" in 3:21–4:25. Joseph Fitzmyer aptly expresses matters when he writes: "The affirmation of the part played by Christ's death and resurrection in the objective redemption of humanity forms a fitting conclusion to part A [i.e., 1:16–4:25] of the doctrinal section of Romans."[127]

127. Fitzmyer, *Romans*, 390, citing in support S. Lyonnet, D. M. Stanley, and B. McNeil — and, further, quoting the concluding words of H. Schlier regarding Rom 4:25, the first half of which quotation is particularly pertinent and reads as follows: "With this traditional formula, which is derived probably from Hellenistic Jewish Christianity, the goal of the first major division of the Letter to the Romans is reached, and it is shown that the central affirmations of 3:21-31 about the manifestation of God's uprightness in Jesus Christ and about the justification through faith connected with it were already attested in the Scriptures (of the OT), indeed in the case of Abraham. In his uprightness it is a question of uprightness from faith. Circumcision has in no way any relevance to it, and it became only later its seal, with the result that Abraham became the father of believing Jews *and* pagans. Nor did the law have anything to do with it. God's promise was related to *dikaiosyne pisteos,* to which grace corresponds, whereas law called forth only transgression and the judgment of divine wrath" (Schlier, *Römerbrief,* 137, italics his).

V. Section II: Peace, Reconciliation, and Life "in Christ" (5:1–8:39)

In Section II of the body middle of Romans, that is, in 5:1–8:39, Paul presents what is at the very heart of his concerns in writing to the Christians at Rome. The material of this section is set out in a dominantly positive manner, as was the case in the second part of an ancient λόγος προτρεπτικός ("word [or 'message'] of exhortation"). Paul's purpose here in 5:1–8:39 was evidently to give to the believers in Jesus at Rome what he had referred to in 1:11 as his "spiritual gift" (χάρισμα πνευματικόν) — that is, a précis of his contextualized proclamation of the Christian gospel to pagan Gentiles in his Gentile mission, which in 2:16 and then again in 16:25 he refers to as "my gospel."

Although they included Jews who believed in Jesus, the Christian congregations at Rome were evidently composed mostly of believing Gentiles. So Paul thought of the Roman Christians as being within his God-given mandate as an apostle to the Gentiles. Though ethnically mixed, all those at Rome who confessed Jesus as Lord seem to have been extensively influenced by the theology, ways of thinking, and religious language of Jewish Christianity, as centered in the mother church at Jerusalem. Thus Paul wrote to this ethnically mixed community of Christians and gave them his "spiritual gift," which he sets out theologically here in 5:1–8:39 (with its ethical corollary presented in the general exhortations of 12:1-21 and 13:8-14). And he did this, as he says in 1:12, "in order that you and I may be mutually encouraged by each other's faith" — that is, (1) that he might instruct them further in their understanding and experience of the Christian gospel, as he had experienced it and contextualized it in his Gentile mission, and (2) that they might join him in his proposed outreach to other Gentiles in the western regions of the Roman Empire, both by their prayers and by their financial support.

In this second major section of the body middle of Romans, Paul continues to proclaim his understanding of "God's righteousness" (as set out in 1:16-17 and 3:21-23) — which understanding he believed was also inherent in at least one portion of the church's early confessional materials (as quoted in 3:24-26) — arguing, in effect, that the expression not only refers to God's nature as being righteous and his actions as being just (i.e., the *attributive sense* of the term) but also includes reference to God's gift of righteousness for those who will receive it by faith (i.e., the *communicative sense* of the term).[1] In this section Paul moves beyond the central OT motifs of "repentance" and "forgiveness," which appear prominently in all the NT portrayals of the Christian message as proclaimed to Jews — likewise beyond the traditional Jewish and Jewish Christian soteriological themes of "justification," "redemption," and "propitiation" ("expiation" or "sacrifice of atonement"), which have dominated the first section of this letter — to speak in much more personal, relational, and participatory language (1) of "peace" and "reconciliation" (5:1-11), (2) of what Adam brought about in the history and experience of all people and what Jesus Christ effected on behalf of all people (5:12-21), (3) of the frustrations of all spiritually sensitive people when they attempt to live their lives "under their own steam," (4) of being "in Christ" and "in the Spirit," (5) of "Christ by his Spirit" being "in the believer," and (6) of the major implications of all this for the Christian's new "life in the Spirit." In 8:31-39, Paul closes this major theological section with a triumphal statement of God's everlasting love to believers in Jesus, which acclamation includes a number of statements that appear to have been drawn from one or more of the early Christian confessions — just as he did in closing the first major section of the letter's body middle with a Christian confessional statement in 4:25.

Rom 5:1–8:39 as a Discrete and Distinctive Section of Material. The relation of this second section of the body middle of Romans to the letter's first section, 1:16–4:25, has been a matter of perennial concern for interpreters. Given that what Paul writes in this second section is something of an advance over what he presented in the first section, one common way of understanding that advance has been to view 1:16–4:25 as being about "justification" (i.e., both its need and God's provision) and 5:1–8:39 as being about "sanctification."[2] These two sections could also be viewed as setting out somewhat parallel lines of thought, though with differing emphases and different modes of expression: the first in 1:16–4:25 using judicial and forensic language; the second in 5:1–8:39 using relational, personal, and participatory language — though with both sections speaking of much the same things.[3] The issues are complex and call for

---

1. Cf. Rom 5:17; see also v. 21; 6:13, 16, 18, 19, 20; 8:10.

2. So, e.g., Cranfield, "Preaching on Romans," in his *On Romans*, 77: "8:1-16 tells of the work of the Holy Spirit in the sanctification of believers." Note also Harrison and Hagner, "Romans," 87, who argue for such a distinction on the basis of Paul's use of prepositions: "The emphasis in ch. 5 is on what has been done for the believer *through* Christ and his saving work (5:1-2, 9-11, 17-19, 21; cf. 3:24), whereas in ch. 6 Paul deals with what has happened to the believer together *with* Christ (6:4-6, 8) and what he or she enjoys *in* Christ (6:11, 23). Furthermore, it is in ch. 6 (vv. 19, 22), not in ch. 5, that sanctification (or holiness) first makes its appearance. Nevertheless, it is true that ch. 5 (especially in vv. 12-21) prepares for chs. 6-8 and thus has somewhat of a transitional character."

3. Cf., e.g., Barrett, *Romans*, 108: "Justification and reconciliation are different metaphors describing the same fact. The meaning of the verb 'to reconcile' is determined by the noun 'enemies'; it puts an end to enmity, as 'to justify' puts an end to legal contention."

careful investigation, which is what we will attempt to do in dealing with matters of form and structure and then in explicating the important exegetical and thematic features of Paul's presentation.

Many commentators have understood 1:16-4:25 as continuing on through 5:11;[4] others as continuing on through 5:21.[5] Most scholars today, however, view 5:1-8:39 as a discrete and distinctive section of material.[6] That is because:

1. The example of Abraham as a "proof from Scripture" in 4:1-25 is seen as an appropriate conclusion to all that is presented, both negatively and positively, in 1:16-3:31.

2. The statement of 5:1 is viewed as a literary hinge that summarizes the argument of 1:16-4:25 ("we have been justified through faith") and prepares for what follows in 5:2-8:39 ("let us have peace" [or 'we have peace'] with God through our Lord Jesus Christ").

3. The material of 5:1-11 functions both as a transitional passage (carrying on the function of the statement of 5:1) and as a thesis for all that follows in 5:12-8:39.

4. Many of the themes of 5:1-11 are taken up again in 8:18-39, thereby setting up something of a rhetorical *inclusio* or type of "ring composition" — especially the themes of "hope" (in 5:2 and 8:20-25), of "the glory of God revealed" (in 5:2 and 8:18-21), of "boasting in sufferings" (in 5:3 and 8:35-37), and of "the love of God expressed in the giving of Christ" (in 5:5 and 8:31-39).[7]

5. The word chain shifts from the dominance of the noun δικαιοσύνη ("righteousness"), the noun πίστις ("faith"/"faithfulness"), and the verb πιστεύω ("believe") in 1:16-4:25 (which contains thirty-three occurrences of "faith" and "believe"), to an emphasis on the noun ζωή ("life") and various participial forms of the verb ζάω ("live") in 5:1-8:39 ("life" and "live" occur twenty-four times in this section) — with δικαιοσύνη ("righteousness") also appearing in eight verses of this second section, though always in a *communicative sense*.[8]

6. The tone shifts from argumentative in 1:16-4:25 to a more personally confessional style in 5:1-8:39,[9] with this confessional style most often cast in

4. So, e.g., M. Luther (with 5:12-21 viewed as an excursus), P. Melanchthon, T. Zahn, F. J. Leenhardt, M. Black, and J. A. T. Robinson.

5. So, e.g., J. Calvin, U. Wilckens, O. Kuss, F. F. Bruce, J. D. G. Dunn, and E. F. Harrison and D. A. Hagner — often referring to 1:18-3:20 as "The Need for Salvation" or "The Plight of Humankind"; to 3:21-5:21 as "Justification" or "The Imputation of Righteousness"; and to 6:1-8:39 as "Justification" or "The Impartation of Righteousness."

6. So, e.g., H. Schlier, A. Nygren, O. Michel, C. H. Dodd, N. A. Dahl, C. E. B. Cranfield, E. Käsemann, J. A. Fitzmyer, and D. J. Moo.

7. Cf. Dahl, "Missionary Theology," in his *Studies in Paul,* appendix I, 88-89.

8. Cf., as noted above, 5:17, 21; 6:13, 16, 18, 19, 20; 8:10.

9. The only exception to such a confessional style being the retelling of "the foundational story" of 5:12-21.

the first-person plural "we" in 5:1-11, 6:1–7:7a, and 8:22-39 (though also appearing in the first-person singular "I" in 7:7b-25 and 8:18).

7. There appears throughout 5:1–8:39 the repeated refrain διὰ τοῦ κυρίου ἡμῶν Ἰησοῦ Χριστοῦ ("through our Lord Jesus Christ"), or its cognate wording ἐν Χριστῷ Ἰησοῦ τῷ κυρίῳ ἡμῶν ("in/by Christ Jesus our Lord"), signaling an *inclusio* not only at 5:1 and 8:39, but four times more at the end of certain important units within this larger section at 5:11, 5:21, 6:23, and 7:25.

Commentators have not usually been too concerned about the differing word chains, the *inclusio* nature of a particular refrain or some of the themes, the diverse organizational structures, or the different tones or styles in these two major sections of material. Such formal features have been viewed as being purely circumstantial in nature, without any inferences drawn from their presence. Yet formal patterning and compositional structures (whether the same, similar, or different) have, we believe, immense significance in signaling the relations that exist between the various sections of a Pauline letter — particularly here in relating Section I and Section II of the body middle of Romans to each other, and so in providing a proper context for the interpretation of each of these sections. In what follows, therefore, matters of form and structure will be viewed as being of great importance in providing a proper setting for what Paul has written in 5:1–8:39.

Rom 5:1–8:39 as Distinguishable in Its Infrequent Use of Biblical Quotations. Whereas there appear in 1:16–4:25 some fifteen to eighteen biblical quotations, located at eight or nine places, here in 5:1–8:39 there appear only two. Further, these two biblical quotations are used only somewhat tangentially: in 7:7, in citing in illustrative fashion the tenth commandment, "Do not covet," from Exod 20:17 and Deut 5:21; and in 8:36, in what appears to be an early Christian confessional portion that makes use of Ps 44:22.[10] In fact, to anticipate our discussions of these passages later, this infrequent use of Scripture in 5:1–8:39 is not only different from what can be observed regarding Paul's use of Scripture in 1:16–4:25, it is also different from his use of Scripture in 9:1–11:36 (with some thirty OT quotations in twenty-five or so places) and in 12:1–15:13 (with ten OT quotations).

The two citations of Scripture that appear in 7:7 and 8:36 look, in fact, very much like biblical passages that have been embedded into traditional materials, which the apostle has quoted either (1) to illustrate in a specific manner a general statement or (2) because the text was included in a confessional portion that he quoted. They do not function, however, as did his earlier biblical quotations in 1:16–4:25, either to build bridges of commonality with his addressees or to support his arguments.

10. Cf. R. N. Longenecker, "Prolegomena to Paul's Use of Scripture in Romans," esp. 146-47, 158-67; see also "Paul and the Old Testament," in *idem, Biblical Exegesis,* 2nd ed., 88-116.

Interpreters of Paul have not usually been overly concerned about these differences between the relative lack of biblical quotations in 5:1–8:39 and the extensive use of biblical quotations, allusions, and aphorisms in 1:16–4:25 (as well as in 9:1–11:36; also to an extent in 12:1–15:13) — nor between the various functions of the biblical quotations, allusions, and aphorisms in the four central sections of Paul's letter to Rome, particularly their relative lack of corresponding functions in 5:1–8:39. Where, however, such differences have been recognized, they have sometimes been seen either (1) as later interpolations by an undiscerning Paulinist or (2) as reflecting contradictions in Paul's own thought. Or they have been viewed — as Robin Scroggs once proposed, on the basis of "the rhetorical differences" (including Paul's use and nonuse of Scripture) between what is written in 5:1–8:39 and the materials that now appear in 1:16–4:25 and 9:1–11:36 — as representing two different Pauline sermons: one to a Jewish audience, which was originally composed of materials now in chs. 1–4 and 9–11, but whose parts have somehow become separated; the other to a Gentile audience, which was composed of materials now in chs. 5–8 and for some reason inserted between chs. 1–4 and 9–11.[11]

More likely, it may be legitimately argued that what Paul presents in 5:1–8:39 is what he referred to earlier in the thanksgiving section of his letter as his "spiritual gift" to his Roman addressees for their strengthening (1:11) — that is, that form of the Christian message that he customarily proclaimed to pagan Gentiles in his Gentile mission, which in 2:16 and 16:25 he calls "my gospel" — whereas the previous material of 1:16–4:25, both in its negative and its positive forms, should be understood as that form of Christian proclamation that Paul knew was held in common by all Jewish believers in Jesus.[12] That form of Jewish Christian proclamation, it may be postulated from a close reading of 1:16–4:25, laid stress on such traditional Jewish features as (1) "the righteousness of God," (2) "the witness of the Mosaic law and the OT prophets," and (3) the soteriological terms "justification," "redemption," and "propitiation" ("expiation" or "sacrifice of atonement"), and sought only to focus attention on Jesus as Israel's Messiah and on faith as a person's proper response — which matters the Jewish believers in Jesus understood as being inherent in their OT Scriptures. Further, as inheritors of a Jewish Christian way of understanding their Christian commitment, the Christians at Rome (1) honored the Mosaic law as the God-ordained "pedagogue" for the nation Israel, (2) proclaimed the fulfillment of God's promise to Abraham in Jesus' ministry and the church's message, (3) supported their proclamation of Jesus as God's promised Messiah by a Christocentric reading of Holy Scripture, and (4) cherished the traditions of the Jerusalem church.

11. So Scroggs, "Paul as Rhetorician," 271-98.

12. Cf. Paul's opening statement in the *propositio* of his letter to his own converts in Galatia, where he declares a similar understanding of the Christian gospel: "We who are Jews by birth, and not 'sinners of the Gentiles,' we know that a person is not justified by the works of the law (ἐξ ἔργων νόμου) but by the faith/faithfulness of Jesus Christ (διὰ πίστεως Ἰησοῦ Χριστοῦ), and so we have put our faith in Christ Jesus" (Gal 2:15-16a).

With this form of early Christian conviction Paul seems to have been in essential agreement, and he perhaps even presented the Christian message in this manner himself when occasion demanded. Yet what Paul wanted his Christian addressees at Rome to know and experience was even more than all this. He wanted them to understand and experience in their own lives the message of the Christian gospel as he knew it and had "contextualized" it in a more personal, relational, and participatory manner to Gentiles in the eastern regions of the Greco-Roman empire.

Epistolary, Rhetorical, and Oral Conventions in 5:1–8:39. The presence in 5:1–8:39 of various oral and rhetorical conventions of the day, as well as a few contemporary epistolary features, also has significance for the passage's interpretation.[13] A dozen or so expressions in this section of Romans have often been identified as ancient *epistolary conventions.* These include (1) "verbs of saying," as in τί οὖν ἐροῦμεν, "what then shall we say?" (6:1, 15; 7:7; 8:31); (2) "verbs of speaking," as in γινώσκουσιν γὰρ νόμον λαλῶ, "for I am speaking to those who know the law" (7:1); (3) various "disclosure formulas" using the verbs ἀγνοεῖτε, "you know" (6:3; 7:1), οἴδατε, "you know" (6:16), or οἴδαμεν, "we know" (7:14; 8:22, 28); (4) the vocative noun ἀδελφοί, "brothers and sisters" (7:1, 4; 8:12); and (5) the "confidence formula" πέπεισμαι γὰρ ὅτι, "for I am convinced that" (8:38). Most of these expressions, however, are probably to be related more to particular rhetorical modes of persuasion that were then in vogue than to any then current epistolary convention, and so to be seen as functioning simply to introduce either a question or the two biblical passages cited in 7:7 and 8:36. Yet the expressions at the beginning of 7:1 and in the resumptive address of 7:4 — that is, the "disclosure formula" ἀγνοεῖτε ("you know") of 7:1, the vocative ἀδελφοί ("brothers and sisters") of 7:1, the "verb of speaking" in the statement γινώσκουσιν γὰρ νόμον λαλῶ ("for I am speaking to those who know the law") of 7:1, and the possessive vocative ἀδελφοί μου ("my brothers and sisters") of 7:4 — can all be identified as strictly epistolary phenomena. Further, the disclosure formulas that appear in 6:3, 6:16, 7:14, 8:22, and 8:28 are probably also to be classified as epistolary phenomena.[14] However they are understood, these quasi- or true epistolary expressions often appear at breaks or turning points in the argument of the letter, and so function to signal some type of transition of thought — either (1) from one feature to another feature within the same argument, or (2) from one major discussion to another major discussion.

More important, however, are the *rhetorical conventions* that are reflected in this section, for they quite expressly serve to identify and mark off the various movements in the apostle's argument. Among the more obvious examples of these rhetorical phenomena are the following:

1. *Transitio* (i.e., a statement or paragraph that recalls what has been said

---

13. For an extensive discussion of oral, rhetorical, and epistolary conventions, see R. N. Longenecker, *Introducing Romans,* ch. 6, pp. 164-229.

14. See also a clear use of an epistolary "disclosure formula" in 11:25

and sets forth what is to follow). The sentence in 5:1 is certainly a rhetorical *transitio*. Probably, however, all the material of 5:1-11 functions in this manner.

2. *Extended Anaphora* (i.e., the repetition of a word or expression at the resumption of a discussion that has been interrupted by another section of material). The phrase δικαιωθέντες οὖν ("having therefore been justified") in 5:1, which begins the discussion of 5:1-5 (which is supported by what Paul says or quotes in 5:6-8), and then the phrase δικαιωθέντες οὖν ("having now been justified") in 5:9, which appears at the beginning of the resumption and development of that same discussion in 5:9-11, constitute, in all likelihood, an instance of rhetorical extended anaphora.

3. *Inclusio* (i.e., similar statements, phrases, or clauses placed at the beginning and end of a relatively short unit of text that serve to frame the material presented). The repeated refrain "through our Lord Jesus Christ" (διὰ τοῦ κυρίου ἡμῶν Ἰησοῦ Χριστοῦ) that appears in 5:1b, 11, 21, and 7:25, together with its synonymous expression "in/by our Lord Jesus Christ" in 6:23 and 8:39 (ἐν Χριστῷ Ἰησοῦ τῷ κυρίῳ ἡμῶν), not only frames the entire section at the beginning of 5:1 and the end of 8:39 (as will be noted again below in dealing with oral conventions) but also nicely concludes four of the principal units of material within that section at 5:11, 5:21, 6:23, and 7:25.

4. *Synkrisis* (i.e., the comparison of persons, objects, or things, with deficiencies and superiorities highlighted). The prominent example of *synkrisis* in Romans is in 5:12-21, where Paul sets out in striking fashion what Christ has effected through his obedience vis-à-vis what Adam brought about because of his disobedience.

5. *Enthymeme* (i.e., an imperfect or abbreviated syllogism, whose premises may involve features of character [*ethos*], emotion [*pathos*], or reason [*logos*] but whose conclusion must be supplied by the audience or addressees). This rhetorical convention is undoubtedly involved in the questions of 6:1 ("Shall we go on sinning so that grace may increase?"), 6:2 ("How can we [who died to sin] still live in it?"), 6:15 ("Shall we sin because we are not under the law but under grace?"), and 7:7 ("Is the law sin?") — with the three questions of 6:1, 6:15, and 7:7 each highlighting a main part of the presentation, and that of 6:2 amplifying the first question of 6:1.

6. *Paradeigma* (i.e., a story that provides a pattern or example to be either imitated or avoided, or an argument that is based on the use of an example, whether positive or negative). The story of sin, frustration, and inability recounted in 7:7-25, whether the "I" (ἐγώ) of the narrative is to be understood in personal terms (i.e., referring to Paul's own experience, past or present) or in gnomic terms (i.e., referring to the experience of humanity generally), should probably be understood rhetorically in this light.

Of significance, as well, are the various *oral conventions* of the ancient world that seem to be present in this section. Among the oral phenomena most discernible in 5:1-8:39 are the following:

1. *Acoustical Orientation* (i.e., the repetition of words and phrases that

sound alike). This convention evidently was used as an aid in understanding and remembering what was said. A prominent example appears in 5:12-21 with the use of a series of nouns that end with the Greek letters μ and α: τὸ παράπτωμα ("the transgression") of Adam (vv. 15, 16, 18, and 20); τὸ χάρισμα ("the grace") effected by Jesus Christ (vv. 15 and 16); κρίμα ("depravity") brought about by Adam's sin (v. 16); κατάκριμα ("divine judgment") on sin (vv. 16 and 18); τὸ δώρημα ("the divine gift") that brought justification (v. 16; also implied in v. 15); and τὸ δικαίωμα (literally "the righteous decree"; here used equivalently to δικαίωσις, "justification," and δικαιοσύνη, "righteousness") that leads to "life eternal" (v. 16; cf. v. 21). On a somewhat smaller scale, each of the four clauses of 5:6-8, which passage seems to be inserted as parenthetical material into the larger section of 5:1-11, ends with a form of the verb "he [Christ] died": ἀπέθανεν . . . ἀποθανεῖται . . . ἀποθανεῖν . . . ἀπέθανεν. Such acoustical features suggest that the portions in which they are found, that is, most prominently in 5:12-21 but also in 5:6-8, probably (1) originated either in the early church as part of an early Christian confession or in the context of Paul's oral preaching during the course of his Gentile mission, and (2) should be viewed as having been carried over by the apostle into his letter to Christians at Rome, whether consciously or unconsciously, with these particular features of their original orality still intact.

2. *Framing Statements, Sentences, Phrases, and Words* (i.e., similar linguistic phenomena, whether statements, sentences, phrases, or words, that appear at the beginning and end of a relatively short unit of text and serve to frame the material presented). Because there are similar themes and parallel features in 5:1-11 and 8:18-39,[15] many view these portions as representing what ancient rhetoricians called an *inclusio* — thereby framing what has every appearance of being a distinctive unit of material from 5:1 through 8:39. Likewise, as noted above, throughout these four chapters there appears the repeated refrain "through [or 'by'] our Lord Jesus Christ," with only slight variations in the preposition used (διά or ἐν) and in the case of the phrase that follows the preposition (as governed by the particular preposition). This refrain is found not only at the beginning and end of the entire section at 5:1 and 8:39, thereby functioning as an *inclusio* for all the material within these four chapters, but also at the end of four of the principal units of material within the section, that is, at 5:11, 5:21, 6:23, and 7:25.

3. *Formulaic Confessional Materials* (i.e., early Christian confessional portions, which were, presumably, originally oral, and which appear to have been incorporated, either whole or in part, by the authors of the NT at strategic places in their writings). As noted in the point about acoustical orientation, the statements of 5:6-8 seem to reflect such early Christian confessional material.

---

15. Cf. Dahl, "Missionary Theology," 88-89: "Apart from the climactic chain in Rom. 5:3-4 and the aside in Rom 5:7, all of the major themes in Rom. 5:1-11 reappear in Romans 8: Justification and a restored relationship to God as the basis for the hope of future salvation and glory, in spite of present sufferings; the gift of the Holy Spirit, the death of Christ, and the love of God as warrants for this hope; and a note of exaltation."

Likewise, many of the expressions used within the lyrical and almost defiant affirmations of 8:31-39 also appear to have been drawn from early Christian confessional materials[16] — thereby closing off in dramatic fashion this second section, as the apostle seems to have done earlier in closing off the first section at 4:25 (and will do again in closing off the third section at 11:33-36).

A Summation on the Structure of 5:1-8:39. On the basis of the rhetorical and oral conventions that appear throughout this second section — as well as certain epistolary features, word chains, and uses (or nonuses) of Scripture — the following matters can reasonably be posited:

1. 5:1-8:39 forms a distinguishable and discrete unit of material in Paul's letter to the Christians at Rome.
2. This second section of the letter's body middle differs in many respects from the first section preceding it and from the two sections that follow it.[17]
3. Subunits of material within this second section can be fairly easily determined by the appearance of such epistolary, rhetorical, and oral conventions as framing or *inclusio* techniques, the use of vocatives, the use of verbs of saying, various disclosure formulas, and the use of rhetorical questions.

Further, it can be argued that while most of 5:1-8:39 reflects a number of oral and rhetorical conventions of Paul's day, which suggests that the bulk of its material must have originated in oral environments of devotion and proclamation, 7:1-6 begins in a more epistolary fashion, and so seems to indicate that it had more of an epistolary origin and was composed by its author when Romans as a letter was written — that is, that Paul wrote it and inserted it into the condensed form of his contextualized proclamation to Gentiles, which he had presented to Gentiles in his Gentile mission and was now sending on in his letter to his Christian addressees at Rome.

The structure of this second section, therefore, is probably best understood with respect to its main divisions as follows:

1. A transitional and thesis passage on "peace" and "reconciliation" in 5:1-11
2. The foundational narrative regarding what Jesus Christ effected vis-à-vis what Adam had brought about in 5:12-21
3. Three questions and an interjected illustration and statement regarding the implications of Christ's work (6:1–7:13):
   Question 1: "Should we go on sinning so that grace may increase?" (6:1-14)

---

16. Cf. R. N. Longenecker, *New Wine into Fresh Wineskins*, 19.

17. J. C. Beker referred to "the very different character of Romans 5–8" from what preceded these four chapters and from what follows them (cf. Beker, *Paul the Apostle*, 85), and then restated that observation for emphasis as follows: "There can be no question about the different character of chapters 5–8" (85).

Question 2: "Should we sin because we are not under the law but under grace?" (6:15-23)

An interjected illustration on the extent of the authority of the Mosaic law and a statement regarding a Christian's freedom from the law (7:1-6)

Question 3: "Is the law sin?" (7:7-13)

4. A soliloquy on the tragic plight of people who attempt to live their lives "under their own steam" in 7:14-25

5. No condemnation and new life for people "in Christ Jesus," and therefore "in the Spirit," in 8:1-17

6. New life in the Spirit: both personal and universal; both present and future — a life of suffering and glory, in 8:18-30

7. A triumphal affirmation of God's vindication, care, and eternal love for people who are in Christ, with early Christian confessional materials incorporated, in 8:31-39

Our Thesis regarding the Nature of the Materials in 5:1–8:39. Our thesis is that in 5:1–8:39 Paul sets out the basic features of the Christian gospel as he had contextualized that message in his Gentile mission to those who had no Jewish heritage and no biblical instruction. Highlighted in chs. 5–8 are the themes of (1) peace with God, (2) God's love and grace, (3) being reconciled to God, (4) deliverance from sin and death, (5) the gift of life, (6) being in Christ, (7) being in the Spirit, and (8) being unable to be separated from Christ's love, and therefore unable to be separated from God's love and protection. These themes can be based, by analogy, on God's past dealings with Israel as recorded in the Jewish (OT) Scriptures. They could not, however, be directly demonstrated to Gentiles by specific biblical texts. Nor, it seems, would the quotation of passages from the Jewish Scriptures have been meaningful or appreciated by pagan Gentiles. Rather, such emphases on "peace," "reconciliation," being "in Christ," being "in the Spirit," and "Christ by his Spirit" being in the Christian, as expressed in 5:1–8:39, while confirmed by Holy Scripture, stemmed primarily from (1) the exalted Christ's encounter of Paul on his way to Damascus and (2) Paul's continued spiritual experiences with God through Jesus Christ. So they were proclaimed by Paul in his outreach to pagan Gentiles on the bases of personal encounter and continued spiritual relationship.

1. Transitional and Thesis Passage on "Peace" and "Reconciliation" (5:1-11)

TRANSLATION

⁵:¹*Therefore having been justified by faith, let us have peace with God through our Lord Jesus Christ.* ²*Through him we have gained access by faith into this grace in which we now stand. And we boast in the hope of the glory of God.* ³*Not only this, but also we boast in our sufferings, because we know that suffering produces steadfast endurance;* ⁴*steadfast endurance produces character; and character produces hope.* ⁵*And this hope does not disappoint us, because God has poured out his love into our hearts by the Holy Spirit, whom he has given us.* ⁶*For,*

> *"While we were still weak, still at that time 'Christ died on behalf of the ungodly.'*
> ⁷*For scarcely on behalf of a righteous person will someone die.*
> *Yet on behalf of the good person someone might even dare to die.*
> ⁸*But God demonstrates his own love to us in that while we were still sinners, 'Christ died on behalf of us.'"*

⁹*Having now been justified by his blood, much more then will we be saved from God's wrath through him!* ¹⁰*For if, when we were God's enemies, we were reconciled to him through the death of his Son, much more, having been reconciled, we will be saved through his life!* ¹¹*Not only this, but also we boast in God through our Lord Jesus Christ, through whom we have now received reconciliation.*

TEXTUAL NOTES

5:1 The subjunctive ἔχωμεν ("let us have") is attested by uncials ℵ* A B* C D (also *Byz* K L) and by minuscules 33 1175 1739 (Category I), 81 1962 (Category II), and 61ᶜ 69 181 436 614 621 630 915 1243 1398 1678 1735 1838 1874 1912 1942 2197 2516 (Category III); it is also reflected in itᵇ, ᵈ, ᶠ, ᵍ, ᵐᵒⁿ, ᵒ vg copᵇᵒ arm eth and supported by Marcionᵃᶜᶜ ᵗᵒ ᵀᵉʳᵗᵘˡˡⁱᵃⁿ Origenˡᵃᵗ Chrysostom Theodore Theodoretˡᵉᵐ Ambrosiaster. The indicative ἔχομεν ("we have") is supported by corrected uncials ℵ¹ B² (together with F G P Ψ 0220) and by minuscules 1739 (Category I), 256 1506 1881 2127 2464 (Category II), 6 104 263 365 424ᶜ 459 1241 1319 1573 1852 2200; it is also reflected in itᵃʳ vgᵐˢˢ copˢᵃ.

Although the subjunctive ἔχωμεν is strongly supported by the Greek textual tradition, by a large number of ancient versions, by many of the most important Greek and Latin Church Fathers, as well as by most commentators of the immediately previous generations,[18] the vast majority of translators and commentators today have, for internal

---

18. So, e.g., B. Weiss, *An die Römer,* 217; Lightfoot, *Notes on Epistles of St. Paul,* 284; Sanday

reasons, argued against it — since, as they understand the passage and its context, Paul is not exhorting (as would be the case if the verb were subjunctive) but stating a fact (as would be the case if the verb were indicative).[19] Thus, despite overwhelming textual support for the subjunctive ἔχωμεν, most scholars today understand the verb to have originally been the indicative ἔχομεν, and therefore to be read as declaring that "peace with God" is the possession of those who have been justified.[20] This postulated change in the textual tradition from indicative to subjunctive has usually been credited to some early scribe's inability to distinguish between the pronunciations of the Greek letters omicron (o) and omega (ω); therefore the view that the switch occurred sometime in the text's early transmission. Others, however, have suggested, as did Bruce Metzger, that "when Paul dictated ἔχομεν, Tertius, his amanuensis (16.22), may have written down ἔχωμεν."[21]

This same phenomenon regarding an indicative verb (λογιζόμεθα, "we reckon," "maintain") or a subjunctive verb (λογιζώμεθα, "let us reckon," "maintain") appeared earlier in Paul's letter to Rome in 3:28b. There, however, the matter is far more easily resolved in favor of an indicative reading, for in 3:28b the subjunctive is far less supported in the textual tradition than it is in 5:1.[22] Here in 5:1, however, E. F. Harrison and D. A. Hagner have identified the problem and expressed their own solution: (1) "The textual evidence for the omega, the subjunctive, is sterling"; yet, because of the indicative nature of the context, (2) "This is one of the few places in textual criticism where the strongest possible manuscript evidence has been made to yield to the internal logic of the passage."[23]

Nonetheless, as W. Sanday and A. C. Headlam argued in support of the originality of the subjunctive verb ἔχωμεν, it is very difficult "to overthrow the weight of direct testimony" that appears in the Greek and Latin textual traditions.[24] Further, as we will attempt to explicate in our "Exegetical Comments" below, such a subjunctive form and hortatory understanding fit quite well in the context of Paul's overall presentation throughout Romans — and, of course, fit well in our proposed understanding of relations between the first and second major sections of the body middle of his letter.

2 The expression τῇ πίστει, "by faith" (in the statement "we have gained access by faith"), is attested by uncials ℵ*, 2 C P Ψ (also *Byz* K L) and by minuscules 33 1175 1739 (Category I), 81 256 1506 1881 2127 2464 (Category II), and 5 6 61 69 104 181 218 263 323 326 330 365 424c 436 441 451 459 467 621 623 629 630 917 1241 1243 1319 1398 1505 1573

and Headlam, *Romans,* 120; Lagrange, *Épître aux Romains,* 101; C. H. Dodd, *Romans,* 72; Kuss, *Römerbrief,* 1.201-2.

19. So, e.g., Lietzmann, *An die Römer,* 58; Käsemann, *Romans,* 133; Barrett, *Romans,* 102; Cranfield, *Romans,* 1.257; Wilckens, *An die Römer,* 1.288-89; Moo, *Romans,* 295-96.

20. Cf. Aland and Aland, *Text of the New Testament,* 286. So also the committee (which included K. and B. Aland), sponsored by the United Bible Societies, that established the same text for both the *GNT*[3, 4] and the *NA*[26, 24], which critical texts have been the basis for almost all modern commentaries on Romans; see Metzger, *Textual Commentary,* 452, for comments with respect to the committee's rationale.

21. Metzger, *Textual Commentary,* 452.

22. See "Textual Notes" above on 3:28b.

23. Harrison and Hagner, "Romans," 93.

24. Sanday and Headlam, *Romans,* 120.

1718 1735 1751 1838 1852 1874 1875 1877 1908 1912 1942 1959 2110 2138 2197 2200 2344 2492 2495 2516 2523 2718 (Category III); it is also reflected in it[ar, b, d2, mon, o] vg syr[p, h, pal] cop[bo] and supported by Origen[lat2/5] Chrysostom[1/2]. It is, however, omitted in uncials B D F G 0220, in versions it[d*, f, g] cop[sa] and in Origen[lat3/5] Ambrosiaster. Judging by its attestation in uncorrected Codex Sinaiticus (א*) but its omission in Codex Vaticanus (B), the external MS evidence may be said to be fairly balanced. The sense of the passage, however, is not changed by either the presence or absence of τῇ πίστει here in 5:2, for Paul has already declared in 5:1 that faith is necessary for justification. So it may have been that some copyists simply deleted τῇ πίστει in 5:2 as being superfluous after ἐκ πίστεως of 5:1. The UBS committee, as Bruce Metzger tells us, "preferred to retain the words in the text but to enclose the phrase within square brackets."[25]

The variant ἐν τῇ πίστει ("in the faith") appears in uncials א[1] A, in minuscules 1962 (Category II) and 88 915 1845 2544 (Category III), in a number of MSS of the Vulgate, and is supported by Chrysostom[1/2]. This variant reading, however, "seems to have arisen by dittography after ἐσκηκαμεν."[26]

3 Codex Beza (D 06) adds the nominative singular neuter demonstrative pronoun τοῦτο, which, employed in a substantival fashion, means "this," to the phrase οὐ μόνον δέ ("but not only"), and so has the beginning of 5:3 read "but not only this." The addition of this neuter demonstrative pronoun is undoubtedly secondary, though it does make clear what Paul meant and so is reflected in our translation (also in 5:11; 8:23; 9:10; cf. 2 Cor 8:19).

6 The reading ἔτι γὰρ . . . ἔτι, "for when (we were) still (powerless)," is supported widely by uncials א A C[vid] D* and by minuscules 81 256 1506 2127 (Category II) and 104 263 365 424[c] 459 1241 1319 1573 (Category III); it is also reflected in syr[h] and in Origen[lat] Marcion[acc to Epiphanius]. It is a rather awkward construction, primarily because of its repetition of the word ἔτι. Nonetheless, it is probably to be accepted as original.

Other textual witnesses omit one or the other of the two instances of ἔτι, evidently to avoid the repetition of the word; for example: (1) ἔτι γὰρ . . . *omit* (i.e., omitting the second use of the word), as supported by uncials D[2] K P Ψ, minuscules 6 1175 1739 (Category I), 1881 1962 2464 (Category II), 6 1912 2200 (Category III), and (2) εἰς τί γὰρ . . . ἔτι (i.e., omitting the first use of the word), as supported by uncials F G, by versions it[ar, b, d, f, g, mon, (o)] vg, and by Irenaeus[lat] Ambrosiaster. The major alternative reading εἴ γε . . . ἔτι ("if indeed [when we were] still [powerless]"), which is attested by uncial B, minuscule 945 (Category V), versions vg[mss] cop[sa, (bo)] syr[pal], and Augustine, "possesses," as Bruce Metzger has observed, "a certain inherent fitness," though there seems to be "no adequate reason why, if this reading were original, the others would have arisen."[27]

7 The adverb μόλις ("scarcely," "with difficulty") is strongly attested in the Greek textual tradition. The alternative adverb μόγις ("hardly," "not readily," "only rarely") is supported by uncial א*, minuscule 1739 (Category I), and Origen. The two adverbs are virtually synonymous, resulting, it seems, in what was probably a very early scribal con-

25. Metzger, *Textual Commentary*, 452-53.
26. *Ibid.*, 453.
27. *Ibid.*

fusion between μόλις (presumably the original) and μόγις (its somewhat synonymous look-alike).

8a The articular expression ὁ θεός ("God") is included after the prepositional phrase εἰς ἡμᾶς ("to us") in uncials ℵ A C K P Ψ, which inclusion and placement are supported widely throughout the minuscule tradition. It appears, however, before εἰς ἡμᾶς in uncials D F G (also *Byz* L), minuscules 1241 2197, and Irenaeus[lat]. The omission of ὁ θεός ("God") in Codex Vaticanus (B 03) is probably inadvertent. In all likelihood, the original text included ὁ θεός with its placement after the prepositional phrase εἰς ἡμᾶς.

8b The conditional particle εἰ ("if") appears before the word ἔτι ("while") in uncials D[1] F G, and is reflected in sy[p] and in Ambrosiaster, thereby reading "if while we were yet sinners." This is, however, an addition very weakly supported in the textual tradition, which possibly was meant to downplay the universality of sin as argued in these verses.

9 The particle οὖν ("therefore," "consequently," "then") is omitted in uncials D* F G, in the Old Latin (it), and in Irenaeus[lat] Ambrosiaster. Its presence breaks up the idiomatic expression of πολλῷ μᾶλλον ("much more"), and so could have been easily set aside. Yet the presence of οὖν as original is strongly attested in the Greek textual tradition.

11a As with the addition of the nominative singular neuter demonstrative pronoun τοῦτο ("this") in 5:3, τοῦτο is here added to the phrase οὐ μόνον δέ ("but not only"), making the beginning of 5:11 read "but not only this." Evidently the demonstrative pronoun was added for stylistic reasons. Nonetheless, it makes clear Paul's meaning.

11b The participle καυχώμενοι ("boasting, we boast") is very strongly supported in the textual tradition, and should be accepted as representing the original text. The first-person plural καυχώμεθα ("we boast"), however, is supported by the ninth-century uncial L (020) and by a number of late minuscule MSS; the first-person plural καυχώμεν appears in ninth-century uncials F (010) and G (012) and many late minuscules. These two variants most likely represent scribal efforts to keep Paul from using too many participles, as was his habit, and so to have him speak more plainly by using finite verbs.

11c The inclusion of the name Χριστός in the genitive Ἰησοῦ Χριστοῦ is strongly attested by uncials ℵ A C D F G P Ψ (also *Byz* K L) and the preponderance of minuscules. It is absent, however, in fourth-century Codex Vaticanus (B 03) and in minuscules 1739 (Category I) and 1881 (Category III). This omission was probably accidental, resulting from haplography with the similar-sounding expression δι' οὗ that immediately follows.

FORM/STRUCTURE/SETTING

In 5:1-11 Paul sets out a carefully constructed portion of material. He begins in 5:1 by using the form of a rhetorical *transitio,* which convention was defined by the first-century B.C. anonymous author of *Rhetorica ad Herennium* as a statement that "briefly recalls what has been said, and likewise briefly sets forth what is to follow next."[28] This transitional statement recalls all that had been said in

28 *Rhet Her* 4.26.35; cf. Cosby, "Paul's Persuasive Language in Romans 5," 213; Reid, "Rhetorical Analysis of Romans 1:1–5:21," 94; Jewett, *Romans,* 346.

1:16–4:25, captions all that will be said in 5:2–8:39, and declares that both "justification by faith" and "peace [or 'completeness'] with God" have been brought about by God "through our Lord Jesus Christ."

In 5:2-5 Paul elaborates on his transitional sentence of 5:1, focusing particularly on its final clause, "through our Lord Jesus Christ." He also highlights certain significant implications for the believer's life of what it means to experience "justification by faith" (as in 1:16–4:25) and "peace [or 'completeness'] with God" (as in 5:1–8:39), which have come about through the work of Christ. What he presents first is a Christocentric affirmation that speaks of the Christian's access by faith into God's grace (5:2a). He goes on to emphasize the Christian's newfound ability to "boast in the hope of the glory of God" (5:2b) and the Christian's newfound ability to "boast in sufferings," since believers in Jesus understand that suffering produces perseverance, perseverance produces character, and character produces hope (5:3-4). The apostle concludes this portion of the passage in a distinctly Trinitarian fashion by affirming that this newfound "hope" of believers in Jesus is not only based on the work of Christ, it also has come about because "God has poured out his love into our hearts by the Holy Spirit, whom he has given us" (5:5).

Having set out such Christological and Trinitarian affirmations, with their corollary implications, Paul supports what he has written by a nicely balanced and carefully constructed series of statements in 5:6-8, which give every appearance of having been drawn from some portion of early Christian confessional material.[29] These seemingly traditional statements are held together by (1) the preposition ὑπέρ ("on behalf of"), which appears in each of them, (2) the fourfold repetition of the verb ἀποθνήσκω ("die"), and (3) the adverb ἔτι ("still") at both the beginning and the end of this subunit of material.

In the final three verses of this transitional and thesis material, that is, in 5:9-11, Paul (1) uses a form of rhetorical anaphora (or what may be called an *extended anaphora*), reaching back to recall the theme of "justification by faith" with which he began the passage in 5:1 and here developing it further; (2) invokes a "from the lesser to the greater" type of argument (i.e., an *a minori ad maius* type of Greek rhetorical argumentation, or a *qal waḥomer* form of Jewish hermeneutics) to signal his movement of thought from purely forensic concerns to more personal, relational, and participatory matters; (3) clarifies what "peace with God" means by use of the highly significant term "reconciliation"; (4) trumpets his earlier theme of "boasting in God"; and (5) closes with the frequently repeated refrain "through our Lord Jesus Christ," which here in 5:11 forms an *inclusio* with its first appearance in 5:1 — and which is then, in essence, repeated four times more at 5:21, 6:23, 7:25, and 8:39.

---

29. Cf. Jewett, *Romans*, 346-47, for perceptive comments in support of the thesis that in 5:6-8 there appears "a citation from or an allusion to an early Christian creed."

EXEGETICAL COMMENTS

5:1 There is a growing recognition among commentators today that the material of 5:1 is best understood as a transitional statement that builds on Section I of the body middle of the letter (i.e., on 1:16–4:25) and points forward to Section II (i.e., to 5:1–8:39).[30] As such, it (1) recalls all that had been said in 1:16–4:25, referring to it under the rubric "justification by faith" (δικαιωθέντες ἐκ πίστεως), (2) introduces all that will be said in 5:2–8:39, captioning it under the rubric "peace with God" (εἰρήνην πρὸς τὸν θεὸν), and (3) declares quite forthrightly that both "justification by faith" and "peace with God" have been brought about by God "through our Lord Jesus Christ" (διὰ τοῦ κυρίου ἡμῶν Ἰησοῦ Χριστοῦ).

Some have proposed that not just this sentence of 5:1 — nor even the whole of 5:1-11 (as we believe) — should be understood as transitional material between what precedes and what follows, but that Paul meant all of 5:1-21 to be, in some sense, a transitional bridge from 1:16–4:25 to 6:1–11:36. This understanding has been most ably argued by Neil Elliott:

> Romans 5 is the pivot on which the letter's argument turns. This chapter channels the force of the opposition generated in chs. 1–4 between divine righteousness and human boasting into an insistence that Christians boast "in God" (5.11), specifically in the mode of hope for "the glory of God" (5.2). The reorientation of Christology in 5.12-21 becomes the apocalyptic-theocentric anchor for the extended qualification of the Christian "boast" in Romans 6–11.[31]

While such an argument can be made, it seems more likely that what Paul wrote in 5:1-11 should be viewed as *both* (1) transitional material, which functions as a bridge between Sections I and II, and (2) thesis material, which prepares for all that will be presented in Section II.[32]

The transitional nature of the passage is indicated in its opening statement of 5:1, "Therefore, having been justified by faith, let us have peace with God through our Lord Jesus Christ." The thesis nature of the passage, however, while suggested here in 5:1 and then in the implications set out in 5:2-5, is more explicitly expressed in the passage's closing material of 5:9-11, which repeats the forensic theme of "justification" through Jesus' "blood" and "death" *but also* moves on in a "lesser to greater" type of presentation to speak of personal and relational matters regarding "salvation" from "divine wrath" and unto "life" that

---

30. So esp. Luz, "Zum Aufbau von Röm 1–8," 178; Dahl, "Missionary Theology," 82, and appendix I, 88-90; Wilckens, *An die Römer*, 1.286-87; and Jewett, *Romans*, 346; for variations on this thesis, see also Black, *Romans*, 81; E. P. Sanders, *Paul and Palestinian Judaism*, 486-87; and P. M. McDonald, "Romans 5:1-11 as a Rhetorical Bridge," 81-96.

31. N. Elliott, *The Rhetoric of Romans*, 226-27.

32. Cf. Fitzmyer, *Romans*, 393, where the caption for 5:1-11 is set out in italics as *"Theme Announced."*

are based on relationship with God's Son — with this relationship epitomized by the term "reconciliation," which appears three times in these final verses (first as a verb, then as a participle, and finally as a noun).

The major textual problem of 5:1 is, of course, whether the main verb of the sentence should be read as ἔχομεν (i.e., indicative "we have") or as ἔχωμεν (i.e., subjunctive "let us have").[33] The Church Fathers were almost unanimous in reading the verb as a subjunctive (ἔχωμεν), and thus understood Paul as exhorting the Christians at Rome to take some type of action in their lives. Origen, in the early third century, for example, commented on the verb as follows:

> It is obvious from this [i.e., Paul's use of the subjunctive ἔχωμεν] that the apostle is inviting everyone who has understood that he is justified by faith and not by works to that "peace which passes all understanding," in which the height of perfection consists.[34]

Origen went on to exhort his readers:

> Let us, therefore, have peace, so that the flesh will no longer war with the spirit, nor will the law of God be opposed by the law of our members. Let there not be in us "yes" or "no," but let us all agree, let us all think alike, let there be no dissension either among ourselves or between us and others outside our ranks, and then we shall have peace with God through our Lord Jesus Christ. But let it most definitely be known that anyone in whom the vice of wickedness is found can never have peace. For as long as he is thinking how he can hurt his neighbor, as long as he seeks after ways of causing harm, his mind will never be at peace.[35]

Likewise, Ambrosiaster in the fourth century understood the verb as being subjunctive in form and imperative in function when he wrote: "Paul means here that we should stop sinning and not go back to the way we used to live, for that is to make war with God."[36] And Pelagius, writing in the fifth century, viewed the verb in much the same manner when he commented on Rom 5:1: "Now, having concluded this argument [i.e., on the example of Abraham in 4:1-25], Paul urges both Jews and Gentiles to live at peace."[37]

The discovery in 1950 of a small vellum fragment of some thirty verses of Romans — the so-called Wyman fragment, which has been designated uncial 0220 and can be dated to the latter part of the third century — has often been cited in support of the originality of the indicative ἔχομεν ("we have"). Since this fragment of the Greek text of Romans agrees with Codex Vaticanus (B 03) at

33. See "Textual Notes" above.
34. Origen, *Ad Romanos,* on 5:1, *PG* 14.988.
35. *Ibid., PG* 14.989.
36. Ambrosiaster, *Ad Romanos, ad loc.*
37. Pelagius, *Ad Romanos, ad loc.*

every point in its transmission of the text *except* in its reading of the main verb of the sentence of 5:1 as ἔχομεν and not ἔχωμεν, and since uncial 0220 can be dated earlier than Codex Vaticanus, it has been argued that this small vellum fragment provides a better reading of the main verb of 5:1 than Codex B. Or, at least, as the noted Greek philologist W. H. P. Hatch wrote in 1952: "This evidence for ἔχομεν is probably pre-Hesychian. Therefore the argument for the indicative is greatly strengthened, and the claim of the subjunctive to be the correct reading is correspondingly weakened."[38]

Whatever the original form of the verb in 5:1 (whether ἔχωμεν, "let us have," or ἔχομεν, "we have"), no one disputes that its "variant" reading must also have appeared in some very early texts — whether through a misunderstanding by an early scribe in transcribing Paul's letter for wider circulation and use (which would have been possible) or because of a misunderstanding by Paul's amanuensis Tertius (which seems unlikely, since Paul could be assumed to have checked Tertius's final copy for errors). One cannot, therefore, make a textual decision here merely on the basis of the date of one external witness vis-à-vis that of another external witness. Nor does the frequently repeated observation that in Paul's day the Greek letters omicron (o) and omega (ω) were most likely pronounced and heard in much the same fashion resolve the question at hand. For a misunderstanding of either pronunciation or hearing could go either way.

As for our understanding of this textual situation, we consider it necessary to honor the overwhelming authority of the subjunctive ἔχωμεν ("let us have") in the textual tradition of Rom 5:1 — not because we feel we must bow to our fathers (though, of course, we should always respect our fathers, even when we disagree with them), but because we believe Paul in this second major section of the body middle of the letter is not only building on what he has written in the first major section, but also moving beyond that. Thus a subjunctive verb with its hortatory emphasis fits quite well in this transitional sentence of 5:1, and also, we believe, in the context of Paul's overall presentation in Romans.

The problem in understanding Paul here in 5:1, however, has not so much to do with the form of the main verb of the sentence, but more with appreciating what the apostle had in mind when he dictated the word "peace" (εἰρήνη) to Tertius. For as an ethnic Jew, who had been trained in Jewish ways of thinking and expression — and who was writing to believers in Jesus at Rome, who had been extensively influenced by Jewish Christian thought and language — the apostle undoubtedly used the Greek word "peace" (εἰρήνη) to mean more than just "an absence of conflict" or "a life lived without turmoil." There can, in fact, be little doubt that when he spoke of "peace" and when his Christian addressees at Rome heard the word "peace" read to them, they both understood the Greek word εἰρήνη in terms of the Hebrew expression *shalom* (שלום)[39] — which, of course,

---

38. Hatch, "Recently Discovered Fragment," 83.

39. Cf. J. D. G. Dunn, *Theology of Paul the Apostle* (Grand Rapids: Eerdmans, 1998), 387, who speaks of Paul's use of the term "justification" in 5:1 as meaning "God bestowing the blessing of peace

included such ideas as "an absence of conflict," "tranquility," and "contentment," but primarily carried nuances of "completeness," "fullness of health (including not just physical but also spiritual and mental health)," and "one's overall welfare."[40] Thus translators and commentators need to think of Paul in speaking of "peace with God" here in 5:1 as exhorting believers in Jesus at Rome to an understanding and experience of "completeness" in their relations with God.

In both Eastern and Western philosophical-religious thought, the idea of "completeness" incorporates a variety of nuances. Here in 5:1, Paul is exhorting his Christian addressees at Rome not just to dwell on matters pertaining to "the righteousness of God" as a divine attribute, on the fact of God's "forgiveness" as extended to the truly repentant, and on such soteriological expressions as "justification," "redemption," and "sacrifice of atonement" ("propitiation" or "expiation"), all of which the apostle included under the rubric "justification by faith." He is also exhorting them to accept and experience the validity of his quite distinctive contextualization of the Christian gospel to pagan Gentiles in the Greco-Roman world, which proclamation and instruction have to do with personal, relational, and participatory ways of appreciating the new "life" that has come about "through our Lord Jesus Christ" and is experienced "in Christ" and "in the Spirit" — all of which he thought of in terms of the rubric "peace [i.e., the Hebrew concept of *shalom*, 'completeness'] with God."

To be noted in 5:1, as well, is that Paul's exhortation to "peace" or "completeness" in a believer's relationship with God is set in a distinctly Christological context by the closing statement in the sentence: "through our Lord Jesus Christ" (διὰ τοῦ κυρίου ἡμῶν Ἰησοῦ Χριστοῦ). This Christocentric basis for completeness is highlighted throughout the materials Paul presents in 5:1–8:39; he highlights it by repeating the phrase "through our Lord Jesus Christ" four times more at 5:21, 6:23, 7:25, and 8:39.

5:2-5 Having set out his transitional and thesis statement in 5:1, Paul goes on in 5:2-5 to speak of certain highly significant implications of what it means for the believer in Jesus to experience both "justification by faith" (as in 1:16–4:25) and "peace [or 'completeness'] with God" (as in 5:1–8:39). What he speaks about in these verses highlights, as well, the Christian emphasis on Christology, for such an experience and such realizations have come about "through our Lord Jesus Christ" (5:1b; see also 5:2a: δι' οὗ, "through whom"). The verses also have to do with a Trinitarian understanding of God. For the matters Paul speaks about in them concern not only what Jesus Christ has done, they also pertain to what has come about and is maintained "because God has poured out his love into our hearts by the Holy Spirit, whom he has given us" (5:5).

---

on those who were formerly enemies (5.10)," and then goes on to say that "peace" here has not the Greek nonwar meaning but is filled with "the richer Hebrew concept of *shalom*."

40. Cf. Paul's other uses of εἰρήνη ("peace") in Romans at 1:7; 2:10; 3:17; 8:6; 14:17, 19; 15:13, 33; and 16:20 — ten times total, and all with a primary emphasis on "completeness," "one's overall welfare," or "wholeness." See also the seven uses of εἰρήνη in Ephesians at 1:2; 2:14, 15, 17; 4:3; 6:15, and 23 (plus some twenty-six times elsewhere in the Pauline corpus).

5:2a Here Paul identifies the first important implication of "justification by faith" and "peace (or 'completeness') with God." The wording has sometimes seemed to commentators rather strange, for it expresses matters a bit differently than Paul expressed them in 5:1 — which is not quite what one would expect if 5:2a is understood as Paul's attempt to pick up from and express more fully what he wrote in the immediately previous statement of 5:1. The principal difficulty here is that this statement seems to repeat needlessly the expression "by faith" in 5:2a; this evidently caused some scribes to omit the second "by faith" in their transmission of the text (even though it is strongly attested in the textual tradition).[41] Further, "by faith" is worded somewhat differently in 5:2a (τῇ πίστει) than it is in 5:1 (ἐκ πίστεως), and without any necessary or obvious reason. And, interestingly, there is a nicely honed play on words in 5:2a in the use of the two perfect tense verbs ἐσχήκαμεν ("we have gained access") and ἑστήκαμεν ("we have stood" or "we stand"), which finds no exact parallel in Paul's other letters.

But if we posit on the basis of these linguistic phenomena (which, admittedly, are few, and which, at best, only suggest but do not demand such an understanding) that Paul added this traditional Christian affirmation in 5:2a after his transitional statement of 5:1 because (1) it said what he wanted to say, (2) it began with the prepositional expression δι οὗ ("through whom"), which allowed him to "go off at a word" from the prepositional clause "through our Lord Jesus Christ" (διὰ τοῦ κυρίου ἡμῶν Ἰησοῦ Χριστοῦ) that closed his sentence of 5:1, and (3) it was presumably well known to his Christian addressees at Rome — some resolution, perhaps, can be reached regarding these somewhat diverse linguistic features. For accepting our proposed suggestion that here Paul made use of the wording of an early Christian confessional statement, it may reasonably be argued that his use of such an early confessional statement (1) offers an appropriate explanation for the linguistic differences between 5:1 (Paul's own statement) and 5:2a (an early Christian confessional statement), and (2) suggests a further item of consciousness on Paul's part about what he and his Christian addressees at Rome held in common.

The proclamation "we have gained (ἐσχήκαμεν) access (τὴν προσαγωγὴν) by faith (τῇ πίστει) into this grace (εἰς τὴν χάριν ταύτην) in which we stand (ἐν ᾗ ἑστήκαμεν)" was undoubtedly an important Christian affirmation that was cherished widely among early believers in Jesus. The perfect tense, indicative mood verbs ἐσχήκαμεν and ἑστήκαμεν speak of a past action that has present results, and so should be translated, respectively, "we have gained" and "we now stand."

The noun προσαγωγή ("access," "approach") appears in the NT only three times: here in Rom 5:2a and twice more in Eph 2:18 and 3:12, with its verb προσάγω found transitively in Luke 9:41, Acts 16:20, 1 Pet 3:18, and intransitively in Acts 27:27. The noun προσαγωγή was used by ancient authors in describing a person's approach to a king. So, for example, Xenophon (c. 430-357

41. Cf. "Textual Notes" on 5:2.

B.C.), the Athenian soldier, historian, and essayist, writes in his *Cyropaedia* (an idealized biography of Cyrus the Great in which Xenophon presents his own ideas about the proper education of a ruler) that people who wanted to obtain an audience with the Persian emperor Cyrus "were to court favor as my friends for access (τοὺς ἐμοὺς φίλους δεομένους προσαγωγῆς)."[42] The verb προσάγω ("gain access," "approach") is used in the LXX in the context of approaching God's altar with an offering, as in the directive of Lev 4:14: "The congregation (ἡ συναγωγή) must bring (προσάξει) an unblemished calf of the herd for a sin offering, and bring (προσάξει) it to (παρά) the doors of the tabernacle of witness." Only those who were worthy and unblemished could approach God in this manner[43] — which is a theme that was extensively developed by the Jewish covenanters at Qumran, who believed that the people of their community alone were pure and qualified enough to enjoy access to God.[44] The Christian proclamation of "access" or "approach" to God, as quoted here in 5:2a by Paul, seems, however, to have focused primarily on the two terms "faith" (πίστις) and "grace" (χάρις). And these two expressions, as Robert Jewett has aptly pointed out, "reverse the cultural expectation" of how one is to approach God, for they require not "a high level of purity and clout" but rather proclaim "an unqualified access, open to the shamed as well as the honored without regard to their performance."[45]

Paul uses this highly important noun "faith" (πίστις) in Section II (5:1–8:39) of the body middle of the letter only here in his transitional statement of 5:1 and in his quotation of early Christian confessional material in 5:2a — even though he had used it, together with its various verbal forms, repeatedly throughout Section I (1:16–4:25).[46] He resumes his use of "faith" and its verbal cognates in Section III (9:1–11:36), where he returns to his earlier discussions of Section I regarding "righteousness (δικαιοσύνη) that is by faith (ἐκ πίστεως)."[47] Likewise, though Paul had explicitly connected the themes of "righteousness," "justification," and "faith" in Section I,[48] he does not continue these motifs in Section II except in 5:1 and 5:2a — reserving them for fuller explication in Section III.[49] Rather, he highlights in this first part of 5:2 the theme of "God's grace" into which "we [as believers in Jesus] have gained access" and in which "we now stand" — with that χάρις ("grace") conceptualized as being prior to and foundational for πίστις ("faith") and as having been worked out in human history in the work of "our Lord Jesus Christ," which points underlie all that Paul writes in what follows in Rom 5–9.

---

42. Xenophon, *Cyropaedia* 7.5.45.
43. Cf., e.g., Exod 29:4, 8; Lev 21:18-19; Num 8:9-10.
44. Cf. 1QH 12.20-26.
45. Jewett, *Romans,* 350.
46. Cf. esp. 1:17; 3:22, 26; 4:5, 9, 11-13, 16, 19-20.
47. Cf. esp. 9:30–10:21.
48. Cf. esp. 3:21-26.
49. Cf. again 9:30–10:21.

5:2b A second implication of "justification by faith" and "peace (or 'completeness') with God" listed by Paul is that of being able to "boast in the hope of the glory of God" (καὶ καυχώμεθα ἐπ' ἐλπίδι τῆς δόξης τοῦ θεοῦ). Because of the omega (ω) in its suffix, the verb καυχώμεθα may, at first glance, be read as being subjunctive in mood ("let us boast"), and so seen as parallel to the subjunctive verb ἔχωμεν ("let us have") in 5:1.[50] Actually, however, the form of καυχώμεθα stems from the form of καυχάομαι ("boast," "glory," "rejoice in," "take pride in"), which is a deponent verb (i.e., a Greek or Latin verb that has a middle or passive form but an active meaning). Thus, while its middle or passive suffix, together with its connecting omega (ω), could be taken to signal the subjunctive mood, as a deponent verb the Greek form καυχώμεθα is really active in meaning and indicative in mood, and therefore should be viewed as paralleling the indicative function of the perfect tense verbs ἐσχήκαμεν ("we have gained") and ἑστήκαμεν ("we now stand") of 5:2a.

Although Paul earlier denounced "bragging" about the Mosaic law and "boasting" about one's relationship to God in 2:17–3:20, 3:27, and 4:2, the rightness or wrongness of "boasting," "taking pride in," or "rejoicing" depends on the nature of that boasting, pride, and joy — that is, whether it is (1) an expression of self-confidence and self-glorification or (2) an expression of confidence and thanksgiving to God in response to who he is and what he has done.[51] In what may seem on the surface somewhat paradoxical, the one who "boasts in God" in the biblical and Pauline sense of "boasting" is, as Rudolf Bultmann has observed, the one who "looks away from himself, so that his glorying [or 'boasting'] is a confession of God."[52]

To "boast in God" is to boast in God's glory, to stand in awe of his radiant holiness and transcendent power, and to marvel with respect to his creation and redemption.[53] It has nothing to do with claiming honor for oneself or favor for one's religious or societal group. Rather, it has everything to do with (1) the person and activities of God and (2) our joyful response to him and his working.

The object of the Christian's "boast," "pride," and "glory" is stated by Paul here in 5:2b as "the hope of the glory of God" (ἐπ' ἐλπίδι τῆς δόξης τοῦ θεοῦ). Karl Rengstorf has observed that, while Semitic people generally and Jews in particular were "certainly not unfamiliar with the concept of hope," the literatures of the Semitic world and of the Jews offer "no close parallel to the word ἐλπίς."[54] In the NT, however, and especially in Paul's letters, "hope" is a frequently repeated term and a dominant theme — not just for God's people corporately, but also for individuals who have come into relationship with God.[55]

---

50. So, e.g., Jewett, *Romans,* 351.

51. See also 2:17 above and our "Exegetical Comments" on that verse.

52. Bultmann, "καυχάομαι, καύχημα, καύχησις," 3.647.

53. Cf. Kittel, "δοκέω, δόξα, δοξάζω," 2.247.

54. Rengstorf, "ἐλπίς, ἐλπίζω," 2.523.

55. As seen not only here in 5:2b, but also as expressed in what immediately follows in 5:3-5 and then later in 8:20-25; see also such earlier expressions as 1 Cor 15:19, Gal 5:5, and 1 Thess 2:19.

In fact, as Paul proclaims in 1 Cor 13:13, when all else fails or ceases — and even when God's purposes for his people are fully completed — three things will remain: "faith, hope, and love." For as Rudolf Bultmann has aptly commented on the reason for hope's continuance even after what he calls "the consummation of Christian experience":

> Hope is not concerned with the realization of a human dream of the future but with the confidence which, directed away from the world to God, waits patiently for God's gift, and when it is received does not rest in possession but in the assurance that God will maintain what He has given.[56]

Likewise, Gerhard Kittel has pointed out that in the NT the word δόξα "is used for the most part in a sense for which there is no Greek analogy whatever," with only a few instances of similar biblical usage appearing in the writings of Josephus and Philo.[57] For δόξα in the NT primarily "denotes 'divine and heavenly radiance,' the 'loftiness and majesty' of God, and even the 'being of God' and His world"[58] — in line with OT usage, but certainly not in line with usage in the Greco-Roman world where δόξα commonly connoted "opinion," "repute," or "honor." It is with respect to such nuances of "hope" and "glory" that Paul declares that a second highly significant implication of the Christian message of "justification by faith" (as in 1:16–4:25) and "peace [or 'completeness'] with God" (as will be proclaimed throughout 5:1–8:39) is this: that we as believers in Jesus are now able to "boast in the hope of the glory of God."

5:3-4 A third significant implication of "justification by faith" and "peace [or 'completeness'] with God" is set out here. Contrary to all pagan views of personal suffering — in which suffering is understood as a calamity without meaning and/or a disaster to be avoided, explained away, or simply forgotten — the Christian, because of being "justified by faith" and having "peace [or 'completeness'] with God" through the work of Christ, comes to understand his or her own sufferings as being under the providence of God and allowed by God as a means of gaining "perseverance," "character," and "hope."

Paul came to understand his own sufferings in this manner, as he makes abundantly clear in 2 Cor 11:23-31 in a graphic recital of his sufferings, afflictions, imprisonments, beatings, and physical weaknesses as a "servant of Christ." Here in 5:3-4 he urges his Christian addressees at Rome to realize that their experience of "justification" and "peace/completeness" with God entails, as a result, not just (1) "access" into the divine presence and (2) being able to "hope in the glory of God," but also (3) a totally new understanding of their own personal sufferings, realizing that they all take place under the providence of God and

---

56. Bultmann, "ἐλπίς, ἐλπίζω," 2.532.
57. Kittel, "δοκέω, δόξα, δοξάζω," 2.237.
58. *Ibid.*

are allowed by God to bring about in the life of the believer such qualities as "perseverance," "character," and "hope."[59]

While the first two implications of "justification" and "peace/completeness" given in 5:2 are of great importance, Paul particularly highlights this latter implication in 5:3-4 by introducing it in 5:3a with the expression οὐ μόνον δέ, ἀλλὰ καὶ ("Not only this, but also")[60] and climaxing it in 5:3b-4 with a chain of very important personal qualities — "perseverance," "character," and "hope." The use of the expression "not only this, but also" is a favorite way of Paul to set off something of particular importance. It appears again at the beginning of 5:11, and is repeated at a number of strategic places elsewhere in his letters.[61] Thus, while the first two implications given in 5:2 are of great spiritual significance for the life of a believer in Jesus, this third implication is of great practical relevance for the ongoing daily "life in Christ" — for it provides a distinctly Christian context for the reality of personal suffering, offering to the believer in Jesus an assurance of both meaning and purpose in his or her sufferings.

5:5 Concluding his list of three significant implications of what it means for a believer in Jesus to experience "justification by faith" and "peace [or 'completeness'] with God," Paul, by using the articular expression ἡ ἐλπίς ("this hope"), reaches back to his earlier reference to "the hope of the glory of God" in 5:2b and characterizes all of what he had set out in 5:1-4 as "this [message of] hope." Later, in 8:20-25, he will return to this theme of hope and his characterization of the Christian proclamation as a message of hope. His purpose in 5:5 is to declare that this message of hope regarding "justification by faith" and "peace/completeness with God" — together with the three very significant implications that he enumerates — does not "put to shame" or "disappoint" (οὐ καταισχύνει) the one who puts his or her trust in Christ.

In using the phrase οὐ καταισχύνει ("it does not put to shame [or 'disappoint']"), Paul picks up on the expression of two psalms attributed to David. One is Ps 22:4-5 (LXX 21:5-6), which declares, "In you our fathers put their trust; they trusted and you delivered them. They cried to you and were saved; in you they trusted and were not *put to shame* [or *'disappointed'*]." The other is 25:20 (LXX 24:20), where the psalmist prays, "Guard my life and rescue me! Let me not be *put to shame* [or *'disappointed'*], for I take refuge in you." Both psalms speak of those who "put their trust" or "take refuge" in God not being "put to shame" or "disappointed." The Christians at Rome probably treasured them in the devotional writings and experiences, for they would presumably have understood these passages as not only expressing the religious experience and certainty of pious Israelites but also reflecting their own Christian commitment and resultant certainty.

---

59. Cf. also Rom 8:28, which undoubtedly must be seen as including the sufferings of a believer in Jesus among the "all things" in which "God works for the good of those who love him, who have been called according to his purpose."

60. See "Textual Notes" on the nominative singular neuter demonstrative pronoun "this."

61. Cf. Rom 8:23; 9:10; 2 Cor 8:19.

Likewise, the rationale given in 5:5 for such a certainty is expressed by Paul in the following words: "because *God has poured out his love into our hearts by the Holy Spirit,* whom he has given us." This is the first reference in Romans to God's love being an ἀγάπη type of love (which reference is repeated in 5:8 in what appears to be the confessional material of 5:6-8) — that is, that God's love is an outgoing and self-giving type of love, whose expression always includes the welfare of his people and his whole creation. Such an understanding of "love" on the part of God the Father and of Jesus Christ his Son, as well as on the part of believers in Jesus between themselves and for others, is a distinctive feature throughout all the NT writings — but it is particularly to the fore in Paul's letters.[62] This emphasis on God's ἀγάπη type of love reaches its peak in this section of 5:1–8:39 in the apostle's rather defiant statement of confidence in 8:38-39: "For I am convinced that neither death nor life, neither angels or demons, neither the present nor the future, nor any powers, neither height nor depth, nor anything else in all creation, will be able to separate us from *the love of God that is in Christ Jesus our Lord.*" The importance of such an ἀγάπη type of love by believers in Jesus comes to its most explicit expression in the apostle's expositions on the nature of "the Christian love ethic" in 12:9-21 and 13:8-14.

Robert Jewett has aptly observed with respect to the language of 5:5: "In every detail it is clear that Paul has selected language in this verse that has very wide resonance in early Christianity, and Paul assumes also in Rome."[63] But while he and his Christian addressees at Rome agree on the language of redemption, what Paul goes on to spell out in 5:12–8:39 about his own contextualization of the Christian gospel is somewhat beyond what the Christians at Rome had conceptualized. Thus, in what follows in Section II of the body middle of the letter, Paul should be seen as (1) transposing the traditional Christian proclamation of "good news" into a higher key and (2) inviting his Roman addressees to "sing along with me" in this higher key.

5:6-8 The material of these verses is, at first glance, exceedingly difficult to understand, not only linguistically and structurally but also theologically — despite what seems to have been a familiar Christian confessional statement at its beginning and at its end, which appears in two slightly different forms: "Christ died on behalf of the ungodly" (5:6) and "Christ died on our behalf" (5:8). Often observed is the fact that the adverb μόλις ("scarcely," "hardly," "with difficulty") is not found elsewhere in Paul's letters. More difficult to understand, however, are some of the linguistic formulations and theological nuances that

---

62. The noun ἀγάπη is not found in any extant nonbiblical Greek writings. Classical and koine Greek writings employed three other words for "love": (1) φιλία, which is a general word for love that appears in many contexts; (2) ἔρως, which has to do principally with sexual love; and (3) στοργή, which usually has to do with love among the members of a family. The word ἀγάπη occurs about twenty times in the LXX, although usually without any special meaning. The noun ἀγάπη, however, appears about 120 times in the NT — with 75 of these occurrences being in the Pauline letters.

63. Jewett, *Romans,* 357; citing Wolter, *Untersuchungen zu Röm 5,1-11,* 166.

appear in a somewhat different manner than one would expect in a letter written by Paul. Particularly baffling are (1) the use of ἀσθενής ("weak") in 5:6 as a synonym for ἁμαρτωλοί ("sinners") in 5:8; (2) the three appearances of the adverb ἔτι ("still"), with the second being somewhat redundant in 5:6 and the first and the third appearing at the beginning and end of this subunit of material; (3) the four appearances of the preposition ὑπέρ ("on behalf of"), with one instance in each of the four sentences; (4) the fourfold use of the verb ἀποθνήσκω ("die") as the final word at the end of each of the four sentences; and (5) the expression κατὰ καιρόν ("at that time"), which by its use of the preposition κατά is fairly unusual on Paul's lips.[64]

Further, the two appearances of the single name Χριστός seem somewhat strange in this passage, for this is the first time in the letter that Paul uses this single name for Jesus — and it appears twice in these three verses, at the beginning of 5:6 and at the end of 5:8, being used in almost *inclusio* fashion to mark off the beginning and end of the passage. Even more difficult for an understanding of Paul is (1) his use of δίκαιος ("a righteous person") in a typically Judaic fashion, and (2) his distinction between δίκαιος ("a righteous person"), on behalf of whom scarcely anyone would give his or her life, and ὁ ἀγαθός ("the good person"), on behalf of whom someone might actually dare to die.[65]

It may also be argued that 5:6-8 is in the form of a *chiasmus* — the name rhetoricians give the phenomenon of paired words, statements, or texts arranged in a pattern of inverted symmetry around a focal word, statement, or text. There is undoubtedly a pairing of statements among these four sentences, with (1) the first and fourth proclaiming much the same Christian affirmation, that is, that "Christ died on behalf of the ungodly [i.e., 'us']," and (2) the second and third setting out diametrically opposed parenthetical comments. What is presented here in 5:6-8 may, therefore, be viewed as somewhat comparable to a *chiasmus*:

> A. For while we were still weak, still at that time "Christ died on behalf of the ungodly."
> B. For scarcely on behalf of a righteous person will someone die.
> B. For on behalf of the good person someone might even dare to die.
> A. But God demonstrates his own love to us in that while we were still sinners "Christ died on our behalf."

Yet the focal point of the passage is not to be found in its two middle statements. Rather, the passage's main point is set out in the two parallel statements that

64. Paul usually uses with the noun καιρός the prepositions ἐν ("in"; cf. Rom 3:26; 11:5; 2 Cor 8:14; 2 Thess 2:6); πρό ("before"; cf. 1 Cor 4:5); πρός ("for"; cf. 1 Cor 7:5; 1 Thess 2:17); or περί ("concerning"; cf. 1 Thess 5:1). Only in his quotation of Gen 18:10 in Rom 9:9 does he use κατά with καιρός, but there his wording is controlled by the OT text.

65. On the difficulties posed in 5:7 and the numerous attempts to solve them, see Wisse, "The Righteous Man and the Good Man in Romans V. 7," 91-93.

surround its two middle statements: "While we were still weak [i.e., 'sinners'], Christ died on behalf of the ungodly [i.e., 'us']." So the passage cannot be viewed as a true *chiasmus*. It can be understood as some type of formulaic material, but hardly as a *chiasmus*.

The differences of language, structure, and theological nuancing are of such a nature that some scholars have declared that the materials of 5:6-8 (and especially that of vv. 6-7) were originally one or two glosses that were at some early time written in the margin of the text by a scribe or scribes and later interpolated into the text, and therefore can be discounted as having been written by Paul.[66] Yet the acoustical use of the verb "he [Christ] died" (ἀπέθανεν ... ἀποθανεῖται ... ἀποθανεῖν ... ἀπέθανεν) that appears as the final word in each of the four sentences of 5:6-8 — together with the linguistic disparities, structural peculiarities, and somewhat variant theological nuancing cited above — more plausibly suggests that this subunit of material originated in the early church as part of an early Christian confession. Further, it may be legitimately argued that Paul carried over (whether consciously or unconsciously) this early Christian traditional portion into the letter with these particular features of orality still intact. Or as Robert Jewett has more concisely expressed about the difficulties of this passage: "All of these anomalies could be explained by a theory of Pauline citation of an early Christian confession that may have been employed in Rome."[67]

What Paul appears to be doing here in 5:6-8 is citing an early Christian confessional portion, which was known not only by him but also by his Christian addressees at Rome, in support of his statement of 5:5 that "this hope does not disappoint us, because God has poured out his love into our hearts by the Holy Spirit, whom he has given us." For if God has so acted on behalf of believers in Jesus at a time when they were "still weak" and "still sinners," how much more can he be trusted for the future — that is, how much more can we be assured that "this hope" he has given us will not "disappoint us" or "put us to shame."[68]

5:9-11 The final paragraph of this transitional and thesis passage has a number of linguistic features that suggest the nature of its material. The first is the phrase δικαιωθέντες νῦν ("having now been justified"), which appears as the second linguistic element in 5:9 and picks up from the phrase δικαιωθέντες οὖν ("having therefore been justified") at the beginning of 5:1. Here in a rhetorical *extended anaphora* Paul resumes his discussion of 5:1-5, which was interrupted by his quotation of an early Christian confessional portion in 5:6-8. Such

---

66. So, e.g., Fuchs, *Die Freiheit des Glaubens,* 16-17; Keck, "The Post-Pauline Interpretation of Jesus' Death in Romans 5:6-7," 237-48.

67. Jewett, *Romans,* 359.

68. Probably the postpositive conjunction γάρ ("for") at the beginning of 5:6 should not be viewed as part of the early Christian material quoted; rather, it most likely is to be understood as Paul's introductory formula, which form of introduction he sometimes used not only to introduce biblical quotations (cf. 2:24; 10:13; 11:34-35; see also 1 Cor 2:16; 10:26; 15:27) but also to introduce a biblically based aphorism (cf. Rom 2:11) and certain Christian traditional materials (cf. 2:14-15).

an extended anaphora not only signals the continuation of an earlier discussion, it also suggests a further elaboration and development of that same theme.[69]

The most obvious linguistic feature of the passage, however, and the one Paul evidently wanted particularly to emphasize, is the phrase πολλῷ μᾶλλον ("much more"), which appears at the very beginning of the Greek sentence of 5:9 and is repeated in the second part of the sentence of 5:10. The expression reflects a type of Greco-Roman rhetoric that argues "from the lesser to the greater" *(a minori ad maius)*. It also expresses a form of Jewish argumentation that holds that "what applies in a less important case will certainly apply in a more important case" (קל וחומר, *qal waḥomer*), which is the first of the seven exegetical "rules" attributed to the venerable Jewish teacher Hillel. This "much more" expression highlights the presence of a major emphasis in this final paragraph of the passage. For it functions to announce that Paul's line of argumentation in the rest of Section II will be as follows: if we have been "justified by faith" (as per Section I), how much more should we go on to consider and experience the realities of "peace *(Shalom)* with God" (as per Section II) — which Paul here in 5:10-11 will speak of in terms of his own experience and proclamation of "reconciliation."

A third linguistic feature here is the twice-repeated temporal adverbial particle νῦν ("now"), which is the third item in the opening sentence of 5:9 and closes off the passage in 5:11. Paul's use of νῦν in 5:9 and 5:11, as did also his earlier use of νυνί in 3:21, highlights the fact that the "eschatological now" is a present reality that (1) culminates all of God's earlier redemptive dealings with his people and (2) brings about in a more personal, relational, and participatory manner what God wants his people presently to experience. A fourth highly important linguistic feature of this passage is the distinctly Pauline term "reconciliation," which comes to the fore three times in 5:10-11 — first as the finite verb (κατηλλάγημεν, "we have received reconciliation"), then as a temporal adverbial participle (καταλλαγέντες, "having been reconciled"), and finally as an articular noun (τὴν καταλλαγήν, "the reconciliation"). The passage closes in 5:11 with a statement regarding the true and only legitimate boasting of a Christian — that is, "boasting in God through our Lord Jesus Christ, through whom we have now received the reconciliation."

5:9-10 In these first two verses of the final paragraph of Paul's transitional and thesis passage he highlights the twice-repeated expression πολλῷ οὖν μᾶλλον ("much more then"), which functions to introduce two very important logical inferences that Paul wants his Christian addressees at Rome to appreciate and cherish: (1) that the forensic reality of having been "justified by his [Jesus'] blood" in this present time of eschatological fulfillment (the eschatological "now")[70] also involves the greater personal hope that believers in Jesus

---

69. Cf. the rhetorical *extended anaphora* of 1:16-17 and 3:21-24, where features of continuation, elaboration, and development are all to the fore in the latter part.

70. Note the temporal particle νυν in 5:9 and 5:11; see also its cognate νυνί in 3:21.

"will be saved through him [Jesus] from God's wrath," and (2) that the judicial reality of having been "God's enemies," but now reconciled to God "through the death of his Son," also involves the greater certainty that "we will be saved through his [Jesus'] life."

There is, of course, a tension that appears in Paul's proclamation of the gospel (and in the proclamation of the Christian gospel throughout the NT) with respect to the Christian life in this time of the eschatological "now." This tension is reflected in these two statements of 5:9-10 by the use of first the aorist passive participle δικαιωθέντες ("having been justified") and then the aorist passive participle καταλλαγέντες ("having been reconciled") vis-à-vis the two uses of the future passive verb σωθησόμεθα ("we will be saved"). Commentators, therefore, have frequently found it difficult to determine whether Paul's future tense "we will be saved" refers to the future or refers in a gnomic fashion to the present — or, most likely, to both the future and the present. Likewise, theologians have often found it difficult to determine whether Paul's references to Jesus' ministry have to do primarily with his physical death (i.e., his "passive obedience"), his earthly life (i.e., his "active obedience"), his exalted heavenly ministries (i.e., his interceding before God and working through the Holy Spirit on behalf of his own), or some combination of these factors. So the statement "we will be saved by his life" has been variously interpreted to mean either Jesus' earthly life or his heavenly life, or both.

Paul does not seem too concerned about such distinctions, common as they may be among interpreters today. What he appears to be doing in 5:9-11 is attempting to convince his addressees that there is much more to the Christian gospel than simply the forensic doctrine of *justification* "by the blood of Christ" (ἐν τῷ αἵματι αὐτοῦ) or "through the death of God's Son" (διὰ τοῦ θανάτου τοῦ υἱοῦ αὐτοῦ) — important as that emphasis is in Christian proclamation. What also needs to be considered and experienced is what Christ has effected on behalf of those who respond to him by faith in terms of the "personal," "relational," and "participatory" theme of *reconciliation*. Thus Paul highlights in this passage this theme of reconciliation as he concludes this transitional and thesis passage: first by the use of the finite verb κατηλλάγημεν ("we have received reconciliation") in 5:10a; then the adverbial temporal participle καταλλαγέντες ("having been reconciled") in 5:10b; and finally the articular noun τὴν καταλλαγήν ("the reconciliation") in 5:11 — much as he will later in 11:15 speak of the full expression of God's work of salvation using the phrase καταλλαγὴ κόσμου ("the reconciliation of the world").

EXCURSUS: PAUL'S MESSAGE OF RECONCILIATION

"Reconciliation" is in Paul's proclamation at the very heart of the Christian gospel, rooted as it is in (1) God's love and purpose, (2) Christ's ministry and death, (3) the earliest Christian confessions, and (4) Paul's own religious experience as a Christian. "Reconciliation is," as T. W. Manson once called it, "the keyword of Paul's Gospel."[71] Or, as Joseph Fitzmyer has aptly pointed out with respect to Paul's theology: "The main effect of Christ's passion, death, and resurrection is the reconciliation of man [i.e., 'responsive people'] to a state of peace and union with the Father."[72]

1. *The Language of Reconciliation.* The Greek verbs καταλλάσσω ("reconcile") and διαλλάσσω ("reconcile"; or its deponent διαλλάσσομαι), as well as the Greek noun καταλλαγή ("reconciliation"), are compound forms of the verb ἀλλάσσω ("alter" or "change") and noun ἄλλος ("other"), and so basically mean "to make otherwise" and connote "a change of relationship or situation." They appear frequently in Greek writings to signify a change of circumstances or relationships in the political, social, familial, and/or moral spheres of life. Yet they played no part in the cultic expiatory rites of the Greco-Roman world and are almost entirely absent in Greek religious writings, for pagan religions did not think of relations between divinity and humanity in terms of personal nearness.[73] Only Sophocles, one of the three great tragic poets of the fifth century B.C., in depicting the humiliation and suicide of the warrior Ajax, speaks about a person *reconciling* himself to the gods[74] — but he does not say how that reconciliation was accomplished.

There are no equivalents to the language of reconciliation in Hebrew or Aramaic. The closest terms in the Jewish Scriptures (the Christian OT), as well as in the later rabbinic writings (i.e., the Jewish Talmud and its associated tractates), are the Hebrew verbs כפר, which means "to cover," "cover over," "pacify," or "propitiate," and רצה, which means "to please," "appease," "satisfy," or "placate." When used in the context of a wrongdoer placating by some act of restitution a person who had been wronged, these verbs connote certain features that correspond, at least to some degree, to the idea of "reconciliation" (cf. *m. Yoma* 8:9 — though without any change of personal relationships or emotional feelings being necessarily involved).

The somewhat parallel Greek verb ἐπιστρέφω ("turn," "turn around," "turn back," or "return") is used in a purely secular fashion in Judg 19:3 (LXX) with reference to a Levite who went after his concubine who had left him to go back to her father's home, and who spoke kindly to her "in order to return her (τοῦ ἐπιστρέψαι αὐτήν) to himself." The noun διαλλαγή ("reconciliation") appears in Sir 22:22 and 27:21 with respect to friends being reconciled. Likewise, the second-person, singular, aorist imperative passive verb διαλλάγηθι ("be reconciled") appears in Matt 5:24 with respect to a person being reconciled to a brother or a sister.

2. *"Reconciliation" as a Religious Term among the Jews.* A religious use of the term "reconciliation" appears among Jews first in 2 Macc 1:5, where the writer prays on behalf of his Jewish addressees: "May he [God] be reconciled to you (καταλλαγήσεται ὑμῖν) and not forsake you in the time of trouble." In 2 Macc 5:20 and 7:33 the writer expresses the common Jewish belief that after God has chastened his people because of their sins — and so, in effect, when he becomes reconciled to his people — the Jerusalem temple will be restored to its former glory. Further, after the early successes of Judas Maccabeus against the Seleucids, the same author in 2 Macc 8:29 tells his readers that the Israelite warriors "united in supplication and besought the Lord of mercy to be reconciled (καταλλαγῆναι) to his servants forever." Josephus twice uses the terminology of reconciliation (both as

---

71. T. W. Manson, *On Paul and John,* 50.
72. Fitzmyer, *Pauline Theology,* 43-44.
73. Cf. Büchsel, "ἀλλάσσω . . . καταλλάσσω, καταλλαγή," 1.254.
74. Sophocles, *Ajax* 744.

a noun and as a verb) in a religious manner — first, in *War* 5.415 in telling his Roman readers that he had declared at the close of his address to the Jewish insurgents of his day that "the Deity is reconciled (τὸ θεῖον εὐδιάλλακτον) to those who confess and repent"; then in *Antiquities* 6.143 in speaking of Samuel, at a time of King Saul's "contempt and disobedience," as pleading with God "to be reconciled to Saul (καταλλάττεσθαι τῷ Σαούλῳ) and not be angry with him."

3. *Paul's Use of the Concept and Language of Reconciliation.* It was Paul, however, who focused on the concept of reconciliation in his Christian theology and made the language of reconciliation central in his preaching to Gentiles in the Greco-Roman world. Admittedly, the term itself appears only a few times in the Pauline corpus of NT letters. Yet it appears in very significant portions of his letters and is used by him almost entirely in a theological sense: the verb καταλλάσσω and its participle appearing here in Rom 5:10 and three times more in 2 Cor 5:18, 19, 20; the noun καταλλαγή appearing in Rom 5:11 and three times more in Rom 11:15 and 2 Cor 5:18, 19; and the verb ἀποκαταλλάσσω (an emphatic form, as prefaced by an additional preposition) appearing three times more in Eph 2:16 and Col 1:20, 22 — with only one secular use to be found in his letters, in 1 Cor 7:11, where he exhorts a wife who may have thoughts about separating from her husband: "If she does separate, let her remain unmarried or else let her be reconciled (καταλλαγήτω) to her husband."

Somewhat surprisingly, the language of reconciliation is not found in any of the other writings of the NT. Nor does it appear in any of the extant Christian literature of the second century. It has often, therefore, been considered not only distinctive to Paul among the earliest extant Christian writers but also to have been "coined by him."[75] Some have proposed that Paul picked up the concept and language from various rather general references in the writings of some Greco-Roman authors who spoke about someone effecting peaceful relations between warring groups, quarreling citizens, or alienated marriage partners — citing, in particular, Plutarch's statement in *Opera moralia* 329c that Alexander the Great claimed to be "the reconciler for the whole world (τῆς διαλλάκτης τῶν ὅλων)" and suggesting that such a theme became a feature in the Greco-Roman ruler cult.[76] Others have argued that behind Col 1:15-20 and 2 Cor 5:19 there lies a cosmological tradition of world reconciliation, which appears also in Paul's thinking in Rom 5:10-11.[77] Yet by the form, content, and context in which Paul expresses this concept of reconciliation and its terminology in 2 Cor 5:19 ("In Christ God was *reconciling* the world to himself, not counting their trespasses against them, and entrusting the message of *reconciliation* to us"), it may be postulated that the apostle was in this verse actually quoting a portion of early Christian confessional material. For the statement of 2 Cor 5:19 reflects a number of features in support of such a hypothesis: (1) it suggests a certain balance of structure, (2) it is introduced by the particle ὅτι (i.e., the so-called *hoti recitativum*), which was often used by Paul and other NT writers to introduce a quotation from some traditional material, (3) it incorporates in a formal manner the essence of Christian proclamation, and (4) it serves as the linchpin or central feature of what is said by way of exposition in the verses that immediately surround it, that is, in 2 Cor 5:18 and 20.

75. See, e.g., Büchsel, "ἀλλάσσω . . . καταλλάσσω, καταλλαγη," 1.258.

76. Cf. Hengel, "Kreuzestod Jesu Christi als Gottes souveräne Erlösungstate"; Hahn, " 'Siehe, jetzt ist der Tag des Heils,' " 247.

77. Cf. Käsemann, "Some Thoughts on the Theme," 52-64; Lührmann, "Rechtfertigung und Versöhnung," 437-52.

It is probably best, therefore, to surmise (1) that Paul came to know the concept and language of reconciliation because of its inclusion in some early Christian confessional material, and (2) that he appreciated it as being quite expressive of what he personally had experienced in his relationship with God through the work of Christ and the ministry of God's Spirit. Further, it may be postulated that he made this personal and relational language central in his preaching to Gentiles in the Greco-Roman world simply because he believed it to be (1) more theologically significant, (2) more culturally meaningful, and (3) more ethically compelling than many of the traditional soteriological expressions being used among both Jews and Jewish Christians.

4. *Important Theological Points Made by Paul in His Use of the Language of Reconciliation.* Paul always makes two highly important theological points when he speaks of reconciliation. The first is that — contrary to a Jewish understanding of reconciliation, where God is spoken of as being reconciled to his people or situations (as in the references from the LXX, Josephus, and the rabbinic writings cited above) — Paul always speaks of God as the subject of the verb καταλλάσσω and never as its object. That is, in Paul's proclamation it is God who reconciles "people" and "the world," and never the reverse.[78] The second point Paul always makes in his proclamation is that God's reconciliation of people and the world is based on the work and faithfulness of Jesus Christ, and never on what people might do in their attempts to please God by their own works or faithfulness.[79] Further, Paul's language of reconciliation is inclusive in its applications, for it refers not only to the reconciliation of "people" (2 Cor 5:18; Rom 5:10-11), but also to the reconciliation of "the world" (2 Cor 5:19; Rom 11:15). Likewise, his teaching with respect to reconciliation has reference not only to what God has already accomplished (2 Cor 5:19; Rom 5:10), but also to what he is presently accomplishing in believers' lives (2 Cor 5:17) *and* to what he will yet bring about for both those who have responded positively to him and his entire creation (Rom 5:10-11; 8:19-25).

Yet inherent in Paul's proclamation of reconciliation — which has been provided by God, is presently a reality for those who turn to him in faith, and will be fully brought about for all his people and all his creation — is what may be called "the twofold absurdity" of the Christian gospel: (1) that reconciliation with God comes about by means of death (i.e., objectively, the physical death of Jesus of Nazareth, God's Messiah; but also, subjectively, the "death" of a person's self-reliance before God, and so a turning to God in complete trust in him alone); and (2) that "the ministry of reconciliation," both in its proclamation and in its exemplary practice, has been delegated by God to finite humans, who themselves have been reconciled to God (2 Cor 5:18b, 19b).

5. *The Ministry Component and Ethical Compulsion of Reconciliation.* Involved in Paul's teaching regarding reconciliation is also a ministry component. For God has not only reconciled people to himself, he has also "entrusted the message of reconciliation

---

78. Cf. 2 Cor 5:18: "God reconciled us to himself"; 2 Cor 5:19: "in Christ God was reconciling the world"; Rom 5:10: "we were reconciled to God"; Rom 5:11: "through whom [i.e., 'our Lord Jesus Christ'] we have now received reconciliation"; Rom 11:15: "the reconciliation of the world."

79. Cf. in the context of Paul's discussions of reconciliation such passages as 2 Cor 5:15: "He [Christ] died for all, so that those who live might live no longer for themselves, but for him who died and was raised for them"; 2 Cor 5:21: "He [God] made him [Christ] to be sin who knew no sin, so that in him we might become the righteousness of God"; Rom 5:10: "We were reconciled to God through the death of his Son"; Rom 5:11: "through whom ['our Lord Jesus Christ'] we have now received reconciliation."

to us" (2 Cor 5:18). So those who have been reconciled to God, and therefore have become "Christ's ambassadors," are called by God to "entreat" all people "on behalf of Christ" to be "reconciled to God" (2 Cor 5:20). It is a component that stems directly from the compulsion of the message and the experience of the "good news" of God's reconciliation, with none of the three — that is, not *the message,* nor *the experience,* nor *the compulsion* of reconciliation — ever able to be separated off from the other two, but all three components meant to be part and parcel of the same reality.

Likewise, there is a vitally important ethical compulsion in Paul's teaching about reconciliation. For just as being loved by God we are motivated to love, so being reconciled by God we are motivated "on behalf of Christ" to be agents of reconciliation to people individually and to the world inclusively. God's reconciliation of us to himself and to others compels our involvement in working for the reconciliation of others, whatever their needs and as God directs us. For to divorce an ethic of reconciliation from the doctrine of reconciliation is, sadly, to deny them both.

The traditional forensic soteriological terms "justification," "redemption," and "expiation" were well known in both Jewish and Jewish Christian circles. This is an important understanding that has been brought to the consciousness of Christian scholars and laypeople quite effectively by Ed Sanders and James Dunn.[80] However, the personal, relational, and participationistic soteriological expressions of "peace [i.e., 'completeness,' 'wholeness']," "reconciliation," "life," "being in Christ," and "Christ by his Spirit being in us," which Paul highlights in chs. 5–8 of his letter to Rome, are realities that were known by him (as well as by others today) only through divine encounter and personal Christian experience. This highly significant point has been made by such scholars as James Denney, Howard Marshall, Ralph Martin, and Seyoon Kim.[81] Both the forensic set of terms and the personal, relational, and participatory set of expressions are important for a full understanding of the "good news" of the Christian gospel. Yet at the heart of the Christian message — at least as Paul proclaimed it in his Gentile mission, and so by extension for most people today — is the personal, relational, and participatory proclamation of God's reconciliation to himself of sinful and rebellious people through the work of Christ and the ministry of the Holy Spirit.

5:11 Paul closes off here in 5:11 the second part of his transition and thesis passage of 5:1-11, just as he did the first part in 5:3, with the expression οὐ μόνον δέ, ἀλλὰ καί ("not only [this], but also"). The rationale for this expression of legitimate boasting has often been debated, for it seems not only repetitious but also quite unnecessary. Yet if Paul can accuse the Jews of "bragging" about the Mosaic law and "boasting" about their relationship to God, as he did in 2:17–3:20, 3:27 and 4:2, it seems proper to infer from his πολλῷ μᾶλλον ("much more") statements in 5:9-10 — where he argues that there is much more to the Christian gospel than simply the forensic doctrine of *justification* — that his

---

80. See E. P. Sanders, *Paul and Palestinian Judaism; idem, Paul, the Law, and the Jewish People;* Dunn, *The New Perspective on Paul.*

81. See Denney, *The Christian Doctrine of Reconciliation;* Marshall, "The Meaning of 'Reconciliation,'" 117-32; Martin, "New Testament Theology," 364-68; *idem, Reconciliation; idem,* "Reconciliation," 36-48; and S. Kim, *Origin of Paul's Gospel* (1981), esp. 13-20, 311-15.

words here in 5:11 should be understood (1) as directed against believers in Jesus at Rome who evidently were boasting about their correctness of doctrine, which they believed they had received directly from the Jerusalem church, and (2) as urging his addressees to boast, rather, "in God through our Lord Jesus Christ, through whom we have now received reconciliation." For a Christian boasting about one's correctness of doctrine can be just as disastrous as a Jewish boasting about the Mosaic law and "covenantal nomism." So Paul desires in what follows in Section II to set out for the Christians at Rome a better way, which has to do with what God has done in a more personal, relational, and participatory manner "through our Lord Jesus Christ." The apostle encapsulates all of that "better way" of the Christian proclamation within his favorite soteriological expression "the reconciliation" (τὴν καταλλαγήν) — which he insists is not something that the Christian himself or herself has brought about but is something that "we have received (ἐλάβομεν) through our Lord Jesus Christ."

BIBLICAL THEOLOGY

Tertullian of Carthage (c. 145–c. 220), who trained as a lawyer and a philosopher before his conversion to Christ, but after his conversion excelled as an apologist and theologian, was a highly significant figure in the early development of Christian theology. He was not an exegete — whether the term "exegesis" is defined as (1) an allegorical interpretation of Scripture (as practiced at Alexandria), (2) a historical, contextual interpretation of Scripture (as later practiced at Antioch), or (3) notes ("glosses") and comments ("scholia") on the meaning of a text (as still later practiced by many Catholic and Protestant commentators). The closest that Tertullian came to the exegesis of a passage was in his *Adversus Marcionem* (first edition in 198; third revised edition in 207-8), where he went through Luke's Gospel in book 4 and Paul's letters in book 5, setting out Marcion's interpretations (as well as noting his frequent deletions of the text) and rebutting Marcion from a more orthodox perspective.

Nonetheless, Tertullian was extremely prolific as a Christian apologist and theologian, writing during the middle years of his life literally scores of apologetic and theological tractates. Many of these were kept and cherished, but others were renounced, lost, or forgotten, primarily because Tertullian adopted in the final years of his life a number of the theological views of the sectarian teacher Montanus. Though he did not write commentaries, and though he later came to be labeled a heretic by the rigidly orthodox clerics of Rome, Tertullian's apologetic and theological writings from about 193 to about 205 laid the theological foundations for much of Latin Christianity. In fact, it was the lucidity and profundity of Tertullian's writings during those middle years of his life that put an end to the reproach of the day that Latin Christianity was theologically and literarily barren. More important for our purposes here, it was Tertullian's treatment of the forensic language of Paul, as expressed particularly in Rom 1:16–4:25, that provided the basis for much of the judicial structuring of Christian theology in the Middle Ages — and not only by Roman Catholic theologians, but also, with decidedly different emphases, by the Protestant Reformers and many Christians today.

Slightly over two centuries after Tertullian, however, the great Church Father Aurelius Augustine (354-430), who was a native of Tagaste in North Africa (now Souk-Ahras, Algeria) and had been a student of philosophy at the university at Carthage (which was then the second most important city of the Roman Empire), brought to the fore a further very important feature in Paul's letter to the Christians at Rome. For while learning much from such North African and Italian Christian worthies as Tertullian, Cyprian, Optatus, Tyconius, and Ambrose, Augustine came to understand the Christian gospel as focused particularly in Paul's statements about God's grace in Rom 5–9.

While Augustine was teaching rhetoric at Milan, he came under the influence of Ambrose, the archbishop of Milan. Through the preaching and counsel of Ambrose, coupled with the prayers of his mother Monica, Augustine became dramatically converted to Christ in 386 and was baptized on Easter Sunday in 387. Four years later he returned to North Africa where he was, in fairly rapid succession, ordained a presbyter at Hippo in 391, then a cobishop in 395, and finally bishop in 396. As bishop of Hippo from 396 until his death on August 28, 430, though administratively very busy, he preached constantly and wrote voluminously.

In his mature years, from 400 to 430, Augustine produced his most noteworthy writings, such as *The City of God (De civitate Dei),* a work on the synoptic problem *(De consensu evangelistarum),* and massive commentaries on the Psalms and John's Gospel. Earlier in 391, however, shortly after returning to North Africa and being ordained a presbyter in the diocese of Hippo, he was asked questions about Paul's letter to the Romans by attendees at a conference held in Carthage. He responded by writing a series of short comments on selected passages drawn principally from Rom 5–9, which comments were grouped into eighty-four sections and published in 394 as *Expositio quarundam propositionum ex Epistula ad Romanos.*

On the basis of his comments in the *Expositio,* which amounts to a little commentary on selected passages from these five chapters of Romans, we surmise that this was when Augustine first began to think seriously about the gratuitous nature of God's grace — though his understanding of God's grace developed considerably over the following years, as seems evident from what he wrote to his friend Simplicianus a few years later during 396-398.[82] And it was the topic of God's grace, as first expressed in the Carthage conference of 391, that came to dominate all of Augustine's thinking during the final three decades of his life, until his death in 430, and that redirected much of Christian theology thereafter.

---

82. Augustine, *De diversis quaestionibus ad Simplicianum.*

Thus, from Augustine to the present day, Rom 5–8 (and often also ch. 9) has frequently been viewed as the apex of Paul's presentation in Romans, with Augustine's emphasis on God's sovereign grace in Rom 5–9 setting the tone for a great deal of subsequent Christian theology. This understanding of these four or five chapters at the heart of Paul's letter to Rome has been picturesquely represented by John Robinson in his simile of Romans as a canal that crosses an isthmus with a series of rising and lowering locks — the highest being chs. 5–8, with the watershed in the locks being ch. 8.[83]

Our thesis about the letter is that the essence of what the apostle believed to be uniquely his, and that he wanted his Christian addressees at Rome to understand and appreciate, is what he presents in Section II, in Rom 5:1–8:39. The material of these chapters deals with the central factors of human existence — that is, with sin, death, God's grace, life "in Christ," life "in the Spirit," and personal relationships with God and others. And these are matters, it is further suggested, that Paul found resolved and illuminated by his own conversion experience and by his continued relationship with Christ, with his practice in his Gentile mission being to present these matters to Gentile audiences without any necessary reference to the Jewish (OT) Scriptures. So he sets out in 5:1–8:39 for his Christian addressees at Rome his own contextualized form of the Christian gospel — not as a replacement to what they had previously confessed as believers in Jesus, but as a fuller and more extensive understanding of what they had already accepted.

Further, our thesis about the interpretation of Rom 5:1-11 is that Paul presents in this passage (1) transitional material that seeks, by a "lesser to greater" rhetorical type of argument, to move forward his Christian addressees at Rome in their thinking and experience from a sole acceptance of the Jewish and Jewish Christian forensic motifs of "justification," "redemption," and "propitiation" (or, "expiation" or "sacrifice of atonement") to a more personal, relational, and participatory understanding and experience of their commitment to Jesus Christ, and (2) thesis material that introduces what he will present in 5:12–8:39 regarding such a personal, relational, and participatory understanding and experience — doing so in these eleven verses under the captions of "peace with God" (or, nuanced more accurately, "completeness with God"), "boasting in God through our Lord Jesus Christ," and "reconciliation."

To view the material of 5:1-11 in this light is, in effect, (1) to view the argument of Romans as evidencing certain conceptual, thematic, and expressional developments, and (2) to call on theologians to take these developmental features into account in their constructions of a biblical theology. For the history of Christian theology is not only a story of development in God's revelation, as expressed in both the OT and the NT Scriptures, it is also a story of the developing understanding and experience of God's people, as set out both in the biblical materials and in the annuals of church history.

---

83 Cf J A T Robinson, *Wrestling with Romans*, 9 (but also passim)

CONTEXTUALIZATION FOR TODAY

Contextualizing the transitional and thesis materials of Rom 5:1-11 for today involves both a challenge and a warning. The challenge of this passage has to do with (1) accepting the exhortations of Paul not to dwell only on matters pertaining to "the righteousness of God" as a divine attribute and on such forensic expressions as "justification," "redemption," and "propitiation" (or, "expiation" or "sacrifice of atonement"), all of which he seems to have included under the soteriological rubric of "justification by faith"; and (2) accepting the validity of his contextualization of the gospel to pagan Gentiles in the Greco-Roman world, which form of Christian proclamation has to do with more personal, relational, and participatory ways of appreciating the new "life" that have come about "through our Lord Jesus Christ" — all of which ways he here in 5:1-11 introduces using the rubric "peace [i.e., *shalom*, 'completeness']" and the term "reconciliation."

The warning of this passage is this: if Paul can accuse the Jews of "bragging" about the Mosaic law and "boasting" about their relationship to God, as he did in 2:17–3:20, 3:27, and 4:2 — and, further, if his words regarding boasting in 5:11 can be understood (1) as directed against believers in Jesus at Rome boasting about their correctness of doctrine, which doctrinal tenets they evidently believed stemmed from the original apostolic leaders in the Jerusalem church, and (2) as urging his addressees to boast, rather, "in God through our Lord Jesus Christ, through whom we have now received reconciliation" — the boasting of a Christian today about his or her correctness of doctrine can be just as disastrous as a Jew boasting about the Mosaic law or a believer in Jesus at Rome boasting about having a correct form of doctrine. For whatever we as Christians affirm as being particularly significant in Paul's message and as especially meaningful to us — whether the themes of "the righteousness of God" and "justification by faith" (as in 1:16–4:25) or the motifs of "peace," "reconciliation," "life in Christ," "life in the Spirit," "Christ by his Spirit in us," and "adoption by God into his family" (as in 5:1–8:30) — there is no room for boasting about one's own Christian beliefs or about the human source (or sources) from which they have come. Our only boast as Christians, whatever our understanding and experience of that new reality might be, must always be about what we have received "through our Lord Jesus Christ" (5:1). Thus our boasting can only be "in God through our Lord Jesus Christ, through whom we have now received reconciliation" (5:11).

2. The Universal and Foundational Redemptive Story: What Jesus Christ Effected vis-à-vis What Adam Brought About (5:12-21)

TRANSLATION

[5:12]*Therefore, just as through one man sin entered the world, and through that sin came death, and thus death permeated all humanity, on the basis of which all have sinned —* [13]*for before the law was given, sin was in the world. But sin is not taken into account when there is no law.* [14]*Nevertheless, death reigned from Adam to Moses, even over those who did not sin in the same way by breaking a command as did Adam, who is a type of the one to come.*

[15]*The gift, however, is not like the trespass. For if the many died by the trespass of the one man, how much more did God's grace and the gift that came by the grace of the one man, Jesus Christ, overflow to the many!* [16]*Again, the gift of God is not like the result of the one man's sin: The judgment followed one sin and brought condemnation, but the gift followed many trespasses and brought righteousness.* [17]*For if, by the trespass of the one man, death reigned through that one man, how much more will those who receive God's abundant provision of grace and of the gift of righteousness reign in life through the one man, Jesus Christ.*

[18]*Consequently, just as through one trespass there has resulted condemnation for all people, so also through one act of righteousness there will result acquittal that brings life for all people.* [19]*For just as through the disobedience of one man the many were made sinners, so also through the obedience of one will the many be made righteous.*

[20]*The law was added so that the trespass might increase. But where sin increased, grace increased all the more —* [21]*in order that, just as sin reigned in death, so also grace might reign through righteousness unto eternal life through Jesus Christ our Lord.*

TEXTUAL NOTES

5:12a The presence of a second use of the articular noun ὁ θάνατος ("the death") as the subject of διῆλθεν ("it came," "went," "went through," "permeated") is strongly attested by uncials ℵ A B C P Ψ 0220[vid] [also *Byz* K L] and by minuscules 33 1175 1739 (Catetory I), 81 1506 1881 1962 2127 2464 (Category II), and 6 69 88 104 181 323 326 330 365 424[c] 436 451 614 629 630 1241 1243 1319 1573 1735 1874 1877 2344 2492 (Category III); it is also reflected in it[ar, dem, x, z] vg syr[p, h*, pal] cop[sa, bo] and supported by Origen[gr, lat]. A few MSS, however, omit it, as do uncials D F G and minuscules 1505 2495 (Category III); likewise, it is omitted in it[d, e, f, g] syr[h] and by Ambrosiaster and

Augustine. These are mostly Western readings. Since the articular noun ὁ θάνατος is present in the former clause, it was evidently argued that this second appearance of ὁ θάνατος is redundant and therefore to be omitted. Yet the widespread support in the textual tradition for this second ὁ θάνατος strongly suggests that it was original and so should be retained.

12b The verb διῆλθεν ("it came," "went," "went through") is very widely attested in the textual tradition. The verb εἰσῆλθεν ("it came into," "went into") appears in minuscule 1881 (Category II), but is probably a scribal assimilation to εἰσῆλθεν in the first part of the verse.

13 There appear in the textual tradition a number of variant spellings and forms in connection with the verb ἐλλογέω ("charge to an account," "taken into account"). Rather than the strongly supported third-person singular aorist indicative passive ἐλλογεῖται ("it is taken into account"), the following variants exist: (1) ἐλλογᾶται in uncial ℵ[1] and minuscule 1881 (Category II), (2) ἐλλογᾶτο in uncial A, (3) ἐλλογεῖτο in minuscules 1505 2495 (Category III), (4) ἐνελογεῖτο in uncial ℵ* and as reflected in it vg[d], and (5) ἐνλογεῖτο in uncials ℵ[2] D F G. All these variants, however, must be judged as secondary scribal changes that were intended, for one reason or another, as improvements to the text.

14a The negative μή ("not") in the participial phrase τοὺς μὴ ἁμαρτήσαντας ("those who did *not* sin") is omitted by minuscules 1739 (Category I) and 6 424[c] 614 2495 (Category III), in some MSS of the Vulgate, and by Origen[lat] and Ambrosiaster, probably because Latin translators and commentators thought of sin as only a repetition of Adam's transgression.

14b The second preposition ἐπί ("on," "upon," "in") is replaced by ἐν ("in," "on") in Codex Vaticanus (B 03) and minuscules 365 1505 1573 2495 (Category III), evidently for the sake of clarity, so as not to confuse it with the first use of ἐπί four words earlier.

15a The inclusion of καί ("also") in the phrase οὕτως καί ("so also") is strongly supported throughout the Greek textual tradition. Its omission in B is probably an attempt to remove a perceived redundancy.

15b The omission of the preposition ἐν ("in," "by") in uncials F and G, which seems a rather obvious mistake, is probably due to haplography with the numeral ἑνός ("one") that follows it four words later.

16a The aorist masculine participle ἁμαρτήσαντος ("[through the one] sinning") is strongly supported in the textual tradition, whereas the genitive singular noun ἁμαρτήματος ("[through one] sin") appears in uncials D F G and is reflected in versions vg[d] and sy[p]. The variant genitive singular noun is probably a Western type of improvement of an otherwise difficult reading.

16b The addition of the genitive noun ζωῆς ("of life") at the end of 5:16 (thereby reading εἰς δικαίωμα ζωῆς, "unto the justification of life") by Codex Beza (D* 06), as also reflected in vg[mss], is probably an assimilation to εἰς δικαίωσιν ζωῆς ("unto the righteousness of life") at the end of 5:18. It may be a correct understanding of what Paul was writing, but it is nonetheless extraneous and should be omitted.

17a The reading τοῦ ἑνός ("of the one [man]") at the beginning of 5:17 is very well attested, though other variant readings also appear in the textual evidence: (1) ἐν ἑνός ("in one") in minuscules 1739 (Category I) and 1881 (Category II), vg[st], and Origen; (2) ἐν ἑνί ("in one") in uncials A F G; and (3) ἐν τῷ ἑνί ("in the one") in uncial D. The textual evidence, however, favors τοῦ ἑνός ("of the one ['man']").

17b The genitive τῆς δωρεᾶς ("of the gift") is strongly supported by P[46] (which papyrus MS is not here extant until the word δωρεᾶς), by uncials ℵ A C D F G P Ψ [also *Byz* K L], and by minuscules 1175 1739 (Category I), 81[vid] 1881 1962 (Category II), and 6 33 69 104 181 323 326 330 365 424[c] 436 614 629 630 1241 1877 (Category III); it is also reflected in it[d, e, f, g] cop[bo, fay]. Evidently because such a reading results in a piling up of three genitives in the statement "how much more will those who receive the abundance 'of the grace' and 'of the gift' 'of righteous' reign in life," some scribes (1) altered τῆς δωρεᾶς to the accusative τὴν δωρεάν, as appears in minuscules 6 88 104 (Category III) and Origen[lat], or (2) added καί ("and") after τῆς δωρεᾶς, as appears in uncials Ψ 0221 and minuscules 2127 (Category II), 330 365 451 2492 2495 (Category III); also as reflected in it[ar (vid), dem, r(3), x, z] vg syr[p, h] and supported by Theodoret, or (3) simply omitted τῆς δωρεᾶς, as in uncial B, as reflected in cop[sa], and as supported by Irenaeus[lat] Origen and Ambrosiaster.

17c The genitive τῆς δικαιοσύνης ("of righteousness") is attested throughout the textual tradition, with only Codex Ephraemi Rescriptus (C 04) omitting it. The omission was undoubtedly accidental.

17d The order in the name Ἰησοῦ Χριστοῦ ("Jesus Christ") at the end of 5:17 is reversed in Codex Vaticanus (B 03) to read Χριστοῦ Ἰησοῦ ("Christ Jesus"), probably for the sake of stylistic improvement so as not to repeat the order "Jesus Christ" in 5:15.

18a The addition of ἀνθρώπου ("man") after ὡς δι᾽ ἑνός (thereby reading "as through one man") by Codex Sinaiticus (ℵ* 01) is probably only an attempted stylistic improvement.

18b The inclusion of the articular nominative τὸ παράπτωμα ("the transgression") in uncials F and G and in minuscule 69 (Category III), rather than the strongly attested anarthrous genitive παραπτώματος, appears to be an attempted grammatical improvement that makes "the transgression" the subject of the sentence.

18c The reading τὸ δικαίωμα ("the righteous decree") in uncials D F G and in minuscule 69 (Category III), rather than the very strongly attested δικαιώματος, appears also to be an attempted grammatical improvement.

19 The addition of ἀνθρώπου ("man") in the second clause of the verse by uncials D* F G and by Irenaeus, thereby reading "through the obedience of the one man," is an obvious attempted stylistic improvement in order to provide a closer correspondence to "through the disobedience of the one man" in the first clause.

FORM/STRUCTURE/SETTING

From patristic times to the present, one of the most extensively discussed passages in Paul's letters has been Rom 5:12-21. Most often it has been to the fore in the church's consciousness because of (1) its treatment of Adam's sin, (2) its statements regarding death as having pervaded all of God's created universe, and (3) its direct association of human sin with the sin of Adam. What has not as often been appreciated, however, is that the primary thrust of the passage has to do not with Adam's sin — nor even with how Adam's sin has affected the human condition — but with what God has brought about by his "grace" through the "obedience" of Jesus Christ, which has resulted in "the gift of God" and "eternal life" being made available to all people.

A great deal of attention has been paid to 5:12 — particularly to (1) the significance of the chain of causality that is set out from Adam's sin to the sin of people today, (2) the meaning of ἁμαρτία ("sin"), particularly in its articular form ἡ ἁμαρτία ("the sin"), (3) the meaning of θάνατος ("death"), particularly in its articular form ὁ θάνατος ("the death"), (4) the translation of the phrase ἐφ' ᾧ (with a variety of possibilities, depending on how one understands the preposition ἐπί and the pronoun ᾧ), and (5) the translation of πάντες ἥμαρτον ("all sinned"). Numerous tractates, articles, and volumes have been written on these matters, purposing such views as (1) a "realist" or "seminal union" theory (i.e., the collective whole of humanity actually sinned "in Adam"), (2) a "representative" or "federal headship" theory (i.e., the whole of humanity was represented "by Adam in his sin"), (3) an "influence" or "example" theory (i.e., humanity has been influenced for the worse "by Adam's sin"), or (4) an "inherited depravity and mediated guilt" theory (i.e., all people have inherited the depraved condition brought about by Adam's sin and have become personally guilty by their own expression of that inherited state of depravity). Yet most of these theological treatises, important as they are in their own right, have failed to highlight the really important matters of 5:12-21, which have to do with "the grace of God," "God's free gift of righteousness," and "the obedience of Jesus Christ" — all of which have been brought about by God so that "this grace might reign through righteousness unto eternal life through Jesus Christ our Lord."

Rhetorical Features. Rom 5:12-21 may be classified rhetorically as a *synkrisis* (i.e., a comparison of persons, objects, or things, with deficiencies and superiorities highlighted) in which Paul sets out in striking fashion what God effected through his grace and what Jesus Christ brought about through his obedience on behalf of all people vis-à-vis what Adam brought about in human experience because of his disobedience. The central portion of the passage also reflects an *acoustical orientation* or what might be called a *rhetorical assonance* (i.e., the repetition of words and phrases that sound alike) in its use of a series of nouns that end with the Greek syllable μα — that is, the articular and anarthrous nouns τὸ παράπτωμα ("the transgression") in 5:15, 16, 18, and 20; τὸ χάρισμα ("the gift of grace") in 5:15 and 16; κρίμα ("depravity") in 5:16; κατάκριμα ("condemnation") in 5:16 and 18; τὸ δώρημα ("the divine gift") in 5:16; and τὸ δικαίωμα (literally "the righteous decree"), which in 5:16 is used equivalently to δικαίωσις ("justification") and δικαιοσύνη ("righteousness"). Ancient speakers often repeated words and phrases that sound alike as an aid to their listeners, enabling them to understand and remember better what was said, and speakers today do the same thing. So this acoustical use of Greek nouns suggests some type of oral background for at least what appears in 5:15-17, which material may have stemmed either from an early Christian tradition or from Paul's own preaching, or both.

Further, the passage presents a shift in personal pronouns from the first person in 5:1-11 to the third person in 5:12-21, with then the first person taken up again throughout 6:1–8:39 — which also suggests, though does not demand, that much of this material of 5:12-21 may have been rooted in early Christian tradition and then used by Paul in his preaching to Gentiles (as well as here in reporting to his Christian addressees at Rome the content of what he proclaimed in his Gentile mission). Likewise, there appears in 5:12 what may be described as an elementary chiastic structure that moves from "the sin of one man" to "the dominance of death over all people" in its first two lines and then moves from "the universal dominance of death" back to the reality that "all people sinned" in its second two lines — though, of course, much depends in the identification of any true *chiasmus* on the intentionality of the author, that is, whether the writer (whether some early Christian or Paul himself) used such a chiastic construction purposefully or rather unconsciously.

The passage closes in 5:21b with the refrain "through Jesus Christ our Lord" (διὰ Ἰησοῦ Χριστοῦ τοῦ κυρίου ἡμῶν), which is clearly comparable to the refrain "through our Lord Jesus Christ" (διὰ τοῦ κυρίου ἡμῶν Ἰησοῦ Χριστοῦ) with which the transitional and thesis material of 5:1-11 both opened in 5:1 and closed in 5:11. That refrain is then taken up again in cognate fashion at the end of two further important subsections, that is, in 6:23 and 7:25, and it appears again at the end of Section II, in 8:39.

Exegetical Issues. Rom 5:12-21 is chock-full of important exegetical issues that have given rise to a number of interpretive issues. These may be enumerated as follows:

1. The significance of the vernacular expression διὰ τοῦτο ("therefore") at the very beginning of the passage, raising the question of how 5:12-21 relates to what has gone before and to what follows.
2. The significance of the chain of causality that appears in 5:12, with particular attention paid to the meanings of the articular expressions ἡ ἁμαρτία ("the sin") and ὁ θάνατος ("the death") in that verse.
3. The use of the comparative particles ὥσπερ and ὡς ("just as," "as") vis-à-vis καὶ οὕτως in 5:12 (though without the latter in this verse), 15, 16, 18, 19, and 21, raising the question of how the more intensive comparative expression πολλῷ μᾶλλον ("much more") in 5:15 and 17 relates to them.
4. The meaning and significance in 5:12b of the prepositional phrase ἐφ᾽ ᾧ, of the nominative substantival adjective πάντες ("all people"), and of the third-person plural aorist verb ἥμαρτον ("they sinned").
5. A rationale for the *anacoluthon* (an incomplete sentence) that exists between the statements of 5:12 and the explanatory comments of 5:13-14.
6. The form and meaning of the explanatory comments in 5:13-14, with particular attention to the presence and significance of the οὐκ . . . ἀλλά construction in 5:13-14.
7. The nature of the parallelism set out throughout the passage between what

579

Jesus Christ has effected in human history and what Adam had earlier brought about, with particular attention given to matters of both universalism and particularism.

8. The nuancing of the negative expressions κρίμα and κατάκριμα in 5:16 and 18, which are roughly synonymous in meaning, but by the addition of the prepositional prefix κατά in the latter, evidently connote some type of intensification in their usage.

9. The meaning of such positive expressions as ἡ χάρις ("the grace") in 5:15b, 20, and 21; τὸ χάρισμα ("the gracious gift") in 5:15a and 16 (cf. also 5:17); ἡ δωρεὰ ἐν χάριτι ("the gift by grace") in 5:15c; δικαίωμα ("the righteous decree") in 5:16; and ἡ δωρεὰ τῆς δικαιοσύνης ("the gift of righteousness") in 5:17.

10. The significance of the colloquial expression ἄρα οὖν ("so then") at the beginning of 5:18.

11. The verbs that are understood, but not expressed, in the two elliptical statements of 5:18.

12. The emphasis on and significance of the expressions διὰ τῆς ὑπακοῆς τοῦ ἑνός ("through the obedience of the one") in 5:19 and διὰ δικαιοσύνης ("through righteousness") in 5:21.

13. The meaning of the terms ζωή ("life") in 5:17b, δικαίωσιν ζωῆς ("righteousness of life") in 5:18b, and ζωὴ αἰώνιον ("eternal life") in 5:21b, which are spoken of as being a believer's possession "through Jesus Christ our Lord."

The Relation of 5:12-21 to 5:1-11 and to What Follows in 6:1-8:39. A major problem for almost all commentators has been how to relate 5:12-21 to what Paul wrote immediately prior in 5:1-11 and to what he wrote later in 6:1-8:39. Martin Luther spoke of 5:12-21 as an appendix or excursus (a *lustigen Spaziergang*) between 5:1-11 and 6:1-8:39.[1] Philipp Melanchthon viewed the large central section of Romans as set out in three major parts: (1) "The Principal Argument" *(praecipua disputatio)* in 1:16–5:11; (2) "A Quasi-New Book" *(quasi novus liber)* in 5:12–8:39, which focuses on the concepts of "sin," "law," and "grace"; and (3) "A New Argument" *(nova disputatio)* in 9:1–11:36, and so treated 5:12-21 as beginning the "Quasi-New Book."[2] John Calvin understood chs. 1–5 as dealing

---

1. See M. Luther, "Preface to Paul's Epistle to the Romans," in his *Lectures on Romans: Glosses and Scholia*, in *Luther's Works*, vol. 25.

2. P. Melanchthon sustained a lively interest in Romans throughout his life, mounting five or six series of university lectures on the letter and reworking his published commentary materials a number of times. See his *Theologica Institutio in Epistulam Pauli ad Romanos* ("Theological Introduction to Romans") of 1519; his *Loci Communes Theologici* ("Common Theological Topics") of 1521; his *Annotationes in Epistolam Pauli ad Romanos* of 1522 (i.e., his lecture notes on Romans, which Luther arranged to be published on his behalf and which he later disowned; trans. into German in 1527); his *Dispositio Orationis in Epistolam ad Romanos* of 1529 (i.e., his rhetorical analysis of Romans); and his *Commentarii in Epistolam Pauli ad Romanos* (i.e., his full-blown commentary on Romans) of 1532, which he thoroughly revised and extensively expanded in 1540 (from about 80,000 words in his 1532 edition to about 135,000 words in his revised 1540 edition).

with "justification and its results" and chs. 6–8 with "the Christian life," and therefore viewed 5:12-21 as Paul's endeavor "to enlarge on the same doctrine [as in 5:1-11] by a comparison of opposites."[3]

Among modern commentators, some have viewed 5:12-21 as the first portion of what Melanchthon called the "Quasi-New Book" of 5:12–8:39 — usually interpreting (1) the postpositive particle οὖν ("therefore") of 5:1 as connecting 5:1-11 with all that preceded it in 1:16–4:25 and (2) the opening expression διὰ τοῦτο ("therefore") of 5:12 as signaling in some manner a new section of material in 5:12–8:39.[4] Others, following Calvin's understanding of Rom 1–5 as dealing with "justification and its results" and Rom 6–8 with "the Christian life" — and thus understanding 5:12-21 as presenting an enlargement of "the same doctrine" as in 5:1-11 "by a comparison of opposites" — have accepted 5:12-21 as the final portion of all that Paul wrote in chs. 1–5.[5] Most commentators today, however, view the materials of the central theological sections of the body middle of Romans, and particularly what appears in chs. 1–8, as grouped in terms of what is presented in 1:16–4:25 and what is set out in 5:1–8:39 — with 5:1-11 and 5:12-21 constituting the opening passages of that second section.

Whatever view of the compositional structure of Romans is adopted — especially if 5:1-11 and 5:12-21 are understood as intrinsically joined together (either as the closing portion of the first section of the letter's body middle or as the opening portion of the second section) — questions arise as to how 5:1-11 and 5:12-21 are related and how they function together. For, while 5:1-11 and 5:12-21 contain a number of verbal and thematic similarities (particularly in their emphases on "the grace of God" and "the work of Christ," as well as in their common refrain "through our Lord Jesus Christ" that concludes each passage), the rhetoric and style of the two passages have often been seen as somewhat different — particularly in their respective uses of the first-person plural pronoun in 5:1-11 and the third-person singular pronoun in 5:12-21.

A few scholars, of late, have proposed that 5:12-21 illustrates what Paul had declared in 5:1-11 — just as the example of Abraham in 4:1-25 functions to illustrate what Paul proclaimed earlier about righteousness and faith in 3:21-31. Such an understanding, it is suggested, goes far to explain the differing rhetorical and stylistic features between 5:12-21 and 5:1-11, just as it did between 4:1-25 and 3:21-31. Others have argued that 5:12-21 should be seen as a Greek *diatribe*, and so the rhetoric of 5:12-21 is different from that of 5:1-11.[6] But neither of these proposals has "caught on" among commentators, and for what we believe are good reasons.

Our Proposal regarding the Material of 5:12-21. Our thesis, as stated at

3. J. Calvin, *Romans*, in *Calvin's New Testament Commentaries*, 8.111.

4. So, e.g., T. Zahn, F. J. Leenhardt, M. Black, and J. A. T. Robinson.

5. So, e.g., Cranfield, *Romans*, 269: "Verses 12-21 indicate the conclusion to be drawn from the previous sub-section"; see also O. Kuss (1957), F. F. Bruce (1963), U. Wilckens (1978), and J. D. G. Dunn (1988).

6. Cf., e.g., S. E. Porter, "Argument of Romans 5," 655-77.

various times earlier, is that in the materials of 5:1–8:39 Paul sets out for his Christian addressees at Rome the essence of what he had been proclaiming as the Christian gospel in his Gentile mission — that is, his contextualization of the Christian message in a manner that resonated with pagan Gentiles who did not think in Jewish ways, and so had no preparation for that message from previous Jewish or Jewish Christian instruction. It was, as his missionary experience had demonstrated, a way of proclaiming the Christian gospel that had proven to be both meaningful and significant for Gentiles — with the result that many Gentiles, through the ministry of Paul and the working of God's Spirit, had turned from paganism to personal faith in Jesus Christ.

For Jewish believers in Jesus, who understood and proclaimed the "good news" of the Christian message in the context of the OT story of God's deliverance of Israel from Egypt, the presentation of the work of Jesus in terms of a "new exodus" was very meaningful and highly significant. Likewise, the traditional Jewish themes of "justification," "redemption," and "sacrifice of atonement" ("propitiation" or "expiation") carried with them profound theological importance. For Paul in his missionary outreach to Gentiles, however, the story of the exodus and such themes as justification, redemption, and sacrifice of atonement were, it may be postulated, not always understood or appreciated by pagan Gentiles who had no Jewish background and no personal contact with Jewish believers in Jesus. So in proclaiming the gospel to Gentiles, Paul (1) spoke of "peace" and "reconciliation" with God "through our Lord Jesus Christ" (5:1-11), (2) told the universal and foundational redemptive story of how sin, death, and condemnation entered the world by "one man," but how grace, life, and righteousness have been brought about "through Jesus Christ our Lord" (5:12-21), (3) spelled out relationships of sin, death, and the law, on the one hand, and grace, life, and righteousness, on the other (6:1–7:13), (4) expressed the plight of all people in their attempts to live by their own insights and strength, using imagery drawn not only from Jewish experiences but also from a familiar tragic soliloquy in Greek literature (7:14-25), (5) highlighted the new relationships that come about when one is "in Christ" and "in the Spirit" (8:1-30), and (6) closed with a triumphal declaration of God's love and care for his own "in Christ Jesus our Lord" (8:31-39).

We propose, therefore, that what Paul presents in 5:12-21 is not the usual Jewish story of God's deliverance of his people from Egypt,[7] which Jewish Christians used as the antitype of God's "new exodus" of redemption from sin through the person and work of Jesus Christ, but the more universal foundational story of sin, death, and human depravity, which have been countered by God's grace as expressed through the "obedience" and "righteousness" of Jesus Christ.[8] It is not a story about "the wrath of God" being directed against "all the

7. Cf. esp. Exod 13:3-16 regarding the importance of commemorating the Exodus.
8. For a somewhat similar thesis, cf. Beker, *Paul the Apostle*, 85: "In my opinion Rom. 5:12-21 is both a summary of 1:18–5:11 and a transition to 6:1–8:39: it sums up in apocalyptic, typological

godlessness and wickedness of people who suppress the truth by their wickedness," as was evidently drawn by many Jews of Paul's day from *1 En* 13:1–14:31 — and was echoed by Paul himself earlier in Rom 1:18-32 when addressing those who had been extensively influenced by Jewish Christian ways of thinking.[9] Nor is it a story about the two *yetzers* ("impulses") that God places in every person at the time of his or her birth, which understanding evidently arose among various sectarian groups during the period of "early Judaism" and was later used by rabbinic teachers to explain how people can be attracted to evil and why they sin.[10] Rather, it is the story drawn by Paul from Gen 3 about sin and death brought about by Adam's sin — a story usually neglected by rabbinic Judaism, but which seems to have been more and more brought to the fore in a number of nonconformist Jewish circles as a primary explanation for human depravity and sin.[11]

Yet Paul does not simply repeat the OT and Jewish versions of this story. He makes no reference, for example, to such features in the story as the temptation of the serpent, the tree of the knowledge of good and evil, the response of Eve, the interaction between Eve and Adam, or God's action of banishing Adam and Eve from the garden. In fact, as Paul begins the story he refers only to "the one man" who sinned and through whom sin entered human history, with the result that death permeated the entire world. In effect, Paul universalizes the biblical story of Adam's sin and its disastrous results — naming, of course, this "one man" as "Adam" in 5:14 (and thereafter throughout the passage), but using the figure of Adam more as a universal personage in a manner that Gentiles could readily identify with. More importantly, he also universalizes the person of Jesus Christ in contrasting what Adam brought about by the far greater story of how "God's grace," "eternal life," and "righteousness" have been brought about "through Jesus Christ our Lord."

---

language the plight of humankind *before* Christ and its new life *in* Christ. But it is also a transition, because Paul shifts in 5:12-21 to the universal, ontological, and eschatological dimensions of Christian life that dominate 6:1–8:39 ('death,' 'life,' 'the flesh,' the power of 'sin,' the 'Spirit').... The Jewish argument of Rom. 1:18–4:25 has been transcended, and we find ourselves on a new ontological level, the level of existence in Adam and in Christ, which 5:1-11 introduced. Because of 'the new age' of 'life' that has come in Christ, the difference between Jew and Gentile is neutralized, for both belong equally to 'the old age' that Christ has undone."

9. Differing diagnoses of the "human predicament" have often been noted in 1:18-32 and 5:12-21. For in depicting the sinful situation of humanity apart from God, 1:18-32 unfolds in terms of humanity's decline during the course of history into idolatry and immorality, without any reference to Adam's sin, whereas in 5:12-21 the focus is on "the disobedience of the one man" and how his one act of transgression has affected all human beings.

10. Cf. Sir 15:14: "God created man from the beginning, and placed him in the hand of his *yetzer*. If you desire, you can keep the commandment, and it is wisdom to do his good pleasure." On the presence of this motif at Qumran, see R. E. Murphy, "Yeṣer in the Qumrân Literature," *Bib* 39 (1958) 334-44. For discussions of rabbinic teaching on the two *yetzers,* or "impulses," see S. Schechter, *Aspects of Rabbinic Theology* (New York: Schocken Books, 1969), 242-92, and Moore, *Judaism,* 1.479-96.

11. Cf., e.g., Sir 25:24; 4 Ezra 3.7-8, 21-22; 2 Bar 23:4; 48:42-43; 56:5-6

What Paul is doing in 5:12-21 is presenting his own version of Gen 3 in a more universalistic manner. He starts in his account of salvation history neither with Abraham (as he did in 4:1-25) nor with Israel's exodus from Egypt (as was commonly done among the Jewish people of his day). Rather, he sets out matters that have been true from the beginning of human history: "sin," "death," and "divine condemnation" — matters that he knows his Gentile hearers know about and have experienced. And he contrasts all that with what a gracious God has provided for all people through the person and work of Jesus Christ. It is a foundational narrative that (1) carries on the motifs of "grace," "righteousness," and "life" that were prominent in the transitional and thesis passage of 5:1-11, and (2) provides the basis for all that Paul will proclaim more expressly regarding "peace ('completeness')," "reconciliation," "life," "being in Christ," "Christ by his Spirit in us," and the impossibility of ever being separated "from the love of God that is in Christ Jesus our Lord" in 6:1–8:39.

The Compositional Structure of 5:12-21. The materials of 5:12-21, however, are not just set out in terms of a "plot" or "linear sequence of events" for either (1) the story of Adam's sin and its results or (2) the story of God's grace through the obedience of Jesus Christ and its resultant effects. Rather, Paul's use of the stories of these two primal persons in human history is fashioned in terms of his own reflections on the apostolic accounts of the person and work of Jesus Christ vis-à-vis the Gen 3 account of Adam.

Drawing on Northrop Frye's differentiation between *mythos* (i.e., "plot" or "sequence of events") and *dianoia* (i.e., "theme" or "reflective discourse" on the meaning of particular events), Richard Hays has aptly set out an understanding of relations between (1) the "plot" of a story that provides the "narrative substructure" for the exposition of an NT letter writer and (2) an NT writer's "reflective discourse" on that narrative substructure, as follows:

1. There can be an organic relationship between stories and reflective discourse because stories have an inherent configurational dimension *(dianoia)* that not only permits but also demands restatement and interpretation in nonnarrative language.
2. The reflective restatement does not simply repeat the plot *(mythos)* of the story; nonetheless, the story shapes and constrains the reflective process because the *dianoia* can never be entirely abstracted from the story in which it is manifested and apprehended.
3. Hence, when we encounter this type of reflective discourse, it is legitimate and possible to inquire about the story in which it is rooted.[12]

So with respect to the narrative substructure that underlies an NT letter writer's exposition, Hays has proposed a twofold procedure: "We may first identify

---

12. Cf. Hays, *The Faith of Jesus Christ* (with its revealing subtitle *An Investigation of the Narrative Substructure of Galatians 3:1–4:11*), 28.

within the discourse allusions to the story and seek to discern its general out-lines; then, in a second phase of inquiry, we may ask how this story shapes the logic of argumentation in the discourse."[13] And this is particularly the case in our understanding of Paul's comparisons and contrasts between (1) "the story of Adam's disobedience," which has brought about sin, death, and condemnation, and (2) "the story of Jesus Christ's obedience," which has countered all that Adam brought into human history by effecting the real possibility of people experiencing God's grace, righteousness, and eternal life.

Thus, while Rom 5:12-21 intertwines two narrative substructures that have to do first with Adam and then with Jesus Christ, the material of the passage is, in reality, a "reflective discourse" that compares and contrasts these two primal persons of human history. It is a reflective discourse that lies at the heart of Paul's proclamation of the Christian gospel to Gentiles, and so, in effect, re-flects a fundamentally new foundational Christian narrative. And while it begins historically with what the first primal person of the comparison has done, its emphasis is on the person and work of the second person, who has by his "obe-dience" and "righteousness" effected an entirely different situation and future for a believer's life.

Paul's reflective discourse in 5:12-21 may be structured in terms of the following four parts:

1. Sin and death have come into the experience of all people through the first man, Adam (in 5:12-14).
2. God's grace through Jesus Christ abounds "much more" and is given as a gift to all who will receive it (in 5:15-17).
3. Conclusion: The effects of the obedience and righteousness of Jesus Christ vis-à-vis the disobedience and condemnation brought about by Adam (in 5:18-19).
4. An addendum on the personified figures of "law," "sin," and "death," as countered by "God's grace" at work "through Jesus Christ our Lord" (in 5:20-21).

This compositional outline will structure our exegetical comments that follow.

EXEGETICAL COMMENTS

I. Sin and Death Have Come into the Experience of All People through the First Man, Adam (5:12-14)

5:12a The idiomatic expression διὰ τοῦτο ("therefore," "on this account") at the beginning of this passage is used by Paul elsewhere in Romans to signal a logical

---

13. Hays, *The Faith of Jesus Christ*, 28 (2nd ed., 29).

connection between what precedes and what follows.[14] Commentators have often, however, been at a loss to identify exactly what connection Paul was attempting to make when he used διὰ τοῦτο here in 5:12a. Many have argued that he had in mind all of what he wrote in 1:16–5:11;[15] others that he was thinking of the statement at the end of 5:11 regarding believers in Jesus having "received reconciliation . . . through our Lord Jesus Christ," with 5:12-21 intended to spell out in more detail how the work of Jesus brought that reconciliation about.[16] Some have proposed that he used διὰ τοῦτο here merely as a transitional expression, without any logical link implied with what precedes it.[17] More likely, however, by his use of "therefore" at the beginning of 5:12, Paul wanted to build on what he had said in 5:1-11 about "grace," "righteousness," and "life,"[18] and so in 5:12-21 to begin to spell out these matters in a "reflective discourse" on the story that underlies all of Christian proclamation.

The expression ὥσπερ ("just as," "as") was used widely in Greek writings to signal the *protasis* (i.e., the first or introductory part) of a comparative statement, with καὶ οὕτως ("so also," "so") used to identify the *apodosis* (i.e., the following or main part) of the statement. Thus, by using ὥσπερ ("just as," "as") at the start of 5:12, it seems evident that Paul had intended to set out a full comparative statement somewhat as follows: "*Just as* (ὥσπερ) sin entered the world through one man, and through that sin came death, and so death permeated all humanity, on the basis of which all have sinned, *so also* (καὶ οὕτως) righteousness entered the world through one man, and through that righteousness came life." But Paul "goes off at a word" in declaring that "all have sinned" (πάντες ἥμαρτον), and he only takes up the comparison again at 5:15 — focusing on its comparable and contrastive features throughout 5:15-21.

What Paul does in 5:12a, however, is to set out a chain of causality that exists between the sin of the first man (Adam) and the depraved and sinful condition of all the descendants of that first man, whatever their location, situation, or claimed status. He does not spell out in this verse the biblical details of how sin entered the world — though later in the passage he speaks of Adam's "transgression" (5:14), "trespass" (5:15, 17-18), and "disobedience" (5:19). But by using the nominative articular ἡ ἁμαρτία in the first line of the verse, as well as twice later in 5:20-21, Paul personifies "sin" as a malevolent force that both is hostile to God and alienates human beings from God. Further, because he uses the genitive articular τῆς ἁμαρτίας in the second line of 5:12, it may legitimately be argued that he was referring to "the sin of the first man" or "that sin" he had just spoken about. And by his two uses of the articular ὁ θάνατος ("the death") here in 5:12, as well as three times later in 5:14, 17, and 21, "death" is personified

---

14. In addition to 5:12, see also 1:26; 4:16; 13:6 (and 15:9 in a quoted OT passage).

15. So, e.g., Godet, *Romans,* 1.202; Wilckens, *An die Römer,* 1.307; Dunn, *Romans,* 1.272.

16. So, e.g., H. A. W. Meyer, *Romans,* 1.240; Morris, *Romans,* 228.

17. So, e.g., Lietzmann, *An die Römer,* 60-61; Schlier, *Römerbrief,* 159; Bultmann, "Adam and Christ," 153.

18. So, e.g., Cranfield, *Romans,* 1.271; Fitzmyer, *Romans,* 411; Jewett, *Romans,* 373.

as a cosmic force that (1) brings to an end the material life and personality of a human being, and (2) separates people from God, both during their earthly lives and throughout eternity.[19]

Modern scholars have usually not attempted to explicate much further Paul's articular use of ὁ θάνατος in 5:12. Reformation commentators, however, frequently spoke of "the death" that resulted from Adam's "transgression," "trespass," or "disobedience" as *inherited depravity,* which became the basis for every person's sins and personal guilt. John Calvin, for example, in commenting on the words "sin entered into the world" of 5:12, insisted that we need to "note the order which he [Paul] follows here," for "he says that sin had preceded and that death followed sin" — and so Calvin argued that as descendants of Adam we do not die "merely because he [Adam] had as it were sinned for us," but because we express "the *natural depravity*" inherited from Adam, which has "*corrupted, vitiated, depraved,* and *ruined* our *nature.*"[20] Calvin went on to say with respect to Adam's sin and its result:

> Having lost the image of God, the only seed which he [Adam] could have produced was that which bore resemblance to himself. We have, therefore, all sinned, because we are all imbued with *natural corruption,* and for this reason are wicked and perverse . . . the allusion here is to *our innate and hereditary depravity.*"[21]

5:12b What Paul is saying in his use of (1) the prepositional phrase ἐφ' ᾧ, (2) the substantival adjective πάντες, and (3) the aorist verb ἥμαρτον has been the focus of a great deal of scholarly attention and debate down through the centuries. Joseph Fitzmyer, however, has done a masterful job in bringing together centuries of discussion on these matters in his 1993 Anchor Bible commentary on Romans, setting out and evaluating the major interpretive proposals that have been offered from patristic times to the present and offering his own position.[22] Fitzmyer's discussion of eleven ways in which the prepositional phrase ἐφ' ᾧ has been (and is today) understood may be condensed to four major positions with their respective refinements:

1. The pronoun in the expression should be understood as masculine in a genuine relative clause, and so translated "in whom" (Latin: *in quo*) with the meaning "in Adam." This position has been commonly attributed to Augustine (as well as, more lately, to that mysterious Latin commentary writer of the fourth century whom Erasmus dubbed "Ambrosiaster"), and

---

19. Cf. Rom 6:16, 21, 23; 7:5, 10, 13, 24; 8:2, 6, 38; see also 1 Cor 3:22; 2 Cor 7:10.

20. J. Calvin, *Romans,* in *Calvin's New Testament Commentaries,* 8.111.

21. *Ibid.,* 8.112 (italics mine); see Erasmus's comments to the same effect on Rom 5:12 in *Collected Works of Erasmus,* 42.34-35.

22. See Fitzmyer, *Romans,* 413-17, much of whose investigation and presentation is reflected in our exegetical comments here.

has been generally followed by Roman Catholic theologians as well as by some Protestant commentators. It has often been explained in terms of the OT idea of corporate personality or solidarity.[23] However, as Fitzmyer points out: "If Paul had meant 'in whom' (in the sense of incorporation), he would have written *en hō,* as he does in 1 Cor 15:22; cf. Heb 7:9-10. Moreover, *Adam* as the personal antecedent of the rel. pron. is too far removed in the sentence from the pronoun."[24] Several Greek Fathers have read the preposition ἐπί rather elliptically to mean "because of whom,"[25] and some modern scholars have also read it elliptically to mean "because of the one by whom."[26] A few commentators today, realizing that a masculine pronoun needs to match a corresponding masculine noun, have attempted to relate the pronoun ᾧ to some masculine noun that is closer to it than ἑνὸς ἀνθρώπου ("one man") in the first line of 5:12a or than Ἀδάμ (the indeclinable name "Adam") in the first line of 5:14a — and so have proposed that either θάνατος ("death"), a masculine noun that precedes it,[27] or νόμος ("law"), a masculine noun that follows it,[28] should be understood as the logical antecedent of this masculine pronoun. But neither of these proposals has been viewed as valid by most contemporary NT scholars.

2. The pronoun in the expression should be understood as being neuter in a genuine relative clause, and so translated "on the basis of which" or "under which circumstances," with the antecedent being all that is said regarding sin entering the world and death permeating humanity in the immediately preceding clauses of the verse.[29] Some early Greek Fathers seem to have understood the expression in this fashion, and so translated the entire clause as "to the extent that all have sinned."[30] On this position — especially in the form that Theodor Zahn argued it in his Romans commentary of 1910 — Joseph Fitzmyer expresses himself as follows: "Of the relative-pronoun understandings of *eph' hō,* this one makes the best sense, and it has extrabiblical parallels."[31]

3. The preposition ἐπί in the expression should be understood as equivalent to the causal conjunction διότι ("because")[32] — or, perhaps, to the

---

23. Fitzmyer, *Romans,* 414.

24. *Ibid.*

25. So, e.g., John Chrysostom, Theodoret of Cyrrhus, John Damascene, and Theophylact.

26. Fitzmyer cites in support L. Cerfaux, *Christ in the Theology of St. Paul* (New York: Herder and Herder, 1959), 232.

27. Fitzmyer cites in support J. Héring, *Le Royaume de Dieu et sa Venue* (Paris: Alcan, 1937), 157; also E. Stauffer, *New Testament Theology* (London, 1955), 270 n. 176.

28. Fitzmyer cites in support F. W. Danker.

29. Fitzmyer credits this position principally to Zahn, *An die Romer,* 263-67.

30. Fitzmyer cites Cyril of Alexandria for this translation.

31. Fitzmyer, *Romans,* 415.

32. Cf. Rom 8:21; 1 Cor 15:9; Phil 2:26; 1 Thess 2:8; 4:6; see also Heb 11:5 (quoting Gen 5:24), 23; Jas 4:3.

phrase ἐπὶ τοῦτο ὅτι ("in this that" or "because") — and therefore translated "since," "because," or "inasmuch as." This is the view accepted by the
vast majority of scholars and commentators today.[33] Fitzmyer's response
to this understanding, however, is as follows: "The trouble with this interpretation is that there are almost no certain instances in early Greek
literature wherein *eph' hō* is used as the equivalent of causal *dioti*. Most of
the examples cited by BAGD (287) or B-A (582) are invalid. . . . Moreover,
alleged examples in the Pauline corpus itself, apart from 5:12, are far from
certain."[34] Thus Fitzmyer questions the common assertion that "myriad
examples of this phrase in the causal sense can be found," and argues that
some other understanding must be posited; he favors among those already
proposed Theodor Zahn's translation "on the basis of which" or "under
which circumstances," but goes on to argue for what he believes is an even
better position (as set out immediately below in #4).[35]

4. The prepositional phrase ἐφ' ᾧ should be read as being equivalent to the
consecutive conjunction ὥστε ("for this reason," "so that") and translated as follows: "with the result that" or "so that." This is the meaning
for the expression that Fitzmyer finds validated in such ancient writers as
Plutarch, Athenaeus, Cassius Dio, and Diogenes Laertius, which evidence
he has spelled out more extensively in his 1993 article "The Consecutive
Meaning of ἐφ' ᾧ in Romans 5.12."[36] Thus Fitzmyer sets out his own proposal as follows: "*Eph' hō,* then, would mean that Paul is expressing a
result, the sequel to Adam's baleful influence on humanity by the ratification of his sin in the sins of all individuals. He would thus be conceding
to individual human sins a secondary causality or personal responsibility
for death. Moreover, one must not lose sight of the adv. *kai houtōs,* 'and
so' (5:12c), which establishes the connection between the sin of 'one man'
and the death and sins of 'all human beings.' Thus Paul in v. 12 is ascribing
death to two causes, not unrelated: to Adam and to all human sinners.
The fate of humanity ultimately rests on what its head, Adam, has done
to it. The primary causality for its sinful and mortal condition is ascribed
to Adam, no matter what meaning is assigned to *eph' hō,* and a secondary
causality to the sins of all human beings."[37]

Joseph Fitzmyer has researched and argued his position well, and there
can be little doubt that his understanding will be increasingly judged by NT
scholars as better than almost all the other views proposed to date. Yet I continue to believe that Theodor Zahn's translation of ἐφ' ᾧ in 5:12b as "on the basis
of which" — with the antecedent of the neuter pronoun being the immediately

33. Fitzmyer lists over thirty who have proposed this position.
34. Fitzmyer, *Romans,* 415.
35. *Ibid.,* 415-16.
36. Fitzmyer, "The Consecutive Meaning of ἐφ' ᾧ in Romans 5.12," 321-39.
37. Fitzmyer, *Romans,* 416.

preceding clauses that speak of how sin entered into the world and of how death has permeated all humanity — is more accurate linguistically and makes better sense contextually.

With respect to the substantival adjective πάντες ("all") and the aorist verb ἥμαρτον ("have sinned") that follow the prepositional clause ἐφ᾽ ᾧ, there is no way that Paul can be made to say "*some* have sinned." He is clear in 3:23, which closes off his expanded thesis statement of 3:21-23, that "all people have sinned (πάντες ἥμαρτον) and fall short of the glory of God." Likewise, there is no legitimate way in which Paul can be made to say that "all have sinned *collectively*" or that "all have sinned *in Adam.*" Such understandings would be, as Fitzmyer rightly insists, "additions to Paul's text."[38] Rather, the πάντες ("all") is emphatic and cannot be toned down; and the constative use of the third-person aorist indicative verb ἥμαρτον ("have sinned") signals the actual sins of individual people throughout the course of human history.[39]

What Paul presents in 5:12 is a declaration of the twofold nature of human sin, human responsibility, and divine judgment — that is, (1) the irrevocable history of all human beings in the disastrous situation that Adam has brought about by his sin, which may be defined as "inherited depravity," and (2) the inevitable response that all people have made to that inherited situation, which results in their own personal sins and their coming under God's judgment. It is a declaration much like that of the prophet Ezekiel, who in ch. 18 of his written prophecy declares on behalf of Yahweh: "What do you people mean by quoting this proverb about the land of Israel: 'The fathers have eaten sour grapes, and the children's teeth are set on edge'?" — and then goes on to use three illustrative father-son relationships to proclaim that (1) the Israelites of the prophet's day had indeed inherited the conditions that their fathers brought on them, but (2) God judges each person within those inherited conditions as to how he or she responds to God, whether negatively or positively.

Ezekiel's message proclaims individual responsibility within inherited depravity. For while it acknowledges the inherited conditions of the day, which had much to do with conditioning the thoughts and actions of the people, it also insists that God judges people not on the basis of what they have inherited from their ancestors, but on the basis of how they have responded to him and acted within those inherited conditions.

Likewise, this first part of Paul's "reflective discourse" on "the universal and foundational story" of the Christian gospel regarding "the two primal persons of human history" is very similar, not only in tone and temper but also in wording, to what is said in some of the nonformist Jewish writings of Paul's day about (1) the inherited spiritual conditions of people and (2) people's responsibilities before God in those conditions. *2 Baruch (Apocalypse of Baruch)*, which was written about A.D. 100-120, is most explicit along these lines in declaring:

38. Fitzmyer, *Romans,* 417.
39. Cf. in Romans also 2:12; 3:23; 5:14.

For though Adam first sinned and brought untimely death upon all, yet of those who are born from him each one of them has prepared for his own soul torment to come, and, again, each one of them has chosen for himself glories to come. . . . Adam is, therefore, not the cause, save only of his own soul; but each of us has been the Adam of his own soul.[40]

This understanding of the twofold nature of sin — that is, as rooted in humanity's inescapable history of depravity, but judged by God with respect to how people respond to him and act within those depraved conditions — appears a number of times in other Jewish sectarian writings that both predate and postdate Paul's time. Thus, for example, in Sirach (so-called Ecclesiasticus), composed about 200-175 B.C., we read (1) "From a woman did sin originate, and because of her we all must die,"[41] but also (2) "God created man from the beginning, and placed him in the hand of his impulse *(yetzer).* If you desire, you can keep the commandment, and it is wisdom to do his good pleasure."[42] Also significant is 1QH (the Qumran *Psalms of Thanksgiving*), column 4, where the author speaks of people being "steeped in sin from the womb *and* guilty of perfidy [i.e., a deliberate breach of faith] unto old age," and concludes with the statement: "When I call to mind all my guilty deeds *and* the perfidy of my sires — when wicked men oppose your covenant, and forward men your word, trembling seizes hold on me and quaking."[43]

It seems best, therefore, to understand Paul's words in 5:12 as speaking of such a twofold understanding of (1) *inherited depravity,* which stems from one man's sin and the resultant experience of death that has permeated all human history, and (2) *actual sins of every person down through the course of history,* which are the inevitable expressions of people's inherited depravity and add by accumulation to the weight of that depravity. This would be a very sad story regarding human history and people's experience if that were all that could be said about people's lives and their relationship with God. But Paul's purpose in referring to this sad story is to counter it by proclaiming the "good news" of the Christian message, and it is this triumphant account of God's grace through the person and work of Jesus Christ that he emphasizes in 5:12-21.

Paul obviously intended to set out in contradistinction to this introductory part of his comparative statement (i.e., the *protasis*) a second and much greater main part of his comparison (i.e., the *apodosis*). But he "goes off at a word" in declaring at the close of 5:12 that "all have sinned" (πάντες ἥμαρτον) and so fails to complete the sentence as intended, which constitutes a syntactical *anacoluthon* (i.e., a shift in the grammar of a sentence or an unfinished

40. *2 Bar* 54:15 and 19.
41. Sir 25:24 (quoted without accepting the antifeminist polemic of the passage).
42. Sir 15:14 (quoted without accepting the "two-impulse" theory of the passage).
43. Cf. *1 En* 41:1-2 (longer recension A); *4 Ezra* 7:116-26; and *2 Bar* 23:4; 48:42-43; 56:5-6 (italics mine, to highlight the twofold nature of the discussion).

sentence). But he takes up his intended comparisons and contrasts and spells them out with consistency in 5:15-21.

5:13-14 Many have viewed what is written in 5:13-14 as a series of rather tortuous, perhaps even incoherent, statements, and all sorts of interpretations have been given. Without attempting to list and evaluate all that has been said about these verses — for, after all, they are of the nature of a digression on the apostle's part, and the history of exegesis on them has not always been helpful in understanding the flow of Paul's argument — we offer the following exegetical comments, realizing that there are many other proposals, some of which leave matters at a dead end.

What Paul is elucidating in 5:13-14 is his previous statement at the close of 5:12 that πάντες ἥμαρτον ("all have sinned"), by which he evidently meant "all people have sinned throughout the course of history."[44] He justifies that affirmation by the explanatory comment of 5:13a, ἄχρι γὰρ νόμου ἁμαρτία ἦν ἐν κόσμῳ ("for before the law was given, sin was in the world") — which is followed by what many have seen as a difficult line of argumentation in 5:13b-14. Paul's explanatory comment of 5:13a was evidently meant to demonstrate that since "sin was in the world" before the Mosaic law was given,[45] it may legitimately be said that "all people have sinned throughout the course of history." And his argument of 5:14 seems to have been given to highlight that death "reigned" over everyone during the time before Moses, and therefore to draw the legitimate conclusion that everyone indeed sinned even before the giving of the Mosaic law.

The principal difficulty that most commentators have seen in these two verses has to do with Paul's statement of 5:13b: ἁμαρτία δὲ οὐκ ἐλλογεῖται μὴ ὄντος νόμου ("But sin is not taken into account when there is no law"). In the context of what he has been explaining and arguing in these two verses, 5:13b has often been viewed as somewhat incongruous. How can Paul say that "sin is not taken into account when there is no law" when he has just insisted that "all people have sinned throughout the course of history" and attempted to justify that claim by declaring that "before the law was given, sin was in the world"?

Some aid in understanding Paul's argument here may be offered by 2 Corinthians, where Paul uses the following pattern of argumentation: (1) when Paul deals with accusations against him or with views he doesn't agree with, he frequently uses the negative οὐ ("not") in referring to them, but (2) when he speaks of his own position in countering those accusations and erroneous views, he uses the much stronger adversative conjunction ἀλλά ("rather," "nevertheless").[46] This pattern of antithetical grammatical construction in 2 Corinthians (however we evaluate the evidence regarding the structures and unity of this canonical letter) needs, we believe, to be taken into account when reading

---

44. As seems evident from his reference in 5:13-14 to a period of time "before the law," i.e., a period of time "from Adam to Moses," that is contrasted to the time after Moses.

45. Paul often omits the definite article before the noun νόμος when it refers to the Mosaic law, as he does here.

46. Cf. 2 Cor 1:12, 24; 2:17; 3:3, 5; 4:5; 5:12; 7:12; 10:13; 12:14.

his parenthetical comments of 5:13-14 — particularly because what appears in canonical 2 Corinthians was written shortly before the apostle wrote Romans, and therefore similar patterns of argumentation might reasonably be viewed as carried over from one set of materials to another.

Accepting the likelihood of such an antithetical grammatical patterning in 5:13-14, we suggest that these two verses should be read as follows:

1. Paul justifies his statement at the end of 5:12 that "all have sinned [in the course of history]" by pointing out that "before the [Mosaic] law was given, sin was in the world."
2. An objection that he knows could be raised against his justifying comment is given: "But sin is not (δὲ οὐκ) taken into account when there is no law."
3. The apostle rebuts this objection: "Nevertheless (ἀλλά), death reigned from Adam to Moses, even over those who did not sin in the same way by breaking a command as did Adam." This rebuttal draws attention to the fact that people died before the Mosaic law was given, and so implies that since death, which came into the world because of sin, was a reality for everyone prior to the time of Moses, the sin of all people was also a reality throughout all of human history.

The reference at the end of 5:14 to Adam as "a type of the one to come" (ὅς ἐστιν τύπος τοῦ μέλλοντος) has posed a number of problems for commentators, for Adam and Jesus Christ are presented in 5:15-21 as being far more antithetical than similar. The basic meaning of τύπος, however, has to do with "form," "mold," "pattern," or "model," whose variations as to what is produced by that "mold" or "pattern" are determined by the nature of the materials or the subject of the discussion involved.[47] Frédéric Godet's comment on Adam as a type of Christ, therefore, is probably most accurate and sufficient: "Adam is the type of the Messiah, inasmuch [as], to quote Ewald, 'each of them draws after him all mankind,' so that 'from what the one was to humanity we may infer what the other is to it.'"[48]

II. God's Grace through Jesus Christ Abounds "Much More" and Is Given as a Gift to All Who Will Receive It (5:15-17)

5:15a Having stated at the end of 5:14 that Adam is a "type" (τύπος; "pattern" or "model") of "the one to come," Paul takes pains throughout 5:15-17 to point out that there is no comparison between what Adam has brought about in human history and what Jesus Christ has effected on behalf of all humanity. That

47. Cf. Paul's use of τύπος in 1 Cor 10:6; Phil 3:17; 1 Thess 1:7; and 2 Thess 3:9.
48. Godet, *Romans*, 1.361, quoting in support G. H. A. Ewald, *Die Sendschreiben des Apostels Paulus* (1857).

is why he begins 5:15 with the very strong negative ἀλλά ("rather," "however"), which functions to draw attention to the facts that (1) there is a very great difference between Adam, "the first man" of 5:12a, and Jesus Christ, "the one to come" of 5:14c, and (2) "the gift of grace" brought by "the one to come" is far greater than "the trespass" of "the first man." Throughout 5:15-17, as well as in the concluding portion of the passage in 5:18-21, there is the proclamation of the Christian message (1) that God's grace through Jesus Christ abounds "much more" than Adam's sin and (2) that it is given as a gift to all who will receive it.

The wording of 5:15a has often been seen as somewhat awkward. Literally, the sentence reads: ἀλλ᾽ οὐχ ὡς τὸ παράπτωμα, οὕτως καὶ τὸ χάρισμα ("But not as the trespass, so also the gift of grace" [which we have translated more colloquially as "The gift, however, is not like the trespass"]). That awkwardness has come about partly because in Greek comparative clauses in the indicative mood, the negative οὐ (here οὐχ since the comparative particle ὡς that follows begins with a vowel) always appears not within but before the clause that represents the *protasis*, with the *apodosis* that follows usually making a positive point.[49] But also because Paul wanted to restate the antithetical comparison in the form that he began it in 5:12 — where he set out the *protasis* but was diverted by his own "going off at a word" from spelling out the *apodosis* — yet also wanted to highlight "the gift of grace" as being far greater than "the trespass."

In his emphasis on the far greater importance of "the gift of grace" vis-à-vis "the trespass," Paul uses a number of Greek nouns, both articular and anarthrous, that end with the syllable μα. Here in 5:15a that greater importance of the one over the other is spelled out by the use of the terms τὸ χάρισμα ("the gift of grace") as being far superior to τὸ παράπτωμα ("the transgression"). This rhetorical assonance of nouns ending with the Greek syllable μα is continued throughout the passage, as witnessed in τὸ χάρισμα ("the gift of grace") in 5:16; τὸ παράπτωμα ("the transgression") in 5:16, 18, and 20; κρίμα ("depravity") in 5:16; κατάκριμα ("condemnation") in 5:16 and 18; τὸ δώρημα ("the divine gift") in 5:16; and τὸ δικαίωμα ("the righteous decree") in 5:16. All these noun endings of μα were evidently meant to enable the hearers of his oral preaching to Gentiles in the eastern regions of the Roman Empire, as well as his Christian addressees at Rome, to feel the impact of his message and recognize its importance.

5:15b Paul's use of "the many" at the beginning (the nominative οἱ πολλοί) and end (the accusative τοὺς πολλούς) of this statement is not to be read as expressing any limitation on the number of those who "died by the trespass of the one man," as though "the many" means "some," "the majority," or even "most." The basic premise in the *protasis* of his conclusion to this passage, that is, in the first part of his comparative statement of 5:18, is that because of one trespass

49. Cf. *ATRob*, 1159.

the impending disaster of "condemnation" (κατάκριμα) hangs like a legendary "sword of Damocles" over "all people" (εἰς πάντας ἀνθρώπους).[50]

Notable as well in 5:15 is the phrase πολλῷ μᾶλλον ("much more"), which carries on the "much more" emphases in the transitional and thesis material of 5:1-11 — particularly in the explicit use of πολλῷ μᾶλλον ("much more") in 5:9-10. The expression reflects a type of Greco-Roman rhetoric that argues "from the lesser to the greater" *(a minori ad maius)*. It also expresses a form of Jewish argumentation that argues that "what applies in a less important case will certainly apply in a more important case" (קל וחומר, *qal waḥomer*), which is the first of the seven exegetical "rules" attributed to the venerable Jewish teacher Hillel.

The foci in 5:15, however, are on (1) "God's grace and the gift that came by the grace of the one man, Jesus Christ," and (2) how what God accomplished through Jesus has affected for their good the spiritual milieu of all people. It is this emphasis that Paul will continue to highlight in the rest of his reflective discourse on this foundational story of the Christian gospel.

5:16-17 The structure and meaning of the first sentence of 5:16 are very much like those of the first sentence of 5:15, and so we have translated these two first sentences, both in structure and meaning, alike — thus reading 5:15a: "But not as the trespass, so also the gift of grace" (or more colloquially, "The gift, however, is not like the trespass"), and reading 5:16a: "Again, the gift of God is not like the result of one man's sin" (with that similarity of structure and meaning being signaled at the very beginning of 5:16a by the insertion of the conjunction καί, which we have translated as "again"). Further, as in the first sentence of 5:15 "the gift of grace" (τὸ χάρισμα) is emphasized, so here in the first sentence of 5:16 the emphasis is on "the divine gift" (τὸ δώρημα); and as in the first sentence of 5:15 "the gift of grace" counters "the transgression" (τὸ παράπτωμα), so here in the first sentence of 5:16 "the divine gift" counters "the sin of the one man" (δι᾽ ἑνὸς ἁμαρτήσαντος).

The very great difference between what Adam brought into the world and what Jesus Christ effected by his obedience on behalf of all people is spelled out quite graphically in two statements in 5:16b-17, with both statements beginning with the conjunction γάρ ("for") that is used in explanatory fashion. The first statement in 5:16b declares that Adam by his transgression brought into the world the disastrous feature of "depravity" (κρίμα) that results in "condemnation" (κατάκριμα). The terms κρίμα and κατάκριμα are roughly synonymous, though with the addition of the preposition κατά, the meaning of κατάκριμα is intensified. But that first statement of 5:16b goes on to proclaim the focus of the

---

50. Cf. the equivalent uses of "all" and "many" in the Synoptic accounts of Jesus' healing the sick in Galilee, where Mark 1:32, 34 says people brought "all who were sick" to Jesus and he healed "many" of them; Matt 8:16 says they brought "many" to him and he healed "all" of them; and Luke 4:40 reads that they brought to him "all" the sick and he healed "everyone." Note also the use of "the many" (οἱ πολλοί) in Rom 5:19 for both (1) all those affected by Adam's sin and (2) all those who receive God's gift of grace through the obedience of Jesus.

NT gospel story, which is a far greater message than contained in the story of what Adam brought about in world history: that God's "gift of grace" (χάρισμα) through the work of Jesus Christ brings about God's "decree of righteousness" (δικαίωμα) — all of which is in contradistinction to "the many trespasses" that have resulted from Adam's transgression.

The second statement regarding the differences between what Adam brought into the world and what Jesus effected by his obedience appears in 5:17. It speaks of the fact that "by the trespass of the one man, death reigned through that one man." But it counters all that Adam brought into the world by the proclamation: "How much more (πολλῷ μᾶλλον) will those who receive God's abundant provision (τήν περισσείαν) of his grace (τῆς χάριτος) and of his gift of righteousness (τῆς δωρεᾶς τῆς δικαιοσύνης) reign in life through the one man, Jesus Christ." The comparison in this *apodosis* of 5:17 again invokes the Greco-Roman argument *a minori ad maius* ("from the lesser to the greater"); it also reflects Hillel's seventh exegetical rule, "what applies in a less important case will certainly apply in a more important case."

III. Conclusion: The Effects of the Obedience and Righteousness of Jesus Christ vis-à-vis the Disobedience and Condemnation Brought About by Adam (5:18-19)

5:18-19 The conclusion to Paul's discourse on the foundational stories of (1) Adam's sin and its results and (2) God's grace through the obedience of Jesus Christ and its resultant effects is set out in 5:18-19. Twice in these two verses the comparison is expressly made between Adam and Jesus Christ using the comparative particles ὡς or ὥσπερ ("as," "just as") in the *protasis* and the expression οὕτως καί ("so also") in the *apodosis*. The joining of the inferential particles ἄρα ("so," "then," "consequently") and οὖν ("so," "therefore," "consequently") to indicate the conclusion of a matter being discussed occurs about fifty times in the Synoptic Gospels, Acts, the Pauline corpus, and Hebrews. Paul is especially fond of using ἄρα οὖν in this manner.[51]

The first of the two comparative statements of Paul's conclusion to his reflective discourse, which uses the comparative particles ὡς ("as," "just as") in the *protasis* and οὕτως καί ("even so") in the *apodosis,* is set out in 5:18: Ἄρα οὖν ὡς δι᾽ ἑνός παραπτώματος εἰς πάντας ἀνθρόπους εἰς κατάκριμα, οὕτως καί δι᾽ ἑνὸς δικαιώματος εἰς πάντας ἀνθρώπους εἰς δικαίωσιν ζωῆς ("Consequently, just as through one trespass [there has resulted] condemnation for all people, so also through one act of righteousness [there will result] acquittal that brings

---

51. In addition to Paul's use of ἄρα οὖν here in 5:18, see also later in 7:3, 25b; 8:12; 9:16, 18; and 14:12, 19. In 8:1, however, he writes ἄρα νῦν ("therefore now"). In Rom 7:21 and Gal 2:21 he uses ἄρα singly, simply to enliven the statement by the expression "so then" or "then" — though ἄρα used singly is often not translated in modern translations.

life for all people"). It may be debated whether the genitive ἑνός is masculine (and so refers to the "one man" Adam) or neuter (and so refers to the "one trespass"). The clauses of both the *protasis* and the *apodosis* in 5:18 are elliptical, and therefore depend for their intelligibility on the context of the passage. Yet while ἑνὸς ἀνθρώπου of 5:12a is certainly masculine — and while the discussion of 5:12 to 5:17 has to do with Adam's trespass as countered by God's grace through the work of Jesus Christ — the reference in the *apodosis* of 5:18 to what Christ effected that counters Adam's transgression is expressed in the phrase ἑνὸς δικαιώματος ("the one act of righteousness"), and so ἑνός in this *apodosis* must be viewed as neuter. Thus, since the *protasis* and *apodosis* of a verse need to match linguistically, Paul in 5:18 should be seen as not reiterating the idea of "the first man Adam" (masculine) as the type of "the one who is to come" (masculine), but as contrasting "the one trespass" (neuter) by "the one act of righteousness" (neuter).

Rom 5:18 is elliptical because a finite verb has been omitted in both its *protasis* and its *apodosis*. These omissions are understandable, for in a concluding statement Paul would have not wanted to repeat the obvious. The following two verbs, therefore, based on contextual considerations, may legitimately be supplied: (1) the third-person, singular, aorist, indicative, active verb ἀπέβη ("it has resulted") in the first clause, and (2) the third-person, singular, future, indicative, middle ἀποβήσεται ("it will result") in the second,[52] both of which derive from the figurative meaning of ἀποβαίνω ("become," "lead to," "result in").

The second comparative statement of this concluding paragraph in 5:19 reads as follows: ὥσπερ γὰρ διὰ τῆς παρακοῆς τοῦ ἑνὸς ἀνθρώπου ἁμαρτωλοὶ κατεστάθησαν οἱ πολλοί, οὕτως καὶ διὰ τῆς ὑπακοῆς τοῦ ἑνὸς δίκαιοι κατασταθήσονται οἱ πολλοί ("For just as through the disobedience of one man the many were made sinners, so also through the obedience of one will the many be made righteous"). The statement begins with the postpositive conjunction γάρ, which in this case is used both to signal continuation and to offer an explanation of the first statement in 5:18. It uses the comparative expressions ὥσπερ ("just as," "as") in the *protasis* and οὕτως καί ("even so") in the *apodosis*. More significantly, Paul here defines (1) "the one trespass" of 5:18 as τῆς παρακοῆς τοῦ ἑνὸς ἀνθρώπου ("the disobedience of one man [i.e., Adam])" and (2) "the one act of righteousness" in 5:18 as τῆς ὑπακοῆς τοῦ ἑνός ("the obedience of one [i.e., Jesus Christ]"). Further, reversing the parallels between the two verses, (1) he twice uses οἱ πολλοί ("the many") in 5:19 as being equivalent to the two appearances of the noun πάντας ("all") in 5:18; (2) he associates "sinners" (ἁμαρτωλοί) in 5:19 with "condemnation" (κατάκριμα) in 5:18; and (3) he identifies "having been made righteous" (δίκαιοι κατασταθήσονται) in 5:19 with "righteousness of life" (δικαίωσιν ζωῆς) in 5:18.

52. The future tense of ἀποβήσεται in the *apodosis* of 5:18 would thereby parallel the future tense of κατασταθήσονται in the *apodosis* of 5:19, as well as correspond to the aorist subjunctive mood of βασιλεύσῃ in the *apodosis* of 5:21.

"The climax in the paragraph," as Joseph Fitzmyer has rightly observed, is in the *apodosis* of 5:19: "through the obedience of one (τῆς ὑπακοῆς τοῦ ἑνός) will the many be made righteous (δίκαιοι κατασταθήσονται οἱ πολλοί)."[53] "The obedience of Jesus" is at the heart of the early church's "Christ hymn," which Paul quotes in Phil 2:6-11 and uses as the basis for his exhortations to his converts at Philippi — focusing on the statement of 2:8: γενόμενος ὑπήκοος μέχρι θανάτου ("he became obedient even to the extent of death").

We have earlier argued (1) that in 3:22, which lies at the heart of his repeated thesis statement of 3:21-23, Paul both explicated and developed the rather cryptic expression ἐκ πίστεως εἰς πίστιν, which he used earlier in 1:17 in his original thesis statement of 1:16-17, and (2) that in so doing he proclaimed the highly important point that God's gift of righteousness in this period of the eschatological "now" has been brought about "through the faithfulness of Jesus Christ."[54] It is the theme of "the obedience of one [i.e., Jesus Christ]" that here in 5:19 functions as the focal point of Paul's conclusion to his reflective discourse on the stories of Adam and of Jesus Christ in 5:12-21. Thus the theme of "the obedience of Jesus" should be viewed as a cognate theme to Paul's references to "the faithfulness of Jesus" — and so, in concert, be understood as expressing a fundamental Christological conviction not only of Paul but also of the earliest believers in Jesus.[55]

IV. Addendum on "Law," "Sin," and "Death" as Countered by "God's Grace" at Work "through Jesus Christ Our Lord" (5:20-21)

5:20-21 Following Paul's conclusion of 5:18-19, the final two verses of the passage constitute an addendum that not only nicely summarizes what has gone before in 5:12-19 but also anticipates what will be expressed more fully about these matters and their relations in 6:1–8:39. Along with the personifications of "sin" (ἡ ἁμαρτία) and "death" (ὁ θάνατος) in 5:12 (and in 5:21), Paul here in 5:20 personifies the Mosaic law (νόμος, which hardly ever needs the article either to identify it or personify it). These are the actors that have "strutted their stuff" on the stage of human history in opposition to God and his will — though, of course, Paul qualifies his attitude toward the Mosaic law vis-à-vis sin later in 7:7-12 (just as he had earlier qualified his attitude toward the Mosaic law vis-à-vis God's promises and righteousness in Gal 3:21-24). But while Paul can call the law "holy, righteous and good" in its function of pointing out sin, as he does in Rom 7:12 — and even appreciate in retrospect the conflicts that it brings about

---

53. Fitzmyer, *Romans*, 421, quoting Michel, *An die Römer*, 191: "His whole life was determined by this obedience, and this obedience has won lawful and theological significance for the humanity of the eschatological period" (Fitzmyer's translation).

54. See our "Exegetical Comments" above on 3:21-23 (also on 3:24-26).

55. Cf. R. N. Longenecker, "The Foundational Conviction of New Testament Christology," 122-44.

in a person's life in exercising its proper function of exposing sin as the awful reality that it really is, as in Rom 7:13-25 — here in 5:20 he speaks of the Mosaic law as having "slipped in" (παρεισῆλθεν).

The only other use of this verb in the NT is Paul's derogatory use of it in Gal 2:4-5 with respect to "some false brothers who had infiltrated" the company of true believers in Jesus at Jerusalem and "to whom we did not give in for a moment." It also appears in Greek literature and in the Jewish writings of Second Temple Judaism as denoting illegitimate or objectionable entry into an area in which someone or something didn't belong.[56] The apostle, however, probably used παρεισῆλθεν here in 5:20 in the sense of "it was added" — that is, that "it came in as a side issue" and so "has no primary place in the Divine Plan."[57] For while in Gal 2:4-5 he denounced "the false brothers" who were seeking "to make slaves" of people and pervert "the truth of the gospel," Paul never in his letters equated their actions with the true intent of the Mosaic law — and so a somewhat different nuance must be attributed to the verb's use in Rom 5:20 vis-à-vis its earlier appearance in Gal 2:4.

Thus in this addendum of two verses, Paul declares that while God's "strange work" of exposing sin through the law continues — with people even increasing their sin in opposition to God, often using their increased knowledge of sin to go on sinning even more — God's "proper work" of "grace" has "increased all the more." And he concludes his reflective discourse of 5:12-21 with the proclamation that resides at the very heart of the Christian message of "good news," which proclamation is incorporated into the structural pattern of "just as" (ὥσπερ) . . . "so also" (οὕτως καί) that dominates the whole passage: "Just as sin reigned in death, so also [God has provided that] grace might reign through righteousness unto eternal life through Jesus Christ our Lord."

BIBLICAL THEOLOGY

Scholarly study of the NT has been enriched by (1) the explicit recognition that underlying the propositional statements of the NT letters are certain foundational "narratives" or "stories," whether one central story, used somewhat differently on different occasions for differing purposes, or multiple narratives or stories, which possessed something of a common "sense of center" even though they were expressed at times somewhat differently; (2) a lively realization that these foundational stories were generative for early Christian theologizing, proclamation, and counseling, and therefore that they undergird all that the NT writers of letters wrote; and (3) a developed consciousness that the NT writ-

56. Cf. Polybius, *Histories* 2.55.3: "He slipped inside these walls secretly at night"; see also 1.7.3; 1.8.4; 3.18.11; Plutarch, *De genio Socratis* 596a; *Marcius Coriolanus* 23.1; *Publicola* 17.2; *De sollertia animalium* 980b; Lucian of Samosata, *Call* 28; *Dial* 12.3; also Philo, *De Abrahamo* 96; and *T Jud* 16·2

57. Quoting *BAG*, 630, col. 1; cf. Gal 3:19: "It was added because of transgressions."

ers were actually building on, arguing from, and using for their own purposes this substratum of narrative material. So to understand more fully what the NT writers are saying in their respective letters, one needs some appreciation for how their various statements function to "tease out" (or, as in some cases, "disentangle"), interpret (or "reinterpret"), and apply the principal features of that basic narrative material.

Such a narrative approach is, of course, not new to biblical study. It has often been used with respect to the historical materials of the OT, that is, (1) the patriarchal narratives of Gen 12–50, (2) the accounts of the exodus and the wilderness experience of Israel in Exod 1–40, (3) the histories of the fledgling nation of Israel from the conquest of Canaan through to the fall of Jerusalem in Joshua through 2 Chronicles, and (4) the stories of the people's return from Babylonian captivity in the records of Ezra and Nehemiah — with these narratives or stories underlying all the prophetic and proverbial statements of the OT and providing the backdrop for the psalmists' praise to God. Likewise, Christians have always viewed as foundational to their faith (1) the portrayals of Jesus' ministry in the Gospels and (2) the accounts of the ministries of Peter and Paul in the Acts of the Apostles, with most of the rest of the NT writings being based, in some manner, on the events presented in the canonical Gospels and Acts. "For the most part, however," as Bruce Longenecker has rightly pointed out, "the Pauline corpus has been relatively immune from narrative study for obvious reasons: Paul wrote letters, not narratives."[58]

However, in the early 1980s the letters of the NT began to be studied as also encapsulating and reflecting an underlying narrative or set of stories, which was known not only to the various authors of the NT letters but presumably also, at least to some extent, to their respective addressees. Much of the impetus for the narrative analysis of NT letters must be credited to Richard Hays in his 1983 publication *The Faith of Jesus Christ,* with its revealing subtitle, *An Investigation of the Narrative Substructure of Galatians 3:1–4:11.*[59] While Hays may be criticized for finding, at times, more "allusions" to Jesus' life in the letters of Paul than the evidence may warrant — and while some scholars may put too much of their own "spin" on Israel's story, and so fail to do justice to the degree that Paul moves beyond the story of Israel to the broader story of the situation and hopes of all humanity — a narrative approach to his discourse in Rom 5:12-21 on the two primal persons of human history is a fruitful one, rightly recognizing the extent to which Paul operates within the story-centered worldviews of his day.

Recalling the major points that Paul has made in 5:12-21, the following matters need always to be included in any truly Christian biblical theology:

1. The "dark side" of every person's life has to do with "sin," "death," and being under "divine condemnation." These are the mocking specters that

58. B. W. Longenecker, *Narrative Dynamics in Paul,* 3.
59. (1983; 2nd ed. 2001).

permeate every facet of human experience and invade every corner of human consciousness. They are, in fact, the major factors that constitute the basic components of the universal "human predicament" — and so in his proclamation of the Christian gospel to pagan Gentiles in the Greco-Roman world, Paul struck a responsive chord in the hearts and minds of many of his spiritually sensitive hearers.

2. At the heart of the Christian gospel are such vitally important matters as "God's grace," "righteousness as a gift from God," Jesus' "one principal act of righteousness" (i.e., his death on the cross), and the provisions of "life," "righteousness of life," and "eternal life" that are offered to all people. Ignore or minimize these central features of the Christian proclamation, and one has "no gospel," that is, no "good news," at all, but only moral platitudes or psychological analyses of the human situation.

3. The focal point of Paul's proclamation in this period of the eschatological "now" is on "the obedience" of Jesus Christ, as he declared in 5:19 of his conclusion to his whole presentation of 5:12-21; this emphasis lies at the heart of the "Christ hymn" that he quotes in Phil 2:6-11. It also appears in cognate forms in Romans in both the development of his teaching on "the faithfulness" of Jesus Christ[60] and his use of the titles "Son" and "Son of God."[61]

4. The law (whether a so-called natural law or the Mosaic law) has no part in bringing about "life," "righteousness of life," or "eternal life" — other than revealing sin, and so, because of people's perverted response to God in their increased knowledge of sin, actually increasing sin.

5. The universalism of God's grace, which has been made effective "through Jesus Christ our Lord," has to do with what God has provided on behalf of all people. It does not, however, as seen in the future tense ("will be") of the verbs (both expressed and implied) in 5:18-19 and the subjunctive mood ("may" or "might") of the verb in 5:21, assure inevitability, but rather speaks of what God has graciously provided, to which people need to respond positively.

These are doctrinal matters that need always to be included in any truly Christian biblical theology and proclamation. But there are also the important themes of "how much more" and of "how grace has increased all the more" in 5:12-21. These are highly significant themes that declare how much more God has done "through Jesus Christ our Lord" in contradistinction to (1) what Adam brought about in human history and (2) the continued reign of sin in the world. They are themes of triumph, victory, and joy that also characterized Paul's Christian contextualized message — and that need, as well, to be incorporated into the theology and proclamation of believers in Jesus today (though without any extraneous expressions of "triumphalism" or "superiority").

60. Cf. esp. 1:1/; 3.22 and 25-26
61. Cf. 1:3-4, 9; 5:10; 8:3, 29, 32.

CONTEXTUALIZATION FOR TODAY

Paul's reflective discourse on the two primal persons in human history, highlighting what Jesus Christ effected vis-à-vis what Adam had brought about in human history, may seem rather familiar to the great majority of Christians today. Its familiarity is largely because of the intensive study the passage has received from biblical scholars and theologians down through the centuries, with special attention focused on the nature and results of Adam's sin, and its rather common use in the church and in society today, whether as a truth of Scripture or as some ancient tradition that has unfortunately been carried over to our modern culture. Our proposal, however, is that when Paul used this material in his outreach to pagan Gentiles in the Greco-Roman world, he was "breaking new ground" — not, of course, by inventing a new story for either the first man Adam or the far more important man Jesus, but by bringing the OT story of Adam and the apostolic story about Jesus together in a comparative and universalistic fashion.

In effect, in his mission to Gentiles Paul set aside the exodus story of redemption, which had been employed extensively within the Jewish world and among the Jewish believers in Jesus of his day, using instead this new form of foundational redemptive narrative. In so doing, he "contextualized" the message of the Christian gospel in a manner that may have seemed to some a bit novel — and which some believers in Jesus at Rome may have viewed as unacceptable because it was not traditional. Paul himself, however, evidently considered such a presentation, which set out matters of sin and salvation in much more universal terms than did the story of the Jewish exodus from Egypt, not only better suited to the understanding and appreciation of pagan Gentiles but also truer to the thrust of God's salvation history as portrayed in the OT narrative about Adam and in the apostolic proclamation about Jesus of Nazareth.

Many Christians are fearful of anything having to do with developments of doctrine, with variations in ecclesiastical practice, and/or with differences of ethical behavior — usually without realizing how much such development has gone on before them and how much they are themselves the products of those developments. But the Scriptures, both OT and NT, evidence a number of developments of theological thought, of ecclesiastical practice, and of ethical behavior, and church history is a record of a great many such developments as well. The question is not whether developments of thought and practice have taken place — nor whether such developments should take place. The real question for Christians today is this: Are the developments that are proposed — whether individually or as a body of doctrine or practice — in line with what is presented and what is anticipated in our revelational base, that is, in the OT and the NT?[62]

62. For my own treatments of development in Paul's thought and letters, see R. N. Longenecker, "On the Concept of Development in Pauline Thought," in *Perspectives on Evangelical Theology,* ed. K. S. Kantzer and S. N. Gundry (Grand Rapids: Baker, 1979), 195-207; *idem, New Testament*

Paul's presentation of the Christian gospel in terms of a universal and foundational story about what Jesus has done on behalf of all people vis-à-vis what Adam had brought about in human history has much to tell us about our own situation as humans and about "God's grace" at work on our behalf "through Jesus Christ our Lord." So it deserves careful exposition and heartfelt thanks in response. But Paul's contextualization of the Christian gospel in Rom 5:12-21 also provides a paradigm for how the Christian witness and contextualization of the gospel can take place in various contemporary situations. And under the guidance of God's Holy Spirit, as well as in continuity with the contents and thrust of Holy Scripture, we need to be constantly open in our day to similar contextualizations of the same Christian gospel, so as to be able to minister meaningfully to people in their specific situations and with their own particular understandings.

Much, of course, needs to be worked out with respect to these matters. At the beginning of all our attempts to proclaim the Christian message in our day, however, we need to be both challenged and informed by the paradigm that Paul sets out for us in Rom 5:12-21 with respect to doing something similar in the varied cultural context(s) within which we as Christians live and minister today.

Social Ethics for Today; idem, "Is There Development in Paul's Resurrection Thought?" in *Life in the Face of Death: The Resurrection Message of the New Testament,* ed. R. N. Longenecker, MNTS 3 (Grand Rapids: Eerdmans, 1998), 171-202; and *idem,* "A Developmental Hermeneutic," 22-36.

3. Three Important Questions, with an
Interjected Illustration and Statement (6:1–7:13)

Commentators have sometimes been at a loss to understand how Rom 6 and 7 — and particularly the materials of 6:1–7:13 — are related to the presentations of Rom 5 and 8. Nils Dahl stated the matter concisely: "The problems raised and discussed in chapters 6 and 7 cause some difficulties for analysis since they are not directly related to the main positive argument set forth in chapters 5 and 8."[1] Earlier in his writings Dahl had spoken of 6:1–7:6 and 7:7-25 as "two digressions" in Paul's argument,[2] building on remarks by Joachim Jeremias, Jacques Dupont, and Bent Noack.[3] Other commentators have also viewed much of this material as something of a "digression" or "excursus" in Paul's line of argumentation.[4]

Most interpreters of Romans today, however, while acknowledging that what Paul writes in chs. 6 and 7 is somewhat parenthetical to the main points of his argument in chs. 5 and 8, are prepared to speak, as did Nils Dahl in his later writings, of "the units introduced by the questions in 6:1, 6:15, 7:1 and 7:13 as refutations of objections against Paul's doctrine and thus as integral parts of his argument"[5] — or, at least, as ad hoc answers to questions that Paul viewed as possibly arising from his previous presentations, but without any clear structures or logical connections except as delineated by their respective rhetorical questions. It is this understanding of 6:1–7:13 that will, in the main, be expressed in our exegetical comments below.

Further, commentators have been divided on how to structure their comments about the materials contained in Rom 6 and 7. Some have organized their treatments in terms of the indicative statements Paul gives about what God has brought about through the work of Jesus and what believers in Jesus have experienced vis-à-vis the imperative exhortations he gives to Christians to experience all that God has provided on their behalf.[6] Others have treated the material in terms of the rhetorical questions asked in 6:1, 6:15a, 7:1, 7:7a, and 7:13a.[7] It is this latter way of structuring 6:1–7:13 that will be set out in

---

1. Dahl, "Missionary Theology," 83.

2. Cf. Dahl, "Two Notes on Romans 5," 5, 41 n. 22.

3. See Jeremias, "Zur Gedankenführung in den paulinischen Briefen," 146-54; Dupont, "Le problème de la structure littéraire de l'Épître aux Romains," 365-97; Noack, "Current and Backwater in the Epistle to the Romans," 155-66.

4. See, e.g., Schmithals, *Römerbrief,* 18-21, who viewed all of 6:1–7:16 as an excursus, and Byrne, "Living Out the Righteousness of God," 562-63, who understands all of 6:1–8:13 as an extended "ethical excursus."

5. Dahl, "Missionary Theology," 83.

6. So, e.g., M.-J. Lagrange (1916), J. Huby (1940), O. Kuss (1957), J. Murray (1959), M. Black (1973), E. Käsemann (1980), J. D. G. Dunn (1988), and J. A. Fitzmyer (1993).

7. So, e.g., A. Nygren (1949), C. K. Barrett (1957), F. J. Leenhardt (1961), C. E. B. Cranfield

our exegetical comments that follow. We will treat (1) the three questions of 6:1, 6:15a, and 7:7a (all of which begin with the deliberative question τί οὖν ἐροῦμεν; "What then shall we say?")[8] as introducing the major presentations of the passage, (2) the question of 7:1a (which is expressed somewhat differently) as introducing an interjected illustration and statement on matters pertaining to the Mosaic law and Christian freedom, and (3) the question of 7:13a (which is also expressed somewhat differently than the three questions of 6:1, 6:15a, and 7:7a) as introducing an extension of the question of 7:7a and a final comment on the issues dealt with in 7:7-13.

Our treatment of 6:1–7:13, therefore, will be in terms of the three major questions that Paul asks in 6:1, 6:15a, and 7:7a — together with his interjected illustration and statement of 7:1-6.

1. Question One: "Should we continue in sin so that grace might increase?" in 6:1-14.
2. Question Two: "Should we sin because we are not under the law but under grace?" in 6:15-23.
3. An interjected illustration on the extent of the authority of the Mosaic law and a statement regarding a Christian's freedom from the law in 7:1-6.
4. Question Three: "Is the law sin?" in 7:7-13.

We will also take into account the three epistolary "disclosure formulas" in this section of the letter, that is, at 6:3 (ἀγνοεῖτε ὅτι; "Do you not know that . . . ?"), at 6:16 (οὐκ οἴδατε ὅτι; "Do you not know that . . . ?"), and at 7:1 (ἀγνοεῖτε; "Do you not know . . . ?"). Such conventional epistolary formulations appear frequently in Greek letters of Paul's day at the beginning of new sections or subsections, thereby identifying for readers where the authors intend a new section or subsection of material to begin. That is how they function in Paul's letters generally and in his letter to the Christians at Rome in particular.[9]

(1975), U. Wilckens (1978), P. J. Achtemeier (1985), B. Byrne (1996), D. J. Moo (1996), and R. Jewett (2007).

8. The question of 6:15 is expressed as τί οὖν; ("What then?"). This is, however, only an elliptical form of τί οὖν ἐροῦμεν; ("What then shall we say?"), which appears in 6:1 and 7:7.

9. For other epistolary "disclosure formulas" in the body middle of Romans (i.e., in addition to those in 6:3, 16, and 7:1), see 7:14; 8:22, 28; 11:25.

QUESTION ONE: "SHOULD WE CONTINUE IN SIN SO THAT GRACE MIGHT INCREASE? (6:1-14)

TRANSLATION

⁶:¹*What, then, shall we say? Should we continue in sin so that grace might increase?* ²*Certainly not! Since we died to sin, how can we still live in it?*

³*Do you not know that all of us who were baptized into Christ Jesus were baptized into his death?* ⁴*We were therefore buried with him through baptism into death in order that, just as Christ was raised from the dead through the glory of the Father, so also we might live a new life.* ⁵*For if we have been united with him like this in his death, we will also certainly be united with him in his resurrection.* ⁶*This we know because our old self was crucified with him so that the body of sin might be done away with, that we should no longer be slaves to sin —* ⁷*for anyone who has died has been freed from sin.*

⁸*Now if we died with Christ, we believe that we will also live with him.* ⁹*For we know that since Christ was raised from the dead, he cannot die again; death no longer has mastery over him.* ¹⁰*The death he died, he died to sin once for all; but the life he lives, he lives to God.* ¹¹*So also consider yourselves to be dead indeed to sin but alive to God in Christ Jesus.*

¹²*Therefore do not let sin reign in your mortal body so that you obey its evil desires.* ¹³*Do not offer the parts of your body to sin, as instruments of wickedness, but rather offer yourselves to God, as those who have been brought from death to life; and offer the parts of your body to him as instruments of righteousness.* ¹⁴*For sin shall not be your master, because you are not under the law but under grace.*

TEXTUAL NOTES

6:1 The present subjunctive verb ἐπιμένωμεν ("should we remain," "persist," or "continue") is strongly attested by uncials A B C D F G Ψ (also *Byz* L) and by minuscules 33 (Category I), 81 1506 (Category II), and 104 326 424ᶜ 630 1241 1735 1874 (Category III); it is, as well, reflected in copˢᵃ ᵇᵒ and supported by Ambrosiaster. It is changed, however, to the present indicative ἐπιμένομεν ("we remain" or "continue") in uncials ℵ P 0221ᵛⁱᵈ (also *Byz* K) and in minuscules 1175 1739 (Category I), 1881 2464 (Category II), and 6 330 365 1243 1319 1573 1874 (Category III), and is reflected in copᵇᵒ ᵐˢ and Tertullian. Further, in a few textual witnesses it is changed to the future indicative ἐπιμένουμεν ("we shall remain" or "continue"), as appears in minuscules 69 323 614 1505 2495 614 945 2495 (Category III) and as reflected in itᵐˢˢ. The present indicative may be due to the interchange of the Greek letters omicron (ο) and omega (ω), as has often been proposed for the verb in 5:1; the future indicative gives much the same sense as the present subjunctive in 6:2.

2 The future indicative verb ζήσομεν ("we will/can live") in the clause "how will/

can we still live in it [sin]?" has strong external support, being attested by uncials ℵ A B D P 0221 (also *Byz* K) and by minuscules 1175 1739 (Category I), 1881 (Category II), and 6 69 323 424^c 614 1241 1319 1505 1573 2495 (Category III); it is reflected, as well, in the majority of the Latin MSS. The aorist subjunctive ζήσωμεν ("we should live"), however, appears in P^46, uncials C F G Ψ (also *Byz* L), and minuscules 33 (Category I), 81 2464 (Category II), and 1241 (Category III). The aorist subjunctive verb is possibly due either (1) to an unconscious exchange of the Greek letters omicron (o) and omega (ω) or (2) to a conscious desire to conform to the subjunctive verb ἐπιμένωμεν ("let us remain") in 6:1 (or, perhaps, to both).

4a The postpositive particle οὖν ("therefore") is strongly supported by uncials ℵ A B C D F G P Ψ 0221 and by minuscules 33 1175 1739 (Category I), 81 256 1881 1962 2127 2464 (Category II), and 6 104 (Category III). It thus connects v. 4 to v. 3 and provides a reason for what is said in v. 3. Some scribes evidently were uncertain about the appropriateness of οὖν ("therefore") and so substituted γάρ ("for"), as appears in minuscule 1506^vid (Category II) and is reflected in it^ar, b, mon, o, r vg and Origen^gr, lat4/8 Jerome^1/3 Augustine^4/15. A few textual witnesses, however, omit any connective whatsoever, as do syr^p cop^bo ms arm geo and Origen^lat4/8 Jerome^2/3 Augustine^3/15.

4b The phrase διὰ τῆς δόξης τοῦ πατρός ("through the glory of the Father") is widely attested in the textual history of the passage. It was omitted, however, by Irenaeus^lat and Tertullian. It was probably omitted because the phrase does not appear elsewhere in Paul's letters in association with his resurrection statements.

5 The connecting particles ἀλλὰ καί ("but also," "but also . . . certainly") are extremely well supported in the textual tradition. The variant expression ἅμα καί ("at the same time"), which appears in ninth-century uncials F and G, is probably a result of certain scribes misreading the uncial letters, as Kurt and Barbara Aland have suggested.[10]

6 Codex Vaticanus (B 03) adds καί ("and") at the start of the sentence before τοῦτο ("this"), evidently for stylistic reasons. The addition of the conjunction, however, is not supported elsewhere in the textual tradition.

8a The particle δέ ("but") at the start of the verse is attested by uncials ℵ A B C D Ψ and minuscules 1175 1739 (Category I), 81 256 962 2127 2464 (Category II), and 6 104 181 (Category III). The variant reading γάρ ("for") appears in P^46 and uncials F G, and is reflected in it^ar, o vg^mss syr^p, evidently in an endeavor to match the wording of v. 7.

8b The future indicative verb συζήσομεν ("we will live") is widely attested in the textual tradition. The subjunctive verb συζήσωμεν ("we might/should live"), however, is supported by uncials C K P and by minuscules 2464 (Category II) and 104 326 330 614 1735 1874 (Category III). Probably the use of the subjunctive συζήσωμεν was meant to bring this verse into line with the variant subjunctive ζήσωμεν ("we might/should live") in 6:2.

8c The dative αὐτῷ ("in him") is well attested in the textual tradition. The variant reading τῷ Χριστῷ ("in the Christ" or "in Christ"), however, appears in uncials D* F G and is reflected in vg^st and sy^p. The variant is probably an attempt to be more specific, but is not sufficiently supported by the MSS to warrant serious consideration.

---

10. Aland and Aland, *Text of the New Testament*, 283.

11a The presence of the present infinitive εἶναι ("to be"), as well as its placement after the reflexive pronoun ἑαυτούς ("yourselves"), is strongly supported by P⁹⁴⁽ᵛⁱᵈ⁾, uncials ℵ* B C, and minuscules 1739 (Category I), 81 104 1506 1881 (Category II), and 365 1319 1573 (Category III). Its inclusion, though after νεκροὺς μέν ("dead indeed"), is supported by uncials ℵ² D¹ P Ψ (also *Byz* K L) and by minuscules 1175 (Category I), 2464 (Category II), and 6 69 88 323 326 330 424ᶜ 614 1241 1243 1505 1735 1874 2495 (Category III). This present infinitive, however, is entirely omitted by P⁴⁶⁽ᵛⁱᵈ⁾, by uncials A D* F G, by minuscules 33ᵛⁱᵈ 2344, and by Tertullian. The presence of the infinitive εἶναι is not absolutely necessary, and its absence may produce a smoother reading. Though its omission is supported by some very good textual evidence, the better textual support is in favor of its retention and of its positioning after the reflexive pronoun ἑαυτούς ("yourselves").

11b The phrase ἐν Χριστῷ Ἰησοῦ ("in Christ Jesus") is the final feature of v. 11 in P⁴⁶, in uncials A B D F G, and in minuscules 1739 (Category I) and 2200 (Category III); it is also reflected in itᵃʳ, ᵇ, ᵈ, ᶠ, ᵍ, ᵐᵒⁿ, ᵒ vgʷʷ, ˢᵗ syrʰ copˢᵃ and supported by Origenᵍʳ, ˡᵃᵗˡ/¹¹ Theodoret and Tertullian¹/². The additional phrase τῷ κυρίῳ ἡμῶν ("our Lord") appears in P⁹⁴ ᵛⁱᵈ, in uncials ℵ C P (also *Byz* K L), and in minuscules 33 1175 1739 (Category I), 81 256 1506 1881 1962 2464 (Category II), and 6 104 [omitting Ἰησοῦ] 459 [also omitting Ἰησοῦ] 263 365 424ᶜ 436 1241 1319 1573 1908 1912 1942 1959 2110 2127 2138 2464 (Category III); it is also reflected in vgᶜˡ, syrᵖ, ᵖᵃˡ, copᵇᵒ and supported by Origenˡᵃᵗˡ/¹¹ Chrysostom Ambrosiaster. A few early Latin witnesses, however, omit ἐν Χριστῷ Ἰησοῦ, such as itʳ Irenaeusˡᵃᵗ Origenˡᵃᵗ⁹/¹¹. The words τῷ κυρίῳ ἡμῶν were probably drawn from a liturgical expression that was in turn derived from 6:23. For as Bruce Metzger has pointed out: "If they were original, no good reason can be found why they should have been deleted from such weighty witnesses [as those cited above]."[11]

12 The phrase ταῖς ἐπιθυμίαις αὐτοῦ ("its desires") is strongly supported by P⁹⁴, by uncials ℵ A B C*, and by minuscules 1739 (Category I), 81 256 1506 1881 1962 2127 (Category II), and 6 263 365 424ᶜ 436 1319 1573 1852 2200 (Category III); it is also reflected in itᵃʳ, ᵈ², ᵐᵒⁿ, ʳ vg syrᵖ copˢᵃ, ᵇᵒ and supported by Origen⁽ᵍʳ⁾, ˡᵃᵗ⁶/⁷ Ambrosiaster Pelagius Augustine. It is, however, replaced by the simple pronoun αὐτῇ ("it") in several textual witnesses, as in P⁴⁶ and such Western witnesses as uncials D F G, versions itᵇ, ᵈ*, ᶠ, ᵍ, ᵒ, and Irenaeusˡᵃᵗ Origenˡᵃᵗˡ/⁷ Tertullian Ambrosiaster — "probably," as Bruce Metzger suggests, "under the influence of the repeated mention of ἁμαρτία in the following verses."[12] The TR, following uncials C³ P Ψ (also, of course, *Byz* K L) and minuscules 33 1912 104 459 1175 1241 2464, and supported by Chrysostom, conflates the two readings to read αὐτῃ ἐν ταῖς ἐπιθυμίαις αὐτοῦ ("in it in its evil desires").

13 The accusative plural present participle ζῶντας ("those brought alive") is widely attested by the textual evidence. The nominative form ζῶντες appears in P⁴⁶ and in uncials D* F G, but lacks sufficient support elsewhere in the textual evidence to be considered original.

---

11. Metzger, *Textual Commentary,* 454.
12. *Ibid.*

FORM/STRUCTURE/SETTING

Paul raises three questions in 6:1–7:13 with respect to what he earlier presented in 5:1-11 (i.e., his "transitional and thesis material," which stands over all he presents in chs. 5–8) and 5:12-21 (i.e., his "universal and foundational story" regarding the two primal persons in human history); both earlier subsections were focused on the overwhelming greatness of God's grace as expressed through the ministry of Jesus Christ vis-à-vis human sin, universal death, and any supposed redemptive powers of the Mosaic law. The questions need not have been raised by some "external objector" or "postulated questioner" during Paul's past missionary activities — nor need they have been asked, as has often been argued, by some "imaginary interlocutor" inserted into a diatribe form of argumentation that the apostle is supposedly using. Rather, they are best understood in terms of an internal debate that Paul knew could very well arise from what he had written in 5:1-11 and 5:12-21 about the greatness of God's grace as expressed "through Jesus Christ our Lord." As Frédéric Godet long ago said in his treatment of the four rhetorical questions of 3:1-8 — which comments, as well, have relevance for the questions here in 6:1–7:13:

> There is no need of expressly introducing an opponent, as many commentators have done. Paul does not here make use of the formula: *But some one will say.* The objections arise of themselves from the affirmations, and Paul puts them in a manner to his own account.[13]

The major theological issue that comes dramatically to the fore in 6:1-14 is how to resolve the tension in Paul's statements between (1) the "already" or "realized" dimension of the Christian gospel and (2) the "not yet" or "futuristic" factors that still exist in every Christian's experience. Christiaan Beker has ably stated the problem as follows:

> Paul seems caught in an insoluble problem. How can he as a Christian-apocalyptic theologian interpret the death and resurrection of Christ as "the already" of God's new age and yet leave room for the "not yet"? How can he allow for an "interim time," in which the "already" and "not yet" are not fused, when his logic seems to compel their necessary conflation? For if sin and death *have been* overcome in Christ's death and resurrection, spiritual tension must yield to the spiritual bliss of the *beati possidentes* ("blessed possessors"), with their conviction, "we have arrived, because the powers

13. Godet, *Romans,* 1.220; see also J. Denney on 6:1: "The question was one sure to be asked by someone; Paul recognizes it as a natural question in view of his doctrine, and asks it himself" (Denney, *Romans,* in EGT 2.632). On Paul's use of diatribe styling in 2:1-5 and 2:17-24 (as well as later in 9:19-21 and 11:17-24), but not in 3:1-8 — and for suggested literary criteria for making such distinctions — see our comments in the "Form/Structure/Setting" section that precedes our "Exegetical Comments" on 3:1-8.

of sin and death *have been* overcome." Paul's Christological center seems to leave no other option but to drown his apocalyptic theology in a realized eschatology.[14]

Beker elaborates further on this problem in saying:

> In view of the twofold fact that Christ "died to *sin,* once for all" (Rom. 6:10) and that "*death* no longer has dominion over him" (Rom 6:9), the relation between the apocalyptic power of sin and the apocalyptic power of death becomes an urgent problem for the interpreter of Paul. Does Paul give us any guidelines for understanding the relation of sin to death? How does he account for death's continuing reign through suffering and cosmic evil in the historical existence of believers, if "the new creation" has come about in Christ's victory over sin and death? Moreover, does Paul believe that cosmic evil can be attributed to sin, or does he leave other possibilities open? And how is the eschatological destiny of the created order related to all this?[15]

EXEGETICAL COMMENTS

6:1-2 The three questions of 6:1; 6:15a; and 7:7a all begin with the same deliberative future expression τί οὖν ἐροῦμεν, "What then shall we say?" (with the second question, in 6:15a, stated elliptically as simply τί οὖν, "What then?"). Further, the first two questions of 6:1 and 6:15 include (in 6:3 and 6:16 respectively) rather traditional "disclosure formulas" (i.e., variations of the question "Do you not know?") — as does also the first verse of 7:1-6 — with these epistolary conventions of the day functioning to identify for the reader where new sections or subsections of a letter begin.

The present subjunctive verb ἐπιμένωμεν here in 6:1 carries with it the nuance of a present continuing action, and so is best translated "Should we continue ('remain' or 'persist') in sin?" The aorist subjunctive verb ἁμαρτήσωμεν used later in 6:15 suggests by its aorist tense a punctiliar (i.e., "point-type") action, and so is best translated "Should we sin?" Both questions amount to much the same thing, with the difference in the tense of the verbs evidently being only to drive home the question without needless redundancy.

Earlier in Rom 3:8 Paul had expressed his consciousness that some Christians (perhaps even some of the believers at Rome) were claiming that his preaching really boiled down to some such axiom as "Let us do evil that good might result." His response to this assertion is the briefest of his responses to the four matters dealt with in 3:1-8; he rebuts his accusers with the bombas-

---

14. Beker, *Paul the Apostle,* 213-14 (italics his).
15. *Ibid.,* 214 (italics his).

tic statement: "Their condemnation is deserved" (ὧν τὸ κρίμα ἔνδικόν ἐστιν). Here in 6:2, in contradistinction to any inference that might be drawn from his statements regarding "God's grace" vis-à-vis "sin" and "death" in human experience, Paul simply bursts out against any possible suggestion that believers in Jesus "should continue in sin so that grace might increase" with the emotionally charged and highly negative response μὴ γένοιτο (literally "Let it not be!" or, more colloquially expressed, "Certainly not!").[16]

The reason why those who are true believers in Jesus — that is, those who have truly experienced God's grace "through Jesus Christ our Lord" — cannot "continue in sin" is expressed concisely in the following statement: because they have "died to sin," and therefore they "cannot still live in it." One of the "special uses" of the relative pronoun ὅστις ("whoever," "everyone," "who") at the start of a relative clause is to signal cause, purpose, or result.[17] Thus the relative pronoun ὅστις with the first-person plural aorist indicative ἀπεθάνομεν ("we died") and the dative of advantage τῇ ἁμαρτίᾳ ("with respect to sin") is legitimately translated "*since* we died to sin." And the question that derives from that fact quite legitimately follows: "How can we still live in it [i.e., 'in sin']?"

6:3-4 In these two verses Paul highlights in rhetorical fashion a matter of great importance in the proclamation of the Christian gospel: all who have been baptized into Christ "were baptized into his death" "so that, just as Christ was raised from the dead through the glory of the Father, we too might live a new life." The particle ἤ ("or") occurs frequently in koine Greek either (1) to separate mutually exclusive opposites or (2) to relate similar terms or expressions, with the second term or expression supplementing the first — perhaps even taking the place of the first. And that is how it usually functions in the NT as well.

Yet the particle ἤ ("or") is also used in both secular and biblical Greek as an opening rhetorical feature in an interrogative sentence simply to highlight the question being asked — and so may be either translated or not, depending on how a translator or commentator understands the need for such a rhetorical device in his or her own receptor language.[18] Thus Paul's use of ἤ ("or") at the beginning of the question in 6:3, as well as at the beginning of the question in

---

16. On Paul's use of μὴ γένοιτο, see our discussion on 3:4. In addition to that earlier use in 3:4 and here in 6:2, see also Rom 3:6, 31; 6:15; 7:7, 13; 9:14; 11:1, 11; 1 Cor 6:15; Gal 2:17; 3:21 (perhaps also 6:14). The expression in an absolute sense appears in the NT almost exclusively in Paul's major missionary letters, being found elsewhere in the NT only once, in the response of "the people" reported in Luke 20:16. It also appears with other linguistic components in the writings of such Greek authors of the koine period as Aeschylus, Euripides, Herodotus, and Epictetus; likewise in the LXX.

17. Cf. *ATRob,* 960: "As in Latin, the relative clause may imply cause, purpose, result, concession, or condition, though the sentence itself does not say this much. This is due to the logical relation in the sentence. The sense glides from mere explanation to ground or reason. . . . This is clearly true in Ro. 6:2, οἵτινες ἀπεθάνομεν τῇ ἁμαρτίᾳ."

18. Cf., e.g., Matt 26:53, where Jesus' question to Judas at his betrayal begins in Greek with the particle ἤ ("or"), but is usually translated without it: "Do you think that I cannot call on my Father, and he will at once put at my disposal more than twelve legions of angels?"

7:1,[19] may or may not be thought necessary in a contemporary translation. We believe that in this particular context the translation of ἤ ("or") is not only unnecessary in English but also a bit cumbersome.

In explicating the reason why those who are true believers in Jesus cannot "continue in sin" — that is, because they have "died to sin" and so "cannot still live in it" — Paul highlights the newness of a Christian's life that has been brought about by God through the agency of Christian baptism. These statements of 6:3-4 constitute the principal discussion of Christian baptism in Paul's letters.[20]

Paul, of course, thought of himself as a Christian apostle and evangelist, whose ministry was to proclaim the Christian message and to bring people to the experience of faith in Christ. He did not, however, think of himself as a church official, whose ministry was confined to the local church and whose function included officiating at the Christian ordinances of baptism and the Lord's Supper. Thus he could write to his converts in the church at Corinth, who were attaching themselves to the names of one or another of the early Christian worthies, the following:

> I am thankful that I did not baptize any of you except Crispus and Gaius, so no one can say that you were baptized into my name. (Yes, I also baptized the household of Stephanas; beyond that, I don't remember if I baptized anyone else.) For Christ did not send me to baptize, but to preach the gospel. (1 Cor 1:14-17a)

But that does not mean that Paul disparaged in any way Christian baptism. Rather, as evidenced by his statements here in 6:3-4, he used Christian baptism as the basis for his exhortations to believers in Jesus to live a new life in Christ and as the primary illustration of what it means for one to live such a new life.

Although there are many references in the Jewish (OT) Scriptures to the purification of people and things by the use of water,[21] the baptism of a person in water as an initiatory religious rite is not spoken of at all in the OT. Some have argued that the origin of baptism as a religious rite stemmed from the ancient Near Eastern cults of Mithra (the Persian god of light) and Isis (the Egyptian goddess of nature, who was the wife and sister of Osiris).[22] But that thesis is thoroughly discounted today.[23]

---

19. In addition to the rhetorical ἤ ("or") at the beginning of the questions in 6:3 and 7:1, see also its use in Rom 3:29; 11:2; 1 Cor 6:9, 16, 19; 10:22; and 2 Cor 11:7.

20. See also the Pauline statements regarding baptism in 1 Cor 6:11; 10:1-2; 12:13; 2 Cor 1:22; Gal 3:27-28; Eph 1:13; 4:30; 5:14, 26; Col 2:11-12; and Titus 3:5.

21. Leviticus, e.g., is filled with exhortations regarding how ritually unclean things and people must be cleansed by the use of water (see not only Lev 17:15 and 22:6, but also whole sections in chs. 14–16). In a real sense, the flood portrayed in Gen 6–8 is depicted as God's ritual cleansing of his created earth.

22. Cf. Bousset, *Kyrios Christos*, 158-72 and 223-27; Reitzenstein, *Hellenistic Mystery-Religions*, 20-21, 40-42, 78-79, 85-86.

23. Cf. the extensive treatments of the subject by H. A. A. Kennedy, *St. Paul and the Mystery*

Jews of the first century A.D. constructed and used for religious purification purposes a rather large number of ritual baths (singular *miqveh;* plural *miqvoth*), as we now know from excavations at the southern end of the Temple Mount at Jerusalem and throughout southern Judea[24] — as did the Essene covenanters in their community northwest of the Dead Sea, as seen by the excavated remains of their system of ritual baths at Qumran. All these types of ritual washings evidently gave rise to the practice of "proselyte baptism" during the period of "early" or "formative Judaism," that is, of baptizing Gentiles who had converted to Judaism.[25] Likewise, John the Baptist is portrayed as calling people to a "baptism of repentance" and baptizing them in the Jordan River at some place near the city of Jericho (Matt 3:1-6; Mark 1:4-6; Luke 3:2-6; see also John 1:31). And Jesus was baptized by John in the river Jordan (Matt 3:13-17; Mark 1:9-11; Luke 3:21-22; see also John 1:29-34).

Much more investigation needs to be undertaken, and much more could be said, about Jewish ritual bathing and initiatory baptism. Suffice it here to point out that (1) the earliest Jewish believers in Jesus, in line with their understanding of Jewish purification rites and practices, were physically "baptized into Jesus Christ," (2) Paul drew his understanding of Christian baptism from his own Jewish background and from the early Christian tradition that existed before him, (3) Paul in his Gentile mission expected that his converts to Christ would be baptized (even though, as he says in 1 Cor 1:14-17 regarding his early experience at Corinth, he himself baptized only Crispus, Gaius, and "the household of Stephanas," who were presumably the first converts to Christ in that city), and (4) Paul left the performance of this Christian religious rite to others who had become leaders in the local congregations of the cities he evangelized.

Further, Jesus is recorded in Mark 10:38-39 and Luke 12:50 as referring to his approaching death as his "baptism," thereby bringing into association ideas of "baptism" and "death" — and, by extension, the correspondence of "resurrection" and "new life." Paul evidently picked up on this imagery in urging the Christians at Rome to view their Christian baptism as representing their union with Jesus in both his death and his resurrection — and therefore, just as death meant the end to Jesus' earthly life and resurrection meant the commencing of Jesus' new life, so these believers were to consider themselves dead to the sins of their past lives and alive to the transforming features of their new lives. Thus he declares to his Roman addressees: "We were buried with him through

---

Religions (1914); Wagner, *Pauline Baptism and the Pagan Mysteries;* and Wedderburn, *Baptism and Resurrection;* see also the briefer treatments by Wedderburn, "The Soteriology of the Mysteries and Pauline Baptismal Theology," 53-72, and Dunn, *Romans,* 1.308-11.

24. Cf. Avigad, "Jewish Ritual Baths," 139-43; E. Mazar and B. Mazar, *Excavations in the South of the Temple Mount* (Jerusalem: Institute of Archaeology, Hebrew University of Jerusalem, 1989).

25. On Jewish "proselyte baptism," see S. Zeitlin, "A Note on Baptism for Proselytes," *JBL* 52 (1933); G. Vermes, "Baptism and Jewish Exegesis: New Light from Ancient Sources," *NTS* 4 (1958) 309-19; T. F. Torrance, "Proselyte Baptism," *NTS* 1 (1954); *idem,* "The Origins of Baptism," *SJT* 11 (1958) 158-71; T. M. Taylor, "Beginnings of Jewish Proselyte Baptism," *NTS* 2 (1956).

baptism into death in order that, just as Christ was raised from the dead through the glory of the Father, so also we might live a new life."

6:5-7 Paul declares here: "For if we have been united with him like this in his death, we will also certainly be united with him in his resurrection. This we know because our old self was crucified with him so that the body of sin might be done away with, that we should no longer be slaves to sin — for anyone who has died has been freed from sin"). In so doing, the apostle speaks of "the great conundrum" of the Christian religion — that is, the most intricate and difficult problem of the Christian faith, which, on the face of it, seems to lack any real resolution. It is an apparent contradiction that resides at the very heart of the Christian proclamation: (1) that believers in Jesus *"have been united with him"* and *"crucified with him"* in Jesus' death, and so *"will also certainly be united* with him" in Jesus' coming again, and yet (2) that at the present time believers in Jesus live their lives in the hope, which has been given by God, *"that the body of sin will be done away with"* and *"that we should no longer be slaves to sin."*

Indeed, there is in the Christian gospel the proclamation of (1) God's grace as expressed "through Jesus Christ our Lord" on behalf of all people, (2) Jesus' dealing with sin and defeating death in his earthly ministry, and (3) people who trust in God and what he has provided through the person and work of Jesus being accepted as righteous before God. All this is part and parcel of the "good news" of the Christian message, which declares an end to the old human tensions relating to "sin," "death," and "condemnation," because of "peace with God," "righteousness," and "life" brought about through the person and work of Jesus Christ. Yet in coming to God "through Jesus Christ our Lord," believers in Jesus, while finding the disastrous effects of sin, death, and condemnation done away with — and therefore experiencing relief from the former fears and tensions of their "old life" — have come to experience a new tension in their lives, which has come about because they have become members of "the age to come" (αἰὼν μέλλον) while still living in "this age" (αἰὼν οὗτος). For in this time of the eschatological "now" of God's working, the experience of a believer in Jesus involves the dual features of (1) having become righteous by God's grace "through Jesus Christ our Lord," yet also awaiting "the hope of righteousness" (Gal 5:5); (2) having been raised to the new resurrection life, yet also awaiting being "united with him in his resurrection" (Rom 6:5); and (3) having been "crucified with Christ" and so "freed from sin," yet also needing to be urged to be no longer "slaves to sin" (Rom 6:6-7).

In the Christian proclamation, therefore, there exists a basic tension between "this age" and "the age to come" — that is, between the "already fulfilled" and the "not yet completed." It is an important aspect of the Christian message of which Martin Luther has said "no sophisters will admit, for they know not the true manner of justification."[26] Further, it is the tension that, as Oscar Cullmann has argued, "contains the key to the understanding of the entire New

---

26. M. Luther, *Galatians,* commenting on Gal 3:6.

Testament."[27] For while Judaism proclaimed that "this age" of sin, rebellion, and condemnation would come to an end, and following it would be "the age to come" when the Messiah would bring about a time of righteousness and God's blessings, the Christian gospel speaks of the overlapping of the two ages — with the result that believers in Jesus now live between "this age," with all its sin, death, and condemnation, and "the age to come," with its righteousness and blessings. So as members of both ages, Christians need always to be conscious of both (1) what they have "already" received and are by God's grace, and (2) what they have "not yet" experienced, but have been promised by God, and of what they will finally receive and be delivered from in the future.

6:8-11 In the first three verses of this paragraph, 6:8-10, Paul expands further on (1) the significance of Christ's death, (2) the significance of Christ's resurrection, and (3) the importance of these two factors in the Christian's life here and now in "this age" — that is, in "the present age" in which "the age to come" has been inaugurated by Jesus through his earthly ministry, death, and resurrection but has not yet been culminated, vis-à-vis the future "age to come" when sin and death will come to an end and God's promises will reign supreme. Then, in 6:11 Paul exhorts his addressees with "consider yourselves to be dead indeed to sin but alive to God in Christ Jesus."

The particle δέ ("but") at the start of 6:8 is amply attested in the textual tradition, in contradistinction to the variant reading γάρ ("for") that was evidently added to match the beginning of 6:7 (see "Textual Notes"). The particle δέ usually functions in koine Greek as a mild adversative. But it was also used at times in a correlative manner to resume a discourse, which is how it seems to function here — and so here it can be translated "now."

All the writers of the NT (including Paul) share this doctrine of "the two ages," which resides at the core of all their ethical thinking: that believers in Jesus presently live out their lives in the context of two ages, not one age — that is, that "the age to come," with its distinctive powers for righteous living, has been inaugurated by Jesus, even though "this age," with its negative powers, still exists and continually attempts to thwart the effects of that inaugurated new age.[28] The Christian life, according to Paul and the other writers of the NT, is lived between the polarities of "already" or "realized eschatology," on the one hand, and of "not yet" or "futuristic eschatology" on the other hand — and so within the context of both "this age" and "the age to come."

The old age has been judged and is passing away; the new age, however, while inaugurated, has not yet been fully brought about. The condemnation of sin has been dealt with and the compulsion of sin has been broken, but sin is still present to tempt and to frustrate. The tyranny of death has been crushed, but mortality and depravity remain. The dominion of the law is ended, but forms of legalism and humanity's perverted desire to gain in divine favor by one's own

---

27. Cullmann, *Christ and Time,* 199.
28. Cf. *ibid.,* esp. 47-48, 81-93, and 222-30.

efforts still exist. The supernatural antagonistic powers have been defeated and disarmed, but they are not yet destroyed and they continue to try to ambush God's own. Indeed, those who have been made righteous by God still await righteousness; those who have been identified as God's children still await their full reception as God's children; those who have been raised to newness of life still await resurrection; and those who have known Christ's first coming still await his future return.

It is this temporal tension between the "already" and the "not yet" that lies at the heart of the Christian gospel and that contains the key to a proper understanding of the ethical teaching of the NT. For it is in the midst of this overlapping of "the age to come," which has been inaugurated by Christ, and "this age," which has yet to be terminated, that believers in Jesus live out their lives and experience the powers of both ages. Thus Paul in 6:8-11 calls on his own converts in his Gentile mission, as well as on his Christian addressees at Rome, to be consciously aware of both (1) what God "through Jesus Christ our Lord" has effected for them and (2) how they should live as citizens of the inaugurated "age to come" in the midst of "this age."

Further, Paul emphasizes in 6:8-11 that believers in Jesus should live out their lives in the present relationship of being "in Christ Jesus" (ἐν Χριστῷ Ἰησοῦ), as he says at the end of 6:11 — with that present relationship of intimacy expressed in the context (1) of having died "with Christ" (σὺν Χριστῷ) in his death (as stated in the aorist tense) and (2) of having the firm conviction that we will also live "with him" (αὐτῷ) in his resurrection (as stated in the future tense), as he declares at the beginning of 6:8. We will say more about these matters when we discuss ἐν Χριστῷ Ἰησου and its cognate concepts in 8:1-17. Suffice it here to observe (1) that this phraseology of being ἐν Χριστῷ Ἰησου is fairly unique to Paul, not appearing in the Synoptic Gospels (though it can possibly be derived from certain teachings of Jesus in the Fourth Gospel regarding relationships between himself and God the Father, as well as about relationships between Jesus and his followers),[29] and (2) that Paul in his major missionary letters states this relationship in terms of a believer being ἐν Χριστῷ Ἰησοῦ[30] (not in terms of being "in Jesus" or even "in Jesus Christ"), thereby signaling an intimate relationship with the exalted and heavenly "Christ." However, this motif of being ἐν Χριστῷ Ἰησοῦ is expressed by Paul in his letters, either explicitly or implicitly, in the context of a "two-age" understanding of the Christian life that has to do with (1) a realization of the overlapping of "this age" and "the age to come," and (2) a consciousness that believers in Jesus in these days of the eschatological "now" live out their lives in a tension between the "already" (or "realized" dimension of the Christian gospel) and the "not yet" (or "futuristic" factor that still exists in every Christian's experience).

29. Cf. esp. John 6:56; 14:20; 15:4-7; 16:33; 17:21.

30. Cf. the earlier appearances of the phrase in Gal 3:26 and 28; see also Rom 6:23 and our discussion and extended excursus at Rom 8:1-2.

6:12-14 In the final three verses of this subsection, Paul exhorts believers in Jesus, because they have died with Christ to sin, to no longer allow sin to dominate their lives. Rather (ἀλλά), they are to live in response to God and what he has done in bringing them to himself. He exhorts them again, this time in quite functional terms, to understand the rationale of the Christian's new life in this present time of God's salvation history: "sin shall not be your master, because you are not under the law but under grace."

The expression "in your mortal body" (ἐν τῷ θνητῷ ὑμῶν σώματι) is Paul's way of referring to the state that exists for all Christians in this present time between the "already" and the "not yet"[31] — that is, in this time of the eschatological "now," with its overlapping of the inaugurated "age to come" and the end of "this age." Paul does not mean that Christians have become sinless or incapable of sinning because of their faith or because of their baptism. Believers in Jesus are still members of "this age," and so they are still able to be tempted by sin and can even be dominated by sin. Therefore, the apostle's exhortations to all believers in Jesus are these: "Do not let sin reign in your mortal body so that you obey its evil desires!" and "Do not allow sin to be your master!" — and he further insists that Christians must never try to justify their sinful actions on some such perverted pretexts as "We should continue in sin so that grace might increase" or "We are not under the law but under grace."

QUESTION TWO: "SHOULD WE SIN BECAUSE WE ARE NOT UNDER THE LAW BUT UNDER GRACE?" (6:15-23)

TRANSLATION

[6:15]*What then? Should we sin because we are not under the law but under grace? Certainly not!* [16]*Do you not know that when you offer yourselves to someone as obedient slaves, you are slaves to the one whom you obey — whether to sin, which leads to death, or to obedience, which leads to righteousness?* [17]*But thanks be to God that, though you used to be slaves to sin, you have obeyed from the heart the form ("type") of teaching to which you were entrusted ("handed over")*[18] *— and having been set free from sin, you have become slaves to righteousness.*

[19]*I put this in human terms because you are weak in your natural selves. Just as you used to offer the parts of your body as enslaved to impurity and to ever-*

---

31. Cf. Rom 8:11: "He [God] who raised Christ from the dead will also give life to your mortal bodies (τὰ θνητὰ σώματα ὑμῶν) through his Spirit, who lives in you"; see also 2 Cor 4:11: "We who are alive are always being given over to death for Jesus' sake, so that his life may be revealed in our mortal flesh (ἐν τῇ θνητῇ σαρκὶ ἡμῶν)."

increasing wickedness, so now offer them as enslaved to righteousness leading to holiness. [20]*When you were slaves to sin, you were free from the control of righteousness.* [21]*What benefit did you reap at that time from the things you are now ashamed of? Those things result in death!* [22]*But now that you have been set free from sin and have become slaves to God, the benefit you reap leads to holiness, and the result is eternal life.* [23]*For the wages of sin is death, but the gift of God is eternal life in Christ Jesus our Lord.*

TEXTUAL NOTES

6:15 The aorist subjunctive verb ἁμαρτήσωμεν (in the question "should we sin?") is very widely attested in the textual tradition. The future indicative ἁμαρτήσομεν ("shall we sin?), however, appears in minuscules 6 323 424[c] 614 629 630 1319 (all of which are Category III MS) and is reflected in vg[cl], but lacks sufficient external support to be classed as anything other than a secondary reading. The aorist indicative ἡμαρτήσαμεν ("we have sinned") is found in the ninth-century uncials F and G, reflected in a number of Latin translations, and supported by Ambrosiaster. But in all likelihood, this use of the aorist indicative verb is simply a scribal error.

16a The particle ἤ ("or") is added at the beginning of this verse by sixth-century Codex Beza (D* 06) and the ninth-century uncials F G, and is reflected in some Vulgate and Syriac versions, evidently in order to correspond with the use of the same Greek particle at the beginning of 6:3 and 7:1.

16b The phrase εἰς θάνατον ("unto death") is widely attested by uncials ℵ A B C G P Ψ (also *Byz* K L) and by minuscules 33 1175 1739[mg] (Category I), 81 1506 1881 1962 2127 2464 (Category II), and 6 69 104 181 323 326 330 365 424[c] 436 451 614 629 1241 1243 1319 1505 1573 1735 1846 1874 1877 2344 2492 2495 (Category III); it is also reflected in it[mss] vg[cl] syr[h, pal] cop[bo] and supported by Chrysostom Theodoret. It is, however, omitted by Codex Beza (D 06) and by minuscule 1739* (Category I), with that omission also reflected in it[d, e, r3] vg[ww] syr[p] cop[sa] arm and in Origen[lat] Ambrosiaster. Since the phrase seems to have been intended as a parallel to the phrase εἰς δικαιοσύνην ("unto righteousness") that follows, the omission of εἰς θάνατον ("unto death") in some textual witnesses is probably to be understood as an unintentional oversight.

17 Fifth-century Codex Alexandrinus (A 02) adds the adjective καθαράς ("pure") to the noun καρδίας ("heart"), but this seems to be an attempted moralistic improvement of the passage that is without support elsewhere in the textual tradition.

19 The two uses of the accusative plural neuter term δοῦλα ("enslaved") in the expressions "enslaved to impurity and to ever-increasing wickedness" and "enslaved to righteousness leading to holiness" are strongly supported in the textual tradition. The two variant uses of the infinitive δουλεύειν ("to be enslaved") in ninth-century uncials F and G, as well as in a number of Latin versions and sy[p], are too weakly supported by the textual tradition to be accepted, and so must be judged as attempted stylistic improvements.

21 After the explanatory conjunction γάρ ("for"), some MSS add the affirmative particle μέν ("indeed") and so read "for indeed." This addition is supported by the late-fifth- to early-sixth-century papyrus portion P^{94vid}, by uncials ℵ^2 A C D* F G, and by minuscules 1505 2495 (Category III); it is also reflected in sy^h. The absence of μέν, however, is better attested by its omission in uncials ℵ* B D^2 P Ψ (also *Byz* K L) and in minuscules 33 1175 1739 (Category I), 1506 1881 2464 (Category II), and 6 69 88 104 323 326 330 365 424^c 614 1241 1243 1319 1573 1735 1874 2344 (Category III). Evidently the addition was meant to highlight the antithesis in the text with the particle δέ that starts v. 22, thereby reading γὰρ μέν ("for indeed") in the last sentence of v. 21 and νυνὶ δέ ("but now") at the start of v. 22.

FORM/STRUCTURE/SETTING

The second question of 6:15a, "Should we sin because we are not under law but under grace?" which dominates all the material of 6:15b-23, stems from two previous statements of Paul: the first, from what he said in 5:20 about the Mosaic law having been "added so that the trespass might increase," which appears at the end of his "universal and foundational story" of the two primal persons in human history of 5:12-21; the second, from what he said about the believer in Jesus being "not under law but under grace" in 6:14, which appears at the end of his answer to the first question of 6:1-14. As he did in 6:2a in response to the first question of 6:1, so Paul responds immediately here in 6:15b to the second question of 6:15a with the highly negative and emotionally charged expression, "Certainly not!" (μὴ γένοιτο). In the rest of his answer in 6:16-23 he uses the analogy of the institution of slavery by way of contrasting (1) "enslavement to impurity that leads to ever-increasing wickedness," which people always experience in their commitment to the world apart from God, and (2) "enslavement to righteousness that leads to holiness," which Christians experience in their commitment to God through the person and work of Jesus Christ.

The analogy and language of slavery — with enslavement to only one master, but never to two; and with never any assumed neutrality between the claims of two masters — would have been immediately understood by, and highly significant for, the pagan Gentiles Paul was attempting to reach for Christ in the Greco-Roman world of his day. Likewise, it would have been understood by Paul's Christian addressees at Rome. For slavery was not only a practice condoned within Greco-Roman society, but also an institution legally protected.[32] It is estimated that slaves accounted for more than one-third of the population of the Roman Empire, and were from three to five times more numerous than Roman citizens; slaves and former slaves ("freedmen") constituted the majority of the population. Seneca the Younger (c. 4 B.C.-A.D. 65), the Roman Stoic philosopher, speaks of the defeat in the Roman Senate of legislation to compel slaves to wear a particular type of clothing to distinguish them from free men

---

32. Cf. Gülzow, *Christentum und Sklaverei in den ersten drei Jahrhunderten;* Brockmeyer, *Antike Sklaverei;* Bartchy, "Slavery (Greco-Roman)," 68-78.

because it was feared that slaves would then recognize how large and powerful a group they were, and so might revolt.[33]

The major sources for slaves, at least prior to the first century A.D., were warfare and piracy. Slave traders followed the armies and served as middlemen for returning marauders in disposal of their booty. With the cessation of Rome's wars of conquest and the establishment of the empire, however, these sources of supply were almost eliminated. Thereafter the major source was children who had been either abandoned by their parents or sold into slavery. Slave breeding was also practiced. And though laws forbade it (from as early as 326 B.C.), some people were still sentenced to slavery because of indebtedness; others were made slaves as punishment for their crimes.

Slavery was a recognized part of the Greco-Roman economy of Paul's day, and it was increasing rather than declining during the first century A.D. The lives of the middle and upper classes could hardly have gone on without it, so ingrained was it in the fabric of society. Slave trading was an accepted profession, and slave revolts were seldom successful in the prevailing climate of opinion. Fear of mortal reprisal kept most slaves subservient.

Household slaves were often treated humanely, with many faring better than lower-class free men in matters of food, housing, clothing, education, and spending money. There is considerable evidence that a large number of household slaves received their freedom because of the beneficence of their masters, and that as freedmen many of them became artisans, people of commerce, and even civic leaders. Yet slavery was an oppressive thing for most people of antiquity, shot through with fear, malice, and resentment.

Many slaves, however, were severely ill-treated, particularly those who worked in the fields and in mines. And to judge by the statements regarding slavery and the stress on freedom that appear in the *Dissertations* of the Stoic philosopher Epictetus (flourished about A.D. 100), who himself had been a slave, many of them would have preferred suicide — if only they had the nerve — to continued slavery. The most oppressive thing about slavery, of course, was that a slave was considered merely "a thing" *(res),* "a mortal object" *(res mortale),* a "chattel" *(mancipium),* but not a person, and so had no personal or even human rights except as permitted by his or her master.

Slavery was also an accepted part of the fabric of Jewish society, with roots in the legal provisions of the Pentateuch. It was, however, less extensive and less exploitative among the Jews than in the Roman Empire generally. Because of Israel's memory of the agony of her own slavery in Egypt, slaves were generally treated with a greater degree of kindness by Jewish masters, and some human rights were built into the system.

On the basis of Lev 25:39-55, Judaism made a distinction between Jewish slaves and Gentile slaves. A Jew might become a slave in restitution for thievery (Exod 22:3) or because of insolvency (Lev 25:39). But a Jewish slave was to be

---

33. Seneca (Lucius Annaeus), *De clementia* 1.24.1 (addressed to the emperor Nero).

treated by his or her Jewish master "as a hired worker or a temporary resident" (Lev 25:40, 53) — not ruthlessly, but in the fear of God, with respect because he or she was a fellow Israelite, a fellow servant of God, and one delivered from Egyptian bondage (Lev 25:42-43, 55). All Jewish slaves, in fact, whether male or female, were to be released at the beginning of the Year of Jubilee, which occurred every fifty years, with compensation given to them for their years of service rendered (Lev 25:40-41, 54). And Jews who sold themselves into slavery were to be released by their Jewish masters in the Sabbath year, after no more than six years of service (Jer 34:14).

There were other grounds for release as well. A female slave, for example, who had been sold on the understanding that she would be married to the master's son, was to be set free if her promised husband refused her or if he married another wife in addition without providing her "food, clothing and marital rights" (Exod 21:7-11). Likewise, a relative could redeem a Jewish slave by paying the price of the service yet outstanding; or Jewish slaves could redeem themselves on the same basis if they could acquire enough money (Lev 25:47-52). Gentile slaves of Jewish masters, however, entertained no such hopes for release. Their service was perpetual, and their condition was inherited by their children (Lev 25:44-46). While they could expect to be treated with greater kindness under Jewish masters than under Gentile masters, they were nonetheless still considered property and could be used in any way their masters saw fit. Only if they were seriously maimed by their masters were they to be automatically set free. Otherwise, the laws governing slavery in the Roman Empire pertained, and they were treated accordingly.

EXEGETICAL COMMENTS

6:15-16 As noted above in commenting on 6:1, the questions of 6:1; 6:15a; and 7:7a all begin with the same deliberative future expression τί οὖν ἐροῦμεν, "What then shall we say?" — though the second question, which appears here in 6:15, is stated elliptically as simply τί οὖν, "What then?" The first two questions of 6:1 and 6:15a go on (in 6:3 and 6:16 respectively) to express rather traditional "disclosure formulas" (i.e., variations of the question "Do you not know?") — as does the first verse of 7:1-6 — with these epistolary conventions of the day functioning to identify for the reader where new sections or subsections of a letter begin.

The aorist subjunctive verb ἁμαρτήσωμεν here in 6:15 suggests by its aorist tense a punctiliar (i.e., "point-type") action, and so is best translated "Should we sin?" Both questions, however, amount to much the same thing; the difference in the tense of the verbs occurs only to drive home the question without redundancy. Paul's immediate answer to this second question is exactly like his answer to the first question: the highly negative and emotional response "Certainly not!" (μὴ γένοιτο; literally "Let it not be!")

Using the analogy and language of slavery in the ancient world, Paul goes on to argue in 6:16 that the reason why believers in Jesus cannot presume that they can continue in sin — since, as is true, they are "not under law but under grace" — is that a commitment to one master never allows (1) the serving of two masters or (2) some type of assumed neutrality between the claims of two masters. So he argues: "When you offer yourselves to someone as obedient slaves, you are slaves to the one whom you obey — whether to sin, which leads to death, or to obedience, which leads to righteousness." Thus a commitment to sin and a commitment to obedience to God[34] are mutually exclusive — without the possibility of any supposed claim to neutrality, such as would allow "sin" and "God" to be somehow amalgamated. Or, as John Calvin has rephrased what Paul says here in 6:16:

> There is such a great difference between the yoke of Christ and that of sin that no one can bear them simultaneously. If we sin, we give ourselves up to the service of sin. Believers, on the other hand, have been redeemed from the tyranny of sin in order to serve Christ. It is, therefore, impossible for them to remain bound to sin.[35]

The notion of the possibility of dual commitments has, sadly, often been entertained by God's people. But it has always had disastrous results for those who think in such ways and have attempted to live their lives accordingly. Commitment to two masters would never have been allowed in the ancient world of slavery. And for someone to attempt to live his or her life in service both to sin and to God not only would be untenable but also would result in dire consequences. For what a person does in practice reveals, in fact, where his or her commitments really are and who is really that person's master.[36]

6:17-18 Although Paul warns against divided loyalties, he is confident about the commitment of those who responded positively to the proclamation of the Christian gospel — whether as he proclaimed it to pagan Gentiles or as the believers in Jesus at Rome had responded to the Christian message proclaimed to them. So he thanks God (1) that they "have obeyed from the heart the form ('type') of teaching to which they were entrusted ('handed over')," and (2) that they "have become slaves of righteousness."

The expression εἰς ὃν παρεδόθητε τύπον διδαχῆς, which reads literally "unto which type ['form,' 'imprint,' or 'pattern'] of teaching you were handed

---

34. Understanding Paul's reference to "obedience" (ὑπακοῆς) as metonymy for "obedience to God," for, as Calvin argues: "His use of the word without any addition indicates that it is God alone who has authority over the consciences of men. Although God's name is not mentioned, obedience is nevertheless referred to God, since it cannot be a divided obedience" (J. Calvin, *Romans*, in *Calvin's Commentaries*, 8.132). Cf. also Paul's use of "righteousness" (δικαιοσύνη) vis-à-vis "sin" (ἁμαρτία) in 6:18 and 6:20 and his direct reference to "God" (θεός) vis-à-vis "sin" (ἁμαρτία) in 6:22.

35. J. Calvin, *Romans*, in *Calvin's Commentaries*, 8.131.

36. Cf. Jesus' statement as reported in John 8:34: "Everyone who sins is a slave to sin."

over," has been notoriously difficult to translate and understand. Its use of the noun τύπος ("type," "form," "imprint," or "pattern") has been puzzling; its syntax has been seen as extremely awkward; and its statement about people being "handed over" (παρεδόθητε) to some "type" or "form of teaching" (τύπον διδαχῆς) seems contrary to the usual Pauline and early Christian thrust of "teaching" or "tradition" being "passed on" or "handed down" to people.[37] Further, the phraseology of the expression has seemed to some to disrupt the "clear antithetical parallelism" between 6:17a and 6:18 and to spoil the important dialectic statements regarding freedom and slavery in these verses by a "rather trivial remark" about obedience to a teaching. Thus some NT scholars have viewed the expression as an early marginal gloss that somehow became interpolated directly into the text, and so may be safely deleted.[38]

A number of other NT scholars, however, have argued for the authenticity of εἰς ὃν παρεδόθητε τύπον διδαχῆς ("unto which type of teaching you were handed over"), but have often been at a loss as to how to interpret it.[39] Among the numerous proposals that have accepted these words as written by Paul and have attempted to interpret what he meant by them, the following are the most prominent and the most important:

1. They speak of a Jewish form of teaching that Jewish Christians had been "given over to" prior to their conversion to Christ.[40]
2. They refer to a "rule" or "pattern" of early Christian teaching, which instruction was probably given at the time of a new convert's Christian baptism — and so, it may be said, the newly baptized believer was "entrusted" or "turned over" to a set "rule" or "pattern" of Christian doctrine and ethical practice.[41]
3. The phrase τύπος διδαχῆς connotes a particular "type," "kind," or "specific form" of Christian teaching that was somewhat different from other forms of Christian teaching. This type of teaching expressed itself in such distinctly Pauline statements as "not under law but under grace," "free from sin and slaves to righteousness," and/or "dying with Christ and rising with Him."[42]

---

37. On the latter point, see 1 Cor 11:2, 23; 15:3; cf. also Luke 1:2; Acts 16:4; 2 Pet 2:21; Jude 3.
38. So, e.g., Bultmann, "Glossen im Römerbrief," 283, who called it a "stupid insertion" ("stupiden Zwischensatz"); see also, among others, Furnish, *Theology and Ethics,* 197-98; Zeller, *An die Römer,* 127-28; and Schmithals, *Römerbrief,* 199-200.
39. For significant discussions of the great variety of proposals that have been advanced and the many scholars who have proposed them, see Käsemann, *Romans,* 180-84, and Gagnon, "Heart of Wax and a Teaching That Stamps," 667-87.
40. So, e.g., C. Lattey, "A Note on Rom. VI. 17,18," *JTS* 29 (1928) 381-84; *idem,* "A Further Note on Romans vi. 17-18," *JTS* 30 (1929) 397-99; M. Trimaille, "Encore le 'typos Didaches' de Romains 6,17," in *La vie de la Parole: De l'Ancien au Nouveau Testament* (Paris: Desclée, 1987), 278-80.
41. So, e.g., Moffatt, "The Interpretation of Romans 6:17-18," 237; also Fitzmyer, *Romans,* 449-50.
42. So, e.g., B. Weiss, *An die Römer* (1881); also Lietzmann, *An die Römer* (1906), 70

4. Because "τύπος in the Pauline corpus almost always had a personal reference," the expression τύπον διδαχῆς ("pattern" or "model of teaching")
should be seen as having in mind "Christ as the pattern for Christian pare-
nesis or the model for Christian conduct."[43]

In the conclusion to his article of 1993, which focuses principally on the
meaning of the phrase τύπον διδαχῆς that he translates as "the imprint stamped
by teaching," Robert Gagnon argues negatively that (1) Paul is not speaking
about "the set 'pattern' of early Christian teaching, or the 'fixed form' of baptismal instruction, or even the *imitatio* Christ" — nor should the full expression
be thought of as an interpolated gloss or a reference to his addressees' "pre-
Christian life"; but, rather, positively, (2) the expression εἰς ὃν παρεδόθητε
τύπον διδαχῆς simply "reaffirms through the use of another piece of imagery,
the centrality of Paul's thinking of the prior, inner transformation of the believer
accomplished by gospel and Spirit, as well as the concomitant requirement
of obedience."[44] While Gagnon's argument, both negative and positive, must
be considered both generally true and aptly said, questions remain regarding
(1) from whence Paul derived this seemingly strange "another piece of imagery"
in speaking about Christian obedience, (2) how central this way of expressing
matters was in Paul's thought and proclamation, and (3) why he used this way of
representing the "inner transformation of the believer accomplished by gospel
and Spirit, as well as the concomitant requirement of obedience," in writing to
his Christian addressees at Rome.

For my part, I tend to favor the thesis of Bernhard Weiss and Hans Lietzmann that the expression εἰς ὃν παρεδόθητε τύπον διδαχῆς — and particularly
the phrase τύπος διδαχῆς — reflects a particular "type," "kind," or "specific
form" of Christian teaching that was somewhat different from other forms of
Christian teaching.[45] Admittedly, such a thesis lends itself to the nineteenth-
century claim that "Paulinism" was a different type of Christianity than that
proclaimed by the earliest Christian apostles. If it is understood in this fashion,
James Denney was certainly right (1) to insist that such an understanding of
Rom 6:17b is an "anachronism," (2) to assert that "it is only modern eyes that
see distinct doctrinal types in the N.T.," and (3) to point out that "Paul, as far
as he knew (1 Cor. xv.3-11), preached the same Gospel as the other Apostles."[46]
Nonetheless, while Paul always insisted that his proclamation of the Christian

---

43. So Dunn, *Romans*, 1.334, 343-44, 353-54.

44. Gagnon, "Heart of Wax and a Teaching That Stamps," 687.

45. See option 3 listed above, citing in support B. Weiss (1881) and H. Lietzmann (1906).
Note also F. Godet's comment on this matter in his *Romans* (1880), 1.436: "The choice of so exceptional a term, and so unique as that which he thinks good to use here, leads us . . . to think of a
special and precisely defined form of Christian teaching. The reference is to that *gospel of Paul* (ii.16,
xvi.25)" — though Godet goes on to define that "gospel of Paul" as being the gospel "which the first
propagators of the gospel at Rome had preached there" *(ibid.)*.

46. Denney, *Romans*, in EGT 8.635.

gospel incorporated the same message as that proclaimed by the earliest apostles of Jesus, he also (1) recognized a difference between the Christian mission to Jews and his own Christian mission to Gentiles (as his statements in Gal 2:6-10 clearly evidence) and (2) thought of his own proclamation of the Christian message to Gentiles as "contextualized" in a somewhat different fashion than that of a Jewish Christian proclamation (as his references to "my gospel" in Rom 2:16 and 16:25 suggest, and as our explications of 1:16–4:25 vis-à-vis 5:1–8:39 have attempted to demonstrate).

Thus, while it may generally be said, as have many commentators, that this "unusual way" of speaking of Christians as having "obeyed from the heart the form ('type') of teaching to which [they] were entrusted ('handed over')" amounts to much the same thing as being "obedient to God" and accepting the "good news" of Christian teaching, it may also more explicitly be argued that this form of expression reflects a figure of speech used by Paul in his proclamation of the Christian gospel to Gentiles in his Gentile mission. It was, it may legitimately be theorized, a form of expression that was not only appropriate but also highly significant for Paul's Gentile converts. For slavery to only one master or to another, but never to two masters at the same time, was an ever-present reality, and being "given" or "handed over" to one master or to another master may be presumed to have been a well-known way of expressing such a master-slave relationship. Further, in the context of Paul's attempt to set out for his Roman addressees a précis of his contextualized Christian gospel to pagan Gentiles of the Greco-Roman world, it would have been appropriate for him to use this contextualized manner of speaking with regard to people who had formerly been "slaves to sin" but now were "obedient to God" — that is, former "slaves to sin" now obeying "from the heart the form ('type') of teaching to which [they] were entrusted ('handed over')."

The postpositive particle δέ at the start of 6:18 is one of the most commonly used connectives in koine Greek generally, as well as in biblical Greek in particular. Usually δέ appears between two clauses or statements to signal some type of mild contrast between them, though frequently the contrast is scarcely discernible. At other times it appears simply as a connecting particle, without any contrast being implied. That is how δέ seems to function here — without any contrast being implied, such as would signal some type of antithetical parallelism between 6:17 and 6:18, but rather as a connecting particle, which would suggest that what is said in 6:18 was meant to be understood as an explication of the previous, rather enigmatic statement of 6:17. Further, the aorist passive participle ἐλευθερωθέντες ("having been set free") is probably to be understood as a circumstantial adverbial participle, and therefore expresses an attendant thought or circumstance — that is, it serves to express an additional idea or fact, which is best translated into English by the conjunction "and" that is followed by a finite construction. Understood in this manner, what Paul writes in 6:18 is best understood as a parallel statement to and explication of what he has just said in 6:17: that Christians have been "set free from sin" and become "slaves to righteousness."

6:19-23 Paul begins the last half of his response of 6:15b-18 to the question posed in 6:15a ("Should we sin because we are not under law but under grace?") with an apology for the all-too-human nature (1) of his analogy of slavery in illustrating a Christian's relationship with God and (2) of his language of slavery in speaking of relationship with God as an enslavement to obedience and righteousness. Clearly, the analogy and language of slavery "fit like a glove" the relations of a person to sin. But just as certainly, such an analogy and language fall far short with respect to a Christian's "obedience to God" and "moral living." Nonetheless, the analogy and language of slavery have this in their favor: they speak of a person's total commitment, total "belongedness," total obligation, and total accountability — whether to sin, with its resulting "death" and "condemnation," or to God, with its resultant features of "righteousness," "holiness," and "eternal life."

In his outreach to pagan Gentiles, Paul evidently came to realize the impact that the analogy and language of slavery had in conveying the Christian message dramatically to his pagan hearers. Yet he seems also to have felt the criticism — which may have been leveled against him by some people during his Gentile mission, but certainly could be presumed to have been directed his way by the more "theologically oriented" believers in Jesus at Rome — that a slave analogy and slave language were not only unworthy but also demeaning and repulsive when speaking about one's relationship with God.

In Gal 3:15 Paul acknowledges, "I am speaking [only] humanly" (κατὰ ἄνθρωπον λέγω; i.e., "using an analogy from everyday life"); and in 1 Cor 9:8 he uses three analogies drawn from "everyday life" in speaking about the rights of a Christian apostle, and then asks the two questions: "Do I say these things [only] humanly (μὴ κατὰ ἄνθρωπον ταῦτα λαλῶ)? Does not the law say the same thing (ἢ καὶ ὁ νόμος ταῦτα οὐ λέγει)?" Here in Rom 6:19, however, while he employs the similar expression "I am speaking [only] in a human fashion" (ἀνθρώπινον λέγω), he goes on to say that he is doing so "because you are weak in your natural selves" (διὰ τὴν ἀσθένειαν τῆς σαρκὸς ὑμῶν) — thereby not only recognizing the inferiority of such an analogy and language (particularly in speaking about the relationship of Christians to God), but also identifying the reason he thinks it necessary to put matters in such terms as his hearers' lack of understanding.

Nevertheless, Paul continues in 6:19b-23 to do just as he did in 6:16-18 — to use the analogy and language of slavery to depict not only the relationship of people to sin but also the relationship of Christians to God. At the beginning of his continued use of the analogy of slavery, in 6:19b, he again uses the comparative phraseology ὥσπερ ("just as") . . . οὕτως καί ("so also") that he used in his "foundational story" of 5:12-21[47] — though here he joins the eschatological νῦν ("now") with οὕτως ("so"), thereby reading "so now," rather than using merely the conjunction καί ("and" or "also"), which in comparative fashion

---

47. See esp. 5:12a, 15, 18, 19, 21.

would read only "so also." In 6:22 he concludes his use of this slave analogy by calling on believers in Jesus to offer themselves "now" to God "as enslaved to righteousness leading to holiness," and in 6:23 he climaxes everything in a closing statement that lifts the whole discussion out of the demeaning context of slavery and into the exalted realms of "God's gift," "eternal life," and being "in Christ Jesus our Lord."[48]

Interjected Illustration on the Extent of the Authority of the Mosaic Law and Statement regarding a Christian's Freedom from the Law (7:1-6)

TRANSLATION

[7:1]*Do you not know, brothers and sisters — for I am speaking to those who know the law — that "the law has authority over a person as long as he or she lives"? [2]For a married woman is bound by law to her husband as long as he is alive; but if her husband dies, she is released from the law of her husband. [3]Consequently, if she marries another man while her husband is still alive, she is called an adulteress. But if her husband dies, she is released from that law and is not an adulteress, even though she marries another man.*

[4]So, my brothers and sisters, you also died to the law through the body of Christ that you might belong to another, to him who was raised from the dead, in order that we might bear fruit to God. [5]For when we were controlled by the sinful nature, the sinful passions aroused by the law were at work in our bodies, so that we bore fruit for death. [6]But now, by dying to what once bound us, we have been released from the law so that we serve in the new way of the Spirit, and not in the old way of the written code.

TEXTUAL NOTES

7:3 The phrase τοῦ ἀνδρός ("of the [her] husband"), after the expression ἀπὸ τοῦ νόμου ("from the law"), appears in minuscules 330 629 2344 (all Category III MSS) and is reflected in vg^ww. It lacks, however, sufficient textual support to be entertained seriously, and so must be viewed as an explanatory addition inserted by some later scribe.

48. On Paul's use of the expression "in Christ Jesus" (ἐν Χριστῷ Ἰησοῦ), see his earlier uses in Gal 3:26, 28, and in Rom 6:11; note especially his use in Rom 8:1-2 and our "Excursus: Paul's Use of 'in Christ Jesus' and Its Cognates" at that passage.

6a The participle ἀποθανόντες ("having died"), after the statement κατηργήθημεν ἀπὸ τοῦ νόμου ("we have been released from the law"), is extensively attested by uncials ℵ A B C P Ψ (also *Byz* K L) and by minuscules 33 1175 1739 (Category I), 1506 1881 1962 2127 2464 (Category II), and 6 69 88 104 181 323 326 330 365 424ᶜ 436 451 614 629 1241 1243 1319 1505 1573 1735 1874 1877 2344 2492 2495 (Category III); it is also reflected in vgʷʷ. The variant τοῦ θανάτου ("of death"), however, appears in its place in uncials D F G, is reflected in it and vgᶜˡ, and supported by Origenˡᵃᵗ ᵐˢˢ and Ambrosiaster. This latter reading is not only far less supported in the textual tradition, it also is, as Bruce Metzger points out, the easier reading in speaking of release "from the law of death," and does not have to deal with the awkwardness of the participle ἀποθανόντες.[49]

6b The pronoun ἡμᾶς ("we") after the infinitive δουλεύειν ("to serve") is strongly supported by uncials ℵ A B C P Ψ (also *Byz* K L) and by minuscules 33 1175 1739 (Category I), 1506 1881 2464 (Category II), and 6 69 88 104 323 326 330 365 424ᶜ 614 1241 1243 1319 1573 1735 1874 2344 (Category III). It is omitted, however, by Codex Vaticanus (B 03) and ninth-century uncials F and G, as well as by minuscule 629 (Category III); and it is changed to ὑμᾶς ("you") by minuscules 1505 and 2495 (both Category III). Apart from its omission in Codex Vaticanus, the textual evidence seems overwhelming in favor of the inclusion of the pronoun ἡμᾶς ("we").

FORM/STRUCTURE/SETTING

The material of Rom 7:1-6 has been variously evaluated. Some have called it an allegory; others a parable; others a metaphor or analogy; and still others an illustration — or, in the words of C. H. Dodd, an "illustration, or metaphor, or allegory, or whatever it is."[50] There has also been a vigorous debate among commentators as to what legislation Paul is here referring to — whether to Jewish marital law, Roman civil law, or both Jewish and Roman law. Likewise, there has been uncertainty regarding exactly whom Paul is addressing in saying "I am speaking to those who know the law," whether Jewish believers in Jesus who know the Mosaic law, Gentile Christians who have come in some way to know at least the rudiments of Jewish law, or Jewish and Gentile Christians who know both Jewish and Roman legislation. Also, various solutions have been offered to the apparent dilemma of how Paul can speak of a woman's husband as dying, equating the husband's death with the demise of the law (as in 7:2-3), and draw from that analogy or illustration the conclusion that "so you also died to the law" and "have been released from the law" in order that you may "serve in the new way of the Spirit and not in the old way of the written code" (as in 7:4-6).

C. H. Dodd's comments about this dilemma have become memorable in the minds of many interpreters, and so have often been repeated:

49. Metzger, *Textual Commentary*, 524.
50. C. H. Dodd, *Romans*, 101.

The illustration, however, is confused from the outset. . . . Here it is not the dead husband, but the living wife, who is freed from the obligations of the law. She is therefore free to marry again. . . . To make confusion worse confounded, it is not Law, the first husband, who dies; the Christian, on the other hand, is dead to the Law. The illustration, therefore, has gone hopelessly astray. The only *tertium comparationis* that remains is the bare fact that, in one way or another, death puts an end to obligations. We shall do best to ignore the illustration as far as may be, and ask what it is that Paul is really talking about in the realm of fact and experience.[51]

Dodd attributed such "confusion" to Paul's lack of "the gift for sustained illustration of ideas through concrete images," which was "probably" based in "a defect of imagination."[52] Charles Gore suggested that it entered the letter "as a result of Paul's dictation."[53] Many commentators during the twentieth century, therefore, have argued that "the illustration is not happy, for the law does not die" — but that Paul's general message of Christian freedom from the Mosaic law is clear in any case.[54]

Bo Reicke, however, argued that instead of Paul having only one thought in mind in 7:1-6, which he rather ineptly expressed in two ways, "two different motifs become blended in the argument" of the passage: (1) that the Mosaic law has died to the Christian, and (2) that the Christian has died to the law.[55] Reicke's argument for this blending of two motifs is based on the fact that at a number of places earlier in Romans Paul had closely associated "sin," "death," and "the flesh" with "the Mosaic law," and so these expressions became intimately related in his mind and come to the fore again in (1) his illustration of the death of a husband that results in freedom for his wife (as in 7:1-3) and (2) his statement regarding believers in Jesus being dead to the decrees of the Mosaic law (as in 7:4-6).[56] Yet Reicke did not want anyone to misinterpret Paul's illustration of the death of a husband as the death of the law with regard to its proper functions of revealing God's righteous standards and condemning all that opposes God and his will. So he added: "When the Law in the first figure [i.e., 'as a husband who dies and thereby sets his wife free'] is said to be dead, it is, in the context of the history of redemption, precisely the same as that the sinful body is dead."[57] Likewise, Martin Luther in his Galatians commentary, while upholding the law's functions of revealing God's righteous standards and condemning sin, spoke of a Christian's relationship to the law in terms of two motifs: "The law, therefore,

---

51. C. H. Dodd, *Romans,* 100-101.

52. *Ibid.,* 103.

53. Gore, *Romans,* 1.240.

54. Quoting and then paraphrasing W. Manson, "Notes on the Argument of Romans," 160-61.

55. Reicke, "The Law and This World according to Paul," 266-67, citing in support Lietzmann, *An die Römer* (1928), 2nd ed., 71-72.

56. Reicke, "The Law and This World according to Paul," 267-68.

57. *Ibid.,* 267.

is bound, dead and crucified unto me; and I again am bound, dead and crucified unto it."[58]

It is also an understanding of "two motifs" in 7:1-6 that will be spelled out in our exegetical comments that follow. We will highlight a number of matters in the passage that seem to suggest that Paul has interjected the illustration and statement of 7:1-6 into the broader context of 5:1–8:39. He evidently thought 7:1-6 would speak more directly to the Christians at Rome in a manner that they would appreciate and understand. Likewise, we will call attention to (1) the two appearances of the vocative ἀδελφοί ("brothers and sisters") in 7:1 and 4, (2) the concluding expression ἄρα οὖν ("consequently") in 7:3, and (3) the distinctive, though not unprecedented, use of the conjunction ὥστε in 3:4; all three of these linguistic phenomena seem not only to structure the passage, but also to lend credence to a thesis of two motifs being consciously expressed in it. Further, we will deal directly with the illustration and its application in 7:2-3, which has to do with the extent of the authority of the Mosaic law, and then with the statement in 7:4-6, which has to do with a Christian's freedom from the law.

Indeed, Rom 7:1-6 has within it a number of rather obvious exegetical and interpretive difficulties, and so this subsection of material has been treated in various ways. It is our thesis, however, that (1) when the passage is understood as an interjected portion of material that was addressed specifically to the Christians at Rome (as were the materials of 1:16–4:25), whereas its immediately surrounding context of 5:1–8:39 (minus 7:1-6) represents a précis of Paul's "contextualized" Christian proclamation to pagan Gentiles in his Gentile ministry, (2) when the two appearances of the vocative ἀδελφοί in 7:1 and 4 are taken into account, (3) when the expression ἄρα οὖν at the beginning of 7:3 is recognized as signaling the conclusion of Paul's illustration in 7:1-3, and (4) when the conjunction ὥστε is understood as introducing a second associated motif, and not the conclusion to the illustration presented — much of the mystery of what Paul is doing and saying here in 7:1-6 becomes somewhat resolved.

EXEGETICAL COMMENTS

7:1 The materials of 7:1-6 begin with an epistolary "disclosure formula," which here is expressed in the one word ἀγνοεῖτε ("Do you not know?") — thereby indicating, as also in 6:3 and 6:16, the beginning of a new subsection of Paul's letter. Four further matters need also to be observed in 7:1. The first has to do with Paul's use of the vocative expression ἀδελφοί ("brothers ['and sisters']"), which he earlier used in 1:13 in addressing the Christians at Rome and had not used since in the letter — but which occurs, with rather dramatic effect, in 7:1 (ἀδελφοί, "brothers and sisters") and in more intensified form in 7:4 (ἀδελφοί μου, "my brothers and sisters"). Paul's practice in this letter appears to have been

---

58. M. Luther, *Galatians,* trans. P. S. Watson (London: Clarke, 1953), 167 (on Gal 2:20).

to use ἀδελφοί as a vocative of address primarily in those sections where he was speaking directly to the Christians at Rome,[59] but not to use it — or, at least, not to use it very often — in the second section of the letter, that is, in 5:1–8:39, where (as we have argued) he is setting out a précis of the message that he had been proclaiming to pagan Gentiles in his Gentile mission.[60] The very nature of this direct form of address in 7:1 and 4, therefore, suggests (though, of course, does not demand) that in 7:1-6 Paul is interjecting into a summarized form of his "contextualized" proclamation of the Christian gospel to pagan Gentiles in 5:1–8:39 a specific message for his Christian addressees at Rome.

Second, Paul addresses his audience of 7:1-6 as "those who know the law." The "law" in question is undoubtedly the Mosaic law. In 7:1a Paul used the anarthrous form νόμος ("law"), that is, without the definite article — whereas here in 7:1b (in what may be understood as quoted material), as well as throughout 7:2-6, he uses the articular ὁ νόμος ("the law"). No distinctions, however, can be made in Paul's letters between the anarthrous and articular forms of νόμος with respect to the Mosaic law. Earlier in Romans he often referred to the Mosaic law using only the anarthrous form νόμος.[61] And his references to νόμος and ὁ νόμος here in 7:1-6 — situated as they are between (1) his earlier discussions of the inability to gain righteousness by means of "the works of the law" in 2:12–3:20 and his references to "God's righteousness" as a "gift" given "apart from the law" in 3:21–4:25, on the one hand, and (2) his expositions of the Christian gospel in relation to the Mosaic law and the hope of Israel in 9:1–11:36, on the other hand — clearly are to be understood as referring to the Mosaic law, whether in anarthrous or articular form. Further, while Paul's identification of his addressees as "those who know the Mosaic law" would hardly have been appropriate in addressing pagan Gentiles in his Gentile mission, it would have been an apt characterization of the Christians at Rome, whether ethnic Jews or ethnic Gentiles — and, in fact (as we believe and have proposed), believers in Jesus in the capital city of the Roman Empire would have taken pride in being so recognized and identified.

Third, the statement "the law has authority over a person as long as he or she lives" is introduced by what appears to be a "ὅτι *recitativum,*" which Paul uses a number of times in his letters to introduce a biblical passage or a biblically based Jewish aphorism — as he did earlier in Romans at 3:10 (a catena of biblical passages) and at 2:2 and 3:19 (two biblically based aphorisms).

Fourth, the statement that follows this introductory use of ὅτι is not only generally in line with biblical teaching about the Mosaic law, it also has an almost verbatim parallel in the teaching of Rabbi Johanan (a "fourth generation" Tannaitic Jewish rabbi of c. A.D. 140-165), who in both *b. Shabbat* 30a and *b. Niddah*

59. In addition to his earlier use in 1:13 and his two uses here in 7:1 and 4, see also his later uses of ἀδελφοί in directly addressing the Christians at Rome in 10:1; 12:1; 14:10, 13, 15, 21; 15:14, 30; 16:17.

60. The only other possible exception to his nonuse of the vocative ἀδελφοί in 5:1–8:39 (in addition, of course, to his use here in 7:1 and 4) is in 8:12, though see our exegetical comments on this usage below *(ad loc.).*

61. So, e.g., in 2:12-14, 23, 25; 3:20, 21, 28, 31; 4:13; 5:13, 20; 6:14, 15.

61b is quoted as saying: "When a man dies, he is free from the law and the commandments" — which teaching he based on Ps 87:5 (LXX): a deceased man is "free among the dead" (ἐν νεκροῖς ἐλεύθερος).[62] Admittedly, Rabbi Johanan's statement in these two *gemaras* of the Talmud represents Jewish teaching at a time later than when Paul wrote to the Christians at Rome. Yet the Mishnah ("halakic rules"), the Babylonian and Jerusalem *gemaras* ("expositions"), the earlier midrashim (exegetical interpretations or "Rabbah"), the Tosefta ("additions"), and the collections of "sayings" of individual teachers all claim to be codified remembrances of what was taught earlier by Jewish teachers and not new instruction — and so, at least in this case, may legitimately be used in support of what we believe should be viewed as a biblically based aphorism, which, in all likelihood, circulated among both Jews and Jewish Christians.

These four points, in concert, suggest that here in 7:1-6 Paul has shifted his attention from setting out for his addressees at Rome a précis of the "contextualized" gospel message he had been proclaiming to pagan Gentiles in his Gentile mission, to speaking directly to the Christians at Rome in a manner he believed would be appropriate to their understanding and appreciated by them. It may be that in reporting to his Christian addressees at Rome what he had been preaching in his Gentile mission that Paul was somewhat embarrassed about his use of the analogy and language of slavery in that missionary outreach — that is, of using such an analogy and language not only with respect to people's relations to sin but also in explicating a Christian's relationship to God, as he did in 6:15-23. So he may have wanted to assure his Christian addressees at Rome — particularly those he believed might criticize him for presenting the Christian gospel to Gentiles in an all-too-human fashion and without sufficient theological content — that he could also argue theologically and from a Jewish perspective. More than that, however, he seems to have wanted to expand further on the topics he raised in the immediately previous question of 6:15a regarding "human sin," "the Mosaic law," and "God's grace" — and to do so in a way that was not only suited to the understanding of pagan Gentiles (as in 6:15b-23) but also would be acceptable to the sensibilities of those who prided themselves in "knowing the Mosaic law" (as here in 7:1b-6). Thus we may surmise that Paul interjected into that summarized version of his "contextualized" message in 5:1–8:39 two motifs in 7:1-6 of particular importance to his Christian addressees at Rome: an illustration on the extent of the authority of the Mosaic law in 7:1-3, the presentation of which he began with the vocative expression ἀδελφοί ("brothers and sisters"); and a statement regarding the freedom of a Christian in 7:4-6, the presentation of which he began with an expanded and more personalized form of the same direct address, that is, ἀδελφοί μου ("my brothers and sisters").

---

62. Cf. *b. Shabb.* 151a; *Pesiq. R.* 51b; and *y. Kilaim* 9:3. See also the teaching of R. Tanhum of Neway (a district in northern Palestine), who is also cited in *b. Shabbat* 30a as teaching: "Let a man always engage in Torah and good deeds before he dies, for as soon as he dies he is restrained from Torah and good deeds."

7:2-3 In his response to the first two rhetorical questions of this section, Paul spoke of "having died to sin" (as in 6:1-7) and of "being no longer under the Mosaic law" (as in 6:15-18). These two themes seem to have been very closely associated in the apostle's mind. And here in 7:1-6 he writes of them again (though in reverse order) — first in his illustration of the death of a husband, which results in freedom for his wife (as in 7:2-3); then in his statement regarding believers in Jesus being dead to the law (as in 7:4-6).

The illustration Paul gives in 7:2-3 stems from what is probably a biblically based Jewish aphorism, which form of traditional teaching he gave immediately before in 7:1b: "The law has authority over a person as long as he or she lives." He applies that aphorism in 7:2 to the illustration of a husband who dies and so frees his wife from her marital ties (i.e., ἀπὸ τοῦ νόμου τοῦ ἀνδρός; literally "from the law of her husband" or "the law of marriage"). The conclusion the apostle presents on the basis of the aphorism and the illustration is stated in 7:3, which begins with the joining of the inferential particles ἄρα ("so," "then," "consequently") and οὖν ("so," "therefore," "consequently").

The expression ἄρα οὖν ("therefore," "consequently") appeared earlier in the letter in 5:18 to signal the conclusion of his argument there, and it will function in much the same fashion later in 7:25 and 8:12. So the joining of these inferential particles in 7:3 needs to be seen (1) as also signaling the conclusion of the apostle's illustration and, further, (2) as alerting his addressees to his implied application: that just as a wife is released from "the law of her husband" at his death, and therefore free to marry another man, so the believer in Jesus, being freed from sin by Jesus' death and identified with him by Christian baptism (as in 6:2-11 and 6:18, 22), is free from the directives of the Mosaic law, which in the outworking of God's program of salvation history have come to an end, and is therefore free to live in a new relationship with Christ.

The major problems with understanding these verses in this fashion have to do with the facts that in 7:3 — which begins with the expression ἄρα οὖν ("therefore," "consequently"), and so suggests that a conclusion to his illustration will immediately follow[63] — Paul (1) does not expressly relate "the death of the husband" to "the death of the Mosaic law" with respect to righteousness before God (as he will do later in Rom 10:4 in declaring that "Christ is the end of the law in its connection with righteousness for everyone who believes"), and (2) does not relate this termination of the law "in its connection with righteousness" to the law's past function as a "pedagogue" of God's people or to its continuing functions in expressing God's holy standards and condemning sin (as he did earlier in Gal 3:19–4:7). Rather, he leaves all these matters open and only here implies from his illustration of the death of a husband and the resultant freedom of his wife the corresponding motifs of the death of the law and a Christian's freedom from its dictates.

---

63. On the idiomatic expression ἄρα οὖν as signaling the conclusion of a matter, see also 5:18 earlier and 7:25; 8:12; 9:16, 18; 14:12, 19 later.

It is likely that the Christians at Rome — having (1) inherited from their early Jewish Christian teachers a reverence for the Mosaic law and (2) accepted from the mother church at Jerusalem a type of Jewish Christian theology, ethics, and piety[64] — were somewhat "overly honoring" the Mosaic law, and so would have been offended had Paul spoken more directly here in 7:1-3 about God's termination of that body of instruction (Torah) "in its connection with righteousness" and as a "pedagogue" for his people. Yet, having written about the inability of the law to produce righteousness (as he did in 2:17–3:20), having said "righteousness" and "faith" in this time of the eschatological "now" were "apart from the law" (as he did in 3:21–4:25), and having set out matters regarding "law" and "grace" rather graphically (as he did in 6:23) — and, further, planning to speak much more explicitly about all these matters in 9:1–11:36 — Paul evidently felt that the implications that could be drawn from his illustration of a husband's death and the resultant freedom of his wife would be fairly obvious to his Roman addressees. So at this point in his argument, and without wanting here needlessly to offend, Paul simply indicates the conclusion to his illustration by the inferential particles ἄρα οὖν ("therefore," "consequently") and allows his Christian addressees at Rome to spell out for themselves the evident implications.

7:4-6 Paul's conclusion to his illustration regarding the death of a husband, which results in freedom for his wife, is not only seminal for all that he will later state by way of explanation in Rom 9:1–11:36, it also expresses the crux of the matter with respect to his Christian proclamation vis-à-vis the message of Judaism: "So, my brothers and sisters, you also died to the law through the body of Christ in order that you might belong to another — to him who was raised from the dead, in order that we might bear fruit to God. For when we were controlled by the flesh, the sinful passions aroused by the law were at work in our bodies, so that we bore fruit for death. But now we have been released from the law, having died to what once bound us, so that we might serve in the new way of the Spirit, and not in the old way of the written code."

The conjunction ὥστε (which stems from the joining of the particles ὡς and τε) is used frequently in the NT in an illative manner (i.e., consequentially or inferentially) to signal the conclusion that follows from what has been said before.[65] However, Paul also used it a few times to introduce a statement, clause, or even question that set out matter in addition to the immediately previous exposition, statement, or clause. One obvious example of this appears in his question of Gal 4:16: "Have I become your enemy by telling you the truth?" (ὥστε ἐχθρὸς ὑμῶν γέγονα ἀληθεύων ὑμῖν;). This follows immediately after his exhortations of Gal 4:12-15, not as a conclusion to what he had been exhorting

---

64. Cf. our comments regarding "the addressees" in our "Introduction to the Commentary." For a fuller discussion of the letter's addressees, see R. N. Longenecker, *Introducing Romans*, ch. 4.

65. As, e.g., in Matt 12:12; 19:6; Mark 2:28; Rom 7:12; 13:2; 1 Cor 7:38; 11:27; 14:22; 2 Cor 5:16; Gal 3:9, 24; 4:7.

but simply to introduce an additional inquiring comment. Another example of this linguistic phenomenon appears in the second of his two uses of ὥστε in 2 Cor 5:16-17, where the first ὥστε that begins 5:16 is used in an illative fashion ("consequently") and the second ὥστε that begins 5:17 adds a further important statement (here evidently quoting an early Christian confessional portion) to that previous statement.

And this is what we believe Paul is doing here in 7:1-6. He is first setting out in 7:1-3 an illustration that is drawn from a biblically based Jewish aphorism and letting his Christian addressees at Rome draw from it the obvious implications for their lives; second, he is adding in 7:4-6 a statement of great significance regarding how believers in Jesus (1) "have died to the law through the body of Christ" so that they might "bear fruit for God" and (2) "have been released from the law" so that they might "serve in the new way of the Spirit, and not in the old way of the written code." In so doing, Paul is not exactly "blending two different motifs" as Bo Reicke has proposed — especially if one means by "blending" an intermingling of motifs and by the adjective "different" certain matters that are unlike one another in nature, form, or quality. Rather, reaching back to his previous questions of 6:1 and 6:15a, and presenting the essence of his earlier responses to these two questions in a form that he believed his Christian addressees at Rome would better appreciate and understand, Paul here in 7:1-6 deals with the same questions and responses he did in 6:1-23 (though in reverse order) — not in a strictly blended fashion, but by presenting first an illustration that had obvious implications for the question of the authority of the Mosaic law over a Christian and then a statement that spoke directly to the question of a Christian's freedom from the Mosaic law.

The means by which (1) freedom from the power and mastery of sin, (2) freedom from the condemnation of death, and (3) release from the lordship of the Mosaic law have been accomplished by God have been "through the body of Christ" (διὰ τοῦ σώματος τοῦ Χριστοῦ). Jesus' earthly life and ministry were indeed of great importance in God's work of salvation and reconciliation. But the acclamation in Phil 2:8b of Jesus being "obedient to the extent of death" (to which Paul seems to have added the awe-filled expression "even death on a cross!"), which resides at the very heart of the early Christian confessional hymn quoted in Phil 2:6-11, dominated all of early Christian preaching. Further, it is this emphasis on Jesus' death on a cross that Paul viewed as central in his own proclamation of the Christian gospel[66] and that he focused on in his response of 6:2-14 to the rhetorical question of 6:1.[67] Thus, just as Paul spoke of Jesus' death by Roman crucifixion, coupled with our identification with him by faith,

66. Cf. esp. 1 Cor 1:23, "We preach Christ crucified," and 1 Cor 2:2, "I resolved to know nothing while I was with you except Jesus Christ and him crucified."

67. Cf. esp. Rom 6:3: "All of us who were baptized into Christ Jesus were baptized into his death"; 6:5: "We have been united with him in his death"; 6:6: "Our old self was crucified with him"; 6:8: "If we died with Christ, we believe that we will also live with him"; and 6:10: "The death he died, he died to sin once for all."

as freeing believers in Jesus from the power and mastery of sin (6:6-7, 11-14a), the judgment of death (6:9-10), and the lordship of the Mosaic law (6:14b), so here in 7:4 when he speaks of Christians having "died to the law through the body of Christ" — and then in 7:6 of believers "dying to what once bound us" and so being "released from the law" — he certainly must be understood as meaning by "the body of Christ" the bodily death by crucifixion of Jesus, Israel's promised Messiah.

Of great significance in Paul's gospel is the fact that "dying to the law through the body of Christ" is not to be viewed only negatively; that is, the law is not some controlling factor that believers in Jesus have been released from and thereby allowed to go their own way and live out their lives in their own fashion. Rather, Jesus' bodily death and physical resurrection have two very important positive purposes — and so for the believer in Jesus today two very significant results: (1) that the people of faith in Jesus *belong* to the risen Christ and (2) that Christians *bear fruit* to God. Both purposes are introduced in 7:4 by an expression that is best translated "in order that": the first, that of *belonging* to the risen Christ, by the preposition εἰς with the articular infinitive τὸ γενέσθαι, which construction commonly indicates purpose; the second, that of *bearing fruit* to God, by the conjunction ἵνα, which also commonly denotes purpose. In these two statements Paul has captured the entire essence of what it means to be a Christian — that is, (1) *belonging* to Christ Jesus, "who was raised from the dead," and (2) *bearing fruit* to God, who has effectively brought about on behalf of believers in Jesus (as Paul earlier proclaimed in 6:22) both "holiness" (ἁγιασμόν) and "eternal life" (ζωὴν αἰώνιον).

In 7:5 Paul uses for the first time in the letter the word σάρξ ("flesh") as a theological expression; the term functions as an important theological concept for the apostle and one that he will develop extensively in 7:14-25 and 8:1-13. Paul, of course, used σάρξ ("flesh") in Romans as a locution for "person" in 3:20, and he used the fuller expression κατὰ σάρκα ("according to the flesh") in the sense of "physical descent" or "human nature" in 1 Cor 10:18; Gal 4:23, 29; and Rom 1:3 and 4:1 — and he will continue these more mundane uses in Rom 9:3, 5, 8, and 11:14, as well as other forms of the expression elsewhere in his letters, to represent the external features of human life. But his theological use of σάρξ ("flesh") here in 7:5, as well as throughout 7:14-25 and 8:1-13, connotes a person as "the willing instrument of sin" who "is subject to sin to such a degree that wherever flesh is, all forms of sin are likewise present, and no good thing can live."[68]

Important also in 7:5 is Paul's direct association of the Mosaic law with "the sinful passions" of "the flesh." Earlier in Romans he spoke of the law in the more passive roles of defining sin (3:20) and showing sin to be sin (4:15). Here in 7:5, however, Paul presents the law as playing an active part in actually "arousing" people's "sinful passions," which, as a result, "bear fruit for death" —

68. So the definition in *BAG*, 751, col. 2.

that is, that the law played (and continues to play) an active part in bringing to the fore the sinful passions of people, which result in both spiritual and physical death. What Paul means by the law's active association with sin and death will be spelled out more fully (1) in 7:7-13, where he deals with the question "Is the law sin?" and (2) in his portrayal of humanity's condition apart from God in 7:14-25, where he sets out the dire plight of people who attempt to live their lives "under their own steam," that is, by their own endeavors. Here in 7:5, however, as James Dunn has appropriately summarized Paul's point: "The intended inference seems to be that the law reinforces the connection between sin and death; the law has, as it were, a greenhouse effect, forcing the growth of sin to bring forth the fruit of death."[69]

In 7:6 Paul closes his interjected statement of 7:4-6 with (1) a declaration of believers in Jesus as being presently in the time of the eschatological "now," which change of situation in the progress of God's salvation history has brought about a tremendous difference in how they are to relate to God; (2) a proclamation that Christians in this changed situation have "died to what once bound us"; and (3) an exhortation to serve God in this new redemptive situation "in the new way of the Spirit, and not in the old way of the written code." By the expression "in the new way of the Spirit" (ἐν καινότητι πνεύματος) Paul highlights the facts (1) that this present time of the eschatological "now" is characterized by the presence and work of God's Holy Spirit (as he proclaimed in Gal 3:1-5) and (2) that believers in Jesus in this new era of God's salvation history are to live their lives as guided by that selfsame Holy Spirit (as he insisted in his exhortations of Gal 5:13-25, which close with the plea: "Let us keep in step with the Spirit"). And by the expression "in the old way of the written code" (παλαιότητι γράμματος; literally "in the obsolete way of the letter"), Paul refers to the Mosaic law that was given to the people of Israel as a "pedagogue" to guide them in divinely ordained nomistic ways (i.e., God's prescribed ordinances for his people) in the living out in practice of their commitment to and continued faith in God (as he stated in Gal 3:23-24) — but which Paul went on to declare in Gal 3:25: "But now that the faith [i.e., 'faith in Christ Jesus'] has come (ἐλθούσης δὲ τῆς πίστεως), we are no longer under a pedagogue [i.e., under the supervision of the law] (οὐκέτι ὑπὸ παιδαγωγόν ἐσμεν)."

Admittedly, the structure of Rom 7:1-6 is notoriously difficult to understand. Is it a confused illustration and application, whose "general message of Christian freedom from the Mosaic law is clear in any case" (as per W. Manson's reading; likewise, that of the vast majority of interpreters today)? Or is it an illustration and application that have in mind "two different motifs," which have become "blended in the argument" (as per Bo Reicke's reading)? Or is it, as we have proposed, (1) an illustration that implies that in this present time of God's program of salvation history the law has come to an end "in its connection with righteousness," both as a means of acceptance before God and as a response

69. Dunn, *Romans,* 1.371-72.

of one's faith in God and continued commitment to God, and (2) a statement that proclaims that believers in Jesus have, through the death and resurrection of Christ Jesus, entered into a new relationship with God, and so have not only died to the law in matters of righteousness before God (i.e., contra "legalism") but have also died to the law in matters pertaining to the expression of their faith and the living out of their lives in response to God's grace and love (i.e., contra "nomism"). However we understand the passage's structure, its message is abundantly clear: the death and resurrection of Jesus have brought about (1) a decidedly new relationship with God and (2) a decidedly new way of living a life of righteousness and justice, both before God and among people in society.

QUESTION THREE: "IS THE LAW SIN?" (7:7-13)

TRANSLATION

[7:7] *What, then, shall we say? Is the law sin? Certainly not! Indeed, I would not have known what sin was except through the law. For I would not have known what coveting really was if the law had not said, "Do not covet."* [8] *But sin, seizing the opportunity afforded by the commandment, produced in me every kind of covetous desire. For apart from law, sin is dead.*

[9] *Once I was alive apart from law. But when the commandment came, sin sprang to life and I died.* [10] *I found that the very commandment that was intended to bring life actually brought death.* [11] *For sin, seizing the opportunity afforded by the commandment, deceived me, and through the commandment put me to death.* [12] *So then, the law is holy, and the commandment is holy, righteous and good.*

[13] *Did that which is good, then, become death to me? Certainly not! But in order that sin might be recognized as sin, it produced death in me through what was good, so that through the commandment sin might become utterly sinful.*

TEXTUAL NOTES

7:7 The wording of the question ὁ νόμος ἁμαρτία; ("Is the law sin?") is very widely attested in the textual tradition. The particle ὅτι ("that"), however, appears before ὁ νόμος in minuscules 33 1175 (Category I) and 88 (Category III), as well as in Marcion's text (à la Tertullian in *Against Marcion* 5). Evidently the addition of ὅτι was meant as a *hoti recitativum* to introduce a direct quotation. But this variant reading is weakly attested in the textual tradition, and so must be viewed as only an attempt to improve the text.

8 The understanding of an implied ἐστιν ("it is") in the statement χωρὶς γὰρ νόμου ἁμαρτία νεκρά ("for apart from the law sin [is] dead") is widely attested throughout

the textual tradition. The past tense ἦν ("it was"), however, appears before νεκρά in the ninth-century uncials F G [also *Byz* K] and is reflected in various Latin texts, sy[P] bo — evidently to correspond with the past tense of κατειργάσατο ("it was working") previously in the verse.

12 The last statement of this verse, that is, "the commandment" is ἀγαθή ("good"), is very well attested in the textual tradition. Only minuscule 1908 (Category III) replaces ἀγαθή ("good") by θαυμαστή ("wonderful"), but that seems to be simply a pious attempt on the part of some scribe to elevate the status of the law.

FORM/STRUCTURE/SETTING

The material of 7:7-13 has often been connected with what Paul writes in 7:14-25.[70] But the question asked in 7:7a is so similar in form to the earlier two questions of 6:1 and 6:15a — -and the response given in 7:7b-13 so similar in content to what Paul wrote in his two earlier responses of 6:2-14 and 6:15b-23 — that 7:7-13 must be seen as connected directly with what precedes it in 6:1–7:6, and not as an introduction to what follows in 7:14-25. Further, as many have pointed out, "there is a significant difference between vv. 7-13 and vv. 14-25 in that the tenses of vv. 7-13 are past, whereas in vv. 14-25 the present tense is used," so these two passages must be treated as discrete units of material.[71] In addition, 7:14 begins with the disclosure formula οἴδαμεν γὰρ ὅτι ("for we know that"), which is a traditional epistolary convention that Paul often uses to start a new section or subsection in his letters.[72] Thus, it seems best to understand 7:14 as beginning a new section or subsection in the development of the apostle's presentation here in Rom 7.

Paul's close association of (1) believers in Jesus "having died to sin" (cf. esp. 6:2b and 6:18a) and (2) believers in Jesus "being no longer under the Mosaic law" (cf. esp. 6:14-15) — which themes are reiterated (in reverse order) in his illustration of the death of a husband, which results in freedom for his wife (7:1-3), and his statement regarding Christians being dead to the law (7:4-6) — could very well raise in some minds the objection that Paul has actually equated sin and the Mosaic law. Likewise, his comment in 7:5 that the Mosaic law played an active part in "arousing" people's "sinful passions," with the result that they "bear fruit for death," could have reinforced such an equation of sin and the law

---

70. So, e.g., Dunn, *Romans,* 1.376-77 (basing his position largely on Paul's uses of γάρ in 7:14-15); Jewett, *Romans,* 440-41 (basing his view largely on Paul's use of the first-person singular "I" throughout 7:7b-25).

71. Quoting the conclusion of Cranfield, *Romans,* 1.342, about the relation of these two passages.

72. Cf. Paul's earlier uses of such a disclosure formula in Romans at 6:3, 6:16, and 7:1, as well as his later uses in 8:22, 8:28, and 11:25 (probably also in 8:18 and 8:26) — all of which function as transitional expressions at the head of a new section or subsection of the letter, and so alert the reader as to where a new part begins.

among both his hearers in his Gentile mission and his addressees at Rome. Paul seems to recognize that his hearers and his addressees could respond in this way, and he wants to counter quite explicitly any such false inferential suggestion. So he deliberately raises the question himself: "Is the law sin?" — that is, from all that he has written in 6:1–7:6, can it be concluded that the law is to be equated with sin? And he answers that spurious understanding of his message with a resounding "Certainly not!" (μὴ γένοιτο) — going on from that brief and rather bombastic answer to spell out the relationship of the law to sin and to cite his own experience as an example of what he is saying.

At the close of his third question and response of 7:7-13, that is, in 7:13, Paul (1) asks a further question that is worded not quite in the manner of his three major questions of 6:1, 6:15, and 7:7, but seems to function as an extension of the question of 7:7, and (2) responds to that further question with his typical emotionally charged negative statement "Certainly not!" (μὴ γένοιτο). In effect, the two questions of 7:7a and 7:13a set up something of an *inclusio* that brackets the material of 7:7-13. And what Paul says in brief about the purpose of the law in that last sentence of 7:13 functions (1) to epitomize all that he has written about sin, death, and the law in 6:1–7:12 (as well as also earlier in 2:17–3:20), and (2) to close off not only the subsection of 7:7-13 but also the larger context of material in 6:1–7:13.

EXEGETICAL COMMENTS

7:7-8 Paul begins the first two verses of 7:7-13 with a question, an answer, and an explanation. Two linguistic features in these two verses appeared earlier in Paul's letter to Rome (and will continue to appear throughout this passage and beyond): (1) Paul uses νόμος ("law") and ὁ νόμος ("the law") interchangeably to mean the Mosaic law, using the noun twice in its anarthrous form and twice in its articular form in these two verses, and (2) he uses ἁμαρτία ("sin") and ἡ ἁμαρτία ("the sin") as a personified power that has come into human experience through Adam and is in opposition to God and his will.[73] Two other distinctive linguistic features are highlighted in these verses for the first time: (1) Paul's particularizing "the law" by his focus on a specific "commandment" (ἡ ἐντολή), which speaks against "covetousness" or "covetous desire" (ἐπιθυμία), and (2) his references to himself in a specifically personal manner by his use of the first-person singular aorist verb ἔγνων (from γινώσκω, "I know"), the first-person singular pluperfect verb ἤδειν (from οἶδα, "I know"), and the first-person dative singular personal pronoun ἐμοί ("in me"), with these uses of the personal pronoun "I" and its verbal suffixes developed more fully in 7:9-13 (and then more fully still in 7:14-25).

The negative answer that Paul expresses in 7:7a declares in the strongest

---

73. Cf. esp. Rom 5:12, 21, and 6:1.

terms possible that just because God's law has a role to play with respect to human sin, it can never be said that "the law is sin" or "part of our human predicament." On the contrary, he insists in 7:7b-8a, using his own experience to illustrate his point, that the law was given by God *to reveal sin* for what it really is before God and in a person's life. For, as he argues, "I would not have known what sin was except through the law" and "I would not have known what coveting really was if the law had not said, 'Do not covet.'" The first statement regarding the God-given purpose of the law is expressed using the aorist verb ἔγνων ("I would not have known") and declares that such a knowledge of sin is generally available "through the law" (διὰ νόμου). The second statement regarding the law's purpose is expressed more intensively using the pluperfect verb ἤδειν, which expresses results in past time with more force than could be done with the aorist tense (though in English a pluperfect verb can only be translated as a simple past) and speaks of that knowledge of sin as having come about through the particular "commandment" (ἡ ἐντολή) that prohibits "covetousness" or "covetous desire" (ἐπιθυμία).[74]

The final statement in Paul's explanation here, his statement in 7:8a that "apart from the law, sin is dead," must not be understood in the sense that "if the law were not present, people would not be troubled by sin." That would be just as obviously false as the statement "the law is sin." Paul is using dramatic and forceful language, and one must not take too literally the reference to sin being dead. Expressed in more prosaic language, what Paul evidently meant by "sin is dead," as Joseph Lightfoot translated the apostle's meaning, was that apart from the law sin is "as the apparently lifeless stock of a tree, it gives no signs of activity."[75] Or, as understood by Archibald Robertson, sin apart from the law is "Inactive, not non-existent. Sin in reality was there in a dormant state."[76] Or, perhaps, as translated and interpreted by Joseph Fitzmyer, sin without the law is "as good as dead" in that it is "lifeless" — "a corpselike being, powerless to make the evildoing of humanity a flagrant revolt against God's will."[77] Or, in

---

74. To some interpreters, the fact of Paul's reference to the tenth commandment, which prohibits ἐπιθυμία ("covetousness"), is evidence that the apostle is here in 7:7 not only speaking autobiographically but also referring to his adolescent life when sexual passions began to assert themselves (cf., e.g., C. H. Dodd, *Romans*, 110; F. Watson, *Agape, Eros, Gender: Towards a Pauline Sexual Ethic* [Cambridge: CUP, 2000], 154; and R. H. Gundry, "The Moral Frustration of Paul before His Conversion: Sexual Lust in Romans 7:7-25," in *Pauline Studies: Essays Presented to Professor F. F. Bruce on His 70th Birthday,* ed. D. A. Hagner and M. J. Harris [Grand Rapids: Eerdmans, 1980], 228-45). But this is not a necessary inference from Paul's statement in 7:7. A theme of many ancient rabbis was "one is never safe from the snares of especially sexual temptation" (cf. C. G. Montefiore and H. Loewe, eds., *A Rabbinic Anthology* [London: Macmillan, 1938], 35), and preaching on this most inward prohibition, "you shall not covet," as the essence of the negative commands of the Decalogue, is not uncommon to either ancient or modern preachers (cf., e.g., 4 Macc 2:1ff., and M. Luther, "A Treatise on Christian Liberty," in *Works of Martin Luther,* vol. 2, trans. W. A. Lambert [Philadelphia: Holman, 1916], 317).

75. Lightfoot, *Notes on Epistles of St. Paul,* 302.

76. Robertson, "Epistle to the Romans," 4.368.

77. Fitzmyer, *Romans,* 467.

the more common vernacular of our day: apart from God's law, sin is relatively powerless and ineffective — for, as Lightfoot insisted, "definite prohibition is necessary in order to produce definite transgression, in whatever form this definite prohibition may be given."[78]

7:9-12 Paul's use of dramatic and forceful language, which he inaugurated in 7:8 in declaring that "apart from the law, sin is dead," continues in his statements of 7:9-12. For here in 7:9-11 he speaks (1) of a personified ἐγὼ ("I") as having been "once alive apart from the law," (2) of sin as "springing to life through the commandment," (3) of this "I" as having been "deceived by sin," and (4) of this "I" as having been "put to death" and having "died" because of sin's use of God's commandment. And in 7:12 he speaks of God's law (ὁ νόμος) as being "holy" and characterizes the commandment (ἡ ἐντολή) that prohibits covetousness as "holy, righteous and good."

Who is this "I" that is spoken of in this passage, and to what time is the passage referring? Later in 7:14-25 we will argue that Paul uses the first-person pronoun "I" in a more "gnomic" or general sense of people who attempt to live out their lives in their own strength, but who find in those attempts not only frustration but also spiritual schizophrenia and personal disaster. Here in 7:7-12, however, his language is so personal and so related to a time in the past that it seems necessary to posit that Paul is recounting his own experiences as a Jewish Pharisee prior to being encountered by the risen and exalted Christ. Thus, in agreement with John Calvin, we argue that Paul's statements in 7:7-12 should be understood as his recollections of (1) a time when as a Pharisee he thought that by keeping the law "sin became dead" in his own life and he became "spiritually alive," but also, conversely, (2) a time in his life when "sin sprang to life through the commandment" against covetousness — and, more importantly, (3) a time when he began to understand, under the guidance of God's Spirit, that God's law is not just "letters" in a body of legislation, but divine instruction that condemns sin and points beyond itself to the God who gave it.[79]

The conjunction ὥστε ("so then") in 7:12 is certainly used in an illative manner (i.e., consequentially or inferentially) to signal the conclusion that follows from what was said in 7:7-11. It is a conclusion that Paul evidently came to learn well during his time as a Jewish Pharisee — that is, that the law (ὁ νόμος) as a whole is "holy" (ἅγιος); and, in particular, that the specific commandment (ἡ ἐντολή), which spoke against covetousness, is "holy, righteous and good" (ἁγία καὶ δικαία καὶ ἀγαθή). Further, it is a conclusion that would have well prepared Saul of Tarsus for Christ's encounter with him on his way to Damascus — and it is a conclusion that well prepares people for God's further working by his Spirit in their lives.

7:13 At the close of his third question of 7:7-13, Paul asks in its final verse a further question: Τὸ οὖν ἀγαθὸν ἐμοὶ ἐγένετο θάνατος; ("Did that which is

78. Lightfoot, *Notes on Epistles of St. Paul,* 302-3.
79. Cf. Calvin, *Romans,* in *Calvin's New Testament Commentaries,* 8.144-45.

good, then, become death to me?"). This question is worded somewhat differently than his three major questions of 6:1a, 6:15a, and 7:7a, and it appears to function somewhat differently than those earlier three questions. For this question of 7:13a does not introduce a further related subject but, rather, (1) functions as an extension of the question of 7:7a, (2) sets up, together with the question of 7:7a, something of an *inclusio* that brackets the material of 7:7-13, and (3) closes off this subsection of 7:7-13. And to this further question, the apostle responds in a very definite negative fashion and explains in a quite clarifying manner: μὴ γένοιτο· ἀλλὰ ἡ ἁμαρτία, ἵνα φανῇ ἁμαρτία, διὰ τοῦ ἀγαθοῦ μοι κατεργαζομένη θάνατον· ἵνα γένηται καθ' ὑπερβολὴν ἁμαρτωλὸς ἡ ἁμαρτία διὰ τῆς ἐντολῆς ("Certainly not! But in order that sin might be recognized as sin, it produced death in me through what was good, so that through the commandment sin might become utterly sinful").

In this final sentence of 7:13 Paul summarizes what he wanted both his pagan Gentile audiences in the Roman Empire and his Christian addressees at Rome to understand about the purpose of the law — that is, that God gave the law "in order that sin might be recognized as sin" and "so that sin might become utterly sinful." It is the same message that he emphasized in Gal 3:19-22 in answer to the specific question "Why then the law?" (though in answer to that question he also spoke in Gal 3:23-25 of the Mosaic law as a "pedagogue" that God put in charge of his people until faith in Christ would be brought about by God, but that "now that this faith has come we are no longer under the supervision of the law"). And it is the same message that Paul proclaimed earlier in Romans in his concluding statement of 3:20: "Therefore no one will be declared righteous in his [God's] sight by 'works of the law,' for *through the law is the consciousness of sin.*"

BIBLICAL THEOLOGY (ON ROM 6:1-7:13 AS A WHOLE)

In Luke's portrayals of Paul's proclamation of the Christian gospel, the verbs πείθω ("persuade" or "urge"), διαλέγομαι ("reason"), διανοίγω ("explain"), and παρατίθημι ("prove") are used frequently to characterize the apostle's manner of preaching and teaching.[80] And this is what we see taking place in the questions Paul raises and the answers he gives in 6:1-23 and 7:7-13 — together with the illustration and statement he interjects in 7:1-6. For in his proclamation of the Christian gospel Paul didn't just announce and proclaim, he also interacted with his hearers and addressees by "persuading," "reasoning," "explaining," and "proving" in a manner they would be able to appreciate and understand.

The materials of 6:1–7:13 are not structured in any standard format of Christian proclamation or instruction. Rather, they are set out in the form of contextualized answers to certain rhetorical questions that the apostle viewed as

---

80. Cf. esp. Acts 13:43; 17:2-4, 17; 18:4, 19; 19:8-10; 20:9; 24:25; 26:28, and 28:23.

quite likely to arise from his previous presentations of 5:1-11 and 5:12-21, without any clear pedagogical structures or logical connections being evident — except, of course, as set by the topics themselves and as delineated by the questions raised. Much of what appears in this section of the letter is, in fact, comparable in form to Martin Luther's rather colloquial responses to questions asked by his associates and friends, which were written down in various notebooks and later published by his associates and friends as Luther's "Table Talk."[81] So it is somewhat difficult to organize what Paul has written in 6:1–7:13 in any formal fashion. Nonetheless, his comments on the topics of "the Mosaic law," "the obedience of Jesus Christ," "God's gift of righteousness and eternal life *through* (and/or *in*) Christ Jesus our Lord," and "the freedom of the believer in Jesus" are forceful and to the point — and, even more basic, his rooting of all salvation history in "God's grace" is clear. It is, therefore, absolutely necessary to highlight these highly significant matters in any contemporary Christian biblical theology.

Suffice it here, however, simply to cite the following explanatory comments on these important topics, given by some of the most perceptive Christian commentators in church history and expressed in much the same manner as Paul stated them here in Romans:

> Martin Luther: "For Christ, toward whom this law [i.e., the Mosaic law] was directed, has clean abolished it by His Passion and Resurrection; He slew it and buried it forever, rent the veil of the Temple in twain, and then broke and destroyed Jerusalem, with priesthood, princedom, law, and everything."[82]

> Adolf Harnack: "No part of the law [as Paul proclaimed matters] had been depreciated in value by any noiseless, disintegrating influence of time or circumstance; on the contrary, the law remained valid and operative in all its provisions. It could not be abrogated save by him who had ordained it — i.e., by God himself. Nor could even God abolish it save by affirming at the same time its rights — i.e., he must abolish it just by providing for its fulfillment. And this was what actually took place. By the death and resurrection of Jesus Christ, God's Son, upon the cross, the law was at once fulfilled and abolished."[83]

Thus the Mosaic law with respect to its God-ordained covenantal obligations — that is, "in connection with righteousness" (εἰς δικαιοσύνην), as Paul will say later in Rom 10:4 — has come to an end. It has, as Paul graphically stated

---

81. See *Selections from the Table Talk of Martin Luther,* trans. H. Bell, ed. H. Morley (London: Cassell, 1886); also *The Table Talk of Martin Luther,* trans. T. S. Kepler (Cleveland: World, 1952).

82. M. Luther, "On the Councils and the Churches," in *Works of Martin Luther,* vol. 5, trans. C. M. Jacobs (Philadelphia: Holman, 1916), 184.

83. A. Harnack, *The Mission and Expansion of Christianity in the First Three Centuries,* trans. J. Moffatt (London: Williams & Norgate, 1908), 1.54.

matters, been "torn down" (Gal 2:18) and it has "died" (Rom 7:1-3) — not because it evolved into something better or different, but because God has established a new covenant wherein "commandments" and "ordinances" have been abolished (Eph 2:1-5) and the distinction between God's covenanted people Israel and the Gentiles has ceased (Eph 2:11-18). It is because Christ in his person and work has brought an end to the old covenantal purpose of the Mosaic law that Paul could expect his "placarding of Jesus Christ as having been crucified" to settle once and for all the question whether righteousness in the new covenant is "through the Mosaic law" or "in Christ" (cf. Gal 3:1). The statement "It is finished" is, in fact, just as much a part of Paul's proclamation as it was a cry of Jesus on the cross (John 19:30; cf. Rom 10:4; Gal 3:13).

The Christian in the new covenant, therefore, ceases to regard righteousness in terms of law at all. The believer in Jesus, as Anders Nygren has observed, is "neither condemned nor justified by it. He hopes for nothing from the law, and fears nothing. For him the law is completely eliminated, as far as righteousness and freedom, condemnation and the wrath of God are concerned."[84] For the one who believes in Jesus has found that "the gospel of Christ is *the very righteousness of God.*"[85] Or, as Martin Luther has expressed matters, the believer in Jesus has found that "no external thing, whatsoever it may be, has any influence whatever in producing Christian righteousness or liberty. . . . One thing and one only is necessary for Christian life, righteousness and liberty. That one thing is the most holy Word of God, the Gospel of Christ."[86]

CONTEXTUALIZATION FOR TODAY

Paul's statements in 6:1–7:13 are set entirely within the context of God's grace as expressed "through Christ Jesus our Lord" vis-à-vis the Mosaic law (1) as a supposed means of attaining righteousness before God (i.e., "legalism") or (2) as a God-ordained way, and therefore a necessary way, for believers in Jesus to express their faith in God and their thanks to God (i.e., "covenantal nomism"). His statements are directly relevant in their negative exhortation to many "Christians" today who view their relationship with God in either a legalistic or a nomistic fashion — for they exhort believers in Jesus "not [to serve God] in the old way of the written code" (as expressly stated in 7:6b).

Yet Paul's words in the entire statement of 7:6, "But now, by dying to what once bound us, we have been released from the law so that we serve in the new way of the Spirit, and not in the old way of the written code," are probably even more important today for many who attempt to live their lives by their own stan-

---

84. Nygren, *Romans,* 310-11.
85. *Ibid.,* 303 (italics his).
86. M. Luther, "A Treatise on Christian Liberty," in *Works of Martin Luther,* vol. 2, trans. W. A. Lambert (Philadelphia: Holman, 1916), 313-14.

dards and in a manner that is both personally virtuous and socially acceptable. For as Martin Luther has aptly contextualized Paul's exhortation to live "not in the oldness of the letter" (7:6b):

> By "letter" the Apostle means all doctrine which prescribes what belongs to a virtuous life. If that is understood and impressed upon the memory without the Spirit of grace, then it is an empty letter and the death of the soul. So also St. Augustine says in the fourth chapter of his book *Concerning the Spirit and the Letter:* "The doctrine through which we receive the commandment to lead an abstinent, virtuous life, is the letter. This kills unless there is with it the Spirit, which makes alive."[87]

Much of what Paul says here in Rom 6:1-7:13 he said earlier in a somewhat similar contextualized form in Gal 5:1-26. The following exhortations of that earlier passage are particularly relevant not only (1) to those who attempt to live righteously before God in either a "legalistic" or a "nomistic" fashion, but also (2) to those who attempt to live a virtuous life before others either by their own standards or by the norms of their particular society:

> Gal 5:1 — "For freedom Christ set us free! Stand fast, therefore, and do not let yourselves be burdened again by a yoke of slavery."
> Gal 5:13 — "You, brothers and sisters, were called to be free! Only do not use your freedom as an opportunity for the flesh, but through love serve one another."
> Gal 5:16 — "Live by the Spirit and you will not carry out the desires of the flesh."
> Gal 5:18 — "Since you are led by the Spirit, you are not under the law."
> Gal 5:25 — "Since we live by the Spirit, let us keep in step with the Spirit."

These important tenets regarding (1) freedom from the law, (2) life guided by the Spirit, and (3) serving others through love — as expressed in Gal 5:1-26 and Rom 6:1-7:13 in different contexts, in somewhat differing ways, but with the same content — need always to be included in our own contextualized proclamation and practice of the Christian gospel today.

---

87. M. Luther, *Commentary on the Epistle to the Romans,* trans. J. T. Mueller, 110; quoting Augustine, *De spiritu et littera (On the Spirit and the Letter)* 4.6.

4. Soliloquy on the Tragic Plight of Those Who Attempt to Live Their Lives Apart from God, "under Their Own Steam" (7:14-25)

TRANSLATION

¹⁴*We know that the law is spiritual; but I am fleshly, having been sold [as a slave] under [the control of] sin.* ¹⁵*I do not understand what I am bringing about. For, "what I want to do, I do not do; but what I hate, this I do."* ¹⁶*If then I do what I do not want to do, I agree with the law that it is good.*

¹⁷*But now [the situation is this]: No longer am I bringing matters about; rather, it is sin living in me.* ¹⁸*For I know that nothing good lives in me, that is, in my sinful nature. The desire is present in me, but the ability to bring about what is good is not.* ¹⁹*For, "not the good that I want to do, but the evil that I do not want to do, this is what I keep on doing."* ²⁰*And if I do what I do not want to do, it is no longer I who brings it about; rather, it is sin that lives in me.*

²¹*So then, I find this law [at work in my life]: When I want to do good, evil is right there with me.* ²²*For in my inner being I delight in the law of God.* ²³*But I see another law in the members of my body that is waging war against the law of my mind and making me a prisoner by the law of sin within my members.*

²⁴*"What a wretched person I am!" Who will rescue me from this body of death?*

²⁵*But thanks be to God, [deliverance is] through Jesus Christ our Lord!*

Consequently, I of myself, in my mind I am indeed a slave to the law of God, but in my human existence a slave to the law of sin.

TEXTUAL NOTES

7:14a The first-person plural οἴδαμεν ("we know") is supported by uncials ℵ A B* C D* F G P Ψ and by minuscules 1175 1739 (Category I), 81 256 1506 1881 1962 2127 2464 (Category II), and 6 104 263 365 424ᶜ 436 459 1241 1319 1573 1852 1912 2200 (Category III); it is also reflected in itᵐˢˢ vg syrᵖ, ʰ copˢᵃ, ᵇᵒ and supported by Origenᵍʳ, ˡᵃᵗ Chrysostom Theodore Theodoret Ambrosiaster Augustine and Jerome⁹ᐟ¹⁰. A few copyists and Church Fathers (as well as some recent scholars), influenced by Paul's frequent use of the first-person singular "I" throughout 7:7-25, have preferred to divide οἴδαμεν so as to read οἶδα μέν ("I know indeed") — as attested by minuscule 33 (Category I), reflected in versions armᵐˢ slav and in lectionary 883, and argued by Jerome in *Contra Jovin* 1.37. But as Bruce Metzger has pointed out, such a reading "overlooks the need at this point in Paul's argument for a statement that would command the general assent of his readers — such as he has the habit of introducing by using οἴδαμεν."[1] Moreover, Paul's contrast in 7:14-25 is not between a supposed "I know" and the following "I am," but between "the law as spiritual" and "the human self as fleshly."

14b The adjective σάρκινος ("fleshly," "made of flesh"), which is used here in substantival fashion, is widely attested by uncials ℵ* A B C D F G Ψ and by minuscules 33 1739 (Category I), 81 1506 1881 (Category II), and 6 69 (Category III). The variant σαρκικός ("fleshly," "belonging to the order of earthly things," "material") appears in uncials ℵ² P [also *Byz* K L] P and in minuscules 1175 (Category I), 2464 (Category II), and 88 104 323 326 330 365 1241 1243 1319 1505 1573 1838 1874 2495 (Category III). The terms are roughly synonymous, though σαρκικός is often considered a "softer" expression. The Greek textual tradition, however, far better supports σάρκινος, and so it should be accepted as original. The variant σαρκικός may have been due either to (1) an error in hearing or (2) to an attempt to reduce the possibility of understanding Paul as speaking of "fleshly" in only a physical sense.

15 The inclusion of the neuter demonstrative pronoun τοῦτο ("this") in the expression "this I do" at the end of the verse is very well supported in the textual tradition and therefore should be accepted. It is, however, omitted by uncials D F and G, probably in an attempt to remove a perceived redundancy between the demonstrative use of the article ὁ ("that which") and the demonstrative pronoun τοῦτο ("this").

16 The preponderance of textual evidence is without the verb ἐστίν ("it is") in the statement "it is good." Only ninth-century uncials F and G read καλός ἐστίν ("it is good"). But an elliptical use of καλός includes the idea of the verb ἐστίν, and is rightly translated as "it is good."

18a The ninth-century uncials F and G add the article τό ("the") before the noun ἀγαθόν ("good," "what is right"), but that appears to be an attempted grammatical improvement.

18b The abrupt ending of the sentence with the negative οὔ ("not") — thereby reading "the desire is present in me, but the ability to bring about what is good is not" — is strongly supported by uncials ℵ A B C and by minuscules 1739 (Category I), 81 1881 (Category II), and 6 424ᶜ 436 1852 1908 220 (Category III); it is also reflected in copˢᵃ, ᵇᵒ and attested by Jerome²ᐟ⁵ Augustine¹⁸ᐟ³⁸ and Augustine. The strangeness of ending a sentence with a negative evidently prompted a number of early scribes to append some kind of supplemental verbal expression, either (1) οὐχ εὑρίσκω ("I do not find"), which appears in uncials D F G P Ψ (also *Byz* K L) and in minuscules 33 1175 (Category I), 1506 1962 2464 (Category II), and 104 424* 459 1241 1912 (Category III); it is also reflected in it⁽ᵃʳ⁾, ᵇ, ᵈ, ᶠ, ᵍ, ᵐᵒⁿ, ᵒ vg syrᵖ, ʰ and supported by Irenaeusˡᵃᵗ Origenˡᵃᵗ Chrysostom and Jerome³ᐟ⁵, or (2) οὐ γινώσκω ("I do not know"), which appears in minuscules 256 2127 (Category II) and 263 1319 1573 (Category III). The shorter, elliptical reading οὔ, however, is to be preferred as original.

19 The phrase οὐ θέλω ("I do not want") in the second part of the verse is very widely attested in the textual tradition. The variant μισῶ ("I hate") appears in uncial F

---

1. Metzger, *Textual Commentary*, 454. Note Paul's other uses of οἴδαμεν ("we know") in Romans at 2:2; 3:19; 8:22, and 28; cf. 1 Cor 8:4 and 2 Cor 5:1, 6.

and is reflected in vg^s. It evidently arose in order (1) to mitigate the redundancy of two οὐ θέλω phrases in the verse, (2) to parallel the use of οὐ θέλω and μισῶ earlier in v. 15, and/or (3) to lay emphasis on a logical progression from "I do not want" to "I hate." It is not, however, sufficiently supported by the external MS evidence to be accepted.

20 The textual evidence for the presence or absence of the first ἐγώ ("I") of the verse is rather evenly balanced. Including this first ἐγω are uncials א A P Ψ (also *Byz* K L), minuscules 33 1175 1739 (Category I), 81 1881 1962 (Category II), 6 69 88 323 326 330 424^c 459 614 1505 1838 1874 1912 2200 2495 (Category III), versions syr^h cop^{bo}, and the Church Fathers Clement Origen^{lat} Chrysostom Jerome$^{2/4}$ Augustine$^{8/15}$. Omitting it are uncials B C D F G, minuscules 256 1506 2127 2464 (Category II), 104 263 1241 1243 1319 1573 1735 1852 (Category III), versions it^{mss} vg cop^{sa}, and the Church Fathers Theodore Ambrosiaster Pelagius Augustine$^{7/15}$. Bruce Metzger has aptly summarized the debate and noted the most probable conclusion: "From the point of view of transcriptional probability, ἐγώ might have been either accidentally omitted through parablepsis or deliberately added for emphasis in conformity with the following ἐγώ. Accordingly, the Committee decided to retain the word but to enclose it within square brackets."[2]

22 The scribe of Codex Vaticanus (B 03), evidently influenced by the phrase τῷ νόμῳ τοῦ νοός in v. 23, seems to have inadvertently replaced θεοῦ with νοός in v. 22.[3]

23 The preposition ἐν ("in," "of," "to," or "by"), which appears before τῷ νόμῳ ("the law"), is supported by uncials א B D G [K] P Ψ and by minuscules 33 (Category I), 1881 (Category II), and 88 (Category III); it is also reflected in it$^{ar, d, dem, e, f, g, t, x, z}$ vg cop$^{sa, bo}$ and supported by Clement Origen^{lat} Ambrosiaster Theodoret. It is, however, omitted in uncials A and C, in minuscules 1739 (Category I), 81 1962 2127 (Category II), and 104 326 330 436 451 614 629 630 1241 2127 2495 (Category III), and by Chrysostom. The textual evidence for its inclusion is somewhat better than that for its exclusion. Further, its inclusion represents the more difficult reading, for it is unnecessary and even somewhat intrusive in the phrase αἰχμαλωτίζοντά με ἐν τῷ νόμῳ τῆς ἁμαρτίας. The majority of the UBS committee for *GNT*^{3}, therefore, preferred to retain ἐν, explaining its absence in some witnesses as the result of harmonization with τῷ νόμῳ in the previous line (ἀντιστρατευόμενον τῷ νόμῳ τοῦ νοός μου), and gave its inclusion a B rating. Probably its deletion arose from an attempt at stylistic improvement.

25a The reading χάρις δὲ τῷ θεῷ ("but thanks be to God!") is attested externally by uncials א C^2 and by minuscules 33 (Category I), 81 256 1506 2127 (Category II), and 104 263 365 436 459 1319 1573 1852; it is also reflected in cop^{bo} and a number of other versions. Internally, this reading seems to account best for the use of all the other possible readings. The postpositive δέ is missing in Codex Vaticanus (B 03), in cop^{sa}, and in Origen Methodius Epiphanius and Jerome$^{1/6}$, which probably represents, as Bruce Metzger suggests, "a natural development in light of liturgical usage (δέ is present in the same ascription at 6.17; 2 Cor 2.14; 8.16; and in some witnesses at 2 Cor 9.15)."[4] Further, as Metzger goes on to suggest: "The reading εὐχαριστῶ τῷ θεῷ (א* A K 614 1739 *Byz*

---

2. Metzger, *Textual Commentary*, 455.
3 Cf. *ibid.*
4. *Ibid.*

Lect) seems to have arisen through transcriptional error involving the reduplication of several letters, του [ευ] χαρις [τω] τω θεω."[5]

Two "Western" readings — that is, (1) ἡ χάρις τοῦ θεοῦ ("the grace of God"), which appears in Codex Beza (D 06), is reflected in it[ar, b, d, mon, o] vg, and is supported by Origen[lat2/3] Theodoret Ambrosiaster Jerome[4/6], and (2) ἡ χάρις κυρίου ("the grace of the Lord"), which appears in uncials F and G and is reflected in it[f, g] — provide an immediate answer to the question of 7:24: τίς με ῥύσεται; ("Who will rescue me?").

25b The inclusion of the particle μέν ("indeed") is widely attested in the textual tradition. It is omitted, however, in Codex Sinaiticus (ℵ* 01) and in the ninth-century uncials F and G. This omission should probably be viewed as reflecting certain scribal uncertainties as to how v. 25b, particularly in its negative statement about being "a slave to the law of sin," should be understood as following the triumphal affirmation that immediately precedes it in v. 25a (which is a matter that needs to be treated more fully in our discussions of 7:24-25 below).

FORM/STRUCTURE/SETTING

Numerous questions have been raised regarding the structure, rhetoric, content, parallels, and purpose of 7:14-25 — particularly regarding who is depicted in the passage and what type of experience is described. Most commentators have treated the passage as a continuation of the discussion regarding the Mosaic law in 7:7-13 and life lived under that law — and so have focused (1) positively on references in 7:14-25 to the law being "spiritual" (πνευματικός) in v. 14, "good" (καλός) in v. 16, and "the law of God" (ὁ νόμος τοῦ θεοῦ) in vv. 22 and 25b, though also (2) negatively on the frustrations of trying to live one's life guided by law, no matter how worthy and noble such legislation might be. In what follows, however, I will interpret 7:14-25 as representing Paul's "soliloquy" or "dramatic monologue" on the subject of what results when people attempt to live their lives "under their own steam," that is, in terms of their own resources and abilities. The account of such a life, as epitomized by the expression "left to myself" (αὐτὸς ἐγώ), is countered by the apostle's contextualized Christian proclamation in 8:1-39 of what it means to live one's life "in Christ Jesus" (ἐν Χριστῷ Ἰησοῦ) and by the enablement of God's Spirit (κατὰ πνεῦμα).

Rom 7:14-25 as a Discrete Unit of Material, as Identified by Its Epistolary Formulas and Elliptical Style. This passage opens in 7:14a with the epistolary disclosure formula "we know that" (οἴδαμεν ὅτι). Such disclosure formulas were commonly used in antiquity to signal the start of a new section or subsection within the structure of a Greek letter — and so should be understood as intended by its author to alert the one who read the letter, as well as those who heard it read, that a new section or subsection was beginning. Paul used them at a number of places in his letters, and particularly in his letter to Rome,

---

5. Metzger, *Textual Commentary,* 455.

thereby identifying where he begins a new section or subsection.[6] Likewise, the passage closes in 7:25b with the idiomatic concluding formulation "so then" or "consequently" (ἄρα οὖν), which Paul uses elsewhere in Romans to indicate where a conclusion to an argument begins[7] — or, at least, where an intermediate conclusion in his overall argument begins, as here at the end of Rom 7, with that intermediate concluding formulation "consequently" of 7:25b being contrasted by the opposing formulation "nevertheless, therefore now" (οὐδὲν ἄρα νῦν) of 8:1a.

Much of what is presented between the opening disclosure formula "we know that" (οἴδαμεν ὅτι) of 7:14a and the concluding formulation "so then" or "consequently" (ἄρα οὖν) of 7:25b is set out in an elliptical style — that is, (1) with a number of nouns, pronouns, and verbs being omitted, though with their intended presence recognizable from their respective contexts, and (2) with relationships expressed in a brisk and extremely brief manner.

Such formal features suggest that 7:14-25 is probably best understood as a discrete body of material that functions in its own right within its author's overall purpose. It may, of course, be noted (1) that the passage follows on from, as well as echoes, much of what Paul wrote about the Mosaic law in 6:1–7:13, (2) that it continues the apostle's use of the first-person pronoun ἐγώ ("I") in 7:7-13, and (3) that it presents material that will be contrasted by what he writes in 8:1-39. Despite these rather obvious similarities of words and expressions, which serve to connect the passage with what precedes and what follows, the tone and temper of 7:14-25 are quite different from what precedes it and what follows it. So we propose that these formal features of an opening "disclosure formula" in 7:14a and a "concluding formulation" in 7:25b, coupled with the passage's elliptical style, signal the discrete nature of what Paul writes in 7:14-25.

Further, we suggest (1) that this passage is best understood as Paul's "soliloquy" or dramatic monologue on the "the tragic plight of people who attempt to live their lives apart from God and by means of their own resources and abilities (i.e., 'under their own steam')," and (2) that this series of terse reflections on the human situation "apart from God" has been strategically placed by Paul as a dramatic conclusion to all that he has written about God's grace, the Mosaic law, and people's responses in 6:1–7:13, *and* as a preparation for what he will write about being "in Christ," about being "enabled by God's Spirit," and about "the love of God that is in Christ Jesus our Lord" in 8:1-39.

Who Is Depicted in 7:14-25 and What Type of Experience Is Described? Two major questions have repeatedly been raised regarding the material of 7:14-25: (1) the identity of who is depicted in the passage, and (2) the type of experience that is described. No part of Romans, in fact, has been the object of

---

6. Other epistolary "disclosure formulas" in Romans appear in 2:2; 3:19; 6:3, 16; 7:1, 14; 8:22, 28 (probably also 8:18 and 26); and 11:25.

7. In addition to Paul's use of ἄρα οὖν here in 7:25b, see also 5:18; 7:3; and 8:12.

so much scrutiny and the source of so much confusion as what Paul writes in 7:14-25, with these two matters being to the fore in every exegetical treatment.

1. Traditional Understandings. Interpreters of the passage have traditionally espoused one or the other of two main schools of thought. For one school, the passage refers primarily to Paul's own experience under the law before he became a follower of Jesus Christ. For the other, Paul is describing the struggle that goes on in his own life as a Christian and within the dual nature of every believer in Jesus — that is, between what believers are "in Adam" and what they are and shall become more fully in the future "in Christ." In both interpretations, what Paul writes in 7:14-25 is understood autobiographically: in the first, as reflections on his own preconversion experience, and that of others, under the Mosaic law; in the second, as his own confessions, and those of others, with respect to continuing struggles as a Christian living in the dual situation of (1) inherited depravity and inherent fleshly passions vis-à-vis (2) new life "in Christ" and guidance "by God's Spirit."

From very early times of Christian interpretation, these two understandings have been debated. Origen and most of the Greek Fathers viewed this passage as Paul's reminiscence of his experience under the Mosaic law before he became a follower of Christ.[8] This preconversion view has been advanced by such proponents as John Wesley, Adolf Deissmann, Henry St. John Thackeray, Arthur S. Peake, James S. Stewart, C. H. Dodd, and Douglas J. Moo. On the other hand, Augustine and the Latin Fathers interpreted the passage as reflecting Paul's postconversion experience as a Christian, which finds analogy in the inner conflicts of every true believer in Jesus.[9] Agreement with this postconversion position has been voiced by Martin Luther, Philipp Melanchthon, and John Calvin, together with most theologians who have looked to these prominent Protestant Reformation interpreters as prototypes of their respective positions. And it has been defended exegetically by such modern commentators as Anders Nygren, C. E. B. Cranfield, James D. G. Dunn, John Murray, Leon Morris, and C. K. Barrett.

The preconversion view stresses (1) the past tense of the verbs in 7:7-13; (2) the definite contrast between chs. 7 and 8, as signaled in the emphatic "now" (νῦν) of 8:1; (3) the absence of Christian expressions in ch. 7 (at least until v. 25a), and the abundance of references in ch. 8 to Christ Jesus, the Spirit, and the Christian life; (4) the expressions in ch. 7 that are definitely contrary to Paul's presentation of the Christian life, as, for example, "sold under sin" in v. 14 and "wretched man" in v. 24; (5) the logical argument that redemption by Christ

8. For extensive treatments on the understandings of this passage by the Church Fathers, see Schelkle, *Paulus*, 242-48, and Kuss, *Römerbrief*, 2.462-85; for the views of not only the early Church Fathers but also the Protestant Reformers and German scholarship to 1929, see Kümmel, *Römer 7 und die Bekehrung des Paulus*, 74-109.

9. Augustine had earlier understood the apostle as speaking in the name of the unregenerate person (cf. *Expositio quarundam propositionum ex epistola ad Romanos*, PL 35.2071); later, however, he argued that Paul was speaking in his own name as a Christian (cf. his *Retractationes* 1.23.1 and 2.1.1; *PL* 32.620-21 and 32.629-30).

is no redemption at all if this is a picture of the Christian life; (6) the experiential argument that such a preconversion struggle has been not uncommon to many, both in the past and in our present day; and (7) the pragmatic argument that a threefold division of Paul's life — that is, "childhood innocence," "struggle under the law," and "freedom in Christ" — "fits like a glove" what we know about Judaism and Paul's life. On the other hand, the postconversion interpretation emphasizes (1) the present tense of the verbs in 7:14-24; (2) the fact that Rom 7 is set in the context of Rom 5, 6, and 8, which speak of the Christian life; (3) that a preconversion interpretation is inconsistent with what Paul says of his former life in Phil 3:6; (4) that an interpretation of the passage as representing the tension that exists within the life of a Christian between the old and the new creations is consistent with portrayals of similar tensions within the Christian life as depicted in Rom 8:23 and Gal 5:17; and (5) that such a view is consistent with what we know of the Christian life in both past and present days, as it is lived between the old and the new aeons of God's salvation history. The arguments for these two positions have appeared to some almost equally convincing, and various interpreters often assumed that the interpretation of Rom 7 had arrived at something of a stalemate.

2. Understanding the "I" (ἐγώ) of 7:14-25 as a Stilform *of Speech and Writing.* The understanding of Paul's use of the personal pronoun "I" (ἐγώ) in 7:7-25, however, changed quite dramatically for many scholars with the publication in 1929 of Werner Kümmel's study of what 7:7-25 actually says about Paul's religious and ethical experiences.[10] For Kümmel argued that there is evidence that ancient Judaism and Paul did not always use the first-person singular pronoun in a strictly biographical sense, but at times employed "I" as a rhetorical and literary *Stilform* ("stylistic form") in the presentations of their respective teachings — that is, the first-person singular pronoun was not always intended to portray the situation of the teacher himself who was giving the teaching, but was often meant to be understood in a gnomic or general sense as including all people. And Kümmel's view of Paul's gnomic use of "I" in 7:7-25 has been supported by such scholars as Günther Bornkamm, Ernst Fuchs, Karl Kertelge, Jan Lambrecht, Ernst Käsemann, and Otto Kuss.[11]

Kümmel cited three early texts from the Jewish Talmud where general teaching by rabbis is given or illustrated by the use of the first-person singular pronoun "I": (1) in *m. Berakot* 1:3, where Rabbi Tarfon relates his dangerous experience of reciting the Shema while lying down in the presence of robbers; (2) in *m. Abot* 6:9, where Rabbi Jose ben Kisma describes an encounter with a Gentile while out walking; and (3) in *b. Berakot* 3a, where Rabbi Jose recounts a conversation he had with an appearance of Elijah.[12] While evidence from the

---

10. Kümmel, *Römer 7 und die Bekehrung des Paulus.*

11. Cf. also R. N. Longenecker, *Paul, Apostle of Liberty,* 86-97, much of which has been reproduced in slightly revised form in what follows.

12. Kümmel, *Römer 7 und die Bekehrung des Paulus,* 128-32

Mishnah and the Babylonian *gemaras* is important in illustrating a Jewish use of the first-person pronoun "I" in a general or gnomic fashion, the value of such material is somewhat mitigated because of (1) its late date, since all three examples cited above are credited to third-generation Tannaitic rabbis, who taught during A.D. 120-140, and (2) the imaginative or conjured character of the statements. A possibly more significant example of a stylistic use of "I" is Philo's change from the first-person plural "we" to the first-person singular "I" in *De somniis* 1.177. The context of the passage concerns the relationship of the mind and the body; in that short section, without the general nature of the thought changing, the first-person singular "I" is used in both its dative and its accusative forms.

More recent evidence on this question has come from the Dead Sea Scrolls from Qumran. These offer the most significant outside aid to understanding Paul's use of the first-person pronoun in Rom 7, particularly in 7:14-25. For in columns 10 and 11 of 1QS, the so-called Manual of Discipline, there is a recitation of the eternal possession and privileges of those God has chosen. In the midst of this description of the gifts of salvation, that is, the gifts of "knowledge," "righteousness," "strength," and "glory," there is the sudden cry:

> But I belong to wicked humanity and to the assembly of perverse flesh. My iniquities, my transgressions, my sin — together with the perversities of my heart — belong to the assembly of worms and of things that move in darkness.[13]

In the "ethical dualism" of the Qumran texts, such a cry of despair could possibly be attributed to those "who are of wickedness and darkness." And Theodor Gaster's caption to columns 10 and 11 as "The Hymn of the Initiants" might lead someone to believe that these are the words of an initiant *before* his admittance into "the elect of God." But the context of the passage, as well as the frequency of similar utterances in the hymns and psalms of the community,[14] demand that these words be viewed as the expression of a Jewish sectarian who was fully conscious of his election by God and his acceptance in the community. The significance of this passage for Rom 7, therefore, has been well stated by Karl Georg Kuhn:

> We have in this text the same "I" as in Rom. 7; it is the same "I" not only in regard to style, but especially in regard to theological connotation: "I" is here, just as in Rom. 7, not meant individually or biographically; it is gnomic, descriptive of human existence. The "I" in this Qumran passage, as in Rom. 7, signifies the existence of mankind, which is flesh.[15]

13. 1QS 11.9-10a, in W. H. Brownlee, trans., *The Dead Sea Manual of Discipline: Translation and Notes*, BASORSup 10-12 (New Haven: American Schools of Oriental Research, 1951).

14. E.g., 1QH 1.21-23 and 3.24-36.

15. K. G. Kuhn, "New Light on Temptation, Sin, and Flesh in the New Testament," in *The Scrolls and the New Testament*, ed. K. Stendahl (New York: Harper, 1957), 102.

We do not need, however, to resort entirely to analogous writings. Despite the many places in his letters where Paul's use of "I" clearly refers to himself (both by the use of the first-person personal pronoun and as incorporated in his verbal suffixes), he also uses the first-person singular "I" (ἐγώ) in a gnomic or general fashion in his letters. Rom 3:7 is an example: "If the truth of God is enhanced unto his glory by my falsehood (ἐν τῷ ἐμῷ ψεύσματί), why am I also still condemned (τί ἔτι κἀγὼ κρίνομαι) as a sinner?" In context, Paul definitely renounces this as his teaching, much less his personal practice — though, of course, the abounding grace of God amidst human deceit is the experience of all who know God, Paul included.

Of even greater significance for our discussion here is the use of the first-person singular pronoun "I" in 1 Cor 13, the so-called Hymn of Love, which begins in 13:1-3 with the following words:

> If I speak in the tongues of men and of angels, but have not love, I am only a resounding gong or a clanging cymbal. If I have the gift of prophecy and can fathom all mysteries and all knowledge, and if I have a faith that can move mountains, but have not love, I am nothing. If I give all I possess to the poor and surrender my body to the flames, but have not love, I gain nothing.

The inadequacy of all without love, as portrayed in these verses, is meant neither as a strictly personal experience nor as a strictly personal realization. It is gnomic, aphoristic, meant to be taken as a general truth — though certainly Paul would insist that such a general truth has also been experienced and realized in his own life.

In 1 Corinthians, therefore, Paul uses the personal pronoun "I" in both (1) a self-referential fashion, as in 1 Cor 9:1-27 where he speaks about his own situation and his own experiences vis-à-vis those of others, and (2) a gnomic or general manner, as in 1 Cor 13:1-13. This passage begins in 13:1-3 with a list of worthy qualities and actions that the "I" in question could very well exemplify, but denies the efficacy of such qualities and actions because of the absence of love (ἀγάπη) in the life of the one personified, and then characterizes in 13:11 the "I" in question as speaking, thinking, and reasoning as a child when he was a child, but now that he is a grown man he has put away "such childish ways." As Luke Timothy Johnson has rightly said with respect to Paul's use of "I" in 1 Cor 13:

> Paul neither claims to have all the qualities listed in 13:1-3, nor to entirely lack *agape*! Likewise, his "when I was a child, I spoke as a child" (13:11) can scarcely be taken as specific self-revelation; it is first-person speech used to make a point vividly and personally. The first-person discourse is less a window giving access to Paul's personality than it is a mirror for the reader's reflection and self-examination.[16]

16. L. T. Johnson, *Reading Romans*, 115.

So also the rhetorical question of 1 Cor 6:15, "Shall I make the members of Christ the members of a harlot?," with its emphatic negative response, "Certainly not!" (μὴ γένοιτο), should be understood as a general maxim couched in the dramatic first-person singular. Likewise, Gal 2:18 ("If I rebuild what I destroyed, I prove that I am a lawbreaker") should be viewed in a similar fashion; probably also 1 Cor 14:11, 14-15 ("If I do not grasp the meaning of what someone is saying, I am a foreigner to the speaker, and he is a foreigner to me. . . . If I pray in a tongue, my spirit prays, but my mind is unfruitful. So what shall I do? I will pray with my spirit, but I will also pray with my mind; I will sing with my spirit, but I will also sing with my mind"). The indefinite pronoun "one" (τις) could just as easily have been used in all these instances, though with considerable loss to the power and graphic character of the passages.

Parallels to 7:14-25 in Greco-Roman Tragic Soliloquies and "Speeches in Character." Commentators have usually been almost exclusively concerned with the identity of the speaker and the type of experience described in 7:7-25 — and particularly as set out in 7:14-25. But important studies have also focused on (1) parallels of content and expression between 7:14-25 and certain Greco-Roman tragic soliloquies regarding the lack of personal self-mastery[17] and (2) parallels of rhetorical technique, particularly those of a "speech in character," between 7:14-25 and speeches that appear in a number of extant ancient monologues, soliloquies, addresses, and dialogues.[18]

1. Parallels of Content and Expression. The text most often cited as a parallel to Paul's cry of despair in Rom 7:15, "What I want to do, I do not do; but what I hate, this I do" — and then again in 7:19, "Not the good that I want to do, but the evil that I do not want to do, this is what I keep on doing" — is the tragic soliloquy that the Greek poet Euripides (c. 484-406 B.C.) puts on the lips of Medea, who was a woman driven by rage against her unfaithful husband Jason and who conceived a plan of vengeance that included the murder of his new bride and the killing of her own children who had been fathered by him:

> I am being overcome by evils (νικῶμαι κακοῖς). And I know, indeed, that what I am about to do is evil (καὶ μανθάνω μὲν οἷα). But passion is stronger than my reasoned reflection (θυμὸς δὲ κρείσσων τῶν ἐμῶν βουλευμάτων). Such is the cause of the worst evils to humans (ὅσπερ μεγίστων αἴτιος κακῶν βροτοῖς).[19]

---

17. See esp. Hommel, "Das 7 Kapitel des Römerbriefs im Licht Antiker Überlieferung," 90-116; Theissen, *Psychological Aspects of Pauline Theology,* 211-19; and Stowers, *A Rereading of Romans,* 260-66.

18. See esp. Stowers, *A Rereading of Romans,* 16-21.

19. Euripides, *Medea* 1077b-80 (written c. 431 B.C.). Cf. Epictetus's paraphrase of Medea's lament some four and one-half centuries later in his *Discourses* 1.28.7: "And now, indeed, I am learning what horrors I intend (καὶ μανθάνω μὲν οἷα δρᾶν μέλλω κακά), but passion masters my sober thought (θυμὸς δὲ κρείσσων τῶν ἐμῶν βουλευμάτων)."

Twice before uttering such an awful lament, Medea, as portrayed by Euripides, reflects on the fact that another course of action would be far better.[20] Nonetheless, though recognizing how heinous her murder of Jason's new wife and the killing of her own children would be, Medea declares that her desire for revenge "is stronger than my reasoned reflection" — and she bemoans this fact of her humanity.

Euripides expressed a similar lament regarding the human condition in more prosaic fashion in his earlier *Hippolytus,* where Phaedra, the wife of King Theseus, comments on her adulterous relations with Hippolytus and on humanity's general lack of personal self-mastery as follows:

> During long nights I have often thought about what wrecks our human life. I do not think that lack of understanding is the root of all evil (οὐ κατὰ γνώμης φύσιν πράσσειν κάκιον). Most people lack nothing by way of insight. Rather, the cause must lie elsewhere: We know and recognize the good (τὰ χρήστ' ἐπιστάμεσθα καὶ γιγνώσκομεν), but we do not do it (οὐκ ἐκποιοῦμεν δ') — some from laziness; others preferring pleasure more than goodness.[21]

Likewise Ovid (c. 43 B.C.-A.D. 17/18), the Roman poet, in his *Metamorphoses* places on the lips of the daughter of King Aeëtes a lament regarding her lack of self-mastery in her illegitimate longing for Jason, which lament parallels the lament of Euripides' Medea:

> Oh wretched one *(Infelix)!* Drive out these flames that you feel from your maiden breast if you can. If I could, I should be more reasonable. But some strange power holds me back against my will. Desire counsels me one way; reason another. I see and approve the better course, but I follow the worse.[22]

Stanley Stowers sets out a number of Greco-Roman texts in support of the thesis that tragic soliloquies on the subject of humanity's lack of personal self-mastery — and particularly "the famous Medean saying" — were widely known in Paul's day, and that they occurred "not only in drama and philosophers' debates, but also in such contexts as letters and public orations."[23] Stowers discusses the pertinence of these ancient tragic writings to Paul's soliloquy of Rom 7:14-25:

> These texts illustrate how versions of the saying found in 7:15 and 19 played a central role in the Greek moral tradition. The words of Euripides' *Medea*

---

20. Cf. Euripides, *Medea* 1040-48 and 1056-58.
21. Euripides, *Hippolytus* 375-83 (written c. 428 B.C.).
22. Ovid, *Metamorphoses* 7.17-21 (published c. A.D. 7).
23. Stowers, *A Rereading of Romans,* 260; he cites and quotes materials regarding this Greco-Roman tragic tradition in 260-63.

were widely cited in this connection. In philosophy and literature alike the words were variously interpreted in discussions about the roles of the emotions, deliberation, and knowledge of good and evil in moral psychology.[24]

2. Parallels in the Use of a "Speech in Character" Rhetorical Technique. Stanley Stowers has also demonstrated the place and importance of the "speech in character" rhetorical technique in ancient oratory and written composition,[25] which technique was a form of rhetoric that was in Greek called προσωποποιία and in Latin labeled *fictiones personarum.* He quotes the Roman rhetorician Quintilian (c. A.D. 35-95), who, when speaking about various "figures" or forms of rhetoric in his day, refers to this convention as follows:

> This technique adds wonderful variety and animation to oratory. With this figure we present the inner thoughts of our adversaries as though they were talking with themselves. . . . Or without diminishing credibility we may introduce conversations between ourselves and others, or of others among themselves, and give words of advice, reproof, complaint, praise or pity to appropriate persons.[26]

Stowers has pointed out that Paul's despairing outburst of Rom 7:24, "What a wretched man I am!" (ταλαίπωρος ἐγὼ ἄνθρωπος), reflects "almost as a parody" (1) Seneca's account of Medea's cry of despair regarding how her will to do the good has been overpowered by her anger, "What, wretched woman, have I done?"[27] (2) Epictetus's statements about people who lament that they are "wretched," who, as Epictetus believed, decry their situation because they admire external things, using Medea in her anguish as his chief example,[28] and (3) the widespread lament, "O wretch that I am," of the ancient tragedians and comedians, which was drawn from Euripides' *Medea.*[29]

Stowers cites Homer, the classic Greek poet of the eighth century B.C., as the principal early practitioner of a "speech in character" rhetorical technique

---

24. Stowers, *A Rereading of Romans,* 263-64. It is certainly true that "these alleged parallels do not really represent statements *conceptually* equivalent to Paul's" (as Huggins, in his "Alleged Classical Parallels," 153 [italics mine], has pointed out in an attempt to discredit such evidence as has been drawn from these ancient tragic soliloquies). Stowers's central points, however, remain valid: (1) that "versions of the saying found in 7:15 and 19 played a central role in the Greek moral tradition," (2) that "the words of Euripides' *Medea* were widely cited" by tragic poets, dramatists, and playwrights of Paul's day, (3) that these tragic expressions "were variously interpreted" in the moral discussions of antiquity, and (4) that Paul seems here in Rom 7:14-25 to reflect some of these same expressions — employing them, as we would argue, in a prolegomenon fashioned to his own contextualized version of the Christian gospel.

25. Stowers, *A Rereading of Romans,* 16-21, 269-72.

26. Quintilian, *Institutio oratoria (On the Education of the Orator)* 9.2.30-33.

27. Seneca, *Medea* 989.

28. Epictetus, *Discourses,* esp. 2.17.19-22; see also 1.28.7-9 and 4.13.15.

29. Stowers, *A Rereading of Romans,* 271-72.

— noting that "earlier [Greek] grammarians had emended many passages in the Homer epics, the Bible of the Greeks, that they considered too immoral for Homer to have written," but that "Aristarchus [of Samothrace; c. 217-145 B.C.] restored many of these [difficult 'I' passages] by emphasizing that words spoken by persons in the narrative represented their views and not necessarily Homer's."[30] Stowers also says such Latin and Greek authors as Cicero, Quintilian, Theon, Hermogenes, and Aphthonius provide "the best evidence from the rhetorical tradition for προσωποποιία in the early [Roman] empire."[31]

In introducing his discussion of ancient "speech in character" rhetoric, Stowers suggests that this rhetorical convention is present in many places in Romans and should be considered by the interpreter; he cites as examples 2:1-5, 3:1-9, 3:31–4:2, and "other texts in Romans."[32] Some of these passages, of course, could be debated. With respect to what we believe to be Paul's soliloquy in 7:14-25, however, such an understanding of what Paul is doing is highly laudatory and needs to be taken into account in our exegesis of the passage.

A Summation and Working Hypothesis. Contrary to a number of earlier scholarly analyses, we propose (1) that 7:7-25 should not be treated as one continuous passage, even though there are some similarities of word and expression throughout, (2) that 7:14-25 is a discrete unit of material, which is best understood as Paul's "soliloquy" or "dramatic monologue" on the subject of "the tragic plight of people who attempt to live their lives apart from God, that is, by means of their own resources and abilities ('under their own steam')," and (3) that this material was originally presented orally by Paul to his Gentile audiences in his Gentile mission and then included here in written fashion to his Christian addressees at Rome. The difference between 7:7-13 in its use of past tenses and 7:14-25 in its use of present tenses should have alerted all previous commentators to the differing purposes and functions of these two passages. The disclosure formula "we know that" (οἴδαμεν ὅτι), which Paul uses in his letters to signal the beginning of a new section of material, should have done the same. As for the apostle's use of (1) the personal pronoun "I" in 7:7-13 to refer to himself and (2) the personal pronoun "I" in 7:14-25 to refer in gnomic fashion to the plight of all humanity, such a dual usage can now be understood as an essential part of Paul's overall rhetoric — especially when one notes his use of "I" in 1 Cor 9:1-27, where the pronoun refers to him personally, vis-à-vis his use in 1 Cor 13:1-13, where "I" is used as a literary *Stilform* ("stylistic form") to heighten the dramatic impact of what he writes.

In Section II of the body middle of Romans, that is, here in 5:1–8:39, Paul shares with his Christian addressees at Rome the essence of what he had been proclaiming as the Christian gospel in his Gentile mission — that is, his contextualization of the Christian message in a manner that resonated with

---

30. Stowers, *A Rereading of Romans,* 19.
31. *Ibid.,* 17.
32. *Ibid.,* 16.

Gentiles who had no preparation for that message by Jewish or Jewish Christian teaching, and so did not think in Jewish categories. It was, as his missionary experience clearly evidenced, a way of proclaiming the "good news" that (1) had proven to be highly significant and meaningful for Gentiles and (2) had resulted, by the work of God's Holy Spirit, in many Gentiles turning from paganism to personal faith in Jesus Christ. And this particular passage of 7:14-25 needs to be seen as an important part of that contextualized message. For as a soliloquy on the human situation "apart from God," it dramatically concludes all that Paul has said about God's grace, the Mosaic law, and people's responses in 6:1–7:13 *and* it effectively prepares for all that he will proclaim about being "in Christ," about being "enabled by God's Spirit," and about "the love of God that is in Christ Jesus our Lord" in 8:1-39.

The Structure of Paul's Soliloquy in 7:14-25. For purposes of analysis, the course of Paul's presentation in 7:14-25 may be set out under the following six headings:

1. Truths commonly known and experienced regarding humanity's lack of personal self-mastery in 7:14-16
2. The presence of the malevolent forces of "sin" (ἡ ἁμαρτία) and "one's own sinful nature" (ἡ σάρξ μου) frustrating every person's best intentions in 7:17-20
3. The dysfunctional experience of knowing what is good but doing what is evil (7:21-23)
4. The human cry of despair and a call for rescue (7:24)
5. A parenthetical interjection: "But thanks be to God, deliverance is through Jesus Christ our Lord!" (7:25a)
6. The conclusion of the matter with respect to people's attempts to live their lives apart from God, that is, by means of their own resources and abilities (7:25b)

This series of headings, with their respective materials, will structure our exegetical comments below.

EXEGETICAL COMMENTS

I. Truths Commonly Known and Experienced regarding Humanity's Lack of Personal Self-Mastery (7:14-16)

7:14-15 The use of a disclosure formula, whether οἴδαμεν γὰρ ὅτι ("for we know that") or οἴδαμεν δὲ ὅτι ("and/now we know that"), was a common way for Paul to begin a new section or subsection in his letters. It was also, it seems, intended by him to highlight the fact that what immediately follows in his presentation was a matter of common ground between himself and his audience (as in his oral preaching) or himself and his addressees (as in his written letters).[33] So what Paul says in this opening paragraph of his soliloquy about humanity's lack of personal self-mastery should be viewed as matters that he believed both pagan Gentiles in his Gentile mission and Jewish-Gentile Christians at Rome would acknowledge as true, and thus would agree with him about.

These commonly known and experienced truths are as follows: (1) that "the law is spiritual" (ὁ νόμος πνευματικός); but (2) that "I am fleshly" (ἐγὼ δὲ σάρκινός εἰμι), and (3) that "I have been sold [as a slave] under sin" (πεπραμένος ὑπὸ τὴν ἁμαρτίαν). The first truth, that "the law is spiritual," goes beyond what Paul has said about the law in 7:12, that is, that "the law is holy, and the command-ment is holy, righteous, and good." To speak of the law as "spiritual," as Robert Jewett has pointed out, is "unparalleled" and a bit "innovative" in early Jewish and early Christian literature.[34] For, as Jewett has observed, while in his letter to Rome Paul had "referred to the spiritual blessing of the Gospel (Rom 1:11), a theme to which he will return in 15:27" — and while earlier in 1 Corinthians and Galatians "he frequently referred to other features of the new age as 'spiritual' (eleven times in 1 Corinthians; once in Galatians)" — "never did he or anyone else prior to this moment . . . ever connect the word 'law' with the adjective 'spiritual.'"[35] In the OT and the writings of Second Temple Judaism, as Jewett goes on to argue, "pro-phetic and wisdom literature are thought to be expressions of the divine Spirit, but it was not until the early rabbinic period that a spiritual origin was claimed for the entire Jewish Scripture."[36] Jewett further notes that while "early Chris-tians were making similar claims about their sacred writings [i.e., that they were expressions of the divine Spirit]" in such passages as Matt 22:43, Mark 12:36, Acts 1:16, 4:25, 28:25, and 2 Pet 1:21, they did so "without using the terms Paul employs here [i.e., πνευματικός and its association with ὁ νόμος]."[37]

Paul's attribution of spirituality to the law may indeed be somewhat inno-vative in form. Nonetheless, the coupling of the adjective πνευματικός with the articular noun ὁ νόμος is highly appropriate in Paul's theological understanding and his Christian proclamation, for it speaks of (1) the law's divine origin as having been given by God's Spirit, (2) the law's authority as being inherent in the fact that it expresses God's will for humanity, and (3) the law as being never able to be properly understood or put into practice except by the enablement of the same Spirit by whom it was given.[38] "The law," as Joseph Fitzmyer has aptly

---

33. Cf. Stowers, *Diatribe and Paul's Letter to the Romans,* 94. See Paul's use in Romans of other disclosure formulas at 2:2; 3:19; 6:3, 16; 7:1; 8:22, 28 (probably also 8:18 and 26); and 11:25.

34. Jewett, *Romans,* 460-61.

35. *Ibid.,* 460, evidently having in mind Paul's earlier use of "spiritual" in such passages as 1 Cor 2:13, 15; 3:1; 9:11; 10:3-4; 12:2; 14:1, 37; 15:44, 46; and Gal 6:1.

36. *Ibid.,* citing in support Erik Sjöberg, "πνεῦμα, πνευματικός . . . in Palestinian Judaism," *TDNT* 6.381-82.

37. Jewett, *Romans,* 460.

38. Cf. Cranfield, *Romans,* 1.355-56; Schlier, *Römerbrief.* See particularly 1 Cor 2:10-16 and Rom 8:4 on this latter point of "the enablement of the same Spirit by whom it was given" as being necessary for a proper understanding and practice of God's law.

rephrased what Paul is saying, "does not belong to the world of earthbound, natural humanity. As *pneumatikos,* the law belongs to the sphere of God, to the sphere of the Spirit of God; it is an expression of God's will"[39] — and as such, "it is opposed to what is *sarkinos,* 'carnal, belonging to the sphere of flesh.' "[40]

The second truth that Paul evidently believes to be rather self-evident among all people is connected with his gnomic or general use of the first-person pronoun "I" (ἐγώ) and is expressed in very brief and antithetical fashion: "But I am fleshly" (ἐγὼ δὲ σάρκινός εἰμι). Paul's earlier use in 1 Cor 3:1-3 of the plural substantival adjective σαρκίνοις ("those who are fleshly," i.e., "those controlled by the sinful nature"), together with its roughly synonymous cognate σαρκικοί ("those who are fleshly," i.e., "those who belong only to the order of earthly things") — as well as his use in Rom 7:5 of the expression ἐν τῇ σαρκί ("in the flesh," i.e., "controlled by the sinful nature") — suggests that Paul here in 7:14, by a *Stilform* use of the personal pronoun ἐγώ coupled with the substantival adjective σάρκινος, is not speaking simply of the material composition of human beings, but rather of the control of all people by their inherited sinful nature. And Paul's highlighting of the gnomic first-person pronoun ἐγώ ("I") by the addition of the first-person verb εἰμι ("I am") functions to lay emphasis on this universal situation of all people.

The participial clause πεπραμένος ὑπὸ τήν ἁμαρτίαν ("having been sold under sin"), which appears at the close of 7:14 and incorporates the third truth that Paul states in this verse, directs attention to the primary problem that confronts every human being in his or her human existence — that is, being a slave to sin and so controlled by one's sinful nature. Paul evidently believed this was also rather self-evident among all people — or, at least, would be acknowledged by almost all spiritually sensitive people, whatever their religious backgrounds; humanity has been "sold [as a slave] under [the control of] sin."

The expression "sold under sin" would have been understood by Paul's pagan audiences in his Gentile mission — as well as by his Christian addressees at Rome — as a religious use of the language of slavery, as we have noted earlier in our discussion of Paul's use of the analogy and language of slavery in 6:15-23. Here in 7:14 Paul uses that same language, but this time to awaken in the consciousness of those who heard him preach (as well as those who will read his Roman letter or hear it read) what he believed they already knew in their hearts but were reticent to put into words: that all people have inherited a condition of death and depravity, which may be characterized as "having been sold [as a slave] under [the control of] sin" — which inherited condition has perverted their best intentions and affected all their actions. Paul's use of the articular τὴν ἁμαρτίαν ("the sin") suggests that he is here in 7:14 (as well as later in 7:17, 20, and 23) personifying "sin" as a malevolent force that is both hostile to God and alienates people from God — just as he did earlier in his use of ἡ ἁμαρτία ("the

---

39. Fitzmyer, *Romans,* 473.
40. *Ibid.*

sin") in 5:12 and 20-21, which verses constitute the beginning and the conclusion of his "foundational narrative" of 5:12-21.

Thus using a "speech in character" rhetorical style, which employs in a gnomic fashion the first-person pronoun "I" (ἐγώ), Paul in 7:15 highlights the fact that this truth regarding people's lack of personal self-mastery, which stems from humanity's heritage of "having been sold under sin," has been known and experienced by most spiritually perceptive people. Further, quoting in paraphrastic fashion laments that Euripides, the Greek poet, placed on the lips of the women Medea and Phaedra, and that Ovid, the Roman poet, put on the lips of one of his characters,[41] Paul suggests that "I do not know (οὐ γινώσκω) what I am bringing about (ὅ κατεργάζομαι)" has become the sad realization of a great many spiritually sensitive people. And by using the verb μισέω or μισῶ ("I hate," "abhor," "detest"), which appears only here in the apostle's extant NT letters, he seems to be acknowledging that what he is saying about the realization and experience of people generally has been drawn from certain ancient Greek and Roman poets — which statements, as Stanley Stowers has pointed out, "played a central role in the Greek moral tradition" and "were variously interpreted in discussions about the roles of the emotions, deliberation, and knowledge of good and evil in moral psychology."[42]

7:16 From such "commonly known and experienced truths" regarding "humanity's lack of personal self-mastery" as expressed in 7:14-15, Paul, as both a Jew and a Christian, draws in 7:16 the following important observation: "If then I do what I do not want to do, I agree with the law that it is good (καλός)." He made this point previously in 7:12 in declaring that "the law is holy, and the commandment is holy, righteous and good (ἀγαθή)" — with its goodness being evident, as he argued in 7:13, in the fact that the law of God reveals sin to be "utterly sinful" (ὑπερβολὴν ἁμαρτωλός). And he will make it again in 8:3, arguing that "the law's inability" (τὸ ἀδύνατον τοῦ νόμου) to set people free from sin and death is not because the law itself is deficient or evil, but rather because the law as given by God has been in its reception seriously "weakened by the sinful nature" (ἠσθένει διὰ τῆς σαρκός) of people.

II. The Presence of the Malevolent Forces of "Sin" and "One's Own Sinful Nature" Frustrating Every Person's Best Intentions (7:17-20)

7:17-20 While the phrase νυνὶ δὲ ("but now") is used in 3:21; 6:22; 7:6; and 15:23 and 25 in a temporal sense to signal the contrast God has brought about through the work of Christ and the ministry of the Holy Spirit, either in the course of salvation history or in the life of a believer (or both),[43] it is also sometimes used

---

41. As cited above in the "Form/Structure/Setting" section.
42. Stowers, *A Rereading of Romans*, 263-64.
43. Cf. also 2 Cor 8:22; Eph 2:13; and Phlm 9, 11

by Paul in a logical or inferential sense rather than a temporal sense[44] — and therefore, at times, should be understood along the lines of the expression "but now the situation is this." And that is how we believe νυνὶ δὲ ("but now") is best understood here in 7:17, that is, as logically connecting the statements of 7:17-20 in an inferential manner with those just previously set out in 7:14-16.[45]

Thus in support of the truths set out in 7:14-16 regarding humanity's lack of personal self-mastery, Paul goes on in 7:17-20 to focus on the real problem that lies at the heart of humanity's tragic situation: the presence of the malevolent forces of "the sin" (ἡ ἁμαρτία) that have permeated all of human history and "one's own sinful nature" (ἡ σάρξ μου) and that frustrate every person's best intentions. In so doing he characterizes in 7:18 the experience of every spiritually sensitive person as (1) knowing that "nothing good lives in me" and (2) recognizing that "the desire is present in me, but the ability to bring about what is good is not." Then in support of such a universal experience and recognition, he paraphrases in 7:19 the lament expressed in Ovid's formulation of Medea's dilemma: "I see and approve the better course, but I follow the worse."[46] This same lament appeared in various forms among many of the dramatists and moralistic writers of Paul's day. And shortly after Paul's time, it was picked up by the Stoic philosopher Epictetus in his evaluation of the human situation: "Every sin involves a contradiction; for since he who sins does not wish to sin, but to be right, it is clear that he is not doing what he wishes."[47]

While the tragic plight of humanity may have been expressed somewhat similarly by Greek and Roman poets, by ancient dramatists and playwrights, and by Stoic philosophers, the Christian solution to this universal lament was decidedly different. For while the ancient poets and philosophers proposed some form of enlightenment as a cure for this central human predicament, for Paul, as Robert Jewett has aptly pointed out, "the situation of being 'sold under sin' involved an unacknowledged hostility against God and thus required a much more fundamental cure."[48] What Paul preached in his Gentile mission — and what he reported to the Christians at Rome about it — was that the Christian gospel proclaims not just some new understanding of one's own self and some new path of enlightenment to be followed to gain acceptance by God and personal wholeness, but rather (1) a much more radical understanding of the human predicament, which stems from "hostility against God," and (2) a much more radical appreciation of what God has provided through the person and ministry of Jesus Christ, which alone can bring about "reconciliation" with God and "wholeness" in a person's life.

Here in 7:17-20, therefore, Paul sets out the basic problem of humanity as

44. Cf. esp. 1 Cor 12:18 and 13:13.
45. So, e.g., Kuss, *Römerbrief,* 2.454; Käsemann, *Romans,* 204; Moo, *Romans,* 457; and Jewett, *Romans,* 467.
46. Ovid, *Metamorphoses* 7.21.
47. Epictetus, *Dissertations* 2.26.1-2.
48. Jewett, *Romans,* 464.

being "the sin that lives in me" (7:17 and 20: ἡ οἰκοῦσα ἐν ἐμοὶ ἁμαρτία) — that is, what "I" know and have experienced "in my sinful nature" (7:18: ἐν τῇ σαρκί μου). He will (1) elaborate further in 7:21-23 on this matter and its consequences for one's life, (2) utter in 7:24 the human cry of despair and a cry for rescue, and (3) state in 7:25b his conclusion to what he has here presented regarding humanity's tragic plight — all of which (except, of course, the interjected statement "Thanks be to God, [deliverance is] through Jesus Christ our Lord!" in 8:25a, which statement is developed more fully in Rom 8) will be countered in 8:1-39 by Paul's proclamation of what God has done on behalf of people through the person and ministry of Christ Jesus and because of their being "in Christ" and thus also "in the Spirit."

III. The Dysfunctional Experience of Knowing What Is Good but Doing What Is Evil (7:21-23)

7:21-23 Paul then goes further by portraying the dysfunctional reality that every person experiences in knowing what is good but doing what is evil. The post-positive particle ἄρα ("so," "then"), which later in 7:25b is incorporated into the expression ἄρα οὖν ("therefore," "consequently"),[49] was used in koine Greek not only in an illative or inferential fashion (i.e., to draw an inference from what precedes), but also to enliven a statement or question. Josephus, for example, in recounting David's response to Saul's offer to give his daughter Michal in marriage to him, starts off David's reply with the question: "So then (ἄρα), does it seem to you a small thing to become a king's son-in-law?"[50] It is with that same colloquial particle ἄρα ("so," "so then") that Paul here in 7:21 begins his statements about the dysfunctional reality that every person experiences in knowing what is good but doing what is evil[51] — evidently with the intention of enlivening the force of those statements in 7:21-23, reserving the use of ἄρα four verses later in the expression ἄρα οὖν ("therefore," "consequently") of 7:25b to signal the presence of an inferential conclusion.

However, the attention of commentators has usually been focused on the repeated use in 7:21-23 of "law" (νόμος) and on what Paul means by "the law" (ὁ νόμος) — for in these three verses he speaks (1) of "the law" or "this law" (τὸν νόμον) in v. 21; (2) of delighting in his inner being "in the law of God" (τῷ νόμῳ τοῦ θεοῦ) in v. 22; and (3) of "another law" (ἕτερον νόμον) at work in the members of his body, which is opposed to "the law of my mind" (τῷ νόμῳ τοῦ νοός μου) and has made him a prisoner "by the law of sin" (ἐν τῷ νόμῳ τῆς ἁμαρτίας), in v. 23. The question often posed is this: Is there a single, unified

---

49. Cf. also Paul's use of ἄρα οὖν ("therefore," "consequently") in 5:18; 7:3; and 8:12.

50. Josephus, *Antiquities* 6.200a.

51. In Gal 2:21 Paul also uses ἄρα singly in the *apodosis* of a conditional sentence simply to enliven the statement by some such expression as "so then" or "then" — though ἄρα here in this verse is often not translated in modern translations.

sense in which νόμος is used five times in these verses? Or is Paul in 7:21 using νόμος in the sense of a "rule" or "principle," then in 7:22 in the sense of the Mosaic law, and finally in 7:23 in the sense of a "set of principles" or "body of teaching" that is opposed to God's law?

Admittedly, the vast majority of occurrences of ὁ νόμος and νόμος in Paul's letter to Rome — with the exceptions of the phrases "the law of faith" in 3:27b, "the law of the Spirit of life" in 8:2a, and "the law of sin and death" in 8:2b[52] — refer to the Mosaic law, and so many commentators have argued that reference to the Jewish Torah needs also, in some fashion, to be understood throughout 7:21-23.[53] On the other hand, the use of νόμος in the sense of a "rule," "principle," or "body of teaching" was not uncommon in Paul's day.[54] And even if Paul's varied uses of νόμος in Rom 3:27b, 8:2a, and 8:2b (as well as in Gal 6:2 and 1 Cor 9:21) are, for some reason, discounted, here in 7:14-25 (as we have proposed) Paul is setting out for his Christian addressees at Rome the substance of a soliloquy that he originally used in his preaching to pagan Gentiles in his Gentile mission — and therefore it need not be viewed as strange that Paul used νόμος in that soliloquy not only in the sense of "the law of God" but also in ways that his Gentile audiences would understand as connoting a "rule," "principle," or "body of teaching."

It has often been claimed that such a dysfunctional experience of "knowing what is good but doing what is evil" was a new discovery by Paul, which came to him at the time of his turning in repentance to God and his acceptance of Jesus as Israel's promised Messiah. Robert Jewett, for example, expresses such a view in saying that "the contradiction between willing the good and actually performing it" was "a new insight that had been unavailable to Paul prior to his conversion."[55] I have argued, however, (1) that such an awareness is an abiding realization of most spiritually sensitive people, and (2) that it takes specific form in the lives of the most earnest and pious, whatever their philosophical or religious commitments.[56] It is this awareness of the basic human predicament that Paul seems to have built on in his proclamation of the Christian gospel to pagan Gentiles in his Gentile mission, the essence of which preaching he sets out for his Christian addressees at Rome.

IV. The Human Cry of Despair and a Call for Rescue (7:24)

7:24 Here in this verse appears one of the most sorrowful cries ever uttered by any human being: ταλαίπωρος ἐγὼ ἄνθρωπος· τίς με ῥύσεται ἐκ τοῦ σώματος

---

52. Cf. also Gal 6:2 ("the law of Christ") and 1 Cor 9:21 ("being 'in-lawed' to Christ").

53. Cf., e.g., Dunn, *Romans*, 1.392-93 (with Dunn denying that 3:27 is a true exception).

54. Cf. Räisänen, *Paul and the Law*, 50 n. 34, which is expanded with extensive detail in *idem*, "Paul's Word-Play on νόμος: A Linguistic Study," in his *Jesus, Paul, and Torah*, 69-94. So also Godet, *Romans*, 2.42-43; Kuss, *Römerbrief*, 2.455-56; Käsemann, *Romans*, 205; Cranfield, *Romans*, 1.362.

55. Jewett, *Romans*, 469, citing in support H. Preisker, "εὑρίσκω," *TDNT* 2.769.

56. Cf. R. N. Longenecker, *Paul, Apostle of Liberty*, 96-97.

τοῦ θανάτου τούτου; (" 'What a wretched person I am!' Who will rescue me from this body of death?"). This cry of despair echoes, as we have noted above,[57] (1) Seneca's account of Medea's final cry of despair, "What, wretched woman, have I done?"[58] (2) Ovid's placement on the lips of the daughter of King Aeëtes the self-loathing appellation, "Oh wretched one!"[59] (3) Epictetus's statements about people who lament that they are "wretched,"[60] and (4) the lament "O wretch that I am," which was drawn from the words Euripides placed on the lips of Medea — and was later used by various tragedians and comedians — to epitomize the essential contradiction and resultant realization of many spiritually sensitive people regarding human life.[61] And this call for deliverance, "Who will rescue me?" Paul sees as inherent in that universal cry of despair.

Set as they are in the context of a "speech in character" — and using the gnomic first-person singular "I" — this cry of despair and this call for rescue express the anguish and yearning of not just Paul alone. Nor do such a cry and call depict people in either their preconversion state or their postconversion condition. Rather, it is Paul uttering humanity's cry of its own inability and giving voice to the call for rescue of many spiritually sensitive people. These are, of course, deeply felt human feelings of Paul himself. But more than that, they represent humanity's basic recognition that — because of our corporate history and our own personal experiences — all of us as human beings have become so bound by depravity and sin that there can be rescue and deliverance only by divine intervention. This is not the recognition of the legalist. It is the abiding realization of the spiritually sensitive, and it is felt most keenly by those who are closest to God.

The Christian, knowing God more intimately and his salvation more personally than did most of God's people under Israel's old covenant (or, for that matter, under any other religious system or teaching), is in a position to realize his or her own inability to a far greater extent than could have been known or experienced under the Jewish law. But that does not mean that a spiritually sensitive Jew under the old covenant, as represented in Israel's canonical psalms and prophetic writings — or even a spiritually sensitive Gentile, as possibly depicted in Rom 2:14-15 — could not have been aware of his or her own inadequacy before God and cry out for God's intervention. Further, the repeated insistences in the Qumran literature on the inability of all flesh of itself to stand before God[62] strikingly reveal, as Millar Burrows has pointed out, that "the point at which the very roots of Paul's theology and that of the Dead Sea Scrolls are intertwined is the experience of moral frustration, with the resulting conviction

57. See above in the "Form/Structure/Setting" section.
58. Cf. Seneca, *Medea* 989.
59. Cf. Ovid, *Metamorphoses* 7.17.
60. Cf. Epictetus, *Discourses* 1.28.7-9; 2.17.19-22; 4.13.15.
61. Stowers, *A Rereading of Romans,* 271-72.
62. Cf. esp. 1QH 1.21-23; 3.24-36; 4.5-40; and 1QS 11.9-10.

of man's hopeless sinfulness."[63] The writer of *4 Ezra* shares this conviction of the inability of human beings to stand before God and do his will by their own efforts and resources[64] — though, of course, the solution given to this basic human problem by the writer of *4 Ezra,* as well as that given by the teachers at the Qumran community, differs from that proclaimed by the apostle Paul.

The cry of despair and the call for rescue in 7:24, therefore, cannot be understood only in terms of Paul's preconversion or postconversion experiences. They are, rather, the universal human cry and human call, which have come to expression because of the corporate history and personal experience of all people — a cry and call that have been, and continue to be, known and experienced by every spiritually sensitive person of every race and nation throughout the course of all human history. Though Paul's intimate and personal relationship with God "through Jesus Christ our Lord" brought about a more intensive realization and expression of this inherited condition of death, depravity, and sin, it would be quite erroneous to suppose that he was entirely unaware of such matters during his earlier Judaistic days. The testimony of such texts as cited above from the Dead Sea Scrolls and *4 Ezra* stands as a warning against such an assumption.[65] And Paul's use in his Gentile mission of this soliloquy, which he here in 7:14-25 sets out for his Christian addressees at Rome, suggests that he believed that such a cry of despair and such a call for rescue were known by many of the more spiritually sensitive pagan Gentiles of the ancient Greco-Roman world.

The expression ἐκ τοῦ σώματος τοῦ θανάτου τούτου has been often understood somewhat differently by NT commentators. Grammatically, the demonstrative pronoun τούτου ("this") could be taken with τοῦ σώματος ("the body"), and so read "*this* body of death,"[66] or taken with τοῦ θανάτου ("the death"), and so read "the body of *this* death."[67] Charles Cranfield has aptly set forth the rationale that has usually been given for each of these two grammatically possible views as follows — proposing in the process his own preferred translation as being the former, that is, "this body of death":

> The fact that there have been references to a death in vv. 10, 11, and 13, and the possibility of regarding vv. 14-23 as explanatory of that death, have inclined some commentators to prefer the latter alternative [i.e., "the body of *this* death"]. But, since an equivalent of σῶμα has twice been used in v. 23 (the repeated ἐν τοῖς μέλεσίν μου) and since vv. 14-23 may perhaps rather

63. M. Burrows, *More Light on the Dead Sea Scrolls* (New York: Viking Press, 1958), 119.
64. Cf. esp. *4 Ezra* 8:31-36.
65. Cf. again 1QH 1.21-23; 3.24-36; 4.5-40; 1QS 11.9-10; and *4 Ezra* 8:31-36.
66. So NIV, NRSV, NJB, and TEV; cf. also Cranfield, *Romans,* 1.366-67; Fitzmyer, *Romans,* 436 (and 476); and Jewett, *Romans,* 472 (with such earlier commentators as A. Schlatter, E. Gaugler, and J. Murray taking this view as well).
67. So KJV and NASB; cf. also Käsemann, *Romans,* 209, and Moo, *Romans,* 466 (with such earlier scholars as H. Lietzmann, W. Kümmel, M.-J. Lagrange, and O. Kuss interpreting the expression in this way as well).

more naturally be considered a drawing out of the meaning of bodily life (note the prominence of σάρκινος in v. 14), we judge it better to take τούτου with σώματος [i.e., "*this* body of death"].[68]

Agreeing with Cranfield regarding the *immediate grammatical antecedents* of the expression, but also drawing attention to its *broader conceptual context,* I would point out that Paul begins his "foundational narrative" of 5:12-21 by first setting out in 5:12 a chain of causality, which includes both (1) the sin of the first man Adam *and* (2) the inherited death, depravity, and sinful condition of all the descendants of that first man, whatever their location, situation, or claimed status. And in that chain of causality Paul personifies both (1) "sin" as a malevolent force that is hostile to God and alienates human beings from God, using the articular ἡ ἁμαρτία ("the sin") in 5:12 (as well as in 5:20-21), and (2) "death" as a cosmic force that not only brings to an end the physical life and personality of a human being, but also — and far more importantly — separates people from God during their earthly lives and finally throughout eternity, using the articular ὁ θάνατος ("the death") in 5:12 (as well as three times later in 5:14, 17, and 21).[69]

At the very beginning of the passage here in 7:14-25, in 7:14b, Paul speaks of humanity "having been sold under sin" — by which he evidently means that all people have inherited the condition of "death" and "depravity," which has perverted even their best intentions and affected all their actions.[70] It is, we believe, in this context — as depicted in 5:12 and 7:14, as well as everything he writes throughout 5:1–7:25 about the presence of "sin" (i.e., what Adam brought about, which has been a factor throughout human history) and "death" (i.e., humanity's inherited depravity, which has been ratified by the thoughts and actions of people throughout human history) — that Paul's reference here in 7:24 regarding "deliverance from *this body of death*" should be understood.

Thus we propose that in 7:24b the expression τοῦ σώματος . . . τούτου is best viewed in a metaphorical sense to signify "this sum total," "substance," or "reality" — much as translators have come to understand τὸ σῶμα ("the body") in Col 2:17, in opposition to the term σκιά ("a shadow"), as signifying "the totality," "substance," or "reality"[71] — and that the phrase τοῦ θανάτου has reference to humanity's inheritance of "death" and "depravity," which have seriously affected the thoughts and actions of all people. And so, though it would be both awkward and cumbersome to translate the expression exactly in this manner, we believe it necessary to understand the expression "this body of death" as a

---

68. Cranfield, *Romans*, 1.367.

69. Cf. Rom 6:16, 21, 23; 7:5, 10, 13, 24; 8:2, 6, 38; see also 1 Cor 3:22; 2 Cor 7:10.

70. See our "Exegetical Comments" above on 7:14.

71. On τὸ σῶμα ("the body") in Col 2:17, note the translation "the substance" in Moffatt, RSV, NRSV, and NAS — though probably better is the translation "the reality" in JB, NEB, and NIV. Cf. also a somewhat similar metaphorical usage in the papyrus materials of the second century A.D. in *P Fay* 34.20: "I, Heron, the above-mentioned, have written *the body* of the contract and agreed to all the aforesaid terms as is aforesaid"; see also *P Lond* 1132 *b.* 11 (cf. *M-M,* 621).

shorthand or cryptic way (that is, as characterized by a somewhat perplexing brevity) of speaking of deliverance from "this sum total (i.e., 'substance' or 'reality') of human sin and depravity."

V. Parenthetical Interjection (7:25a)

7:25a Many commentators have understood the opening words of 7:25a, χάρις δὲ τῷ θεῷ διὰ Ἰησοῦ Χριστοῦ τοῦ κυρίου ἡμῶν ("But thanks be to God, [deliverance is] through Jesus Christ our Lord!"), as Paul's positive conclusion to all that he wrote negatively about the inadequacies of human abilities and resources in 7:7-24. So, for example, after treating 7:25a, Anders Nygren wrote: "Paul has reached the conclusion of his discussion."[72] Thus also Charles Cranfield spoke of these words of thanksgiving ("but thanks be to God") and deliverance ("through Jesus Christ our Lord") in 7:25a as "an indirect answer to the question in v. 24."[73]

Yet it has frequently been asked: Why, after giving thanks to God for deliverance in 7:25a (which seems to present a positive conclusion to all that has been expressed in 7:14-24), should Paul revert back in this final lament of 7:25b to speaking about the inability and futility of human action to do good apart from divine intervention (which continues the negative laments of 7:14-24)? C. H. Dodd has stated the problem that many have found in the passage: "It is scarcely conceivable that, after giving thanks to God for deliverance, Paul should describe himself as being in exactly the same position as before."[74]

Thus, although there is no external evidence in the textual tradition that would support their views, a number of NT interpreters have resorted to one or another of the following expedients: (1) to reverse the positions of the material in 7:25a (the seeming conclusion) and the material in 7:25b (the final lament of the passage),[75] (2) to declare that 7:25b "is very likely a gloss, which, in addition, has landed in the text at the wrong place; it belongs to vs. 23,"[76] (3) to suggest that 7:25b can safely be eliminated, since it appears to be an interpolation or an error that has crept into the text in the process of dictation,[77] or (4) to argue that not only is 7:25b rightly placed when it precedes 7:24-25a, but that 8:2 must also be transposed to follow immediately after 7:25a.[78] C. H. Dodd in 1932 gave voice to the basic understanding of all these interpreters on this matter when

---

72. Nygren, *Romans,* 302.

73. Cranfield, *Romans,* 1.367.

74. C. H. Dodd, *Romans,* 114-15.

75. So, e.g., *ibid.;* J. Moffatt, *An Introduction to the Literature of the New Testament* (Edinburgh: T. & T. Clark, 1912), 143.

76. So, e.g., Bultmann, "Glossen im Römerbrief," 198-99; *idem,* "Christ the End of the Law," 40; Käsemann, *Romans,* 212: "Here if anywhere we have the gloss of a later reader, which presents the first Christian interpretation of vv. 7-24."

77. So, e.g., Lietzmann, *An die Römer,* 39.

78. So, e.g., Müller, "Zwei Marginalien im Brief Paulus an die Römer," 249-54.

he wrote: "We do seem to have here one of the cases . . . where a primitive corruption of the text has affected all our surviving MSS., and we cannot avoid trusting our own judgment against their evidence."[79]

It is, however, far better to understand the exclamatory statement of 7:25a, "But thanks be to God, [deliverance is] through Jesus Christ our Lord!" as a "parenthetic interjection"[80] that Paul inserted into his "speech in character" presentation of 7:14-25. For this exclamation of 7:25a is in line with his earlier exclamation of 6:17, "But thanks be to God" (χάρις δὲ τῷ θεῷ), which he interjected between his statements in 6:16-20 regarding the former condition of his addressees as having been "slaves to sin, which leads to death."[81]

VI. The Conclusion of the Matter with Respect to People's Attempts to Live Their Lives Apart from God, That Is, "by Means of Their Own Resources and Abilities" (7:25b)

7:25b The joining of the inferential particles ἄρα ("so," "then," "consequently") and οὖν ("so," "therefore," "consequently") to indicate the conclusion of a matter being discussed occurs (as we noted in our exegetical comments on 5:18 and 7:3) about fifty times in the Synoptic Gospels, Acts, the Pauline letters, and Hebrews, with Paul evidently being fond of using ἄρα οὖν in this manner.[82] Therefore — despite (1) suggestions that the exclamatory statement of 7:25a provides the conclusion to the presentation of 7:14-24, (2) proposals to the effect that the material in 7:25b is either a gloss or an interpolation, which could therefore be ignored altogether, or (3) arguments that 7:25b should be relocated to a position after 7:23 and before 7:24 — the probability is high that the material of 7:25b, which begins with this heightened inferential expression ἄρα οὖν, should be understood as the true conclusion to Paul's soliloquy of 7:14-25.

In 1954 C. L. Mitton asked with respect to the then-current scholarly hab-

79. C. H. Dodd, *Romans*, 115. Cf. also the varied statements of the problem and the various solutions that have been proposed by such representative scholars as J. Weiss, "Beiträge zur paulinischen Rhetorik," 232-33; Kuss, *Römerbrief*, 2.461; O'Neill, *Romans*, 131-32; Schlier, *Römerbrief*, 235; Wilckens, *An die Römer*, 2.96-97; and Jewett, *Romans*, 456-58 and 476.

80. Cf. Stowers, *A Rereading of Romans*, 281 — though Stowers includes 7:25b in this "parenthetic interjection" and proposes that the "speech in character" material continues on to the end of 8:2; see also Jewett, *Romans*, 456, who speaks of "the ejaculation in vv. 24-25a." In 1964 I used the expressions "anticipatory exclamation," "interjected parenthesis," "anticipatory interjection," and "anticipatory ejaculation" (cf. R. N. Longenecker, *Paul, Apostle of Liberty*, 113-15) for what I now prefer simply to call, accepting Stowers's phraseology, Paul's "parenthetic interjection".

81. Cf. Paul's similarly worded exclamations in 1 Cor 15:57; 2 Cor 2:14 and 8:16; perhaps also in 2 Cor 9:15.

82. In addition to Paul's use of the idiomatic expression ἄρα οὖν here in 7:25b, see also his earlier concluding use at 5:18 and 7:3 and his further usage in 8:12; 9:16, 18; and 14:12, 19. In 8:1, however, he writes ἄρα νῦν ("therefore now"). In Rom 7:21 and Gal 2:21 he uses ἄρα singly, simply, as it seems, to enliven the statement by the expression "so then" or "then" — though ἄρα used singly is usually not translated in modern translations.

its of disregarding or transposing the position of 7:25b and failing to appreciate the import of the pronouns αὐτὸς ἐγώ in the verse: "Are we not in reality
setting aside the key to the passage?" — and he answered that question in the
affirmative.[83] Mitton pointed out that the pronouns when combined together
are "exceedingly emphatic," and, further, that when joined together they sum
up all the previous occurrences of ἐγώ in the chapter. Thus he insisted that 7:25b
is neither to be ignored nor to be relocated, but should be regarded as the summary of the whole chapter — and, further, that the true contrast between chs.
7 and 8 is to be found in the αὐτὸς ἐγώ expression of 7:25b and the ἐν Χριστῷ
Ἰησοῦ expression of 8:1.[84] It is with Mitton's treatment of 7:25b and its relation
to both what precedes it and what follows it that I agree.

The expression αὐτὸς ἐγώ certainly signifies more than simply the "Ich"
of Luther's German Bible or the "I" of the JB English translation; likewise, it
connotes more than "I myself" of the KJV, NEB, NIV, TNIV, and NET. And
certainly it should not, because of its difficulty of translation, be simply left untranslated, as was done by the translators of the NRSV. Moffatt's "left to myself,"
TEV's "by myself," and Phillips's "in my own nature" are undoubtedly better.
Probably, however, the best concise translation is "I of myself" of the ASV and
RSV, and that is how we have translated it above — though even that translation
needs to be understood more expansively along the lines of some such phraseology as "I by means of my own resources and abilities, apart from God" (or,
more colloquially, "I under my own steam").

When ἄρα οὖν is understood as signaling the conclusion to the apostle's
soliloquy of 7:14-25 and αὐτὸς ἐγώ is taken as the key to all that he has presented
in the passage, what then is Paul saying in 7:25b that summarizes the message
of his "speech in character" rhetorical material of 7:14-24? It is this: human
beings, because of their inherited depravity and their own sins, have become
spiritually and personally schizophrenic — that is, all people contain within
their persons and express in their actions contradictory attitudes and qualities
that, apart from divine intervention, keep them from doing the good things
that they know to be right (which spring from their knowledge of "the law of
God") and are always being driven to do those evil things that they know to be
wrong (which arise from their servitude to "the law of sin"). Or, as C. L. Mitton
has paraphrased 7:25b:

> This then is the conclusion to which I have been leading: when I rely on
> my own resources, and cease to depend on God, then this is what happens
> — I continue to acknowledge with my judgment the authority of God's
> commands, but in my thoughts and actions it is the authority of sin which
> holds sway.[85]

83. Mitton, "Romans vii," 132-35.
84. *Ibid.*
85. *Ibid.*, 134.

Or, perhaps better, as William Sanday and Arthur Headlam have paraphrased Paul's meaning in this passage:

> Without His intervention — so long as I am left to my own unaided self — the state that I have been describing may be briefly summarized: In this twofold capacity of mine I serve two masters: with my conscience I serve the Law of God; with my bodily organism the Law of Sin.[86]

BIBLICAL THEOLOGY

Rom 7:7-25 is not to be viewed as Paul's evaluation of either his preconversion Jewish experience or his postconversion Christian experience. Nor do these verses express the lament of only a Jew under the Mosaic law or the cry of only a Christian who slips back into a legalistic attitude toward God. Rather, this awful lament should be understood as Paul's rhetorical soliloquy, which he sets out in a "speech in character" rhetorical form, regarding the tragic plight of all people who attempt to live their lives by their own natural abilities and acquired resources, apart from God. And it expresses the realization of both Paul and all spiritually sensitive people that, because of humanity's corporate history and our own personal experiences, we have become so bound up by depravity and sin that there can be deliverance only through divine intervention.

This is not the recognition of a religious legalist or crass materialist. It is, rather, the abiding realization of the spiritually sensitive of whatever time, race, or geographical locality. It seems, in fact, to be a consciousness that is felt most intensely by those who are the closest to God. Thus, prior to his contextualized Christian message of 8:1-39, which form of the Christian gospel he had proclaimed to Gentiles in his Gentile mission and here reports to his Christian addressees at Rome, Paul presents in the form of a soliloquy what he knows to be true from Scripture and what he has confirmed from his own observations of the human predicament — and, further, what he believes pagan Gentiles also understand from their knowledge of God as drawn from God's creation all around them, from human history, and from their own experiences: that people, in their minds, are aware of what is good and right, and so seek to serve "the law of God," but in their everyday existences they all too often do what is evil and wrong, and so serve "the law of sin," thereby giving evidence of being spiritually and personally schizophrenic and in desperate need of divine salvation.

In reading Romans, therefore, we need to appreciate how Paul has used such a common human realization and consciousness as preparation for his contextualized proclamation of the Christian gospel. Likewise, in our Christian biblical theology we need to incorporate that same realization and consciousness

---

86. Sanday and Headlam, *Romans*, 178.

into our endeavors to understand, describe, and proclaim — humbly accepting that we lack resources and abilities, and so rely entirely on God and his Spirit. And in our living, there is, as well, the constant need to be aware of our human frailties and liabilities — thus seeking always to walk humbly before God and others, being conscious of God's abiding presence, of new life and hope given through the work of Christ Jesus, and of the enablement that God provides through the ministry of his Spirit.

CONTEXTUALIZATION FOR TODAY

The soliloquy of 7:14-25 not only teaches us something about how Paul, "the apostle to the Gentiles," used the literary forms, rhetorical techniques, classical themes, and current expressions of his day as prolegomena to the message of the Christian gospel. It also suggests some things about the pagan audiences he addressed in his Gentile mission, as well as his Christian addressees at Rome for whom he wrote this soliloquy. Further, it alerts us to the need to couch our communication of the Christian gospel to people of our day and society in a way that incorporates the forms, techniques, themes, and expressions that would be meaningful to them. Paul in his Christian ministry seems to have been a master at such contextualization of the Christian message. And his letter to the Christians at Rome, as we have suggested at a number of places earlier in this commentary, sets a paradigm for the contextualization of the same gospel proclamation today.

Christians have always been involved in contextualizing the Christian message when it comes to "worship," "proclamation," "doctrinal formulation," and "ethics."[87] For if the message of the kingdom of God as focused in Jesus is to be communicated effectively and worked out in practice appropriately, it must always be proclaimed in ways that are relevant to the worldview and culture of those being addressed. A great part of Paul's genius is that he was conscious of such a need and took pains to contextualize the "good news" of God's redemption through Christ Jesus in both his oral preaching and his written letters. We could wish that we knew more of how he preached in various situations. His letters, however, which are the most numerous of any NT writer, give us some indications of how he adjusted the form of his teaching and of his pastoral counsel to fit the various situations that he addressed and to speak meaningfully to somewhat different people. And here in his letter to Rome, and particularly in 7:14-25 of this letter, we observe how he contextualized his approach in presenting the gospel to pagan Gentiles — offering Christians today not a form that must always be followed in its specifics, but a paradigm that points the way to more effective communication and more appropriate application.

87. Cf. R. N. Longenecker, *New Wine into Fresh Wineskins,* esp. part 3 and the epilogue, 132-76.

5. No Condemnation and New Life for People "in Christ Jesus" and Therefore "in the Spirit" (8:1-17)

___

TRANSLATION

^{8:1} *So then, there is now no condemnation for those who are in Christ Jesus.* ²*For, "the law of the Spirit of life in Christ Jesus has freed you from the law of sin and death."* ³*For what the law was powerless to do in that it was weak on account of the sinful nature, "God has done by sending his own Son in the likeness of sinful humanity" — and with respect to sin, he condemned sin in our sinful nature* ⁴*in order that the righteous requirement of the law might be fulfilled in us, who live not according to the sinful nature but according to the Spirit.*

⁵*People who live according to the sinful nature have their minds set on what that nature desires; but people who live in accordance with the Spirit have their minds set on what the Spirit desires.* ⁶*The mind controlled by the sinful nature is death, but the mind controlled by the Spirit is life and peace.* ⁷*The sinful mind is hostile to God. It does not submit to God's law, nor can it do so.* ⁸*People who are controlled by the sinful nature cannot please God.*

⁹*You, however, are not controlled by the sinful nature but by the Spirit, since the Spirit of God lives in you. (If anyone does not have the Spirit of Christ, that person does not belong to Christ.* ¹⁰*And if Christ is in you, your body is indeed dead because of sin, but your spirit is alive because of righteousness.)* ¹¹*Since then the Spirit of "the One who raised Jesus from the dead" is living in you, "he who raised Christ from the dead" will also give life to your mortal bodies through his Spirit, who lives in you.*

¹²*Therefore, brothers and sisters, we are obligated not to the sinful nature to live according to the sinful nature.* ¹³*For if you live according to the sinful nature, you are destined to die. But if by the Spirit you put to death the practices of the body, you will live.*

¹⁴*"All who are led by the Spirit of God, they are sons and daughters of God."* ¹⁵*For you did not receive a spirit that makes you a slave again to fear. Rather, you received a spirit of adoption as sons and daughters, by which we cry out "Abba, Father."* ¹⁶*The Spirit himself testifies with our spirit that we are children of God.* ¹⁷*And since we are children, then are we also heirs — heirs indeed of God and co-heirs with Christ, since we share in his sufferings in order that we may also share in his glory.*

TEXTUAL NOTES

8:1a The postpositive expression ἄρα νῦν ("so then now") is widely attested by the extant MS evidence. The adverb νῦν ("now"), however, is omitted in sixth-century

Codex Beza (D* 06) and in minuscule 1908^{mg} (Category III); it is also missing in sy^p. But the omission of νῦν is too weakly supported in the textual tradition to merit real consideration. It was probably deleted simply to reduce the number of adverbs and conjunctions in the passage.

1b The kerygmatic statement οὐδὲν κατάκριμα τοῖς ἐν Χριστῷ Ἰησοῦ ("[there is] no condemnation to those who are in Christ Jesus"), without any qualifying addition(s), is supported by uncials B C^2 D* (also F G, though with space left for a possible addition) and by minuscules 1739 (Category I), 1506 1881 (Category II), and 6 424^c (Category III); it is also reflected in it$^{b, d*, g, mon2}$ cop$^{sa, bo}$ and supported by Marcion$^{acc\ to\ Adamantius}$ Origen^{lat} Athanasius Ambrosiaster and Augustine. Certain MSS, however, have after the name Ἰησοῦ one or both of the additional qualifying clauses, which seem to have been drawn from 8:4: either (1) the shorter μὴ κατὰ σάρκα περιπατοῦσιν ("who walk not according to the flesh"), which appears in uncials A D^1 Ψ, and in minuscules 81 256 2127 (Category II), and 263 365 [with the exchange of τοῖς for μή] 1319 1573 1852 (Category III); it is also reflected in versions it$^{d2, f, mon2}$ vg syr^p and by Chrysostom and Jerome; or (2) the longer μὴ κατὰ σάρκα περιπατοῦσιν ἀλλὰ κατὰ πνεῦμα ("who walk not according to the flesh but according to the Spirit"), which appears in uncials א^2 D^2 P [also *Byz* K L], and in uncials 33^{vid} 1173 (Category I), 1962 2464 (Category II), and 104 424* 436 [though omits μή] 459 1241 1912 2200 (Category III); it is also reflected in versions it$^{ar, o}$ syr^p. The concise statement οὐδεν κατάκριμα τοῖς ἐν Χριστῷ Ἰησου, however, apart from either of these qualifying additions, is far better supported in the textual tradition. Further, its acceptance best explains the inclusion of the two variants.

2 The object of the freeing action of "the law of the Spirit of life in Christ Jesus," whether με ("me"), σε ("you" [singular]), or ἡμας ("us"), is somewhat difficult to determine. The pronoun με ("me") is attested by uncials A D P (also *Byz* K L), and by minuscules 1175 1739c (Category I), 81 256 1506^c 1881 1962 2127 2464^{vid} (Category II), and 6 104 263 365 424^c 436 459 1241 1319 1573 1852 1912 2200; it is also reflected in it$^{d, mon}$ vg syr^h cop^{sa} and supported by Origen^{lat} Didymus Chrysostom Theodore Theodoret Tertullian$^{1/2}$ Jerome Augustine$^{3/10}$. The pronoun σε ("you" [enclitic singular]) is attested by uncials א B F G and by minuscules 1739* (Category I) and 1506* (Category II); it is also reflected in it$^{ar, b, f, g, o}$ syr^p and supported by Tertullian$^{1/2}$ Ambrosiaster Augustine$^{10/13}$. Because of its inclusion by both Codex Sinaiticus (א 01) and Codex Vaticanus (B 03), the external MS support for the singular σε ("you") must be judged the strongest. The pronoun ἡμᾶς ("us"), which is attested by the eighth- and ninth-century uncial Ψ, reflected in syr^{pal} cop^{bo} eth, and supported by Marcion$^{acc.\ to\ Adamantius}$ Methodius and Basil, is probably a later modification inserted to make a more general application.

On the choice between the pronouns με ("me") and σε ("you" [singular]), Bruce Metzger argues: "The latter, as the more difficult reading, is more likely to have been replaced by the former (which harmonizes better with the argument in chap. 7) than vice versa. On the other hand σε may have originated in the accidental repetition of the final syllable of ἠλευθέρωσεν when the terminal -ν, represented by a horizontal line over the ε, was overlooked."[1] The difficulty in determining what was probably the original reading

---

1. Metzger, *Textual Commentary,* 456.

is evident when one notes that *GNT*² accepted με with a C evaluation, *GNT*³ accepted σε with a D evaluation, and *GNT*⁴ accepted σε with a B evaluation. We also accept the second-person singular pronoun σε ("you") as having been original, with an additional internal reason suggested below in our exegetical comments on 8:2.

3 The phrase καὶ περὶ ἁμαρτίας ("and concerning [or 'with respect to'] sin"), which appears after σαρκὸς ἁμαρτίας ("sinful flesh/humanity"), is extremely well attested in the textual tradition. It is, however, omitted in minuscule 1912 (Category III), evidently in an effort to smooth out the text.

10 The insertion of the copula ἐστίν ("it is") after τὸ μὲν σῶμα ("the [your] body indeed"), which appears in ninth-century uncials F and G and in minuscule 629 (Category III), and is supported by Ambrosiaster, represents an effort to improve the text. Such an insertion, however, would have been hardly necessary in idiomatic Greek.

11a The article τόν before Ἰησοῦν is attested by uncials ℵ* A B, and by minuscules 1739 (Category I), 1881 (Category II), and 6 630 1505 2495 (Category III); it is, however, omitted in ℵ² C D F G P Ψ (also *Byz* K L), in minuscules 33 1175 (Category I), 1506 2464 (Category II), and 69 88 104 323 326 330 424ᶜ 614 1241 1243 1319 1573 1735 1846 1874, and by Clement and Epiphanius. With codices Sinaiticus (ℵ 01), Vaticanus (B 03), and Alexandrinus (A 02) in support, the probability is high that τὸν Ἰησοῦν should be viewed as original, with the omission of the article considered an attempted stylistic improvement.

11b The phrase Χριστὸν ἐκ νεκρῶν ("Christ from the dead") is attested by Codex Vaticanus (B 03), as well as by uncials Dᶜ G, by minuscule 2127 (Category II), and by Marcion Methodius Epiphanius. It was accepted as the preferred reading by *GNT*² and as a D reading by *GNT*³. Some MSS, however, have the article τόν before Χριστόν, as do uncials ℵ³ P Ψ (also *Byz* K) and minuscules 33 (Category I), 88 181 326 2495 (Category III); also supported by Theodoret — perhaps as a "scribal parallelization" to the foregoing τὸν Ἰησοῦν.² Many other variants also appear, e.g., (1) Ἰησοῦν for Χριστόν, (2) the use of the full name Ἰησοῦν Χριστόν, (3) the reordering of the phrase, and even (4) the omission of the entire clause ὁ ἐγείρας Χριστὸν ἐκ νεκρῶν, as in minuscules 436 629 (Category III) and as reflected in itᵃʳ. In all likelihood, Χριστὸν ἐκ νεκρῶν ("Christ from the dead") is to be accepted as original.

11c The adverbial use of καί ("also," "likewise") is widely attested in the textual tradition, and so to be accepted. It is, however, omitted in Codex Sinaiticus (ℵ 01) and Codex Alexandrinus (A 02), and in minuscules 1739 (Category I), 1881 (Category II), and 326 630 (Category III). Evidently the omission of καί was a localized Alexandrian attempt to smooth out the text.

11d The preposition διά followed by the genitive construction τοῦ ἐνοικοῦντος αὐτοῦ πνεύματος ("through his indwelling Spirit" or "through his Spirit who lives in you") is attested by uncials ℵ A C Pᶜ, and by minuscules 81 256 1506 1962 2127 (Category II) and 104 263 436 1319 1573 1852 (Category III); it is also reflected in itᶠ, ᵐᵒⁿ syrʰ copˢᵃ, ᵇᵒ and supported by Clement Jerome[1/3] Augustine[28/43]. The preposition διά followed by the accusative construction τὸ ἐνοικοῦν αὐτοῦ πνεῦμα ("because of his indwelling Spirit" or

---

2. Cf. Metzger, *Textual Commentary,* 456.

"because of his Spirit who lives in you") is attested by uncials B D F G P* Ψ (also *Byz* K L), and by minuscules 33 1175 1739 (Category I), 1881 2464 (Category II), and 6 424^c 459 1241 1912 [which omits αὐτοῦ] 2200; it is also reflected in it$^{ar, b, d, g, o}$ vg syr$^{p, (pal)}$ and supported by Irenaeus^{lat} Origen$^{gr, lat}$ Chrysostom Tertullian Ambrosiaster Jerome$^{2/3}$ Augustine$^{15/43}$.

Internal considerations do not favor one reading over the other. The accusative reading suggests that God will raise the mortal bodies of those possessing the Spirit because the Spirit is essentially a Spirit of life. The genitive reading points to the idea that the Spirit is the direct and personal agent of God's action in raising bodies. External support, likewise, seems quite evenly balanced — though, as Bruce Metzger has pointed out, the weight of Codex Vaticanus (B 03) in support of the accusative construction is lessened by a "Western" infusion, as evidenced by the association of B with D and G.^{3} The UBS committee, therefore, preferred the genitive construction. In addition, this reading receives broad support from Alexandrian (ℵ A C and 81), Palestinian (syr^{pal} Cyril-Jerusalem), and "Western" (it$^{61?}$ Hippolytus) text types.

13 The expression τοῦ σώματος ("of the body") in the second part of the verse is widely attested in the textual tradition, and so merits acceptance. The variant τῆς σαρκός ("of the flesh") appears in uncials D F G and in minuscule 630 (Category III); it is also reflected by a number of Latin texts and supported by Iren^{lat}. This variant reading was evidently inserted so as to correspond more exactly with κατὰ σάρκα ("according to the flesh" or "the sinful nature") in the first part of the verse; the repetition of the same wording was preferred over the use of an equivalent expression.

14 The final three words of 8:14 are set out in the Greek textual tradition in four ways, with the first two most frequently attested and the last two weakly supported: (1) υἱοὶ θεοῦ εἰσιν (literally "sons of God they are"), as attested by uncials ℵ A C D, and by minuscules 1739 (Category I), 81 1506 (Category II), and 88 630 1319 1573 (Category III); and (2) υἱοί εἰσιν θεοῦ (literally "sons they are of God"), as attested by uncials B F G and by Origen Pelagius — also (3) εἰσιν υἱοὶ θεοῦ (literally "they are sons of God"), as in uncials P Ψ (also *Byz* K L) and a host of Byzantine minuscules, and (4) εἰσιν θεοῦ υἱοί (literally "they are of God sons"), as in minuscule 326 (Category III). A difference of meaning between these options, however, is inconsequential, with translations usually obscuring any possible difference.

16 Codex Beza (D 06), and as reflected in the Syriac Peshitta (sy^p), begins this verse with the conjunction ὥστε ("for this reason"). But this variant reading is weakly supported in the textual tradition, and appears to be an insertion made to strengthen the argument.

17 The adverbial use of καί ("also," "likewise") between ἵνα ("in order that") and συνδοξασθῶμεν ("we may share in his glory") is strongly attested in the textual tradition. Its omission is supported only by Byzantine MSS. Thus καί ("also," "likewise") should be retained as original, thereby reading "in order that we may also share in his glory."

---

3. Cf. Metzger, *Textual Commentary,* 456.

678

FORM/STRUCTURE/SETTING

In the second major section of the body middle of Romans, here in 5:1–8:39, Paul presents to the Christians at Rome his "spiritual gift" that he had promised to give them earlier in 1:11 — that is, he sets out the essence of his contextualized form of the Christian gospel that he proclaimed to pagan Gentiles in his Gentile mission, which he called "my gospel" in 2:16 and will refer to again as "my gospel" in 16:25. It is a section that builds on — though also moves beyond — the themes of "righteousness," "justification," "redemption," and "propitiation" ("expiation" or "sacrifice of atonement") in Section I of the body middle of his letter (i.e., in 1:16–4:25). It highlights the personal, relational, and participatory features having to do with (1) "peace" and "reconciliation," (2) relationships "in Adam" and "in Christ," (3) being "in Christ" and "in the Spirit," and (4) "Christ by his Spirit being in the believer." The section comes to its theological climax in ch. 8 with the presentation of the following three matters:

1. Paul's contextualized proclamation of the Christian message, as set out in 8:1-17 — with particular attention being given to the pronouncement of "no condemnation" for those who are "in Christ Jesus," to the themes of new "life in Christ Jesus" and new "life in the Spirit," to statements regarding "Christ by his Spirit being in and controlling the Christian," to the metaphor of believers in Jesus having been "adopted" by God into his family as sons and daughters, and to the exhortation to live as children of God who are guided by God's Spirit.
2. What this new "life in Christ Jesus" and new "life in the Spirit" involves, as set out in 8:18-30 — with attention given not only to personal features but also to universal implications, and not only to the present but also to the future.
3. A triumphal affirmation of God's love as expressed in Christ Jesus and the believer's resultant confidence, as spelled out in 8:31-39 — with that affirmation including various portions of early Christian confessional material in support.

Likewise, it is in this major section that the three basic features of ancient rhetoric come most fully to expression: *logos* (content or argument), *ethos* (the personal character of the speaker or writer), and *pathos* (the power to stir the emotions). And it is in Rom 8, using John Robinson's analogy of "a journey by canal across an isthmus" with its "series of locks" rising to and then falling away from "a central ridge," that "the heights of the epistle are reached" and there occurs "a sustained climax which takes the argument across the watershed."[4]

The Unified and Distinctive Nature of 8:1-17. Our immediate concern here, however, is the first part of Paul's presentation in ch. 8 — that is, his pro-

---

4. J. A. T. Robinson, *Wrestling with Romans*, 9.

nouncement that "there is now no condemnation for those who are in Christ Jesus," with his themes of life "in Christ Jesus" and life "in the Spirit," with his emphasis on "Christ by his Spirit being in the Christian," with his use of the metaphor "adoption," and with the implications he draws from these distinctive matters. These are the basic features of Paul's contextualized proclamation of the Christian gospel. It is with this pronouncement, these themes, this emphasis, and this metaphor — together with their respective implications — that Paul has come to the high-water mark of all that he proclaimed to pagan Gentiles in the Greco-Roman world of his day.

Most commentators have viewed this first part of Paul's presentation in ch. 8 as contained in 8:1-11.[5] Others have understood the first part as expressed in 8:1-13.[6] But Paul's emphasis on the Spirit — which (1) appears as early as 8:2 in the phrase "the Spirit of life," (2) is repeated a dozen or so times more throughout the passage, and (3) comes to a climax in 8:16 in the statement "the Spirit himself testifies with our spirit that we are children of God" — unifies all the material of 8:1-17, and therefore suggests that these seventeen verses should be held together to constitute the first portion of Rom 8. Likewise, the contrast between life lived "according to one's sinful nature" (κατὰ σάρξ) and life lived "in accordance with the Spirit's direction" (κατὰ πνεῦμα), which is a major feature in 8:1-11 and is continued in 8:12-17, provides additional thematic support for understanding 8:1-17 as a unified portion of material.

Also, at the close of 8:17 Paul anticipates his discussion of "present suffering" and "future glory" in 8:18-30 by appending the comment "if [or, as we will propose later, 'since'] we share in his [Christ's] sufferings in order that we may also share in his glory," and in 8:18 he formally introduces that presentation of "suffering and glory" in 8:18-30 by using the singular form of a traditional epistolary "disclosure formula," that is, he uses the expression λογίζομαι ὅτι ("I calculate that" or "consider that") — which anticipatory comment of 8:17 and disclosure formula of 8:18 function together to indicate that there exists in Paul's line of argument in Rom 8 a minor break between 8:17 and 8:18.

Epistolary and Rhetorical Conventions. The particle ἄρα ("so," "then") was used in koine Greek not only in an illative or inferential fashion (i.e., to draw an inference from what precedes), but also simply to enliven and highlight a statement or question that follows ("so then," or some such colloquial expression as "you see") — and so to draw particular attention to its message.[7] That is how Paul uses ἄρα ("so then," "you see") here at the beginning of 8:1 — to draw attention to his pronouncement that "there is now no condemnation for those who are in Christ Jesus." Further, the combining of the particles ἄρα and οὖν to form the expression ἄρα οὖν ("consequently," "therefore") was used by Paul

---

5. So, e.g., Godet, *Romans*, 2.57; Michel, *An die Römer*, 248; Käsemann, *Romans*, 212; Cranfield, *Romans*, 1.372; Dunn, *Romans*, 414.

6. So, e.g., Lagrange, *Épître aux Romains*, 200; Wilckens, *An die Römer*, 2.120; Fitzmyer, *Romans*, 479; Moo, *Romans*, 470.

7. As noted above in our "Exegetical Comments" on 7:21.

to signal the conclusion of a section or subsection of material.[8] And that is how he uses the idiomatic expression ἄρα οὖν at the beginning of 8:12, that is, to signal the start of a concluding paragraph in this first subsection of material in Rom 8. Thus in the structuring of his soliloquy on the dire situation of all human beings in 7:14-25 and in the structuring of his contextualized proclamation in 8:1-17, Paul sets out these two passages in a noticeably similar fashion by using these particular particles, both singly and in combination — thereby not just balancing the two presentations, but also countering the portrayal of 7:14-25, which speaks about the inability of people to do good and be acceptable before God by their own resources, by the proclamation of 8:1-17, which announces what a person is "in Christ Jesus" and "in the Spirit."

Paul uses the vocative ἀδελφοί ("brothers and sisters") in 8:12 of this proclamation section. Just as he earlier used this epistolary convention in 1:13, 7:1, and 7:4, he uses it here as an affectionate form of address.[9]

The Prominence of Terms for "Life" and "Living" and of References to the Spirit. In our earlier discussions of this second major section of the body middle of Romans (i.e., 5:1–8:39) we noted that the word chain shifts from (1) the dominance in 1:16–4:25 of the nouns δικαιοσύνη ("righteousness") and πίστις ("faith"), together with the verb πιστεύειν ("to believe"), to (2) the prominence in 5:1–8:39 of the noun ζωή ("life"), the verb ζῆν ("to live"), and the various participial forms of ζάω or ζῶ ("live"), in contradistinction to the repeated use of the nouns ἁμαρτία ("sin") and θάνατος ("death").[10] This feature is particularly obvious in 8:1-17 — what with the noun ζωή ("life") being explicitly used in 8:10; the present infinitive ζῆν ("to live") used in 8:12; the second-person plural present indicative verb ζῆτε ("you are living") in 8:13a; and the second-person plural future indicative verb ζήσεσθε ("you will live") in 8:13b. In addition, various synonymous expressions for "life" and "living" appear in this passage, such as τοῖς περιπατοῦσιν ("those walking about") in 8:4, οἱ ὄντες ("those being" or "living") in 8:5 and 8, and οἰκεῖ ("he dwells") in 8:9 and 11.

There are also a number of references in 8:1-17 to God's Spirit as the agent who brings about new realities and new relationships in the lives of those committed to Christ Jesus. This theme appears as early as 8:2 in the phrase "the Spirit of life," is repeated a dozen or so times more throughout 8:2-16, and comes to a climax in 8:16 in the statement "the Spirit himself testifies with our spirit that we are children of God" — with applications of that statement of 8:16 made in 8:17 with respect to both (1) a Christian's new status before God (i.e., "children" and "heirs") and (2) a Christian's new lifestyle (i.e., "suffering" and "glory").

---

8. As noted above in our "Exegetical Comments" on 5:18, 7:3, and 7:25b.

9. See our "Exegetical Comments" on Paul's use of ἀδελφοί at 1:13 and 7:1 and ἀδελφοί μου at 7:4; note also his later uses of ἀδελφοί in directly addressing the Roman Christians at 10:1; 12:1; 14:10, 13, 15, 21; 15:14, 30; and 16:17.

10. Though with δικαιοσύνη also appearing in various contexts in eight verses of this second section of the body middle at 5:17, 21; 6:13, 16, 18, 19, 20; and 8:10.

Explicit and Allusive Uses of Early Christian Confessional Materials.
We observed earlier that this second major section of the body middle of the
letter (5:1–8:39) is distinguishable from the letter's first major section (1:16–
4:25) and its third major section (9:1–11:36) — and even from its fourth major
section (12:1–15:3) — by its lack of biblical quotations used in support of Paul's
statements and the development of his arguments.[11] Such a nonuse of biblical
quotations is particularly evident in his kerygmatic statement of 8:1 and his further presentations in 8:2-17. Rather, what appear in 8:1-17 (as well as elsewhere
throughout Rom 8) are explicit and allusive uses of early Christian confessional
materials in support of the apostle's contextualized Christian proclamation and
the development of its basic themes.

Such early Christian confessional materials are recognizable by the kerygmatic nature of their contents and the formal styling of their structures. They can
also be identified by Paul's use of the postpositive particle γάρ ("for") to introduce them — much as he, at times, uses γάρ elsewhere in his letters to introduce
not only OT passages but also traditional Jewish axiomatic affirmations, classical
Greco-Roman statements, and various Jewish Christian confessional materials.[12]

Here in 8:1-17 these identifiable features of kerygmatic content, formal
styling, and an introductory use of the conjunction γάρ ("for") come together
most obviously in the following two verses:

8:2 — For, "the law of the Spirit of life in Christ Jesus has freed you from
the law of sin and death" (ὁ γὰρ νόμος τοῦ πνεύματος τῆς ζωῆς ἐν Χριστῷ
Ἰησοῦ ἠλευθέρωσέν σε ἀπὸ τοῦ νόμου τῆς ἁμαρτίας καὶ τοῦ θανάτου).

8:14 — For, "all those who are being led by the Spirit of God, they are children of God" (ὅσοι γὰρ πνεύματι θεοῦ ἄγονται, οὗτοι υἱοὶ θεοῦ εἰσιν).

Two or three other statements in 8:1-17 may also be legitimately viewed as allusive quotations of early Christian confessional materials. Each of these four or
five possible confessional portions — whether identified by their content and
structure, or by the introductory use of γὰρ — needs to be investigated in our
exegetical treatments below.

The Structure of Paul's Presentation in 8:1-17. The structure of Paul's presentation in 8:1-17 may be set out under the following five headings:

1. "No condemnation" for people "in Christ Jesus," and thus also "in the
   Spirit," in 8:1-4

---

11. See our treatment of the subject in the introductory section to 5:1–8:39. Cf. also R. N.
Longenecker, "Prolegomena to Paul's Use of Scripture in Romans," esp. 146-47, 158-67; *idem*, "Paul
and the Old Testament," in *Biblical Exegesis*, 2nd ed., 88-116.

12. For other instances in Romans where γάρ functions to introduce biblical quotations,
Jewish axioms, Greco-Roman statements, and/or Christian confessional materials, see 2:11, 14, 24;
5:6; 7:15, 19; 10:13; 11:34-35. Cf. also 1 Cor 2:16; 10:26; 15:27.

2. Two diametrically opposed mind-sets and modes of human existence, and their respective results, in 8:5-8
3. People who are "in Christ," and therefore controlled "by the Spirit," are people who have life, in 8:9-11
4. An exhortation to live not "according to the sinful nature" but "by the Spirit" in 8:12-13
5. Additional statements regarding the status of believers in Jesus as God's sons and daughters, with an emphasis on the Greco-Roman metaphor of "adoption," in 8:14-17

This series of headings, with their respective materials, will structure our exegetical comments below.

EXEGETICAL COMMENTS

I. No Condemnation (8:1-4)

Rudolf Bultmann argued that 8:1 should be viewed as a non-Pauline marginal gloss that had somehow found its way into the text,[13] and a number of commentators have followed him in this opinion. Friedrich Müller suggested that 8:1 and 8:2 should be reversed, for logically the statement "the law of the Spirit of life in Christ Jesus has freed you from the law of sin and death" in 8:2 provides the basis for the pronouncement of "no condemnation" in 8:1 and not the result.[14] There is, however, no support in the Greek textual tradition for such a proposal or such a suggestion.

Further, to call 8:1 a marginal gloss is to ignore the contextual consideration that the pronouncement in 8:1 of "no condemnation" (οὐδὲν κατάκριμα), which is what Christ effected for those who are committed to him, reaches back to statements in 5:16 and 18 about the "condemnation" (κατάκριμα) that Adam brought about in the lives of all his descendants — with that earlier presentation of humanity's awful situation before God being here in 8:1 declared to have come to an end for "those who are in Christ Jesus." It is also to ignore that this pronouncement in 8:1 of "no condemnation" is set in the immediate context of Paul's statements about "sin, seizing the opportunity afforded by God's commandment, deceived me, and through the commandment put me to death" in 7:7-13; his statements about the inability of people to gain personal self-mastery, and so to be acceptable before God, by their own resources and abilities in 7:14-25; and his statements about the powerlessness of the law because of sin in 8:2-4. Likewise, to reverse the order of 8:1 and 8:2, thereby reading 8:2 first and then 8:1, seems highly implausible because of the tight verbal connections

13. Bultmann, "Glossen im Römerbrief," 197-202.
14. Müller, "Zwei Marginalien im Brief Paulus an die Römer," 249-54.

that exist between 8:2 and 8:3. For in 8:2 "the law of the Spirit of life in Christ Jesus" is contrasted to "the law of sin and death," and then in 8:3 that same contrast is set out again, though in reverse order, by references to "the law that was powerless" and to what "God has done by sending his own Son in the likeness of sinful humanity."[15]

8:1 The opening statement of this great central passage of 8:1-17 is a highly significant declaration: οὐδὲν ἄρα νῦν κατάκριμα τοῖς ἐν Χριστῷ Ἰησοῦ ("So then, [there is] now no condemnation for those who are in Christ Jesus"). The statement is devoid of a finite verb, and so should be understood as reflecting a theological pronouncement: "No condemnation for those who are in Christ Jesus."[16] The significance and force of the statement are emphasized by the postpositive particle ἄρα ("so then," "you see"), which was used in koine Greek not only in an illative or inferential fashion but also to enliven a statement or question — and thus to highlight a statement or message.[17] In this first verse of ch. 8, therefore, introducing as it does the central theological pronouncement of the passage, the particle ἄρα is probably to be understood as an intensified "you see," and so best translated "so then." The adverb νῦν ("now") could possibly connote only a logical contrast, and thus be viewed along the lines of the expression "but now here is the situation." Νῦν here, however, most likely — in line with Paul's usual usage elsewhere in his letters, but particularly his earlier uses of νῦν in Romans at 3:21 and 7:6 — has a temporal significance, and therefore should be seen as referring to this present time of the eschatological "now" of salvation history, which has been inaugurated by Christ's death and resurrection.[18]

The pronouncement "no condemnation" (οὐδὲν κατάκριμα) is presented here in 8:1 in the broader context of what Paul spoke about earlier in 5:12-21, particularly in 5:16 and 18 where the only two other uses of the intensified noun κατάκριμα appear in the Pauline corpus (and, for that matter, in the rest of the NT) — that is, about Adam's sin having as its final result God's "judgment (κρίμα) unto condemnation (εἰς κατάκριμα)" on all human beings. Here in 8:1 that awful heritage of Adam's sin, humanity's inherited depravity and people's own resultant sins, which together have brought about the universal sentence of "judgment unto condemnation" (κρίμα εἰς κατάκριμα), is countered by God's wondrous grace through the work of Jesus of Nazareth and the proclamation of "no condemnation for those who are in Christ Jesus" (οὐδὲν κατάκριμα τοῖς ἐν Χριστῷ Ἰησοῦ).

8:2 The pronouncement of "no condemnation" of 8:1 is supported by

---

15. Cf. Jewett, *Romans*, 477-78, who argues for the unity of 8:1-17 on a rhetorical basis, citing, in particular, "the alternation between parallelism and climax" that exists throughout this passage.

16. E. Käsemann speaks of it as "a dogmatic sentence," which "parallels" in converse fashion the statement of 7:25b and "is to be understood as a foundation" for what follows (*Romans*, 214).

17. As noted in our "Exegetical Comments" on 7:21.

18. Cf. the nontheological temporal uses of νῦν later in Romans at 15:23, 25; see also 2 Cor 8:22; Eph 2:13; Phil 1:5; Phlm 9, 11.

the explanatory statement here in 8:2: "For the law of the Spirit of life in Christ Jesus has freed you [singular] from the law of sin and death." Paul likely drew this supporting statement from some early Jewish Christian confessional material. Such a background can be postulated because of the statement's distinctive kerygmatic content and its formal styling. Likewise, Paul's use of the conjunction γάρ ("for") to introduce this statement — much as he used γάρ earlier in the letter to introduce not only biblical passages but also traditional Jewish axioms, classical Greco-Roman statements, and other Jewish or Christian confessional materials[19] — seems to support such a thesis. Further, it may be argued that such an understanding of Paul's use of γάρ here at the beginning of 8:2, which is followed by his use of γάρ again at the beginning of 8:3, provides a likely explanation for these two uses in such close proximity to each other: the first, in 8:2, functions in an introductory fashion; the second, in 8:3, functions in an explanatory manner. In support of our thesis that the statement of 8:2 was drawn from some early Christian confessional material is the appearance of the second-person singular personal pronoun σε ("you"), which is better attested in the text tradition than the first-person singular με ("me") or the first-person plural ἡμᾶς ("us")[20] — and which differs from Paul's own use of second-person plural personal pronouns and second-person plural verbal suffixes throughout the rest of 8:1-17.[21]

Many commentators have noted the fairly nice linguistic balance in 8:2 between the clause "the law of the Spirit of life in Christ Jesus" and the clause "the law of sin and death" — even though the contents of these two clauses are set out in opposition to one another. Most interpreters have also seen in the two uses of the articular expression ὁ νόμος ("the law") not a "Jesus code of regulations" in the first instance or a "Moses code of regulations" in the second instance, but in both situations a broader reference to "principles" or "matters that pertain to" these two contrasting clauses — that is, principles or matters that have to do with "life in Christ Jesus" and "the ministry of the Spirit" vis-à-vis principles or matters that have to do with "sin" and "death."[22] And if this

---

19. See our translations and treatments of 2:11, 14, 24; 5:6; and 7:15, 19. Note also Rom 10:13; 11:34-35; 1 Cor 2:16; 10:26; 15:27.

20. See "Textual Notes" above on 8:2.

21. Note Paul's dominant use in 8:1-17 of such first- and second-person plural pronominal expressions as "in us" (ἐν ἡμῖν) in 8:4; "in you" (ἐν ὑμᾶς) in 8:9, 10, 11 (twice); "your" (ὑμῶν) in 8:11; and "our" (ἡμῶν) in 8:16 — as well as the numerous first- and second-person plural verbal suffixes — throughout the rest of the passage.

22. Cf. esp. C. H. Dodd, *Romans,* 119; Leenhardt, *Romans,* 201; Ziesler, *Romans,* 202; Räisänen, "Paul's Word Play on νόμος," in his *Jesus, Paul, and Torah,* 90 — though James Dunn objects, arguing with respect to "the law of sin and death" here in 8:2b: "Despite reservations on the part of some commentators . . . it is most unlikely that νόμος was intended here in some more general sense. Paul has already linked the law, that is, the Torah, too closely with sin and death to allow readily of any other conclusion (5:12-14, 20; 7:5, 9-11, 13, 23-24). The words here simply sum up these earlier descriptions of the interplay of sin, death, and the law in a single forceful phrase" (Dunn, *Romans,* 1.418-19).

statement, with its linguistically balanced but content-contrasting clauses, is understood as having been originally composed and used as an early Christian affirmation in a Jewish Christian context, three features regarding the statement and Paul's use of it need particularly to be noted: (1) that its wording reflects Jewish Christian ways of expressing matters, particularly the terms "law," "sin," and "death"; (2) that its references to "the Spirit" and "life in Christ Jesus" reflect distinctive Christian theology; and (3) that in its emphasis on "freedom" as a dominant feature of the Christian message, the statement strikes an important note that was particularly appreciated by Paul.[23] So, it may be speculated, Paul had a special interest in using this early Jewish Christian confessional statement in support of his own contextualized proclamation that "there is no condemnation for those who are in Christ Jesus."

The expression "in Christ Jesus," together with its cognates, was a favorite way for Paul to signal the personal, local, and dynamic relations of a Christian believer vis-à-vis his or her Savior, Christ Jesus. To say that it was a favorite expression of Paul is not, however, to rule out its use by early Jewish believers in Jesus or by Jewish Christian leaders before Paul. For if Gal 3:26 is accepted as an early Christian "sayings" statement and Gal 3:27-28 is viewed as a portion of an early Christian confession, both of which include the expression "in Christ Jesus"[24] — and if in Rom 8:2 Paul also brings into play an early Jewish Christian confessional statement that includes the expression "in Christ Jesus" in support of his pronouncement of 8:1, as we are here proposing — then, while it may legitimately be said that Paul develops this theme of "in Christ Jesus" in fairly distinctive ways, it cannot also be said that he was the first to use it or that it was unique to him.

EXCURSUS: PAUL'S USE OF "IN CHRIST JESUS" AND ITS COGNATES

The expression "in Christ Jesus" (as well as its cognates "in Christ," "in the Lord," "in the Lord Jesus," "in him," and "in whom," together with a few other individual variations) has been counted by Adolf Deissmann as appearing some 164 times in Paul's letters[25] — though Deissmann's count includes a few debatable inclusions, such as Tertius's statement of having "written down" Paul's letter to Rome "in the Lord" (Rom 16:22). It also excludes 8 further appearances in the Pastoral Epistles, all of which use the phraseology "in Christ Jesus."[26] Following out Deissmann's count, the appearances of the expression and its cognates in Paul letters are as follows: ἐν Χριστῷ Ἰησοῦ ("in Christ Jesus"), 42 times, plus another 8 times in the Pastorals; ἐν Χριστῷ ("in Christ"), 26 times; ἐν κυρίῳ ("in the Lord"), 47 times; ἐν αὐτῷ ("in him"), 19 times; and ἐν ᾧ ("in whom," all in Ephesians and Colossians) a few other times — with also such other variations as ἐν τῇ

---

23. Cf. my highlighting of this theme in R. N. Longenecker, *Paul, Apostle of Liberty*.
24. Cf. R. N. Longenecker, *Galatians*, 152.
25. See Deissmann, *Die neutestamentliche Formel "In Christo Jesu."*
26. See 1 Tim 1:14; 3:13; 2 Tim 1:1, 9; 2:1, 10; 3:12, 15.

ζωῇ αὐτοῦ ("in his life") appearing in Rom 5:10; ἐν Χριστῷ Ἰησοῦ τῷ κυρίῳ ἡμῶν ("in Christ Jesus our Lord") in Rom 6:23; ἐν τῷ Χριστῷ ("in the Christ") in 1 Cor 15:22; ἐν κυρίῳ Ἰησοῦ ("in the Lord Jesus") in Phil 2:19; and ἐν τῷ Ἰησοῦ ("in Jesus") in Eph 4:21.

1. Past Attempts to Understand Paul's "in Christ" Expression. On the basis of his survey, Deissmann argued in his *Die neutestamentliche Formel "In Christo Jesus"* of 1892 that at the heart of all that Paul proclaimed and did was a consuming consciousness of an intensely personal relationship that existed between the exalted Christ and himself — which was assumed to be present also in all those who were truly committed to and followers of Jesus Christ. It is a consciousness of a relationship between Christ and believers in Christ that is, in fact, so close, lively, and personal that it can properly be called "Christian mysticism."

Building on Deissmann's thesis (though without acknowledgment to him), Albert Schweitzer asserted in his *Mysticism of Paul the Apostle* of 1910 (German ed.; ET 1931) that central to the "developed" thought of Paul, and therefore the main theme in his letter to the Romans, was not "justification by faith" — which Schweitzer called "a subsidiary crater" in the Pauline landscape "formed from the rim of the main crater" — but "the mystical doctrine of redemption through being-in-Christ."[27] Ever since Deissmann's original thesis, as well as its somewhat aberrant employment by Schweitzer, NT interpreters have frequently spoken of Paul's theology as being "personal," "relational," "participationistic," and even "mystical" — sometimes (1) setting out the apostle's "personal," "relational," and "participationistic" language in contrast to his "forensic" soteriological statements; at other times (2) viewing his "in Christ Jesus" or "in Christ" expressions as extensions or elaborations of his forensic statements; but usually (3) simply allowing the "personal," "relational," "participationistic," and/or "mystical" features to reside side by side with the "forensic" features of his message, without any attempted resolution.

Another understanding of Paul's "in Christ" language during the first half of the twentieth century was that it was a carryover from the Greek mystery religions. Wilhelm Bousset and Richard Reitzenstein argued that this phraseology was one of the many items that the Christian apostle borrowed, not only in form but also in content, from the Greek mystery religions.[28] Going further along these lines, Alfred Loisy and Kirsopp Lake claimed that "Christianity has not borrowed from the Mystery Religions, because it was always, at least in Europe, a Mystery Religion itself";[29] and Erwin Goodenough, agreeing with the Hellenistic nature of the expression, insisted that there was no need for Paul to have borrowed directly from any pagan source since the synagogues of Diaspora Judaism themselves had become homes for the mysteries — as seen in the writings of Philo of Alexandria.[30] Thus it was argued that Paul's "in Christ" or "in Christ Jesus" expression carried with it connotations found in the Greek mystery religions — that is, sacramental initiation, absorption into divinity, mystic identity, ecstatic experience, and all. Such an understanding, however, has failed to carry conviction among today's NT scholars for both methodological and comparative reasons.

Methodologically, the question of Greek influence on Paul — at least with respect

---

27. Schweitzer, *Mysticism of Paul the Apostle,* 225.

28. Bousset, *Kyrios Christos,* 104-20; Reitzenstein, *Die Hellenistischen Mysterienreligionen,* 333-93.

29. Quoting Lake, *The Earlier Epistles of St. Paul,* 215; see also Loisy, "The Christian Mystery," 50-64.

30. Goodenough, *By Light, Light,* passim.

to his "in Christ Jesus" expression — can never be settled in the affirmative as decisively as its advocates earlier claimed, for information concerning the ancient mystery religions is both meager and late of date. The dangers are (1) to be more precise than the evidence allows[31] and (2) to assume uncritically that the influence between the mysteries and Christianity always moved in only one direction.[32] Most scholars today recognize that the question to be asked is not only how much was Christianity influenced by Greek thought and culture, but also how much were the Greek mystery religions aberrations of early Christianity.

Comparatively, the differences between Paul's "in Christ Jesus" and the concept of union with divinity in the mystery religions are most convincing against the view that Paul incorporated the religious speculations and forms of the latter into Christianity. For in addition to the fact that he does not proclaim a sacramental initiation, Paul does not advance the fundamental salvific tenet of the Greek mystery religions, that is, the ultimate absorption of the personhood of a devotee into whatever is viewed as the divine. Similarly, while the mystery religions present a salvation that is solely individualistic, Paul's "in Christ Jesus" motif is both personal and corporate. Further, the following matters need also to be taken into account: (1) that while salvation in the mystery religions is freedom from fate, Paul accepted creatureliness and proclaimed a salvation from sin and its results; (2) that while faith is intellectual acceptance in the mystery religions, it is personal and ethical commitment with the apostle; and (3) that while ecstatic rapture is the goal of the mysteries, the ecstatic is only reluctantly spoken of by Paul and is not considered characteristic of the Christian life.

Even the form of the phrase "in Christ Jesus," while similar to that of the Greek mystery religions, cannot with certainty be attributed to that milieu for its occurrence in Paul. For the question must always be asked: Is the similarity of phraseology a true "genealogical" parallel, which has resulted from direct borrowing, or is it merely an "analogical" parallel, and so to be regarded as arising from a more or less similar religious experience and temper? The facts (1) that Paul's Jewish background included the reciprocal concepts of God's identification with his people and his people's identification with him, (2) that his Christian experience was one of personal fellowship with the exalted Christ, and (3) that he probably knew at least something about Jesus' teaching regarding an intimate relationship existing between himself and his own, as later recorded in John's Gospel[33] — all these factors make it highly likely that his "in Christ Jesus" theology and

31. As E. Bevan has caustically commented: "Of course, if one writes an imaginary description of the Orphic mysteries, as Loisy, for instance, does, filling in the large gaps in the picture left by our data from the Christian eucharist, one produces something very impressive. On this plan, you first put in the Christian elements, and then are staggered to find them there" ("Mystery Religions and Christianity," in *Contemporary Thinking about Paul: An Anthology,* ed. T. S. Kepler [New York: Abingdon-Cokesbury, 1950], 43).

32. For a significant discussion of such methodological considerations, see B. M. Metzger, "Considerations of Methodology in the Study of the Mystery Religions and Early Christianity," *HTR* 48 (1955) 1-20.

33. Note the "abide in me and I in you" motif that appears repeatedly as a feature of Jesus' teaching in John's Gospel — most prominently in (1) John 6:48-58, the discourse on the bread of life, which draws to a close in the words "he who eats my flesh and drinks my blood abides in me and I in him"; (2) John 14:20, where Jesus is reported as telling his disciples, "In that day you shall know that I am in my Father and you in me and I in you"; (3) John 15:1-11, the analogy of the vine and the branches, whose imagery focuses a number of times on the exhortation "abide in me as

proclamation were rooted primarily in his Jewish and Christian backgrounds and his own religious experience. It will always remain a question regarding just how Hellenistically orientated so-called Hellenistic Judaism and Hellenistic Jewish Christianity really were. But the argument that Paul's "in Christ Jesus" expression reflects the thought and language of the Greek mystery religions has fallen into disrepute among scholars today, and rightly so.

Adolf Deissmann argued that "in Christ" should be interpreted as a literal local dative of personal existence in the pneumatic Christ. Further, he proposed that Paul viewed the Spirit as a semiphysical, ethereal entity — and so by equating the resurrected Christ with the ethereal Spirit, he could quite easily think of the Christian life as being "in Christ Jesus" and of Christ "by his Spirit living in us." Deissmann's favored analogy was that of air, of which it can be said that "we are in it" and "it is in us." But while Deissmann's treatment of Paul's "in Christ" expression was a significant advance in NT studies, he also left the discussion open to two quite unwarranted assertions: (1) that since Paul so closely equated the Spirit and Christ, what is true of the Spirit as a semiphysical and nonpersonal being must also, at least to some extent, be true of Christ; and (2) that in advocating the incorporation of a person into the ethereal and semiphysical substance of the pneumatic Christ, Paul has shown himself to be a very primitive metaphysical thinker.

Thus Johannes Weiss, while agreeing in the main with Deissmann, argued that Deissmann did not go far enough, for while what is true of Christ is true of the Spirit, what is true of the Spirit is also true of Christ.[34] This association of Christ with the Spirit, insisted Weiss, is one place where "it cannot be denied that Paul's Christology is inclined, upon one side, to abandon the firm lines laid down by concrete ideas of a definite personality"[35] — for here Paul enters into "abstract speculation" and effects "the sublimation and dissolution of personality."[36] Going further, and in opposition to Deissmann's literal local thesis, Friedrich Büchsel asserted that to view Paul's "in Christ" as a local dative is to degrade both the Pauline presentation of Christ, representing him as "ein halb sachliches Fluidum,"[37] and the person of Paul himself, portraying him as a "primitiver Denker."[38] And indeed, it is at these points that Deissmann's interpretation fails to do justice to Paul's understanding of Jesus.

Many scholars, in reaction to Deissmann's local interpretation, have proposed that Paul's "in Christ" expression must be viewed as simply a dative of instrumentality, causality, or source. Büchsel, for example, concluded that "es ist instrumental, kausal, modal und im übertragenen Sinne lokal gebraucht"[39] — that is, that while a figurative

---

I abide in you"; (4) John 17:21, where Jesus' prayer to God his Father includes the request for his own: "that they also may be one in us"; (5) John 17:23 and 26, which include the expression "I in them"; and (6) John 16:33, where Jesus uses locative language in telling his disciples: "In me you may have peace; in the world you have tribulation" (cf. also the language of close relationship in Jesus' statements in Matt 18:20 and 25:40-45).

34. Cf. J. Weiss, *Primitive Christianity,* ed. F. C. Grant (London: Macmillan, 1937), 2.464.

35. J. Weiss, *Paul and Jesus,* trans. H. J. Chaytor (New York: Harper & Bros., 1909), 22.

36. *Ibid.,* 24; cf. *idem, Primitive Christianity,* 2.464-71.

37. F. Büchsel, "'In Christus' bei Paulus," *ZNW* 42 (1949) 146.

38. Büchsel, "'In Christus' bei Paulus," 152. Somewhat similarly, H. Lietzmann referred to Paul's "in Christ" motif as "a plastically conceived mysticism" in his *The Beginnings of the Christian Church,* trans. B. L. Woolf (London: Nicholson & Watson, 1937), 183.

39. Büchsel, "'In Christus' bei Paulus," 156.

sense may at times be found, the primary meaning is more adequately expressed by ap-plying the instrumental idea "by Christ" to Paul's phrase "in Christ,"[40] and the dynamic idea "through the empowerment of Christ" to his formulation "Christ in us."[41]

Such an understanding often, of course, yields a perfectly intelligible and theo-logically sound meaning. No one would disagree that Paul, whatever he exactly meant by the expression, did not exclude the ideas of Christ as the source, cause, and power of the Christian's life. But the question that stands over all of Büchsel's work — and the question he neglects to raise — is this: Why, then, didn't Paul just continue to use the Greek constructions διὰ Χριστοῦ and ἐκ Χριστοῦ, and not also use the expression ἐν Χριστῷ, if he desired to express only the ideas of instrumentality, causality, and/or source? And further, Why did he use all three expressions within a single presentation when, according to Büchsel, his thought was roughly singular?

Similarly in opposition to Deissmann's local interpretation is the view that un-derstands the phrase as simply a metaphor of personal communion with Christ. It is not that this position desires to minimize the personal element of intimate relation between Christ and the Christian contained in the expression, but it considers it "hazardous to press the 'local' significance of the formula."[42] It accepts the more general, but still pro-found, truth that Paul proclaims regarding a close and personal communion with Christ, but it shies away from trying to be more explicit in the exposition of that relationship by an emphasis on the form of the term. In its insistence that the metaphor stands for the believer's "supremely intimate relation of union with Christ,"[43] this understanding has certainly caught the main theme of the apostle's teaching. Nonetheless, as William Bar-clay has aptly observed, "the cumulative effect of all Paul's uses of the phrase 'in Christ' demands something even more than this."[44]

During the twentieth century there has also arisen to prominence a different type of objection to Deissmann's interpretation. This position agrees with the local emphasis but interprets ἐν Χριστῷ not as denoting an individual or personal relationship with Christ but as being a locution for corporate communion in the Christian church. The Roman Catholic Church, of course, has always taken this position, asserting that to be in the living Christ is to be in "the Church with its centre in Rome."[45] In reaction to various types of religious individualism, and with the rediscovery of "corporate personality" in the Scriptures, many non-Romanists have also viewed the phrase as speaking primarily of corporate life in the body of Christ — that is, in the organic church. Albert Schweitzer, for example, argued that " 'being-in-Christ' is the prime enigma of the Pauline teach-ing"[46] if we view it as "an individual and subjective experience" rather than "a collective and objective event."[47] Thus he insisted that "the expression 'being-in-Christ' is merely brachyology for being partakers in the Mystical Body of Christ."[48] And while "in Christ" language may be common in Paul's letters, it is, Schweitzer asserted, not the most appro-

40. Büchsel, " 'In Christus' bei Paulus," 146.

41. *Ibid.,* 152.

42. So H. A. A. Kennedy, *The Theology of the Epistles* (London: Duckworth, 1919), 121.

43. *Ibid.,* 124.

44. W. Barclay, *The Mind of St. Paul* (London: Collins, 1958), 128.

45. So the Roman Catholic biblical scholar C. Cary-Elwes, *Law, Liberty, and Love* (London: Hodder & Stoughton, 1949), 247.

46. Schweitzer, *Mysticism of Paul the Apostle,* 3.

47. *Ibid.,* 123.

48. *Ibid.,* 122-23.

priate expression for union with Christ. It becomes the most usual, not only because of its shortness but primarily because of the facility it offers for forming antitheses with the analogous expressions "in the body," "in the flesh," "in sin," and "in the spirit," thereby providing the mystical theory with a series of neat equations.[49]

Likewise, Rudolf Bultmann argued that " 'in Christ,' far from being a formula for mystic union, is primarily an ecclesiological formula," and thus "to belong to the Christian Church is to be 'in Christ' or 'in the Lord.' "[50] In Britain, this position was strongly advanced by John A. T. Robinson and L. S. Thornton as a corollary to their insistence that "the Church as literally now the resurrection 'body' of Christ" was the dominant motif in the proclamation of Paul.[51]

2. The Significance of the Expression "in Christ Jesus" in Paul's Letters. Endless debate will probably continue to gather around Paul's expression "in Christ Jesus," for it signifies a central feature of the Christian life that is better experienced than explained. Further, the more confident we are that we have reduced the phrase to the cold prose of the psychologist's laboratory, the more assured we can be that we have lost its central significance. The inexplicable must always remain in a truly personal relationship. Yet personal relationships can be intellectually understood and expressed up to a point — and it is to that point, and I trust only to that point, that I would seek to go in understanding Paul's "in Christ" phraseology.

It is true that there are many places in Paul's letters where the expression could be viewed as being synonymous with the noun and adjective "Christian." For example, in greeting his addressees in his letters by such phraseology as "to all the saints 'in Christ Jesus,' " Paul could simply mean "to all the Christians."[52] Likewise, in his reference to "the dead 'in Christ,' " he need not be seen as meaning anything more than "the Christian dead";[53] and in his mention of certain individuals who were "in Christ" or "in the Lord," his use of the phrase could be only in order to identify them as Christians.[54] Similarly, there are a host of passages where διὰ Χριστοῦ or ἐκ Χριστοῦ could just as well have been written as ἐν Χριστῷ and a perfectly intelligible meaning would emerge. The most prominent examples of such a possible conflation of meaning are the following:

> 2 Cor 3:14, where Paul speaks of the veil that "is done away ἐν Χριστῷ" (RSV: "through Christ"; AV, NIV, NRSV: "in Christ").
>
> Rom 5:10, which speaks of being "saved ἐν τῇ ζωῇ αὐτοῦ" (AV, ASV, RSV, NRSV: "by his life"; NIV: "through his life").
>
> Rom 14:14, where Paul says, "I know and am persuaded ἐν κυρίῳ 'Ιησοῦ" (AV: "by the Lord Jesus"; RSV, NIV, NRSV: "in the Lord Jesus").
>
> Phil 4:13, where Paul asserts that he "can do all things ἐν τῷ ἐνδυναμοῦντί με" (AV: "through Christ which strengtheneth me"; RSV: "in him who strengthens me"; NRSV: "through him who strengthens me"; NIV: "through him who gives me strength").

---

49. Schweitzer, *Mysticism of Paul the Apostle*, 123.

50. Bultmann, *Theology of the New Testament*, 1.311.

51. J. A. T. Robinson, *The Body: A Study in Pauline Theology* (London: SCM, 1957), 51; also L. S. Thornton, *The Common Life in the Body of Christ* (London: Dacre, 1941), passim.

52. So Phil 1:1; cf. Eph 1:1 and Col 1:2.

53. So 1 Thess 4:16; cf. 1 Cor 15:18.

54. E.g., Rom 16:7, 11.

Nonetheless, the fact that in the following passages Paul distinguishes ἐν from διά and ἐκ with respect to Christ suggests that he used these prepositions somewhat more exactly than he has at times been thought to have done:

> 2 Cor 1:20: "All the promises of God have their 'Yes' ἐν αὐτῷ. Wherefore also we utter the 'Amen' δι' αὐτοῦ to the glory of God."
> 2 Cor 2:17: "As ἐκ θεοῦ in the presence of God we speak ἐν Χριστῷ."
> Col 1:16: "ἐν αὐτῷ were all things created. . . . All things were created δι' αὐτοῦ and εἰς αὐτόν."
> Col 1:19-20: "ἐν αὐτῷ it was considered proper for all the fullness of God to dwell, and δι' αὐτοῦ to reconcile all things to himself."

Moreover, in most of those passages where it is possible that Paul used "in Christ Jesus," "in Christ," "in the Lord," or "in him" only as a synonym for the noun or adjective "Christian" — or where it is asserted that an instrumental, causal source or dynamic idea was uppermost in his thought — the local designation, if it were not for the revulsion of the interpreter to the seeming crudity of the idea, could just as easily be seen. The following instances certainly possess a local flavor:

> Rom 8:1: "There is therefore now no condemnation for those who are ἐν Χριστῷ Ἰησοῦ."
> 2 Cor 5:17: "If anyone is ἐν Χριστῷ, that person is a new creation."
> 2 Cor 5:19: "God was ἐν Χριστῷ reconciling the world to himself."
> Eph 1:20: "God's work was accomplished ἐν τῷ Χριστῷ when he raised him from the dead."
> Phil 3:9: "That I might gain Christ and be found ἐν αὐτῷ."

Thus, while not assenting to all of Adolf Deissmann's positions, nor insisting that there be a unitary exegesis of the expression, it seems that one must recognize that Paul's "in Christ Jesus" motif frequently carries a quite definite local flavor.[55] It is not just a bit of "verbal ingenuity."[56] Nor is it one of many metaphors subservient to the controlling concept of "the body of Christ."[57] Rather, "in Christ Jesus" is the dominant expression of Paul for the intimate and personal relationship that exists between the exalted Christ and those who have committed themselves to him. And while the expression certainly has corporate overtones and social implications, it is used so often[58] and in such individualistic settings[59] that it must be understood as much more than just an extension of meaning from a more fundamental concept of corporeity or instrumentality.[60]

55. As argued by E. Best, *One Body in Christ* (London: SPCK, 1955), passim.
56. As asserted by Schweitzer, *Mysticism of Paul the Apostle,* 117.
57. As claimed by J. A. T. Robinson, *The Body,* esp. 58-67.
58. A total of 164 times in ten of the Pauline letters, according to the count of Deissmann, *Die neutestamentliche Formel "in Christo Jesu,"* 1-2, 118-23.
59. Cf. esp. 2 Cor 5:17; Phil 3:9.
60. Of two books written during the heyday of scholars' interest in Paul's use of the expression "in Christ," E. Best's title and treatment in his *One Body in Christ* of 1955 is much more representative of Paul's thought than is J. A. T. Robinson's *The Body* of 1957, for Best recognizes the personal emphasis contained in the expression "in Christ" while also stressing the corporate nature

3. Paul's Use of "in Christ" in Romans. Paul uses the expression "in Christ" — as well as its cognates "in Christ Jesus," "in Christ Jesus our Lord," "in the Lord Jesus," and "in the Lord" — a number of times in his letter to the Christians at Rome.[61] In 8:1-11, however, he focuses particular attention on this theme in speaking of believers in Jesus as being "in Christ Jesus" and of Christ by his Spirit being "in the believer." The question arises, however, regarding how Paul in his use of such local terminology understood the intermingling of personalities — that is, of believers being "in Christ Jesus" and of Christ by his Spirit being "in believers."

Deissmann wrestled with this question and proposed that Paul must have thought along the lines of the joining of an ethereal Spirit and a pneumatic Christ, into which union the Christian lives in a sort of rarefied air — and which could also, as can air, indwell the believer. But such an analogy is not really Pauline. Rather, Paul seems to have thought of the exalted Christ as a cosmic, redemptive, and eschatological "Universal Personality,"[62] as his statements regarding Jesus Christ, "the Son/the One whom he [God] loves," in Col 1:15-20 and Eph 1:3-14 suggest.[63]

As Gen 15:6 says regarding Abraham: "And he trusted in Jahweh" (והאמן ביהוה), and as the various writers of the OT Scriptures often used that same Hebrew preposition ‎ב ("in") rather than the more usual relational Hebrew preposition ‎ל ("to," "for," "in regard to") when speaking about people either trusting or not trusting God[64] — and, further, as Jesus is reported to have spoken of his relationship to the Father as being that of "the Father in me" (ἐν ἐμοὶ ὁ πατήρ) and "I in the Father" (κἀγὼ ἐν τῷ πατρί) without diminishing in any way the personality either of God or of Jesus[65] — so Paul with his high Christology could speak of being "in Christ" without suggesting softening or dissolving the personality either of Christ or of the Christian. To be forced to give a psychological analysis of this relationship would probably have left Paul speechless. Yet he was convinced that he had experienced just such an intimacy with the exalted Christ.

In accepting such an intimate, local, and personal meaning for the expression "in Christ Jesus," one is of course acknowledging some form of mysticism in Paul's thought. But this need not be abhorred if, by the term "mysticism," we mean "that contact be-

---

of the Christian life as contained in the metaphor "the body of Christ," whereas Robinson subdues everything under the corporate concept of "the body."

61. Cf. Rom 6:11, 23; 8:1-2, 39; 9:1; 14:14; 15:17; 16:2, 11-13.

62. A. Oepke, "ἐν," *TDNT* 2.542 (translating Oepke's cosmic and eschatological term "Universalpersönlichkeit" in *TWNT* 2.538).

63. Note especially the following Christological statements in these passages: "In him all things were created in heaven and on earth, things visible and invisible" (Col 1:16); "In him all things consist" (Col 1:17); "In him it was considered proper for all the fullness of God to dwell" (Col 1:19); God "has blessed us in the heavenly realms with every spiritual blessing in Christ" (Eph 1:3); "In him we have redemption through his blood, the forgiveness of sins" (Eph 1:7); God "made known to us the mystery of his will according to his good pleasure, which he purposed in Christ" (Eph 1:9); and "in him" God's plan for the fullness of time will be brought to completion in "bringing to summation all things in the Christ, things in heaven and on earth" (Eph 1:10).

64. See 2 Kgs 18:5-6 (of Hezekiah, who "trusted *in* the Lord"); Ps 78:22 (of Israel's lack of "trust *in* God"); Prov 28:25 (of the person who "trusts *in* the Lord"); Isa 50:10 (on the prophet's call for Israel to "trust *in* the name of the Lord"); Jer 17:5-7 (on the blessedness of the person who "trusts *in* the Lord"); Nah 1:7 (on God's care for the person who "trusts *in* him"); and Zeph 3:12 (on meek and humble people who "trust *in* the name of the Lord").

65. Cf. John 10:38; 14:10, 11, 20; 17:21.

tween the human and the Divine which forms the core of the deepest religious experience, but which can only be felt as an immediate intuition of the highest reality and cannot be described in the language of psychology."[66] It is not the pagan mysticism of absorption, for the human "I" and the divine "Thou" of the relationship retain their identities. Rather, it is fellowship between the human "I" and the divine "Thou" at its highest, which for Paul epitomizes the essence of personal relations between the exalted Christ and those who believe in and are committed to him. And this is how Paul uses "in Christ Jesus" and its cognates here in 8:1-2, which usage is reflected also elsewhere in the letter at 6:11, 23; 8:39; 9:1; 14:14; 15:17; and 16:2, 11-13.

8:3-4 In these two verses Paul declares what God has done in sending his own Son, Christ Jesus, on behalf of all people. The statement begins with an explanatory use of the conjunction γάρ ("for"), which follows closely after an introductory use of the same conjunction at the beginning of 8:2.[67] The meanings of a number of terms and expressions in this declaratory statement, however, have been viewed by various scribes and commentators down through the centuries as not only complex but also in need of explanatory comment or linguistic improvement.

Problems of interpretation have arisen with respect to these important questions:

1. What is meant by the substantive use of the adjective ἀδύνατον ("powerless," "impotent")? Is it to be understood in the active sense of "unable" or in the passive sense of "impossible"?
2. Why is a verb lacking in the statement "God . . . by sending his own Son in the likeness of sinful humanity"?
3. What is the significance of the "sending" motif for an understanding of relations between "God" and "his own Son"?
4. What is the relation of the clause καὶ περὶ ἁμαρτίας ("and with respect to sin") to what precedes it in 8:3a and what follows it in 8:4?
5. What is the meaning of τὸ δικαίωμα τοῦ νόμου ("the righteous requirement of the law")?
6. What is signified by the expression πληρωθῇ ἐν ἡμῖν ("fulfilled in us"), and how is that fulfillment worked out in the lives of those "who do not live according to the sinful nature but according to the Spirit"?

Many of these matters regarding Paul's argument and its form in 8:3-4 are, we believe, clarified — at least to some extent — by Eduard Schweizer's theses. He contends (1) that there arose within Alexandrian Judaism certain speculations about the equation and eternality of God's "Torah," God's "Wisdom," and God's "Logos"; (2) that some early followers of Jesus in the Greco-

---

66. Kennedy, *Theology of the Epistles,* 122.
67. Note also this same phenomenon at the beginnings of both 8:14 and 8:15.

Roman world picked up on that equation of terms, as well as that emphasis on eternality, applying those understandings to Christ as God's Son; (3) that there was developed among some early believers in Jesus a "sending formula" that spoke of Jesus as having been "sent by God," just as Torah, Wisdom, and Logos had been; (4) that such a christianized "sending formula" was known in certain circles of early believers in Jesus; and (5) that it is alluded to by Paul in Gal 4:4-5 and Rom 8:3-4 and by John in John 3:16-17 and 1 John 4:9.[68]

Without necessarily advocating all that Schweizer has argued about the historical and religious background of such a "sending formula," at least his conclusions — that a christianized version of a Jewish "sending formula" was known in at least some circles of early Christianity and was alluded to by Paul in Gal 4:4-5 and Rom 8:3-4 and by John in John 3:16-17 and 1 John 4:9 — seem plausible and offer a significant approach toward a proper understanding of what Paul writes here in 8:3-4. For in positing that Paul is alluding to a known "sending formula," which in its essence was probably expressed along the lines of "God sent his Son (ἐξαπέστειλεν ὁ θεὸς τὸν υἱὸν αὐτοῦ) in order to redeem (ἵνα . . . ἐξαγοράσῃ)" — with, in all likelihood, various other statements being included in the ἵνα clause to fill out the formula as the occasion demanded — a number of the problems that interpreters have found in the structure and terminology of this important statement in the letter may be seen to be somewhat clarified.

If the central statement of 8:3, "God . . . by sending his own Son in the likeness of sinful humanity," reflects in allusive fashion an early Christian "sending formula," then its lack of an explicit verb would certainly be understandable — just as it was understandable in Paul's earlier quotation of a Christian confessional portion in 8:2. Conversely, if some of the terms and expressions of 8:3-4 were originally associated with such an early Christian "sending formula," and if Paul continues their usage in this passage, it may be somewhat difficult to determine the precise theological nuances that were understood in some of these expressions when first used in their original context and then when Paul continues their usage here in 8:3-4. For Christian confessional and formulaic materials may be assumed to have been generally more devotional in nature than theologically precise. So commentators have often been at a loss to determine exactly what is meant in 8:3-4 by (1) the substantive term "powerless" (ἀδύνατον), which may be understood in either an active sense of being "unable" or a passive sense of being "impossible" (or, perhaps, both); (2) the nominative singular masculine aorist participle "sending" (πέμψας), which may carry with it a number of nuances with respect to Jesus' relation to God the Father; (3) the clause "in the likeness of sinful flesh" (ἐν ὁμοιώματι σαρκὸς ἁμαρτίας), which may suggest various connotations with respect to Jesus' person; (4) the

68. See E. Schweizer, "Zum religionsgeschichtlichen Hintergrund der 'Sendungsformel,'" *ZNW* 57 (1966) 199-210. Cf. my earlier evaluation and use of Schweizer's thesis for the interpretation of Gal 4:4-5 (R. N. Longenecker, *Galatians,* 167-69); note also L. E. Keck's use of this thesis with respect to the interpretation of Rom 8:3-4 in his "The Law and 'the Law of Sin and Death,'" 43-44.

expression "the righteous requirement of the [Mosaic] law" (τὸ δικαίωμα τοῦ νόμου), which may suggest somewhat different meanings in different contexts, and (5) the comment that the righteous requirement of the law is "fulfilled in us" (πληρωθῇ ἐν ἡμῖν), that is, in "those who do not live according to the sinful nature but according to the Spirit." The clause "and with respect to sin" (καὶ περὶ ἁμαρτίας), which appears in 8:3b, I take to be not part of the "sending formula" that Paul has allusively used, but rather, the beginning of an additional comment that continues to the end of 8:4.

There are, therefore, a number of uncertainties about (1) the structure of what is presented in 8:3-4 and (2) the nuancing of some of the terms and expressions used in the passage. What seems to be reasonably clear, however, is that here in 8:3-4 Paul is attempting to add additional support to his contextualized proclamation that "there is now no condemnation for those who are in Christ Jesus" by his use of such a traditional "sending formula." He did this earlier and explicitly in 8:2 by quoting the central portion of some early Christian confessional material. And he seems to have done it in 8:3-4, by what appears to be an allusive reference to some christianized version of such a traditional "sending formula."

This twofold support — as first drawn explicitly from some early Christian confession in 8:2 and then echoing in allusive fashion some traditional sending formula in 8:3-4 — serves to highlight the importance of what Paul is proclaiming in 8:1. For in that statement that "[there is] now no condemnation for those who are in Christ Jesus," Paul sets out the crux — that is, the central or main features — of his contextualized Christian proclamation to the Gentile world.

II. Two Diametrically Opposed Mind-sets and Modes of Human Existence and Their Respective Results (8:5-8)

8:5-8 Paul brought the first part of his proclamation section of 8:1-17 to a close with the statement in 8:4 about those who are in Christ Jesus "not living their lives" (from the verb περιπατεῖν; literally "to go about," "walk around")[69] "according to the sinful nature" (κατὰ σάρκα), but rather "according to the Spirit" (κατὰ πνεῦμα). Here in 8:5-8 he develops this theme of how one lives one's life by speaking of two diametrically opposed mind-sets and two quite different modes of human existence, that is, of (1) living "controlled by the sinful nature" or (2) living "controlled by the Spirit." The two mind-sets and modes of existence are expressed in two quite different forms of behavior, which result in either "death" or "life and peace." Each of the sentences in 8:5-8 is introduced by one or another of the conjunctions γάρ ("for"), διοτι ("because"), or δέ ("but,"

---

69. Cf. 6:4 for an earlier metaphorical use of περιπατεῖν with reference to someone's way of life or moral conduct in Paul's letter to Rome; see also Rom 14:15; Eph 2:2; as well as Mark 7:5 and 2 John 6, for the use of περιπατεῖν with κατά in similar contexts.

"and").[70] All the conjunctions, however, appear to be used simply to express ideas of continuation or connection in spelling out what is involved with respect to these two different mind-sets and modes of existence — and therefore do not need to be translated, for in English the juxtaposition of sentences is often sufficient by itself to signal ideas of continuation or connection.[71]

Here in 8:5-8 Paul highlights the fact that the thoughts and actions of "people who live according to the sinful nature" (οἱ κατὰ σάρκα ὄντες, as in v. 5a) — or, as expressed in slightly different words, "people who are controlled by the sinful nature" (οἱ ἐν σαρκὶ ὄντες, as in v. 8a) — have as their end result the judgment of "death" (θάνατος, as in v. 6). For such a way of thinking and such a manner of living are "hostile to God" (ἔχθρα εἰς θεόν, as in v. 7), and people who think and live like that are "unable to please God" (θεῷ ἀρέσαι οὐ δύνανται, as in v. 8).

The question frequently asked by interpreters regarding Paul's presentation in 8:5-8 is this: Is the apostle describing the contrast that exists between a non-Christian and a Christian, or is he speaking not only about the situation of nonbelievers in Jesus but also about the situation of Christians who retreat back into a way of thinking and a manner of living that is controlled again by their sinful nature? The fact that Paul could exhort those who seem to have been among his best Christian converts (that is, the believers in Jesus at Philippi) to have a mind-set like that of Christ Jesus (as he does in Phil 2:5: "Your attitude/mind-set should be the same as that of Christ Jesus," and by his quotation of the "Christ hymn" of Phil 2:6-11) — and, further, that he could exhort them: "Join with others in following my example, brothers and sisters, and take note of those who live according to the pattern we gave you" (as he does in Phil 3:17) — clearly suggests that he regarded it as necessary to speak to both nonbelievers in Jesus and true Christians regarding these diametrically opposed mind-sets and modes of existence. For thinking and living "according to the fleshly nature" is not only the situation of the unregenerate, it is also a real possibility, as well as a sad reality, for many who claim to be Christ's own.

III. People "in Christ" and Therefore Controlled by the Spirit Are Those Who Have Life (8:9-11)

8:9-11 In this third paragraph of his proclamation section of 8:1-17, Paul declares: "You, however, are not controlled by the sinful nature but by the Spirit, since the Spirit of God lives in you. [If anyone does not have the Spirit of Christ, that person does not belong to Christ. And if Christ is in you, your body is indeed dead because of sin, but your spirit is alive because of righteousness.]

---

70. Γάρ ("for") in 8:5a, 6a; διότι ("because") in 8:7a; and δέ ("but," "and") in 8:8a, all appearing in their usual postpositive positions in their respective sentences.

71. Cf. Paul's four similar uses of the postpositive conjunction γάρ in 1 Cor 9:16-17

Since then the Spirit of 'the One who raised Jesus from the dead' is living in you, 'he who raised Christ from the dead' will also give life to your mortal bodies through his Spirit, who lives in you." Three matters immediately stand out in this declaration regarding the Christian's new life "in Christ" and "in the Spirit":

1. The use of the plural pronoun "you" throughout these three verses: the nominative plural "you" (ὑμεῖς) at the very beginning of the passage; the genitive possessive plural "your" (ὑμῶν) in its concluding verse; and the dative plural expression "in you" (ἐν ὑμῖν), which appears four times in these three verses — all of which suggests that Paul is addressing a group of people and speaking about their status as believers in Jesus.
2. Paul's focus in this passage is not on the Christian being "*in* Christ," as he proclaimed in 8:1-2, but on Christ by his Spirit being "*in* the Christian" — thereby highlighting that these two features of Christian existence are both true and reciprocal in nature.
3. The ease with which Paul, in speaking of "Christ by his Spirit" being "*in* the Christian," brings together all three persons of the Trinity as agents of such a personal relationship — speaking first in 8:9a of "the Spirit" and "the Spirit of God" as living in the believer; then in 8:9b-10 of "the Spirit of Christ" and "Christ" as being present in the believer; and finally in 8:11 of God, "the One who raised Jesus from the dead," as living in believers and giving life to their mortal bodies.

A major problem in understanding what Paul is writing in these three verses, however, is how to interpret the conditional particle εἰ ("if") and its related conjunction εἴπερ ("if indeed," "if after all," "since") — with the conjunction εἴπερ appearing at the beginning of the second clause of the statement in 8:9a and the particle εἰ heading up the three statements that follow in 8:9b-11. Both εἰ and εἴπερ could be read as expressing either (1) a condition, and therefore a warning, or (2) a note of assurance, and therefore an encouragement. The uses of the particle εἰ ("if") at the beginning of the statement in 8:9b ("If anyone does not have the Spirit of Christ, that person does not belong to Christ") and at the beginning of the statement in 8:10 ("If Christ is in you, your body is indeed dead because of sin, but your spirit is alive because of righteousness") seem best understood as expressing a condition, and so as involving something of a warning. Yet the use of εἴπερ at the beginning of the second clause of the first statement of 8:9a (i.e., εἴπερ πνεῦμα θεοῦ οἰκεῖ ἐν ὑμῖν) is far better understood as a word of assurance, and so to be read as "*since* the Spirit of God lives in you" — just as Paul earlier used εἴπερ ("if indeed," "if after all," "since") in 3:30 ("*since* there is only one God"), as he will use εἴπερ again at the close of this section in 8:17 ("*since* we share in his sufferings in order that we may also share in his glory"),[72] and as

---

72. Cf. Cranfield, *Romans*, 1.407: "εἴπερ συμπάσχομεν ἵνα καὶ συνδοξασθῶμεν is not to be understood as introducing a condition, but rather as stating a fact which confirms what has just been

he had earlier used εἴπερ in 1 Cor 15:15 ("*since* it is preached that Christ has been raised from the dead, how can some of you say there is no resurrection of the dead?") and in 2 Thess 1:6 ("*since* God is just, he will pay back, etc.").[73] Likewise, because the statement of 8:11 is basically a repetition of the opening statement of 8:9a (though, of course, with expansions of both phraseology and content), the particle εἰ ("if") that begins the statement of 8:11 should probably also be understood as continuing the note of assurance given in the second clause of the first verse of the passage, and so be read as "*since* the Spirit of 'the One who raised Jesus from the dead' is living in you."

Because of such linguistic uncertainties, Paul's line of argumentation in these three verses has frequently been viewed by commentators as somewhat jumbled. Without attempting to set out the various possible readings of the passage, which are numerous, we propose that the course of Paul's argument is here in this passage best understood in terms of:

1. A main thesis that is given at the beginning of the passage in 8:9a: "You are not controlled by the sinful nature but by the Spirit, *since* the Spirit of God lives in you."
2. A parenthetical comment of pertinence that is given in 8:9b, which has to do with the essential relations between "the Spirit of Christ" and "Christ" himself: "*If* anyone does not have the Spirit of Christ, that person does not belong to Christ."
3. A second parenthetical comment in 8:10, which speaks of the results of Christ being in the Christian: "*If* Christ is in you, your body is indeed dead because of sin, but your spirit is alive because of righteousness."
4. The repetition in 8:11 of the original thesis of 8:9a — though in an expanded form and twice using what seems to have been an early Christian attributive formula for the simple term "God": "*Since* the Spirit of 'the One who raised Jesus from the dead' [i.e., God] is living in you, 'he who raised Christ from the dead' [i.e., God] will also give life to your mortal bodies through his Spirit, who lives in you."

On such an understanding of the flow of Paul's argument in 8:9-11, a clear note of assurance resounds in the thesis statement of 8:9a and then again in the expanded form of that statement in 8:11 — though Paul inserts into 8:9b and 8:10, in parenthetical fashion, two conditional comments, which function to warn Christians who might take such assuring statements for granted and fail to rely on the Spirit in their actual thinking and their practice.

By the inclusion in 8:10 of the particle μέν — one of the most common

said. As in v. 9, εἴπερ means here 'seeing that' (cf. Old Latin 'si quidem'), and is roughly equivalent to γάρ"; see also 1.388.

73. See also, to the same effect, the treatments of Kuss, *Römerbrief,* 2.501; Leenhardt, *Romans,* 206-7; Schlatter, *Romans,* 178; Morris, *Romans,* 308; Moo, *Romans,* 490; and Jewett, *Romans,* 489.

particles in both classical and koine Greek (as an affirmative particle: "indeed"; as a concessive particle: "though") that can be found at least 180 times in the NT — the second clause of this verse, which may be read "your body is *indeed* dead because of sin," points back to something Paul wrote earlier in this second major section of the body middle of the letter. For by his use of μέν ("indeed") Paul is likely recalling his earlier discussion in 5:12-21 regarding the sin of "the one man, Adam," which brought depravity and death into the experience of all humanity. And so we should understand the Christian situation in this present era of salvation history as (1) experiencing all that is involved in the expression "dead because of sin," but also (2) realizing in an inaugurated fashion all that is connoted by the statement "your spirit is alive because of righteousness."

Likewise, in the expanded form of his main thesis, as expressed in 8:11, Paul seems to be alluding to a Christian formulation that was used as a locution for God by believers in Jesus before him — perhaps first by Jewish followers of Jesus, who used the locution "*the One who* raised *Jesus* from the dead" in speaking of God; then by Gentile Christians, who probably would have reworded such a Jewish Christian locution for God as follows: "*He who* raised *Christ* from the dead."[74]

Of primary importance in this passage, however, are the repeated uses of the dative expression "in you" (ἐν ὑμῖν), which appears four times in these three verses. Together, the "in Christ Jesus" (ἐν Χριστῷ Ἰησοῦ) formula of 8:1-2 and the four "in you" (ἐν ὑμῖν) formulations of 8:9-11 constitute, in brief, the two reciprocal polarities of Paul's contextualized Christian message, which he proclaimed to Gentiles in his Gentile mission and which he wanted his Christian addressees also to appreciate and experience. It is a message that focuses on the personal, relational, and participational features of the Christian gospel — and it is a message that Paul was convinced would radically change lives for the better by its acceptance.

IV. Exhortation to Live Not "according to the Sinful Nature" but "by the Spirit" (8:12-13)

In his proclamation of "no condemnation" and "new life" for those who are "in Christ Jesus," and therefore are "in the Spirit," Paul takes pains to highlight the ethical imperative that is always involved in the proclamation of the Christian gospel. For the Christian life according to Paul (and as portrayed by the other writers of the NT) is lived between the polarities of an "already" or "realized eschatology," on the one hand, and a "not yet" or "futuristic eschatology" on the other hand. Oscar Cullmann has aptly stated the situation of believers in Jesus as follows: Christians live out their lives in the context of two ages, not just one

---

74. Cf. our discussion of what seems to have been Paul's use of a Christological "sending formula" in 8:3. See also our treatments of his use of early Christian confessional materials in 8:2 and in 8:14.

age — that is, in the context of (1) "the age to come," with its positive powers for righteous living, which was inaugurated by Jesus, and (2) "this age," with its negative powers, which still exists and continually attempts to thwart the effects of that inaugurated new age.[75]

8:12-13 Here in these two verses Paul calls on his converts in his Gentile mission (who were the original recipients of his proclamation) — as well as on his Christian addressees at the capital city of Rome (who heard his contextualized proclamation of the Christian gospel read and explained to them) — to be not only vitally aware about what God has done for them because of the work of Christ Jesus and the ministry of the Spirit, but also aware of how they should live as citizens of this newly inaugurated "age to come" in the midst of "this age":[76] "Therefore, brothers and sisters, we are obligated not to the sinful nature to live according to the sinful nature. For if you live according to the sinful nature, you are destined to die. But if by the Spirit you put to death the practices of the body, you will live."

The apostle begins this portion of his proclamation by joining the particles ἄρα ("so," "then") and οὖν ("so," "therefore") to form the idiomatic expression ἄρα οὖν ("consequently," "therefore"), thereby signaling here at 8:12a the beginning of the conclusion of his central proclamation section of 8:1-17 — just as he did previously at 5:18a, 7:3a, and 7:25b to identify for his original hearers (in his Gentile mission) and for his present addressees (in his letter to Rome) where his conclusions in those earlier portions began. Further, here at the beginning of 8:12 he employs the vocative ἀδελφοί ("brothers and sisters"), an affectionate form of direct address to those he was speaking to (in his Gentile mission) and is now addressing (in his letter to Rome) — just as he earlier used ἀδελφοί ("brothers and sisters") in 1:13 and 7:1, as well as the somewhat more affectionate expression ἀδελφοί μου ("my brothers and sisters") in 7:4.[77]

The expression "we are obligated" (ὀφειλέται ἐσμέν) is reminiscent of Paul's statement "I am obligated" (ὀφειλέτης εἰμί) in 1:14. And just as the apostle's obligation was not to any material concerns or human interests, but was directed (1) to God himself, who had called him to a prophetic ministry as an apostle to the Gentiles (cf. 1:1a, 5), and (2) to the proclamation of the Christian gospel, for which he had been set apart by God (cf. 1:1b, 9), so the obligation of the believer in Jesus has nothing to do with matters pertaining to "the sinful nature," but is (1) in response to God himself, who has provided in the work of Jesus Christ for the believer's release from the condemnation and power of sin, (2) in accordance with the believer's new position of being "in Christ Jesus" and "in the Spirit," and (3) in line with his or her new status as a "son or daughter of God," to whom God has given his Holy Spirit to guide and empower.

---

75. Cf. Cullmann, *Christ and Time,* 47-48, 81-93, and 222-30.

76. Cf. our earlier "Exegetical Comments" on 6:8-11.

77. Cf. also Paul's use of the vocative ἀδελφοί in addressing the Christians at Rome in 10:1; 12:1; 14:10, 13, 15, 21; 15:14, 30; 16:17.

Paul goes on to explain, using as introduction the conjunction γάρ ("for"): "For if you live according to the sinful nature, you are destined to die. But if by the Spirit you put to death the practices of the body, you will live." In support of these words of explanation that have to do with putting to death the sinful practices of the body and entering by God's Spirit into real life, he quotes what has every appearance of having been an early Christian confessional statement, which he introduces by the conjunction γάρ ("for"): "All those who are being led by the Spirit of God, they are sons and daughters of God (οὗτοι υἱοὶ θεοῦ εἰσιν)."[78]

V. Additional Statements regarding the Status of Believers in Jesus as God's Sons and Daughters, with an Emphasis on the Greco-Roman Metaphor "Adoption" (8:14-17)

8:14-17 The postpositive conjunction γάρ, which appears at the beginning of 8:14, is used not to introduce an explanation but simply to connect these additional proclamation statements of 8:14-17 with the material set out in 8:1-13. Paul's proclamation of 8:1-11 had been building up to the theme of believers in Jesus being "children of God" (τέκνα θεοῦ). The hortatory material of 8:12-13, however, while vitally important, has somewhat broken the fuller development of that theme. So here in 8:14-17 Paul fills out the details of that important theme by (1) quoting what appears to be an early Christian confessional affirmation: "All who are led by the Spirit of God, they are sons and daughters of God (οὗτοι υἱοὶ θεοῦ εἰσιν)," (2) referring to the Greco-Roman laws of "adoption" and using that socio-legal family situation of antiquity as a metaphor for the God-given status of a believer in God's family, (3) highlighting the work of the Spirit in bringing about the believer's new status as a child of God and in witnessing to the believer of the reality of this new family relationship, and (4) speaking about the results of being God's sons and daughters as including being "heirs of God and co-heirs with Christ" and as sharing "in his [Christ's] sufferings in order that we may also share in his glory."

A major contribution to an understanding of the Christian's new status, which has been established by God through the work of Jesus Christ and the ministry of the Spirit, was set out by Joachim Jeremias in his concise little book *The Central Message of the New Testament* of 1965 and his more extensive and detailed monograph *Abba: Studien zur neutestamentlichen Theologie und Zeitgeschichte* of 1966.[79] For Jeremias observed (1) that while the word "father" (אָב in both Hebrew and Aramaic) was used widely among Jews for ancestors and

---

78. Understanding υἱοὶ θεοῦ as referring inclusively to both males and females.

79. J. Jeremias, *The Central Message of the New Testament* (London: SCM; New York: Scribner's, 1965); *idem, Abba: Studien zur neutestamentlichen Theologie und Zeitgeschichte* (Göttingen: Vandenhoeck & Ruprecht, 1966).

other respected persons, the emphatic vocative form of "father" (אבא in Aramaic) was used by Jewish children in an affectionate manner for their own human fathers, (2) that Jesus used this form of address in his Gethsemane prayer to God his Father in Mark 14:36, and (3) that this use of "Abba" by Jesus provides the key to the new relationship that exists between God and his people throughout the NT presentations of the Christian gospel.[80] Further, (1) the fact that in Mark 14:36, Rom 8:15, and Gal 4:6 the Aramaic term "Abba" (אבא) is immediately followed by the Greek term "Father" (πατήρ) indicates that such an affectionate consciousness of intimate relationship with God was widespread among early believers in Jesus, whether Aramaic- or Greek-speaking, and (2) the fact that the Greek form of the expression is articular, that is, that it reads ὁ πατήρ ("the father"), suggests that the Greek form of the expression, as well as its Aramaic counterpart, should be understood as a vocative of address that carries an emphatic nuance.[81]

In such a family relationship, with God as Father and all believers in Jesus as God's adopted "sons and daughters," everything changes! Picking up from his use of the imagery and language of slavery in 6:16-18 and 7:14, Paul declares here in 8:15: "You did not receive a spirit that makes you a slave again to fear. Rather, you received a spirit of adoption by God as his sons and daughters, by which we cry out 'Abba, Father.'"

Paul's two uses of πνεῦμα ("spirit") in the two clauses of this verse may be viewed (either or both) as referring to God's Holy Spirit, and so capitalized. More likely, however, they should both be understood as signifying "the activating or essential principle influencing a person,"[82] and therefore not capitalized. Thus the believer in Jesus lives his or her life in an entirely new environment — that is, no longer activated by the principle of "slavery to sin," which results only in fear, but activated by the principle of υἱοθεσία, that is, by the reality of having been "adopted by God as his sons and daughters." This new factor of life makes all the difference in one's Christian experience — not that "of slavery again unto fear" (δουλείας πάλιν εἰς φόβον), but that "of adoption (υἱοθεσίας) as his [God's] sons and daughters."

The term υἱοθεσία ("adoption") appears only five times in Paul's letters: here in 8:15; earlier in Gal 4:5; later in Rom 8:23 and 9:4; and then again in Eph 1:5. It is not found in the Jewish (OT) Scriptures (either in the Greek LXX or in any cognate expression of the Hebrew MT). Nor does it appear in the literature of Second Temple Judaism or elsewhere in the non-Pauline writings of the NT.

---

80. See Jeremias, *Central Message of the New Testament,* esp. 9-30; *idem, Abba,* esp. 15-67 (ET: *The Prayers of Jesus,* SBT 2.6 [London: SCM, 1967], 11-65); cf. also *idem, New Testament Theology,* vol. 1, *The Proclamation of Jesus,* trans. J. Bowden (London: SCM, 1971), 61-68, 197.

81. On Αββα ὁ πατήρ as an emphatic vocative, see H. D. Betz, *Galatians,* 211; also D. Zeller, "God as Father in the Proclamation and in the Prayer of Jesus," in *Standing before God: Festschrift J. M. Oesterreicher,* ed. A. Finkel and L. Frizzell (New York: Ktav, 1981), 122-25.

82. Quoting definition 5a of the word "spirit" in *Merriam Webster's Deluxe Dictionary,* Tenth Collegiate Edition.

It may be said, therefore, that the use of the word "adoption" to characterize the relationship of God's people to God himself was unique to Paul — though the presence of the term in the "sending formula" of Gal 4:5, as well as in what seems to be a traditional listing of features (beginning with ὧν ἡ υἱοθεσία, "theirs is the adoption") that constitute the special status of Jews in Rom 9:4-5, suggests that υἱοθεσία as characterizing the relationship of God's people to himself would have been understood by both Jewish and Gentile believers in Jesus.

There have been a number of highly significant studies on the laws pertaining to the adoption of children (especially male children) in Greco-Roman society vis-à-vis the appearance of the metaphor of υἱοθεσία in three of Paul's letters.[83] The following features are particularly important to note for an appreciation of Paul's use of the term υἱοθεσία here in 8:15:

1. An adopted son was taken out of his previous situation and placed in an entirely new relationship to his new adopting father, who became his new *paterfamilias.*
2. An adopted son started a new life as part of his new family, with all his old debts canceled.
3. An adopted son was considered no less important than any other biologically born son in his adopting father's family.
4. An adopted son experienced a changed status, with his old name set aside and a new name given him by his adopting father.

Undoubtedly most (if not all) of these features pertaining to the adoption of a son into a Gentile family of the Greco-Roman world would have come to the fore in the consciousness of Paul's hearers in his mission to pagan Gentiles in the eastern portion of the Roman Empire when they heard him speak about a Christian's new status as being "adopted" by God. Likewise, it may be presumed that they would have come to the fore in the consciousness of his Christian readers at Rome, as well as in the consciousness of his own converts to whom he wrote in the province of Galatia and the city of Ephesus.

Further, it needs to be noted (1) that "adoption is fundamentally a relational and familial [i.e., related to a family] metaphor," and (2) that the term υἱοθεσία is one that "Paul borrowed from the Roman sociolegal context of his

83. See, esp., W. J. Woodhouse, "Adoption (Roman)," in *Encyclopedia of Religion and Ethics,* ed. J. Hastings (Edinburgh: T. & T. Clark, 1908), 111-14; W. W. Buckland, *A Textbook of Roman Law from Augustus to Justinian* (Cambridge: Cambridge University Press, 1963), 124-28; J. M. Scott, *Adoption as Sons of God: An Exegetical Investigation into the Background of HUIOTHESIA in the Pauline Corpus,* WUNT 2.48 (Tübingen: Mohr, 1992); A. Berger, B. Nicholas, and S. M. Tregarri, "Adoption," in *The Oxford Classical Dictionary,* ed. S. Hornblower and A. Spawforth (Oxford: Oxford University Press, 2003), 12-13, 54-57; J. Stevenson-Moessner, *The Spirit of Adoption: At Home in God's Family* (Louisville: Westminster John Knox, 2003); T. J. Burke, *Adopted into God's Family: Exploring a Pauline Metaphor* (Downers Grove, Ill.: InterVarsity, 2006); and *idem,* "Adopted as Sons (ΥΙΟΘΕΣΙΑ): The Missing Piece in Pauline Soteriology," in *Paul: Jew, Greek, and Roman,* ed. S. E. Porter (Leiden: Brill, 2008), 259-87.

day."[84] The adoption of a child was not a Jewish practice, and therefore Paul would presumably not have taken over the word υἱοθεσία from either his Jewish heritage or his Jewish Christian background. Nonetheless, he used it here in Rom 8:15 (and again in 8:23) as a metaphor for what God has done through the work of Jesus Christ, evidently believing that it would be particularly meaningful to pagan Gentiles in the eastern part of the empire. Likewise, Paul seems to have believed that as a metaphor of relationship the expression υἱοθεσία was known and understood by his Christian addressees at Rome (cf. Rom 9:4) — as well as his converts in Galatia (cf. Gal 4:5), and in Ephesus and its environs (cf. Eph 1:5).

In this new relationship of having been adopted by God into his family, as believers in Jesus "we cry out" (κράζομεν) in response to God: "Abba, Father" (Αββα ὁ πατήρ). There have been numerous attempts to identify exactly what Paul had in mind when he spoke of Christians as "crying out" to God as "Father." Some have suggested that this "crying out to God as Father" should be understood in the context of the early Christians praying the "Lord's Prayer," which begins with the familial affirmation "Our Father."[85] Others, however, have postulated that Paul had in mind (1) some portion of an early Christian confession, (2) some early Christian baptismal formula, (3) some other early Christian liturgical formulation of his day, or (4) some prominent ecstatic utterance that had been expressed in early Christian worship. But, as Charles Cranfield has quite rightly observed in stating his own opinion:

> The true explanation is surely rather the simple one that κράζειν is used again and again in the LXX of urgent prayer, being so used in Psalms alone more than forty times (e.g., 3.4 [LXX: 5]; 4.3 [LXX: 4]; 18.6 [LXX:17.7]; 22.2, 5 [LXX: 21.3, 6]; 34.6 [LXX: 33.7]). It is used to represent several different Hebrew words. So here it is best taken to denote an urgent and sincere crying to God irrespective of whether it is loud or soft (or even unspoken), formal or informal, public or private.[86]

Paul closes this final paragraph of his contextualized proclamation in 8:1-17 with the following twofold declaration: (1) that it is "the Spirit himself" (αὐτὸ τὸ πνεῦμα) who "testifies with our spirit" (συμμαρτυρεῖ τῷ πνεύματι ἡμῶν) that "we are children of God" (ἐσμὲν τέκνα θεοῦ), as he says in v. 16; and (2) that "since we are children" (εἰ τέκνα), we are "also heirs of God" (καὶ κληρονόμοι θεοῦ) and "co-heirs with Christ" (συγκληρονόμοι Χριστοῦ), as he states in v. 17. Thus, as those who are "in Christ Jesus," and therefore also "in the Spirit," believers in Jesus have come to experience a more intimate and far more truly

---

84. Quoting two of T. J. Burke's concluding statements in the "summary" section of his book *Adopted into God's Family*, 194.

85. So, e.g., Cullmann, *Christology of the New Testament*, 208-9; G. Kittel, "ἀββᾶ," *TDNT* 1.6; Jeremias, *New Testament Theology*, 1.191-97; as well as a host of others.

86. Cranfield, *Romans*, 1.399.

filial relationship with God than they could ever have experienced under the "covenantal nomism" of the religion of Israel that God provided for his people, as expressed in the Jewish (OT) Scriptures. For now, as God's own people, who are "in Christ Jesus" and live "by the Spirit," Christians can address God directly as "Father" (Αββα ὁ πατήρ) and are able to enjoy all the benefits of being "children of God" (τέκνα θεοῦ) — as well as being, as Paul will go on to speak about in 8:18-30, involved in the advance of God's program of salvation history by "sharing in his [Christ's] sufferings in order that we may also share in his [Christ's] glory."

BIBLICAL THEOLOGY

In Rom 8:1-17 Paul sets out the basic features of his contextualized proclamation of the Christian gospel to pagan Gentiles in the Greco-Roman world. It is a passage that emphasizes (1) the pronouncement of "no condemnation" for those who are "in Christ Jesus," (2) the themes of life "in Christ Jesus" and life "in the Spirit," (3) statements regarding "Christ by his Spirit" being in and controlling the Christian, (4) an ethical imperative that is always involved in the proclamation of the Christian gospel and in a person's commitment to Jesus Christ, and (5) the additional Greco-Roman metaphor of "adoption," which highlights the fact that a believer's relationship with God is not a "natural" one but a relationship brought about because of the will of God the Father, the work of Jesus Christ, and the ministry of the Spirit. These are the matters that Paul sets out as his "spiritual gift" to the Christians at Rome — not denying the validity of what they already knew and had earlier experienced as believers in Jesus, which understandings and commitments had been extensively influenced by their ties with the mother church at Jerusalem, but desiring to bring the Roman believers in Jesus into the orbit of his own personal, relational, and participatory understanding of what it means to be a Christian or Christ follower.

Paul presents much more in his letters of his own contextualized version of the Christian gospel — not only in this letter to believers in Jesus at Rome, but also in his pastoral letters to his own converts that are included within the NT. Further, there was undoubtedly much that he agreed on with Jewish believers in Jesus about the life, death, and resurrection of Jesus of Nazareth — not only with those in Jerusalem and other localities of Palestine, but also with those living in Jewish Christian enclaves elsewhere in the Greco-Roman world. Certainly Paul understood Jesus as the climax of Israel's story, just as they did. Likewise, as an ethnic Jew who had been trained as a Jewish teacher and then came to believe in Jesus as the Jewish Messiah, Paul (1) understood the significance of the central forms and practices of Judaism, as he evidences in Rom 2:1–3:20, and (2) appreciated the Jewish and Jewish Christian uses of such highly significant forensic terms as "righteousness," "justification," "redemption," and "propitiation" ("expiation" or "sacrifice of atonement"), as he evidences particularly in

Rom 3:21–4:25. But, as Douglas Moo has aptly pointed out about Paul's Christian theology and his contextualized proclamation: "Jesus Christ is the climax not only of Israel's story but also of humanity's story" — and therefore, as Moo goes on to insist: "Renewed attention to the Jewish matrix of Paul's thinking should not blind us to the fact that Paul's vision of Christ ultimately transcends the story of Israel. Paul may begin with the narrative of Israel, but he does not end there."[87]

Christian biblical theology has most often focused (1) on the message of the NT as being the fulfillment of the religion of Israel in the OT, (2) on the person and work of Jesus as Israel's promised Messiah, and (3) on the soteriological expressions "righteousness," "justification," "redemption," and "propitiation" ("expiation" or "sacrifice of atonement") as expressing the essence of Christian proclamation. These matters have constituted the central themes in the theologies and writings of not only the Church Fathers of the first five centuries of Christian history, but also the Protestant Reformers of the sixteenth and seventeenth centuries — as well as, of course, the vast majority of orthodox Christian theologians, preachers, teachers, and writers of today. These are, in fact, the foundational themes of earliest Christian proclamation, which are expressed at many places and in various ways throughout the whole of the NT. They certainly, therefore, must be viewed as having been of great importance to the earliest Jewish believers in Jesus, to those influenced by early Jewish Christianity (as were the Christians at Rome), and to various other Christians scattered throughout the ancient world (as were the believers in Jesus in Ethiopia and elsewhere in North Africa). Further, they have been central features in the theologies of most of the "established" churches of the Western world, whether Roman Catholic, Eastern Orthodox, or Protestant.

However, while Paul fully agrees with all these important matters (as we have attempted to highlight in our explications of his statements in 3:21–4:25), what he presents in Section II of the body middle of the letter, that is, in 5:1–8:39, is what he considered his "spiritual gift" to his Roman addressees, which he gave them "so as to make you [i.e., them] strong" (1:11) and "so that we [i.e., the believers in Jesus at Rome and Paul] may be mutually encouraged by each other's faith, both yours and mine" (1:12) — which form of Christian proclamation he viewed as uniquely his (cf. again his use of the expression "my gospel" in 2:16 and 16:25). And that "spiritual gift" has to do, we propose, with understanding and experiencing the "good news" of the Christian gospel also in terms of its personal, relational, and participatory features.

Paul is not presenting some type of "second blessing," "deeper life," or "higher life" theology, as has been often advocated for Christians in certain circles today. Rather, he is calling on believers in Jesus (1) to understand and experience the Christian gospel not just in the traditional manner of Judaism and early Jewish Christianity, that is, in a highlighting of the forensic terms

---

87. Moo, "Christology of the Early Pauline Letters," 177.

"righteousness," "justification," "redemption," and "propitiation" ("expiation" or "sacrifice of atonement"), as, evidently, the Christians at Rome were doing — but, building on the truths of these forensic realities, (2) to move on in their Christian lives to an understanding of what "peace (i.e., *shalom*, 'completeness') with God" and "reconciliation to God" really mean (as he set out in 5:1-11), and therefore (3) to appreciate and experience the vitally important personal, relational, and participatory features of the Christian message of "life in Christ Jesus," "life in the Spirit," and "Christ by his Spirit" being in and controlling them (as he sets out here in 8:1-17).

There is no doubt that Christians today need (1) to understand the roots of their Christian faith in the OT Scriptures, (2) to see the lines of continuity that can be drawn between the proclamation of the Christian gospel, as declared in the NT, and God's dealings with his people in the religion of Israel, as portrayed in the OT, and (3) to appreciate the basic meanings and further NT developments of such soteriological terms as "righteousness," "justification," "redemption," and "propitiation" ("expiation" or "sacrifice of atonement"), both in Judaism and in early Jewish Christianity. Such topics and such studies are certainly of great importance for all contemporary believers in Jesus. Yet the Christian religion is not just to be understood as the fulfillment of Jewish expectations about a promised Messiah and a Christocentric explication of OT teachings.

What Paul is proclaiming in his letter to believers in Jesus at Rome is that the Christian message comes to its apex in what he is presenting to them as his "spiritual gift" in 5:1–8:39 — with, in particular, his proclamation in 8:1-17 of (1) "no condemnation" for those who are "in Christ Jesus," (2) new life "in Christ Jesus" and "in the Spirit," (3) "Christ by his Spirit" being in and controlling the Christian, (4) the ethical imperative that must always be understood as part and parcel of a Christian proclamation and of commitment to Jesus Christ, and (5) believers in Jesus as having been adopted by God into his family. It is this personal, relational, and participatory message that Paul proclaimed to pagan Gentiles in his missionary activities throughout the eastern regions of the Roman Empire; that he wanted believers in Jesus at Rome to appreciate and accept into their own Christian experience; and that he hoped, on the basis of their acceptance of such an understanding of the Christian gospel, they would join by offering their prayers and financial support in a further outreach to Gentiles in Spain (and probably elsewhere in the western regions of the Roman Empire). And it is such a personal, relational, and participatory message that ought also to be at the heart of Christian proclamation today, and so be a major feature in a truly Christian biblical theology.

CONTEXTUALIZATION FOR TODAY

The Pauline letters of the NT contain instructions, rebukes, and encouragements (1) to particular churches or groups of churches within the orbit of Paul's missionary outreach to Gentiles in the Greco-Roman world or (2) to certain individuals associated in some manner with Paul in his ministry. The addressees of Paul's letters were largely evangelized by the apostle himself (or, in the case of his letter to believers at Colossae, by one of his converts) — the letter to the Christians at Rome being the notable exception. All of Paul's letters, as well as all the other canonical letters (also the canonical Gospels, Acts, and the Apocalypse), evidence a bipolar relationship between the various circumstances, orientations, and needs of the people being addressed and the Christian gospel as proclaimed by the NT authors for the particular people they addressed. Paul's letter to the believers in Jesus at Rome, however, exhibits four such polarities:

1. That of the mixed group of Gentile and Jewish believers in Jesus in the various Christian congregations at Rome, as Paul speaks to them in a manner that he believed they would understand and appreciate in 1:16–4:25 and then again in 9:1–11:36.
2. That of early Jewish Christianity, which was centered in the mother church at Jerusalem, a portion of whose confessional material Paul quotes in 3:24-26 and at various other strategic places in the letter.
3. That of Paul himself, as expressed in the body opening and body closing sections of the letter, as well as in the "spin" and "development" that he gives to all the traditional material that he sets out throughout the letter.
4. That of Paul's contextualized form of the Christian message that he proclaimed to pagan Gentiles in the Greco-Roman world of his day, which he presents in its essential features in Romans, that is, in the letter's theological section of 5:1–8:39 and then in its ethical section of 12:1–15:13.

This latter matter regarding Paul's contextualized Christian message to pagan Gentiles is clearly evident in the proclamation section of 8:1-17, particularly in his use of such personal, relational, and participatory language as that of being "in Christ Jesus," being "in the Spirit," and "Christ by his Spirit" being in the believer — which expressions he saw as characterizing his own relationship with God as a believer in Jesus and which realities he desired to be true for his Christian addressees at Rome as well. His contextualized Christian message to pagan Gentiles also comes to the fore in this passage in his metaphorical use of the Greco-Roman sociological-legal practice of adoption — which, it may be assumed, he became aware of during his missionary travels in the eastern portion of the Roman Empire and which Pauline application to the Christian life his Gentile audiences would have understood and appreciated.

Paul's letter to the Christians at Rome, therefore, is not only a highly significant NT letter because of the knowledge of Christian doctrine that it presents (i.e., what it teaches). It is also important (1) for an appreciation of how the Christian message was contextualized among various groups of people in Paul's day (i.e., how the Christian gospel was somewhat differently understood and expressed by different groups of early believers in Jesus) and (2) as a template for an understanding of how the Christian gospel may be more effectively contextualized today (i.e., how it can be more effectively expressed in our day in various cultures and to people of somewhat differing mind-sets). As a template for the contextualization of the Christian gospel today, Paul's letter offers both (1) an ecumenical challenge in our endeavors to understand and appreciate other believers in Jesus, and (2) a missionary encouragement to present the "good news" of the Christian gospel to others in a manner that is both true to the apostolic proclamation of the NT and meaningful to those being addressed. And it is this passage of Rom 8:1-17, where Paul highlights the central thrust of his proclamation of the Christian gospel to pagan Gentiles, that needs always to take a prominent place in our own endeavors as Christians to speak and to act meaningfully with respect to the Christian message, which focuses on what God has done on behalf of all people by means of the work of Jesus Christ and what he continues to do by means of the ministry of his Spirit.

6. Life in the Spirit, Both Personal and Universal and Both Present and Future: A Life of Suffering and Glory (8:18-30)

TRANSLATION

⁸:¹⁸*I consider that our present sufferings are not worth comparing to the destined glory that is to be revealed in us.* ¹⁹*The creation waits in eager expectation for the children of God to be revealed.* ²⁰*For the creation was subjected to its present frustration, not by its own choice, but by the will of the One who subjected it — in the hope* ²¹*that the creation itself will be set free from its bondage to decay and brought into the glorious freedom of the children of God.*

²²*We know that the whole creation has been groaning together and suffering agony together right up to the present time.* ²³*Not only the creation, but also we ourselves, who have the firstfruits of the Spirit, we groan inwardly as we eagerly await our adoption as sons and daughters, the redemption of our bodies.* ²⁴*It is in this hope that we have been saved. But hope that is seen is no hope at all. For who hopes for what one already has?* ²⁵*And if we hope for what we do not have, we wait for it with steadfast endurance.*

²⁶*Likewise, the Spirit also helps us in our weakness. For, what should we pray for as we ought? We do not know! The Spirit himself, however, intercedes for us with groans that words cannot express.* ²⁷*And "the One who searches our hearts [i.e., God]" knows the mind of the Spirit, because the Spirit intercedes on behalf of God's "holy ones" in accordance with God's will.*

²⁸*Further, we know that for those who love God, he ["God"] works all things together for good — that is, on behalf of those who are called according to his purpose.* ²⁹*Because,*

> *"Those he foreknew he also predestined*
>   *to be conformed to the likeness of his Son,*
>   *in order that he might be the firstborn among many brothers and sisters;*
> ³⁰ *Those he predestined, he also called;*
> *Those he called, he also justified; and,*
> *Those he justified, he also glorified."*

TEXTUAL NOTES

8:19 The phrase τῆς κτίσεως ("of the creation") is extensively attested in the Greek textual tradition. The variant τῆς πίστεως ("of the faith"), which appears only in ninth-century minuscules 2464 (Category II) and 69 (Category III), is certainly a scribal error.

20a The expression οὐχ ἑκοῦσα ("not willingly," "not by its own choice") is also extensively attested in the textual tradition. The variant οὐ θελοῦσα ("not desiring"), which appears in ninth-century uncials F (010) and G (012), is either a scribal error or an attempt to replace a less common phrase with a more common one.

20b The expression ἐφ' ἑλπίδι ("in hope") is well supported by P[46] (second century) and uncials א B* D* F G. The variant ἐπ' ἑλπίδι ("upon hope"), however, appears in P[27] (third century), uncials A B[2] C D[2] P (also *Byz* K L), and minuscules 33 1175 1739 (Category I), 1506 1881 2464 (Category II), and 6 69 88 104 323 326 330 424[c] 614 1241 1243 1319 1505 1573 1735 1874 2495 (Category III). While ἐπ' ἑλπίδι ("upon hope") has fairly extensive support from the third century onward, it is most likely an attempted early correction of the better attested ἐφ' ἑλπίδι ("in hope").

21a The particle ὅτι ("that") — which appears at the beginning of v. 21 in our relatively modern versification, but actually continues the clause begun at the end of v. 20 with the phrase ἐφ' ἑλπίδι (so reading "in [the] hope that") — is attested by P[46], by uncials A B C D[2] P Ψ (also *Byz* K L), and by minuscules 33 1175 1739 (Category I), 81 256 1506 1881 1962 2464 (Category II), and 6 104 263 424[c] 436 459 1319 1573 1852 1912 2200 (Category III); it is also reflected in syr[p] and supported by Origen Methodius Eusebius Chrysostom and Theodoret. The variant διότι ("because") appears in uncials א D* F G and minuscule 2127 (Category II); it is also reflected in syr[h, pal] and found throughout the Byzantine textual tradition. Bruce Metzger states the opinion of most text critics and commentators today: "Apparently διότι arose accidentally by dittography, ΕΛΠΙΔΙΟΤΙ becoming ΕΛΠΙΔΙΔΙΟΤΙ."[1]

21b The third-person future passive ἐλευθερωθήσεται ("it will be set free") is widely attested in the textual tradition. The third-person present middle passive ἐλευθεροῦται ("it is freed"), however, appears in corrected P[27] and is reflected in vg[ms], probably to conform with the other present tenses in the passage. However, while it appears in P[27], it is not supported elsewhere in the Greek textual tradition, and so is probably not original.

23a The phrase καὶ αὐτοί ("also ourselves") at the beginning of the verse, together with the similar expression ἡμεῖς καὶ αὐτοί ("we also ourselves") that appears later in this same verse, seems to have caused some confusion among copyists. Thus instead of καὶ αὐτοί ("also ourselves"), some uncial MSS read καὶ ἡμεῖς αὐτοί (so D F G); a few minuscule MSS read καὶ αὐτοί ἡμεῖς (so 104 and probably 630, both Category III); while P[46] omits the phrase entirely. And instead of ἡμεῖς καὶ αὐτοί ("we also ourselves"), the variant readings are (1) καὶ αὐτοί (so uncial B and Epiphanius); (2) ἡμεῖς καὶ αὐτοί (so P[46], uncials א A C, and minuscules 1739 [Category I], 81 1506 1881 [Category II]); (3) αὐτοί (so uncials D F G and vg[ms]); (4) ἡμεῖς αὐτοί (so uncial Ψ, it[d*, g] and Ambrosiaster); and (5) καὶ ἡμεῖς αὐτοί (so the *Byz* tradition; also probably reflected in syr[h]).

23b The term υἱοθεσίαν ("adoption") is extensively attested by uncials א A B C P Ψ and by minuscules 33 1175 1739 (Category I), 81 256 1506 1881 1962 2127 2464 (Category II), and 6 104 263 424[c] 436 459 1241 1319 1573 1852 1912 2200 (Category III); it is also reflected in it[ar, b, mon] vg syr[p, h] cop[sa, bo] and supported by Origen[lat] Chrysostom Theodore[lat]

---

1. Metzger, *Textual Commentary,* 456.

and Augustine. It is, however, omitted by P[46 vid], by uncials D F G, by minuscule 614 (Category III), by it[d, f, g, o, t], and by Ambrosiaster. Its omission was most likely, as Bruce Metzger has suggested, because copyists found the word to be "clumsy in the context and dispensable, as well as seeming to contradict ver. 15."[2]

24a The interrogative pronoun τίς ("who") in ὃ γὰρ βλέπει τίς ἐλπίζει; ("For who hopes for what he sees?") is attested by P[27 vid] and P[46], by uncial B*, and by minuscule 1739[mg] (Category I); it is also reflected in it[mon]* cop[bo] and supported by Origen. Three variant readings and their support are as follows: (1) τις . . . τί ("For what anyone sees, why does he [yet] hope?"), as in uncials B[1] D F G, versions it[ar, d, f, g, mon2, o] vg [syr[p]], and Origen[gr, lat] Ambrosiaster Augustine[42/51]; (2) τις . . . καί ("For what anyone sees he also hopes for"), as in uncial ℵ, minuscules 1739* (Category I) and 459 (Category III), and arm[ms]; and (3) τις . . . τί καί ("For what anyone sees, why does he also hope [for it]?"), as in uncials ℵ[2] A C P Ψ (also *Byz* K L), minuscules 33 1175 (Category I), 81 256 1506 1881 1962 2127 2464 (Category II), and 6 104 263 424[c] 436 1241 1319 1573 1852 1912 2200 2464 (Category III); it is also reflected in it[b] syr[h] cop[sa] and supported by Clement Didymus Chrysostom Theodoret Augustine[9/51]. Bruce Metzger writes about these possibilities: "A majority of the [UBS] committee, impressed by the weight of the combination of P[46] B* 1739[mg] cop[bo] Origen, preferred the reading τίς and regarded the other readings as expansions of a strikingly terse and typically Pauline type of question. The expansions may have been introduced by copyists because of the lack of punctuation (after βλέπει) and the ambiguity of ΤΙΣ (interrogative or indefinite) in unaccented script."[3]

24b The third-person singular present indicative active verb ἐλπίζει ("he hopes") is widely attested by P[46], by uncials ℵ[2] B C D F G P Ψ (also *Byz* K L), and by minuscules 33 1175 1739* (Category I), 81 256 1506 1881 1962 2127 2464 (Category II), and 6 104 263 424[c] 436 459 1241 1319 1573 1739[c] 1852 1912 2200; it is also reflected in it[ar, b, d, f, g, mon, o] vg syr[h] cop[bo ms] and supported by Clement Origen[gr, lat] Chrysostom Theodoret Ambrosiaster Augustine. The verb ὑπομένει ("it endures," "awaits"), however, is found in uncials ℵ* A and in minuscule 1739[mg]; it is also reflected in syr[p] cop[sa, bo] and supported by Origen and Ephraem. Bruce Metzger reports that although ὑπομένει "may appear to be the more difficult reading and therefore deserving of adoption, a majority of the [UBS] committee was unwilling to base the text upon such limited support, especially in view of the early and very diversified testimony for ἐλπίζει (P[46] B C D G Ψ 33 81 614 1739* it[d, g] vg syr[p h] arm eth cop[bo ms] Clement Origen[gr, lat] Cyprian *al*). Furthermore, although the verb ὑπομένειν with object ('to await something') is rather common in the Septuagint, no example of this use can be cited from the New Testament except the present variant reading. On balance, therefore, it is probable that the presence of ὑπομονή in the following verse prompted an early copyist to substitute ὑπομένει for ἐλπίζει."[4]

26 The third-person singular present indicative active verb ὑπερεντυγχάνει ("he intercedes") is strongly attested by uncials ℵ* A B D F G and by minuscules 1739 (Category I), 81 256 1506 1881 2127 (Category II), and 6 263 424[c] 1319 1573 (Category III); it

2. Metzger, *Textual Commentary,* 457.
3. *Ibid.*
4. *Ibid.*

is also reflected in it[b, d*, g] and supported by Origen Epiphanius[1/4] and Augustine[14/17]. It is, however, supplemented by ὑπὲρ ἡμῶν ("for us") in uncials א[2] C P Ψ (also *Byz* K L) and minuscules 33 1175 (Category I), 1962 2464 (Category II), and 104 436 459 1241 1852 1912 (Category III); with that supplement being reflected in it[ar, d2, f, mon, o] vg syr[h] cop[sa, bo] and supported by Origen[lat] Eusebius Chrysostom Theodore Ambrosiaster Jerome and Augustine[3/17]. It seems most likely, however, that ὑπὲρ ἡμῶν should be viewed as a later scribal addition inserted in an attempt to make explicit what was already implied by ὑπερεντυγχάνει.

28a The clause πάντα συνεργεῖ — understanding either (1) the neuter πάντα as the subject of the sentence (so reading "*all things* work together") or (2) the subject of the sentence expressed in the suffix of the verb, whether masculine (so reading "*he* [i.e., 'God'] works all things together") or neuter (so reading "*it* [i.e., 'the Spirit'] works all things together" — is very widely attested by uncials א C D F G P Ψ (also *Byz* K L) and by minuscules 33 1175 1739 (Category I), 256 1506 1881 1962 2127 2464 (Category II), and 6 104 263 424[c] 436 459 1241 1319 1573 1852 1912 2200; it is also reflected in it[ar, b, d, f, g, mon, o] vg syr[p, h] cop[bo] and supported by Clement Origen[gr, lat] Eusebius Theodoret Ambrosiaster Jerome and Augustine. The reading πάντα συνεργεῖ ὁ θεός ("*God* works all things together"), however, is attested by P[46] (though P[46] reads πάν as the predicate of the sentence rather than πάντα, which is evidently a scribal error), uncials A and B, minuscule 81 (Category II), versions cop[sa] eth, and Origen[gr2/5]. The testimonies of P[46] and Codex Vaticanus (B 03) in favor of the inclusion of ὁ θεός after the verb συνεργεῖ, together with those of Codex Alexandrinus (A 02) and two Greek recensions of Origen's commentary on Romans, are important. Nonetheless, these comparatively few witnesses in support of the inclusion of ὁ θεός provide a rather narrow basis for the determination of the original text, especially in view of the fact that πάντα συνεργεῖ (without ὁ θεός) has far more extensive and diversified support (as cited above). Thus, since the verb συνεργεῖ itself suggests a third-person singular subject — and since the immediate antecedent of that third-person singular subject is τὸν θεόν ("God") — the suffix of συνεργεῖ should most likely be viewed as being masculine, with the phrase then being read as "*he* [i.e., 'God'] works all things together." The inclusion of ὁ θεός in the text was probably, as Bruce Metzger has proposed, "a natural explanatory addition made by an Alexandrian editor."[5]

28b The use of the substantive noun ἀγαθόν ("good") is abundantly attested in the Greek textual tradition. The addition of the article τό in the ninth-century uncial L (020) and the ninth-century minuscule 945 (both of which MSS have been classified by Kurt and Barbara Aland as Category V materials), while evidently thought to be a linguistic improvement, is entirely unnecessary.

30 The third-person singular aorist indicative προώρισεν ("he predestined") in the first part of the verse is widely attested in the Greek textual tradition. Codex Alexandrinus (A 02), however, reads προέγνω ("he foreknew"), which evidently harkens back to προέγνω in the earlier part of 8:29 — but here in 8:30 the reading "he foreknew" is contextually unlikely.

5. So Metzger, *Textual Commentary,* 458.

FORM/STRUCTURE/SETTING

Having proclaimed in 8:1-17 the new relationships of believers in Jesus as (1) being "in Christ," (2) being "in the Spirit," (3) "Christ by his Spirit" being in the believer, and (4) having been "adopted" by God into his family, Paul in 8:18-30 sets out the major implications of these relationships for Christ's own people, for "the whole creation," and for both the present and the future — with emphases on the themes of (1) suffering and glory, (2) hope for the future, (3) the help and intercession of the Spirit, and (4) a Christian's assured confidence in God.

The Extent of the Passage. Where the passage begins and ends has been often debated. Some understand it as beginning at 8:14 and ending at 8:30;[6] others as beginning at 8:17 and ending at 8:30;[7] others as starting at 8:18 and concluding at 8:25;[8] others as starting at 8:18 and concluding at 8:27;[9] and still others as extending from 8:18 through to the end of 8:39.[10]

Most interpreters today say the passage begins with the statement of 8:18, "I consider that our present sufferings are not worth comparing with the glory (δόξαν) that will be revealed in us," and concludes in 8:29-30 with the quotation of Jewish or Jewish Christian catechetical or liturgical statements (or, possibly, the quotation of a portion drawn from an early Christian confession), which affirms that "those whom God foreknew . . . predestined . . . called . . . and justified, he also glorified (καὶ ἐδόξασεν)"[11] — with that unit of material followed by a series of rhetorical questions and answers in 8:31-36 and a triumphal affirmation in 8:37-39, which bring to a close Section II of the body middle of Paul's letter.

Douglas Moo has pointed out that the theme of "glory" marks the boundaries of this subsection that sets out the major implications of being "in Christ" and "in the Spirit," with the noun δόξα in 8:18 and the verb δοξάζω in 8:30 functioning as *inclusio* markers for the passage — and with the expression τὴν ἐλευθερίαν τῆς δόξης ("the freedom of the glory" or "the glorious freedom") in 8:21 serving, as well, to highlight that same theme in the very midst of the passage. For, as Moo argues:

> Although "glory" is mentioned only three times in vv. 18-30, it is the overarching theme of this passage. Occurring at both the beginning (v. 18 — "the glory that shall be revealed in us") and at the end (v. 30 — "these he glorified"), this concept frames these verses, furnishing us with an important indicator of Paul's central concern.[12]

6. So, e.g., von der Osten-Sacken, *Römer 8*, 137-39.
7. So, e.g., Cranfield, *Romans*, 1.403-5; see also *idem,* "Sanctification as Freedom," in his *On Romans*, 46-47.
8. So, e.g., Nebe, *"Hoffnung" bei Paulus*, 93.
9. So, e.g., Balz, *Heilsvertrauen und Welterfahrung*, 33.
10. So, e.g., Lewis, "A Christian Theodicy," 405.
11. So, e.g., Käsemann, *Romans*, 231-32; Moo, *Romans*, 508-10.
12. Moo, *Romans*, 508.

Henning Paulsen has also drawn attention to the centrality of the theme of "the hope of glory" in the passage, citing its importance not only at the beginning and end of the passage, but also in Paul's use of this theme in his statement of 8:21 that "the creation itself will be liberated from its bondage to decay and brought into the glorious freedom of the children of God."[13]

Epistolary and Rhetorical Conventions. Most prominent among the epistolary and rhetorical conventions present in 8:18-30 are the two occurrences of the epistolary disclosure formula οἴδαμεν ὅτι ("we know that"); they appear at the beginning of 8:22 and 8:28. Probably λογίζομαι ὅτι ("I consider that") at the beginning of 8:18 should also be viewed as a cognate form of the more usual disclosure formula οἴδαμεν ὅτι ("we know that").

Also evident in the passage is the rhetorical manner in which the themes of 8:18-30 (together with those that follow in 8:31-39) reach back and echo many of the themes that earlier dominated the transitional and thesis subsection of 5:1-11, thereby setting up something of a rhetorical *inclusio* or type of "ring composition." Most noticeable in this regard are the themes of "hope" in 8:20-25 (cf. 5:2), "the glory of God revealed" in 8:18-21 (cf. 5:2), "boasting in sufferings" in 8:35-37 (cf. 5:3), and "the love of God expressed in the giving of Christ" in 8:31-39 (cf. 5:5).[14]

A Probable Use of Common Aphoristic Teaching and of Jewish and/or Jewish Christian Catechetical Instruction. The fact that the statement of 8:28 is set out in what appears to be a carefully constructed form and is introduced by the disclosure formula οἴδαμεν ὅτι ("we know that") suggests that it incorporates a christianized form of rather common aphoristic teaching. Further, the material of 8:29-30 is introduced by what appears to be a *hoti recitative,* that is, a special use of the particle ὅτι ("for," "because") that often serves in Paul's letters to introduce a quotation of some traditional aphorism or biblical teaching; also, the material presents a "golden chain" of spiritual blessings that stem from God and pertain to "those who love God and have been called according to his purpose," that is, the expressions "foreknown," "predestined," "called," "justified," and "glorified" — with this list of blessings (apart from a comparable listing in Eph 1:3-14) being not particularly characteristic of Paul's usual manner in writing to his own Christian converts in his other NT letters.

For these reasons, it has often been suggested that Paul has incorporated into this passage (1) a christianized version of rather common aphoristic teaching in 8:28, and/or (2) a portion of Jewish or Jewish Christian catechetical or liturgical instruction in 8:29-30[15] — perhaps even material drawn from some early Christian confession.[16] Charles Cranfield theorized: "The language used and the fact that Jewish parallels can be adduced make it likely that he [Paul] is deliberately incorporating a piece of traditional teaching";[17] and Ernst Käse-

---

13. Paulsen, *Überlieferung und Auslegung in Römer 8,* esp. 107.
14. Cf. Dahl, "Missionary Theology," appendix I, 88-89.
15. So, e.g., Michel, *An die Römer,* 273; Zeller, *An die Römer,* 163-64.
16. So, e,g., H. W. Schmidt, *An die Römer, ad loc.*
17. Cranfield, *Romans,* 1.424.

mann proposed: "The careful rhetorical construction of the members, which are linked in a mounting chain, and a vocabulary not typical of the apostle, indicate that we have here a traditional liturgical piece."[18] Somewhat similarly, Robert Jewett has argued that "the language of this verse reflects Paul's adaptation of traditional Jewish teaching."[19]

The Structure of the Passage. Paul focuses in 8:18-30 on the major implications of what it means to live one's life positionally "in Christ" and experientially "in the Spirit." The topics of the passage have to do with (1) the present sufferings and future glory of the Christian, as paralleled by the present frustrations and future freedom of the creation (8:18-21); (2) the hope given by God to all believers in Jesus, who have "the firstfruits of the Spirit," as well as the hope given to "the whole creation" (8:22-25); (3) the prayers of a Christian, as enabled by the Spirit's help and intercession (8:26-27); and (4) the assurance of believers in Jesus that God works all things together for good for those who love him and are called according to his purpose (8:28-30). These four topics are set out in four paragraphs, three of which are introduced by an epistolary disclosure formula of the day (or a cognate version of such a formula) — most obviously, the disclosure formula οἴδαμεν ὅτι, "we know that" (as in 8:22 and 8:28), and also the singular cognate formula λογιζομαι ὅτι, "I consider that" (as in 8:18).[20] These topics in their respective paragraphs provide the structure for Paul's presentation in 8:18-30. They will serve as the organizational structure for our exegetical comments below.

EXEGETICAL COMMENTS

I. The Present Sufferings and Future Glory of the Christian as Paralleled by the Present Frustrations and Future Freedom of Creation (8:18-21)

8:18 "I consider that our present sufferings are not worth comparing to the destined glory that is to be revealed in us" — as well as all the statements in 8:19-30 — is not to be understood as either correcting or amplifying what Paul wrote earlier in 8:1-17. Rather, building on his proclamation of the Christian message in 8:1-17, the apostle here in 8:18-30 goes on to highlight a number of the most important implications of what it means to live one's life "in the Spirit." What he writes in this first verse of the passage functions as something of a thesis statement for all that he will present in 8:19-30.[21]

---

18. Käsemann, *Romans*, 244.

19. Jewett, *Romans*, 526.

20. Cf. the usual disclosure formula οἴδαμεν ὅτι that appears earlier in 2:2; 3:19; 7:14; see also other cognate disclosure formulas in Romans at 6:3, 16; 7:1; 11:25.

21. Cf. C. E. B. Cranfield: "In fact, the whole of vv. 19-30 may be said to be in one way or another support for, and elucidation of, v. 18" (*Romans*, 1.410); see also C. H. Talbert, though closing off the section at 8:27: "The thesis statement for 8:18-27 comes in v. 18" (*Romans*, 213).

The postpositive conjunction γάρ appears in koine Greek, as well as throughout the NT, not only to introduce an explanation, a cause or reason, or an inference, but also to indicate some sort of continuation of thought between what immediately precedes and what follows. And this is how γάρ is used here — to signal that what appears in 8:18-30, while not the same as what appears in 8:1-17, continues that proclamation by highlighting certain of its most important implications for the Christian.[22]

The expression λογίζομαι ὅτι ("I consider that") functions in an epistolary fashion to highlight Paul's own conviction, which he desires would also become the abiding realization of his hearers and readers: that for God's people, "our present sufferings (τὰ παθήματα τοῦ νῦν καιροῦ; literally 'the sufferings of the now time') are not worth comparing (οὐκ ἄξια) to the destined glory (πρὸς τὴν μέλλουσαν δόξαν) that is to be revealed (ἀποκαλυφθῆναι) in us (εἰς ἡμᾶς)." It is an understanding that Paul learned well from his reading of the Jewish (OT) Scriptures — as expressed particularly in the story of Job, in the praise and declarations of the psalmists, and in the prophets' interpretations of God's dealing with his people. It is also a consciousness that resided at the heart of Jewish messianic expectations in Paul's day. More specifically, however, it is a conviction that became focused for Paul as a believer in Jesus and a proclaimer of the Christian gospel. For the message of the earliest Jewish believers in Jesus had at its core the proclamation that through suffering, death, resurrection, and ascension, Jesus of Nazareth was accredited by God as Israel's promised Messiah and humanity's glorified Lord — with the result that all who believe in him, though they die, will themselves experience resurrection, immortality, and eternal glory.

The expression τὰ παθήματα τοῦ νῦν καιροῦ ("the sufferings of the now time") is a general reference that includes everything that believers in Jesus suffer, whether as finite and fallible humans under the curses of sin and depravity or as Christians in their witness for God and the gospel. The term ἄξιος, when used of things, connotes "comparable worth" or "equal value," and so appears here with the negative particle οὐκ to put into proper perspective the relative insignificance of a Christian's "present sufferings" vis-à-vis his or her "destined glory." The aorist infinitive passive verb ἀποκαλυφθῆναι ("to be revealed") directs attention to the future, and so to the time of Christ's parousia when believers in Jesus will be raised "in glory" and become "immortal" (1 Cor 15:42-57). And the phrase εἰς ἡμᾶς, which may be translated "to us" or "for us,"[23] is probably best understood here in the sense of "in us" (thereby equating the prepositions εἰς and ἐν, as is frequently done in the NT).[24]

22. A. T. Robertson comments on the use of γάρ in 8:18-24 as follows: "Paul begins every sentence with γάρ in Ro. 8:18-24. . . . The precise relation between clauses or sentences is not set forth by γάρ. That must be gathered from the context if possible" (*ATRob*, 1191).

23. So "to us" (RSV, NRSV, TEV, NET) or "for us" (NEB, Phillips, JB); also the more awkward expression "to usward" (ASV).

24. So "in us" (KJV, NIV, TNIV); cf. the Vulgate translation "in nobis."

8:19-21 Paul speaks in poetic imagery and apocalyptic language here (and continuing on through 8:22). His purpose in aligning "the present frustration and future freedom" of God's creation, as here in 8:19-22, with "the present sufferings and future glory" of those who are "in Christ" and "in the Spirit," as in the opening statement of 8:18, was evidently to support the latter by way of a parallel phenomenon. So (1) the sufferings and glory of believers in Jesus in 8:18 and (2) the frustration and freedom of the creation in 8:19 are set out in parallel fashion, with the second given, as Charles Cranfield has aptly noted, "as support for the statement made in v. 18."[25] It may be presumed that the postpositive conjunction γάρ functions here in 8:19 just as it did earlier in 8:18 — not to introduce an explanation, a cause, or a reason, nor even an inference, but simply to signal that a close relationship exists between what has immediately preceded and what follows.

More importantly, however, by bringing the present frustration and future deliverance of the creation (as in 8:19) into his discussion of the present sufferings and destined glory of the believer in Jesus (as in 8:18), the apostle is able (1) to support the first statement by the analogy of the second, and (2) to suggest something regarding the breadth of God's salvation through the work of Jesus Christ and the ministry of God's Spirit. Yet, as Cranfield has gone on to point out: "Once introduced [as in 8:19], it itself [i.e., the statement of support] requires expansion and elucidation [as in 8:20-21]."[26]

What exactly Paul had in mind by his use of ἡ κτίσις ("the creation") three times in 8:19-21 — and then its expanded form πᾶσα ἡ κτίσις ("the whole creation") in 8:22 — has been variously understood among Christian interpreters from the time of the Church Fathers to the present.[27] Among contemporary NT interpreters, who have often aligned themselves with the various understandings of the Church Fathers, the following positions have been proposed:

1. That κτίσις refers in an all-encompassing fashion to all of God's creation — that is, not only to the subhuman creation (both animate and inanimate), but also to all humans (both believing and unbelieving) and to the heavenly angels (though not the fallen angels).[28]
2. That κτίσις refers to created subhuman earthly life, both animate and inanimate — that is, to "the nonrational creation" or what people today call "nature," as differentiated from people (whether believing or nonbelieving) and angels (whether heavenly or fallen).[29]

---

25. Cranfield, *Romans*, 1.410.

26. *Ibid.*

27. See the extensive survey of positions set out by Biedermann, *Die Erlösung der Schöpfung beim Apostel Paulus.* Note, as well, the condensed versions of that history of interpretation given by Cranfield, *Romans*, 1.411-12, and Fitzmyer, *Romans*, 506-7.

28. So, e.g., Michel, *An die Römer*, 173; Barrett, *Romans*, 166; Gerber, "Röm viii.18ff als exegetisches Problem," 64-68; and Gibbs, "Pauline Cosmic Christology," 471.

29. So, e.g., Godet, *Romans*, 2.89-90; Sanday and Headlam, *Romans*, 207; Zahn, *An die Römer*, 400; Cranfield, *Romans*, 1.411-12; *idem*, "Some Observations on Romans 8.19-21," 225; Fitz-

3. That κτίσις signifies "all of humanity" or "the entire human race" (in line with Augustine's understanding), but not the subhuman creation (animate or inanimate) and not angels (heavenly or fallen) — with the term being used in this passage, as Adolf Schlatter spoke of it, as "humanity's honorific name," which signals "a homogenous [or 'uniform'] closed circle" of created people.[30]

4. That κτίσις here should be understood to refer to believers in Jesus; for while Paul used an apocalyptic fragment that originally referred to the world of nature as awaiting transformation, it seems that in these verses he changed the meaning of κτίσις in order to speak of believers who are awaiting the glory that is "not yet" theirs.[31]

5. That κτίσις here refers to the created body of a believer in Jesus, and so should be translated "creature" and not "creation"; that Paul used the word "simply as a metaphor for the body"; and "that Romans 8:21 is an affirmation of the bodily resurrection of believers, no more and no less"; in support of this view are Irenaeus's comments on 8:19-22 in his *Against Heresies*.[32]

6. That the term here has in view unbelievers.[33]

7. That the term here refers to both the subhuman creation and unbelieving humanity, though not angels, demons, or believers.[34]

8. That the term here refers to angels.[35]

Among modern commentators, C. E. B. Cranfield has most cogently, as well as most concisely, evaluated the above proposals — ruling out those positions that seem unlikely and concluding by a process of elimination in favor of what he believes to be most supportable.[36]

---

myer, *Romans,* 506; Murray, *Romans,* 303; Morris, *Romans,* 322; Dunn, *Romans,* 1.469; and Talbert, *Romans,* 214. This is, in fact, the most widely held position among NT commentators today.

30. So Schlatter, *Romans,* 184-87; cf. also T. W. Manson, "Romans," 966; and Gager, "Functional Diversity in Paul's Use of End-Time Language," 328-29. In support of this understanding, Augustine is often quoted on "the creation" in 8:19-22: "This is not to be understood simply as meaning that trees, vegetables, stones and the like sorrow and sigh — this is the error of the Manichaeans — nor should we think that the holy angels are subject to vanity or that they will be set free from the slavery of death, since they are immortal. Here 'the creation' means the human race" (*Expositio quarundam propositionum ex epistola ad Romanos,* Prop. LIII, *PL* 35.2074; see also Augustine on Romans, 23).

31. So, e.g., Reumann, *Creation and New Creation,* 98-99; Hommel, "Das Harren der Kreatur," 7-23; see also H. W. Schmidt, *An die Römer,* 145; Vögtle, "Röm 8,19-22," 351-66; and *idem, Zukunft des Kosmos,* 183-207.

32. So Michaels, "The Redemption of Our Body," 92-114, crediting in support Irenaeus, *Against Heresies* 5.32.1 and 36.3.

33. So E. Brunner, *Revelation and Reason: The Christian Doctrine of Faith and Knowledge* (Philadelphia: Westminster, 1946), 72 n. 16.

34. So Foerster, "κτίζω, κτίσις," 3.1031; Leenhardt, *Romans,* 219; Käsemann, *Romans,* 232-33.

35. So Fuchs, *Die Freiheit des Glaubens,* 109.

36. Cranfield, *Romans,* 1.411.

1. "Believers must almost certainly be excluded, since in v. 23 they are contrasted with the creation."

2. The expression οὐχ ἑκοῦσα ("not willingly" or "not by its own choice") "seems to rule out mankind generally; for, if Paul meant to include mankind when he used κτίσις here, he can hardly have intended to exclude Adam, the created man *par excellence* (had he intended to make so strange an exception, he must surely have indicated it), and Adam at any rate clearly cannot be said to have been subjected οὐχ ἑκών to ματαιότης."

3. "Against the suggestion that only unbelieving mankind is referred to, it may be urged that this would involve an extremely unnatural distinction; for, while it is understandable that κόσμος should sometimes be used to denote unbelievers in contrast with believers, it is very hard to imagine a NT writer using κτίσις in this way, a term specifically indicating a relation to God, which is not only one in which Christians stand no whit less than non-Christians but is also one which they above all men must acknowledge and delight in."

4. "A reference to angels seems not very likely." Likewise, "the use of κτίσις to denote the angels alone and the use of it to denote the angels in addition to sub-human nature with mankind excluded would seem about equally unlikely." Further, "it is hardly possible to give any really convincing interpretation of τῇ ... ματαιότητι ... ὑπετάγη, οὐχ ἑκοῦσα in respect of the angels."

Thus Cranfield concludes: "The only interpretation of ἡ κτίσις in these verses which is really probable is surely that which takes it to refer to the sum-total of sub-human nature both animate and inanimate."[37] This is position 2 above. It is this understanding that we believe to be the proper one, and so we will build on it in our exegetical comments below.

It has sometimes been argued that the expressions ἀποκαραδοκία ("eager expectation"), ματαιότης ("frustration"), ἑκοῦσα ("willingly" or "by choice"), ἐλπίς ("hope"), συστενάζει ("groaning together"), and συνωδίνει ("suffering together") connote "conscious volitional motivations" that "represent personal actions" of people, and are not to be viewed as "fanciful personifications" ascribed to the subhuman creation. Therefore, interpreters of 8:19-22 need to take seriously into account the probability that Paul had principally people, that is, God's "created humanity," in mind when speaking of "the creation" in 8:19-22.[38] But the personification of subhuman entities in the natural world, whether animate or inanimate, appears a number of times in the Jewish (OT) Scriptures, particularly in the poetry of the Psalms and the writings of the prophets.[39] And

37. Cranfield, "Some Observations on Romans 8:19-21," 225; also *idem, Romans*, 1.411-12 (with only slight changes in the wording from "is surely" in his earlier article to "seems to be" in his commentary and from ἡ κτίσις in his article to κτίσις in his commentary).

38. So, esp., Schlatter, *Romans*, 184-86.

39. Cf., e.g., Pss 65:12 13; 98:7-9; Isa 14:7-8; 24:4, 7; 55:12; Jer 4:28; 12:4.

although 8:19-22 is not set out in the structure or rhythm of poetry, the passage reflects many features of biblical poetry and prophecy. Thus, as Cranfield has observed:

> This sub-section will hardly be properly understood, unless the poetic quality displayed in it, particularly in vv. 19-22, is duly recognized. What is involved in these verses is not what belongs to the outward form of poetry, such things as artistic arrangement and rhythm, but rather those things which belong to its inner essence, imaginative power (to be seen, for instance, in the use of images), feeling for the richly evocative word, a deep sensitivity, catholicity of sympathy, and a true generosity of vision and conception.[40]

Understanding ἡ κτίσις ("the creation") in 8:19-21 to refer to what we would today call "nature" — that is, God's subhuman creation, both animate and inanimate — we can best understand Paul here in 8:19 as affirming that "the world of nature," both animate and inanimate, waits in eager expectation (ἡ ἀποκαραδοκία) for the children of God to be revealed. Although the verb ἀποκαραδοκέω appears in classical Greek writings of the fifth and sixth centuries B.C., as well as in various koine Greek writings of the second century B.C.,[41] the noun ἀποκαραδοκία has not been found in any extant Greek texts prior to Paul.[42]

Paul, however, uses the noun ἀποκαραδοκία twice in his letters: here in Rom 8:19 ("the creation waits in *eager expectation*") and again in Phil 1:20 ("It is my *eager expectation* and hope that I will in no way be put to shame"). Both uses are associated with ἐλπίς ("hope"), which suggests that in his mind the noun ἀποκαραδοκία includes the nuance of confident expectation.

By placing the dative articular noun τῇ ματαιότητι ("to its present frustration") at the beginning of the compound sentence of 8:20-21, Paul signals that his attention in these verses is on nature's present bondage to frustration and decay — that is, how it all came about and when God's subhuman creation, both animate and inanimate, will be set free. Likewise, his use of the third-person singular aorist passive verb ὑπετάγη ("it was subjected") highlights the facts (1) that a particular past event is in mind (so the aorist tense) and (2) that someone beyond the realm of creation itself was the originator of nature's present condition (so the passive voice). And while not stated explicitly, there can be little doubt that the event in mind is the judgment related in Gen 3:17-19, which includes the statement of v. 17: "Cursed is the ground." Nor can there be any doubt that it was God himself who brought about the present condition of

---

40. Cranfield, *Romans*, 1.404-5; cf. also C. H. Dodd, *Romans*, 133.

41. Cf. *LSJM*, 877.

42. Cf. *M-M*, 63, col. 2. In noting that ἀποκαραδοκία is "peculiar to Paul," J. H. Moulton and G. Milligan went on to suggest that the noun form of the verb "may possibly have been his [Paul's] own formation."

his own subhuman creation, doing so, as Gen 3:17 also emphasizes, "because of you" — that is, because of humanity's sin.

Charles Talbert has aptly expressed Paul's understanding in his comment: "Paul could no more think of persons apart from their environment than he could of them apart from their bodies."[43] So in 8:19-21 the apostle speaks about both the sufferings of God's people and the present frustrations of God's subhuman creation, supporting the sufferings of God's people by calling attention to the frustrations of God's subhuman creation. More importantly, however, he is convinced of a promised future glory for both God's people and God's subhuman creation — not only from his knowledge of the Jewish (OT) Scriptures[44] and various noncanonical Jewish writings of his day,[45] but preeminently from the proclamation of the Christian gospel.[46] Thus here in 8:20b-21, as based primarily on the good news of the Christian gospel, Paul extends that promised hope for God's people (as he set it out earlier in 1 Cor 15:35-57) to include all of God's creation — apart, of course, from the fallen angels and from people who have rejected Christ and so have refused God's salvation.

John Chrysostom, commenting on Rom 8:20, was thoroughly in line with Paul's teaching regarding "the present sufferings" vis-à-vis "the future glory" — not only for believers in Jesus, but also for the whole subhuman creation — when he said:

> Paul means by this that the creation became corruptible. Why and for what reason? Because of you, O man! For because you have a body which has become mortal and subject to suffering, the earth too has received a curse and has brought forth thorns and thistles [i.e., as stated in Gen 3:18]. . . . The creation suffered badly because of you, and it became corruptible, but it has not been irreparably damaged. For it will become incorruptible once again for your sake. This is the meaning of "in hope."[47]

II. The Hope God Gives to Believers in Jesus and to "the Whole Creation" (8:22-25)

In 8:22-25 Paul elucidates more fully this theme of "hope" — speaking of it with regard to both (1) people who have come to God through the work of Jesus Christ and the ministry of the Spirit, and so have been given by God "the first-fruits of the Spirit," and (2) God's subhuman creation.

43. Talbert, *Romans,* 214.
44. Cf. esp. Isa 11:6-9; 65:17, 25; 66:22.
45. Cf. esp. *Jub* 1:29; *1 En* 24:1–25:7; 91:16-17; *Sib Or* 3:744-52, 788-95.
46. Cf. such later NT statements as 2 Pet 3:13; Rev. 21:1-5 (though articulated most clearly by Paul himself in 1 Cor 15:35-57 and here in Rom 8:19-21).
47. Chrysostom, "Homilies," in *Nicene and Post-Nicene Fathers,* 11.444.

8:22-23 The postpositive conjunction γάρ at the beginning of 8:22 signals a continuation of thought between what precedes it and what follows it, just as it did at the beginning of 8:18 and 8:19. The epistolary disclosure formula οἴδαμεν ὅτι ("we know that") suggests that the apostle was sure that those to whom he proclaimed the Christian gospel in his Gentile mission — as well as all of his addressees at Rome — would agree with him regarding nature as "groaning together and suffering agony together right up to the present time."[48]

Paul would have known of nature's decay and corruption from his reading of Isa 24:4-7, where the prophet laments that "the earth dries up and withers, the world languishes and withers," and "a curse consumes the earth" — as well as from his knowledge of Hos 4:1-3, which speaks of the earth as languishing, mourning, and polluted because of human sin. A similar consciousness of the world's decay and corruption appears also in Greek literature, going back as far as the eighth-century didactic poet Hesiod, who sketched out a theory of the world's decline in which nature's corruption was linked to human failings.[49] And from the Jewish prophets and the Greek poets eventuated such Hellenistic Jewish portrayals of the state of the world and its people as found in *Sib Or* 3:752, which speaks of the earth being "convulsed with deeply drawn groans," and in *4 Ezra* 5:50-55, where an angel declares that "creation has already grown old and is already past the strength of youth"; this latter passage uses the specious analogy of younger children in a family being always born inferior to their older siblings, with the result that the beauty, vigor, and ability of one's immediate posterity inevitably declines.

In the Roman world, the poet Vergil (70-19 B.C.) wrote during 42-37 B.C. his *Eclogues* (or *Bucolics*), which consisted of ten poems that were generally on pastoral themes. In *Eclogues* 4.11.41 he prophesied that a regent would appear on the scene of human history who would restore the world's lost golden age — at which time nature would produce plentifully without any human endeavor and the blight of human impiety would no longer pollute the earth. Only a few decades later, Caesar Augustus (63 B.C.–A.D. 14), sole ruler of the Roman Empire for forty-four years, was proclaimed by pagan priests and various Roman citizens as the one who, because of his glorious accomplishments, actually fulfilled Vergil's prophecy — though others, particularly his detractors and people from the lower classes, seem to have withheld such an acclamation.

Paul's message, however, was not about Caesar Augustus (or any other human emperor or king), but about Jesus of Nazareth, who had been accredited by God as humanity's Lord in resurrecting him from the dead — and through whom not only are believers in Jesus brought into a right relationship with God and given the sure promise of a glorious future, but also "the creation itself will be set free from its bondage to decay and brought into the glorious freedom of

---

48. Cf. Paul's use of οἴδαμεν ὅτι earlier in Romans at 2:2, 3:19, 7:14; and then later in this same section of material at 8:28.

49. Hesiod, *Works and Days* 109-201.

the children of God." Nonetheless, Paul seems to have been confident that those who heard him preach and those who would read this letter — having lived during the turbulent times that followed the reign of Caesar Augustus — would agree with him that "the whole creation has been groaning and suffering agony together right up to the present time." So he begins this second paragraph that elucidates this topic of "hope" with the epistolary disclosure formula οἴδαμεν ὅτι ("we know that").

Paul's use of the expression πᾶσα ἡ κτίσις ("the whole creation") includes the entire range of animate life and inanimate things on the earth. The verb στενάζω ("cry out," "groan"), used here in 8:22 in its compound form συστενάζω ("cry out intensely," "groan together"), appears in the LXX in Job 31:38-40, where Job acknowledges the relationship that was established by God in Gen 3:17-19 between a person's sin and nature's retribution. The verb ὠδίνω ("be in travail" "suffer agony"), which also appears in this verse in its compound form συνωδίνει ("be in travail together," "suffer agony together"), was used figuratively by Paul earlier in Gal 4:19 and then literally in Gal 4:27 with respect to a woman's "labor pains" at childbirth.[50]

Largely because of his use of the articular substantive adverb τοῦ νῦν ("the now") in the phrase ἄχρι τοῦ νῦν (literally "until the now"), a number of commentators have proposed that Paul had in mind here in 8:22 the eschatological "now" of which he spoke in 2 Cor 6:2 ("Behold, *now* is the time of God's favor; behold, *now* is the day of salvation") and which he emphasized at the beginning of Rom 3:21 ("But *now,* apart from the law, the righteousness of God has been revealed, being attested by the law and the prophets").[51] Yet Paul also used νῦν ("now") in a mundane, nontheological sense in Romans, as well as in his other letters, to mean simply "at present" or "the present time."[52] And that is how, it seems, he used the articular substantive adverb at the end of 8:22 — and so the expression ἄχρι τοῦ νῦν here is probably best understood as "right up to the present time" or "until now without having ceased."[53]

Paul's emphasis in this passage, however, is not simply on the present frustrations and future freedom of God's subhuman creation, even though he has spoken of these matters in illustrative fashion in the four verses of 8:19-22. Rather, his focus is on the believer's confident hope for the future, which he introduced earlier in his thesis statement of 8:18 and which he spells out more

---

50. Cf. Isa 66:7 (LXX); Mic 4:10 (LXX); Rev 12:2; see also the noun ὠδίν (or ὠδίς) in Mark 13:8 and Matt 24:8 as referring to the "messianic woes," that is, the terrors and torments that are prophesied to precede the coming of the messianic age.

51. Cf., e.g., Barrett, *Romans,* 166: "the decisive moment, when God's purposes are fulfilled"; Käsemann, *Romans,* 236: "the eschatological moment . . . which precedes the parousia"; Dunn, *Galatians,* 1.473: "the 'now' of eschatological salvation in which the process of salvation is being worked out." See such other uses in Romans of the eschatological "now" in 7:6 and 8:1.

52. Cf. Rom 15:23, 25; 2 Cor 8:22; Eph 2:13; Phil 1:5.

53. So Cranfield, *Romans,* 1.417: "The words ἄχρι τοῦ νῦν serve to emphasize the long continuance (until now without having ceased) of this groaning and travailing (cf. Phil 1.5)."

fully here in 8:23-25 as a major implication of what it means for a person to be "in Christ," "in the Spirit," and "adopted by God" into his family — and, reciprocally, to have "Christ by his Spirit being in the believer." Thus he proclaims in 8:23: "We ourselves, who have the firstfruits of the Spirit, we groan inwardly as we eagerly await our adoption as sons and daughters, the redemption of our bodies."

So that his hearers and readers might not become so enraptured with the illustration (i.e., the future of God's subhuman creation) that they miss what it supports and explicates (i.e., the future of those "in Christ" and "in the Spirit"), the apostle prefaces what he really wants to emphasize by inserting the contrasting formula οὐ μόνον δέ, ἀλλὰ καί ("not only, but also"). While earlier in 8:15 he had proclaimed that "the spirit of adoption" (πνεῦμα υἱοθεσίας) is presently the possession of all believers in Jesus, here in 8:23 he speaks of believers having "the firstfruits of the Spirit" in anticipation of their future "adoption as sons and daughters" — both of which realities are true, living as every Christian does in this time of "inaugurated eschatology" between "D Day" and "V Day" in the working out of God's salvation history.[54]

The word ἀπαρχή ("firstfruits") appears in such fifth-century classical Greek writers as Herodotus and Euripides, where it denotes the first of a person's property given as a sacrifice to a pagan deity or as the first portion of a sacrificial offering.[55] It appears in the LXX also in a cultic context to mean the firstborn son of a Jewish family, as well as the firstborn male of their cattle and sheep; all firstborn males were considered God's own possessions, and so either to be offered as a sacrifice to God or redeemed by a blood sacrifice, on the eighth day (Exod 22:29-30). Likewise, the first portion of all the grain in the fields and of all the fruit on the trees or on the ground were to be offered as "firstfruits" to God (Exod 23:19; Num 18:12-13; Deut 18:4). The term is also occasionally found in a figurative sense in the LXX to refer to the best portion of a tract of land (Deut 33:21) or the best young men of a nation (Pss 78:51 [LXX 77:51]; 105:36 [LXX 104:36]). In a cultic context, however, the biblical use of ἀπαρχή signals (1) dedication to God, (2) personal holiness, and (3) the promise of future fertility. The term, therefore, is used a number of times in the NT, both of Jesus as "the firstfruits of those who have fallen asleep" (1 Cor 15:20, 23) and of believers in Jesus as dedicated to God, considered holy, and providing assurance by their very presence of an increase in the future of their numbers.[56]

The most interesting and significant feature of the use of ἀπαρχή in Rom 8:23, however, is this: Paul uses the term not with reference to a sacrifice offered by a person to God, but as a gift given by God to his people as a pledge of

---

54. See our earlier discussion on 6:5-11 regarding the "apparent contradiction" or "great conundrum" of the Christian religion, which lies at the very heart of Christian proclamation.

55. Cf. Herodotus, *History* 1.92; Euripides, *Orestes* 96.

56. Cf. Rom 11:16; 16:5; Jas 1:18; Rev 14:4; perhaps also 2 Thess 2:13, where either the word ἀπαρχήν (as in Codex Vaticanus [B 03], etc.) or the phrase ἀπ' ἀρχῆς (as in Codex Sinaiticus [א 01], etc.) is to be accepted as original.

something even greater yet to come. In effect, Paul's use of ἀπαρχή in this verse is similar to his use of ἀρραβών ("a first installment," "deposit") in 2 Cor 1:22, 5:5, and Eph 1:14 — that is, as a "down payment" or "pledge" that guarantees a promised future action.

What believers in Jesus groan for inwardly, and what they wait for as God's own people, is the full manifestation in their lives of God's promises, that is, "the destined glory that is to be revealed in us," as the thesis statement of 8:18 announces — which, in effect, means the glorified existence of God's people, as the purpose of all of God's redemptive actions is declared to be in 8:29-30. This full manifestation of "our adoption as sons and daughters" is related directly to "the redemption of our bodies," that is, to Christ's parousia ("coming"), the resurrection of those who are his, and the transformation of all believers in Jesus from merely mortal followers of Jesus here on earth to immortal companions of their Lord throughout eternity (as proclaimed by Paul earlier in 1 Cor 15:42-57).

8:24-25 In the second part of the paragraph contained in 8:22-25, Paul goes on to declare and extol the hope of the Christian — that is, "the destined glory that is to be revealed in us" (as his statement of 8:18 proclaims), which focuses on the Christian's resurrection at the time of Christ's parousia when those who are committed to Jesus will fully experience "our adoption as sons and daughters, the redemption of our bodies" (as his explication in 8:23 states). Connecting 8:24-25 with 8:22-23 is the postpositive conjunction γάρ, which has been used at the beginning of every sentence throughout 8:18-24. But as Archibald Robertson long ago observed: "The precise relation between clauses or sentences [in 8:18-24] is not set forth by γάρ. That must be gathered from the context if possible."[57] So because of its context, we have elected to treat the conjunction γάρ at the beginning of 8:24 as only signaling a connection of thought between what precedes it and what follows it (just as it did at the beginning of 8:18, 8:19, and 8:22), and therefore we have not translated it. Also note in our translation of 8:24 the following two matters: (1) that having elected not to translate the conjunction γάρ, we have begun the sentence with what seems from the context to be the understood third-person singular present indicative verb ἐστί ("it is"), and (2) that since the definite article in the expression τῇ γὰρ ἐλπίδι refers to the hope just mentioned in the previous verse, we have understood τῇ ἐλπίδι as "in this hope." Thus we have translated the first sentence of this verse as "It is in this hope that we have been saved."

Paul's use of the aorist passive verb ἐσώθημεν ("we have been saved") may seem somewhat surprising, particularly in a context that lays heavy emphasis on a Christian's hope for the future.[58] But here again — as with the tension between "the spirit of adoption" (πνεῦμα υἱοθεσίας) as a present possession of the believer (as in 8:15) and "our adoption as sons and daughters" (υἱοθεσίαν) as a

---

57. Quoting again *ATRob*, 1191, as in n. 22 on 8:18 above.

58. Cf. also Rom 5:10; 13:11; 1 Cor 3:15; 5:5; and 1 Thess 5:8, where the noun σωτηρία ("salvation") and the verb σώζω ("save") are used by Paul primarily in a future, eschatological sense.

future experience (as in 8:23) — the tension between "we have been saved" and "we will be saved" continues to exist in the life of every Christian[59] and comes to resolution only at Christ's parousia, when believers in Jesus will be resurrected and glorified, and thus become immortal.

The question remains, however, as to why Paul included in this verse (1) the very brief comment, "Hope that is seen is no hope at all," which is a rather obvious thing to say, and (2) the quite brief question, "For who hopes for what one already has?" which is also a rather obvious query to raise. Neither the comment nor the question supports or explains the statement just given, that "it is in this hope that we have been saved." Nor would anything be lost in the flow of Paul's argument if such an obvious comment and obvious question were absent. One could, in fact, read the first sentence of 8:24 and then the entire sentence of 8:25 — omitting both the comment and its accompanying question — without losing anything of Paul's argument. In all likelihood, therefore, this comment and question should be seen as only serving a particular rhetorical purpose in Paul's presentation. And probably, as may be postulated, the apostle's purpose in speaking in this manner was simply to lighten the intensity that would have been created by the joining of the two profound statements in the passage: the pronouncement at the beginning of 8:24, "It is in this hope that we have been saved," and the concluding statement of the passage, with its implied exhortation, in 8:25, "And if we hope for what we do not have, we wait for it with steadfast endurance."

Further, it may reasonably be suggested that such a rhetorical break of intensity would have been more relevant for Paul when preaching orally to a pagan audience than when writing a formal letter to Christians at Rome. One could, therefore, with only a slight stretch of one's imagination, envision a bit of joviality in the crowd when hearing such an obvious statement and such an obvious question. Such a rhetorical break of intensity could well have served the dual purposes of (1) aiding to seal the pronouncement of 8:24 in his audience's mind, and (2) preparing his audience, both mentally and emotionally, for the implied exhortation of 8:25. Nonetheless, for whatever reason, Paul appears to have included in his letter to the Christians at Rome this rhetorical break when portraying to them the nature of his proclamation of the Christian gospel to pagan Gentiles — even though he might have appreciated that they did not need it to understand the flow of his argument (and might have considered it somewhat superficial).

The statement of 8:25, which constitutes the final sentence of the second paragraph of this section of 8:18-30, carries with it an implied exhortation in saying: "If we hope for what we do not have, we wait for it with ὑπομονή." The noun ὑπομονή was used widely in both classical and koine Greek to signify such

---

59. Or the tension of a threefold deliverance, as in 2 Cor 1:10: (1) "he [God] has delivered us" (the aorist ἐρρύσατο ἡμᾶς); (2) "he will deliver" (the future ῥύσεται); and (3) "he will continue to deliver" (the present ἔτι ῥύσεται).

personal qualities as "patience," "endurance," "steadfastness," "fortitude," and "perseverance" as drawn from human strength and bravery. However, in the LXX, the literature of Second Temple Judaism, and the NT, these qualities are based on one's faith in God. And in the Pauline letters, as Friedrich Hauck points out, the term ὑπομονή is "most richly sketched [out]" and "draws its power from religious faith, and here especially from Christian hope."[60]

English versions of the NT have translated ὑπομονή in 8:25 (as well as elsewhere in Romans where it appears: in 2:7, 5:3-4, and 15:4-5) a number of ways. Most often it has been translated by the noun "patience" (e.g., KJV, RSV, NRSV, JB, TEV, Phillips) or by the adverb "patiently" (e.g., Moffatt, BV, NIV, TNIV) — sometimes even by such expansive translations as "patience and composure" (Amplified Bible) or "patiently and confidently" (NLT). Other translators have rendered it "endurance" (e.g., NEB, Knox, NET), "persistently" (Goodspeed), or "perseverance" (NAS). Likewise, there has been a similar variety of translations in the commentaries on Romans, with "patience" again being the most common[61] — though with such cognate expressions as "patiently,"[62] "patient endurance,"[63] or "patient fortitude"[64] also proposed. Still other commentators have translated the word as "endurance,"[65] "perseverance,"[66] "constancy and fortitude,"[67] or "steadfast perseverance."[68]

Friedrich Hauck has probably best captured Paul's meaning by his translation of ὑπομονή in Romans as "steadfast endurance." For the noun "endurance," which connotes the ability of a person to remain firm under suffering, opposition, or misfortune, without yielding — coupled with the adjective "steadfast," which signals the idea of being firmly fixed in one's belief, determination, or adherence — seems to suggest more of what Paul meant by ὑπομονή than does the word "patience" (whether as a noun, an adjective, or an adverb), which has frequently evoked only "a theology of Christian resignation."[69] For just as God's people in the old covenant were to remain firmly fixed in their commitment to God and their obedience to the Mosaic law — and so because of their "*steadfast*

---

60. On the use of ὑπομονή in classical and koine Greek generally, in the LXX and other Jewish Greek writings, and in the NT, see F. Hauck, "ὑπομένω, ὑπομονή," *TDNT* 4.586-88. In addition to its use here in 8:25, note as well its other appearances in Romans at 2:7; 5:3-4 (twice); and 15:4-5 (twice). See also 2 Cor 6:4; 1 Thess 1:3; 2 Thess 1:4; 1 Tim 6:11; 2 Tim 3:10; and Titus 2:2; similarly Heb 10:36; Jas 1:3-4 (twice); 2 Pet 1:6; and Rev 2:2-3 (twice), 19.

61. So, e.g., Calvin, *Romans*, in *Calvin's Commentaries*, 8.176-77; Godet, *Romans*, 1.99-100; Käsemann, *Romans*, 230; and Dunn, *Romans*, 1.476.

62. So C. H. Dodd, *Romans*, 135.

63. So Barrett, *Romans*, 168.

64. So Moo, *Romans*, 522.

65. So Fitzmyer, *Romans*. 516.

66. So Jewett, *Romans*, 521.

67. So Sanday and Headlam, *Romans*, 210.

68. So Cranfield, *Romans*, 1.147.

69. As Jewett, *Romans*, 521, has characterized the frequent use of the translation "patience," and so has argued for the more active translation "perseverance."

endurance in doing good" to receive from God "glory, honor, and immortality" (as Paul characterized Jewish religiosity in Rom 2:7) — so the apostle's implicit exhortation here in 8:25 is that Christians are to await with "steadfast endurance" the promised hope proclaimed in the gospel, that is, to remain firmly fixed in times of suffering, opposition, or misfortune, without yielding, in "eager expectation" of "the destined glory that is to be revealed in us."

III. Christian Prayers as Enabled by the Spirit's Help and Intercession (8:26-27)

Here Paul continues his listing of the most important implications of being "in Christ" and of living one's life "in the Spirit." In these two verses he focuses not on the eschatological future, but on the prayers of Christ's own people here and now. The question may legitimately be asked: Why does Paul focus on prayer when he speaks of the Spirit's help for Christians in their human weakness? Kingsley Barrett offers two quite different understandings of Paul's rationale here in 8:26-27: (1) "Possibly because prayer is the most elementary of religious duties: we are so weak that we do not even know how to pray"; or, perhaps more likely, (2) to parallel, and so displace, "the language of gnostic religion," where a person "does not know the secret prayers which alone can give him access to God; when he has been initiated, the divine Spirit speaks through his mouth the correct formula, which may never be communicated to, and indeed would not be understood by, the public."[70] Our own proposed rationale for why Paul uses prayer as his chief example of human weakness, and so of the necessity for the Spirit to help in our lives, is this: because it is in prayer that one's most fervent desires are expressed (whether directly or allusively), one's hierarchy of values is revealed (whether consciously or unconsciously), and one's resources for life are affirmed (whether openly or in veiled fashion). Thus here in 8:26-27 the apostle speaks of the Spirit's help in the prayers of a Christian as being a vitally important implication of living one's life "in the Spirit" — with the immediate subject being that of Christian prayer, but with the implications of his statements having to do much more broadly with all of a believer's desires, values, and acclaimed resources for life.

8:26 At the head of these two verses appear the adverb ὡσαύτως and the postpositive particle δέ, which — either the adverb alone or the adverb and particle together — have been variously translated as "likewise," "in like manner," "in the same way," "in a similar way," or "similarly." Translators and commentators have often attempted to draw certain comparisons between what Paul writes here in 8:26-27 and what he wrote earlier in 8:18-25 — that is, between (1) the expression "waiting with steadfast endurance" in 8:25b and the statement that "the Spirit helps us" in 8:26, (2) the thought that our hope sustains us in

---

70. Barrett, *Romans,* 168.

8:24-25 and the statements regarding the Spirit sustaining us in 8:26, or (3) the "groanings" of nature and God's people in 8:22-23 and the Spirit's "groaning" in 8:26. So they have translated the adverb, with or without its accompanying particle, by some such expression as "in the same way," "in a similar way," or "similarly."[71]

However, all Paul seems to have really wanted to signify by his use of ὡσαύτως is that he was here moving on in his presentation of the major implications of a Christian's "life in the Spirit" to a further, highly important matter — one that complements the first two but need not be seen as either explaining or developing them. And in line with this understanding of Paul's purpose in 8:26-27 — that is, that he wanted in these two verses only to speak about a further significant implication of "life in the Spirit," without any necessary paralleling of words or expressions in the passages — we have translated ὡσαύτως (with or without δέ) as "likewise."[72]

In this first sentence of 8:26, Paul acknowledges that "human weakness" (ἀσθένεια) is a dominant feature in the lives of all people, including every believer in Jesus. Such a weakness stems not only from the fact that as creatures we are finite and frail, but also from our irrevocable history of sin and depravity. More disastrously, it becomes a controlling factor in all our lives because of our personal choices in confirming our irrevocable human history by our own sinful thoughts and actions. So in our prayers — which reflect our desires, express our values, and reveal what we believe to be our resources — we are not insightful enough to know what we ought to pray for. And what is true about what should be the subject of our prayers is also true, Paul seems to imply, about the living of our lives generally. Thus in this first sentence of the passage Paul sets out his thesis with respect to this third implication of being "in Christ" and of living one's life "in the Spirit": "the Spirit also helps us in our weakness."

The third-person present indicative active verb συναντιλαμβάνεται ("he helps," "aids") is a double compound verb, whose prepositions σύν and ἀντί may have functioned in Paul's day simply to intensify the action of the verb. Etymologically, however, λαμβάνεται ("he received," "took into his possession"), together with the prefixes σύν ("with") and ἀντί ("against," "facing"), could have connoted to Paul's pagan audiences in his Gentile mission (as well as to his Christian addressees at Rome) a reading similar to Archibald Robertson's rather paraphrastic translation of this first sentence of 8:26: "The Holy Spirit lays hold of our weakness along with (σύν) us and carries his part of the burden facing us (ἀντί), as if two men were carrying a log, one at each end."[73] The verb was used three times in this double compound form by the translators of the LXX in Exod 18:22, Num 11:17, and Ps 89:21 (LXX 88:21), and it appears twice

71. So, e.g., NAS, NEB, TEV, NIV, TNIV, NET.
72. So, e.g., KJV, RSV, NRSV; note also variations of this translation in Moffatt, "So too," and in JB, "The Spirit too."
73. ATRob, 573.

in this form in the NT — here in Rom 8:26 and then again in Luke 10:40. It also appears in Josephus in participial form as συλλαμβανομένου, though with only the one prepositional prefix σύν.[74]

Because it was considered somewhat strange for a Greek verb to have two prepositional prefixes, the compound verb συναντιλαμβάνεται was in earlier times often viewed as an isolated phenomenon, which was likely coined by the translators of the LXX and then used once by Paul and once again by the Evangelist Luke. Adolf Deissmann, however, has effectively argued that συναντιλαμβάνομαι was probably used "throughout the whole extent of the Hellenistic world of the Mediterranean," and therefore this particular compound verb may be taken as an "example of the unity and uniformity of the international Greek vocabulary."[75] If we accept Deissmann's thesis, we may presume that συναντιλαμβάνεται ("he helps," "aids") was a common verb of the day — and so the expression would have been known by both Paul's pagan audiences in his Gentile mission and his Christian addressees at Rome.

The postpositive conjunction γάρ ("for") at the beginning of the sentence of 8:26b, while often used in 8:18-24 to suggest only a continuation of thought between what has preceded and what follows, appears here to introduce all that follows in 8:26b-27 as incorporating Paul's explanation of how the Spirit "helps us in our weakness." The sentences that follow this postpositive γάρ in 8:26b, however, have presented commentators with a number of linguistic, exegetical, and interpretive problems. Chief among these are (1) Paul's use of the neuter article τό at the beginning of the second sentence of the passage; (2) what Paul had in mind when he used the neuter interrogative pronoun τί; (3) why he cast his opening remarks regarding prayer in the form of an indirect question ("What should we pray for as we ought?"), which is followed by a brief exclamation ("We do not know!"); and (4) what he was referring to in speaking of "groans that words cannot express" in the final portion of the verse.

The first matter, regarding the presence of the neuter article τό at the beginning of the second sentence, is a purely linguistic phenomenon, which carries on the classical idiom of a neuter article appearing before an indirect question.[76] This construction is found in the NT principally in Luke's writings,[77] but it also appears in Paul's letters in 1 Thess 4:1 (τὸ πῶς) and here in Rom 8:26 (τὸ τί).

What Paul had in mind when he used the neuter interrogative pronoun τί ("what") is somewhat more difficult to determine. Does τί here refer to the

74. Cf. Josephus, *Antiquities* 4.198, using the single prefix verb.

75. Deissmann, *Light from the Ancient East*, 87-88 — citing evidence not only from (1) the Greek historian Diodorus of Sicily in his *Universal History*, which originally consisted of forty books (with only seven being extant, though with large sections of many of the remaining books also preserved) and covered the history of the then-known world from earliest times to the death of Alexander the Great, but also from (2) two Greek wall inscriptions that dated from the third century B.C. and (3) a Greek papyrus letter, which can be dated about 238 B.C.

76. Cf. *ATRob*, 739, 1045-46; see also *LSJM*, 1195, VIII.B.5.

77. See Luke 1:62 (τὸ τί); 9:46 (τὸ τίς); 22:4 (τὸ τῶς); Acts 4:21 (τὸ πῶς); and 22:30 (τὸ τί).

object or objects of a person's prayers — that is, *what we are to pray for* (as in Mark 11:24)?[78] Does it refer to the content of a person's prayers — that is, *what we are to pray* (as in Luke 18:9-14)?[79] Or should it be understood as dealing with the manner or form of a person's prayers — that is, *how we are to pray* (as in Mark 11:25)?[80] The first two options may be understood as virtually synonymous. The third, however, while able to be interpreted broadly as the same as the first two, lends itself much too easily to matters that have simply to do with a proper manner or form of prayer. Thus, as Charles Cranfield has rightly argued: (1) "τί is not to be reduced to a virtual equivalent of πῶς,"[81] and (2) "the words τί προσευξώμεθα κατὸ δεῖ are not to be understood as indicating two distinct things as unknown, namely, what to pray for (or what to pray) and how to present our prayers to God, but one thing, namely, what it is right, i.e. according to God's will (καθὸ δεῖ is parallel to κατὰ θεόν in v. 27), for us to pray for (or to pray)."[82]

The third problem confronting the interpreter of 8:25-27 — that is, why Paul cast his opening remarks regarding prayer in the form of an indirect question ("What should we pray for as we ought?"), which is followed by an exclamation ("We do not know!") — is probably impossible to answer with any assurance. Such a linguistic phenomenon is not a common feature in a formal letter. All we can postulate is that Paul likely used such an indirect question and exclamation here in 8:26 for a reason somewhat similar to that which motivated him in 8:24 to offer the obvious comment "Hope that is seen is no hope at all" followed by the obvious question "For who hopes for what one already has?" — that is, for some rhetorical reason that probably should be related to his oral proclamation of the Christian gospel to his pagan audiences in his Gentile mission, which rhetorical flare he then simply incorporated at a later time into his more formal letter to his Christian addressees at Rome.[83]

The fourth interpretive problem in 8:26 — what Paul had in mind in saying that the Spirit himself intercedes for us "with groans that words cannot express" (στεναγμοῖς ἀλαλήτοις) — has seemed to many interpreters difficult to resolve. Some significant NT scholars, such as Horst Balz, Ernst Käsemann, and Gordon Fee, have argued extensively that the expression στεναγμοῖς ἀλαλήτοις refers to the charismatic experience of praying in "angelic" or "ecstatic tongues."[84] And a

---

78. So, e.g., KJV: "what we should pray for"; NIV, TNIV: "what we ought to pray for." Cf., e.g., Cranfield, *Romans,* 1.421; Moo, *Romans,* 522; Jewett, *Romans,* 522.

79. So Barrett, *Romans,* 161 and 168: "what are the proper prayers to offer."

80. So, e.g., RSV, NEB, TEV: "how we ought to pray"; NRSV: "how to pray as we ought"; Phillips: "how to pray worthily"; Moffatt: "how to pray aright"; NET: "how we should pray." Cf., e.g., Sanday and Headlam, *Romans,* 213; Lagrange, *Aux Romains,* 211-12; and Huby, *Aux Romains,* 303.

81. Cranfield, *Romans,* 1.421.

82. *Ibid.*

83. See our "Exegetical Comments" regarding this matter on 8:24.

84. Balz, *Heilsvertrauen und Welterfahrung,* 80-92; Käsemann, *Romans,* 240-42; *idem,* "The Cry for Liberty in the Worship of the Church," 122-37; Fee, *God's Empowering Presence,* 577-86.

number of other commentators, such as Theodor Zahn, Archibald Hunter, Paul Althaus, and Dieter Zeller,[85] have voiced their support for this understanding — which goes back to Origen and Chrysostom,[86] and so has a venerable history.

Nonetheless, a number of frequently made observations seem to stand against such an understanding:

1. The στεναγμοί ("groanings") in this passage clearly have to do with bringing the needs and petitions of Christians before God, and so the utterances of charismatic glossolalia, which is a phenomenon preeminently used in worshipful praise, are not likely to be in mind.[87]

2. The adjective ἀλάλητος ("unspoken," "unexpressed," or "wordless") does not mean "ineffable," that is, incapable of being expressed in human language — which makes it almost impossible to identify the "groans" of this passage with glossolalia, since tongues are verbalized utterances even if not understandable.[88]

3. The groans in this passage are not the believer's groans but the Spirit's.[89]

It seems best, therefore, to translate the dative noun στεναγμοῖς with its adjective ἀλαλήτοις as "with groans that words cannot express," and so to understand that phrase, as Douglas Moo has expressed matters, as referring to "the Spirit's own 'language of prayer,' a ministry of intercession that takes place in our hearts (v. 27) in a manner imperceptible to us."[90]

The strong adversative ἀλλά at the beginning of this final sentence of 8:26 is best rendered by the adverbial negative expression "however." The subject of the sentence is "the Spirit himself" (αὐτὸ τὸ πνεῦμα) — translating the neuter phraseology in personal terms. The verb ὑπερεντυγχάνει ("he pleads," "intercedes") is the activity of the Holy Spirit on behalf of the Christian. And while ὑπὲρ ἡμῶν ("on behalf of us" or "for us") is most likely a scribal addition inserted to make explicit what was already implied by the verb ὑπερεντυγχάνει (see "Textual Notes"), the inclusion of "for us" in our translation is legitimate because it is implied by the verb.

8:27 Not only does the apostle speak in 8:26 of the Spirit helping Christians know what to pray for and interceding on their behalf before God, but Paul in 8:27 goes on to speak of God knowing the mind of the Spirit and of the Spirit interceding on behalf of God's holy ones in accordance with God's will. In effect, therefore, though a Christian's prayers are translated by the Spirit into

---

85. Zahn, *An die Römer,* 412-13; Hunter, *Romans,* 84; Althaus, *An der Römer,* 84; Zeller, *An die Römer,* 163.

86. Origen, *Ad Romanos, PG* 14.1120; Chrysostom, *Homilia XXXII in Epistolam ad Romanos, PG* 60.533.

87. Paraphrasing Cranfield, *Romans,* 1.423.

88. Paraphrasing Moo, *Romans,* 525.

89. Paraphrasing *ibid.*

90. Moo, *Romans,* 525-26.

his own "language of prayer," there is nothing lost in the translations (1) from the prayerful words of a Christian to the groans of the Spirit or (2) from the Spirit's groans before God to God's gracious response to the Spirit's prayers on behalf of a Christian. It is in this confidence that the Christian prays — that is, in the confidence that "life in the Spirit" includes (1) the work of the Holy Spirit to teach us what we should pray for, (2) the translation by the Spirit of our words into his own language of prayer, (3) the presentation by the Spirit of our requests to God in accordance with God's will, and (4) God's knowing the mind of the Spirit, and therefore his answering a Christian's prayer in terms of his own will.

The expression "the One who searches our hearts" echoes such OT statements as God's words to the prophet Samuel in 1 Sam 16:7 regarding his selection of David as Israel's king: "The Lord does not look at the things a human being looks at. A human looks at the outward appearance, but *the Lord looks at the heart*"; and as the proverb of Prov 20:27 states: "The lamp of the Lord searches the spirit of a person; *it searches out his or her inmost being.*"[91] Reference to God as "the One who searches our hearts" had evidently become quite widely proverbial, as seen in Wis 1:6, *"God is the witness of a person's reins and a true overseer of his heart,"* and Sir 42:18, *"God searches out the deep and a person's heart, and all their secrets he surveys."*[92] It may, therefore, be presumed that the expression would have been known both by Paul's pagan audiences in his Gentile mission and by his Christian addressees at Rome as (1) having God as its subject ("the One who") and (2) signaling the depth of God's knowledge of all human beings ("who searches our hearts").

The final clause of 8:27 begins with the conjunction ὅτι, which in this case may signal either a causal connection (i.e., providing an explanation of what God knows in his knowing the intention of the Spirit)[93] or an explicative connection (i.e., describing the nature of or giving a reason for the Spirit's intercession).[94] Because the phrase κατὰ θεόν ("according to [the will of] God") comes at the beginning of this final clause of the verse (which is where in a Greek sentence the emphasis most often appears, while in an English sentence an emphasis or climax is usually reserved for the end of a sentence), it is probably best to understand ὅτι as introducing the reason for Paul's statement that "God who searches our hearts knows the mind of the Spirit" — that is, "*because* the Spirit intercedes on behalf of God's holy ones *in accordance with God's will* (κατὰ θεόν)."

91. Cf. 1 Kgs 8:39; 1 Chr 28:9; 29:17; Pss 7:9; 17:3; 26:2; 44:21; 139:1-2, 23; Prov 15:11; 17:3; 24:12; Jer 11:20; 12:3; 17:10; 20:12.

92. Cf. Acts 1:24; 15:8.

93. So, e.g., Cranfield, *Romans*, 1.424: "ὅτι is better taken to mean 'that' than 'because' or 'for,' since the clause it introduces explains not *why* God knows the Spirit's intention but *what* He knows in knowing it"; Käsemann, *Romans*, 242: "The ὅτι clause is not explicative but causal"; cf. also Godet, *Romans*, 2.103; Wilckens, *An die Römer*, 3.161.

94. So, e.g., Sanday and Headlam, *Romans*, 214: "It seems best to make ὅτι describe the nature of the Spirit's intercession"; Moo, *Romans*, 527: "The emphatic position of 'in accordance with [the will of] God' suggests that Paul is giving a reason for the first statement"; cf. also Kuss, *Römerbrief*, 3.644; Jewett, *Romans*, 525.

These two verses of 8:26-27 deal with matters regarding (1) our human weakness in not knowing what to pray for, (2) our experiencing the aid of God's Spirit in knowing what to pray for, (3) our being conscious that the Spirit "intercedes for us with groans that words cannot express" and "in accordance with God's will," and (4) our being convinced that "God knows the mind of the Spirit," and thus that he answers our prayers in accordance with the Spirit's intercession and not just in terms of the words we might use in expressing them. The "good news" of Paul's presentation in these two verses, therefore, is that those who are "in Christ," and therefore also "in the Spirit," have a highly significant resource — especially for their praying, but also, as implied, for the living out of their present earthly lives — that is far greater than anything that those who are apart from Christ and the Spirit possess: "the help" of God's Spirit and "the intercession" of that same Holy Spirit on their behalf before God.

IV. The Assurance of Believers in Jesus That God Works All Things Together for Good on Behalf of Those Who Love Him and Are Called according to His Purpose (8:28-30)

8:28 The opening statement of 8:28-30, which sets out a fourth and final implication of the Christian's "life in the Spirit," begins with the postpositive conjunction δέ, which was a common particle used by Greek writers to connect one clause with another. Frequently δέ appears when some contrast is to be seen between sentences or clauses — though at other times it functions simply as a connecting conjunction without any nuance of contrast. Earlier, in 8:23 and 24, the particle δέ functioned in a contrasting manner. In 8:25, 26, and 27, however, it was used only to connect one sentence or clause to another — and later in 8:30 it will appear again in this same fashion. Thus, here at the beginning of 8:28, surrounded by its use simply to connect the sentences of 8:25, 26, 27, and 30, δέ should most likely also be viewed as simply connecting this material of 8:28-30 with that given in 8:26-27 — and therefore, because of its enumerative context, it is probably best translated by some such expression as "in addition," "moreover," or "further."

Paul's use of the epistolary "disclosure formula" οἴδαμεν ὅτι ("we know that") at the beginning of 8:28 suggests that what he writes in the rest of this verse is what he believed all discerning people would recognize as being true — not only Jews and Christians, but also the philosophically acute and all religiously devout people. Charles Talbert has cited a number of axiomatic statements drawn from the Greek classical philosophers (principally Plato, c. 428/427–348/347 B.C.) and from certain Greco-Roman Stoic philosophers (principally Seneca the Younger, c. 4 B.C.–A.D. 65) to the effect that "all that comes from the gods turns out for the best for the one who is dear to the gods" (so Plato) and "all things are good to a god-fearing person, even things that others find evil" (so Seneca).[95] In a similar vein, Jesus ben Sira, a prominent Jewish teacher of the first quarter of the second century B.C., wrote at sometime during 180-175 B.C.: "All things to the godly are for their good";[96] and Rabbi Akiba, a prominent third-generation Tannaitic rabbi active during A.D. 120-140, is quoted in the Talmud as having taught: "All that the Almighty does, He does for good."[97]

Paul's use here in 8:28 of such a widespread sentiment in justification of the actions of the divine (whether of the Jewish-Christian God or of other so-called gods) — which expresses in aphoristic fashion (i.e., using a terse formulation of truth or sentiment) an elemental theodicy (i.e., a defense of divine goodness and omnipotence in view of the existence of evil) — has often been viewed as difficult to spell out with precision (see "Textual Notes" above). The Greek text of the verse has been read in at least four ways:

1. That the plural neuter adjective πάντα ("all things"), which is used as a substantive noun, is nominative, and therefore the subject of the sentence — with the third-person singular suffix of the verb συνεργεῖ, when used with a neuter subject, being translated as either "it" or "they," depending on the singular or plural number of the sentence's subject. On such an understanding, Paul is declaring that "*all things* work together for good to those who love God," which seems to echo in somewhat fatalistic fashion the aphoristic statements of the ancient philosophers.

2. That the plural neuter πάντα ("all things") is accusative, and therefore the predicate of the sentence — with the third-person singular suffix of the verb συνεργεῖ functioning as the subject of the sentence, and so, understood as a neuter verbal suffix, has as its antecedent the neuter noun τὸ πνεῦμα ("the Spirit") that appears earlier in the passage at 8:23 and 8:26-27. On such an understanding, Paul has here in mind God's Holy Spirit as the subject of the sentence, and thus is declaring that "*it* [i.e., 'the Spirit'] works all things together for good to those who love God."

3. That the plural neuter noun ("all things") is accusative, and therefore the predicate of the sentence — with the third-person singular suffix of συνεργεῖ being viewed as masculine, and so picking up on the immediately preceding masculine noun τὸν θεόν ("God") in 8:28. On such an understanding, Paul has here in mind God himself as the subject of the sentence, and thus is declaring that "*he* [i.e., 'God'] works all things together for good to those who love God."

4. That the plural neuter noun ("all things") is accusative, and therefore the predicate of the sentence — with the third-person singular suffix of

95. Talbert, *Romans,* 222-23.
96. Sir 39:25; cf. also 39:27: "all of these things [i.e., 'water,' 'fire,' 'iron,' 'salt,' 'wheat,' 'milk,' 'honey,' 'grapes,' 'oil' and 'clothing'] prove to be good to the godly."
97. *b. Bcr.* 60b.

συνεργεῖ being viewed as masculine and kept from any possible ambiguity by the insertion (whether in the original text or by a later scribe) of ὁ θεός ("God") as the One in mind in the suffix of the verb συνεργεῖ. On such a reading, Paul is here explicitly declaring that "*God works* all things together for good to those who love him."

While scholars may never agree unanimously about the verse's precise wording or syntax, it seems best to understand πάντα συνεργεῖ εἰς ἀγαθόν as constituting the sentence's original form, with (1) the suffix of the verb συνεργεῖ understood as the subject of the sentence and as being masculine ("he") and (2) the substantive noun πάντα ("all things") viewed as accusative and therefore the sentence's predicate — thereby reading "*he* [i.e., 'God'] works all things together for good" (i.e., option 3 above), with that statement introduced by the clause "to those who love God" and followed by the clause "to those called according to his purpose." This reading should probably be accepted as original because of its extensive and diversified textual support (see "Textual Notes"). Yet the reading πάντα συνεργεῖ ὁ θεὸς εἰς ἀγαθόν ("*God* works all things together for good"), which explicitly identifies "God" as the One in mind in speaking of "he" in the suffix of the verb, also carries a high degree of probability (i.e., option 4 above) because of its attestation by P[46], Codex Alexandrinus (A 02), Codex Vaticanus (B 03), and two Greek recensions of Origen's commentary on Romans.

Such a reading of 8:28 (whether option 3 or option 4 above) not only (1) understands the subject of the principal statement of the verse as being "God" and (2) views the predicate of the sentence as being "all things," but also (3) considers the rationale for the positioning of πάντα ("all things") at the beginning of the sentence as being for the sake of emphasis — that is, it was placed there to highlight the fact that everything that occurs in the life of a Christian, whether viewed from a human perspective as being either "good" or "bad," is under God's sovereign supervision, and so should be viewed by believers in Jesus as in some way good in the course of the fulfillment of God's purpose for their lives, both presently and in the future. Or, as Joseph Fitzmyer has aptly rephrased Paul's statement in this verse: "Everything that happens to Christians in earthly life is somehow governed by God's providence. Nothing in this life can harm Christians, whether it be suffering or the attack of hostile evil powers, for all of these things can contribute to the destiny to which Christians are called."[98]

Further, the two qualifying clauses that appear before and after the affirmation "he [God] works all things together for good" — that is, the clauses "for those who love God" and "for those who are called according to his purpose" — are not given in this fashion so as to allow the second to correct the first.[99]

---

98. Fitzmyer, *Romans*, 522.

99. As Calvin has suggested, in commenting on the clause "for those called according to his

Rather, the two clauses are given, one before Paul's affirmation and the other after it, to explicate in a twofold and highly dramatic manner the subjects of God's providential care in "working together" all the events of their lives.

8:29-30 In these two verses Paul sets out the reason why Christians can be confident that God works all things together for good for those who love him and are called according to his purpose: because those who have responded positively to God's love, mercy, and grace — as expressed through the person and work of Jesus Christ and the continued ministry of the Spirit — have become personally involved in the working out of God's salvation history, and thus have the assurance that what God ordains and allows in their earthly lives will result in their becoming more and more "conformed to the likeness of his Son" (as in 8:29) and in their finally being fully "glorified" (as in 8:30), which are the ultimate purposes of all of God's redemptive actions on their behalf.

The stages of a believer's life as God works out his salvation in it, as seen from the divine perspective, are set out with five significant expressions: "foreknown" . . . "predestined" . . . "called" . . . "justified" . . . "glorified." These stages, however, as Joseph Fitzmyer has rightly warned, "should not be too facilely transposed into the *signa rationis* of later theological systems of predestination."[100] For while Paul in Rom 9 speaks of God's choice of people even before they are born and God's selection of events even before they occur — and while he uses the verb προορίζω ("decide beforehand," "predestine") with respect to God's decisions on behalf of believers in Jesus even "before time began" in 1 Cor 2:7 (cf. also Eph 1:5, 11) — here in Rom 8:29-30 Paul's purpose in setting out these five stages seems not simply to present a divine "order of salvation," but rather to emphasize that God's salvation of people (1) is based in his "foreknowledge" and his "predestination," (2) is effected by his "calling" and his "justification," and (3) will result for those who respond positively to him in their ultimate "glorification." So in support of his statement that believers in Jesus can be assured that God works all things together for good for those who love him and are called according to his purpose, the apostle lists these five significant stages in the course of God's working in a Christian's life — which stages include God's supervision of all the circumstances and events in a Christian's life.

It may be that Paul drew this list from Jewish or Jewish Christian instruction, whether catechetical or liturgical — or, perhaps, from some portion of early Christian confessional material. If so, it should probably be theorized that in repeating the list Paul included his own emphases after the term "predestined," in order to highlight the two major purposes that he sees God having in the outworking of his program of salvation history — that is, (1) so that those who respond to him in a positive manner might be "conformed to the likeness of

---

purpose": "This clause seems to have been added by way of correction. No one is to think that, because believers love God, they obtain the advantage of deriving so much fruit from their adversities by their own merit" (Calvin, *Romans,* in *Calvin's Commentaries,* 8.179).

100. Fitzmyer, *Romans,* 524-25.

his Son," and (2) "in order that he [Jesus Christ, his Son] might be the firstborn among many brothers and sisters."

Further, with respect to the much-disputed features of the relations between God's "foreknowledge" and his "predestination," as well as to the extent of his predestination, Paul's positive statements on these matters should not be turned into negative statements about God's rejection and applied to those who have rejected God's love, grace, and mercy; refused the work of Christ Jesus on their behalf; and so resisted the ministry of God's Spirit. For the counterpart of God's foreknowledge and predestination of people who love him is not his predestination of those who reject him. People have rejected God, his Son, and his Spirit apart from God's desires; their rejection stems from them alone. As Origen in the third century aptly wrote with respect to God's foreknowledge and predestination:

> In Scripture, words like *foreknew* and *predestined* do not apply equally to both good and evil. For the careful student of the Bible will realize that these words are used only of the good. . . . When God speaks of evil people, he says that he *never knew* them [Matt 7:23; Luke 13:27]. . . . They are not said to be foreknown, not because there is anything which can escape God's knowledge, which is present everywhere and nowhere absent, but because everything which is evil is considered to be unworthy of his knowledge or of his foreknowledge.[101]

On the basis of the structure and language of 8:28-30, therefore, it may legitimately be proposed that Paul has incorporated into these final verses of this section certain materials that he drew from various portions of Jewish and/or Jewish Christian instruction — perhaps even from an early Christian confession — all of which he redacted for his own purposes. He evidently wanted to use this material to bring to a fitting conclusion both (1) his central proclamations of "no condemnation," "new life," being "in Christ," being "in the Spirit," "Christ by his Spirit" being in the Christian, and believers in Jesus having been "adopted" by God into his family (as in 8:1-17), and (2) the major implications that he has spelled out on what it means to live one's life "in the Spirit" (as in 8:18-30).

BIBLICAL THEOLOGY

The implications of what it means to live one's life "in the Spirit," which Paul has highlighted here in 8:18-30, are of great significance both for Christian biblical theology and for Christian living. They are, in fact, as Charles Cranfield has observed with regard to "the Christian hope" as set out in this passage, "something far more wonderful and more generous than at most times our preoccupation

---

101. Origen, *Ad Romanos*, CER 4.86, 88, 90.

with ourselves and the feebleness of our concern for God's glory allow us to conceive."[102] For basic to all Christian thought and all Christian living are:

1. An understanding of how the present sufferings of Christians and the present situation of God's creation relate to the destined glory of believers in Jesus, both in this life and in the future, and the promised future freedom of creation (as in 8:18-21).
2. A vital conviction regarding the hope given by God to all believers in Jesus, who have "the firstfruits of the Spirit," and given in derivative fashion to "the whole creation" (as in 8:22-25).
3. A lively realization of the Spirit's help and intercession before God on behalf of those who are God's people, particularly with respect to prayer but also with regard to all the facets of the lives of Christians (as in 8:26-27).
4. The assurance of Christians that God "works all things together" for good to those who love him and are called according to his purpose (as in 8:28-30).

Everything else in the thought and life of a Christian is dependent on the consciousness and experience of these primary truths.

CONTEXTUALIZATION FOR TODAY

Paul had earlier exhorted his converts in the Roman province of Galatia to "live by the Spirit" (Gal 5:16, 25a) and to "keep in step with the Spirit" (Gal 5:25b). Here in Rom 8, however, we have, as James Dunn has rightly noted, "Paul's most sustained exposition of the work of the Spirit."[103] And while much is presented in the NT Gospels, and particularly in the Fourth Gospel, regarding (1) the person and work of God's Spirit, (2) the relation of God's Spirit to Jesus, God's Son, and (3) the spirituality of those who are believers in Jesus, here in Rom 8:18-30 we have in Paul's words what it means to live one's life as a Christian "in the Spirit" — with, in particular, reference to the themes of (1) suffering and glory, (2) hope for the future, (3) the help and intercession of the Spirit, and (4) a Christian's assured confidence in God as being foundational for his or her life and spirituality. Indeed, as Joseph Fitzmyer has emphasized in his *Spiritual Exercises Based on Paul's Epistle to the Romans,* "Paul's epistle to the Romans, if read critically yet meditatively, is a tremendous source for prayer and reflection on the human condition and about the Christian's relationship to God."[104]

It remains for us as believers in Jesus, therefore, to reflect critically and meditatively on what it means to live both positionally "in Christ" and expe-

102. Cranfield, "Some Observations on Romans 8:19-21," 230.
103. Dunn, "Spirit Speech," 82.
104. Fitzmyer, *Spiritual Exercises,* 3.

rientially "in the Spirit" — and so to live our lives by means of "Christ by his Spirit" living in us. As citizens of the Western world and members of our modern cultures, we are often quite expert at proposing programs for living a healthy life and focusing on what we see as some type of true spirituality. What we as Christians need, however, is to contemplate (1) what it really means to be "in Christ," "in the Spirit," and to have "Christ by his Spirit" living in us, and (2) what impact these realities are meant by God to have on our thinking and on our living — that is, to consider seriously what these "new life realities" are meant to have on our outlook, on our hopes, and on our actions. And this is what Paul here in 8:18-30 calls on us as believers in Jesus to consider thoughtfully, to work out in our own lives appropriately, and to express effectively in our actions by means of the Spirit's guidance and enablement.

7. A Triumphal Affirmation of God's Vindication, Care, and Eternal Love for People "in Christ Jesus," with Early Christian Confessional Materials Incorporated (8:31-39)

TRANSLATION

8:31*What, then, shall we say in response to these things? If God is for us, who can be against us?* 32*"He who even did not spare his own Son, but gave him up for us all, how will he not also along with him graciously give us everything else?"* 33*Who will bring any charge against God's elect? "God is the One who justifies!"* 34*Who can condemn? "It is Christ Jesus who died — more than that, who was raised to life — who is at the right hand of God and is also interceding for us!"*

35*What can separate us from the love of Christ — "trouble or hardship or persecution or famine or nakedness or danger or sword?* 36*As it is written, 'For your sake we face death all day long; we are considered as sheep to be slaughtered.'"* 37*In all of these things, however, "We are more than conquerors through him who loved us!"*

38*For I am convinced that neither death nor life, neither angels nor demons, neither things present nor things to come, nor any powers,* 39*neither height nor depth, nor anything else in all creation, will be able to separate us from the love of God that is in Christ Jesus our Lord.*

TEXTUAL NOTES

8:34a The double name Χριστὸς Ἰησοῦς appears in uncials ℵ A C F G L Ψ (also *Byz* L) and in minuscules 33 (Category I), 81 256 1962 2127 (Category II), and 6 104 365 424[c] 436 1319 1573 1852 (Category III); it is also reflected in it[b, f, g] vg syr[h] cop[bo] and supported by Origen[lat] Augustine[3/4]. The single name Χριστός, however, appears in uncials B D (also *Byz* K) and in minuscules 1175 1739 (Category I), 1506 1881 2464 (Category II), and 263 459 1241 1912 2200 (Category III); it is also reflected in it[d2, mon] syr[p] cop[sa] and supported by Irenaeus[lat] Chrysostom Ambrosiaster Augustine[1/4]. The clause ἅμα δὲ Χριστὸς Ἰησοῦς ("but at the same time it is Christ Jesus"), which includes the name Ἰησοῦς, is found in P[46vid] — though ἅμα δὲ ("but at the same time") does not appear in this verse elsewhere in the Greek textual tradition. Support for and against the inclusion of Ἰησοῦς in the double name Χριστὸς Ἰησοῦς is so evenly balanced in the textual tradition that the UBS committee decided to retain it but to enclose it in square brackets.

34b The verb ἐγερθείς ("was raised") is amply attested by P[27vid] and P[46], by uncials ℵ[a] B D G (also *Byz* K), and by minuscules 1739 (Category I), 1881 2127 (Category II), and 1241 2495 (Category III); it is also reflected in it[ar, d, dem, e, f, g, t, x, z] vg syr[p, h] and supported by Irenaeus[lat] Origen[lat]. Some witnesses add ἐκ νεκρῶν ("from the dead") — as do uncials ℵ*, c A C Ψ, minuscules 33 (Category I), 81 1506 1962 (Category II), and 104 326 436 (Category III); the phrase is also reflected in cop[sa, bo] and supported by Chrysostom. This longer reading, however, is probably an explanatory gloss.

35 The name Χριστοῦ ("Christ") by itself after the phrase τῆς ἀγάπης ("the love of") is attested by uncials C D F G Ψ (also *Byz* K L) and by minuscules 33 1175 1739 (Category I), 81 256 1881 1962 2127 2464 (Category II), and 6 104 263 424[c] 436 459 1241 1319 1573 1852 1912 2200 (Category III); it is also reflected in it[ar, b, f, g, mon, o] vg syr[p, h] cop[bo] and supported by Origen[gr, lat3/11] Chrysostom[2/3] Theodoret Tertullian Ambrosiaster Jerome[1/7] and Augustine[24/25] (Codex Alexandrinus [A 02] is illegible). The reading τῆς ἀγάπης θεοῦ τῆς ἐν Χριστῷ Ἰησοῦ ("the love of God that is in Christ Jesus"), which appears in Codex Vaticanus (B 03) and Origen[lat4(1)/11], is probably a scribal harmonization to the same phrase later in 8:39. The phrase τῆς ἀγάπης θεοῦ ("the love of God"), as in Codex Sinaiticus (ℵ 01) and minuscules 365 1506 (also reflected in cop[sa] and supported by Hippolytus Origen[gr mss, lat3/11] Eusebius[3/4] Chrysostom[1/3] and Augustine[1/25]) — rather than τῆς ἀγάπης Χριστοῦ ("the love of Christ") — is probably a partial echo of 8:39.

38-39 Paul's list of potential obstacles to "the love of God that is in Christ Jesus our Lord" — which appears between the clause "neither angels (ἄγγελοι) nor demons (ἀρχαί)" in 8:38 and the clause "neither height (ὕψωμα) nor depth (βάθος)" in 8:39 — is found in a variety of sequences in the textual tradition. The reading οὔτε ἐνεστῶτα οὔτε μέλλοντα οὔτε δυνάμεις ("nor things present, nor things to come, nor powers") has decisive support in P[27vid] and P[46] (using δύναμις), in uncials ℵ A B F G, and in minuscules 1739 (Category I), 1506 1881 1962 2127 (Category II), and 365 1319 1573 (Category III); it is also reflected in it[ar, d, f, g, o] vg[ww, st] cop[sa, bo] and supported by Origen[gr, lat2(2)/9] Eusebius Jerome[l(6)/7] (Augustine[5/8]). Apparently some scribes viewed the arrangement of Paul's list, particularly with respect to angelic beings, as needing improvement, and so the following sequences (among others) are attested: (1) "nor powers, nor things present, nor things to come," as in *Byz* uncials K L and minuscules 33 1175 (Category I), 2464 (Category II), and 6 424[c] 1241 1912 2200 (Category III); also reflected in it[b, mon] and supported by Origen[lat2/9] Chrysostom Theodore[vid] Theodoret Ambrosiaster and Augustine[1/8]; (2) "nor rulers (ἐξουσίαι), nor things present, nor things to come, nor powers," as in uncial C and minuscules 81 256 (Category II), 104 263 459 (Category III); also reflected in vg[cl] syr[h with *] cop[bo mss] and supported by Origen[lat2/9]; and (3) "nor rulers (ἐξουσίαι), nor powers, nor things present, nor things to come," as in minuscules 436 and 1852 (both Category III) and as reflected in syp[p].

FORM/STRUCTURE/SETTING

In these nine verses of 8:31-39, Paul brings to a dramatic climax Section II of the body middle of his letter to the Christians at Rome — that is, he sets out a fervent, triumphant, even defiant conclusion to what he presented in 5:1–8:30. What the apostle has written in this section of the body middle of his letter is, as we have proposed, what he earlier referred to as his "spiritual gift" (χάρισμα πνευματικόν) to his addressees at Rome,[1] with that gift understood as a précis of his more personal, relational, and participatory form of the Christian message that he proclaimed to Gentiles in various cities and towns of the eastern regions of the Roman Empire. Further, this more relational, personal, and participatory form of the Christian gospel is (1) what he characterized as "my gospel" (τὸ εὐαγγέλιόν μου),[2] (2) what he felt Christians at Rome needed to know to understand his Gentile mission more accurately and the content of his proclamation more appreciatively, (3) what he wanted the Roman believers in Jesus to accept as being a more developed understanding of the Christian gospel, and (4) what he desired they would respond to positively by their prayers and financial support for his proposed extension of that same Christian message to pagan Gentiles in Spain.[3]

The Nature of This Closing Passage. Because of what has been viewed as the passage's poetic language and/or because of its confessional echoes, 8:31-39 has often been understood as a hymn[4] or a doxology.[5] At times, because of its extensive use of questions and answers, it has also been understood as styled in the form of a Greek diatribe.[6] Though this passage concludes with a triumphal affirmation of the impossibility that God's people can ever be separated from God's love as expressed in Christ Jesus, a "poetic beauty" is difficult to spell out — and though it includes Christian confessional materials (particularly in vv. 32-34; probably also in vv. 35-37), it goes far beyond the evidence to understand the passage as a Christian doxology. Further, the suggestion that 8:31-39 (or at least the materials of vv. 31-37) should be understood as a Christian diatribe is unsupportable.[7]

In ch. 4 of the letter, Paul introduced his exposition of Abraham as the example par excellence of faith by asking the rhetorical question, "What, then, shall we say?" (τί οὖν ἐροῦμεν;) in 4:1. And in ch. 3 he used a number of variations of this basic rhetorical question, as in 3:1 ("What advantage, then, is there in being a Jew?"), 3:3 ("What if some did not have faith?"), 3:5 ("What shall we say?"), 3:8 ("Why not say?"), and 3:9 ("What, then, shall we conclude?"). In each instance Paul used forms of this basic rhetorical question to highlight his

---

1. Cf. 1:11-12 and our exegetical comments on this passage.

2. Cf. 2:16 and 16:25 and our exegetical comments on these passages.

3. Cf. 1:13 and 15:24 and our exegetical comments on these passages.

4. So, e.g., J. Weiss, "Beiträge zur paulinischen Rhetorik," 195-96.

5. So, e.g., Balz, *Heilsvertrauen und Welterfahrung,* 116.

6. So, e.g., Käsemann, *Romans,* 246: "The interplay of question and answer, objection and response, shows that we again have a Christian diatribe with an approximation to the rhythmic prose of antiquity."

7. S. K. Stowers, in his often perceptive work *The Diatribe and Paul's Letter to the Romans,* does not even list 8:31-39 as a possible example of a diatribe in Romans. And when he does refer to Käsemann's treatment of Paul's use of diatribe styling in Romans, he says: "Käsemann's interpretation is certainly under the influence of Bultmann's idea that the diatribe style in Romans is a reflection of Paul's unplanned, spontaneous preaching style" (122-23) — which thesis Stowers has repudiated.

arguments that follow — with the implied premise for each question rooted in what he had written earlier and his responses stated in rather cryptic and dramatic fashion.[8] It seems reasonable, therefore, to conclude that Paul's use of such a rhetorical question here in 8:31-39 should be seen as similar to his use of rhetorical questions and Christian answers earlier in chs. 3 and 4 — without postulating that the passage expresses some sort of hymn, doxology, or diatribal styling.

One can, with only a slight extension of one's imagination, understand 8:31-39 as a faithful representation of how Paul must have often closed off his oral proclamation of the gospel to non-Jewish audiences in various eastern cities and towns of the Roman Empire. Features of triumph, assurance, and even defiance reverberate throughout these final verses — with, as well, an implied invitation to Paul's Gentile hearers to respond positively to "the love of God that is in Christ Jesus our Lord."

Likewise, one can appreciate why Paul would have wanted to include these highly dramatic and fervently expressed closing words of 8:31-39 in his letter to Christians at Rome. For not only did he desire to set before them a précis of what he had been proclaiming to pagan Gentiles, as he did in 5:1–8:30, he also wanted them to respond positively to the relational, personal, and participatory features of the Christian gospel as he had proclaimed them — and so, experiencing such matters for themselves, to join with him by their prayers and financial support in a further extension of this form of Christian proclamation to non-Jewish people in Spain.

The Repeated Use of the Interrogative Pronoun τίς *("Who") in the Passage.* Because Greek was written without punctuation, it is sometimes difficult to tell whether a statement in Paul's letters (as well as elsewhere in the NT) should be read as declarative or interrogative. That is why a question in the NT is often signaled by an interrogative pronoun, frequently by τί ("what") but more often by τίς ("who"). At a number of places in the NT, however, no interrogative pronoun is present to alert the reader that a question follows, and so interpreters must decide from the context how a statement was intended to be understood — as, for example, in 1 Cor 1:13, whose three statements could be read, when divorced from their context, as either declarative or interrogative: μεμέρισται ὁ Χριστός ("Christ is divided" or "Is Christ divided?"); μὴ Παῦλος ἐσταυρώθη ὑπὲρ ὑμῶν ("Paul was not crucified for you" or "Was not Paul crucified for you?"); and εἰς τὸ ὄνομα Παύλου ἐβαπτίσθητε ("You were baptized into the name of Paul" or "Were you baptized into the name of Paul?").[9] Grammar itself cannot tell us; context alone must suffice.

This closing passage of 8:31-39 has not only the neuter interrogative pronoun τί ("what") at its beginning, it also includes a fourfold repetition of the masculine interrogative pronoun τίς ("who") in 8:31c, 8:33a, 8:34a, and 8:35a.

---

8. See our discussions on these passages in chs. 3 and 4 above.
9. Cf. also John 16:31; Rom 14:22; 1 Cor 1:22; 2 Cor 3:1; Heb 10:2; Jas 2:4.

The immediate recognition of such a pattern of rhetorical questions followed by distinctive Christian responses would have been, it may be assumed, of great importance in Paul's oral preaching to pagan Gentiles in his evangelistic endeavors in the eastern portion of the Roman Empire. Further, it may be presumed that it would have been of continued relevance in his presentation of that proclamation in written form to his Christian addressees at Rome. So, it seems, Paul four times incorporated the interrogative pronoun τίς ("who") into his statements of 8:31c-35 in order to make clear, both to his original hearers and to his readers at Rome, how to understand a central feature of the structure of his presentation — that is, as structured in terms of four rhetorical questions that are followed by four Christian confessional responses. And amidst struggles by many present-day translators and commentators about how to punctuate and structure the materials of this passage, Paul's use of the masculine interrogative pronoun τίς ("who") offers, we believe, some guidance for a proper understanding of what he presents.

The Use of Early Christian Confessional Materials in the Passage. Many contemporary commentators hold that Paul, in some form or fashion, made use of various Christian confessional materials in 8:31-39 — particularly in 8:32-37. With reference to the statements in 8:32-33 about God giving up his Son for us all, graciously giving us everything in addition, and justifying his own people against the charges raised against them by other people, Ernst Käsemann has commented: "As is almost universally recognized today," these matters "come to expression . . . in confessional fragments."[10] On the statements in 8:34 about the death, resurrection, and intercession of Christ, Käsemann has further written: "A reminiscence of formulated material is probably also present in the expression about his own Son."[11]

Likewise, it may be argued that in response to Paul's rhetorical question of 8:35a, "Who shall separate us from the love of Christ?" the apostle incorporates in 8:35b-37 at least two early Christian formulaic pieces, which function to first dramatically focus on the question asked and then defiantly express the Christian response to that question. He first lists in 8:35b such highly antagonistic features as "trouble, hardship, persecution, famine, nakedness, danger, or sword," which list probably included in its earliest Christian form the citation of Ps 44:22 (LXX 43:22) in support, as appears in 8:36, and he then cites in 8:37 what may be assumed to have been a foundational Christian conviction: "We are more than conquerors through him who loved us."

The Structure of the Passage. Most translators and commentators have treated 8:31-39 in one of three ways: (1) as one extended paragraph; (2) as a thesis statement in 8:31, followed by two sets of questions and answers in 8:32-34 and 8:35-37 and then a concluding triumphal affirmation in 8:38-39; or (3) as

---

10. Käsemann, *Romans,* 247; cf. Cranfield, *Romans,* 1.436: "The traditional language of the primitive Church is echoed here."

11. Käsemann, *Romans,* 247.

three sets of rhetorical questions and their Christian answers, which appear in 8:31-32, 8:33-34, and 8:35-37, with a concluding affirmation in 8:38-39. All these proposals for the passage's structure have some merit, and all can be validated by various selected features in the material.

Rhetorically, however, the passage can be divided into two basic forms of ancient Greek oral speech and prose writing, which Aristotle (384-322 B.C.) called in his *Art of Rhetoric:* (1) the "extended," "continuous," or "running" (εἰρομένη) style, and (2) the "periodic" (ἐν περιόδοις) or the "contracted" or "compact" (κατεστραμμένη) style.[12] The "extended," "running," or "continuous" style is the most common rhetorical styling in the extant prose of ancient Greek authors (as well as in the prose materials of the NT), and appears in this final passage of Section II of the body middle of Paul's letter in 8:31-37. The second form is found in 8:38-39.[13]

The passage is most naturally divided into two subsections on the basis of subject matter: the first, in 8:31-34, asks such judicial questions as "Who can be against us?" "Who will bring any charge against God's elect?" and "Who can condemn?"; the second, in 8:35-39, begins with the rhetorical question, "What shall separate us from the love of Christ?" and concludes with a triumphant affirmation that nothing in heaven or on earth, as well as nothing in the whole range of human experience, "will be able to separate us from the love of God that is in Christ Jesus our Lord." Further, this final subsection of the passage begins in 8:35a by explicitly asking the question about any possible "separation" from "the love of Christ" and concludes in 8:39b by asserting that nothing in all creation is able to "separate" Christians from "the love of God that is in Christ Jesus our Lord" — with such a similarity of wording functioning as a literary *inclusio* that brackets all of what Paul writes in 8:35-39.[14] It is this understanding of the rhetorical features of the passage together with its somewhat differing subject matters — that takes into account not only the rhetorical styling of the passage but also its somewhat diverse subjects — that will guide our treatment of 8:35-39 in the exegetical comments that follow.

EXEGETICAL COMMENTS

Archibald Robertson has characterized 8:31-39 as "a brilliant oratorical passage, worthy of any orator in the world. . . . Here we have oratory of the highest kind with the soul all ablaze with great ideas."[15] In this passage we enter not only into the *logos* (i.e., the argument) of Paul's preaching to pagan Gentiles in the eastern

12. See Aristotle, *Rhetoric* 3.9 (1409a-b).

13. Cf. *ATRob,* 432; citing in support F. Blass, *Greek of the NT,* 275. See our development of this observation in the "Exegetical Comments" on 8:38-39 that follow.

14. So Balz, *Heilsvertrauen und Welterfahrung,* 117-18; Moo, *Romans,* 538-39.

15. *ATRob,* 1198, citing such other passages as Rom 6; 7; 9; 10; 11; 1 Cor 3; 4; 8; 9; 12; 13; 15; and 2 Cor 2; 3; 4; 5; 8; 10; 11; 13 as "almost equal to it," but not surpassing it.

part of the Roman empire, but also quite expressly into the *ethos* (i.e., the character of the speaker or writer) and the *pathos* (i.e., the power to stir emotions) of the apostle's presentation. He referred to this form of the Christian message as "my gospel" in 2:16 and 16:25, set it out in its basic features for his Christian addressees at Rome in 5:1–8:30, and wanted the believers in Jesus at Rome to accept it as a legitimate contextualization of the Christian gospel, and so join with him by their prayers and their financial support in his proposed mission to pagan Gentiles in Spain.

I. God's Vindication of and Care for People "in Christ Jesus" (8:31-34)

8:31-32 Paul begins this closing portion of Section II of the body middle of his letter to Rome with the same rhetorical question that he began the closing portion of Section I — τί οὖν ἐροῦμεν; ("What, then, shall we say?"). He used it in 4:1a to begin his presentation of Abraham as the example par excellence of faith,[16] and he uses it again here in 8:31a. Such a paralleling of rhetorical questions serves to highlight, even by itself, something about the purpose and the function of this twofold use of the question. Likewise, such a formal patterning suggests something about the concluding and hortatory nature of these two bodies of material that this same question introduces[17] — though more data on the concluding and hortatory nature of 8:31-39 will need to be taken into account in our exegetical comments on the passage itself, just as was done in our exegetical comments on Paul's treatment of Abraham in 4:1-24.

The use of the phrase πρὸς ταῦτα ("to these things" or "in response to these things") in 8:31a has sometimes been viewed as difficult to interpret. For the preposition πρός with an accusative noun usually expresses the idea of "motion to," as it does some 678 other times in the NT.[18] Yet, as Charles Moule has observed with respect to the meaning of πρός with the accusative ταῦτα here in 8:31a (as well as in a dozen other verses in the NT where the preposition is used with an accusative noun or pronoun): "In transferred senses, it means *tending towards, leading to, concerning, against, in view of.*"[19] Thus πρὸς ταῦτα in this verse denotes some such translation as "concerning" or "in view of these things" — though in the context of a passage that not only affirms but also exhorts, the

---

16. Cf. our discussion of Paul's use in this letter of this rhetorical question and its cognates in the introductory section ("Form/Structure/Setting") to Section I.

17. In discussing the relation of 8:31-39 to the materials earlier in 4:23-25 and those that appear later in 11:33-36, A. H. Snyman has aptly noted: "It seems to be a stylistic or *dispositio* feature that Paul often signals the end of a major section by inserting a perorative conclusion" ("Style and Rhetorical Situation of Romans 8:31-39," 228).

18. Cf. *Moule*, 52.

19. *Ibid.*, 53 (italics his). Professor Moule goes further in pp. 53-54 to identify the other twelve "transferred senses" of πρός with the accusative in the NT as being in Matt 19:8//Mark 10:5; Mark 12:12; Acts 23:30; Rom 8:18; 15:2; 1 Cor 6:1; 12:7; 2 Cor 5:10; Gal 2:14; Eph 4:14; and Heb 4:13.

phrase is probably even more accurately understood as connoting the idea of "*in response to* these things."

The question "What, then, shall we say in response to these things?" has as its premise what Paul has written earlier. Further, it functions to set up his answers that follow. It remains, however, to ask exactly what "things" Paul had in mind when he called on his pagan audiences in his Gentile mission — and his Christian addressees at Rome — to respond appropriately to "these things." Many interpreters have understood the apostle as here urging an appropriate response either (1) to his immediately previous statements in 8:28-30 (which speak about how God works all things together for good on behalf of his own people, because in responding positively to him through the work of Christ Jesus and the ministry of his Spirit they have become part of his eternal plan of salvation), or (2) to his much fuller proclamation of the Christian gospel as he has presented it throughout all of 1:16–8:30 (or, at least, in 3:21–8:30) — or both. Charles Cranfield has expressed his own view of the matter, as well as that of many other commentators down through the course of Christian history, in declaring:

> While the primary reference of "these things" in v. 31a is, no doubt, to what has just been said in vv. 29 (or 28)-30, it is clear from the contents of vv. 32-34 that it has also a wider reference, and that this sub-section serves not only as the conclusion of section V.4 [i.e., of Cranfield's outline of the letter, which section he identifies as 5:1–8:39] underlining the certainty of the Christian hope (the occurrence of the formula "in Christ Jesus our Lord" in v. 39 is a pointer to its being an integral part of V.4 [i.e., of Cranfield's outline] — compare 5.1, 11, 21; 6.23; 7.25), but also as a conclusion to the whole course of the theological exposition up to this point. The words "God is for us" in v. 31b are a concise summary not only of vv. 28-30 but also of 1.16b–8.30 (or, at the least, of 3.21–8.30).[20]

Our answer to this question regarding "the things" (ταῦτα) focuses on what we have identified as Paul's "spiritual gift" to his Christian addressees at Rome — that is, on his contextualized version of the Christian gospel, which he set out in its basic form in 5:1–8:39 (including these nine verses of affirmation and exhortation in 8:31-39). We have earlier argued that Section I (i.e., 1:16–4:25) and Section II (i.e., 5:1–8:39) of the body middle of Romans are not only distinguishable sections of his letter, but also discrete units of material. Likewise, we have observed that both Section I and Section II use the same rhetorical question, "What, then, shall we say?" in 4:1a and 8:31a to introduce their respective conclusions in 4:1b-24 and 8:31b-39 — which formal patterning carries with it certain implications regarding the respective nature and function of these two major sections of Paul's letter to Rome. Further, it has often

20. Cranfield, *Romans*, 1.434.

been pointed out that many of the themes in the transitional and thesis passage of Section II (i.e., in 5:1-11) are taken up again in the concluding units of that same major section of the letter (i.e., in 8:18-30 and 8:31-39), thereby setting up something of a rhetorical *inclusio* or type of "ring composition" — particularly the themes of "hope" (in 5:2 and 8:20-25), "the glory of God revealed" (in 5:2 and 8:18-21), "boasting in sufferings" (in 5:3 and 8:35-37), and "the love of God as demonstrated in the giving of Christ Jesus" (in 5:5 and 8:31-39).[21]

Thus we believe it best to understand Paul's reference to "these things" (ταῦτα) in 8:31a as having particularly in mind those relational, personal, and participatory features that he set out in the course of his presentations in 5:1–8:30 — which matters he viewed as constituting his own unique emphases in the proclamation of the Christian gospel, and therefore spoke of them in 2:16 and 16:25 as together constituting "my gospel" — that is, his proclamation of:

1. "Peace (i.e., 'completeness') with God," with "reconciliation" being a distinctive feature of the Christian experience (5:1-11).
2. The "grace" and "obedience" of "the one man, Jesus Christ" as countering the "sin" and "disobedience" of "the first man, Adam," thereby providing "righteousness" as a divine gift that is available to all who respond positively to God and what he has effected through Christ (5:12-21).
3. Being "in Christ" and "in the Spirit," with "Christ by his Spirit" being also in the believer (8:1-13).
4. Being "adopted by God" into his family, with all the rights and privileges of naturally born sons and daughters (8:14-17).
5. "Life in the Spirit," that is, life lived under the control of God's Spirit — with this new relationship bringing about a number of important implications for a Christian's understanding and living (8:18-30).

There can be little doubt that Paul himself believed in — and must have, as well, actually proclaimed in various Jewish Christian contexts (as evidenced particularly in 1:16–3:20) — such important themes as (1) "righteous" and "righteousness" being not only descriptive of God's person and actions, but also characteristic of what God gives as a gift to people who respond to him positively; (2) "justification," "redemption," and "propitiation" ("expiation" or "sacrifice of atonement"), which were important in the theology of Judaism and continued to be of great significance in the hearts and minds of all Jewish believers in Jesus; (3) the "faithfulness" of Jesus, Israel's Messiah and humanity's Lord, to God his Father; and (4) the necessity of "faith" and "faithfulness" by God's people, as exemplified by Abraham the man of faith par excellence. All these motifs Paul seems to have believed were present — at least in embryonic fashion — in the consciousness of the earliest believers in Jesus, in the theology of the mother church at Jerusalem, and in the thinking of his Christian addressees at Rome.

21. Cf. esp. Dahl, "Missionary Theology," appendix I, 88-89.

Yet it is the themes highlighted in Section II, that is, in 5:1–8:30, that he seems primarily to have had in mind when he asked those to whom he proclaimed the Christian gospel in his Gentile mission, as well as those to whom he wrote at Rome, to respond positively to in their thinking and in their living.[22]

Paul's own answer to his rhetorical question, "What, then, shall we say in response to these things?" is set out in a brief, straightforward, and rather defiant two-part conditional statement: "If God is for us, who can be against us?" The first part *(protasis)* of his statement is, in essence, a summation of all that he wrote in 5:1–8:30 — which, with the interrogative particle εἰ ("if") set in the context of an indicative statement, expresses the established fact that "God is for us!" It is a consciousness that the apostle wanted not only his own Gentile converts, but also all the Christians at Rome, to appreciate with clarity and to realize fully in their new lives "in Christ." For to have God "for us" (ὑπὲρ ἡμῶν) changes everything in one's life — not only in the lives of pagan Gentiles in the Roman Empire and the lives of believers in Jesus at Rome, but also in the lives of Christians today, who have come to God through the work of Christ Jesus and the ministry of God's Spirit.

The root meaning of the preposition ὑπέρ is "over," and so with an accusative noun or pronoun it is usually translated in the NT with some such idea included as "over," "above," or "beyond." With a genitive noun or pronoun, however, ὑπέρ is commonly translated "for," "for the sake of," "for the benefit of," "on behalf of," or "instead of" another. Yet in most of its NT uses the preposition ὑπέρ with a genitive noun or pronoun also incorporates the idea of "someone taking another's place" — though such a connotation "depends on the nature of the action" involved and not just on the preposition itself.[23] Thus while ὑπέρ ὑμῶν may quite rightly be translated as simply "for us" or "on our behalf," the context of the passage calls on the reader to understand "for us" or "on our behalf" in a more expanded fashion to mean "God has acted for us (or 'on our behalf') by taking our place."

The second part (or *apodosis*) of Paul's answer to the opening question is the further question, "Who can be against us?" which calls for an implied and rather defiant answer, "Nobody!" This assertion of question and implied answer is also a summation of all that the apostle wrote earlier in 5:1–8:30. And Paul supports that affirmation in 8:32 by what has every appearance of being a quotation drawn from some early Christian confessional portion, which expressed matters more fully by its own focused and challenging statement: "He [God] who even did not spare his own Son, but gave him up for us all, how will he not also along with him graciously give us everything else!"

Christians of the second and third centuries recognized in the wording

---

22. So a number of major commentators have also concluded, though for somewhat different reasons. See, e.g., Zahn, *An die Römer,* 422; Michel, *An die Römer,* 183; C. H. Dodd, *Romans,* 146; Schlier, *Römerbrief,* 276; Wilckens, *An die Römer,* 2.172; Käsemann, *Romans,* 246; Fitzmyer, *Romans,* 530; Moo, *Romans,* 539; and Jewett, *Romans,* 535.

23. Cf. *ATRob,* 630.

of 8:32a, God "did not spare his own Son" (τοῦ ἰδίου υἱοῦ οὐκ ἐφείσατο), an allusion to the statements of Gen 22:12 and 16, that Abraham "did not spare his beloved son" (οὐκ ἐφείσω τοῦ υἱοῦ σου τοῦ ἀγαπητοῦ).[24] Likewise, at least some early believers in Jesus seem to have viewed Isaac and his "sacrifice" as an anticipatory type of Jesus and his sacrifice on the cross.[25] Further, viewing this relationship from an explicitly Jewish perspective, Hans Joachim Schoeps proposed in 1946 that early Jewish believers in Jesus made use of a vicarious and substitutionary emphasis that appears in early rabbinic teaching on the *Akedah Isaac* ("Binding of Isaac") in which Isaac was viewed as a sacrifice Abraham willingly offered to God on behalf of the Jewish people — and from which rabbinic teaching the earliest Jewish Christians developed their own version of Jesus of Nazareth as God's promised Messiah who suffered vicariously for his people.[26]

The allusion in the wording of 8:32a to the statements of Gen 22:12 and 16 must be judged, we believe, as being at least "highly probable," as many contemporary commentators have suggested[27] — though some have viewed it as not at all likely, and others have simply ignored it. It does not follow, however, that accepting the presence of such an allusion necessarily supports the view that the earliest believers in Jesus saw Isaac as a prototype of Jesus — though the second-century writer of the *Epistle of Barnabas* 7:3 evidently saw it that way, as do also some earnest Christians today. Although a number of late-twentieth-century scholars have accepted, in varying degrees of commitment, the thesis of Hans Schoeps (1) that an early Jewish understanding of the *Akedah Isaac* included a vicarious, substitutionary atonement motif, and (2) that this feature was picked up by the earliest Jewish believers in Jesus and applied to their Messiah's sacrifice on the cross,[28] interpreters today are far less ready to accept such an understanding of relationships and developments.

Mainly because of the studies of Alan Segal and Joseph Fitzmyer, this thesis of Schoeps has been largely rejected. For Segal and Fitzmyer have not only documented the lack of any vicarious atonement features in early Jewish references to the biblical story of Isaac — that is, in references to the biblical story of Isaac in (1) the apocryphal and apocalyptic writings of Second Temple Judaism, (2) the philosophically oriented theological tractates of Philo, (3) the

24. Cf. Origen, *Homiliae in Genesim* 8 (*PG* 12.208); such a paralleling of expressions appears, as well, in Clement of Alexandria, Tertullian, and Irenaeus.

25. Cf. *Barn* 7:3: "He also Himself was to offer in sacrifice for our sins the vessel of the Spirit, in order that the type established in Isaac when he was offered upon the altar might be fully accomplished."

26. Cf. Schoeps, "The Sacrifice of Isaac in Paul's Theology," 385-92; see also *idem, Paul,* 141-49.

27. So, e.g., Cranfield, *Romans,* 436: "quite probably an intentional echo"; Wilckens, *An die Römer,* 2.172: "it cannot be contested"; Moo, *Romans,* 540 n. 18: "Paul may well intend an allusion to the Isaac incident."

28. Cf. esp. Dahl, "The Atonement," 15-29; see also Wood, "The Isaac Typology in the New Testament," 583-89; Wilcox, " 'Upon the Tree,' " 98-99; R. J. Daly, "The Soteriological Significance of the Sacrifice of Isaac," *CBQ* 39 (1977) 67.

polemically oriented historical works of Josephus, and (4) the teachings of the early Tannaitic rabbis recorded in the later Talmud and its associated rabbinical compositions — they have also pointed out that such vicarious motifs in the Isaac story can be found in Jewish writings only in the Amoraic period of rabbinical Judaism that dates about A.D. 200-500. Thus it cannot be claimed that such later Jewish speculations on the biblical story of Abraham "not sparing his beloved son" had any influence on the development of early Christian theology.

Joseph Fitzmyer has aptly summarized the situation as follows: "The real problem is whether Jewish teaching about the 'Aqedah (lit., the 'binding') was already understood with a vicarious soteriological connotation in pre-Christian Judaism. Was Isaac ever seen as a prototype of the Messiah? Of a Messiah who suffered vicariously for his people?" — and to these questions, Fitzmyer has answered "No!"[29] Further, Alan Segal, with whom Fitzmyer agrees, has suggested: "The amoraic tradition of the death and ashes of Isaac and his subsequent resurrection can be reasonably understood as an attempt to enrich Judaism with a figure that was as colourful as the one known to Christian exegesis."[30]

Two further, seemingly small exegetical features in 8:32, which have often been viewed as rather incidental, need also (at least briefly) be considered here, for they are both of real significance for a proper understanding of this statement. The first is the use of the enclitic particle γε at the beginning of 8:32. In its thirty other uses in the NT, γε appears in association with conjunctions or other particles and functions either (1) to limit or question the word or expression with which it is associated or (2) to intensify and highlight that associated word or expression. Thus γε serves in these cases to convey more of an emotional nuance than a strictly grammatical meaning, and so when translated (though often it is simply omitted) it is usually rendered by some such English particle as "still" or "even."

Here in 8:32, however, appears the only instance in the NT where the particle γε is associated with the masculine relative pronoun ὅς ("who," "he who"). By the joining of the two (whether it was done by some early Christian author or by Paul himself), this small particle inserts into the passage the emotional idea of "even" with respect to God's action of not sparing his own Son but giving him up for us all — that is, it functions to lay emphasis on how great was God's gift of his own Son on humanity's behalf. Such a highlighting of God's action was evidently of great importance not only to the earliest believers in Jesus but also to Paul — and it continues to be of significance for Christians today.

A second, somewhat small yet important exegetical feature in 8:32 is the use at the end of the verse of the articular neuter plural phrase τὰ πάντα, which appears to be an idiomatic expression of that day and so must be understood in

---

29. Fitzmyer, *Romans*, 531.

30. Segal, "He Who Did Not Spare His Own Son," 183. Cf. also Davies and Chilton, "The Aqedah," 46, who argue that "the conception [of a vicarious feature in the story of Isaac] is post-Tannaitic."

terms of its immediate context. The neuter singular phrase τὸ πᾶν, which signals some such meaning as "the whole" or "the totality," is found only a couple of times in the NT. The plural τὰ πάντα, however, which is based on the singular τὸ πᾶν, appears a number of times elsewhere in Romans and in the Corinthian letters to signify "the sum total of things" or "everything" — with the context of each passage needing to be taken into account to identify the expression's reference.[31] Here in 8:31-32 the context has to do with God being "for us" *in the present* because of what he has already done "for us all" through the work of Christ *in the past* — and the focus of Paul's presentation in the material that immediately follows in 8:33-34 is also on *the present*, with that discussion being about God's *present* justifying of his people against all human charges and about Christ's *present* intercession "for us" before God.[32] Thus the articular phrase τὰ πάντα here in 8:32, which can be translated simply as "everything," should probably be more accurately understood — based on what God has already done for humanity in the past — as connoting "everything else" that God desires to give to his people and do for them.[33]

8:33-34 The second series of questions and answers, in 8:33-34, restates in other words the question of 8:31c ("Who can be against us?") and expands more fully the answer of 8:32 regarding God's gift of his own Son and "along with him" also "everything else." The two rhetorical questions of 8:33a ("Who will bring any charge against God's elect?") and 8:34a ("Who can condemn?") both carry with them, as did the rhetorical question of 8:31c, the implied answer "Nobody!" And their two respective, confessional answers of 8:33b and 8:34b explicate matters more fully regarding both God and Christ Jesus. Thus these questions and answers of 8:33-34 must be tied closely to the question and answer of 8:31c-32, for together they serve the same purpose and function in the same manner.

A major issue about the focus of 8:33-34 has been whether the two questions and answers of this passage have to do with (1) a future, eschatological judgment scenario, where Satan — as well as, perhaps, one's own sins — makes accusations against believers in Jesus and God defends them,[34] or (2) the present opposition and oppression by nonbelievers against Christians vis-à-vis God's defense of his own people on the basis of the past and present work of Christ Jesus.[35] Of importance in determining this matter, as Robert Jewett has aptly pointed out, are the facts that (1) the legal term ἐγκαλεῖν ("to impeach," "bring charges against") is "used elsewhere in the NT only in public trials depicted

31. Cf. Rom 11:36; 1 Cor 11:12; 12:6 and 19.

32. See our exegetical comments on 8:33-34 below.

33. So NRSV: "everything else"; see also Moffatt: "everything besides"; Phillips: "everything else that we can need."

34. So, e.g., Leenhardt, *Romans*, 237; Barrett, *Romans*, 173; Schlier, *Römerbrief*, 277; Dunn, *Romans*, 1.502; Stuhlmacher, *Romans*, 138; Moo, *Romans*, 541-42.

35. So, e.g., Käsemann, *Romans*, 248: "The future is not eschatological but logical"; cf. also Jewett, *Romans*, 539.

in Acts 19:38, 40; 23:29; 26:2, 7," and (2) "nowhere else in the OT, the NT, or associated literature is this verb employed in connection with eschatological judgment."[36] Thus it may legitimately be argued that the focus in 8:33-34, just as it was in 8:31-32, is on *the present* — with the two rhetorical questions and their two respective confessional responses having to do with God's *present* justifying of his own people against all human opposition and charges.

In the question of 8:33a ("Who will bring any charge against God's elect?") there appears for the first time in the letter the designation ἐκλεκτοὶ θεοῦ ("the elect/chosen ones of God" or "God's elect") with application to believers in Jesus — though (1) earlier in 8:30 Paul had spoken of Christians as those "God has called" (ἐκάλεσεν), with the stems of the verb in 8:30 and the substantival adjective in 8:33a being closely associated; (2) later in 16:13 he will identify Rufus as τὸν ἐκλεκτὸν ἐν κυρίῳ ("elect/chosen in the Lord"); and (3) still later in the Pauline corpus of NT letters, as well as in some other NT letters, the expression ἐκλεκτοὶ θεοῦ ("the elect/chosen ones of God" or "God's elect") will be used as a title for believers in Jesus.[37] The title was, of course, used in the Jewish (OT) Scriptures for those who had been chosen by God as his special people, that is, the people of Israel.[38] In his letter to Rome, however, Paul begins to use "the elect/chosen ones of God" or "God's elect" as applicable to all believers in Jesus, whatever their ethnicity. This use of such a revered title may have been somewhat offensive to Jewish believers in Jesus, as well as to some Christian congregations composed of both Jewish and Gentile believers who had been extensively influenced by Jewish Christianity (as were the Christians at Rome, as we have proposed). So in Section III of the body middle of the letter (9:1–11:36), Paul considers it necessary to spell out in some detail (1) the relations that exist between these two communities of "God's elect/chosen ones," and (2) how matters are to be understood in the working out of God's salvation history.

II. The Impossibility of Ever Being Separated from the Love of Christ and Therefore from the Love of God (8:35-39)

8:35-37 The final rhetorical question of 8:31-39 begins with the masculine interrogative pronoun τίς ("who"), just as did the earlier rhetorical questions of 8:31c, 8:33a, and 8:34a. Yet, since the adversities listed in 8:35b are all expressed in English as neuter features that are opposed to a person's well-being (i.e., "trouble," "hardship," "persecution," "famine," "nakedness," "danger," and "sword"), it is necessary to translate the Greek masculine interrogative pronoun τίς in 8:35a by the English neuter interrogative pronoun "what."

---

36. Cf. Jewett, *Romans,* 539; citing, in particular, Exod 22:9 (LXX); Prov 19:3 (LXX); and Zech 1:4 (LXX), as well as Sir 46:19 and 2 Macc 6:21, which speak of humans making charges against their fellow humans; also Wis 12:12, which refers to humans attempting to impeach God.

37. See Col 3:12; 2 Tim 2:10; Titus 1:1; cf. also 1 Pet 1:1; 2:9; 2 John 13.

38. So, e.g., in 1 Chr 16:13; Ps 89:3; 105:6, 43; Isa 65:9, 15, 23.

The list of personal difficulties set out in 8:35b can be paralleled by Paul's list of adversities in 1 Cor 4:9-13 ("condemned to die," "made a spectacle," "fools for Christ," "considered weak," "dishonored," "hungry," "thirsty," "in rags," "brutally treated," "homeless," "cursed," "persecuted," "slandered," and "considered the scum of the earth, the refuse of the world") — likewise by his listing of afflictions and distresses in 2 Cor 11:23-29 ("in prison," "flogged," "exposed to death," "lashed," "beaten with rods," "stoned," "shipwrecked," "in danger from rivers," "in danger from bandits," "in danger from my own countrymen," "in danger from Gentiles," "in danger in the city," "in danger in the country," "in danger at sea," "in danger from false brothers," "hungry," "thirsty," "cold," "naked," and "being concerned for all the churches").[39] Such lists of personal hardships were, it seems, rather common among the philosophers, the sages, and religious teachers of Paul's day. They were set out not only by Greco-Roman Stoic, Epicurean, and Cynic philosophers, but also by Jewish rabbis and sectarian writers — to highlight both their own virtues and the divine power that lay behind their teachings.[40] Paul's lists of adversities and afflictions, however, were not for the purpose of self-praise or self-aggrandizement; rather, they were "to demonstrate his congruence with the suffering Christ."[41]

Here in 8:35-37 Paul uses a pattern of question and answer that is similar to the pattern he used in 8:31-34 (as well as the one he often used in Section I of the body middle of the letter in such subsections as 2:3-11, 3:1-8, 3:9-18, and 4:1-8) — that is, first he states a question mainly in his own words and then a response drawn largely from earlier traditional material. Such a patterning is not always rigidly expressed. Yet Paul seems to think generally in this fashion. So here in 8:35-37 it may be postulated that:

1. The rhetorical question of 8:35a, "What can separate us from the love of Christ?" is stated in Paul's own words.
2. The list of potential obstacles to "the love of God that is in Christ Jesus our Lord" in 8:35b (i.e., "trouble or hardship or persecution or famine or nakedness or danger or sword") is drawn from some early Christian confessional portion.
3. The biblical material in 8:36 (i.e., "for your sake we face death all day long; we are considered as sheep to be slaughtered"), which is drawn from Ps 44:22 (LXX 43:22) in support of the immediately previous list of potential obstacles, was included in that early Christian confessional portion and simply quoted by Paul as he found it.
4. The introduction to the confessional response given in 8:37a (i.e., "in all of these things, however,") is expressed in Paul's own words.

39. Cf. also the briefer lists of adversities and distresses in 2 Cor 6:4-5 and Phil 4:12.
40. For an extended discussion of such ancient endeavors, with appropriate bibliographies, see Jewett, *Romans*, 544-46.
41. *Ibid.*, 545, citing H. D. Betz's analysis of such "catalogues of hardship" in his *Der Apostel Paulus und die sokratische Tradition*, BHT 45 (Tübingen: Mohr Siebeck, 1972), 74-89.

5. The concluding statement of 8:37b, "We are more than conquerors through him who loved us!" is a triumphal affirmation that Paul quotes from some other early Christian confessional material.

However one analyzes the structure of 8:35-37, the two most important points that come to the fore in these verses are:

1. The reality of a Christian's personal identification with the suffering Christ, as experienced both by Paul and by all Christians. This is signaled by the plural personal pronoun "we" (ἡμᾶς) in 8:35 and by the plural pronominal suffixes "we" in the verbs θανατούμεθα ("we face death") and ἐλογίσθημεν ("we are considered") in 8:36.
2. The triumphal note in response to such an awesome catalogue of personal adversities, with that triumph in the face of all sorts of hardships and difficulties having been experienced by Paul himself and available to all believers in Jesus as well: "We are more than conquerors through him who loved us!" This is highlighted by the plural pronominal suffix "we" in the verb ὑπερνικῶμεν ("we are more than conquerors") and by the plural personal pronoun "us" (ἡμᾶς) in 8:37.

The expression ὑπερνικάω ("I am more than conqueror" or "a supervictor") is a heightened form of the noun νίκη ("victor," "conqueror," or "prevailer") and the verb νικάω ("I am victor," "conqueror," or "prevailer") — which word with its preposition ὑπέρ appears only here in the NT at 8:37 (though later in 12:2 Paul will use the roughly synonymous dative singular ἀνακαινώσει, "be transformed," as a strong word of exhortation). The aorist participial phrase διὰ τοῦ ἀγαπήσαντος ἡμᾶς ("through the One who loved us") has in mind the love of God the Father as expressed particularly in his own Son's death on the cross — as referred to earlier in 8:32 ("He who even did not spare his own Son, but gave him up for us all!") and in 8:34a ("It is Christ Jesus who died!"). A Christian's confidence in the face of personal adversity, therefore, as well as one's ability to be a victor in the midst of opposition and oppression, is not based on one's own human skills or strategic actions, but rests entirely in the hands of "the One [God] who loved us" so much as to "not spare his own Son, but gave him up for us all!"

8:38-39 Paul writes here an excellent example of what Aristotle called a "periodic" (ἐν περιόδοις) and "contracted" or "compact" (κατεσταμμένη) style of Greek rhetoric, whether spoken or written[42] — that is, a rhetorical styling that incorporates a series of parts or units (so "periodic") that are closely joined together in a manner that is neither diffuse nor verbose (so "contracted" or "compact"). This form of expression would have been highly memorable for pagan Gentiles who heard Paul preach and for believers in Jesus at Rome who

---

42. Aristotle, *Rhetoric* 3.9 (1409a-b), as noted above in "The Structure of the Passage" in our introductory section "Form/Structure/Setting."

read his letter — as well as for a vast number of Christians down through the centuries who have viewed 8:38-39 as the apex of Paul's message in this his most famous letter. His closing reference to "the love of God that is in Christ Jesus our Lord" in 8:39b is very similar to his reference to "the love of Christ" in the opening question of 8:35a. It may, in fact, be reasonably argued that these two statements — together with the use of the verb χωρίζω ("divide," "separate") in both verses — form something of a rhetorical *inclusio,* and therefore that this subsection of 8:35-39 (even though part of the passage is written in one rhetorical style and part in another) is best understood as constituting one unit of concluding material.

The enumeration of potential obstacles to God's never-ending love for people who are "in Christ Jesus" — that is, nine quite expansive matters that have to do with "death," "life," "angels," "demons," "things present," "things to come," "powers," "height," and "depth," which are followed by a tenth all-inclusive matter that has to do with "anything else in all creation" — gives to Paul's affirmation what Archibald Robertson has called "a kind of solemn dignity."[43] Such a listing has rhetorically been called a *polysyndeton.*[44] Some ancient scribes evidently thought the matters cited and/or their sequence in Paul's list needed improvement, so they proposed a few other matters and some other sequences between "neither angels (ἄγγελοι) nor demons (ἀρχαί)" and "neither height (ὕψωμα) nor depth (βάθος)" (see "Textual Notes"). But the better papyrus, uncial, and minuscule manuscripts, and such early Church Fathers as Origen, Eusebius, Jerome, and Augustine, seem decisively to favor the list as commonly set out in contemporary translations and as represented in our translation above. Further, while in Gal 1:6b-7a Paul makes a distinction between the adjectives ἄλλος ("other" or "another [of the same kind]") and ἕτερος ("other" or "another [of a different kind]"),[45] here in 8:39 the plural adjective ἑτέρα, which is used in substantive fashion, means not "another of a different kind" but "anything else of the same kind."[46]

The message of this final, periodic, and personalized affirmation that Paul sets out in 8:38-39 is, as Joseph Fitzmyer has expressed matters, the underlying conviction of all truly Christian thought, life, and proclamation:

> The love of God poured out in the Christ-event is the basis of Christian life and hope. No created being or force can unsettle that foundation. In all of the uncertainty of human, earthly life there is something fixed and certain, [that is,] Christ's love and God's election. These are unshakable; and Christians must learn to trust in them and take them for granted.[47]

43. *ATRob,* 427.
44. Cf. similar uses of *polysyndeton* in Rom 9:4; see also Matt 15:19; 1 Tim 1:9-10; Rev 5:12; 7:12.
45. So also 2 Cor 11:4.
46. So also Gal 1:19 and 1 Cor 15:39-41.
47. Fitzmyer, *Romans,* 536.

Such a proclamation provides a fitting conclusion to all that Paul preached to pagans in his Gentile mission and to all that he wrote to Christians in Section II of the body middle of his letter to Rome. More than that, it offers to believers in Jesus today the heart and soul of the Christian message and calls on us to live out our lives in the context of this God-given reality.

BIBLICAL THEOLOGY

In reading Romans, interpreters of various Christian denominations, allegiances, and commitments have frequently (1) highlighted one particular theme or motif in the letter, (2) understood that theme or motif as being the central, organizing feature of everything in the letter (as well as in many of Paul's other NT letters), and (3) declared that central theme or motif to have been the primary and controlling factor in all his Christian theology. Such a focusing on one central theme or organizing motif has been done with respect to what Paul has written in Section I of the body middle of the letter (i.e., in 1:16–4:25) — particularly highlighting one or another of such matters in that section as: (1) his use of the terms "the righteousness of God," "righteous," and "righteousness" (as in 1:17; 3:5; 3:21-26); (2) his employment of the expression "salvation" (as in 1:16; see also 10:10; 11:11; 13:11); (3) his picking up of the Jewish and Jewish Christian forensic metaphors of "justification," "redemption," and "propitiation/expiation/sacrifice of atonement" in speaking of the situation of believers in Jesus (as in 3:24-25; 5:1, 9); (4) his teaching that relationship with God is "now apart from the law" (as in 3:20 and 21); and/or (5) his insistence on "faith" as the only proper response to God's love, mercy, and grace (as in 3:26; 3:27-31; 4:1-24). Likewise, such a focusing has been done with respect to what the apostle wrote in Section II (i.e., in 5:1–8:39) — laying emphasis on one or another of such matters in that section as: (1) his reference to "peace" (as in 5:1); (2) his use of the metaphor "reconciliation" (as in 5:10-11); (3) his emphasis on the "grace" and "obedience" of Christ Jesus as countering the "sin" and "disobedience" of Adam, thereby providing righteousness as a divine gift available to all who respond positively to God and to what he has effected through the work of Christ and the ministry of the Spirit (as in 5:12-21); (4) his exposition on being "in Christ" and "in the Spirit," with "Christ by his Spirit" being also in the believer (as in 8:1-13); (5) his use of the Greco-Roman legal and familial term "adoption" to characterize the Christian's status in the family of God, including all the rights and privileges of naturally born sons and daughters (as in 8:14-17); and/or (6) his teaching on "life in the Spirit," that is, life lived under the control of God's Spirit — with this new relationship bringing about a number of important implications for a Christian's understanding and life (as in 8:18-30). Such a highlighting of individual themes or motifs has also been done by a number of interpreters for Section III (9:1–11:36) and Section IV (12:1–15:13) of the body middle of the letter; these will be pointed out in the "Exegetical Comments" on these two sections that follow.

Many interpreters of Romans have either (1) atomized what Paul writes in this his most famous letter, bringing everything under only one particular theme or motif (or, one set of themes or motifs) that he sets out in the letter, or (2) been somewhat at a loss to understand the coherence of what he has written, highlighting only a certain theme or motif (or, a certain set of themes and motifs) in his letter and tending to pass over much else that appears in it. Ernst Käsemann, however, has quite appropriately commented on the overall unity of Paul's presentations in the letter: "Notwithstanding widespread views to the contrary, the apostle constructed the epistle very carefully and structured it systematically."[48] It is to such a "careful construction" and such a "systematic structuring" that we must look as we attempt to spell out what Paul has written in Romans and to build on that exegesis for our own biblical theology today.

At the conclusion of each of the subsections in Section II we have commented on the need to incorporate the themes and motifs that appear in that particular subsection into our own constructions of Christian theology today. Here in these affirmations of 8:31-39 Paul not only sets out in dramatic fashion the conclusion to all that he has presented in the second major section of his letter's body middle, he also identifies the basic convictions that underlie all of what he has written throughout 5:1–8:30:

1. God is not a deity who needs to be — or, in fact, can be — propitiated by any human endeavor or religious activity (as he has denounced throughout 2:1–3:20), but rather, "God is for us" (as he proclaims in 8:31b).
2. God has demonstrated his great concern for all people by the fact that "he even did not spare his own Son, but gave him up for us all" (as expressed in Jesus' life of faithfulness and his sacrificial death on the cross) — and further, by "graciously giving us, along with him, everything else that we need" (as he proclaims in 8:32).
3. No one can "bring any charge against" or "condemn" God's people, for it is "God himself who justifies [them]" and it is "Christ Jesus who has died, been raised to life, and now is at the right hand of God interceding [for them]" (as he proclaims in 8:33-34).
4. No circumstance, event, or person "in all creation" is able to separate God's "elect people" who are "in Christ" from "the love of God that is in Christ Jesus our Lord" (as he proclaims in 8:35-39).

These are the basic convictions — as well as the resultant conclusions — that must underlie, provide the framework for, and come to expression in every Christ-centered biblical theology.

48. Käsemann, *Romans,* 246; though, of course, his thesis is in some of its details quite different from mine.

CONTEXTUALIZATION FOR TODAY

In writing to the Christians at Rome, Paul focused in 5:1–8:39 on the soterio-logical themes of "peace with God," "reconciliation," "being in Christ," "being in the Spirit," "Christ by his Spirit being in the Christian," and "adopted by God into his family" — evidently believing (1) that this language of "peace," "reconciliation," being "in Christ," being "in the Spirit," and "adoption" connoted features that were both more theologically profound and more ethically significant, and (2) that these ways of proclaiming the message of the Christian gospel resonated better with non-Jews in his Gentile mission than the more traditional soteriological language of the Jews or the Jewish Christians. Yet, while it seems that in his Gentile mission Paul preferred to proclaim such personal, relational, and participatory themes as "peace," "reconciliation," "being in Christ," "being in the Spirit," and "adoption by God," it also appears — to judge by Luke's portrayals of his preaching in Acts and his own use of Scripture in at least one instance in Section I of the body middle of the letter — that he had no aversion in particular circumstances to call for people's "repentance" and to proclaim God's "forgiveness" — as seen in (1) his sermon to members of a Jewish synagogue at Antioch of Pisidia (cf. Acts 13:24, 38); (2) his denunciation of pagan idolatry at Athens (cf. Acts 17:30); (3) his words to Agrippa, who was a Roman ruler who knew something about the Jewish (OT) Scriptures and had been influenced by Jewish thought and customs (cf. Acts 26:18, 20); and (4) his quotation of Ps 32:1-2 to the Christians at Rome, who had been extensively influenced by the theology and language of Jewish Christianity (cf. Rom 4:7-8).

God's forgiveness of repentant sinners is a central theme in the OT. At Mount Sinai God proclaimed himself "merciful and gracious, slow to anger, and abounding in steadfast love and faithfulness, . . . *forgiving* iniquity and transgression and sin" (Exod 34:6-7). Levitical legislation had as its purpose God's forgiveness of his people's sins (cf. Lev 4:20, 26, 31, 35; 5:10, 13, 16, 18; 6:7; 19:22; Num 15:25, 26, 28). The OT psalmists repeatedly praise God because he forgives his people's sins (cf. Pss 86:5; 102:2-3; 130:4). The cry of Israel's prophets often incorporated some such request as "O Lord, hear; O Lord, *forgive;* O Lord, listen and act and do not delay!" (Dan 9:19), or "O Lord God, *forgive,* I beg you!" (Amos 7:2). And the prophetic vision of "a new covenant" that God would make with his people, as expressed in Jer 31:31-34, concludes with this significant promise: "I will *forgive* their iniquity, and remember their sin no more" (v. 34).

In the Synoptic Gospels, the themes of "repentance" and "forgiveness" appear frequently as highly important features in the stories of Jesus and his ministry. They are, for example, to be found in (1) the prophecy of Zechariah about the future ministry of his infant son John, which includes the statement that God "will give knowledge of salvation to his people by the *forgiveness* of their sins" (Luke 1:77); (2) the characterization of the ministry of John the Baptist as proclaiming "a baptism of *repentance* for the *forgiveness* of sins" (Mark 1:4// Luke 3:3; cf. Matt 3:7-8, 11; Acts 13:24; 19:4); (3) the prayer that Jesus taught his disciples to pray (the so-called Lord's Prayer), which includes the coupling together of God's *forgiveness* of sins and his people's *forgiveness* of others (cf. Luke 11:4//Matt 6:12); (4) Jesus' ethical teaching, which includes the specific commands "If there is *repentance,* you must *forgive!*" and "If a person sins against you seven times a day, and turns back to you seven times and says, 'I *repent,*' you must *forgive!*" (Luke 17:3-4); (5) Jesus' words at the Last Supper, as given in Matthew's Gospel: "This is my blood of the covenant, which is poured out for many for the *forgiveness* of sins" (Matt 26:28); (6) Jesus' prayer on the cross for those who crucified him, as expressed in Luke's Gospel: "Father, *forgive* them; for they do not know what they are doing" (Luke 23:34); and (7) Jesus' postresurrection words to his disciples, as also depicted in Luke's Gospel: "Thus it is written, that the Messiah is to suffer and to rise from the dead on the third day, and that *repentance* and *forgiveness* of sins is to be proclaimed in his name to all nations, beginning from Jerusalem" (Luke 24:46-47).

These twin themes also appear prominently in the Acts of the Apostles — as, for example, in Peter's preaching on the Day of Pentecost, which concluded with an appeal and a promise: "*Repent,* and be baptized every one of you in the name of Jesus Christ so that your sins may be *forgiven;* and you will receive the gift of the Holy Spirit" (Acts 2:38); as well as in the second defense of Peter and "the apostles" before the Jewish Sanhedrin, which includes the following significant proclamation: "God exalted him [Jesus] at his right hand as Leader and Savior that he might give *repentance* to Israel and *forgiveness* of sins" (Acts 5:31). Further, Peter's message to Cornelius and his household closes with the significant affirmation: "All the prophets testify about him [Jesus] that everyone who believes in him receives *forgiveness* of sins through his name" (Acts 10:43).

In the Johannine literature, however, the term "forgive" (in its verbal form) appears only in the words of Jesus in John 20:23 and then twice more in 1 John 1:9 and 2:12. Paul's letters also are almost devoid of references to "repentance" (the noun appears only in Rom 2:4, "God's kindness is meant to lead you to *repentance,*" and in 2 Cor 7:9, "your grief led to *repentance*"); likewise, his letters are almost devoid of references to "forgiveness" (the noun appears only in the quotation of Ps 32:1 in Rom 4:7, and then later in Eph 1:7 and Col 1:14). Yet, in a number of places in Luke's depictions of Paul's ministry in Acts, Paul is portrayed as (1) calling for "repentance" (Acts 13:24; 17:30; 26:20), (2) proclaiming God's "forgiveness" through the work and person of Jesus (Acts 13:38; 26:18), and (3) speaking generally of his preaching of the Christian gospel as a proclamation of "repentance" (Acts 20:21).

In speaking of God's salvation, Paul used such Jewish and Jewish Christian forensic expressions as "justification" and "righteousness" (which in Hebrew and Greek are the same word; cf. esp. Rom 1:17; 3:21-22, 25; 5:1a, 16-21; 2 Cor 5:21). But he also viewed his own personal, relational, and participatory experiences of "peace with God" (cf. Rom 5:1b, passim), "reconciliation" (cf. Rom 5:11; 11:15; 2 Cor 5:18-20), being "in Christ Jesus" and "in the Spirit" (cf. Rom 8:1-17; Gal 3:26-28, passim), and being "adopted" by God into his family (cf. Rom

8:15, 23; 9:4; Gal 4:5; Eph 1:5) as more theologically significant, more personally compelling, and more ethically life changing than the Jewish and Jewish Christian soteriological, forensic metaphors of "justification," "redemption," and "propitiation" (or, "expiation" or "sacrifice of atonement") — and as being even more important for his Gentile audiences than the traditional religious themes of "repentance" and "forgiveness."

Thus Paul must be seen in his Gentile mission — as he himself has reported here in this second major section of the body middle of the letter (i.e., in 5:1–8:39) — as having presented the Christian message in a manner that was particularly meaningful to his non-Jewish audiences. It is a contextualization of the Christian message that was (1) founded on the basic truths of the Christian gospel and (2) presented in terms of the understanding, situation, and needs of those being addressed — just as he had earlier proclaimed and developed the gospel message in the first section of the body middle of the letter (i.e., in 1:16–4:25) in a manner that would be understood and meaningful to believers in Jesus at Rome, who, it appears, had been extensively influenced by the theological understandings and religious language of Jewish Christianity as centered in the mother church at Jerusalem. And the apostle's somewhat different modes of Christian proclamation in these two instances provide both a paradigm and a challenge for our own Christian proclamation today — that is, for a proclamation of the Christian message that is (1) founded on the essentials of the Christian gospel and (2) contextualized for the understanding, situation, and needs of those being addressed.

VI. Section III: The Christian Gospel
vis-à-vis God's Promises to Israel (9:1–11:36)

The third major section of the body middle of Paul's letter to the Christians at Rome, that is, 9:1–11:36, has often been viewed as a discrete and self-contained body of material. Further, questions have frequently been asked regarding (1) the provenance of the material that appears in these three chapters and (2) how this section of Paul's letter is related to the earlier theological sections of 1:16–4:25 and 5:1–8:39, as well as to the following hortatory section of 12:1–15:13.

Some have speculated that 9:1–11:36 was originally a separate letter or a tractate of Paul that was in some way physically associated with the apostle's letter to Rome in an early "copy book" kept by one of his friends or amanuenses, either appearing immediately after Romans in that copy book or exhibiting a similar handwriting, or both — and that this letter or tractate was later inserted by some undiscerning scribe into what we now have as "To the Romans."[1] Others have postulated that 9:1–11:36 was an interpolation by Paul himself into the text of his letter to Rome; it was originally a sermon he preached orally at some earlier time or a treatise he wrote earlier for some reason that he had with him when he wrote Romans — but which in its present placement has no necessary connection with what he wrote elsewhere in the letter.[2] A variant of this latter understanding has been offered by Robin Scroggs, who argued (1) that 9:1–11:36, because of its rhetorical similarity to 1:16–4:25 (including a similar use of OT Scripture), should most likely be viewed as having been originally joined with 1:16–4:25, with these two sections together representing an early sermon by the apostle to a Jewish audience, but (2) that the

---

1. À la Deissmann's "copy book" thesis in his *Light from the Ancient East,* 235-36; see also 206 n. 1.

2. So, e.g., C. H. Dodd, *Romans,* 148: "Chaps. ix-xi form a compact and continuous whole, which can be read quite satisfactorily without reference to the rest of the epistle, though it naturally gains by such reference, just as other parts of the epistle gain by being read alongside Galatians or I Corinthians." Cf. also A. M. Hunter, *Introduction to the New Testament* (London: SCM, 1945), 96: "Paul may have written this section earlier as a separate discussion of a vexed question. It forms a continuous whole and may be read without reference to the rest of the letter"; see also J. A. T. Robinson, *Wrestling with Romans,* 6 and 108-10.

connection between these two parts of Paul's Jewish-oriented sermon was at some early time (and for some unknown reason) broken, with the result that what now appears as 9:1-11:36 became coupled with what is written in 5:1-8:39 — and having been brought together, was circulated among various early Christian communities as two parts of Paul's letter to believers in Jesus at Rome.[3] Most interpreters from patristic times to the present, however, have viewed 9:1-11:36 as having been always an integral part of Paul's letter to the Christians at Rome and as always positioned in its present location. Yet opinions have varied regarding (1) how what is set out in this section of the letter should be understood and (2) how this section is related to what has gone before and to what follows.

The usual ways of interpreting 9:1-11:36 by commentators today — and particularly the ways of interpreting what the apostle has written in 9:6-29 — may be set out as follows:

1. A *theological* understanding that highlights God's "sovereign grace" in the salvation of people, as can be found especially in the writings of Augustine during the final decade of the fourth century and the first three decades of the fifth century[4] — coupled with an emphasis on God's predestination of

---

3. Cf. Scroggs, "Paul as Rhetorician," 271-98.

4. Aurelius Augustine (354-430) is best known for his mature writings during the latter three decades of his very prolific life — such as *The City of God,* a work on the Synoptic problem *(De consensu evangelistarum),* and massive commentaries on the Psalms and John's Gospel. Earlier in 391, however, shortly after he was ordained a presbyter in the diocese of Hippo, North Africa, Augustine was asked a number of questions about Romans by attendees at a conference held in Carthage. He responded by giving a series of short exegetical comments on the topic of "God's sovereign grace" that were based principally on Paul's statements in Rom 5-9, which comments he later grouped into eighty-four sections and published in 394 as *Expositio quarundam propositionum ex Epistula ad Romanos* (PL 35.2063-88).

So enraptured was Augustine by Paul's teaching on God's grace that he determined to undertake a full-blown commentary of Romans, which he began also about 394. It seems that he planned to write a fairly extensive commentary on the letter, for his exposition of the salutation in 1:1-7 takes up about eighteen columns in Migne's *Patrologia Latina* (see his *Epistulae ad Romanos inchoata expositio, PL* 35.2087-2106). But after commenting on these first seven verses, Augustine felt unable to proceed further. The project, he said, was just too large for him, and therefore he would return to "easier tasks" (see his *Retractationes* 1.25). Yet, while a careful exegesis of the whole of Romans would undoubtedly have been of great importance for all his subsequent life and teaching, Augustine was, as David Bentley-Taylor has aptly noted, "no doubt right in thinking that his talent was for the pastoral application of Scripture rather than for detailed, scholarly exposition, for which his ignorance of Hebrew and limited knowledge of Greek were severe handicaps" (D. Bentley-Taylor, *Augustine: Wayward Genius* [Grand Rapids: Baker, 1981], 70).

In late 396 or early 397 Augustine wrote two extended letters to his friend Simplicius on the subjects of God's sovereign grace and the predestination of the elect, which letters evidence how his understanding of God's grace and predestination was developing (cf. his *De diversis quaestionibus ad Simplicianum, PL* 40.102-47). It was this topic of God's grace that continued to dominate all of Augustine's thought and all of his mature writings until his death in 430 — and which, of course, redirected much of Christian theology thereafter.

"the elect," as set out in Augustine's later writings and developed further by John Calvin in the sixteenth century.

2. A *theological* understanding that highlights the theme of humanity's God-given "free will," as appeared in the writings of Origen in the third century, John Chrysostom in the fourth century, and Jacob Arminius in the sixteenth century.

3. A *salvation history* understanding, which views these chapters as Paul's presentation of the course of redemptive history vis-à-vis that of Judaism or Jewish Christianity, as proposed by Oscar Cullmann and Johannes Munck (though in quite different ways).

4. A *history of religions* or *comparative religions* understanding, which interprets these chapters as proclaiming that the existence of both Judaism and Christianity is in accord with God's will and under his approval, as proposed by Krister Stendahl.

5. An *apologetic* understanding that treats these chapters as Paul's vindication of God's actions in redeeming some people and condemning others (i.e., a "theodicy"), which understanding has occasionally been argued separately[5] but has also been frequently incorporated into one or more of the other positions cited above.

Without denying the validity of some of the highlighted matters in the understandings cited above, I propose that the course of Paul's argument in 9:1–11:36 — and particularly the expository materials of 9:6–11:32, which appear at the heart of Section III of the body middle of the letter — is best understood when seen in terms of a Jewish and/or Jewish Christian remnant theology, which incorporates a particular use of biblical texts in support and a distinctive type of remnant rhetoric in its presentation.[6] Further, my thesis includes the suggestions (1) that an argument based on remnant theology would have been understood and would have been meaningful not only to Jewish believers in Jesus but also to Gentile Christians who had been extensively influenced by the theology, ways of thinking, and religious language of Jewish Christianity, as centered in the mother church at Jerusalem, and (2) that because remnant rhetoric has been largely foreign to both ancient and contemporary Western mentalities, Paul's argument in 9:1–11:36 (and particularly in the subsections of 9:6–11:32) has often failed to resonate with Christian interpreters, and thus the thrust and significance of this section in the apostle's letter have all too often not been appreciated — not only as to why Paul incorporated the material of these three chapters into his letter, but also as to what he wanted his addressees at Rome to understand. It is this thesis and its corollaries that will be explicated in our treatments of this section below.

---

5. As, e.g., by Piper, *The Justification of God,* esp. 73-79 (and as explicated in chs. 6–8).

6. Cf. my discussion "The Rhetorical Genres of Romans" above in the "Introduction to the Commentary"; see also "Remnant Theology and Rhetoric," in R. N. Longenecker, *Introducing Romans,* 247-53 and 413-21.

The Placement and Function of 9:1-11:36 in Paul's Letter to Rome. Paul's letter to Rome should be understood rhetorically (we have argued) as a "protreptic word [or 'message'] of exhortation" (λόγος προτρεπτικός), which was an ancient diachronic form of rhetoric used in both oral and written communication by various Greco-Roman speakers and writers, as well as by certain Jews during the Hellenistic period, to convey their messages of rebuke and exhortation; Paul employed this rhetorical form for his own purposes in writing to his Christian addressees at Rome.[7] The apostle may have used the structure of Greco-Roman protreptic discourse with deliberate intent in order to make the greatest possible rhetorical impact on his Roman addressees. More likely, however, he used it simply because it was well known both to him and to his Roman addressees, and so provided an appropriate vehicle for what he wanted to say to these particular addressees in this particular letter. Yet Paul was not a slave to any of the rhetorical or literary conventions of his day. Thus, while Greco-Roman protreptic discourse had its own structures and its own strictures, the apostle filled this ancient form of rhetoric with Christian content. Further, he felt free to alter and expand the structures he used in order to accomplish his own purposes when writing to believers in Jesus at Rome.

Most often Greco-Roman speakers and writers set out a "protreptic word [or 'message'] of exhortation" in three recognizable major parts or sections: (1) a negative section, which critiqued a rival position or understanding; (2) a positive section, which presented the truth claims of the speaker or author; and (3) a hortatory section, which appealed to the hearers or addressees to accept and put into practice the message given in the second major section. In Paul's use of such a protreptic rhetorical structure, however, he employed the first section not only to critique certain legalistic views that he opposed (which he evidently believed his Christian addressees at Rome also opposed, at least in theory if not always in practice), but also to develop more fully the themes of (1) "the righteousness of God," (2) "the faithfulness of Jesus," and (3) "faith" or "trust" in God. He was convinced these themes were rooted in the foundational convictions of all believers in Jesus, though he seems also to have been aware that all believers in Jesus in his day did not sufficiently understand them. Most obvious with regard to the structure of the letter (and most important for our purposes here) is the fact that Paul expanded the usual threefold structure of protreptic discourse by including in 9:1-11:36 an additional major section of material in which he explored "the Christian gospel vis-à-vis God's promises to Israel." That additional material was placed between 5:1-8:39, where he provides for his Roman addressees a précis of his own form of Christian proclamation to pagan Gentiles, and 12:1-15:13, where he calls on his readers to accept and put into practice the message he proclaimed in 5:1-8:39.

7. Cf. "The Rhetorical Genres of Romans" above; see also "Diachronic Rhetorical Analysis," in R. N. Longenecker, *Introducing Romans*, 196-200.

Yet questions remain regarding (1) why this material of 9:1–11:36 was set out by Paul immediately after the material of 5:1–8:39, and (2) how these chapters were meant to function in that location. As noted above in our comments on 8:33a, where the apostle asks the rhetorical question, "Who will bring any charge against God's elect?" there appears in that question for the first time in this letter the designation ἐκλεκτοὶ θεοῦ ("the elect/chosen ones of God" or "God's elect") with application to believers in Jesus. This was an identifying expression used in the Jewish (OT) Scriptures only for those who had been chosen by God as his own special people; it was used as a title only for the people of Israel. In Romans, however, Paul begins to apply this title to all believers in Jesus, whatever their ethnicity.

Such a use of "God's elect/chosen ones" for Gentile believers was undoubtedly offensive to Jews generally. It may also have been offensive to certain Jewish believers in Jesus — as well as somewhat troubling to some of the Jewish-Gentile Christian congregations in Rome, whose members had been, it seems, extensively influenced by the theology, ways of thinking, and religious terminology of Jewish Christianity as centered in Jerusalem (as we have proposed). So here in 9:1–11:36, it seems, Paul considered it necessary to spell out (1) the relations that exist between these two communities of "God's elect/chosen ones" and (2) how matters are to be understood in the working out of God's salvation history, both in this present time and in the future.

Jewish and/or Jewish Christian Remnant Theology and Rhetoric in 9:1–11:36. We believe it is important for an understanding of his presentation in 9:1–11:36 to appreciate Paul's use of Jewish and/or Jewish Christian remnant theology, which comes to the fore in these three chapters in what appears to be his own christianized version of remnant rhetoric. It is a type of thought and expression that (1) stems from a "chosen," "elect," or "survivor" understanding of God's people in the Jewish (OT) Scriptures, (2) comes to expression most explicitly in the works of the writing prophets of the canonical OT, (3) was used by the earliest Jewish Pharisees, by the Dead Sea covenanters, and by other Jewish sectarian groups to justify their existence, (4) was prominent in the ministry of John the Baptist in calling the Jewish people to repentance and in baptizing them, (5) was present in the ministry of Jesus in inviting people to follow him, referring to those who became his followers as his "little flock" and calling them "my sheep" — and, further, that (6) became a prominent feature in the self-consciousness of the earliest Jewish believers in Jesus.[8]

Gottlob Schrenk and Volkmar Herntrich have aptly set out the essential features of a Jewish remnant theology, which we summarize as follows:[9]

---

8. For significant treatments of "remnant theology" and "remnant rhetoric" see especially M. A. Elliott, *The Survivors of Israel: A Reconsideration of the Theology of Pre-Christian Judaism* (Grand Rapids: Eerdmans, 2000). The thesis stated here is given fuller treatment in R. N. Longenecker, *Introducing Romans*, 247-53 (bibliography in n. 23 on pp. 247-48).

9. Cf. Schrenk and Herntrich, "λεῖμμα, ὑπόλειμμα, καταλείπω," 4.203-14.

1. The remnant is sovereignly established by God alone.
2. The remnant may be small, but also envisioned is its greatness.
3. The remnant is both a present and a future entity.
4. The concept of the remnant is related to God's election of Israel.
5. The remnant is commonly associated with Zion, the city of Jerusalem.
6. While God establishes the remnant, the other side of that establishment is a response of faith and faithfulness on the part of those whom God has elected.
7. Not only is there a remnant of Israel, but also envisioned is a remnant that God gathers from among the Gentiles.
8. There are diverse opinions regarding the gathering of the Gentiles, that is, whether on a proselyte basis or on a missionary basis, with the expectation that Gentiles will be received on a proselyte basis being most often expressed.
9. The gathering of the remnant is not the final goal of God; rather, God's final goal is the readoption and salvation of all Israel.
10. Just as there is a close relationship between God's "chosen (or 'elected') remnant," the people of Israel, and the city of Zion, so there will be a close relationship between the remnant and God's promised Messiah.

While certain important characteristics of a Jewish — as well as of a Jewish Christian — remnant theology can be identified, it needs always to be recognized, as Gottlob Schrenk points out, that "The prophetic concept of the remnant is growing and adaptable. Its application changes with changing situations."[10]

Not every feature of a remnant understanding cited above can be found either in the extant sectarian writings of "early Judaism" or in the Jewish Christian writings of the NT. Nor, for that matter, can every feature of such a widespread remnant perspective be found in Paul's letter to believers in Jesus at Rome, whatever their ethnic backgrounds — that is, to believers in Jesus who had been extensively influenced by Jewish Christianity, whose mother church was in Jerusalem (as we have suggested was true of the Christians at Rome). But enough appears in all these materials to make a remnant theology and remnant rhetoric frequently quite recognizable.

It certainly cannot, for instance, be said that Paul understood remnant theology and used remnant rhetoric only with regard to the election of the people of Israel (as in point 4 above). Nor did he associate remnant theology only with the present city of Jerusalem (as in point 5) or think of an outreach to Gentiles only on a proselyte basis (as in point 8). His contextualized message of "new life in Christ Jesus" — which honored what God had done for the people of Israel under the old covenant, but was not confined to the people, places, or

---

10. Schrenk and Herntrich, "λεῖμμα, ὑπόλειμμα, καταλείπω," 4.209, which observation he makes at the beginning of his treatment of "The Remnant in Romans 9–11."

practices of the Jewish nation — went far beyond the previous "old covenant" theology and lifestyle. Yet it cannot be doubted (1) that Paul knew various forms of a Jewish-based remnant theology, as held both by Jews themselves and by Jewish believers in Jesus, and (2) that he recognized that some form of remnant theology existed among the believers in Jesus at Rome (whatever their ethnic mix), influenced as they had been by the theology, ways of thinking, and religious language of Jewish Christianity. So it may legitimately be proposed that what Paul is seeking to do here in 9:1–11:36 is to "christianize" in a more appropriate manner a Jewish and/or Jewish Christian remnant theology — speaking specifically, in light of God's "new covenant" as founded on the work of Christ Jesus and as carried out by the ministry of God's Spirit, regarding (1) how the Christian gospel relates to God's promises to Israel and (2) how matters are to be understood in the overall course of God's salvation history.

The Possible Presence of a Few Greco-Roman Epistolary Conventions in 9:1–11:36. Paul's exposition on "the Christian gospel vis-à-vis God's promises to Israel" in 9:1–11:36 is an important part of this letter. So one might expect that what he writes in this third major section of the body middle of his letter to Rome would be comparable in many ways, particularly in its use of Greco-Roman epistolary conventions, to what appears in the body middle of his other NT letters and in the specifically epistolary portions of this present letter. Yet what Paul writes in 9:1–11:36 differs in many respects from what he has written earlier (and will write later), not only in his other NT letters but also in the other sections of this letter. And it differs not only in content but also in its use (or, rather, its nonuse) of then-current epistolary conventions. For not only does Paul base what he writes in this section of the letter on a Jewish and/or Jewish Christian remnant theology and rhetoric — which, we propose, is the major rhetorical feature of his presentation in these three chapters, and therefore differs somewhat in content from what he writes elsewhere in the letter (esp. in 5:1–8:39) — he also sets out a different structure and styling for the materials of this section, which differs in many ways from what he has presented in his earlier NT letters and from some of the other portions of this present letter.

The Greco-Roman epistolary conventions that appear in this letter are found primarily in the beginning sections (i.e., the "salutation" of 1:1-7, the "thanksgiving" of 1:8-12, and the "body opening" of 1:13-15) and in the closing sections (the "body closing" of 15:14-32; the "peace benediction," "commendation," and "greetings" of 15:33–16:16) — as well as in the "personal subscription" of 16:17-23, which contains additional exhortations, a typical "grace benediction," and further greetings. An extremely small cluster of epistolary phrases and expressions is also present in 12:1 (i.e., a *request formula* and a *vocative of direct address*) and in 12:3 (i.e., a *verb of saying*); this seems to be a logical place for such a cluster, where Paul is moving from exposition in 1:16–11:36 to exhortation in 12:1–15:13. In this third major section of the body middle of the letter, however, the only traditional epistolary conventions that seem to appear are the following:

9:1 — Attestation statement: ἀλήθειαν λέγω ἐν Χριστῷ, οὐ ψεύδομαι, "I am speaking the truth in Christ, I am not lying."

9:14 — Verb of saying: τί οὖν ἐροῦμεν;, "What then shall we say?"

9:30 — Verb of saying: τί οὖν ἐροῦμεν;, "What then shall we say?"

10:1 — Vocative of direct address: ἀδελφοί, "brothers and sisters."

11:1 — Verb of saying: λέγω οὖν, "I say then . . ."

11:11 — Verb of saying: λέγω οὖν, "I say then . . ."

11:13 — Verb of saying/speaking: ὑμῖν δὲ λέγω τοῖς ἔθνεσιν, "Now, I am speaking to you Gentiles."

11:25 — Disclosure formula and vocative of direct address: οὐ γὰρ θέλω ὑμᾶς ἀγνοεῖν, ἀδελφοί, "I do not want you to be ignorant, brothers and sisters."

Many of Paul's other NT letters contain in their body middle sections a relatively large number of Greco-Roman epistolary features, which introduce, connect, and close off the various parts of their respective subsections. The body middle of Paul's letter to Rome, however, is different in this regard, and this difference is particularly evident in 9:1–11:36. We have observed earlier about the differing uses of such proposed epistolary conventions, (1) that at least some of the material within the body middle of Romans, and particularly its second major section of 5:1–8:39, should be viewed as having had an earlier oral and rhetorical history before being cast into its present epistolary form, and therefore, (2) that these materials should be evaluated more in terms of their oral and rhetorical functions than in terms of any epistolary features they may reflect. Such observations are particularly appropriate when evaluating what has seemed to many to be rather traditional epistolary conventions in this third major section of the letter's body middle, which features in an original oral form of the material would have served a strictly rhetorical function — though in both their original oral forms and their subsequent letter forms, these same features, whether rhetorical or epistolary, would have functioned similarly to signal certain introductory and concluding breaks in these two modes of presentation.[11]

On the Presence of Only a Few Greco-Roman Synchronic Rhetorical Conventions in 9:1–11:36. With respect to the rhetoric of 9:1–11:36, not only is this section dominated by the structures and argumentation present in Jewish and/or Jewish Christian remnant theology and rhetoric, it also reflects, at least to some extent, a few of the synchronic rhetorical features that were widely prevalent in the Greco-Roman world of Paul's day. This seems to be true in what appears to be the apostle's minimal use in 9:1–11:36 of (1) chiastic structures, (2) diatribe styling, (3) the framing of certain sections by the repetition of particular phrases or words, and (4) metaphor.

Chiasmus is the name modern rhetoricians have given to the phenomenon

---

11. On ancient oral, rhetorical, and epistolary conventions, with application to the materials within Romans, see R. N. Longenecker, *Introducing Romans,* 169-235.

of paired words, statements, or texts that are arranged in a pattern of inverted symmetry around a focal word, statement, or text. The name is a transliteration of the postclassical Greek word χιασμός, which means "crossing." But the term is more directly derived from the Greek letter "χ," and so used for the structure's basic A-B-A' pattern of arrangement.

Most scholars have no problem believing that Paul retained the chiastic structures of some of the OT passages he quoted in this section of the body middle of Romans, especially in 10:19 (quoting Deut 32:21), in 11:3 (quoting 1 Kgs 19:10), and in 11:10 (quoting Ps 69:23). But there remains a rather high degree of uncertainty among many contemporary commentators about where and how the apostle used a chiastic structure elsewhere in 9:1–11:36. At times it has been seen in 10:9-10 ("If you *confess with your mouth* 'Jesus is Lord' and *believe in your heart* that God raised him from the dead, you will be saved; for it is *with your heart that you believe* and are justified, and it is *with your mouth that you confess* and are saved") and in 11:30-31 ("Just as you who were at one time disobedient to God have now received *mercy* as a result of their *disobedience,* so they too have now become *disobedient* in order that they too may now receive *mercy* as a result of God's mercy to you") — with the doxological statements of 11:33-35 being sometimes viewed in this light as well.

"Diatribe" is the designation assigned to a lively dialogical style that makes use of direct address to an imaginary interlocutor, hypothetical objections, and false conclusions. The clearest and most sustained use of this rhetorical convention in the NT appears in Paul's letter to Rome, particularly in 2:1-5 and 2:17-24.[12] Of late, a diatribe structure has also been seen in 3:1-8 (perhaps including v. 9) and 3:27-31 (perhaps including 4:1-2);[13] likewise, in 14:4-11. Here in 9:1–11:36 diatribe styling seems to be reflected, at least to an extent, in the statements of 9:19-21 and 11:17-24, which we will consider more carefully in our exegetical comments below.

Inclusio is the term used in rhetorical parlance when speaking of certain relatively short sections of oral or written communication that seem to be framed by the repetition of the same or similar words, terms, phrases, or clauses at their beginning and at their end, and therefore may be viewed as rather distinctive units of material. Such a feature seems to have been somewhat common in antiquity, not only in oral speech generally but also in formal rhetoric and everyday letter writing. It appears in Rom 9–11 particularly in the use of the word σπέρμα ("seed," "descendants"), which is used three times in 9:6-8 to begin the subsection of 9:6-29 and once again in 9:29b to close off that subsection (with such an *inclusio* also possibly discernible elsewhere in the following subsections of these three chapters).

The term "metaphor" is used with respect to a word, a group of words, or a sentence that stands for something different than its literal reference, but which

12. See my earlier comments on these passages *ad loc.*
13. See my earlier comments on these passages *ad loc.*

is linked to its literal meaning by some perceivable similarity and therefore suggests a likeness or analogy between its figurative usage and its literal reference. It is an appropriate rhetorical designation for Paul's references to (1) "the first-fruits" and "the whole batch" in 11:16a, (2) "the root" and "the branches" in 11:16b, and (3) "the natural branches" and "the engrafted wild branches" in 11:17-21 — which metaphors must be spelled out later in our exegetical comments on the passage.

On the Probable Presence of Narrative Substructures in 9:1–11:36. A narrative approach to Paul's letters has been proposed by a number of NT scholars during the past few decades, has been developed in various ways, and is today the subject of rather intense scrutiny and critical assessment.[14] Such an approach is particularly important for a study of what Paul wrote earlier in the letter about (1) Abraham as the example par excellence of faith in 4:1-24 and (2) what Adam brought about in human experience and what Christ has effected on behalf of humanity in 5:12-21. But it is also, it seems, of importance for an analysis of what he says about (3) relations between Israel and the church in 9:6–10:21 and (4) the course of God's salvation history in 11:1-31.

As interpreters of what Paul has written in his letters, we need always to read the texts with an appreciation of the narrative substructures that underlie what is written. Such narrative substructures had a profound impact on the theologizing of the earliest believers in Jesus, which took the form of "early Christian confessions," as expressed in hymns, formal statements, and condensed sayings, and on the eventual composition of the four canonical Gospels, which brought these narratives together in a more formalized fashion. They also had a profound effect on what Paul wrote about the message of the Christian gospel in his letters. And so we should be aware of such narrative substructures underlying 9:1–11:36 — particularly about them underlying what the apostle writes about relations between Israel and the church and about the course of God's salvation history.

Early Christian Confessional Materials. In addressing the Christians at Rome, Paul used a number of early Christian confessional materials, whether in whole or in part. He used them in at least two ways: (1) to support and focus his arguments (as he did earlier in 1:3-4 and 3:24-26 and will use them later in 14:9) and (2) to summarize and bring to a climax his presentations (as he did in 4:25 and 8:33-39). Likewise, Paul incorporated into 9:1–11:36 certain traditional aphorisms and various then-existing Jewish and/or Jewish Christian devotional and catechetical materials for much the same reasons, even though these latter materials may be less commonly recognized or discussed. The exegetical detail that is necessary to identify properly and to spell out adequately the apostle's use of these confessional affirmations and other traditional materials in this passage must be left for our exegetical comments that follow. Suffice it here to

---

14. Cf., e.g., the collection of articles and responses in B. W. Longenecker, *Narrative Dynamics in Paul*.

say (as we have argued earlier at many places about such matters in 1:16–4:25) that (1) the pre-Pauline affirmations and materials that appear in 9:1–11:36 were presumably known (whether in whole or in part) by Paul's Christian addressees at Rome (whether ethnically Jews or Gentiles), and (2) he used them to build bridges of commonality with his Roman addressees, thereby instructing them in ways that they would understand and appreciate.

The Prominence of Biblical Quotations. Out of a total of 45 explicit biblical quotations in Romans, with 55 to 60 OT passages being quoted (if one disengages the conflated texts and separates the possible dual sources), about 30 of these biblical quotations appear in twenty-five or so places in 9:1–11:36 — that is, about two-thirds of the quotations of Scripture in Romans are found in this third major section of the body middle. Such a heavy concentration of OT quotations in 9:1–11:36 is similar to — and even goes beyond — the use of biblical quotations in 1:16–4:25, where 18 explicit biblical quotations appear in eight or nine places. Likewise, this concentration of biblical quotations goes far beyond what can be found in the other Pauline letters of the NT, with only 15 explicit OT quotations appearing in 1 Corinthians, 7 in 2 Corinthians, 10 in Galatians, 4 in Ephesians, 1 in 1 Timothy, and 1 in 2 Timothy — and none at all in 1 Thessalonians, 2 Thessalonians, Philippians, Colossians, Philemon, or Titus. Further, only 2 biblical quotations appear somewhat tangentially in Rom 5:1–8:39, only 10 more are found (and that with a somewhat different usage) in the ethical exhortations of 12:1–15:13, and only 1 OT citation is present in the body closing of 15:14-32.

This pattern in the distribution of biblical quotations in Paul's letters — and particularly in Romans — is frequently ignored. And when it is observed, it is most often considered a rather inconsequential phenomenon. Adolf Harnack, however, highlighted this pattern of biblical usage in the Pauline corpus; and from this pattern he developed a circumstantial understanding of Paul's use of Scripture, arguing that the apostle quoted the Jewish (OT) Scriptures in his letters only when confronting "Jewish opposition" — by which he meant opposition from "the Judaizers."[15] Though we deny Harnack's insistence on a "Judaizing" opposition as the major factor motivating Paul to quote the Jewish (OT) Scriptures, we affirm that his observations regarding the uneven pattern in Paul's use of biblical quotations in his letters remain valid — particularly with respect to the uneven pattern of Paul's use of OT quotations in his letter to Rome.

In explanation of this quite distinctive pattern of OT usage highlighted by Harnack, we propose (in contradistinction to Harnack) that (1) when Paul speaks directly to those who had been influenced by Jewish or Jewish Christian theology, ways of thinking, and religious language (as had been the ethnically mixed congregations of believers in Jesus at Rome), he uses OT quotations,

---

15. A. Harnack, "Das alte Testament in den paulinischen Briefen and in den paulinischen Gemeinde," *Sitzungsberichte der Preussichen Akademie der Wissenschaften zu Berlin* (1928) 124-41.

OT allusions, and biblically based aphorisms to support his arguments and his presentations (as in 1:16–4:25 and 9:1–11:36); but (2) when he reports to his Christian addressees at Rome what he had been proclaiming as "his gospel" to pagan Gentiles in the eastern part of the Roman Empire, he represents himself as speaking in more personal, relational, and participatory language — doing so without the support of any biblical quotations, biblical allusions, or biblically based aphorisms (as in 5:1–8:39). Exceptions to this thesis have been seen in Paul's use of the two biblical quotations in 7:7 and 8:36 in the second major section of the body middle of Romans (i.e., in 5:1–8:39), his use of ten OT quotations in the fourth major section of the letter's body middle (i.e., in 12:1–15:13), and his one further OT quotation in 15:21 of the letter's body closing (i.e., in 15:14-32). But in the biblical citations of 7:7 and 8:36 in the second major section and in the ten biblical quotations in the letter's fourth major section, Paul uses OT texts somewhat differently (as we have argued earlier with respect to the first two and will argue later with respect to the following ten) than he does in either 1:16–4:25 or 9:1–11:36 — though his use of a biblical quotation in 15:21 is in line with his use of biblical texts in Sections II and IV of his letter's body middle, and for much the same circumstantial reason.[16]

On the Distinctive Structure, Style, Literary Features, and Content of 9:1–11:36. While it may legitimately be claimed that the material of 9:1–11:36 is an integral part of the letter, the structure, style, and literary features of this third major section of the body middle of Romans are unique when compared with the other three major sections in the body middle. The first thing one notes is that the section begins with an "introduction" in 9:1-5, which closes with a liturgical "Amen," and concludes with a "doxology" in 11:33-36, which also closes with a liturgical "Amen." A second matter, and one that almost immediately strikes most careful readers, is that the material in these chapters "has a character of its own,"[17] which character is much more that of "a preacher than a writer" and more "conversational" in nature.[18] Further, there is no explicit grammatical connection between this third major section and what has preceded it in Section II — even though there is the quite definite thematic connection between Paul's statement of 8:33a, where he applies for the first time in the letter the highly honored appellative ἐκλεκτοὶ θεοῦ ("the elect/chosen ones of God" or "God's elect") to believers in Jesus, and his treatment of relations that exist between the people of Israel as "God's elect/chosen ones" and believers in Jesus as "God's elect/chosen ones," as he sets out in 9:6–11:32. Likewise, as William Sanday and Arthur Headlam have noted, in chs. 9–11 "St. Paul does

16. On the OT quotations in 7:7 and 8:36, the ten quotations in the ethical exhortations of the fourth major section of the body middle of the letter, and the one further quotation in 15:21, see our exegetical comments on these verses.

17. Using C. H. Dodd's apt characterization, as expressed in his *Romans*, 148.

18. So, again, *ibid.*: "Almost everywhere in Paul's writings we overhear the tones of the living voice, as is natural in one who was much more a preacher than a writer; but in this section the conversational note is very clear."

not here follow his general habit of stating the subject he is going to discuss (as he does for example at the beginning of chap. iii [and elsewhere]), but allows it gradually to become evident."[19] If we are right in claiming that the course of Paul's argument in 9:1–11:36 is dominated by his use of a Jewish and/or Jewish Christian form of remnant theology and rhetoric, which comes to the fore in his own version of remnant rhetoric (as proposed above), these three chapters must be judged as being fairly distinctive in their content as well.

Such differing structural, stylistic, literary, and content phenomena may be seen as buttressing certain speculations about an earlier oral provenance for the materials of 9:1–11:32, most likely Paul's preaching and teaching in congregations in Antioch (cf. Acts 11:25-26), as I will suggest in my treatments of 9:6-29; 9:30–10:21; and 11:1-32 below. Or as Sanday and Headlam speculated: "Perhaps there has been a pause in writing the Epistle, the amanuensis has for a time suspended his labours"[20] — that is, that while Sections I, II, and IV of the letter's body middle may be understood as having been written by Paul using one of his friends as his amanuensis, here in Section III the apostle writes without any such secretarial assistance. But whatever rationale may be proposed to explain these particular features, there is nothing of substance in what is written in 9:1–11:36 that requires a decision one way or the other on any earlier provenance for these three chapters, and so all conjectures on the subject must remain just that — simply conjectures.

Nonetheless, the overall structure of 9:1–11:36 seems fairly easy to identify. The beginning and the end of the section are clearly marked by an opening introduction in 9:1-5 and a concluding doxology in 11:33-36, with both passages including as their final item a closing "Amen." And while Paul's argumentation between these two rather obvious units of material may be viewed as somewhat subtle, complicated, and even convoluted — and, further, while commentators have often analyzed somewhat differently this material that appears between 9:1-5 and 11:33-36 — we believe that what is presented in 9:6–11:32 is best understood as incorporating three parts of an exposition that has to do with the overall theme "The Christian Gospel vis-à-vis God's Promises to Israel." We propose that these three parts may be set out as follows:

> Part I: God's promises given to "the remnant," with biblical passages cited in support in 9:6-29
> Part II: Israel's present situation of unbelief vis-à-vis the situation of believing Gentiles in 9:30–10:21
> Part III: The course of God's salvation history, as expressed with respect to (1) a present remnant within Israel, but also with respect to (2) a present remnant among the Gentiles, and (3) the future salvation of "all Israel" in 11:1-32

19. Sanday and Headlam, *Romans,* 226.
20. *Ibid.*

The exegetical and thematic features that seem to necessitate the recognition of five subsections in 9:1–11:36 — that is, an opening introduction, a three-part exposition, and a concluding doxology — will be explicated in our exegetical discussions that follow. This proposal of five subsections in chs. 9–11 will provide the basic outline for our treatment of what Paul presents here in Section III of the body middle of his letter to the Christians at Rome.

1. Introduction: Paul's Great Desire for His People, Israel's Heritage, and Israel's Messiah, with a Closing "Amen" (9:1-5)

TRANSLATION

⁹:¹I speak the truth in Christ — I am not lying, my conscience confirms it by the Holy Spirit — ²I have great sorrow and unceasing anguish in my heart! ³For I could wish that I myself were cursed and cut off from Christ for the sake of my brothers and sisters, my own people according to the flesh. ⁴They are Israelites. To them belong the adoption as God's own children, the divine glory, the covenants, the giving of the law, the worship of God, and God's promises. ⁵To them also belong the patriarchs. And from them, as far as human descent is concerned, has come the Christ ["the Messiah"], who is supreme over all as God blessed forever! Amen.

TEXTUAL NOTES

9:1 The expression ἐν Χριστῷ ("in Christ") is well attested in the Greek textual tradition. The variant ἐν Χριστῷ Ἰησοῦ ("in Christ Jesus"), which appears in uncials D* F C and is reflected in arm vgˢ, must be considered a secondary scribal reading.

3a The preposition ἀπό (reading "*from* Christ") is well attested in the textual tradition. The variant ὑπό (reading "*by* Christ"), which appears in uncials D G and minuscule 1505 (Category III), as well as the variant ὑπέρ (reading "*on behalf of* Christ"), which appears in uncial Ψ, are far less supported and seem to be only attempts to minimize the severity of being "cut off *from* Christ" — and thus are to be rejected.

3b The possessive pronoun μου ("my") is missing after τῶν ἀδελφῶν ("of the brothers") in P⁴⁶, while the entire phrase τῶν ἀδελφῶν μου ("of my brothers") is absent from uncorrected Codex Vaticanus (B*). Although P⁴⁶ and uncorrected B are important witnesses in any textual evaluation, here their omissions are probably to be judged as accidental.

4a The plural αἱ διαθῆκαι ("the covenants") is well attested by uncials ℵ C Ψ (also *Byz* K) and by minuscules 33 1175 1739 (Category I), 81 256 1506 1881 [also 1962, which omits αἱ] 2127 2464 (Category II), and 6, 104 263 365 424ᶜ 436 459 1241 1319 1573 1912 2200 (Category III); it is reflected in itᵈ, ᶠ, ᵍ, ᵐᵒⁿ, ᵒ vgʷʷ, ˢᵗ syrᵖ, ʰ (ʰ ᵍʳ) copᵇᵒ and supported by Origenˡᵃᵗ Epiphanius Chrysostom Ambrosiaster Jerome⁴ᐟ⁷ Augustine⁵ᐟ⁶. The singular ἡ διαθήκη ("the covenant"), however, is also well attested by P⁴⁶, by uncials B D F G, and by minuscule 1852 (Category III); it is also reflected in itᵃʳ, ᵇ vgᶜˡ copˢᵃ, ᵇᵒ ᵐˢˢ eth and supported by Theodore Jerome³ᐟ⁷ Augustine¹ᐟ⁶. The textual evidence seems almost equally divided. Nonetheless, the plural αἱ διαθῆκαι ("the covenants") is probably to be preferred for the following reasons: (1) because copyists were more likely to change a plural to a singular than a singular to a plural; and (2) because the idea of "plural covenants," as Bruce Metzger has observed, "may have appeared to involve theological difficulties, and therefore the expression was converted to the singular number."[21]

4b The plural αἱ ἐπαγγελίαι ("the promises") is attested by uncials ℵ C Ψ (also *Byz* K) and by minuscules 33 1739 (Category I), 81 (Category II), and 614 (Category III); it is also reflected in it[d, g], vg syr[p, h, hgr] cop[bo] goth arm. The singular (ἡ) ἐπαγγελία ("the promise"), however, appears in P[46], in uncials D F G, and is reflected in it[a] cop[bo mss]. The plural reading αἱ ἐπαγγελίαι ("the promises") is somewhat better externally attested in the textual tradition than the singular reading (ἡ) ἐπαγγελία ("the promise). More important, however, is the fact that the internal rationale given above for preferring the plural αἱ διαθῆκαι ("the covenants") over the singular (ἡ) διαθήκη ("the covenant") applies here as well.

5 Variant textual readings are not at issue in the interpretation of this verse. Differences of interpretation have stemmed mainly from proposed differences of punctuation, and vice versa. The earliest MSS, however, are without any systematic punctuation, and so modern editors, translators, and commentators have been forced to insert such punctuation as seems appropriate to their understanding of the syntax and meaning of what Paul has written here.[22]

FORM/STRUCTURE/SETTING

Most Jews of the first century undoubtedly viewed Paul as a traitor to his people, for he proclaimed (1) that Jesus of Nazareth is God's promised Messiah, (2) that Israel's prerogatives as the exclusive people of God have come to an end, and (3) that pagan Gentiles who turn to God by faith in Jesus have the same claims to acceptance by God and salvation as righteous Jews. Further, many Jews must have viewed Paul's "failure" to use the Jewish (OT) Scriptures in his evangelistic preaching to Gentiles and his "refusal" to relate his Gentile converts to the teachings of the Jewish law as constituting, in effect, a renunciation of the Mosaic law and a repudiation of all that Judaism had taught regarding God and a God-ordained lifestyle. Even some Jewish believers in Jesus, while accepting the person, ministry, and redemptive work of Jesus as the fulfillment of God's ancient promises to his people, seem to have had misgivings about some of these matters — particularly about Paul's seeming renunciation of Israel's prerogatives and his refusal to relate his Gentile converts to the practices specified in the Jewish law.

These accusations were probably frequently raised by Jews against Paul and his evangelistic endeavors. In all likelihood, many of these objections were also raised against him by Jewish believers in Jesus who had doubts about the

21. Metzger, *Textual Commentary*, 459.
22. For a brief summary of the major positions taken with regard to the punctuation and interpretation of 9:5b, see *ibid.*, 459-62. See also "Exegetical Comments" below on the passage.

validity of his Gentile mission. And probably the apostle's responses to these accusations and objections were given in some such fashion as he sets out here in 9:1–11:36. Thus, in writing to believers in Jesus living in Rome, who had been extensively influenced (as we believe) by the theology, ways of thinking, and religious language of Jewish Christianity, it may be assumed (or, perhaps, only "conjectured") that Paul reused some of the materials, whether oral or written, that he had earlier used in speaking to Jewish opponents and Jewish Christian objectors during his missionary endeavors throughout the eastern regions of the Roman Empire — with the result that this third major section, 9:1–11:36, in the body middle of the letter carries on many of the same features of content, structure, and style of those earlier presentations to Jewish opponents and Jewish Christian questioners.

EXEGETICAL COMMENTS

Karl Schelkle has spoken of Paul's response to the Jewish rejection of Jesus as Israel's Messiah — together with all the spiritual and personal implications that resulted from that rejection — as "the one lasting, great and grievous sorrow of his [Paul's] life."[23] Likewise, William Sanday and Arthur Headlam have characterized Paul's reaction to Israel's negative response to Jesus as "a fact which is to him so full of sadness."[24] And it is with such deeply felt sorrow that the apostle writes what he does here in 9:1-5 and throughout the rest of 9:6–11:36 — identifying himself with those he affectionately calls "my brothers and sisters, my kinsmen according to the flesh," yet also criticizing his own people for their lack of spiritual understanding and their failure to accept God's gracious gift of new life in Christ Jesus.

9:1-3 Paul begins his exposition of "the Christian gospel vis-à-vis God's promises to Israel" here in Section III of the body middle of his letter by affirming (1) his love for the people of Israel, (2) his desire for their spiritual welfare, and (3) his willingness (if it were at all possible) to be "cursed and cut off from Christ" for their sake. He introduces that threefold affirmation by his own fervently expressed christianized version of what was in that day a rather conventional "attestation statement": ἀλήθειαν λέγω ἐν Χριστῷ, οὐ ψεύδομαι ("I am speaking the truth in Christ, I am not lying"). Such claims to "truthfulness" and "not lying" can be paralleled in the extant writings of antiquity, and they seem to have carried great weight not only for the speakers themselves but also for the hearers.[25] Yet Paul adds even greater weight as a Christian to these claims by asserting that he affirms such truthfulness "in Christ" and that it is confirmed by his own conscience as guided by the Holy Spirit.

---

23. Schelkle, *Romans,* 149.
24. Sanday and Headlam, *Romans,* 226.
25. Cf. the Greco-Roman parallels highlighted by Jewett, *Romans,* 557-59

This claim of truthfulness is the strongest of all such attestation statements in Paul's NT letters. The fact that it appears here at the very beginning of his exposition in chs. 9–11 — together with the emphasis he places on it by insisting that he speaks "in Christ" and that his conscience as guided by the Holy Spirit confirms it — suggests that during the apostle's outreach to pagan Gentiles in the eastern Roman Empire (and, evidently, even before that Gentile mission), he had not only interacted with Jews who had serious doubts about his devotion to his Jewish heritage but also had been confronted by Jewish Christians who questioned the validity of his form of direct Christian outreach to the heathen world. Further, it suggests that Paul knew that Jewish and/or Gentile believers in at least some of the Christian congregations at Rome questioned his commitment to God's ancient people Israel and were concerned about what they believed were anti-Jewish statements and/or anti-Jewish attitudes on his part — which questions and concerns he probably learned about from one or more of his friends or relatives who lived in Rome at the time.[26]

To all such doubts about his commitment to his Jewish heritage, as well as questions regarding his teachings and attitudes about the people of Israel, Paul answers pointedly. He does not begin his exposition in 9:1–11:36, as Sanday and Headlam have observed, by "stating the subject he is going to discuss . . . but allows it gradually to become evident."[27] What he does do here, however, is align himself with Moses and the great prophetic tradition of the Jewish (OT) Scriptures by echoing the heartfelt desire Moses expresses to God on behalf of Israel: "Please forgive their sin — but if not, then blot me out of the book you have written"[28] — saying, in effect, that such a desire for the people of Israel was his earnest desire as well. Paul, like Moses, knows that one cannot barter with God for the sake of the salvation of others. Yet he uses that extreme expression "cursed and cut off from Christ" for the sake of his own people — as did Moses in requesting God to "blot me out of the book you have written" on behalf of his people — in order to declare at the very beginning of his exposition in these chapters his bond with the people of Israel.

9:4-5 Paul here in these verses sets out seven special features or prerogatives in the life and experience of the Jewish people that highlight their unique relationship with God. The first is introduced by the nominative plural pronoun οἵτινες ("they"), which picks up from the apostle's reference to "my brothers and sisters, my own people according to the flesh" at the close of 9:3. The six that follow are all introduced by a single use of the genitive plural relative pronoun ὧν ("of whom [belong]," or "to whom belong"), with these latter special features connected by the repetition of the simple conjunction καί ("and"). "In

---

26. Perhaps receiving this information from some of those he greets later in 16:3-16.

27. Quoting again Sanday and Headlam, *Romans*, 226.

28. Cf. Exod 32:31-32: "So Moses went back to the Lord and said: 'Oh, what a great sin these people have committed! They have made themselves gods of gold. But now, please forgive their sin — but if not, then blot me out of the book you have written.'"

enumerations," as Archibald Robertson has pointed out, "the repetition of καί gives a kind of dignity and is called *polysyndeton*."[29]

The first prerogative of the Jews that Paul lists is that "they are Israelites."[30] The names "Israel" and "Israelite" occur thirteen times in 9:1–11:36,[31] in contrast to the use of the name "Jew" or "Jews" in the earlier chapters of the letter.[32] The pattern of this usage in Romans suggests that when Paul speaks generally about Jews and/or when he criticizes them from some "outside" position, he refers to them as simply "Jews" (as he does earlier in his letter to Rome) — but when he identifies with his people and agonizes over them because of their rejection of Jesus as God's promised Messiah, he calls them "Israelites." That is, as James Dunn has aptly observed, he uses "his people's own view of themselves, as himself an insider rather than as one looking in from outside."[33] Further, as Dunn goes on to infer, the names "Israel" and "Israelite" here in chs. 9–11 are "deliberately chosen by Paul to evoke his people's sense of being God's elect, the covenant people of the one God."[34]

It is this highly significant feature or God-given privilege that Paul cites first in his listing of the prerogatives of Jewish life and experience. Most important in the apostle's view of the Jews is the spiritual dimension of their existence, that is, their relationship with God. For, as Walter Gutbrod has characterized the Jewish situation from the Pauline perspective: "Israel is not just the totality of its individual members; it is the bearer of the promise and the recipient of its fulfillment."[35]

The second God-given privilege that Paul lists is ἡ υἱοθεσία, which may legitimately be translated "the adoption as God's own children." The word υἱοθεσία ("adoption," which literally may be translated "sonship") appears only five times in Paul's letters — earlier in this letter at 8:15 and 23 with application to Gentile believers in Jesus and here in 9:4 with application to the Jewish people; also once in Gal 4:5 and once more in Eph 1:5. The term is not found in the Jewish (OT) Scriptures, either in the Greek LXX or in any cognate expression of the Hebrew MT. Nor is it found in the extant literature of Second Temple Judaism or in any of the non-Pauline writings of the NT. It may be said, therefore, that the use of "adoption" as a metaphor to characterize the relationship

29. *ATRob*, 472. See also Paul's repetitive use of the negative conjunction οὔτε in the enumeration of potential obstacles to God's love that he cites in 8:38-39.

30. On the derivations, meanings, and uses of the names "Israelities," "Hebrews," and "Jews," see "Exegetical Comments" on 2:17.

31. The name "Israel" occurs eleven times in Romans: in 9:6, 27 (twice), 31; 10:1, 19, 21; 11:2, 7, 25, 26 (also in 1 Cor 10:18; 2 Cor 3:7, 13; Gal 6:16; Eph 2:12; Phil 3:5); the name "Israelite" occurs two times in Romans: in 9:4 and 11:1 (also in 2 Cor 11:22).

32. The name "Jew" (or its plural "Jews") occurs earlier in Romans in 1:16; 2:9, 10, 17, 28, 29; 3:1, 9, 29; it is used also in 9:24 and 10:12 in contrasting Jews and Gentiles. It appears often, as well, in 1 and 2 Corinthians and in Galatians; likewise, once in Col 3:11 and once in 1 Thess 2:14.

33. Dunn, *Romans*, 2.526.

34. *Ibid.*

35. W. Gutbrod, "Ἰσραήλ, κτλ," *TDNT* 3.387

of God's people to himself was unique to Paul — though (as we noted above in our "exegetical comments" on 8:15) the presence of this term in the "sending formula" earlier in Gal 4:5, as well as here in 9:4 in what appears to be a rather traditional listing of features that constitute the prerogatives of the people of Israel, suggests that υἱοθεσία as characterizing the relationship of God's people to himself would have been understood by both Jewish and Gentile believers in Jesus.[36] And while Paul seems to have picked up this term from the Greco-Roman socio-legal practice of his day — and while he used it in 8:15 and 23 as a metaphor for the family relationship that Gentile believers in Jesus now have with God through the historical work of Jesus and the continuing ministry of the Holy Spirit — he was convinced, as Robert Jewett has expressed the apostle's firm belief, that

> The sonship" [i.e., ἡ υἱοθεσία, which, contra Jewett, we have translated "the adoption"] discussed in 8:15, 23 belongs first to Israel. Believers who do not have Jewish blood become sons and daughters of God (8:15, 23; 2 Cor 6:18) and thus enter into the family of Israel.[37]

The third God-given privilege of the Jewish people that Paul cites in 9:4, that is, ἡ δόξα ("the divine glory"), highlights a particularly meaningful matter. For the Jewish (OT) Scriptures frequently speak of "the glory of the Lord" as having been present with the people of Israel in their experiences and in their worship — as, for example, in the desert (Exod 16:7, 10), in the wilderness tabernacle (Exod 40:34-35; Lev 9:6; Num 14:10; 16:19, 42), in the giving of the law on Mount Sinai (Exod 24:16-17), in their prophetic visions (Ezek 1:28), and in the Jerusalem temple (1 Kgs 8:11). Its presence is also promised to all people in the future when "all the earth will be filled with the glory of the Lord" (Num 14:21). It is this resplendent divine presence that Paul refers to with this expression "the glory" (ἡ δόξα). And while the apostle does not go on to elaborate, his simple expression "the glory" would signal to all Jewish and Christian hearers "the splendor of the divine presence" among his people.[38] Thus to experience "the divine glory" in one's life — whether as Israelites, as the remnant of Israel, or as believers in Jesus of whatever ethnicity — is to have a treasure of great worth, which well deserves an early billing in any list of special features in the lives and experiences of God's people.

Debate exists over whether the original text for the fourth Jewish prerogative listed, αἱ διαθῆκαι (the possession of "the covenants"), reads the plural αἱ διαθῆκαι ("the covenants") or the singular ἡ διαθήκη ("the covenant"). Both readings are almost equally supported by the Greek textual tradition (see "Tex-

---

36. For a bibliography of significant works on the social-legal understanding of "adoption" in the Greco-Roman world and Paul's use of the term as a metaphor to characterize the relation of God's people to himself, see our exegetical comments and footnotes on 8:15 and 23.

37. Jewett, *Romans*, 563.

38. So NEB: "the splendor of the divine presence."

tual Notes" above). Yet, for internal reasons, the plural αἱ διαθῆκαι is most likely to be preferred, simply because (1) copyists were more likely to have changed a plural to a singular than a singular to a plural, and (2) the idea of "plural covenants may have appeared to involve theological difficulties, and therefore the expression was converted to the singular number."[39] Further, a reference to plural covenants in Israel's history is not at all unusual among Jewish writers[40] — though, at times, a similar textual ambiguity exists in some Jewish materials,[41] and probably for much the same reason. In all likelihood, therefore, Paul had in mind by his use of the plural αἱ διαθῆκαι God's covenants with Abraham (Gen 15:18; 17:2, 7, 9); with Isaac (Gen 26:3-5; Exod 2:24); with all three of the patriarchs, Abraham, Isaac, and Jacob (Exod 6:4-5; Lev 26:42); with Moses (Exod 24:7-8); and with David (2 Sam 23:5).

The fifth special feature of Israel's life and experience is what Paul identifies as ἡ νομοθεσία, which literally means "the lawgiving." The Greek noun νομοθεσία could refer to the *giving* of the law by God, to the *reception* of the law by the people, to the *promulgation* of the law by Israel's teachers — or, in a passive sense, to the *collection* of the divine instructions by the Jewish rabbis, that is, to later *formulated legislation.* Earlier in 3:1 Paul had asked the rhetorical question, "What advantage is there in being a Jew?" The apostle immediately answers this by his confident insistence of 3:2: "Much in every way! First of all, they [the Jews] were entrusted with the words of God." So here in 9:4 his use of ἡ νομοθεσία as a prerogative of Israel must be understood as having principally in mind God's *giving* of his "words" or "instructions for living" to his people Israel. Thus, as Joseph Fitzmyer has characterized this special feature in the lives and experience of the people of Israel: "Israel had as its instructor God himself, and because of that *tôrāh* Israel possessed an unparalleled wisdom, an educative force and guide for its life."[42]

The sixth Israelite prerogative cited by Paul in 9:4 is ἡ λατρεία, which we have translated as "the worship of God." Many commentators have understood ἡ λατρεία here to mean "the OT sacrificial system."[43] That is how λατρεία is used in the LXX in describing the Passover in Exod 12:25-26 and in speaking of Israel's worship of God "at his sanctuary" in the presentation of the people's "burnt offerings, meat offerings, and peace offerings" in Josh 22:27. Yet in Rom 1:9, the apostle had used the verb λατρεύω ("I worship") with reference to his

---

39. Metzger, *Textual Commentary,* 459.

40. Cf., e.g., Wis 18:22, where it is said that Aaron's intercession stayed a plague "by bringing to remembrance God's oaths and *covenants* made with the fathers"; 2 Macc 8:15, which speaks of "the *covenants*" made with Israel's fathers; and *4 Ezra* 5:29, where Ezra questions God regarding "why those who denied your promises have been allowed to tread under foot those who have believed your *covenants.*"

41. Note the differing readings of plural and singular covenants in Sir 44:12, 17-18.

42. Fitzmyer, *Romans,* 546.

43. So, e.g., Käsemann, *Romans,* 259; Dunn, *Romans,* 2.527-28; Fitzmyer, *Romans,* 547; Moo, *Romans,* 564; Schreiner, *Romans,* 484.

"serving God" (literally "worshiping") with his whole heart "in the gospel of his Son" — and, further, he used the aorist tense of this verb when he spoke of godless people a few verses later in 1:25, declaring that they "worshiped and served created things rather than the Creator." And in Phil 3:3, Paul counters certain Jewish Christians who had insisted on the circumcision of his Gentile Christian converts by asserting that "we (i.e., believers in Jesus) are the true circumcision, that is, those who worship (λατρεύοντες) by the Spirit of God and who glory in Christ Jesus."

Such references as these suggest that in Paul's understanding, as well as in that of his Roman addressees, "worship" had a broader reference than merely Jewish sacrificial worship as prescribed in the OT. Rather, Paul's use of ἡ λατρεία here in 9:4 should likely be understood, as Robert Jewett has proposed, more generally as "including temple sacrifices, home services, the observation of the Sabbath, the recitation of the Shema, and also the Lord's Supper and other forms of early Christian worship."[44]

Christian worship has its roots in the religion of Israel, and Paul never wants to break or deny that worship connection between a real Christian and a true Israelite. But he also does not want his addressees to think of Israel's sacrificial system — even though ordained by God himself and appropriate for God's people at that time — as the only true way to worship God. So, while always understanding Christian worship as connected with the worship of the religion of Israel, Paul also speaks of the true worship of God as being broader and more boundless than the prescribed forms set out for Israel in the Jewish (OT) Scriptures.

The seventh prerogative of the people of Israel that Paul highlights in 9:4 is that to Israel belong αἱ ἐπαγγελία ("God's promises"). The question whether the plural αἱ ἐπαγγελίαι ("the promises") or the singular (ἡ) ἐπαγγελία ("the promise") should be understood as the original reading is somewhat similar to the question above whether the original text read "the covenants" or "the covenant" — though in this case the plural "the promises" is better supported by the textual tradition than is the singular "the promise" (see "Textual Notes" above). More important, however, is the fact that the internal rationale given above for preferring "the covenants" over "the covenant" applies here as well, and thus favors the acceptance of αἱ ἐπαγγελίαι ("the promises") over (ἡ) ἐπαγγελία ("the promise") as the original reading.

Paul had written earlier in Romans, in 4:1-24, regarding "the promise" that God gave to Abraham in Gen 15:5, referring four times to that promise by the explicit use of the singular ἡ ἐπαγγελία in 4:13, 14, 16, and 20. And even earlier in his letter to his converts in Galatia, Paul highlighted in Gal 3:6-9 and 4:21-31 the patriarch Abraham, who based his faith on God's singular promise of Gen 15:5, and so became the prototype for all Christian believers. Undoubtedly, therefore, it was that singular topic and that singular form of the expression

44. Jewett, *Romans*, 565.

that motivated a number of scribes down through the centuries to change αἱ
ἐπαγγελίαι ("the promises") to (ἡ) ἐπαγγελία ("the promise") here in 9:4. Yet
Paul also speaks later in Rom 15:8 about God having confirmed "the promises
given to the patriarchs" (τὰς ἐπαγγελίας τῶν πατέρων), which plural reference
would include all the promises God gave to Abraham (Gen 12:2-3; 13:14-17;
15:4-5; 17:4-8, 16-21; 21:12-13; 22:16-18), to Isaac (Gen 26:3-5), and to Jacob (Gen
28:13-15), as well as the promises he gave to Moses (Deut 18:18-19) and to David
(2 Sam 7:8-16). Further, Paul goes on in 9:6-29 to refer to the "remnant" of Israel
as "the children of promise" (9:8) and to speak of both Sarah and Rebecca as
recipients of God's promises (9:9-13).

In effect, then, as Robert Jewett has rightly theologized: "All of the promises received by the congregations in Rome belong first and foremost to Israel.
Sympathy with Israel's tragic plight is therefore required by the multitude of
divine promises on which the life of these congregations depends."[45] But it is
also a fact that Jews and Christians have understood and responded to God's
promises as recorded in the OT quite differently. Therefore in this third section
of the body middle of his letter Paul seeks to clarify matters from a Christian
perspective regarding (1) how the Christian gospel relates to God's promises to
Israel and (2) how matters are to be understood in the overall course of God's
salvation history.

Paul's listing of this seventh prerogative of the people of Israel, where he
declares "to them belong God's promises," leads him directly into his presentation in 9:6-29 of God's promises to the remnant of Israel — which is the first part
of his three-part exposition of what we have captioned "The Christian Gospel
vis-à-vis God's Promises to Israel" in 9:6–11:32. Yet before developing that three-
part exposition, Paul adds two further matters of great importance — not as an
afterthought, but as the climax of all that he has been leading up to. These two
crowning special features of the people of Israel concern persons and not just
privileges given or events experienced: the first, that of their having Abraham,
Isaac, and Jacob as their forefathers; the second, that of Israel having been the
matrix "as far as human descent is concerned" of God's promised Messiah.

The first of the two is introduced by a resumption of the genitive plural
relative pronoun ὧν ("of whom [belong]," or "to whom belong"), which had appeared at the beginning of the six special features of Israel's life and experience
in 9:4 and here introduces the first of the prerogatives of the people of Israel at
the beginning of 9:5. Because of the repetition of ὧν ("to whom belong"), we
have translated this special feature of Israel's life and experience as "to them *also*
belong the patriarchs." The second God-given special privilege of the people of
Israel is introduced by the prepositional phrase ἐξ ὧν ("from whom"), thereby
signaling by its somewhat differing phraseology something different about the
listing of this prerogative. Thus we have translated this final special feature of
Israel's life and experience — which from Paul's perspective is the most import-

45. Jewett, *Romans*, 566.

ant prerogative listed — as follows: "And *from them* [i.e., 'the people of Israel'], as far as human descent is concerned, has come the Christ ['the Messiah']."

For Paul, as well as for all Jewish believers in Jesus, the two great figures in God's redemptive program are the patriarch Abraham and God's promised Messiah Jesus. The apostle set forth their importance earlier in 3:21–4:25 — which passage in 3:21-31 and 4:25 focuses first on the faithfulness and redemptive work of Jesus in 3:21-31, and then in 4:1-21 highlights the example of Abraham's trust in God as the prototype for all believers in Jesus.[46] For Jews, the most important figures in the nation's history were Moses, to whom God gave the Torah ("Instructions for Living"), and the patriarchs Abraham, Isaac, and Jacob, from whose experiences one can derive spiritual and practical lessons for one's own life. In Paul's listing of the prerogatives of the people of Israel here in 9:4-5, however, he does not refer directly to Moses — even though he included ἡ νομοθεσία (literally "the lawgiving," i.e., God's "giving the law") in 9:4 as a special feature of Israel's history. Rather, he cites only "the patriarchs" (οἱ πατέρες) and "the Christ" (ὁ Χριστός), understanding the first as epitomized in the life and faith of Abraham and the second as embodied in Jesus of Nazareth, God's promised Messiah.

Scholars down through the centuries have never had any doubts regarding the wording of the text of 9:5b. They have often, however, had questions about the punctuation of this latter portion of the verse and therefore its meaning. For since the earliest MSS of this verse (and all the other texts of the NT) are without any systematic punctuation, both ancient scribes and contemporary editors have been forced to insert such punctuation as has seemed most appropriate to them, as based on their own understanding of the syntax and meaning of what Paul has written.

In the main, two seemingly minor — though significantly different — options for the punctuation of 9:5b have been proposed and extensively discussed, with this difference resulting in two quite different translations:

1. *The Christological Option,* which punctuates the text with a comma after the word σάρκα, thereby reading καὶ ἐξ ὧν ὁ Χριστὸς τὸ κατὰ σάρκα, ὁ ὢν ἐπί πάντων θεὸς, εὐλογητὸς εἰς τοὺς αἰῶνας, ἀμήν (literally "And from them is the Christ according to the flesh, who is God over all, blessed forever! Amen").[47]

---

46. Cf. also Gal 3:6-9 and 4:21-31.

47. The most comprehensive exegetical, contextual, and theological defense of Rom 9:5b as a Christological affirmation is that by M. J. Harris, *Jesus as God,* 143-72. The position has also been argued by such scholars as Godet, *Romans,* 341-44; B. Weiss, *An die Römer,* 396; Zahn, *An die Römer,* 342-43; Sanday and Headlam, *Romans,* 233-38 (with an extensive list of earlier advocates); H. W. Schmidt, *An die Römer,* 158; Schlatter, *Romans,* 202; Murray, *Romans,* 2.245-48 (appendix A: "Romans 9:5"); Michel, *An die Römer,* 296-98; Schlier, *Römerbrief,* 287-88; Cranfield, *Romans,* 2.464-70; Morris, *Romans,* 349-50; Fitzmyer, *Romans,* 548-49; Moo, *Romans,* 565-67; and Jewett, *Romans,* 566-69.

2. *The Theological Option,* which punctuates the text with a period after the word σάρκα, thereby reading καὶ ἐξ ὧν ὁ Χριστὸς τὸ κατὰ σάρκα. ὁ ὢν ἐπὶ πάντων θεὸς, εὐλογητὸς εἰς τοὺς αἰῶνας, ἀμήν (literally "And from them is the Christ according to the flesh. May God who is over all be blessed forever! Amen").[48]

Within these two basic punctuation options there have been proposed a number of other translation options — perhaps as many as eight ways of reading the latter portion of this verse.[49]

The debate among biblical scholars during an earlier generation has been almost equally divided. Of late, however, scholarly opinion in favor of the Christological interpretation seems to have become dominant.[50] The principal reasons why many earlier and some modern scholars preferred the theological option for the translation of 9:5b are as follows:

1. Paul does not elsewhere in his letters refer to Jesus as God[51] — though, as Robert Jewett has quite properly responded: "Phil 2:6 is a prominent example of his doing so and in many of the other instances where Paul refers to Jesus as 'Lord,' divinity is implied."[52]
2. The phrase "God over all things" is too extensive a claim to make for Christ[53] — yet, as Jewett goes on to point out: "there are instances in

48. The most comprehensive exegetical, contextual, and theological defense of Rom 9:5b as a doxology in praise of God is that by Ezra Abbot, "On the Construction of Romans ix.5," 87-154. The position has also been argued by such scholars as H. A. W. Meyer, *Romans,* 2.117-20 (with an extensive list of earlier advocates); Lietzmann, *An die Römer,* 90; C. H. Dodd, *Romans,* 152; Käsemann, *Romans,* 260; Kuss, *Römerbrief,* 3.678; Wilckens, *An die Römer,* 2.189; Ziesler, *Romans,* 239; Zeller, *An die Römer,* 174; Dunn, *Romans,* 2.528-29; Stuhlmacher, *Romans,* 146; L. T. Johnson, *Reading Romans,* 147; and Byrne, *Romans,* 288.

49. See, e.g., the various translations discussed earlier by Abbot, "On the Construction of Romans ix.5," 87-154; *idem,* "Recent Discussions of Romans ix.5," 90-112; note also the more recent (as well as more abbreviated) discussions of Cranfield, *Romans,* 2.465-70; Moo, *Romans,* 565, and M. J. Harris, *Jesus as God,* 150-55.

50. As witness, e.g., the editors of *NA*[26&27] and *GNT*[3&4], as well as the translators of the NRSV, whose preferred translation now reads (though with alternative readings in the footnotes): "From them, according to the flesh, comes the Messiah, *who is over all, God blessed forever.* Amen" — which is a significant reversal of the earlier critical texts and the RSV-preferred translation: "Of their race, according to the flesh, is the Christ. *God who is over all be blessed for ever.* Amen." Note also the preferred translation of the NIV: "From them is traced the human ancestry of Christ, *who is God over all, forever praised!* Amen"; as well of the TNIV: "From them is traced the human ancestry of the Messiah, *who is God over all, forever praised!* Amen" (with also alternative readings in the footnotes).

51. So, e.g., H. A. W. Meyer, *Romans,* 2.118-19; Käsemann, *Romans,* 260; Kuss, *Römerbrief,* 3.678; Dunn, *Romans,* 2.529.

52. Jewett, *Romans,* 567; citing in support Hurtado, *Lord Jesus Christ,* 108-18.

53. So, e.g., H. A. W. Meyer, *Romans,* 2.120.

789

which Paul makes such a claim for Christ by referring to him as 'Lord' over all."[54]

3. The reverential expression εὐλογητός ("blessed," "praised") is used only as an ascription of God himself in the OT[55] and by Paul elsewhere in his letters,[56] as well as by other writers of the NT[57] — which Jewett acknowledges is a matter that "must be explained," but to which he also offers the following probable explanation: "The preceding reference to Christ as stemming from Israel 'insofar as the flesh is concerned' is a delimitation that invites an antithesis, which the doxology to Christ provides, thus bringing this passage into correlation with the opening confession: 'from David's seed according to the flesh, appointed son of God in power according to the Spirit of holiness' (1:3-4)."[58]

The major exegetical feature that favors "the Christ" (ὁ Χριστός) as being ascribed as "God" (ὁ θεός) in 9:5b is, as Murray Harris has expressed it, the following Greek syntactical pattern that appears throughout the LXX and elsewhere in the NT:

> Throughout the Greek Bible, whenever εὐλογητός occurs in an independent or asyndetic doxology, it always precedes the name of God. Thus, for instance, εὐλογητος ὁ θεὸς ὁ ὕψιστος (Gen. 14:20) and εὐλογητὸς ὁ θεὸς καὶ πατὴρ τοῦ κυρίου ἡμῶν ᾽Ιησοῦ Χριστοῦ (2 Cor. 1:3; Eph. 1:3; 1 Pet. 1:3). But in Romans 9:5 εὐλογητός follows θεός. If normal biblical word order for independent doxologies were followed in Romans 9:5, one would expect either εὐλογητὸς θεὸς εἰς τοὺς αἰῶνας, ἀμήν (if ὁ ὢν ἐπὶ πάντων is construed with ὁ Χριστός) or εὐλογητὸς ὁ θεὸς ὁ ὢν ἐπὶ τοὺς αἰῶνας, ἀμήν.[59]

The major theological and contextual arguments that favor "the Christ" (ὁ Χριστός) as being ascribed "God" (ὁ θεός) in 9:5b, as Robert Jewett has summarized them from a vast body of literature on the subject, are as follows:

---

54. Jewett, *Romans*, 567; citing Rom 10:12; 14:9; Phil 2:10; cf. also Col 1:15-17.
55. Cf., e.g., Gen 14:20; 2 Chr 2:12; 6:4; Ps 72:18 (LXX 71:18).
56. Cf. Rom 1:25; 2 Cor 1:3; 11:31; Eph 1:3.
57. Cf. Mark 14:61; Luke 1:68; 1 Pet 1:3.
58. Jewett, *Romans*, 568; citing in support Cranfield, *Romans*, 2.468.
59. M. J. Harris, *Jesus as God*, 161. See also "Blessed be the Lord" (εὐλογητὸς Κύριος) in Gen 9:26; 24:27; Exod 18:10; 1 Sam 25:32; and Ps 41:13 (LXX 40:13). There is an apparent exception to this exegetical pattern in the Septuagint at Ps 68:19 (LXX 67:19) (Κύριος ὁ θεὸς εὐλογητός, "Blessed be the Lord God"), but this is evidently, by comparison with the MT, a gloss that was added to the real doxology of Ps 68:20 (LXX 67:20). Further, see Cranfield, *Romans*, 2.464-70, who on page 468 speaks of this exegetical pattern as being "in itself almost conclusive." Also note Harris, 161-63, who has gone on to cite and evaluate a number of ways this "extraordinary inversion (on the assumption that v. 5b is a doxology to God the Father)" has been explained by earlier and contemporary advocates of the theological option.

1. "The ascription of divinity to Christ was the principal barrier against Jewish acceptance of Jesus as the Messiah, so a doxology to him as God is relevant to Paul's argument."

2. "The participle ὤν makes excellent sense in reference to Christ, with the connotation 'who is really God,' reflecting the controversial point [of the passage]."

3. "The preceding reference to Christ as stemming from Israel 'insofar as the flesh is concerned' is a delimitation that invites an antithesis, which the doxology to Christ provides, thus bringing this passage into correlation with the opening confession: 'from David's seed according to the flesh; appointed son of God in power according to the Spirit of holiness' (1:3-4)."[60]

We therefore agree with the evaluation of the evidence as proposed by Oscar Cullman in the middle of the twentieth century: "We conclude that it is quite probable, if not certain, that Paul designates Jesus Christ as 'God' in Rom. 9:5"[61] — as well as the conclusion expressed by Murray Harris in 1992: "Given the high Christology of the Pauline letters, according to which Jesus shares the divine name and nature, exercises divine functions, and is the object of human faith and adoration, it should generate no surprise if on occasion Paul should refer to Jesus by the generic title θεός."[62]

The ἀμήν ("Amen") that appears at the end of 9:5 calls for a response of solemn ratification (as in an affirmation of faith) or hearty approval (as in an assertion of agreement). It was used by speakers and writers in anticipation of the response they wanted to evoke, as well as expressed as an affirmative response by those who heard or read what those speakers or writers said or wrote. Paul in 1 Cor 14:16 refers to people saying "Amen" to expressions of thanksgiving in the various Christian churches; John "the Seer" in Rev 5:14 speaks of "the four living creatures" in heaven saying "Amen" in response to the praise that had been presented by all creation "to the one seated on the throne and to the Lamb." As the people's response, it was also used in Jewish and Christian prayers.[63] And it appears repeatedly as the final liturgical affirmation in Christian doxologies.[64]

More pertinent to the situation here in 9:5b, however, is the fact that a liturgical "Amen" was often turned into a literary call for an affirmative response by the readers — as in Paul's closing statements in his earlier letter to his own Christian converts in Galatia in 6:18 ("May the grace of our Lord Jesus Christ be with your spirit, brothers and sisters. Amen!"), and then later in this more

60. Jewett, *Romans*, 568.

61. Cullmann, *Christology of the New Testament*, 313.

62. M. J. Harris, *Jesus as God*, 171, which is the final entry and probably the most significant of Harris's list of six exegetical, contextual, and theological conclusions.

63. Cf. Schlier, "ἀμήν," 1.335-38.

64. So, e.g., in Paul's letters "Amen" appears at the conclusion of creedal affirmations and doxologies in Rom 1:25; 11:36; 16:27; Gal 1:5; Eph 3:21; Phil 4:20; 1 Tim 1:17; 6:16; 2 Tim 4:18; see also Heb 13:21; 1 Pet 4:11; 5:11; Jude 25.

formal letter to the Christians in Rome in 15:33 ("The God of peace be with all of you. Amen!"). Thus here in 9:5b Paul calls on his Christian addressees at Rome to respond affirmatively to his proclamation of "the Christ," that is, "the Messiah" of God's promise to Israel, who is "supreme over all as God blessed forever" — and whom he has proclaimed to pagan Gentiles as humanity's Lord and Savior. Further, as Robert Jewett has rightly observed: "By uttering their assent, the congregations in Rome take the first step to overcome their cultural chauvinism and open themselves to the mission that Paul wishes to advance."[65]

BIBLICAL THEOLOGY

In any reading of Rom 9:1-5, the following three features come immediately to the fore:

1. The passion of Paul for the welfare of his own people (as well as the welfare of all people, as evidenced elsewhere in all his letters) in his proclamation of the Christian gospel (in 9:1-3).
2. The recognition by Paul that what God brought about on behalf of Israel in the past has had a large part in effecting the conditions for God's program of salvation and reconciliation through Christ Jesus on behalf of all people in the present (in 9:4-5a).
3. Paul's focus in his proclamation on Jesus, who (a) "as far as human descent is concerned," is thoroughly Jewish; (b) as far as his place in his nation's history is concerned, is God's promised Messiah; and (c) as far as his work and person in the outworking of God's salvation history are concerned, is "supreme over all as God blessed forever" (in 9:5b).

These three features — that is, (1) a passion for the welfare of one's own people (as well as for all people); (2) a recognition of God's working in past history, and particularly within another culture and societal framework, as providing the divinely ordained setting for the present course of salvation history; and (3) a focus on the work and person of Jesus in Christian proclamation — need to be incorporated into a biblical theology that is truly Christian.

Yet, while it may legitimately be claimed that here in 9:5b Paul declares that Jesus is not only "the Christ" (i.e., the Jewish "Messiah") but also the One "who is supreme over all as God blessed forever," the somewhat surprising fact is that elsewhere in his NT letters Paul seldom (if ever) uses θεός ("God") as a Christological title — that is, as an ascription of Jesus. The only two times he does are found in Titus 2:13, which reads τοῦ μεγάλου θεοῦ καὶ σωτῆρος ἡμῶν Χριστοῦ Ἰησοῦ and most likely is to be translated "our great God and Savior, Christ Jesus," and in 2 Thess 1:12, which reads τοῦ θεοῦ ἡμῶν καὶ κυρίου Ἰησοῦ

65. Jewett, *Romans*, 569.

Χριστοῦ and could be translated "our God and Lord, Jesus Christ." In both passages a single article is used to connect the two nouns of the same case that follow; such a phenomenon suggests to most grammarians and lexicographers, as well as to many NT translators, NT commentators, and writers on NT theology, that the two descriptive nouns that follow that one article have to do with the same person.[66]

Such a pattern is especially clear in Titus 2:13 (as it is also in 2 Pet 1:1). A major problem in interpreting 2 Thess 1:12 in this manner, however, is the fact that the immediate context of this verse is bipartite, that is, the context speaks of both "our God" and "our Lord Jesus Christ" — which has led many NT scholars to conclude that in this verse Paul must also be speaking in a bipartite manner of both "our God" and "the Lord Jesus Christ."[67] An appeal to 1 Tim 3:16 as also supporting a Christological use of θεός is illegitimate, for reading the text as "who (ὅς) was manifested in the flesh" has much stronger support in the textual tradition than does the variant "God (θεός) was manifested in the flesh."

In addition to θεός being used by Paul as a title for Jesus here in 9:5b — as well as most likely in Titus 2:13 (and perhaps, though with a question about the bipartite nature of the verse's immediate context, in 2 Thess 1:12) — it needs to be noted (1) that θεός as a Christological title appears a further six times in the NT, in John 1:1, 18; 20:28, 1 John 5:20; Heb 1:8; and 2 Pet 1:1, and (2) that all six of these occurrences are found in writings representative of a Jewish Christian cycle of witness — three times in John's Gospel; once in the sermonic materials of Hebrews, quoting Ps 45:6; and once each in 1 John and 2 Peter. The problem of why Paul in his letters so seldom ascribed θεός to Jesus, however, is a real one, which calls for some explanation. Little explanation can be offered along theological lines. For Paul, if anyone among the early believers in Jesus, undoubtedly thought of Jesus in terms of what may be called a "high Christology." Certainly he understood him as divine. Further, Paul used the associated title κύριος ("Lord"), which was employed frequently in the Jewish (OT) Scriptures as equivalent to "God," more frequently than did all the other writers of the NT.

In all likelihood, it may be postulated that Paul did not usually use θεός with reference to Jesus in his outreach to pagan Gentiles because of the confusion such an ascription would have caused among many in the Gentile world — which was, of course, the philosophical and religious world in which he ministered. To use θεός with respect to Jesus in a Jewish setting would have generated one of two quite opposite reactions: (1) a rethinking of traditional monotheism

66. Though sometimes disputed, it is nonetheless a generally reliable exegetical rule that "when the copulative καί connects two nouns of the same case, if the article ὁ or any of its cases precedes the first of the said nouns or participles, and is not repeated before the second noun or participle, the latter always relates to the same person that is expressed or described by the first noun or participle; that is, that it denotes a further description of the first-named person." This "rule" is usually attributed to Granville Sharp.

67. Cf., e.g., Cullmann, *Christology of the New Testament*, 313; L. Morris, *First and Second Epistles to the Thessalonians* (Grand Rapids: Eerdmans, 2009), 212.

in an attempt to include the idea of a plurality of persons within a unity of Divine Being, or (2) a charge of blasphemy. It would hardly have caused Jews to think along the lines of polytheism. Everything in Israel's history and consciousness militated against that. But to use θεός as a title for Jesus in a Gentile milieu, without in some way indicating its relationship to monotheism, would have invariably resulted in the proclamation of Jesus as "one god among many," and thus would have undermined the basic structure of the apostle's proclamation of the Christian message. Thus it may be postulated that in order to proclaim the absolute lordship of Jesus, and yet protect the proclamation of Jesus from being accepted as yet another polytheistic presentation, Paul in his Gentile mission usually used the bipartite confession "God the Father" and "the Lord Jesus Christ" — employing the title "God" to signal the note of monotheism and the title "Lord" to designate the supremacy of Christ Jesus, though for the apostle himself the ascriptions "God" and "Lord" were broadly equivalent.

Nonetheless, just as the confession of the early church that "Jesus is Lord" (as later in Rom 10:9) appears in his letters, so Paul's consciousness of the nature of his "Lord Jesus Christ" also occasionally expressed itself in the direct assertion that "the Christ" is "supreme over all as God blessed forever!" (as here in 9:5). Such a wording of this basic Christological conviction might not have been understood by Paul's Gentile audiences in his evangelistic preaching. It would certainly, however, have been understood and appreciated by his Christian addressees at Rome. And so in this introduction to his three-part exposition of 9:6–11:32, Paul contextualizes his presentation in a manner that would resonate clearly and most accurately with his Jewish-Gentile Christian readers in the Christian congregations of Rome.

CONTEXTUALIZATION FOR TODAY

Much in this introductory material of 9:1-5 is of importance as a paradigm for believers in Jesus today — that is, as a paradigm for their lives as Christians and for their ministries to others on behalf of Christ. Certainly the passion that Paul had for the welfare of his own people (as well as for all people) sets the standard for a similar passion as motivating all of us who claim to be followers of Christ Jesus and who desire to serve him in some type of ministry to others. So also Paul's recognition of the validity of Israel's prerogatives in the course of God's redemptive program on behalf of his people vis-à-vis his understanding of the culmination of God's program of salvation and reconciliation through Christ Jesus on behalf of all people should not be seen as a tension in one's theological understanding, but, rather, needs to be understood as integrating and vitalizing realities in a Christian's thought and action. And, just as certainly, Christians today need to focus their lives and their witness on Jesus as a Jew, as Israel's promised Messiah, and as the One "who is supreme over all as God blessed forever."

Christians also need to learn from the paradigms Paul exhibits in his ministry regarding how to contextualize the Christian gospel in a manner that would be understood and appreciated by people today, all of whom live out their lives in the context of their own cultures and in terms of their own modes of perception. Much of what we can learn from Paul in this regard has already been observed in what he has written earlier in Romans (as well as in his other NT letters). But here in Rom 9:1-5, and particularly in the latter portion of v. 5, we are able to learn something more about how Paul used the most significant topics and most appropriate language in addressing his various audiences — not only in speaking to pagan Gentiles of his day, as presented in précis form in 5:1–8:39, but also in writing to believing Christians at Rome who had been extensively influenced by Jewish Christianity and had a working knowledge of the Jewish (OT) Scriptures.

2. Part I of Paul's Exposition:
God's Promises Given to "the Remnant" of Israel, with OT Passages Cited in Support (9:6-29)

TRANSLATION

⁹:⁶*It is not that God's word has failed. For not all those who are from Israel are Israel. ⁷Nor because they are the seed of Abraham are they all his children. Rather, "It is through Isaac that your seed will be reckoned." ⁸That is, it is not the children of the flesh who are God's children, but the children of the promise who are regarded as Abraham's seed. ⁹For the word of the promise is this: "At the appointed time I will return and Sarah will have a son."*

¹⁰*Not only that, but also Rebecca had sexual intercourse with only one man, our father Isaac. ¹¹Yet before the twins were born or had done anything good or bad — in order that God's purpose in election might stand: ¹²not by works but by him who calls — she was told, "The older will serve the younger." ¹³Just as it is written: "Jacob I loved, but Esau I hated."*

¹⁴*What then shall we say? "Is there injustice with God?" Certainly not! ¹⁵For he says to Moses:*

"I will have mercy on whomever I am merciful,
and I will have compassion on whomever I am compassionate."

¹⁶*Therefore it does not depend on a person's desire or a person's effort, but, rather, on the mercy of God. ¹⁷For the Scripture says to Pharaoh: "I raised you up for this very purpose, that I might display my power in you and that my name might be proclaimed in all the earth." ¹⁸Therefore God has mercy on whomever he desires to have mercy, and he hardens whomever he desires to harden.*

¹⁹*You will say to me then: "Why [then] does he still blame us? For who resists his will?" ²⁰O mere human, on the contrary, who are you to talk back to God? Shall what is molded say to him who molded it, "Why did you make me like this?" ²¹Does not the potter have the right to make out of the same lump of clay some pottery for noble purposes and some for common use?*

²²*And what if God, choosing to show his wrath and make his power known, bore with great patience the objects of his wrath, which are prepared for destruction? ²³What if he did this in order to make the riches of his glory known to the object of his mercy, whom he prepared in advance for glory — ²⁴even to us, whom he also called, not only from the Jews but also from among the Gentiles?*

²⁵*As he says also in [the book of] Hosea:*

"Those who were not my people I will call 'my people,'
and her who was not beloved I will call 'beloved.'"

²⁶*And,*

"In that very place where it was said to them, 'You are not my people,' there they will be called 'sons and daughters of the living God.' "

²⁷*Isaiah cries out concerning Israel:*

"Though the number of the sons and daughters of Israel is as the sand
by the sea,
only the remnant will be saved.
²⁸*For the Lord with rigor and finality will carry out his word*
['of judgment'] on the earth."

²⁹*And just as Isaiah has earlier said [in his prophecies]:*

"Unless the Lord Almighty had left us seed ['surviving descendants'],
we would have become like Sodom and
we would have been similar to Gomorrah."

TEXTUAL NOTES

9:6a The inclusion of ὅτι ("that") in the phrase οὐχ οἷον δὲ ὅτι (literally "it is not the situation that") is well attested in the textual tradition. Its omission in P⁴⁶, in versions it and sy^p, and by Ambrosiaster is probably best understood as an attempt to provide an easier and more colloquial reading.

6b The statement οὐ γὰρ πάντες οἱ ἐξ Ἰσραήλ οὗτοι Ἰσραήλ ("for not all those who are from Israel are Israel") is widely attested in the textual tradition. The plural Ἰσραηλῖται ("Israelites"), however, is found in uncials D (06) F G, in minuscules 1881^c (Category II) and 88 330 614 (Category III), and is reflected in vg^{ww}. Though the variant reading Ἰσραηλῖται leaves no doubt regarding Paul's meaning, its inclusion is too weakly attested in the textual tradition to be accepted as original, and thus it must be viewed as an attempted linguistic improvement.

7 The causal conjunction ὅτι ("because," "since") is very strongly supported in the textual tradition. The abstract nominative plural adjective ὅσοι ("all those who," "as many as"), however, is found in Origen^{gr} and reflected in the Latin *qui* ("who") of it^{a b} and vg^{cl}. Both of these variants appear to be only attempted efforts at stylistic improvement.

11 The substantival adjective φαῦλον ("worthless," "bad," "evil"), which appears only four or five times elsewhere in the NT (in addition to here in 9:11, also in John 3:20; 5:29; 2 Cor 5:10; and Titus 2:8; and perhaps also Jas 3:16), is attested by uncials ℵ A B and by minuscules 1739 (Category I), 81 1506 1881 (Category II), and 6 69 365 424^c 630 1243 1319 1573 (Category III). The much more frequently used word κακόν ("bad," "worthless," "evil"), however, appears in P⁴⁶, in uncials D F G Ψ (also *Byz* K L), and in minuscules 1175 (Category I), 2464 (Category II), and 88 104 323 326 330 424^c 614 1241 1735 1846 1874 2344 (Category III). The words κακόν and φαῦλον are synonyms, and so nothing of any substance is at stake in the choice of one over the other. Yet κακόν should probably be understood as the variant reading in this verse, and therefore viewed as a scribal substitution for the much more infrequently used φαῦλον. Further, as has been often pointed out, κακόν would bring Paul's usage into conformity with his usual antithesis between ἀγαθός ("good," "fit") and κακός ("bad," "evil"),[1] and so it may be surmised that later scribes felt free to substitute it for the more infrequently used φαῦλον.

12 The feminine dative pronoun αὐτῇ ("to her") is very well attested in the textual tradition. It does not, however, appear in P^{46} or in uncial D*; nor is it reflected in vg or sy^p or supported by Origen or Ambrosiaster. Its omission, being far less supported in the textual tradition, must be viewed as a scribal attempt at stylistic improvement and therefore secondary.

13 The adverb καθώς ("just as") is strongly supported by P^{46}, by uncials ℵ A D F G P Ψ (also *Byz* K L), and by minuscules 33 1175 1739 (Category I), 1506 1881 2464 (Category II), and 6 69 88 104 323 326 330 365 424^c 614 1241 1243 1319 1505 1573 1735 1874 2495 (Category III). Its synonym καθάπερ ("just as"), which appears in the NT only in Paul's letters, is found only in Codex Vaticanus (uncial B) and is supported only by Origen, and so must be viewed as secondary.

18 The addition of ὁ θεός ("God") by uncial D, and as reflected in numerous Latin versions and supported by the commentator Ambrosiaster, has every appearance of being a needless attempt to clarify the third-person singular suffix "he" in the four verbs of the two sentences — and thus should be viewed as being secondary.

19 The inclusion of οὖν ("then") in the phrase τί οὖν ("why then") is attested by P^{46} and by uncials B D F G; it is also reflected in it and vg^{mss}. The omission of this second οὖν ("then") in the verse, however, is supported by uncials ℵ A P Ψ (also *Byz* K L) and by minuscules 33 1175 1739 (Category I), 1506 1881 2464 (Category II), and 6 69 88 104 323 326 330 365 424^c 614 1241 1243 1319 1505 1573 1735 1874 2495; it is also reflected in the majority of the vg versions and in the sy. The matter of originality is difficult to determine on the basis of the evidence from the textual tradition alone. C. E. B. Cranfield is probably right to argue for the omission of this second οὖν on the grounds that the frequent repetition of τί οὖν ("what then?") in Romans would have provoked a copyist's error here in 9:19. Yet the frequency of the expression may also be used to support the legitimacy of its repeated appearance in this verse. We will, therefore, include this second οὖν ("then") in our translation, but note the problem by placing it in parentheses.

20a The reading ὦ ἄνθρωπε μενοῦνγε ("O man ['mere human'], on the contrary") is attested by uncials ℵ A B and by minuscules 1739 (Category I), 81 1506 1881 (Category II), and 69 630 (Category III); it is also supported by Origen. The omission of μενοῦνγε ("on the contrary"), however, is found in P^{46}, in uncials D* F G, and in minuscule 629 (Category III); it is also reflected in the Latin versions. Further, the reversal of the sequence to μενοῦνγε ὦ ἄνθρωπε ("on the contrary, O man ['mere human']") appears in uncials ℵ^2 D^2 P Ψ (also *Byz* K L) and in minuscules 33 (Category I), 2464 (Category II), and 6 88 104 323 326 330 1735 2495 (Category III); and it is reflected in sy^p. The use of μενοῦνγε ("on the contrary") after the expression ὦ ἄνθρωπε ("O man ['mere human']") was probably surprising to some ancient scribes, and therefore either deleted

---

1. Cf., e.g., Rom 3:8; 7:19 (though in 2 Cor 5:10 ἀγαθόν and φαῦλον are contrasted).

or placed before ὦ ἄνθρωπε. Yet, though ὦ ἄνθρωπε μενοῦνγε may have surprised some scribes, its inclusion and order are better attested, and so this "more difficult reading" deserves to be considered original.

20b The second-person singular aorist active verb ἐποίησας ("you made") in the question asked at the end of the verse is very strongly supported in the textual tradition. The variant ἔπλασας ("you molded"), which appears in D and is reflected in sy^p, is far less supported and thus undoubtedly a later scribal reading.

23a The inclusion of καί ("and") at the beginning of the verse is very widely attested by P^46, uncials ℵ A D F G P Ψ (also *Byz* K L), and minuscules 33 1175 1739 (Category I), 81 256 1506 1881 1962 2127 2464 (Category II), and 88 104 181 263 323 330 365 451 459 614 629 1241 1243 1319 1505 1573 1735 1846 1852 1874 1877 2344 2492 2495 (Category III); it is also reflected in a number of it and vg versions, as well as in sy^p, h, cop^bo, eth, geo, and slav, and is supported by Chrysostom Ambrosiaster Pelagius and Augustine. The conjunction καί at the beginning of the verse does not, however, appear in Codex Vaticanus (B 03) or in minuscules 6 69 326 424^c 436 1912 (Category III), with its possible deletion being also noted in 1739^mg; nor does it appear in Origen^gr, lat. In all likelihood, as Bruce Metzger has suggested, this omission of καί on the part of certain scribes came about because of "translational freedom, and not a different underlying Greek text"[2] — i.e., because of their attempt, whether conscious or unconscious, to eliminate the presence of an additional καί in the sentence of 9:22-24.

23b The phrase τῆς δόξης ("of his glory") is very widely attested in the textual tradition. The variant τῆς χρηστότητος ("of his kindness"), however, appears in its place in uncial P and is reflected in sy^p. Just why such a replacement of the noun occurred is impossible to say. Nonetheless, it is too weakly supported to be accepted as original.

25 The inclusion of the preposition ἐν ("in") in the expression "*in* [the book of] Hosea" is strongly supported throughout most of the textual tradition. It is omitted, however, by P^46(vid) and Codex Vaticanus (B 03). Since the dative case does not require a preposition, the preposition was probably deleted for stylistic reasons. But the meaning remains the same with or without the preposition.

26a The genitive singular relative pronoun οὗ ("of which") is well attested in the textual tradition. The dative singular relative pronoun ᾧ ("in which") appears in P^46, in uncial ℵ*, and is supported by Irenaeus^lat(vid). Either οὗ ("of which") or ᾧ ("in which") would represent acceptable Greek syntax. Probably the substitution of ᾧ for οὗ was made by P^46 and uncorrected ℵ in order to avoid any possible confusion with the negative οὐ ("not") that appears immediately following in the same sentence.

26b The phrase ἐρρέθη αὐτοῖς ("it was said to them") is strongly supported by uncials ℵ A D F G P Ψ (also *Byz* K L), and by minuscules 33 1175 1739 (Category I), 1506 1881 2464 (Category II), and 6 69 88 104 323 326 330 365 614 1241 1243 1319 1505 1573 1735 1838 1874 2344 2495 (Category III); it is also reflected in vg sy^h cop versions. The dative pronoun αὐτοῖς ("to them"), however, is omitted in Codex Vaticanus (B 03) and by Irenaeus^lat(vid). More importantly, the variant reading ἐὰν [or ἄν] κληθήσονται ("if they are called") appears in P^46, in uncials F and G, and is reflected in a number of Latin versions

2. Metzger, *Textual Commentary*, 462.

and the Syriac Peshitta (sy^p). In all likelihood, ἐὰν [or ἄν] κληθήσονται ("if they are called") is a scribal error, which came about by assimilation with the verb κληθήσονται that follows in the quotation.

26c The pronoun ὑμεῖς ("you") in the statement "*You* are not my people" is widely attested in the textual tradition. It does not appear, however, in P^{46}; nor is it reflected in it and sy^p or supported by Irenaeus^{vid}. The omission of ὑμεῖς ("you") is probably to be viewed as an early scribal error.

27 The noun ὑπόλειμμα ("remnant") is attested by uncials א* A B and by minuscules 81 (Category II) and 1739^c (a corrected Category I minuscule); it is also supported by Eusebius. Its synonym κατάλειμμα ("remnant"), however, is much more widely attested by uncials א^1 D F G P Ψ (also *Byz* K L) and by minuscules 33 1175 1739* (Category I), 256 1881 1962 2127 2464 (Category II), and 6 61 69 88 104 181 218 263 323 326 330 365 436 451 459 614 621 623 629 630 917 1241 1243 1319 1398 1505 1563 1573 1678 1718 1735 1751 1838 1845 1852 1874 1875 1877 1912 1942 2138 2197 2200 2344 2492 2495 2516 2523 2544 (Category III). There is no essential difference in meaning between ὑπόλειμμα and κατάλειμμα. Yet the text-critical rule that favors the "more difficult reading" has led most text critics to accept ὑπόλειμμα ("remnant") as original.

28 The comments of Bruce Metzger on the additional words ἐν δικαιοσύνῃ, ὅτι λόγον συντετμημένον in the TR (which the KJV translated "in righteousness, because a short work will the Lord make upon the earth") are both appropriate and helpful: "The Textus Receptus, following א* D G K P Ψ 33 88 326 614 1241 *Byz Lect* Old Latin vg sy^h goth arm *al*, has filled out the quotation from the Septuagint Is 10.22-23 by inserting ἐν δικαιοσύνῃ, ὅτι λόγον συντετμημένον. Considered in itself, the absence of these words from P^{46vid} א* A B 1739 1881 syr^p cop$^{sa, bo}$ eth *al* could be explained as arising when the eye of a copyist accidentally passed from συντέμνων to συντετμημένον. But it is not credible that Paul, who in ver. 27 does not follow the Septuagint closely, should in ver. 28 have copied verbatim a sentence that is so opaque grammatically."[3]

FORM/STRUCTURE/SETTING

It is difficult to deal with matters regarding the form, structure, and setting of any passage of Scripture unless we have some idea of the major issues that the passage deals with and its basic thrust. This is true of what Paul presents in 9:6-29. For this passage has received a great variety of treatments, with its form, structure, and setting being variously explicated. It is necessary, therefore, even before attempting to exegete this subsection of material, to have some understanding of how 9:6-29 has been understood in the past and some idea regarding how it should be properly treated today.

Major Interpretations of 9:6-29 Proposed. In their classic commentary on Romans in the original ICC series, William Sanday and Arthur Headlam sketched out in a seven-page appendix, "A History of the Interpretation of Rom.

---

3. Metzger, *Textual Commentary,* 462.

ix.6-29," a condensed but highly appropriate review of the major interpretations of the passage that have been proposed from the earliest days of Christian exposition to the time of the Protestant Reformation, together with rather full documentation for the positions advanced.[4] At the beginning of their review they declare: "The difficulties of the ninth chapter of Romans are so great that few will ever be satisfied that they have really understood it"[5] — which may be one of the more obvious *under*statements ever uttered by biblical scholars. In their history of the various understandings of what Paul is teaching here in 9:6-29 — with some of the positions advanced being directly opposed to other positions espoused — Sanday and Headlam have identified the following major types of treatment of the passage:

1. That of the "Christian" Gnostics of the first two centuries A.D., who read 9:6-29 — and particularly Paul's teaching in 9:14-18 on God's election — as expressing "their own exclusive religious pretensions."[6]

2. That of Origen (185-254), who, in reacting strongly against such a Gnostic interpretation, set out in his comments on this passage a "strenuous defense of freewill." For Origen declared in his treatment of the subject that "God calls men because they are worthy, not that they are worthy because they are called." And his defense of the free will of humans as based on Rom 9 was followed, "in the main," by such Eastern Church Fathers as Diodore of Tarsus (325-393), John Chrysostom (347-407), and Theodore of Mopsuestia (350-428) — as well as by such Western Church Fathers as Jerome (347-420) and Pelagius (354-420).[7]

3. That of John Chrysostom (who in his youth had been a student of Diodore of Tarsus, as was also Theodore [later bishop of Mopsuestia]), who understood 9:6-29 as an apostolic proclamation of the free will of humans — which understanding gained widespread acceptance in Chrysostom's own day and was espoused throughout the eastern regions of the Christian church. His very popular *Thirty-two Homilies on Paul's Epistle to the Romans* "became supreme in the East," with the result that Chrysostom's understanding of 9:6-29 (as derived from Origen and Diodore of Tarsus) became dominant among all later Greek commentators — not only in the writings of Theodore of Mopsuestia, but also in the commentaries of John of Damascus, Photius, Oecumenius, Theophylact, and Euthymius Zigabenus.[8]

4. That of Augustine (354-430), who wrote in his first letter to his friend Simplicius in 397 what Sanday and Headlam have identified as "the most complete exposition of the ninth chapter of Romans," with "all the leading

---

4. Sanday and Headlam, *Romans*, 269-75.
5. *Ibid.*, 269.
6. *Ibid.*
7. *Ibid.*, 269-70.
8. *Ibid.*, 270-71.

points in this exposition" being repeated elsewhere in his later writings — that is, and most importantly for our purposes here, Augustine's insistence (1) that what appears in 9:14-19 is to be ascribed to Paul himself and represents his own opinions, "thus correcting the false exegesis of Origen and Chrysostom," and (2) that Paul's purpose in so writing "is to prove that works do not precede grace but follow it, and that Election is not based on foreknowledge, for if it were based on foreknowledge then it would imply merit." Augustine's understanding of 9:6-29 became dominant in the Middle Ages, being accepted and advanced by such important Roman Catholic scholars as Peter Abelard (1079-1144) and Thomas Aquinas (1224-1274).[9]

5. The quite diverse interpretations of 9:6-29 proposed by John Calvin (1509-1564), who built on Augustine's interpretation, and by Jacob Arminius (1560-1609), who opposed the Augustine-Calvin understanding during the period of the Protestant Reformation. On the positions of Calvin and Arminius, Sanday and Headlam have commented as follows: "The antithesis which was represented among patristic commentators by Augustine and Chrysostom was exaggerated at the Reformation by Calvin and Arminius. Each saw only his own side. Calvin followed Augustine, and exaggerated his hardest teaching [i.e., on the predestination of the damned]; Arminius showed a subtle power of finding Freewill even in the most unlikely places."[10] Earnest discussions of "predestination" and "free will" generally — as well as fervent discussions regarding a "proper" interpretation of Rom 9:6-29 in particular — continued on throughout Christian history and appear frequently today, with numerous scholarly volumes written on these matters that often express quite diverse opinions.[11]

In closing their review of interpretations of 9:6-29, Sanday and Headlam have quite rightly said: "It would be impossible to enumerate all the different varieties of opinion in the views of modern scholars."[12] Yet, despite their caveat — which, of course, includes an implied warning against any further attempts to multiply such interpretations — we believe it important for contemporary interpreters of 9:6-29 to recognize that Paul is here (1) basing his presentation on a Jewish and/or Jewish Christian type of remnant theology and (2) constructing his arguments in a then-current Jewish Christian form of remnant rhetoric. Or, perhaps more correctly stated, the apostle is here setting out his own version of such a Jewish Christian form of remnant theology and remnant rhetoric. Thus in what follows in the remainder of "Form/Structure/ Setting," as well as in our "Exegetical Comments," it is this thesis with respect

9. Sanday and Headlam, *Romans*, 271-73.
10. *Ibid.*, 273-74.
11. On the variety of treatments in their day, see *ibid.*, 274-75.
12. *Ibid.*, 275.

to the passage's remnant theology and remnant rhetoric — together with the major issues of such an approach and the passage's basic thrust — that will be developed more fully.

EXCURSUS: ON THE TERMS FOR "REMNANT" IN THE OT SCRIPTURES (MT AND LXX), AS WELL AS THE USE OF "REMNANT" IN THE RABBINIC TRACTATES OF FORMATIVE JUDAISM AND THE JEWISH NONCONFORMIST WRITINGS OF THE FIRST TWO CENTURIES B.C.

There are four Hebrew root words used in the Jewish (OT) Scriptures that express the concept of "remnant" — that is, the basic idea of "what is left" or "remains" or of "having escaped" or "survived." The most common of these root words is שאר — which, with its derivatives, occurs in the MT some 220 times. As a noun it is used in both the singular (25 times) and the plural (66 times) to refer to something or someone that is "left," "remains," or "survives"; as a verb it means in the niphal "to be left remaining" and in the hiphil "to leave remaining." In Gen 7:23b, for example, the root שאר is used in the statement "only Noah [and his family] remained alive." And in 1 Kgs 19:18 this same root word appears in God's statement to the prophet Elijah that there continue to be seven thousand people in Israel whom he has reserved (השארתי, "my remnant") — that is, "all whose knees have not bowed down to Baal and all whose mouths have not kissed him."

The root word יתר with its derivatives, which can be found approximately 103 times in the MT of the Jewish (OT) Scriptures, is used mainly as a synonym for שאר. In Ezek 6:8, for example, the prophet Ezekiel, employing יתר as a verb in its hiphil form, speaks on behalf of God in saying: "I *will leave a remnant,* for some of you will escape the sword when you are scattered among the lands and the nations." The root word פלט with its derivatives is found in the Hebrew Scriptures about 80 times. As well as referring to the remnant in a religious sense, פלט often connotes simply the idea of "escape" or "deliverance" — blending, at times, both the religious and the secular motifs. In Isa 10:20, for example, the prophet proclaims: "In that day *the remnant* (שאר) of Israel, *the survivors* (פליטת) of the house of Jacob, will no longer rely on him who struck them down, but will truly rely on the Lord, the Holy One of Israel" — and then goes on to declare in Isa 10:21-22a: "*a remnant* (שאר) will return, *a remnant* (שאר) of Jacob will return to the mighty God; though your people, O Israel, be like the sand by the sea, only *a remnant* (שאר) will return." The root word שרד with its derivatives occurs in the MT about 29 times, often with the nuances of fear and flight being to the fore. In Josh 10:20, for example, it is written: "So Joshua and the Israelites destroyed them [i.e., the Amorites] completely — almost to a man — but *the few who were left* (השרידים שרדו) reached their fortified cities."

Frequently these root words are combined or function as parallel expressions in Jewish (OT) Scripture, both in its prose statements and in its poetic passages. Most often these Hebrew roots and their derivatives are used in historical and secular contexts. The corporate noun שאר and its plural form שארית, however, are the most important theologically among these four root words, for a number of times שאר and שארית appear with reference to "the remnant" of God's people who have survived some disaster or have been blessed by God in a particular fashion — as, for example, with reference to the Jews who survived under Hezekiah (2 Kgs 19:4; Isa 37:4), or to those who remained in the land under Josiah (2 Chr 34:21), or to those who remained in Jerusalem after the deportation of 597 under Zedekiah (2 Kgs 25:11; Jer 24:8; 52:15; Ezek 9:8; 11:13; 2 Chr 36:20). Likewise in the deportation of Jews to Babylon in 586, those who remained in the land under Gedaliah are spoken of as "the remnant" (הֹשְׁאִיר; 2 Kgs 25:22; Jer 40:6, 11, 15; 41:10, 16; 42:2, 15, 19; 43:5; 44:12, 28). And those who returned to Judea from Babylonian exile are also called "the remnant" (הֹשְׁאִיר; Ezra 9:8, 13, 14, 15; Neh 1:2-3; Hag 1:12, 14; 2:2; Zech 8:6, 11, 12).

In the LXX the verb λείπω ("left behind," "remain"), together with its prepositionalized cognates, is the word most often used to translate the four above-cited Hebrew root words and their derivatives. The noun λεῖμμα ("remnant") is found only once in the LXX, in 2 Kgs 19:4, where Hezekiah requests prayer for "the remnant that is left" (τοῦ λείμματος τοῦ εὑρισκομένου) — with the Greek articular noun τοῦ λείμματος (here in the genitive) being the LXX translation of the Hebrew noun שְׁאֵרִית. The adjective λοῖπος appears in the LXX more than 120 times, mostly to represent the Hebrew root word יתר and its derivatives — though about 10 times it translates the root שאר. The most frequent use in the LXX of this concept of "what is left," "remains," or "survives," however, with nearly 300 instances occurring, is represented by the verb καταλείπω along with its cognate nouns καταλεῖπος and καταλεῖμμα.

With respect to the understanding of "the remnant" in the later rabbinic tractates of "formative Judaism" — that is, in the Mishnah and the Babylonian *gemaras* (which together constitute the Talmud), the Palestinian *gemaras,* the Tosefta (the "Additions"), the *midrashim* (exegetical tractates on the OT writings), and the collected teachings of individual rabbis — Rudolf Meyer has quite rightly pointed out that:

> In Rabb. theology the remnant concept is secondary to the expectation that the people as a whole will partake of salvation. The few Jews who are eternally rejected, and the small number of righteous from among the nations, hardly count in comparison.[13]

The word "remnant" in the developing traditions of so-called formative Judaism was most often used by the earlier Tannaitic rabbis with reference to (1) food that was left over from a family's table or (2) offerings at the temple that were not presented or consumed, and so was usually equated with "refuse" or "uncleanness."[14] Only a few times was the idea of a "remnant" used favorably in a theological context by the Jewish teachers of the first two or three centuries A.D. And where employed positively, the concept seems always to have been expressed with reference to the people of Israel as a whole — as it was, for example, by Joshua ben Hananiah, a prominent Jewish rabbi who flourished during the second century A.D. and is quoted in *m. Berakot* 4:4 as saying: "He who journeys in a place of danger should pray a short prayer [i.e., should pray only the essence of the 'Eighteen Benedictions'], saying 'Save, O Lord, *the remnant* (שְׁאֵרִית) of Israel [i.e., the whole of the people of Israel, who exist as only a remnant among the Gentile nations], at their every crossroad let their needs come before you!'"

The Hasidim of early rabbinic times, who were devoted to a strict observance of the law, evidently spoke of themselves as "the remnant of Israel" — as do those Jews today

---

13. R. Meyer, "λεῖμμα, ktl," *TDNT* 4.212.

14. See, e.g., the Mishnah statements in the tractates *Pesahim* ("Feast of Passover") 10:9; *Nedarim* ("Vows") 1:3; *Makkot* ("Stripes") 3:3; *Hullin* ("Animals Killed for Food") 8:6; *Keritot* ("Extirpation") 1:1; 3:2; 4:2; *Meilah* ("Sacrilege") 1:2; 2:9; 4:3, 4; and *Teharot* ("Cleannesses") 3:4.

who call themselves the "Hassid" (i.e., the ultra-orthodox and mystical sect founded in Poland about 1750, in opposition to the rationalism and ritual laxity that they perceived as characterizing the mainstream of Judaism in their day). As well, such nonmainstream Jewish religionists as the authors of *4 Ezra* (a late first century A.D. composition) and of *Apocalypse of Abraham* (a first to second century A.D. apocalyptic tractate) employed the concept in a decidedly theological manner in referring to "the remnant" as those persons in the coming eschatological age who will be devoted to the Messiah.[15] But mainline Jewish rabbis of the past — as well as Jews today, whether Orthodox, Reform, or Conservative — have most often regarded the entire community of Jews, which has throughout the centuries endured great suffering and intense persecution by various Gentile nations, as the "remnant of Israel." Thus they have used (and continue to use) the term "remnant" not as a description of a particular portion of the Jewish people, but as a designation that is fully appropriate for the whole community of Jews amidst all the world's non-Jewish nations — in line with God's promise given in Lev 26:36-45 regarding "those of you who are left" and on whose behalf their heavenly Father "will remember his covenant with their ancestors whom he brought out of Egypt."

The Concept of "Remnant" in the Writings of the Old Testament Prophets. The numerous references to "remnant" in the Jewish (OT) Scriptures, whether in Hebrew (MT) or in Greek (LXX), have at times been more confusing than revealing. Indeed, the account in Gen 6:1–9:28 speaks of Noah and his family having been separated from all the other people of the earth — specifically pointing out that "only Noah [and his family] *remained* alive." Likewise, the story of the prophet Elijah in 1 Kgs 18:1–19:18 focuses on the importance of one particular person who spoke and acted for God amidst national apostasy — closing with God's statement regarding seven thousand others in Israel who also *remained* true to Yahweh. Yet a word-study approach to the concept of "the remnant," as James Barr has pointed out, may prove to be as much a hindrance as a help for the study of the concept of a "righteous remnant" in the Jewish (OT) Scriptures and the other Jewish writings, since there are so many references to "remnant" and "the remnant" in these bodies of literature that (1) have merely a secular meaning, (2) are used with respect only to some particular historical situation, or (3) have only a rather neutral nuance.[16] In fact, a relatively fixed theological nuance for the word "remnant" and the concept of a "righteous remnant" — that is, one that includes the quality of righteousness and does not have just a numerical quantity in mind — seems not to have come about in Jewish thinking until the time of Israel's writing prophets, whose messages are included in the Jewish (OT) Scriptures. Thus the idea of a "righteous remnant" in the OT, as well as in the writings of "Second Temple Judaism," is best dealt with as a theme or motif, simply because it is not always expressed in those passages where the term itself (together with its derivatives or cognates) appears.

The eighth-century prophet Amos spoke of a "remnant" on a number of occasions, writing in his prophecy of such matters as (1) a remnant of the women in Samaria (Amos 4:1-3), (2) the remainder of Israel's fighting men (5:3), and (3) one survivor of ten men in a house (5:3). In each case where Amos uses the remnant motif, however, it is to infer the meaninglessness and ineffectiveness of the remaining survivors for the future existence of Israel as a national entity. For example, in 3:12 of his prophecy, Amos writes:

---

15. Cf. *4 Ezra* 6:25; 7:27, 28; 9:7; 12:34; 13:24, 26, 48, 49; *Apoc Ab* 29:17.
16. Cf. Barr, *Semantics of Biblical Language,* 263 65.

This is what the Lord says: "As the shepherd rescues from the mouth of a lion only two leg bones or a piece of an ear, so will the people of Israel be rescued, those who sit in Samaria on the edge of their beds and on the corner of their couches."

In effect, the prophet Amos first of all used the idea of a "remnant" to dispel the notion that Israel was automatically, as a result of its divine election, assured a future. His employment of the remnant motif was to shake the people of Israel out of their complacency, and so to cause them to realize their desperate situation before God and return to him.

But Amos also challenges his people to "seek Yahweh" in order that they might "live" (5:4-6). The promise of divine salvation is conditioned by Israel's response, so that if there would be a remnant from Israel it would be a remnant that is faithful to God. Thus the prophet proclaims in 5:15 the following message to his people: "Hate evil, love good; maintain justice in the courts. Perhaps the Lord God Almighty will have mercy on the remnant (שארית) of Joseph."

With regard to this "eschatological remnant" portrayed by Amos, there is little evidence that the prophet was referring to a future national destination as much as to a religious quality of life. This can be seen by his reference in 9:11-12 to "the remnant of Edom," which will participate with the remnant of other nations in the promises that God gave to King David:

"In that day I will restore David's fallen tent, I will repair its broken places, restore its ruins, and build it as it used to be, so that they may possess the remnant of Edom and all the nations that bear my name," declares the Lord, who will do these things.

The prophet Amos, therefore, should be understood as using the remnant concept in the following three ways:

1. To refute the claim that all the people of Israel constitute "the remnant," for he uses it as a motif within his larger pronouncement of judgment and doom for the nation as a whole.
2. To show that there will be a surviving remnant that exists within Israel by the fact that destruction will come to those other people of Israel who do not return to God — which pronouncement of judgment also entails the idea of salvation for those who choose to return to God.
3. To enlarge by his inclusion of the "remnant of Edom," along with his allusion to neighboring nations, the remnant concept to include all those who will be recipients of God's promises to David.

Thus the prophet understands "the remnant" not as referring to some sort of Jewish national dominance, but as highlighting a subgroup of people within Israel — as well as a subgroup of people within Edom and the other nations — who are of religious importance to God and will experience a future prepared by God himself.

The context for Joel's prophecy is a locust plague that disrupted the nation's economy and consequently affected all levels of Israel's society. So great was the plague that the continuance of the sacrificial offerings, which were vital to the religious ceremonies, was threatened. In these catastrophic circumstances the prophet proclaimed the judgment of God on the people of Judah for taking God's blessings for granted. Moral decadence had become the norm, and Joel informed his listeners that the plague of locusts was a warning of a far greater judgment that was imminent unless they repented and turned to God.

In his use of the expression "the day of the Lord" in 1:15, 2:1, and 2:11-13, Joel proclaimed that God will judge his people when sin takes over in their lives. This judgment came about by means of (1) a natural disaster, that is, by a plague of locusts, and (2) invasions by other nations, which God used to bring punishment on his people. Yet the prophet goes on to proclaim that, while God allows other nations to chastise Israel on his behalf, he has reserved a remnant of people within Israel for himself, on whom he will pour out his Spirit and will manifest himself with marvelous signs (2:28-32) — after which he will "restore the fortunes of Judah and Jerusalem" (3:1).

For the prophet Joel, therefore, the one who truly trusts in God is to "call on the name of the Lord" in believing faith. His message for those who have faith in God is that they will not only be physically delivered but will also be rewarded; this will occur when the repentant people of Jerusalem and Judah are gathered together as *the remnant* of Israel.

It is the prophet Isaiah, however, who used the concept of "the remnant" most extensively in his message. Assyria's invasion of 701 B.C. had left Judah as a decimated state, with "the Daughter of Zion," that is, the capital city of Jerusalem, "left like a shelter in a vineyard, like a hut in a field of melons, like a city under siege" — with only "some survivors" left in the land (Isa 1:2-9). The remnant concept appears right at the beginning of Isaiah's prophecy in speaking of the survivors of a past historical catastrophe. Later, however, the prophet will also use that remnant concept in speaking of a future portion of the nation's people who will inhabit the land and be blessed by God. Throughout the prophet's message there is the continued intertwining of a historical use and an eschatological use of this "remnant" or "survivor" concept.

Isaiah preached against the apostasy of his people in the hope of drawing them back to God (5:1-7). He entertained the hope that God's dealings with his people in judgment would serve a purging purpose, causing them to renounce their old ways and so bring about the fruition of God's promises for their future under his divine blessing. The prophet's assertion that God was "hiding his face from the house of Jacob" (8:17) should, therefore, be understood in the context that some inhabitants (including the prophet himself) continued to put their trust in God — that is, people who served as "signs and symbols in Israel from the Lord Almighty, who dwells on Mount Zion," and so constituted "the righteous remnant" within the nation of Israel (8:18).

Isaiah responds to God's "hiding his face" from his people with the question, "How long, O Lord?" (6:11a). It is a question that both (1) highlights Isaiah's love for his people and (2) suggests that the prophet thought of God's acts of judgment as conditioned by a desire for the salvation and good of his people. And in response to Isaiah's question "How long?" God answers as follows:

> Until the cities lie in ruin and are without inhabitant; until the houses are left deserted; until the Lord has sent everyone far away and the land is utterly forsaken. And even though *a tenth part remains* in the land, it will again be laid waste. But as the terebinth and oak leave stumps when they are cut down, so *the holy seed* [i.e., "the surviving remnant"] will be the stump in the land. (6:11b-13)

Here Isaiah presents quite explicitly the remnant motif using the imagery of trees to symbolize both the destruction of the nation and its resurgent life, which will grow out of "the holy seed" — that is, "the surviving remnant" that will function as "the stump in the land." Thus God punishes in order to save; he destroys in order to rebuild. God's ultimate purpose is not destruction but salvation. Isaiah himself, in fact, is a representative of that future remnant, for he is confronted by God's holiness and emerges as cleansed and purified (cf. Isa 6) — and so the prophet presents his own experience of being cleansed and purified as a symbol of God's cleansing and forgiveness of the people of Israel.[17]

During the Syro-Ephraimite war, Isaiah used the remnant motif again in his confrontation with King Ahaz, in exhorting the king and his people to return to God by faith. The name Shear-Jashub, which the prophet gave to his son at his birth, means "a remnant will return." It is Isaiah's use of that name that epitomizes the content of his message to Ahaz. For within that name is expressed both (1) a message of doom for those who make decisions only on the basis of political expediency and (2) a message of salvation for those who make decisions on the basis of their trust in God (7:2-9). It is, therefore, faith that distinguishes the remnant that survives from the greater body of people that will perish. Confidence and trust in God on the part of Israel will create the conditions for God to intervene on behalf of his people and for a righteous remnant to emerge from a catastrophe. Thus in Isaiah's prophecies the ideas of remnant and faith become inseparable.

Later in his career Isaiah expressed a message that was probably directed to Hezekiah at a time when he planned to make an alliance with Egypt; it was a prophetic exhortation to the king of Judah to decide for God rather than to rely on Egypt. This message highlights the thesis that "the remnant of his people" will have its power, security, and glory not because of any political alliance but because of its faith in God:

> In that day the Lord Almighty will be a glorious crown, a beautiful wreath for *the remnant* of his people. He will be a spirit of justice to him who sits in judgment, a source of strength to those who turn back the battle at the gate. (28:5-6)

Then, in closing his message to Hezekiah, the prophet declares:

> This will be the sign for you, O Hezekiah: "This year you will eat what grows by itself, and the second year what springs from that. But in the third year sow and reap, plant vineyards and eat their fruit. Once more *a remnant* of the house of Judah will take root below and bear fruit above. For out of Jerusalem will come *a remnant,* and out of Mount Zion a band of *survivors.* The zeal of the Lord Almighty will accomplish this." (37:30-32)

From the very beginning of Isaiah's ministry to its end, therefore, the remnant concept played an important part in the prophet's message. He uses the remnant motif both (1) in a negative sense to speak of dire judgment and (2) in a positive sense to exhort repentance and instill hope. And he uses ideas of a "holy" and "purified" remnant, which will emerge as a result of God's breaking into history, as a way of introducing God's future eschatological blessing. But Isaiah's main concern was to call Israel back to God and to create the condition by which some of the people would become members of that future remnant — that is, some of them would become the "holy" and "purified" eschatological remnant. Thus the remnant motif in Isaiah is associated with both a call to repentance and a call for faith. It is no wonder, then, that Paul in Romans quite expressly, as well as often, refers to the preaching of Isaiah as he also attempts to bring his "own people according to the flesh" to faith in the Messiah by means of the ministry of "the remnant"

---

17. Cf. Harrelson, *Interpreting the Old Testament*, 232.

that believes in Jesus the Christ (which remnant includes "the remnant of Israel," "the remnant of Gentiles," and Paul himself).[18]

The prophet Micah also used the remnant motif in his preaching, primarily in a negative sense with regard to God's punishment of Samaria and Jerusalem for their rebellion against him. Nonetheless, he also proclaimed that God does not give up on his people entirely, for God forgives the sins of those who are repentant and put their trust in him. Thus Micah closes his prophecy with the following awe-inspiring affirmation about the nature of Israel's God:

> Who is a God like you, who pardons sin and forgives the transgression of *the remnant* of his inheritance? You do not stay angry forever but delight to show mercy. You will again have compassion on us, you will tread our sins underfoot and hurl all our iniquities into the depths of the sea. You will be true to Jacob, and show mercy to Abraham, as you pledged on oath to our fathers in days long ago. (Mic 7:18-20)

The message of Zephaniah is also one of both judgment and hope. In the first two and one-half chapters of his prophecy, the prophet sets out in graphic terms God's judgments that will come on Judah, Philistia, Moab, Ammon, and Cush because of their wickedness. In the latter half of ch. 3, however, he speaks of a future time when a remnant will be gathered on God's holy hill — a people that will not be put to shame, because the sources of their shame ("pride" and "haughtiness") will be abolished.

Instead of being haughty, the remnant will be "meek and humble" and will "trust in the name of the Lord." Regarding this future remnant, Zephaniah says: "The remnant of Israel will do no wrong; they will speak no lies, nor will deceit be found in their mouths. They will eat and lie down and no one will make them afraid" (Zeph 3:13). As for the future welfare of this remnant of God's people, the prophet closes his message with the divine promise: "At that time I will gather you; at that time I will bring you home. I will give you honor and praise among all the peoples of the earth when I restore your fortunes before your very eyes" (3:20).

The prophet Jeremiah was a contemporary of Zephaniah, but his ministry extended several years beyond that of Zephaniah. In the introductory three verses to his numerous prophecies, not only is he identified as "Jeremiah son of Hilkiah, one of the priests at Anathoth in the territory of Benjamin," but the extensive length of his ministry is chronicled, beginning in "the thirteenth year of the reign of Josiah son of Amon king of Judah," continuing on throughout "the reign of Jehoiakim son of Josiah king of Judah," and coming to a close in "the fifth month of the eleventh year of Zedekiah son of Josiah king of Judah, when the people of Jerusalem went into exile." This entire period was a time of rampant immorality and apostasy throughout the kingdom of Judah. And so the message of Jeremiah is much more judgmental and his use of the remnant motif far more somber than were those of any of the other writing prophets in the Jewish (OT) Scriptures.[19]

Yet even amidst all his proclamations of judgment, Jeremiah proclaims a bit of hope for "the remnant" that survives God's destruction of Judah: " 'Even in those days,' declares the Lord, 'I will not destroy you completely!' " (Jer 5:18). And in the latter chap-

---

18. Cf. esp. Paul's explicit uses of the prophecy of Isaiah in the conclusion of this section of Rom 9:6-29 — i.e., his use of Isa 10:22-23 in Rom 9:28 and of Isa 1:9 in Rom 9:29 (as well as a number of times elsewhere throughout the remainder of chs. 9–11).

19. Cf., e.g., the express statements regarding "the remnant" in Jer 6:9; 8:3; 11:23; 24:8.

ters of Jeremiah's prophecy there are such statements as the following, which promise
that God will in a future day act on behalf of his people and restore them:

> "In that day [i.e., the prophesied future time]," declares the Lord Almighty, "I will
> break the yoke off the necks of the people of Judah and will tear off their bonds;
> no longer will foreigners enslave them. Instead, they will serve the Lord their
> God and David their king, whom I will raise up for them. So do not fear, O Jacob
> my servant," declares the Lord. "I will surely save you out of a distant place, your
> descendants from the land of their exile. Jacob will again have peace and security,
> and no one will make him afraid. I am with you and will save you," declares the
> Lord. "Though I completely destroy all the nations among which I scatter you, I
> will not completely destroy you. I will discipline you but only with justice; I will
> not let you go entirely unpunished." (30:8-11)

> "Do not fear, O Jacob my servant, for I am with you," declares the Lord. "Though I
> completely destroy all the nations among which I scatter you, I will not completely
> destroy you. I will discipline you but only with justice; I will not let you go entirely
> unpunished." (46:28; see also v. 27)

In the prophecy of Jeremiah, therefore, even though the prophet's overall message
is much more somber and judgmental than any of the earlier writing prophets of the OT,
the promise of God to preserve and bless a remnant of the people of Israel who will be
true to him is also in evidence. Further, the data in his prophecy include two important themes: (1) God is always interested in "the remnant" and provides for them, and
(2) those who proclaim God's message must always cherish and seek to support those
"remnant" people who are true to him.

***Paul's Use of Biblical Themes and Quotations, as well as Certain Rather
Common Greco-Roman Rhetorical Conventions, in 9:6-29.*** Similar to his earlier
use of OT quotations in 1:16-4:25, Paul here in 9:6-29 uses a number of biblical
themes and passages in support of his remnant thesis[20] — as he will continue
to do somewhat more extensively throughout 9:30-10:21, as well as somewhat
less frequently (though just as significantly) in 11:1-32. It is in his use of biblical
themes and passages that Paul reflects a typically Jewish type of "midrashic"
exegesis, which involves the reading of a text of Scripture not only with attention to its literal meaning but also with respect to relationships that are set up,
nuances that are implied, and implications that are suggested — with the intent
of answering the important question, "What does all of what the Scriptures say
mean for us today?"[21]

---

20. See the apostle's use of the biblical accounts of God's sovereign choices of Isaac (not
Ishmael) and Jacob (not Esau), and thus his quotations of Gen 21:12 (in 9:7); Gen 18:10, 14 (in 9:9);
and Gen 25:23 (in 9:12). Also with respect to specific points in his exposition, note his uses of Mal
1:2-3 (in 9:13); Exod 33:19 (in 9:15); Exod 9:16 (in 9:17); Hos 2:23 [MT 2:25] (in 9:25); Hos 1:10 [MT
2:1] (in 9:26); Isa 10:22-23 (in 9:27-28); and Isa 1:9 (in 9:29).

21. The Hebrew verb דרש literally means "to resort to" or "seek"; figuratively it connotes
"to read repeatedly," "study," or "interpret."

In Jewish hands midrash interpretation often included what has been called "pearl stringing," a method of not only highlighting the unity of God's instruction in the "written Torah" but also spelling out the meaning of a particular biblical passage by bringing to bear on one point made in that passage certain other passages from other parts of the Jewish (OT) Scriptures in support.[22] And "pearl stringing" appears here in 9:6-29 in support of the apostle's argument regarding the presence of a "remnant" of people throughout history, with particular emphases on (1) God's sovereign selection of such a "remnant" and (2) God's promises as always having been given to "the remnant." This collection of themes and passages is comparable to what appeared earlier in 3:10b-18.[23]

Likewise, there may be found in 9:6-29 certain rather common Greco-Roman rhetorical conventions of the day, which were "in the air" in Paul's day and so available to many speakers and writers. In 9:19-21, for example, the apostle uses the second-person singular future indicative verb ἐρεῖς ("you will say") and the vocative noun expression ὦ ἄνθρωπε ("O man," "human"); these forms of direct address were fairly common in Greco-Roman diatribes. Further, there appears at the beginning and end of this passage the word σπέρμα ("seed," "descendant") — three times in the thesis statement of 9:6-8 and once more in the concluding materials in Isa 9:27-29, with the latter occurrence in 9:28 paralleled by the synonymous term τὸ ὑπόλειμμα ("the remnant") in 9:27. Such a use of similar words, phrases, or clauses to begin and end a relatively short unit of material, whether in speech or in writing, has been given in rhetorical parlance the name *inclusio.* It was a rather common rhetorical convention of Paul's day, and seems, whether consciously or unconsciously, to be reflected at the beginning and end of 9:6-29.

The Structure of Paul's Exposition in 9:6-29. A question that commentators have often struggled with is this: Should the first section of Paul's exposition in ch. 9 — that is, the material that begins at 9:6 (after the introduction of 9:1-5) — be understood as coming to a close at the end of 9:13[24] or as continuing to the end of 9:18?[25] Or should it be seen as extending to the end of 9:29?[26] Usually a

---

22. Cf. R. N. Longenecker, *Biblical Exegesis,* 2nd ed., 99-100.

23. Cf. also Rom 11:8-10; 15:9-12; Gal 3:10-13; as well as, though to a more limited extent, Rom 4:1-8; 9:33; 1 Cor 3:19-20; 15:54-55; and 2 Cor 6:16-18.

24. So, e.g., Michel, *An die Römer,* 298-304; Schlier, *Römerbrief,* 289-93; Käsemann, *Romans,* 260-67; Wilckens, *An die Römer,* 2.191-97; Fitzmyer, *Romans,* 558-63l; and Moo, *Romans,* 570-99.

25. So, somewhat tentatively, Jewett, *Romans,* 570-86, citing in support J. P. A. Louw, *A Semantic Discourse Analysis of Romans,* 2 vols. (Pretoria: University of Pretoria Press, 1979), 2.99-100.

26. So, e.g., Cranfield, *Romans,* 2.471, and Dunn, *Romans,* 2.536-37, both of whom view this major section as being subdivided into the "two parts" or subsections of 9:6-13 and 9:14-29. See Augustine, who speaks in his letter *Ad Simplicianum* 1.2.1 of the material in 9:6-29 as being unified, though also somewhat obscure. Note also the argument of J.-N. Aletti for the unity of 9:6-29 on the basis of what he perceives to be a chiastic structure in Paul's argument of these verses (cf. his "L'Argumentation paulinienne en Rm 9," 42-45) — which *chiasmus,* however, Aletti sets out rather artificially, and thus has been judged debatable.

determination of this question is based solely on the identification of the topics or themes present in the verses themselves — which, of course, is always an important consideration in the analysis of any extended passage. So, what is written in this subsection of Rom 9–11 has most often been separated into two or three distinguishable units of material.

Our thesis, however, is that attention to the *formal patterning* of any particular written text — taking into account whatever traditional rhetorical and epistolary conventions seem to appear in that particular author's material — must always go hand in hand with a *thematic analysis* of what is written in determining a passage's *compositional structure.* Keeping that literary rubric in mind, we note that the noun σπέρμα ("seed," "descendants") is used three times in 9:6-8 and is repeated in 9:29 — with the roughly synonymous articular noun τὸ ὑπόλειμμα ("the remnant") appearing just two verses earlier in 9:27. This use of σπέρμα in 9:7-8 and then in 9:29 (together with τὸ ὑπόλειμμα in 9:27) suggests the presence of a rhetorical *inclusio*[27] — which *inclusio* should probably be viewed as a conscious attempt by the apostle to inform his Roman addressees (as well as his readers today) that the material in 9:6-29 constitutes a discrete and unified subsection in the overall argument of these three chapters.

Further, though 9:6-29 is best understood as a discrete and unified subsection of material (as we believe and have here proposed), in this first part of Paul's argument there appears in 9:14 the rhetorical question, "What, then, shall we say?" (τί οὖν ἐροῦμεν), which Paul uses seven times in his letter to Rome (and only in this letter of the NT Pauline corpus) to introduce a particular section or subsection of material.[28] So we suggest that this rhetorical question of 9:14 should also be seen as part of the formal patterning of this first subsection (i.e., what we have called "Part I") of Paul's three-part exposition in Rom 9:6–11:32; it is used to introduce a further subunit of material in 9:14-18 within the larger section of 9:6-29.

Likewise, within this larger section of 9:6-29 is to be found in 9:19-20a what appears to be a reflection of an ancient diatribe form of direct address in its uses of the second-person singular pronominal verbal suffix ἐρεῖς ("you will say"), the vocative form of address ὦ ἄνθρωπε ("O man," or "O mere human"), and the personal pronoun συ ("you") — which forms of direct address are followed by the questions of 9:19b, 9:20b, 9:20c, 9:22, and 9:23. This use of "you" (as both a verbal suffix and a personal pronoun) and "O man" is in line with

---

27. Cf. Hays, *Echoes of Scripture,* 65, who, in speaking of Paul's use of Gen 21:12 in Rom 9:7, says: "The key terms of this programmatic quotation ('In Isaac shall be *called* for you a *seed*') are recapitulated in quotations from Hosea and Isaiah (in Rom. 9:25-29) that create an *inclusion* encompassing verses 6-29." See also Jewett, *Romans,* 604, who aptly notes that "The reiteration of the term σπέρμα ('seed') from the initial proof text of Gen 21:12 provides an inclusio that brings the midrash [of 9:6-29] to an effective conclusion."

28. In addition to its appearance here at 9:14, see also its other appearances in Romans, i.e., at 3:5; 4:1; 6:1; 7:7; 8:31; and 9:30.

Paul's similar use of such a diatribe form of address in 2:1 and 2:3. Its use here suggests that what is written in 9:19-26 should also be viewed as a subunit of material within the larger section of 9:6-29.

This first section of Paul's argument in 9:6-29 closes in 9:27-29 with two very significant biblical quotations; both are drawn from the prophet Isaiah and function together to form a conclusion to this first part of his presentation. The following two sections of his overall three-part argument, 9:30–10:21 and 11:1-32 (as well as, for that matter, his doxology in 11:33-36), also incorporate very similar quotations from Isaiah in their concluding statements. Thus, while it may not be conclusive for the identification of the concluding portion of each of these latter two subsections of Paul's argument in Rom 9–11, the apostle's use of quotations from Isaiah is in line with our thesis regarding the discrete and unified character of 9:6-29 — and also in line with our later proposals with respect to the discrete and unified character of the materials in 9:30–10:21 and 11:1-32.

Taking into consideration all the above-cited features of "formal patterning" in the passage, as well as undertaking a "thematic analysis" of its material, our understanding of the structure of 9:6-29 (Part I of Paul's three-part exposition in Rom 9–11) is expressed in terms of the following outline:

1. Thesis statements on the presence of a "remnant" in Israel's history (as well as within other non-Jewish nations) and on the fact that God's promises are given only to his remnant people — both of which truths are illustrated in the biblical accounts of Israel's patriarchs (9:6-13)
2. An exposition on the mercy of God in choosing a "remnant" for himself and God's justice in using other people negatively for his own purposes, quoting biblical passages in support (9:14-18)
3. An elemental theodicy with respect to God's election of some people and his hardening of other people, with both Jews and Gentiles in view (9:19-26)
4. The conclusion of the matter, using the words of two passages from the prophet Isaiah to state that conclusion (9:27-29)

EXEGETICAL COMMENTS

In 9:6-29, the first part of his three-part exposition, Paul sets out a twofold thesis: (1) that there has always been (and continues to be) a "righteous remnant" in Israel's history, and (2) that God's promises are given only to those "remnant" people whom he has sovereignly chosen — both of which truths can be seen in the biblical accounts of the nation's patriarchs. Throughout this first portion of his exposition the apostle gives evidence of his recognition that there is not only a "remnant of Israel" but also a remnant from among the Gentiles.

I. Thesis Statements on the Presence of a "Remnant" in Israel's History and on the Fact That God's Promises Are Given Only to His Remnant People — Both of Which Truths Are Illustrated in the Biblical Accounts of Israel's Patriarchs (9:6-13)

9:6-8 The rather unusual expression οὐχ οἷον ὅτι ("it is not that"), which begins these verses, is a mixture of two Greek idioms: οὐχ οἷον and οἷον ὅτι, both of which can be translated "it is not that" or "it is not as if." The bringing together of these two idioms into one compound expression suggests that Paul wanted, at the very beginning of his three-part argument in Rom 9–11, to stress that whatever he had just written in 9:2-3 about his own "great sorrow and unceasing anguish" with respect to the situation of the Jews, whom he describes as "my own people according to the flesh," should not in any way be taken as implying that God himself or his promise to Abraham and his descendants has somehow failed. And his use of the conjunction δέ in the midst of this idiomatic expression supports such an understanding. For the postpositive δέ must certainly here be viewed in an adversative fashion, and thus understood as signaling the exclusion of any such false impression regarding the failure of God or his promise because of the Jewish rejection of Jesus as Israel's promised Messiah.

The statement ἐκπέπτωκεν ὁ λόγος τοῦ θεοῦ ("God's word has failed") was, in all likelihood, an assertion that Paul had heard many times throughout his ministry — particularly from some Jews living in the Diaspora who had given up believing in God and his promises to Abraham and the people of Israel because of the adverse circumstances they were personally experiencing. Perhaps, as well, he had heard such an assertion uttered by some Christians, whether ethnically Jews or Gentiles, in support of their denigration of the Jewish people, whether in a particular locality or generally.

Paul, however, disclaims in 9:6a such a gross misunderstanding of the situation. And in support of his disclaimer he makes a distinction in 9:6b between οἱ ἐξ Ἰσραὴλ οὗτοι ("those who are from Israel") and Ἰσραήλ ("true Israelites"). Further, in 9:7 he explicates his meaning: first in writing negatively, "Nor because they are the seed [or 'descendants'] of Abraham (σπέρμα Ἀβραὰμ) are they all his children"; then in saying quite positively, using the words of Gen 21:12: "It is through Isaac that your seed ['descendants,' 'offspring'] will be reckoned." Finally in 9:8-9, the two concluding verses of this opening thesis paragraph, Paul sets out his own concluding comment: "That is (τοῦτ' ἔστί), it is not the children of the flesh who are God's children, but the children of the promise who are regarded as Abraham's seed (σπέρμα, 'descendants')" — which he supports by quoting God's promise given to Abraham as recorded in Gen 18:10 and 14 regarding his wife Sarah and his promised son Isaac: "At the appointed time I will return and Sarah will have a son."

"Ambrosiaster," the anonymous late-fourth-century Latin commentator on the Pauline letters (whom Erasmus in the sixteenth century dubbed by that name), has aptly summarized what Paul has written here:

What Paul wants us to understand is that not all are worthy because they are children of Abraham, but only those who are children of the promise, that is, whom God foreknew would receive his promise, whether they are Jews or Gentiles.[29]

And John Chrysostom, the great Greek commentator, preacher, and statesman of roughly the same period, has quite appropriately contextualized Paul's message in these verses as follows:

> What Paul means is something like this: Whoever has been born in the way that Isaac was born is a son of God and of the seed of Abraham. . . . For Isaac was born not according to the law of nature nor according to the power of the flesh, but according to the power of the promise.[30]

This first portion of Paul's argument in 9:6-29 is clearly based on the remnant theology of Israel's writing prophets, and so must be considered an important example of a Christian form of remnant rhetoric. Also, just as the apostle used the patriarch Abraham as the example par excellence of righteousness and faith in 4:1-24, so he uses the story of Abraham and Sarah in the birth of Isaac as his primary biblical illustration that God's promise was given only with respect to the birth of Isaac, the child of promise, and not with respect to the birth of Ishmael, who was born to him by his handmaid Hagar (Gen 16:1-16) — or, for that matter, with respect to his other sons born to him by his second wife Keturah or his various concubines (Gen 25:1-6). These verses of 9:6-8 provide the twofold thesis for all that Paul will set out in his three-part argument that follows in the rest of Rom 9–11.

9:10-13 It may be argued, of course, that God's selection of Isaac over Ishmael was because Isaac was Abraham's natural son whereas Ishmael was the son of a slave woman — or, perhaps, that God's selection of Isaac was because Abraham's numerous other sons were born to him by his second wife Keturah and his various concubines. But such an understanding based on the circumstances of one's birth is quickly dispelled by Paul in his midrashic argument of 9:10-13 with respect to God's selection of Jacob over his brother Esau. The point he makes is that Rebecca had sexual intercourse with only one man, that is, only with Isaac.[31] So Esau and Jacob had the same parents and were born as the twin

---

29. Ambrosiaster, *Ad Romanos, CSEL* 81.309.

30. Chrysostom, "Homilies," in *Nicene and Post-Nicene Fathers,* 11.463. Charles Cranfield has aptly expressed in somewhat more prosaic terms what was understood by Ambrosiaster and Chrysostom, as well as by almost all commentators: that Paul's conclusion in 9:8 "does not mean to imply that the children of God are not also children of the flesh — Isaac was, of course, just as much a child of the flesh, i.e., a child of Abraham by natural birth, as was Ishmael — but to indicate that the mere fact of being physically children of Abraham does not by itself make men [i.e., people] children of God" (*Romans,* 2.475).

31. The noun κοίτη generally means "bed" and specifically refers to the "marriage bed." It was

sons of their parents in the same short period of time. Yet God proclaimed even before their birth: "The older will serve the younger! [Gen 25:23b]. Just as it is written: 'Jacob I loved, but Esau I hated' [Mal 1:2-3]." It is not, therefore, that God's promises were (and are) given on the basis of the circumstances of one's birth. Rather, as Ambrosiaster has quite rightly commented: God's promises are given "only to those who are children of the promise, that is, who God fore-knew would receive his promises, whether they are Jews or Gentiles"[32] — that is, God's promises are given only to those people who he knows will receive his promises, irrespective of the circumstances of their birth or their ethnicity.

II. Exposition on the Mercy of God in His Choice of a "Remnant" for Himself and in His Justice in Using Other People Negatively for His Purposes, Quoting Biblical Passages in Support (9:14-18)

9:14-18 Having denied the premise that "God's word ('promise') has failed" — arguing, rather, that God's promises are given to those people who he knows will receive his promises, and citing in support the biblical accounts of the births of Isaac and of Jacob, which accounts highlight God's sovereign selection and not any particular circumstance regarding their birth — Paul now asks, "What, then, shall we say? Is there injustice with God?"

As we mentioned above, the introductory phrase τί οὖν ἐροῦμεν ("What, then, shall we say?") appears seven times in the letter. Each of the other six instances (as well as its appearance here) introduces a particular section or sub-section of material.[33] So we propose that this introductory question should be viewed as part of the formal patterning of this first subsection of Paul's argument in Rom 9–11, and that it introduces a subunit of material in 9:14-18 within the larger section of 9:6-29.

The rhetorical question μὴ ἀδικία παρὰ τῷ θεῷ; ("Is there injustice with God?") begins with the strong adversative particle μή, which functions to alert the reader to the impossibility of any idea of injustice on the part of God. In an English translation, however, such a negative particle is hardly necessary in view of the question's context. For Paul immediately answers that question with the emphatic negative response μὴ γένοιτο ("Certainly not!").[34] And, like the

---

also used euphemistically by the ancients to connote "sexual intercourse" (cf. Lev 15:21-24 [LXX] and Wis 3:13, 16; see also the plural κοίταις as a locution for "sexual excesses," "sexual immorality," or "licentiousness" in Rom 13:13).

32. Quoting again Ambrosiaster, *Ad Romanos, CSEL* 81.309.

33. In addition to its appearance here at 9:14, see those other places in Romans where this exact rhetorical question appeared; in 3:5; 4:1; 6:1; 7:7; 8:31; and 9:30.

34. The negative particle μή with the optative γένοιτο means literally "Let it not be!" More colloquially, however, it is probably best translated "By no means!" or "Certainly not!" See Paul's other uses of μὴ γένοιτο in Romans in 3:4 (particularly noting our discussion there), 31; 6:2, 15; 7:7, 13; and 11:1, 11; also in 1 Cor 6:15 and Gal 2:17; 3:21. Cf. also Luke 20:16.

assertion "God's word has failed" of 9:6a, the question "Is there injustice with God?" of 9:14, which is voiced as an accusation against the person and work of God, was probably also sometimes expressed by Paul's opponents during his ministry — whether by Jewish, Jewish Christian, or pagan Gentile opponents.[35]

There can, however, be no doubt that the idea and theme of God's sovereign choice of people, events, and circumstances are fundamental to all that is proclaimed and presented in the Jewish (OT) Scriptures — nor can there be any doubt that God has sovereignly chosen the people of Israel as his own people. This choosing of Israel is clearly expressed in such passages from the Law, the Psalms, and the Prophets (to engage in a bit of "pearl stringing" ourselves), as follows:

> Deut 7:6 — "You are a people holy to the Lord your God. The Lord your God has chosen you out of all the peoples on the face of the earth to be his people, his treasured possession."
>
> Ps 135:4 — "The Lord has chosen Jacob to be his own, Israel to be his treasured possession."
>
> Isa 41:8-9 — "You, O Israel, my servant; Jacob, whom I have chosen; you descendants of Abraham, my friend — I took you from the ends of the earth, from its farthest corners I called you. I said, 'You are my servant'; I have chosen you and have not rejected you."

Most Jews of Paul's day, however, understood God's election of Israel as an irrevocable covenant that could never be invalidated, superseded, or set aside; witness the following statements from various pious Jewish teachers who wrote about the same time as Paul:

> *Pss Sol* 9:17-18 — "You chose the seed of Abraham before all the nations, and you set your name before us, O Lord; and you will abide among us forever."
>
> *Pss Sol* 14:3 — "The planting of them [God's chosen people] is rooted forever; they will not be plucked out all the days of the heavens. For the portion of the Lord and the inheritance of God is Israel."
>
> *4 Ezra* 6:55 — "Israel is the end of the Divine action; for Israel was the world created."
>
> *2 Bar (Apocalypse of Baruch)* 48:20-24 — "This is the nation you have chosen, and these are the people with whom you have found no equal. . . . Your law is with us, and we know that we will not fall as we keep your statutes. For all time we are blessed at all events in this: that we have not mingled with the Gentiles. For we are all one celebrated people, who have received one law from One. And the law which is among us will aid us; the surpassing wisdom that is in us will help us."

---

35. So Schelkle, *Paulus*, 341-43, and Wilckens, *An die Römer*, 2.299, who cite Origen, Diodorus, Theodore of Mopsuestia, and John Chrysostom in support.

Paul, however, saw in the patriarch Abraham the example par excellence of righteousness and faith (as in Gal 3:6-9 and Rom 4:1-24). Further, he understood the promise(s) of God as having been given only to those who were "the children of the promise," that is, who were "remnant" people, and not just to anyone who claimed on the basis of birth or nationality to be a child of God (as he argues here in Rom 9:6-13). Such boasting, therefore, was for him a perversion of God's intention in his selection of the people of Israel and a distortion of God's purpose in giving Israel his written Torah. Rather, quoting the words that God spoke to Moses in revealing his glory to him in the wilderness, the apostle argues that the divine principle in dealing with all people is this: "I will have mercy on whomever I will have mercy, and I will have compassion on whomever I will have compassion" (Exod 33:19).

Paul's conclusion to all these matters regarding God's choice of people, events, and circumstances is expressed in 9:16 as follows: "Therefore (ἄρα οὖν) it does not depend on a person's desire or a person's effort, but, rather, on the mercy of God." And as a corollary to God's mercy, Paul quotes in 9:18 the words of God given by Moses to Pharaoh after the plague of boils had covered the land of Egypt: "I raised you up for this very purpose, that I might display my power in you and that my name might be proclaimed in all the earth" (Exod 9:16) — and he draws from these words of God the further conclusion: "Therefore (ἄρα οὖν) God has mercy on whomever he desires to have mercy, and he hardens whomever he desires to harden" (Rom 9:18).[36]

It cannot, therefore, be said either (1) that "God's word has failed" or (2) that "there is injustice with God." For God's promise has always been given (and continues to be given) only to "the remnant" of Israel (as well as to those whom God considers "the righteous remnant" among the various non-Jewish nations), and God's mercy has always been expressed (and continues to be expressed), both positively and negatively, to those he chooses to express it.

III. Elemental Theodicy with Respect to God's Election of Some People and His Hardening toward Others, with Both Jews and Gentiles in View (9:19-26)

Having addressed assertions regarding the supposed "failure of God's word" as expressed in 9:6 and the supposed "injustice of God" as expressed in 9:14 — and having answered them by reference to certain pivotal events and statements of Scripture — Paul here in 9:19-26 interacts with a further question

36. In addition to Paul's use of ἄρα οὖν here in 9:16 and 18, see also his previous uses of this idiomatic expression to signal a conclusion in his letter to Rome in 5:18; 7:3, 25b; 8:12; and his later uses to this effect in 14:12, 19. In 8:1, however, he writes ἄρα νῦν ("therefore now"); while in 7:21 and Gal 2:21 he uses the particle ἄρα singly, evidently only to enliven the statement by the expression "so then" or "then" — though the singular ἄρα is not usually translated in contemporary English translations.

regarding God's dealings with humanity. The question asks why God finds fault with people when he himself has had a part, at least to some extent, in bringing about their hardness of heart and their evil actions. In all probability, this was an accusing query that was also thrown back at the apostle during his ministry by various Jews, Jewish Christians, and/or pagan Gentiles who had heard him preach in their synagogues, marketplaces, or lecture halls (as was the claim of 9:6 that "God's word has failed!" and the question of 9:14 "Is there injustice with God?," which two matters he responded to earlier in 9:6-13 and 9:14-18).

9:19-21 In dealing with this third matter regarding the justice of God in dealing with people — which is introduced by the twofold rhetorical question "Why then does God still blame us? For who resists his will?" — Paul sets out an elemental theodicy, that is, a basic and rather undeveloped defense of divine justice, mercy, and goodness with respect to God's selection of some people and his hardening of other people. In so doing the apostle employs a diatribe style of presentation, which makes use of direct address to an imaginary or real interlocutor, hypothetical objections, and false conclusions; this diatribe styling is particularly evident in his use of the second-person future indicative verb ἐρεῖς ("you will say"), his direct form of address ὦ ἄνθρωπε ("O man" or "O mere human"), and his continued use (both explicit and implied) of the personal pronouns μοι and με ("to me" and "me") and σύ ("you").[37]

In typical Jewish midrashic fashion, Paul first buttresses his answer with biblical support, making use of the familiar OT imagery of a potter working with a lump of clay to form what he desires.[38] And he argues from that traditionally accepted OT imagery, which speaks of the relationship of God as the Creator to human beings whom he has created, that a question as to why God does what he does in his selection of some people and his rejection of other people is far too inappropriate a question to ever be asked.

9:22-23 Then the apostle sets out two rhetorical questions of his own, which together propose a rationale for what God does in his selection of one person and his rejection of another person. The first is expressed in 9:22: "What if God, choosing to show his wrath and make his power known, bore with great patience the objects of his wrath, which are prepared for destruction?" — suggesting, thereby, that by not dealing immediately with evil people and their evil actions, God has actually been expressing his patience, and doing so in the hope that evil people will repent of their evil and respond positively to his divine mercy. The second of Paul's rhetorical questions, in 9:23, is this: "What if God did this in order to make the riches of his glory known to the object of his mercy, whom he prepared in advance for glory?" — suggesting that God's patience has

37. Cf. Paul's earlier uses of diatribe styling in 2:1-5 and 2:17-24, as well as his later use in 11:17-24. Other uses of a diatribe form are often seen in 3:1-8 (possibly including 9); 3:27-31 (possibly including 4:1-2); and 14:4-11, though see our comments on these passages in rebuttal.

38. Cf. Job 10:9; Isa 29:16; 41:25; 45:9; 64:8; Jer 18:1-12; see also Wis 15:7-17; Sir 27:5; 33:13; 38:29-30; 1QS 11.22; 1QH 1.21; 3.23-24; 4.29; 11.3; 12.26, 32; 18.12.

been a major factor in people turning to him, and so not immediately being "prepared for destruction" but rather in the extended time given by God being "prepared in advance for glory." Thus with these two rhetorical questions Paul proposes the very real possibility that one must always take into account the fact that what "mere humans" all too often view as acts of divine injustice are, in reality, to be understood as acts of divine mercy, which are brought about by God on behalf of the eternal welfare of people.

In these responses of 9:20-23 to these assertions against the justice of God's judgments, Paul sets out (as we have noted earlier) only the rudiments of a Christian theodicy — that is, only the elemental or basic features of the subject, without developing the matter further in a manner that has often been attempted in the philosophical theologizing of Christian theologians down through the centuries. Yet the apostle's references in 9:23 to "the riches of his [God's] glory" (τὸν πλοῦτον τῆς δόξης) and to people being "prepared in advance [by God] for glory" (ἃ προητοίμασεν εἰς δόξαν) — as well as his immediately following references in 9:24-26 to people being "called" by God, using the verbs "he called" (ἐκάλεσεν), "I will call" (καλέσω), and "they will be called" (κληθήσονται) — reflect a number of those five features or stages of a believer's life in the course of God's salvation history, as seen from the divine perspective, that Paul referred to earlier in 8:28-30 when speaking about God's plans and purposes for "those who love him, who have been called according to his purpose" (τοῖς κατὰ πρόθεσιν κλητοῖς οὖσιν).[39] For in sketching out the divine plan and purpose for his people in those earlier verses of ch. 8, Paul presents the basic factors involved in God's working out of his salvation history in the lives of those who respond to him by faith — and he does so in terms of what appear to be, at least in broad outline, the logical and chronological stages of that divine plan and purpose as follows:

1. God's *foreknowledge* of all the possible responses and actions that might transpire in a person's life in the exercise of his or her own God-given free will, and of all the corresponding events that might occur.
2. God's *predestination* of a person's actual responses and actions, as well as all the events that will take place — which he sovereignly selects from among all the foreknown possibilities and ordains both for the good of the person himself or herself and for the advance of his own divine plans and purposes.
3. God's *call* of people to himself whom he foreknew and predestined.
4. God's *justification* of those people whom he calls.
5. God's *glorification* of those people whom he has justified — with the themes of glory and glorification, both present and future, being to the fore in all of God's plans and purposes.

39. On the provenance and Paul's use of these five features or stages in 8:29-30, see our exegetical comments on these verses.

It may therefore be surmised that should Paul have gone further in his response to the questions he reproduces in 9:19 — which, in effect, accuse God for humanity's evil thoughts and rebellious acts — he might possibly have said (assuming that the apostle would have thought in such philosophically oriented ways): "If blame is to be assigned, it must be assigned solely to the person himself or herself who has exercised his or her own God-given freedom in rebellious and evil ways; but if mercy and grace are experienced in the life of a person, it is to be credited solely to God, who, it may be presumed, has selected the best of all the foreknown possibilities of a person's thoughts and actions and has sovereignly chosen the best of those potentialities and possibilities, with those divine choices being not only best for the person and situation in question, but also best for God's overall plans and purposes."

9:24-26 Leaving such speculations aside, what is much more significant for our purposes here is that Paul brings to a close his statements regarding "the riches of his glory," "the object of his mercy," and people being "prepared for glory" by referencing in 9:24 the recipients of God's salvific graciousness as not only himself and the remnant people of Israel (those ἐξ Ἰουδαίων), as might be expected, but also a remnant of people from among the non-Jewish nations (i.e., people ἐξ ἐθνῶν). The legitimacy of including this reference to such a remnant of righteous people who exist among the Gentiles is validated by biblical statements that the apostle draws from "the [book of] Hosea" (ὡς καὶ ἐν τῷ Ὡσηὲ λέγει; literally "as also in the Hosea he says"):[40]

Hos 2:23: "Those who were 'not my people' (οὐ λαόν μου) I will call 'my people' (λαόν μου), and her who was 'not beloved' (οὐκ ἠγαπημένην) I will call 'beloved' (ἠγαπημένην)."

Hos 1:10: "In the very place where it was said to them, 'You are not my people,' there they will be called 'sons and daughters of the living God.'"

Many commentators have drawn attention to the fact that at the end of this major section of 9:6-29 there appear (1) two quotations in 9:25-26 from the prophet Hosea (i.e., Hos 2:23 and 1:10), both of which speak of non-Jewish people, who were not traditionally considered God's people, as being at some time in the future actually called "the people of God," and (2) two quotations in 9:27-29 from the prophet Isaiah (i.e., Isa 10:22-23 and 1:9), both of which have to do with Israel and a "righteous remnant" that existed (and continues to exist) within the nation. Some commentators have drawn from this seeming balance of quoted OT prophetic statements certain implications that have to do not only with God's acceptance of a "righteous remnant" within Israel but also with his

40. This way of referring to an OT writing appears also in Mark 1:2: καθὼς γέγραπται ἐν τῷ Ἠσαΐα τῷ προφήτῃ ("even as it is written in the [book of] Isaiah the prophet"). See also Rom 11:2b: ἐν Ἠλίᾳ τί λέγει ἡ γραφή ("what the Scripture says in [the passage about] Elijah")

acceptance of a body of people drawn from among the Gentiles. Much can be commended about these observations and implications, for they are certainly in line with Paul's thought as expressed elsewhere in this passage. Further, they express far better the apostle's purpose in quoting these four OT statements than do many of the more usual comments on 9:25-29 — such as those that merely note (1) that there are "a number of quotations from the O.T." that Paul includes at the end of 9:6-29, (2) that these biblical quotations are "introduced somewhat irregularly so far as method and arrangement go," and (3) that these quotations function "to recall the fact that this Divine plan, which we shall find eventually worked out more fully, had been foretold by the O.T. prophets."[41]

Paul, however, seems not just to have wanted to close off 9:6-29 with sets of quotations from Hosea and Isaiah — the first set dealing with God's acceptance of certain people from among the Gentiles; the second set highlighting his acceptance of a "righteous remnant" from within Israel. If that had been all he wanted to do, one would expect him to have written first of God's acceptance of a "righteous remnant" *within Israel* and then of God's acceptance of a body of people *from among the Gentiles*. But Paul does not set out matters quite in that fashion.

Rather, the two quotations of Hos 2:23 and 1:10 are given in support of the apostle's final statement of 9:24b, where he says God has chosen to make "the riches of his glory known" not only to the apostle and a "righteous remnant" of Jews within Israel, but also to people "from among the Gentiles" (ἐξ ἐθνῶν). Undoubtedly his reference to those "from the Jews" (ἐξ Ἰουδαίων) has in mind Jewish believers in Jesus of Paul's day. Such an identification may legitimately be assumed from what he said earlier in 9:6b-9 about "the true seed of Abraham" and from what he will say later in 11:1-7a about "a righteous remnant" within Israel. Likewise, his reference to people "from among the Gentiles" (ἐξ ἐθνῶν) has in mind Gentile believers in Jesus who will be accepted by God, and so come to know the same "riches of his glory" as Jewish believers — even, in fact, who will be called by God himself "my people" (as in Hos 2:23a), "my loved one" (as in Hos 2:23b), and "sons and daughters of the living God" (as in Hos 1:10).

IV. The Conclusion of the Matter, Using the Words of Two Passages from Isaiah (9:27-29)

9:27-29 Paul's quotations of two passages from Isaiah here in 9:27-29, however, do more than merely balance out the two quotations from Hosea in 9:25-26. It may legitimately be argued that the apostle used the passages from Isa

---

41. Quoting Sanday and Headlam, *Romans,* 267, whose rather general comments on Paul's quotations of these four OT passages have been repeated in various forms by many contemporary commentators.

10:22-23 and Isa 1:9 mainly because they contain the highly important terms τὸ ὑπόλειμμα ("the remnant") and σπέρμα ("seed" or "surviving descendants") — which encapsulate, each in its own way, (1) all that Paul wrote earlier about God's promise and sovereign choice with respect to the births of Isaac and Jacob in 9:6-13, and (2) much of what is implicitly involved in what he wrote about God's election in 9:14-24. Thus they function as concluding statements to what is presented in this first major section, that is, in 9:6-29, of the apostle's three-part exposition in Rom 9–11.

This rather distinctive use of these two passages from the book of Isaiah to provide an appropriate conclusion to a whole section of material is signaled, it seems, by the way in which Paul introduces each passage. For the quotation of Isa 10:22-23 in Rom 9:27 is introduced by the third-person singular present indicative verb κράζει ("he [Isaiah] cries out") — which intensive verb reflects one significant way in which teachers and writers of Paul's day, both Jewish and Christian, provided summary conclusions to what they had earlier said or written.[42] And the quotation of Isa 1:9 in Rom 9:29 is introduced not only by the frequently used adverb καθώς ("just as"), but also by the third-person singular perfect indicative verb προείρηκεν ("he has already [or 'earlier'] said [i.e., in the same writing or document]") — which expression was often set out in contrast to the present tense and functioned to highlight a further important summary statement that was meant to explicate some earlier concluding statement.[43] These two ways of introducing quotations of the Scriptures were not the usual ways for Paul to introduce biblical statements in either Romans (where the greater part of his OT quotations appear) or his other NT letters.[44] So they suggest some type of difference in the use of OT biblical passages that requires not only notice but also explanation.

It remains to inquire, however, regarding (1) how the second part of Isa 10:22-23 should be read and (2) how Paul understood and used that latter part of the prophet's statement here in 9:28, for both of these matters have frequently been viewed as somewhat perplexing. Charles Cranfield has summarized quite well the first question regarding how Isa 10:23 should be read in the MT, in the LXX, and in Paul's quotation of it:

42. Cf., e.g., the summation of John the Baptist's message in John 1:15-18, which begins with the introductory statement "he cried out saying" (κέκραγεν λέγων); see also the summaries of Jesus' teaching in John 7:28-29, 37-38, and 12:44-46, each of which begins with the aorist verb "he cried out" (ἔκραξεν) followed by "saying" (λέγων) or "and he said" (καὶ εἶπεν). Note also Josephus, *Antiquities* 10.117, where the Jewish historian writes in summary fashion of the message of the prophet Jeremiah, who, even in prison, "did not remain quiet but 'cried out' (ἐκεκράγει)" his message for the people to surrender to the Babylonian king.

43. Cf. Paul's use of προείρηκα ("I have said before") in 2 Cor 7:3.

44. Cf. my listing of Paul's eighty-three explicit quotations of OT passages (whether single or conflated) in the corpus of his NT letters (forty-five of which are found in Romans) in R. N. Longenecker, *Biblical Exegesis,* 2nd ed., 91-95. This list includes all the "introductory formulas" he used to introduce these various biblical quotations, but also notes that these two ways of introducing a biblical passage are different from his others.

ROMANS 9:6-29

The Hebrew of Isa 10.23 is difficult, and the LXX translators were apparently
baffled by the details. Nevertheless, both the LXX rendering and Paul's ab-
breviation of it, though differing considerably from the MT, give the general
idea of the original quite correctly.[45]

On the second matter, how the apostle understood and used Isa 10:23 at Rom
9:29, Cranfield is also probably right in saying that in Paul's understanding the
prophet's statement that "the Lord with rigor and finality will carry out his word
['of judgment'] on the earth" functions to explain "how it will come about that
only a remnant of Israel will be saved," which prophetic declaration Paul had
just quoted in 9:27.[46]

Thus in concluding our exegetical comments on this first major section
of the apostle's three-part exposition in Rom 9–11, we need only observe again
that Paul in 9:27-29 provides a highly appropriate biblical conclusion to all that
he has written in 9:6-26 — and that he does so by using two highly significant
quotations from the prophet Isaiah. This first major section of 9:6-29 is a vitally
important portion of material in which Paul sets out his thesis for everything
that he will argue in 9:30–11:32. And it is the prophetic statements in Isa 10:22-23
and 1:9, which he sees as encapsulating and explicating a true form of remnant
theology, that he quotes as the conclusion to this very important passage of 9:6-
29 regarding the essential features of Christian consciousness and life.

BIBLICAL THEOLOGY

Rom 9:6-29 has often been viewed as an important passage in the construction
of a Christian biblical theology. Origen in the third century, Chrysostom in the
fourth century, and Arminius in the sixteenth century used this passage in their
defenses of humanity's "free will." Conversely, Augustine in the fifth century
and Calvin in the sixteenth century based their teachings with respect to God's
"predestination" and "sovereign election" on this same passage. More recently,
and particularly in today's discussions, what appears in 9:23-26 has received
increasing attention, what with its message of God's desire to make known "the
riches of his glory" not only to Paul and to Jewish believers in Jesus, but also to
people "from among the Gentiles" — with this message of God's salvation for
both Jews and Gentiles being supported by two quotations from the prophecy
of Hosea.

However, the principal thrust of 9:6-29 has to do with God's promises
being given only to a "righteous remnant" of people who live among the various

45. Cranfield, *Romans*, 2.502. On our rejection of the words ἐν δικαιοσύνη, ὅτι λόγον
συντετμημένον at the end of 9:28 (which appear in the TR and were translated by KJV as "in righteousness, because a short work will the Lord make upon the earth"), see the "Textual Notes" above.
46. *Ibid.*

824

national, ethnic, and societal groupings of the world — with that "remnant" being uniquely present within the people of Israel, but also present in some God-ordained fashion among their neighboring non-Jewish peoples. This proclamation includes many (if not all) of the essential features of our traditional theological discussions about "God's sovereignty," "predestination," "election," and "humanity's free will" (however these matters are brought together). And it includes most of the important aspects of God's salvation as having been provided for both Jews and Gentiles. Further, it is a message that (1) needs to be highlighted in any truly Christian "biblical theology" (whatever our own particular theological proclivities) and (2) must be proclaimed by both word and action in all our Christian churches (whatever their somewhat varied doctrinal stances and specific denominational affiliations).

Paul was not opposed to organizational structures, established institutions, or human attempts to develop specific systems of belief. Nor are structures, institutions, or systems renounced in either the OT or the NT. Such objective factors are necessary, whether in a corporate or a personal context, so that people might live out their lives properly and think in a constructive manner. Nonetheless, what Paul proclaims, and what all the biblical materials support, is this: at the heart of every structure, institution, or system must be the all-important factor of "righteousness" — that is, (1) God's own attributive righteousness, which is the primary attribute of his person and character, (2) God's communicative righteousness, which is the gift that he gives to those who commit themselves to him, and (3) the righteousness of God's people, which is what they have received from God as a gift and what they are to express to others by the direction of his Holy Spirit.

Thus here in 9:6-29 Paul focuses on God's promises as being given only to a "righteous remnant" of people, who exist first of all within Israel and also may be found among other non-Jewish national, ethnic, and societal groups of people. His desire is that all believers in Jesus, whatever their national, ethnic, or societal backgrounds — as well as whatever their ecclesiastical and denominational preferences — both (1) incorporate such an understanding of themselves into their biblical theology and (2) actually think and act in terms of a Christian remnant theology.

CONTEXTUALIZATION FOR TODAY

Rom 9:6-29 highlights the fact that two portions of the Jewish (OT) Scriptures functioned for the apostle Paul as the principal biblical bases for his Christian proclamation to believers in Jesus at Rome: (1) the accounts in Genesis of God's promise given to Abraham (and extended to his son Isaac and grandson Jacob), and (2) the clarification of that divine promise by the prophet Isaiah, who proclaimed that all the promises of God were given (and continue to be given) only to a "righteous remnant" of people within Israel and among the Gentiles. These were undoubtedly passages and topics of great importance to Paul himself. And while his Christian proclamation to both Jews and Gentiles always focused on God's abounding love and mercy, Jesus' ministry in accomplishing the work of salvation for all people, and the ministry of God's Spirit in actively working for the good of all people — and while he earlier presented in 5:1–8:39 a précis of the Christian message that he proclaimed in his mission to pagan Gentiles in the non-Jewish world — here in 9:6-29 (as well as in the remainder of Rom 9–11) Paul addresses the Christians at Rome who had been extensively influenced by the theology, ways of thinking, and religious language of Jewish Christianity, as centered in the mother church at Jerusalem. And so he speaks to them in a way that they would appreciate and understand — that is, not only in citing biblical incidents and using biblical quotations, but also in clothing his presentation in a christianized form of Jewish remnant theology.

Paul's presentation of the Christian gospel here in 9:6-29 is, in form and content, much like that which he presented earlier in 1:16–4:25. It differs somewhat, however, not only in form but also in content and emphasis, from what he has just written in 5:1–8:39. These two forms of the Christian gospel, while somewhat different, are to be understood as entirely complementary. Yet they represent two rather distinctive contextualizations of the same Christian message as proclaimed to two somewhat different culturally conditioned mind-sets, with both contextualizations having a place in the one letter written by one Christian evangelist to one group of Christian people. And as such they present us not only with two sets of compatible early Christian teachings, but also with two templates or patterns for how as Christians today we are to represent ourselves and proclaim the Christian message in somewhat differing cultural and religious contexts.

3. Part II of Paul's Exposition: Israel's Present Failure and the Gentiles Blessed, with OT Passages Cited in Support (9:30–10:21)

TRANSLATION

⁹:³⁰*What, then, shall we say? That Gentiles, who did not pursue righteousness, have attained righteousness — a righteousness that is by faith;* ³¹*but the people of Israel, who are pursuing a law of righteousness [i.e., a "legalistic" or "nomistic" form of righteousness] in connection with the Mosaic law, have not attained [it].* ³²*Why so? Because [they are pursuing it] not by faith, but, rather, as if [it could be attained] on the basis of works. They stumbled over "the stumbling stone."* ³³*As it is written:*

"See, I lay in Zion a stone that causes people to stumble
  and a rock that makes them fall,
and the one who believes in him will not be put to shame."

¹⁰:¹*Brothers and sisters, my heart's desire and prayer to God for the people of Israel is, indeed, with respect to their salvation.* ²*For I can testify about them that they are zealous for God, but their zeal is not based on knowledge.* ³*For being ignorant of the righteousness of God, and seeking to establish their own righteousness, they did not submit to God's righteousness.* ⁴*For "Christ is the end of the law in connection with righteousness for everyone who believes."*

⁵*For Moses writes regarding the righteousness that comes from the law: "The person who does these things will live by them."* ⁶*But the righteousness that is by faith says: "Do not say in your heart, 'Who will ascend into heaven?' (that is, to bring Christ down)* ⁷*or 'Who will descend into the deep?' (that is, to bring Christ up from the dead)."* ⁸*But what does it say? "The word is near you; it is in your mouth and in your heart" — that is, the word of faith that we are proclaiming:* ⁹*that if you confess with your mouth "Jesus is Lord" and believe in your heart that God raised him from the dead, you will be saved.* ¹⁰*For it is with the heart that you believe and are justified, and it is with the mouth that you confess and are saved.* ¹¹*For as the Scripture says, "Everyone who believes in him will never be put to shame."* ¹²*For there is no difference between Jews and Gentiles — for the same Lord is Lord of all and richly blesses all who call on him.* ¹³*For, "everyone who calls on the name of the Lord will be saved."*

¹⁴*How, then, can they call on the one they have not believed in? And how can they believe in the one of whom they have not heard? And how can they hear without someone preaching to them?* ¹⁵*And how can they preach unless they are sent? As it is written, "How beautiful are the feet of those who bring good news!"*

¹⁶*But not all [of the people of Israel] have accepted the good news. For Isaiah*

says, "Lord, who has believed our message?" ¹⁷Thus faith comes from hearing the message, and the message is heard through the word of Christ.

¹⁸But I ask: Did they not hear? Of course they did!

"Their voice has gone out into all the earth;
 and their words to the ends of the world."

¹⁹Again I ask: Did Israel not understand? Moses is the first one to say,

"I will provoke you to jealousy by those who are not a people;
 I will provoke you to jealous anger by a nation without understanding."

²⁰Isaiah is bold and says,

"I was found among those who are not seeking me;
 I made myself known to those who did not ask for me."

²¹But concerning the people of Israel he says, "All day long I held out my hands to a disobedient and obstinate people."

TEXTUAL NOTES

9:30 The accusative noun δικαιοσύνην ("righteousness") in all three appearances in this verse is anarthrous, and it is this use of δικαιοσύνην without the definite article that is amply attested in the textual tradition. But the article τήν before this first use of the accusative δικαιοσύνην in this verse (thereby reading "the righteousness") is found in P⁴⁶ and in uncial G. Probably the inclusion of τήν before this first appearance of the accusative δικαιοσύνην was meant to signal that here in 9:30-33, as well as in all that follows in 10:1-21, Paul was reaching back to and resuming his treatment of δικαιοσύνη ("righteousness") that he earlier had set out in 1:16–4:25. Yet such a relationship between what appears here in 9:30–10:21 and what Paul wrote earlier in 1:16–4:25 is already contextually implied, and therefore the insertion of an article before δικαιοσύνην ("righteousness") in 9:30 would be unnecessary. Thus because of its weak MSS support, coupled with the lack of any necessity for its appearance here (certainly not in any earlier oral delivery by Paul, and just as certainly not in his letter to the Christians at Rome), the presence of τήν before this first use of the accusative noun δικαιοσύνη is best understood as a variant reading inserted by some early scribe.

31a The phrase εἰς νόμον ("in connection with the law" or "with respect to the law") is attested by P⁴⁶ᵛⁱᵈ, by uncials ℵ* A B D G, and by minuscules 1739 (Category I), 81 1506 2464 (Category II), and 6 424ᶜ (Category III); it is also reflected in the Coptic versions and supported by Ambrosiaster. The omission of εἰς νόμον, however, is supported by minuscule 33 (Category I) and some Byzantine minuscules, but this omission should most likely be discounted.

31b The expanded phrase εἰς νόμον δικαιοσύνης ("in connection with the law *of righteousness*") is found in uncials ℵ² F P Ψ (also *Byz* K L) and in minuscules 1175 (Category I), 1881 2464ᵛⁱᵈ (Category II), and 69 88 104 323 326 330 365 1241 1243 1319 1505

1573 1735 1836 1874 2344 2495 (Category III). This addition of the noun "righteousness," however, has every appearance of being a later attempt at consistency of expression and so a stylistic improvement.

32 The prepositional phrase ἐξ ἔργων ("from works" or "on the basis of works") is attested by P⁴⁶ᵛⁱᵈ, by uncials ℵ* A B F G, and by minuscules 1739 (Category I), 1881 (Category II), and 6 424ᶜ 2200 (Category III); it is also reflected in itᵃʳ, ᵇ, ᶠ, ᵍ, ᵐᵒⁿ, ᵒ vg copˢᵃ, ᵇᵒ and supported by Origenˡᵃᵗ Ambrosiaster Pelagius Jerome and Augustine. The addition of the word νόμου ("of the law") to ἐξ ἔργων ("by works"), thereby reading "by works of the law," is supported by uncials ℵ² D P Ψ (also *Byz* K L) and by minuscules 33 1175 (Category I), 81 256 1506 1962 2127 2464 (Category II), and 104 263 365 436 459 1241 1319 1573 1852 1912 (Category III); it is also reflected in itᵈ vgᵐˢ syrᵖ, ʰ, ᵖᵃˡ and supported by Diodoreᵛⁱᵈ and Chrysostom. The shorter reading ἐξ ἔργων ("by works"), however, is better attested in the textual tradition, and so should most likely be considered original — with the addition of νόμου ("of the law") being probably an assimilation to Paul's earlier use of this fuller expression in 3:20 and 28 (cf. also Gal 2:16 [3x]; 3:2, 5, and 10).

33a The articular phrase ὁ πιστεύων ("the one who trusts" or "believes") is attested by uncials ℵ A B D F G and by minuscules 81 1506 1881 (Category II); it is also reflected in itᵇ, ᵈ*, ᶠ ᵍ, ᵐᵒⁿ, syrᵖ, ᵖᵃˡ copˢᵃ, ᵇᵒ and supported by Origenᵍʳ, ˡᵃᵗ Ambrosiaster and Augustine. The presence of the substantival adjective πᾶς ("whoever," "everyone who") after καί ("and"), which expresses the heightened sense "everyone who believes," is supported by uncials P Ψ (also *Byz* K L) and by minuscules 33 1175 1739 (Category I), 181 256 1962 2127 2464 (Category II), 6 69 88 104 263 323 326 330 365 436 614 1241 1243 1319 1505 1573 1735 1852 1874 1877 1912 2200 (Category III); it is also reflected in itᵃʳ, ᵈ², ᵒ vg syrʰ and supported by Chrysostom and Theodore. This appearance of πᾶς here in 9:33b is most likely to be understood as a scribal assimilation to Paul's citation of the same quotation in 10:11, where all MSS read πᾶς ὁ πιστεύων ("everyone who believes" or "trusts").

33b The third-person, singular, future, indicative, passive verb καταισχυνθήσεται in the statement "he will not be shamed" or "put to shame" is amply attested in the textual tradition. The third-person, singular, aorist, subjective, passive καταισχύνθη, however, appears in uncials D F G — which form of the verb causes the statement to be read as "he is not shamed." But this variant form is most likely a scribal attempt to have Paul's quotation of Isa 28:16 correspond exactly with the LXX reading of the verse.

10:1 The genitive (of reference) plural pronoun αὐτῶν ("for them") following ὑπέρ (in the phrase "my prayer to God for them [i.e., 'the people of Israel']") is amply attested by P⁴⁶, by uncials ℵ* A B D F G, and by minuscules 1739 (Category I), 256 1506 1881 1962 2127 (Category II), and 6 365 1319 1573 1912 (Category III); it is also reflected in itᵈ*, ᶠ, ᵍ, ᵐᵒⁿ syrᵖ, ᵖᵃˡ cop ˢᵃ, ᵇᵒ and supported by Ambrosiaster and Augustine⁵ᐟ⁹. The addition of ἐστιν ("it is"), which appears in uncials ℵ² P Ψ and in minuscules 33 (Category I) and 263 1852 (Category III), as well as reflected in itᵃʳ, ᵇ, ᵈ², ᵒ vg and supported by Origenˡᵃᵗ Chrysostom and Augustine⁴ᐟ⁹, was probably inserted for clarification, since otherwise the sentence has no verb. Likewise, the longer reading τοῦ Ἰσραήλ ἐστιν ("for Israel is") that appears in Byzantine uncials K L, as well as in minuscules 1175 (Category I), 81 2464 (Category II), and 104 436 459 1241 [1319 omits ἐστιν] 2200 (Category III), being also supported by Marcionᵃᶜᶜ ᵗᵒ ᵀᵉʳᵗᵘˡˡⁱᵃⁿ, was probably inserted not only to clarify the grammar but also to restate from 9:31 that it is "the people of Israel" who are the object of Paul's concern. This longer reading may have been added, as B. M. Metzger has suggested, "when this verse was made the beginning of a lesson read in church services (cf. the reference to Israel in 9:31)."[1]

3 Whether the word δικαιοσύνην ("righteousness") should or should not be included after τὴν ἰδίαν ("their own") is difficult to determine. It is omitted in uncials A B D P and in minuscules 1739 (Category I), 81 1506 1881 (Category II), and 365 629 630 (Category III); it is also omitted in it[a] vg cop[sa, bo] and by Clement. It is present, however, in P[46], in uncials ℵ F G Ψ (also *Byz* K L), and in minuscules 33 1175 (Category I), 1962 2464 (Category II), and 5 6 61 88 104 181 218 323 326 330 436 441 451 459 467 614 621 623 915 917 1241 1243 1398 1505 1718 1735 1751 1838 1845 1874 1875 1877 1912 1942 1959 2138 2197 2344 2492 2495 2516 2523 2544 2718 (Category III); it is also reflected in it[(b), d*] and supported by Marcion and Irenaeus[lat]. Because of their uncertainty, the editors of *GNT*[3, 4] and *NA*[26, 27] decided to place this occurrence of δικαιοσύνην after τὴν ἰδίαν in square brackets, thereby changing the earlier editorial decision to omit the word in previous editions of *GNT* and *NA*.

It remains, of course, always a possibility that δικαιοσύνην in the middle of 10:3 was viewed by some scribes as redundant, and so they deleted it. Yet the MSS evidence is slightly in support of the view that δικαιοσύνην did not originally appear with the phrase τὴν ἰδίαν ("their own"). In the exegetical comments that follow, therefore, while we accept the presence of δικαιοσύνην at both the beginning and the end of the verse, we will not include this noun as having originally appeared in the middle of the verse — even though the idea of "righteousness" is clearly implied by the context.

5a The position of the particle ὅτι is disputed. Its appearance at the end of the statement Μωυσῆς γράφει τὴν δικαιοσύνην τὴν ἐκ τοῦ νόμου ("Moses writes regarding the righteousness that comes from the law") is attested by P[46], by uncials ℵ[2] B D[2] G P Ψ, and by minuscules 33[c] (Category I corrected copy), 1962 2127 (Category II), and 104 326 436 1241 2495 (Category III); it is also reflected in it[ar, d, e, f, g] syr[(p), h, pal ms] and supported by Ambrosiaster Chrysostom and Theodoret. In this positioning at the end of the statement, the particle ὅτι functions in an introductory fashion to prepare the reader for the words quoted from Lev 18:5 that follow — just as it did earlier in 8:36 and as it does elsewhere in the NT.[2] Some textual witnesses, however, have ὅτι between Μωυσῆς γράφει and τὴν δικαιοσύνην, thereby reading "Moses writes *that* [i.e., 'about,' 'concerning'] the righteousness [that comes from the law]." This positioning of ὅτι appears in uncials ℵ* A and D* and in minuscules 1739 (Category I), 81 1506 1881 (Category II), and 630 (Category III). Further, some minuscules avoid the issue entirely by simply omitting the particle ὅτι, as do 424[c] (Category III) and the distinctly Byzantine minuscules 1827 and 1984. But the positioning of ὅτι as introducing the words taken from Lev 18:5 is somewhat better supported by the external MS evidence, and so will be favored in our "Exegetical Comments" below.

5b The statement ὁ ποιήσας αὐτὰ ἄνθρωπος ζήσεται ἐν αὐτοῖς ("the one ['per-

---

1. Metzger, *Textual Commentary*, 463.
2. Cf. also Matt 2:23; 21:16; Luke 2:23; John 10:34; 1 Cor 14:21; Heb 11:18.

son'] who does these things will live by them") is attested by P⁴⁶, by uncials ℵ² P Ψ (also *Byz* K), and by minuscules 1962 2127 (Category II) and 88 104 326 451 1241 2495 (Category III); it is also reflected in it^d* syr^h and supported by Theodoret. The word ἄνθρωπος ("man," "person"), however, is omitted by uncial G, which omission is reflected in it^f, g syr^p and supported by Ambrosiaster Chrysostom — most likely because it seemed unnecessary with ὁ ποιήσας αὐτά ("the one ['person'] who does these things").

Further, αὐτά ("these things") is sometimes omitted, as by uncials ℵ* A D^gr, by minuscules 1739 (Category I) and 81 (Category II); this omission is reflected in it^dem, z vg cop^sa? bo? and supported by Origen^gr, lat. Likewise, αὐτοῖς ("them") in the phrase ἐν αὐτοῖς ("by them") is sometimes replaced by αὐτῇ ("these things"), as by uncials ℵ* A B, by minuscules 33^c 1739 (Category I), 81 1506 1881 (Category II), and 436 630 (Category III); and as reflected in versions it^dem, x, z vg cop^sa? bo? and supported by Origen^gr, lat — probably because the context contains no antecedent to which the plural refers.

8 The neuter pronoun τί ("it") in the question ἀλλὰ τί λέγει; ("But what does it say?") is amply attested in the textual tradition. The variant ἡ γραφή ("the Scripture"), however, is found in uncials D F G and in minuscules 33 (Category I) and 88 104 326 365 629 1319 1573 1735 2344 (Category III); it is also reflected in ol^ar vg^cl and cop^bo and is supported by Ambrosiaster. The substitution of ἡ γραφή for the simple pronoun τί, while providing an acceptable explanatory function, is clearly secondary.

9a The phrase ἐν τῷ στόματί σου κύριον Ἰησοῦν ("with your mouth, 'Jesus is Lord'") is quite strongly attested by P⁴⁶, by uncials ℵ D F G P Ψ (also *Byz* K L), and by minuscules 33 1739 (Category I), 1881 1962 2127 (Category II), and 104 436 1241 2495 (Category III); it is also reflected in it^(ar), d, dem, e, f, g, x, z vg syr^p, h cop^bo and supported by Irenaeus^lat Ambrosiaster Chrysostom and Theodoret. Some Alexandrian witnesses, such as Codex Vaticanus (B 03), cop^sa, and Clement, however, add the clarifying expression τὸ ῥῆμα ("the word"). Other textual witnesses, such as uncial A, and as reflected in it^t, add Χριστόν to the name Ἰησοῦν (thereby reading "Christ Jesus"). But both of these additions appear to be simply assimilations to expressions used earlier in the passage.

9b The accusative phrase κύριον Ἰησοῦν ("Jesus is Lord") is very strongly supported by P⁴⁶, by uncials ℵ B D F G P Ψ (also *Byz* K L), and by minuscules 33 1175 1739 (Category I), 81 1506 1881 1962 2127 2464 (Category II), and 6 69 88 104 181 323 326 330 365 424^c 436 451 614 629 630 1241 1319 1505 1573 1735 1874 1877 2344 2492 2495 (Category III); it is also reflected in all the Latin and Coptic versions and supported by Origen^lat. The fuller expression ὅτι κύριος Ἰησοῦς (i.e., the addition of ὅτι, together with the title and name being in the nominative case), which appears in Codex Vaticanus (B 03) and in minuscules 81 1506 (both Category II), is most likely a secondary addition that was done to render the formulation closer to the standard form of this early Christian confession.

15 The quotation of Isa 52:7 appears here in two forms, the shorter reading being Ὡς ὡραῖοι οἱ πόδες τῶν εὐαγγελιζομένων τὰ ἀγαθά ("How beautiful are the feet of those who are proclaiming good news!"), which is attested by P⁴⁶, by uncials ℵ* A B C, and by minuscules 1739 (Category I), 81 1506 1881 (Category II), and 1912 2200 (Category III); it is also reflected in it^ar cop^sa, bo and supported by Clement and Origen^gr, lat. A number of other textual witnesses, however, have πόδες ("feet") after the phrase τῶν εὐαγγελιζομένων εἰρήνην ("of those who are proclaiming peace"), which reading appears in uncials ℵ² D F G P Ψ (also *Byz* K L) and in minuscules 33 1175 (Category I), 256 1962 2464 (Category II), and 6 104 263 365 436 459 1241 1319 1573 1852 (Category III); it is also reflected in it[b, d, f, g, o] vg syr[p, h] and supported by Marcion[acc to Tertullian], Irenaeus[lat] Chrysostom Ambrosiaster Jerome and Augustine. While it is possible that the shorter reading originated because a scribe's eye passed from τῶν εὐαγγελιζομένων to τῶν εὐαγγελιζομένων, it is more probable that the longer phrase with the insertion of πόδες (as in uncials ℵ² D F G P Ψ, etc.) was added to make the quotation correspond more fully to the reading of the Septuagint (see Isa 52:7; Nah 1:15 [LXX 2:1]).

17 In the clause ἡ δὲ ἀκοὴ διὰ ῥήματος Χριστοῦ ("and what is heard comes through the word of Christ"), the genitive form of the name Χριστοῦ is attested by P[46vid], by uncials ℵ* C[vid] D*, and by minuscules 1739 (Category I), 81 1506 (Category II), and 6 1852 (Category III); it is also reflected in it[ar, b, d] cop[sa, bo] and supported by Origen[lat] and Augustine. The genitive θεοῦ, however, replaces Χριστοῦ (thus reading "the word of God") in uncials ℵ¹ A D¹ P Ψ (also *Byz* K L) and in minuscules 33 1175 (Category I), 256 1881 1962 2127 2464 (Category II), and 104 263 365 436 459 1241 1319 1573 1912 2200 (Category III); it is also reflected in syr[p, h] and supported by Clement Chrysostom Theodore and Jerome. A few "Western" witnesses omit any reference either to "Christ" or to "God" (as do uncials F G; also as reflected in it[f, g, o] and in Hilary Ambrosiaster Pelagius), which omission was most likely the result of scribal carelessness at some stage in the text's transmission.

As for the two most possible readings, the phrase ῥῆμα Χριστοῦ ("the word of Christ") occurs only here in the NT, whereas ῥῆμα θεοῦ ("the word of God") is the more familiar expression (cf. Luke 3:2; John 3:34; Eph 6:17; Heb 6:5; 11:3), which would support the more difficult reading "the word of Christ" — so we accept "the word of Christ" as having been original, which was replaced by the more usual phrase "the word of God."

20a The third-person singular, present, indicative, active ἀποτολμᾷ ("he is bold"), coupled with the conjunction καί ("and," "even"), constitutes a difficult expression, since this is the only time that the verb ἀποτολμάω appears in the LXX or the NT. Yet the phrase ἀποτολμᾷ καί ("he is bold and") is well attested in the textual tradition. Its omission in only uncials D* [and c] F and G is too weakly supported to be considered original.

20b The presence of the preposition ἐν ("in," "by," "among") after the verb εὑρέθην ("I was found") is attested by P[46], by uncials B D* F G, and by minuscule 1506[vid] (Category II); it is also reflected in it and vg[cl]. It is, however, omitted in uncials ℵ A C D¹ P Ψ (also *Byz* L) and in minuscules 33 1175 1739 (Category I), 1881 2464 (Category II), and 6 69 104 323 326 330 365 614 1241 1243 1319 1505 1573 1735 1874 2344 2495 (Category III); its omission is also reflected in vg[st]. Determination regarding the inclusion or omission of ἐν ("in," "by," "among") is difficult on an external basis alone. Internal matters with respect to context and sense must prevail (see "Exegetical Comments" below, where we suggest an acceptance of the preposition as original and translate it as "among"). Its omission may be explainable as assimilation to the wording of the LXX.

20c The presence of the preposition πρός ("to") after the clause ἐμφανὴς ἐγενόμην ("I made myself known") is amply attested in the textual tradition. The preposition ἐπί ("upon"), however, appears in its place in Codex Bezae (D 06), but that reading is much too weakly supported to be considered original.

FORM/STRUCTURE/SETTING

Earlier in Part I of his three-part exposition, that is, in 9:6-29, Paul dealt with "God's promises and people's responses" from the perspective of God's sovereign will and election in the giving of his promises. Here in Part II, in 9:30–10:21, the apostle continues to discuss God's promises and people's responses, but (1) he focuses on people's responses, dealing particularly with the Jewish rejection of Jesus, and (2) he refers to certain positive responses to God by some Gentiles, which responses he characterizes as expressions of faith.

The Materials of 9:30–10:21 as Constituting a Discrete and Unified Passage. Many interpreters have viewed 9:30-33 as either a summary, with biblical support, of what Paul has just written in 9:6-29,[3] or a transitional passage, with biblical support, which introduces what he will write in 10:1-21[4] — or, somewhat more commonly, a passage that functions in both a summary and a transitional fashion.[5] James Dunn, however, is certainly correct in observing that "the impression that vv. 30-33 are transitional is probably in large part due to the modern chapter division."[6] And Douglas Moo has rightly argued that although "at first glance it seems natural to follow the chapter divisions in isolating the next major stage of Paul's argument, . . . our first glance is in this case misleading; a more fundamental break comes at 9:30."[7]

Disregarding, therefore, the relatively modern chapter division that has been inserted between 9:30-33 and 10:1-21, we propose that 9:30–10:21 is a discrete and unified passage.[8] We do so for the following reasons, which have to do with features of *formal patterning* that appear in this subsection and function to highlight its distinctive and coherent nature:

1. The rhetorical question τί οὖν ἐροῦμεν; ("What then shall we say?") of 9:30a, which includes the epistolary convention of a "verb of saying,"[9] functions to signal the start of a distinguishable subsection of material —

3. See, e.g., Sanday and Headlam, *Romans,* 278: "The οὖν, as is almost always the case in St. Paul, sums up the results of the previous paragraph"; it asks the question, "What then is the conclusion of this discussion?" Note also C. K. Barrett's first words at the beginning of his exegetical comments on 9:30-33: "The sum of the matter is this, . . ." (*Romans,* 192).

4. See, e.g., Fitzmyer, *Romans,* 576: "Verses 30-33 are transitional to chap. 10, where the second step in his argument is mainly developed."

5. See, e.g., Michel, *An die Römer,* 319; Schlier, *Römerbrief,* 305; Wilckens, *An die Römer,* 2.210-11; Schmithals, *Römerbrief,* 365.

6. Dunn, *Romans,* 2.579.

7. Moo, *Romans,* 616.

8. So also such commentators as C. H. Dodd, *Romans,* 161-72, and Käsemann, *Romans,* 276-98, who understand this subsection of material as the second part of what Paul sets out in his three-part exposition of 9:6–11:32 — with the first part appearing in 9:6-29, the second part in 9:30–10:21, and the third part in 11:1-32.

9. On Paul's use of "verbs of saying [or 'speaking']" in this section of Romans, see also 9:14; 11:1, 13. Note how the apostle uses verbs of saying at various turning points in the development of his argument in Galatians (cf. Gal 3:15; 17; 4:1, 21; 5:16).

just as it did earlier in 9:14 and its five other appearances in Paul's letter to Rome.[10]

2. Paul's statements in 9:30-32 about Gentiles "attaining" righteousness, but the people of Israel failing to do so because they are not "pursuing" God's gift of righteousness "by faith" (as well as the biblical support for those statements in 9:33, which is drawn from a conflation of Isa 28:16 and 8:14) — together with his extended quotation in 10:20-21 of Isa 65:1-2, which speaks about Gentiles as "finding" God but the people of Israel failing to do so because of their "disobedience" and "obstinacy" — form a quite recognizable *inclusio* that functions to alert the Christians at Rome (as well as readers today) that what appears in 9:30–10:21 is to be understood as a discrete and unified section of material.[11]

3. The nouns δικαιοσύνη ("righteousness") and πίστις ("faith"), together with the verb πιστεύω ("believe"), are prominent — in fact, are central — throughout the subsection of 9:30–10:21,[12] even though they were not present in the earlier subsection of 9:6-29 and will be almost entirely absent from the later subsection of 11:1-32 (as well as not appearing in either the introduction of 9:1-5 or the doxology of 11:33-36).

4. Paul's quotation of Isa 65:1-2, which appears in two parts in 10:20-21 (that is, at the end of this second subsection of his exposition), gives every appearance of functioning very much like his quotation of passages from Isa 10:22-23 and 1:9 earlier in 9:27-29 (that is, at the conclusion of the first subsection of his exposition), thereby suggesting that in these two concluding passages of 9:27-29 and 10:20-21 the apostle brings to a close the points he has been making in each of their respective subsections of material, first in 9:6-29 and then in 9:30–10:21 — doing so by quoting the express words of the great Israelite prophet Isaiah.

Paul's Use of Biblical Quotations in 9:30–10:21. Earlier in 1:16–3:20 Paul employed a rather large number of biblical quotations, biblical allusions, and traditional Jewish aphorisms based on the OT Scriptures in support of his arguments. Likewise, in 9:6-29 he made use of certain important statements drawn from the patriarchal narratives in Genesis and numerous OT quotations in support of his presentation. And the apostle will employ a number of additional OT quotations in what follows in 11:1-32.

But what is not often realized, is that here in 9:30–10:21 (i.e., in Part II of

10. In addition to its appearance earlier in 9:14 and here in 9:30, see also Rom 3:5; 4:1; 6:1; 7:7; and 8:31 where Paul uses this same rhetorical question to signal the start of other sections or subsections of material.

11. On 9:30-33 and 10:20-21 as a rhetorical *inclusio*, see Aletti, "L'Argumentation paulinniene en Rm 9," 42-43; Dunn, *Romans*, 2.579; and Moo, *Romans*, 617.

12. Cf. Paul's use of δικαιοσύνη in 9:30 (3x), 31; 10:3 (2x), 4, 5, 6, 10; see also the occurrences of πίστις/πιστεύω in 9:30, 32, 33; 10:4, 6, 8, 9, 10, 11, 14, 16, 17 (with the noun πίστις appearing elsewhere in this three-part exposition of the apostle only in 11:20).

his three-part exposition), Paul uses even more OT quotations, biblical allusions, and proverbial materials based on OT Scripture in support of his statements than he does anywhere else in his letter to Rome — even more than in 9:6-29.[13] In fact, as Ernst Käsemann has aptly noted with respect to the presentation of 9:30–10:21 (though, perhaps, expressed a bit too expansively): "The organization of the section is governed by the fact that a biblical text rounds off each thought."[14]

The thrust of 9:30–10:21 has to do with the situation of unbelieving Jews of Paul's day, and so his biblical quotations are given in support of his overall argument — which may be expressed, as Joseph Fitzmyer has stated matters, as follows: "What has happened to Israel is not contrary to God's direction of history, because its infidelity had been foreseen and even recorded in its Scriptures."[15] However, the apostle also refers to believing Gentiles, comparing their situation before God with that of the people of Israel. And in support of his assertion that in God's sight "there is no difference between Jew and Gentile, for the same Lord is Lord of all and richly blesses all who call on him," Paul uses statements drawn from the ancient Israelite prophets Isaiah and Joel.

In all the biblical passages quoted in support of his arguments regarding the people of Israel vis-à-vis Gentiles, Paul uses a Jewish form of midrashic exegesis. This type of interpretation had to do not only with the particular points, whether explicit or implied, that can be extracted from the biblical texts (i.e., exegesis), but also with the form and wording of those texts (i.e., text criticism). At times, in opposition to Jewish teachers who claimed to be basing their lives and instructions on what Moses had written, Paul even uses statements from this same great Jewish lawgiver in support of his own understanding of the relationships that God has brought about in this new epoch of salvation history — that is, new relationships that are (1) based on the ministry, death, and resurrection of Jesus of Nazareth, together with his promises for the future, and (2) brought about in the lives of believers in Jesus by the ministry of God's Spirit.

The Structure of 9:30–10:21. In Part I of his three-part exposition, that is, in 9:6-29, Paul discussed the topic of "God's promises and people's responses" from the perspective of God's sovereign will and election. Here in Part II, 9:30–10:21, however, he deals with that same subject from the point of view of humanity's responses. In this second part of his exposition he focuses principally on the Jewish rejection of Jesus of Nazareth, whom the Christians proclaimed as God's promised Messiah. But he also alludes to some Gentiles having received from God "a righteousness that is by faith" — which implies that at least certain

---

13. Note Paul's quotations (or, perhaps, proverbial use) of Isa 28:16 and 8:14 (in 9:33); Lev 18:5 (in 10:5); Deut 30:12-14 (in 10:6-8); Isa 28:16 again (in 10:11); Joel 2:32 [MT and LXX 3:5] (in 10:13); Isa 52:7 (in 10:15); Isa 53:1 (in 10:16); Ps 19:4 [MT 19:5; LXX 18:5] (in 10:18); Deut 32:21 (in 10:19); and Isa 65:1-2 (in 10:20-21).

14. Käsemann, *Romans,* 284 (though Käsemann specifically applies his observation only to what appears in 10:8, 11, and 13).

15. Fitzmyer, *Spiritual Exercises,* 165.

Gentiles during the course of human history (as well as, of course, during the apostle's own Gentile mission) responded to God and his saving mercies in a positive fashion, even though they did not have the same knowledge about God and his redemptive actions as did the people of Israel. So while the same overall topic of "God's promises and people's responses" is dealt with in the first two parts of the apostle's three-part exposition, because of their differing foci of attention — Part I on "God's sovereign will, choice, and election," and Part II on "humanity's responses" — Paul's presentation here in 9:30–10:21 is somewhat different from his presentation in 9:6-29.

Though the particular matters dealt with in these two passages are different, their formal structures are very similar. What is written in 9:6-29 may be outlined under four captions or headings: (1) opening thesis statements, which are supported by certain features in the patriarchal accounts of Genesis; (2) an exposition on God's mercy and justice in his choice of people, with supporting biblical data; (3) an elemental theodicy in defense of God's election of some people and his hardening toward others, with support from traditional reasoning and the Scriptures; and (4) a conclusion of the matter, using the words of two OT passages drawn from the prophet Isaiah. What appears in 9:30–10:21 is also structured in terms of four quite similar captions or headings:

1. Thesis statements about Israel's present situation of unbelief vis-à-vis the situation of believing Gentiles, with confirming data regarding Israel's situation drawn from two passages in the prophecy of Isaiah (9:30-33).
2. An exposition on the focus of God's program of salvation history — explicating the thesis statements of 9:30-33, setting out what appears to be a quasi-confessional affirmation in 10:4, and quoting OT passages and biblically based proverbial material in support (10:1-13).
3. Two sets of rhetorical questions and direct responses regarding the situation of unbelieving Jews, with further OT passages cited in support (10:14-19).
4. Concluding statements drawn from the prophet Isaiah, which Paul understands as God speaking about revealing himself to certain Gentiles who did not "seek" or "ask for" him, but finding no response from "disobedient and obstinate" Jews (10:20-21).

These comparable features of "formal patterning" between 9:6-29 and 9:30–10:21 could be used to argue for an earlier oral provenance for at least Parts I and II of Paul's exposition in this third major section of his letter to Rome. Such a view is similar to that proposed by C. H. Dodd, which he based on his observation that the material of Rom 9–11 "has a character of its own" — that is, that these chapters are more expressive of "a preacher than a writer" and more "conversational in nature."[16] This similarity of structures between the two

---

16. C. H. Dodd, *Romans*, 148. Dodd has spelled out these observations further to suggest

parts may stem from Paul's earlier Christian preaching and teaching in various Jewish synagogues and/or in certain Jewish Christian gatherings[17] — with what he presents in 11:1-32 as constituting the climactic conclusion to that three-part oral exposition. Nonetheless, while we believe that such a proposal is highly likely, it must always remain largely conjectural. For it is supported mainly by such inferences as can be drawn from the tone and form of what appears in Part I (9:6-29) and Part II (9:30–10:21) — with, as may be argued, further support by (1) certain features of form and nature as may be postulated for the apostle's quite dramatic statement in 10:4; (2) the seemingly proverbial nature of his quotation of Deut 30:12-14 in 10:6b-8a, which may be attributable to a popular, midrashic treatment of an OT passage in his Christian oral proclamation; and (3) such other matters having to do with oral provenance as may be claimed for what appears in 11:1-32 — all of which matters will be dealt with more fully in our "Exegetical Comments" on these passages that follow.

EXEGETICAL COMMENTS

Paul's use of a Christian version of Jewish remnant rhetoric was clearly to the fore in the first part of his exposition in 9:6-29 — particularly in (1) his employment of certain important features in the patriarchal narratives of Genesis as illustrating God's choice of certain people and not of others, (2) his emphasis on God's sovereignty in working out his will in the lives of people and the events of human history, (3) his elemental theodicy in defense of God's sovereignty in his election of certain people and their actions, and (4) his repeated references to the words of the great Israelite prophet Isaiah, who was the most prominent proclaimer of remnant theology in the OT religion of Israel. He even used statements from this great OT prophet, which included some of the most significant terms and expressions of Jewish remnant theology, to provide the conclusion to what he wanted to say in 9:6-29. Paul continues to use remnant theology and remnant rhetoric in 9:30–10:21 — particularly in (1) his emphasis on the necessary response of faith to God by those who have been elected and called, (2) his explicit statements regarding God's blessings on "all who call on him" as including Gentiles, (3) his allusions to the close relations that exist between

---

the following twofold proposal: (1) that throughout Rom 9–11 "we get the impression that we are listening to Paul preaching . . . the kind of sermon that Paul must often have had occasion to deliver in defining his attitude to what we may call the Jewish question," and (2) that "it is quite possible that he kept by him a MS of such a sermon for use as occasion demanded, and inserted it here" (149).

17. Luke refers to Paul as preaching in various Jewish synagogues in Acts 9:20-22, 29; 13:14-41, 44-47; 14:1-3; 17:1-4, 10-11, 17; and 18:4-6. He also notes that Paul taught "for a whole year," along with Barnabas, "a great number of people" in various meetings of Jewish believers in Jesus (including, evidently, former Gentile proselytes to Judaism who had become believers in Jesus) at Antioch of Syria in Acts 11:25-26 — and, further, that he discussed briefly the nature of his ministry and theology with James and "all the elders" at Jerusalem in 21:17-19.

God's Son, who is Israel's promised Messiah and humanity's Lord, and "everyone who calls on the name of the Lord," and (4) his further use of statements drawn from the prophet Isaiah to support his own Christian proclamation of remnant theology and his own form of remnant rhetoric.

There are also certain recognizable differences between Part I (9:6-29) and Part II (9:30–10:21). The most obvious are:

1. The omission of any explicit remnant history or remnant vocabulary in Part II, even though that theme and its vocabulary were to the fore in Part I in the apostle's use of the patriarchal narratives of Genesis, his treatment of God's sovereign election of both people and events, and his explicit use of the terms "remnant" and "seed" — and with such a remnant theme and vocabulary reoccurring in Part III (11:1-32).
2. The prominence of the terms "righteousness," "faith," and "belief" in Part II, even though those expressions did not appear in Part I, where the vocabulary regarding God's "election" and the theme of "God's sovereign choice" were particularly dominant — and with the language of God's election and the theme of his sovereign choice coming again to the fore in Part III.
3. The strong accusatory tone and accusations expressed in Part II, which are somewhat different from the declaratory tones and statements in Parts I and III — and, further, even more expressly accusatory than Paul's earlier statements about the Jews in 2:1–3:20 of the letter.[18]

I. Thesis Statements about Israel's Present Situation of Unbelief vis-à-vis the Situation of Believing Gentiles, with Confirming Data regarding Israel's Situation from Two Passages in Isaiah (9:30-33)

9:30-32a Paul begins his thesis statements about Israel's present situation of unbelief with the question τί οὖν ἐροῦμεν; ("What, then, shall we say?"). The apostle is not here responding to an objection by some opponent, whether imaginary or real (as has sometimes been proposed). Rather, he is highlighting the discussion that follows by the use of a rhetorical question, just as he did with this same rhetorical question six times earlier in this letter (and only in this letter of his collected NT letters). He did this in all these instances to draw attention to what he believed was (1) a very important point in the course of a particular argument or (2) a highly significant section or subsection of material in his presentation.[19]

---

18. The tone of this material in Part II is more comparable to Stephen's accusatory tone and defiant statements as reported in Acts 7:51-53, to which the Jewish leaders took great offense, and thus arranged for this early Christian leader's death by stoning.

19. Cf. Paul's earlier uses of this rhetorical question in 3:5; 4:1; 6:1; 7:7; 8:31; and 9:14.

In these statements Paul focuses on the present situation of Israel's unbelief. He does so by contrasting the unbelief of most Jews of his day with the situation of certain Gentiles who had actually "attained righteousness" on the basis of their positive responses to God — even though they (1) did not "pursue righteousness" in the way that the Jews did, (2) had no revealed knowledge of God as the Jews had, and (3) were not conscious of God as a righteous Deity who gives the gift of righteousness to those who respond to him "by faith," as the people of Israel were called on to understand and experience.

The anarthrous plural noun ἔθνη ("Gentiles") represents a qualitative use of the term as descriptive of the nature of the people referred to. It is used here in 9:30 to describe non-Jewish people whom the Jews viewed as "pagans" or "heathen." It does not, however, have in mind any particular group of non-Jewish people or any particular non-Jewish nation. Nor does Paul's use of ἔθνη without the article suggest that all "Gentiles" are people of faith.

Yet it seems evident from his reference here in 9:30 to Gentiles who have "attained righteousness, a righteousness that is by faith" — as well as from his earlier references in 9:22-24 to Gentiles being the objects of God's mercy, called by him, and recipients of "the riches of his glory" (as supported in 9:25-26 by quotations from Hos 2:23 and 1:10, which speak of Gentiles being accepted by God as "his people," "his beloved," and "his sons and daughters") — that for Paul an understanding of God's divine mercy and saving grace was broader than what we as Christians usually assume. For from the apostle's statements and quotations in these passages, it may legitimately be inferred that for him God's mercy and saving grace include (to some extent and in some manner) not only God's acceptance of (1) a "righteous remnant" within Israel, (2) Jewish believers in Jesus as God's promised Messiah, and (3) Gentile converts to Christ, who had come to God through belief in Jesus on the basis of the Christian gospel as proclaimed by Paul himself or some other Christian preacher — but also (4) some adherents of other religions and some seemingly secular or "pagan" Gentiles (who have sometimes been identified as "those of insider movements" or "churchless believers in Jesus"), to whom God has revealed himself in mercy and saving grace (in ways known only to God himself) and who have responded to him by their trust of him and their commitment to Jesus (in ways appropriate to their own cultures or circumstances), and so have been accepted by God as his own people.

We may not as Western Christians be able to conceptualize either the circumstances or the content of such a trust in God and commitment to Jesus on the part of such other "believing" religionists, seeming secularists, or so-called pagans (whether living in an Eastern or a Western culture). Further, we may never have experienced any such acts of mercy and saving grace by God through his Spirit as have sometimes been claimed (such as transforming visions, direct divine interventions, or miraculous circumstances).[20] Nonetheless, we can still

20. Paul himself, of course, claimed that divine interventions, transformative visions, and

believe, as has been eloquently expressed by Frederick William Faber in the first and third stanzas of his 1862 hymn:

> There's a wideness in God's mercy like the wideness of the sea;
> there's a kindness in his justice, which is more than liberty.
>
> . . .
>
> For the love of God is broader than the measure of man's mind;
> and the heart of the Eternal is most wonderfully kind.

Here in 9:30b-32 Paul declares that the situation of most Jews of his day was in direct contrast to the situation of certain Gentiles, as known only to God himself, who responded positively to divine mercy and grace by putting their trust in God. The apostle highlights this contrast (1) by beginning his statements about Israel in 9:31 with the adversative particle δέ ("but"), and then (2) by increasing the negativity of that first statement by inserting into the following statement of 9:32 the stronger adversative particle ἀλλά ("but rather"). Likewise in 9:30b-32 he sets out a sharp difference between believing Gentiles and unresponsive Jews by his contrasting use of the verb διώκω ("strive for," "seek after," "pursue"), on the one hand, and the verbs καταλαμβάνω ("seize," "make one's own," "attain") and φθάνω ("arrive," "reach," "obtain," "attain"), on the other hand — doing so explicitly twice in 9:30b-31 and then implicitly again in 9:32a.[21]

The thesis statements of speakers and writers are often quite elliptical; they frequently contain an economy of speech or writing expression, with that brevity of expression, together with the obscurity engendered by such brevity, being more fully explicated in what follows. And this feature of both oral and written communication is present in Paul's statements of 9:30-32 — particularly in his accusatory statement of 9:31, that is, in (1) his use of the corporate name "Israel," which, though grammatically singular, has reference to the plurality of "the people of Israel"; (2) his grammatically consistent use of the nominative *singular* present active participle διώκων ("who are pursuing") and the third-person *singular* aorist verb ἔφθασεν ("he/she/it has not attained"), which appear after the corporate name "Israel," when he actually has in mind the great majority of "the people [plural] of Israel"; (3) his notoriously difficult wording with respect to what exactly the people of Israel "are pursuing," that is, "a law of righteousness (νόμον δικαιοσύνης) in connection with (εἰς) the law (νόμον)"; and (4) his omission at the end of this verse of what exactly the people of Israel "did not attain," which he evidently expected would be understood from

---

miraculous circumstances were vitally important factors in radically changing his own religious commitments, his own understanding of life, and his own resultant ministry (cf. esp. Acts 26:1-23 and 2 Cor 12:1-10) — and while as a believer in Jesus he proclaimed the supremacy of Christ (the Messiah) Jesus, he continued to honor his own Jewish heritage (cf. esp. Phil 3:3-11).

21. This pairing of the verbs διώκω ("strive for," "seek after," "pursue") and καταλαμβάνω ("seize," "make one's own," "attain") also appears in Phil 3:12-14, where Paul speaks of his own "pursuing" and not yet "attaining" all that is involved in knowing Christ.

the context as being "righteousness" (and so the necessity of inserting a third-person singular pronoun "it" into our English translation).

Points 1, 2, and 4 (above) have to do with purely grammatical issues, and therefore can be understood on the basis of common grammatical usage and the passage's context. The rather strange phraseology νόμον δικαιοσύνης εἰς νόμον (point 3 above) is, as Ed Sanders has quite rightly observed, "an almost incomprehensible combination of words." Yet, the clause's wording is nonetheless, as Sanders points out, used by Paul as "the thrust of the passage" in his proclamation that "the only ground of salvation" is "faith in Christ, which is available to all without distinction . . . and which excludes the law as a way to 'righteousness.'"[22]

Working backward in our own understanding of this rather strangely worded clause of 9:31 (that is, dealing first with what appears to be the more easily determined interpretive feature at its end, and then moving forward to the more difficult matters that precede it), I propose that this rather cryptic phraseology should be understood as follows:

1. The accusative noun νόμον, which appears at the end of the clause, refers not to some "general law" or some "legal principle," but specifically to "the Mosaic law."
2. The preposition εἰς, which precedes the accusative noun νόμον, is used as a "consecutive and final εἰς," and so should be translated "with reference to" or "in connection with" (as understood earlier in 1:16 and later in this same subsection of material in 10:1 and 4).[23]
3. The phrase νόμον δικαιοσύνης, which appears at the beginning of the clause, is a paraphrastic expression that would connote the concept of "a 'legalistic' or 'nomistic' form of righteousness" to people who had a Jewish background (i.e., Jews and Jewish believers in Jesus) — as well as to Gentile believers in Jesus who had been extensively influenced by Jewish Christian forms of expression (as we have argued was true of all the believers in Jesus at Rome, whatever their ethnicity).

It seems best, therefore, to understand Paul in his rather elliptical phraseology of 9:31 as declaring: "The people of Israel are pursuing a 'legalistic' (or 'nomistic') form of righteousness in connection with the Mosaic law, but they have not attained it." Such a statement, it may be assumed, would have been understood by both Jews and Jewish believers in Jesus who heard Paul proclaim

22. E. P. Sanders, *Paul, the Law, and the Jewish People*, 42.

23. Cf. Stauffer, "εἰς," 2.429, where Stauffer discusses what he refers to as a "consecutive and final εἰς" — that is, where: "The preposition denotes the direction of an action to a specific end." See also our treatments of such a "consecutive and final εἰς" earlier at 1:16 ("with respect to salvation") and later in this present passage at 10:1 ("with respect to their salvation") and 10:10 ("in connection with righteousness"); cf. also the somewhat similar uses of εἰς in Rom 9:17; 14:9; 2 Cor 2:9; Eph 6:22; and Col 4:8.

the Christian message in their synagogues or meeting places. It would probably also have been understood by the apostle's Christian addressees at Rome (whatever the ethnic mix in their various "house churches" or congregations). For all the believers in Jesus at Rome, whatever their various ethnicities, seem to have been acquainted with Jewish Christian forms of thought and expression (as we have proposed). And whatever history this rather strangely worded clause may have had in Paul's earlier preaching and teaching, "the thrust of the passage is clear"[24] — with the result that this statement, however it is worded, "excludes the law as a way to 'righteousness.'"[25]

In 9:32a Paul asks the rhetorical question Διὰ τί; ("Why so?"). And he answers it with a further elliptically expressed accusatory statement: Ὅτι οὐκ ἐκ πίστεως ("because [it is] not by faith"), ἀλλ' ὡς ἐξ ἔργων ("but as if from works") — which, more expansively, may be read as follows: "Because the people of Israel are pursuing it not by faith, but, rather, as if it could be attained on the basis of works." William Sanday and Arthur Headlam have aptly observed that the particle ὡς before the phrase ἐξ ἔργων "introduces a subjective idea," and thus the clause ὡς ἐξ ἔργων in this verse should be translated "as if from works."[26] They go on to explain the reason for Paul's subjective usage here as follows:

> St. Paul wishes to guard himself from asserting definitely that ἐξ ἔργων was a method by which νόμος δικαιοσύνης might be pursued. He therefore represents it as an idea of the Jews, as a way by which they thought they could gain it.[27]

9:32b-33 In this same vein, Paul goes further in 9:32b-33 to declare that "they ['the people of Israel'] stumbled over 'the stumbling stone,'" which causes people to stumble and fall. In so doing, he uses imagery drawn from the OT in support of his declaration about Israel's stumble and fall — but also in anticipation of his proclamation that "the one who believes in him [i.e., the 'stone' or 'rock' in question] will not be put to shame."

There are a number of references in the OT to a "stone" or "rock" that will be prominent in the final days of God's eschatological salvation. Ps 118:22-23 is probably the earliest of these "stone" passages: "The *stone* that the builders rejected has become the *capstone;* the Lord has done this, and it is marvelous in our eyes." In Isa 8:14 the prophet Isaiah announces that God will become "a sanctuary" for his remnant people, but "for both of the houses of Israel he will be a *stone* that causes people to stumble and a *rock* that makes them fall — a trap and snare for the inhabitants of Jerusalem." In Isa 28:16 the prophet reports the words of the Lord God as follows: "See, I am laying in Zion a *foundation stone,*

---

24. Using E. P. Sanders's expression in *Paul, the Law, and the Jewish People,* 42.
25. *Ibid.*
26. Sanday and Headlam, *Romans,* 280, citing 2 Cor 2:17, 11:17, and Phlm 14 in support of such a subjective understanding of ὡς.
27. *Ibid.*

a *tested stone*, a *precious cornerstone*, a *sure foundation;* the one who trusts will never be dismayed." And in Dan 2, which relates the story of Daniel's interpretation of Nebuchadnezzar's dream, the interpretation given in vv. 44-45 of *"the crushing rock"* that was cut out of "a mountain, but not by human hands," has to do with a time in the future when "the God of heaven will set up a kingdom that will never be destroyed, nor will it be left to another people; it will crush all those kingdoms and bring them to an end, but it will itself endure forever."

Much of this "stone" imagery of the OT seems to have been rather enigmatic to most Jews during the time of Jesus and Paul — though it may have been understood, at least to some extent, by certain Israelites of Second Temple Judaism as having some sort of messianic import.[28] A distinctly Christological use of this OT stone imagery, however, appears prominently throughout the NT writings. Jesus is reported in all three Synoptic Gospels to have quoted the words of Ps 118:22, which speak of "the *stone* that the builders rejected" being "the *capstone*" of God's whole program of salvation history, as having reference to his own person and ministry[29] — thereby using these words of the psalmist to foretell his rejection by the people of Israel, his vindication by God, and his eschatological redemptive victory. In all probability, as J. Rendall Harris has aptly characterized the situation, it was Jesus himself who "set the stone rolling" in the consciousness of the earliest believers in Jesus.[30]

Elsewhere in the NT there appear three variations of this Christological use of OT stone imagery among the earliest believers in Jesus, with three different biblical texts used in support: (1) the *"rejected stone* that has become *the capstone,"* as based on Ps 118:22; (2) the *"precious cornerstone* for a sure foundation,"* together with the exhortation that "the one who trusts will never be dismayed," as based on Isa 28:16; and (3) the *"stone of stumbling* and *rock of offense,"* as based on Isa 8:14. The first is found in Acts 4:11 and 1 Pet 2:7, and the second in Eph 2:20 and 1 Pet 2:6 (as well as implicitly in 1 Cor 3:11). The third use, which speaks

28. Some support for a possible messianic use among certain Jews of OT stone imagery may be found in (1) Josephus's account in *War* 5:270-74 regarding the siege of Jerusalem by the Roman Tenth Legion, particularly about how when nearing the close of that siege the Roman army began catapulting large stones over the city's walls in order to break up the city's buildings and kill the people, and how the Jewish watchmen in the towers of the city's walls would alert the people by crying out ἡ πέτρα φέροιτο ("the stone [or 'rock'] is in transit") — but when things got to their worst and the stones kept being catapulted over the city's walls, the watchmen would cry out ὁ υἱὸς ἔρχεται ("the son is coming"), and (2) the similar spelling of the Hebrew words אבן ("stone") and בן ("son"), which allowed some Jews of Second Temple Judaism to associate the two words. Cf. M. Black, "The Christological Use of the Old Testament in the New Testament," *NTS* 18 (1971) 11-14; see also R. N. Longenecker, *Christology of Early Jewish Christianity,* 50-53. The Jewish covenanters at Qumran viewed themselves as "a tested bulwark" and "a precious cornerstone" (1QS 8.7, using the language of Isa 28:16) and viewed their community as God's "structure on a rock," with "its rafters truly positioned" and "its stones well laid" (1QH 6.26-27).

29. Cf. Mark 12:10-11 and its parallels in Matt 21:42 and Luke 20:17-18.

30. J. R. Harris, *Testimonies,* 2 vols. (Cambridge: Cambridge University Press, 1916, 1920), 2.96; so also K. Stendahl, *The School of St. Matthew and Its Use of the Old Testament* (Lund: Gleerup; Philadelphia: Fortress, 1958), 69, 212.

of "the *stone of stumbling* and *rock of offense*," appears here in Rom 9:33 (to which is joined the hortatory second part of Isa 28:16) and in 1 Pet 2:8.[31]

Such a widespread use of OT stone imagery in the NT — which, as we have noted, was applied by Jesus to his own person and ministry and was then used with respect to him by a number of NT writers — suggests that a christianized version of it had become fairly well known among the earliest believers in Jesus. Further, it also seems evident, judging by the way these OT passages and their variations on the "stone imagery" are brought together in 1 Pet 2:6-8, that a joining together of these three biblical passages and their respective themes was a significant feature in early Jewish Christian proclamation. So it need not be thought too unusual (1) that Paul focused at the close of his thesis statements in 9:30-33 on the accusation that the Jews have "stumbled over 'the stumbling stone,'" and (2) that he supported that accusation by a collation of statements drawn from Isa 8:14 ("a stone that causes people to stumble and a rock that makes them fall") and Isa 28:16b ("the one who trusts will never be dismayed") — even christianizing the Greek pronoun αὐτῷ to read not as a neuter personal pronoun "it" (that is, reading "the one who trusts in *it*," i.e., the "stone" or "rock") but as a masculine personal pronoun "him" (that is, reading "the one who trusts [or 'believes'] in *him* [Christ Jesus] will not be put to shame").[32]

II. Exposition on the Focus of God's Program of Salvation History Explicating the Thesis Statements of 9:30-33, Setting Out What Appears to Be a Quasi-Confessional Affirmation in 10:4, and Quoting OT Passages and Biblically Based Proverbial Material in Support (10:1-13)

Immediately obvious in any scanning of 10:1-13 is the fact that γάρ ("for") appears a total of nine times in thirteen verses. The particle γάρ is, of course, a common Greek conjunction, which was used by Paul and other NT writers in a variety of ways — principally (1) to indicate the continuation of an earlier presentation, (2) to introduce a statement regarding cause, (3) to suggest an inference, (4) to introduce an explanatory statement, and (5) to signal that what follows is a biblical quotation, a biblical allusion, or a biblically based aphorism or proverbial statement. The conjunction is employed three times in 10:1-4, to introduce the three accusatory statements of 10:2-3, which function to spell out more explicitly the apostle's quite elliptical thesis statements of 9:30-33. Then in the nine verses of 10:5-13 it appears six times more to introduce biblical quotations, biblical allusions, and what seems to be a proverbial statement

---

31. For a helpful and extensive survey of "Christ as λίθος" in the NT, see Jeremias, "λίθος," *TDNT* 4.271-79.

32. As Barrett has quite rightly noted in his *Romans*, 192 n. 1: "The Greek pronoun (αὐτῷ) could equally be translated 'him.'"

based on Scripture, all of which are set out in support of Paul's quite dramatic "Christ-Torah antithesis" of 10:4.

Such a concentration of γάρ in 10:1-13 — without that conjunction appearing in the materials that either immediately precede or immediately follow this passage — suggests that Paul intended his readers (1) to view these two paragraphs of 10:1-4 and 10:5-13 as together constituting one unified and discrete subsection of material (with the four questions that follow in 10:14-15 signaling the beginning of a further subsection of material), and (2) to understand these two paragraphs as containing explanatory materials, whose function was, first of all, to spell out more fully his elliptically expressed thesis statements of 9:30-33, but also to elucidate his rather dramatic statement of 10:4.

10:1-4 Paul begins his explanatory statements of 10:1-4 with the plural noun ἀδελφοί ("brothers and sisters"), which functions here as a vocative of direct address. Paul uses this vocative of address, with all its family imagery, not only as a respectful and honorific gesture to other believers in Jesus, but also as an epistolary convention of the day to signal the beginning of an important portion of material that he did not want his addressees to misunderstand or be offended by. Likewise, Paul includes at the beginning of these explanatory statements the postpositive particle μέν, a common particle of the Greek language that was used either to reaffirm something that had just been said (i.e., "indeed") or to interject some sort of concession with regard to something that had previously been said (i.e., also "indeed"). Paul uses μέν here in 10:1 to reaffirm his "heartfelt desire and prayer" for his own people, the people of Israel — just as he had expressed his deep concern for them earlier in 9:3 in speaking of "my brothers and sisters, those of my own race, the people of Israel." So by his use of both the vocative of direct address ἀδελφοί and the affirming particle μέν, the apostle is (1) expressing familial respect and honor to his Christian addressees at Rome, (2) introducing material that he did not want his addressees either to misunderstand or be offended by, and (3) reaffirming his heartfelt desire and prayer for his own people, the people of Israel.

Three very serious accusations, however, are made in 10:1-4, which serve to explicate more fully what Paul had earlier stated in elliptical fashion in 9:30-33 about Israel's present situation of unbelief — that is, (1) that the people of Israel "are zealous for God, but their zeal is not based on knowledge," (2) that they "are ignorant of the righteousness of God," and (3) that they "seek to establish their own righteousness," and therefore "have not submitted to God's righteousness." Paul concludes this paragraph with what appears to be his own dramatic confessional statement, which springs from the heart of the Christian message: τέλος νόμου Χριστὸς εἰς δικαιοσύνην παντὶ πιστεύοντι ("Christ is the end of the law in connection with righteousness for everyone who believes").

This dramatic and forceful affirmation must have arisen in a milieu where matters having to do with the focus of the Christian message were especially to the fore. These issues concerned (1) how the person and work of Jesus were to be understood in the context of the OT religion of Israel, (2) how commitment to Jesus as Israel's Messiah and humanity's Lord affected one's understanding of the Mosaic law, (3) what emphasis should be placed on the person and work of Jesus vis-à-vis the teachings of the Mosaic law, and (4) where the focus of Christian proclamation should be seen, whether on the person and work of Jesus or on the instructions of the Mosaic law — or, perhaps, on some amalgamation of the teachings and work of Jesus *and* the legislation of the Mosaic law. The Christian message was understood by many early Jewish believers in Jesus in a bifocal fashion, with dual emphases on the person and work of Jesus of Nazareth *and* on the instructions given for righteous living in the Mosaic law. This seems to have been true of the earliest Jewish believers in Jesus whom James and "the elders" of the Jerusalem church had in mind when they told Paul about "how many thousands of Jews have believed, and all of them are zealous for the law" (Acts 21:20) — and then went on to counsel him regarding how he should act in Jerusalem to assuage such fears on the part of Jewish believers about him (Acts 21:21-25). It was certainly true of those "certain men who came from James" who confused the believers in Jesus (even Peter) at Antioch of Syria (see Gal 2:11-21). And this matter of a proper Christian focus continued to be an issue of great concern when a Jewish-Christian teacher came into the province of Galatia and attempted to tell Paul's Gentile converts there that they had to take on certain Jewish regulations in living out their Christian convictions (Gal 1:6-10 and 3:1–5:26).

It may legitimately be argued that this matter of focus in the Christian message — that is, whether on Christ alone or on both Christ *and* the Mosaic law — had been a prominent feature of discussion among believers in Jesus in the ethnically diverse city of Syrian Antioch.[33] Further, it may be conjectured

---

33. Cf. my article "Antioch of Syria," 16-17:

Apart from Jerusalem, no city of the Roman empire played as large a part in the early life and fortunes of the Christian church as Antioch of Syria. The book of Acts tells us that it was Hellenistic Jewish Christians who, on fleeing Jerusalem, first brought the gospel to Antioch, preaching first only to Jews but soon including Gentiles as well. With the increase of believers at Antioch, the Jerusalem church sent Barnabas to check on the situation. It was through his efforts that the Christian community at Antioch was joined to the Christian community at Jerusalem, thereby preventing any possible alienation or split because of Antiochene Christianity's rather unusual beginnings. Further, it was through Barnabas' efforts that Saul of Tarsus became involved in the ministry at Antioch.

First-century Antioch was a fertile place for various philosophies, cults, and religions. It was a city that prided itself on its toleration, with even its Jewish population more open to Gentiles than anywhere else in the Jewish Diaspora or Palestine. Yet many Antiochenes were looking for a more significant religious experience and more meaning to life than paganism offered. Many Gentiles, in fact, were associated in one way or another with the Jewish synagogues of the city, being impressed with the monotheism and ethics of Judaism. So when the Christian gospel came to Antioch, it was received not only by Jews but also by Gentiles who had been mentally and spiritually prepared by Judaism.

A great number of people at Antioch, Acts tells us, accepted the gospel message and committed themselves to Jesus. Since, however, this group was made up of both Jews and Gentiles, the city's officials had to find a name for them that would distinguish them from

that it was Paul himself — who taught, along with Barnabas, "great numbers of people" during "a whole year" (Acts 11:25-26) — who played a prominent part in these discussions, and so should be credited with having a major role not only (1) in the fact that "the disciples were first called Christians at Antioch" (Acts 11:26b), but also (2) in the composition of this very important and quite dramatic statement of 10:4 that "Christ is the end of the law in connection with righteousness for everyone who believes."

Here in 10:1-4, therefore, Paul expresses three matters of great significance about his own ministry (as well as Christian ministry generally): (1) pathos for one's own people (i.e., the people of Israel) "with respect to their salvation" (v. 1); (2) a perceptive analysis of the wayward religious situation of others (vv. 2-3), and (3) what seems to be a quasi-confessional statement that encapsulates the crux of the matter with respect to the focus of the Christian message vis-à-vis that of Judaism — as well as, of course, between the message of the Christian gospel and the messages of all other religions, which set out a path to be followed rather than proclaim a person to whom one is committed, that is, the crucified, risen, exalted, and "coming again" Messiah and Lord, Jesus Christ (v. 4).

In their paraphrase of 10:1-4, William Sanday and Arthur Headlam have captured the basic thrust (though, perhaps, not all the specific details or nuances) of these four verses, rephrasing the apostle's words in rather vernacular fashion (though also somewhat archaically) as follows:

> [1]Let me pause for a moment, brethren. It is a serious accusation that I am bringing against my fellow-countrymen. I repeat that I do it from no feeling of resentment. How great is my heart's good will for them! How earnest my prayer to God for their salvation! [2]For indeed as a fellow-countryman, as one who was once as they are, I can testify that they are full of zeal for God. That is not the point in which they have failed; it is that they have not guided their zeal by that true knowledge which is the result of genuine spiritual insight. [3]Righteousness they strove after, but there are two ways of attaining it. The one was God's method: of that they remained ignorant. The other was their own method: to this they clung blindly and willfully. They refused to submit to God's plan of salvation.
>
> [4]Their own method was based on a rigid performance of legal enactments. But that has been ended in Christ. Now there is a new and a better way, one which has two characteristics: it is based on the principle of faith, and it is universal and for all men alike.[34]

Jews and all the devotees of the various pagan religions of the city. So they nicknamed them Christians, which means "Christ Followers" or "People of Christ." And it is this name, rather than the earlier self-designation "Those of the Way," that stuck, simply because it was seen by the Christians themselves to be highly appropriate.

34. Sanday and Headlam, *Romans*, 276-77.

What Sanday and Headlam have done in first giving a paraphrase of what Paul wrote in this subsection of 10:1-4 (as they also did in their commentary for the rest of the apostle's letter to Rome) was to follow the example set by Erasmus in the early sixteenth century in his treatment of the NT writings — who, in turn, followed the practice of certain earlier secular interpreters of the Greek and Roman classical writers.[35] This practice of seeking to understand the biblical materials by first preparing (whether consciously or unconsciously; whether formally or informally) a paraphrase of what a particular biblical author has written is commonly done (whether explicitly or simply assumed) by many interpreters and commentators today prior to getting on with the more strenuous tasks of textual criticism, exegetical comments, and biblical theology.

The crucial exegetical and theological issues in 10:4 have to do with what Paul meant in saying τέλος νόμου Χριστός ("Christ is the end of the law"). The placement of the predicate nominative expression τέλος νόμου ("the end of the law") at the beginning of the statement suggests that one must deal very seriously with what "the end of the law" means and implies. The true subject of the sentence, Χριστός ("Christ"), which appears at the end of its first clause,

---

35. Desiderius Erasmus (c. 1466-1536), the Dutch religious humanist, was trained as a Roman Catholic theologian but worked principally as a Latin and Greek linguist. He was a very important linguist and biblical commentator in the Europe of his day, serving also as professor of divinity at Cambridge University from 1509 to 1514. He is best known today for having established, based on only four or five late manuscripts, a critical Greek text of the New Testament (or *Novum Instrumentum*), which was comparable in many ways to what in the seventeenth century came to be called the "received text" (Textus Receptus), with accompanying textual notes and Latin translation. In his day, however, Erasmus was more applauded — though often also criticized — as a paraphraser of the NT, appropriating a method of interpretation used by the Greek rhetorician Quintilian (late first century) and the Latin rhetorician Themistius (fourth century) on the writings of the classical authors and applying that method to the writings of the NT. For, as Erasmus argued, to paraphrase a text was to improve its clarity, and so to facilitate its translation from one language to another.

Sometime around 1499 Erasmus began a paraphrase of Romans. But he gave it up when he realized that his Greek was insufficient for the task. Then, after years of intensive study of the Greek language and the Greek NT, which culminated in the publication of the first edition of his Greek New Testament in 1516, he returned in 1514 to paraphrasing Paul's letter to Rome. And in 1517 he published his *Paraphrase on Romans* — which he dedicated to Cardinal Marion Grimani, a fellow religious humanist who himself published in 1542 a commentary on Romans. Following his paraphrase of Romans, Erasmus published during 1519-1524 paraphrases of all the rest of Paul's letters, the General Epistles (except for the Johannine letters), Hebrews, each of the four Gospels, and finally the Acts of the Apostles. All these paraphrases were undertaken by Erasmus in support of his work as a biblical translator. They were, however, also done in preparation for what he hoped would be his own full-scale commentaries on these NT materials — though, sadly, he never got around to writing such commentaries.

Erasmus's paraphrases were widely read and quite influential, being immediately popular on the Continent and later in Britain. Because of his passionate desire to reform the church through his biblical scholarship — especially his text critical work and his NT paraphrases — it may legitimately be said that "Erasmus laid the egg that Luther hatched" (as has become a rather common cliché). He has also, however, inspired and set a paradigm for a number of biblical commentators who have followed him (including Sanday and Headlam on Romans).

also requires that interpreters take seriously into account the work of Christ in God's unfolding program of salvation history.

The noun τέλος had a rather wide range of meaning in both classical and koine Greek, signifying not only "termination," "end," or "cessation" but also such theologically significant matters as "purpose," "goal," and "fulfillment," and more mundane ideas such as "performance," "event," "validity," "task," or "duty." In the history of the interpretation of this verse, the nuances of "goal," "purpose," "fulfillment," "termination," and/or "end" have been often intertwined and quite diversely spelled out. The literature on how this short statement should be understood is voluminous.[36]

A decision about how to understand what Paul meant by τέλος in 10:4 has always been extensively influenced by each interpreter's own understanding of the course of God's salvation history — that is, whether (1) in a Marcionite fashion (which was declared by the better theologians of the early church to be heretical, yet still exists in various forms today), (2) on the basis of an Alexandrian perspective (which may be credited to the hermeneutical principles and writings of Origen and Clement of Alexandria in opposition to Marcion's claims, has remained dominant during most of the first eighteen centuries of Christian history, and continues in many quarters today), or (3) in terms of an Antiochean understanding (which may be credited particularly to the preaching and writings of John Chrysostom in the late fourth century and Martin Luther in the first half of the sixteenth century, has been to the fore in the "biblical theology movement" of the past century, and is the position that I believe is the best and most defensible one).[37]

The issues involved in the interpretation of Rom 10:4 are complicated and have been discussed at great length. However, in at least three other highly important passages in Galatians and Romans — which have every appearance of being parallel passages to 10:4 — there resonates the nuance of believers in Jesus having experienced (1) the closing of a former relationship, which had been ordained by God for the lives of his people, and (2) the beginning of a new relationship, which was established by God himself by the redemptive work of Jesus Christ and the ministry of the Holy Spirit and was set forth as a distinctly new feature in the Christian proclamation. These three important passages in Galatians and Romans are:

1. Gal 3:23-25 — where, while readily acknowledging that a custodial function for the Mosaic law had been ordained by God for the supervision of his people under the old covenant, Paul also insists that in the new cov-

36. For brief and perceptive treatments of the issues involved (together with important bibliographies on the subject), see Käsemann, *Romans*, 282-83, and Moo, *Romans*, 636-43. For more extended treatments, see, e.g., Bultmann, "Christ the End of the Law," 36-66; Stuhlmacher, "Das Ende des Gesetzes," 14-39; and Mussner, "Christus, des Gesetzes Ende zur Gerechtigkeit für Jeden der Glaubt (Röm 10.4)," 31-44.

37. Cf. R. N. Longenecker, "Three Ways of Understanding," 22-32.

enant, established by God by means of the person and work of Jesus Christ and the ministry of his Spirit, the people of God are no longer under such a "supervisory guardian" — that is, they are no longer under the Mosaic law as the necessary means for the living out of their new life in Christ Jesus.

2. Rom 3:21-4:25 — where, in developing the essence of the Christian gospel to believers in Jesus at Rome, the apostle begins in 3:21 with the statement "but now, apart from the law (νυνὶ δὲ χωρὶς νόμου), the righteousness of God has been revealed, being attested by the law and the prophets."[38]

3. Rom 7:1-6 — where Paul interjects the illustration of the death of a husband resulting in freedom for his wife from her husband's control (in 7:1-3) — and then applies that illustration to the status of believers in Jesus as having died to the Mosaic law (in 7:4-6).

Thus, while concepts having to do with "purpose," "goal," and "fulfillment" may quite legitimately be seen as being implied in Paul's use of τέλος here in 10:4, the feature the apostle highlights is "termination," "end," or "cessation" of the Mosaic law in any positive or custodial fashion in this new age of salvation history, which is characterized by the Lordship of Christ and the ministry of God's Holy Spirit. To illustrate the apostle's meaning in this dramatic affirmation of 10:4, Douglas Moo has aptly set out the following analogy or comparable scenario:

> The analogy of a race course (which many scholars think *telos* is meant to convey) is helpful: the finish line is both the "termination" of the race (the race is over when it is reached) and the "goal" of the race (the race is run for the sake of reaching the finish line). Likewise, we suggest, Paul is implying that Christ is the "end" of the law (he brings its era to a close) and its "goal" (he is what the law anticipated and pointed toward). The English word "end" perfectly captures this nuance; but, if it is thought that it implies too temporal a meaning, we might also use the words "culmination," "consummation," or "climax."[39]

Two qualifying phrases follow this highly significant affirmation that "Christ is the end of the law." Both must be taken into account for any proper understanding of it. The first is the phrase εἰς δικαιοσύνην, which, with the telic use of the preposition εἰς ("in connection with" or "with respect to"), specifies exactly what has come to an end by the person and work of Jesus Christ, that is, the Mosaic law "in connection with righteousness."[40] The second is the phrase

38. On the expressions "but now" (νυνὶ δέ) and "apart from the law" (χωρὶς νόμου), see our earlier "Exegetical Comments" on 3:21; see also our comments on the phrase "through the faith/faithfulness of Jesus Christ" (διὰ πίστεως Ἰησοῦ Χριστοῦ) in 3:22.

39. Moo, *Romans*, 641.

40. Cf. again Stauffer, "εἰς," 2.429, where Stauffer discusses what he calls a "consecutive and

παντὶ τῷ πιστεύοντι ("for everyone who believes"), which also, following a telic use of the preposition εἰς, identifies those for whom the Mosaic law has come to an end in their Christian experience.

In the religion of Israel as set out in the OT (we repeat here some comments we expressed earlier with regard to Paul's phrase νυνὶ δὲ χωρὶς νόμου in 3:21), relationship with God was based on God's love, mercy, grace, and forgiveness — not on any type of legalistic observance by people of a set of divine laws or instructions. Yet the OT prophets always insisted that the covenantal relationship established by God with his people was to be expressed by them in ways that were prescribed by the ordinances given by God to his servant Moses, that is, by a life governed by "covenantal nomism" as expressed in the Mosaic law.

Paul, however, understood that because of God's provision for humanity in the person and work of Jesus Christ, coupled with the more intensive ministry of the Holy Spirit, a new age in the course of salvation history has dawned — that is, the promised eschatological "now" has been inaugurated by God and is presently being experienced in its beginning stages by his people. Thus the apostle proclaimed that (1) a nomistic faith (that is, "covenantal nomism"), which had served its God-given purpose effectively in the days of the old covenant, has come to an end,[41] and (2) a "new covenant piety" is now by God's ordination in effect. This new form of covenantal piety, as Paul's proclamation of the Christian gospel asserted, is opposed to every form of "legalism" (as the true faith of the OT had always been) — but it has also brought an end to the requirement of expressing one's response to God's love, mercy, and grace in terms of the ordinances and practices of OT "covenantal nomism."

Because of Christ's encounter of the Jewish Pharisee Saul on his journey to Damascus, the Christian apostle Paul came to understand that Jesus of Nazareth, who had been exalted by God, was both Israel's Messiah and humanity's Lord. He also learned in that Damascus Road experience — coupled with the continued ministry of God's Spirit throughout the rest of his life as a believer in Jesus and an apostle ordained by God to a particular Christian ministry — a great deal more about the unfolding nature of God's salvation for all humanity (including, as he insists in Rom 8:19-23, the redemption of "the whole creation"). Further, Paul the Christian apostle came to appreciate — both because of his original commitment to Jesus and as a result of his continued growth by means of the Spirit's ministry — something of great importance with respect to the developing nature of God's redemptive program: that God has been moving forward throughout all of his redemptive activity, bringing that activity to a focus in the person, ministry, and salvific work of Jesus of Nazareth and explicating the implications of what Jesus taught and did through the ministry of the Holy Spirit. So God's people, he believed, needed also to move forward (1) in their

final εἰς" — that is, where "the preposition denotes the direction of an action to a specific end." See also other uses of this "consecutive and final εἰς" in Romans at 1:16, 9:31, 10:1, and 10:10.

41. Cf. R. N. Longenecker, "The End of Nomism," in *Paul, Apostle of Liberty*, ch. 6, pp. 128-55.

understanding of God's redemptive working, (2) in the focus of their faith, and (3) in the manner that they responded to God's love, mercy, and grace in these final days of salvation history.

It was on the basis of such an understanding of the developing nature of God's program of salvation history that Paul rebuked his Gentile converts in Galatia for even thinking about accepting certain "minimal requirements" of the Mosaic law in order to express their Christian faith "better" — and, in particular, doing so by accepting certain Jewish dietary restrictions and certain Jewish cultic practices as not only "God-ordained" for the people of Israel but also as required for the "proper" lifestyle of all believers in Jesus, whatever their ethnicity. Thus it was from this quite distinctive perspective that Paul here in 10:4 declares that "Christ is the end of the law in connection with righteousness for everyone who believes." And with such a distinctive feature of the Christian message highlighted in the apostle's preaching and teaching in Syrian Antioch (which was at that time the third-largest city of the Roman Empire, with an ethnically diverse population that included a large number of Jews), it should not be considered surprising that the people of that multicultural city came to recognize that believers in Jesus were not simply "messianic Jews" — but rather, and much more importantly, that they should be called Χριστιανοί, that is, "Christ followers" or "those of the household of Christ" (cf. Acts 11:26).

10:5-8 "The form of this pericope," as Robert Jewett rightly notes, "is a fusion between a classical 'speech-in-character' and a Hebrew *pesher*."[42] The two "voices" that are contrasted in the "speech-in-character" rhetorical form of 10:5-8 are (1) *what Moses writes* with respect to righteousness in Lev 18:5, and (2) *what the Christian faith declares,* understanding the words of Deut 30:11-14 in what appears to be a proverbial manner. The *pesher* features of the passage come to expression in Paul's use of Deut 30:11-14 and his three uses of the expression τοῦτ' ἔστιν ("that is") in 10:6, 7, and 8.

Usually Paul closely adheres to the original sense of a passage that he quotes from the OT. So in 10:5, at the very beginning of this paragraph, he quotes the words of God given to Moses in Lev 18:5 with respect to τὴν δικαιοσύνην τὴν ἐκ τοῦ νόμου ("the righteousness that comes from [or 'is based on'] the law") — quoting quite strictly the statement ὁ ποιήσας αὐτὰ ἄνθρωπος ζήσεται ἐν αὐτοῖς ("the person who does these things will live by them"). In 10:6-8, however, the apostle appears to quote Deut 30:11-14 without any regard to the passage's original context — arguing that the message of the Christian gospel, that is, "the word of faith that we are proclaiming," is not to be sought in some esoteric manner either in the heavens above or in the depths beneath; rather, that "word [of faith] is near you, in your mouth and in your heart."[43] In Paul's

---

42. Jewett, *Romans,* 622; citing with regard to a "speech-in-character" rhetorical form particularly Bultmann, *Der Stil der paulinischen Predigt,* 87-88, and Stowers, *A Rereading of Romans,* 309, and citing with regard to midrashic *pesher* practices particularly Wilckens, *Romans,* 2.225; Hays, *Echoes of Scripture,* 79; and Fitzmyer, *Romans,* 588.

43. Cf. also (1) Gal 3:16, where the promise of God to Abraham regarding his "seed" (זרע,

use of the statements of God in this OT passage, therefore, the subject matter is dramatically altered from (1) God's "word of instruction" (i.e., Torah) as being very close to his people to (2) "the word of faith that we are proclaiming" (i.e., the Christian gospel) as being very close to all people.

In their commentary on Romans, William Sanday and Arthur Headlam have treated Rom 10:6-8 as a proverbial allusion that uses much of the same wording as found in Deut 30:12-14, but changes both the subject and the message of that OT text. Their argument for the proverbial nature of what Paul writes here is as follows:[44]

1. "The context of the passage shows that there is no stress laid on the fact that the O.T. is being quoted. The object of the argument is to describe the characteristics of δικαιοσύνη ἐκ πίστεως, not to show how it can be proved from the O.T."
2. "The Apostle carefully and pointedly avoids appealing to Scripture, altering his mode of citation from that employed in the previous verse."
3. "The quotation is singularly inexact. An ordinary reader fairly well acquainted with the O.T. would feel that the language has a familiar ring, but could not count it as a quotation."
4. "The words of this O.T. passage had certainly become proverbial, and many instances of them so used have been quoted."[45]
5. "St. Paul certainly elsewhere uses words of Scripture in order to express his meaning in familiar language."[46]

Thus Sanday and Headlam conclude: "For these reasons it seems probable that here the Apostle does not intend to base any argument on the quotation from the O.T., but only selects the language as being familiar, suitable, and proverbial, in order to express what he wishes to say."[47]

It is, of course, extremely difficult to determine the precise intent of any author at the time of his writing. Sanday and Headlam, however, are probably generally correct in viewing Paul's presentation here as more a proverbial use of Scripture than an explicit quotation. The apostle's introductory formula, as noted above, evidences a greater degree of variation than one would expect for a Pauline quotation — focusing on "the righteousness that is by faith" as doing

---

σπέρμα) is not interpreted corporately to refer to the people of Israel, but viewed as referring to Christ; and (2) Eph 4:8, where Ps 68:18 is read "he gave (ἔδωκεν) gifts to people" rather than "he received (לקחת, ἔλαβες) gifts from people." For a discussion of the issues involved in these Pauline passages, together with possible resolutions, see R. N. Longenecker, *Biblical Exegesis,* 2nd ed., 106-8.

44. For the following five points, see Sanday and Headlam, *Romans,* 289.

45. Citing such passages as Philo, *Quod omnis probus liber sit* 10; *4 Ezra* 4:8; *2 Bar* 3:29-30; and *Jub* 24:32; also see Amos 9:2.

46. Citing Rom 10:18 and 11:1.

47. Sanday and Headlam, *Romans,* 289; cf. also Thackeray, *Relation of St. Paul to Contemporary Jewish Thought,* 187-88.

the speaking rather than the OT Scriptures, the law, Moses, or God. Further, the passage in Paul's day, as Sanday and Headlam have noted, was already somewhat proverbial, coming to expression in a number of Jewish contexts.[48] Further, the fact that in 1 Cor 15:32 Paul quotes Isa 22:13 in quite a proverbial fashion, joining it to a Gentile proverb in 1 Cor 15:33, lends some support to the suggestion that he probably did likewise with regard to Deut 30:12-14 here in Rom 10:6-8.

The wording of what appears here in 10:6-8, while evidently used proverbially in Paul's day, conforms in many respects to that of Deut 30:12-14, and therefore the passage has often been viewed as a biblical citation. Yet Paul uses this wording drawn from Scripture quite freely (1) in assigning a decidedly Christian meaning to the OT passage, (2) in entering into a running commentary in the form of a short midrash, with the *pesher* phrase τοῦτ' ἔστιν ("that is") in 10:6, 7, and 8 used to introduce three explications in the passage,[49] and (3) in selecting the form of a saying that best suits his purpose.[50] Thus, rather than being engaged in biblical exegesis, the apostle seems here more to be turning a proverbial maxim to his own use and situating it into what he believed was a more appropriate setting.

10:9-13 In the final five verses of 10:5-13, Paul (1) applies in a Christian manner the difference between *what Moses writes* (as given in 10:5, quoting Lev 18:5) and *what the Christian faith proclaims* (as declared in 10:6-8, using the words of a christianized proverb based on Deut 30:12-14); (2) highlights the focus of the Christian message as being not on the Mosaic law but on the person and work of Jesus; (3) reiterates the recognition of all believers in Jesus that "there is no difference between Jews and Gentiles," thereby denying the spiritual importance of any form of ethnicity (quoting Isa 28:16 in support); and (4) proclaims that "everyone who calls on the name of the Lord will be saved," affirming the significance of the universality of God's gift of salvation (quoting Joel 2:32 in support). The subject of τὸ ῥῆμα ("the word") proclaimed by Paul and his colleagues has to do with the person and work of Jesus Christ, and the truth of his resurrection. The confession of faith, which is made by people who possess δικαιοσύνη ("righteousness") as a gift of God, is κύριος Ἰησοῦς ("Jesus is Lord"). Paul says this radical reorientation of a person's life is both experienced inwardly ("believe in your heart") and expressed outwardly ("confess with your mouth").

---

48. Cf. *Deut. Rab.* 8:6, which may, however, be a rabbinic rebuttal to Paul. See also Thackeray, who cited *Targ Jer I* on Deut 30:12-14: "For the word is nigh you *in your schools*" (italics his).

49. Cf. the same use of the phrase in Heb 2:14; 7:5; and 10:20; see also *b. Ber.* 6a and *Sifra Num.* 139 in later rabbinic literature.

50. Neither the MT nor the LXX of Deut 30:12 reads "Who will descend into the abyss?" Rather, both Hebrew and Greek texts read: "Who will go over the sea for us?" It seems most likely that Paul picked up the text that he uses here from the early church, for ἄβυσσος could mean (1) the depths of the sea, (2) the grave, or (3) the underworld — which would allow the use of a *katabasis-anabasis* ("lower-rising") theme, as was employed in a number of ways by the earliest believers in Jesus (see my *Christology of Early Jewish Christianity*, 60).

III. Two Sets of Rhetorical Questions and Direct Responses regarding the Situation of Unbelieving Jews, with Further OT Passages Cited in Support (10:14-19)

Paul goes on in the six verses of 10:14-19 to set out two sets of rhetorical questions and direct responses regarding the situation of unbelieving Jews, supporting his statements with a number of OT passages. His immediate point of contact is the statement of the prophet Joel in Joel 2:28, which he had just quoted in 10:13: πᾶς ὅς ἄν ἐπικαλέσηται τὸ ὄνομα κυρίου σωθήσεται ("Everyone who calls on the name of the Lord will be saved").

10:14-17 To introduce this further exposition, the apostle first asks a set of four rhetorical questions in 10:14-15a that all begin with the interrogative particle πῶς ("how," "in what way"). These questions function to set out four logical steps (though in reverse chronological order, evidently in order to lay particular emphasis on the last one). These steps are necessary to bring about God's salvation in people's lives: (1) *believing* in "the one they have not believed in," that is, believing in the Lord Jesus Christ; (2) *hearing* the message of the good news, that is, hearing the message of the Christian gospel; (3) the *preaching* of someone who proclaims that Christian gospel, that is, the preaching of Paul and other Christian proclaimers; and (4) the *sending* of preachers who proclaim the Christian gospel, that is, God's sending of those preachers. The quotation in 10:15b of Isa 52:7, "How beautiful [on the mountains] are the feet of those who bring good news," not only adds a prophetic acclamation of acceptance to the four steps, it also (1) highlights the necessary role of preaching in bringing about God's gift of salvation for people and (2) suggests that this fourth prerequisite for the bringing about of divine salvation on behalf of Paul's Jewish kinsfolk has already been met by God in his sending preachers to the people of Israel, who proclaimed to them the good news of the Christian gospel.

The saddest point that Paul makes in all his statements about Israel's present situation is set out quite tersely in 10:16: Ἀλλ' οὐ πάντες ὑπήκουσαν τῷ εὐαγγελίῳ ("But not all [of the people of Israel] have accepted the good news [i.e., the Christian gospel]." This lack of response by the Jewish people, as the apostle declares in 10:16, has been anticipated by the prophet Isaiah in his Servant Song of Isa 52:13–53:12; Paul quotes explicitly the words of Isa 53:1a: "Who has believed our message?" — which biblical statement the apostle interprets in a Christian fashion not only by speaking of the necessity of "faith" in the "message" proclaimed by the preachers sent by God, but, more particularly, by identifying that "message" as "the word of Christ."

10:18-19 In bringing to a conclusion his application of these four rhetorical questions of 10:14-15a, Paul asks a further set of two rhetorical questions in 10:18-19. The first question is this: μὴ οὐκ ἤκουσαν; ("Did they ['the people of Israel'] not hear?"). The form of this question, as well as that of the second question, has frequently been somewhat confusing for interpreters, since both questions include the two negative particles οὐ and μή, either together or in close proximity to one another — and in over seventy instances where οὐ and μή appear in the NT, the negative feature of a statement is strengthened (not, as in English, where a double negative actually destroys the negativity of what is being said, suggesting, rather, something positive).

In these two questions of 10:18-19, however, the particles μή and οὐκ are set out in reverse order from how they usually appear when they are brought together. This reverse order is found in the LXX and the NT only in questions, with μή appearing first and employed as an interrogative particle and with οὐ following, used as the negative of the verb.[51] Further, while the double negative οὐ μή anticipates a negative response of "No," the combination of μή as an interrogative particle and οὐ as a negative particle anticipates the positive response of "Yes."[52] Probably the most significant OT and NT parallels to this order of μή followed by οὐ as anticipating a positive response of "Yes" (as appears here in Paul's introductions to these two questions of 10:18-19) are the following passages drawn from the LXX and from one of Paul's other letters:

> Jer 23:24: μὴ οὐχὶ τὸν οὐρανὸν καὶ τὴν γῆν ἐγὼ πληρῶ; λέγει Κύριος ("'Do I not fill heaven and earth?' says the Lord").
>
> 1 Cor 9:4-5 (twice): μὴ οὐκ ἔχομεν ἐξουσίαν φαγεῖν καὶ πεῖν; μὴ οὐκ ἔχομεν ἐξουσίαν ἀδελφὴν γυναῖκα περιάγειν ὡς καὶ οἱ λοιποὶ ἀπόστολοι καὶ οἱ ἀδελφοὶ τοῦ κυρίου καὶ Κηφᾶς; ("Do we not have the right to our food and drink? Do we not have the right to be accompanied by a believing wife, as do the other apostles and the brothers of the Lord and Cephas?").
>
> 1 Cor 11:22: μὴ οἰκίας οὐκ ἔχετε εἰς τὸ ἐσθίειν καὶ πίνειν; ("Do you not have homes to eat and drink in?").

Further, Paul supports such an expected positive response by quoting in 10:18b the words of Ps 19:4, thereby Christianizing in a typically *pesher* fashion the words of a passage in the Jewish (OT) Scriptures that in their context of Ps 19:1-6 extolled God's revelation of himself through his created world.

In the second rhetorical question in this passage, expressed in 10:19, the apostle asks: μὴ Ἰσραὴλ οὐκ ἔγνω; ("Did Israel not understand?"). Just as in his first question of 10:18, the apostle here again uses μή as an interrogative particle and οὐκ as a negative particle, and so again anticipates the positive response "Yes." Then, in support of such an expected positive response, he quotes the words of Deut 32:21b that reside at the very heart of the "Song of Moses," which the great Jewish lawgiver recited "in the hearing of the whole assembly of Israel" — which words express God's reaction to his people turning away from their

51. Cf. *ATRob*, 1173-74.

52. Contra *BAG*, 519, col. 1, who, despite their recognition of μή as an interrogative particle and οὐ as a negative particle in the questions of Rom 10:18-19 and 1 Cor 9:4-5, go on to state that "the double negative causes one to expect an affirmative answer."

knowledge of him to the worship of idols. Paul introduces this quotation of Deut 32:21b by the statement πρῶτος Μωυσῆς λέγει (literally "First Moses says").

The use of πρῶτος ("first") in this introductory statement has always been somewhat difficult for interpreters to understand, for there appears no explicit reference to a "second" OT statement that follows. Usually, therefore, translators and commentators have assumed that while the apostle intended to present a numerical listing of two or more OT passages, he simply set out the following two quotations from Isa 65:1-2 without a further numerical listing — or, more commonly, that he used the transitional particle δέ ("and," "but," "now") to signal such a numerical identification at the beginning of the first (or both) of the following two portions that he quotes from Isa 65:1-2.[53]

Archibald Robertson, however, has rightly pointed out that πρῶτος is not only used in the NT as an adverb, it also appears as an adjective — and therefore, understood adjectivally, Paul's statement πρῶτος Μωυσῆς λέγει here in 10:19 should be read as follows: "Moses is the first one who says."[54] Or, as Charles Cranfield has expressed Paul's meaning in his use of πρῶτος (though basing his argument on the issue of punctuation): "The point of πρῶτος then is that Moses is the first witness to the fact that Israel has indeed known."[55] Thus, in effect, what Paul is doing here by his introductory phrase πρῶτος Μωυσῆς λέγει is declaring (1) that it was the great Jewish lawgiver Moses, and not anyone else, who first acknowledged that the people of Israel did understand the essence and overall purpose of God's redemptive program as leading up to the coming of their Messiah, Jesus of Nazareth, and (2) that it was Moses himself, to whom the Jewish people looked for guidance, who predicted that God would use those who are "not a people" and "a nation without understanding" as a factor in bringing about Israel's acceptance of Jesus of Nazareth as God's promised Messiah.

There is no doubt that the phrases ἐπ᾽ οὐκ ἔθνει ("by not a people") and ἐπ᾽ ἔθνει ἀσυνέτῳ ("by a nation without understanding") refer to non-Jewish people, that is, to Gentiles, both in Deut 32:21b and in Paul's use of that OT passage. The disputed matter in this verse deals with the nuancing of the two future verbs παραζηλώσω and παροργιῶ in the two statements of the passage. For (1) the verb παραζηλώσω could be translated "I will make jealous [or 'provoke to jealousy']" or "I will make envious [or 'provoke to envy']" — perhaps also "I will make zealous [or 'provoke to zeal in the attainment of a desired goal'])";

<hr/>

53. So, e.g., RSV and NRSV: "*First* Moses says. . . . *Then* Isaiah is so bold as to say"; or as NIV has it: "*First* Moses says. . . . *And* Isaiah boldly says. . . . *But* concerning Israel he says."

54. So *ATRob*, 657, citing adjectival parallels in Matt 5:24; John 1:41; and 1 Tim 1:16. Cf. Jewett, *Romans*, whose translation of 10:19 (p. 634) reads "First Moses says," but in his comments on this verse (p. 644) he writes: "The word πρῶτος, used here . . . without a subsequent 'second,' probably has the sense of 'Moses was the first to say.'"

55. Cranfield, *Romans*, 2.539; though he goes on to assert on the same page that "Isaiah is introduced as a second witness to the fact that Israel has known," thus continuing to understand Paul's use of πρῶτος in 10:19 adverbially.

and (2) the verb παροργιῶ could be translated simply "I will make angry [or 'provoke to anger']." Most recent commentators have understood παραζηλώσω here as expressing the idea of "jealousy,"[56] though other interpreters view the verb as expressing more the nuance of either "envy" or "zeal." Most contemporary commentators have translated παροργιῶ by the word "anger." Richard Bell, however, seems to have best captured the nuances of these two verbs in his translation of παραζηλώσω as "I will provoke to jealousy" and his translation of παροργιῶ as "I will provoke to jealous anger."[57]

IV. Concluding Statements from Isaiah Which Paul Understands as God Speaking about Revealing Himself to Certain Gentiles Who Did Not "Seek" or "Ask for" Him, but Finding No Response from "Disobedient and Obstinate" Jews (10:20-21)

Paul's quotation of Isa 65:1-2, which appears in two parts here in 10:20-21, gives every appearance of functioning very much like his quotation of statements drawn from Isa 10:22-23 and Isa 1:9 earlier in Rom 9:27-29. Such a parallel strongly suggests that the apostle, in 9:27-29 and 10:20-21, brings to a close the points he has been making in each of the respective subsections of material, first in 9:6-29 and then in 9:30-10:21 — that is, bringing to a close both Part I (9:6-29) and Part II (9:30-10:21) of his three-part exposition by quoting words drawn from the great Israelite prophet Isaiah.

10:20-21 The words that Paul quotes here are drawn from Isa 65:1-2. In its OT context, Isa 65:1-2 encompasses God's answer to his people's extended prayer set out in Isa 63:7-64:12. This prayer reminds God of his past blessings given to his people and of his past actions on their behalf, and requests God's present intervention in their current troubles. The immediate point of contact in God's answer, which begins with these quoted words of Isa 65:1-2, is the challenging statement at the close of the people's prayer to God in Isa 64:12: "After all this, O Lord, will you hold yourself back? Will you keep silent and punish us beyond measure?"

Textually, the words of Isa 65:1a that Paul quotes in 10:20 agree substantially with the LXX reading — though with the two statements "I revealed myself to those who did not ask for me; I was found by those who did not seek me" of Isa 65:1a being transposed by the apostle in 10:20 to "I was found among those

---

56. So, e.g., Zahn, *An die Römer,* 493; Godet, *Romans,* 2.388-89; B. Weiss, *An die Römer,* 460; Sanday and Headlam, *Romans,* 300; Schlier, *Römerbrief,* 315; Käsemann, *Romans,* 297; Kuss, *Römerbrief,* 3.779; Cranfield, *Romans,* 2.539; Wilckens, *An die Römer,* 2.231; Dunn, *Romans,* 2.625; Stuhlmacher, *Romans,* 160; Fitzmyer, *Romans,* 599-600; and Moo, *Romans,* 668.

57. Bell, *Provoked to Jealousy,* esp. 39. Terence L. Donaldson has provided an excellent treatment of this whole subject of "Paul's Christ-Torah antithesis," the apostle's characterization of Israel's situation, and God's provoking the people of Israel to jealousy by the positive responses of Gentiles in his 1989 article "Zealot and Convert"; see esp. 668-82.

who are not seeking me; I made myself known to those who did not ask for me." Likewise, the words of Isa 65:2a that the apostle quotes in 10:21 agree quite closely with the LXX reading, except that the phrase "I held out my hands" does not precede the phrase "all day long," as in Isa 65:2a, but follows it, as in "All day long I held out my hands."

Just why and how these transpositions came about is impossible to say. Perhaps differing cultures required somewhat different progressions of thought. Or it may be surmised that Paul is here quoting a proverbial rendition of Isaiah's statements in Isa 65:1-2 — much as he did for the words of Deut 30:12-14 earlier in 10:6-8, with that proverbial rendition having been done earlier by certain Jewish believers in Jesus with whom he was in contact. Such transitions of phrases, however, may be viewed as rather inconsequential.

The major interpretive problem with respect to Paul's quotation of Isa 65:1-2 here in 10:20-21 is that in its OT context God's words are directed to his own people of Israel:

> I revealed myself to those who did not ask for me; I was found by those who did not seek me. (To a nation that did not call on my name, I said, "Here am I, here am I") [Isa 65:1]. All day long I have held out my hands to an obstinate people, who walk in ways not good, pursuing their own imaginations [Isa 65:2].

Paul, however, reads this OT passage as speaking first regarding Gentiles to whom God has revealed himself and who have responded positively to him (in Isa 65:1) and then rebuking the people of Israel for being "disobedient and obstinate people" (in Isa 65:2).

The historical question of when Isa 65:1-2 was first divided into two parts — the first verse speaking about Gentiles who have responded positively to God; the second verse speaking about the people of Israel who have been "disobedient and obstinate" — will probably never be answered. It may have been done by Paul himself here in Rom 10:20-21 — or, perhaps more likely, by some earlier Christian apostle or teacher in the Jerusalem church or in the congregations of Syrian Antioch, and then carried on by Paul in his evangelistic outreach in Syrian Antioch and afterward in his Gentile mission in the eastern Roman Empire (possibly paralleling the proverbial rendering of Deut 30:12-14 that the apostle used earlier in 10:6-8).

Exegetical and historical questions aside, when Paul speaks about Israel's present situation of unbelief vis-à-vis the situation of believing Gentiles, as he does here in Part II (9:30–10:21) of his three-part exposition of 9:6–11:32, he concludes his discussion with words drawn from the great Israelite prophet Isaiah, who was also the most prominent proclaimer of remnant theology in the Jewish (OT) Scriptures — just as he earlier concluded Part I (9:6-29) of the exposition with words drawn from two passages in the prophecies of Isaiah (from Isa 10:22-23 and 1:9). Further, when Paul concludes Part II, he introduces his understanding of the words drawn from Isa 65:1-2 by the statement "Isaiah is bold and says" ('Ησαΐας ἀποτολμᾷ. καὶ λέγει) — which statement is similar to what he wrote earlier in 9:29 when introducing those earlier passages from Isaiah by the statement "Isaiah cries out" (προείρηκεν 'Ησαΐας).

Admittedly, such parallels of *formal patterning* in the use of words from the prophet Isaiah are hardly conclusive in establishing a similar use of statements drawn from the prophecies of Isaiah in 9:27-29 and 10:20-21. They are, however, at least suggestive of Paul's use of biblical quotations drawn from this prominent OT prophet as concluding statements for the first two parts of his three-part exposition in Rom 9–11. Thus it may be legitimately proposed that not only did Paul use material drawn from the prophet Isaiah elsewhere in Parts I and II of his three-part exposition, but he also may have used such Isaian statements as concluding and supportive affirmations for each of these subsections of 9:6-29 and 9:30-10:21. Further, commentators today may also use these parallels of *formal patterning* to support the thesis that what is presented in written form in Parts I and II had an original provenance earlier in Paul's preaching and teaching — whether in the multicultural city of Syrian Antioch or in various eastern towns and cities of the Roman Empire, or in both.

BIBLICAL THEOLOGY

In dealing with the earlier subsection of 2:17-29, which we identified as consisting of "denunciations of Jews and Jewish failures," we commented at the beginning of the "Biblical Theology" section as follows: "There is, admittedly, not much that can be derived positively from a passage that is devoted almost entirely to the denouncing of spiritual and ethical failures." What was true about that subsection of material is even more true about what appears here in 9:30-10:21, which we have captioned "Israel's Present Failure and the Gentiles Blessed, with OT Passages Cited in Support." For what appears here in 9:30-10:21, while it builds on 2:17-29 and analyzes more perceptively from a Christian perspective the situation of the Jews, is more accusatory in its tone and in its accusations than were the apostle's earlier statements about the Jews and their failures in 2:17-29.[58]

The issues present here in 9:30-10:21 go far beyond the mere denouncing of Jews and Jewish failures. It may, of course, be appropriate to spell out more fully Paul's analysis of Israel's present situation of unbelief, doing so from the apostle's Christian perspective. But it is much more significant, as well as far

---

58. Note again the three very serious accusations made against the people of Israel in 10:2-3 (which accusations explicate more fully what the apostle stated in elliptical fashion in 9:30-33, but also spell out more expressly what he wrote much earlier about Jews and Jewish failures in 2:17-29): (1) they "are zealous for God, but their zeal is not based on knowledge," (2) they "are ignorant of the righteousness of God," and (3) they "seek to establish their own righteousness," and thus "have not submitted to God's righteousness."

more necessary for a Christian biblical theology, to highlight here in 9:30–10:21 the following three important matters: (1) Paul's teaching on what has been called "the Christ-Torah antithesis," (2) the apostle's remarks about God's acceptance of "believing Gentiles," and (3) his view of the function of believing Gentiles as a catalyst for faith in Jesus of Nazareth as God's promised Messiah for the Jewish world. We do this while urging that these three matters be considered more extensively in our Christian theological discussions, be expressed more ably in our Christian proclamation, and be worked out more appropriately in our Christian ethics and practice.

1. *The Christ-Torah Antithesis.* Questions regarding the relation of Christ and the Jewish Torah, which we have suggested were especially prominent among believers in Jesus in the Christian congregations of Syrian Antioch, have continued on throughout all of Christian history and are to the fore in many Christian quarters today. These questions are: (1) How are the person and work of Jesus to be understood in the context of the OT religion of Israel? (2) How should commitment to Jesus as Israel's Messiah and humanity's Lord affect one's understanding of the Mosaic law? (3) What emphasis is to be placed in Christian theology on the person and work of Jesus of Nazareth vis-à-vis the teachings of the Mosaic law? (4) Where should the focus of Christian proclamation and Christian living be seen, on the person and work of Jesus or on the instructions of the Mosaic law — or, perhaps, on some amalgamation of the two?

Paul's response to these questions is encapsulated in his dramatic statement of Rom 10:4: "Christ is the end of the law in connection with righteousness for everyone who believes." We have postulated that Paul himself probably formulated — or, at least, had a part in formulating — this quasi-confessional affirmation. But even if he was not involved in its wording, it remains true that Paul proclaimed it here in 10:4, defended it in the verses that immediately follow, and lived out his Christian life and ministry in terms of its teaching. Sadly, it also remains true that this affirmation of 10:4 needs to be taken to heart more extensively in our Christian biblical theology and in our Christian proclamation — as well as expressed more consciously in our lives and in our ecclesiastical experiences as "Christians" (i.e., "Christ followers").

2. *Paul's Remarks with Respect to God's Acceptance of "Believing Gentiles."* In the first part of Section I of the body middle of this letter, particularly in 2:1–3:20, Paul included a number of statements that speak rather favorably of at least certain Gentiles and that seem to imply God's acceptance of those particular Gentiles. The following passages stand out as being especially relevant:

> Rom 2:10-11: "There will be glory, honor and peace for everyone who does good, both for the Jew first and for the Gentile. For, 'There is no favoritism with God.'"
>
> Rom 2:14-15: "Whenever Gentiles, who do not have the law, do by nature the things required by the law, even though they do not have the law, they are a law for themselves, since they show that the work of

the law is written in their hearts, their consciences joining in bearing witness and their thoughts within them now accusing, now even excusing them."

Rom 2:26-27: "If then a man who is not circumcised should keep the law's requirements, will he not be regarded as though he were circumcised? The one who is not circumcised physically, and yet who satisfies the requirements of the law, will condemn you who, even though you have the written code and circumcision, are a lawbreaker."

Here in Section III of the body middle of the letter, where he elaborates more fully on much of what he wrote in 2:1–3:20, Paul expresses similar remarks in Part I (9:6-29) of his three-part exposition with respect to God's outreach to and relationship with "believing Gentiles" — with the following being particularly important:

Rom 9:23-24: "What if he ['God'] did this [i.e., 'bore with great patience the objects of his wrath'] in order to make the riches of his glory known to the object of his mercy, whom he prepared in advance for glory — even to us, whom he also called, not only from the Jews but also from among the Gentiles?"

Rom 9:25-26 (quoting from the prophecy of Hosea in support of the statement above): " 'Those who were not my people I will call "my people," and her who was not beloved I will call "beloved" [Hos 2:23],' and 'In that very place where it was said to them, "You are not my people," there they will be called "sons and daughters of the living God" ' [Hos 1:10]."

In the context of his presentation in 9:6-29, the apostle's remark "whom he also called, not only from the Jews but also from among the Gentiles" of 9:24 — as well as the import of his two quotations from Hosea in 9:25-26 in support of that remark — could very well refer only to the righteous remnant of Gentiles who responded positively to God through the preaching of Paul himself (as did his own Gentile converts) or were introduced to Christ by certain other Christian evangelists (as were the Gentile believers in Jesus at Rome).

However, Paul begins Part II (9:30–10:21) of his three-part exposition by speaking in 9:30 of "Gentiles, who did not pursue righteousness," as having "attained righteousness — a righteousness that is by faith." And he concludes this subsection in an *inclusio* manner by citing in 10:20 words drawn from Isa 65:1, which he evidently understood as referring to Gentiles (contra their function in the prophecy of Isaiah as referring to the "disobedient and obstinate people" of Israel): "I was found among those who are not seeking me; I made myself known to those who did not ask for me."

It therefore seems evident — at least from the apostle's references in 9:30 to Gentiles who have attained "a righteousness that is by faith" and his use in

10:20 of words drawn from Isa 65:1 (as well as from some of his earlier references in Romans, as cited above) — that for Paul the recipients of God's mercy and saving grace included not only (1) a "righteous remnant" within Israel, (2) Jewish believers in Jesus as God's promised Messiah, and (3) Gentile converts to Christ, but also (4) certain Gentiles (whatever their number) to whom God revealed himself in mercy and saving grace (in some way known only to God himself) and who have responded positively to God (in some manner that God understood as being "trust" and "faith" in him), and so have been accepted by God as his own people.

We may not be able to conceptualize either the circumstances or the content of such a trust in God on the part of pagan Gentiles. Yet we can still believe that there exists a "remnant of Gentiles" to whom God has reached out, in some way known only to him, in divine love, mercy, and grace — and who have responded positively, in some manner, in trust and faith. Such an understanding of the scope of divine love, mercy, and grace needs to be incorporated, at least in some fashion, in a contemporary Christian biblical theology.

3. *Paul's Understanding Believing Gentiles as Catalysts for Faith in Jesus among Jews.* Also of importance in 9:30–10:21 is the point made in 10:19 regarding believing Gentiles being catalysts for faith in Jesus among the Jews. It is a point that the apostle declares was first made by Moses, the great lawgiver to whom all the Jews have looked for instruction, when he wrote in Deut 32:21b that God has proclaimed to his people Israel: "I will provoke you to jealousy (ἐγὼ παραζηλώσω ὑμᾶς) by those who are not a people; I will provoke you to jealous anger (παροργιῶ ὑμᾶς) by a nation without understanding." There is little doubt among commentators that the expressions ἐπ' οὐκ ἔθνει ("by not a people") and ἐπ' ἔθνει ἀσυνέτῳ ("by a nation without understanding") refer to non-Jewish people, that is, to Gentiles — both in Deut 32:21b and in Paul's use of that OT passage. The context of Deut 32:21b suggests that these expressions had in mind non-Jewish people and nations who would afflict the people of Israel in carrying out God's punishments of his people, and thus would turn them to repentance. However, it is evident from the context of Paul's quotation that he understood these expressions as referring to "believing Gentiles" whose presence and proclamation would have a significant effect on the people of Israel for good.

Later, in Part III (11:1-32) of his three-part exposition, Paul will speak in 11:11 of "salvation" (ἡ σωτηρία) as having come to the Gentiles "to make Israel jealous" (εἰς τὸ παραζηλῶσαι αὐτούς) — and will say in 11:14 that his own ministry to Gentiles was being carried out "in the hope that somehow (εἴ πως) I will provoke to jealousy (παραζηλώσω) my own people (μου τὴν σάρκα) and save some of them (καὶ σώσω τινὰς ἐξ αὐτῶν)." Much more will be said about how Paul envisioned the salvation of the Gentiles and his own ministry to Gentiles as being witnesses to his own people the Jews. Suffice it here, however, merely (1) to note that the Greek verb παραζηλόω ("provoke to jealousy," "make jealous") not only appears in the words of Deut 32:21b that the apostle quotes here in 10:19, but also comes to the fore quite prominently in the apostle's statement later regarding a particularly important feature of his Christian ministry in 11:14; (2) to highlight the point that "the apostle to the Gentiles" understood that one of the major functions of "believing Gentiles," that is, of those who believed in Jesus as their Savior and Lord whatever their ethnicity, was to function as a catalyst for this same faith in Jesus on the part of Jews, and (3) to urge that Jewish people must always be included by Christians (whatever their respective ethnic heritage) when they attempt to understand the fullness of God's love, mercy, and saving grace, when they construct their biblical theologies, and when they attempt to reach out to others in their witness.

CONTEXTUALIZATION FOR TODAY

Of great importance for any contextualization today of what Paul writes in 9:30–10:21 are the words of God that he quotes in 10:20-21 from Isa 65:1-2, which he sets out as the conclusion of this subsection of material: (1) "I was found among those who are not seeking me; I made myself known to those who did not ask for me" (as drawn from Isa 65:1), and (2) "All day long I held out my hands to a disobedient and obstinate people" (as drawn from Isa 65:2). We may never understand just why Paul (or some early believer in Jesus before him) transposed the statements of Isa 65:1-2 in Rom 10:20-21. Nor may we ever be able to explain when or why God's message to the people of Israel in Isa 65:1-2 was divided into two parts — with the two statements of 65:1 being understood as speaking about "believing Gentiles" and the statement of 65:2 directed to the "disobedient and obstinate" people of Israel. Yet these words written by the great Jewish prophet Isaiah, who was the most prominent proclaimer of remnant theology in the old covenant of the Jewish (OT) Scriptures, need to reverberate always in the minds and in the hearts of all of us who claim to be members of God's "new covenant," constantly reminding us (1) that God has made himself known to people who did not ask for him, and so is to be found among people who have not been seeking him (as in Isa 65:1) and (2) that God has at all times held out his hands in welcome to obstinate people (as in Isa 65:2). As believers in Jesus, we have experienced the truth of all these affirmations about the person and nature of God — which affirmations speak particularly about his love, mercy, and saving grace. And it is such experienced realizations about God that need to motivate and control all our thinking about him and all our actions on his behalf.

Just as important for any legitimate contextualization of the Christian gospel is the quasi-confessional affirmation of Rom 10:4, which declares that "Christ is the end of the law in connection with righteousness for everyone who believes." For Christians today need to cease regarding righteousness in terms of law at all, either in a "legalistic" or a "nomistic" sense. The believer in Jesus, as Anders Nygren has aptly said, is "neither condemned nor justified by it. He hopes for nothing from the law, and fears nothing. For him the law is completely

CONTEXTUALIZATION FOR TODAY

eliminated, as far as righteousness and freedom, condemnation and the wrath of God are concerned."[59] For, as Nygren has gone on to assert: the one who believes in Jesus has found that "the gospel of Christ is *the very righteousness of God.*"[60] Or as Martin Luther has expressed matters, the Christian has found that "no external thing, whatsoever it may be, has any influence whatever in producing Christian righteousness or liberty. . . . One thing and one only is necessary for Christian life, righteousness and liberty. That one thing is the most holy Word of God, the Gospel of Christ."[61]

---

59. Nygren, *Romans,* 310-11.
60. *Ibid.,* 303 (italics his).
61. Luther, "A Treatise on Christian Liberty," 313-14.

4. Part III of Paul's Exposition:
The Course of God's Salvation History: A Remnant within Israel, a Remnant among the Gentiles, the Salvation of "All Israel," and God's Mercy on All People (11:1-32)

TRANSLATION

$^{11:1}$*I ask then: Did God [entirely] reject his people? Certainly not! I am an Israelite myself, a descendant of Abraham, from the tribe of Benjamin.* ^{2}*God did not reject [totally] his people, whom he foreknew! Don't you know what the Scripture says in [the passage about] Elijah — how he appealed to God against Israel:*

> ^{3}*"Lord, they have killed your prophets and torn down your altars;*
> *I am the only one left, and they are trying to kill me."*

^{4}*But what was the response of God to him?*

> *"I have reserved for myself seven thousand who have not bowed the knee to Baal."*

^{5}*So, too, at this present time there continues to exist a remnant chosen by [God's] grace.* ^{6}*And if by grace, then it is no longer by works; if it were, grace would no longer be grace.*

^{7}*What then? What Israel is seeking, it failed to obtain. But those chosen [by God] obtained it, whereas the others were hardened.* ^{8}*Just as it is written:*

> *"God gave them a spirit of stupor,*
> *eyes so that they could not see*
> *and ears so that they could not hear,*
> *to this very day."*

^{9}*And David says:*

> *"May their table become a snare and a trap,*
> *a stumbling block and a retribution for them;*
> ^{10}*May their eyes be darkened so they cannot see,*
> *and their backs be bent forever."*

^{11}*Again I ask: Did they stumble so as to fall beyond recovery? Certainly not! Rather, because of their transgression, salvation has come to the Gentiles to make Israel jealous.* ^{12}*But if their transgression means riches for the world and their loss means riches for the Gentiles, how much greater riches will their fullness bring about!*

^{13}*Now I am speaking [directly] to you Gentiles. Inasmuch as I am in truth*

866

the apostle to the Gentiles, I make much of my ministry [14]*in the hope that I may somehow arouse my own people to envy and save some of them.* [15]*For if their rejection is the reconciliation of the world, what will be their acceptance if not life from the dead?*

[16]*For if the part of the dough offered as firstfruits is holy, then the whole batch is holy! And if the root is holy, so are the branches!*

[17]*Now if some of the branches have been broken off, and you, though a wild olive shoot, have been grafted in among the others and so share in the nourishing sap from the olive root,* [18]*do not boast over those branches. But if you do, consider this: You do not support the root, but the root supports you.* [19]*You will say then, "Branches were broken off so that I could be grafted in."* [20]*Granted. But they were broken off because of unbelief, and you stand by faith. Do not be arrogant, but be afraid.* [21]*For if God did not spare the natural branches, he will not spare you either.*

[22]*Consider, therefore, the kindness and sternness of God: sternness to those who fell, but kindness to you, provided that you continue in his kindness. Otherwise, you also will be cut off.* [23]*And if they do not persist in unbelief, they will be grafted in, for God is able to graft them in again.* [24]*After all, if you were cut out of an olive tree that is wild by nature, and contrary to nature were grafted into a cultivated olive tree, how much more readily will these, the natural branches, be grafted into their own olive tree?*

[25]*I do not want you to be ignorant of this mystery, brothers and sisters, so that you may not be conceited: Israel has experienced a hardening in part until the full number of the Gentiles has come in.* [26]*It is in the following way that all Israel will be saved, just as it is written:*

> *"The Deliverer will come from Zion;*
> *he will turn godlessness away from Jacob.*
> [27]*And this is my covenant with them*
> *when I take away their sins."*

[28]*As far as the gospel is concerned, they are enemies on your account; but as far as [God's] election is concerned, they are loved on account of the patriarchs,* [29]*for God's gifts and his call are irrevocable.* [30]*Just as you who were at one time disobedient to God have now received mercy as a result of their disobedience,* [31]*so they too have now become disobedient in order that they too may now receive mercy as a result of God's mercy to you.* [32]*For God has bound everyone over to disobedience in order that he might have mercy on them all.*

TEXTUAL NOTES

11:1 The articular noun τὸν λαόν ("the people"), which appears in the phrase τὸν λαὸν αὐτοῦ ("his people"), is strongly supported by uncials ℵ A B C D P Ψ (also *Byz* L) and by minuscules 33 1175 1739 (Category I), 81 256 1506 1881 1962 2127 2464 (Category II), and 6 69 88 104 181 263 323 326 330 365 424^c 436 451 459 614 629 1241 1243 1319 1573

867

1735 1852 1874 1874 1877 1912 2200 (Category III); it is also reflected in it[ar, d] vg syr[p, h] cop[sa, bo] and supported by Origen[lat] Eusebius Chrysostom Jerome and Augustine. The reading τὴν κληρονομίαν ("the inheritance"), however, appears in P[46] and in uncials F G; it is also reflected in it[b, f, g, o] and supported by Ambrosiaster. This variant reading has probably been influenced by Ps 94:14 (LXX 93:14): "For the Lord will not cast off his people (τὸν λαὸν αὐτοῦ), neither will he forsake his inheritance (τὴν κληρονομίαν αὐτοῦ)."[1]

2 After ἐντυγχάνει τῷ θεῷ κατὰ τοῦ Ἰσραήλ ("he appealed to God against Israel") at the end of the verse, the nominative singular present participle λέγων ("saying") appears in fourth-century Codex Vaticanus (B* 03) and in ninth-century *Byz* L; it also is found in minuscules 2464 (Category II) and 69 88 104 323 326 330 614 1241 1735 1874 (Category III). The participle λέγων, however, does not appear in uncials א[2] A B[2] C D F G P Ψ or in minuscules 1175 1739 (Category I), 81 1506 1881 (Category II), and 6 365 424[c] 1243 1319 1505 1573 2495; nor is it reflected in Latin or Syriac translations. In all likelihood, the lack of the participle λέγων ("saying") was original. It was probably inserted to make it clear that what follows is a biblical quotation, thereby paralleling λέγει ("it says") at the beginning of 11:4.

4 The second aorist verb κατέλιπον ("I kept" or "reserved") is attested by uncials א B D Ψ and by minuscules 6 69 323 330 365 614 1241 (Category III). The imperfect κατέλειπον ("I have kept" or "have reserved"), however, is somewhat better attested in the textual tradition, being supported by P[46], by uncials A C F G P (also *Byz* L), and by minuscules 1175 1739 (Category I) and 88 104 326 1319 1573 1735 1846 1874 (Category III). The future form καταλείψω ("I will keep," "leave," "reserve"), which appears in minuscules 81 and 1506 (both Category II), has probably been influenced by the LXX reading of 1 Kgs 19:18 (3 Kgdms 19:18): "And *you will leave/reserve* (καταλείψεις) in Israel seven thousand men, all the knees that have not bowed to Baal and every mouth that has not worshipped him."

A decision between the second aorist verb κατέλιπον ("I kept" or "reserved") and the imperfect verb κατέλειπον ("I have kept" or "have reserved") is extremely difficult to make, for there is only a slight difference in spelling, only a slight difference in textual support, and very little difference in meaning between the two forms of the verb. Yet since the imperfect κατέλειπον is somewhat better supported in the textual tradition, it should likely be viewed as having been original.

6 After the second occurrence of the word χάρις ("grace") at the end of this verse, the statement εἰ δὲ ἐξ ἔργων, οὐκέτι ἐστὶ χάρις, ἐπεὶ τὸ ἔργον οὐκέτι ἐστὶν ἔργον ("But if it is by works, it is no longer on the basis of grace; otherwise work is no longer work") appears in corrected Codex Sinaiticus (א[2]) and in the eighth- or ninth-century uncial Ψ, as well as in minuscules 33[vid] 1175 (Category I), 256 (Category II), and 6 104 365 424[c] 436 459 1241 1319 1573 1912 (Category III). Variations on this statement are also to be found (1) in Codex Vaticanus (B 03), which omits the first ἐστί and reads χάρις for the

---

1. M. D. Given, "Restoring the Inheritance in Romans 11:1," *JBL* 118 (1999) 89-96, has argued that τὴν κληρονομίαν ("the inheritance") was probably the original reading, for it is "the harder reading" and provides a number of intertextual echoes. But his argument is somewhat tenuous, and so probably spurious.

final ἔργον, (2) in minuscule 1962 (Category II), which reads ἡ χάρις for ἐστὶ χάρις, and (3) in *Byz* L and minuscules 2127 2464 (Category II), as well as reflected in vg[ms] [syr[p, h]] and supported by Chrysostom, which texts have ἤ for ἐπεί and read οὐκ ἐστιν ἔργον for οὐκέτι ἐστὶν ἔργον. Such variant readings, however, are not attested by P[46], by uncials ℵ* A C D F G P, or by minuscules 1739 (Category I), 81 1506[vid] 1881 (Category II), or 263 1852 2200 (Category III); nor are they reflected in it[ar, b, d, f, g, o] vg cop[sa, bo] or supported by Origen[gr, lat] Ambrosiaster Jerome or Augustine. Bruce Metzger has quite appropriately observed: "There appears to be no reason why, if the words were original, they should have been deleted. The existence of several forms of the addition likewise throws doubt upon the originality of any of them."[2]

7 The third-person singular present indicative active verb ἐπιζητεῖ ("it is seeking") is amply attested throughout the textual tradition. The aorist ἐπεζήτει ("it sought"), which appears in ninth-century uncials F G and in minuscules 104 1846 (both Category III), and is reflected in various Latin and Syriac translations, has weak textual support and seems to have been motivated by an explanatory purpose.

8 The adverb καθώς ("just as," "as") is attested by P[46], by uncials A C D G P Ψ (also *Byz* L), and by minuscules 33 1175 1739 (Category I), 1881 2464 (Category II), and 6 69 88 104 323 326 330 365 614 1241 1243 1319 1505 1573 1735 1874 2344 2495 (Category III). The synonymous adverb καθώσπερ ("as"), however, is attested by uncials A B and minuscule 81 (Category II). There is little, if any, difference between these two adverbs, either in textual attestation or in meaning. Yet the expression καθώς γέγραπται ("just as it is written") is a very common introductory formula used by Paul when quoting an OT passage, and so καθώς here with γέγραπται merits acceptance as being original (as the editors of *NA*[26, 27] and *GNT*[3, 4] also thought is most probable).

12 Codex Alexandrinus (A 02) entirely omits 11:12: "But if their transgression means riches for the world and their loss means riches for the Gentiles, how much greater riches will their fullness bring!" Perhaps the omission came about because some fifth-century scribe (1) considered the verse's use of the word πλοῦτος ("wealth," "riches"), which is twice employed and once implied, overly repetitious, or (2) saw no difference between the expressions "riches for the world" and "riches for the Gentiles," or (3) viewed the verse's elliptical statement πόσῳ μᾶλλον τὸ πλήρωμα αὐτῶν, which appears at its end, as difficult to translate — or perhaps (4) considered this statement redundant in view of the more explicit statement of 11:15: "For if their rejection is the reconciliation of the world, what will their acceptance be but life from the dead?" Whatever the reason or reasons, the inclusion of this verse is abundantly attested in the textual tradition, and so should be viewed as original.

13a The postpositive connecting particle δέ ("but," "and," or "now") is strongly supported by uncials ℵ A B P and by minuscules 1739 (Category I), 81 1506 1881 (Category II), and 104 630 1243 1735 1874 (Category III). The conjunction γάρ (which may be used to express cause, inference, and continuation, or to introduce an explanation), however, appears in its place in uncials D F G Ψ (also *Byz* L) and in minuscules 33 1175 (Category I), 2464 (Category II), and 6 69 88 323 326 330 365 614 1241 1319 1505 1573 2344 2464

2. Metzger, *Textual Commentary*, 464.

2495 (Category III). And the inferential particle οὖν ("so," "therefore") appears in uncial C. On the strength of its textual history, the particle δέ must be viewed as having been original. Perhaps the variant readings of either γάρ or οὖν were substituted in attempts to strengthen the connection between what appears in 11:11-12 and in 11:13-15 — which connection is obvious without the insertion of either of these other connecting particles.

13b The idiomatic expression μὲν οὖν ("indeed then," "in truth") is well attested by P46, by uncials ℵ A B C P, and by minuscules 81 and 1506 (both Category II). It is, however, either (1) replaced by the connective particle δέ ("but," "and") in uncial Ψ (also *Byz* L) and minuscules 33 1175 1739 (Category I), 1881 2464 (Category II), and 6 69 88 323 330 614 1241 1243 1505 1735 1874 2344 2495 (Category III), or (2) eliminated by uncials D F G and by minuscules 326 365 1319 1573 (all Category III). It seems that later scribes were just unable to understand μὲν οὖν as an early oral, vernacular, and poetic idiom, and therefore replaced it by a more literary prose expression or simply eliminated it (see "Exegetical Comments" on this passage below).

13c The future verb δοξάσω ("I will glory" or "make much of") and the future verb δοξάζω ("I will think," "believe," "consider") were, it seems, often confused by scribes in the textual tradition, evidently because of similar sounds in the dictation of the Greek letters σ and ζ. The future verb δοξάσω ("I will glory" or "make much of") is attested by P46, by uncials F G Ψ, and by minuscules 33 1175 (Category I) and 88 1874 2344 (Category III), and so should most likely in its context be accepted as original. The future verb δοξάζω ("I will think," "believe," "consider"), while similar in sound and somewhat similar in meaning, is probably to be viewed as a variant reading, and so to be rejected.

16a The postpositive particle δέ ("but," "and," or "now") at the beginning of the sentence is amply attested throughout the textual tradition. It is, however, replaced by γάρ ("for") in Codex Alexandrinus (A 02). But that worthy fifth-century textual witness cannot overthrow the overwhelming MS support for δέ ("but," "and," or "now").

16b The conditional particle εἰ ("if") in the clause εἰ ἡ ῥίζα ἁγία ("if the root is holy") is amply attested by uncials ℵ A B C D Pᶜ Ψ (also *Byz* L) and by minuscules 33 1175 1739 (Category I), 81 (Category II), and 69 104 181 323 326 330 365 451 614 629 1319 1505 1573 1874 1877 2344 2495 (Category III); it is also reflected in itᵃʳ, ᵈ, ᵈᵉᵐ, ˣ, ᶻ vg syrᵖ, ʰ copˢᵃ, ᵇᵒ and supported by Clement and Ambrosiaster. The particle εἰ ("if"), however, is omitted in P46, in uncials F G P*, and in minuscules 1962 2127 (Category II), and 436 1241 (Category III); its omission is also reflected in vgᶠ, ᵍ and attested by Chrysostom. The omission here of εἰ was probably accidental, since its presence seems necessary to the rhetorical balance of the successive clauses in 11:16.

17 Several different phrases appear in the textual tradition to complete the thought of συγκοινωνὸς . . . ἐγένου ("you became fellow sharers"): (1) τῆς ῥίζης τῆς ἐλαίας, "of the root of the olive tree" (as in the Ethiopic version and Ambrosiaster); (2) τῆς πιότητος τῆς ἐλαίας, "of the sap of the olive tree" (as in P46, uncials D* F G, versions itᵈ, ᶠ, ᵍ copᵇᵒ ᵐˢ, ᶠᵃʸ, and the Church Fathers Irenaeusˡᵃᵗ and Augustine³/⁵); (3) τῆς ῥίζης καὶ τῆς πιότητος τῆς ἐλαίας, "of the root and of the sap of the olive tree" (as in P², uncials A D² P [also *Byz* L], and minuscules 33 1739 [Category I], 81 256 1881 1962 2127 [Category II], and 6 104 263 365 436 459 1241 1319 1573 1852 2200; also reflected in itᵃʳ vg syrᵖ, ʰ and supported by Origenˡᵃᵗ³/⁴ Chrysostom and Augustine²/⁵); and (4) τῆς ῥίζης τῆς πιότητος τῆς ἐλαίας, "of the root of the sap of the olive tree" (as in uncials ℵ B C Ψ, in minuscules 1175 [Category I], 1506 2464 [Category II], and 1912 [Category III]; also reflected in it[b, o] [cop[sa, bo]] and supported by Origen[lat1/4]). Metzger has argued that the fourth option, despite its more limited attestation, "appears to explain best the origin of the other readings, since the widespread introduction of καί and the omission of τῆς ῥίζης (P[46] D* G it[d. g] al) are suspicious as ameliorating emendations."[3]

21 The insertion of μή πως ("perhaps," "lest somehow") before οὐδέ ("not," "neither") is supported by P[46], by uncials D F G Ψ (also *Byz* L), and by minuscules 33 1175 (Category I), 1962 2464 (Category II), and 104 459 1241 1912 (Category III); it is also reflected in it[ar, b, d, f, g, o] vg syr[p, h] and supported by Irenaeus[lat] Chrysostom Ambrosiaster. The shorter text of οὐδέ (i.e., without the insertion of μή πως), however, is supported by uncials ℵ A B C P and by minuscules 1739 (Category I), 81 256 1506 1881 2127 (Category II), and 6 263 365 424[c] 436 1319 1573 1852 2 2200 (Category III); it is also reflected in cop[sa, bo, fay] and supported by Origen[lat] and Augustine. With such strong textual support, the shorter text is most likely original. Perhaps an early copyist (such as the one involved in the production of P[46]) was averse to the blunt statement "neither will God spare you," and so sought to soften it by inserting "perhaps."

"On the other hand, however," as Bruce Metzger has observed, "(a) μή πως is a Pauline expression (it occurs in nine other passages in Paul; only once elsewhere in the New Testament), and (b) copyists may have taken offense at its presence here because of its apparent unrelatedness (Origen substituted the more appropriate πόσῳ μᾶλλον and πόσῳ πλέον — see *in loc.*) and its grammatical inappropriateness with the following future [tense of φείσεται]."[4] The editors of *GNT*[3, 4] and *NA*[26, 27], therefore, have retained μή πως in the text, but enclosed it in brackets. This marks a change from the earlier decision expressed in *GNT*[2] and *NA*[25] to omit μή πως — which we believe is best supported by the Greek textual tradition.

25 The preposition used — or, for that matter, the use of any preposition at all — before the dative plural reflexive pronoun ἑαυτοῖς is disputed. The following positions and textual data are important: (1) the preposition παρ' before the reflexive pronoun ἑαυτοῖς is original, as attested by uncials ℵ C D (also *Byz* L) and by minuscules 33 1175 (Category I), 81 256 1881 1962 2127 2464 (Category II), and 104 263 365 436 459 1241 1319 1573 1912 (Category III); it is also reflected in it[b] and supported by Origen[lat] Chrysostom Theodore and Jerome[1/3]; (2) the preposition ἐν before ἑαυτοῖς is original, as appears in uncials A B and in minuscules 1506 (Category II) and 1852 2200 (Category III); it also is reflected in sy[p, h]; or (3) no preposition before ἑαυτοῖς should be understood as having been original, which omission is supported by P[46], by uncials F G Ψ, and by minuscules 1739 (Category I) and 6 424[c] (Category II); nor is any preposition reflected in it[ar, d, f, g, o] vg cop[sa, bo, fay] or supported by Ambrosiaster Jerome[2/3] or Augustine. The simple reflexive pronoun ἑαυτοῖς (i.e., without any preposition) may have prompted copyists to insert a preposition. On the other hand, παρ' has the strongest support in the textual tradition. Thus *NA*[26, 27] and *GNT*[3, 4] have retained the preposition παρ' in square brackets, thereby

3. Metzger, *Textual Commentary*, 464.
4. *Ibid.*, 464-65.

indicating considerable doubt — which marks a change from the earlier GNT^2 and NA^{25}, which accepted the preposition ἐν.

31 The decision as to which word precedes the verb ἐλεηθῶσιν ("they may receive mercy"), if any, is difficult to make. The options are (1) νῦν ("now"), which is attested by uncials ℵ B D* and by minuscule 1506 (Category II), and is reflected in cop[bo, fay ms]; or (2) ὕστερον ("later"), which appears in minuscules 33 (Category I), 256 1962 2127 (Category II), and 263 365 1319 1573 1852 1912 (Category III); it is also reflected in cop[sa, fay ms] and supported by Ambrosiaster[mss] — or, perhaps, that (3) neither of these two words should be seen as preceding the verb, as in P[46], in uncials A D[2] F G Ψ (also *Byz* L), and in minuscules 1175 1739 (Category I), 81 1881 (Category II), and 6 104 436 459 1241 2200 (Category III); with this omission reflected also in it[ar, b, d, f, g, o] syr[p] Origen[lat] and supported by Chrysostom Ambrosiaster Jerome and Augustine.

The omission of both νῦν and ὕστερον has the preponderance of both early and diverse MS evidence. On the other hand, as Metzger has suggested, "the difficulty in meaning that the second occurrence of νῦν seems to introduce may have prompted either its deletion or its replacement by the superficially more appropriate ὕστερον."[5] External and internal evidence, therefore, has seemed to many textual critics to be quite evenly balanced, and so the UBS editors have retained νῦν but enclosed it in square brackets.

32 The phrase τούς πάντας ("all people" or "everyone") in the clause συνέκλεισεν γὰρ ὁ θεὸς τοὺς πάντας εἰς ἀπείθειαν ("For God has bound everyone over to disobedience") is decisively supported by uncials ℵ A B D[2] Ψ and by minuscules 33 1175 1739 (Category I), 81 256 1506 1881 1962 2127 (Category II), and 6 104 (Category III). A few textual witnesses, however, read the neuter plural τὰ πάντα ("all things"), as do P[46vid] and uncial D* (uncials F G have πάντα but omit the article τά); this variant reading is also reflected in it[ar, b, d, f, g, o] vg and supported by Irenaeus[(gr), lat] Ambrosiaster Jerome[12/17] and Augustine[1/10] — probably as a result of a scribal recollection of Gal 3:22: ἀλλὰ συνέκλεισεν ἡ γραφὴ τὰ πάντα ὑπὸ ἁμαρτίαν ("But the Scripture has bound over all things to sin").

FORM/STRUCTURE/SETTING

What Paul presents in Part III of his three-part exposition, that is, here in 11:1-32, has frequently been viewed by translators and commentators as difficult to understand — particularly with respect to textual criticism (see "Textual Notes" above) and certain features of the interpretation of the text (see "Exegetical Comments" below). If, however, we postulate that what Paul has written in 11:1-32 (together with what he wrote in 9:6-29 and 9:30–10:21) had (1) earlier been proclaimed orally by him in his Christian ministry (perhaps in his preaching and teaching at Syrian Antioch, where, as Acts 11:26 tells us, he ministered along with Barnabas "for a whole year," "taught great numbers of people," and "the disciples were first called 'Christians'"), and then (2) included in episto-

5. Metzger, *Textual Commentary*, 465.

lary form in his letter to Rome, which he sent to the ethnically mixed Christian congregations of the capital city — it may be legitimately proposed that at least some of the textual and interpretive difficulties of this passage can be plausibly explained. Utilizing such an approach in attempting to understand what Paul has written in 11:1-32, translators and commentators today are in a somewhat better position to offer more cogent resolutions to a number of matters that have perplexed many interpreters of the past.

Paul's Remnant Theology and Rhetoric Brought to a Conclusion in 11:1-32. Of greatest importance for an understanding of what is written in 11:1-32 is this basic realization: in this passage Paul brings to a conclusion his remnant theology and his remnant type of rhetoric, which he began in 9:6-29 (Part I of his exposition) and then carried on throughout 9:30–10:21 (Part II). We spoke earlier of ten essential features of a Jewish remnant theology and rhetoric, proposing that the apostle employed most of these features in his own fashion in the third major section of the body middle of the letter (that is, in 9:1–11:36, and particularly in his three-part exposition of 9:6–11:32).[6] Of those ten points, the following eight seem particularly important for an understanding of what the apostle has written here in 11:1-32:

> Point 1: The remnant is sovereignly established by God alone.
>
> Point 2: The remnant may be small, but also envisioned is its greatness.
>
> Point 3: The remnant is both a present and a future entity.
>
> Point 4: The concept of the remnant is related to God's election of Israel — though on this matter Paul argues that God's promises are given only to "the remnant within Israel" and extended through it to "the remnant among the Gentiles."
>
> Point 6: While God establishes the remnant, the other side of that establishment is a response of faith and faithfulness on the part of those whom God has elected.
>
> Point 7: There is not only "a remnant within Israel," but also envisioned is "a remnant" that God elects "from among the Gentiles."
>
> Point 9: The gathering of the remnant is not the final goal of God; rather, God's final goal is the readoption and salvation of all Israel.
>
> Point 10: There is a close relationship between God's "chosen ('selected' or 'elected') remnant" people and God's Messiah.

Epistolary and Rhetorical Conventions in 11:1-32. Rather obvious in 11:1-32 is the presence of a few traditional epistolary expressions. They appear in five verses of the passage and function to identify (1) the start of certain major portions of Paul's presentation and (2) the beginnings of some of his corollary statements:

---

6. Cf. p. 770 above, where we have cited ten points drawn from the article by G. Schrenk and V. Herntrich, "λεῖμμα, ὑπόλειμμα, καταλείπω," *TDNT* 4.203-14.

11:1 — A "verb of saying": λέγω οὖν ("I say/speak/ask then")

11:7 — An abbreviated rhetorical question: τί οὖν; ("What then?")

11:11 — Another "verb of saying": λέγω οὖν ("I say/speak/ask then")

11:13 — A further "verb of saying/speaking," which includes a "dative of direct address": ὑμῖν δὲ λέγω τοῖς ἔθνεσιν ("Now, I am speaking to you Gentiles")

11:25 — A "disclosure formula," which includes a "vocative of direct address": οὐ γὰρ θέλω ὑμᾶς ἀγνοεῖν, ἀδελφοί ("I do not want you to be ignorant, brothers and sisters")

Used in the first two "verb of saying" statements of 11:1 and 11:11 is the rhetorical convention *anaphora,* which is the name rhetoricians give to the repetition of a word or expression at the beginning of two or more sets of statements; the word is repeated at the beginning of a subsequent set (or sets) of statements either immediately following the first set or at some distance from it. The extended use of such a rhetorical anaphora here in the first part of ch. 11 not only indicates a connection between the statements of 11:1-6 and the similar statements a few verses later in 11:11-12, it also suggests that what is presented in the second set of statements is a development from what was presented in the first set — much like the extended rhetorical anaphora that appears in the apostle's thesis statements of 1:16-17 vis-à-vis his statements two chapters later in 3:21-22, which essentially repeat, extend, and develop the earlier statements.[7]

Another traditional convention of both speech and letter writing that appears prominently in 11:1-32 is what rhetoricians call *metaphor.* The term "metaphor" is used with respect to a word, a group of words, or a sentence that stands for something different from its literal reference but is linked to its literal meaning by some perceivable similarity — and thus suggests a likeness or analogy between its literal reference and its figurative usage. And "metaphor" is quite an appropriate designation for Paul's references to (1) "the firstfruits" and "the whole batch" in 11:16a, (2) "the root" and "the branches" in 11:16b, (3) "the natural branches" and "the engrafted wild branches" in 11:17-24, and (4) "a wild olive tree" and "a cultivated olive tree" in 11:24.

Likewise, there are two stylistic features in 11:1-32 that may be understood as comparable to two rhetorical conventions that often appear in Greco-Roman oratory and writing. The first is Paul's use of the pronoun "you" in a direct address fashion in 11:13 (plural "you") and then more fully in 11:17-24 (repeated singular "you"), which closely resembles the use of "you" (whether singular or plural) in Greek *diatribe.* The second comes to the fore in the structuring of the

---

7. For a compact anaphora in Romans, note the repetition of the phrase "God gave them over" in 1:24, 26, and 28; elsewhere in his letters, see the extended anaphora in the repetition of the adage "everything is lawful" (or "permissible") in 1 Cor 6:12-13, which is essentially repeated in 10:23-24. Outside of the Pauline correspondence, note the eighteen appearances of the phrase "by faith" in Heb 11:3-31, the nine occurrences of the expression "blessed" in Matt 5:3-12, and the four times that the words "blessed" and "woe" are used in Luke 6:20-26.

apostle's statement of 11:30-31, which seems to reflect a Greek *chiastic* structuring in its declaration: "Just as you who were at one time disobedient to God have now received *mercy* as a result of their *disobedience,* so they too have now become *disobedient* in order that they too may now receive *mercy* as a result of God's mercy to you."

Diatribe language and chiastic structuring were widely used in the Greco-Roman world of Paul's day. Thus Paul's use of these rather common oratorical and literary conventions (whether expressed consciously or unconsciously) probably means only that he knew how to speak appropriately, both to Jews and to Gentiles, using the traditional conventions of his day — and how to write to an ethnically mixed group of believers in Jesus at Rome in a manner that all would understand.

More important with respect to the rhetorical features of this passage, however, is the narrative substructure that underlies all of what Paul writes in 11:1-32. For while it cannot be said that he presents here a full-blown "philosophy of history," as has sometimes been asserted, the apostle does set out in this passage what may be called the "course of God's salvation history" — dealing in successive stages first with "the remnant within Israel," then with "a remnant among the Gentiles," then with the salvation of "all Israel," and finally with "God's mercy on them all" (that is, on "all people"). Yet even more significant than the recognition of a narrative substructure in this passage is the fact that here in 11:1-32 (as also expressed explicitly in 9:6-29 and implicitly in 9:30–10:21), Paul utilizes a Jewish and/or Jewish Christian remnant theology and remnant rhetoric — which he recasts into a form of his own fashioning and proclaims as being at the heart of the Christian message.

Our overall thesis regarding the formal patterning and compositional structure of this letter is that not only do they (1) provide insights into how Paul constructed his letter, but also they (2) suggest something regarding the function or functions he wanted the various sections and subsections to serve, (3) highlight the importance that he himself placed on the various materials within the letter, and so (4) provide guidance for interpreters on how to understand the course of his argument.[8] Such matters of formal patterning and compositional structure seem to be particularly evident in this passage of 11:1-32, and thus will need to be constantly taken into consideration in our exegetical comments that follow.

Paul's Use of Biblical Statements in 11:1-32. Earlier in 1:16–3:20 the apostle supported his arguments with a large number of biblical quotations, biblical allusions, and traditional Jewish aphorisms based on the OT Scriptures. Likewise in 4:1-24, he used the Jewish patriarch Abraham as the example par excellence to support what he had written about human faith and trust in God earlier in 3:21-31. So, too, in the subsections of 9:6-29 (Part I of his three-part exposition in chs. 9–11) and 9:30–10:21 (Part II), Paul employed certain OT

---

8. See our "Introduction to the Commentary," 20-21.

narratives and statements in support of his presentations — extensively and quite significantly in Part I to introduce his own christianized form of remnant theology, but even more extensively and more freely in Part II when speaking about "Israel's present situation of unbelief vis-à-vis the situation of believing Gentiles." And he will continue to employ here in 11:1-32 (Part III): (1) a notable OT narrative in support of his affirmation regarding the continuing existence of a "righteous remnant" within Israel (in 11:1-6), (2) three highly significant statements drawn from three of Israel's most respected leaders of the past in support of his characterization of the people of Israel in his day (in 11:7-10), and (3) a final conflated quotation drawn principally from the words of the great Israelite prophet Isaiah (and echoed by the prophet Jeremiah) regarding the eternality of God's promises to Israel in support of his affirmation that in the future "all Israel will be saved."

Following that conflated quotation drawn principally from the prophet Isaiah, Paul appends in 11:28-32 what has every appearance of being a postscript. This postscript provides a fitting summary of not only what he wrote in 11:1-27, but also of all that he wrote in 9:6–10:21. Likewise, the material of 11:28-32 reiterates, in brief, a great deal of what Paul wrote very much earlier in the two major theological sections of the body middle of the letter, that is, in Section I (1:16–4:25) and Section II (5:1–8:39) — particularly reiterating in 11:32, in very brief summary fashion, many of the statements that he set out in those two earlier theological sections: συνέκλεισεν γὰρ ὁ Θεὸς τοὺς πάντας εἰς ἀπείθειαν, ἵνα τοὺς πάντας ἐλεήσῃ ("For God has bound everyone over to disobedience in order that he might have mercy on them all").[9]

The Structure and Message of 11:1-32. In any analysis of the structure of 11:1-32, attention must first be given to the epistolary and rhetorical conventions that appear in rather significant places in the major portion of the passage, that is, in 11:1-27:

1. The two "verb of saying" epistolary expressions that appear at the beginnings of 11:1 and 11:11.
2. The abbreviated rhetorical question, "What then?" that functions to introduce a corollary consideration in 11:7-10.
3. The rhetorical anaphora construction that ties together the two subsections of 11:1-10 and 11:11-24, as well as suggests a development in the presentation of the latter.
4. The "verb of saying/speaking" epistolary expression in 11:13 that introduces a further corollary discussion in a subsection of the material in which it appears.
5. The "disclosure formula" and "vocative of direct address," traditional epistolary features that appear prominently at the beginning of 11:25.

9. Cf. Dunn, *Romans,* 2.696, who observes that this epigrammatic statement of only twelve Greek words sums up "the principal themes of the whole letter."

On the basis of these five features having to do with "formal patterning" and "compositional structure," I propose that what is written in 11:1-27 deals with the following topics and presentations:

1. The continuing presence of a "remnant" within Israel vis-à-vis God's hardening of "the others" in Israel, with OT support for the affirmation of a continuing righteous remnant drawn from the Elijah story and quotations in support of statements about God's hardening of Israel drawn from words attributed to Moses, Isaiah, and David (11:1-10).
2. The "stumbling" of Israel, the "reconciliation" of believing Gentiles, and the interaction of these matters in the overall purpose and plan of God (11:11-24).
3. The irrevocable promise of God regarding the salvation of "all Israel" in the context of Israel's present rejection of Jesus as the nation's God-given Messiah and God's present "hardening in part" of his ancient people, with OT support drawn from the prophet Isaiah (11:25-27).

To these three presentations set out in 11:1-27, Paul adds a further paragraph of material in 11:28-32, which functions as a fitting summary of much of what the apostle wrote earlier in the letter (see above). Thus in the "Exegetical Comments" below, we not only will deal with the three subsections of material in 11:1-10, 11:11-24, and 11:25-27, but also will take seriously into account this additional paragraph of 11:28-32.

EXEGETICAL COMMENTS

I. The Continuing Presence of a "Righteous Remnant" within Israel vis-à-vis God's Hardening of "the Others" with Support for the Former from the Story of Elijah and for the Latter from Statements Attributed to Moses, Isaiah, and David (11:1-10)

Commentators have frequently understood 11:1-10 as a discrete and unified portion of material in the larger subsection of 11:1-32.[10] And such an understanding is undoubtedly true. Yet two lines of argument are also present in this passage. The first appears in 11:1-6 and deals with the continuing presence of a "righteous remnant" within Israel, which is introduced by the "verb of saying" λέγω οὖν ("I say/ask then"). The second is found in 11:7-10 and deals with the failure of Israel to obtain righteousness, which is introduced by an abbreviated rhetorical question τί οὖν; ("What then?"). In setting out each of these presentations, Paul

---

10. Cf., e.g., Sanday and Headlam, *Romans,* 307; Schlier, *Römerbrief,* 320-21; Michel, *An die Römer,* 337; Barrett, *Romans,* 206; Cranfield, *Romans,* 2.542; Kuss, *Römerbrief,* 3.784; Wilckens, *An die Römer,* 2.234-35; Dunn, *Romans,* 2:632-34; and Moo, *Romans,* 670-71.

first states his position (doing so rather expansively for the first topic; briefly for the second) and then supports what he has written with materials drawn from the Jewish (OT) Scriptures — though in the first presentation he goes further to highlight at its conclusion his main point: that "at this present time (ἐν τῷ νῦν καιρῷ) a remnant (λεῖμμα) selected by [God's] grace (κατ᾽ ἐκλογὴν χάριτος) continues to exist (γέγονεν)."

11:1-2a The verb of saying λέγω ("I say," "speak," "ask"), coupled with the inferential particle οὖν ("then"), establishes a link between what Paul said earlier in 10:14-21 with respect to the spiritual condition of the great majority of the people of Israel and what he proclaims here in 11:1-2a regarding God's reaction to his people's failure to respond positively to his sending of his Son, Israel's promised Messiah. He does this in good epistolary fashion by connecting this use of a "verb of saying" here in 11:1a with the two earlier uses of a "verb of saying" in 10:18 and 19. Yet, while a connection exists between what Paul writes in 11:1-6 and what he had written immediately before in 10:14-21, the discussions of these two passages have to do with quite diametrically opposed responses: the first passage in 10:14-21 (in response to the questions, "Did they not hear?" and "Did Israel not understand?"), which, by its use of the interrogative particle μή followed by the negative particle οὐ, suggests in idiomatic fashion the positive response, "Of course they did!"; the second here in 11:1-6 (in response to the question, "Did God reject his people [totally]?"), which, by its use of the single negative particle μή, calls for a negative response of "No!" This negative response is highlighted by the fervently expressed and quite emotionally charged negative phrase that immediately follows: μὴ γένοιτο ("Let it not be!"; or, more colloquially, "By no means!" or "Certainly not!").[11]

Paul, as a true Israelite ('Ισραηλίτης),[12] could never say that God has totally rejected the people of Israel. In proof of such a conviction, he cites his own national and spiritual heritage:

1. He is a true "Israelite," that is, a person who not only believes in the one and only true God and acknowledges that God has revealed himself through his "Instructions" (Torah) given to his people through Moses, but has also responded to God's love, grace, and mercy as expressed in the ministry, teaching, and saving work of Jesus Christ — and so by faith has come to God through the work of Jesus of Nazareth, God's promised Messiah, and the continued ministry of the Holy Spirit, with the result that he or she has received from God his gift of righteousness.

---

11. For another nine uses of this dramatic negative expression μὴ γένοιτο in Romans, see 3:4, 6, 31; 6:2, 15; 7:7, 13; 9:14 (i.e., before its appearance here in 11:1) and 11:11 (i.e., after its appearance in 11:1). The expression is found elsewhere in Paul's letters only in 1 Cor 6:15 and in Gal 2:17; 3:21 (perhaps also 6:14); elsewhere in the NT it appears only in Luke 20:16. For a somewhat more extensive treatment of the expression, see our exegetical comments on Rom 3:4.

12. The appellation "Israelite" ('Ισραηλίτης) appears only twice in Romans, earlier in 9:4 and here in 11:1. For a discussion of its significance, see our exegetical comments on 9:4.

2. He is a "descendant of Abraham," the great patriarch of the people of Israel to whom God gave his irrevocable promises.
3. He is a member of "the tribe of Benjamin," which, as James Denney has rightly pointed out, was "the one tribe with which Judah mainly represented the post-exilic theocratic people."[13]

In 11:2a Paul repeats the essence of the conviction he had just expressed in 11:1, doing so in summary fashion by the following affirmation: "God did not reject [totally] his people, whom he foreknew!"[14] It is possible to understand the nature of the first part of this affirmation in any of five ways:

1. As a biblical quotation, with certain slight redactional alterations, of 1 Sam 12:22a (LXX 1 Kgdms 12:22a) and/or Ps 94:14a (LXX Ps 93:14a): "For the Lord will not reject [totally] his people."[15]
2. As an "allusive evocation" or "contextual echo" of either (or both) of these two OT passages.[16]
3. As a Jewish and/or Jewish Christian "aphorism" based on either (or both) of these two OT passages.
4. As a Jewish and/or Jewish Christian confessional portion that had been formulated on the basis of either (or both) of these two OT passages.
5. As an affirmation composed by Paul himself, without any conscious dependence on either (or both) of these two OT passages.

It is obviously true that very little difference of meaning, if any, would occur if one accepted one or another of the foregoing understandings. Yet it is somewhat difficult to argue that Paul is here quoting directly from either 1 Sam 12:22 or Ps 94:14 (or both), since he does not introduce that affirmation by any introductory formula, phrase, or statement — as he does immediately following in 11:2b when quoting material from the story of the prophet Elijah in the OT ("Don't you know what the Scripture says?") and as he does a few verses later in 11:8a ("As it is written") and then in 11:9a ("And David says").[17] It is possible to

---

13. Denney, *Romans*, 2.676. Joachim Jeremias, in his *Jerusalem in the Time of Jesus*, 275-83, has demonstrated that many Jews in the time of Jesus (and Paul) knew their tribal identities and cherished them.

14. Cf. the contrast of Peter's declaration in Acts 3:23, which uses the very strong verb ἐξολεθρευθήσεται ("destroy utterly," "root out"): "Anyone who does not listen to him [i.e., to Jesus, 'the prophet whom the Lord your God will raise up for you from among your own people'] will be completely cut off from the people [of God] (ἐξολεθρευθήσεται ἐκ τοῦ λαοῦ)" — which declaration, drawn from the LXX reading of Deut 18:19, was probably read by some early Gentile Christians in an anti-Jewish fashion.

15. As witness the bold type for the statement οὐκ ἀπώσατο ὁ θεὸς τὸν λαὸν αὐτοῦ in the Nestle-Aland Greek text; cf. also, e.g., Dunn, *Romans*, 2.636.

16. As Hays has argued in his *Echoes of Scripture*, 68-70.

17. And as Paul does a number of times elsewhere in Romans, as well as in some of his other NT letters (cf., e.g., R. N. Longenecker, *Biblical Exegesis*, 2nd ed., 92-95).

understand this affirmation of 11:2a not as a direct biblical quotation but rather, as Richard Hays has proposed, as an "allusive evocation" or "contextual echo" of either (or both) of these two OT passages — in which case it would not require any introductory formula, phrase, or statement.

More likely, however, Paul is here employing a Jewish and/or Jewish Christian aphorism that was based on either (or both) of these two OT passages — which aphorism he knew his earlier audience (perhaps, as we have postulated, the ethnically mixed believers in Jesus at Syrian Antioch) and his Christian addressees at Rome (whatever their particular ethnicities) would accept and appreciate as true. So we propose that here in this first part of 11:2a, in response to the rhetorical question, "Did God [entirely] reject his people?" Paul expresses a widely known aphorism drawn originally from either 1 Sam 12:22 or Ps 94:14 (or both): "God did not reject his people!" The apostle's pattern of response here appears to be very much like what he employed earlier in 2:2, where he supported his argument by citing the aphorism "God's condemnation of those who do such things is based on truth," and also like that a few verses later in 2:11, where he cites the aphorism "There is no favoritism with God." Further, a rather close parallel to such a usage can be found in 2:6-10, where Paul used for the same purpose what appears to be early Christian confessional, devotional, and/or catechetical materials — and likewise a few verses later in 2:14-15, where he seems to have used catechetical materials that evidently had been originally composed in a Jewish and/or a Jewish Christian milieu.[18]

Paul's reference to "those whom he [God] foreknew (ὅν προέγνω)" in the second part of 11:2a picks up on his wording "those he [God] foreknew (οὕς προέγνω)" in the first part of 8:29. In that earlier use in 8:29, the term "foreknown" appears at the beginning of his list of five highly important spiritual stages in a believer's life, that is, "foreknown," "predestined," "called," "justified," and "glorified," which he enumerated in 8:29-30. So it may legitimately be claimed: (1) that the word "foreknown" in 8:29, at the head of that list, was intended by the apostle to function as the caption or heading for those vitally important spiritual realities in the lives of God's people, and (2) that the word "foreknown" here in 11:2a should be viewed as triggering that whole complex of matters having to do with "foreknown," "predestined," "called," "justified," and "glorified" that appeared in 8:29. Thus, in adding the phrase "whom he foreknew" to the biblically based aphorism "God did not reject [totally] his people," the apostle is most likely affirming that since the people of Israel have always been extensively involved in God's program of salvation history — and, just as importantly, since they *continue to be so involved* — God cannot have totally rejected them.

11:2b-6 Paul goes on to cite in support of his affirmation that "God did not reject [totally] his people" the passages about Elijah's despair in 1 Kgs 19:10 and 14 ("Lord, they have killed your prophets and torn down your altars; I am

18. See our earlier exegetical comments on these passages in ch. 2 of the letter.

the only one left, and they are trying to kill me") — as well as, of course, the passage relating God's response in 1 Kgs 19:18 ("Yet I have reserved for myself seven thousand in Israel whose knees have not bowed down to Baal and whose mouths have not kissed him").[19] These passages directly support the apostle's remnant theology. So he speaks expressly in 11:5 of there being "at this present time (ἐν τῷ νῦν καιρῷ) a remnant (λεῖμμα) selected by [God's] grace (κατ' ἐκλογὴν χάριτος)," which remnant of God's people "continues to exist (γέγονεν)"[20] — that is, that true Israelites *continue to exist* within the corporate body of national Israel. There can be no doubt that he had here in mind principally those Jews who had acknowledged Jesus as God's promised Messiah — as well as those Jews who would do so in the future. But it also seems likely from his broadly worded references to "the remnant" in 9:6-18 and 9:22-24 and to "the Gentiles" in 9:30 — as well as from his quotations of Hosea and Isaiah that he used in support of those references to "the remnant" in 9:25-26 and 10:20 — that Paul left to God the more difficult and perplexing questions having to do with the hearts, minds, and commitments of other "remnant people" (as known to God alone) who resided not only within the nation of Israel but also among the Gentiles.[21]

The two-part statement of 11:6 ("And if by grace, then it is no longer by works; if it were, grace would no longer be grace") has seemed to some ancient scribes, as well as to a number of textual critics today, to be somewhat extraneous to Paul's discussion — and therefore could be omitted or would require certain textual emendations (see "Textual Notes" above). But neither the omission of this statement nor its proposed "corrections" are supported by the evidence of the better MSS. Further, as Bruce Metzger has pointed out: "There appears to be no reason why, if the words were original, they should have been deleted. The existence of several forms of the addition likewise throws doubt upon the originality of any of them."[22]

What Paul is evidently doing here in 11:6 is highlighting a matter that

19. Paul's elliptical use in 11:2b of the phrase ἐν Ἠλίᾳ ("in [the passage about] Elijah") is similar to his use in 9:25a of the phrase ἐν τῷ Ὡσηέ ("in [the book] of Hosea"). See also Mark 1:2: ἐν τῷ Ἠσαΐᾳ τῷ προθήτῃ ("in [the book] of Isaiah the prophet").

20. Γέγονεν is in form a third-person singular, perfect, indicative verb (from γίνομαι, "born," "come about," "exist"), and so suggests both a past presence and a continuing existence.

21. Paul's attitude on such matters is very much like that of Peter in Acts 10:34-35 when he was faced by the situation of God's acceptance of the Roman centurion Cornelius: "Now I realize how true it is that God does not show favoritism (προσωπολήμπτης), but accepts those from every nation who fear him and do what is right." See also Peter's quotation in Acts 11:9 of the words of God to him in his explanation to the believers at Jerusalem of what took place at Caesarea: "Do not call anything impure that God has made clean." Further, note Peter's conclusion in Acts 11:17 regarding the significance of that Caesarean event: "So if God gave them [i.e., Cornelius, his family, and his friends] the same gift as he gave us who believed in the Lord Jesus Christ, who was I to think that I could stand in God's way?" Note, as well, Paul's statement in Rom 2:10-11: "Glory, honor and peace for everyone who does good: first for the Jew, then for the Gentile. 'For God does not show favoritism' (προσωπολημψία)."

22. Metzger, *Textual Commentary*, 464.

he made central earlier in the letter — that is, anyone who is accepted by God is accepted on the basis of God's grace (χάρις) and not on the basis of his or her own works (ἔργα).[23] And he is affirming again this central truth in quite a summary fashion. Further, it may be surmised that what the apostle writes in this verse reflects by its elliptical style the form of his earlier oral preaching and teaching — perhaps, as we have postulated, the apostle's earlier preaching and teaching at Syrian Antioch.

11:7-10 The abbreviated rhetorical question τί οὖν; ("What then?") identifies the beginning of the second part of this first subsection of material in 11:1-10. And here in 11:7 Paul speaks to the implicit question that would inevitably arise explicitly with respect to his exposition on "the remnant," with that question being expressed elliptically in the quite direct two-word query "What then?" If this query were spelled out more expansively, it would read: If at this present time there is a remnant selected by God's grace (as stated in 11:5), *what then* is to be said about "the others" of Israel who are not among "the remnant" selected by God? Paul's answer is also given in a very abbreviated and summary fashion: "What Israel is seeking, it failed to obtain; but those selected [by God] obtained it, whereas the others were hardened" — thereby bringing together in this one verse of 11:7 the essence of what the apostle had said in 9:6-29 about "the remnant" and in 9:30–10:21 about what we have captioned "Israel's present situation of unbelief."

Having set out a summary of his earlier teaching regarding "the remnant" and "the others," Paul goes on in 11:8-10 to defend his response to the implied question, "What then about 'the others' (i.e., those who are not 'the remnant' among the people of Israel)?" by citing passages from the three main divisions of the Hebrew canon — from "the Law" (quoting Deut 29:4), from "the Prophets" (quoting Isa 29:10), and from "the Writings" (quoting Ps 69:22-23). In so doing, he seeks in typical Jewish fashion to demonstrate how all the Jewish (OT) Scriptures speak with one voice regarding "the others" within Israel who have refused to respond to God as his believing "remnant" people.

The first OT quotation that Paul sets out, in 11:8, is a conflated quotation drawn from both Deut 29:4 and Isa 29:10. Its basic structure, as well as most of its wording, is taken from Deut 29:4, which is part of the exhortations Moses gave to the people of Israel after their "wilderness wanderings" and before they crossed over the Jordan River to take possession of "the promised land": "God gave them [i.e., 'the people of Israel'] a spirit of stupor, eyes so that they could not see and ears so that they could not hear, to this very day." The leading sentence of this conflated quotation, however, is taken from Isa 29:10, which declares that "the Lord has made you [i.e., 'the people of Israel'] to drink 'a spirit of stupor'" (LXX πνεύματι κατανύξεως, "a spirit of deep sleep") — and goes on to speak of the people's "eyes" and "the eyes of their prophets and their rulers" being "closed" by God to the significance of his working. The resemblances be-

---

23. Cf. esp. Rom 3:21-24 and 5:1-2.

tween Deut 29:4 and Isa 29:10 regarding the people's "stupor" (or "deep sleep"), their "closed eyes," and their failure to understand God's working in the course of salvation history were evidently what first brought these two OT passages together among Jewish and/or early Jewish Christian teachers. So Paul declares in summary fashion — conflating these two highly significant declarations from the great Jewish lawgiver Moses and from the great Jewish prophet Isaiah — that the Jewish people in his day are in a spiritual stupor, with eyes that are closed to God's present working in the course of his salvation history by means of the proclamation of the Christian gospel.

The second OT passage quoted, which appears in 11:9-10, is drawn from Ps 69:22-23: "May the table set before them become a snare; may it become retribution and a trap. May their eyes be darkened so they cannot see, and their backs be bent forever." In all likelihood, this passage was joined by the apostle (or, perhaps, by Jewish believers in Jesus before him) to the previous conflated passages from Deut 29:4 and Isa 29:10 simply on the basis of the similar expressions "darkened eyes," "closed eyes," and "spirit of stupor [or, 'deep sleep']" — without giving any particular attention to the imagery of "a table set before them" or "their backs bent forever." Evidently all that Paul wanted to affirm by his quotations of these biblical passages in 11:8-10 was that the people of Israel, because of their spiritual stupor and spiritual blindness, have failed to obtain the gift of God's righteousness — as declared (1) by Moses, the great Jewish lawgiver, (2) by Isaiah, the great Jewish prophet, and (3) by David, the great Jewish king.

II. The "Stumbling" of Israel, the "Reconciliation" of Believing Gentiles, and the Interaction of These Matters in the Overall Purpose and Plan of God (11:11-24)

Having spoken in summary fashion about the continuing presence of a "remnant" within Israel (11:1-7), and then about God having hardened "the others" of the Jewish people who refused his promised Messiah (11:8-10), Paul now sets out in 11:11-24 the second subsection of Part III of his three-part exposition of 9:6–11:32. Here in 11:11-24 he deals principally with matters having to do with (1) the "stumbling of Israel" (in 11:11-12), (2) the "reconciliation of the world," by which he evidently means the salvation of believing Gentiles, that is, a "remnant" from among the Gentiles (in 11:13-16), and (3) the interaction of these two important features in the overall purpose and plan of God (in 11:17-24). He relates this three-part discussion of 11:11-24 with what he had just written in 11:1-10, (1) by using the epistolary expression λέγω οὖν ("I say/ask then") in 11:11 that he had earlier used in 11:1, thereby signaling a connection between the two passages, and (2) by employing two "verb of saying" epistolary expressions in an anaphoric rhetorical fashion, thereby suggesting that there will be certain developments presented in this second set of statements of 11:11-24 over and beyond what had been stated in the first set of 11:1-10.

11:11-12 With respect to the "stumbling of Israel," Paul declares the following four vitally important points:

1. Israel's "stumbling" does not mean that the people of Israel have fallen "beyond recovery"; it does not mean that the nation's "fall" from God's grace is to be understood as permanent. To such an idea the apostle responds immediately in 11:11 with a highly emotional and entirely negative expression μὴ γένοιτο ("Certainly not!"), which he had employed in 11:1b. Later in this chapter he will declare in 11:25-27, contrary to any idea of a permanent fall, that the people of Israel have experienced a "partial hardening," which will be rectified when "the full number of the Gentiles has come in" and "all Israel will be saved."
2. Israel's rejection of its God-given Messiah, which the apostle refers to as "their transgression" (τῷ αὐτῶν παραπτώματι), has been ordained by God as a factor in bringing "salvation" to the Gentiles.
3. God's acceptance of believing Gentiles has been ordained by God so as "to make Israel jealous" (εἰς τὸ παραζηλῶσαι αὐτούς).
4. If at this present time God is blessing "remnant" people who exist within Israel and among the Gentiles, "how much greater riches will Israel's fullness bring about" (πόσῳ μᾶλλον τὸ πλήρωμα αὐτῶν)!

There is in 11:11-12, however, no thought of God's promises, which had been given to the people of Israel, being redirected (or "transferred") in this present epoch of salvation history to the Christian church, which is understood as "the true, spiritual Israel." Nor had there been any such suggestion in the previous passage of 11:1-10, and certainly no such idea appears in what follows in 11:13-27. The assertion that God's promises have been redirected from the nation of Israel to the Christian church, and so from the Jewish people to believing Gentiles, was stated explicitly by Justin Martyr (c. 100-165), the first great Christian apologist of the postapostolic period, in his *Dialogue with Trypho,* which purports to be a two-day "discussion" between the Gentile Christian Justin, who before his conversion to Christ was a pagan thinker, and a learned Jewish rabbi named "Trypho." Each debater attempts to convince the other of the legitimacy of his position, though, of course, Justin's position is presented as being the only true understanding: "We [i.e., Gentile believers in the Christian church] are the true spiritual Israel!"[24] Such a claim for the transferal of God's promises also appears in a number of other early Christian writings.[25] Further, it has been assumed by many Christian interpreters down through the centuries — whether patristic, Roman Catholic, Eastern Orthodox, or Protestant.

---

24. Justin Martyr, *Dialogue* 11.5; see also 121.4–122.1.

25. So, e.g., *1 Clement* 29:1-3; 30:1; 59:4; *2 Clement* 2:3; *Apocalypse of Peter* 2; Ignatius, *To the Magnesians* 8:1-2; 10:2-3; *Epistle of Barnabas* 4:8; 14:1, 5; 10:12; *Didascalia* 6.5.4-8.

The claim that the Christian church is "the true, spiritual Israel" has frequently been based on the final words of Paul's benediction to his Gentile converts in Gal 6:16: "Peace and mercy be on all those who will follow this rule, *even on the Israel of God.*"[26] But, as W. D. Davies has noted: "If this proposal were correct one would expect to find support for it in Rom. ix–xi where Paul extensively deals with 'Israel' "[27] — particularly here in 11:11-12, but also in the immediately following verses of 11:13-32. Such biblical support, however, is lacking, not only in Paul's letter to Rome but also in his other NT letters.[28]

Respect and honor for those who have gone before us — especially for the church's teachers down through the past twenty centuries — are entirely proper. For we are all as Christians heavily indebted to those who have been our spiritual parents and instructors. In large measure we "stand on one another's shoulders" in our perceptions and our developments of the church's traditional understandings. Yet, while we have profited immensely from our Christian heritage, we have also found it necessary, at times, to recognize the failures of our "fathers" (whether male or female) and our respected teachers — and to forgive their blunders (which is a response that we hope those who follow us will also express as they remember our lives and work). In this case it cannot be said, as a rather large number of interpreters of the Christian proclamation down through the centuries have held, that Paul in Rom 9–11 is redirecting (or "transferring") God's promises, which had been given originally to the people of Israel, to believers in Jesus and the Christian church, which new body of people he considered to be "the true, spiritual Israel" — and, as has also been all too often erroneously thought, leaving to the Jews God's words of judgment and his curses on sin.

Rather, what Paul is doing throughout Rom 9–11, and particularly here in 11:11-12 and in the immediately following paragraphs of 11:13-27, is highlighting the relationship that exists between "the remnant within Israel" and a corresponding "remnant among the Gentiles" — both of whom have responded (and will in the future respond) "by faith" to the love, mercy, and grace of God as expressed in the person and work of Jesus of Nazareth and the ministry of God's Holy Spirit. It is a message that acknowledges that the people of Israel have "stumbled" badly — in fact, that they have "fallen" from God's favor in their rejection of Jesus, God's promised Messiah, which rejection constitutes their primary "transgression" (τὸ παράπτωμα αὐτῶν) against

26. Cf. also 1 Pet 2:9-10: "You are a chosen people, a royal priesthood, a holy nation, a people belonging to God, that you may declare the praises of him who called you out of darkness into his wonderful light. Once you were not a people, but now you are the people of God; once you had not attained mercy, but now you have received mercy."

27. W. D. Davies, "Paul and the People of Israel," *NTS* 24 (1977) 10-11 n. 2.

28. For a highly significant treatment of this bogus motif, which is often claimed as being present in Rom 9–11, see Richardson, *Israel in the Apostolic Church,* 76-80. On Paul's use of "the Israel of God" in Gal 6:16, see Burton, *Galatians,* 357-58, and Dahl, "Der Name Israel," 161-70. Note also R. N. Longenecker, *Galatians,* 296-99.

God. But it is also a message that expresses the certainty that the people of Israel have not stumbled and fallen "beyond recovery" (ἵνα πέσωσιν). For the apostle expresses in 11:11-12 confidence in the following two matters having to do with the spiritually fallen people of Israel: (1) that "because of their transgression, salvation has come to the Gentiles to make Israel jealous" (11:11), and (2) that "if their transgression means riches for the world and their loss means riches for the Gentiles, how much greater riches will their fullness bring about" (11:12)!

Just how God's salvation to the Gentiles will bring about a "righteous jealousy" on the part of the people of Israel, and just how Israel will again experience its promised spiritual riches, Paul does not say in any explicit fashion. Later in this same subsection of material he will speak about repentant Israelites being "grafted into their own olive tree," for "God is able to graft them in again" (in 11:23-24); then in the following three verses he will go on to talk about a future time when "all Israel will be saved" (in 11:25-27). But all these statements in 11:11-27 are proclamation statements, which express the apostle's God-given confidence about the future — and thus seem intended only to inspire confidence about God's dealings with the people of Israel in the future, but not to spell out any cause-and-effect relationships or speak in such detail as interpreters today with their analytical minds might desire.

What Paul writes in 11:11-12 is most likely an important part of the message he had earlier proclaimed in his preaching and teaching to believing Jews and believing Gentiles in Syrian Antioch (as we have speculated), which he here incorporates into his letter to the Christians at Rome (whose congregations included both ethnic Jews and ethnic Gentiles, with the latter being more prominent). The apostle is not, however, attempting in this passage — nor in what immediately precedes or follows it — to spell out a connection that exists between the nation of Israel and the Christian church. And he is certainly not presenting any thesis regarding the redirection or transferal of God's promises from Israel to the Christian church. Rather, he is highlighting the disconnect that exists between believing Gentiles, who have experienced "reconciliation" with God, and unbelieving Jews, who have experienced "rejection" by God. And he is proclaiming the essential oneness that exists between "the remnant within Israel" and "the remnant from among the Gentiles" — with that connection between these two groups of "remnant" people, as well as a consciousness of their oneness, displacing all ethnic differences and all former orientations of both thought and lifestyle.

11:13-15 In this short paragraph of three verses,[29] Paul introduces what

---

29. Some translations (e.g., RSV, NRSV, NIV, and TNIV) and some commentators (e.g., C. H. Dodd, *Romans*, 173; Schreiner, *Romans*, 592, 603) insert a paragraph division between 11:16 and 11:17 (as do *NA*[27] and UBS[4]). Other translations (e.g., TEV and NJB) and most other commentators (e.g., Godet, *Romans*, 2.244; Sanday and Headlam, *Romans*, 319; Michel, *An die Römer*, 344; Käsemann, *Romans*, 307; Wilckens, *An die Römer*, 2.241; Murray, *Romans*, 2.84; Moo, *Romans*, 696-97; and Jewett, *Romans*, 666) view the division of paragraphs as occurring between 11:15 and

will follow more fully in diatribe form in 11:17-24. Notable in 11:13-15 are the following features:

1. The paragraph begins with the second-person plural pronoun of direct address "you" (ὑμῖν) in 11:13, which is a feature that closely resembles the use of "you" (whether singular or plural) in a Greek *diatribe*. Further, the second-person singular pronoun "you" (σύ, σέ, and σοῦ) appears a number of times, coupled once by the second-person singular perfect verbal suffix (-ας), throughout the materials that follow in 11:17-24.

2. There is a repeated use of the common connective particle δέ ("but," "and," "for," or "now"), which began in 11:12 (εἰ δέ, "*but* if"), is prominent here in 11:13 (ὑμῖν δὲ λέγω, "*now* I am speaking to you"), and continues on throughout the two following paragraphs in 11:16 (εἰ δέ, "*for* if"), 11:17 (εἰ δέ, "*but* if" or "*now* if"), 11:18 (εἰ δέ, "*but* if"), and 11:23 (δέ ἐάν, "*and* if"). These somewhat varied uses of δέ suggest that all of 11:11-24 should be understood as a connected body of material on basically the same topic.

3. Paul employs in this paragraph the expression μὲν οὖν (literally "indeed then"; idiomatically "in truth"), which is well attested in the Greek textual tradition (see "Textual Notes" above). Μὲν οὖν is what A. T. Robertson has referred to as "the old idiom," which "survived best in the vernacular and in poetry"[30] — but which seems to have been inscrutable to a number of later scribes, and therefore replaced with a more literary expression or simply eliminated.[31]

4. The apostle's earnest desire was that his Gentile mission would be used by God "to somehow" (or "in some way") arouse the Jews of his day ("my own people") "to envy" and so "save some of them." His use of the enclitic particle πως ("somehow," "in some way," "perhaps"), however, suggests that he was not sure just how such an arousing of the Jews would (or "could") come about. Nonetheless, his desire remained constant that God would in some way use his mission to pagan Gentiles as a factor in bringing about a positive response by the people of Israel to the message of the Christian gospel.

11:16. The latter position is the better of the two, simply because the metaphors of 11:16 (i.e., "first-fruits" and "the whole batch," which is followed by "root" and "the branches") are closely related in Paul's argument to his use of similar metaphors in 11:17-24 (i.e., "the natural branches" and "the engrafted wild branches") and in 11:24 (i.e., "a wild olive tree" and "a domestic olive tree"). Yet, since Paul's aphoristic use of the metaphors of 11:16 is so distinctly his own (as will be proposed in what follows), these two statements are probably best viewed as constituting a separate paragraph that expresses the essence of the apostle's proclamation in metaphorical fashion (as our translation above treats them).

30. *ATRob,* 1151.

31. Such an older and more prominent use of μὲν οὖν in "the vernacular and in poetry" suggests an earlier oral provenance for the apostle's statement here in 11:13b: "Inasmuch as I am *in truth* the apostle to the Gentiles."

5. Paul characterized the situation of the majority of Jews of his day with the word "rejection" (ἀποβολή; as used in the phrase ἡ ἀποβολὴ αὐτῶν, "the rejection of them") — which condition, though he insisted earlier in 11:1-6 and 11:11-12 that it was not total or permanent, is certainly spiritually serious and sadly quite terrible.

6. Paul characterized the situation of believers in Jesus, God's promised Messiah, with the word "reconciliation" (καταλλαγή; i.e., in the phrase καταλλαγὴ κόσμου, "the reconciliation of the world"). This is the same term he used in 5:10-11 to characterize the situation of people who respond positively to God, whether ethnic Jews or ethnic Gentiles — and which he also had used in 2 Corinthians in speaking of the essential nature of God's salvation and of the essence of his own ministry and message (principally, of course, to Gentiles, but also to Jews).

7. Paul's earnest desire for his compatriot Jews was that they would ultimately experience "life from the dead," which he hoped would "somehow" or "in some way" come about through his ministry to Gentiles when "the full number of the Gentiles has come in" (11:25) — yet more importantly, as he will proclaim in 11:26-27, that he was convinced the people of Israel would experience when "the deliverer will come from Zion and will turn godlessness away from Jacob" and "all Israel will be saved."

11:16 In the context of his earlier statement in 11:5 that *"a remnant"* (λεῖμμα) "having been *chosen* by [God's] grace" (κατ᾽ ἐκλογὴν χάριτος) "continues to exist" (γέγονεν) — which is followed by the apostle's phraseology in 11:7: *"those chosen* obtained ['righteousness']" (ἡ ἐκλογὴ ἐπέτυχεν) — Paul's metaphorical statements here in 11:16 should be understood as carrying on that discussion of God's "chosen remnant" by (1) highlighting the inseparable connection that exists between "the remnant within Israel" and "a remnant among the Gentiles" and (2) proclaiming the essential oneness of these two groups of "remnant" people. This verse "does not," as Ernst Käsemann has rightly observed, "express a strong sense of Jewishness"[32] — that is, it does not speak of a direct identity that exists between the Christian church and Israel. Rather, because of its context, it must be viewed as expressing Paul's own distinctive thesis regarding how matters stand before God with respect to "a remnant among the Gentiles" vis-à-vis "the remnant within Israel." Thus, while he employs imagery that is drawn from the OT Scriptures, Paul's use of that imagery here in 11:16 should not be viewed as speaking about connections between the Christian church and Israel, but, rather, as highlighting the connections and the oneness that exist with respect to "a remnant among the Gentiles" vis-à-vis "the remnant within Israel."

The first of these aphoristic statements in 11:16 ("If the part of the dough

---

32. Cf. Käsemann, *Romans*, 307 (citing in support the understanding of E. Kühl in his 1913 commentary *Der Brief des Paulus an die Römer*).

offered as firstfruits is holy, then the whole batch is holy!") recalls instructions given by God to Moses in Num 15:18-21:

> When you enter the land into which I bring you, then it shall come to pass, when you eat of the bread of the land, that you shall separate a wave-offering, a special offering to the Lord, the "firstfruits" (ἀπαρχήν) of your dough. You shall offer your bread as a heave-offering: as a heave-offering from the threshing floor, so shall you separate it — even the "firstfruits" (ἀπαρχήν) of your dough — and you shall give the Lord a heave-offering throughout your generations.[33]

The second statement ("If the root is holy, so are the branches!") employs imagery that was used in Jewish writings, both canonical and postbiblical, with respect to the spiritual situations of people — as, for example, in:

> Job 18:16: "His [i.e., 'a wicked person's'] roots dry up below and his branches wither above."

> Sir 40:15: "A branch that springs from violence has no tender twig, for an impious root is on the point of a crag [i.e., 'is on a sharp fragment of rock, which possesses no nourishment']."[34]

Yet, while the imagery of "firstfruits," "the whole batch [of dough]," "the root," and "the branches" was undoubtedly familiar to his first-century hearers and readers, Paul's use of this imagery has frequently been viewed as being difficult to understand. Origen and many of the early Church Fathers understood "the firstfruits" and "the root" as speaking of Christ, whose own "holiness" guarantees blessings for his people — with "the whole batch" and "the branches" understood as those united with Christ and therefore members of his body, the Christian church universal.[35] Many Christian interpreters down through the centuries have agreed with them, as do many today.[36]

Other Church Fathers, however, as well as most commentators today, have understood the metaphors of "firstfruits" and "root" as having in mind the patriarchs of Israel (whether all three or Abraham alone) — with "the whole

---

33. See also Lev 23:14: "You must not eat any bread, whether baked or new grain, until the day you bring this offering to your God. This is to be a lasting ordinance for the generations to come, wherever you live!" Note Josephus, *Antiquities* 4.70: "The [Jewish] people are required to offer to God firstfruits (ἀπαρχήν) of all the produce of the soil"; cf. Philo, *De specialibus legibus* 1.27-28.

34. For additional uses of the imagery of "root" and "branches" in canonical and postbiblical passages, see, e.g., Jer 17:8; Hos 9:16; Sir 1:20.

35. Origen, *Ad Romanos* 8.11 (*PG* 14.1193); see also Theodore of Mopsuestia, *Ad Romanos*, *PG* 66.858.

36. So today, e.g., P. von der Osten-Sacken, *Christian-Jewish Dialogue: Theological Foundations* (Philadelphia: Fortress, 1986), 106-7; Elizabeth E. Johnson, *The Function of Apocalyptic and Wisdom Traditions in Romans 9–11*, SBL.DS 109 (Atlanta: Scholars, 1989), 90.

batch" and "the branches" referring to Israel onto which the Christian church has been grafted.[37] Such understandings have frequently been based exegetically on the facts that (1) earlier in 9:5 the apostle evidenced that he was particularly interested in the patriarchs of Israel as being very important foundational persons in Israel's history, and (2) only a few verses after these statements of 11:16 he will speak in 11:28 of the people of Israel being "loved on account of the patriarchs." It is this understanding that has been dominant throughout most of Christian history — with a number of contemporary commentators pointing out that in some postbiblical Jewish writings the patriarchs of Israel (whether all three or only one) are referred to as "the root" or "a plant of righteousness" for all the generations of the earth.[38]

However, a few interpreters of 11:16 have viewed Paul's metaphors of "firstfruits" and "root" as being in continuity with — and therefore as carrying on — his references to "a remnant chosen ('selected' or 'elected') by [God's] grace" in 11:5 and to "those chosen ('selected' or 'elected')" in 11:7. So they have understood "firstfruits" and "root" as having in mind a believing "remnant within Israel."[39] Further, some within this rather small group of interpreters have attempted to combine two or more of the various understandings of these metaphors in somewhat different ways — as does, for example, Joseph Fitzmyer in his endeavor to "divide the images," with "the first handful of dough representing the 'remnant,' which has already accepted Christ, and the root representing the 'patriarchs,' especially Abraham."[40]

Obviously, there is an extensive degree of disagreement among interpreters today about what exactly Paul meant in these two metaphorical statements of 11:16. Certainly there can be little doubt that in other contexts the apostle could (1) speak of Jesus Christ as the basis for the new lives of Christians, (2) refer to God's covenantal relations with Israel as providing a paradigm for his relations with believers in Jesus, and (3) highlight Abraham as the example par excellence of faith. It may be rather easy, therefore, to view Christ, Israel, and/ or Abraham — or some combination of these important prototypical people or features — as being in some vital ways "the firstfruits" and "the root" of the religious experience of Christians.

Here in the context of Rom 11, however, where Paul explicates his understanding of relations between "the remnant of Israel" and "the remnant among Gentiles," he uses these metaphors of "firstfruits," "the whole batch," "the root,"

---

37. So Chrysostom, *Homilia XXXII ad Romanos*, PG 60.588; see also, e.g., Godet, *Romans,* 2.244-45; Cranfield, *Romans,* vol. 2 on 11:16; and Moo, *Romans,* 700-701.

38. See, e.g., *Jub* 21:24 (Abraham's words to his son Isaac); *1 En* 93:5 (Enoch's prophecy regarding God's election of Abraham); Philo, *Quis rerum divinarum heres sit* 279 (in speaking about Abraham).

39. So, particularly, B. Weiss, *An die Römer,* 4th ed., on 11:16; Kühl, *An die Römer,* 385; and Barrett, *Romans,* 216-17 — though with that remnant within Israel usually seen as "the pledge of the eventual salvation of all Israel" (quoting Barrett, 216).

40. Fitzmyer, *Romans,* 614.

and "the branches" (1) to highlight the inseparable connection that exists between "the remnant within Israel" and "the remnant among Gentiles," (2) to proclaim the intrinsic oneness of these two groups of "remnant" people, and (3) to announce that in God's eyes both groups of remnant people possess the quality of "holiness" (ἄγια) as a gift from God — which gift alters entirely their standing before God and is meant to dramatically affect their lifestyles and their relations with others.[41]

11:17-24 In the final paragraphs of this subsection of material, Paul "goes off at a word" with respect to the metaphors of "root" and "branches" (which he had just used in his statement of 11:16), refashioning these metaphors somewhat in his statements of this passage in order to warn the believing "remnant among the Gentiles" (i.e., the "engrafted branches") against any adverse attitudes or actions expressed toward the "remnant within Israel" (i.e., toward those "natural branches" who, because of their positive response to Jesus, remained firmly connected to their God-ordained "root" and "stock"). It may be conjectured that some Gentile Christians of Paul's day looked disparagingly on those Jews who had accepted Jesus of Nazareth as Israel's promised Messiah, but who had incorporated (at least in the opinion of those Gentile believers) far too much Jewish "baggage" into their Christian experience — as did, for example, the second-century Gentile Christian teacher Marcion, who came to prominence in the small town of Sinope, in the Roman province of Pontus in northeastern Asia Minor. Further, it may be speculated that certain disparaging attitudes toward Jews who believed in Jesus were present, as well, among some of the believing Gentiles in the Christian congregations at Rome — as seen in the fact that Paul had to admonish his addressees in Romans with regard to relations between "the Strong" and "the Weak" in 14:1–15:12. Further, it may be assumed that certain disparaging attitudes (perhaps even certain adverse actions) were expressed by some of the Gentile "Christ followers" against Jewish believers in Jesus in the Christian congregations of Syrian Antioch — if, as we have postulated, the message of these verses had been earlier proclaimed by Paul in his yearlong ministry of preaching and teaching in that great metropolitan city.

The apostle expresses his warning to believing Gentiles, that is, to "the remnant among the Gentiles," in two sets of metaphorical statements that have to do with (1) "the engrafted wild branches" vis-à-vis "the natural branches" and (2) "a wild olive tree" vis-à-vis "a domestic olive tree." And he employs the form

41. To a large extent, Paul's metaphor of a wild olive branch that is grafted onto the root or stock of a domestic olive tree is similar in its theological meaning and existential significance to his metaphor of a boy who is adopted by a patrician father into his family, which appears in Rom 8:15, 23; 9:4 (as well as in Gal 4:5 and Eph 1:5). For in both of these metaphors, the engrafted branch and the adopted son (1) are taken out of their previous situations and placed into an entirely new relationship, (2) begin a new life with much greater resources in that new relationship, (3) are considered no less important than the other natural branches or the other biologically born sons, and (4) experience a radically changed status with far greater privileges and greater opportunities than were theirs before (cf. "Exegetical Comments" on Rom 8:15 above).

of a Greek diatribe expressly in 11:17-24, which language is directed principally to Gentile believers in Jesus. The diatribe form began with the plural address "to you Gentiles" (ὑμῖν ἔθνεσιν) in 11:13a and continued in a more sustained fashion by the use of the second-person singular "you" (συ, σε, and σου) and the second-person singular verbal suffix "you" (-ας) here in 11:17-24.[42]

Two matters regarding the imagery of the metaphors used in 11:17-24 have frequently been discussed by commentators. The first has to do with Paul's choice of an olive tree to fill out the imagery of a "root" and its "branches," as set out in 11:16. The apostle could, of course, have used almost any tree or growing plant to make his point when speaking about relations between a root and its branches. In all likelihood, however, he used the olive tree because (1) it was used as a symbol of the nation Israel in the Jewish (OT) Scriptures,[43] and so would be most fitting with reference to a "righteous remnant" within Israel (i.e., true "Israelites"), and (2) olive trees were widely planted and cultivated throughout the Mediterranean region,[44] and therefore would be very well known to everyone to whom Paul preached and wrote.

A second matter has to do with Paul's speaking about "wild branches" from a "wild olive tree" being grafted onto the root or stock of a "cultivated" or "domestic olive tree." For, as has sometimes been argued, such a procedure is just the opposite of the normal horticultural practice of antiquity, where a nonproducing branch of a domestic olive tree was grafted onto the root or stock of a wild olive tree in order to capture the strength of the wild olive root, thereby channeling that strength into the production of olives on the formerly unproductive branch. Some interpreters, in fact, following comments by Hans Lietzmann (in 1906) and C. H. Dodd (in 1932), have viewed Paul's metaphor of the grafting of a "wild olive branch" onto a "domestic olive tree" as something of a faux pas ("false step" or blunder) — which displays Paul's ignorance of horticultural practice of his day, and thus, quite inadvertently, betrays his urban background.[45]

42. For Paul's other uses of a Greek diatribe form in Romans, see particularly 2:1-5 and 2:17-24 where a diatribe styling most assuredly appears. Note also its likely presence in 9:19-21. Probably, however, a diatribe form cannot be supported for the materials of 3:1-8 (perhaps including 3:9) and 3:27-31 (perhaps including 4:1-2); further, diatribe form falls far short of certainty in 14:4-11 (see our treatments of these disputed passages, *ad loc.*).

43. Cf. esp. Jer. 11:16: "The Lord called you [i.e., 'Israel'] a thriving olive tree with fruit beautiful in form. But with the roar of a mighty storm he will set it on fire, and its branches will be broken." Note also Hos 14:5-6: "I will be like the dew to Israel; he will blossom like a lily. Like a cedar of Lebanon he will send down his roots; his young shoots will grow. His splendor will be like an olive tree, his fragrance like a cedar of Lebanon."

44. Some have proposed that Paul's metaphorical use of an olive tree and its branches was influenced by the fact that one of the Jewish funerary inscriptions discovered in the Jewish catacombs at Rome refers to a Jewish synagogue in the city named Eleas, which means "olive tree." Eleas, however, most likely refers to the location of that particular synagogue in Rome, without any nuance with respect to the character of its worshipers. On "Jewish Funerary Inscriptions at Rome," see R. N. Longenecker, *Introducing Romans,* 64-66.

45. Cf. esp. C. H. Dodd, *Romans,* 180, where Paul's imagery of a wild olive branch being

On the other hand, some interpreters have followed the lead of William M. Ramsay, the venerated NT historian of an earlier generation, who argued that it was fairly common in the ancient Mediterranean world "to reinvigorate an Olive-tree which is ceasing to bear fruit, by grafting it with a shoot of the Wild-olive, so that the sap of the tree ennobles this wild shoot and the tree now again begins to bear fruit."[46] And there is a reference from a contemporary of Paul named Columella, who spoke of a mode of engrafting "a green slip taken from a wild olive tree," putting it into a hole made in the root or stock of an old cultivated olive tree, and so reviving the old domestic olive tree to the production of olives again.[47]

It is exceedingly difficult, as many interpreters have noted, to match in any exact fashion Paul's metaphorical use of "root" and "branches" with his thesis regarding the connection between, as well as the oneness of, "the remnant within Israel" and "the remnant among the Gentiles." Yet the theological points that he makes remain valid. For, as Douglas Moo has stated with respect to the use of metaphors generally and the apostle's use here in particular:

> Writers and speakers frequently transgress the natural boundaries of a metaphor in their application of it. We should therefore be content to recognize that Paul has allowed the theological process he is illustrating to affect the terms of his metaphor. We cannot be sure, then, whether he knows he is citing an actual arboricultural practice or not; and we certainly cannot draw any theological conclusions from the fact.[48]

Paul's warnings to Gentile believers in Jesus in 11:17-20, that is, to "the remnant among the Gentiles," are expressed in the following negative admonitions:

1. "Do not boast over the natural branches," for "you do not support 'the root' (understood as 'the remnant within Israel') but 'the root' supports you ('the remnant among the Gentiles')."
2. Do not say that "the natural branches (understood as 'the unbelieving people of Israel') were broken off so that you could be grafted in," for "they were broken off because of unbelief, and you stand by faith."

---

grafted on to the root or stock of a domestic olive tree is characterized as "A truly remarkable horticultural experiment!" — and evokes the inference that "Paul had the limitations of the town-bred man." See also Lietzmann, *An die Römer, ad loc.*

46. Ramsay, "The Olive-Tree and the Wild Olive," 223, quoting Theobald Fischer, who had traveled extensively throughout Palestine.

47. Columella, *De re rustica* 5.9.16. Further on this "reverse" horticultural procedure, see Baxter and Ziesler, "Paul and Arboriculture," 25-32 — though such a procedure, when used metaphorically, would speak of reviving the old "root" by grafting onto it a "wild branch," not of nourishing a wild branch by grafting it onto a domestic olive root or stock.

48. Moo, *Romans,* 703, citing in support such commentators as Godet, Murray, Käsemann, Barrett, and Cranfield.

3. Do not be arrogant, but be afraid, for "if God did not spare the natural branches ('the unbelieving people of Israel'), he will not spare you ('the remnant people from among the Gentiles') either."

Such boasting, such expressions of supremacy, and such arrogance are entirely unbecoming — worse yet, they are extremely dangerous spiritually — for those who have experienced God's saving grace and received by faith his gift of holiness. For, as the apostle points out in 11:21: "If God did not spare the natural branches, he will not spare you either."

Further, Paul urges his hearers and readers in 11:22-24 to be constantly cognizant of both God's "kindness" and his "sternness" — that is, sternness toward those who have rejected his provisions of grace, but kindness to those who have responded positively to God and "continue in his kindness." He closes this subsection of material with the assurance that even those who have rejected God's grace (as expressed in the work of Jesus the Messiah), and so were "cut off" from the stock of their own "domestic olive tree," can be "grafted in" again, for "God is able to graft them in again" — since (continuing the imagery of the olive trees and their branches), if God can graft wild olive branches into a cultivated, domestic olive tree, "how much more readily will these, the natural branches, be grafted into their own olive tree?"

In all these metaphorical presentations, as first set out in his pronouncements of 11:16 and then refashioned in slightly different ways in 11:17-24, Paul's main points have to do with (1) the inseparable connection of "the remnant among the Gentiles" with "the remnant within Israel," (2) the intrinsic oneness of these two groups of "remnant" people, (3) God's gift of holiness that resides in all believers in Jesus, both in "the remnant within Israel" and in "the remnant among the Gentiles," and (4) warnings to Gentile believers in Jesus not to boast about their relationship with God because of God's present rejection of the majority of Jewish people, but to stand in reverent awe because of God's saving grace and to respond to both God and the people of Israel appropriately.

III. The Irrevocable Promise of God regarding the Salvation of "All Israel" in the Context of Israel's Present Rejection of Jesus as the Nation's God-Given Messiah and God's Present "Hardening in Part" of His Ancient People, with OT Support from Isaiah (11:25-27)

11:25-27 A major point in Paul's presentations of 9:6–11:32 — one, in fact, that he has been building up to throughout his three-part exposition in these passages — is that God's promises to the people of Israel are irrevocable, and therefore they will be fulfilled in the future at a time of God's own choosing. It is this point that he proclaims here in 11:25-27: that at some time in the future, as ordained by God, "all Israel will be saved!" And the apostle proclaims this message with assurance, despite (1) the widespread Jewish rejection of Jesus as

God's promised Messiah and (2) God's present "hardening in part" of the great majority of Jewish people.

This is a highly significant feature in Paul's overall Christian message. It was based on his convictions regarding the person of God and the trustworthiness of his promises — which convictions were part and parcel of his Jewish heritage and continued in his Christian commitments. More particularly, however, they came to birth in his heart and mind because of (1) his new understanding of the course of God's salvation history, as brought about by his conversion to Christ and the Spirit's continued teaching, (2) his Christian rereading of the great Israelite prophet Isaiah, who was the most prominent preacher of remnant theology in the OT, and (3) his Jewish and Jewish Christian *pesher* exegetical methods, which allowed him to reinterpret some of the difficult passages in the Jewish (OT) Scriptures and spell out their somewhat obscure meanings in a fuller and more explicit sense. Thus here in 11:25-27 Paul affirms "that the gathering of the remnant [whether 'the remnant of Israel' or 'the remnant from among the Gentiles,' or both] is not the final goal of God; rather, God's final goal is the readoption and salvation of 'all Israel'" (which we have cited above as point 9 of a Jewish and/or Jewish Christian remnant theology).

The importance of God's ultimate goal in the outworking of his love, mercy, and grace as being the readoption and salvation of "all Israel" is highlighted by Paul in his use of the epistolary "disclosure formula" that appears in 11:25a: "I do not want you to be ignorant, brothers and sisters" (οὐ θέλω ὑμᾶς ἀγνοεῖν, ἀδελφοί). This rather traditional disclosure formula draws particular attention to the highly important features that he sets out in 11:25-27. Further, the apostle's use of the term "mystery" (μυστήριον) with reference to the salvation of "all Israel" — as well as with reference to certain associated matters having to do with the culmination of the course of God's salvation history — was evidently meant to signal to his addressees that he wanted in this relatively short passage of only three verses to speak to them about some hitherto little-known features (or, perhaps, some "inadequately known" aspects) having to do with God's saving activity in the future.[49]

What Paul meant by a "mystery" that has now become "more fully known" (or, perhaps, "clarified") has certainly to do with the three matters that he sets out in 11:25b-26a regarding (1) Israel's present "hardening in part" by God,

---

49. On Paul's use of "mystery" as having a Semitic background (particularly in the Jewish Scriptures and apocryphal writings) — and not, as some scholars of the nineteenth and twentieth centuries have proposed, a Hellenistic mystery cult background — see R. E. Brown, "The Semitic Background of the New Testament *Mysterion*"; also R. E. Brown, *The Semitic Background of the Term "Mystery" in the New Testament.* In the Pauline canonical letters, the word "mystery" (μυστήριον) appears twenty times, the majority of which refer to the nature of the gospel message that the apostle proclaimed (see esp. Rom 16:25-26; also note 1 Cor 2:6-13; 4:1; 15:51; Eph 3:3-10; 6:19; Col 1:26-27; 2:2; 4:3). The statement in Eph 5:32 with respect to marriage ("The two shall become one; this is a great *mystery,* and I take it to mean Christ and the church") uses the word "mystery" to mean only "intrinsically difficult to understand."

(2) Israel's "hardening" as continuing "until the full number of the Gentiles has come in," and (3) the salvation of "all Israel" as the concluding episode in the course of God's salvation history. Most likely, however, the apostle thought this "mystery" had to do also with the two further matters that he cites in 11:26b-27, which matters he drew from the words of the prophet Isaiah in Isa 59:20-21 and 27:9 regarding (4) "the deliverer who will come from Zion" as "turning godlessness away from Jacob" and (5) God's covenantal promise that he will "take away their [his people's] sins." All these statements are not of equal weight or importance. Nonetheless, Paul seems to have viewed all of them as being quite definitely associated in the complex of events having to do with the culmination of the course of God's salvation history — and so all of them are important in a Christian's understanding of the future:

1. At this present time "Israel has experienced a hardening in part" (11:25b).
2. This "hardening" by God will continue "until the full number of the Gentiles [i.e. 'the believing remnant from among the Gentiles'] has come in" (11:25c).
3. When these matters regarding "Israel's hardening in part" and "the full number of believing Gentiles" have been completed, "all Israel will be saved" (11:26a).
4. The salvation of "all Israel" will take place at some time in the future when "the Deliverer will come from Zion" and "will turn godlessness away from Jacob."
5. All of this will occur because of God's assured (i.e., "irrevocable" [as in 11:29]) promise to his ancient people Israel, with God himself taking away the sins of the people of Israel.

Exactly "when" and "how" all these matters will come about, Paul does not say. Interpreters down through the centuries of Christian history have frequently attempted to "fill in the blanks" of these apocalyptic statements. Paul himself, however, only speaks of having a hope that "somehow" or "in some way" (πως) his own mission to pagan Gentiles would be used by God as a factor in the future salvation of some of his Jewish compatriots (as he says in 11:14). With respect to the other weighty matters he sets out in these three verses — both those he expresses in his own statements of 11:25b-26a and those he draws from the prophet Isaiah in 11:26b-27 — the apostle simply does not provide any specifications regarding "when" or "how" they will occur. What he is doing in these verses is proclaiming what he knows to be at the heart of the Christian message with respect to the culmination of the course of God's salvation history. He has come to understand this central message regarding the future from a Christian *pesher* reading of Isaiah's prophecy in the conflated texts of Isa 59:20-21 (as he condenses these verses in 11:26b) and of Isa 27:9 (as he condenses this verse in 11:27).

What Paul sets out in 11:25-27 are apostolic pronouncements — not "cause and effect" or "means to an end" statements. They are given in order (1) to rebuke Gentile Christians who might consider themselves to be the primary focus of God's attention in the course of his salvation history, (2) to encourage believers in Jesus, both "the remnant within Israel" and "the remnant among the Gentiles," to enlarge their vision with respect to God's redemptive outreach and salvific working, and (3) to provide an assured hope for the continued working of God on behalf of the people of Israel in the future. And while a number of proposals and suggestions have been put forward by both scholars and laypeople regarding how readers are to understand the details set out by Paul in 11:25-27, such matters seem not to be at the heart of the apostle's concerns.

Discussion has most often been focused, however, on Paul's statement in 11:26a that "all Israel will be saved," and quite rightly so. The most common understanding of the adjective "all" coupled with the noun "Israel" is that the phrase is a popular and rather hyperbolic (that is, "extravagant" or "exaggerated") way of referring to a large number of Jews (similar, in fact, to such hyperbolic statements as "the whole school turned out to see the football game" and "the whole nation was outraged by the incident"). *m. Sanhedrin* 10:1a has frequently been cited as a later Jewish parallel:

> *All Israelites* have a share in the world to come, for it is written [quoting Isa 60:21]: "*All* your people will be righteous, and they will possess the land forever. They are the shoot I have planted, the work of my hands, for the display of my splendor."

This rabbinic statement summarizes the official Jewish understanding of the people of Israel vis-à-vis "the world to come." Yet immediately following this statement, in *m. Sanhedrin* 10:1b-3, there are a number of rather fulsome paragraphs that identify "those people [mainly those of the 'people of Israel'] who have no share in the world to come"; among those without hope are (1) "he that says that there is no resurrection of the dead prescribed in the Law," (2) "he that says that the Law is not from Heaven," and (3) "an Epicurean."

What Paul meant by the pronouncement "all Israel will be saved" (πᾶς Ἰσραὴλ σωθήσεται) in 11:26a has been variously understood. Principally, it has been understood to mean that (1) all the people of Israel throughout all human history will in some way experience God's salvation in "the world to come," or (2) all Jews living at the time when God brings to culmination the course of salvation history will experience God's salvation, or (3) all the people who are known by God as belonging to "spiritual Israel" (i.e., the Christian church) will experience the fulfillment of God's salvation — whether ethnic Jews or ethnic Gentiles; whether those of the old covenant or those of the new covenant. My own view is that Paul is here speaking of the salvation of Jewish people who will be alive when the course of God's salvation history is brought by God himself to its culmination. Further, I propose that Paul's pronouncement that "all Israel will be saved" in 11:26a is in line with the second part of the "Christ hymn" of

Phil 2:6-11, which the apostle evidently quoted from the worship of earlier believers in Jesus — whose second part reads as follows (italics mine):

> God exalted him [i.e., "Jesus"] to the highest place,
>   and gave him the name that is above every name;
>   *that at the name of Jesus every knee should bow,*
>   *in heaven and on earth and under the earth,*
>   *and every tongue acknowledge that Jesus Christ is Lord,*
>   *to the glory of God the Father.* (Phil 2:9-11)

Particularly relevant for this discussion are the statements here regarding the purposes of God in having "exalted Jesus to the highest place" and having "given him the name that is above every name" — that is, that (1) "at the name of Jesus every knee should bow, in heaven and on earth and under the earth," and (2) "every tongue acknowledge that Jesus Christ is Lord, to the glory of God the Father." It is the same apostle Paul who quoted with unbridled approval this early Christian hymn of Phil 2:6-11 — which lauds in its second part the future worship of Jesus by all people — who declares here in Rom 11:26 that at the culmination of the course of God's salvation history "all Israel will be saved."

The "Christ hymn" of Phil 2:6-11 — in both its two parts of 2:6-8 and of 2:9-11 — is of the nature of an early Christian proclamation, open to all sorts of legitimate questions regarding "when" and "how" and all sorts of further issues regarding "substance" and "results." Paul's pronouncement that "all Israel will be saved" is of the same nature, and therefore raises many of the same types of questions and issues. Yet, while containing some rather perplexing matters regarding "when" and "how," it must be concluded that Paul's conviction regarding the future salvation of "all Israel" was very much a part of his Christian proclamation. His whole ministry to pagan Gentiles was in fact conditioned by such a positive expectation for the people of Israel — with that expectation, as he believed, coming to realization at some time in the future (as he affirmed earlier in 11:13-15). Thus Christians today need, as well, always to live in the expectation that God himself, in bringing about the culmination of the course of salvation history, will also bring about the situation where "all Israel will be saved." Yet we need always to leave to God and his future salvific activity those perplexing human questions regarding "when" and "how."

There is, however, one particular thesis about "how" "all Israel will be saved" that has been set forth and developed during the past thirty or forty years by a number of prominent NT scholars.[50] It is a proposal that builds on

---

50. Franz Mussner argued in 1976 and 1977 for a "two-covenant" understanding of Paul's soteriology, dealing first with Rom 11:26 and then with Rom 10:4. He proposed that these two verses, in their respective contexts, speak of two forms of divine salvation: (1) belief in Christ as the required basis for Gentiles to receive God's gift of righteousness, but also (2) obedience to God's Torah ("instructions") given in the Mosaic law as the required basis of righteousness for Jews (see F. Mussner, " 'Ganz Israel wird gerettet werden' (Rom 11,26): Versuch einer Auslegung," *Kairos*

898

the observation that within the materials of 11:1-32 — and especially in 11:25-27 — there is an absence of specific Christological language. Rather, in 11:26b-27 Paul employs the words of the OT prophet Isaiah, as drawn from Isa 59:20-21 and Isa 27:9, to support his affirmation of 11:26a that "all Israel will be saved" — with the agent of that salvation in those two Isaiah passages being God himself (i.e., "the Deliverer" who "will come from Zion") and the means of bringing about that salvation of the people of Israel being "God's covenant," without any reference to the person or work of Jesus Christ. So, on the basis of such observations, some NT scholars have argued (1) that what they can identify as a lack of Christological emphasis in 11:1-32 has every appearance of being deliberate on the apostle's part, and (2) that what Paul is actually proclaiming with respect to the people of Israel is that God's salvation of them will come about in a "special way" or by means of a "separate path" (a *Sonderweg*) — that is, by means of obedience to God's covenant as expressed in the Mosaic law, which is a different way than having "faith in Christ Jesus," as required of Gentiles.

A number of other NT scholars, however, have expressed opposition to such a "two-covenant" or *Sonderweg* understanding of what Paul has written in 11:26-27. Their opposition is mainly because (1) it is at odds with what Paul has quite clearly set out elsewhere in his letter to Rome (even in chs. 9–11, when rightly understood) and his other NT letters, and (2) it attempts to interpret Paul's statements in 11:26-27 apart from his more explicit soteriological statements elsewhere in his writings, playing on what is not said rather than invoking the overall contexts in which his statements appear.[51] Robert Jewett, for example, has quite rightly pointed out with respect to the third-person future verb σωθήσεται in 11:26: "There is little doubt that the verb σωθήσεται ('they shall be saved') refers to evangelical conversion, as in 5:9-10; 10:9-13; and 11:14. There is no indication in Paul's formulation that Jewish conversion constitutes a *Sonderweg* ('separate path')."[52] And Ed Sanders's evaluation of a *Sonderweg*

---

18 [1976] 241-55; and *ibid.*, "Christus, des Gesetzes Ende zur Gerechtigkeit für Jeden der Glaubt (Röm 10.4)," 31-44). Such a "two-covenant theology" has been the underlying premise for most of the Jewish-Christian discussions of the past decades. And Mussner's thesis has been accepted and developed by a number of other NT scholars into somewhat differing versions of a *Sonderweg* ("special way," "separate path") thesis with respect to Paul's soteriology as appears in Romans. For major presentations of such a *Sonderweg* understanding as expressed particularly here in 11:26-27, see K. Stendahl, "Christ's Lordship and Religious Pluralism," in his *Meanings: The Bible as Document and as Guide* (Philadelphia: Fortress, 1984), 233-44; J. G. Gager, *The Origins of Anti-Semitism: Attitudes toward Judaism in Pagan and Christian Antiquity* (Oxford: Oxford University Press, 1983), 261-64; Haacker, "Das Evangelium Gottes und die Erwählung Israels," 70-71; and O. Hofius, "Das Evangelium und Israel. Erwägungen zu Röm 9–11," *ZTK* 83 (1986) 319-20; further, see O. Hofius, "'All Israel Will Be Saved': Divine Salvation and Israel's Deliverance in Romans 9–11," *PSBSup* 1 (1990) 19-39.

51. Particularly insightful rebuttals to such a *Sonderweg* understanding of Paul's soteriology in 11:26-27 are presented by E. P. Sanders, "The Salvation of Israel," in his *Paul, the Law, and the Jewish People*, 192-98; Hvalvik, "A 'Sonderweg' for Israel," 87-107; and Moo, *Romans*, 725-26.

52. Jewett, *Romans*, 702, citing in support Cranfield, *Romans*, 2.577; Fitzmyer, *Romans*, 623; and W. Radl, "σώζω," *EDNT* 3 (1993) 320.

understanding of 11:26-27 — which interprets "the Deliverer" who comes "from Zion" as being God himself rather than Christ who comes at "the end" before the kingdom is handed over to God (cf. 1 Cor 15:24) — is entirely appropriate:

> It matters little whether he [Paul] understands "the Deliverer" to be God or Christ; for it is incredible that he thought of "God apart from Christ," just as it is that he thought of "Christ apart from God." This is where the interpretation of Rom. 11:25f. as offering two ways to salvation seems to me to go astray. It requires Paul to have made just that distinction. By the time we meet him in his letters, however, Paul knew only one God, the one who sent Christ and who "raised from the dead Jesus our Lord" (Rom. 4:24). To suppose that "the Deliverer" could be for Paul "God apart from Christ" seems to expect from him an unthinkable abstraction. . . . There should be no hard distinction between "theocentric" and "christocentric" strains in Paul's thought. . . . It is God's will that all be saved through Christ. It is God who hardened part of Israel, it is God whose word will not fail (Rom. 9:6), and it is God who will see to it that all Israel is saved, though this does not happen apart from Christ.[53]

Further, I believe it legitimate to point out that in presentations where Paul focuses on remnant theology and remnant rhetoric — as he does in all three parts of his exposition in 9:6–11:27 (see our treatment below on the somewhat different nature of the materials in 11:28-32) — we would expect to find in the closing verses of the third part of that exposition, that is, in 11:25-27, the following important feature: "that there is a close relationship between God's chosen ['selected' or 'elected'] remnant people and God's Messiah" (as we have earlier identified that feature as point 10 of a Jewish and/or Jewish Christian remnant theology). It is my contention, therefore, that Paul's original hearers (perhaps, as we have speculated, the Jewish and Gentile believers in Jesus at Syrian Antioch), as well as his Christian addressees at Rome, would have accepted a close connection between God the Father and Jesus Christ the Son, and so would have understood the apostle's proclamation "all Israel will be saved" to express both theological and Christological nuances.

IV. A Postscript That Brings to a Fitting Close Much of Paul's Three-Part Exposition and That Highlights Matters of Particular Significance in Sections I and II of the Body Middle of the Letter (11:28-32)

11:28-32 There is, as many commentators have noted, no Greek conjunction (nor any Greek particle that might function as a conjunction) between what Paul presented in 11:1-27 and what he now writes in 11:28-32. In fact, the mate-

---

53. E. P. Sanders, *Paul, the Law, and the Jewish People*, 194.

rial that the apostle has set out in Part III of his three-part exposition (11:1-27) seems to be brought to a conclusion in vv. 26b-27 by the quotation of conflated and condensed passages drawn from the OT prophet Isaiah — as was also the case in both Part I (9:6-29), which comes to a close in 9:29 with a quote from the prophet Isaiah, and in Part II (9:30–10:21), which comes to a close in 10:20-21 with words drawn from the same prophet. So, while some type of thematic connection must be assumed to have been intended by the apostle, there is a linguistic *asyndeton* (i.e., a "not connected" feature) between what he wrote in 11:1-27 and what he writes here in 11:28-32.

This linguistic *asyndeton* is, of course, a relatively minor matter in the overall "formal patterning" and "compositional structure" of Paul's letter to Rome. Yet such a "not connected" feature at the close of each part of the apostle's three-part exposition — coupled with the observations (1) that he concluded each part with quoted materials drawn from the prophet Isaiah, and (2) that the length of these three subsections of material is almost exactly the same — suggests (though certainly does not "prove") that these three subsections were reproduced by Paul as three parts of one discrete unit of material, which was at some earlier time proclaimed orally by the apostle in his preaching and/or teaching (perhaps, as we have speculated, at Syrian Antioch).

Further, it may be postulated, particularly when this observation of a linguistic *asyndeton* is combined with other observations regarding the nature of the contents of this paragraph, that:

1. The materials of 11:28-32 constitute an "appended postscript," which was positioned by the apostle himself following the close of Part III of his three-part exposition of these chapters (i.e., following 11:1-27) — and, of course, is also positioned after that three-part exposition had been set out in full (i.e., after 9:6–11:27), as well as positioned near the very end (with only the doxology of 11:33-36 being then added) of his three large theological sections (i.e., Section I in 1:16–4:25, Section II in 5:1–8:39, and Section III in 9:1–11:27).
2. Paul added this postscript with the intention of bringing to a fitting close much of what he had proclaimed in 11:1-27 and much of what he had set out earlier in 9:6-29 and 9:30–10:21 — as well as to highlight certain matters of great significance that he had set out in the course of his argument in the previous two major sections of his letter, that is, in 1:16–4:25 and 5:1–8:39.

The apostle emphasizes in 11:28-31 a number of matters: (1) the present situation of the Jews as being not only "enemies of the Christian gospel and of Christians" but also "loved by God on account of the patriarchs," (2) God's "election" ("choice" or "selection") of people, (3) the "irrevocability" of God's promises to his people, (4) the disobedience of all people with respect to their basic response to God, (5) the righteous judgments of God against all human disobedience, and (6) the purpose of God in expressing his mercy as being that everyone who turns to him in obedience might receive mercy — all of which is summed up in the final declaration of 11:32 (that is, in what we here identify as point 7): "For God has bound everyone over to disobedience in order that he might have mercy on them all." These are matters that Paul proclaimed in various degrees of detail at many points throughout his theological presentations in his letter to Rome, which have come to culmination in his own Christian version of remnant theology as set out in his three-part exposition of 9:6–11:27. And in the final statement of this appended postscript of 11:28-32 the apostle declares that undergirding the entire course of God's salvation history — that is, undergirding all his continued acceptance of a "remnant within Israel," all his present acceptance of a "remnant from among the Gentiles," and all his future salvation of "all Israel" — is God's desire to "have mercy on them all" (i.e., on all people, whatever their ethnic heritage, their geographical location, and their particular situation or circumstance).

BIBLICAL THEOLOGY

In Part I of his three-part exposition in Rom 9–11, that is, in 9:6-29, Paul argued that God's promises have been given only to a "righteous remnant" of people; that remnant has existed and continues to exist "within Israel," but is also present "by faith" (as known only to God) "among the Gentiles." In Part III of the exposition, in 11:1-27, the apostle sets out more expressly his own understanding of the course of God's salvation history.

In so doing, he argues neither (1) that Gentiles are accepted by God by becoming Jewish proselytes (as most Jews believed) nor (2) that Jews are accepted by God by being united to the institution of the Christian church (as many Christians have asserted throughout the past twenty centuries of Christian history). Rather, Paul proclaims the following:

1. There continues to exist a "remnant within Israel," even though the great majority of Jews have rejected Jesus as their Messiah and God has hardened their hearts.
2. There also exists at this present time a "remnant among the Gentiles."
3. Following that time when "the full number of Gentiles has come in" — and particularly when "the Deliverer will come from Zion" — it will come about by divine action that "all Israel will be saved."

Further, the apostle proclaims in this appended postscript of 11:28-32 that throughout all the course of salvation history, despite the disobedience of both his people Israel and the Gentiles generally, God's desire has been — and continues to be — "that he might have mercy on them all [i.e., on all people]," whatever their ethnicity, location, situation, or circumstance.

It is a message that focuses on "the remnant within Israel" (i.e., those from among "the natural branches") and "the remnant among the Gentiles" (i.e., "the engrafted branches") — with these two bodies of "remnant people" being (1) inseparably connected, (2) intrinsically one, and (3) given the same quality of holiness before God. Paul is not attempting to relate the Christian church to the nation of Israel; nor is he transferring God's promises to Israel to the Christian church (but leaving his curses on Israel alone). He is not even speaking about Israel or the Christian church as corporate entities. Rather, his concern is with the "righteous remnant" that exists — because of God's sovereign election and on the basis of people's response of faith — among all groups of people and within various forms of human institutions.

Thus, in our attempts as Christians to construct a biblical theology, as well as in all our ecclesiastical and ecumenical discussions, it is of great importance to emphasize this very significant "remnant" feature of the Christian religion, and not just focus on matters having to do with organizational structures and inherited forms. Structures and forms, as well as human attempts to develop systems of doctrinal belief, are all important — not only for us individually but also for believers in Jesus corporately — principally so that we might be able to think constructively and live out our lives in a proper and helpful fashion. Yet all too often we as Christians become so structured in our thinking and so institutionalized in our practice that we forget that we are really "remnant people" — that is, that we are God's "chosen people" in a non-Christian, religiously pluralistic, and quite secular world. Thus we need at all times (1) to incorporate into our thinking, as well as into our more formal biblical theology, an understanding of ourselves as God's "remnant people," and (2) to act in terms of that Christian "remnant" understanding in our personal and corporate lives.

CONTEXTUALIZATION FOR TODAY

A great deal of our difficulty today in understanding 11:1-32 results from the facts (1) that Romans 10 has often been read simply as Paul's "thrashing" (i.e., "beating soundly over and over again") the people of Israel for their refusal to accept Jesus as their God-given Messiah, and (2) that Romans 11 has frequently been viewed as dealing with the relation of the Christian church to the nation of Israel — with that relationship usually spelled out in terms of God's promises as originally given to Israel but now transferred to the Christian church. Such readings, however, disregard the explicit statements in Paul's appended postscript of 11:28-32, which speak of (1) the people of Israel being "loved [by God] on account of the patriarchs" (11:28b), (2) "God's gifts and his call" to the people of Israel as being "irrevocable" (11:29), and (3) the present disobedience of the people of Israel being, at some time in the future, dramatically changed by God himself, with the result that then "all Israel will be saved" (11:31, picking up from what was said and quoted in 11:26-27). What we as Christians need to do today, therefore, in order to contextualize Paul's statements in 11:1-32, is to think more clearly and walk more humbly before God (not arrogantly, as Paul feared that Gentile Christians might do), realizing (1) that we are by God's grace a "remnant people" who have been "chosen" ("elected," "selected") mainly "from among the Gentiles," despite our own former lives of disobedience and sinfulness; (2) that as a "remnant people from among the Gentiles" we are inseparably connected and intrinsically one with the "remnant people within Israel"; and (3) that the holiness that has been given us by God has come to us historically through "true Israelites" of the OT religion of Israel and by means of the witness of "remnant people" of God within the nation of Israel. Ours is, in fact, the need to conceptualize our own spiritual existence in terms of our being the chosen "remnant people" of God — not just in terms of our ecclesiastical structures or institutions.

Also of importance for a contextualization of Paul's message today are the patterns that the apostle sets out with respect to his contextualizations of the Christian gospel to those of his own day; these patterns function in many ways as paradigms for our contextualizations today of that same Christian gospel. For in the three large theological sections of the body middle of the letter — that is, in Section I (1:16–4:25), Section II (5:1–8:39), and Section III (9:1–11:36) — the apostle sets out three somewhat different ways of understanding and explicating the Christian gospel:

1. That presented in Rom 1:16–4:25 (Section I) to believers in Jesus (both Gentiles and Jews ethnically) who had been extensively influenced by Jewish Christian ways of understanding and expressing the message of the Christian gospel, which presentation speaks in forensic language of God's salvation through the work of Christ and seeks to develop that forensic understanding in more explicitly Christian ways.
2. That set out in Rom 5:1–8:39 (Section II) with respect to how the apostle proclaimed the Christian gospel to pagan Gentiles, which presentation emphasizes the relational and personal features of God's salvation through the work of Christ and the ministry of the Spirit.
3. That inserted into his overall rhetorical structure of a "message of exhortation" (λόγος προτρεπτικός) in Rom 9:1–11:36 (Section III) — a section of material that appears to have been drawn from the apostle's earlier oral preaching and teaching (perhaps to Jewish and Gentile believers in Jesus at Syrian Antioch) and then sent in epistolary form to his Christian addressees at Rome — which presentation particularly emphasizes the factors of God's sovereign election of his people and the remnant nature of believers in Jesus.

These three ways of understanding and presenting the message of the Christian gospel may seem, at first glance, to be "somewhat different ways." They are, however, not competing or contradictory ways. Nor do they represent three different gospels. Rather, they set before us crucial features having to do with the fullness of Paul's understanding and proclamation of the Christian gospel. Further, they echo many of the stages and emphases that we as believers in Jesus have experienced in our own thinking, living, and Christian service. And still further, they provide paradigms for meaningful Christian proclamation and service today.

5. Doxology: A Hymn of Praise to God for His Wisdom and Knowledge, Incorporating Early Christian Confessional Materials (11:33-36)

TRANSLATION

[11:33] Oh, the depth of the riches of the wisdom and knowledge of God!
How inscrutable are his judgments,
and how unable to be traced out are his ways!
[34] "Who has known the mind of the Lord?
Or who has been his counselor?"
[35] "Who has ever given to God,
that God should repay the gift?"
[36] For from him and through him and for him are all things.
To him is the glory forever! Amen.

TEXTUAL NOTE

11:33 The inclusion of the first καί (which is, evidently, an explicative καί that was used to signal the ideas of "even" or "that is") in the opening expression of praise, "O the depth of the riches *even* [or *'that is'*] of the wisdom and knowledge of God!" is widely attested in the textual tradition. Only Greek uncial 321 and the Latin vg omit it. Its inclusion enhances the statement regarding "the depth of [God's] riches" by identifying specifically God's "wisdom" and God's "knowledge" as evidencing "the depth of [God's] riches" — though it is difficult to translate such an enhancement into either Latin or English without overweighting the poetic flow of the passage.

FORM/STRUCTURE/SETTING

Paul often closes off major sections in his letters with a doxology, a hymn, or an early Christian confessional statement that functions to bring to a fitting conclusion what he has just presented. He did this earlier in his letter to Rome in 4:25 (a confessional statement) and then in 8:31-39 (a mixture of confessional and doxological statements); and he will do it again in closing off the letter in 16:25-27 (a doxology).[1] Here in Rom 11:33-36 he sets out a doxology that ex-

---

1. See also the doxologies in praise of God in Gal 1:5; Eph 3:20-21; Phil 4:20; 1 Tim 1:17; and 2 Tim 4:18b.

presses rhapsodic praise to God for (1) his wisdom, which goes beyond human comprehension and (2) his knowledge, which cannot be contained in any human system of thought.

The Provenance of the Passage. This passage of 11:33-36 has often been viewed as an important example of artistic language and hymnodic expression in the NT.[2] Its provenance — that is, whether (1) composed entirely by Paul himself, (2) quoted by him from some earlier Christian confessional material, or (3) quoted by him in 11:33 and 36 as two strophes from some early Christian doxological confession, with his insertion in 11:34-35 of two supporting biblical quotations drawn from the prophet Isaiah and the book of Job — has been frequently and extensively debated. Of late, many NT scholars have argued that Paul was the sole author of this entire hymnodic passage[3] — taking over expressions and statements from various Jewish biblical and apocryphal passages (in 11:33), from two widely known OT passages (in 11:34-35), and from what appears to have been an often quoted Hellenistic Jewish teaching (in 11:36). While it cannot be proven, this is how the provenance of 11:33-36 should most likely be understood.[4]

The Structure and Message of the Passage. Paul's doxology of praise to God is structured in terms of three short strophes. The first strophe, in 11:33, speaks of "the riches of the wisdom and knowledge of God," highlighting the facts that his judgments are "inscrutable" and his ways are "unable to be traced out!" The second, in 11:34-35, quotes statements drawn from the prophet Isaiah and the book of Job to the effect that God's wisdom and knowledge are far beyond anything possessed by humans, and therefore they can never be said to be dependent on human wisdom, knowledge, or actions. And the third, in 11:36, declares that since "all things" (τὰ πάντα) are "from him" (ἐξ αὐτοῦ) and "through him" (δι' αὐτοῦ) and "for him" (εἰς αὐτόν), to God alone belongs "the glory" (ἡ δόξα) "forever" (εἰς τοὺς αἰῶνας).

In these three short strophes, therefore, Paul brings to a close what he has proclaimed in 9:6–11:32 of his letter about (1) God's election of people and events, (2) his choosing ("election," "selection") of both "a remnant within Israel" and "a remnant from among the Gentiles," (3) his present rejection of

---

2. Eduard Norden, who inaugurated the modern critical study of early Christian prayers and hymns, used this passage as the first of five passages (four in Paul's letters and one in the Gospel of Matthew) that seemed to him the most obvious materials for the study of *antike Kunstprosa* within the NT (see Norden, *Agnostos Theos*).

3. So, e.g., Bornkamm, "The Praise of God," 105; Käsemann, *Romans*, 381; Cranfield, *Romans*, 2.589; Dunn, *Romans*, 2.698; Fitzmyer, *Romans*, 633; and Moo, *Romans*, 740. Jewett, however, in *Romans*, 714, argues that "the lack of explicitly Christian elements [in 11:33 and 36] and the indications of later redaction [in the use of two OT passages in 11:34-35]" make it more likely that Paul is quoting an early Christian confessional portion in 11:33 and 36, into which he inserts two statements from Isaiah and Job in 11:34-35.

4. On the position that Paul composed this hymn himself after the manner of contemporary hymns of praise, see esp. Deichgräber, *Gotteshymnus und Christushymnus in der frühen Christenheit*, 61-64.

the majority of the people of Israel because of their disobedience, which has been expressed principally in their refusal to receive Jesus as their promised Messiah, (4) his present salvation for "the remnant of Israel" and "the remnant from among the Gentiles," and (5) his future salvation of "all Israel" at a time when "the full number of Gentiles has come in" and "the Deliverer comes from Zion." Yet this doxological hymn of 11:33-36 does not bring to a close only Paul's three-part exposition of 9:6–11:32. As Joseph Fitzmyer has aptly pointed out,

> This hymn also forms the conclusion to the whole of the doctrinal section of Romans (1:16–11:36). For not only God's dealings with Israel are unsearchable and manifest his uprightness and mercy to his chosen people, but all God's dealings with humanity are so. No one holds God in his debt. God's ways of dealing with human beings are quite different from what humans might calculate. What they receive from God is not merited; their justification and salvation stem from his grace and his mercy. Moreover, God constantly makes use of human sinfulness and disobedience to achieve his own ends.[5]

EXEGETICAL COMMENTS

11:33 The interjection "Oh" (ὦ) is not here an expression of fear or surprise. Rather, it is a response of overwhelming wonder, heartfelt gratitude, and reverent awe. And it functions to introduce a matter that goes far beyond all human comprehension — that is, the response of wonder, gratitude, and awe that is a prominent feature in the heart and mind of every person who seriously considers "the depth of the riches of the wisdom and knowledge of God!"[6]

The OT canonical and apocryphal passages that Paul may have had in mind when writing the second part of 11:33 could very well be Job 9:10 ("He [God] performs wonders that cannot be fathomed, miracles that cannot be counted") and Wis 17:1 ("Great are your judgments and hard to interpret, therefore undisciplined people have gone astray"). That such statements about God's wisdom and knowledge were widespread as proverbial maxims within the Jewish world of Paul's day is suggested by the more expansive and more flowing statements of the Jewish writer of 2 Bar 14:8-9, as expressed only a half-century or so after the time of the apostle:

> Who, O Lord, my Lord, will comprehend the workings of your judgment? Or who will be able to search out the depths of your way? Or who can search

---

5. Fitzmyer, *Romans*, 633.

6. With that wonder, gratitude, and awe enhanced in the Greek text by the inclusion of an explicative καί ("even") after the phrase βάθος πλούτου ("the depth of the riches") — though (as stated above in our "Textual Note") it is difficult to translate that enhancement into either Latin or English without overweighting the poetic flow of the passage, and so we have not translated it.

out the profundity of your path? Or who can describe your unfathomable counsel? Or who of those that are born has ever found the beginning or end of your wisdom?

11:34-35 In support of his affirmation about "the riches of the wisdom and knowledge of God" — and, in particular, with respect to his exclamatory statements that God's "judgments are unsearchable" and God's "ways are unable to be traced out" — Paul goes on to quote two OT passages. The first is Isa 40:13 ("Who has understood the mind of the Lord, or instructed him as his counselor?"); the second is most likely drawn from the question asked in Job 35:7 ("What do you give to him ['God'], or what does he receive from your hand?"). It is sometimes argued that these questions can hardly be viewed as Pauline quotations of Scripture, for Paul's habit in his letters is to introduce OT quotations by the introductory formula καθὼς γέγραπται ("as it is written") or some such introductory expression. But the material of these verses is given in the form of a hymn, as are the materials of 11:33 before it and 11:36 after it. Further, it may very well be that Isa 40:13 and the latter part of Job 35:7 had become proverbial in Paul's day, for which an introductory formula would be only pedantic.

11:36 Paul concludes his rhapsodic hymn of praise with the declaration that since "all things" (τὰ πάντα) are "from him" (ἐξ αὐτοῦ) and "through him" (δι' αὐτοῦ) and "for him" (εἰς αὐτόν), to God alone belongs "the glory" (ἡ δόξα) "forever" (εἰς τοὺς αἰῶας). And he closes that declaration with the affirming liturgical formula "Amen" (ἀμήν), which functioned among Jews, Paul, and all other NT writers to confirm and strengthen an immediately previous doxology, benediction, or significant statement.[7] Thus Paul's doxology of 11:33-36 closes with the declaration that everything that was created and exists has its *origin* in God, has its *support* from God, and has as its *goal, end,* and *purpose,* to praise God. That overall program of divine action includes — as the apostle argued just previously in his three-part exposition of 9:6–11:32 — not only (1) God's ancient promises to Israel, but also (2) his past and present dealings with "the remnant within Israel," (3) his concerns for and outreach to "the remnant among the Gentiles," and (4) his future salvation of "all Israel."

BIBLICAL THEOLOGY AND CONTEXTUALIZATION FOR TODAY: A CONCLUDING AND "UNSCIENTIFIC" NOTE OF IMPORTANCE

Constructing a biblical theology is far more than simply accumulating biblical statements and arranging them in a "proper" order, whether that order is based

---

7. For Paul's use of ἀμήν elsewhere in Romans, see 1:25; 9:5; 15:33; and 16:27 (also in the textually disputed 16:24). For his use at the end of doxologies and benedictions elsewhere in his canonical NT letters, see Gal 1:5; 6:18; Eph 3:21; Phil 4:20, 23; 1 Tim 1:17; 6:16; and 2 Tim 4:18.

on logical, pastoral, or existential considerations. Logical, pastoral, and existential considerations are vitally important in any Christian endeavor. Nonetheless, every attempt to construct a biblical theology — as well as to express such a theological construct for living one's life and for outreach to others — must primarily be done as an expression of praise to God and as an act of worship.

In his own life, in his evangelistic outreach to others, and in all his NT letters, Paul epitomizes, in quite a unique fashion, his own fervent desires to praise God and to worship him. And these matters of praise and worship are quite clearly expressed here in the apostle's hymn of praise to God for his wisdom and knowledge. Yet the following conviction needs to be instilled into our consciousness as believers in Jesus: our praise to God and our worship of him need always be reflected, in some appropriate fashion, not only in our Christian lives but also in our respective formulations of a biblical theology.

VII. Section IV: Exhortations, Both General and Specific (12:1–15:13)

Ancient "messages of exhortation" (λόγοι προτρεπτικόι; literally "words of exhortation") comprised a negative section of censure and correction and a positive section in which the writer presented his own truth claims in a quite structured manner — with a third section frequently included in which the author exhorted in a more loosely structured manner the acceptance and implementation of what he had just presented in his second section of material.[1] Although Paul expands the first two sections of a typical "protreptic" discourse into three major theological sections in the body middle of this letter — paralleling the form of the first two sections of a traditional "message of exhortation" in his two sections of 1:16–4:25 and 5:1–8:39, but going further by inserting an additional section of theological exposition in which he presents his own Christian understanding of remnant theology in 9:1–11:36 — the fourth major section of the body middle of his letter to Rome, that is, 12:1–15:13, parallels in many ways the third section of hortatory materials often included in an ancient "message of exhortation" in (1) calling for a response to what has been earlier presented and (2) setting out exhortations and appeals in a somewhat loosely structured fashion.

Certain Unique Features of 12:1–15:13. Every letter of Paul written to a particular church or group of churches contains (1) a theological section (or sections), which is rather well organized, and (2) a hortatory section, which is somewhat less structured.[2] This practice of the apostle in closing the body middle of a letter with a hortatory section, however, appears most expressly and most extensively in his letter to the Christians at Rome, whose congregations in the capital city he viewed as being within his God-given mandate to Gentiles because of the preponderance of Gentile believers in them. Thus, after setting out

---

1. Paraphrasing Aune, *Westminster Dictionary*, 385. For summary statements regarding the nature and structure of "protreptic discourse" in Romans (with references to the scholarly literature in support), see R. N. Longenecker, *Introducing Romans*, 197-200. Note also our treatment of this diachronic rhetorical genre beginning on p. 15 above.

2. Paraphrasing White, *Form and Function of the Body of the Greek Letter*, 87-88.

the three large theological sections of 1:16–4:25, 5:1–8:39, and 9:1–11:36, Paul brings to a close the body middle of Romans with this section of hortatory material. And here in 12:1–15:13 he sets out (1) general exhortations, which include his exposition on the topic of "the love ethic of a Christian," which is presented in two parts, and (2) specific appeals, which first deal with a Christian's attitude toward Roman governmental authorities and taxation (in 13:1-7) and then speak of some troubling attitudes and actions by certain believers in Jesus in at least some of the Christian congregations of that city (in 14:1–15:13) — with both of these matters evidently causing divisions among the Christians at Rome.

The section of exhortations and appeals of Romans is not only presented in a more express and extensive manner than that found in any of Paul's other NT letters, it is also set out in a somewhat different form and a much more inclusive manner than appears in any of his other letters. For (1) the admonitions of 12:1-8 regarding "dedication, commitment, and discernment," which are followed by "appeals for humility and mutual service," speak directly to the core of every Christian's thought and life; (2) the general exhortations of 12:9-21 and 13:8-14 incorporate the basic features of an all-encompassing "Christian love ethic," which the apostle calls on all believers in Jesus to emulate and express in every aspect of their lives; and (3) the specific appeals of 13:1-7 and 14:1–15:13 deal with certain ecclesiastical concerns of the Christians at Rome and provide paradigms for Christians today in dealing with similar issues in our own contemporary circumstances and situations (whether or not such wider applications were actually envisioned by Paul when he wrote to the Christians at Rome). Thus these hortatory materials of this final section of the body middle of the letter have immense importance for "Christ followers" today, not only as individuals but also as members of society and as coreligionists within the Christian church. And so these passages are not only important for our understanding of a "Christian personal ethic," but they are also of vital significance in the construction of a "Christian social ethic" (which, as disciplines of study, can be distinguished for purposes of analysis, but may never in practice be separated from one another) — as well as being of great relevance for the corporate experience of every truly Christian congregation.

Further, this section of 12:1–15:13 contains material that Paul viewed as an integral part of his "spiritual gift" (χάρισμα πνευματικόν) to the Christians at Rome, which he referred to earlier in 1:11-12 as his gift to them in order to strengthen and encourage them. The gift was (1) his relational and personalized contextualization of the message of the Christian gospel that he proclaimed to pagan Gentiles in various eastern provinces of the Roman Empire (the essence of which he reproduced for his Roman addressees earlier in 5:1–8:39) and (2) his "Christian love ethic" that he taught to his own converts regarding what it means to live as those who are "Christ followers," the essence of which he presents in two parts, in 12:1-21 and in 13:8-14. The apostle seems to have included such a presentation of Christian ethics in his own distinctive contextualization of the Christian gospel — which built on the forensic truths that were accepted by all earlier Jewish believers in Jesus and proclaimed by Jewish Christian preachers, but were developed by him in more relational and personal ways in his proclamation of this same message of "good news" to pagan Gentiles — as his references to "my gospel" in 2:16 and 16:25 suggest. When this general ethical teaching of 12:1-21 and 13:8-14 is joined by the specific appeals of 13:1-7 and 14:1-15:13, this section of exhortations and appeals provides both ethical content and ethical paradigms for Christians today that are not only relational and personal but also societal and ecclesiastical in the multiplicities of their dimensions.

Epistolary Conventions in 12:1-15:13. One looks hard to find the usual epistolary features of an ancient Greek letter in this fourth hortatory section of the body middle of Romans — particularly epistolary features like those that appear in the letter's opening sections of 1:1-15, its body-closing section of 15:14-32, and its concluding sections of 15:33-16:27. In many ways, 12:1-15:13 compares more in its rhetorical and formal features with the three preceding theological sections of 1:16-4:25, 5:1-8:39, and 9:1-11:36 — with Section I (1:16-4:25) and Section II (5:1-8:39) being most comparable to Greek "protreptic" speeches and writings, and Section III (9:1-11:36) being most comparable to the type of argumentation employed in Jewish and Jewish Christian "remnant" theology and rhetoric. A few epistolary conventions of the day, however, do appear in 12:1-15:13, and these features provide some aid for interpreters in analyzing this final major section of material.

First of all, it is clear that the "request formula" παρακαλῶ οὖν ὑμᾶς ("I urge you") and the "vocative of direct address" ἀδελφοί ("brothers and sisters") at the beginning of 12:1 identify the hortatory section of Paul's letter as beginning at 12:1. It is also clear that the "verb of saying" λέγω γάρ ("for I say") of 12:3 signals the start of a new subsection of material. It may also reasonably be argued that the "confidence formula" οἶδα καὶ πέπεισμαι ἐν κυρίῳ Ἰησοῦ ὅτι ("I know and am convinced by [or 'in'] the Lord Jesus that") of 14:14 functions as the start of another new epistolary subsection following the οὖν ("therefore") of 14:13. The verse 14:13 is then understood as (1) bringing to a close the apostle's admonitions of 14:1-12 and (2) setting out his final two appeals of that unit of material in 14:1-13. Likewise, it may be postulated that the two "prayer wishes" of 15:5-6 and 15:13 were intended by Paul to bring to a close the exhortations that precede them — whether those exhortations are understood (1) as the material that appears immediately before each of these two "prayer wishes," that is, the material of 15:1-4 and then the material of 15:7-12; or, more broadly, (2) as the exhortations regarding "the Strong" and "the Weak" in 14:1-23, or, even more broadly, (3) as bringing to a close all the exhortations throughout 12:1-14:23, together with those of 15:1-4 and 15:7-12.[3]

Structures and Content of 12:1-15:13. It has frequently been proposed that there are two sets of hortatory materials in this final ethical section of the

---

3. "Prayer wishes" appear elsewhere in Paul's letters to close off certain sections or subsections of material — as in 1 Thess 3:11-13, 2 Thess 2:16-17; 3:5; 3:16a (perhaps also in 2 Cor 13:14).

body middle of Paul's letter to Rome. The first set, as is often argued, appears in 12:1–13:14 and includes (1) an opening statement in 12:1-2 on dedication, commitment, and discernment, (2) an appeal in 12:3-8 for humility and mutual service among believers in Jesus, (3) general exhortations in 12:9-21 having to do with the main features of "the Christian love ethic," (4) specific admonitions in 13:1-7 to the Christians at Rome to be subject to their civic leaders and to pay their rightful taxes, and (5) a further series of general exhortations in 13:8-14 that continues the theme of "the Christian love ethic." A second set of ethical exhortations, as frequently proposed, appears in 14:1–15:12 and has to do with relations between "the Strong" and "the Weak" about dietary matters within the Christian congregations at Rome and expresses admonitions of rebuke to those who consider themselves to be "the Strong" in the conflict. A closing "prayer wish" or "doxological benediction" follows in 15:13. On such an understanding, each set of exhortations exists very much on its own[4] — with (1) Paul's admonitions regarding respect for civic authorities and the paying of taxes in 13:1-7 set between the two passages of 12:9-21 and 13:8-14 that present a "Christian love ethic," and therefore are probably to be understood as specific applications of that love ethic, and (2) the apostle's exhortations in 14:1–15:13 about dietary matters in the Christian congregations at Rome. The exhortations of 14:1–15:13 are often viewed as (1) analogous to what Paul wrote in 1 Cor 8:1–11:1 to the believers in Jesus at Corinth and (2) best illuminated by studies of various cultural circumstances and dietary practices in the Roman world.

Such an understanding of two sets of exhortations in 12:1–15:13 is, of course, possible. For hortatory sections of Paul's NT letters are typically less structured than are the theological sections that precede them, and therefore allow variations in the understandings of interpreters with respect to the interrelations that exist between the general exhortations and the specific appeals that appear in this hortatory section. Yet it remains just as possible that Paul intended his general "love ethic" statements of first 12:9-21 and then 13:8-14 each to function as the basis for his specific appeals that immediately follow; that is, Paul intended (1) the general exhortations of 12:9-21 to be foundational for his specific appeals regarding the civic and taxation matters that he sets out in 13:1-7, and (2) the general exhortations of 13:8-14 to be foundational for his specific appeals regarding the dietary dispute that he discusses in 14:1–15:12.

Because of the less structured nature of the ethical materials of 12:1–15:13 — which prohibits interpreters from spelling out with certainty some of the passage's inner relations — our "Exegetical Comments" below will deal with the individual subsections of the passage *ad seriatim* (i.e., one after another in regular order). We will, of course, offer some suggestions for how the general

---

4. Cf., e.g., such separate treatments of these two sets of exhortations as those (1) by Cranfield, *A Commentary on Romans 12–13,* and (2) by Reasoner, *The Strong and the Weak.* Note also the statement by Käsemann, *Romans,* 323: "The arguments of this part of the epistle comprise general exhortation in chs. 12–13 and a clearly separate set of teaching directed to the Christians at Rome in 14:1–15:13."

exhortations and the specific appeals of this major section should most likely be viewed in relation to each other. But we will do so (1) in a cumulative fashion, building our particular thesis as we move along in treating the various materials of this major section, and (2) without attempting to spell out in any precise manner the exact nature of these relationships.

On the Christian Way of Thinking and Acting Ethically vis-à-vis the Ways of a Jewish Rabbi or a Gentile Philosopher. Of greatest importance for an understanding of the ethical exhortations and appeals in 12:1–15:13 is to recognize that what Paul writes here has to do with (1) the basic factors involved in the formation of a Christian ethical consciousness, (2) the essential motivations of a Christian's ethical thinking and action, (3) questions regarding how a believer in Jesus is to determine how he or she should think and act in the various personal, societal, and ecclesiastical situations of life, and (4) the need to put all these matters into practice. These are highly significant matters that the apostle seems to have earlier included in his preaching and teaching to Gentiles in the eastern provinces of the Roman Empire and that he evidently wanted believers in Jesus at Rome to appreciate more fully as well — whatever their pre-Christian understandings of ethical thought and action might have been, whether as religious Jews or as pagan Gentiles.

With respect to those with a Jewish background — and those who had been extensively influenced by Jewish and/or Jewish Christian theology and modes of expression (as were, it seems, the believers in Jesus at Rome, whatever their ethnic backgrounds) — Pheme Perkins has aptly pointed out in discussing the broad outline of Pauline ethics that:

> Paul does not provide an exposition of ethics as interpretation of the Law and its obligations, as one might have expected in a Jewish context. Exhortation follows rather from proclamation of the gospel (Rom. 12:1; 1 Thess. 4:1; Gal. 5:1). The Christian lives in or for the Lord (1 Cor. 7:39; 11:11; Phil. 4:4; Rom. 14:9). Pauline ethics presupposes that a new community of moral discernment has come into being in Christ. Paul can presume that its members are able to discern the truth of his exhortation in relationship to the Lord (Rom. 13:8). He expects that they will act in accord with their internal standard of faith (Rom 14:22-23).[5]

Ten OT quotations appear in this major hortatory section.[6] Yet the biblical quotations in 12:1–15:13 are used in a somewhat different manner than were the many biblical quotations employed by Jewish rabbis in their collected teachings — and in a different manner than Paul himself employed earlier in 1:16–4:25 and 9:1–11:36, where he used biblical texts, allusions, and aphorisms quite ex-

---

5. Perkins, "Paul and Ethics," 269.
6. See our discussion "The Distribution of Biblical Quotations in Romans," in R. N. Longenecker, *Introducing Romans,* 239-41.

tensively as the basic support for all that he argued in his presentations. Here in 12:1–15:13, Paul bases his exhortations and his appeals on (1) implications drawn from the message of the Christian gospel and (2) the teachings and example of Jesus — with OT quotations being drawn into the presentations not as the primary basis for the ethical thinking and living of Christians, but rather to demonstrate that Christian ethics, as based on the message of the Christian gospel and the teachings and example of Jesus, are in line with the instructions given by God in the Jewish (OT) Scriptures.

Further, though Paul may at times have adopted for his own purposes — or, as might be said, "rebaptized" for his own use — various philosophical resources and expressions of his day in exhorting believers in Jesus to pursue the good, he "never," as Pheme Perkins has gone on to point out, "substitutes ethics as philosophic *paideia*" (that is, as "primary philosophic instruction" or "an elementary body of training").[7] Rather, when he speaks in 12:1–15:13 regarding the basic factors involved in the formation of a Christian ethical consciousness, he highlights such matters as "God's mercy," the message of "the Christian gospel," the "transformation" of a person through divine salvation, and God's continued "renewing of the mind" of a believing person. Likewise, when Paul speaks about motivations in Christian ethical thought and action, he principally has in mind the response of a believing person to God's work of salvation through Jesus Christ, which comes to expression in terms of "the Christian love ethic" and is significant only when brought about by genuine Christian concern for others. And when he speaks in 12:1–15:13 about guidance in determining what a Christian should think and do in certain personal, societal, and ecclesiastical spheres of life, he refers to (1) the implications inherent in the Christian gospel and (2) the pattern set by Jesus in his teachings and example.

7. Perkins, "Paul and Ethics," 277.

1. Opening Appeals and a Statement regarding Dedication, Commitment, and Discernment (12:1-2)

TRANSLATION

¹²:¹*Therefore, I urge you, brothers and sisters, in view of the [afore-stated] mercies of God, to present yourselves as living sacrifices, holy and acceptable to God. This is your proper act of worship as rational people. ²Do not conform to this present age, but be transformed by the renewing of your mind. Then you will be able to test and approve what God's will is — that is, his good, pleasing, and perfect will.*

TEXTUAL NOTES

12:2a The second-person plural imperative middle or passive verb συσχηματίζεσθε ("conform yourselves" or "be conformed") and the second-person plural imperative middle or passive verb μεταμορφοῦσθε ("transform yourselves" or "be transformed") are attested by P46, by uncials B* P [also *Byz* L], and by minuscules 1739 (Category I) and 104 365 1241 (Category III). The present middle or passive infinitive συσχηματίζεσθαι ("to conform yourselves") and present middle or passive infinitive μεταμορφοῦσθαι ("to be transformed"), however, appear in uncials A B² D* F G Ψ and in minuscules 1175 (Category I), 81 1506 (Category II), and 630 2495 (Category III). The external MSS evidence leaves the question somewhat open. But on internal grounds, as based on the imperative nature of the context, it is more likely that the second-person plural imperative middle or passive verbs were original and that a later scribe (or scribes) changed them to aorist middle or passive infinitives in order to parallel the aorist infinitive verb παραστῆσαι ("to present") of 12:1 — thereby completing the sense of the expression παρακαλῶ ὑμᾶς ("I urge you") of that previous verse — rather than the reverse of changing infinitive verbs to imperative verbs.

2b The phrase τοῦ νοός ("of the mind" or "of your mind") is attested by P⁴⁶, by uncials A B Dᵍʳ* F G, and by minuscules 1739 (Category I) and 6 424ᶜ 1881 (Category III); as well as supported by Clement Origen and Cyprian. The addition of ὑμῶν ("of your") following τοῦ νοός ("of the mind") appears in uncials ℵ D² P Ψ (also *Byz* L) and in most minuscules, and is reflected in itᵈ, ᵍ vg syrᵖ, ʰ. The shorter text, which is "supported by early and good witnesses," is to be preferred not only because of the weight of the external evidence, but also because of "the likelihood that ὑμῶν would have suggested itself to scribes as a fitting parallel to its occurrence in ver. 1."[8]

---

8. Metzger, *Textual Commentary*, 466.

FORM/STRUCTURE/SETTING

The first two verses of this extended passage of ethical exhortations and appeals have frequently been characterized as containing "the main theme,"[9] "the introduction,"[10] "a summary,"[11] or a kind of title paragraph[12] for all that follows in 12:3–15:13. More than that, however, Paul sets out in this opening paragraph the vitally important factors that are involved in the formation of a Christian ethical consciousness: (1) "God's mercies," (2) the message of "the Christian gospel," (3) the "transformation" of a person by means of divine salvation, and (4) God's continual "renewing of the mind" of a believing person.

EXEGETICAL COMMENTS

12:1 The postpositive οὖν ("therefore"), though frequently used in the NT as simply a transitional particle, is here employed by Paul to reach back to what he has written before about the mercies of God (thus our translation above includes in brackets the word "afore-stated") and to build on those prior theological proclamations in his exhortations that follow. The question inevitably arises, however, regarding how far back in his theological presentations Paul reaches as the basis for what he exhorts in 12:1–15:13. Some interpreters have proposed that he reaches back to the immediately previous section of 9:1–11:36, where he set out a "remnant" type of Christian theology. Others assume that he had in mind his presentations of 1:16–4:25, where he (1) developed a traditional Jewish *attributive* understanding of "the righteousness of God" to include a distinctively Christian *communicative* understanding of righteousness as being God's gift of righteousness to repentant sinners, (2) highlighted the forensic concepts of "justification," "redemption," and "propitiation" (perhaps better translated as "expiation" or "sacrifice of atonement"), and (3) argued for basing a person's relationship with God not on the person's "works" of righteousness but on the person's "trust" in God and his or her reception "by faith" of what God has provided in the work of Christ and the ministry of the Holy Spirit. Most commentators today, however, argue that Paul — because he used the particle οὖν ("therefore") at the beginning of 12:1, and used the plural word "mercies" in the phrase διὰ τῶν οἰκτιρμῶν in what almost immediately follows in 12:1 — probably had here in mind all that he had previously written about God's love, mercy, and saving grace in the three major theological sections of the body middle of his letter (i.e., in 1:16–4:25, 5:1–8:39, and 9:1–11:33).

It is this latter understanding with which I generally agree — though with

---

9. So, e.g., Käsemann, *Romans,* 323.
10. So, e.g., Cranfield, *Romans,* 2.595.
11. So, e.g., Dunn, *Romans,* 2.707.
12. So, e.g., Michel, *An die Römer,* 365.

the addition of the following statement: "principally in the materials of Section II of the body middle of Paul's letter (i.e., 5:1–8:39)." I propose the inclusion of this additional statement for two reasons: (1) because in the format of a "message of exhortation" (λόγος προτρεπτικός), which is the rhetorical structure that the apostle seems to have employed in the writing of the letter, Section II contains the positive presentation that functions as the basis for the hortatory section that follows (whether that hortatory section be viewed as Section III, as was often included in a λόγος προτρεπτικός; or as Section IV, as in Paul's letter to Rome), and (2) because Section II presents the Christian's relations with God in a highly relational and personal manner, which type of language and understanding of relations seems to also underlie the exhortations and appeals here in Section IV (12:1–15:13).

The verb παρακαλῶ ("I urge," "exhort," "encourage") was used in a number of ways, both in official correspondence and in private letters of the Greco-Roman period, to introduce something requested by the writer of his addressees.[13] Probably the closest parallel outside of the NT to Paul's request here is the request made by the Syrian-Greek ruler Antiochus IV (so-called Epiphanes, who reigned during 175-164 B.C.) of his recently conquered Jews, as recorded in 2 Macc 9:26 — which (though hardly comparable in content with any of the apostle's letters) begins with the same three Greek words as appear in Paul's request in Rom 12:1:

"Therefore, I urge you (παρακαλῶ οὖν ὑμᾶς) and implore that you remember the public and private benefits you have received [from me] and that you preserve, each of you, your present goodwill toward me and my son."

This same Greek expression παρακαλῶ οὖν ὑμᾶς appears later in Paul's letter to Rome in 15:30 and in 16:17, with very comparable wording to be found also in 2 Cor 2:8, 6:1, Eph 4:1, Phil 4:2, and Titus 2:6.[14] Thus, on the basis of this same or comparable wording — as well as the apostle's ease of variation with regard to the form of this wording — it may be said that Paul often used the verb παρακαλέω (or its contracted spelling πααρακαλῶ) to introduce to his Christian addressees his exhortations and appeals regarding their thinking and their living as "Christ followers."

The preposition διά ("through," "because of," "in view of") is used here to indicate the reason why something happens — that is, that it is "in view of [or 'because of'] the mercies of God" that believers in Jesus are able to respond positively to God. For it is God, and no one else, who in his love, mercy, and saving grace has opened the way for the reconciliation of people who believe in Jesus to himself. The plural expression "the mercies" (οἱ οἰκτιρμοῖ, which

13. Cf. Bjerkelung, *PARAKALÔ,* who has cited a variety of uses.
14. See also slightly different forms of the verb in 1 Cor 1:10; 16:15-16; 2 Cor 8:6; 1 Thess 4:1; and 2 Thess 3;12.

919

appears here in the genitive because of the controlling factor of the preposition διά) suggests a number of deeds of divine mercy rather than just the abstract idea of mercy — with all these deeds of God's mercy directly connected with the proclamation of the Christian gospel, as presented throughout Sections I, II, and III of the body middle of the letter (i.e., in 1:16–11:36) and as particularly set out in Section II (i.e., in 5:1–8:39).

The aorist infinitive παραστῆσαι ("to present," "offer," "dedicate") is drawn from the language of sacrifice and connotes an act of personal devotion. Paul describes this act as a presentation of oneself, using the expression "your bodies" (τὰ σώματα ὑμῶν) as a locution for the reflexive pronoun "yourselves." The presentation of oneself to God is depicted in cultic terms as "a living sacrifice" (θυσίαν ζῶσαν) — that is, not a killed, bloody, or dead sacrifice, as were the animal sacrifices at the Jewish tabernacle and temple, but as the sacrifice of one's entire person in all its created vibrancy and aliveness. Further, this "living sacrifice" is described by the adjectives ἁγίαν ("holy") and εὐάρεστον ("pleasing," "acceptable") to God, which adjectives signal that Christians are to present themselves to God as those (1) who are committed entirely to his purposes, (2) who accept at all times his continued cleansing of their lives, and (3) who endeavor always to act in ways that are consistent with his will.

Paul concludes 12:1 by inserting a statement that he evidently thought highlighted what he wrote in the first part of the verse — that is, τὴν λογικὴν λατρείαν ὑμῶν (which I have translated: "This is your proper act of worship as rational people"). Translating this statement has proven to be notoriously difficult, which is demonstrated most obviously by perusing the following English versions: (1) "which is your reasonable service" (KJV, NET); (2) "which is your spiritual service" (ASV); (3) "which is your spiritual service of worship" (NASB); (4) "which is your spiritual worship" (RSV, NRSV, NIV); (5) "worship him in a way that is worthy of thinking beings" (JB); (6) "this is your proper worship as rational beings" (TNIV), (7) "an act of intelligent worship" (Phillips), (8) "the worship offered by mind and heart" (NEB), (9) "that is your cult, a spiritual rite" (Moffatt); and (10) "this is the true worship that you should offer" (TEV). Commentators have also varied in their understandings of this statement of 12:1, as is evident by the following few examples of their interpretative translations: (1) "a service to God such as befits the reason, i.e., a spiritual sacrifice and not the offering of an irrational animal" (W. Sanday and A. C. Headlam); (2) "your cult, a spiritual rite" (C. H. Dodd); (3) "the spiritual worship you owe him" (C. K. Barrett); (4) "this is your spiritual worship" (E. Käsemann); (5) "the intelligent understanding of worship, that is, the worship which is consonant with the truth of the gospel" (C. E. B. Cranfield); (6) "the worship to which our [i.e., Paul's] argument leads" (N. T. Wright); (7) "a cult suited to your rational nature" (D. J. Moo); and (8) "your reasonable worship" (R. Jewett).[15]

---

15. Sanday and Headlam, *Romans,* 353; C. H. Dodd, *Romans,* 189-91 (employing Moffatt's translation); Barrett, *Romans,* 230-32; Käsemann, *Romans,* 325 and 329; Cranfield, *Romans,* 601-5; N. T.

Also, Paul employs cultic terminology in 12:1, (1) in urging his addressees to present themselves as "living sacrifices, holy and acceptable to God" (θυσίαν ζῶσαν ἁγίαν εὐάρεστον τῷ θεῷ) and (2) in calling such a presentation an "act of worship" (λατρείαν) — just as he will do in 15:16 by the metaphorical use of cultic language in referring to his own God-ordained ministry to Gentiles as his "priestly duty" (ἱερουργοῦντα; literally "holy service performed as a priest") of proclaiming the gospel of God so that Gentile believers in Jesus might become "the offering" (ἡ προσφορά) that is "acceptable" (εὐπρόσδεκτος) to God.[16] This cultic language suggests that in our understanding of the statement τὴν λογικὴν λατρείαν ὑμῶν in 12:1 — as well as in our translation of that Greek wording — we need always to bring to the fore the fact that the Christian life is lived out in terms of a believer's worship of God. Further, although the adjective λογικός ("rational") never appears in the LXX, it was a favorite term of many ancient Greek philosophers, and appears particularly in the writings of Aristotle, Plato, and the later Stoics.[17] The word's widespread usage in antiquity suggests that λογικός ("rational") had become a "coin of the realm," and thus would have been understood by Gentiles, by Jews, and by believers in Jesus (whatever their ethnicity and wherever their residence in the Greco-Roman world).

The close association of the adjective λογικός ("rational") and the adjective πνευματικός ("spiritual") in Philo's writings (and perhaps also in 1 Pet 2:2 and 2:5) seems to provide rather clear evidence that the two terms were closely aligned in Hellenistic Jewish thought. It goes, however, far beyond the evidence to claim that they were understood in Paul's day as being synonymous terms. If Paul had wanted to say "your spiritual worship" here in 12:1, he could have simply written πνευματικὴν λατρείαν ὑμῶν (rather than, as he did, λογικὴν λατρείαν ὑμῶν) — for the πνεῦμα word group appears frequently in his letters, being found particularly just a few chapters earlier in 8:1-30, whereas the adjective λογικός occurs only here in all his NT letters. Contextually, the understanding of λογικὴν λατρείαν ὑμῶν as "your rational worship" (rather than "your spiritual worship") corresponds well with the apostle's appeal in 12:2 that believers in Jesus be transformed "by the renewing of your minds" (τῇ ἀνακεινώσει τοῦ νοός). So for both linguistic and contextual reasons, it seems best to understand Paul's statement here in 12:1 as follows: that it is eminently reasonable, both intellectually and spiritually, for believers in Jesus, because they experienced "the [aforestated] mercies of God," to dedicate themselves wholly to God — in fact, "this is your proper act of worship as rational people."

12:2 The relationship between what Paul writes here in 12:2 and what he wrote in 12:1 could be viewed in either of two ways: (1) as two *coordinate* sets of exhortations — that is, as two parallel but separate sets of exhortations, or

Wright, "The Messiah and the People of God," 224; Moo, *Romans,* 637 and 640; Jewett, *Romans,* 729-31.

16. See also Paul's metaphorical use of cultic terms in 2 Cor 2:14-16 and Phil 2:17; 4:18.

17. See the summary given by Cranfield, *Romans,* 2.602-4, of the articles by G. Kittel, *TWNT* 4.145-47, and J. Behm, *TWNT* 3.186-89 (not in *TDNT,* as sometimes cited).

(2) as this second set of exhortations being *subordinate* to the first — that is, the exhortations of 12:2 state the means by which believers in Jesus are to carry out the sweeping exhortations of 12:1. Joseph Fitzmyer, for example, argues that these two verses are set out in coordinate fashion: "the first expressing the somatic [i.e., 'bodily' or outward] aspect of Christian life; the second, the noetic [i.e., 'intellectual' or inner]."[18] On the other hand, Douglas Moo suggests that the imperatives of 12:2 explicate how the call to dedication and commitment to God in 12:1 is to be brought about — and comments further regarding a believer's discernment of God's will that will then result.[19] Most likely the imperatives of 12:2, in line with Moo's suggestion, explicate how what is requested in 12:1 is to be brought about — with the resultant situation of testing and approving God's will, which are matters of very great importance in every believer's life, being then actuated in his or her life.

Because the verb συσχηματίζεσθε (from συσχηματίζω, "form by," "conform to," or "guide by") is in the present tense and middle voice (probably not here in the passive voice) — as well as because συσχηματίζεσθε is preceded by the negative particle μή ("not"), which negative particle frequently appears in intensive prohibitions — some interpreters have viewed this appeal as exhorting the Christians at Rome to "Stop conforming to [the thinking and practices of] this present age!" — which translation of μή as "stop" would imply that such a conforming of thought and practice was what Paul believed the Christians at Rome were actually doing. Later in 15:14, however, at the very beginning of the closing sections of the letter, the apostle assures his Roman addressees: "I am myself convinced concerning you, my brothers and sisters, that you are full of goodness, filled with knowledge, and competent to instruct one another." Thus the negative exhortation here in 12:2a should, in all likelihood, not be understood as a specific rebuke of the existing thought and actions of his addressees at Rome, but rather as a general exhortation that Paul would express to every believer in Jesus: (1) Gentile believers he himself had brought to God during his Gentile mission, (2) Gentile and Jewish believers who had been evangelized by other Christians and were now living at Rome, as well as all who profess to be "Christ followers" in both the apostle's day and ours today: "Do not conform to [the thinking and practices of] this present age!"

Such a refusal to "conform to this present age" is an important factor for every Christian who desires to know what the will of God is for him or her. In exhorting believers in Jesus to not conform themselves "to this present age" (τῷ αἰῶνι τούτῳ), Paul is picking up on his doctrine of "the two ages" (which understanding also resides at the core of the ethical thinking of all the NT writers). This teaching holds that believers in Jesus are to live their lives in the context of "the age to come," with its distinctive powers for righteous living, which has

---

18. Fitzmyer, *Romans*, 638-39, citing in support H. D. Betz, "Foundation of Christian Ethics according to Romans 12:1-2," 61.

19. Moo, *Romans*, 754-55, citing in support Zahn, *An die Römer, ad loc.*

been inaugurated by Jesus' earthly ministry, death, and resurrection, but also in the context of "this present age," with its negative powers, which still exist and continually attempt to thwart the effects of that inaugurated new age.[20]

J. B. Phillips's famous paraphrase of 12:2a, "Don't let the world around you squeeze you into its mold," has effectively captured the ethos of Paul's negative exhortation, and therefore must be credited as being helpful for an understanding of the apostle's desire for all Christians in whatever time and whatever circumstance — even though such a paraphrastic rendering fails to "translate" the apostle's appeal in terms of its ideological background, its distinctive linguistic forms, and its specific language. And this evaluation is true with respect to a number of other current paraphrastic "translations" of the Bible — as, for example, that of the *New International Reader's Version,* which as a children's translation renders 12:2a as follows: "Don't live any longer the way this world lives."

Yet even more important than this negative injunction for believers in Jesus not to live their lives according to the ways of thinking and the practices of the people of "this present age," Paul exhorts all his hearers and readers of that day — as well as all of us today who profess to be Christians — as follows: "But be transformed by the renewing of your mind" (ἀλλὰ μεταμορφοῦσθε [the form of the verb here being passive] τῇ ἀνακαινώσει τοῦ νοός). This remarkable "metamorphosis" that Paul speaks of here is not some pattern of external decorum or form of outward expression that believers in Jesus are to accept by way of a makeover of their lives and practices. Rather, it is a complete inner change of thought, will, and desires that Christians are to allow God by means of the ministry of his Holy Spirit to bring about in their lives, resulting in a recognizable external change of actions and conduct. It is a metamorphosis of a person's inner being such as Paul evidently had in mind earlier in 8:12-13 when he wrote: "Therefore, brothers and sisters, we have an obligation — but it is not to the sinful nature, to live according to it. For if you live according to the sinful nature, you will die; but if by the Spirit you put to death the misdeeds of the body, you will live." It is, in fact, the renewal of a believer's mind that is brought about by God's Spirit, as also expressed in such later Pauline passages as Eph 4:23 (Christians are "to be made new" in their thoughts and attitudes); Col 3:10 (the believer's "new self" is "being renewed [by God's Holy Spirit] in knowledge in the image of its Creator"); and Titus 3:5 (God has "saved us through the washing of rebirth and renewal by the Holy Spirit").

The result of this inner renewal of the believer's mind, which is brought about by the work of God's Spirit, is this: "Then you will be able to test and approve what God's will is — his good, pleasing, and perfect will." This statement of result is grammatically introduced by Paul's use of the preposition εἰς ("into," "unto") with the articular infinitive τὸ δοκιμάζειν ("to prove by testing" or "approve") — with such a use of εἰς with an articular infinitive signaling the idea

---

20. See Cullmann, *Christ and Time,* esp. 47-48, 81-93, and 222-30. Note also "Exegetical Comments" on Rom 6:5-11.

of purpose or result (literally translated "in order to"). What the apostle means by his use of the three articular substantival adjectives τὸ ἀγαθόν ("the good," "what is good," "the right"), τὸ εὐάρεστον ("the pleasing," "the acceptable"), and τὸ τέλειον ("the perfect," "the complete") — which he uses in characterizing the nature of God's will that the Christian, by means of the renewing actions of the Holy Spirit on the believer's mind, comes to experience — can be aptly summarized as "that kind of life which the renewed mind of the Christian person can see to be good in itself, satisfying, and complete."[21]

BIBLICAL THEOLOGY

The ethics of a Christian are not set out in any moral code, whether that given by God in the OT for the guidance of his people Israel or that proposed by some philosophical system of thought, either ancient or modern. Nor are Christian ethics a matter of (1) being in conformity to the ethical norms of the day, (2) being conditioned by one's own inherited family values, or (3) following out the dictates of one's own conscience. All these are factors that can be helpful in certain situations. But at the heart of the matter, Christian ethical thought and life spring from the new resurrection life that has been given to us by a loving God. Thus the Christian life, while awaiting a future resurrection, must always be understood as the present expression of our newly inaugurated resurrection life — which new life (1) has been given to us by God through the work of Christ and the ministry of God's Spirit, and (2) is to be lived out in ways that glorify God, respond to the work of Christ, are guided by the Holy Spirit, and serve others as representatives of our resurrected Christ. Therefore Paul's opening appeals to believers in Jesus with respect to the topics of "dedication," "commitment," and "discernment" in 12:1-2, which appear at the very beginning of Section IV (i.e., 12:1–15:13) of the body middle of the letter, are to be understood as being significant not only for his own converts to Christ in his Gentile evangelistic mission and not only for his Christian addressees at Rome, but also in any attempt to construct a Christian biblical theology today.

CONTEXTUALIZATION FOR TODAY

In any contextualization of Paul's ethical teaching, the following matters regarding the formation of a Christian ethical consciousness must always be highlighted at the very beginning of that treatment: (1) a calling to mind of "God's mercies," (2) a remembrance of the message proclaimed in "the Christian gospel," (3) the "transformation" of a person by means of divine salvation,

21. C. H. Dodd, *Romans*, 193 (though adjusting Dodd's language to speak of a "Christian person" rather than a "Christian man").

and (4) God's continual "renewing of the mind" of a believing person by the ministry of his Spirit — with the result that the believer in Jesus has (5) the ability "to test and approve what God's will is" — that is, "his good, pleasing, and perfect will." The Christian ethic (1) has to do with a believer's new moral discernments and moral commitments more than just external guidance and practices, and (2) is generated and expressed in response to what God has done and is doing redemptively through the work of Jesus Christ and the ministry of the Holy Spirit. Further, it is rooted in the basic features of "transformation" and continued "renewal" of those who have come to God through faith in Christ. So Christian ethics have to do with attitudes, thoughts, and actions that have been (and are being) brought about in the hearts, minds, and lives of such "trans-formed" and "renewed" people, both individually and in community. And it is such a contextualization of God's love, mercy, and grace, as expressed in the Christian gospel, that believers in Jesus are called on to express more adequately and more extensively today.

2. Appeal for Humility and Mutual Service among Believers in Jesus (12:3-8)

TRANSLATION

¹²:³*For I say to every one of you by virtue of the grace given me: Do not think of yourself more highly than you ought to think, but think of yourself with a sound mind, in proportion to the amount of faith that God has granted each of you. ⁴For just as each of us has one body with many members, and these members do not all have the same function, ⁵so we, though many, form one body in Christ, and each of us belongs to all the other members.*

⁶We have different gifts, according to the grace given to each of us. If your gift is prophesying, then prophesy in accordance with your faith; ⁷if it is serving, then serve; if it is teaching, then teach; ⁸if it is to encourage, then give encouragement; if it is giving, then give generously; if it is to lead, do it diligently; if it is to show mercy, do it cheerfully.

TEXTUAL NOTES

12:3a The phrase διὰ τῆς χάριτος τῆς δοθείσης μοι ("through" or "by virtue of the grace given me") is strongly attested in the textual tradition. The possessive τοῦ θεοῦ ("of God") after διὰ τῆς χάριτος, however, appears in *Byz* uncial L and in minuscules 81 1506 (Category II) and 69 323 330 1241 1735 (Category III); it is also reflected in vg^ms and sy^h. The possessive "of God" is certainly contextually appropriate. Yet because of its very weak textual support, it must be judged a secondary expansion of the text.

4 The order of the words πολλὰ μέλη ("many members") is amply attested by P⁴⁶ (also P³¹) and by uncials ℵ B D F G. The reversal of this order to μέλη πολλά ("members many"), however, appears in uncials A P Ψ (also *Byz* L) and in minuscules 33 1175 1739 (Category I), 1506 1881 (Category II), and 6 69 88 104 323 326 614 1243 1319 1505 1573 1874 2344 2495 (Category III). The meaning of the words in either order is, of course, the same. Yet the sequence πολλὰ μέλη ("many members") is, most likely, the original reading because of its stronger textual attestation.

5a The omission of the verb ἐσμεν ("we are") in ninth-century uncials F and G is probably a scribal error.

5b The neuter definite article τό in the idiomatic expression τὸ δὲ καθ' εἷς ἀλλήλων ("but each belongs to all the others") is amply attested by P⁴⁶ (also P³¹), by uncials ℵ A B D* F G P, and by minuscules 1739 (Category I), 81 1506 (Category II), and 6 365 1243 1319 1573 (Category III). The masculine definite article ὁ, however, appears in place of the neuter article τό in uncials D² and Ψ (also *Byz* L) and in minuscules 33 1175 (Category I), 1881 (Category II), and 69 88 104 323 326 614 1241 1505 1735 1874 2495

(Category III). In all likelihood, the neuter article τό, because of its stronger textual attestation, is to be preferred as having been the original.

FORM/STRUCTURE/SETTING

Frequently during his ministry Paul seems to have found it necessary to appeal to the Christians of his day not to be arrogant or conceited because of their relationship with God, but rather (1) to be humble, (2) to serve others by their God-given gifts, and (3) to allow others by their God-given gifts to minister to them. Such an attitude of arrogance and conceit on the part of believers in Jesus vis-à-vis unbelieving Jews was earlier referred to in 11:17-25a, with the following explicit statements being directed to such professing "Christ followers": "Do not be arrogant, but be afraid!" (11:20b) and "Do not be conceited!" (11:25a). These same attitudes of arrogance and conceit appear to have been carried over into relations between at least some of the Christians in the congregations of Rome, and the apostle had to speak directly to those who considered themselves "the Strong" in their attitudes and actions regarding certain dietary matters vis-à-vis those they viewed as "the Weak," as follows: "May the God who gives endurance and encouragement give you the same attitude of mind toward each other that Christ Jesus had!" (15:5) and "Accept one another just as Christ accepted you, in order to bring praise of God!" (15:7).

Arrogance and conceit are, sadly, quite common human failures, which all too often have been carried over into the Christian church in both blatant and covert fashion. These rather perverse features actually result in a denial of what we as "Christ followers" proclaim in our Christian theology: that we have "the same attitude toward each other that Christ Jesus had" and that we "accept one another just as Christ accepted us." This was, it seems, such a serious problem in at least some of the Christian congregations at Rome that Paul thought it necessary to speak to it at the very beginning of his ethical exhortations in 12:1–15:13 — that is, immediately after his opening appeals and his statements regarding "dedication, commitment, and discernment" in 12:1-2 and before setting out the first part of his "Christian love ethic" in 12:9-21. This problem of arrogance and conceit is a human failing that needs to be addressed in every Christian ethical agenda and renounced in all our contemporary thinking and action as believers in Jesus today.

EXEGETICAL COMMENTS

12:3-8 Paul begins his exhortations of this passage with the rather conventional "verb of saying" phraseology λέγω γάρ ("for I say") of 12:3a, which functions to signal the start of a new subsection of material. Yet, because of the inclusion of the postpositive γάρ ("for"), which seems here to convey a sense of continuation, there is signaled something of a continuation of the topic of being "transformed by the renewing of your mind" in 12:2 in what is then exhorted in 12:3-8 regarding a new kind of "thinking" about oneself and about others and a new type of "sound mind."

In 12:3b the apostle plays on the verb φρονεῖν ("to think") four times to declare: "*do not think* [of yourselves] (μὴ ὑπερφρονεῖν) *more highly than what you ought to think* (παρ᾽ ὃ δεῖ φρόνεῖν), *but think* [of yourselves] (ἀλλὰ φρονεῖν) *with a sound mind* (εἰς τὸ σωφρονεῖν)." His emphasis in this verse on a new kind of "thinking" and his appeal for a new type of "sound mind" with regard to oneself are specifically related to the exhortation of 12:2, in which he declared that believers in Jesus are to be transformed by "the renewing of your mind" — with this new kind of thinking and this new type of sound mind being credited to God himself, who has granted to every Christian an appropriate measure of faith and calls on all believers to think and act in proportion to the amount of faith God has granted them.[22]

While at many places in his other NT letters Paul makes distinctions between (1) his speaking as an apostle and (2) his own understanding of a particular matter — which personal understanding, of course, he firmly believes to be a proper evaluation of the situation he is addressing (as he did most explicitly in his statements regarding the married lives of God's people in 1 Cor 7)[23] — here in 12:3, about matters of arrogance and conceit, he speaks as an authoritative apostle (διὰ χάριτος τῆς δοθείσης μοι; "by virtue of the grace given to me," which expression undoubtedly refers to his God-given apostleship to the Gentiles). And he directs his exhortation to all his addressees (παντὶ τῷ ὄντι ἐν ὑμῖν; literally "to everyone who is among you"), thereby signaling that what he says immediately following is not to be dismissed or taken lightly; rather, it is to be received as an apostolic denouncement of an all-too-common human failing, which, if allowed to continue, would have very adverse consequences for growth in the Christian life and for the health of every Christian congregation, and therefore needs to be taken with great seriousness.

In 12:4-5 Paul illustrates what he has admonished by the use of the metaphor of a healthy human body, which possesses both a unity in its existence and a diversity of function among its members or parts — all of which results in

---

22. The interpretation of the final statement of 12:3 is notoriously difficult (see Cranfield, *Romans*, 2.613-16, for a list of possible interpretations). Probably here πίστεως ("faith") should be understood as "the act of believing" and μέτρον ("measure") as "the amount of this gift of faith that one has received" — with the result that the apostle would then be saying that each one is to think in proportion to the amount of the gift of believing that God has granted.

23. Note such statements in 1 Cor 7 as (1) "I say this as a concession, not as a command" (v. 6); (2) "To the married I give this command (not I, but the Lord); . . . [But] to the rest I say this (I, not the Lord)" (vv. 10 and 12); (3) "This is the rule that I lay down in all the churches" (v. 17b); (4) "Now about virgins: I have no command from the Lord, but I give a judgment as one who by the Lord's mercy is trustworthy" (v. 25); (5) "I am saying this for your own good, not to restrict you, but so that you may live in a right way in undivided devotion to the Lord" (v. 35); and (6) "In my judgment she [i.e., a widow] is happier if she stays as she is — and I think that I too have the Spirit of God" (v. 40).

a unity of the various parts, a recognition of the importance of each part, and the mutual service of each part on behalf of the health and welfare of the whole body. Thus Paul urges believers in Jesus to recognize that despite their differences of God-given gifts and functions — as well as their differences of inherited attitudes — they all together form "one body in Christ." And so the idiomatic expression of the day, τὸ δὲ καθ' εἷς ἀλλήλων ("but each [part] belongs to all the others"), is true not only of the parts of a person's physical body but also with respect to the members of Christ's body.[24]

Paul concludes his appeal for humility and mutual service among believers in Jesus by setting out in 12:6-8 seven gifts of God that are given for the benefit of the whole "body of Christ," the church universal as expressed in each of its local manifestations. These seven gifts are listed as follows:

1. "Prophesying," which signifies here not the predicting of the future but inspired Christian preaching (as in 1 Cor 12:10, 28; 13:2; 14:1, 3-6, 24, 39; 1 Tim 4:14);

2. "Serving," by which the apostle probably had in mind all the activities meant to build up the Christian community (as in 1 Cor 12:5; 2 Cor 4:1; 11:8; and Eph 4:12);

3. "Teaching," which has to do with teaching the truths of the Christian gospel (as in 1 Cor 12:28-29, where teachers are also mentioned third in the listing of those gifted by God);

4. "Encouraging," which most likely has to do with helpful counsel (as in Phil 2:1; 1 Thess 5:11; cf. also Heb 13:22);

5. "Giving," which undoubtedly has to do with sharing one's private wealth for the needs of others and for the advance of the gospel (as in Job 31:17; Luke 3:11; Eph 4:28);

6. "Leading," which has to do with presiding, directing, or ruling as a leader or official in a local congregation or a group of churches (as in 1 Thess 5:12-13); and,

7. "Showing mercy," which seems to mean principally the actions of those who care for the sick, but could also refer to all sorts of kindness and helpfulness directed toward others (as, for example, providing for the poor, caring for the unemployed, burying the dead, and supplying what is needed for disabled, incapacitated, and imprisoned persons).

This list of gifts given by God to his people in 12:6-8 is very much like the list of "the gifts of the Spirit" that Paul set out earlier in 1 Cor 12:4-11 (and then later summarized briefly in Eph 4:11). The list here, however, is not meant to be exhaustive but only representative. And none of the gifts referred to are cited

---

24. Cf. Sanday and Headlam, *Romans,* 355-56, where appearances of the neuter definite article τό in this idiomatic expression are cited in Greek and Roman writings, in the NT, and in Eusebius's *Ecclesiastical History.*

in order to authorize or support the institution of particular offices or officers in the early Christian congregations. Rather, by speaking of these seven gifts Paul is simply declaring that believers in Jesus (1) function differently in terms of their God-given gifts, and (2) are to be judged only on the basis of their God-given gifts and their use of these gifts — not on the basis of certain personal characteristics or features, and certainly not on the basis of wealth, status, or prominence. What matters in our evaluations of both other believers in Jesus and ourselves has to do with (1) the gifts that God has given to each of us by his grace and in response to his mercy and (2) what we as his people have done with these God-given gifts, which are given on behalf of the welfare of Christ's body.

BIBLICAL THEOLOGY

Frank Matera has aptly characterized the thrust of Rom 12:3-8 as follows: "By exhorting the Romans to think in a new way that will allow them to live as one body in Christ, Paul provides a concrete example of what it means to be 'transformed by the renewal of your minds.'"[25] It is a message the apostle had evidently proclaimed to his own Gentile converts in his earlier evangelistic ministries in Asia Minor. And it is a proclamation he wanted believers in Jesus at Rome to understand as well: (1) that basic to all our thinking and acting as believers in Jesus is the need to appreciate more fully, both individually and corporately, that God has given each of us as "Christ followers" certain gifts for the welfare of "the body of Christ," (2) that we individually as Christians are judged by God in accordance with our response to and our expression of these God-given gifts, and (3) that our judgments with respect to others and our evaluations of ourselves are to be based not on such external matters as personal appearance, wealth, status, or prominence, but on the respective gifts that God by his grace and mercy has given his people and on what both we and other believers in Jesus have done with these God-given gifts. It is such a consciousness of (1) God's good gifts to his people and (2) his people's faithful expression of God's gifts that must underlie all our Christian living, both individually and corporately — as well as all our attempts to construct and express a true and vital biblical theology.

CONTEXTUALIZATION FOR TODAY

New life in Christ requires new attitudes and new perspectives, as provided by God through his Spirit in response to our God-given faith — not only with respect to our own lives but also with respect to others. Thus, as declared by Paul in broad terms, we as Christians are to allow God by his Spirit to transform our

25. Matera, *Romans,* 290.

minds and to renew constantly that transformation by that same Holy Spirit. And in quite specific terms, we are to appreciate (1) that God by his Spirit has given a variety of spiritual gifts to all his people, (2) that we are to evaluate our own lives on the basis of the gift or gifts God has given each of us and how ably we are expressing that gift or those gifts, and (3) that we are also to judge others only on the same basis of the gift or gifts that God has given them and their expressions of their particular God-given gift or gifts.

3. The Christian Love Ethic, Part I (12:9-21)

TRANSLATION

[12:9]*Christian love must be genuine! Abhor what is evil; cling to what is good.* [10]*Be devoted to one another with mutual affection. Honor others above yourselves.*

[11]*Never be lacking in zeal, but keep your spiritual fervor, serving the Lord.* [12]*Be joyful in hope, patient in affliction, faithful in prayer.* [13]*Share with God's people who are in need. Practice hospitality.*

[14]*Bless those who persecute you; bless and do not curse them.* [15]*Rejoice with those who rejoice; mourn with those who mourn.* [16]*Live in harmony with one another. Do not be haughty, but be willing to associate with people of low position. Do not think of yourselves in a conceited fashion.*

[17]*Do not repay anyone evil for evil. Take care to do what is right in the eyes of everybody.* [18]*If it is possible, so far as it depends on you, live at peace with everyone.*

[19]*Do not take revenge, beloved ones, but leave room for God's wrath, for it is written: "It is mine to avenge; I will repay, says the Lord."* [20]*On the contrary:*

"If your enemies are hungry, feed them;
if they are thirsty, give them something to drink.
In so doing you will heap burning coals on their heads."

[21]*Do not be overcome by evil, but overcome evil with good.*

TEXTUAL NOTES

12:9 The nominative plural present participle ἀποστυγοῦντες ("abhorring," "hating") is attested by a wide range of MSS. It is, however, replaced by the plural present participle μισοῦντες ("hating") in ninth-century uncials F (010) and G (012), and it is reflected in various Latin and Syriac translations. Yet ἀποστυγοῦντες is far better supported by the evidence from the textual tradition. So it seems best to understand ἀποστυγοῦντες as original — even though it is a *hapax legomenon* that appears only here in 12:9 in the entire NT — and, further, to theorize that μισοῦντες ("hating"), whose basic verbal form μισέω ("I hate") is fairly common in the NT, was substituted by later scribes simply because it was more commonly known by their readers.

11 The reading τῷ κυρίῳ ("the Lord") in the phrase τῷ κυρίῳ δουλεύοντες ("to the Lord giving service" or "serving the Lord") is amply attested by P[46], by uncials ℵ B D[2] Ψ [also *Byz* L], and by minuscules 33 1175 1739 (Category I), 81 256 1506 1881 1962 2127 (Category II), and 6 104 263 365 436 459 1241 1319 1573 1852 2200 (Category III). The reading τῷ καιρῷ ("in the right ['proper,' 'favorable'] time"), however, is attested, as Bruce Metzger has pointed out, "chiefly by Western witnesses (D* F G it[d*, g] Origen[lat]

Cyprian Ambrosiaster Jerome *al*)" — and further, as Metzger has gone on to suggest, this variant reading "probably arose from a confusion of κω [line over] and κρω (the *nomen sacrum* κυρίω was customarily contracted to κω [line over], and the καί compendium was written κ")."[26]

14 The inclusion of the dative personal pronoun ὑμᾶς ("you") in the admonition εὐλογεῖτε τοὺς διώκοντας ὑμᾶς ("Bless those who persecute you") is attested by uncials ℵ A [and D in another position] (also *Byz* L) P Ψ and 33[vid], by minuscules 1175 (Category I), 81 256 1506 1881 1962 2127 (Category II), and 104 263 365 436 459 1241 1319 1573 1852 1912 2200 (Category III); it is also reflected in it[(b), d, s] vg[cl] syr[p, h] cop[sa, bo, fay] and supported by Origen[lat] and Chrysostom. This pronoun ὑμᾶς, however, is omitted in P[46], in uncials B and 6, in minuscules 1739 (Category I) and 424[c] (Category III), with this omission being reflected in vg[ww, st] and supported by Clement. "It is difficult," as Bruce Metzger has observed, "to decide whether ὑμᾶς was deleted to broaden the range of the exhortation, or whether copyists, recalling the sayings in Mt 5.44 and Lk 6.28, added the pronoun" — and so Metzger reported on the decision taken by the UBS committee as follows: "Since both readings are fairly evenly supported in the witnesses, a majority of the Committee preferred to print [ὑμᾶς]" (that is, to retain ὑμᾶς but enclose it in square brackets)."[27]

Some MSS omit the whole clause εὐλογεῖτε τοὺς διώκοντας ὑμᾶς, as do uncials F G and as reflected in it[ar, f, g, o] syr[pal]. But that is probably because of a presumed *homoioteleuton*, since εὐλογεῖτε is repeated in the next clause.

17 To the admonition προνοούμενοι καλὰ ἐνώπιον πάντων ἀνθρώπων ("Take care to do what is right in the sight of everybody"), several scribes, evidently under the influence of Prov 3:4 and 2 Cor 8:21, inserted after καλά either (1) ἐνώπιον τοῦ θεοῦ καί ("in the sight of God and"), as does corrected Codex Alexandrinus (A[c] 02), or (2) οὐ μόνον ἐνώπιον τοῦ θεοῦ ἀλλὰ καί ("not only in the sight of God but also"), as do uncials F G and minuscule 629 (Category III); and as reflected in it[g] vg and as supported by Ambrosiaster.

Likewise, a few textual witnesses omit πάντων, as do minuscules 181 (Category II) and 436 (Category III), with that omission reflected in it[d, g]. This omission was probably due to transcriptional oversight. Further, some textual witnesses have replaced πάντων by the article τῶν, as do P[46] and uncials A[1] D* F[gr] G (also such later uncials as 056 and 0142), with that replacement of πάντων by τῶν being also reflected in some Latin versions and supported by Ambrosiaster. But as Bruce Metzger has aptly noted: "The word πάντων, however, is necessary to give balance to the earlier μηδενί."[28]

FORM/STRUCTURE/SETTING

Opinions are diverse regarding the nature, structure, development of thought, and intended purpose of Paul's hortatory statements in 12:9-21 (as well as in his

26. Metzger, *Textual Commentary,* 466.
27. *Ibid.*
28. *Ibid.*

corresponding hortatory statements in 13:8-14). Much of what has been said (or can be said) about these matters is conjectural. Yet certain "informed conjectures" are better than others, and therefore certain issues with respect to these matters need to be dealt with here.

The Nature of Paul's Hortatory Materials Generally and His Exhortations in 12:9-21 (and in 13:8-14). In the first half of the twentieth century, Martin Dibelius identified the hortatory materials of the NT and of early postcanonical Christian writings as a distinctive type of material that he called "paraeneses," which he claimed were made up of *topoi* or stock treatments of moral subjects that were frequently strung together without any direct relation to the matters discussed elsewhere in the particular piece of writing in which they appeared.[29] Thus he proposed that the hortatory sections of Paul's letters (1) differ in style from the argumentation sections, (2) lack immediate relevancy to the issues at hand, (3) serve only the general requirements of the churches, and, in fact, (4) have "nothing to do with the theoretic foundation of the ethics of the Apostle, and very little with other ideas peculiar to him."[30] Many interpreters of Paul have generally agreed with Dibelius, and so have tended to view all the apostle's ethical sections in his letters as being (1) substantially traditional in content (that is, as using rather stock moral aphorisms and clichés drawn from the ancient world and from early Christian usage), (2) largely stylistic in presentation and arrangement, and (3) basically interchangeable from one letter to another, without any direct relevance to the particular issues addressed in his various letters.

In my commentary on Galatians, however, I have pointed out that Paul's exhortation section of Gal 5:1–6:10 speaks directly to the issues that he argued in the previous four chapters of that letter. And many quite reputable commentators have demonstrated how the hortatory sections of Paul's other NT letters spell out important ethical implications of the earlier theological sections of those letters.

While the themes of "love" and "service to others" reverberate throughout the exhortations of Gal 5:13–6:10 — with the opening exhortation "through love serve one another" of 5:13 and the closing exhortation "do good to all people" of 6:10 functioning as a rhetorical and literary *inclusio* for this unit of material[31] — Paul's two-part presentation of "the Christian love ethic" in Rom 12:9-21 and Rom 13:8-14, while similar in some ways to his earlier "love ethic" statements in Galatians, is considerably different in other ways. The differences in the two exhortations are most obviously in form and styling. They are also, however, somewhat different in content (esp. with regard to the inclusion of the work of the Spirit in Gal 5:13–6:10 but the omission of references to the Spirit in Rom

29. M. Dibelius, *A Fresh Approach to the New Testament and Early Christian Literature* (London: Nicholson & Watson, 1936), 217-37.

30. M. Dibelius, *From Tradition to Gospel,* trans. B. L. Woolf (New York: Scribner, 1965), 238-39; see also his *Commentary on the Epistle of James,* Hermeneia (Philadelphia: Fortress, 1976), 1-11, where Dibelius sets out his thesis with reference to the NT Epistle of James.

31. Cf. R. N. Longenecker, *Galatians,* esp. 236-37.

12:9-21 and 13:8-14); these differences are explainable on a circumstantial basis of different matters being discussed, different forms being used, and different purposes being involved.

It must therefore be concluded that there is no *a priori* reason to presume that the two major ethical passages on "the Christian love ethic" in Rom 12:9-21 and 13:8-14 should be viewed as representing only *topoi* or "stock treatments" of various moral issues that were common among the early believers in Jesus (à la the thesis of Dibelius). Rather, it is far better to begin our discussions of these two hortatory passages on the assumption that they speak in a manner that is (1) in line with the theological presentations that precede them and (2) consistent with the purposes of the materials into which they are embedded.

The Structure and Development of Thought in the Exhortations of 12:9-21. There is very little agreement among commentators, however, regarding the internal structure and the development of thought in 12:9-21. Charles Cranfield, for example, captions this passage "A Series of Loosely Connected Items of Exhortation,"[32] and James Dunn speaks of the passage as "loosely constructed."[33] Conversely, Robert Jewett regards 12:9-21 as being "artfully constructed for rhetorical impact and closely related to the tensions between Christian groups in Rome."[34]

Yet, while certain matters of interpretation may be somewhat unsettled and some issues regarding the passage's overall structure are in flux, there is a growing perception among interpreters that there is evident in 12:9-21 "a minor break between 12:13 and 12:14."[35] In form, this "minor break" can be recognized by the facts that (1) Paul employs in 12:9-13 a series of independent (or "absolute") participles, which function as regular verbal imperatives, and then (2) he uses in 12:14-21 both independent (or "absolute") participles together with independent (or "absolute") infinitives, and independent (or "absolute") participles with regular imperative verbs, which all function in the same imperatival manner as did the participles alone in the first series.[36] Further, this "minor break" seems to be evident in the change of subject matter from (1) "those who are the people of God" and how they are to be treated, as set out in 12:9-13, to (2) "those who persecute you" and how they are to be treated, as dealt with in 12:14-21.[37]

---

32. Cranfield, *Romans,* 2.628-29.

33. Dunn, *Romans,* 2.737; see also Barrett, *Romans,* 239-43; Talbert, "Tradition and Redaction in Romans 12:9-21," 83-93.

34. Jewett, *Romans,* 756.

35. So, e.g., Matera, *Romans,* 290.

36. A. T. Robertson has noted: this confluence of independent (or "absolute") participles and independent (or "absolute") infinitives in 12:9-21 is "the most outstanding example of its kind in the NT" (*ATRob,* 946).

37. So, e.g., Cranfield, *Romans,* 2.629: "With v. 14 the construction changes, and this change seems to mark something of a new beginning. In vv. 9-13 Paul has been concerned mainly at any rate with the relations of Christians with their fellow Christians. In vv. 14-21 he is at any rate mainly concerned with the relations of Christians with those outside the Church."

EXEGETICAL COMMENTS

The exhortations that appear here in 12:9-21 (as well as in 13:8-10) have all to do with "the Christian love ethic" of a believer in Jesus, for which the apostle uses the Greek word ἀγάπη. The noun ἀγάπη is not found in any extant Greek writing. Both the extant classical and koine Greek writings employ three other words for "love": (1) φιλία, which is a general word for love that appears in many contexts; (2) ἔρως, which has to do principally with sexual love; and (3) στοργή, which usually has to do with love among members of a family. The word ἀγάπη, however, does occur about 20 times in the LXX, though most often without any specialized meaning. The noun ἀγάπη appears about 120 times in the NT, 75 of which are found in the Pauline corpus of letters. The word itself cannot be claimed to be uniquely Christian. Yet because of Paul's repeated use of its articular form, coupled with the particular contexts in which it appears in his various letters, it may be claimed that the expression ἡ ἀγάπη in the apostle's letters — and particularly here in his letter to the Christians at Rome — connotes a distinctive Christian flavor as being principally in mind: (1) the love that God the Father and Jesus Christ our Savior and Lord have for us (as in Rom 5:5, 8; 8:35), and (2) the love that Christians are to have in response to God and to Christ Jesus, are to have for one another, and are to express to those who have never claimed to be "Christ followers" (as here in Rom 12:9-21 and then later in Rom 13:8-10).

12:9-13 The series of exhortations in vv. 9-13 are devoid of regular verbs — particularly of verbs with the second-person plural imperative suffix ἔστε ("you must be" or "need to be").[38] Rather, the exhortations of these five verses are dominated by a number of independent (or "absolute") participles, which could be viewed by themselves as being either indicative or imperative in mood. Greek participles are technically neither indicative nor imperative. Thus, without a governing regular verb to indicate either indicative or imperative nuances, the context of the passage in which they appear must decide their modal qualities.[39] And there can be little doubt that here in 12:9-13 the context is decidedly set out in the imperative mood.

The first exhortation of 12:9a, which heads the list of exhortations in 12:9-13, functions as the thesis statement for what follows in these five verses: ἡ ἀγάπη ἀνυπόκριτος (literally "the love must be without hypocrisy"). An article in Greek is not always required to make a Greek noun definite. Often, however,

---

38. As A. T. Robertson has pointed out: "The imperative shows a few examples of the dropping of ἔστε as with the participles in Ro. 12:9, though, of course, the context can decide between the indicative and imperative" (*ATRob,* 396).

39. Cf. *ibid.:* "The participle in itself is never imperative nor indicative, though there seem to be examples in the N.T., as in the papyri, where, because of ellipsis [an omission of one or more words that must be understood in order to make a construction grammatically complete] or anacoluthon [a syntactical inconsistency or incoherence within a sentence], the participle carries on the work of either the indicative or the imperative" (*ATRob,* 1133).

it is used with a substantive noun in a particular context to highlight a certain distinction or to make a certain point. In the present context Paul, by using the article ἡ ("the") with the noun ἀγάπη ("love"), not only appears to have in mind the generic subject of "love," but, more importantly, he appears to be making the point that what he is talking about here is God's love as expressed in and through the life of a Christian.[40] And while the negative word ἀνυπόκριτος means literally "apart from" or "without hypocrisy," it is probably best to understand the term in 12:9a in the sense of the more positive expression "genuine" (which is the essence of being "without hypocrisy"). Thus we have viewed this hortatory statement of 12:9a as not only the thesis statement for the series of exhortations that follows in 12:9b-13, but also as declaring that *"Christian love* must be *genuine!"*

Paul exhorts those who profess to be "Christ followers" to have love that is "genuine" (that is, "without hypocrisy"). And this genuine love the apostle spells out in a series of brief exhortations that use only independent (or "absolute") Greek participles (i.e., without the presence of any Greek imperative verbs) — which, in context, urge that Christians, in their thinking, lifestyle, and actions, must always:

1. "Abhor what is evil and cling to what is good."
2. "Be devoted to one another with mutual affection."
3. "Honor others above yourselves."
4. "Never be lacking in zeal, but keep your spiritual fervor, serving the Lord."
5. "Be joyful in hope, patient in affliction, faithful in prayer."
6. "Share with God's people who are in need."
7. "Practice hospitality."

This list of admonitions was not given as a "checklist" of Christian duties, which are to be expressed in some legalistic fashion. Rather, these exhortations function as an explication of what it means to love genuinely (i.e., "without hypocrisy") as one of God's children. The focus of a Christian's attention is not on some list of responsibilities or duties. The Christian's focus must always be on the personal relationship with God that God himself has brought about through the person and work of Christ Jesus and the ministry of God's Spirit — with all these seven listed matters flowing quite "naturally" (or, rather, "supernaturally") from the relationship that God has established between himself and his people. Yet there are times in every Christian's life when he or she needs to be reminded about the responsibilities of the people of God. Thus Paul proclaimed at an

---

40. The use of the word ἀγάπη for "love" is, at best, severely restricted in pagan Greek writings. It appears occasionally in Jewish writings, as in the LXX (see esp. Song of Solomon; note also *Pss Sol* 18:3; *Let Aris* 229; Philo, *Quod Deus sit immutabilis* 69; *T Gad* 4:7; 5:2; *T Benj* 8:2; *Sib Or* 2, 65). In the NT, however, ἀγάπη is used repeatedly with reference to God's love, Christ's love, and the responding love of God's people to God, to Christ Jesus, and to other people. See also Paul's two uses of ἡ ἀγάπη ("the love") in the statements of 13:10.

earlier time, as may be conjectured, this message of Christian responsibility to his own Gentile converts in the eastern provinces of the Roman Empire — and then he included this same ethical emphasis in his letter to the Christians at Rome. And so by the mercy, love, and grace of God, we as believers in Jesus have received these same exhortations today.

12:14-21 Throughout Paul's proclamation of the first part of "the Christian love ethic" in 12:9-21, a number of independent (or "absolute") participles come to the fore in what seems to be an almost unending series of such occurrences. They appeared in rapid succession in 12:9-13, as noted above, without any regular verbal association. In 12:14-21, however, independent (or "absolute") participles are not only associated with other such participles, they also appear with independent (or "absolute") infinitives — as well as, of course, with regular imperative verbs, as participles usually do.

In 12:14 there appears the fairly common Greek syntactical pattern of the articular participle τοὺς διώκοντας ("those who persecute") in association with the second-person plural present imperative verb εὐλογεῖτε ("You must bless!") — and then in association with the second-person plural present imperative negative verbal phrase μὴ καταρᾶσθε ("Do not curse!"). In 12:15, however, the independent (or "absolute") participle χαιρόντων ("those who rejoice") appears with the independent (or "absolute") infinitive χαίρειν ("Rejoice!") and the independent (or "absolute") participle κλαιόντων ("those who mourn") is associated with the independent (or "absolute") infinitive κλαίειν ("Mourn!"). Likewise, in 12:16 the independent participle φρονοῦντες ("think alike" or "live in harmony") is set out in association with the independent participial negative injunction μὴ τὰ ὑψηλὰ φρονοῦντες ("Do not be haughty" or "proud") — as well as with the regular negative imperative verbal statement μὴ γίνεσθε φρόνιμοι παρ' ἑαυτοῖς ("Do not think of yourselves in conceited fashion"). Further, in 12:17-18 the independent participle ἀποδιδόντες ("being careful" or "taking care") is associated with such other independent participles as προνοούμενοι ("taking into consideration" or "having regard for") and εἰρηνεύοντες ("living at peace").

In all these instances in 12:14-18, the independent (or "absolute") participles and the independent (or "absolute") infinitives are equivalent to the regular imperative verbs that appear in the passage. In 12:19-21, however, imperative verbs — that is, imperative verbal constructions without any independent participles or independent infinitives — dominate what is written. The phenomena of both this usage and this variety of relationships in 12:14-21 have caused A. T. Robertson, as well as many interpreters of his generation and ours, to say somewhat in despair: "These various gradations in the use of the participle are not always clearly defined."[41]

My own understanding of this phenomenon in 12:14-21 of independent (or "absolute") participles being associated with other independent (or "absolute") participles, as well as associated with a few independent (or "absolute")

41. *ATRob*, 340.

infinitives — together, of course, with the more normal association of participles with imperative verbal constructions — may be set out as follows:

1. In 12:14a, 17a, 19-20, and 21, which are the four places in the passage where imperative verbal constructions appear, Paul should be understood as paraphrasing four "sayings of Jesus" that had been enshrined in the consciousness of at least some of the earliest Christian congregations (that is, as had been incorporated in a "Logia [i.e., a 'Sayings']" or so-called Q collection, which evidently existed before the teachings of Jesus were set out in the narrative context and the verbal form that they presently have in our Synoptic Gospels) — and, further, in three of these paraphrastic renderings of the "sayings of Jesus" that Paul here sets out, the wording is very similar to that used later in the Synoptic Gospels, that is, as appears in the "saying" of 12:14a (cf. Matt 5:44//Luke 6:27-28), in the "saying" of 12:17a (cf. Matt 5:39-42//Luke 6:29-30), and in the "saying" of 12:21 (cf. Matt 5:38-48//Luke 6:27-36).[42]

2. The exhortation "Do not take revenge, beloved ones, but leave room for God's wrath" given in 12:19a — together with the OT materials of 12:19b-20 quoted from Deut 32:35 ("It is mine to avenge; I will repay") and Prov 25:21-22a ("If your enemy is hungry, give him food to eat; if he is thirsty, give him water to drink. In doing this, you will heap burning coals on his head") — should also be viewed as most likely drawn from some earlier "Logia" or "Q" collection of "sayings of Jesus." Matthew and Luke chose not to include this exhortation and these OT passages as "sayings of Jesus" in their Gospels, probably because they considered the metaphor of "heaping burning coals on an enemy's head" as somewhat too difficult for their readers to understand. Paul, however, writing earlier than the canonical Evangelists, seems to have felt no hesitancy to include this figure of speech — along with its context of a "saying" of Jesus and the OT passages that he quotes — in his list of the four dominical sayings that he sets out in this passage.

3. The independent participles and the independent infinitives that appear in 12:14-18 are all to be found in Paul's two sets of his own related exhortations (i.e., in vv. 15-16 and vv. 17b-18), which follow the first two "sayings of Jesus" cited by him in vv. 14 and 17a — with the function of these inde-

---

42. This matter regarding Paul's use of the teachings of Jesus is only part of a much larger question that has long divided NT scholars (for a helpful survey of issues and stances from the early nineteenth century through the latter part of the twentieth century, see Furnish, "The Jesus-Paul Debate," 342-81). Without attempting to delineate the contours of that very long discussion, whether past or present, I would here only state my agreement with Allison, "The Pauline Epistles and the Synoptic Gospels," 25: "The persistent conviction that Paul knew next to nothing of the teaching of Jesus must be rejected. Jesus of Nazareth was not the faceless presupposition of Pauline theology. On the contrary, the tradition stemming from Jesus well served the apostle in his roles as pastor, theologian, and missionary."

pendent participles and independent infinitives in vv. 15-16 and vv. 17b-18 being evidently intended by him to be equivalent to the imperative verbs that appear in the first two "sayings of Jesus" in vv. 14 and 17a.

4. The exhortation of 12:21, which paraphrases the teaching of Jesus as presented later in Matt 5:38-48 and Luke 6:27-36, "may be said," as Charles Cranfield has written, "to sum up the whole subsection 12:14-21; for the theme of these verses is precisely the victory of the believer, of the man who is held fast by the good of the gospel, over the evil of the world."[43]

Thus we propose that in attempting to understand Paul's exhortations in 12:14-21, the structure of the passage should be viewed as follows:

12:14-16: A paraphrastic rendering of a "saying of Jesus" in 12:14: "Bless those who persecute you; bless and do not curse them!" (cf. Matt 5:44//Luke 6:27-28) — which is followed in 12:15-16 by Paul's own expository exhortations: "Rejoice with those who rejoice; mourn with those who mourn." "Live in harmony with one another." "Do not be proud, but be willing to associate with people of low position." "Do not be conceited."

12:17-18: A paraphrastic rendering of a "saying of Jesus" in 12:17a: "Do not repay anyone evil for evil" (cf. Matt 5:39-42//Luke 6:29-30) — which is followed in 12:17b-18 by Paul's expository exhortations: "Take care to do what is right in the eyes of everybody." "If it is possible, so far as it depends on you, live at peace with everyone."

12:19-20: A paraphrastic rendering of a "saying of Jesus" in 12:19a: "Do not take revenge, beloved ones, but leave room for God's wrath" — which is followed in 12:19b-20 not by further expository exhortations given by Paul but by OT support drawn by Jesus himself from Deut 32:35 and Prov 25:21-22 (including the notoriously difficult metaphor of Prov 25:22 regarding "heaping burning coals on a person's head"), with these OT quotations evidently having been included in an earlier "Logia" or "Q" collection of "sayings of Jesus" (though not reproduced by either Matthew or Luke in their Gospels).

12:21: A paraphrastic rendering of a "saying of Jesus" in this final verse of the passage: "Do not be overcome by evil, but overcome evil with good" (cf. Matt 5:38-48//Luke 6:27-36) — which "saying" Paul did not develop in any way, but let stand as a conclusion to his whole discussion of 12:14-21.[44]

43. Cranfield, *Romans*, 2.650.

44. On such a consciousness of Jesus' teachings and example among early Christians, see our chapter "Christological Materials in the Early Christian Communities," which is ch. 3 in R. N. Longenecker, ed., *Contours of Christology in the New Testament*, 61-68. In addition to the important article cited earlier by Allison, "The Pauline Epistles and the Synoptic Gospels," see also the significant presentations by D. M. Stanley, "Pauline Allusions to the Sayings of Jesus," 26-39; Stuhlmacher,

The most perplexing problem of interpretation in this second set of exhortations in 12:14-21 is how to understand the metaphor in 12:20b of "heaping" or "carrying coals of fire" on a person's head — not only in its OT usage and its possible employment by Jesus, but also in Paul's usage here. This figure of speech may be understood in the Hebrew (MT) text of Prov 25:22a to refer to "*removing* coals of fire [i.e., judgment] *from* an enemy." But that interpretation cannot be supported by the Greek of the LXX nor by its use here in Rom 12:20b. Most commentators, therefore, have understood "coals of fire" as a symbol of "burning pangs of shame";[45] others, however, have interpreted it as a symbol of "a more noble type of revenge."[46]

In 1953 and in 1975, however, the Egyptologist Siegfried Morenz called attention to an Egyptian ceremonial ritual of the priests of Memphis in which an enemy would express genuine repentance for the offenses he had committed by coming before those he had wronged "with a forked stick in his hand and a censer of fire upon his head."[47] This Egyptian ritual is from the third century B.C., and thus later than the composition of the OT book of Proverbs. Nevertheless, its reference to "a censer of fire upon his head" may reflect an earlier Egyptian ritual practice that became something of a metaphor or figure of speech connoting the idea of repentance in the ancient world — with the likelihood that it was so understood (1) by the writer of Prov 25:22, (2) by Jesus (if Prov 25:22 was included in an early "sayings of Jesus" collection), and (3) by Paul in Rom 12:20b (quoting Jesus, as we believe is most likely the case).

BIBLICAL THEOLOGY

What Paul presents here in 12:9-21 is ethical material (1) that he was convinced was an integral part of the Christian gospel, and so must accompany every proclamation of the Christian message; (2) that he viewed as representing the essential features of his ethical teaching, and therefore needed to be included in his presentation to the Christians at Rome to inform them more fully of the nature of his message to Gentiles in the Greco-Roman world; and (3) that he considered an important feature of his "spiritual gift" he was presenting to the Christians at Rome in order "to make them strong" and so that both they and he "might be mutually encouraged by each other's faith" (as he promised his addressees earlier in 1:11-12).

We have treated 12:9-21 as a rather formal exposition of Christian ethics; it has a quite distinctive rhetorical and literary form that would have lent itself

---

"Jesustradition im Römerbrief?" 140-50; Wenham, "Paul's Use of the Jesus Tradition," 7-37; Dunn, "Paul's Knowledge of the Jesus Tradition," 193-207; and M. B. Thompson, *Clothed with Christ,* passim.

45. So, e.g., Origen, Ambrosiaster, Augustine, Jerome, and many modern commentators.

46. So, e.g., Chrysostom, Theophylact, and some contemporary commentators.

47. Morenz, "Feurige Kohlen auf dem Haupt," 187-92, as cited and discussed by Klassen, "Coals of Fire," 337-50; see also *idem,* "Love Your Enemy," 147 71 (cap. 161 63).

to both oral and written proclamation. In fact (to repeat the observation of A. T. Robertson cited earlier): the confluence of independent (or "absolute") participles and independent (or "absolute") infinitives that appears in this passage is "the most outstanding example" of its kind in the NT.[48] Further, we have captioned this portion of ethical material "The Christian Love Ethic: Part I," for (1) the articular expression ἡ ἀγάπη ("the love") appears at the very beginning of this passage and (2) there is spelled out in these verses an understanding of how "the love [of the people of God]" is to express itself with respect to "those who are God's people" (in 12:9-13) and then to "those who oppose God's people" (in 12:14-21). Later in 13:8-14 the apostle will present "The Christian Love Ethic: Part II," in a somewhat different style and for a somewhat different purpose. Here in 12:9-21, however, he presents the basic core of his teaching regarding the Christian love ethic, which he evidently included in his evangelistic outreach to pagan Gentiles — thereby proclaiming not only (1) his distinctive theological message of peace, reconciliation, and life "in Christ," as he spelled it out in a personal, relational, and participatory fashion in 5:1–8:39, but also (2) his unique ethical teaching on what it means to live a new life of love "in Christ," as previously set out in his admonitions of 12:1-8 but particularly highlighted in these more formally patterned exhortations of 12:9-21.

The pattern of Paul's ethical preaching and teaching comes especially to the fore here in 12:9-21, that is, in his presentation of "The Christian Love Ethic: Part I" — though certain features of this pattern also appear in his previous admonitions of 12:1-8; in "The Christian Love Ethic: Part II," of 13:8-14; and in his still later applications of these ethical statements to actual practice within the Christian congregations at Rome in 14:1–15:13. This pattern of Paul's ethical preaching and teaching lays particular emphasis on (1) the ethical implications that are inherent in the Christian proclamation of the gospel and (2) the religious teachings and ethical example of the historical Jesus. Later in 13:8-14 Paul will also speak of "the genuine love of the people of God" as being "the fulfillment of the [Mosaic] law"; still later he will draw attention in 14:1–15:13 to how the ethical implications of the gospel proclamation and the teachings and example of Jesus are in line with the ethics of the OT.

In the foregoing passages of 12:1-2, 12:3-8, and 12:9-21, however, as has often been pointed out, there is no reference to God's Holy Spirit as guiding, controlling, or empowering the ethical thought and life of a believer in Jesus — at least no explicit reference to this effect. Earlier in 5:1–8:39 the apostle had spoken extensively regarding the Holy Spirit in the life of the Christian — doing so most expressly with reference to (1) the Spirit having been given to believers in Jesus, who have been made righteous and have experienced the love of God poured out into their hearts (in 5:5); (2) Christians being able to "serve in the new way of the Spirit, and not in the old way of the written code" (in 7:6); (3) "the law of the Spirit [or 'the spirit'] of life" having freed believers from "the

---

48. Citing again, *ATRob*, 946.

942

law of sin and death" (in 8:2); (4) God's purpose in freeing believers from the (Mosaic) law being so "that the righteous requirements of the law might be fully met in us, who do not live according to the sinful nature but according to the Spirit" (in 8:4); (5) Christians not being controlled by "the sinful nature" but "by the Spirit" (in 8:9); (6) "the Spirit" giving "life because of righteousness" (in 8:10); (7) God giving life to "the mortal bodies" of believers "because of his Spirit who lives in them" (in 8:11); (8) "the children of God" being "led by the Spirit of God" (in 8:11); (9) believers in Jesus having received "adoption" as God's children by the work of God's Spirit and so being able to address God as "Father" by that same Holy Spirit (in 8:15); (10) "the Spirit" testifying to a Christian's spirit that he or she is a child of God (in 8:16); (11) "the Spirit" interceding on behalf of believers in Jesus before God "with groans that words cannot express" (in 8:26); and (12) God knowing "the mind of the Spirit" on behalf of God's people "because the Spirit intercedes for God's people in accordance with the will of God" (in 8:27). Luke Timothy Johnson has quite appropriately written about the problem involved here:

> Reading Romans to this point one could easily conclude that God's Holy Spirit was most actively and intimately involved in the moral life of believers. Everything in Paul's argument leads the reader to this expectation. Yet when Paul turns in 12:1 to the moral consequences of his argument (note the οὖν, "therefore"), such language about the Holy Spirit virtually disappears.[49]

Yet in discussing relations between Paul's religious language that is "explicitly and obviously religious in character," which "aligns human agency with a transcendental spiritual power" (as earlier in 1:16–11:36), and his hortatory language that is "moral or paraenetic in character," which "advocates the practice of virtue and the avoidance of vice" (as here in 12:1–15:13), Luke Timothy Johnson has argued (1) that there is an intrinsic link between these two modes of discourse in Paul's letter to Rome, (2) that Paul himself indicates that there is such a link, and (3) that such a connection is to be inferred from the previous religious language (as found explicitly in 5:5, 7:6, and especially 8:1-30) that the apostle himself does not explicate in these three passages of 12:1-21.[50] And Johnson supports his thesis regarding the theory and form of Paul's ethical statements first in 5:1–8:39 and then in 12:1-21 by comparing them to the theory and form of Aristotle's ethical statements in his *Nicomachean Ethics*[51] — though

---

49. L. T. Johnson, "Transformation of the Mind and Moral Discernment in Paul," 217.

50. As Johnson has set out in question form in *ibid.*, 215, which he then explicates throughout all of pp. 216-36.

51. *Ibid.*, 221-25. On relations between Paul and Aristotle, Johnson quite clearly states: "I do not suggest that Paul was writing with a copy of the *Nicomachean Ethics* in hand, or that Aristotle was a direct influence. I am suggesting that Paul's language about moral discernment follows a strikingly similar kind of logic" (225).

Johnson also highlights the difference of Paul vis-à-vis Aristotle in his explicit Christological content and his implied pneumatic understanding, which functioned to bathe all the apostle's ethical teaching and practice.[52]

Accepting Johnson's overall thesis, together with most of its specific points, we can quite appropriately say that in any truly Christian ethical thought and practice certain features need always to be emphasized: (1) the implications of the Christian gospel; (2) the teaching and example of the historical Jesus; (3) the acknowledgment that what can be drawn from the ethical implications of the gospel message and from the teaching and example of Jesus is in line with the proclamation of the Israelite prophets of the OT; and (4) the necessity for the direction given by these first three factors to be actualized in a Christian's personal and corporate living by the guidance, control, and empowerment of God's Spirit. Thus by taking into consideration all four of these matters, there is the real possibility of constructing a truly biblical theology that deals effectively with both "personal ethics" and "social ethics."

CONTEXTUALIZATION FOR TODAY

As Paul presents matters in 12:1-2, the formation of a Christian ethical consciousness is based on (1) a recollection of "God's mercies," (2) the acceptance of the message of "the Christian gospel" and its implications, (3) God's "transformation" of a person by means of divine salvation, and (4) God's continual "renewing of the mind" of a believing person. Here in Part I of his exposition on "the love of the people of God" in 12:9-21 (as well as later in Part II of that same topic in 13:8-14 *and* his specific appeals to the Christians at Rome with respect to a division among believers regarding certain dietary matters in 14:1-13), the apostle goes on to speak of a Christian's ethical thinking and actions as being directed by (1) the implications that can be drawn from the message of the Christian gospel and (2) the teachings and example of the historical Jesus — with OT quotations being drawn into the presentations not as the primary basis for the ethical thinking and living of Christians, but simply to demonstrate that Christian ethics, as based on implications drawn from the message of the Christian gospel and the teachings and example of Jesus, are in line with the revelation given by God in the Jewish (OT) Scriptures. And although the Christian life is often thought of and expressed in a way that all too often resembles some type of Jewish legalism or some form of Greek Stoicism, its essential theocentric, Christocentric, and pneumatic nature needs always today to be recaptured, highlighted, and contextualized in the thinking and actions of believers in Jesus individually and of the Christian church corporately.

---

52. L. T. Johnson, "Transformation of the Mind and Moral Discernment in Paul," 225-29. See also Johnson's conclusion in the final paragraphs of 235-36.

4. Exhortations regarding Christians and the State (13:1-7)

TRANSLATION

[13:1]*Let everyone be subject to the governing authorities. For there is no authority except that which God has established — and those that exist have been appointed by God.* [2]*So whoever rebels against the authority is rebelling against that which God has instituted, and those who do so will bring judgment on themselves.*

[3]*For rulers hold no terror with respect to good work; rather, with regard to what is evil. Do you want to be free from fear of the one in authority? Then do what is right and you will be commended.* [4]*For the one in authority is God's servant to each of you for the purpose of the good. But if you do wrong, be afraid. For rulers do not bear the sword for nothing. They are God's servant, an agent of wrath to bring punishment on those who do evil.* [5]*Therefore, it is a necessity to submit yourselves [to human governmental authorities], not only because of [possible] punishment but also because of conscience.*

[6]*This is also why you pay taxes, for the authorities are God's servants who give their full time to governing.* [7]*Give to everyone what you owe: If you owe taxes, pay taxes; if revenue, then revenue; if respect, then respect; if honor, then honor.*

TEXTUAL NOTES

13:1a The exhortation πᾶσα ψυχὴ ἐξουσίαις ὑπερεχούσαις ὑποτασσέσθω ("Let everyone [literally 'every soul' or 'every person'] be subject to the governing authorities") is widely attested by uncials ℵ A B D² P Ψ [also *Byz* L] and by minuscules 33 1175 1739 (Category I), 81 256 1506 1881 1962 2127 (Category II), and 5 6 61 69 88 104 218 263 323 326 330 365 436 441 451 459 467 614 621 623 629 630 915 917 1241 1243 1319 1398 1505 1563 1573 1678 1718 1735 1751 1838 1845 1852 1874 1875 1877 1908 1912 1942 1959 2110 2138 2197 2200 2344 2492 2495 2516 2523 2544 2718 (Category III). An early variant, however, omits πᾶσα ψυχή ("everyone"; literally "every soul" or "every person") at the beginning of the verse and inserts the dative plural πάσαις ("to all") before ἐξουσίαις ὑπερεχούσαις ὑποτάσσεσθε (thereby reading "Be subject to *all* the governing authorities"). This variant reading seems to have first entered the Greek textual tradition about A.D. 200 through a scribe responsible for P⁴⁶. It was then taken over in fourth- and fifth-century Latin translations it^(ar, b, d*, f, g, t) vg^(mss) and is supported by such Western commentators as Irenaeus^(lat) Hippolytus (Tertullian) and Ambrosiaster. Later it reappeared in the Greek textual tradition in sixth-century uncial D* (06) and ninth-century uncials F and G.

In both its omission and its insertion, this variant reading seems to represent an attempt to expand the significance of the phrase ἐξουσίαις ὑπερεχούσαις from referring to "the city officials *at Rome*" to including "*all governing authorities wherever and when-*

ever they might rule." On the other hand, it may have been introduced by the scribe of P[46] — then carried on by a number of Old Latin translators, Vulgate editors, and Western commentators — because of its "less formal style" or "in order to avoid the Hebraic idiom involved in the phrase πᾶσα ψυχή."[1]

1b The prepositional expression ὑπὸ θεοῦ ("by God") is amply attested in the Greek textual tradition. The variant ἀπὸ θεοῦ ("from God"), however, receives support from uncials D* F G and from minuscules 1506 (Category II) and 69 88 323 629 1573 (Category III). Yet textual support for ἀπὸ θεοῦ ("from God") is far too weak for that variant reading to be accepted. The substitution of ἀπὸ θεοῦ for ὑπὸ θεοῦ was probably done to effect a linguistic improvement that would more ably signify "that which God has established." But whatever the reason for its displacement in some Greek MSS, the expression ὑπὸ θεοῦ ("by God") quite ably connotes "that which God has established."

1c The text with only the plural article αἱ ("those"), that is, without the repetition of ἐξουσίαι ("authorities"), is supported by uncials ℵ A B D F G P and minuscules 1739 (Category I), 81 1506 1881 (Category II), and 6 88 330 365 424[c] 1319 1573 (Category III); it also is reflected in Latin and Coptic versions and is supported by Irenaeus[lat] and Origen. The addition of the noun ἐξουσία, however, appears in uncials D[2] P Ψ (also *Byz* L) and in minuscules 33 1175 (Category I) and 69 104 323 326 424[c] 614 1241 1243 1505 1735 1874 2344 2495 (Category III), but is a secondary and quite unnecessary addition.

1d The omission of the article in the phrase ὑπὸ θεοῦ ("by God") of the final clause of this verse is amply attested by uncials ℵ* A B D F G P and by minuscules 1739 (Category I), 81 1506 1881 (Category II), and 69 88 104 365 1243 1319 1573 (Category III); this omission is also supported by Origen. The appearance of the article τοῦ before θεοῦ ("the God") is supported by uncial ℵ[c] (also *Byz* L) and by minuscules 33 1175 (Category I) and 6 323 326 330 614 1241 1505 1735 1874 2344 2495 (Category III), but is most likely a secondary addition for stylistic purposes.

3a The phrase τῷ ἀγαθῷ ἔργῳ ("with respect to good work") is attested by P[46], by uncials A B D* F[c] G, and by minuscules 1739 (Category I), 256 1506 1881 (Category II), and 6 424[c] 630 1319 1573 1852 2110 2523 (Category III); it also is reflected in Latin and Coptic versions and is supported by Irenaeus[lat] and Clement. The variant plural genitive phrase τῶν ἀγαθῶν ἔργων ("of good works"), however, appears in uncials D[2] and Ψ (also *Byz* L) and in minuscules 33 1175 (Category I), 81 1962 2127 (Category II), and 5 61 69 88 104 181 218 263 323 326 330 365 436 441 451 459 467 614 621 623 629 915 917 1241 1398 1505 1563 1678 1718 1735 1751 1838 1845 1874 1875 1877 1908 1912 1942 1959 2138 2200 2344 2492 2495 2516 2544 2718 (Category III); it also is reflected in various Syriac versions. This variant phraseology likely represents an attempt to improve the sentence both grammatically and stylistically. Likewise, the variant τῷ ἀγαθοεργῷ ("with respect to the one doing good"), which is found in ninth-century uncial F (010), is probably also an attempted grammatical and stylistic improvement.

4a The second-person dative singular pronoun σοί ("you," which we have translated "to each of you") is very widely attested in the textual tradition. This singular pronoun, however, is omitted in ninth-century uncials F (010) and G (012) and in minuscule

---

1. As suggested by Metzger, *Textual Commentary,* 467.

2344 (Category III); it is also not reflected in bo^ms — probably because it was thought that a singular pronoun was inappropriate in an exhortation that begins with such an expansive phrase as πᾶσα ψυχή ("everyone," "every soul," or "every person").

4b The article τό ("the") in the purpose clause εἰς τὸ ἀγαθόν ("for the purpose of the good") is almost universally accepted in the Greek textual tradition. It is, however, omitted in fourth-century Codex Vaticanus (B 03), probably due to a scribal error or because of an attempted stylistic improvement.

4c The word order of ἔκδικος εἰς ὀργήν (literally "an avenger for wrath") is amply attested by P^46, by uncials ℵ^c A B P Ψ* and fifth-century 048 [also *Byz* L], and by minuscules 1739 (Category I), 81 1506 1881 (Category II), and 6 69 88 104 326 330 365 630 1243 1319 1505 1573 2495 (Category III); it is also supported by Irenaeus^lat. The prepositional expression εἰς ὀργήν ("for wrath"), however, is omitted in uncials D* F G. Also to be noted is the reversed word order εἰς ὀργὴν ἔκδικος ("for wrath the avenger") that appears in uncials ℵ* D^2 Ψ^c and in such minuscules as 33 1175 (Category I) and 323 614 1241 1319 1735 1874 2344 (Category III). But neither of these two variant readings has sufficient MS support to be accepted as original.

5 The presence of the present middle infinitive ὑποτάσσεσθαι ("to submit your-selves") is very widely attested by uncials ℵ A B P Ψ and fifth-century 048, as well as by minuscules 33 1175 1739 (Category I), 81 1506 1881 1962 2127 (Category II), and 88 104 181 323 326 330 365 436 451 614 629 630 1241 1505 1573 1735 1877 2492 2495 (Category III). This form of the verb is also reflected in Latin, Syriac, and Coptic versions. The second-person plural present imperative ὑποτάσσεσθε ("you must submit yourselves"), however, ap-pears in P^46, in uncials D F G, and in minuscules 6 69 1243 1319 1874 2344 (Category III); it also is reflected in the Old Latin version it and is supported by Irenaeus^lat and Ambrosiaster. But a second-person plural present imperative suffix -εσθε ("you must") is not sufficiently attested in the textual tradition to displace the present middle infinitive suffix -εσθαι as having been original. Evidently certain scribes in their transcription of 13:5 were influenced by the use of imperative verbs earlier in the paraphrasing of the "sayings of Jesus" in 12:14a, 12:17a, 12:19-20, and 12:21.

FORM/STRUCTURE/SETTING

Paul's exhortations on "Christians and the state" in 13:1-7, both in their content and in their form, have appeared to many interpreters to be somewhat "out of keeping" with his "Christian love ethic" as set out in 12:9-21 (and continued in a somewhat different form in 13:8-14). For his appeals here in 13:1-7 seem, at least at first glance, to be rather different from their immediate context in that (1) they are specific in scope and application, whereas the exhortations that surround them in chs. 12–13 are much more sweeping and general; (2) their argument is based on what God has established by his sovereign choice, whereas prominent throughout the rest of the presentations in chs. 12–15 are the motivational fac-tors having to do with Christology, eschatology, and love (ἀγάπη); and (3) they break the apparent continuity of the apostle's "Christian love ethic" as set out in

12:9-21 and 13:8-14. But the apostle's letter was written to Christians who lived in the capital city of the Roman Empire. Thus it would be rather strange if he did not say something in it about how those Christians were to evaluate and relate to the governmental authorities of that major capital city.

Indeed, amidst conditions of civic and political unrest in Rome in the middle and late 50s — which seem (1) to have arisen because of the rapacious practices of those who were collecting the city's taxes, revenues, and tolls, and (2) to have come to a head at the very time the apostle was completing this letter in A.D. 58[2] — it would be strange if the apostle did not write something about how believers in Jesus should respond to the conditions of turmoil in the city. For events that were then taking place at Rome, together with the response of the believers in Jesus to those events, would have had very serious repercussions for both (1) the lives and witness of the Christians living in Rome and (2) the thinking and actions of nascent Christianity within the whole of the Roman Empire generally with respect to this continually pressing subject of "Christians and the state."

Or stating matters in a more theological manner, it would be quite strange if in writing to believers in Rome the apostle did not attempt to provide some pastoral counsel to those who were then, as it seems, psychologically torn between (1) experiencing the inauguration of "the age to come" and rejoicing in their "new life in Christ" and (2) being called by God to live out their lives in a suitable manner as members of "this age."[3] For even though the Christians at Rome were new people "in Christ," whose lives had been changed by the message of the Christian gospel and the ministry of God's Spirit among them, they were also confronted by troubling concerns of a civic and political nature that were of great practical importance to them both as people living in the capital city and as believers in Jesus who were attempting to express in a faithful manner a Christian witness to a secular and essentially pagan culture — with all these issues being focused for them in the very "down to earth" concerns of (1) whether or not they should continue to pay taxes, revenues, and tolls to their local civic officials, and (2) to what extent they should respect and honor their city's governmental authorities.

It may always be debated exactly how this passage of seven verses relates to what the apostle wrote immediately before it and immediately after it in chs. 12–13. For there are no connecting particles or conjunctions in 13:1, as well as none in the following verses of 13:2-7, that would link in any direct manner 13:1-7 to what appears immediately before it in 12:9-21. Nor are there any such particles or conjunctions between this passage and 13:8-14. Yet, while accepting the integrity of the passage, it may legitimately be argued that Paul himself (1) viewed his appeals of 13:1-7 as highly significant contextualizations of his "Christian Love

2. Cf. Friedrich, Pöhlmann, and Stuhlmacher, "Zur historischen Situation und Intention von Röm 13,1-7," 342-81. Note our discussions of the relevancy of their proposal in R. N. Longenecker, *Introducing Romans*, 49-50, 121-22, and 145; see also "Exegetical Comments" below.

3. On "this age" and "the age to come" in Paul's thought and throughout the NT generally, see esp. Cullmann, *Christ and Time*, 47-48, 81-93, and 222-30.

Ethic: Part I," which he had just set out in 12:9-21, and (2) believed that these ethical appeals would be particularly relevant for believers in Jesus at Rome in their present situation. So he exhorts his addressees to be subject to their governing authorities; to pay their legitimate taxes, revenues, and tolls; and to respect and honor their city officials.[4]

The more general message of Christian civic responsibility that appears in the first portion of this passage, in 13:1-5, was probably earlier proclaimed by the apostle during his Gentile mission in cities and towns in the eastern provinces of the Roman Empire. For Paul's Gentile Christian converts who lived in such other localities under Roman rule would have undoubtedly been confronted by many of these same issues. Here in 13:1-7, however, Paul seems to have desired not only to contextualize his proclamation of the Christian gospel by writing in rather broad strokes regarding the attitude of believers in Jesus toward human governments generally (as he probably did elsewhere in his Gentile mission, and as he reported the essence of that message to his Christian addressees here at Rome in 13:1-5) but also to give specific advice as a Christian apostle to believers in Rome regarding their response to the civic and political matters that were at that time troubling them (as he does in 13:6-7) — even though his more general hortatory statements of 13:1-5 (which he may have given a number of times to his Christian converts during his Gentile mission) and his quite specific advice of 13:6-7 (which deals directly in quite specific fashion with a proper Christian response to the specific matters that were then occurring in Rome) might have seemed to some Church Fathers of only a few centuries later (as well as to many NT commentators today) as rather discordant in comparison to his much more sweeping statements regarding "the Christian love ethic" presented in 12:9-21 (in one form) and in 13:8-14 (in another form).

Diverse Understandings of the Occasion and Purpose of the Exhortations and Appeals of 13:1-7. From the earliest Christian readings of 13:1-7 to readings of the passage today, there have been diverse views regarding the occasion for and the intended purpose of the exhortations and appeals in this passage. A widespread understanding among the early Church Fathers was (1) that there existed in the Christian congregations at Rome some "overly enthusiastic" or "extremist" believers in Jesus who thought that the gospel message of "new life in Christ" and "God's inauguration of a new age in human history" required a rejection of everything that had to do with "this age" and "the old world," which would have included their rejection of all forms of human government and their refusal to pay taxes and tolls levied by any human authority, and (2) that Paul was in this passage endeavoring to counter such a perversion of the Christian

---

4. Or, concomitantly, it may be argued that, having based his general ethical exhortations on the teachings of Jesus in 12:14, in 12:17 (also in 12:19-20, as seems most likely), and in 12:21 — as well as having included a further "Jesus saying" in what immediately follows in 13:8 — the apostle simply interjected this material of 13:1-7 into the larger context of his more general exhortations regarding a "Christian love ethic," since both his exhortations of 12:9-21 and his appeals of 13:1-7 are based, in one way or another, on the teachings of the historical Jesus.

message.[5] This understanding of the occasion and purpose of 13:1-7 has been accepted by a number of interpreters of fairly recent times.[6]

Other interpreters have argued that the edict of Claudius in A.D. 49, which expelled a large number of Jews from Rome "because the Jews constantly made disturbances at the instigation of Chrestus"[7] — coupled with a possibly earlier edict of Claudius in 41, which allowed the Jews of Rome to continue their "traditional mode of life" but ordered them "not to hold meetings"[8] — was remembered with both anguish and resentment by the Christians at Rome (especially by Jewish believers, but also by many Gentile believers). So it is argued that Paul's exhortations of 13:1-7 were intended to stifle any continuing resentment against Rome and its officials by believers in Jesus, in order to ward off any possible recurrence of official antagonism by the city's authorities that would be prejudicial against the "Christ followers" of the city — who were, in all likelihood, still viewed by the city's officials as a Jewish sect because of their claim to be believers in Jesus of Nazareth, whom they viewed as the Jewish Messiah.[9]

Both of these understandings have been proposed, in various ways (whether separately or together), by NT commentators in earlier times and today — with John Calvin's comments on these two understandings often quoted in support (on the first explicitly, but also on the second allusively, since Calvin was unable to use modern scholarly studies of Jewish Zealotism or critical assessments of Rome's suppression and expulsion of the Jews). In his opening comments on 13:1-7 in his Romans commentary, Calvin wrote as follows:

> Paul's careful treatment of this passage in his instructions concerning the Christian life seems to have been forced on him by some great necessity, which the preaching of the Gospel was able to occasion in that age in particular, although at all times this is involved in it. There are always some restless spirits who believe that the kingdom of Christ is properly exalted only when all earthly powers are abolished, and that they can enjoy the liberty which He has given them only if they have shaken off every yoke of human slavery. This error, however, possessed the minds of the Jews more than others, for they thought it a disgrace that the offspring of Abraham, whose Kingdom

---

5. See, e.g., the analyses of Schelkle, "Staat und Kirchen in der patristischen Auslegung von Röm 13:1-7," 223-36; Blank, "Kirche und Staat im Urchristentum," 9-28; and K. Aland, "Das Verhältnis von Kirche und Staat in der Frühzeit," 60-246.

6. So, e.g., Nygren, *Romans,* 426-27; H. Schlier, "The State according to the New Testament," in his *The Relevance of the New Testament* (New York: Herder and Herder, 1968), 229-30 (reprinted in his *Römerbrief, ad loc.*); Wilckens, "Römer 13.1-7," 226-30; Ridderbos, *Paul,* 320-23; Fitzmyer, *Romans,* 663; and Moo, *Romans,* 792-94.

7. Cf. Suetonius, *Claudius* 25.4 (see our discussion in *Introducing Romans,* 67-69).

8. Cf. Cassius Dio, *Historia Romana* 60.6.6-7.

9. So, e.g., Borg, "A New Context for Romans xiii," 205-18; R. A. Culpepper, "God's Righteousness in the Life of His People: Romans 12–15," *RevExp* 13 (1976) 456-57; E. Bammel, "Romans 13," in *Jesus and the Politics of His Day,* ed. E. Bammel and C. F. D. Moule (Cambridge: Cambridge University Press, 1984), 366-75; and J. Moiser, "Rethinking Romans 12–15," *NTS* 36 (1990) 571-82.

had flourished greatly before the coming of the Redeemer, should continue in bondage after His appearing.

There was also another thing, which alienated the Jews as much as the Gentiles from their rulers. These rulers not only all detested true godliness, but also persecuted religion with feelings of utmost hostility. It seemed absurd, therefore, to acknowledge as lawful masters and rulers those who were contriving to snatch the kingdom from Christ, the only Lord of heaven and earth.

It is probable that these reasons led Paul to establish the authority of the magistrates with the greater care. He first of all lays down a general precept which briefly summarizes what he intends to say, and then adds further statements which help to explain and prove the precept.[10]

On the other hand, a number of NT text critics during the past two centuries have credited 13:1-7 to the work of a later redactor, and so have declared this passage to be a "gloss" or an "interpolation," mainly because of the lack of any explicit Christological or eschatological features in it[11] — though also because of the omission of any obvious linguistic connections with the theme of "love" that resonates throughout 12:9-21 before it or that appears in 13:8-14 after it.[12] Nonetheless, as Ernst Käsemann has pointed out:

> There is no reason to dispute the authenticity of the text . . . on either external or internal grounds. The fact that Irenaeus quotes it first (*Adv. Haer.* v.24.1) in opposition to the Gnostic misinterpretation of the authorities as angelic powers means nothing in face of the fact that the same tradition, which is obviously Jewish-Christian, is used already in 1 Pet 2:13-17. Possibly this passage might even be regarded as the first commentary on our text, although that remains problematic. At any rate, the great antiquity of the tradition is secured by its appearance in the framework of the household table in 1 Peter 2.[13]

And as Käsemann has quite rightly gone on to say: "There can be no denying that the entire general exhortation [of 13:1-7] is bracketed by 12:1f. and 13:8ff., so that it does in fact receive a Christian impress."[14]

10. Calvin, *Romans*, in *Calvin's Commentaries*, 8.280.
11. Often discounting any use by Paul of a "sayings of Jesus" tradition, whether oral or written, since his letter to Rome was written earlier than were the canonical Gospels.
12. So, e.g., Schmithals, *Römerbrief*, 458-62; O'Neill, *Romans*, 207-9; J. Kallas, "Romans XIII.1-7: An Interpolation," *NTS* 11 (1964-1965) 365-74; and W. Munro, "Romans 13:1-7: Apartheid's Last Biblical Refuge," *BTB* 20 (1990) 161-68. See also our discussion "Glosses and Interpolations" in the letter in R. N. Longenecker, *Introducing Romans*, 16-19, where a rather large number of earlier claims with respect to the presence of "glosses" and/or "interpolations" in Romans (including 13:1-7) are discussed.
13. Käsemann, *Romans*, 351.
14. *Ibid.*, 352.

Even more significant with respect to the historical context and Paul's purpose in writing 13:1-7, however, is the thesis proposed by Johannes Friedrich, Wolfgang Pöhlmann, and Peter Stuhlmacher, which they presented in a coauthored article of 1976: that the specific appeals of 13:6-7 regarding the payment of taxes, revenues, and tolls to civic authorities (at Rome) — as well as the exhortations of 13:1-5 (rephrased in 13:6-7) that urge that respect and honor be extended to human governmental authorities generally — are to be understood against the background of a growing unrest during the mid-50s among the people of Rome against the rapacious practices of government officials who were in charge of collecting the city's taxes, revenues, and tolls.[15] Tacitus (c. 56–c. 120), the Roman historian and orator who was at one time a praetor (i.e., a magistrate with judicial functions) of the city of Rome, reports that during the year 58 there was such an outcry by the people of Rome against the city's taxation system that the emperor Nero (who reigned from 54 to 68) was forced to intervene, though he did not abolish the city's taxes, revenues, or tolls but only ordered that the collectors be more strictly regulated.[16] Likewise, Suetonius (c. 69–c. 122), the Roman biographer, historian, and teacher of rhetoric, who was for a time the private secretary of the emperor Hadrian, speaks of Nero as having mitigated during his reign the most grievous burdens of Rome's system of taxes, revenues, and tolls.[17]

As Friedrich, Pöhlmann, and Stuhlmacher have pointed out, instructions regarding the payment of taxes are not only absent in Paul's other NT letters, they are also rarely found in other extant Jewish and Greco-Roman writings of Paul's day. Thus the fact that Paul probably wrote Romans during the winter of 57-58[18] — that is, at the very time when popular agitation was coming to a head in Rome against the rapacious practices of governmental officials in collecting the city's taxes, revenues, and tolls — suggests that 13:6-7, as well as 13:1-5, is best understood as the apostle's counsel to his Christian addressees on how they should respond in this particular situation, given at the precise time when the apostle's counsel was sorely needed. And if that is so (as we believe it to have been), it seems necessary to accept the following conclusions as voiced by Alexander Wedderburn: (1) that at least 13:6-7 evidences "a surprisingly intimate knowledge by Paul, not only of the circumstances within the Roman church, but also of the situation in which its members had to live, and of the social, economic and political environment that surrounded them," and (2) that Paul's advice to his Christian addressees "was written in light of that knowledge, and is to be interpreted by us in the light of that situation."[19]

15. Friedrich, Pöhlmann, and Stuhlmacher, "Zur historischen Situation und Intention von Röm 13,1-7," 131-66. See also F. Laub, "Der Christ und die staatliche Gewalt: Zum Verständnis der 'politischen' Paränese Römans 13,1-7 in der gegenwärtigen Diskussion," *MTZ* 30 (1979) 257-65; and Dunn, *Romans,* 2.759; *idem,* "Romans 13:1-7," 66.

16. Tacitus, *Annals* 13.50-51.

17. Suetonius, *Nero* 10.1.

18. See our discussion of "Date" in R. N. Longenecker, *Introducing Romans,* 46-50.

19. Wedderburn, *Reasons for Romans,* 63.

Proposals with Regard to the Historical Context and Literary Connections of 13:1-7, as well as regarding Paul's Purpose in Writing This Passage. There can be little doubt that some first-generation believers in Jesus were "overly enthusiastic" (or even "extremist") in their understanding of the Christian message of "new life in Christ" and "God's inauguration of a new era in history," and therefore would have viewed with suspicion whatever had to do with the "old era" or "old world" — including all forms of human government and all attempts by governmental officials to collect taxes, revenues, and tolls. The "saying of Jesus" later incorporated into the canonical Synoptic Gospels in Mark 12:17, Matt 22:21b, and Luke 20:25, "Render to Caesar the things that are Caesar's, and to God the things that are God's" — as well as the conflict situation reported by the three Synoptic Evangelists in which this saying appears — clearly suggests that anti-Roman views existed among Jesus' Jewish audiences, and that Jesus spoke about these matters. Likewise, 1 Tim 2:1-4, Titus 3:1-2, and 1 Pet 2:13-17 (whose exhortations with respect to a Christian's attitude toward human governments and their officials are in many respects similar to the appeals expressed here in Rom 13:1-7) suggest that such antigovernment attitudes were also present among early believers in Jesus. The fact that a number of early Church Fathers — who lived at some distance from one another, not only geographically but also temporally and theologically — understood the apostle's appeals of 13:1-7 as expressing his endeavor to counter such antigovernment tendencies among believers in Jesus, suggests that such an understanding of relations (or, rather, of "nonrelations") between the Christians at Rome and the officials of the city was rather widely known throughout the Roman Empire, and so could have existed among some of the "overly enthusiastic" or "extremist" believers in Jesus who lived in Rome at the time Paul was writing his letter to them.

Further, it is not too difficult to believe that the edict of Claudius in 49 (as well as the possibly earlier edict of Claudius in 41) was well remembered by both Jewish and Gentile believers of Rome.[20] So it may be argued that the Christians at Rome, both Jewish and Gentile believers, had embedded in their religious psyches a certain residual antagonism toward Roman authority, which would have served to support the theological extremism that resided among at least some of the Christians who then lived in the capital city. And both of these factors — that is, (1) an "overly enthusiastic" or "extremist" understanding of the Christian message that tended to reject anything having to do with "the old era" and "the old world," and (2) a lingering remembrance of Rome's attempts first to stifle Jewish gatherings (as with the edict of 41) and then to exterminate all Jewish debates by the deportation of a large body of Jews and Jewish sympathizers from the city (as with the edict of 49) — would have remained as residual memories in the minds and hearts of a great many of the Christians at Rome, whether ethnically Jews or Gentiles.

---

20. On our discussions of the edict of Claudius of 41 and Claudius's much more serious expulsion edict of 49, see R. N. Longenecker, *Introducing Romans*, 67-69.

These two factors undoubtedly affected the attitudes of the Christians at Rome toward the city's government and its officials — even though such antagonistic feelings toward human governments generally, as well as toward Rome's governing officials in particular, may have been somewhat dormant or resided in a veiled fashion in the minds and hearts of most of the "Christ followers" in their respective Christian congregations of the city. But while dormant and veiled, such views and antagonisms probably continued to exist among Roman believers in Jesus — much like dry brush and decaying trees that lie about on a forest floor without much notice, but become suddenly aflame when struck by a bolt of lightning or ignited by a match or some type of "spark."

The igniting spark that set aflame this dormant extremism and veiled antagonism in Rome's "Christ followers" appears to have been provided by the unscrupulous actions of the city's tax collectors in extracting exorbitant revenues and tolls from the people of the city — with the resultant tide of resentment, repulsion, and thoughts of revolt rising among the city's general population during the mid-50s and cresting sometime in 58. It may be conjectured that at least some of the believers in Jesus at Rome were prepared to express their support of such revolutionary thoughts and possible actions on the part of the city's populace by also renouncing their support of Rome's governing authorities and doing so by refusing to pay their assigned taxes, revenues, and tolls. Thus Paul, knowing in some way about the civic and political situation at Rome (probably from letters received from one or more of the people he will greet in 16:3-15), used the occasion of writing his letter to counsel them on how they should respond to the city's authorities generally and to the immediately pressing situation of their payment of taxes, revenues, and tolls to such unscrupulous city tax officials. Further, it may also be conjectured that when Paul set out his exhortations and appeals of 13:1-7, he saw himself contextualizing for his addressees such earlier statements as now appear toward the close of his "Christian Love Ethic, Part I" of 12:9-21 — that is, as found in 12:17-19 (which, as we have proposed, are most likely quoted "sayings of Jesus"): "Do not repay anyone evil for evil. Be careful to do what is right in the eyes of everyone" (12:17); "If it is possible, as far as it depends on you, live at peace with everyone" (12:18); and "Do not take revenge, beloved ones, but leave room for God's wrath" (12:19).

The Structure of 13:1-7. The exhortations of Paul in 13:1-7 can be set out as four subunits of material:

1. An opening exhortation in 13:1a: "Let everyone be subject to the governing authorities," which functions as the thesis statement for 13:1b-7.
2. The primary theological argument of 13:1b-2, which is set out in support of the opening hortatory thesis statement of 13:1a — with that primary supporting argument focused on God's establishment of human governmental authority and his judgment on those who oppose what he has instituted.
3. A series of further "logical" and "practical" supporting arguments in

13:3-5, which urge subjection to "the governing authorities" in order that Christians might avoid "possible punishment" and be true to their own "conscience" as based on the message of the Christian gospel and enlivened by God's Spirit.

4. The specific application in 13:6-7 of Paul's hortatory statements of 13:1-5, with particular reference to the controversial matters that were then confronting the Christians at Rome: (a) the paying of the city's taxes, (b) the paying of other tolls and governmental revenues, (c) respect owed to governmental authorities generally, and (d) honor owed to the city's officials in particular.

The structure of 13:1-7 suggests that the apostle has brought together in this passage two units of hortatory material that originated in his apostolic ministry. The first unit, as set out in 13:1-5, consists of a rather stock (i.e., "commonly used" or "often brought forward") body of exhortations regarding "Christians and the state," which Paul probably included in his ministry to his Gentile converts during his earlier missionary outreach to the eastern regions of the Roman Empire. The second unit, as set out in 13:6-7, contains specific appeals to believers in Jesus at Rome, in which he (1) speaks directly about the rising civil and political unrest taking place in the city, (2) seeks to dissuade the Christians there from aligning themselves with antigovernment rebellion, and (3) quotes in support the essence of a known "saying of Jesus" — which was of particular significance for the Christians at Rome in the situation confronting them during the middle and late 50s (accepting the thesis proposed by Friedrich, Pöhlmann, and Stuhlmacher).

EXEGETICAL COMMENTS

I. Opening Exhortation Functioning as the Thesis Statement for What Follows (13:1a)

13:1a The opening exhortation of 13:1a functions as the thesis statement for all that follows in the passage. Interpreters of this hortatory thesis statement, however, are immediately confronted by a number of rather perplexing issues that have a great deal to do with how one understands what is being exhorted in the rest of the passage in 13:1b-7 — that is, they are immediately faced by the following questions:

1. Where should the adjective "all" or "every" appear in the first part of 13:1 — that is, at the beginning of the exhortation in the nominative phrase πᾶσα ψυχή ("everyone"; literally "every soul") or as the first feature in the dative phraseology πάσαις ἐξουσαις ὑπερεχούσαις ("to all governing authorities")?

955

2. Whom did Paul have in mind by his use of the expression πᾶσα ψυχή ("everyone"; literally "every soul")? Was it "all of the believers in Jesus at Rome" or "all Christians generally" — or, perhaps, "all people everywhere"?
3. What did the apostle mean by the dative phrase ἐξουσίαις ὑπερεχούσαις ("the governing authorities")? Was it the civic officials at Rome or was it spiritual (or angelic) powers that he viewed as standing behind and acting out their desires in the decisions and actions of human officials — or, perhaps, both?

The first question is probably the most easily answered, since the reading "Let *everyone* (πᾶσα ψυχή; literally 'every soul') be subject to the governing authorities" is far better attested in the Greek MSS tradition than is the variant reading "Be subject *to all the governing authorities* (πάσαις ἐξουσίαις ὑπερεχούσαις)," which variant reading, while first appearing in the usually respected P[46], is mainly attested in the earlier portion of the textual tradition by fourth- and fifth-century Latin translations and some Western Church Fathers (see "Textual Notes" above). Further, it seems fairly obvious that by deleting πᾶσα ψυχή from the beginning of the thesis exhortation of 13:1a and adding πάσαις to the closing clause of the exhortation, some early Greek scribe (as represented by P[46]) sought to expand the expression ἐξουσίαις ὑπερεχούσαις ("to the governing authorities") so as not to have it refer to a particular local governmental authority (i.e., *the city officials at Rome*) but, rather, to include all human governmental authorities (i.e., *all government officials, whenever and wherever they rule*) — with this scribal adjustment of P[46] being carried on principally by Old Latin translators and Latin Vulgate editors, as well as by some fourth- and fifth-century Western commentators, and then by a few later Greek uncial MSS.

The second question — whom Paul had in mind by his use of the nominative phrase πᾶσα ψυχή — also seems fairly easy to answer. For any answer to this question must be based principally on a contextual reading of what appears in 13:1a, and not just on a strictly textual consideration. On this matter Charles Cranfield is quite right in declaring that πᾶσα ψυχή refers "in the context of Romans" to "every Christian (in Rome)." The exhortation may be applied in paradigmatic fashion to other believers in Jesus in other cities and other circumstances. Here in 13:1a, however, the apostle's exhortation (as well as his appeals that follow in 13:1b-7) should most likely be understood as having primary reference to the Christians then living in the capital city of the Roman Empire.

The third question — "what" or "whom" Paul had in mind by the dative phrase ἐξουσίαις ὑπερεχούσαις ("to the governing authorities") — has often been discussed by NT scholars during the past century. Martin Dibelius, in 1909, was the first NT scholar in contemporary biblical scholarship to argue that the Greek plural noun ἐξουσίαι ("authorities" or "powers") in 13:1 has reference not just to "human governmental authorities," but has in mind both "human authorities" and "angelic or spiritual powers" — understanding "human authorities" as being guided and empowered by the "angelic or spiritual powers" that stood behind them and supported them.[21] During the last half of the twentieth century, this understanding of ἐξουσίαις ὑπερεχούσαις in 13:1a was taken up and developed by a number of NT expositors — including Günther Dehn, Karl Schmidt, Karl Barth, and Oscar Cullmann (as well as by Charles Cranfield in his earlier writings on the subject).[22]

The arguments both pro and con for such a "double reference" interpretation of Paul's expression ἐξουσίαις ὑπερεχούσαις here in 13:1a were best summarized by Cranfield in his ICC Romans commentary of 1979 (which was reprinted in 1981, 1983, 1986, and 1989 with a number of "corrections") — with all these editions of his later full-blown Romans commentary dealing with the expression in quite a different manner than he dealt with it earlier in his publications of 1960, 1962, and 1965. For in summarizing in his later Romans commentary the arguments presented by Oscar Cullmann in support of a double reference interpretation of ἐξουσίαις ὑπερεχούσαις, Cranfield first lists the following five principal points of Cullmann's argument (which Cranfield accepted in his earlier publications of the 1960s but rejected in his 1979 Romans commentary):

1. In every other place in the Pauline epistles where ἐξουσία occurs in the plural or the plurally used singular with πᾶσα (apart from Titus 3:1), it clearly signifies invisible angelic powers (1 Cor 15:24; Eph 1:21; 3:10; 6:12; Col 1:16; 2:10, 15; cf. 1 Pet 3:22).

2. The conception of the angel powers and of their subjection by Christ is of central importance in Paul's letters and also in the thought of the early church generally, as is indicated by the fact that these powers are mentioned in most of the primitive confessional formulae, in spite of their brevity.

3. The expression τῶν ἀρχόντων τοῦ αἰῶνος τούτου in 1 Cor 2:8, with regard to which there is strong support among exegetes both for a reference to invisible powers and for a reference to human rulers, is best explained as carrying just such a double reference as is proposed for ἐξουσίαις in Rom 13:1.

21. See M. Dibelius, *Die Geisterwelt im Glauben des Paulus* (Göttingen: Vandenhoeck & Ruprecht, 1909). Later, however, Dibelius abandoned this position; cf. his article "Rom und die Christen in ersten Jahrhundert," *SHAW* (1941-1942), esp. 7 n. 2; see also the second volume of Dibelius's collected articles entitled *Botschaft und Geschichte: Gesammelte Aufsätze II* (Tübingen: Mohr, 1956), 2.177-228.

22. G. Dehn, "Engel and Obrigkeit," in *Theologische Aufsätze Karl Barth zum 50. Geburtstag,* ed. E. Wolf (Munich, 1936), 90-109; K. L. Schmidt, "Das Gegenüber von Kirche und Staat in der Gemeinde des Neuen Testaments," *TB* 16 (1937), cols. 1-16; K. Barth, *Church and State* (London: Macmillan, 1939); ET of *Rechtfertigung und Recht* (Zollikon-Zurich, 1938); O. Cullmann, "Zur neuesten Diskussion über die ἐξουσίαι in Röm. 13,1," *TZ* 10 (1954) 321-36; ET in *The State in the New Testament,* 93-114; on Cranfield's earlier views on the interpretation of ἐξουσίαις ὑπερεχούσαις in 13:1, see his "Some Observations on Romans 13:1-7," 241-42; *idem,* "The Christian's Political Responsibility according to the New Testament," 176-92, and *idem, Commentary on Romans 12–13, ad loc.*

4. The mention of angels in 1 Cor 6:3 in connection with the question of litigation by Christians in the civil courts is best explained by reference to the conception of the civil authorities as the executive agents of angel powers.

5. Early Christianity shared with "late" Judaism (more aptly referred to today as "early" or "formative Judaism") belief that invisible powers were at work behind earthly phenomena (with Cullmann connecting references to the στοιχεῖα τοῦ κόσμου in Gal 4:3, 9 and Col 2:8, 20 to an individual's angel in Matt 18:10 and Acts 12:15, as well as to the angels of the churches in Rev 2 and 3; also to 1 Cor 4:9 and Eph 6:12, and finally to a late Jewish belief in angels as directing nations).[23]

After setting out in his 1979 Romans commentary the basic points of Cullmann in support of his "double reference" interpretation of ἐξουσίαις ὑπερεχούσαις in 13:1a, Cranfield presents five "weightier objections" that speak against such a double reference understanding — which objections he approves of, in opposition to his earlier acceptance of such a double reference theory in his writings of the 1960s:

1. The reference of ἐξουσία in the plural to spiritual powers or civil author- ities depends on its linguistic and substantial context, and the linguistic context of the occurrence in Rom 13:1 differs from that of all the other occurrences in Paul's writings in that here alone it is not accompanied by ἀρχή and does not form part of a list of (at least two) terms, while the substantial context differs in that here alone there is no reference to Christ.

2. Cullmann's interpretation of 1 Cor 2:8 draws too much out of the text.

3. The NT affords no evidence in support of the contention that hostile spir- itual powers were recommissioned, after being subdued, to a positive ser- vice of Christ.

4. Paul nowhere else gives any indication that the subjection of the powers to Christ involved their being placed over believers; on the contrary, it is affirmed that in Christ believers are no longer subject to the spiritual powers of the world.

5. Paul's teaching in 13:1-7 rests squarely on the OT prophetic, apocalyptic, and wisdom tradition of God's appointment and use of human rulers for his own purposes.[24]

In his ICC Romans commentary of 1979, therefore, contra his earlier writ- ings on the subject during the 1960s, Cranfield understood Paul as not employ-

23. Cranfield, *Romans*, 2.657-58 (though understanding his references to "late Judaism" as having reference to what is more aptly today called "early Judaism" or "formative Judaism").
24. *Ibid.*, 2.658-59.

958

ing a "double reference" understanding of ἐξουσίαις ὑπερεχούσαις here in 13:1a, but rather, as using the expression with reference only to the city government at Rome and its officials, whom believers in Jesus were to respect and offer their submission. Thus Cranfield translated this opening thesis exhortation as follows: "Let every [Christian] person [living in Rome] be subject to the governing authorities [of the empire's capital city]." And with this understanding I agree — recognizing (1) that thesis statements of speakers and writers, both of antiquity and today, are often expressed in a highly condensed fashion, and (2) that Paul expected that the overall content of his letter to believers in Jesus at Rome would provide for his readers an obvious understanding regarding those to whom he wrote, as well as much of what he had in mind, in this thesis statement.

II. The Primary Theological Argument for the Thesis Statement (13:1b-2)

13:1b-2 The principal reasons that Paul gives in 13:1b in support of his hortatory thesis statement of 13:1a are theological: (1) he sets it out quite clearly in a proclamation manner by stating that "There is no [human] authority except that which God has established," and (2) he repeats and emphasizes it by declaring that "Those [human authorities] that exist have been appointed by God." These primary reasons are introduced by the explanatory conjunction γάρ ("for") and twice employ the prepositional phrase ὑπὸ θεοῦ ("by God"), thereby laying particular emphasis on God's sovereignty in the "appointment" and "establishment" of human governments and their officials.

Such a conviction that "there is no [human] authority except that which God has established," which is repeated in the explicative statement that "those [human authorities] that exist have been appointed by God," was rooted for the Christian apostle in his Jewish heritage. For such an understanding of divine sovereignty in all the activities of human beings — including the formation by God's created people of human governments, with their respective decisions and actions — is (1) basic to the teachings of the Jewish (OT) Scriptures and (2) continues on in many of the noncanonical Jewish writings, as seen in such passages as the following:

> Jer 27:5-6 (with respect to the rule of Nebuchadnezzar of Babylon): "It is I [the Lord God] who by my great power and my outstretched arm have made the earth — with the people and animals that are on the earth — and I give it to whomever I please. Now I have given all these lands into the hand of King Nebuchadnezzar of Babylon, my servant, and I have given him even the wild animals of the field to serve him."
>
> Dan 4:17, 25, and 32 (being the proclamation of "the Holy Watcher" in Nebuchadnezzar's dream, which is repeated in Daniel's response to the king and spoken again from heaven to the king): "The Most High

is sovereign over the kingdom of mortals, and he gives it to whomever he will."

Dan 5:21 (with respect to the rule of Belshazzar of Babylon): "The Most High God has sovereignty over the kingdom of mortals, and he sets over it whomever he will."

Sir 10:4-5 (with respect to rulers and commanders generally): "The rule over the world is in the hands of God, and at the right time he sets over it one that is worthy; in the hand of God is the rule of every man, and he invests the commander with his dignity."

Wis 6:3 (with respect to the rulers and judges of this world): "Your dominion is given you from the Lord; your sovereignty is from the Most High."

The somewhat surprising feature in Paul's principal argument of 13:1b, however, is that, even though such an understanding of God's sovereignty in the appointment and establishment of human governments and their officials was ingrained in the religious psyches of Jews (including that of the apostle himself, as well as of all other Jewish believers in Jesus), he does not himself quote here any OT text in support of his affirmation that God has sovereignly "established" and "affirmed" human governments and their officials. Using the Jewish (OT) Scriptures would not only have been acceptable to Paul's Christian addressees at Rome, it would also have been highly approved by them — influenced as they had been by Jewish Christian thought, language, and interpretive habits (as we have argued, based on the manner in which he wrote to the Christians of Rome earlier in 1:16–4:25).

But if the materials of 13:1-5 had been originally formulated by Paul in the context of his missionary outreach to Gentiles, with his pagan Gentile audiences knowing very little (if anything) about the Jewish (OT) Scriptures and next to nothing about the teachings of Judaism — and if he was attempting in his theological presentations of Section II (5:1–8:39) and his general exhortations of Section IV (as appear in 12:1-21 and 13:8-14) to set out for believers in Jesus at Rome the essentials of what he had been proclaiming in his outreach to Gentiles in the Roman world — then it should not be thought too strange that Paul did not here in 13:1-5 include any OT "proof texting" in support of his hortatory statements of 13:1-5 (nor in the climax of this section of exhortations in 13:6-7).

For Paul, a lively consciousness of God's sovereignty in the affairs of nations corporately — as well as of all people individually — had been ingrained in him from his Jewish heritage. This consciousness had also been reinforced by Christian teaching generally and by his own religious experiences as a "Christ follower" and a Christian apostle in particular. He may even have been convinced that "what may be known about God" through the revelation of himself in his creation (which he spoke about earlier in Rom 1:19-20 as being "plain" to all people) includes a basic understanding of the one true God as being sovereign over all human decisions and in the course of all human actions, whether good or evil.

Thus, however such matters regarding origins and parallels may be understood, it needs here to be noted (1) that when in 13:1b Paul sets out his principal rationale in support of his hortatory thesis statement of 13:1a, he does so by means of the theological axiom that "There is no authority except that which God has established," (2) that in 13:1c he goes on to lay emphasis on this primary theological rationale by repeating it: "Those that exist have been appointed by God," and (3) that in 13:2 he brings to conclusion all that he has just said about divine sovereignty in the establishment of human governments and their officials with the dire warning: "So whoever rebels against the authority is rebelling against that which God has instituted, and those who do so will bring judgment on themselves."

III. Further "Logical" and "Practical" Supporting Arguments That Urge Subjection to the Governing Authorities So That Christians Might Avoid "Possible Punishment" and Be True to Their Own "Conscience" (13:3-5)

13:3-4 Following the principal theological reason that Paul set out in 13:1b-2 in support of his hortatory thesis statement of 13:1a, here in 13:3-4 the apostle presents other "logical" and "practical" reasons for the people of God at Rome to be "subject" to their city officials — which may be summarized as follows:

1. Since the ultimate purpose of human governments and human rulers is the welfare of those they govern, Christians need not fear them but are to be submissive to them (13:3).
2. Since human governments and their officials have a mandate to promote "the good" on behalf of those they govern, Christians need to support and encourage them (13:4a).
3. Human governments and human rulers have a God-given authority to "bear the sword" and to function as "agents of wrath" in punishing people who do "the evil." Christians are not to take retributive justice into their own hands, but rather are to submit to the God-established governmental authorities in these matters (13:4b) — that is, as the apostle has earlier exhorted in the closing verses of his "Christian Love Ethic, Part I": believers in Jesus (1) are not "to repay anyone evil for evil," but rather are "to live at peace with everyone" (12:17-18), and (2) are not "to take revenge" on anyone who has harmed them, but rather are "to leave room for God's wrath," for God himself has declared, "It is mine to avenge; I will repay" (12:19).

What Paul writes here in 13:3-4, however, as Joseph Fitzmyer has aptly observed, "has created a major problem in modern theological discussion, because

Paul's teaching has at times been invoked to justify any sort of human govern-ment."[25] For, as Fitzmyer has gone on to point out about 13:1-7, but especially about the apostle's positive characterizations of human government in 13:3-4:

> The supposition running through vv. 1-7 is that the civil authorities are good and are conducting themselves rightly in seeking the interests of the politi-cal community. Paul does not envisage the possibility of either a totalitarian or a tyrannical government or one failing to cope with the just rights of indi-vidual citizens or of a minority group. He insists merely on one aspect of the question: the duty of subjects to duly constituted and legitimate authority. He does not discuss the duty or responsibility of civil authorities to the peo-ple governed, apart from one minor reference (13:4). Moreover, the concept of legitimate civil disobedience is beyond his ken. Paul is not discussing in exhaustive fashion the relation of Christians to governing authorities.[26]

A number of interpreters down through the centuries of Christian history have understood Paul's statements in 13:3-4 (and his surrounding exhortations of 13:1-2 and 13:5-7) in an "absolutist" fashion. Eusebius of Caesarea (c. 260-339), for example, employed this passage as biblical support for the largely beneficial, thirty-one-year reign (306-337) of the emperor Constantine over his so-called Holy Roman Empire. And certain "liberal Christian" theologians and preachers in Germany during the late 1930s and early 1940s used this passage to support the maniacal rule of Hitler — whose terribly misguided nationalistic and ra-cial theories resulted in (1) the brutal deaths of many European civilians for political reasons, (2) the awful Jewish "Holocaust" for racial reasons, and (3) a series of devastating "blitzkrieg" invasions of neighboring nations, with avowed intentions for further worldwide warfare, for purely nationalistic and personal aggrandizement reasons.

Conversely, many Christian scholars, preachers, teachers, and laypeople down through the centuries (and today) have had great difficulty accepting the thesis that because God has sovereignly established human governments, the people of God must always submit to the judgments and actions of their respective human governmental officials. Origen (185-254), who was in many ways a genius of his day and one of the most significant of the early Church Fathers — whose own father had been martyred as a Christian by Egyptian governmental officials; who during his life was often opposed and threatened by both secular and ecclesiastical "authorities"; and who throughout the final five years of his life experienced quite intense persecution and even physical torture in the city of Tyre (where in 254 he died, suffering a fate similar to that of Christian martyrdom) — was forced to admit, based on his own numerous experiences of adverse decisions and actions by both secular governments and

---

25. Fitzmyer, *Romans,* 664-65.
26. *Ibid.,* 665.

ecclesiastical officials, that the apostle's quite positive characterization of human governments and their officers as "ministers of God" greatly disturbed him.[27] Thus Origen found it necessary to understand Paul's words here in 13:3-4 as referring only to matters having to do with murder and theft — and so he viewed the legitimacy given by God to human governments to "bear the sword" and to function as "agents of wrath" as having to do only with the two moral evils of murder and theft.

Likewise, Karl Barth in the mid–twentieth century reacted strongly to the liberal theology of his day in Germany when he observed that many of his teachers of Christian theology were using Paul's statements of 13:1-7 (and particularly those in 13:3-5) to legitimize Hitler's quite perverse racial and nationalistic policies, which culminated in the Jewish Holocaust and his "blitzkrieg" invasions during World War II. For in Barth's view, the apostle's teachings with respect to ethics, governmental officials, and politics are summed up not in his exhortations of 13:1-7, but rather in the concluding verse of his "Christian love ethic" of 12:9-21 — that is, in 12:21: "Do not be overcome by evil, but overcome evil with good!"[28]

Many Christians today have also had difficulty in understanding Paul's exhortations of 13:1-7 — and particularly his statements of 13:3-4 — as "God's final word" on the subject of "Christians and the state." There can be no doubt that God has sovereignly decreed that human governments and human officials have a legitimate authority in the lives of God's people (as stated in 13:1b-2). And there are, just as certainly, a number of logical and practical reasons why believers in Jesus should not attempt "to take matters into their own hands" with respect to matters of retributive justice (as set out in 13:3-4). But to assume that in 13:1-7 Paul is presenting in full-blown form a Christian theology regarding "Christians and the state" (as has been often argued) — or that here in 13:3-4 he is justifying the existence of all human governments and the actions of all their officials (as has also sometimes been asserted) — is not only to ignore, but also to misrepresent, the purpose and particularity of his hortatory statements in these passages.

A great many scholars have attempted to spell out the historical context and the apostle's purpose in writing 13:1-7 — and particularly in writing 13:3-4.[29]

27. Cf. Origen, *Commentarium in epistulam b. Pauli ad Romanos* (Rufinus's abridged Latin translation), *PG* 14.1227, which Thomas Scheck translated as "Paul troubles [me] by these words, that he calls the secular authority and the worldly judgments as ministers of God; and he does this not merely one time, but he even repeats it a second and third time. I would like to endeavor to ascertain the sense in which a worldly judge is a minister of God" (Origen, *Commentary on the Epistle to the Romans,* trans. Scheck, 2.224). None of the extant fragments of Origen's Greek commentary on Romans includes any material from Rom 13. It is only in Rufinus's Latin translation of 405 that we have Origen's treatment of Paul's words in 13:1-7.

28. See K. Barth, *Römerbrief* in its numerous edited editions and English translations, *ad loc.*

29. For a listing of scholarly views regarding the context and purpose of 13:1-7 (and particularly of 13:3-4), together with respective bibliographies, see Jewett, *Romans,* 785-86.

In my opinion, Robert Jewett's understanding of these matters has most ably set the direction that our own understanding should take:

> Romans 13:1-7 was not intended to create the foundation of a political ethic for all times and places in succeeding generations — a task for which it has proven to be singularly ill-suited. Believing himself to be a member of the end-time generation Paul had no interest in the concerns that would later burden Christian ethics, and which continue to dominate the exegetical discussion. His goal was to appeal to the Roman audience as he conceived it, addressing their concerns in a manner that fit the occasion of his forthcoming visit.[30]

Paul most likely expressed his positive statements regarding governmental authorities — which begin with the explanatory assertion: "For rulers hold no terror with respect to good work; rather, with regard to what is evil" (13:3a), and conclude with the explanatory claims: "For the one in authority is God's servant to each of you for the purpose of the good" and "They are God's servants, agents of wrath, to bring punishment on the wrongdoer" (13:4) — during the first half of Nero's fifteen-year reign (54-68) as Roman emperor. For it was during those early years of his reign that Nero was honored by the people of Rome for his clemency and justice — largely because he had restored "the rule of law" in the Roman Senate, had corrected many abuses and inequities among the people, and had provided a time of peace for most of the provinces within the Roman Empire. In 63, however, the Romans lost the province of Armenia, and in 64 a fire destroyed a large part of the city of Rome. Nero blamed the fire on the Christians of the city in an attempt to divert attention from himself, but most residents of Rome accused him of starting it in order to have the occasion to rebuild the capital city of the empire in a more grandiose fashion. After these events, matters went "from bad to worse," with Nero himself dramatically "falling apart" in his own personal relationships and finally committing suicide outside of his beloved city of Rome on June 9, 68.

Writing during the winter of 57-58 to the Christians at Rome — during the early favorable years of Nero's reign, when he was well received by the people of Rome and his reign was viewed with favor by most of his subjects throughout the empire — Paul speaks quite positively of the city's "governing authorities."[31] It is a characterization of Rome's civic governance that the apostle had probably used earlier in his Gentile mission in various eastern regions of the Roman Empire. And here in 13:3-4 he seems to have written the essence of that charac-

---

30. Jewett, *Romans*, 786-87.

31. For this thesis regarding the background of Paul's positive view of the state in 13:3-4, cf. esp. M. Theobald, *Römerbrief* (Stuttgart: Katholisches Bibelwerk, 1992-1993), 2.88; W. E. Pilgrim, *Uneasy Neighbors: Church and State in the New Testament* (Minneapolis: Fortress, 1999), 28-29.

terization in order "to avoid any gesture of disloyalty that might jeopardize the peaceful extension of the Christian mission."[32]

13:5 Paul also, however, knew (1) that believers in Jesus, whether Jewish or Gentile, were viewed throughout the Roman world as constituting a sect of Judaism and (2) that the Christian message was associated by pagan Gentiles with whatever they knew about the teachings of Judaism. This was simply because the Christian religion had its roots in the country of the Jews and because its adherents worshiped Jesus, a Jewish carpenter from the town of Nazareth in Galilee, whom they claimed was the Jewish Messiah. Further, Paul must have realized, as did most Jews and non-Jews of the empire, that Jews and Romans were on something of a "collision course" — with the result that the Christians of Rome needed always to take into consideration how they represented themselves and their message to their non-Christian neighbors. Or, as Marcus Borg has more dramatically expressed the situation that Paul and the Christians of his day faced — and which they always had to respond to in their daily lives:

> When Paul wrote this passage to the Christians in Rome, Judaism was on the brink of catastrophe as a result of its longstanding resistance to Roman imperialism. An emerging Christianity, founded by a Jew whom the Romans had crucified — regarded still by Rome as a Jewish sect, and inextricably implicated, by history and culture, by ideology and associational patterns, in the Jewish world — was inevitably caught up in the crisis of Jewish-Roman relations. What was the right posture to adopt toward Rome? This was a burning question for Diaspora and Palestinian communities alike, one certain to underlie any theoretical interest in the status of civil authorities.[33]

Thus the apostle concludes the "logical" and "practical" reasons that he sets out in 13:3-4 with the appeal of 13:5: "Therefore it is necessary to submit (διὸ ἀνάγκη ὑποτάσσεσθαι), not only because of punishment (τὴν ὀργήν), but also because of conscience (τὴν συνείδησιν)." The elliptical Greek sentence διὸ ἀνάγκη ὑποτάσσεσθαι ("therefore it is necessary to submit") is a contraction of the much fuller statement "therefore it is necessary for believers in Jesus to submit to the governmental authorities at Rome, who have been established by God."[34] The articular phrase τὴν ὀργήν ("the wrath") here in 13:5 is, undoubtedly, to be defined by the description of human governmental authority that

32. As Jewett, *Romans,* 786, has summarized the positions of Wengst, *Pax Romana and the Peace of Jesus Christ,* 102-4; K. Haacker, "Der Römerbrief als Friedensmemorandum," *NTS* 36 (1990) 25-41; and D. A. Cineira, *Die Religionspolitik des Kaisers Claudius und die paulinische Mission* (Freiburg: Herder, 1999), 403.

33. Borg, "A New Context for Romans xiii," 218.

34. Cf. similar uses of the verb ὑποτάσσω ("to subject oneself," "to be subordinate to," "to obey") in other Pauline contexts in Rom 8:7, 20; 10:3; 1 Cor 14:32, 34; 15:27-28; 16:16; Eph 1:22; 5:21-22; Col 3:18; and Titus 2:5, 9.

had just been given at the end of 13:4 — that is, θεοῦ διάκονός ἐστιν ἔκδικος εἰς ὀργήν ("God's servant, who is 'the agent of wrath' or 'the one who punishes'"). Or, as Peter Stuhlmacher has expressed matters, this "first reason" of the two reasons given "for loyal submission to the power of the state" is this: because of "the reality of God's judgment of wrath upon evildoers as representatively carried out by the state courts."[35] And the second reason Paul gives for submission to the Roman authorities is set out both briefly and simply by the articular phrase τὴν συνείδησιν ("the conscience"), which most likely has principally in mind matters regarding the "transformation" and "renewal" of the mind of a Christian earlier highlighted in 12:2b. Such a transformation of outlook and renewal of thinking is promised to bring about in a believer's experience an understanding of "what God's will is," that is, what God's "good, pleasing, and perfect will" is in all the circumstances of life — including, it seems evident, what God's will is in the particular civic and political situation that was facing the Christians at Rome.

So in writing to the Christians at Rome in 13:5 about how they should think and act in response to the civic and political turmoil that was then developing all around them in the capital city of the empire, Paul sets out in abbreviated form and somewhat cryptic fashion the two major human factors that must come into play in all the decisions and practices of every believer in Jesus: (1) an evaluation of the situation in which one finds oneself (here, that of rising societal and political turmoil), and (2) the guidance provided by one's own transformed and renewed mind to think and act appropriately — with such a transformed and renewed mind brought about in a person's life by the Holy Spirit.

It is this message that Paul must have proclaimed to his Christian converts during his evangelistic outreach to Gentiles in eastern provinces of the Roman world (before writing to the Christians at Rome), with that message being set out here in 13:1-5 in abbreviated fashion to the believers in Jesus at Rome. For both Gentile and Jewish believers in Jesus lived under Roman governmental authority, and therefore were both in need of apostolic instruction regarding how the new people of God, that is, believers in Jesus, should live out their lives in a secular and quite pagan society.

IV. Specific Application of the Exhortations of 13:1-5 with Particular Reference to Civic and Political Issues Facing the Christians at Rome (13:6-7)

13:6-7 The specific application of Paul's hortatory statements in 13:1-5 appears here in 13:6-7. It has to do with the civic and political issues then confronting the Christians at Rome — that is, with (1) the paying of city taxes, (2) the paying of other tolls and governmental revenues, (3) respect owed to governmental

---

35. Stuhlmacher, *Romans*, 203.

authorities generally, and (4) honor owed to the city officials of Rome in particular. What the apostle sets out in these final two verses of the passage was what he obviously believed was of great immediate importance for the believers in Jesus at Rome in the situation that was then confronting them (accepting the thesis proposed by Friedrich, Pöhlmann, and Stuhlmacher).

In the narrowly directed appeals of the final two verses of this passage, the apostle continues to characterize the Roman government and its officials in a positive manner as being "servants of God (λειτουργοὶ θεοῦ) who give their full time to governing." This characterization in 13:6 is very similar to how he spoke of them earlier in 13:4 — that is, as "God's servant" (θεοῦ διάκονος), who by divine decree has been appointed (1) to bring about "the good" (τὸ ἀγαθόν) for its people and (2) to deliver "punishment (ὀργήν) on those who do evil (τῷ τὸ κακὸν πράσσοντι)." Paul evidently referred in this manner to Rome's government and its officials for much the same reasons we suggested were present in his thinking when he first spoke and then wrote what he did in 13:1-5 — that is, because (1) he joined with others in applauding the many beneficial actions of the emperor Nero on behalf of people living throughout the Roman Empire during the early years of his reign and (2) he wanted to avoid any gesture of political disloyalty that might jeopardize the peaceful extension of the Christian mission.[36]

Paul's counsel to the Christians at Rome is quite explicit and pointed: "Give to everyone what you owe: If you owe taxes, pay taxes; if revenue, then revenue; if respect, then respect; if honor, then honor." Such advice is in line with God's instruction given through the prophet Jeremiah to the people of Israel in their experience of exile in Babylon: "Seek the peace and prosperity of the city where I have carried you into exile. Pray to the Lord for it, because if it prospers, you too will prosper" (Jer 29:7).[37]

More particularly, however, the apostle's exhortations of 13:7 reflect a central teaching of Jesus that most likely was included in a "sayings of Jesus"

---

36. See again my summary comments on 13:3-4, as well as the bibliography cited in support of those comments, where I have proposed the following: writing during the winter of 57-58 to the Christians at Rome — that is, during the early favorable years of Nero's reign, when he was well received by the people of Rome and his reign was viewed with favor by most of his subjects throughout the empire — Paul speaks quite positively in 13:3-4 of the city's "governing authorities." It is a characterization of Rome's civic governance that the apostle had probably used earlier in his Gentile mission in various eastern regions of the Roman Empire. And here in 13:3-4 he seems to have incorporated the essence of that characterization in order "to avoid any gesture of disloyalty that might jeopardize the peaceful extension of the Christian mission" (using the phraseology of Robert Jewett, as cited earlier).

37. Cf. the advice expressed to God's people in Bar 1:11: "Pray for the life of Nebuchadnezzar, king of Babylon, and for that of his son Belshazzar, that their days on earth may endure as the heavens; and pray that the Lord may give us strength and clear understanding so that we may lead our lives under the protection of Nebuchadnezzar king of Babylon and of his son Belshazzar, and by our long service win their favor." See also Prov 8:15; Dan 2:21; Sir 17:17; Wis 6:3-4; *Let Aris* 196, 219, 224.

or so-called Q collection, which evidently circulated within a number of early Christian congregations[38] and was known by both Paul and his Christian addressees at Rome. This is the epigrammatic "Jesus saying" that was later incorporated by all three Synoptic Evangelists into their respective Gospels in Mark 12:17, Matt 22:21, and Luke 20:25: "Give to Caesar what is Caesar's and to God what is God's!" This "saying" of the Christians' Teacher and Lord may also have motivated the central exhortations of 1 Pet 2:13-17 — particularly (1) those of the first part of this Petrine passage that speak of "submission to every authority instituted among people, whether to the Emperor as the supreme authority or to governors sent by him," and (2) those of the final portion of the passage that urge Christians "to show proper respect to everyone" and "to honor the Emperor." The same saying probably underlies much of the exhortation addressed to the apostle's "loyal child in the faith" in Titus 3:1-2: "Remind them [i.e., those under the pastoral care of Titus] to be subject to rulers and authorities, to be obedient, to be ready for every good work, to speak evil of no one, to avoid quarreling, to be gentle, and to show every courtesy to everyone."

Paul's use of this "saying" of the historical Jesus here in Rom 13:7, however, while similar to the Petrine and Pauline uses cited above, has particularly to do with the civic and political issues then confronting the Christians at Rome, that is, with matters that had to do with the believers in Jesus at Rome actually (1) paying their assigned city taxes, (2) paying other legitimate governmental tolls and revenues, (3) respecting governmental authorities generally, and (4) honoring their city officials in particular. Thus what the apostle sets out in the final two verses of 13:1-7 is what he believed was of immediate relevance for the Christians at Rome, living, as they did, in the highly charged civic and political situation that was rising in the capital city of the Roman Empire during the middle to late 50s (as per the thesis proposed by Friedrich, Pöhlmann, and Stuhlmacher).

BIBLICAL THEOLOGY

The questions always asked regarding this passage of 13:1-7 are these: Did Paul intend in these verses to express a definitive understanding of a Christian's relation to all human governments, and so to be obeyed by believers in Jesus in whatever situation or circumstance they might live in or encounter (as had often been taken for granted in Western Christianity)? Or were the hortatory statements of these seven verses meant to give guidance to believers in Jesus at Rome at a specific time and under a specific set of conditions, and meant only to exhort the Roman Christians on how to respond to the particular conditions of their day — though perhaps also functioning in a paradigmatic fashion for how Christians today should respond to similar societal and political circumstances,

38. See my article "Christological Materials within the Early Christian Communities," 47-76.

with attention also directed to such other relevant NT passages as Mark 12:13-17 par., Acts 5:29, 1 Pet 2:13-17, and Rev 13?

Peter Stuhlmacher has briefly characterized Paul's argument in his hortatory statements of Rom 13:1-7 as follows:

> Paul summons the Christians at Rome to the greatest possible loyalty toward the existing power of the state and sees in it an ordinance of God. In harmony with the will of God, which created and graciously sustains the world, the state institutions are to promote the good and restrain evil (with the power of the police). Christians should be the first to recognize this with gratitude. They should also not refuse the state's demands for dues and taxes.[39]

Yet Stuhlmacher goes on to qualify, in a brief and quite appropriate fashion, what many other NT interpreters have more expansively spoken about with respect to Paul's exhortations here in 13:1-7 — calling on all Christian commentators, teachers, preachers, and laypeople today to recognize:

1. That "in spite of the undeniably idealistic tone in which Paul writes, he is not intending to speak timelessly 'of the divinely established nature and mandate of the government.' . . . Rather, he is merely calling for an appropriate respect of those who bear the power of the Roman state and who exercise their governing authority according to God's ordinance."
2. That, "like all powers on the earth, they too must answer before God's throne in the final judgment."
3. That this passage "is by no means the only New Testament text that deals with the relationship of Christians to the state, but only one of several equally important passages: Mk. 12:13-17 par.; Acts 5:29; (Rom. 13:1-7) 1 Pet. 2:13-17; Revelation 13."
4. That "Christians must regard the state as a form of government which, in accordance with God's ordinance and his will, restrains chaos."
5. That "for Christians, there can be no question of toying with the idea of anarchy."
6. That "Christians must also continue to expect that the power of the state will take on demonic features. These impulses can confront them with the decisive question of whether they desire to confess Christ or give their allegiance to the bearers of political power who claim for themselves divine dignity and authority."
7. That in all situations where "the testimony of the gospel is prohibited or essentially limited," the response of Peter before the Jewish Sanhedrin is the Christian's only possible attitude: "We must obey God rather than human beings!"

39. Stuhlmacher, *Romans*, 206.

8. That "all of the New Testament texts dissuade one from violent opposition against the power of the state."
9. That "the possibility that the Christians, who were completely without influence politically, could one day successfully insist upon a humane form of government which corresponds to the claims of the gospel, and then go on to bring it about, did not yet even exist within the field of vision of the New Testament texts."[40]

Stuhlmacher concludes his important exegetical treatment of Paul's exhortations in 13:1-7 with the following observation and set of hermeneutical proposals:

> While during the biblical period Christians could not exert any substantial influence on the state and its exercise of power, today Christian citizens have the possibility of influencing the state institutions directly and indirectly in many countries and of taking upon themselves the responsibility of governing. Under these circumstances Christians need principles which can be discussed and which will make it possible for them to combine their Christian faith with their responsibility as citizens of the state. Measured by the biblical texts and presuppositions, such principles are to be evaluated on the basis of whether they maintain the difference between the church (as the body of Christ) and the civil community, whether they adequately bring to bear God's will in Christ on both forms of life, and whether they relate church and state positively to one another.[41]

Further, it may legitimately be said, based only on Rom 13:1-7, that Christians need always to work out a biblical theology for the subject of "Christians and the state" in terms of at least three considerations: (1) an overriding conviction regarding God's sovereignty in the affairs of all nations and all people — even though we may not always understand how God's will is being expressed in any given situation or circumstance (as implied in 13:1-2 and passim); (2) the necessity to respond positively to governmental authorities, wherever possible, with respect to matters both human and religious — so as to avoid such governmental reactions as would adversely affect the outreach of the Christian gospel and the ongoing mission of the Christian church (as implied in the phrase "because of punishment" in 13:5a); and (3) the necessity to allow God's Spirit through a Christian's "transformed" and constantly "renewed" mind to make proper judgments in particular matters of civic and political concern (as implied in the phrase "because of conscience" in 13:5b). These three considerations are basic to any biblical theology having to do with Christians and the state, and therefore need to be at the heart of all Christian thought and action on these matters.

---

40. Stuhlmacher, *Romans*, 206-7.
41. *Ibid.*, 207.

CONTEXTUALIZATION FOR TODAY

Much could be said regarding the "contextualization for today" of Paul's teaching on Christians and the state in 13:1-7. Following all that we have set out exegetically and theologically above, it is probably both redundant and unnecessary to go any further here. Nonetheless, the following general points are of particular importance in any theoretical discussion of Christians and the state and in every attempt to live one's life as a believer in Jesus in a particular societal and political situation:

1. Christian proclamation must always include, among its other components, some instruction regarding how those who have experienced the inauguration of "the age to come," and so are rejoicing in their "new life in Christ," are to live out their lives as members of "this age" — with particular reference to matters regarding how "Christ followers" are today to evaluate and relate to their respective human governments and governmental officials.
2. Basic to all Christian thought and action, including matters having to do with all societal and political concerns (both local and worldwide), is the conviction that God is sovereignly working out his will and his purpose — even though God's will and purpose are often quite difficult to discern or to spell out in detail.
3. In every situation of life, the specific circumstances that confront believers in Jesus (whether immediately or as might follow from certain actions) need to be carefully analyzed by God's people — at least as far as is humanly possible.
4. Christians in every situation of their lives need to turn to God for guidance, which is given through his Holy Spirit by means of the "transformed" and "renewed" mind of a "Christ follower" (as highlighted earlier in 12:2). For such a transformation of outlook and renewal of thinking is promised to bring about in a believer's experience an understanding of "what God's will is," that is, what God's "good, pleasing, and perfect will" is in all the varying circumstances of life — including the societal and political circumstances that confront Christians today.

This hortatory passage of 13:1-7, therefore, should not be viewed as presenting a set of timeless statements regarding what has been called "the divinely established nature and mandate of human governments." Rather, Paul here should be understood as (1) setting forth certain principles that believers in Jesus need always to keep in mind when dealing with matters regarding Christians and the state, and (2) applying those principles to the specific matters that were then facing believers in Jesus at Rome. The passage does not settle every question that may arise with respect to relations between Christians and their respective human governments and governmental officials. But it sets out a paradigm for Christian thought and action in similar situations. And when combined with other NT passages on closely related matters (such as Mark 12:13-17 par.; Acts 5:29; 1 Pet 2:13-17; Rev 13), this passage functions as an important biblical text for use by God's Spirit in guiding the thinking and actions of God's people, who may be in similar societal and political circumstances today.

5. The Christian Love Ethic, Part II (13:8-14)

TRANSLATION

^{13:8}*Owe no one anything, except to "Love one another!" For whoever loves someone other [than himself or herself] has fulfilled the law.* ⁹*The biblical commandments "Do not commit adultery," "Do not murder," "Do not steal," "Do not covet" — and whatever other ethical decrees there may be — are summed up in this one word of instruction: "Love your neighbor as yourself." *¹⁰*Christian agape love does no harm to one's neighbor. Therefore, Christian agape love is the fulfillment of the law.*

¹¹*And do this, understanding this present time. Because the hour has already come for you to wake up from your slumber. For now our salvation is nearer now than when we first believed. *¹²*The night is nearly over; the day is almost here. So let us put aside the deeds of darkness and put on the armor of light. *¹³*Let us behave decently, as in the daytime, not in orgies and drunkenness, not in sexual immorality and debauchery, not in dissension and jealousy. *¹⁴*Rather, clothe yourselves with the Lord Jesus Christ, and do not think about how to gratify the desires of the sinful nature!*

TEXTUAL NOTES

13:8 The second-person plural present imperative ὀφείλετε ("you owe," "are indebted," "are obligated") is amply attested in the textual tradition. The nominative plural present participle ὀφείλοντες ("owing," "being obligated"), however, appears in Codex Sinaiticus (ℵ* 01), thereby relating the exhortations of 13:8 to the commands of 13:7 to "pay to everyone what you owe" — that is, "taxes," "revenues," "respect," and "honor." The subjunctive form ὀφείλητε ("you ought to owe," "ought to be indebted," "ought to be obligated") appears in a corrected version of Codex Sinaiticus (ℵ²). But these variant readings of ℵ* and ℵ² seem to be only attempted stylistic improvements, and therefore should probably not be considered original.

9 The inclusion and order of the commandments οὐ κλέψεις ("You shall not steal") and οὐκ ἐπιθυμήσεις ("You shall not covet") are amply attested by P⁴⁶, by uncials A B D F G Ψ, and by minuscules 33 1175 1739 (Category I), 1881 (Category II), and 6 1241 2200 (Category III). Some textual witnesses, however, insert between these two commandments the command οὐ ψευδομαρτυρήσεις ("You shall not bear false witness"), as do uncials ℵ [P] 0150 and minuscules 81 256 1506 1962 2127 (Category II) and 104 365 436 459 1319 1573 1852 1912 (Category III); also as reflected in it^{ar, b} vg^{cl} syr^{(h), pal} cop^{bo} and supported by Origen^{lat1/6}. This insertion was evidently done under the influence of Exod 20.15-17 and Deut 5:19-21. Other readings, as well, came about in the course of transmission — some through omission; others through a rearrangement of the commandments (evidently based on the fact that the LXX manuscripts vary among themselves and from the MT). The twofold shorter reading οὐ κλέψεις, οὐκ ἐπιθυμήσεις, however, has the better MS support, and thus is to be accepted as original.

11 The pronoun ὑμᾶς ("you") in the phrase ὅτι ὥρα ἤδη ὑμᾶς . . . ἐγερθῆναι ("because the hour is already present *for you* to wake up") is attested by uncials ℵ* A B C P and by minuscules 81 1881 1962 2127 (Category II) and 365 1319 1852 (Category III); it is also reflected in it[ar, b, d, f, g, o] vg cop[bo] and supported by Clement Ambrosiaster Jerome Augustine. On the other hand, the pronoun ἡμῶν ("us") is supported by P[46 vid], by uncials ℵ[2] D F G Ψ 0150 (also *Byz* L), and by minuscules 33 1175 1739 (Category I), 256 1506 (Category II), and 6 104 263 436 459 1241 1573 1912 2200 (Category III); it is also reflected in syr[p, pal] cop[sa] and supported by Chrysostom. Both readings have rather strong support. Yet on internal grounds ὑμᾶς ("you") is probably to be preferred, for it is more likely that ὑμᾶς ("you") was changed to ἡμῶν ("us") in order to conform to the person ἡμῶν ("us") in the next clause than that ἡμῶν ("us") was changed to ὑμᾶς ("you"). A few textual witnesses omit the pronoun entirely (as reflected in syr[h] eth and supported by Origen[lat]).

12a The first-person plural aorist subjunctive middle verb ἀποθώμεθα ("let us put aside") in the clause ἀποθώμεθα οὖν τὰ ἔργα τοῦ σκότους ("Therefore *let us put aside* the works of darkness") receives decisive support from uncials ℵ A B C D[2] P Ψ 0150 (also *Byz* L) and from minuscules 33 1175 1739 (Category I), 81 256 1506 1881 1962 2127 (Category II), and 6 104 263 365 436 459 1241 1319 1573 1852 1912 2200; it is also supported by Clement Chrysostom and Theodoret. Several Western textual witnesses, however, read ἀποβαλώμεθα ("let us cast off"), as do P[46] and uncials D*[, 3] F G; also as reflected in eth. But ἀποθέσθαι is the verb normally used in such formulas of renunciation. Moreover, the verb ἀποβάλλειν appears nowhere else in Paul's letters.

12b The contrasting, correlative, or transitional particle δέ ("rather," "so," "now," "then," or "therefore"), which is attached to the verb ἐνδυσώμεθα ("let us put on") in the final clause of this verse, is somewhat controverted. Some textual witnesses omit the particle altogether (as do P[46 c], uncials ℵ* and P, and minuscule 6; also as suggested by cop[mss]). Others place the conjunction καί before the verb ἐνδυσώμεθα (as do uncials ℵ[c] C[3] D[2] F G Ψ and minuscules 33 326; see also versions it vg syr). P[46] of about A.D. 200 has οὖν following the verb — though most textual witnesses have δέ immediately after the verb (as do uncials A B C* D* P 1506 and minuscules 1739 1881; also supported by Clement). The *GNT*[3, 4] accepts δέ as immediately following ἐνδυσώμεθα, but places it in square brackets to indicate some doubt.

FORM/STRUCTURE/SETTING

As with the hortatory statements of 12:9-21, so a number of diverse opinions have been expressed by commentators with respect to the nature, structure, development of thought, and purpose of Paul's hortatory statements here in 13:8-14 — though usually interpreters have been content simply to spell out the derivations and meanings of the words used by the apostle. Much of what has been said (and can be said) regarding the form, structure, development of thought, and purpose of this passage has been conjectural. Yet some "informed conjectures" are better than others, and so we offer what we believe to be better conjectures in what follows.

A Proposal regarding the Original Formulation and Present Purpose of 13:8-14. It may reasonably be speculated that Paul drew the exhortations set out in 13:8-14 from his earlier teaching and preaching as a Christian apostle — whether (1) from his teaching "for a whole year" in the Christian congregations at Antioch of Syria, which were made up of various ethnically mixed groups of believers, and/or (2) from his proclamation of the Christian gospel during his evangelistic outreach to pagan Gentiles in other cities, towns, and regions of the eastern provinces of the Roman Empire.

Further, it may be postulated that the apostle's purpose for including the material of 13:8-14 in his letter was much like his purpose for including his earlier hortatory material of 12:9-21 — that is, to set out certain important Christian axioms that would provide ethical guidance for specific circumstances that believers in Jesus at Rome were then encountering. Or, stating matters and their rationales somewhat more explicitly: it may be presumed that just as (1) Paul's ethical axioms in his "Christian Love Ethic: Part I" of 12:9-21 are best understood as general Christian axioms intended to serve as foundational considerations for his specific exhortations of 13:1-7 having to do with certain concerns of a civic and political nature, which matters were of great practical importance to the believers in Jesus then living in Rome, so (2) the hortatory statements of his "Christian Love Ethic: Part II" here in 13:8-14 should most likely be seen as intended to serve as foundational considerations for his contextualized exhortations of 14:1–15:13 regarding a troubling matter that had arisen within at least some of the Christian congregations at Rome. To some extent, such a paralleling of passages may be justified (as we believe) by recourse to our thesis regarding the importance of "formal patterning" and "composition structures" in the interpretation of an NT letter.[1] It also, however, appears to be the most likely hypothesis to resolve the constantly recurring "conundrum" (that is, a perennially arising question that seems to have only a conjectural answer) regarding (1) why Paul separated these passages of similar materials in 12:9-21 and 13:8-14, and (2) how the apostle intended these passages to function in their respective contexts.

Paul's statements regarding an ἀγάπη type of love — which topic permeates all of his "Christian Love Ethic: Part I" of 12:9-21 and then reappears in the opening portion of the hortatory statements of his "Christian Love Ethic: Part II" of 13:8-14, that is, in the first and third verses of 13:8-10 — are rooted in

---

1. See our introductory statements regarding "formal patterning" and "compositional structures" in our "Introduction to the Commentary" (pp. 20-21 above); also note our application of this thesis to the materials in Romans that we believe represent the substance of three earlier sermons drawn by the apostle from his earlier Gentile mission on the subject of "A Christian Remnant Theology" in 9:6-29; 9:30–10:21; and 11:1-32.

early Christian tradition, as seen in the remembrance of the earliest believers in Jesus that their Master had given his disciples "a new commandment" (ἐντολὴν καινήν) to "love one another" (ἀγαπᾶτε ἀλλήλους), as later recorded in John 13:34-35. They also call to mind Paul's emphasis on an ἀγάπη type of love as being the principal quality of a Christian ethic in Gal 5:14 ("Love your neighbor as yourself") and in Gal 5:22 ("The fruit of the Spirit is [first of all] love)." And they carry on the thrust of the apostle in his lyrical composition of 1 Cor 13:1-13, where in quite rhapsodic fashion he concludes that poetic homily by citing the three great attributes of the Christian life as being "faith" (πίστις), "hope" (ἐλπίς), and "love" (ἀγάπη) — and then adds the highly significant statement: "But the greatest of these is an *agape* type of love (μείζων δὲ τούτων ἡ ἀγάπη)."

It must therefore be concluded that an emphasis on a self-giving and personal ἀγάπη type of love was a major feature of the Christian message among the earliest believers in Jesus. And there can be little doubt that it was, as well, a major feature in Paul's evangelistic mission to pagan Gentiles — with his repetition of this theme here in 13:8-10 being intended to assure his Christian addressees at Rome that this theme of ἀγάπη love functioned as the foundational feature in all his ethical teaching (as it did also in 12:9-21).

Likewise, Paul's insistence in 13:11-14 on "the present time" as being of very great significance in the eschatological course of God's salvation history — which material he inserts at the close of this unit of axiomatic materials in 13:8-14 — functioned as a theme that undergirded all of early Christian thought and served as a basic tenet of the Christian message proclaimed by the apostle in his Gentile mission.[2] Here in 13:11-14 Paul employs this theme both (1) to reassure his Roman addressees that such an emphasis on "the present time" in the course of God's salvation history was also a prominent feature in his Gentile ministry, and (2) to insist, with particular reference to the ecclesiastical problem that was at that time evidently "tearing apart" the unity of the Christians at Rome (which matter he will deal with specifically in 14:1–15:13), that how believers in Jesus dealt with these matters and how they treated each other with respect to these concerns must always be viewed in the context of where they as God's "new covenant people" were now living in the course of God's salvation history. A compelling case, therefore, can be made that these two themes of (1) "Christian ἀγάπη love" and (2) "the importance of 'this present time' in God's salvation history" (as set out in these two paragraphs of 13:8-10 and 13:11-14) were drawn by Paul from his previous preaching and teaching during his earlier Gentile mission and were seen as foundational for all that he exhorts and urges in his appeals of 14:1–15:13.

On the other hand, Paul's reference in 13:9 to four of the Ten Commandments of the Mosaic law (including his allusion to "whatever other command-

---

2. On the prominence of the relation of "this age" and "the age to come" in early Christian thought, with an emphasis on the overlapping of the ages at "the present time" in NT eschatological thought, see esp. Cullmann, *Christ and Time*, 47-48, 81-93, and 222-30.

ments there may be") — as well as his need to insist, as he does in 13:10, that an ἀγάπη type of love by a Christ follower is "the fulfillment of the [Mosaic] law" — was probably not representative of the thrust of his preaching to converted Gentile converts during his Gentile mission. For most Gentiles were probably generally unaware of the ethical instructions of the OT and had little knowledge of the ethical teachings of Judaism.

It was in Paul's earlier teaching ministry to an ethnically mixed body of believers in Jesus who worshiped in the Christian congregations of Syrian Antioch — which, according to Luke in Acts, occurred before the apostle's celebrated Gentile mission — that issues regarding relations between the ethics of believers in Jesus and the ethics of Judaism became important. And by the way Luke in Acts 11:26 associates that yearlong ministry of Barnabas and Saul at Antioch, where they "taught great numbers of people" and "the disciples were first called Χριστιανοί (that is, 'Christ followers')," it is probably best to postulate (1) that Paul had been extensively involved in those earlier discussions among the believers in Jesus at Antioch regarding relations between the ethics of a believer in Jesus and the ethics of a Jew, and (2) that it was the apostle's teaching at Antioch that was largely responsible for believers there being identified not just as "people of the Way" who accepted Jesus of Nazareth as the Jewish Messiah and took their directions for living from the Mosaic law, but, rather, more accurately being characterized as "Christ followers" (Χριστιανοί) in both their allegiance and their style of life — whether such an appellative was originally used in derision by the Jews and Gentiles of the city who were not believers in Jesus and then was accepted by Jewish and Gentile believers in Jesus as being an appropriate characterization, or was first declared by both Jewish and Gentile believers as being the most apt identification for their basic convictions and their different style (or "styles") of life.

Paul may have dealt with this matter in other contexts in his evangelistic outreach to pagan Gentiles during his later Gentile mission. In all likelihood, however, his emphasis here in 13:8-10 on "Christian ἀγάπη love" as being the "fulfillment of the Mosaic law" (1) represents a feature of the apostle's earlier preaching and teaching in the ethnically mixed groups of believers in Jesus in Syrian Antioch, (2) highlights a matter of great ethical significance that was also of concern to the Christians at Rome (who constituted, as well, an ethnically mixed group of believers in Jesus), and (3) is brought into the presentation here in 13:8b-10 as an extremely important Christian principle that has direct relevancy to the ecclesiastical and practical concerns that were then disrupting relations between groups of believers in the Christian congregations at Rome.

On the Purpose and Structure of the Materials of 13:8-14. Our proposal is that Paul set out the two hortatory paragraphs of 13:8-10 and 13:11-14 as two sets of concisely stated theological materials to serve as the theological foundation for his appeals in 14:1–15:13 about the troubling ecclesiastical matter existing within at least some of the Christian congregations at Rome. (The exhortations might also function in the broader context of the apostle's theological and ethical presentations throughout the entire body middle of the letter, that is, from 1:16 to these two paragraphs of 13:8-10 and 13:11-14, as something of an epigrammatic conclusion to what he had previously presented in the body middle.) The first paragraph carries on in an explicit manner the theme of "the Christian ἀγάπη love ethic" that was prominent in 12:9-21; the second highlights in a complementary fashion the important theme of "the nature of 'this present time' of God's salvation history." These two themes played important roles in all of Christian thinking and Christian living of that day (and need to function similarly in Christian thought and action today). The "Exegetical Comments" on this material that follow will be presented under the following two captions:

> Christian *Agape* Love as the Fulfillment of the Mosaic Law (13:8-10)
> The Nature of Christian Ethics in "This Present Time" of God's Salvation History (13:11-14)

EXEGETICAL COMMENTS

I. Christian *Agape* Love as the Fulfillment of the Mosaic Law (13:8-10)

The exhortations in the first paragraph of Paul's "Christian Love Ethic: Part II" of 13:8-14, that is, in 13:8-10, have to do with what it means for believers in Jesus to be motivated and directed by an ἀγάπη type of love in their dealings with others. What Paul presents in this first paragraph is set out in the context of the following implicit — though also highly significant — questions: How is a believer in Jesus to be guided in his or her ethical decision making and practice? Is such direction to be gained by a reverent submission to and Spirit-led expression of the instructions ("Torah") of the OT commandments? Or is *agape* love, which characterizes all of God's dealings with his creation and his people — as well as being foundational for all of God's commandments and all of Jesus' ethical teaching — to be understood as the fundamental factor in the ethical thinking and actions of a Christian?

13:8 The verb ὀφείλω ("owe," "indebted," "obligated") was a common term in the ancient Greek world, being frequently employed in matters of finance and legal jurisprudence. It was also used as a metaphor with respect to (1) relationships between people and (2) relationships between people and their gods or God.[3] In the LXX, which expresses in Greek the Jewish law as set out in the Hebrew OT, this metaphorical conception of indebtedness (ὀφείλειν) to God "proceeds partly from the [people's] relation to God, partly from the given facts of creation, and partly from the divine Law or sacred custom."[4] In Phlm 18, Paul uses ὀφείλει ("he owes") quite literally when referring

---

3. Cf. Hauck, "ὀφείλω," 5.559-60.
4. *Ibid.,* 5.561.

to any possible misuse of finances on the part of Philemon's servant Onesimus. Elsewhere in his letters, however, as well as here in 13:8, Paul speaks metaphorically of the debt or obligation owed by believers in Jesus to God and to others — which indebtedness is deduced as flowing from the salvation that God himself has brought about by means of the salvific work of Jesus and the ministry of God's Spirit.

The idiom εἰ μή, which brings together the conjunction εἰ ("if") and the negative particle μή ("not"), is frequently used in the NT to mean "unless" or "except." And the neuter article τό in the first sentence of this paragraph, which has often been either ignored or treated in a substantive fashion by translators and commentators, should most likely be viewed as introducing some sort of quotation[5] — not a biblical quotation but probably a quotation from the teaching of the historical Jesus. Thus we have inserted quotation marks and an exclamation point in translating what we believe to be the essence of the content of Jesus' ethical teaching quoted here: "Love one another!"

Further, when Paul elaborates on this first sentence of 13:8, he writes, "whoever loves (ὁ ἀγαπῶν) someone other [than himself or herself] (τὸν ἕτερον) has fulfilled the law (νόμον πεπλήρωκεν)" — with the articular term "the love" (ἡ ἀγαπή) used in a distinctly Christian fashion; the expression "the other" (τὸν ἕτερον) employed generically and with a contrasting nuance to mean "someone other [than himself or herself]"; and the statement "he or she has fulfilled the law" (νόμον πεπλήρωκεν) as signaling the relation of the Christian type of ἀγάπη love ethic vis-à-vis the Jewish type of a nomistic ethic, with the latter being rooted in the Mosaic legislation of the OT. As noted earlier, Greek writers of both the classical and koine periods used three words for "love" in their writings: (1) φιλία, which is a general word for "love" and "friendship" that appears in many contexts; (2) ἔρως, which has to do principally with "sexual love"; and (3) στοργή, which usually was used in contexts that had to do with "love among members of a family." The word ἀγάπη, however, is not found in any extant nonbiblical Greek writing. Yet ἀγάπη ("love") occurs about twenty times in the LXX, though usually without any specialized meaning. Thus because of its twenty or so uses in the LXX, the word itself cannot be claimed to be uniquely Christian.

The noun ἀγάπη, however, appears about 120 times in the NT — 75 of which occur in the letters of Paul. Because of Paul's repeated use of ἀγάπη in its articular form, coupled with the particular contexts in which it appears in his NT letters, it may be claimed that ἡ ἀγάπη in the apostle's letters — and particularly here in Romans — connotes a distinctive Christian flavor as being principally in mind: (1) the love that God the Father and Christ Jesus have for their own people (as in 5:5, 8; 8:35), (2) the love that Christians are to have in response to God and to Christ Jesus, (3) the self-giving love that believers in

---

5. As A. T. Robertson has pointed out: "One way of expressing a quotation was by τό, as in Ro. 13:8" (*ATRob*, 243).

Jesus are to have for one another, and (4) the personal and self-giving type of love that Christians are to express to other people who have never claimed to be "Christ followers."

13:9-10 In v. 9 Paul quotes four commands contained in the Decalogue (i.e., "The Ten Words of Instruction" or "The Ten Commandments" of the Mosaic Law), as presented in Exod 20:1-17 and Deut 5:6-21 of the Jewish (OT) Scriptures. As these four commandments are presented in the Hebrew MT text, they appear as (1) the seventh commandment ("Do not commit adultery"), the sixth commandment ("Do not murder"), the eighth commandment ("Do not steal"), and the tenth commandment ("Do not covet") — though the apostle sets them out here in 13:9 in the order of MS B of the Greek LXX (note LXX Exod 20:13, 14, 15, 17). Paul argues that all four OT commandments, as well as "whatever other ethical decrees there may be," are "summed up in this one word of instruction" (ἐν τῷ λόγῳ τούτῳ ἀνακεφαλαιοῦται): "Love your neighbor as yourself" (ἀγαπήσεις τὸν πλησίον σου ὡς σεαυτόν). This command (1) underlies all of God's commandments as given to his people in the OT,[6] (2) was considered "the great summation of the Law" or "the greatest commandment" by a number of prominent Jewish rabbis in the days of Jesus and Paul,[7] (3) appears as a major teaching of Jesus in the NT Gospels,[8] (4) was called by James "the royal law of Scripture,"[9] and (5) was highlighted by Paul in Galatians as "the summary in a single command of the whole law."[10]

Further, in v. 10 Paul argues that "Christian *agape* love does no harm to one's neighbor," for, as seems obvious, "*agape* love" is a self-giving and personal type of love that always has the welfare of "someone other than oneself" in view. Likewise, he insists that "Christian *agape* love is the fulfillment of the OT law," since, as Joseph Fitzmyer has quite rightly pointed out:

> If Christ is "the end of the Law" (10:4), the goal toward which it [the Mosaic law] was aimed in the history of human salvation, then "love," which motivated his [God's] whole existence and soteriological activity (8:35), can be said to be the fulfillment of the law itself.[11]

What Paul is proclaiming in 13:8-10, as Fitzmyer has gone on to write, is the following:

---

6. As witness particularly Lev 19:18b and Deut 6:5.

7. Cf. *Str-Bil,* 1.357, 907-8; see also I. Abrahams, "The Greatest Commandment," in his *Studies in Pharisaism and the Gospels,* 1st ser. (Cambridge: Cambridge University Press, 1917), 18-29.

8. So the "Jesus saying" reported later by all three canonical Evangelists in Mark 12:31a, Matt 22:39a, and Luke 10:27b. Cf. P. Borgen, "The Golden Rule: With Emphasis on Its Use in the Gospels," in his *Paul Preaches Circumcision and Pleases Men* (Trondheim: Tapir, 1983), 99-114.

9. Cf. Jas 2:8.

10. Cf. Gal 5:14. See also Col 3:14: "Above all, clothe yourselves with love (τὴν ἀγάπην), which binds everything together in perfect unity."

11. Fitzmyer, *Romans,* 679.

That Christians, living by faith that works itself out through love, fulfill the very aspiration of those who have tried to live by the Mosaic law. He is not proposing the fulfillment of the Mosaic law as an ideal for Christian life. He is only reformulating what he already said in 8:4, Christian love does what the law requires.[12]

Or to state matters a bit more colloquially: though the ethic of a believer in Jesus must always be in line with the basic thrusts, intentions, and aspirations of the ethical commands of the OT Scriptures, a Christian "*agape* love" actually "trumps" (that is, "overrides" by bringing to a fitting conclusion) all the ethical commands of the OT, as well as whatever other ethical prescriptions are set out by any other religious or secular philosophy.[13] So *agape* love must always be understood and practiced by Christ followers of whatever gender, age, and period in time as a major and decisive factor in their ethical decision making and actions.

II. The Nature of Christian Ethics in "This Present Time" of God's Salvation History (13:11-14)

Paul brings to a close his "Christian Love Ethic: Part II" of 13:11-14 with an appeal that calls on believers in Jesus (1) to recognize this period of time in which they are now living as of great eschatological significance, for it is the time when God is inaugurating "the age to come" in "this present existing age," (2) to realize the implications of living in this time of the overlapping of "the age to come" and "this age," and (3) to think and act responsibly in this epoch of salvation history. It is, in fact, the promised epoch of God's salvation history[14] when believers in Jesus are to be guided and directed (1) by the implications of the Christian gospel, (2) by the teachings and example of the historical Jesus, (3) by God's Spirit in applying the message of the Christian gospel, the teachings of Jesus, and the example of Jesus to matters of Christian living, and (4) by God's continual "renewal of the mind" of a believer in Jesus, which comes about by means of the ministry of God's Spirit. It is the "new covenant" guidance that all the commandments of the "old covenant" looked forward to. It is not simply obedience to the commandments of God as set out in the OT, as laudatory as that might seem to many pious people. Yet new covenant guidance and direction

---

12. Fitzmyer, *Spiritual Exercises,* 197 (reformulating a bit more explicitly what he had written in *Romans,* 679a).

13. Or, as Fitzmyer somewhat similarly writes in his *Spiritual Exercises,* 189, with respect to what Paul has presented in 14:1–15:13: "As it [the passage] stands in this epistle, it implies that Mosaic legal prescriptions may no longer be the norm for Christian conduct, but there are, nonetheless, demands made of Christians. The principle at work in all of them is love or charity (13:8-10), which flows from the faith evoked by the gospel."

14. As proclaimed by the prophet Jeremiah in Jer 31:33-34 (with that biblical passage being later explicitly referred to by the writer of Hebrews in Heb 10:15-17).

must always be understood as being "in line with" the basic thrust, intentions, and aspirations of the old covenant commandments (even when dealing with matters beyond the purview of the OT writers), and thus the fulfillment of the OT commandments.[15]

13:11-12a In the first verse and a half of the second paragraph of this passage, that is, in 13:11-12a, Paul uses a number of common eschatological expressions of his day to introduce his exhortations of 13:12b-14 — that is, he employs the expressions "the [present] time" (τὸν καιρόν), "the [future] hour" (ὥρα), "the [future] salvation" (ἡ σωτηρία), and the contrast of "the night" being "nearly over" vis-à-vis "the day" being "almost here" (ἡ νὺξ προέκοψεν, ἡ δὲ ἡμέρα ἤγγικεν). This catena of eschatological expressions corresponds to the postbiblical Jewish phrases "this age" and "the age to come"[16] — with references to "this age" or "the present age," as well as references to "the age to come," appearing also in the NT canonical Gospels[17] and in some of the other non-Pauline NT writings.[18] In addition to his allusions to "this age" and "the coming age" here in 13:11, Paul uses equivalents of these terms about a dozen times elsewhere in his letters.[19]

Previously, in writing to his converts living in the Roman province of Galatia, the apostle contrasted in Gal 3:1-5 the era of the Mosaic law and the era of the Spirit — arguing that having experienced the new age of the Spirit through the proclamation of the Christian gospel, they must not go back to the law in order to bring about some sort of completion in their new life, which had been brought about by the Spirit. Rather, he urged his converts in Gal 5:16 "to live by the guidance of the Spirit," promising them in the following portion of that verse that in so doing they "will not carry out the desires of the flesh." And in Gal 3:23–4:7 he contrasted in extensive fashion (1) God's present guidance of his people through the ministry of his Spirit vis-à-vis (2) his earlier guidance of the Israelites by means of the Mosaic law — arguing in Gal 3:23-25, which serves as the thesis paragraph for all that the apostle presents in what follows, that:

> Before the coming of "this faith (τὴν πίστιν; i.e., 'the Christian faith')" we were held in custody under the law, locked up "until the faith that was to come (εἰς τὴν μέλλουσαν πίστιν)" would be revealed. So the law was put

---

15. Cf. our earlier "Exegetical Comments," "Biblical Theology," and "Contextualization for Today" with respect to the exhortations of 12:2 that appear above on pp. 921-25.

16. On "this age" and "the age to come" in the NT see especially Cullmann, *Christ and Time*, 47-48, 81-93.

17. On the appearance of the expression "this age" / "the present age" in the canonical Gospels, see Matt 13:22, 39, 40, 49; 24:3; 28:20; Luke 16:8; 20:34, 35; on the appearance of "the age to come," see Mark 10:30; Luke 18:30; on the use of both terms in the same context, see particularly Matt 12:32 and Luke 20:34-35.

18. On "the age to come" apart from the Pauline letters, see particularly Heb 6:5, "the powers of 'the coming age' (μέλλοντος αἰῶνος)."

19. In addition to Rom 13:1-2a, see also Rom 12:2; 1 Cor 1:20; 2:6, 8; 3:18; 2 Cor 4:4; Eph 1:21; 2:2; 1 Tim 6:17; 2 Tim 4:10; and Titus 2:12.

in charge of us until Christ came that we might be justified by faith. But now with the coming of "this faith (τῆς πίστεως; i.e., 'the Christian faith')," *we are no longer under the pedagogical supervision of the law* (οὐκέτι ὑπὸ παιδαγωγόν ἐσμεν).

Throughout Galatians, Paul sets out, in fact, two eras or epochs of God's salvation history, using the language of what is quite properly called "apocalyptic eschatology"[20] and urging the Galatian believers in Jesus (1) to recognize the present time in which they were now living as being a highly significant period of time in the course of God's salvation history, (2) to realize the implications of living in this time of the overlapping of "this age" and "the age to come," and (3) to think accurately and act responsibly in this present epoch of God's salvation history. And so he does here in his exhortations of Rom 13:11-12a in urging the Christians at Rome to "understand this present time."

13:12b-14 Specific exhortations regarding how Christians are to live in "this present time" of God's salvation history are set out in 13:12b-14. The tone of the first set of these exhortations in vv. 12b-13 suggests that this hortatory material was first addressed to newly converted believers in Jesus during Paul's outreach to pagan Gentiles. For those to whom he speaks are urged to "put aside the deeds of darkness" — such external matters as "orgies," "drunkenness," "sexual immorality," and "debauchery," but also such more inward matters as "dissension" and "jealousy." The exhortations conclude in 13:14, however, with an appeal that is most important for all the apostle's addressees — whether recently converted pagans brought to Christ by him in his Gentile missions or professing Christians of both Jewish and Gentile heritage in the congregations at Rome (as well as, of course, believers in Jesus in our various Christian denominations and churches today): "Clothe yourselves with the Lord Jesus Christ, and do not think about how to gratify the desires of the sinful nature!" For, as Joseph Fitzmyer has most aptly characterized Paul's desires and intention in writing:

> Christians must realize that they are living in the *eschaton,* for the two ages (that of the Torah and that of the Messiah) have met (as Paul puts it in 1 Cor 10:11). Christ Jesus, by his passion, death, and resurrection, has inaugurated the new aeon: Salvation is at hand. So Christians must respond to the age in which they now live. This is the explanation of why Christians must not conform themselves to this world (12:2), but must be in harmony with the new aeon. They must be looking forward to the day when salvation fully arrives. Salvation is said to be nearer, but it is still a thing of the future. Yet the time in which Christians live is critical, and Paul seeks to awaken from slumber and exhorts them to vigilance.[21]

---

20. See Boer, *Galatians,* 31-35, for an extended exposition on the significance of "apocalyptic eschatology" in Galatians.

21. Fitzmyer, *Spiritual Exercises,* 197-98.

BIBLICAL THEOLOGY

Paul's two paragraphs of 13:8-10 and 13:11-14 are best understood (we believe) to be two sets of highly significant ethical exhortations that he had previously used in his preaching and teaching, and which in Romans he used again as important theological foundations for his specific appeals regarding the troubling ecclesiastical matter that existed within at least some of the Christian congregations at Rome (which matter he will deal with specifically in his immediately following appeals of 14:1–15:13). However, they also serve in the letter in the broader context of his earlier theological and ethical presentations in the body middle of the letter (that is, from 1:16 to these two paragraphs of 13:8-10 and 13:11-14) as something of an epigrammatic conclusion to the entire body middle. For both of these reasons, these two brief paragraphs of 13:8-10 and 13:11-14 provide important ethical materials for a Christian biblical theology today.

An emphasis on a self-giving and personal ἀγάπη type of love — which characterizes all of God's thought and action, was a major feature of the Christian message among the earliest believers in Jesus, and is highlighted here in the apostle's exhortations of 12:9-21 and 13:8-10 — must always be included in any truly Christian biblical theology. Likewise, it is important that Paul's insistence in 13:11-14 on "the present time" as being of very great significance in the course of God's salvation history undergird all our Christian thinking and actions today.

It is with these two highly significant emphases that Paul brings to a close his theological presentations in his most famous and most widely read letter of that day and today. Whatever else is to be incorporated into a contemporary Christian biblical theology, these two features of (1) an *agape* type of Christian love and (2) the nature of Christian ethics in this present epoch of God's salvation history must always permeate the whole of what is discussed, presented, and enacted — if, indeed, a Christian biblical theology is to be understood as being Christian at all.

CONTEXTUALIZATION FOR TODAY

As believers in Jesus today, we need constantly to experience God's gracious *agape* love and constantly to reflect that same type of *agape* love to others. The Christian life is not just a life of commitment to God and serious theological thought. It is also to be a life of loving response to God and loving action on behalf of others. In all our thinking and all our actions as Christians, there must be the presence of an *agape* type of love if our thinking and our actions are to be valid, constructive, and helpful. That is the highly important matter that Paul highlights in this closing portion of the body middle of his letter — and that is an emphasis that must always be to the fore in any contextualization of the Christian gospel today.

Likewise, we must always recognize the importance of "the present time" (that is, the present era or epoch in the course of God's salvation history) in which we as believers in Jesus are now living. Are we living in the era of the Mosaic law? Or are we now living in the epoch of Jesus, the Jewish Messiah and humanity's Savior and Lord? Paul's answer in his final exhortations of 13:8-14 is this: we are living in "this present time" under the lordship of Jesus! And thus his final exhortation of 13:14 is stated as follows: "Clothe yourselves with the Lord Jesus Christ, and do not think about how to gratify the desires of the sinful nature!"

6. On Relations among the Christians at Rome (14:1–15:13)

TRANSLATION

^{14:1}*Accept those among you whose faith is weak, without passing judgment on disputable opinions.* ²*One person's faith allows the eating of everything, but another person, whose faith is weak, eats only vegetables.* ³*The one who eats everything must not look down on the one who does not; and the one who does not eat everything must not condemn the one who does, for God has accepted that person.* ⁴*Who are you to judge someone else's servant? To their own master they stand or fall. And they will stand, for the Lord is able to make them stand.*

⁵*One person, indeed, considers one day more sacred than another; but another considers every day alike. Each one of you should be fully convinced in his or her own mind.* ⁶*Likewise, the one who regards one day as special does so in relation to the Lord. The one who eats meat does so in relation to the Lord, for he or she gives thanks to God. And the one who does not eat meat does so in relation to the Lord and gives thanks to God.*

⁷*For we do not live in relation to ourselves alone and we do not die in relation to ourselves alone.* ⁸*If we live, we live in relation to the Lord; and if we die, we die in relation to the Lord. So whether we live or die, we belong to the Lord.* ⁹*It is for this reason that Christ died and returned to life, in order that he might be the Lord of both the dead and the living.*

¹⁰*You, then, why do you judge your brother or sister? Or why do you look down on your brother or sister? For everyone will stand before God's judgment seat.* ¹¹*For it is written:*

" 'As surely as I live,' says the Lord,
  'every knee will bow before me;
  every tongue will confess to God.' "

¹²*Therefore each of us will give an account of ourselves to God.*

---

¹³*Let us then stop passing judgment on one another. Instead, make up your mind not to place a stumbling block or obstacle in the way of a believing brother or sister.* ¹⁴*I know and am persuaded by the Lord Jesus that no food is unclean of itself. But if anyone regards something as unclean, then for that person it is unclean.* ¹⁵*If your brother or sister is distressed because of what you eat, you are no longer acting in love. Do not by your eating destroy your brother or sister for whom Christ died.*

¹⁶*So do not allow what you consider to be good to be spoken of as evil.* ¹⁷*For the kingdom of God is not a matter of eating and drinking, but of righteousness,*

peace and joy in the Holy Spirit, [18]*because anyone who serves Christ in this way is pleasing to God and receives human approval.*

[19]*Therefore let us make every effort to do what leads to peace and the building up of one another.* [20]*Do not destroy the work of God for the sake of food. All food is clean, but it is wrong for a person to eat anything that causes someone else to stumble.* [21]*It is better not to eat meat or drink wine or to do anything else that will cause your brother or sister to stumble.* [22]*So you should keep whatever you believe about these things between yourselves and God — with the realization that "Blessed are those who do not condemn themselves by what they approve."* [23]*Yet the one who has doubts is condemned if he or she eats, because their eating is not from faith — since "Everything that does not come from faith is sin."*

[15:1]*We who are "the Strong" ought to bear with the failings of "the Weak" and not please ourselves.* [2]*Each of us should please our neighbors for their good in order to build them up.* [3]*For even Christ did not please himself but, as it is written:*

"The insults of those who insult you have fallen on me."

[4]*For everything that was written in the past was written to teach us, so that through steadfast endurance and the encouragement of the Scriptures we might have hope.*

[5]*May the God who gives steadfast endurance and encouragement give you a spirit of unity among yourselves as you follow Christ Jesus,* [6]*so that with one heart and mouth you may glorify the God and Father of our Lord Jesus Christ.*

---

[7]*Thus accept one another just as Christ accepted you, in order to bring praise to God.* [8]*For I tell you that Christ became a servant of the Jews on behalf of God's truth, to confirm the promises made to the patriarchs* [9]*so that the Gentiles might glorify God for his mercy.*

As it is written:

"On account of this I will praise you among the Gentiles;
    and I will sing praise to your name."

[10]*And again,*

"Rejoice, O Gentiles, with his people."

[11]*And again,*

"Praise the Lord, all you Gentiles,
    and let all the people sing praise to him."

[12]*And again, Isaiah says,*

"The root of Jesse will spring up,
one who will arise to rule over the nations;
and the Gentiles will hope in him."

[13]*May the God of hope fill you with all joy and peace as you trust in him, so that you will overflow with hope by the power of the Holy Spirit.*

TEXTUAL NOTES

14:1 The word διαλογισμῶν (i.e., with the prefix δια) suggests the idea of "disputable opinions," with this reading being widely attested in the Greek textual tradition. It is, however, replaced by λογισμῶν (i.e., without the prefix δια) in such minuscule MSS as 1175 (Category I), 81 (Category II), and 69 1874 2344 (Category III), which would suggest simply the idea of "thoughts." But this variant reading is too weakly supported to be accepted as original.

2 The third-person singular present indicative active verb ἐσθίει ("he eats") is amply attested by uncials ℵ A B C D² 048 [also *Byz* L] and by minuscules 33 1175 1739 (Category I), 1506 1881 (Category II), and 6 69 104 326 330 365 614 9 1241 1243 1319 1505 1573 1735 1874 2344 2495 (Category III); it is also reflected in vg, syr and cop versions, and is supported by Tertullian and Clement. The imperative verb ἐσθιέτω ("let him eat"), however, appears in P⁴⁶ and in uncials D* F G; it is also reflected in some versions of it and vg. But this latter imperatival form, while supported to an extent in the textual tradition, is too weakly attested to be considered original.

3 The clause ὁ δὲ μὴ ἐσθίων ("and/but the one who does not eat"), which parallels in reverse fashion the opening expression of 14:3 (ὁ ἐσθίων, "the one who eats"), is attested by P⁴⁶, by uncials A B C D* 048*, and by such minuscules as 1506 (Category II) and 5 623 2110 (Category III); it is also supported by Clement. The clause καὶ ὁ μὴ ἐσθίων ("and/also the one who does not eat"), however, appears in uncials ℵᶜ D² P Ψ [also *Byz*] and in a number of later minuscule MSS. Likewise, οὐδὲ ὁ μὴ ἐσθίων ("nor the one who does not eat") is found in various Byzantine MSS. But both of these latter readings lack sufficient support in the Greek textual tradition to be accepted as original.

4 The appearance of ὁ κύριος ("the Lord") in the final statement of this verse ("For *the Lord* is able to make them stand") is amply attested by P⁴⁶, by uncials ℵ A B C P Ψ, and by minuscule 1852 (Category III); it is also reflected in [syrᵖ] copˢᵃ, ᵇᵒ goth arm eth and supported by Augustine¹ᐟ⁶. A number of other MSS, however, read ὁ θεός ("God"), as do uncials D F G 048 0150 [also *Byz* L] and minuscules 33 1175 1739 (Category I), 81 256 1506 1881 1962 2127 (Category II), and 6 104 263 365 436 459 1241 1319 1573 1912 2200 (Category III); it is also reflected in itᵃʳ, ᵇ, ᵈ, ᶠ, ᵍ, ᵒ vg syrʰ and supported by Origenˡᵃᵗ Chrysostom Ambrosiaster Jerome and Augustine⁵ᐟ⁶. Probably, as Bruce Metzger has suggested with respect to this latter reading, "the copyists" were "influenced by θεός in ver. 3."[1]

---

1. Metzger, *Textual Commentary*, 468.

5 The omission of γάρ ("for") in the phrase ὅς μέν ("some person indeed") is attested by P⁴⁶, by uncials ℵᶜ B D F G Ψ 048 [also *Byz* L], and by minuscules 33 1175 1739 (Category I), 81 1881 1962 (Category II), and 6 436 1241 1912 2200 (Category III); it is also reflected in syrᵖ, ʰ copˢᵃ and supported by Origenˡᵃᵗ Chrysostom Jerome Augustine²ᐟ³. The inclusion of γάρ ("for"), however, is attested by uncials ℵ* A P 0150 and by minuscules 256 1506 2127 (Category II) and 104 365 459 1319 1573 1852 (Category III); it is also reflected in itᵃʳ, ᵇ, ᵈ, ᶠ, ᵍ, ᵒ vg copᵇᵒ and supported by Ambrosiaster Augustine¹ᐟ³. External evidence slightly favors the omission of γάρ as having been original. Bruce Metzger, however, commenting on the deliberations of the UBS committee, (1) suggests that ancient scribes probably did not appreciate the continuative function of the conjunction γάρ, and so, since it does not express a causal relation, were inclined to delete it, yet (2) notes that the UBS committee decided to include γάρ, but to place it in square brackets to indicate uncertainty.²

6 After the sentence ὁ φρονῶν τὴν ἡμέραν κυρίῳ φρονεῖ ("The one who regards one day as special does so in relation to the Lord"), a number of textual witnesses add the sentence καὶ ὁ μὴ φρονῶν τὴν ἡμέραν κυρίῳ οὐ φρονεῖ ("and the one who does not regard one day as special does not observe it to the Lord"), as do uncials C³ P Ψ [also *Byz* L] and most minuscules; as reflected also in syrᵖ, ʰ, arm. But as Metzger has pointed out: "This is a typical Byzantine gloss, prompted by the desire to provide a balanced statement after the model of the clause καὶ ὁ μὴ ἐσθίων later in the verse."³

9 The reading ἀπέθανεν καὶ ἔζησεν ("he [Christ] died and returned to life") is amply attested by uncials ℵ* A B C 0150 and by minuscules 1739 (Category I), 256 1506 (1881 καὶ ἀπέθανεν) 2127 (Category II), and 365 1319 1573 1852 (Category III); it is also reflected in (vgˢᵗ) copˢᵃ, ᵇᵒ and supported by Origenˡᵃᵗ⁽¹ᐟ²⁾ Chrysostom¹ᐟ² and Augustine²ᐟ⁶. Certain ancient scribes, however, evidently influenced by 1 Thess 4:14 (Ἰησοῦς ἀπέθανεν καὶ ἀνέστη, "Jesus died and rose again"), attempted to explain more clearly the meaning of ἔζησεν, either (1) by replacing it with ἀνέστη, as do uncials F G and minuscule 629; also as reflected in it⁽ᵈ²⁾, ᶠ, ᵍ vgᶜˡ, ⁽ʷʷ⁾, or (2) by combining ἀνέστη with two cognate verbs in various sequences and sometimes adding an initial καί (e.g., καί ἀπέθανεν καὶ ἀνέστη καὶ ἔζησεν), as do uncials ℵ² D¹ 0209ᵛⁱᵈ and minuscules 1175 (Category I) and 6 81 424ᶜ (Category III); or as does D*, ², which employs all three verbs ἔζησεν καὶ ἀπέθανεν καὶ ἀνέστη.

10 The genitive θεοῦ ("of God") in the phrase βήματι τοῦ θεοῦ ("judgment seat of God") is strongly supported by uncials ℵ* A B C* D F G (cf. also τῷ θεῷ of uncial 0150) and by minuscules 1739 (Category I), 1506 (Category II), and 1852 2200 (Category III); it is also reflected in itᵃʳ, ᵇ, ᵈ, ᶠ, ᵍ, ᵒ vgʷʷ, ˢᵗ copˢᵃ, ᵇᵒ and supported by Origenˡᵃᵗ⁵ᐟ⁶ Jerome¹ᐟ³ and Augustine¹ᐟ⁶. The genitive Χριστοῦ ("of Christ"), however, supplants the genitive θεοῦ in many textual witnesses, as in uncials ℵ² C² ᵛⁱᵈ P Ψ 048 0209 [also *Byz* L] and in minuscules 33 1175 (Category I), 81 256 1881 1962 2127 (Category II), and 6 104 263 365 436 459 1241 1319 1573 1912 (Category III); it is also reflected in vgᶜˡ syrᵖ, ʰ and supported by Polycarp Marcionᵃᶜᶜ ᵗᵒ ᵀᵉʳᵗᵘˡˡⁱᵃⁿ Origenˡᵃᵗ¹ᐟ⁶ Chrysostom Ambrosiaster Jerome²ᐟ³ Augus-

2. Metzger, *Textual Commentary*, 468.
3. *Ibid.*

tine[5/6]. This change from θεοῦ ("of God") to Χριστοῦ ("of Christ") probably came about under the influence of the wording of 2 Cor 5:10 (ἔμπροσθεν τοῦ βήματος τοῦ Χριστοῦ).

12 Whether or not τῷ θεῷ ("to God") at the end of the statement ἕκαστος ἡμῶν περὶ ἑαυτοῦ λόγον δώσει τῷ θεῷ ("each of us will give an account [of ourselves] *to God*") is original is somewhat difficult to determine. The inclusion of τῷ θεῷ is attested by uncials ℵ A C D P Ψ 048 0150 0209 [also *Byz* L] and by minuscules 33 1175 (Category I), 81 256 1506 1962 2127 (Category II), and 104 263 365 436 459 1241 1319 1573 1852 1912 (Category III); this inclusion is also reflected in it[ar, b, d, gue] vg syr[p, h] cop[sa, bo] and supported by Origen[lat] Chrysostom Augustine[2/8]. The omission of τῷ θεῷ at the end of the verse, however, is attested by uncials B F G and by minuscules 1739 (Category I), 1881 (Category II), and 6 424[c] 2200 (Category III); it also is reflected in it[f, g, o, r] and is supported by Polycarp Ambrosiaster Augustine[6/8]. External textual evidence strongly favors the inclusion of τῷ θεῷ ("to God"). Yet internal considerations make it rather easy to understand how, if the words were originally absent from the text, scribes would have added them to clarify the reference of the verb δώσει. The UBS committee decided to retain τῷ θεῷ, but to enclose it in brackets to indicate some doubt.

13 The prohibition τὸ μὴ τιθέναι πρόσκομμα τῷ ἀδελφῷ ἢ σκάνδαλον ("to not place a stumbling block or obstacle in the way of a believing brother or sister") is very strongly supported throughout the textual tradition. The word πρόσκομμα ("stumbling block") and the particle ἤ ("or"), however, are omitted in Codex Vaticanus (fourth-century uncial B, 03), with this omission reappearing in minuscule 365 (Category III) — either by mistake or because of an attempt by some early scribe to eliminate what appeared to him to be an awkward redundancy in speaking of both "a stumbling block" and "an obstacle."

14 The reflexive pronoun ἑαυτοῦ ("of himself," "of itself") is attested by uncials ℵ B C[2] 048 and by such minuscules as 1739 (Category I), 81 1506 (Category II), and 6 69 104 330 365 1319 1505 1573 2495 (Category III). The genitive personal pronoun αὐτοῦ ("of him" or "because of him"), however, appears in certain Alexandrian and Western texts such as uncials A C* D F G P Ψ 209 [also *Byz* L] and in minuscules 33 1175 (Category I), 1881 (Category II), and 88 323 326 614 1241 1243 1735 1846 1874 2344 (Category III), thereby suggesting the translation "because of Jesus nothing is unclean." The textual evidence with respect to this matter is almost equally divided. Yet while the latter may be more Christologically significant, it seems highly improbable that scribes would have changed "because of him [i.e., Christ Jesus]" to a simple "of itself [i.e., the food in question]." Rather, it is more likely that some early scribe changed the simple reflexive pronoun ἑαυτοῦ ("of itself") to the more significant personal pronoun ἑαυτοῦ ("of himself"). Thus it may reasonably be postulated that the reflexive pronoun ἑαυτοῦ ("of itself"), which referred to "the food in question," was original.

16a The inclusion of the transitional conjunction οὖν ("so," "therefore," "consequently," "then") is widely attested by P[46], by uncials ℵ A B C D P Ψ 048 [also *Byz* L], and by minuscules 33 1175 1739 (Category I), 1506 1881 (Category II), and 6 69 88 104 323 326 330 365 614 1241 1243 1505 1573 1735 1874 2344 2495 (Category III); its inclusion is also reflected in it vg sy[h] cop and supported by Clement and Ambrosiaster. The particle οὖν, however, is omitted by uncials F G and by minuscule 1319, with this omission reflected in syᵖ. Yet the inclusion here of οὖν is strongly supported in the Greek textual tradition, and its omission seems to be only an attempted stylistic improvement.

16b The second-person possessive plural ὑμῶν ("of you," "your") in the clause μὴ βλασφημείσθω οὖν ὑμῶν τὸ ἀγαθόν ("do not allow *your* good to be spoken of as evil") is amply attested by uncials ℵ A B C P 048 0209 and by minuscules 33 1739 (Category I), 81 1881 1962 2127 (Category II), and 104 326 436 451 1241 2495 (Category III). The first-person possessive plural ἡμῶν ("our"), however, is attested by uncials D G Ψ, is reflected in itᵃʳ, ᵈ, ᵉ, ᵍ vg syrᵖ copˢᵃ, and is supported by Clement Origenˡᵃᵗ Ambrosiaster and Augustine. Either word makes good sense, though ὑμῶν ("of you," "your") fits the immediate context somewhat better (see the second-person references that appear immediately earlier in v. 15, whereas the first-person word κρίνωμεν appears much earlier in v. 13). Moreover, the weight of external textual support favors the second-person possessive ὑμῶν ("of you," "your") as having been original.

18 The prepositional phrase ἐν τούτῳ ("in this way" or "manner") appears in uncials ℵ* A B C D* F G P 048 0209 and in minuscules 1739 (Category I), 81 1506 1881 (Category II), and 326 330 1243 (Category III). The phrase ἐν τούτοις ("in these matters"), however, appears in uncials ℵ¹ D² Ψ [also *Byz* L] and in minuscules 33 1175 (Category I) and 6 69 88 104 323 365 614 1241 1319 1505 1573 1735 1838 1874 2344 2495 (Category III). The external textual evidence is somewhat in favor of ἐν τούτῳ ("in this way" or "manner"). Further, ἐν τούτῳ is probably "the more difficult reading," since its antecedent may be viewed as being somewhat unclear. Thus the phrase ἐν τούτῳ ("in this way") should probably be viewed as original and ἐν τούτοις ("in these matters") as only an attempted improvement.

19 The textual question of this verse is whether Paul, in describing the Christian ideal of pursuing "the things of peace," does so (1) by the use of the first-person, present, indicative verb διώκομεν ("we are pursuing"), as in uncials ℵ A B F G P 048 0150 0209 [also *Byz* L] and in minuscules 6 263 2200*ᵛⁱᵈ (Category III), or (2) by the use of the hortatory first-person, present, subjunctive verb διώκωμεν ("let us pursue"), as in uncials C D Ψ and in minuscules 33 1175 1739 (Category I), 81 1506 1881 256 1962 2127 (Category II), and 104 365 436 459 1241 1319 1573 1852 1912 2200ᶜ ᵛⁱᵈ; also as reflected in itᵃʳ, ᵇ, ᶠ, ᵍ, ᵍᵘᵉ, ᵒ, ʳ vg syrᵖᵃˡ copˢᵃ, ᵇᵒ and supported by Origenˡᵃᵗ Chrysostom Ambrosiaster and Augustine. A few lectionaries have here the second-person plural imperative διώκετε ("you should pursue"). Bruce Metzger has reported as follows: "Despite the slightly superior uncial support for διώκομεν . . . and despite the circumstance that elsewhere in Romans the phrase ἄρα οὖν is always followed by the indicative (5.18; 7.3, 25; 8.12; 9.16, 18; cf. 14.12), the Committee felt that, on the whole, the context here calls for the hortatory subjunctive (cf. the imperatives in ver. 13 and ver. 20)."[4]

21 The appearance of the verb προσκόπτει ("he/she stumbles") as the final word in the sentence ("It is better not to eat meat or drink wine, or to do anything else that will cause that your brother or sister stumbles") is supported by uncials ℵ¹ A C 048 0150 and by minuscules 1506 (Category II) and 6 88 1735 1852 (Category III); it is also reflected in itʳ syrᵖ copᵇᵒ and supported by Origenᵍʳ, ˡᵃᵗ Augustine³/⁵. Some other MSS, however, add

4. Metzger, *Textual Commentary,* 469.

the clause ἢ σκανδαλίζεται ἢ ἀσθενεῖ ("or he/she is scandalized or weakened"), as do uncials א² B D F G Ψ 0209 [also *Byz* L] and minuscules 33^vid 1175 (Category I), 256 1881 1962 2127 (Category II), and 104 263 365 436 459 1319 1573 1912 2200 (Category III). This more expansive reading is also reflected in it^ar, b, d, f, g, o vg syr^h, (pal) cop^sa and supported by Chrysostom^1/2, (1/2) Ambrosiaster Augustine^2/5. The verb προσκόπτει is replaced by λυπεῖται ("he/she is grieved") in uncial א* and replaced by λυπεῖται ἢ σκανδαλίζεται ἢ ἀσθενεῖ ("he/she is grieved or scandalized or weakened") in uncial P. Such variant readings suggest that the original reading was modified by scribes who recalled the wording of 1 Cor 8:11-13.

22 The text question here is whether the relative pronoun ἥν was original in the clause σὺ πίστιν ἥν ἔχεις ("as for you, the faith that you have"). Its presence is supported by uncials א A B C 048; it is also reflected in it^ar, r vg^mss and supported by Origen^lat Augustine^3/4. The relative pronoun ἥν, however, is omitted in uncials D (F) G P Ψ 0150 0209^vid and in minuscules 1175 1739 (Category I), 81 256 1506 1881 1962 2127 (Category II), and 6 104 263 365 436 459 1241 1319 1573 1852 1912 2200 (Category III); it is also omitted in it^b, d, f, g, o cop^sa, bo and by Chrysostom Ambrosiaster Augustine^1/4. Without the relative pronoun ἥν, the clause can be read as either a statement or a question. The latter option makes for a more lively style, thereby allowing what is written to be translated: "So whatever you believe about these things, keep it between yourself and God." If ἥν was originally absent, it is possible that it was inserted to relieve a certain abruptness. Conversely, if ἥν was originally present, it probably was omitted because of an itacism after πίστιν (for in later Greek the letters HN and IN were pronounced alike). The UBS committee decided to retain the relative pronoun ἥν as original because of its attestation in uncials א A B C, but to enclose it in brackets.

23 Some textual witnesses place the doxology of 16:25-27 (i.e., as appears at the end of ch. 16) here at 14:23b (i.e., at the close of ch. 14). This placement appears in seventh-century uncial 0209 and ninth-century uncial P [also in ninth-century *Byz* uncial L]. It also appears at the close of ch. 14 in minuscules 1881 (Category II) and 181 326 330 451 614 1241 1877 2492 2495 (Category III); it is also reflected in syr^h (an early-seventh-century version) and supported by such fifth-century Church Fathers as Cyril of Alexandria and Theodoret of Cyrus, as well as by the eighth-century Arab Christian John of Damascus. Early support, however, is lacking in the Greek textual tradition for the placement of this doxology at the close of ch. 14 — with far better textual support available for its location at the end of ch. 16 (as will be argued later in our discussion of 16:25-27).

As Bruce Metzger has quite rightly pointed out: "A full discussion of the problems of the termination of the Epistle to the Romans involves questions concerning the authenticity and integrity of the last chapter (or of the last two chapters), including the possibility that Paul may have made two copies of the Epistle."[5] For an overall treatment of these issues, see my "The Form of the Original Letter," in R. N. Longenecker, *Introducing Romans,* 19-30. For more intensive treatments of the textual evidence that pertains to the end of Romans, see Gamble, *The Textual History of the Letter to the Romans,* esp.

---

5. Metzger, *Textual Commentary,* 470.

56-95; K. Aland, *Neutestamentliche Entwürfe*, 284-301; Lampe, "Zur Textgeschichte des Römerbriefes," 273-77; and Metzger, *Textual Commentary*, 470-77.

15:2 The use of the genitive first-person plural pronoun ἡμῶν ("of us") in the exhortation "Each *of us* should please our neighbors for their good in order to build them up" is amply attested by uncials ℵ A B C D*[and 2] Ψ [also *Byz* L] and by minuscules 33 1175 1739 (Category I), 1506 (Category II), and 6 88 323 1241 1243 1319 1573 1874 2344 (Category III). The genitive second-person plural pronoun ὑμῶν ("of you"), however, appears in uncials D[1] F G P 048 0209[vid] and in minuscules 1506 1881 (Category II) and 69 104 326 330 365 614 630 1505 2495 (Category III). The reading ἡμῶν ("of us") is better attested in the Greek textual tradition, and so should be accepted as original. The variant ὑμῶν ("of you") may have come about through a scribe's attempt to avoid any possible contradiction with Paul's evident identification of himself with "the strong" in the preceding verse.

7 The pronoun ὑμᾶς ("you") at the end of the clause καθὼς καὶ ὁ Χριστὸς προσελάβετο ὑμᾶς ("just as Christ also accepted *you*") has better and more diversified textual support, as represented by uncials ℵ A C D[2] F G Ψ and by minuscules 33 1175 1739 (Category I), 81 256 1881 1962 2127* (Category II), and 6 263 365 436 1241 1319 1573 1912 2200 (Category III); also as reflected in it[d2, f, g, gue] vg syr[p, h] cop[bo] and supported by Origen[lat] Chrysostom Ambrosiaster, than does the pronoun ἡμᾶς ("us"), as represented by uncials B D* P 048 0150 and by minuscules 1506 2127 (Category II) and 104 459 1852 (Category III); also as reflected in it[ar, b, d*, r, o] vg[ms] cop[sa] and supported by Theodoret[lem]. Further, the pronoun ὑμᾶς ("you"), as Bruce Metzger has pointed out, "is in harmony with the other instances of the second person plural in the context (verse 7)."[6]

8 The perfect passive infinitive γεγενῆσθαι ("has become") is attested by uncials ℵ A C[2] D[1] P 048 (also *Byz* L) and by minuscules 33 1175 (Category I), 1506 (Category II), and 6 69 88 104 323 326 330 365 614 1241 1243 1319 1505 1573 1735 1874 2344 2495 (Category III). The aorist infinitive γενέσθαι ("became"), however, appears in uncials B C* D* F G Ψ and in minuscules 1739 (Category I), 1881 (Category II), and 630 (Category III). On external textual considerations alone, the decision between the two readings is difficult. Yet on theological grounds the perfect passive infinitive γεγενῆσθαι ("has become") is the more difficult reading, for it could be understood as implying that Jesus during his earthly ministry was not "a servant of the Jews" but that as the exalted Christ he became "a servant of the Jews" — whereas the aorist infinitive γενέσθαι ("became") makes only the point that the historical Jesus "was" a servant of the Jews, without any implication arising from the verb itself with respect to his present situation. It is probably best, therefore, to view the perfect passive γεγενῆσθαι as the original reading and the aorist γενέσθαι as a scribal emendation, which variant emendation attempts to prevent any possible implication that might be drawn from the original reading.

11a The use of the phrase καὶ πάλιν ("and again") to introduce another biblical quotation here in 15:11 — that is, without the use of the verb λέγει ("it says") — is widely attested by uncials ℵ A C P Ψ [also *Byz* L] and by minuscules 33 1175 1739 (Category I), 1506 1881 (Category II), and 6 69 88 104 323 326 330 365 614 1241 1243 1319 1573 1874 2344 (Category III); it is also reflected by Jerome in his vg. On the other hand, the fuller

---

6. Metzger, *Textual Commentary*, 473.

introductory wording καὶ πάλιν λέγει ("and again, it says") is supported by uncials B D F G and by minuscules 1505 1735 2495 (Category III); with this use of λέγει also reflected in it sy and supported by Ambrosiaster. The difference is, of course, of no great importance for an understanding of 15:10 in its context. Yet the textual evidence seems to support the simple phrase καὶ πάλιν ("and again") without the use of the verb λέγει ("it says") — just as appears in the introductory phrase καὶ πάλιν ("and again") in the following verse of 15:11 (as well as, to an extent, the introduction to the passage from Isaiah that is quoted in 15:12).

11b   The third-person plural, aorist, imperative, active ἐπαινεσάτωσαν ("let them sing praise") is amply attested by P[46], by uncials A B C D Ψ, and by minuscules 1739 (Category I), 81 1506 1881 (Category II), and 88 326 365 1319 1505 1573 2495 (Category III). The second-person plural imperative ἐπαινέσατε ("you should praise"), however, appears in uncials F G P [also *Byz* L] and in minuscules 33 1175 (Category I) and 6 69 104 323 330 614 1241 1243 1735 1874 2344 (Category III). The third-person plural, aorist, imperative, active ἐπαινεσάτωσαν ("let them sing praise") of P[46] and uncials A B C D Ψ is better supported in the textual tradition, and so should be considered original.

FORM/STRUCTURE/SETTING

Throughout 14:1–15:13 Paul sets out a number of exhortations and appeals that have to do with how the believers in Jesus at Rome are to relate to one another. These exhortations and appeals are presented in two fairly large sections of hortatory materials in 14:1-12 and 14:13-23. These two large sections are then followed by two very brief sections of appeals in 15:1-6 and 15:7-13; these short sections are somewhat more direct, somewhat more revealing about the situation being addressed, and somewhat repetitious of what had just been presented in the two larger sections. Each of the two smaller sections is brought to a close by a concluding "prayer wish," first in 15:5-6 (at the end of 15:1-6) and then in 15:13 (at the end of 15:7-13).

On the Specificity of the Matters Dealt with by Paul in 14:1–15:13. Commentators have at times understood these particular hortatory appeals of 14:1–15:13 as having been abstracted by Paul from his previous letters written to his converts at Corinth, since similar appeals about dietary matters appear in 1 Cor 8:1–11:1. Yet the apostle's references here to vegetarianism (as in 14:2, 6c, and 21) and to the observance of special holy days (as in 14:5-6a), as well as his allusions to abstinence from wine (as in 14:17 and 21), find no parallel in his Corinthian letters. So most commentators today do not understand 14:1–15:13 as a set of exhortations on Christian liberty generated in the apostle's mind by certain circumstances he encountered at Corinth during his Gentile mission, but rather as exhortations and appeals directed to a specific situation then existing within at least some of the Christian congregations at Rome.

In fact, the majority of NT interpreters today have generally agreed with Paul Minear regarding this matter of specificity in the exhortations of 14:1–15:13:

> It is true that Paul often incorporated into his letters didactic material which was typical of what he taught in all the churches. Chapters 12 and 13 [of Romans] contain material which is probably of this sort. . . . There is, however, a change in literary style between ch. 13 and 14 [of Romans]. The apostle moves from general injunctions embodied in traditional oral forms of parenesis, to the consideration of a specific set of problems. The nearest analogy is 1 Corinthians (8.1-13; 9.19-23; 10.23–11.1). No one doubts that in Corinth he was wrestling directly with a specific situation. Why then should we doubt that this was also true in Rome?[7]

I agree with Professor Minear (and those who agree with him) about the specificity of the issues dealt with in Rom 14:1–15:13. For I believe (as I have earlier proposed) that Paul is here spelling out in quite a pragmatic fashion (i.e., with respect to very "practical affairs") the two important Christian convictions that he presented in his immediately previous section of 13:8-14, and doing so with respect to a particularly troubling matter that had arisen within at least some of the Christian congregations in Rome — much as he did earlier in 13:1-7 in contextualizing for the believers in Jesus at Rome his quite significant Christian ethical pronouncements of 12:1-21 (and particularly those of vv. 9-21) in a way that was especially relevant for them in their civic and societal situation.

On the Issues Involved and the People in View in 14:1–15:13. It is, however, difficult to determine exactly how the issues involved and the people in view should be understood, on the basis of what Paul writes about the situation then existing at Rome. For at the time he wrote this letter, the apostle had never been to Rome. He seems, in fact, to have known personally only a few of the Christians of the city — and most of those only from previous contacts in other cities and towns of the Roman Empire. More important, it seems that most (if not all) of what he knew about the situation at Rome came to him by hearsay (i.e., from the Christian "grapevine") or from a letter (or letters) sent to him from one (or more) of the people he greets later in 16:3-15.

Nonetheless, it may be deduced from what Paul writes in 14:1–15:13 that there were believers in Jesus at Rome who viewed themselves as being "the Strong" (οἱ δυνατοί) in their Christian faith, and from their supposedly superior stance were judging and looking down on other believers in Jesus whom they characterized as "the Weak" (οἱ ἀδύνατοι). Further, it may reasonably be inferred that they were doing so because the supposedly "weaker" group of believers was taking a quite restrictive stance on the eating of various kinds of food, the veneration of certain religiously significant days, and the drinking of wine at meals. And it may also reasonably be conjectured (1) that "the Strong" group was largely (if not entirely) made up of Gentile Christians, who had no commitment to any Jewish scruples about the propriety or impropriety of certain foods, the sanctity of certain days, and the drinking of wine; whereas the group that "the

7. Minear, *The Obedience of Faith,* 22.

Strong" identified as "the Weak" was composed mainly (if not entirely) of Jewish believers in Jesus, who had been raised to view the appropriateness or inappropriateness of eating certain kinds of food; the necessity of considering certain times, seasons, and days as particularly sacred; and the propriety or impropriety of drinking wine; (2) that Paul in his appeals to the Christians of Rome spoke primarily to those who thought of themselves "the Strong" believers, and that he was urging them to initiate reconciliation with those they identified as "the Weak" believers; and (3) that the apostle's purpose in all his exhortations was to restore peace and unity within the Christian congregations at Rome, and so to enhance an accurate expression of the Christian gospel in the city.

Some NT scholars, however, have gone a bit further in identifying the issues and persons involved in this rather difficult ecclesiastical situation at Rome — and some have gone quite a lot further in analyzing the situation and Paul's purpose in writing 14:1–15:13. Paul Minear, for example, went somewhat beyond his own general approach to the questions of the issues and the people involved (as in his statement quoted above) to suggest that the divisions among the Christians at Rome were likely much more complex than usually thought and to propose as many as five different groups of believers in Jesus represented in 14:1–15:13 who were arguing with one another.[8] And Francis Watson has gone a great deal further in arguing that Paul's exhortations and appeals of the passage (1) are directed to "the Weak" rather than to "the Strong," and (2) should be understood as urging Jewish believers in Jesus to separate from the Jewish community of the city and its commitment to the Jewish law, and thus be in a position to unite with the Gentile believers in their distinctly Christian convictions.[9]

It is difficult from what Paul writes in 14:1–15:13 to know exactly what was taking place within the Christian congregations at Rome and to evaluate with any precision what was being argued. Undoubtedly the Christians at Rome knew the situation and understood what was urged, both pro and con. Likewise, Paul probably had no doubt about the accuracy of his information, however received. As interpreters today, however, we may never really know the exact circumstances or arguments.

Nonetheless, it seems fairly obvious that in his exhortations and appeals Paul is (1) asking those who considered themselves "the Strong" to accept other believers that they seem to have viewed as "the Weak," (2) teaching that believers in Jesus need to exercise Christian liberty with respect to matters that could generally be classed as *adiaphora* (i.e., matters neither required of nor prohibited to Christians), (3) urging mutual edification among believers in Jesus, without condemning the conscience of others or rebuking one's own self, and (4) pleading for unity and peace within the Christian congregations at Rome.

---

8. Minear, *The Obedience of Faith,* 8ff.

9. F. Watson, "The Two Roman Congregations: Romans 14:1–15:13," in *Paul, Judaism, and the Gentiles,* 94-105; reprinted in K. P. Donfried, ed., *The Romans Debate: Revised and Expanded Edition* (Peabody: Hendrickson, 1991), 201-15.

On the Theological Bases for Paul's Exhortations and Appeals in 14:1–15:13. In the apostle's contextualization of the Christian gospel here in Section IV of the body middle of his letter to Rome, that is, in 12:1–15:13, Paul incorporates a number of highly significant theological and ethical emphases that function as the bases for his exhortations and appeals. At the very beginning of this major hortatory section, that is, in 12:1-2, he argues that Christian ethics must always be based on (1) a calling to mind of "God's mercies," (2) a remembrance of the message proclaimed in "the Christian gospel," (3) the "transformation" of a person by means of divine salvation, and (4) God's continual "renewing of the mind" of a believing person by means of the ministry of his Spirit. Further, in 12:3-8 he asks the Christians at Rome not to think of themselves more highly than they ought to — that is, with arrogance and conceit, assuming that because God has graced them with his presence and his salvation that their persons and opinions are to be viewed as being of particular importance — but rather, to think of themselves "with a sound mind," that is, in proportion to the faith and the gifts that God has granted to each of them. And in 12:9-21 he spells out the essence of his Christian ethical teaching by presenting a rather formalized body of material about "the *agape* love of the people of God," which type of love responds to God's own *agape* love and is to be expressed to all people. Thus Christian ethics have to do with attitudes, thoughts, and actions that have been (and are being) brought about by God in the hearts, minds, and lives of "transformed" and "renewed" people, both individually and in community.

But most significant for the troubling ecclesiastical situation in at least some of the Christian congregations at Rome are the two important convictions that Paul sets out in 13:8-14:

1. While the ethics of a believer in Jesus must always be "in line" with the basic thrusts, intentions, and aspirations of the commandments of the OT Scriptures, a Christian "*agape* love" ethic trumps all the ethical commands of the OT (as well as all other ethical prescriptions proposed by any other religious or secular philosophy).
2. At "this present time" in the course of God's salvation history, believers in Jesus are to live under the lordship of Jesus and not under the lordship of the Mosaic set of instructions (i.e., the Jewish "Torah").

And so the apostle sets out in this final set of exhortations in 13:8-14 his concluding appeal of v. 14, which presents matters in a distinctly Christocentric fashion: "Clothe yourselves with the Lord Jesus Christ, and do not think about how to gratify the desires of the sinful nature!"

On the Christological Support That Paul Gives for His Exhortations and Appeals of 14:1–15:13. To anticipate our exegetical comments that follow, we note how the apostle supports his own exhortations and appeals by employing (1) a number of allusions to "sayings of Jesus" and (2) a number of Jesus' actions during his earthly ministry that were remembered by the early Christians as paradigms for Christian action. Most obvious of the teachings of the historical Jesus that Paul alludes to in this passage are the following:

> 14:10: "Why do you judge your brother or sister?" (cf. Matt 7:1; Luke 6:37).
>
> 14:13: "Let us, therefore, stop passing judgment on one another. Instead, make up your mind not to put a stumbling block or obstacle in the way of your brother or sister" (cf. Matt 18:7; Mark 9:42; Luke 17:1-2).
>
> 14:14: "I know and am persuaded by the Lord Jesus that no food is unclean of itself" (cf. Matt 15:11; Mark 7:15).[10]

Likewise, references to the example of Jesus as setting the paradigm for Christian behavior are to be found in 15:1-13, where, as Michael Thompson has aptly observed, "the Christological direction of Paul's paraenesis comes most plainly into view":[11]

> 15:3: "For even Christ did not please himself."
>
> 15:5: "May the God who gives steadfast endurance and encouragement give you a spirit of unity among yourselves as you follow Christ Jesus."
>
> 15:7b-9a: "Accept one another just as Christ accepted you. . . . For I tell you that Christ became a servant of the Jews on behalf of God's truth, to confirm the promises made to the patriarchs so that the Gentiles may glorify God for his mercy."

On Paul's Citation of Biblical Passages, Which Are Used Here to Show That His Exhortations and Appeals of 14:1–15:13 Are "in Line" with the Proclamation of the OT Scriptures. Also present in Paul's exhortations of 14:1–15:13 are a number of biblical quotations that are introduced by the standard Pauline introductory formula γέγραπται ("it is written") — or by the simple expression πάλιν ("again"), which carries on the nuance of the more formal expression γέγραπται that precedes it — with that introductory formula, in both its formal and abbreviated forms, signaling a definite note of divine authority:

> 14:11: " 'As surely as I live,' says the Lord, 'every knee will bow before me; every tongue will confess to God' " (quoting Isa 45:23).
>
> 15:3: "The insults of those who insult you have fallen on me" (quoting Ps 69:9 [MT 69:10; LXX 68:19]).
>
> 15:9: "On account of this I will confess you among the Gentiles; and I will sing praise to your name" (quoting Ps 18:49 [MT 18:50; LXX 17:49]).

---

10. Cf. Paul's earlier paraphrasing of "sayings of Jesus" in 12:14a, 17a, 19-20, and 21; see also our discussions in 13:8 and 13:9-10 on Paul's use of Jesus' historical teachings.

11. M. B. Thompson, *Clothed with Christ,* 208 (see also the other possible allusions to Jesus' example as identified by Thompson).

15:10: "Rejoice, O Gentiles, with his people" (quoting Deut 32:43).

15:11: "Praise the Lord, all you Gentiles, and let all the people praise him" (quoting Ps 117:1 [LXX 116:1]).

15:12: "The root of Jesse will spring up, the one who will arise to rule over the nations; and the Gentiles will hope in him" (quoting Isa 11:10).

Yet, like his earlier uses of OT quotations in 12:3-21 and 13:8-14, Paul does not use these biblical passages as the primary basis for his Christian exhortations and appeals. Rather, he employs them to suggest that his exhortations and appeals of 14:1–15:13 — which are based on (1) the message of the Christian gospel, (2) the teachings of the historical Jesus, and (3) the remembrance of how Jesus lived his earthly life and carried out his earthly ministry — are "in line" with the major thrusts, intentions, and aspirations of the ethical commands and hortatory statements of the OT Scriptures.

On the Structure of the Materials in 14:1–15:13. The structure of this section has seemed to many translators and interpreters somewhat difficult to discern. For this reason, commentators have frequently treated what Paul writes in this passage as being rather loosely expressed — or, as Joseph Fitzmyer once stated as his own opinion (as well as that of many others): "This hortatory section [of 14:1–15:13] is not exactly an ethical treatise, for it is *quite unsystematic and rambles.*"[12] Everyone, however, recognizes that throughout the passage the apostle is exhorting and appealing to the Christians at Rome about the same general topic — their response to the troubling situation that had arisen within at least some of their congregations. Yet how to analyze what Paul presents in 14:1–15:13 with respect to that ecclesiastical situation at Rome and its various features — including how to represent the contours of his presentation by even such formal matters as appropriate captions and paragraphing — has always been a problem for translators and commentators.

Among contemporary English translations, the editors of JB (who relied on the French translation of 1961) captioned all the material of 14:1–15:6 under one heading, "Charity towards the Scrupulous," and divided this rather extensive body of material into the five paragraphs of 14:1-12, 13-15, 16-21, 22-23; 15:1-6. They captioned the additional material of 15:7-13 "An Appeal for Unity," which they set out in the two paragraphs of 15:7-12 and 15:13. The RSV translators basically agreed, placing 14:1–15:13 under the one general heading "Welcome One Another," and setting out the material in seven paragraphs of 14:1-4, 5-9, 10-12, 13-23; 15:1-6, 7-12, and 13. The NRSV, however, put the passage under the following four headings: "Do Not Judge Another" (which is developed by four paragraphs in 14:1-4, 5-6, 7-9, and 10-12); "Do Not Make Another Stumble" (which is expressed in the one paragraph of 14:13-23); "Please Others, Not Yourselves" (which is stated in the one paragraph of 15:1-6); and "The Gospel for Jews and Gentiles Alike" (which is expressed in the one paragraph of 15:7-13).

12. Fitzmyer, *Spiritual Exercises*, 189 (italics mine).

The NIV and its TNIV revision placed all of 14:1–15:13 under only one heading, "The Weak and the Strong"; both translations set out Paul's presentation in ten paragraphs: 14:1-4, 5-8, 9-12 (though NIV's paragraphing of 14:5-8 and 9-12 is changed in TNIV to 14:5-9 and 10-12), 13-18, 19-21, 22-23; 15:1-4, 5-6, 7-12, and 13.

Among English commentators, Kingsley Barrett dealt with 14:1–15:13 in terms of three major sections (14:1-12, 13-23; 15:1-13);[13] Ernst Käsemann, Joseph Fitzmyer, and Douglas Moo understood it as set out in four major sections (14:1-12, 13-23; 15:1-6, 7-13);[14] and Charles Cranfield viewed the passage in terms of five parts (14:1-12, 13-23; 15:1-6, 7-12, 13).[15] It is with the division of the materials of this passage into four major subsections (as proposed by Käsemann, Fitzmyer, and Moo) that I agree.

My argument is based on both the form and the content of the passage. With respect to form, it needs to be noted (1) that the first subsection of this extended passage, 14:1-12, is brought to a close at the beginning of v. 12 with the joining of the inferential particles ἄρα ("so," "then," "consequently") and οὖν ("so," "then," "therefore," "consequently") and (2) that the second subsection of the passage, 14:13-23, is brought to a close at the beginning of its final paragraph in vv. 19-23 in the same manner, that is, by joining these same inferential particles at the beginning of v. 19. This joining of ἄρα and οὖν to indicate the conclusion of a section or subsection of material occurs about fifty times in the Synoptic Gospels, the Acts, the Pauline letters, and Hebrews — with Paul being especially fond of using the resultant idiomatic expression ἄρα οὖν in this fashion.[16] Further, both of the two final subsections of material in 15:1-6 and 15:7-13 are brought to a close with a "prayer wish," first in 15:5-6 (at the end of 15:1-6) and then in 15:13 (at the end of 15:7-13). These two "prayer wishes" function quite clearly to bring to a conclusion their respective portions of material.

Not only can these four subsections of 14:1–15:13 be identified by certain epistolary and rhetorical conventions, they can also be identified by their respective contents — and particularly by the way Paul develops his presentation. In 14:1–15:13 the apostle's argument seems to be set out in four phases of development:

1. Guidelines regarding relations between believers in Jesus (14:1-12).
2. Specific exhortations and appeals to the Christians at Rome (14:13-23).
3. The obligation of "the Strong" to care for the welfare of "the Weak" (15:1-6).

---

13. Barrett, *Romans,* 255-73.

14. Käsemann, *Romans,* 365; Fitzmyer, *Romans,* 686-708; Moo, *Romans,* 826-84.

15. Cranfield, *Romans,* 2.698-99.

16. In addition to Paul's use of ἄρα οὖν here in 14:12 and 19, see also his previous use of this idiomatic expression in his letter to Rome in 5:18; 7:3, 25b; 8:12; and 9:16, 18. In 8:1, however, he writes ἄρα νῦν ("therefore now"); while in 7:21 and Gal 2:21 he uses the particle ἄρα singly, evidently only to enliven the statement by the expression "so then" or "then" — though the singular ἄρα is not usually translated in contemporary English translations.

4. A conclusion that summarizes Paul's inclusive Christian ethic, with the example of Jesus in his earthly ministry cited in support and biblical passages quoted to show how Paul's inclusive Christian ethic is "in line" with the OT Scriptures (15:7-13).

This structure of four phases in the apostle's presentation of 14:1–15:13 will guide our "Exegetical Comments" below.

EXEGETICAL COMMENTS

I. Guidelines regarding Relations between Believers in Jesus (14:1-12)

In the first phase of his presentation in 14:1–15:13, the apostle presents in 14:1-12 certain guidelines for the relations between believers in Jesus at Rome — doing so with reference to the particular matters then causing division within at least some of the Christian congregations at Rome.

14:1 The thesis that dominates Paul's guidelines is presented in the first verse of this subsection of hortatory material: "Accept those among you whose faith is weak, without passing judgment on disputable opinions." The second-person plural present imperative middle verb προσλαμβάνεσθε ("you are to accept [another person]"; or, simply, "accept [another person]") has to do not just with a toleration of other people or an acceptance of them in some formal fashion. Rather, the verb προσλαμβάνω connotes the much more significant nuance of "thinking about and receiving other people as being within one's circle of friends and as members of one's society" — and so suggests in this context that believers in Jesus are to accept and welcome all other professing "Christ followers" as having been similarly blessed by God, and so to be thought of and treated as brothers and sisters "in Christ." Thus Paul is urging his Christian addressees at Rome to accept and welcome all other professing believers in Jesus, particularly in situations where there are differences of understanding or practice about matters having to do primarily with social background, personal opinion, or personal preference — that is, with the so-called *adiaphora,* or matters that are neither required of nor prohibited to believers in Jesus.

14:2-6 From the guidelines that Paul sets out in these verses, it may be inferred that the matters causing divisions among the Christians at Rome had to do with (1) certain dietary issues pertaining to whether believers in Jesus should eat only λάχανα ("garden plants," "herbs," or "vegetables")[17] and abstain from eating κρέα (literally "meats"),[18] and (2) certain religious concerns regarding

---

17. Note the use of the plural word λάχανα in Matt 13:32; Mark 4:32; and Luke 11:42; see also Josephus, *War* 5.437.

18. Note Paul's later exhortation in 14:21, "It is better not to eat κρέα (pl. 'meats') or drink wine or do anything else that will cause your brother or sister to stumble." See also Josephus, *An-*

the particular sanctity of certain times, seasons, and days (or day) of the week (as in 14:5-6a). Later, in 14:13-23, Paul seems to include the appropriateness or inappropriateness of drinking wine with one's meals as a matter of debate among the Christians at Rome (as in 14:17 and 21).

The dietary issues being debated were certainly not gluttony or drunkenness — which probably would not have been defended by any of the Roman believers. Rather, they evidently had to do with the appropriateness or inappropriateness of Christians eating meat and drinking wine at their meals. The calendar concerns seem not to have been just regarding the appropriateness of worshiping God at certain times and seasons of the year — nor regarding which day of the week was to be considered the most sacred in a Christian's worship of God. Rather, they were probably focused on questions about how Jewish and Gentile believers in Jesus should relate their new Christian experience to the events and occasions of their respective pasts as either observant Jews or pagan Gentiles, with the question for Jewish believers in Jesus most likely being whether they should observe both the Jewish Sabbath on Saturday and the Christian Lord's Day on Sunday.[19]

To each of these matters Paul sets out a quite inclusive response: (1) with respect to the dietary issues, he declares: "The one who eats everything (i.e., including 'meats') must not look down on the one who does not; and the one who does not eat everything (i.e., is a 'vegetarian') must not condemn the one who does, for God has accepted that person" (14:3); and (2) with respect to the calendar concerns, he writes: while "one person, indeed, considers one day more sacred than another" and "another considers every day alike," it is necessary that "each of you should be fully convinced in his or her own mind" (14:5). With respect to both matters, the apostle relates the decisions and actions of a Christian to his or her own relationship to Christ Jesus, their Lord. For, as he says of believers in Jesus in these two paragraphs (and will expand on further in the immediately following paragraph of 14:7-9): (1) "to their own master they stand or fall; and they will stand, for the Lord is able to make them stand" (14:4), and (2) in their actions they act "in relation to the Lord" (14:6).

14:7-9 Earlier in 14:4 the apostle compared the Christian to a slave who is dedicated to and controlled by his or her master. Here in 14:7-8 Paul applies that analogy of slave and master to the thoughts and actions of "the Strong" believers and "the Weak" believers at Rome — even to their seemingly mundane thoughts and actions regarding the appropriateness of including meat and wine in their daily meals and to their religious veneration of certain days, times, and seasons

---

tiquities 10.261; cf. 1 Cor 8:13, "If what I eat causes my brother or sister to fall into sin, I will never eat κρέα ('meats') again, so that I will not cause them to fall into sin."

19. Paul's two theses of 13:8-14, "Christian *Agape* Love as the Fulfillment of the Mosaic Law (13:8-10)" and "The Nature of Christian Ethics in 'This Present Time' of God's Salvation History (13:11-14)" — which we have proposed are generally foundational for what he exhorts and urges here in 14:1–15:13 — seem to be largely in mind throughout the apostle's specific exhortations of this extended ethical passage.

of the calendar year. The apostle's argument in these matters is that a Christian's thoughts and actions are not to be controlled by his or her particular heritage or personal preference — though these need always to be respected — but by the will and direction of his or her exalted Lord Jesus Christ. So Paul declares in 14:9, as a final statement of this present paragraph, that "it was for this reason that Christ died and returned to life, in order that he might be the Lord of both the dead and the living." And so, in effect, he teaches the believers in Jesus at Rome that with respect to these particular dietary and calendar matters — as well as, by extension, all other matters having to do with one's background and personal preferences — there is the need to be guided by (1) the message of the Christian gospel, (2) God's continued renewal of their minds by his Spirit, and (3) the early church's remembrances of the teaching and example of Jesus.

14:10 The final paragraph of the subsection of 14:1-12 begins in v. 10 with a direct challenge to the Christians at Rome that repeats the rebuke given earlier in this subsection of material in 14:4. This rebuke of the arrogant judgment of certain believers in Jesus on the thinking and actions of other believers in Jesus was also given by James, the titular leader of all Jewish believers in Jesus, in Jas 4:12: "Who are you to judge your neighbor (σὺ τίς εἶ ὁ κρίνων τὸν πλησίον)?" And it may reasonably be argued that this challenge by James and Paul to any such supposedly "Christian" judging of other Christians is based on the teachings or "sayings" of Jesus, which were remembered and passed on in either oral or written fashion (or both) by the earliest believers in Jesus[20] and then recorded by the canonical Evangelists in:

> Luke 6:37: "Do not judge, and you will not be judged. Do not condemn, and you will not be condemned."
>
> Matt 7:3-5: "Why do you look at the speck of sawdust in someone else's eye and pay no attention to the plank in your own eye? How can you say, 'Let me take the speck out of your eye,' when all the time there is a plank in your own eye? You hypocrite, first take the plank out of your own eye, and then you will see clearly to remove the speck from the other person's eye."

There may be uncertainty about exactly whom the apostle had in mind in some of his other exhortations and appeals that follow in 14:13-23. Here in the rebuking guidelines of 14:4 and 10, however, where he denounces professing Christians who considered themselves to be rightful judges of other professing Christians, Paul quite clearly has in mind both those who viewed themselves as "the Strong" and those whom "the Strong" seem to have characterized as "the Weak" — for (1) he writes inclusively in 14:3 of both "the one who eats every-

---

20. Cf. R. N. Longenecker, "A Logia or Sayings Collection," in *Contours of Christology in the New Testament,* 61-68; reprinted in *ibid., Studies in Hermeneutics, Christology, and Discipleship,* 104-12.

thing" and "the one who does not eat everything," (2) he speaks inclusively in 14:10 of "everyone" (πάντες) being required in the future to stand before God in judgment, and (3) he continues to write in such an inclusive fashion when he warns in 14:12 that "each of us" (ἕκαστος ἡμῶν) will be called on in that final day of judgment "to give an account of ourselves to God."

14:11-12 In 14:11 Paul asserts that what he has just proclaimed in his declaration "We will all stand before God's judgment seat!" — as well as, implicitly, what he writes in the present passage about the arrogant judgments of so-called Christ followers against other professing Christ followers — is directly "in line" with the pronouncement of God expressed much earlier through the prophet Isaiah to the people of Israel in Isa 45:23. For the apostle, the most important remnant preacher of the OT religion of Israel, as well as one of the most prominent forerunners of the Christian faith, was the prophet Isaiah. That was quite clearly demonstrated in his three remnant theology homilies or sermons presented earlier in 9:6–11:32 (which, as we have proposed, were probably first proclaimed to believers in Jesus at Antioch of Syria, and then set out in essence for the Christians at Rome, as well as highlighted in his doxology that closes off that section of sermons in 11:33-36).[21] Thus in 14:11, in conflated fashion, the apostle quotes from Isa 49:18 the divine oath formula "As surely as I live!" and from Isa 45:23 the divine declaration "Every knee will bow before me; every tongue will confess to God!"

In quoting the words of the prophet Isaiah, Paul seems only to be seeking to demonstrate the continuity of his words with those OT prophetic statements. Yet, in using words drawn from Isaiah, he is also declaring the biblically based and ominous reality that confronts all who would arrogantly judge and condemn others — and, in particular, all who would judge and condemn others about matters of heritage, personal opinion, and/or preference — that is, such people, even though believers in Jesus themselves, will be called on by God himself at the final judgment to give an account of their judgmental thoughts toward and condemning actions against other believers in Jesus! And so in this final statement of his guidelines of 14:1-12, Paul gives the following warning to the Christians in Rome, as well as to all believers in Jesus today: "Each of us will give an account of ourselves to God" (ἕκαστος ἡμῶν περὶ ἑαυτοῦ λόγον δώσει τῷ θεῷ).

II. Specific Exhortations and Appeals to the Christians at Rome (14:13-23)

What exactly was being said by one group of believers in Jesus against another group (or groups) of believers in Jesus at Rome — and, more importantly, how each of these groups argued its respective position — are questions we cannot

---

21. See our earlier discussions of Paul's use of the prophecies of Isaiah in Rom 9:27-28 (Isa 10:22-23); 9:29 (Isa 1:9); 9:33 (Isa 28:16; 8:14); 10:11 (Isa 28:16); 10:15 (Isa 52:7); 10:16 (Isa 53:1); 10:20-21 (Isa 65:1-2); 11:8 (Isa 29:10); 11:26-27 (Isa 59:20-21; 27:9). Note also his employment of statements drawn from Isaiah in his doxology of Rom 11:34-35.

answer with precision from what Paul writes in his exhortations and appeals of 14:13-23. The Christians at Rome undoubtedly knew the situation and understood what was then being argued, both pro and con (as we have postulated above). Likewise, Paul seems to have had no doubt about the accuracy of his information, however received. But as interpreters today, we may never really know the exact composition of the various groups nor be able to trace out the precise lines of their respective arguments.

Nonetheless, accepting the thesis that Paul's earlier ethical pronouncements of 12:9-21 function as the theoretical basis for his specific exhortations and appeals of 13:1-7, we believe it is legitimate to suggest that his statements of 13:8-14 — first of all about "Christian *agape* love as the fulfillment of the Mosaic law" (in vv. 8-10); then about "the nature of Christian ethics in 'this present time' of God's salvation history" (in vv. 11-14) — should also be understood as functioning as the theological foundation for the exhortations and appeals he sets out in 14:1–15:13 about the troubling dietary and calendar issues in Rome. So we propose that the apostle intended his readers to understand the drawing together of certain theological and foundational statements in 13:8-14 and certain specific exhortations and appeals in 14:1–15:13 as another example of "formal patterning" in the structure of the letter — thereby setting out a parallel of "compositional structures" with respect to the materials presented in these latter two portions of 13:8-14 (on theological foundations) and 14:1–15:13 (on specific exhortations and appeals) vis-à-vis the materials presented earlier in 12:9-21 (on ethical foundations) and 13:1-7 (on specific exhortations and appeals).[22]

Such a scenario of "formal patterning and compositional structure," as observed above in the materials of 12:9-21 and 13:1-7, should, in all likelihood, also be seen as being paralleled in the theological and ethical statements of 13:8-14 and the exhortations and appeals of 14:1–15:13. So what Paul writes about in both 13:8-14 and 14:1–15:13 should most likely be understood as dealing with the following two related issues that were of great concern to the Christians at Rome: (1) how believers in Jesus are to be guided in their thinking and actions, whether by the commands of the Mosaic law or by implications drawn from the message of the Christian gospel, by the teachings and example of the historical Jesus, and by the guidance given by the Holy Spirit, and (2) how believers in Jesus during "this present time of salvation history" are to live out their new life in Christ, whether by means of a nomistic lifestyle (as it seems the more Jewish-oriented members of the Christian church were supporting) or by a Christ-based response to the Spirit's guidance (as it seems the non-Jewish-oriented believers were advocating).

14:13-14 The appeal that dominates all of Paul's exhortations with respect to relations among the Christians at Rome is set out in the opening verse of this

---

22. See "Formal Patterning and Compositional Structures" in the "Introduction to the Commentary," pp. 20-21. Note also this feature as it appears prominently in the three "homilies" or "sermons" of 9.6–11.32.

subsection of hortatory material, that is, in 14:13: "Let us stop passing judgment on one another. Instead, make up your mind not to place a stumbling block (πρόσκομμα) or an obstacle (σκάνδαλον) in the way of a believing brother or sister." The noun πρόσκομμα, which most often is translated "a stumbling block," means literally "a hindrance" or "an occasion to take offense"; the noun σκάνδαλον, which usually is translated "an obstacle," signifies quite literally "a temptation to sin" or "an enticement to apostasy." This appeal by Paul to his Christian addressees at Rome echoes a historical teaching of Jesus, which presumably was incorporated into an early "sayings of Jesus" collection — and so known not only by Paul but also by the Christians of the city: "Woe to the world on account of temptations to sin (ἀπὸ τῶν σκανδάλων)! Such things must come, but woe to the person through whom they come!"[23]

The apostle then buttresses his appeal to the Christians at Rome that they "not place a stumbling block or obstacle in the way of a believing brother or sister" by alluding to a further remembrance of an early "saying of Jesus," which was later incorporated by two of the canonical Evangelists into their Gospel portrayals (first by Mark in 7:15-23 and then by Matthew in 15:11-20). Both of these Synoptic Evangelists tell their readers that Jesus himself explained privately to his disciples what he wanted them to understand from what he was teaching them — that is, that "Nothing that enters you from the outside can defile you," but, rather, "What comes out of you is what defiles you. For from within, out of your hearts, come evil thoughts, sexual immorality, theft, murder, adultery, greed, malice, deceit, lewdness, envy, slander, arrogance and folly. All these evils come from inside and defile you." The Evangelist Mark, however, after reporting Jesus' statement that "Nothing that enters you from the outside can defile you," declares in parenthetical fashion in Mark 7:19b the particularly relevant point, which undoubtedly many of the earliest Jewish believers in Jesus had picked up: "In saying this, Jesus declared all foods clean." And this teaching of Jesus that "Nothing that enters you from the outside can defile you" is, it seems, what Paul had in mind when he wrote in 14:14, "I know and am persuaded by the Lord Jesus that no food is unclean of itself."

Admittedly, the first part of this affirming statement, "I know and am persuaded by the Lord Jesus" — and particularly its prepositional phrase ἐν κυρίῳ Ἰησοῦ — has frequently been understood somewhat differently than I am proposing. Most common among the major English versions of our day are the following renderings:

> JB — "I am perfectly well aware, and I speak *for the Lord Jesus.*"
> NEB — "I am absolutely convinced, *as a Christian.*"
> ASV, RSV, NRSV — "I know and am persuaded *in the Lord Jesus.*"
> NIV — "As one who is *in the Lord Jesus* I am fully convinced."
> TNIV — "I am convinced, being fully persuaded *in the Lord Jesus.*"

23. So Matt 18:7; cf. also Mark 9:42 and Luke 6:37.

Also representative of various other understandings of what Paul is saying here in 14:14a are those of:

J. Moffatt — "I know, I am certain *in the Lord Jesus.*"
R. F. Weymouth — "I know and feel assured *in the Lord Jesus.*"
E. J. Goodspeed — "I know and *as a follower of the Lord Jesus* I am convinced."
C. G. Williams — "I know, and *through my union with the Lord Jesus* I have a clear conviction."
Berkeley Version (G. Verkuyl) — "*In union with the Lord Jesus* I know and am convinced."
J. B. Phillips — "I am convinced and I say this *in the presence of Christ Himself.*"
TEV or "Good News for Modern Man" (R. G. Bratcher) — "My *union with the Lord Jesus* makes me know for certain."

The exegetical problem that confronts every translator and every commentator who deals with 14:14a is how to understand the apostle's use of the preposition ἐν. It is beyond doubt that ἐν was the most common preposition of ancient koine Greek, appearing at least 2,245 times in the LXX and some 2,698 times in the NT (though ἐν as a preposition has disappeared in modern Greek, evidently due to its previous use as "a maid of all work" — which, all too often, led to uncertainties about its meaning, and eventually brought about its demise and final disuse). Later in 15:16 Paul will use the preposition ἐν in an instrumental fashion in speaking of Christians as being sanctified "by the Holy Spirit" (ἐν πνεύματι ἁγίῳ). And probably his use of ἐν κυρίῳ Ἰησοῦ here in 14:14 should also be understood instrumentally to mean "by the Lord Jesus."

Over four centuries ago the translators of the KJV translated ἐν κυρίῳ Ἰησοῦ in 14:14 in an instrumental fashion to read "by the Lord Jesus" — without at that time being able to profit from any of today's studies with respect to a collected group of "sayings of Jesus" that circulated (whether orally or in writing) among the earliest Christian congregations. In our day, however, with scholars being able to draw together (in, of course, something of an inferential fashion) such a "sayings of Jesus" collection, it is reasonable to believe that Paul most likely had in mind, by his use of the prepositional phrase ἐν κυρίῳ Ἰησοῦ in 14:14, a remembered teaching of Jesus circulating among at least many early congregations of believers in Jesus — and so to posit that the apostle is alluding to one of Jesus' historical teachings, which he believed the Christians at Rome not only knew but also would find particularly meaningful for the dietary matters being debated within at least some of their congregations.

Thus Paul affirms, on the authority of Jesus himself, that "no food is unclean of itself." Yet he also knows that some of the Christians at Rome were making distinctions between what they considered "clean food" and "unclean food" — distinctions evidently based on what they had been taught in the past as faithful Jews (or perhaps, though less likely, as pagan Gentiles). But Paul expresses no direct rebuke of those believers in Jesus at Rome who may have had restrictive views regarding "clean" and "unclean" foods. For Christians, as he implies throughout this passage, are free to make up their own minds and to express their own preferences with respect to such matters. Rather, the apostle (1) directs his attention to those "stronger" Christians who looked down on or disdained those they viewed as being overly narrow and too restrictive about what a believer in Jesus should or should not eat and drink at meals, (2) urges the supposedly "stronger" Christians to "act in love" toward those they viewed as "weaker" Christians in these matters, and not cause them to be "distressed" because of what the self-identified "stronger" Christians ate and drank, and (3) asks the supposedly "stronger" Christians "not to destroy your brother or sister for whom Christ died" by what they ate and drank. It is an appeal that emphasizes "*agape* love" and mutual respect among the believers in Jesus at Rome, just as the apostle had earlier in 13:8a called on all the Christians at Rome to "owe no one anything, except to 'Love one another!'"

14:16-18 In these three verses Paul basically repeats his exhortations of the previous three verses — though here he places matters in a slightly different context of understanding. For here in 14:16-18 he sets out the overriding concerns of "righteousness," "peace," and "joy in the Holy Spirit" as being the basic and essential matters having to do with "the kingdom of God" — that is, with a truly Christian experience. And he does so in opposition to those thoughts, comments, and actions that were dominating what was then going on in Rome — that is, the thoughts, comments, and actions that focused on past rules, personal preferences, ingenious debates, and the outclassing of others in both theory and practice. The apostle's injunction in these three verses is that believers in Jesus should not twist matters regarding "the kingdom of God" into "a matter of eating and drinking," but, rather, they should focus in their thinking and living on "righteousness, peace, and joy in the Holy Spirit." His assurance to his readers is that "anyone who serves Christ in this way is pleasing to God and receives human approval."

14:19-23 Paul concludes this second portion of his extended exhortations in 14:1–15:13 with quite specific appeals to the believers in Jesus at Rome in 14:19-23. He begins this concluding set of appeals with the joining of the inferential particles ἄρα ("so," "then," "consequently") and οὖν ("so," "then," "therefore," "consequently") in 14:19a, thereby indicating that in setting out this paragraph of 14:19-23 he has come to the close of this second part of his overall presentation regarding relations between the Christians at Rome — just as he had previously used the same idiomatic expression ἄρα οὖν in 14:12a to signal the close of the first part of this subsection of hortatory material.

What Paul desires for all the Christian congregations of his day — as well as for all Christian congregations today — are the two most highly significant features of (1) "peace" (εἰρήνη; שָׁלוֹם, which means not just "an absence of conflict," "tranquility," and "contentment," but also "completeness," "overall welfare," and "wholeness")[24] and (2) "the building up of one another" (τὰ τῆς οἰκοδομῆς τῆς εἰς ἀλλήλους). As Robert Jewett has aptly pointed out with respect to this second feature of "the building up of one another":

> The use of οἰκοδομή for congregational edification is a typical Pauline metaphor for congregational work (1 Cor 3:9-10; 14:3, 5, 12, 26; 2 Cor 10:8; 12:19; 13:10). While the LXX uses this metaphor to describe God's building of Israel (Jer 12:16; 38:4, 28; 40:7; 45:4; 49:10; 51:34), the clearest parallels to the idea of building a congregation of believers are found in Qumran. For example, in 1QS 8:5-10 the Qumran community is described as the "eternal planting of a holy house for Israel and a circle of the Most High" whose task is to witness to the truth of the law, to "make atonement for the land and to judge the Godless." In the pesher on Ps 37 found at Qumran, it is the Teacher of Righteousness whom God "appointed to build for him the congregation" (הכינו לבנות לו עדת, 4Qp 37 III.16). Although the metaphor is the same, the nature of the early Christian communities is very different and the responsibility for upbuilding is much more widely shared than in Qumran.[25]

As Jewett has gone on to point out with respect to the apostle's use of the phrase τὰ τῆς οἰκοδομῆς τῆς εἰς ἀλλήλους ("the building up of one another"), "Paul has the whole community of God in mind."[26]

Thus the apostle pleads with the Christians at Rome as follows: "Do not destroy 'the work of God' for the sake of food!" The expression "the work of God" (τὸ ἔργον τοῦ θεοῦ) evidently pertains to both (1) all that has been accomplished through the witness of faithful believers in Jesus in their proclamation of the Christian gospel in Rome and (2) all that the Christians at Rome had experienced by faith and their continued faithful response to that early gospel proclamation.

Paul's appeal is to both those who thought of themselves as "the Strong" and those who apparently were identified by others (presumably, by the self-proclaimed "stronger" group of believers) as "the Weak." And while he continues to insist that "all food is clean" (as he did earlier in 14:14 and does here in 14:20b), the apostle goes on to counsel the Christians at Rome (1) to realize in their thinking that "it is wrong for a person to eat anything that causes someone else to stumble" (14:20c) and (2) to express in their actions that "it is better not to eat meat or drink wine or to do anything else that will cause your brother or sister to stumble" (14:21).

Further, Paul enjoins all the parties in these debates about dietary and

---

24. See Paul's uses of εἰρήνη ("peace") not only here in his exhortations of 14:17, 19, and 15:13, but also earlier in 1:7; 2:10; 3:17; 8:6, and then later in 15:33 and 16:20 — all with a primary emphasis on "completeness," "overall welfare," and "wholeness."

25. Jewett, *Romans*, 865, citing for his Qumran references Cranfield, *Romans*, 2.721.

26. Jewett, *Romans*, 866, citing in support such commentators as Schlatter, *Romans*, 258, and Michel, *An die Römer*, 436.

calendar concerns, which evidently were issues of contention among the Christians at Rome in the apostle's day (and, sadly, remain so among many believers in Jesus today), to (1) "keep between yourselves and God whatever you believe about these things," with the realization that "Blessed are those who do not condemn themselves by what they approve,"[27] and (2) recognize that "the one who has doubts is condemned if he or she eats, because their eating is not from faith," since "Everything that does not come from faith is sin."[28]

III. The Obligation of "the Strong" to Care for the Welfare of "the Weak" (15:1-6)

In the previous two subsections of the hortatory materials of 14:1–15:13 — that is, in (1) "the guidelines" of 14:1-12 and (2) "the specific exhortations and appeals" of 14:13-23 — Paul appears to have said everything he wanted to say to the Christians at Rome regarding the dietary and calendar issues being rather hotly debated. What more could he say about these matters than what he had already said? Yet the apostle goes on to speak further about these very troubling concerns. And he does this by inserting two smaller sections of specific appeals in 15:1-4 and in 15:7-8 — with then a number of biblical passages cited in 15:9-12 as being in line with the apostle's understanding.

These two brief sets of appeals in 15:1-4 and 15:7-8 are somewhat more direct, somewhat more revealing about the situation being addressed, and somewhat repetitious of what had been presented previously in 14:1-12 and 14:13-23. And Paul adds a "prayer wish" at the end of each of these two shorter sets of appeals, that is, in 15:5-6 (after the appeals of 15:1-4) and in 15:13 (after the appeals and biblical citations of 15:7-12).

These two brief sets of appeals, with their accompanying "prayer wishes," have been treated by interpreters in a great variety of ways. The ecclesiastical editor of the "short form" of Romans, who seems to have wanted to "catholicize" (that is, to make more "universal" or "general") Paul's letter for use in the worship of the early church, evidently felt free to cut off 15:1-13 from what preceded it in 14:1-23. The doxology of 16:25-27, which had appeared as the concluding feature of the "long form" of the apostle's letter, was often transposed to appear

---

27. I have set this statement off in quotation marks, believing it to have probably been a proverbial statement that was common in Paul's day — as seen, for example, in the proverbial statement given by the Greek Stoic philosopher Epictetus (who was active during the latter part of the first century and the early part of the second century A.D.) in *Dissertationes* 4.3.11: "Guard your own good in everything" (τήρει τὸ ἀγαθὸν τὸ σεαυτοῦ ἐν παντί).

28. I have set this statement off in quotation marks, believing it to have probably stemmed from some such common Jewish religious aphorism as expressed by Philo (the Hellenistic Jewish philosopher-theologian of Alexandria, who was born c. 30 B.C. and died c. A.D. 45) in *De Abrahamo* 18: "Whatever is done apart from being mindful of God is unprofitable" (ἐπεὶ τὸ ἄνευ θείας ἐπιφροσύνης ἀλυσιτελές).

after the exhortations and appeals of 14:1-23 in this "short form" of Romans.[29] Probably much of that early editor's reasoning for eliminating 15:1-13 was because (1) the passage seems to add very little to what the apostle had already written in 14:1-23, (2) it possesses some syntactical difficulties or convoluted expressions, and (3) it includes two prayer wishes, whereas a prayer wish appears only once elsewhere in the apostle's letters at the conclusion of certain sections or subsections.

For such reasons, a number of nineteenth-century interpreters, as well as some present-day scholars, teachers, and preachers, have treated 15:1-13 as some sort of interpolation or misplaced intrusion, and so, in effect, have attempted to divert attention away from it. The most extreme example of such a treatment has been that of Walter Schmithals, who made much of these problematic matters in his *Der Römerbrief als historisches Problem* (of 1975) and his *Der Römerbrief. Ein Kommentar* (of 1988) and thus declared that what appears in 15:1-13 is a conflation of two earlier conclusions of two earlier versions of Paul's letter to Rome — that is, the conclusion to the apostle's "Letter A" (as reconstructed by Schmithals) and then the conclusion to his "Letter B" (as reconstructed by Schmithals), with these two conclusions being later brought together in the canonical version (or "long form") of Paul's letter.

In my opinion, however, both an interpolation hypothesis and speculations about the bringing together of two earlier conclusions are highly improbable. Nonetheless, the problem of why these two brief subsections of 15:1-6 and 15:7-13 appear as they do in the longer (and canonical) form of the letter is a real one. But rather than view 15:1-13 as an interpolation or as a conflation of two earlier sets of closing materials, it seems far better to understand 15:1-6 and 15:7-13 as having been original in both their present content and context — and, further, to suggest a more appropriate rationale (1) for the nature of their contents as being a repetition of much of what the apostle has already written in 14:1-23, (2) for the syntactical problems that many interpreters have seen in their expressions, and (3) for the presence of two prayer wishes that bring to a conclusion each of these two subsections of material.

What is necessary, as I here propose, is to recognize that while the dietary and calendar debates in the Christian congregations at Rome may not have been "earthshaking" on a global scale, they were of great spiritual concern to Paul and had an immense emotional impact on him — not only as a believer in Jesus himself, but also as a God-ordained Christian apostle to the Gentile world. For if there were not present among the believers in Jesus at Rome, the capital city of the Roman Empire, both of the highly important features of (1) "peace" (that is, "an absence of conflict," "tranquility" and "contentment," and even more important, an atmosphere of "completeness," "wholeness," and "concern for the welfare of others") and (2) an earnest desire to "build up one another" (that

---

29. For a discussion of "short," "intermediate," and "long" forms of Romans, see my *Introducing Romans*, 19-30.

is, "mutual concern and care for each other"), then — at least in the apostle's estimation — "the work of God" would be "destroyed."

This situation of conflict between believers in Jesus at Rome appears to have been of "great anguish of heart" to Paul. So his repetition of appeals in 15:1-4 and 15:7-9a of what he had already written in ch. 14, his somewhat tortured syntax, and his two concluding prayer wishes most likely reflect his own personal anguish — for anguish of heart often results in the repetition of one's thoughts, in jumbled forms of one's verbal and written statements, and in repeating one's own wishes and desires. Yet, whatever the cause and the circumstance, Paul does restate the substance of his appeals in the two short sections of 15:1-6 and 15:7-13 and adds two prayer wishes — which appeals and prayer wishes he sets out not only with regard to the welfare of the Christians at Rome, but also with regard to the continued extension of his own Gentile mission in Spain (and perhaps other western regions of the Roman Empire).

15:1-2 In the first two verses of the brief hortatory section of 15:1-6, Paul begins by being somewhat more direct, somewhat more revealing, yet also somewhat repetitive in what he declares about the situation he addressed throughout 14:1-23. It is in 15:1, in fact, that he first explicitly speaks of the conflict among the Roman believers as being between "the Strong" (οἱ δυνατοί) and "the Weak" (οἱ ἀδύνατοι) — with the appellation "the Strong" evidently having been coined by one group as a self-designation and that of "the Weak" attributed to the other group by others (probably by the so-called strong group) in derision. We may never, however, be able to determine the exact composition of these two groups.[30] Nonetheless, it seems most likely (1) that the group that spoke of itself as "the Strong" was made up largely (if not entirely) of Gentile Christians, who had no commitment to any Jewish scruples about the propriety or impropriety of certain foods, the sanctity of certain days, and the drinking of wine, and (2) that the group that others (probably "the Strong" group) identified as "the Weak" was composed mainly (if not entirely) of Jewish believers in Jesus, who had been taught as Jews to distinguish the appropriateness or inappropriateness of eating certain kinds of food; the necessity of considering certain times, seasons, and days as particularly sacred; and the propriety or impropriety of drinking wine at their meals.[31] Yet Paul, who was ethnically a

30. Sanday and Headlam, in an "excursus" in their ICC *Romans* commentary, 399-403, which is entitled "What Sect or Party Is Referred to in Rom XIV?" have given special attention to this question of the composition of "the Strong" group of Christians at Rome. Though their study is dated, their identifications are widely drawn and their comments highly significant.

31. Cf. Cranfield, "Preaching on Romans," in his *On Romans,* 78: "It is not at all easy to determine precisely what was at issue between the 'weak' and the 'strong,' and different explanations are offered. My guess is that the weak were Christians (mainly Jewish Christians presumably) who, while (unlike the Judaizers to whom Galatians refers) neither thinking they were putting God in their debt by their observance nor wanting to force all Christians to conform to their way, yet felt strongly that, as far as they themselves were concerned, they could not give up the observance of the ceremonial requirements of the Old Testament law with a clear conscience. The strong, on the other side, were Christians who had recognized that now that he, who is the very substance

Jew and had been trained as a Jewish Pharisee, explicitly identifies himself in his declaration of 15:1a ("We who are 'the Strong'") as being at one with the basic convictions of those who called themselves "the Strong." History is replete with stories of converts from one religious persuasion to another who either attempt to incorporate their old practices into their new understanding or want to judge their old practices by their new convictions. The lines of demarcation, therefore, are not easily drawn as to just how the Jewish believers in Jesus and the Gentile Christians at Rome would have aligned themselves with respect to "the Strong" and "the Weak," whether as self-ascribed or as attributed by others.

Yet, whatever the composition of the group that appears to have called itself "the Strong," the apostle in 15:1 considers himself to hold similar views as they do and he exhorts them "to bear with the failings of 'the Weak' and not please ourselves." Further, he goes on in 15:2 to expand on that exhortation by appealing to his addressees at Rome as follows: "Each of us should please our neighbors for their good in order to build them up" — thereby repeating, in essence, the thrust of his previous exhortation in 14:19: "Let us make every effort to do what leads to peace and the building up of one another."

15:3-4 In 15:3-4 Paul supports his appeals of the previous two verses by citing the church's remembrance of the example of Jesus during his earthly ministry, which he summarizes in the statement: "For even Christ did not please himself!" This example of Jesus, as the apostle seeks to make clear, was "in line" with the words of Ps 69:9, where the psalmist spoke of his experience as a God-fearing person as follows: "The insults of those who insult you [God] have fallen on me." So Paul supports his appeals "to bear with the failings of the weak, and not to please ourselves" and "to please our neighbors for their good, to build them up" (as in 15:1-2) by reminding his readers of the remembered example of Jesus and the written example of the consciousness of the OT psalmist. He states that by such thoughts and actions having to do with the "building up" of a supposedly "weaker" believer in Jesus, the "stronger" Christians will experience "steadfast endurance" (ὑπομονή),[32] "encouragement" (παράκλησις), and "hope" (ἐλπίς).

15:5-6 After speaking of "steadfast endurance" (ὑπομονή) and "encouragement" (παράκλησις) in the immediately previous verse, Paul expresses the following "prayer wish" for his Christian addressees at Rome:

> May the God who gives steadfast endurance and encouragement (ὁ θεὸς τῆς ὑπομονῆς καὶ παρακλήσεως) give (δῴη; optative mood) you a spirit of unity among yourselves as you follow Christ Jesus, so that with one heart and mouth you may glorify the God and Father of our Lord Jesus Christ.

---

of the law, the One to whom all along its ceremonies had been pointing, has come, it is no longer necessary to obey the ceremonial requirements literally." With these comments I generally agree, though without focusing principally on matters regarding "the ceremonial requirements" of OT law.

32. On ὑπομονή as "steadfast endurance," see F. Hauck, "ὑπομένω, ὑπομονή," *TDNT* 4.586-88. Cf. also the use of the noun earlier in Romans at 2:7; 5:3-4; and 8:25.

This is not a doxology, whether drawn from earlier Christian confessional materials or composed by Paul himself. Rather, it is a prayer wish, comparable to what can be found elsewhere in Paul's letters in 1 Thess 3:11-13, 5:23, 2 Thess 2:16-17, 3:5, 3:16a, 2 Tim 4:16b, and perhaps 2 Cor 13:14.[33] A prayer wish usually employs the optative mood for its major verb. And it often serves in the apostle's letters to signal the climax of a section or subsection, and therefore functions as a concluding feature for the section or subsection of material in which it appears.

Paul's prayer wish for his Christian addressees at Rome is that they might have "steadfast endurance" and "encouragement," as given by God, so that they might express "a spirit of unity among themselves." This unity in caring for the welfare of others takes as its pattern the example of Jesus in identifying with others during his earthly ministry and resulting in the glorification of "the God and Father of our Lord Jesus Christ." Thus concern and care for others are expressions of the new life of a believer in Jesus. Yet even more importantly, such new attitudes and actions on behalf of others are rooted in the new family relationships established by God himself in his "adoption" of people into his family and giving them new family responsibilities.[34]

IV. Conclusion: Summary of Paul's "Inclusive Christian Ethic," Supported by the Example of Jesus and by OT Passages (15:7-13)

15:7 In the first verse of this subsection, Paul states the essence of all his appeals in 14:1–15:13 to his Christian addressees at Rome: "Accept one another just as Christ accepted you, in order to bring praise to God."[35] Such acceptance of everyone who calls on Christ and professes relationship to him (1) receives its impetus and pattern from Christ's acceptance of all who call on him and profess relationship to him, whatever their other views or practices, and (2) should be seen as bringing about "praise to God," which must be the ultimate desire of all Christians. And it repeats in summary fashion the first verse of this entire section of exhortations in 14:1–15:13, as set out in 14:1: "Accept those among you whose faith is weak, without passing judgment on disputable opinions."

15:8-9a In the immediately following verse and a half, in 15:8-9a, the apostle goes on to fill out what he had in mind by referring to "the pattern of Christ" and "the bringing about of praise to God." In so doing he alludes (1) to Jesus during his earthly ministry becoming a servant of others (particularly, "a servant of the Jews"), which he did "to confirm the promises made to the patriarchs,"

33. Cf. R. N. Longenecker, "Prayer in the Pauline Letters," 222-23.

34. Cf. Paul's use of the Greco-Roman metaphor of "adoption" in speaking of the Christian's new status and new relationships in the family of God in Rom 8:15, 23, and 9:4; see also Gal 4:5 and Eph 1:5.

35. Understanding the comma in the sentence to be placed after the simple pronoun ὑμᾶς ("you") rather than earlier after the reciprocal pronoun ἀλλήλους ("one another").

and (2) to Jesus' own faithfulness to God his Father and to God's instructions ("Torah") as given in the OT, which he accomplished in order that "the Gentiles might be able to glorify God for his mercy."

15:9b-12 Then in 15:9b-12 Paul cites the following four biblical passages:

1. Ps 18:49 (LXX 17:49) as quoted in 15:9b: "On account of this I will praise you among the Gentiles; and I will sing praise to your name."[36]
2. Deut 32:43 as quoted in 15:10: "Rejoice, O Gentiles, with his people."
3. Ps 117:1 (LXX 116:1) as quoted in 15:11: "Praise the Lord, all you Gentiles."
4. Isa 11:10, as quoted in 15:12: "The root of Jesse will spring up, one who will arise to rule over the nations; and the Gentiles will hope in him."

All four biblical passages contain references to "the Gentiles," and so reflect important features that have to do with Paul's own understanding of both the Christian gospel and his God-given Gentile mission. Important to note, as well, is that the first three passages speak of praise being offered to God from among or by the Gentiles; the second passage associates Gentiles with God's people Israel; and the fourth includes Gentiles who "will hope" in the Jewish "root of Jesse" — that is, in the Messiah. Paul closes his enumeration of these important "proof texts" with a quotation from the prophet Isaiah, whom he names explicitly — and whom, as seems evident by his repeated use of passages drawn from Isaiah in Section III of the body middle of the letter,[37] he considered the most explicit "remnant preacher" of the OT religion of Israel and one of the most important forerunners of Christian proclamation. So all four quoted biblical passages contain features of great significance to Paul in support of his own consciousness regarding both the message of the Christian gospel and his own God-given mission to the Gentile world.

Yet Paul's purpose in quoting these four biblical passages here seems not to have been to support his mission and message to pagan Gentiles. Rather, he uses them to show how his "ethic of inclusion and concern for others" is "in line" with the basic thrusts, intentions, and aspirations of the OT Scriptures — and, in particular, how it supports the Christian recognition that there are varieties of people and various practices to be found within the family of God. His appeal to the Christians at Rome is that they should also be inclusive in their understanding and their concern for others who proclaim themselves to be "Christ followers" but who may have somewhat differing understandings and practices in the expression of their Christian faith — for such an acceptance of and concern for the spiritual welfare of "Christ followers" who express

---

36. In both of the Greek texts of Ps 18:49 and 2 Sam 22:50, the exalted title Κύριε ("Lord") appears, though Paul omits it in his quotation.

37. See again our earlier discussions of Paul's use of the prophecies of Isaiah in Rom 9:27-28 (Isa 10:22-23); 9:29 (Isa 1:9); 9:33 (Isa 28:16; 8:14); 10:11 (Isa 28:16); 10:15 (Isa 52:7); 10:16 (Isa 53:1); 10:20-21 (Isa 65:1-2); 11:8 (Isa 29:10); 11:26-27 (Isa 59:20-21; 27:9). Note also his employment of statements drawn from Isaiah in his doxology of Rom 11:34-35.

their faith "in Christ" in somewhat different ways is "in line" with God's own intentions and purposes.

15:13 In the final verse of his second brief subsection of 15:7-13, Paul expresses his final "prayer wish" for his Christian addressees at Rome: "May the God of hope fill you with all joy and peace as you trust in him, so that you may overflow with hope by the power of the Holy Spirit." It is a prayer wish that has in mind the apostle's basic appeals for the acceptance of other believers in Jesus. These appeals (1) are based on the example of Jesus in his earthly ministry, (2) suggest that variations in certain dietary and calendar matters should be seen as largely matters of inherited practice and/or personal preference, and (3) suggest that such variations of Christian liberty should be viewed as being "in line" with four OT passages that make reference to the bringing together of both Gentiles and Jews into the one family of God's people. Most explicitly, however, Paul here in 15:13 speaks of the unifying factors that exist for all believers in Jesus; these are "glorifying God for his mercy," "singing God's praises," "rejoicing with all of God's people," and "having hope for all that God has promised." In this final prayer wish of this concluding verse of the entire body middle (i.e., 1:16–15:13) of the letter, God is portrayed as "the God of hope" (ὁ θεὸς τῆς ἐλπίδος), who (1) promises hope (ἐλπίς) for the future, (2) fills his people in the present with "all joy and peace" (πάσης χαρᾶς καὶ εἰρήνης) "in their trust" (ἐν τῷ πιστεύειν) of him and his promise, and (3) enables his people "to overflow" (εἰς τὸ περισσεύειν) "with this hope" (ἐν τῇ ἐλπίδι) "by the power of the Holy Spirit" (ἐν δυνάμει πνεύματος ἁγίου). What Paul sets out here in 15:13 is, in fact, the essence of all that he proclaimed in his mission to pagan Gentiles, of all that he wrote to the believers in Jesus at Rome, and of all that, by being canonized in our NT, is being spoken to Christians today.[38]

---

38. As a word of personal testimony, my own appreciation of the importance and centrality of "hope" for the future — as grounded in "the God of hope," the work of Jesus Christ, and the ministry of God's Holy Spirit — was rather unexpectedly heightened some years ago (in what was for me a quite overwhelming and emotionally draining experience) when I was walking by the old city cemetery that is located just north of the main campus area of Yale University, New Haven, Connecticut, where in large letters there appears in the black metal grating over the central gate of that cemetery the caption: "IN HOPE OF THE RESURRECTION." For in a flash of understanding there was burned into my consciousness the fact that "In Hope of the Resurrection" is the basic conviction that supports all of Christian living and that undergirds everything that pertains to the death of a believer in Jesus. Later, in arranging for the placement of a headstone for our family burial plot (which gravesite presently includes my maternal grandparents, my mother and father, and will at some time in the future include my dear wife and me), I had these same words "In Hope of the Resurrection" engraved into that headstone as the final word of our family — just as it was Paul's final word of his extensive theological and ethical presentations in Rom 1:16–15:13 and the final word many years ago of those dear Christian people in New Haven.

BIBLICAL THEOLOGY

In his general ethical expositions of 12:1-21 and 13:8-14 regarding the nature of Christian ethics — as well as in his specific exhortations and appeals of 14:1–15:13 about a certain troubling situation among the Christians at Rome — Paul spoke of a Christian's ethical thinking and action as being directed by (1) the transformed and renewed mind of a believer in Jesus, (2) implications drawn from the message of the Christian gospel, and (3) the church's remembrances of the teaching and example of the historical Jesus. He also used some OT quotations in those presentations. He did not, however, employ those biblical commands as the primary basis for a Christian's ethical thinking and living. Rather, he used OT quotations to point out that Christian ethics are "in line" with the revelation given by God in the Jewish (OT) Scriptures. Although the Christian life is often thought of and expressed in ways that all too often resemble some type of Jewish "nomism," some form of Greek classical "ethicism," or some features of Greek Stoicism, its essential theocentric, Christocentric, and pneumatic nature needs always to be highlighted and contextualized in the thinking and actions of professing Christians in their structuring of a biblical theology for today.

As Luke Timothy Johnson has summarized matters in comparing the ethics of Paul and the ethics of Aristotle (384-322 B.C.):

> While Paul's moral logic is remarkably similar to the character ethics of Aristotle — so much so that some of the assumptions that Paul leaves unexpressed can helpfully be supplemented by reference to the *Nicomachean Ethics* — the framework for the logic [of the apostle] is pervasively colored by his religious convictions. Human prudential reasoning and testing is demanded, but it is informed not only by one's own mind but also by the mind of Christ. The capacity to see truly and to act appropriately is enabled by the Holy Spirit. The point of prudence is not only one's own interest but above all the good of the community that is the body of Christ. The measure of sound moral reasoning is not hitting "the mean" which is virtue, but corresponding to the faith of Christ which is spelled out in lowly service to others. In short, the habits Paul seeks to shape in his readers are the habits of Jesus; the character he seeks to mold in his communities is the character of Jesus Christ.[39]

And as Johnson argued earlier in this same article with regard to Paul and his treatment of ethics:

> Paul understands the process of moral discernment within the [Christian] community to be exercised not only within the measure of faith, but specifically within the "faith of Christ" . . . that was demonstrated by Jesus'

---

39. L. T. Johnson, "Transformation of the Mind and Moral Discernment in Paul," 235-36.

obedience to God and loving self-disposition toward others. The transformation of believers "in the renewal of mind" means therefore their "putting on" the mind of Christ, so that the process of φρόνησις ["way of thinking"] is aligned with the ἀρχαί ["elementary Christian teachings"] apprehended by their νοῦς ["mind," "intellect"] thus renewed and informed.[40]

It is such a theocentric, Christocentric, and pneumatic ethic that must always permeate our thinking as "Christ followers" (i.e., our biblical theology) and our living as believers in Jesus (i.e., our Christian ethics) today, not only personally but also ecclesiastically and societally. For the Christian life, while awaiting a future resurrection, must always be understood as the present expression of our newly inaugurated resurrection life — which new life (1) has been given to us by God through the work of Christ and the ministry of God's Spirit, (2) is to be lived out in ways that glorify God in response to the work of Christ and the guidance of the Holy Spirit, and (3) is intended by God for us to serve others as representatives of our resurrected Christ.

CONTEXTUALIZATION FOR TODAY

Paul's exhortations and appeals in 14:1–15:13 are directed to a particular situation that was then occurring among the Christians at Rome in at least some of their congregations. So there is a specificity of matters dealt with — as well as an apostolic nuance that is embedded — in all the exhortations and appeals that Paul as the God-appointed apostle to the Gentiles sets out. As readers today of his letter to the Christians at Rome of that day, we cannot be exactly sure regarding either (1) the nature or the content of the issues dealt with or (2) the precise identification of the people involved. Nor can we speak or write with the apostolic authority that Paul possessed.

Nonetheless, we can understand some things about vegetarian diets, about the veneration of certain holy days and seasons, and about drinking wine. Further, we all have our own family heritage from which we have derived certain personal preferences — which have often grown into personal convictions. And we can all understand, at least to some extent, the propensity of people (even Christian people) to magnify such inherited preferences or convictions into some form of theory or theology that will guide one's thinking and regulate one's life — and, as we often take for granted, guide the thinking of all other people and regulate all of society.

Paul, however, does not set out "rules" that he wants his readers to impose on themselves or others in any comparable situation that may be confronted by a believer in Jesus today. Rather, he provides Christians with a paradigm (that is, an "archetype" or "prototype") for dealing with matters that might (or,

---

40. L. T. Johnson, "Transformation of the Mind and Moral Discernment in Paul," 229.

"could" or "may") be classified by them (or by others) as *adiaphora* concerns (that is, matters neither required of Christians nor prohibited to them). The following verses that begin each of the subsections of the apostle's exhortations and appeals in 14:1–15:13, as well as at least one of the subsumed paragraphs of the passage, are surely appeals that he would want Christians today to take to heart in their relations with and responses to other Christians — as well as in their attitudes and actions within their own Christian congregations:

1. "Accept those among you whose faith is weak, without passing judgment on disputable opinions" (14:1).
2. "Let us stop passing judgment on one another. Instead make up your mind not to place a stumbling block or obstacle in the way of a believing brother or sister" (14:13).
3. "Let us make every effort to do what leads to peace and the building up of one another" (14:19).
4. "We who are 'the Strong' ought to bear with the failings of 'the Weak' and not please ourselves. Each of us should please our neighbors for their good in order to build them up" (15:1-2).
5. "Accept one another just as Christ accepted you, in order to bring praise to God" (15:7).

What Paul has said in the above statements is straightforward and quite clear. What remains is (1) clarity in our differentiating between matters that are important for the sake of the Christian gospel and for a healthy human existence and matters that represent only *adiaphora* concerns, and (2) a will on our part to take what we know to be appropriate action in a particular circumstance, as based on a mind that has been transformed by God and is being constantly renewed by his Spirit, in concert with other such transformed and renewed minds in the various congregations of God's people — with both clarity of mind and readiness of will being always dependent on God's Holy Spirit for specific direction and sufficient strength.

C. Body Closing

VIII. "Apostolic Parousia" (15:14-32)

TRANSLATION

¹⁵:¹⁴*I myself am convinced, my brothers and sisters, that you yourselves are full of goodness, complete in knowledge, and competent to admonish one another.* ¹⁵*Nonetheless, I have written to you rather boldly on some points, as if to remind you of them again, because of the grace that was given to me by God —* ¹⁶*[which grace God gave me] for the purpose of being a minister of Christ Jesus to the Gentiles, with the priestly duty of proclaiming the gospel of God so that the Gentiles might become an offering acceptable to God, sanctified by the Holy Spirit.*

¹⁷*Therefore I boast in Christ Jesus with respect to my service for God.* ¹⁸*I will not venture to speak of anything except what Christ has accomplished through me in leading the Gentiles to obey God by what I say and what I do —* ¹⁹*as accompanied by the power of signs and miracles, through the power of God's Spirit. So from Jerusalem all the way around to Illyricum, I have fully proclaimed the gospel of Christ.* ²⁰*It has always been my ambition to preach the gospel where Christ was not known, so that I would not be building on someone else's foundation.* ²¹*Rather, as it is written:*

> *"Those who were not told about him will see,*
> *and those who have not heard will understand."*

²²*That is why I have frequently been hindered from coming to you.*

²³*But now not having a place [to minister] in these regions, and since I have been longing for many years to see you,* ²⁴*I plan to do so whenever I go to Spain. I hope to visit you while passing through [on my way to Spain] and to have you assist me on my journey there, after I have enjoyed your company for a while.*

²⁵*Presently, however, I am on my way to Jerusalem to serve the saints there.* ²⁶*For the believers in Jesus of Macedonia and Achaia were well pleased to make a contribution to the poor among the saints in Jerusalem.* ²⁷*They were well pleased to do so — and, indeed, they are their debtors. For since Gentile believers in Jesus share in the spiritual blessings of believing Jews, they owe it to believing Jews to minister to them in material matters.* ²⁸*Then after completing this task and mak-*

ing sure that they have received this fruit, I will go to Spain and visit you on the way. [29]*And I know that when I come to you, I will come in the full measure of the blessing of Christ.*

[30]*I urge you, brothers and sisters, by our Lord Jesus Christ and by the love of the Spirit, to join me in my struggle to aid the impoverished believers in Jesus at Jerusalem by praying to God for me.* [31]*Pray that I may be rescued from the unbelievers in Judea and that my service in Jerusalem may be acceptable to the saints there,* [32]*so that by God's will I may come to you with joy and together with you be refreshed.*

TEXTUAL NOTES

15:14a The genitive singular personal pronoun μου ("my"), which appears here in the expression ἀδελφοί μου ("*my* brothers and sisters"), is amply attested by uncials א A B C D² P Ψ [also *Byz* L] and by minuscules 33 1175 (Category I), 1506 (Category II), and 6 69 88 104 323 326 330 365 614 1241 1243 1319 1505 1573 1735 1874 2344 2495 (Category III); it is also reflected in the major vg and syr versions. It is, however, omitted in P⁴⁶, in uncials D* F G, and in minuscules 1739 (Category I) and 1881 (Category II); it is also omitted in it (i.e., the Old Latin version) and by Ambrosiaster. Its omission was probably occasioned by the church's desire to "catholicize" (i.e., "make general") the message of Romans for public reading in its worship services — as seems also to have been the motivation for the "short form" of the letter (i.e., 1:1–14:23).

14b The inclusion of the expression καὶ αὐτοί ("also yourselves" or "you yourselves") is very widely attested in the Greek textual tradition. It is, however, omitted in P⁴⁶ and in uncials D F and G; its absence also is reflected in it (i.e., the Old Latin version). This omission of καὶ αὐτοί is probably due, at least in part, to a desire to "catholicize" Romans by deleting references to any special relationship between Paul and the believers in Jesus at Rome.

14c The inclusion of the genitive ἀγαθωσύνης ("of goodness"), which appears in the phrase μεστοί ἐστε ἀγαθωσύνης ("you are full *of goodness*"), is amply attested in the Greek textual tradition. The genitive ἀγάπης ("of love"), however, is found in its place in uncials F and G, while the genitive ἁγιωσύνης ("of holiness") appears as a substitute in minuscule 629 (Category III). But these much more weakly attested variants cannot displace the originality of the far better supported genitive ἀγαθωσύνης ("of goodness") — even though one or more ancient scribes might have (1) thought that speaking "of love" (ἀγάπης) or "of holiness" (ἁγιωσύνης) was more appropriate for the apostle Paul or (2) simply confused these words because of their somewhat similar spellings.

14d The genitive article τῆς ("of the"), which appears in the clause πεπληρωμένοι πάσης [τῆς] γνώσεως ("filled with" or "complete in *the* knowledge"), is omitted in P⁴⁶, in uncials A C D F G [also *Byz* L], and in minuscules 33 1175 (Category I) and 69 88 104 323 326 365 614 1241 1319 1505 1573 1735 1874 2495 (Category III). It is included, however, by uncials א B P Ψ and by minuscules 1739 (Category I), 1506 1881 (Category II), and 6 330 1243 2344 (Category III). With the omission of the article, the phrase reads "filled with all knowledge" or "complete in knowledge"; if the article were included, it would most likely have in view some particular kind of knowledge as represented by the expression "*the* knowledge."

The MS evidence is almost equally divided. Yet there seems to be no reason why τῆς, if it had been original, would have been deleted. Further, since the textual evidence somewhat favors the omission of τῆς, the clause should probably be read without the article, and so be translated "filled with all knowledge" or "complete in knowledge."

14e The reciprocal pronoun ἀλλήλους ("one another"), in the expression ἀλλήλους νουθετεῖν ("to instruct *one another*" or "to admonish *one another*"), is strongly supported by P[46], by uncials א A B C D F G P Ψ, and by minuscules 1175 1739 (Category I), 1506 1881 (Category II), and 88 326 630 1243 1505 2495 (Category III); it is also reflected in all the Latin versions and in syr[h]. The variant plural pronoun ἄλλους (which usually signifies "others" who are different from the person speaking or writing), however, appears in its place in the ninth-century *Byz* uncial L and in minuscules 33 (Category I) and 6 69 104 323 330 365 614 1241 1319 1573 1735 1874 2344 (Category III); it is also reflected in syr[p]. This variant reading was evidently inserted by later scribes in order either (1) to catholicize further the import of Paul's words or (2) to heighten the authority of the church at Rome vis-à-vis that of all other Christian congregations of the day — or, perhaps, both.

15a The adjective τολμηρότερον ("boldly"), which appears as the first word of this verse, is amply attested by P[46], by uncials א[2] C D F G P Ψ [also *Byz* L], and by minuscules 33 1175 1739 (Category I), 1881 (Category II), and 6 69 88 104 323 326 365 614 1241 1243 1319 1505 1573 1735 1874 2344 2495 (Category III). The adverbial form τολμηροτερῶς ("boldly"), however, appears in uncials A G and in minuscules 1506 (Category II) and 330 629 (Category III). While there is no essential difference in their meanings, and while the adverbial τολμηροτερῶς may be considered by scholars today as more grammatically suitable, the adjective τολμηρότερον is to be preferred as having been original simply because of its better attestation in the textual tradition.

15b Following the phrase ἔγραψα ὑμῖν ("I have written to you") there is no appearance of the word ἀδελφοί ("brothers ['and sisters']") in uncials א* A B C or in minuscules 1739 (Category I), 81 1881 (Category II), and 218 630 2495 (Category III); this omission is also reflected in cop[sa, bo] and supported by Origen Chrysostom and Augustine. Many Greek MSS, however, have ἀδελφοί immediately after ἔγραψα ὑμῖν, as does P[46], as do uncials א[c] D F G P Ψ [also *Byz* L] (though with ἀδελφοί appearing after the phrase ἀπὸ μέρους in the seventh-century uncial 0209) and as do most minuscules; the presence of ἀδελφοί in the original Greek text is also reflected in it[d, g] vg syr[h, pal] cop[sa mss] arm.

This question regarding the omission or inclusion of ἀδελφοί here in 15:15 is difficult to resolve, simply because the MSS evidence seems to be so evenly balanced. Yet Bruce Metzger is probably correct in arguing (1) that if ἀδελφοί had been original, there would have been no reason why the word would have been dropped, and (2) that ἀδελφοί was probably inserted at some time in the lectionary use of the letter.[1] We have, therefore, concluded that the word ἀδελφοί at this point in Paul's letter was probably not original, and so have not included it in our translation.

1. Cf. Metzger, *Textual Commentary*, 473.

15c The textual evidence is almost equally strong for either (1) ὑπὸ τοῦ θεοῦ ("by God"), which is attested by P⁴⁶, by uncials ℵ² A C D G P Ψ [also *Byz* L], and by minuscules 33 1175 1739 (Category I), 1506 1881 (Category II), and 69 88 323 326 330 365 614 1241 1243 1319 1505 1573 1735 1874 2344 2495 (Category III), or (2) ἀπὸ τοῦ θεοῦ ("from God"), which is supported mainly by uncials ℵ* B F. Both ὑπό and ἀπό may connote much the same meaning. Yet ὑπό is somewhat better supported in the Greek textual tradition, and so is most likely to have been original.

16a The preposition εἰς ("unto," "for the purpose of being") at the beginning of v. 16 is widely attested in the textual tradition. P⁴⁶ has in its place, however, the preposition διά ("on account of"). But this variant, which appears only in P⁴⁶, is probably best judged an idiosyncratic reading of a particular scribe or simply a scribal error.

16b The phrase εἰς τὰ ἔθνη ("to the Gentiles") is extremely well attested in the Greek textual tradition. Its omission in Codex Vaticanus (B 03) was most likely accidental.

16c The aorist subjunctive verb γένηται ("it might become") is well attested in the Greek textual tradition. The aorist passive γενήθη ("it became"), however, appears in Codex Vaticanus (B 03) and in minuscule 1881* (Category II), but probably should be viewed as a retrospective evaluation of Paul's mission by a later scribe.

17a There are three possible Greek wordings for the opening expression of this verse: (1) ἣν ἔχω καύχησιν ("which boast I have"), which appears in P⁴⁶; (2) ἔχω οὖν καύχησιν ("therefore I have a boast"), which appears in uncials ℵ A P Ψ [also *Byz* L] and in minuscules 33 1175 1739 (Category I), 1881 (Category II), and 6 104 323 326 614 1241 1243 1505 1874 2495 (Category III); and (3) ἔχω οὖν τὴν καύχησιν ("therefore I have the boast"), which is attested by uncials B Cᵛⁱᵈ D F G and by minuscules 81 1506 (Category II) and 69 330 365 1319 1573 1735 (Category III). All three options have been proposed to be original, yet all three options can rather colloquially be translated "therefore I boast (or 'glory')."

17b The phrase ἐν Χριστῷ Ἰησοῦ ("in Christ Jesus") appears in this same place very widely throughout the Greek textual tradition. The name Ἰησοῦ, however, is omitted by P⁴⁶, by minuscule 323 (Category III), and by Ambrosiaster — which omission is somewhat difficult to understand.

18a The future verb τολμήσω ("I will make bold," "presume," "venture") is widely attested in the Greek textual tradition. The present tense verb τολμάω ("I make bold," "presume," "venture"), however, appears in uncials ca² and B. Probably the future τολμήσω is to be preferred as having been original — not only because of the preponderance of external MS evidence in its favor but also because a future verb seems somewhat out of place amidst all the present and past tense verbs of the passage, and so must be credited as being "the more difficult reading."

18b The expression δι᾽ ἐμοῦ ("through me") is strongly supported throughout the textual tradition. The reading δι᾽ ἐμοῦ λόγων ("through my words"), however, appears in Codex Vaticanus (B 03). This expanded reading is evidently a fourth-century attempt to set out more fully the meaning of the apostle's expression "through me." Yet, though attested by Codex Vaticanus (B 03), this expanded reading δι᾽ ἐμοῦ λόγων ("through my words") seems unable to displace the extensive textual support for the simple expression δι᾽ ἐμοῦ ("through me").

18c The phrase ὑπακοὴν ἐθνῶν ("the obedience of the Gentiles") is also strongly attested in the Greek textual tradition. In place of ὑπακοήν ("obedience"), however, Codex Vaticanus (uncial B 03) reads ἀκοήν ("hearing"). But like the situation cited above in 18b, this reading of ἀκοήν ("hearing") cannot displace the more extensive MS support for the originality of ὑπακοὴν ἐθνῶν ("the obedience of the Gentiles").

19 In considering the phrase ἐν δυνάμει πνεύματος ("by the power of the Spirit"), it needs to be noted that many important textual witnesses also have the possessive qualifier θεοῦ (thereby reading "by the power of the Spirit *of God*"), as attested by P⁴⁶, by uncials ℵ D¹ P Ψ 0150 [also *Byz* L], and by minuscules 1175 (Category I), 1506 (Category II), and 6 436 1241 1912 (Category III); this reading is also reflected in it^b syr^{p, h} and supported by Origen^{lat2/3} Chrysostom. A number of other MSS have the adjectival qualifier ἁγίου (thereby reading "by the power of the *Holy* Spirit"), as supported by uncials A D*'² F G and by minuscules 33 1739 (Category I), 81 104 256 1881 1962 2127 (Category II), and 263 365 459 1319 1573 1852 2200 (Category III); this reading of the adjectival qualifier ἁγίου is also reflected in it^{ar, d, f, g, mon, o} vg syr^{h mg, pal} cop^{sa, bo} and supported by Origen^{latl/3} Ambrosiaster Augustine. Further, a number of Byzantine MSS have both θεοῦ and ἁγίου (reading ἐν δυνάμει ἁγίου πνεύματος θεοῦ).

The inclusion of both θεοῦ and ἁγίου should, in all likelihood, be viewed as later conflations of the two options cited above that attempt to solve this textual problem. Only Codex Vaticanus (B 03) has the word πνεύματος by itself — which raises the question whether the attestation by uncial B alone, despite the overall excellence of this important fourth-century MS, is enough to answer the question of originality (as was thought to be the case by the editorial committee of *GNT*²). Bruce Metzger reports that the UBS committee that sought to establish the Greek texts of *GNT*³ and *GNT*⁴ decided (in "compromise" votes) to follow here the earliest MS witness, that is, the witness of P⁴⁶, but to enclose θεοῦ in brackets to indicate considerable doubt.² This decision marks a decided change from the acceptance of the reading of Codex Vaticanus (B 03) alone, as expressed in *GNT*². It is this decision to accept the witness of P⁴⁶ as primary with which we agree, and so have incorporated the possessive qualifier θεοῦ into our translation — though acknowledging that there are legitimate grounds for disputing such a judgment.

22 The articular τὰ πολλά ("many times") is amply attested by uncials ℵ A C P Ψ [also *Byz* L] and by minuscules 33 1175 1739 (Category I), 1506 1881 (Category II), and 6 69 88 104 323 326 365 614 1241 1243 1319 1505 1573 1735 2344 2495 (Category III). The adverb πολλάκις ("many times," "often," "frequently"), however, is attested by P⁴⁶, by uncials B D F G, and by minuscule 330 (Category III). The resultant meanings are much the same. Yet it may be surmised (1) that the adverb πολλάκις ("often," "frequently") was original (in line with the testimony of P⁴⁶) and (2) that the articular noun τὰ πολλά ("many times") was later inserted in its stead because it was deemed to be more polished syntactically.

23 Paul declares that he had longed to see the Romans "for many years." The word πολλῶν ("many") is amply attested by P⁴⁶, by uncials ℵ A D F G Ψ [also *Byz* L], and by minuscules 33 1739 (Category I), 1881 (Category II), and 104 436 451 1241 2495 (Category

---

2. Metzger, *Textual Commentary*, 473.

III); it is also supported by Chrysostom Theodoret. The idea of "many," however, is expressed by the word ἱκανῶν ("sufficient," "large number," "many in number") in uncials B C P and in minuscules 81 1962 2127 (Category II) and 326 (Category III). But πολλῶν has better and more diversified support, and therefore should most likely be viewed as having been original. The word ἱκανῶν is a more polished term, which, as may be surmised, was substituted by some Alexandrian editor to soften what could have been viewed by readers as an exaggeration of the apostle's statement.

24 Probably because the sentence in 15:23-24a lacks a finite verb (following the double use of the participle ἔχων), some ancient scribe(s) inserted the statement ἐλεύσομαι πρὸς ὑμᾶς ("I will come to you"), which additional sentence appears in uncial ℵ² [also *Byz* L] and in minuscules 33 1175 (Category I), 256 2127 (Category II), and 6 104 263 365 436 459 1241 1319 1573 1912 (Category III); it is also reflected in syr^h. But the shorter text, which reads simply ὡς ἂν πορεύωμαι εἰς Σπανίαν ("whenever I go to Spain," without the further statement "I will come to you"), already implies what the scribes of those weaker textual witnesses seem to have wanted to make abundantly clear. More important, the shorter text is rather decisively attested by P^46, by uncials ℵ* A B C D F G P Ψ 0150, and by minuscules 1739 (Category I), 81 1506 1881 1962 (Category II), and 2200 (Category III); it is also reflected in it^ar, (b), d, f, g, mon, o vg syr^p cop^sa, bo and supported by Origen^lat Chrysostom Ambrosiaster Jerome. Thus this shorter reading should be accepted as original.

25 The present participle διακονῶν ("serving") is widely attested by uncials ℵ^c A B C P Ψ [also *Byz* L] and by minuscules 33 1175 1739 (Category I), 1506 1881 (Category II), and 6 69 88 104 323 326 330 365 614 1241 1243 1319 1505 1573 1735 1874 2344 2495 (Category III). Uncial ℵ*, however, has the aorist participle διακονήσων ("having served"), while P^46 and uncials D F G have the aorist infinitive διακονῆσαι ("to serve"). The first of these possibilities is rather awkward, though it is the most widely supported of the above three options. But the reading of P^46 and the "Western" uncials D F and G seems to incorporate best the apostle's purpose in going to Jerusalem, that is, "to serve the saints" of the city of Jerusalem. Therefore, for both internal and external reasons, it seems best to give priority to the aorist infinitive διακονῆσαι ("to serve") of P^46, and so to translate Paul's statement here as follows: "I am on my way to Jerusalem *to serve* the saints there."

26a The name Μακεδονία ("Macedonia") is amply attested in the textual tradition. The plural Μακεδόνες ("Macedonians"), however, appears in uncials F G; it is also reflected in it and syr^p and supported by Ambrosiaster. This variant reading evidently sought to make it quite clear that the apostle's reference here is to "the people of Macedonia." Yet the name "Macedonia" in this context already implies "the people of Macedonia" — and, in particular, "the believers in Jesus of Macedonia." Thus such an explication by the translators of the Old Latin translation and by the commentator Ambrosiaster — as well as by the scribes of uncials F and G — seems quite unnecessary.

26b The third-person plural aorist verb εὐδόκησαν ("they were pleased") is also extensively attested in the textual tradition. The third-person singular aorist verb εὐδόκησεν ("he/she was pleased"), however, appears in its place in P^46, in Codex Vaticanus (B 03), and in minuscule 1241 (Category III). This use of the third-person singular εὐδόκησεν in P^46 and uncial B is grammatically in line with the singular use of the name Μακεδονία that appears very widely in the Greek textual tradition. Yet the plural verb εὐδόκησαν conceptually carries the implied plurality of people that exists in the name "Macedonia" (i.e., "the people of Macedonia"), which in this context signifies "the believers in Jesus of Macedonia." Either could be accepted without disrupting the sense of the sentence.

27 The somewhat grammatically awkward expression εὐδόκησαν γὰρ καὶ ὀφειλέται εἰσίν ("for they were pleased and they are debtors") is amply attested by uncials ℵ A B C P Ψ [also *Byz* L] and by minuscules 33 1175 1739 (Category I), 1506 1881 (Category II), and 6 69 88 104 323 326 330 365 614 1241 1243 1319 1505 1573 1735 1846 1874 2344 2495 (Category III); it is also reflected in vg syr cop. There are, however, a few other MSS that read simply (1) ὀφειλέται γάρ εἰσιν ("for they are debtors"), as do P⁴⁶, uncials F and G, and Ambrosiaster, or (2) ὀφειλέται εἰσίν ("they are debtors"), as does uncial D (06). A determination of originality between the more widely accepted reading of the textual tradition and the simpler readings of P⁴⁶ (c. A.D. 200) and D (sixth century A.D.) is not easy to make. Yet, because of the awkwardness of the expression εὐδόκησαν γὰρ καὶ ὀφειλέται εἰσίν, which is "the more difficult" reading (and so, according to the rubrics of contemporary textual criticism, more likely the original reading) — coupled with the fact of its widespread appearance in the Greek textual tradition — it should probably be judged that εὐδόκησαν γὰρ καὶ ὀφειλέται εἰσίν ("for they were pleased and they are debtors") was original.

28 The particle οὖν ("then"), which in a historical narrative serves to resume a subject that has in some way been interrupted, is widely attested in the textual tradition. The ninth-century uncials F and G, however, add immediately after οὖν the additional particle ἄρα (thereby reading "so then"). But this addition of ἄρα appears to be only a stylistic improvement, and so its originality is probably to be discounted.

29a The expression οἶδα δέ ("but I know" or "and I know") is also widely attested in the textual tradition. Uncials F and G, however, have in its place the phrase γινώσκω γάρ ("for I know"), which reading is also reflected in Jerome's Vulgate and supported by the Latin commentator Ambrosiaster. This replacement of οἶδα δέ ("but I know") by γινώσκω γάρ ("for I know") appears (1) to have been an attempt to minimize whatever uncertainty might possibly be seen in Paul's use of the particle δέ ("but") and/or (2) to speak more positively about the apostle's assured conviction by the use of the verb γινώσκω. Yet this variant reading γινώσκω γάρ ("for I know") lacks sufficient MS support to be accepted as original.

29b The dative noun πληρώματι ("in fullness") is widely attested throughout the textual tradition. Uncials F and G, however, have in its place the noun πληροφορία ("with full assurance," "with certainty") — which expresses the same connotation as "in fullness," but is far less supported by the MS evidence of the textual tradition.

29c The clause ἐν πληρώματι εὐλογίας Χριστοῦ ἐλεύσομαι ("in the full measure of the blessing of Christ I will come") is amply attested by P⁴⁶, by uncials ℵ* A B C D F G P, and by minuscules 1739 (Category I), 81 1506 1881 (Category II), and 6 424ᶜ 629 630 1243 2200 (Category III); it is also reflected in vgʷʷ ᵇᵒ geoˡ and supported by Clement Origenˡᵃᵗ Ambrosiaster Pelagius. A number of other MSS, however, add the phrase τοῦ εὐαγγελίου τοῦ ("of the gospel of") before Χριστοῦ, thereby reading "in the full measure of the blessing *of the gospel of* Christ." This addition is supported by uncials ℵ² and Ψ [also

Byz L] and by minuscules 33 1175 (Category I), 256 1506 1962 2127 (Category II), and 5 61 69 88 104 181 218 323 326 330 365 436 441 451 459 467 614 621 623 915 917 [though with Ἰησοῦ for Χριστοῦ] 1241 1319 1398 1505 1563 1573 1678 1718 1735 1751 1838 1845 1846 1874 1875 1877 1908 1912 1942 1959 2110 2138 2344 2492 2495 2523 2544 2718 (Category III); it is also reflected in vg^cl syr^{p, h} geo². But this variant reading cannot supplant the far better attested shorter reading.

30a The inclusion of the word ἀδελφοί ("brothers [and sisters]") in the opening appeal of the final paragraph of this subsection of material (thus reading "I urge you, *brothers and sisters*) is amply attested by uncials א A B C D F G P [also *Byz* L] and by minuscules 33 1175 1739 (Category I), 1506 1881 (Category II), and 6 69 88 104 323 326 330 365 614 1241 1243 1319 1505 1573 1735 1874 2344 2495 (Category III); it is also reflected in the major Latin, Syriac, and Coptic versions. The word ἀδελφοί, however, is lacking in P⁴⁶ and in Codex Vaticanus (B 03).

This omission of ἀδελφοί in both P⁴⁶ and uncial B is extremely difficult to explain — so much so that many commentators have included it simply because it was a common practice of Paul to include ἀδελφοί in his other hortatory appeals. So the editors of *NA*²⁶, ²⁷ and *GNT*³, ⁴ consistently included it, though they placed it in square brackets to indicate uncertainty. And thus we have included it in our translation — even though we are unable to give any reason for its omission in P⁴⁶ and Codex Vaticanus (B 03).

30b The use of the preposition διά ("through," "by") in the expression "through" or "by the Lord Jesus Christ" is strongly supported throughout the textual tradition. The addition of the phrase ὀνόματος τοῦ ("of [or 'by'] the name of"), thereby reading "I urge you, brothers and sisters, by *the name of* the Lord Jesus Christ," however, appears in *Byz* uncial L and in minuscule 1881 (Category II). But this variant reading is far too weakly attested in the textual tradition to merit consideration as original.

31a The word διακονία ("service," "ministry") in the expression "my service [or 'ministry'] in Jerusalem" is amply attested by P⁴⁶, by uncials א A C D² P Ψ 0150 [also *Byz* L], and by minuscules 33 1175 1739 (Category I), 81 256 1506 1881 1962 2127 (Category II), and 104 263 365 436 459 1241 1319 1573 1852 1912 2200 (Category III); it is also reflected in it^{d2, f, g} vg^{mss} syr^{p, h} cop^{sa, bo} and supported by Origen^lat Chrysostom. It is, however, replaced by δωροφορία ("the bringing of a gift") in uncials B D* F G; it is also reflected in it^{ar, b, d*} vg and supported by Ambrosiaster. Perhaps the phrase ἡ διακονία μου ἡ εἰς Ἰερουσαλὴμ seemed somewhat odd to later "Western" editors. Or, perhaps, they wanted to articulate the purpose of Paul's journey more clearly by the use of δωροφορία, which appears nowhere else in the NT.

31b The preposition εἰς ("in") in the expression ἡ εἰς Ἰερουσαλὴμ ("which is *in* Jerusalem") is strongly supported by P⁴⁶, by uncials א A C D² P Ψ [also *Byz* L], and by minuscules 33 1175 1739 (Category I), 1881 (Category II), and 6 69 88 104 323 326 330 365 614 1241 1243 1319 1573 1735 1874 2344 (Category III). A number of Western MSS, however, have in its place the preposition ἐν ("in"), as found in uncials B D* F G and in minuscules 1505 and 2495 (Category III). This substitution of ἐν for εἰς most likely came about because of a fear that the preposition εἰς could be read as implying submission to Jerusalem, whereas the preposition ἐν would hardly convey anything other than the idea of location. Yet the reading εἰς ("in") is very amply attested, and so is probably original.

32 The reading of the subordinate purpose sentence ἵνα ἐν χαρᾷ ἐλθὼν πρὸς ὑμᾶς διὰ θελήματος θεοῦ συναναπαύσωμαι ὑμῖν ("in order that by God's will I may come to you with joy and together with you be refreshed") is attested by uncials A C 0150 and by minuscules 33 1739 (Category I), 81 256 1506^{vid} 1881^c [though 1881* reads ἀναπαύσομαι] 2127 [though reading συναναπαύσομαι] (Category II), and 263 365 424^c 1319 1573 1852 [though omitting ἐν χαρᾷ] 2200 (Category III); it is also reflected in cop^{sa} and supported by Origen^{lat}. This reading of v. 32 should probably be accepted as original.

A whole cluster of other readings have to do with both the order of the words and the words themselves that appear in the textual tradition. These variant readings may be listed as follows: (1) the reversal of the word order ἐν χαρᾷ and ἐλθών, as appears in ℵ*; (2) the alteration of words that qualify θελήματος — e.g., Ἰησοῦ Χριστοῦ, as found in ℵ*; or Χριστοῦ Ἰησοῦ, as appears in D* F G, as reflected in it$^{ar, (b) d*, (d2), f, g, mon, o}$ vg^{ms}, and as supported by Ambrosiaster; (3) the appearance of κυρίου Ἰησοῦ, as attested by uncial B in place of the more widely attested θεοῦ; (4) the replacement of the participle ἐλθών by the aorist subjunctive ἔλθω plus the conjunction καί to make a paratactic construction, as in uncials ℵ^2 D* F G P Ψ [also *Byz* L] and in minuscules 1175 (Category I), 1962 (Category II), and 104 436 459 1241 1912 (Category III); as also reflected in it$^{ar, (b) d*, (d2), f, g, o}$ vg syr$^{(p), h}$ cop^{bo} and supported by Chrysostom Ambrosiaster; (5) the replacement of the aorist subjunctive verb συναναπαύσωμαι by the future indicative verb συν)αναπαύσομαι, as in uncials P Ψ and minuscules 1881 2127 (Category II) and 104 459 1241 1319 1912 (Category III) — or by the verb ἀναψύξω, as in uncial D* (and as reflected in it$^{ar, (b) d*, (d2), f, g, o}$ vg^{ms} and supported by Ambrosiaster) or by the verb ἀναψύχω, as in uncials F G; and (6) the substitution of μεθ' ὑμῶν for ὑμῖν, as in uncials D* F G; also reflected in it$^{ar, (b) d*, (d2), f, g, o}$ vg^{ms} and supported by Ambrosiaster. Yet the more accepted reading of this subordinate purpose sentence of 15:32 (as cited above) has sufficient support to be considered original — and, further, it seems to explain most, if not all, of the other variant readings.

An Anticipatory Comment with Respect to Our Treatment of 15:33. It has frequently been claimed that the peace blessing (or, supposedly, the peace benediction) and the "Amen" of 15:33 provide an appropriate conclusion to the original content of Paul's letter to Rome (as per the thesis of a possible "intermediate form" of fifteen chapters for Romans, with or without the doxology of 16:25-27, as having been the original form of the apostle's letter, which thesis was proposed by a number of earlier NT scholars based on their readings of P^{46} and certain important patristic commentators)[3] — or, at least, that the peace blessing (or peace benediction) provides an apt conclusion to the body closing or "apostolic parousia" section of Romans (with parallels being the grace benediction of 1 Cor 16:23 and the peace blessings and grace benedictions of 2 Cor 13:11b and Phil 4:9b and 23). In any case, the separation of 15:33 from what follows in 16:1-27 has become rather traditional among commentators ever since the Scriptures (both OT and NT) were first chapterized in the early thirteenth century and then versified in the mid–sixteenth century, thereby connecting 15:33 with 15:14-32 and separating it from what follows in 16:1-27.

3. Cf. "The Probable Existence of an Early Short Form" and "The Possible Existence of an Intermediate Form" in our *Introducing Romans*, 20-24.

Elsewhere in his NT letters, however, Paul does not conclude a letter or a section of a letter with a peace blessing (or peace benediction). When a peace blessing or wish appears in his other extant letters, it usually *begins* that letter's conclusion (see particularly 1 Thess 5:23; 2 Thess 3:16; and Phil 4:9b; note also 2 Cor 13:11b; Gal 6:16; Eph 6:23a; Phil 4:9b; and 1 Thess 5:23a) — with a grace benediction then given almost immediately after it, or shortly thereafter, closing off that letter's conclusion (as in 1 Thess 5:28; 2 Thess 3:18; Phil 4:23). We will, therefore, postpone our discussion and deal with the material of 15:33 as the opening feature of "the concluding sections" in 15:33–16:27 of the letter.

FORM/STRUCTURE/SETTING

In his body closing or apostolic parousia section of 15:14-32, Paul (1) commends the Christians at Rome (15:14), (2) states his purpose in writing them (15:15-16), (3) refers to his past ministry to pagan Gentiles throughout the eastern parts of the Roman Empire (15:17-22), (4) says his future travel plans include a visit to the believers in Jesus at Rome and then an evangelistic outreach to pagan Gentiles in Spain (15:23-24), (5) declares that presently, however, he must go to Jerusalem "to serve the saints" there, and that only after his ministry there will he be able carry out his desire to go on an evangelistic mission to Spain, and thus to visit the Christians at Rome on his way to Spain (15:25-29), and (6) requests that his Christian addressees at Rome pray for him, asking God for his safety and for the accomplishment of his purpose in going to Jerusalem — as well as praying about his desired visit with them at Rome, after having accomplished his mission on behalf of the believers in Jesus at Jerusalem (15:30-32). Such an enumeration of topics in the passage is fairly obvious.

Some of the language Paul employs in this passage, as well as his use of one passage drawn from the OT prophet Isaiah in support of the missionary stance that he has taken, closely resembles the form and purpose of his statements in Section I of the letter's body middle, that is, in 1:16–4:25. In fact, in both of these sections there is a striking similarity in (1) Paul's use of OT imagery and (2) his use of the OT to support one or more of his statements.

There can be little doubt that Paul, as a Jewish believer in Jesus, would have often thought along these lines. But why, in speaking to Gentile Christians about his Gentile ministry, would he have justified that missionary outreach to them in this manner? It is hard to believe that he would have declared to pagan Gentile audiences (1) that his mission to the Gentile world was a carrying out of *"his priestly duty* of proclaiming the gospel of God *so that the Gentiles might become an offering acceptable to God"* (as in 15:16) or (2) that his desire "to preach the gospel where Christ was not known" was *in fulfillment of the OT prophet Isaiah's words* that "those who were not told about him will see, and those who have not heard will understand" (as in 15:20-21). But those to whom he speaks in this manner in 15:14-32, whatever their varied ethnicities, were (as we have postulated) believers in Jesus who had been extensively influenced by the theology, language, and ways of thinking of Jewish Christianity.

Such a characterization of Paul's ministry (as in 15:16) and such a use of an OT quotation in support of his argument (as in 15:21) do not appear in Section II of the body middle of his letter (i.e., in 5:1–8:39), where Paul sets out a précis of his contextualized Christian message to pagan Gentiles. But this type of language and presentation in 15:16 and 21 conforms quite closely to the content of his message and to his manner of using OT quotations in Section I, where the apostle speaks to an ethnically mixed group of believers who had been extensively influenced by the theology, language, and ways of thinking of Jewish Christianity. Likewise, it parallels the type of language and exegetical support that Paul employs in the development of his Christian remnant theology in Section III, that is, in 9:6–11:32 (which, as we have speculated, probably reflects his earlier preaching in the ethnically mixed Christian congregations of Syrian Antioch). So it may be hypothesized that matters regarding form, method, and even substance were usually contextualized by Paul for the particular audience he was addressing; we will keep this in mind as we analyze this body closing or apostolic parousia section of material.

Nature and Designation of the Passage. Because this passage contains a number of references to Paul's past missionary journeys (v. 19) and his future travel plans (vv. 23-32), it has frequently been called a "travelogue." In 1967, however, Robert Funk coined the expression "apostolic parousia" to designate a section of a Pauline letter that was particularly concerned with the apostle's own presence and plans.[4] The term "apostolic parousia" has frequently been employed today as an appropriate caption for the contents of this "body closing" material of Paul's letter to Rome.

Funk viewed what appears in 15:14-32 (including v. 33, which we believe is better understood as the start of a concluding section of a Pauline letter) as the most complete example of an apostolic parousia in Paul's letters. He also identified other apostolic parousia sections as being 1 Thess 2:17–3:13, 1 Cor 4:14-21 (with a "secondary" apostolic parousia in 16:1-11), Phil 2:19-24 (with a "secondary" apostolic parousia in 2:25-30), Phlm 21-22, and Gal 4:12-20. Each of these other identifications, however, is somewhat debatable, and none of them seems to be particularly relevant to our purpose here.

Epistolary Forms and Features of the Passage. Just as there are a number of forms and features that reflect various epistolary conventions of the day in the beginning sections of Romans (i.e., in the salutation of 1:1-7, the thanksgiving of 1:8-12, and the body opening of 1:13-15), so there can be found a number of rather traditional epistolary forms and features in these latter sections of the letter (i.e., in the body closing or apostolic parousia of 15:14-32 and the concluding sections of 15:33–16:27). These conventional epistolary features appear in this section of Romans as follows:

4. Cf. Funk, "The 'Apostolic Parousia,'" 249 68.

15:14 — A *confidence expression* coupled with a *vocative of direct address:* πέπεισμαι, ἀδελφοί, "I am convinced, brothers and sisters."

15:15 — A *reminder statement:* ἔγραψα ὑμῖν . . . ὡς ἐπαναμιμνῄσκων ὑμᾶς, "I have written you . . . so as to remind you."

15:22 — A *visit wish:* ἐνεκοπτόμην τὰ πολλὰ τοῦ ἐλθεῖν πρὸς ὑμᾶς, "I have often been hindered from coming to you."

15:23-24 — A *notification of a coming visit:* νυνὶ δὲ . . . ἐλπίζω . . . θεάσασθαι ὑμᾶς, "but now . . . I hope . . . to visit you."

15:29 — A further *confidence expression:* οἶδα δὲ ὅτι ἐρχόμενος πρὸς ὑμᾶς ἐν πληρώματι εὐλογίας Χριστοῦ ἐλεύσομαι, "I know that when I come to you, I will come in the full measure of the blessing of Christ."

15:30 — A *request formula* coupled with a *vocative of direct address:* παρακαλῶ ὑμᾶς, ἀδελφοί, "I urge you, brothers and sisters."

The presence of such a relatively large number of traditional epistolary features in the space of only nineteen verses serves to distinguish (at least, in formal fashion) the materials here in 15:14-32 from the previous four major sections of the body middle of Romans — that is, from the three large theological sections of 1:16–4:25, 5:1–8:39, and 9:1–11:33 and the extensive ethical section of 12:1–15:13, all of which contain a relative paucity of epistolary formulas. For whereas rhetorical conventions of the day tend to dominate the apostle's presentations in the much larger theological and ethical sections of the body middle of his letter, with only a few epistolary features being present (mainly a few vocatives of direct address, a few verbs of saying, and some disclosure formulas, which are located at various strategic places in these four more extensive sections), in this body closing or apostolic parousia section of only nineteen verses, a number of then-current epistolary forms and features appear quite suddenly — with rhetorical conventions of the day being largely absent (though with the probable exception of Paul having reworked in a Christian manner the basic material of 15:14, which, apart from its Christian features and its context, may echo in rhetorical fashion a somewhat conventional and polite apology of the day).

Structure of the Passage. The epistolary forms and features of 15:14-32 serve to highlight in a formal way the structure of this section; this structure, at least in its main divisions, can be set out as follows:

1. A commendation of the Christians at Rome and Paul's purpose in writing them (15:14-16) — which commendation is introduced by a *confidence expression* and a *vocative of direct address* in v. 14 and is followed by a *reminder statement* in v. 15.

2. Paul recounts his past ministries in eastern regions of the Roman Empire, using his involvement in these earlier ministries to explain his inability to visit the believers in Jesus at Rome earlier (15:17-22) — which exposition opens with the postpositive particle οὖν that functions as a transitional conjunction in v. 17.

3. Paul's future travel plans and proposed missionary outreach to Spain, with an intervening ministry to the believers in Jesus at Jerusalem and a promised visit to the Christians at Rome on his way to Spain (15:23-29) — which future travelogue opens with a *visit wish* in v. 23 and a *notification of a coming visit* in v. 24, and then closes with a *confidence formula* in v. 29.

4. A request for prayer (15:30-32), which begins with a *request formula* and a *vocative of direct address* in v. 30.

Presentation of the Passage. The prominence of epistolary forms and features in the beginning sections of the letter and in final portions of the letter — with the four major sections of the body middle dominated by a number of quite significant rhetorical features — has caused some to think of Romans as simply a theological and ethical treatise (or what we would identify as a "protreptic" discourse) set within an epistolary frame.[5] To a large extent, of course, that is true. Yet the materials of this epistolary frame of the letter also function to support the flow and development of the apostle's argument as contained in the much larger body middle of the letter. For as the beginning sections of Romans express in rather condensed fashion Paul's attitudes and concerns when writing, anticipate his primary purposes for writing, and highlight what he wants to develop more fully in the rest of the letter, so the concluding sections recapitulate and unpack more fully many of these same attitudes, concerns, and purposes of the apostle.

Thus at the beginning of the body closing or apostolic parousia of 15:14-32, Paul speaks very well of his addressees: "I myself am convinced, my brothers and sisters, that you yourselves are full of goodness, complete in knowledge, and able to instruct one another" (v. 14). This compares to what he said about them at the beginning of the thanksgiving section of 1:8-12: "First, I thank my God through Jesus Christ for all of you, because your faith is being reported all over the world" (v. 8). So in two important sentences that appear just before and after his protreptic "message of instruction and exhortation" in 1:16–15:13, Paul speaks to his addressees in highly commendable terms — implying by both tone and word that his purpose in writing them was not to rebuke them but to encourage and strengthen them.

Then in 15:15-16 Paul gives one of the clearest statements regarding his purpose in writing to the believers in Jesus at Rome:

> Nonetheless, I have written to you rather boldly on some points, as if to remind you of them again, because of the grace given me by God — [which

---

5. So, e.g., the still important nineteenth-century French commentator Frédéric Godet, professor of theology, Neuchâtel, who declared at the very beginning of what he identified as the "Epistolary Conclusion" of Romans, the following: "The Epistle to the Romans is a didactic treatise, doctrinal and practical, contained in a letter. The treatise is now closed, and the letter begins again. It is easy to show, indeed, that the part about to follow is closely correlated to the epistolary preface which preceded the treatise (i.1-15)" (as translated in the 1881 English edition of his *Commentary on St. Paul's Epistle to the Romans*, 2.364).

grace God gave me] for the purpose of being a minister (λειτουργόν) of Christ Jesus to the Gentiles, with the priestly duty (ἱερουργοῦντα) of proclaiming the gospel of God, so that the Gentiles might become an offering that is acceptable (ἡ προσφορά . . . εὐπρόσδεκτος) to God, sanctified by the Holy Spirit.

Here the apostle directly connects what he has written in the body middle of his letter (i.e., in 1:16–15:13) with his apostolic responsibility to preach the gospel to the Gentiles — as he said in more compact form in 1:5b-6, 13b, and 15. Further, in 15:15-16 he claims that he has received grace from God to be a minister of Christ Jesus, which is a claim to authority that echoes the more condensed statements of 1:1 and 1:5a. And he asserts that his addressees, predominantly Gentile believers in Jesus, should consider themselves within the scope of his divinely mandated ministry, as suggested in his reference to "the Gentiles" in 1:5 and the inclusion of them within the scope of his ministry in 1:13b-15. Thus, in effect, what Paul is saying here in 15:15-16 is that the contents of his letter should (1) be understood by them as an important part in the carrying out of his God-given mandate to proclaim the Christian gospel to Gentiles and (2) be accepted by them as a divinely authorized contextualization of the message of that gospel proclamation.

Likewise in these two verses, as well as throughout 15:17-29 (where he refers to his past ministries and future plans), Paul hints as to how his purpose statement of 1:11-12, which has to do with his proposed visit and present writing ("I long to see you so that I may impart to you some spiritual gift to make you strong — that is, that you and I may be mutually encouraged by each other's faith"), is to be unpacked. For in writing what he has to the Christians at Rome, the apostle wants his addressees to be encouraged by his letter's contents. Further, he wants them to respond to his letter by encouraging him in his proposed mission to Spain — not only by their prayers, as he urges in 15:30-31, but also by their financial support, as he implies in 15:32 (so that "by God's will I can come to you with joy and together with you be refreshed").

Therefore this body closing or apostolic parousia section of Romans must not be viewed as simply a closing portion of the epistolary frame for what the apostle wanted to say in the central body middle of the letter. More importantly, Paul highlights in this closing section certain essential features with respect to his attitudes, concerns, and purposes when writing to the Christians at Rome — which features were first set out in rather compressed fashion in the opening sections of the letter, then spelled out in the four major sections of the letter's body middle, and here in the letter's closing are again highlighted and further unpacked. In effect, whereas Paul's concerns and purposes mentioned in the opening sections of the letter provided something of a rough agenda for what he would write in the letter's body middle, here in the body closing that agenda is again highlighted and brought to a summary conclusion more expressly.

EXEGETICAL COMMENTS

Understanding Paul's statements in this body closing section (with respect to form) or apostolic parousia section (with respect to content) is somewhat difficult because a number of ancient scribes seem to have felt a greater degree of freedom to impose their own readings on the text of 15:14-32 than they considered was proper when dealing with the textual data of the four major theological and ethical sections of 1:16–15:13 (as seen in our "Textual Notes" on 15:14-32 vis-à-vis our "Textual Notes" on the four much more extensive presentations of 1:16–15:13). This attitude of greater freedom seems to have been associated, at least in part, with the early church's desire to "catholicize" Paul's theology and ethics (as seen in the widespread acceptance among many early believers of the "short form" of the apostle's letter). In such a climate of understanding, chs. 1–14 of Romans evidently became for many early believers in Jesus something of an early compendium of Christian theology — with the personal and historical materials of 15:14-32 viewed as being more open to scribal adjustments.

Yet, while textual variants appear relatively often in 15:14-32 — and while they have left many textual critics with a number of unanswerable questions — there is today a rather high degree of confidence among NT scholars that the original readings for this passage can still be generally determined. And we also, based on our own text-critical analyses of the passage, believe it possible to read this body closing or apostolic parousia with a high degree of rather general confidence in its original text — and so we view what appears here in 15:14-32 as representing, at least in the main, what Paul wanted to say to his Christian addressees at Rome (as well as what he would want to say to professing Christians today).

I. Commendation of the Christians at Rome and Paul's Purpose in Writing to Them (15:14-16)

While the situation of conflict between believers in Jesus at Rome, which was dealt with by the apostle in 14:1–15:13, seems to have been of "great anguish of heart" to him personally, what Paul writes here in 15:14-16 strikes a quite different tone in setting out (1) his underlying conviction regarding the true character of his addressees, (2) his own purpose in writing them, and (3) the nature of his ministry to them.

15:14 "I myself am convinced, my brothers and sisters, that you yourselves are full of goodness, complete in knowledge, and competent to admonish one another." This opening "confidence expression" has often been viewed as simply "complimentary flattery," "mere kind words," or "Christian courtesy" expressed by the apostle to his Roman addressees.[6] But, as Stanley Olson has

---

6. So, e.g., Käsemann, *Romans*, 391, who seems to espouse the thesis of "complimentary

shown (and as Robert Jewett, with approval, has summarized from Olson's 1985 article with respect to this verse): "Papyrus letters often contain polite apologies for making requests on the grounds that the recipient is already predisposed by excellent character to perform the duty anyway."[7] So there is here in Paul's commendation of the Roman believers an echo of what appears to be a rather common rhetorical flourish of the day in speaking to someone regarding some matter of discord or disagreement — which rhetorical flourish, it may be presumed, the apostle used and reworked in a Christian manner to commend the lives of his addressees as being "full of goodness, complete in knowledge, and competent to admonish one another."

This commendation of the Christians at Rome compares quite favorably to what Paul wrote earlier in his thanksgiving section of 1:8-12: "First, I thank my God through Jesus Christ for all of you, because your faith is being reported all over the world" (1:8). So in an important statement given in 1:8, which appears just before his extensive four-part "message of instruction and exhortation" in 1:16–15:13 — and then in this opening sentence of 15:14, which appears immediately after those four major sections — the apostle speaks of his addressees in highly commendable terms, implying by both word and tone that his purpose in writing to them was not to rebuke them, but to encourage and strengthen them. His "anguish of heart," therefore, must have to do with the situation that the believers had mistakenly gotten themselves into and which he desired to correct. Yet his confidence remained, even with an anguish of heart, that the Roman Christians were essentially "full of goodness, complete in knowledge, and competent to admonish one another."

15:15-16 Nonethess, despite his confidence in the Christians at Rome, Paul sets out his reasons for speaking "boldly on some points" as being (1) "to remind you [i.e., 'the believers in Jesus at Rome'] of them [i.e., 'of those certain important points'] again" and (2) "because of the grace that was given to me by God" — which grace was given to him "for the purposes of being a minister of Christ Jesus to the Gentiles, with the priestly duty of proclaiming the gospel of God so that the Gentiles might become an offering that is acceptable to God, sanctified by the Holy Spirit."

Of significance in his statement of purpose in 15:15-16 is the imagery that Paul, the God-ordained apostle to the Gentiles, uses in 15:16 with respect to his Gentile ministry — that is, (1) that his ministry to Gentiles was *a priestly ministry* (λειτουργός, a term the apostle used earlier in 13:6 of governmental authorities and that the author of Hebrews would use in Heb 1:7 of angels who minister on behalf of God, but in this context has human priestly connotations);

---

flattery" and sets out a number of other such interpretive proposals and their proponents; note also Cranfield, *Romans*, 2.752, who argues that "What we have here is Christian courtesy, not flattery, though there is no doubt an element of hyperbole in the use of the words μεστοί, πεπληρωμένοι and πάσης."

7. Jewett, *Romans*, 903, paraphrasing Olson, "Pauline Expressions of Confidence," 282-95 (particularly 291).

(2) that his Gentile ministry was "*a priestly service* (ἱερουργοῦντα) of the gospel of God," and (3) that his desire was that through his ministry "the Gentiles might become *an acceptable offering* (ἡ προσφορὰ . . . εὐπρόσδεκτος) [to God]." The syntax of v. 16 is a bit difficult. Yet the priestly and sacrificial imagery is clear. And such imagery has seemed to a number of modern interpreters of Paul as being somewhat strange on the lips of "the apostle to the Gentiles" (or from the pen of one of his amanuenses). On the other hand, other commentators have argued from this text that the apostle had an OT cultic understanding of his role as God's appointed apostle to the Gentiles.[8]

If, however, we understand Paul to be writing to Christians at Rome who had been extensively influenced by the theology, language, and ways of thinking of Jewish Christianity (whatever their own particular ethnicities), it should come as no surprise that he would speak of the nature of his God-given ministry using religious expressions that they would understand and religious imagery that they would appreciate — that is, in speaking to them of his own Gentile mission using the Jewish and Jewish Christian metaphors of "priestly ministry," "priestly service," and "acceptable offering" to characterize that ministry. By way of a parallel employment of terms, Paul had earlier in the letter included the confessional material of 3:24-26, in which are found such Jewish Christian soteriological expressions as "righteousness" (δικαιοσύνη); "redemption" (ἀπολύτρωσις); "propitiation," "expiation," or "sacrifice of atonement" (ἱλαστήριον); and "in his blood" (ἐν τῷ αὐτοῦ αἵματι) when speaking of the work of Jesus Christ to those who had been extensively influenced by Jewish Christian theology, language, and ways of thinking.

Although Paul did not use biblical quotations to support his arguments in Section II of the body middle of Romans, that is, in 5:1–8:39, when representing to believers in Jesus at Rome the nature of his Christian proclamation to pagan Gentiles in the Greco-Roman world — for the material he set out in that second major section of his letter was evidently meant to be a précis or summary account of what he had proclaimed to non-Jews who had no knowledge of the Jewish (OT) Scriptures — his use in 15:21 of Isa 52:15 ("Those who were not told about him will see, and those who have not heard of him will understand") would have been both understood and accepted, just as similar OT passages in Section I (1:16–4:25) and Section III (9:1–11:36) of the body middle of Romans would have been understood and accepted. For in Section I and Section III the apostle is speaking directly to addressees (whatever their various ethnicities) who were rooted and grounded in the Jewish Scriptures. And for the same reason, his use of cultic language in 15:16 and of an OT Isaiah passage in 15:21 demonstrates how he contextualized the Christian gospel when speaking directly to those who had a background in some type of Jewish Christianity and a working knowledge of the Jewish (OT) Scriptures.

---

8. E.g., K. Weiss, "Paulus — Priester der christlichen Kultgemeinde," *TLZ* 79 (1954) 355-64.

II. Paul's Past Ministries in Eastern Regions of the Roman Empire as an Explanation for His Inability to Visit the Christians in Rome Earlier (15:17-22)

15:17 The second part of Paul's apostolic parousia begins with the postpositive conjunction οὖν ("therefore"), which here functions in its usual capacity as a transition particle that takes a reader from one portion of an author's presentation into a further portion of it; the further portion here in 15:17-22 is a summary account for the Christians at Rome of Paul's past ministries in various eastern parts of the Roman Empire, which he uses to explain his inability to visit them previously. Though there are three possible Greek readings for the opening of this verse: (1) ἣν ἔχω καύχησιν ("which boast I have"), which is attested by P[46]; (2) ἔχω οὖν καύχησιν ("therefore I have a boast"), which appears in uncials ℵ A P Ψ; and (3) ἔχω οὖν τὴν καύχησιν ("therefore I have the boast"), which is supported by uncials B C[vid] D F G — with each option seeming to suggest a slightly different emphasis — all three can be rather colloquially translated "therefore I boast" or "I glory" (see "Textual Notes" above).

Paul's "boasting" in 15:17 is quite different from the "boasting" he denounced in 3:27.[9] For rather than being in opposition to God or in competition with God, Paul's boasting in this verse has to do with (1) his being "in Christ Jesus" (ἐν Χριστῷ Ἰησοῦ) and (2) his doing "those things that pertain to God" (τὰ πρὸς τὸν θεόν) — that is, his boasting of a personal relationship "in Christ" and of his service for God.[10]

15:18-19a Paul goes on along this same line to declare in 15:18-19a that all that he has the right to speak about as a Christian apostle has to do with "what Christ has accomplished through me (δι' ἐμοῦ) in leading the Gentiles to obey God by what I have said and what I have done!" Jesus Christ is the focus of Paul's message and the agent of all spiritual and personal change; Paul is only the human instrument that God ordained for that day to bring about spiritual and personal change in the lives of non-Jewish people. Further, all of what the apostle said and did in his Gentile mission was accompanied by signs and miracles — which features of divine presence were brought about by "the power of God's Spirit." And what Paul most earnestly desired in being God's human instrument in his day was "to bring about the obedience ['of faith'] on the part of the Gentiles ['to God'] (εἰς ὑπακοὴν ἐθνῶν),"[11] doing so by both what he said

---

9. On the verb καυχάομαι ("boast," "glory," "pride oneself in"), the neuter noun καύχημα ("boast"), and the feminine noun καύχησις ("boasting") as used in various ways by ancient Greek writers, by the authors of the Jewish (OT) Scriptures, and by Paul elsewhere in Romans and his other NT letters, see our earlier discussion on Rom 3:27, pp. 441-44.

10. Cf. Paul's statements of "boasting" that he expressed earlier in 2 Cor 1:12-14.

11. The phrase εἰς ὑπακοὴν ἐθνῶν (literally "unto the obedience of the Gentiles") resonates with the expression εἰς ὑπακοὴν πίστεως (literally "unto the obedience of faith"), which appears in 1:5 and 16:26. For a discussion of that rather difficult expression εἰς ὑπακοὴν πίστεως, which

and what he did (λόγῳ καὶ ἔργῳ) in carrying out his God-given evangelistic and pastoral Christian ministry.

15:19b The scope of Paul's previous missionary activities — that is, prior to his ministry to "the saints" at Jerusalem; prior to his desired visit with the Christians at Rome; and prior to his proposed evangelistic outreach to pagan Gentiles in Spain — was, as the apostle himself describes it, "from Jerusalem all the way around to Illyricum (ἀπὸ Ἰερουσαλὴμ καὶ κύκλῳ μέχρι τοῦ Ἰλλυρικοῦ)." There has been considerable discussion among commentators whether by using the name Jerusalem (the Jewish capital) and the name Illyricum (the Roman province, which was also called Illyria or Dalmatia, on the seacoast north of Macedonia and west of Thrace) Paul was speaking inclusively — that is, that he had carried on Christian evangelistic outreaches in the city of Jerusalem and in the province of Illyricum — or was speaking in a more exclusive fashion to say that his missionary outreach extended from the limits of the city of Jerusalem to the limits of the Roman province of Illyricum (or Illyria or Dalmatia). There is, of course, no mention in Luke's Acts of Paul ever having ministered in the Roman province of Illyricum. Nonetheless, he seems to have viewed his apostolic ministry in certain eastern regions, cities, and towns of the Roman Empire as being carried on by his local Christian converts into the adjoining regions, cities, and towns, and thus seems to have looked upon those ministries as being legitimate extensions of his own God-given Gentile mission.[12]

Therefore, the following comment by William Sanday and Arthur Headlam still remains a plausible explanation for Paul's geographical statement here:

> A perfectly tenable explanation of the words would be that if Jerusalem were taken as one limit and the Eastern boundaries of Illyria as the other, St. Paul had travelled over the whole of the intervening district, and not merely confined himself to the direct route between the two places. Jerusalem and Illyria in fact represent the limits.[13]

And with respect to the apostle's claim that he has "fully proclaimed the gospel of Christ" in his Christian mission of evangelism "from Jerusalem all the way around to Illyricum," Robert Jewett has aptly commented:

> What Paul claims is not that he has preached the gospel in every conceivable location but that he had fulfilled his specific calling to establish churches in a sufficient number of important centers to make the subsequent mission-

---

relates to this expression εἰς ὑπακοὴν ἐθνῶν in 15:18, see our exegetical comments and footnotes on 1:5, pp. 77-82.

12. Cf. esp. Col 4:7-17, where Paul speaks of a number of his converts as ministering in other nearby cities and areas (even in the city of Colossae itself), with those ministries being viewed by the apostle as extensions of his own ministry.

13. Sanday and Headlam, *Romans*, 407.

izing of their regional hinterlands by local colleagues feasible. He has now discharged his responsibilities in the East and is ready to move on.[14]

15:20-21 Here in 15:20-21 Paul provides a very interesting and quite important glimpse into his own thinking of how a Christian mission of evangelism should be carried on. For in v. 20 he inserts a rather telling statement about his own planning and his own desires with respect to such a Christian outreach: "It has always been my ambition to preach the gospel where Christ was not known, so that I would not be building on someone else's foundation."

During the course of Christian history, Christian ministries have often been built on the foundations that others have provided by their earnest endeavors. That may not always be a bad thing, for God works out his will through his people in many ways. All too often, however, building on the foundation of others has set up certain competitive nuances that (1) have failed to reflect the message of oneness in the Christian gospel and (2) have denied the unity of God's people. Worse yet, some so-called Christian ministries have been carried out by people who seem to have had deep within themselves a driving desire to "build an empire to themselves" — doing so even by such praiseworthy factors as an earnest witness, judicious counseling, exemplary character, and "good works" on behalf of others. Obviously, such an adverse judgment as we have expressed is extremely superficial and ultimately is humanly impossible, for only God knows the thoughts and intentions of a person's innermost being (including our own). Certainly such factors as an earnest witness, judicious counseling, exemplary character, and "good works" must always be viewed as worthy in any well-ordered and well-lived Christian life, and therefore deserve our highest praise. Yet worthy motivations and well-lived lives can also divert believers in Jesus from their primary allegiance to God through Christ and from recognizing and caring for the needs of others — turning instead to the honoring of one's own life and to a primary concern for one's own needs, as those needs have grown amidst the many additional situations and activities that are confronted. And as our lives become more involved and more political in nature, we as Christians often become overly defensive and overly egotistical in our own limited situations. It is a common human failing, which, sadly, seems to become almost inevitable in us as we grow older — even as we grow older in our Christian living and as we take on more and more responsibilities in our own family situations, our own societal circumstances, and our own religious activities!

Yet Paul always wanted (1) to keep a focus in his life on the Lordship of Christ and (2) to keep alive in his thinking and his actions a concern for people who never had the opportunity to respond to God through Christ Jesus and/or who were experiencing real spiritual, economic, or social problems. Further, he believed (1) that God, through the ministry of his Spirit and the appropriate actions of his people, was able to work out all the subsequent details in both his

---

14. Jewett, *Romans*, 914.

own life and the lives of others, and (2) that as God's servant he could trust God to work out all the details of living — both his and theirs — by the guidance of his Spirit and the God-directed actions of his people. Paul viewed his convictions along these lines as supported by the words of the great OT prophet Isaiah, who declared in his Suffering Servant passage of Isa 52:13–53:12: "What they [i.e., the people and kings of many nations] were not told, they will see; and what they have not heard, they will understand" (Isa 52:15b).

15:22 Whether in 15:22 Paul used (1) the articular expression τὰ πολλά ("many times"), as in Codex Sinaiticus (i.e., uncial ℵ of the fourth century) and Codex Alexandrinus (i.e., uncial A of the fifth century), or (2) the adverb πολλάκις ("often," "frequently"), as in P⁴⁶ (c. A.D. 200) and Codex Vaticanus (i.e. uncial B of the fourth century) (see "Textual Notes" above), his point to his Christian addressees at Rome was clear: because of his extensive missionary outreach to Gentiles "over the whole of the intervening district" between "Jerusalem and Illyria,"[15] he had been so intensively involved in his God-mandated Gentile mission that he was unable at any earlier time to visit the Christians at Rome. Further, as he said just previously in v. 20 — and then supported in v. 21 by what he saw as a supporting statement from the prophet Isaiah — he felt no compulsion to minister at the capital city of the Roman Empire, simply because (as he phrased matters) "it has always my ambition to preach the gospel where Christ was not known, so that I would not be building on someone else's foundation."

III. Paul's Future Travel Plans and Proposed Missionary Outreach to Spain, with an Intervening Ministry to the Christians in Jerusalem and a Promised Visit to the Christians in Rome (15:23-29)

15:23-24 Paul begins the presentation of his future travel plans by (1) declaring that he hopes to visit the Christians at Rome soon, (2) saying that he has no further place to minister "in these regions" (that is, from the city limits of Jerusalem to the provincial boundaries of Illyricum), (3) claiming that he has frequently desired to be with them, and (4) giving his promise that he will visit them in the near future, "whenever I go to Spain." His statement in 15:19 that he has "fully proclaimed the gospel of Christ" throughout the region from Jerusalem to Illyricum did not mean that he had preached the Christian gospel in every conceivable location of that area, but rather "that he had fulfilled his specific calling to establish churches in a sufficient number of important centers to make the subsequent missionizing of their regional hinterlands by local colleagues feasible."[16] Thus he tells his Christian addressees at Rome (1) that he is hoping and planning to visit them on his way to Spain, (2) that he wants to

---

15. To quote again the wording of Sanday and Headlam, *Romans,* 407.
16. Quoting again Jewett, *Romans,* 914.

be with them for a while on his way to a ministry in Spain, so that (as he stated earlier in 1:12) "you and I may be mutually encouraged by each other's faith," and (3) that he desires their assistance for his proposed journey to and ministry in Spain — or, as he said earlier regarding his purpose in visiting the Christians at Rome in 1:13b: "in order that I might have a harvest among you, just as I have had among the other Gentiles."

15:25-27 Presently, however (using again the expression νυνί δέ, as previously employed in 15:23 but here translated more idiomatically into English as "presently, however"), Paul declares that he must carry out an intervening mission "to the poor among the saints in Jerusalem" (εἰς τοὺς πτωχοὺς τῶν ἁγίων τῶν ἐν Ἰερουσαλήμ) — that is, to believers in Jesus who were economically impoverished in the Jewish capital city. The Greek of 15:27 is highly elliptical (i.e., marked by an extreme economy of speech or writing, with words and expressions that are obviously to be understood being simply omitted), and so it is necessary to supply these words or expressions drawn from the context in order to make what is said or written understood. My own contextually expanded translation of this verse is as follows: "They were well pleased to do so — and, indeed, they are their debtors. For since Gentile believers in Jesus share in the spiritual blessings of believing Jews, they owe it to believing Jews to minister to them in material matters."

It has frequently been claimed that Paul's theological and ethical statements in his NT letters have little to do with the social structures and economic issues of the day. However, Bruce Longenecker, in his highly significant historical and exegetical study entitled *Remember the Poor: Paul, Poverty, and the Greco-Roman World*,[17] has effectively put an end to such an assertion by demonstrating (1) that concern for economically poor people was integral to the apostle's understanding of the Christian proclamation, and (2) that such a concern should also be of great importance in the thoughts and actions of Christians today. Such an active concern for economically impoverished people is what Paul in Gal 2:10 had earlier insisted — in response to the one request that the leaders of the Jerusalem church asked of him in his carrying out of a Gentile ministry, that is, that he should always "remember the poor" — was "the very thing" that he "had been eager to do all along."

Yet, as Leander Keck has rightly noted, "Paul does not [here in Rom 15:25-27] designate the recipients [of the monetary gift that he is bringing] as 'the Poor' [in some theological or technical sense] but thinks of them as saints who are now distressingly poor."[18] Nor does Paul in his letter to Rome cite any request made by the leaders (or "pillars") of the Jerusalem church to "remember the poor," as reported by him earlier in Gal 2:10. Rather, his forthcoming mission "to serve the saints" at Jerusalem in a financial manner was motivated by the facts (1) that the believers in Jesus at Jerusalem were in dire financial need,

17. (Grand Rapids: Eerdmans, 2010).
18. Keck, "The Poor among the Saints in the New Testament," 122.

and (2) that the Christians of Macedonia and Achaia, since they were spiritually in debt to the Jerusalem believers in Jesus, thought it only right that they share with those believers at Jerusalem their material blessings.

Thus Paul's collection of money from his own Gentile converts for Jewish believers in Jesus at Jerusalem should be understood by his later interpreters — as it was by Paul himself — as an example and paradigm of "the very thing" that as a Christian apostle he "had been eager to do all along." Paul was prepared to carry out such a financial "service to the saints at Jerusalem" with the possibility of great personal loss, and he thought his mission of providing financial aid to economically impoverished believers in Jesus at Jerusalem took precedence over his own desire to visit the Christians at Rome and his plans for an evangelistic mission in Spain.

In addition to providing financial aid to impoverished believers, it may be postulated that Paul wanted to go to Jerusalem to present to the Jewish believers in Jesus of that city the essence of what he had been writing in his letter to the Christians at Rome. There can be little doubt that what he wrote in the four major sections of the body middle of Romans had been consuming his thoughts for a long time — not only in his earlier Christian ministry at Syrian Antioch and then in his much more extensive Christian Gentile mission in various eastern regions of the Roman Empire, but also during the time he was actually composing the letter (with the aid of an amanuensis, but also, quite likely, in response to various comments by his associates and friends from Corinth and its environs to whom he would have read various portions of the letter during its composition). Further, it may be speculated that Paul would have wanted to present to the "Christ followers" of the Jerusalem church some of the matters he considered distinctive to his own proclamation of the Christian gospel and which he had highlighted in his letter to Rome — particularly on such topics as the following:

1. Righteousness as not only a basic attribute of God's person but also God's gift to repentant sinners.
2. Personal relationship with God as resulting from one's positive response of faith in God and trust in what he has provided, and not on any supposed meritorious "works of the Law."
3. The faithfulness of Jesus as the foundational theme in a "new covenant" relationship with God.
4. The faith of Abraham as the paradigm for the type of response that God asks for and accepts.
5. Peace and reconciliation as having been brought about by Jesus Christ.
6. The experience of being "in Christ" and "in the Spirit" as characterizing the new life of a believer in Jesus.
7. The reality of having been "adopted by God into his family" as being true for all believers in Jesus.
8. The realization of what it means to be God's righteous remnant — both theologically and ethically; both for Israel and for believers in Jesus.

9. The recognition that God knows and accepts his own "righteous remnant," wherever such people exist, whatever our own prejudices and perceptions on the matter.
10. Basic principles of a Christian "love ethic," with application of these principles to the civic and societal situations that the Christians at Rome (and probably elsewhere throughout the Roman Empire) were then facing.
11. A further statement with respect to the Christian "love ethic," with application to the ecclesiastical situation that had arisen among at least some of the Christians at Rome (and possibly also existed among many other believers in Jesus elsewhere).

These were matters, it may be postulated, that Paul wanted also to present and discuss in person with the believers in Jesus at Jerusalem. But any hoped-for full and open discussion of these important matters was cut short by his imprisonment at Jerusalem — and then by his more extensive incarceration at Caesarea and his two-year house arrest at Rome. Yet, even during those rather long periods of imprisonment at Caesarea and Rome, it may reasonably be thought that Paul continued to think seriously about these distinctive theological and ethical matters (as well as about many other theological, ethical, and ecclesial concerns, as seen in his "Prison Epistles" of Ephesians, Philippians, Colossians, and Philemon and his later "Pastoral Epistles" of 1 and 2 Timothy and Titus) that he had included in his letter to the Christians at Rome — and which the Roman Christians had read to them by their respective leaders and teachers. And further, even though some Jewish Christian leaders from Jerusalem, then from Caesarea, and finally from Rome were able to visit him in his various imprisonments — and although he had some opportunities while imprisoned to speak with his visitors about many of the distinctive features of his proclamation of the Christian gospel — it may also be surmised that he longed to proclaim his own contextualized version of the Christian message (that is, what he captioned "my gospel" in 2:16 and 16:25) in a much more widespread fashion. So it may be speculated that during at least some of his long periods of confinement in prison, Paul would have been at work editing his own original letter to the Christians at Rome (which at that time had been taken by Phoebe to the Christians at Rome, and, as may be presumed, was being read to them by their local leaders under Phoebe's guidance).[19]

So we may hypothesize that it was during one or more of these rather extensive periods of confinement in prison that Paul himself actually edited — and so "catholicized" for general use — his own letter to Rome by (1) deleting its specific references to the city of Rome in 1:7 and 1:15, (2) closing off the original contents of his letter with the exhortations of 14:1-23, and, perhaps, actually himself (3) relocating the doxology of 16:25-27 to a position immediately after

---

19. See our discussion in 16:1-2 with respect to Phoebe's part in the preparation, delivery, and interpretation of Paul's letter to Rome.

what he had set out in those exhortations of 14:1-23[20] — thereby bringing into existence what has been called the "short form" of Romans, which, it may be postulated, the apostle wanted read among various groups of believers in Jesus to whom he could not speak directly while in prison (and which material seems to have been known and read as the essential message of Paul among various groups of early "Christ followers").

15:28-29 In 15:28-29 Paul returns to the main point that he made earlier in 15:23-24 — that is, that on his way to an evangelistic mission to pagan Gentiles in Spain he will visit the Christians at Rome, so that (1) the Christians at Rome might "assist" him on his journey to Spain and (2) he might "enjoy" their company "for a while." His visit to Rome would not be an attempt to "build on someone else's foundation." Rather, what Paul desired was that the Christians at Rome would function for his Gentile mission in the western regions of the Roman Empire much like the Christians at Antioch of Syria functioned for his Gentile mission in the eastern regions of the empire. For just as the "Christ followers" at Syrian Antioch, who were an ethnically mixed group of Jews and non-Jews, had come to know Paul and his message from his yearlong ministry in their midst, so he wanted the Christians at Rome, who were also an ethnically mixed group of people, to (1) know his distinctive message from the contents of his present letter to them and (2) then come to know him personally from his planned visit with them. Thus, just as the Christians of Syrian Antioch had functioned as the support base for his Gentile mission in the eastern regions of the Roman Empire, assisting him by their prayers and their financial gifts, so he desired the Christians at Rome to function in much the same manner for his proposed evangelistic mission to pagan Gentiles in Spain. Paul concludes his reaffirmation of his plans to visit the Christians at Rome, which visit he promised earlier in 15:23-24, with a christianized epistolary *confidence formula:* "I know that when I come to you, I will come in the full measure of the blessing of Christ."

IV. Request for Prayer (15:30-32)

15:30-32 In closing off this body closing or apostolic parousia subsection of his letter, Paul asks the Christians at Rome to pray for him in his mission to "the saints in Jerusalem." In that request he speaks of his efforts to aid the financially impoverished believers in Jesus at Jerusalem as his "struggle" on their behalf (using the aorist infinitive συναγωνίσασθαι, which stems from the preposition συν and the verb ἀγωνίζομαι, and so may be understood as "a combat in company

---

20. We are told in 2 Tim 4:13 that Paul at one time left "with Carpus at Troas" not only a "cloak" but also his "scrolls" and his "parchments," and that he asked Timothy to bring them to him while he was in prison — thereby implying that "scrolls" and "parchments" were of great importance to him in his imprisonments, and even suggesting something about his possible editing of his own written materials while in prison.

with another person or people," "the exertion of one's strength in association with someone else and/or other people," or "earnestly aiding someone else or other people in a situation"). Thus we may understand the apostle's rather elliptical phraseology here in 15:30b as asking his addressees "to join him" in his "struggle to aid the impoverished believers in Jesus at Jerusalem" by praying for him and his mission. Further, he asks them to "pray that I may be rescued from the unbelievers in Judea and that my service in Jerusalem may be acceptable to the saints there."

The question, of course, arises: Why was Paul so fearful of what might happen to him in his mission of taking a monetary gift to Jewish believers in Jesus at Jerusalem? Why does he ask that he "may be rescued from the unbelievers in Judea" and that his service in Jerusalem "may be acceptable to the saints there"? Who would have opposed anyone bringing a gift of money to certain impoverished Jewish people, whatever their views about Jesus of Nazareth as Israel's Messiah might be?

James Dunn has quite appropriately pointed out:

> Paul was widely regarded [by Jews generally] as a renegade for abandoning the law, and it would seem that little or nothing had been done within or by the Jerusalem church to defend him on this score [citing Acts 21:20-24; despite Acts 16:3 and 18:18]. Then when Paul was arrested and put on trial we hear nothing of any Jewish Christian standing by him, speaking in his defence — and this despite James's apparent high standing among orthodox Jews. . . . Where were the Jerusalem Christians? It looks very much as though they had washed their hands of Paul, left him to stew in his own juice.[21]

Indeed, if the apostle felt it necessary to defend himself in his letter to Rome against certain criticisms of his person and certain misrepresentations of his message,[22] he was even more aware of there being at Jerusalem (1) criticisms of his person, (2) misrepresentations of his message, and (3) charges against him with respect to his missionary outreach to pagan Gentiles — all of which were leveled against him not only by the unbelieving Jews of Jerusalem, but also, as seems evident, by at least some of the believing Jews of the city and its regions, who acknowledged Jesus as Israel's Messiah and humanity's Lord but were ill-disposed to accept some of the features of Paul's preaching and some of his evangelistic methods and practices in his Gentile mission. As Bruce Longe-

---

21. J. D. G. Dunn, *Unity and Diversity in the New Testament* (London: SCM, 1977), as quoted by B. W. Longenecker, *Remember the Poor,* 311 n. 30. For a highly significant discussion of Paul's fears in going to Jerusalem to present this gift of money to "the saints at Jerusalem," on the response of both nonbelieving and believing Jews to this monetary gift, and on the significance of this gift for the apostle and for Christianity generally, see B. W. Longenecker, 310-16.

22. Cf. my *Introducing Romans,* 123-126, for a listing of such possible charges against Paul's person and against his Gentile mission.

necker has characterized the apostle's own thoughts about going to Jerusalem to minister financially to the impoverished Jewish believers in Jesus of that city: "Paul was willing to put his life on the line."[23]

Thus in 15:31 the apostle asks the Christians at Rome to pray for him with respect to two matters: (1) "that I may be rescued from the unbelievers in Judea" and (2) "that my service in Jerusalem may be acceptable to the saints there." In the final verse of his body closing or apostolic parousia, that is, in 15:32, he declares that his earnest desire is that after he delivers the monetary gift to the believers in Jesus at Jerusalem, he will be able "by God's will" to visit the Christians at Rome "with joy" and together with them "be refreshed."

Sadly, however, Paul's mission to the financially impoverished Jewish believers in Jesus at Jerusalem did not turn out as he had desired or expected. We have no knowledge of whether or not the Jewish believers actually accepted the money Paul brought to them. Nor do we have any knowledge of what they did with the monetary gift if they accepted it; nor how they were treated by the Jewish authorities if they accepted it; nor what happened to them and to the money offered if they did not accept it. All we know is what Luke tells us in Acts 21:17–28:31 about some of the details of Paul's arrival in Jerusalem, about his being taken as a prisoner in Jerusalem, about his being imprisoned first in Jerusalem and then in Caesarea, about his defenses before Roman authorities, about his appeal to Caesar, about his journey under guard to Rome, and finally about a two-year house imprisonment in his own rented house where he (1) "welcomed all who came to see him," (2) "proclaimed the kingdom of God and taught about the Lord Jesus Christ," and (3) continued his ministry as God's appointed apostle "with all boldness and without hindrance."

Undoubtedly, Paul continued to think of all the events recorded by Luke in Acts 21–28 as having been within "God's will" — as well as all the subsequent events of his life and Christian ministry as taking place according to "God's will." We are, however, left with only speculations based on certain autobiographical statements in his other NT letters regarding how Paul fared personally after writing his letter to Rome and regarding how he continued to live and minister while imprisoned in his own rented house in the capital city. All of that goes far beyond the purposes of our commentary on Paul's letter to Rome. Further, we have already, perhaps, proposed far too many hypotheses regarding what the apostle wrote to the Christians at Rome. And although we have certain personal opinions about Paul's trial (or trials) at Rome, his possible ministry (or ministries) after what Luke records in Acts 28:30-31, and the nature of his death, we will not set out any further speculations here on those matters — none of which would be of pertinence to a commentary on Romans.

---

23. B. W. Longenecker, *Remember the Poor*, 311, 315.

BIBLICAL THEOLOGY

Rom 1:1–15:13 tells us (1) a number of things about Paul personally, (2) a great deal about the apostle's proclamation of the Christian gospel, and (3) some things having to do with his pastoral ministry. All the material in this letter is of very great importance for the construction of a Christian biblical theology. Yet, what Paul sets out in this body closing or apostolic parousia subsection of 15:14-32 is highly significant for an understanding of (1) his thoughts and actions with respect to his evangelistic ministries, (2) his hopes for an outreach to pagan Gentiles in Spain (and perhaps elsewhere in the western regions of the Roman Empire), and (3) his plans and purposes in delivering a gift of money from Gentile Christians of Macedonia and Achaia to the financially impoverished Jewish believers in Jesus of Jerusalem. His plans and purposes with respect to the monetary gift for "the saints at Jerusalem" express in symbolic fashion Paul's deep-seated concern for all economically impoverished people and his earnest desire that there be a true ecumenical relationship between all professing "Christ followers."

What the apostle Paul evidences in 15:14-32, as Paul Stevens has pointed out in a sermon on 15:29, are three important personal passions that functioned to motivate the apostle throughout all of his Christian ministry: (1) "a passion for the gospel of God" (not only here in this passage, but also throughout the letter), (2) "a passion for the mission of God" (as highlighted here in his proposed future mission to Spain), and (3) "a passion for the unity of the people of God" (as expressed in his collection and delivery of financial aid for "the saints in Jerusalem").[24] In effect, as Stevens has argued, Paul's bringing of a gift of money from Gentile believers in Jesus to financially impoverished Jewish believers in Jesus was an attempt to build "a bridge of unity between Jews and Gentiles, symbolized by this love-gift."[25] And as Stevens goes on to insist:

> It is not too much to say that this bridge-building dominated Paul's sense of mission. He was an ecumenical missionary. Unity is not the means to the end, the precondition for God's people getting God's work done on earth. Unity *is* the end. It is the goal (cf. Eph 4:11-16) since God's mission is ultimately to build community on earth under the headship of Christ.[26]

Or as Bruce Longenecker has written regarding Paul's desire "to serve" the financially impoverished Jewish believers in Jesus of Jerusalem by personally delivering to them a gift of money that had been given by Gentile believers in Jesus of Macedonia and Achaia:

24. Stevens, " 'The Full Blessing of Christ' (Romans 15:29)," 295-303; though see our "Textual Note" on 15:29c above contra Stevens's reading of the first matter as "a passion for *the gospel of God*" rather than *"the blessing of Christ."*
25. *Ibid.*, 301.
26. *Ibid.*

In all probability two goals stood front and center as motivating Paul to bring a collection right into the heart of Jerusalem. First, he hoped that the collection would unleash unifying forces among different streams of the early Jesus-movement. Second (but not unrelated), he hoped that the collection would serve these purposes by removing the offense of the early Jesus-movement's "law-free" mission that targeted the Gentiles. Perhaps two further consequences would follow in the wake of these primary goals: it would assist in the proclamation of the good news to Judeans who were not Jesus-followers, and it would undermine the efforts of any who sought to influence the communities Paul had established in ways that ran contrary to his understanding of the good news.[27]

And as Bruce Longenecker goes on to say in this regard:

An underlying conviction must be seen to lie behind any and all of these possible motivations, and one that intertwines economics and salvation history at every point. For Paul, the fact that Gentile Jesus-followers had given some of their limited resources in an effort to alleviate the needs of the poor is testimony to the working of the Spirit in their midst and of the legitimacy of their acceptance by Israel's all-powerful deity, despite their non-circumcised status.[28]

Thus, in the construction of a true and vital Christian biblical theology, there must always be alive and present (1) "a passion for the message of the Christian gospel," (2) "a passion for the outreach of the Christian gospel," and (3) "a passion for the unity of believers in Jesus" (as has been highlighted, using his own phraseology, by Paul Stevens). Likewise, in the expression of such a true and vital Christian biblical theology, there must always exist (1) a desire to unify differing streams of Christian conviction and expression, (2) a desire to remove existing offenses on the part of one group of Christians against another group of Christians, (3) a desire to free up Christian proclamation from extraneous features and influences, so that it will resonate in the minds and hearts of those who have all-too-long lived apart from Christ, (4) a desire to undermine efforts by those who would divert others from responding positively to God through the work of Jesus Christ and the ministry of God's Spirit, and (5) a willingness to rely ultimately on God's Spirit in meeting the needs of others and in verbalizing "the good news" of the Christian gospel (as brought into focus, in his own way, by Bruce Longenecker). For Christian biblical theology is not just the accumulation of data drawn from the Scriptures (both OT and NT), with guidance provided by church history and by one's own philosophic perspectives. It also has to do with the passions and motivations of Christian

27. B. W. Longenecker, *Remember the Poor,* 313.
28. *Ibid.*

theologians, pastors, teachers, evangelists, and laypeople in all their respective situations and opportunities of life.

CONTEXTUALIZATION FOR TODAY

The immediately previous section about the construction of a true and vital Christian biblical theology summarizes concisely the contextualization of the Christian gospel for today. As believers in Jesus today, however, we should not be concerned so much about learning more about how to do things, but should be willing to rely more and more on God's Spirit to lead us into a better understanding of situations, a greater love for people, and a more effective life of service on behalf of our Messiah and Lord, Jesus Christ. Thus we need to have as an important pattern for our lives, ministries, and service the pattern of life, ministry, and service of Paul himself, as he has set that out for us here in 15:14-32. Likewise, we need to be constantly attuned to the guidance of God's Spirit as he directs God's children in the living of their lives and in the expression of the gospel message that focuses on what God through Christ has brought about for all humanity (and for all of God's creation).

THE CONCLUDING SECTIONS OF THE LETTER

Two matters regarding the length and presentation of the two concluding sections of Rom 15:33–16:16 and 16:17-27 are immediately obvious when one compares them with the closing section or sections of Paul's other NT letters. The first readily observable feature is that these two concluding sections are considerably longer than the closing section or sections of the apostle's other NT letters — though they are rather comparable in length to the two opening sections of Romans in 1:1-7 and 1:8-12. A second easily recognizable feature of 15:33–16:16 and 16:17-27 is that the topics appearing here parallel a number of topics that appear in the closing section or sections of many of his other NT letters. There are, of course, a few differences of wording and differences of purpose, and a number of differences in nuancing, that are found not only here in these concluding sections of Romans but also in the final section or sections of his other letters.

The most obvious of these parallels of presentation in these two concluding sections of Paul's letter to Rome vis-à-vis what appears in the closing section or sections of his other NT letters may be set out as follows:

1. Paul's peace blessing or "peace wish" in 15:33 is paralleled by his peace blessings or "prayer wishes for peace" in 2 Cor 13:11b; Gal 6:16; Eph 6:23a; Phil 4:9b; and 1 Thess 5:23a.
2. His commendation of an associate in 16:1-2 is paralleled by his commendations of associates in 1 Cor 16:10-12, 15-18; Eph 6:21-22; Col 4:7-9; and 2 Tim 4:20.
3. His requests that the Christians at Rome greet a number of his past associates, friends, and acquaintances who were then living at Rome in 16:3-15 may be paralleled, to some extent, by similar requests in 1 Cor 16:20b; 2 Cor 13:12; Phil 4:21a; Col 4:15; 1 Thess 5:26; and Titus 3:15b.
4. His reference to a "holy kiss" in 16:16a is paralleled by three other such references to a "holy kiss" in 1 Cor 16:20b; 2 Cor 13:12a; and 1 Thess 5:26 (cf. also 1 Pet 5:14).
5. His conveyance of greetings from other churches and certain associates

1053

in 16:16b and 16:21-23 is paralleled by similar conveyances of greetings from various associates in 1 Cor 16:19-20a; 2 Cor 13:13; Phil 4:21b-22; Col 4:10-14; 2 Tim 4:21b; Titus 3:15a; and Phlm 23-24.

6. His warning exhortation in 16:17-19 is paralleled by similar warning exhortations in 1 Cor 16:13-14, 22a; 2 Cor 13:10; Eph 6:10-17; and Col 4:17.

7. His use of an "eschatological wish/promise" in 16:20a is paralleled by similar "eschatological wishes/promises" in 1 Cor 16:22b; Gal 6:16; and 1 Thess 5:23-24.

8. His concluding grace benediction in 16:20b is paralleled by concluding grace benedictions in 1 Cor 16:23; 2 Cor 13:14; Gal 6:18; Eph 6:24; Phil 4:23; Col 4:18c; 1 Thess 5:28; 2 Thess 3:18; 1 Tim 6:21b; 2 Tim 4:22b; Titus 3:15c; and Phlm 25.

The fact that these concluding sections of Rom 15:33–16:16 and 16:17-27 contain topics that appear in a somewhat similar fashion to what is said in the closing sections of many of his other NT letters serves to remind readers of the commonality that can be found in all of Paul's letters, whatever their respective historical settings, doctrinal expositions, or ethical exhortations. Yet the more extensive length of 15:33–16:16 and 16:17-27 suggests that interpreters should not be too surprised to find in these sections certain features of importance that go beyond what appear in the apostle's other letters. The similar features in these concluding sections of Romans may be itemized as follows:

1. The extended commendation of Phoebe in 16:1-2.

2. The lengthy set of greetings in 16:3-15 that Paul asks the Christians at Rome to express to his past associates, friends, and acquaintances who were then living at Rome — with greetings also to be expressed to the Christian households and congregations that were associated with some of the people that Paul also greeted.

3. The greetings to the Christians at Rome that Paul conveys in 16:16b on behalf of "all the [Gentile] churches of Christ" that he founded and continued to care for.

4. The additional set of exhortations given in 16:17-20a.

5. The further greetings that Paul himself conveys to the Christians at Rome on behalf of certain of his associates at Corinth and its environs in 16:21 and 23.

6. The inclusion of a greeting from the amanuensis who "wrote down" Paul's letter to Rome in 16:22, which greeting was probably requested and composed by Tertius himself.

7. The rather fulsome doxology presented in 16:25-27, which evidently was intended to highlight certain important themes and emphases that undergirded all of what Paul had written earlier in the letter.

IX. Peace Blessing, Commendation of Phoebe, Requests for Greetings to Be Sent to Paul's Past Associates, Friends, and Acquaintances in Rome and to Certain Christian Households and Congregations, and a Greeting of the Christians at Rome on Behalf of the Churches That Paul Founded and Continued to Supervise (15:33–16:16)

TRANSLATION

[15:33]*The God of peace be with all of you!*

[16:1]*Now I commend to you our sister Phoebe, who is also a deacon of the church at Cenchrea.* [2]*Receive her in the Lord in a way that is worthy of God's people and give her any help she may need from you, for she has been a benefactor to many people, including me.*

[3]*Greet Prisca and Aquila, my co-workers in Christ Jesus.* [4]*They risked their lives for me. Not only I but all the churches of the Gentiles are grateful to them.*

[5]*Greet also the church that meets at their house.*

Greet my dear friend Epenetus, who is the firstfruit of [the province of] Asia for Christ.

[6]*Greet Miriam, who worked very hard for you.*

[7]*Greet Andronicus and Junia, compatriots from my own country who were in prison with me. They are outstanding among the apostles, and they were in Christ before me.*

[8]*Greet Ampliatus, whom I love in the Lord.*

[9]*Greet Urbanus, our co-worker in Christ, and my dear friend Stachys.*

[10]*Greet Apelles, tested and approved in Christ.*

Greet those who belong to the household of Aristobulus.

[11]*Greet Herodion, my fellow countryman.*

Greet those of the household of Narcissus who are in the Lord.

[12]*Greet Tryphena and Tryphosa, those women who work hard in the Lord.*

Greet my dear friend Persis, another woman who has worked very hard in the Lord.

[13]*Greet Rufus, chosen in the Lord, and his mother, who has been a mother to me too.*

^{14}*Greet Asyncritus, Phlegon, Hermes, Patrobas, Hermas, and the other believers who are with them.*

^{15}*Greet Philologus and Julia, Nereus and his sister; as well as Olympas, and all the saints with them.*

^{16}*Greet one another with a holy kiss.*

All the churches of Christ send greetings.

TEXTUAL NOTES

Here in 15:33–16:16 there appears what commentators have sometimes called "a tangle," "an intricate array," or "a complicated intermeshing" of textual variants in the Greek textual tradition. Some of these variants are minor in nature, others reflect bits and pieces of important features of early Christian thought and practice, and still others are rather inexplicable. Further, as with the abundance of textual variants for the body closing or apostolic parousia section of 15:14-32, so here in 15:33–16:16 it seems that some ancient scribes felt a greater degree of freedom to impose their own readings on the Greek text than they considered was proper when dealing with the four major theological and ethical sections of the body middle of Paul's letter — that is, when dealing with the texts of 1:16–15:13 (or, assuming the early existence of a "short form" of Paul's letter to Rome, when dealing with the Greek of the materials that came to an end at 14:23).[1]

15:33 The absence of ἀμήν ("so let it be," "truly," "amen") at the end of the sentence is attested by P^{46}, by uncials A F G, and by minuscules 1739 (Category I), 1506 1881 (Category II), and 330 436 451 630 2200 (Category III); its absence is also reflected in vg^{ms}. The presence of ἀμήν at the end of the sentence, however, is supported by uncials ℵ B C D P Ψ [also *Byz* L] and by minuscules 33 1175 (Category I), 81 256 1962 2127 (Category II), and 6 69 88 104 181 263 323 326 365 459 614 629 1241 1243 1319 1505 1573 1735 1852 1874 1877 1912 2344 2492 2495 (Category III); its inclusion also is reflected in vg syr$^{p, h}$ cop$^{sa, bo}$ arm eth slav and is supported by Origen^{lat} Chrysostom and Ambrosiaster.

The question regarding whether ἀμήν was originally absent or present at the end of the sentence is exceedingly difficult to answer. It is, in fact, almost impossible to answer on the basis of the MS evidence alone. For the Greek textual tradition is about equally divided, with (1) the absence of ἀμήν being principally based on the reading of P^{46} (which is our earliest MS witness of the textual tradition), but with (2) the inclusion of ἀμήν being supported by a rather large number of MSS (with their respective editors evidently accepting its presence as closing off a major portion of Paul's letter to Rome). The difficulties are so great that Bruce Metzger felt it necessary to assert that ἀμήν at the end of this sentence "should be enclosed within square brackets," thereby signaling to readers that considerable doubt exists about its inclusion (though Metzger seems to have

---

1. See "The Probable Existence of an Early Short Form" in my *Introducing Romans*, 20-22 (note also other views on shorter versions of Romans discussed in 22-28). With respect to my own speculations regarding Paul as the one who edited for wider distribution his own original letter to Rome while being confined in various Roman prisons, thereby producing a "short form" of Romans, see pp. 1010-11 of this present commentary.

been outvoted on this matter by his editorial colleagues in their work of "establishing" the Greek texts of $NA^{26/27}$ and $GNT^{3/4}$).[2]

With respect to this very difficult text-critical matter, I believe it best (1) to honor the absence of ἀμήν in P^{46}, which is our earliest MS evidence, and (2) to acknowledge that elsewhere in his NT letters Paul does not *conclude* a letter or a section of a letter with a peace blessing (a peace wish or assumed peace benediction); rather, when a peace blessing appears, it actually *begins* that letter's conclusion (see particularly 1 Thess 5:23; 2 Thess 3:16; and Phil 4:9b; note also 2 Cor 13:11b; Gal 6:16; Eph 6:23a; and 1 Thess 5:23a)[3] — with a grace benediction then following almost immediately after it, or shortly thereafter, in closing off that letter's conclusion (as in 1 Thess 5:28; 2 Thess 3:18; Phil 4:23).[4] So I think it most appropriate to understand Paul's words here in 15:33 ("The God of peace be with all of you!") as an opening peace blessing or peace wish, which was intended by the apostle to *precede* all his concluding statements of 16:1-27 — and not to *conclude* the previous subsection of material in 15:14-32 (or even, as is often postulated, to be viewed as a peace benediction that should be seen as the first part of his final doxology, with other materials intervening between this assumed peace benediction and the apostle's final grace benediction of 16:25-27).

16:1a The particle δέ ("but," "then," "now") is amply attested throughout the Greek textual tradition. It is, however, omitted in uncials D* F and G, with that omission probably best viewed as an attempted stylistic improvement and not original.

1b The pronoun ἡμῶν ("our") in the phrase τὴν ἀδελφὴν ἡμῶν ("our sister") is attested by uncials ℵ B C D Ψ (also *Byz* L) and by minuscules 33 1175 1739 (Category I), 1881 (Category II), and 6 69 88 104 323 326 330 365 614 1241 1243 1505 1573 1735 1874 2344 2495 (Category III); it also is reflected in the vg and most syr versions and is supported by Ambrosiaster. On the other hand, the pronoun ὑμῶν ("your") appears in P^{46}, in uncials A F G P, and is reflected in it (i.e., the Old Latin version) and in cop^{bo}. A similar replacement of the pronoun ἡμῶν ("our") by the pronoun ὑμῶν ("your") is found in uncials F G P for the text of Rom 15:2. In all likelihood, however, the reading τὴν ἀδελφὴν ἡμῶν ("our sister") was original.

1c The presence of καί (evidently used adverbially to signify "even," "likewise," or "also") in the phrase οὖσαν καὶ διάκονον ("who [she] is also a deacon") is supported by P^{46}, by uncials ca[2] B C*, and by minuscules 81 (Category II) and 1243 (Category III); it is also reflected in cop^{bo}. It is absent, however, in uncials ℵ* A C[2] D F G P Ψ (also *Byz* L) and in minuscules 33 1175 (Category I), 1881 (Category II), and 6 69 88 104 323 326 330 365 614 1241 1505 1573 1735 1874 2344 2495 (Category III); this absence is also reflected in all the Latin versions and in cop^{sa}.

The textual evidence for the presence or absence of καί has seemed to many to be evenly divided, as seen in the fact that the editors of $NA^{26/27}$ and $GNT^{3/4}$ placed καί in brackets here at 16:1. Yet the presence of καί in 16:1 is attested by two of our most important textual witnesses: (1) by P^{46}, which is our earliest MS witness (c. A.D. 200),

---

2. Metzger, *Textual Commentary,* 475.
3. See "An Anticipatory Comment with Respect to Our Treatment of 15:33" above.
4. See pp. 1031-32 above

and (2) by Codex Vaticanus (uncial B 03), which was transcribed sometime during the fourth century A.D. — thereby focusing attention on Phoebe's qualification as being that of a διάκονον ("deacon"). Later scribes were probably motivated by a desire to downplay such a leadership role for women in the early church and so simply omitted this adverbial use of καί ("also," "even"). I believe, however, that this adverbial use of καί in 16:1 should be retained, both (1) because it is attested by such major textual witnesses as P⁴⁶ and Codex Vaticanus (B 03), and (2) because it witnesses to a proper understanding of Christian women in leadership roles in the early church (as will be explicated further in "Exegetical Comments" on 16:1-2 below).

2a The word order of αὐτὴν προσδέξησθε ("her you should receive") — that is, with the accusative singular feminine pronoun αὐτὴν placed at the beginning of the sentence and the second-person plural aorist subjunctive verb προσδέξησθε following it — serves to highlight Phoebe's significance in saying to the Christians at Rome: "her [i.e., Phoebe] you should receive." This reading is attested by uncials ℵ A P Ψ [also *Byz* L] and by minuscules 33 1175 1739 (Category I), 1881 (Category II), and 6 69 88 104 323 326 330 365 614 1241 1243 1319 1505 1573 1735 1874 2344 2495 (Category III); it is also reflected in the vg and supported by Ambrosiaster. Likewise, P⁴⁶ seems to support this reading, though this very early and important MS has here only the verb προσδέξησθε — with the pronoun αὐτὴν evidently meant to be understood from the immediately previous verse. The reversal of the word order from αὐτὴν προσδέξησθε ("her you should receive") to προσδέξησθε αὐτήν ("you should receive her"), however, appears in uncials B C D F G (as well as in all the Byzantine minuscules).

Such a reversal of word order may possibly be credited to some scribe's attempted "stylistic improvement." Yet this variant word order moves the feminine accusative pronoun αὐτὴν ("her") from a position of prominence at the beginning of the sentence to a place of lesser emphasis at its end. This change of word order is in line with what appears to have been a scribal deletion of the adverbial use of καί ("also") in 16:1 (see our discussion above).

I believe it best, therefore, to understand αὐτὴν προσδέξησθε ("her you should receive") as the original reading. Thus, while it may seem necessary in an English translation (for purely stylistic reasons) to render Paul's request of 16:2 by some such colloquial translation as "I ask you to receive her," "you should receive her," or "receive her," it needs always to be realized that the apostle, in what we have deemed was probably his original word order, was laying particular emphasis on Phoebe herself in writing to his Christian addressees at Rome: "*her* you should receive."

3a The name Πρεισκαν ("Prisca") appears in P⁴⁶ and Codex Vaticanus (B 03); all the other early Greek MSS set out this name in the slightly contracted form of Πρισκαν ("Prisca"). A number of later minuscule MSS, however, have the diminutive form Πρισκιλλαν ("Priscilla"), as appears in minuscules 81 256 1881ᶜ (Category II) and 104 323 365 614 629 630 1319 1505 1573 1735 1852 2495 (Category III); this diminutive form also is reflected in vgᵐˢˢ syrᵇᵒ and supported by Ambrosiaster. This is consistent with the readings of this lady's name in Acts 18:2, 18, 26; 1 Cor 16:19; and 2 Tim 4:19.

The original form of this name was probably Πρεισκαν (as in P⁴⁶ and Codex Vaticanus) — or, perhaps, the slightly contracted form Πρισκαν (as in all the other early uncial MSS). The diminutive and more colloquial name Πρισκιλλαν ("Priscilla"), as employed by Luke in Acts and Paul in 1 Corinthians and 2 Timothy, has undoubtedly influenced later scribes here in Rom 16:3.

3b The phrase καὶ τὴν κατ᾽ οἶκον αὐτῶν ἐκκλησίαν ("also the church at their house") appears in uncials D* ² F G here at 16:3b (rather than later at 16:5a). But this change of location from the end of 16:5 to the beginning of 16:3 is too weakly supported by the textual tradition to merit serious consideration as having been original. Probably it came about simply because its appearance at the beginning of 16:5 seemed to some early interpreters as something of an afterthought, and so needed to be more closely connected to the persons of Prisca and Aquila. In the ninth-century uncial P the phrase καὶ τὴν κατ᾽ οἶκον αὐτῶν ἐκκλησίαν ("also the church at their house") is omitted in both 16:3 and 16:5 — most likely because of a lack of conviction in that day as to where it should appear, whether at the end of 16:3 or at the beginning of 16:5.

5a The presence and location of the elliptical sentence καὶ τὴν κατ᾽ οἶκον αὐτῶν ἐκκλησίαν ("[Greet] also the church at their house") of 16:5, while somewhat disconnected from the reference to Prisca and Aquila in 16:3, are amply attested by the earlier Greek MSS, and so deserve acceptance as original (see "Textual Note" on 16:3 above).

5b The reference to Paul's "dear friend Epenetus" as being ἀπαρχή . . . εἰς Χριστόν ("the firstfruit . . . for Christ") is amply attested in the textual tradition. The variant ἀπ᾽ ἀρχῆς ("from the beginning"), which appears in P⁴⁶ and in the sixth-century uncial D* (06), is most likely a transcription error, which came about because of the almost identical vocalization of ἀπαρχή ("firstfruit") and ἀπ᾽ ἀρχῆς ("from the beginning").

5c The geographical reference τῆς Ἀσίας ("of [the province of] Asia") is amply attested by P⁴⁶, by uncials ℵ A B C D* F G, and by minuscules 1739 (Category I), 81 256 2127 (Category II), and 6 263 365 424ᶜ 630 915 1319 1573 1852 1912 2110 2200 (Category III). The reading τῆς Ἀχαίας ("of Achaia"), however, appears in uncials D¹ P Ψ [also *Byz* L] and in a great number of Byzantine minuscules. In all likelihood, this variant reading "of Achaia" is a scribal assimilation to Paul's earlier reference in 1 Cor 16:15 to "the firstfruit of [the province of] Achaia."

5d The reading εἰς Χριστόν ("unto Christ" or "for Christ") is strongly supported throughout the earliest MSS. The variant reading ἐν Χριστῷ ("in Christ"), as appears in uncials D F G and in minuscules 1881 (Category II) and 323 1505 (Category III), seems to be a scribal assimilation to Paul's quite distinctive expression "in Christ" or "in Christ Jesus."

6a The lady of 16:6 is called Μαρίαν ("Mary") in uncials A B C P Ψ and in minuscules 1739 (Category I) and 104 365 1505 1573 1735 2495 (Category III); this name is also reflected in the Coptic versions. The feminine name Μαριάμ ("Miriam"), however, is attested by P⁴⁶, by uncials ℵ D F G [also *Byz* L], and by minuscules 1175 (Category I), 1881 (Category II), and 6 69 88 323 326 330 614 1241 1243 1319 1874 2344 (Category III). The evidence from the Greek textual tradition is almost equally divided, and thus interpreters have been almost equally divided with respect to the original reading. Yet because the name Μαριάμ ("Miriam") (1) is attested by P⁴⁶, (2) is a Semitic name, and so is in this context perhaps the "more difficult reading," and (3) is more easily changed to Μαρίαν than vice versa, I believe it probable that Μαριάμ ("Miriam") was original.

6b The expression εἰς ὑμᾶς ("for you") is very amply attested by P[46], by uncials ℵ A B C P Ψ, and by minuscules 1739 (Category I), 81 256 1881 2127 (Category II), and 6 61 263 326 330 365 451 1243 1319 1505 1573 1718 1852 1908 1942 2110 2197 2495 (Category III). The variant ἐν ὑμῖν ("in you" or "among you"), which appears in uncials D F G, is too weakly attested to be considered original — though, of course, it is a quite distinctive Pauline expression, and for that reason was probably thought by some scribe or scribes to be a better reading. Likewise, the variant expression εἰς ἡμᾶς ("for us"), which is found in uncial C[2] [also *Byz* L] and in many Byzantine minuscule MSS, is far too weakly supported in the textual tradition to be considered original.

7 Two matters with respect to the second name given in 16:7 are of importance: (1) the spelling of the name, and (2) the accent to be assigned to the name. As for the original spelling of the name, Ἰουνιαν is attested in the Greek textual tradition by uncials ℵ A B C D F G P. The variant spelling Ἰουλιαν, however, appears in P[46] and in minuscule 6 (Category III); it is also reflected in it[ar, b] vg[mss] cop[bo] eth and supported by Jerome. With such a strong attestation from the Greek uncial MSS (though, admittedly, not from P[46]), there has been little doubt among scholars that the name was originally spelled Ἰουνιαν.

The question regarding how this name should be accented, however, that is, whether as a masculine name (i.e., Ἰουνιᾶν or "Junias") or as a feminine name (i.e., Ἰουνίαν or "Junia"), has become a rather hotly debated matter during the past half-century or so. The difficulty in determining how the name should be accented has been complicated, of course, by the fact that Greek accents for the NT text came into vogue only in the sixth century A.D.; prior to the employment of accents, decisions were made solely on the basis of a word's immediate context. While in the great majority of biblical texts there is no question regarding how a Greek name should be understood in its context, that is, whether as masculine or feminine, where a particular name appears in isolation without a specific context, there have been, at times, legitimate questions whether that name is a man's or a woman's.

It appears from the history of interpretation (1) that patristic commentators usually treated the unaccented name Ἰουνιαν as feminine; (2) that from the thirteenth century to the middle of the twentieth century most commentators understood this name as masculine, and so accented it as Ἰουνιᾶν or "Junias" (a contracted form of the name Junianus); and (3) that since about the middle of the twentieth century the overwhelming text-critical opinion has favored the name as feminine, and so to be accented as Ἰουνίαν or "Junia."[5] And I accept this feminine reading Ἰουνίαν, translated as "Junia,"

5. See esp. the quite concise text-critical treatments of this issue by R. R. Schulz, "Romans 16.7," 109-10; Cervin, "A Note regarding the Name 'Junia(s)' in Romans 16.7," 464-70; and by Epp, *Junia*, 45-46. Many English translations during the past few decades have clearly expressed this interpretive change from understanding this name as a masculine name to understanding it as a feminine name — as seen in the masculine readings of this name as "Junias" in RSV, TEV, NJB, NIV, NASB, but the revised feminine readings of it as "Junia" in NRSV, TNIV, REB (which name the sixteenth-century translators of the KJV seem to have also understood as feminine in translating it as "Junia"). And many of today's major commentators on Romans have argued for a feminine understanding of this name, as, e.g., M.-J. Lagrange (1931), F. F. Bruce (1963), H. Schlier (1977), C. E. B. Cranfield (1979), U. Wilckens (1982), J. D. G. Dunn (1989), J. A. Fitzmyer (1993), D. J. Moo (1996), and R. Jewett (2007).

and understand her as most likely the wife of Andronicus — with the apostle speaking of this Christian couple as being Jewish compatriots from his own country, as at some time earlier being in prison with him (probably in a Roman territorial prison at Caesarea), as "outstanding among the apostles," and as having been believers in Jesus before he was.

8 The masculine name Ἀμπλιᾶτον ("Ampliatus") is attested by P⁴⁶, by uncials ℵ A B* C^vid F G, and by minuscule 1739* (Category I); it is also reflected in all the Latin versions and in cop^bo. The abbreviated masculine form Ἀμλιᾶν ("Amplian"), however, is found in uncials B² D P Ψ (also *Byz* L) and in minuscules 33 1175 (Category I), 1881 (Category II), and 69 88 104 323 326 330 614 1241 1243 1735 1874 2344 (Category III). The feminine name Ἀπλίαν ("Aplian") is found in minuscules 365 1319 1505 1573 2495 (all Category III); it is also reflected in cop^sa. Such a feminine understanding may have been influenced (1) by Paul's statement "whom I love in the Lord," and/or (2) by the fact that this name of v. 8 closely follows the feminine name Ἰουνίαν or "Junia" in v. 7. But the masculine name Ἀμπλιᾶτον ("Ampliatus") is far better supported by such important MSS as P⁴⁶, Codex Sinaiticus (ℵ 01), and Codex Vaticanus (B 03), and thus should be accepted as original.

9 The name Χριστῷ ("Christ") in the expression ἐν Χριστῷ ("in Christ") is attested by P⁴⁶, by uncials ℵ A B P (also *Byz* L), and by minuscules 33 1175 1739 (Category I), 1881 (Category II), and 6 88 104 323 330 614 1241 1243 1505 1573 1735 1874 2344 2495 (Category III); it also is reflected in all the Latin versions and in cop^bo and is supported by Ambrosiaster. The dative use of the title κυρίῳ ("in the Lord"), however, replaces the dative use of the name Χριστῷ ("in Christ") in uncials C D F G Ψ and in minuscules 81 (Category II) and 326 365 630 1319 (Category III). But this variant should probably be understood as having been influenced by the repeated use of the expression "in the Lord" elsewhere in the immediate passage, that is, in 16:2, 11, 12 (twice), and 13, even though the expression "in Christ" here in 16:9 is strongly supported by the MS evidence.

15a The feminine name Ἰουλίαν ("Julia") is attested by uncials ℵ A B C² D P Ψ [also *Byz* L] and by minuscules 33 1175 1739 (Category I), 81 256 1881 1962 2127 2464 (Category II), and 6 69 88 104 181 263 323 326 330 365 436 451 459 614 629 1241 1243 1319 1505 1573 1735 1852 1874 1877 1912 2200 2344 2492 (Category III); it also is reflected in vg syr^p, h cop^sa bo and is supported by Origen^lat and Chrysostom. The name Ἰουνιαν ("Junia") in its unaccented form, however, appears in uncials C* F G. Being unaccented in uncials C* F G, this variant could be read as either masculine or feminine (see "Textual Notes" on 16:7 above). But Ἰουνιαν ("Junia"), whether masculine or feminine, is far too weakly attested by the MS evidence to be here considered original.

15b The two names Ἰουλίαν ("Julia") and Νηρέα ("Nereus") are amply attested by uncials ℵ A B C^c D P Ψ [also *Byz* L] and by minuscules 33 1175 1739 (Category I), 81 1881 1962 2127 2464 (Category II), and 6 69 88 104 181 323 326 330 365 436 451 614 629 630 1241 1243 1319 1505 1573 1735 1874 1877 2492 2495 (Category III); these two Greek names are also reflected in Latin, Syriac, and Coptic versions. In P⁴⁶, however, these two names Ἰουλίαν ("Julia") and Νηρέα ("Nereus") appear as Βηρέα ("Bereus") and Ἀουλίαν ("Aoulia"). The appearance of these two quite different names in P⁴⁶ has always been noticed in text-critical studies, usually without any attempted explanation — though, at times, their presence has been related to a pattern of altering names that some have posited can be found in P⁴⁶.

15c The masculine name Ὀλυμπᾶν ("Olympas") is extensively supported in the Greek MSS of the textual tradition. It is a shortened and more colloquial form of the formal name Ὀλυμπιδα ("Olympida"). This formal name Ὀλυμπιδα, however, appears in the ninth-century uncials F and G, and it is reflected in all the Latin versions by the Latin name Olympiadem. It may be debated which came first in the reading of this person's name by various early scribes — whether referring to him as Olympas or referring to him as Olympiadem. But here in 16:15 Paul uses the shorter and more colloquial name Ὀλυμπᾶν ("Olympas") in referring to this acquaintance to whom he expresses his personal greeting, evidently because he considered him not just an acquaintance but also a friend.

FORM/STRUCTURE/SETTING

A peace blessing or peace wish in 15:33 marks off what follows as being distinct from the body closing or apostolic parousia before it. This peace blessing, together with two rather standard epistolary conventions, functions to signal the beginnings of the first three parts of 15:33, 16:1-2, and 16:3-16a in this section; a further portion of material is attached, which conveys the greetings of all the Gentile churches founded by Paul and under his care to the Christians at Rome in their various local congregations (16:16b).

> 15:33 — A peace blessing or peace wish: ὁ θεὸς τῆς εἰρήνης μετὰ πάντων ὑμῶν, "the God of peace be with you all."
>
> 16:1 — A commendation of the letter carrier: συνίστημι ὑμῖν Φοίβην τὴν ἀδελφὴν ἡμῶν, "I commend to you our sister Phoebe."
>
> 16:3-16a — Requests for the Christians at Rome to greet a number of Paul's past associates, friends, and acquaintances who were then living at Rome, to greet also certain Christian households and congregations of that city, and to "greet one another with a holy kiss": ἀσπάσασθε Πρίσκαν καὶ Ἀκύλαν, etc., "Greet Priscilla and Aquila, etc."
>
> 16:16b — Paul's conveyance of greetings from "all the [Gentile] churches of Christ" to the believers in Jesus at Rome.

The expression παρακαλῶ ὑμᾶς, ἀδελφοί ("I urge ['exhort' or 'encourage'] you, brothers and sisters") of 16:17, which follows the materials set out in 15:33–16:16, functions to separate what follows from what precedes it (cf. the identical use of this same epistolary expression earlier in 12:1 and 15:30).

Thus this subsection of material in 15:33–16:16 should be understood as consisting of the following four parts:

1. A Peace Blessing or Peace Wish (15:33)
2. A Commendation of Phoebe (16:1-2)

3. Requests for the Christians at Rome to Greet a Number Paul's Past Associates, Friends, and Acquaintances Then Living at Rome (as well as Certain Christian Households and Congregations of That City) and to "Greet One Another with a Holy Kiss" (16:3-16a)
4. A Conveyance of Greetings from "All the Churches of Christ" to the Christians at Rome (16:16b)

A peace blessing; a commendation of a particular lady; requests for the Christians at Rome to greet Paul's past associates, friends, and acquaintances then living at Rome; and a rather general conveyance of greetings from Paul's own Gentile-Christian churches to the Christian congregations at Rome may seem, at first glance, rather standard fare for the conclusion of almost any letter written by a Christian leader during the first century, and therefore not of any great significance for an understanding of what Paul sets out in this letter. Yet, intrinsic to each of these four units of this first concluding section of Romans are certain implications that have to do with the situation of the Christian church in Paul's day and with certain features of importance in the apostle's argument of this letter.

EXEGETICAL COMMENTS

I. Peace Blessing or Peace Wish (15:33)

15:33 The reason Paul included the peace blessing or peace wish of 15:33, "The God of peace be with all of you" (ὁ δὲ θεὸς τῆς εἰρήνης μετὰ πάντων ὑμῶν), which appears at the beginning of this passage, was probably not because it was a standard way for a Christian writer to begin a conclusion, but because he wanted to highlight his great desire for peace among the Christians at Rome with respect to certain existing disputes between "the Strong" and "the Weak" that he had dealt with earlier in 14:1–15:13. And because the personal subscription of 16:17-23, which follows immediately after this present section of material, contains (1) further references to "divisions" between believers in Jesus at Rome and to "obstacles" having been erected by some Christians against other Christians (16:17-18) and (2) another peace statement, "The God of peace will soon crush Satan under your feet!" (16:20a) — which two passages appear just before the final grace benediction of the letter (in 16:20b) — it seems legitimate to infer that a concern for both "peace and reconciliation with God" (as expressed earlier in 5:1-11) and "peace and reconciliation among believers in Jesus" (as expressed throughout 14:1–15:13) weighed heavily on the apostle's heart and mind as he was writing this concluding section of his letter. Further, it may be inferred that in this peace blessing of 15:33 Paul was directing his words against every type of antagonistic attitude on the part of professing "Christ followers" toward other believers in Jesus, setting out, instead, an emphasis on the most appropriate feature of "peace" within the Christian community — that is, on "wholeness" or "completeness" of "life in Christ," which brings about "reconciliation" with God and with other believers in Jesus (as set out earlier in his theological presentation of 5:1-11).

II. Commendation of Phoebe (16:1-2)

16:1-2 Conjectures about Phoebe and Paul's commendation of her in 16:1-2 are rampant — dealing with (1) what Paul explicitly says about Phoebe, (2) what part Phoebe had in the delivery of Paul's letter to the Christians at Rome, (3) what part Phoebe had in explaining the contents of the apostle's letter to his Roman addressees, (4) what such words of commendation for Phoebe suggest about Paul's understanding of the attitudes of the Christians at Rome toward him and his own concerns when writing to them, and (5) what role both Paul and Phoebe expected that she would assume in the furtherance of the apostle's Gentile mission to Spain.

From what Paul says about Phoebe, it is clear that, in speaking of her as "our sister Phoebe" (Φοίβην τὴν ἀδελφὴν ἡμῶν), he considered her a true believer in Jesus. Further, he lauds her (1) as being "also a deacon (καὶ διάκονον) of the church at Cenchrea," the harbor port for the city of Corinth, which signals some type of active leadership in a Christian congregation at Cenchrea; and (2) as being a "benefactor" or "patroness" (προστάτις) to him and to many other Christians of the area, which suggests that she had been quite strategically involved in both Paul's ministry and that of other believers in Jesus in Corinth and its environs.

With respect to what part Phoebe had in delivering Paul's letter to the Christians at Rome, it seems evident that she carried the apostle's letter from Corinth to Rome, doing so at her own expense. As for what part she played in presenting and interpreting the contents of that letter to the Christians at Rome, it may legitimately be surmised that not only did she present Paul's letter to the Christian leaders and congregations of Rome, but she also served as their major source of information regarding (1) the apostle's earlier use of the materials that he set out in the letter and (2) his intentions for the use of such materials. For, after all, Phoebe had been Paul's patron during his ministry at Corinth, had most likely heard from his own lips the contents of the letter as it was being formulated, and must have had some part in discussing with Paul and other Christians of that area at least a few portions of the letter — and therefore would have been in a position to explain to the Christians at Rome (1) what Paul was saying in the various sections of his letter, (2) what he meant by what he proclaimed in each of those sections, and (3) how he expected certain important sections of his letter to be worked out in practice in the particular situations at Rome. Probably Phoebe should be viewed as the first commentator to others on Paul's letter to Rome. And without a doubt, every commentator, teacher, or preacher on Romans would profit immensely from a transcript of Phoebe's explanations of what Paul wrote in this letter before actually having to write or speak on it themselves.

With respect to the fourth matter above, what Paul's words in commending Phoebe may suggest about the attitudes of the Christians at Rome toward him and his message, as well as about his concerns when writing to them, it needs to be noted that the fact that the apostle felt such a commendation of Phoebe was necessary suggests (1) that he had some misgivings about how the Christians at Rome would receive his letter and understand what he wrote — but also (2) that he had confidence in Phoebe to clarify whatever might be in question and to represent what he had written in the best light. As for what role both Paul and Phoebe expected that she would play in the furtherance of the apostle's Gentile mission in Spain, it seems legitimate to believe (1) that Phoebe's financial backing would, at least to some extent, be continued in Paul's proposed missionary endeavors to pagan Gentiles in Spain, and (2) that her example of financial support would encourage the Christians at Rome to support the apostle's outreach to Gentiles in that western region of the Roman Empire in a similar way.

Paul says nothing further about Phoebe, for evidently he was confident that her person and her actions at Rome would sufficiently commend her to the Christians of that city so that nothing additional needed to be said. All that the apostle specifically asks of the Christians at Rome with respect to Phoebe is that they "receive her in the Lord in a way that is worthy of God's people and give her any help she may need from you." It is a request couched in diplomatic language and expressed with Christian fervency. Nonetheless, it is a request that would have been understood by all parties in the Christian congregations at Rome as intending to further the advancement of the Christian gospel, both at Rome and in Paul's proposed ministry in Spain.

III. Requests for the Christians at Rome to Greet Paul's Past Associates, Friends, and Acquaintances in Rome and Certain Christian Households and Congregations There and to Greet "One Another with a Holy Kiss" (16:3-16a)

The most noticeable features about the greetings that appear in 16:3-16a are the following:

1. Paul asks the Christians at Rome to express their greetings to a number of his past associates, friends, and acquaintances who were then living at Rome, rather than sending his own greetings (or those of his associates, friends, or acquaintances) to his Christian addressees, as he does in most of his other NT letters.[6]

---

6 Only the request of Phil 4:21a is a possible exception.

2. There are quite a large number of people to whom Paul asks the Christians at Rome to express their greetings.
3. There are highly laudatory descriptions of most of the people to whom the apostle requests the Christians at Rome to send their greetings.
4. These laudatory descriptions relate primarily to their past associations with Paul and his Gentile mission.

In Col 4:10-14 and Phlm 23-24 the apostle sets out similar commendatory descriptions in series of greetings. But those commendations are in the context of Paul's own greetings or his conveyance of the greetings of others. Only at the end of his requested greetings of Rom 16:3-15 — in which the apostle asks the Christians at Rome to express their greetings to many of his past associates, friends, and acquaintances in Rome — does Paul add his more usual exhortation to "greet one another with a holy kiss" (16:16a) and does he convey greetings on behalf of "all the [Gentile] churches of Christ" (16:16b).

All those mentioned in this list were probably Jewish believers in Jesus (or those considered by Roman authorities to be related to Jewish Christians) who had left Rome because of the edict of Claudius in A.D. 49 but had, after the repeal of that edict of expulsion (whether *de facto* before the emperor's death in 54 or *de jure* after his death in 54), either (1) returned to the capital city for family or economic reasons or (2) migrated there for these and other quite personal reasons. Perhaps Paul thought the Christians at Rome would profit from knowing something about these people, and therefore asks them to greet his past associates, friends, and acquaintances. Yet those the apostle asks the Christians at Rome to greet were already involved in one or another of the Christian congregations of Rome, and not just visitors or outsiders. They were, presumably, already well known to Paul's addressees at Rome, and not strangers who needed to be introduced. Thus it seems not ingenuous to believe that, by giving this long list of greetings, Paul primarily wanted to promote his own credibility with the Christians at Rome — and that he does so by highlighting the personal relationships he had with several of the people of their own Christian congregations. Or as Harry Gamble has aptly observed with respect to this long list of requested greetings:

> It is especially striking how, in the descriptive phrases, a heavy emphasis is placed on the relationship between the individuals and Paul himself. He ties them to himself, and himself to them. From these features it can be seen that Paul's commendatory greetings to specific individuals serve to place those individuals in a position of respect vis-à-vis the community, but also, by linking the Apostle so closely to them, place Paul in the same position.[7]

16:3-5a We actually know very little about most of the believers in Jesus that Paul lists in 16:3-15 (though scholars have frequently attempted to fill out

7. Gamble, *Textual History,* 92.

their history or relate them to known people of the same or similar names). The first two early believers in Jesus from Rome cited here in 16:3-5a, the married couple Prisca and Aquila, are undoubtedly the best known today to readers of Paul's NT letters. For Luke tells us in Acts 18:2 that during his second evangelistic outreach to pagan Gentiles living in the eastern regions of the Roman Empire, Paul "met a Jew named Aquila, a native of Pontus, who had recently come from Italy with his wife Priscilla [a colloquial and diminutive form of Prisca], because Claudius had ordered all Jews to leave Rome."[8] The story of relations between Paul and this married couple was one of real friendship and close cooperation, both in secular matters and in Christian ministry.

The fact that Prisca (or, colloquially, "Priscilla") is usually referred to first by both Paul and Luke when speaking of this couple suggests that Prisca came from a higher social class than her husband — or, perhaps, that she was for some other reason considered more important. Probably Aquila was a former Jewish slave who became a "freedman" in Rome and married a local lady who was connected in some way with the Roman family Prisca *(gens Prisca)*, which had Roman citizenship rights. Together, probably through the craftsmanship of Aquila and the status, money, and contacts of Prisca, they seem to have established a tentmaking and leatherworking firm at Rome, with branches of their business at Corinth and at Ephesus (cf. Acts 18:2, 18-19, 26; Rom 16:3; 1 Cor 16:19; 2 Tim 4:19). Prisca and Aquila, however, were also believers in Jesus, having become "Christ followers" (either separately before their marriage or together after their marriage), probably when living at Rome. But because of the edict of the emperor Claudius in A.D. 49, they were forced to leave Rome and continue their business at Corinth.

Luke tells us in Acts 18:1-4 that when "Paul left Athens and went to Corinth . . . he went to see them [Prisca/Priscilla and Aquila] . . . and because he was a tentmaker as they were, he stayed and worked with them." While staying with them he proclaimed the message of the Christian gospel "in the synagogue, trying to persuade both Jews and Gentiles." Later, as Luke tells us further in Acts 18:18-21, after "Paul stayed on in Corinth for some time," he "left the believers and sailed for Syria, accompanied by Priscilla and Aquila" — and during that sea voyage to Syria, Prisca and Aquila left the ship to take up residence at Ephesus (where, it seems, they had another branch of their tentmaking and leatherworking business).

At Ephesus, as Luke goes on to tell us in Acts 18:24-26, Prisca and Aquila heard Apollos proclaim the Christian gospel as he knew it, and after they heard him they "invited him to their home and explained to him the way of God more adequately." Further, we learn from 1 Cor 16:19 that Paul joined Prisca and Aq-

8. Luke's habit was to use the more colloquial and diminutive forms of the names that he mentions in his writings (e.g., Silas, Sopater, Priscilla, Apollos), whereas Paul usually refers to his friends by their more formal names (e.g., Silvanus, Sosipater, Prisca, Epaphroditus) — though in certain situations Paul also speaks of some of his friends in a more colloquial and diminutive fashion (e.g., Apollos, Epaphras).

uila at Ephesus and they carried on a lengthy Christian ministry together. We do not know when Prisca and Aquila returned to their home city of Rome. But it would be only natural that they would have wanted to return after Claudius's decree of Jewish banishment had lapsed or been rescinded, either before or after the emperor's death in 54.

Likewise, we do not know what principally motivated Prisca and Aquila to return to Rome after the edict was no longer in effect. It was probably to resurrect their business in the empire's capital city. But their reason for returning may have included a desire to lend their support to Paul's proposed visit to Rome — which the apostle must have talked with them about at many times, both at Corinth and at Ephesus. Here in 16:3-5a, however, Paul mentions only two matters of special notice with respect to the Christian ministries of these two associates and friends of his: (1) that they risked their lives for him at a previous time in his Gentile ministry (probably in helping to save him from an imminent death during the riot that Luke speaks about in Acts 19:23-41), and (2) that there was a congregation of believers in Jesus that met in their home at Rome. Thus the apostle begins his list of people for whom he asks that greetings from the Christians at Rome be sent by speaking of this Jewish-Christian couple with whom he had very close relations as a friend and as a co-worker in both secular business and Christian ministry — knowing that the Christians at Rome highly respected this married couple and probably hoping that their high esteem of them would, at least to some extent, be transferred to him.

16:5b-6 Two special people whom Paul highlights among those that he asks the Christians at Rome to greet are (1) his "dear friend Epenetus," whom he describes as "the first convert (i.e., 'the firstfruit') of [the province of] Asia," and (2) a lady named Miriam, about whom he says: "She worked very hard for you."[9] While Epenetus and Miriam are not mentioned anywhere else in the NT, we may believe (1) that Paul met each of them at some time and some place during his Gentile mission when they were refugees from Rome after Claudius's edict of 49; (2) that he heard their respective stories as "Christ followers" from not only themselves but also from others; (3) that they returned to Rome at some time after the edict had lapsed or was legally rescinded after Claudius's death in 54; (4) that they were held in high honor by the Christians at Rome because they were two of the original founders of the Christian community there; and (5) that Paul wanted to be identified with them by the Christians at Rome as having the same concerns for not only the growth of the Christian religion in the city but also the extension of the Christian gospel throughout the Roman Empire.

16:7 Paul next asks that greetings be sent to Adronicus and Junia, who were in all likelihood a married couple of special note among the believers in

---

9. On support from the Greek textual tradition for the provincial name Asia and the feminine name Miriam, see our "Textual Notes" above on 16:5c and 6a.

Jesus at Rome.[10] Of this couple Paul says four quite significant things: (1) they were compatriots from his own country (that is, a Jewish couple who emigrated from Judea to Rome); (2) they were "in prison with me" (probably in the same Roman territorial prison at Caesarea); (3) "they are outstanding among the apostles" (probably in carrying out a Christian ministry first in the Jewish homeland and then in Rome); and (4) "they were 'in Christ' before me."

Douglas Campbell is undoubtedly right in positing (1) that belief in Jesus of Nazareth as Israel's Messiah and humanity's Lord originated in Rome earlier than Paul's Gentile mission, (2) that it came about through Jewish believers in Jesus who were from the Roman province of Judea, and (3) that such an understanding probably sheds some light on the life and ministry of this Jewish-Christian couple Adronicus and Junia, who were then living at Rome and about whom Paul speaks so highly:

> The original Christian influence on the Roman community was doubtless both early and Judaean. That community's theological traditions therefore go back to the earliest post-Easter period, probably in a special relation to the apostolic couple Junia and Andronicus (Rom 16:7), who had been Christians and leaders for a longer period even than Paul and hence almost certainly came from Judaea.[11]

If Campbell's understanding of the situation is correct, which we believe it is, we are provided with some insight into why Paul lists this Jewish-Christian couple of 16:7 among those he seems to classify as very significant in the founding and early welfare of Christianity at Rome, and so were highly esteemed among the Christians at Rome — that is, that along with Prisca and Aquila, Epenetus, and Miriam, Paul includes the married couple Andronicus and Junia, whom he refers to as "compatriots from my own country," as having been "in prison with me," "outstanding among the apostles," and among "those who were 'in Christ' before me."

It seems that Prisca and Aquila, Epenetus, Miriam, and Andronicus and Junia were foundational in the establishment of Christianity in the capital city of the Roman Empire. And it was these early Jewish believers in Jesus (1) whom Paul considered his associates, friends, and/or acquaintances from his encounters with them during the period when Jews and Jewish Christians were expelled from Rome (i.e., sometime during 49-54), and (2) whom he believed the Christians at Rome also honored as having been of special importance in the founding and establishment of Christianity in their city. Thus he asks the Christians at Rome to greet each of these people, who had only recently returned to Rome after Claudius's decree of Jewish banishment had lapsed or been rescinded. And he evidently makes such requests with the hope that his

---

10. On the name Ἰουνιαν, whether unaccented or accented, as being feminine, see our extended "Textual Note" above on 16:7.

11. D. A. Campbell, "The Story of Jesus in Romans and Galatians," 116.

association with these Jewish Christian "heroes of faith" — who were most likely still respected by the Christians at Rome, and so could speak on his behalf — would somehow accrue to his benefit.

16:8-15 The list of significant believers in Jesus in 16:3-7, whom, it seems, Paul viewed as some of his most notable past associates, friends, and acquaintances then living at Rome, is supplemented in 16:8-15 by an even longer list of other believers in Jesus at Rome — whom, evidently, the apostle also wanted his Christian addressees at Rome to understand as having been met and known by him during his outreach to pagan Gentiles in the eastern parts of the Roman Empire. He asks the Christians at Rome to greet them as well — identifying them as being of special honor, and desiring that the believers in Jesus at Rome think of him in terms of his relationships with them. For, in terms of the common adage that "A person is known by his or her friends," Paul in these verses seems to be asking the Christians at Rome to accept his person, his proclamation of the Christian gospel, and his Gentile mission by reference to his past associates, friends, and acquaintances — and so to accept him, pray for him, and support him financially in his proposed evangelistic outreach to Spain.

16:16a This long list of greetings that Paul asks the Christians at Rome to give to his past associates, friends, and acquaintances in 16:3-15 is brought to a close in 16:16a by the apostle's request that the Christians at Rome "Greet one another with a holy kiss." In so doing they would, in effect, be united in their thoughts and actions — particularly in their thoughts and actions having to do with Paul personally, his Gentile mission, his contextualized version of the Christian gospel, and his proposed evangelistic outreach to Spain.

IV. Greetings Conveyed from "All the Churches of Christ" to the Christians at Rome (16:16b)

16:16b Paul brings this whole subsection of material to a conclusion in 16:16b by conveying to the Christians at Rome greetings from "all the churches of Christ." These "churches of Christ" were undoubtedly those congregations of believers in Jesus that Paul himself had founded, either directly or through the ministries of his converts, in various eastern regions of the Roman Empire — and with whom he continued to be in contact as their "founding father" through his associates, pastoral letters, and occasional visits. In so speaking, Paul is (1) affirming his authority as God's apostle to the Gentiles to send such greetings, for he had been ordained by God to proclaim the gospel message to the Gentile world; (2) highlighting his relationship with Gentile Christians throughout the eastern portion of the Greco-Roman world, for he had sustained such a particularly significant position with them that he could speak on their behalf; and (3) inviting his Christian addressees at Rome to join with these Gentile churches in acknowledging the appropriateness of his Gentile ministry, the validity of his own particular contextualization of the Christian gospel to Gentiles, and their spiritual oneness that they possess with all the other Gentile believers in Jesus who have been brought to God through his Gentile mission.

As Jeffrey Weima has aptly observed with respect to this greeting:

> Nowhere else does Paul speak so broadly ("all the churches") in passing on the greetings of others. So here, it seems, Paul presents himself to the Romans as one who has the official backing of all the churches in Achaia, Macedonia, Asia, Galatia, Syria and elsewhere in the eastern part of the empire. Furthermore, their support demonstrates that his gospel has a proven track record among believers throughout the Mediterranean world. Consequently, there is in this greeting an implied challenge to believers in Rome that they join these other churches in recognizing the authority of Paul's apostleship and his gospel.[12]

Or as James Dunn has stated matters more concisely, though a bit more mundanely: "The greeting thus has a 'political' overtone: Paul speaks for all these churches, and they are behind him in his mission."[13]

BIBLICAL THEOLOGY

Of particular pertinence for the construction of a biblical theology in this first concluding section of 15:33–16:16 are (1) the apostle's commendation of the lady Phoebe, whom he speaks of as "our sister," "a deacon of the church at Cenchrea," and "a benefactor to many people, including me," and (2) his references to an additional nine Christian women, whom he thought of as his past associates, friends, and respected acquaintances because of their Christian ministries at Rome and then in various cities, towns, and regions where the apostle had carried out his God-given Gentile mission. He evidently met these women personally in his evangelistic outreach to Gentiles, and believed the Christians at Rome also held them in high esteem. They were the seven Christian women he identifies by name (i.e., Prisca, Miriam, Junia, Tryphena, Tryphosa, Persis, and Julia), together with two other women he refers to by their relationships to their son or their brother (i.e., the unnamed "mother of Rufus" and the unnamed "sister of Nereus"). These references to women in Christian ministry reflect the fact that women believers in Jesus were engaged during the earliest days of nascent Christianity in ministries that were just as God-ordained and just as important as the ministries of believing men.

Women played an important role in the early church. And it appears evident from this passage (as well as from other passages in the NT) that Christian ministry in the early church was never confined to men. In fact, it seems that

---

12. Weima, *Neglected Endings*, 227.
13. Dunn, *Romans* 2,899.

this phenomenon of "both men and women" in Christian ministry was what the apostle Peter had in mind when he proclaimed in Acts 2:17 (quoting God's promise regarding his future actions during this final epoch of salvation history, as reported by the prophet in Joel 2:28): "In the last days, God says, I will pour out my Spirit on *all people.* Your *sons and daughters will prophesy,* your young men will see visions, and your old men will dreams."

Peter actually goes somewhat beyond the exact words of Joel 2:28 by interjecting into that OT prophecy his own particular emphasis as found in Acts 2:18, which is expressed in a somewhat repetitive fashion: "Even on my servants, *both men and women,* will I pour out my Spirit in those days, and *they will prophesy.*" It is, in fact, this emphasis on "both men and women" in Christian ministry that Paul's statements here in Rom 15:33–16:16 reflect. And it is this emphasis that needs also to be captured and expressed in our contemporary constructions of a biblical theology.

Likewise, Paul's references to a great number of associates, friends, and acquaintances in this passage (not only ten women, but also some nineteen men) suggest that he did not consider himself a "lone ranger" in carrying out the work of God. At every point in his ministry, Paul drew to himself a significant number of other believers in Jesus who worked along with him in Christian ministry.[14] And this note of collegiality needs also always to be expressed in our theological constructions — in our exegetical treatments, our excurses, our footnotes, our organization of the various materials, and in the nuancing of our statements.

CONTEXTUALIZATION FOR TODAY

Admittedly, we probably do not learn much about Christian theology, Christian proclamation, or Christian living from a peace blessing, a commendation of Phoebe, and a series of greetings that are requested to be sent to others. Somewhat indirectly, however, we may infer that if Paul needed such a body of associates, friends, and associates, so do we. It is, in fact, extremely unhealthy in the Christian life to have no close associates, no real friends, or no group of acquaintances. Likewise, a "lone ranger" approach to Christian ministry carries with it dire implications for one personally — and it all too often results in disastrous consequences for one's ministry.

Ours is a gospel message that highlights both (1) being "in Christ" personally and individually, and (2) being a member of "Christ's body" corporately and in union with others, not only in our thinking as Christians but also in our living and practice as Christians. So in this first concluding subsection of his letter to Rome, Paul draws us as readers into association with himself and into fellowship with all true "Christ followers" — both past and present, as well as all believers in Jesus of the future.

14. Cf. esp. Ellis, "Paul and His Co-Workers," 437-52.

X. Personal Subscription, Appended Greetings, and Appended Doxology (16:17-27)

TRANSLATION

^{16:17}*I urge you, brothers and sisters, to watch out for those who cause divisions and put obstacles in your way that are contrary to the teaching you have learned. Keep away from them.* ¹⁸*For such people are not serving our Lord Christ, but their own appetites. By smooth talk and flattery they deceive the minds of naive people.* ¹⁹*Everyone has heard about your obedience, so I am full of joy over you. I want you, however, to be wise about what is good and innocent about what is evil.* ^{20a}*The God of peace will soon crush Satan under your feet.*

^{20b}*The grace of our Lord Jesus be with you! Amen.*

---

²¹*Timothy, my co-worker, sends you his greetings, as do Lucius, Jason and Sosipater, my relatives.* ²²*[I, Tertius, who wrote down this letter, greet you in the Lord.]* ²³*Gaius, whose hospitality I and the whole church here enjoy, sends you his greetings. Erastus, who is the city's director of public works, and our brother Quartus send you their greetings.*

²⁵*Now to him who is able to establish you by my gospel — that is, the proclamation of Jesus Christ according to the revelation of the mystery hidden for long ages past,* ²⁶*but now revealed and made known through the prophetic writings by the command of the eternal God so that all the Gentiles might believe and obey him —* ²⁷*to the only wise God be glory forever through Jesus Christ!*

TEXTUAL NOTES

16:17-20a and 25-27 In concert with a large number of NT scholars, both past and present, Robert Jewett has most ably argued for the view that the "additional admonitions" of 16:17-20a and the "doxology" of 16:25-27 are "interpolations" (that is, "glosses" or "extraneous materials"), which have been inserted into the text by later scribes or copyists. Jewett's argument for such an interpolation understanding is based on his observations (as well as those of many other NT scholars) that these two passages are (1) inconsistent in their placement with "the remarkable symmetry" of presentation in the apostle's letter to Rome,[1] and (2) "different in style and logical development from the rest of Romans."[2] We believe, however, that what Paul sets out in 16:17-20a and 16:25-27 — while, admittedly, somewhat different from what he writes in the personal subscriptions of his other NT letters — was meant to be understood in ways (1) that relate to his earlier presentations in his letter to Rome, (2) that highlight some of his purposes for his personal subscription of 16:17-27 (minus 16:24), and (3) that summarize, particularly in the doxology of 16:25-27, a number of the major themes and thrusts of what he had earlier written in the letter (which theses we will attempt to explicate in our treatments of these passages below).

20a The positioning of a grace benediction as the second part of 16:20 — whether employing the single name Ἰησοῦ or the compound name Ἰησοῦ Χριστοῦ — is amply attested by P[46], by uncials ℵ A B C Ψ 0150, and by minuscules 33 (Category I), 1881 256 (Category II), and 104 263 436 1319 1573 1852 (Category III); it is also reflected in syr[p]. Some MSS, however, place this grace benediction at the end of 16:23 (that is, as the content of 16:24), as do uncials D F G; this positioning is also reflected in it[d*, f, g, mon, o]. The reason for this placement by these "western" MSS seems to have been to prevent the greetings of 16:21-23 from appearing as an afterthought or appended postscript. Other MSS have this grace benediction at both the end of 16:20 and the end of 16:23 (i.e., as the content of 16:24), as appears in uncial Ψ [also *Byz* L] and in minuscules 1175 (Category I) and 6 365 1241 1912 2200 (Category III); this placement is also reflected in it[ar] syr[h]. But a second appearance of the apostle's grace benediction in what has been versified as 16:24 is far too weakly attested by the Greek MSS to be accepted (see below on v. 24).

Still other MSS have this grace benediction after the doxology of 16:25-27, which positioning is supported by ninth-century uncial P and by minuscules 33 (Category I), 256 (Category II), and 104 263 436 459 1319 1573 1852 (Category III); this placement also is reflected in vg[ms] sy[p] and is supported by Ambrosiaster. Such a positioning was undoubtedly intended to bring the entirety of Paul's letter to a fitting conclusion. Yet, as Bruce Metzger has pointed out with respect to this placement of the grace benediction as the final word to Paul's letter to Rome: "If, however, it stood in this position originally, there is no good reason why it should have been moved earlier."[3]

Much of the discussion regarding the presence and positioning of a grace benediction in Paul's "personal subscription" of 16:17-27 — as well as with respect to the presence and positioning of an affirming "Amen" — depends on what one believes about the so-called short form, intermediate form, and long form of Paul's letter to Rome.[4] The MSS evidence, however, suggests that a grace benediction (whether with the single

1. See Jewett, *Romans*, 50.
2. See *ibid.*, 986-96 (on 16:17-20a) and 997-1011 (on 16:25-27); also note the interpreters that Jewett cites in support of these positions.
3. Metzger, *Textual Commentary*, 476.
4. For our earlier discussions of the form of the original letter, see R. N. Longenecker, *Introducing Romans*, 19-30.

name "Jesus" or the compound name "Jesus Christ") — together with a quasi-liturgical "Amen" — was original in 16:20b (and must be viewed as being highly suspect for what has traditionally been designated as 16:24, as versified in the mid–sixteenth century). Therefore our translation includes both a grace benediction and an affirming "Amen" in 16:20b, but does not include either anywhere else in 16:17-27.

20b The grace benediction of the second part of 16:20 may be understood to employ either the single name Ἰησοῦ ("Jesus") or the compound name Ἰησοῦ Χριστοῦ ("Jesus Christ"). The single name "Jesus" after the title "Our Lord" — that is, ἡ χάρις τοῦ κυρίου ἡμῶν Ἰησοῦ μεθ' ὑμῶν ("The grace of our Lord Jesus be with you!") — is attested by P[46], by uncials ℵ and B, and by minuscule 1881 (Category II). The compound name "Jesus Christ" after the title "Our Lord" — that is, ἡ χάρις τοῦ κυρίου ἡμῶν Ἰησοῦ Χριστοῦ μεθ' ὑμῶν ("The grace of our Lord Jesus Christ be with you!") — is attested by A C P Ψ 0150 [also *Byz* L], by minuscules 33 1175 1739 (Category I), 81 256 2127 2464 (Category II), and 6 104 263 365 459 1241 1319 1573 1852 1912 2200 (Category III); this compound usage is also reflected in it[ar, b, (d2)], vg[p, h] cop[sa, bo] and supported by Origen[lat] and Chrysostom.

At first glance, the MSS evidence may seem somewhat evenly divided. Yet the fact that the single name Ἰησοῦ ("Jesus") is attested by three of our most important MSS of the Greek textual tradition — that is, by P[46], by Codex Sinaiticus (ℵ 01), and by Codex Vaticanus (B 03) — weighs heavily in favor of the single name Ἰησοῦ as having been original. Further, if Χριστοῦ ("Christ") was originally included in the name, "there seems to be," as Bruce Metzger has pointed out, "no reason why a copyist should have deleted it, whereas the general tendency was to expand liturgical formulations."[5] It is most likely, therefore, that the single name "Jesus" was original.

24 As noted above in discussing 16:20b, some MSS have a grace benediction not only at the end of 16:20 but also as the content of 16:24, as do uncials Ψ [also *Byz* L] and minuscules 1175 (Category I) and 6 365 1241 1912 2200 (Category III); this placement is also reflected in it[ar] syr[h]. A second grace benediction also appears in some MSS following 16:27, as it does in ninth-century uncial P and in minuscules 33 (Category I), 256 (Category II), and 104 263 436 459 1319 1573 1852 (Category III); such a second grace benediction also appears after 16:27 in vg[ms] syr[p] cop[bo[ms]] arm eth and is supported at that place by Ambrosiaster. The earliest and best textual witnesses, however, omit entirely a second grace benediction, whether at 16:24 or after 16:27 — as omitted by P[46, 61], by uncials ℵ A B C 0150, and by minuscules 1739 (Category I) and 81 1962 2127 2464 (Category II); this omission is also reflected in it[b] vg[ww, st] cop[sa, bo] and supported by Origen[lat]. Thus in concert with all major contemporary translations and commentaries, we will not include 16:24 or add anything after 16:27 in our "Exegetical Comments" below.

25-27 Bruce Metzger has concisely pointed out: "The doxology ('Now to him who is able to strengthen you . . . be glory for evermore through Jesus Christ!') varies in location; traditionally it has been positioned at the close of chap. 16 (as verses 25-27), but in some witnesses it occurs at the close of chap. 14, and in another witness (P[46]) at the close of chap. 15. Moreover, several textual witnesses have it at the close of both chap.

---

5 Metzger, *Textual Commentary*, 476.

14 and chap. 16, and in others it does not occur at all."[6] And as Metzger has noted with regard to the stance of the UBS committee that endeavored to "establish" the Greek text for all later English translations: "While recognizing the possibility that the doxology may not have been part of the original form of the epistle, on the strength of impressive manuscript evidence (P[61] $\aleph$ B C D 81 1739 it[ar, b, d*, f, o] vg syr[p] cop[sa, bo] eth Clement al) the Committee decided to include the verses at their traditional place in the epistle, but enclosed within square brackets."[7]

Summarizing "the textual evidence for six locations of the doxology," Metzger sets out the following chart with respect to its positioning in the NT textual tradition:[8]

(a) 1.1–16.23 + doxology   P[61 vid] $\aleph$ B C D 81 1739 it[d. 61] vg syr[p]
                                    cop[sa, bo] eth

(b) 1.1–14.23 + doxology +   A P 5 33 104 arm
        15.1–16:23 + doxology

(c) 1.1–14.23 + doxology +   L Ψ 0209[vid] 181 326 330 614 1175
        15.1–16.24   *Byz* syr[h] mss[acc to Origen (lat)]

(d) 1.1–16:24   F[gr] G (perhaps the archetype of D)
                                    629 mss[acc. to Jerome]

(e) 1.1–15.33 + doxology +   P[46]
        16:1-23

(f) 1.1–14.23 + 16.24 +   vg[mss] Old Latin[acc. to capitula]
        Doxology

27 The single word αἰῶνας ("forever") in the final ascription of the doxology is attested by P[46], by uncials B C Ψ (also *Byz* L), and by minuscules 33 1175 1739 (Category I), 256 1506 1881 2127 (Category II), and 6 104[1/2] 263 365 459[1/2] 1241 1319 1573 1912 2200; this single word is also reflected in syr[h] cop[sa] and supported by Eusebius Chrysostom Theodoret and Ambrosiaster. The more developed phrase αἰῶνας τῶν αἰώνων ("forever and ever") is attested by P[61], by uncials $\aleph$ A D P 0150, and by minuscules 81 1962 2464 (Category II) and 104[1/2] 436 459[1/2] 1852; it also is reflected in it[ar, b, d*, f, o] vg syr[p] cop[bo] and supported by Origen[lat] and Augustine. Since it was unusual for scribes to delete any words of a biblical doxology that they viewed as original — but rather common for them to expand doxologies in line with the current ecclesiastical usage of their day — it seems best to accept only the single word αἰῶνας ("forever") as original.

---

6. Metzger, *Textual Commentary*, 470.

7. *Ibid.*, 476-77.

8. *Ibid.*, 473. Metzger also writes in this footnote the following: "It should be pointed out that since $\mathfrak{P}^{61}$ is extremely fragmentary in Romans (preserving only 16.23, 24-27), it could be cited in support of sequence *(b)* as well as *(a)*."

FORM/STRUCTURE/SETTING

Paul usually concluded his NT letters with a personal subscription or postscript that (1) included greetings and admonitions, (2) incorporated at times both a peace blessing and a grace benediction, but always ended in some fashion with a grace benediction, and (3) appeared to have been written in his own hand.[9] And the materials of 16:17-20b — with the appended greetings of 16:21-23 and the appended doxology of 16:25-27 — seem to express such a subscription.

Some scholars have understood the personal subscription portion of Romans as being all of ch. 16, others as starting at 16:21, directly after the grace benediction of 16:20b. We believe that the letter's personal subscription begins at 16:17 with the request formula παρακαλῶ ὑμᾶς ("I urge you") and the vocative of direct address ἀδελφοί ("brothers and sisters"), and ends with a series of greetings sent by the apostle (including also a greeting sent by Tertius in v. 22) on behalf of others in 16:21-23 — without, however, the weakly attested grace benediction of 16:24, but with the addition of the doxology of 16:25-27. Here in this final section of his letter Paul seems to have taken the pen from Tertius, one of his associates at Corinth who served as the amanuensis for his letter, and added a postscript in his own handwriting (though with Tertius taking back the pen to add his own greeting in his own handwriting in 16:22).

All the personal subscriptions in Paul's NT letters have generally been treated in a somewhat cursory fashion, largely because (1) the natural tendency of commentators is to focus on the weightier matters found in the thanksgiving sections and body sections of his letters, and (2) a widespread assumption maintains that the opening salutations and closing subscriptions of his letters are purely conventional in nature, functioning only to establish or maintain contact with their addressees. But as Adolf Deissmann long ago argued (with particular reference to the personal subscription of Gal 6:11-18, though with application to all the subscriptions of Paul's letters): "More attention ought to be paid to the concluding words of the letters generally; they are of the highest importance if we are ever to understand the Apostle."[10] And this thesis has been significantly developed by Ann Jervis and Jeffrey Weima.[11]

What Paul apparently wanted to do in his personal subscription and doxology of 16:17-27 (minus the inclusion of v. 24) was (1) to express some lingering concerns about his Roman addressees by directing further admonitions toward them (so vv. 17-20a), (2) to add a closing grace benediction and final "Amen" to his letter (so v. 20b), (3) to send the greetings of those who were immediately associated with him at Corinth and its environs (so vv. 21-23), and (4) to sum-

9. Cf. Gal 6:11-18; 2 Thess 3:16-18; 1 Cor 16:19-24; Col 4:18; and Phlm 19–25; see R. N. Longenecker, "Ancient Amanuenses and the Pauline Epistles," 282-92.

10. Deissmann, *Bible Studies,* 347; see also G. Milligan, *The New Testament Documents: Their Origin and Early History* (London: Macmillan, 1913), 21-28.

11. Jervis, *The Purpose of Romans,* 132-57; Weima, *Neglected Endings,* 215-30; *idem,* "Preaching the Gospel in Rome," 358-66.

marize in a quasi-liturgical doxology the major thrusts of what he had written in the letter (so vv. 25-27).

Structure of the Section. The first part of Paul's personal subscription, that is, 16:17-23, contains in only seven verses a relatively substantial number of rather common epistolary formulas and conventions of the day:

> 16:17 — A request formula and a vocative of direct address (παρακαλῶ ὑμᾶς, ἀδελφοί): "I urge you, brothers and sisters."
>
> 16:19 — An expression of joy (ἐφ᾽ ὑμῖν χαίρω): "I rejoice over you."
>
> 16:21 — A conveyance of the greetings of others (ἀσπάζεται ὑμᾶς Τιμόθεος ὁ συνεργός μου καὶ Λούκιος καὶ Ἰάσων καὶ Σωσίπατρος οἱ συγγενεῖς μου): "Timothy, my co-worker, greets you, as do also Lucius, Jason and Sosipater, my relatives."
>
> 16:22 — An inserted greeting (ἀσπάζομαι ὑμᾶς ἐγὼ Τέρτιος ὁ γράψας τὴν ἐπιστολήν): "I, Tertius, who wrote [down] this letter, greet you."
>
> 16:23 — A further conveyance of the greetings of others (ἀσπάζεται ὑμᾶς Γάϊος. ἀσπάζεται ὑμᾶς Ἔραστος . . . καὶ Κούαρτος): "Gaius greets you, Erastus greets you, . . . as does also Quartus."

The section also includes a grace benediction and an affirming "Amen" in 16:20b, which features follow the peace statement of 16:20a. The peace statement of 16:20a, however, is not strictly a peace blessing (as in 15:33), but should be seen as "a promise of peace" of what God will bring about with respect to the situation alluded to in 16:17-19.

A second grace benediction, which has been versified since the mid–sixteenth century as 16:24, is too weakly attested in the Greek textual tradition to be viewed as original. Some have wanted to retain it (particularly when they question the integrity of the doxology of 16:25-27) so as to close off the entire letter with a final grace benediction, just as Paul does in his other letters.[12] But textual evidence for a second grace benediction at 16:24 — or as following 16:25-27 — is insufficient for its inclusion at either of those locations, with no support from P[46] or P[61] and none from any of the major uncial MSS. Further, farewell wishes in ancient Greek letters — which usually began with ἔρρωσο or ἔρρωσθε, "farewell," but at times with εὐτύχει or its intensified form διευτύχει, "good luck" or "best wishes" — evidence a rather standard pattern: the first farewell appearing somewhere in the first part of a letter's conclusion, in material written down on behalf of an author by an amanuensis or secretary; the second farewell appearing in the personal subscription of a letter, written by an author himself in his own handwriting. This is the pattern that appears in the concluding sections of Romans: (1) a peace blessing at the beginning of the letter's concluding sections at 15:33, with the first section of that conclusion, 15:33–16:16, having

---

12. As, e.g., Gamble, *Textual History,* 122-24, and Jervis, *The Purpose of Romans,* 138-39, in their otherwise highly credible and rightly acclaimed respective writings.

been "written down" by Tertius at Paul's direction; (2) a grace benediction in the personal subscription section at 16:20b — with the second portion of that conclusion, that is, 16:17-27 (minus v. 24), having evidently been written (at least substantially, minus Tertius's insertion of his own greeting) by Paul himself in his own handwriting.

This personal subscription of Romans has a further set of greetings in 16:21-23, which appears immediately after the grace benediction of 16:20b. This latter set of greetings is different from the first set of requested greetings in 16:3-16. For whereas in the first set the apostle asked the Christians at Rome to send their greetings to a number of his past associates, friends, and acquaintances then living in Rome (16:3-15) — and asked them to "greet one another with a holy kiss" and conveyed greetings from "all the churches of Christ" (16:16) — in this latter set of greetings Paul himself sends greetings from seven of his co-workers, relatives, and friends at Corinth and its environs to the Christians at Rome (16:21 and 23). And, interestingly, there is included a greeting from Tertius (16:22), who served as Paul's amanuensis in the writing of Romans and actually describes himself as "the one who 'wrote down' this letter 'in the Lord'" (ὁ γράψας τὴν ἐπιστολὴν ἐν κυρίῳ) — whatever that rather unique Pauline expression "in the Lord" may have meant to Tertius himself in his work as Paul's amanuensis.

A grace benediction is normally the last item in the personal subscriptions of Paul's NT letters. But personal subscriptions in Paul's letters — as well as in the extant letters of antiquity generally — vary considerably in format. So it may be presumed that the variations that appear in the subscriptions of both ancient letters generally and Paul's letters in particular are the result of, and so reflect, the particular situation that existed when each of those letters was written.

Here in Romans we believe it reasonable to postulate the following scenario as the particular situation that took place at some time (and at some place in or near the city of Corinth) *after* Paul had written the grace benediction and its affirming "Amen" in 16:20b of the letter:

1. Some of the apostle's associates and friends at Corinth and its environs had gathered (or, perhaps, were called together by the apostle himself) to hear Paul's letter read to them (possibly by the apostle himself, but more likely by Phoebe or Tertius, or by a number of readers in the group itself), before entrusting the letter to Phoebe to be carried to Rome.
2. After the letter was read to those who had gathered, some of them asked that their personal greetings be also sent with the letter — not only as an act of cordiality, but, more importantly, to lend support to what Paul had written.
3. Tertius, too, who was Paul's amanuensis at the time, evidently wanted to be included in those greetings and to express his support, and therefore took back the pen from Paul to include his own greeting.
4. After having appended this further set of rather spontaneous and support-ive greetings — and desiring to highlight what he considered the major

thrusts of what he had written — Paul himself closed off his letter with a fairly formal and quite eloquently expressed doxology, which presently appears as 16:25-27 (which the apostle himself composed as an appropriate conclusion to his letter and may have written in his own handwriting rather than dictating it to Tertius).

The individual items in Paul's personal subscription of 16:17-27, therefore, can be set out as follows:

1. Additional admonitions in 16:17-20a, which (a) begin with a *request formula* (παρακαλῶ ὑμᾶς, "I urge you") and a *vocative of direct address* (ἀδελφοί, "brothers and sisters") in 16:17; (b) interject a note of confidence with an epistolary *expression of joy* (ἐφ' ὑμῖν χαίρω, "I rejoice over you") in 16:19; and (c) close with the promise that "the God of peace will soon crush Satan under your feet" in 16:20a.
2. A closing grace benediction with its quasi-liturgical "Amen" in 16:20b.
3. An appended "Further Greetings" from certain of the apostle's associates and friends at Corinth and its environs — who may have been forced to leave Rome at the expulsion of Jews and Jewish Christians from the capital city, continued to remain at Corinth and its environs as exiles from Rome, and were evidently well known by the believers in Jesus at Rome — to the Christians at Rome in 16:21-23.
4. An appended doxology in 16:25-27.

Implied Arguments of the Section. Jeffrey Weima has observed about the function of a Pauline conclusion (which he rightly identifies in Romans as being the materials of 15:33–16:27, minus the weakly attested second grace benediction of 16:24), that:

> Paul commonly shapes and adapts this epistolary unit in such a way that it relates directly to — sometimes, in fact, even summarizes — the major concerns and themes taken up in the bodies of their respective letters. Thus the letter closing functions a lot like the thanksgiving, but in reverse. For as the thanksgiving foreshadows and points ahead to the major concerns to be addressed in the body of the letter, so the closing serves to highlight and encapsulate the main points previously taken up in the body. This recapitulating function of Paul's letter closings suggests that the letter closing of Romans is likewise significant for revealing the central concern(s) of Paul at work in the rest of the letter.[13]

This function of a Pauline conclusion we believe to be true for the first part of the concluding sections of Paul's letter here in 15:33-16:16, which Tertius wrote

13. Weima, "Preaching the Gospel in Rome," 359.

down at Paul's direction — and which includes (1) a peace blessing, (2) a commendation of Phoebe, and (3) a long list of greetings that the apostle requests the Christians at Rome to express to a number of his past associates, friends, and acquaintances who were then living in Rome. This function is also true for the personal subscription section of 16:17-27 (minus v. 24), which, it seems, the apostle himself wrote in his own handwriting (at least in the main, except for Tertius's inserted greeting of 16:22) — that is, (1) the additional admonitions of 16:17-20a, (2) the closing grace benediction with its affirming and quasi-liturgical "Amen" of 16:20b, (3) the appended "Further Greetings" conveyed by the apostle from his associates and friends at Corinth of 16:21-23 (though with Tertius's greeting of 16:22 set out in his own handwriting), and (4) the appended doxology of 16:25-27.

EXEGETICAL COMMENTS

I. Additional Admonitions (16:17-20a)

16:17-20a The additional admonitions of 16:17-20a most likely have in mind the disruptions referred to earlier in 14:1–15:13, which had to do with conflicts between "the Strong" and "the Weak." For here in this additional set of admonitions Paul alludes to "divisions," "obstacles," and those who "by smooth talk and flattery deceive the minds of naive people," characterizing what was taking place as "contrary to the teaching you have learned," and urging the Christians at Rome to "keep away from them" (16:17-18). His admonitions, however, are not simply rebukes of his addressees. For even when speaking of divisions and obstacles within the Christian congregations at Rome, Paul refers to his addressees as "brothers and sisters" (v. 17a), acknowledges that they had received proper teaching (v. 17b), and distinguishes them from those who were causing trouble in the Christian congregations at Rome by "not serving our Lord Christ but their own appetites" (v. 18). In fact, the apostle goes on to praise the Christians at Rome for their "obedience" (16:19a), urges them in a rather nonjudgmental manner to be "wise about what is good and innocent about what is evil" (16:19b), and assures them that "the God of peace will shortly crush Satan under your feet" (16:20a).

The relations between "the Strong" and "the Weak" within the community of Christians at Rome seem to have been of great concern to Paul. It was a situation that he had evidently heard about from others and that he had dealt with in a rather direct manner in 14:1–15:13. Here in 16:17-20a he appears to raise that matter again, admonishing his addressees in a manner that resembles what in certain circles today would be called "advice from a Dutch uncle" (that is, with a sternness of expression but a heart of love). Such a series of admonitions written in Paul's own handwriting suggests that this ecclesiastical matter was not only of concern to the Christians at Rome but also of great pastoral and

1081

emotional concern to the apostle himself, and thus he felt compelled to deal with it again here in 16:17-20a.

Paul's major concerns when writing to the Christians at Rome were (1) that they would understand and appreciate his distinctive manner of contextualizing the Christian message in his Gentile mission (i.e., his "spiritual gift" to them, as referred to in 1:11; cf. also "my gospel" of 2:16 and 16:25) and (2) that both he and they would be able to derive from each other what each of them most urgently needed (as alluded to in 1:12 of the thanksgiving section; cf. also 15:24 and 32 of the apostolic parousia section). Here in 16:17-20a, however, he seems to be aligning himself with his addressees in their particular situation and with one of their major concerns. Yet he speaks affectionately of them as "brothers and sisters" (v. 17a), affirms their proper grounding in the Christian faith (v. 17b), views at least most of them in an entirely different category from certain other divisive persons in their midst (vv. 18-19a), praises them for their obedience (v. 19a), urges them in a nonjudgmental manner to be "wise about what is good and innocent about what is evil" (v. 19b), and assures them that "the God of peace will shortly crush Satan under your feet" (v. 20a) — speaking like this in order to build relations with them.

II. Closing Grace Benediction and Affirming "Amen" (16:20b)

16:20b As noted above in our "Textual Notes," the MSS evidence is decidedly in favor of the positioning of the letter's closing grace benediction and affirming "Amen" here at 16:20b — and not in a supposed 16:24 (as later versified) or immediately after the quasi-liturgical doxology of 16:25-27. Amidst all the speculations of yesterday and today regarding where the original grace benediction and its affirming "Amen" originally appeared, certainly the overwhelming witness of the MS evidence must be respected as primary in our deliberations.

It has often seemed strange to many ancient scribes and to many interpreters today that Paul would have appended two portions of material, that is, a short section of additional greetings in 16:21-23 (minus 16:24) and the doxology of 16:25-27, after pronouncing a final grace benediction and supporting it by an affirming "Amen." But the Greek MS evidence indicates that is most likely what he did. And while ancient scribes and modern interpreters have often shied away from speaking of 16:21-23 and 16:25-27 as "afterthoughts" or "postscripts" (which designations have seemed to some rather pejorative as meaning only "tacked on"), it is difficult to dispute the fact that these two passages present materials that are somewhat different in both their content and their placement from what appear as the final sections of the apostle's other NT letters.

It is our thesis, however, that these two passages of 16:21-23 and 16:25-27 should be understood in light of our proposed scenario of events at the conclusion of Paul's composition of his letter to Rome — that they were composed by the apostle and attached to his letter as appended materials *after* the reading of the letter by his associates and friends at Corinth and *before* the letter was entrusted to Phoebe to be taken to the believers in Jesus at Rome.[14] Admittedly, such a scenario is conjectural. Yet it is a reasonable conjecture that provides interpreters with certain positive results.

III. Appended "Further Greetings" from Paul's Associates and Friends in Corinth and Its Environs (16:21-23)

16:21-23 The further greetings sent by Paul in 16:21-23, as noted above in positing a probable scenario for their inclusion,[15] also serve to build relations with Paul's Roman addressees. They are not just in competition with the earlier set of greetings in 16:3-16, but are a complementary set to that of 16:3-16. For just as the greetings of the earlier set in 16:3-16 (esp. vv. 3-15), which the apostle asks the Christians at Rome to express to his associates, friends, and acquaintances who were at that time living in Rome, should be seen as functioning principally to promote his credibility among the believers in Jesus at Rome by highlighting the personal relationships he had had with several of the people of their community, so this second set of greetings in 16:21-23, which Paul sends from seven of his friends, relatives, and associates at Corinth and Cenchrea (and to which Tertius, who acted as his amanuensis, attaches his greetings), should also be seen as having been included primarily to support his apostolic authority and to enhance the acceptability of his contextualization of the gospel among the Christians at Rome.

IV. Appended Doxology (16:25-27)

16:25-27 The authenticity of the doxology of 16:25-27 has often been contested, both on textual and on literary grounds. The textual tradition exhibits various versions of its placement: (1) after 14:23 (i.e., at the end of the "short" form of the letter); (2) after 15:33 (i.e., at the end of the "intermediate" form of the letter); (3) after 16:23/24 (i.e., at the end of the "long" form of the letter); (4) after both 14:23 and 16:23/24 (e.g., in uncial codices A [02] of the fifth century and P [025] of the ninth century); (5) after both 14:23 and 15:33, with 16:1-23/24 being omitted (i.e., in minuscule 1506); or (6) omitted altogether (e.g., in uncial codices F [010] and G [012] of the ninth century). Many today see the language and style of the doxology as non-Pauline. In fact, the majority of NT scholars today view this quasi-liturgical doxology of 16:25-27 as a post-Pauline addition to Romans

---

14. Note our "proposed scenario" regarding the situation that probably took place at Corinth after Paul had completed his letter to Rome, which, as we believe, would have encouraged the apostle to append "Further Greetings" in 16:21-23 and a doxology in 16:25-27 after the grace benediction and "Amen" of 16:20b (see pp. 1079-80).

15. See again our "proposed scenario" on pp. 1079-80.

that probably originated in the mid–second century during the time of Marcion, who, it is argued, was the one who excised chs. 15–16 — and whose followers would then have composed this doxology as a fitting conclusion to chs. 1–14.

Paul's usual style, as many have observed, was not to finish off a letter with a doxology, but to conclude with a grace benediction. One possible exception is "the love wish" of 1 Cor 16:24, which most likely should be viewed as a postscript penned by Paul himself that appears after the grace benediction of 1 Cor 16:23 — and so may be seen as something of a parallel to the concluding phenomena in Romans where an appended set of further greetings in 16:21-23 and a closing doxology in 16:25-27 appear after the grace benediction of 16:20b. A further problem is that the language of 16:25-27 is quite formal, perhaps even liturgical (so we have used the term "quasi-liturgical"), being more like the so-called deutero-Pauline letters, particularly Ephesians and the Pastorals. But if these later letters are accepted as being in some sense written by Paul — whether as an encyclical letter (as Ephesians) and/or with an amanuensis having been given greater freedom (as the Pastorals) — then this particular phenomenon loses much of its adverse critical value. So, while the above-cited observations regarding the placement and language of the doxology of 16:25-27 are pertinent, conclusions often drawn from them against the authenticity of these three verses are not overly convincing.

More important for any positive evaluation of Paul's authorship of this doxology of 16:25-27 is the fact that his habit in Romans seems to be to close off large sections of important material with a confessional statement or a doxological passage, which is either quoted verbatim or paraphrased in his own words. This is what he did in (1) his Christocentric statement "He was delivered over to death for our sins and was raised to life for our justification" that appears in 4:25, which closes off Section I of the body middle of his letter (i.e., 1:16–4:25), (2) his "Triumphal Affirmation of God's Love in Christ" that appears in 8:31-39, which closes off Section II of that same body middle of his letter (i.e., 5:1–8:39), (3) his "Praise to God for His Wisdom and Knowledge" that appears in 11:33-36, which closes off Section III (i.e., 9:1–11:36), and (4) his doxological statement "May the God of hope fill you with all joy and peace in believing, so that you may abound in hope by the power of the Holy Spirit" that appears in 15:13, which closes off Section IV (i.e., 12:1–15:13). These confessional or doxology passages nicely summarize what was written in their respective sections, but they do it more in a rhetorical fashion than in a strictly instructional fashion. It is plausible, therefore, to believe that this is how Paul intended the doxology at the end of Romans to function as well.

This doxology of 16:25-27, as Jeffrey Weima points out, is "striking for the way in which it recapitulates the concern of Paul" as expressed throughout Romans. In particular, Weima notes:

> The reference to "*my* gospel" recalls well Paul's concern in the letter opening, thanksgiving, letter body and apostolic *parousia* to share his gospel

with the Roman believers. The doxology claims that Paul's gospel will be used by God "to strengthen" (στηρίξαι) the believers in Rome — the same point that was made in the thanksgiving section (1.11, "in order that you may be strengthened" [στηριχθῆναι]). The doxology further highlights the continuity of Paul's gospel with the message of the OT — a matter also stressed in the letter opening (1.2-4). More specifically, the phrase "through the prophetic writings" (16.26, διὰ γραφῶν προφητικῶν) is a deliberate allusion to the opening words of the letter, "through his prophets in the holy writings" (1.2, διὰ τῶν προφητῶν αὐτοῦ ἐν γραφαῖς ἁγίαις). The goal or purpose of making the mystery of the gospel known is "to bring about the obedience of faith for all the Gentiles" (16.26, εἰς ὑπακοὴν πίστεως εἰς πάντα τὰ ἔθνα). This phrase from the doxology provides yet another direct verbal link with the letter opening: "to bring about the obedience of faith for all the Gentiles" (1.5, εἰς ὑπακοὴν πίστεως ἐν πᾶσιν τοῖς ἔθνεσιν). It also recalls Paul's point in the apostolic *parousia* that Christ is working through him "to bring about the obedience of the Gentiles" (15.18, εἰς ὑπακοὴν ἐθνῶν).[16]

And as Weima has additionally observed: "The strong recapitulating character of the doxology serves as yet a further means by which Paul seeks to establish the authority and acceptability of his gospel among the Roman believers."[17]

So we propose that this quasi-liturgical doxology was most likely composed by Paul himself — either (1) at some earlier time during his Gentile ministry in eastern regions of the Roman Empire to express in a paragraph the essence of his ministry in those regions, and then reproduced here at the end of his letter to Rome, or (2) after finishing his letter, and probably at the request of his associates and friends living at Corinth and/or its environs, to highlight in summary fashion what he believed were the major themes and thrusts of the letter — doing so, retrospectively, to ingrain within their minds and hearts those central points. At least five points are highlighted in this summarizing doxology of the apostle's letter:

1. All of what Paul has written in the letter was meant to establish them in their Christian convictions (v. 25a).
2. The focus of his contextualized gospel proclamation ("my gospel") — which he earlier proclaimed in his Gentile mission in eastern regions of the Roman Empire and was now proclaiming in his letter to the believers in Jesus at Rome — has to do with the person and work of Jesus Christ (v. 25b).
3. This proclamation of Jesus Christ, though a "mystery hidden for long ages past," has "now been revealed and made known through the prophetic writings by the command of the eternal God" (vv. 25c-26a).

16. Weima, *Neglected Endings,* 229.
17. *Ibid.*

4. The purpose of all of God's action, all of Jesus' redemptive ministry, and all of Paul's preaching was so that "all the Gentiles might believe and obey God."

5. All praise and glory for whatever has been done (and will be accomplished) in an outreach to Gentiles must be directed "to the only wise God . . . through Jesus Christ."

BIBLICAL THEOLOGY AND
CONTEXTUALIZATION FOR TODAY

It would be repetitious to try to expound on any of these emphases in this doxology of 16:25-27. Paul evidently believed that all these matters were foundational for, and had been expressed by, what he had written in the letter — whether this doxology was (1) composed during his earlier Gentile ministry and then reproduced here at the end of the letter or (2) written after finishing his dictation of the contents of the letter. So it seems best to understand this doxology of 16:25-27, however it came about in the apostle's ministry, as intended by him to be an appended closing and summarizing paragraph of what he had written and what he believed constituted the essence of his God-given ministry.

We cannot improve on such a closing statement. And certainly we must allow Paul to have the final word in concluding his own letter. Nonetheless, at least the following must be emphasized in any contextualization of this doxological utterance in our day: what Paul has highlighted in his doxology of 16:25-27 must also resound in all our attempts today to construct a truly Christian biblical theology — and, further, it needs to be engrained in all our Christian thinking and all our Christian living.

Index of Contemporary Authors

Index of Ancient Sources

Jubilees		*Sibylline Oracles*		8:3	164n43
1:23	318	2:65	937n40		
1:29	723n45	2:73	217n104	*Testament of Reuben*	
2:24	86n219	3:8-45	210	4:4	195n14
3:28-32	212n85	3:185-87	217n104		
5:15	259n71	3:194-95	302n28		
6:19	492	3:499	517n95	**DEAD SEA SCROLLS/**	
12:16-24	210n76	3:594-600	217n104	**QUMRAN**	
15:3-4	367n133	3:744-52	723n45		
15:28	313n64	3:752	724	**CD**	
15:30b-32	447	3:763	217n104	3.2	368n134
16:19	520	3:768-69	510n74	4.17-18	219n107
17:11	86n218	3:788-95	723n45	6.15	308n47
19:9	476n10	4:162	195n14	6.16-17	320n88
21:24	890n38	5:75-76	195n14	7.19	180n105
23:10	368n135, 476, 492	5:386-433	217n104	20.20	164n43
24:32	853n45			20.34	164n43
31:14	86n218	*Testament of Abraham*			
31:19	164n43	13:5	281n143	**1QH**	
33:12	86n218			1.21	819n38
		Testament of Benjamin		1.21-23	654n14, 667n62, 668n65
Letter of Aristeas		8:2	937n40		
152	217n104			3.23-24	819n38
166	215n93	*Testament of Dan*		3.24-36	654n14, 667n62, 668n65
196	967n37	5:10	164n43		
219	967n37			column 4	591
224	967n37	*Testament of Gad*		4.5-40	667n62, 668n65
229	937n40	4:7	937n40	4.29	819n38
254	195n14	5:2	937n40	4.29-31	370n140
		7:1	113n66	6.26-27	843n28
Life of Adam		8:1	164n43	7.6-7	73n153
and Eve	212n85			7.16	370n140
		Testament of Joseph		7.18-19	164n43
Psalms of Solomon		19:11	164n43	9.32	73n153
2:18	259n71			11.3	819n38
8:8-14	320n88	*Testament of Judah*		12.12	73n153
8:11-13	308n47	16:2	599n56	12.19	370n140
8:29	303n29			12.20-26	558n44
9:17-18	817	*Testament of Levi*		12.26	819n38
11:2	140n63	14:4-8	320n88	12.32	819n38
12:6	510n74	14:5	308n47	12.37	173n66
14:3	817	14:5-8	219n107	13.16-17	370n140
15:8	248	14:6	217n104	13.37	173n67
17:21	65n109	17:11	217n104	14.13	73n153
17:23	65n109	18:7	73	16.7	73n153
17:23-51	184n115	18:9	302n28	16.12	73n153
17:49	86n218			18.12	819n38
18:3	937n40	*Testament of Naphtali*		18.14	60
		3:2-4	218		
		4:1	217n104		